INDEX TO SOUTHEAST ASIAN JOURNALS, 1960-1974:

A Guide to Articles, Book Reviews, and Composite Works

Donald Clay Johnson

G. K. HALL & CO., 70 LINCOLN STREET, BOSTON, MASS.

Copyright © 1977 by Donald Clay Johnson

Library of Congress Cataloging in Publication Data

Johnson, Donald Clay, 1940-
    Index to Southeast Asian journals, 1960-1974.

    1. Asia, Southeastern--Periodicals--Indexes.
2. Asia, Southeastern--Book reviews--Indexes.
3. Asia, Southeastern--Indexes. I. Title.
Z3221.J64   [DS501]   016.95   77-3467
ISBN 0-8161-7891-7

This publication is printed on permanent/durable acid free paper
MANUFACTURED IN THE UNITED STATES OF AMERICA

In memoriam, *F. Bernice Field*, 1906-1974,

whose work with serials and cataloging

has made library resources more readily

available to scholarship, and,

who made my years at Yale

such stimulating ones

Contents

Introduction

The purpose of this index is to cite articles and book reviews dealing with Southeast Asia that have appeared in selected journals published from 1960 through 1974, and to cite the contents of selected composite works of identified multiple authorship.

SCOPE

In order to provide access to information on Southeast Asia that is presently beyond bibliographic control, an in-depth subject index of a finite list of scholarly journals dealing either exclusively or extensively with Southeast Asia was prepared. The criteria for selection of journals were:

1. The journal had to be internationally oriented rather than local, regional or national. The chief indicator of this was the use of English, or any other commonly understood international scholarly language.

2. The journal had either to deal with several academic disciplines for a single country of Southeast Asia, or to deal with several countries of Southeast Asia for a single academic discipline.

The journals that met these criteria are listed on pages xiii-xv.

All articles included in the journals that did not deal with Southeast Asia have been excluded. All book reviews dealing with Southeast Asia cited in these journals have been indexed except reviews of new journals and doctoral dissertations. The basic list of composite works of identified multiple authorship was primarily derived from the book reviews within journals. Thus most of the books indexed were published 1960-1974.

ORGANIZATION

Subject terms are based, whenever possible, on the principles and terminology of the subject headings of the Library of Congress. When no guidance regarding standardized terminology was provided by that source, the subject term was usually derived from the article itself. In cases of terminology conflict one term was selected with see reference(s) made from the term(s) not used. One major deviation from Library of Congress practice however, was the consistent use of the present name (i.e. 1976) of the individual countries of Southeast Asia rather than all the names associated with them, e.g. Malaysia vs. Federated Malay States, Unfederated Malay States, Malaya, Malayan Union, Straits Settlements.

The selection of subject terms was designed to provide access to information through several perspectives. Four particular areas of concern were:

1. Broad subject areas of an interdisciplinary nature that are not approached from the constraints of a single academic discipline, e.g. urbanization, land tenure.

2. People. This has several levels:
   a. Cultural, ethnic or linguistic groups of the area.
   b. Individuals of the area who were the subject of an article.
   c. Biographical information on scholars of the area.

3. Geographical units. This also has several levels:
   a. Political entities.
   b. Geographical entities, e.g. islands, rivers.
   c. Linguistic areas.
4. The individual precise subjects of articles.

In several areas of the index there are gathering places that alert users to the numerous aspects of that topic that can be found. Two important ones are found under the terms "Language" and "Literature" which gather or pull together the names of all the individual languages/literatures for the countries of Southeast Asia. The subdivision "Minorities" under each country cites all of the minority groups that have been given attention in articles.

The book review section is arranged by cataloging main entry element as cited in the *National Union Catalog* (NUC). Items not located in NUC are preceded by an asterisk to alert users to the fact that the entry element is based solely upon information in the book review and that either this information was insufficient to identify the work in NUC or that for some reason no copy of the title was reported to NUC. Works in languages not using the Roman alphabet are included if their alphabet is transliterated into the Roman alphabet, but excluded if the title is translated into a western language.

Indexes are provided for the two sections. An author index is given for the article section, and a title index for the book review section.

FORMAT OF ENTRIES

Different bibliographical formats are used to assist in distinguishing book reviews, journal articles and articles from composite works. These formats are:

1. Book reviews. Bibliographic data on the book being reviewed, code identification of journal, volume number, year (within parentheses), inclusive pagination, and reviewer if cited (within parentheses).
   ALFON, ESTRELLA D. Magnificence and other stories. Manila, Regal Printing Co., 1960. PA 35 (1962) 82-3. (D. V. Hart)

2. Journal articles. Author, title of the article, code identification of journal, volume number, year (within parentheses), inclusive pagination.
   SZANTON, DAVID. Art in Sulu, a survey. PS 11 (1963) 463-502.

3. Articles from composite works. Author, title of the article, code identification of composite work, inclusive pagination.
   SINGH, VISHAL. Social development in Southeast Asia. S32 pp. 52-3.

The code identifications for journals and composite works appears on pages xiii-xxiii.

ACKNOWLEDGEMENTS

The basic indexing of materials was done in the following libraries: National University of Malaysia Library, University of Malaya Library, Institute of Southeast Asian Studies Library, University of Singapore Library, Northern Illinois University Library and the University of Wisconsin Library. At each library staff members kindly assisted me whenever possible and patiently endured my bringing to their attention gaps in their serial holdings.

When problems of missing, incomplete, or mutilated issues prevented my seeing complete issues, the following individuals generously either opened their personal libraries or through correspondence answered questions about articles:

Richard Cooler, Marina Dayrit, David Feeny, Donn V. Hart, Lian Tie Kho, Father Robert Suchan, Rosita G. Villanueva, and Zainal Abidin bin Abdul Wahab.

Amin Sweeney rendered invaluable assistance in dealing with the Dutch language. Charles A. Bunge and William L. Williamson made helpful comments regarding format and publishing. The Committee on Research Materials for Southeast Asia (CORMOSEA) of the Association for Asian Studies gave a modest grant to assist in the production of a portion of the manuscript.

Last, but far from least, my parents deserve recognition for so patiently putting up with seemingly endless boxes of cards and portions of the manuscript in great disarray in their basement den during the summers of 1975 and 1976.

Abbreviations

*	Item could not be located in the *National Union Catalog*
**	Consult supplement for additional information
Bd.	Band
Ed.	Edition
Enl.	Enlarged
Fasc.	Fascicule
GPO	Government Printing Office
Min.	Ministry
N.d.	No date
N.p.	No place, no publisher
No.	Number
Nouv.	Nouvelle
Pr.	Press
Pt.	Part
Pub.	Publishing
Rev.	Revised
Ser.	Series
T.	Tome
Trans.	Translated, translator
Uitg.	Uitgave
UP	University Press
Univ.	University
V./Vol.	Volume

List of Indexed Journals

AAS — Asian and African Studies
Dept. of Oriental Studies
Slovak Academy of Sciences
Bratislava, Czechloslovakia
1-10 (1965-1974)

AC — Asian Culture
2-3 (1960-1)
Ceased publication

AF — Asian Forum
Institute for Asian Studies
1750 Pennsylvania Ave., N.W.
Washington, D.C., 20006
1-6 (1969-1974)

AP — Asian Perspectives, the Bulletin of the Far Eastern Prehistory Association
Social Science Research Institute
1914 University Avenue, no. 101
Honolulu, Hawaii, 96822
4-17 (1960-1974)

AQ — Asia Quarterly, a Journal from Europe
Centre d'Etude du Sud-Est Asiatique et de l'Extreme-Orient
Avenue Jeanne, 44
B-1050, Brussels, Belgium
1971-1974
Replaced RSA

AR — Archipel; Etudes Interdisciplinaires sur le Monde Insulindien
Archipel Cedrasemi
43 Rue Cuvier
75 Paris VE
1-8 (1970-1974)

AS — Asian Survey
University of California Press
Berkeley, California, 94720
1-14 (1960-1974)

AST — Asian Studies
Dept. of Asian Studies
University of the Philippines
Quezon City, Philippines
1-11 (1963-1973)

BEF — Ecole Francaise d'Extreme-Orient. Bulletin
Adrien-Maisonneuve
11, rue Saint-Sulpice
Paris 6e
50-61 (1960-10974

BIJ — Bijdragen tot de Taal-, Land- en Volkenkunde
Martinus Nijhoff
Lange Voorhout 9-11
The Hague
116-130 (1960-1974)

BMJ — Brunei Museum Journal
Brunei Museum
Bandar Seri Begawan, Brunei
1-4 (1969-1974)

DR — Diliman Review
College of Arts and Sciences
University of the Philippines
Diliman, Quezon City, Philippines
8-22 (1960-1974)
Not seen: 12 pt. 4 (1964)

EACS — East Asian Cultural Studies
Center for East Asian Cultural Studies
Toyo Bunko
147 Kamifujimae-cho
Komagomo, Bankyo-ku, Tokyo
1-13 (1962-1974)

FA — France Asie/Asia, Revue Francaise des Problemes Asiatiques Contemporains
54, rue de Varenne
Paris 7e
17-24 (1960-1970) and 1974

PHR   Philippine Historical Review
         Philippine Chapter
         IAHA Secretariat
         6th Floor
         National Library Building
         Manila, Philippines
         1-2 (1965-1969)

PS   Philippine Studies
         Box 154
         Manila, Philippines
         8-22 (1960-1974)

PSSHR Philippine Social Sciences and
      Humanities Review
         Arts and Sciences Building
         University of the Philippines
         Quezon City, Philippines
         25-38 (1960-1973)
         Not seen: 32 pts. 3-4; 33
         pts. 3-4; 35 pts. 3-4; 38
         pts. 3-4 (1967-1973)

RSA   Revue du Sud-Est Asiatique
         1963-1970
         Replaced by AQ

RSAS Review of Southeast Asian Studies
         South Seas Society
         P. O. Box 709
         Singapore
         1-4 (1971-1974)
         Not Seen: 4 pts. 3-4 (1974)

SA   Southeast Asia, an International
      Quarterly
         Center for Vietnamese Studies
         Southern Illinois University
         Carbondale, Ill., 62901
         1-3 pt. 3 (1971-1974)

SAA   Southeast Asian Archives
         National Archives of Malaysia
         Jalan Sultan
         Petaling Jaya, Malaysia
         1-2 (1968-9)

SAJSS Southeast Asian Journal of Social
      Science
         University Education Press
         37 Somerset Road
         Singapore 9
         1-2 (1973-4)

SEIB Societe des Etudes Indochinoises.
      Bulletin
         Musee National du Vietnam
         Daila Thong Nhut
         Saigon, Vietnam
         35-49 (1960-1974)

SJ   Silliman Journal
         James W. Chapman Research
         Foundation
         Dumaguete City, Philippines
         7-21 (1960-1974)

SLQ   Saint Louis Quarterly
         1-7 (1963-1969)
         Replaced by SLURJ

SLURJ Saint Louis University Research
      Journal.
         Graduate School of Arts and
         Sciences
         St. Louis University
         P. O. Box 71
         Baguio City, Philippines
         1-5 (1970-1974)
         Replaced SLQ

SMJ   Sarawak Museum Journal
         Sarawak Museum
         Kuching, Sarawak, Malaysia
         9-22 (1960-1974)

SOAS University of London. School of
      Oriental and African Studies.
      Bulletin
         Messrs. Luzac and Co., Ltd.
         46 Great Russell Street
         London, WCl
         23-37 (1960-1974)

UN   Unitas
         Office of the Secretary General
         University of Santo Tomas
         Manila 2806, Philippines
         33-42 (1960-1969)

List of Composite Works Indexed

A28 ABUEVA, JOSE VELOSO. Foundations and dynamics of Filipino government and politics. Editors: Jose Veloso Abueva and Raul P. de Guzman. Manila, Bookmark, 1969.

A41 CONFERENCE ON THE CULTURAL PROBLEMS OF MALAYSIA, KUALA LUMPUR, 1965. Cultural problems of Malaysia in the context of Southeast Asia. Papers presented at the first Conference on the Cultural Problems of Malaysia, held in Kuala Lumpur from the 22nd until the 25th of October 1965. Edited by S. Takdir Alisjahbana, Xavier S. Thani Nayagam and Wang Gungwu. Kuala Lumpur, Malaysian Society of Orientalists, n.d.

A43 Modernization of languages of Asia, papers presented at the Conference of the Malaysian Society of Orientalists held in Kuala Lumpur from the 29th of September until the 1st of October, 1967. Edited by S. Takdir Alisjahbana. Kuala Lumpur, Malaysian Society of Asian Studies, 1970.

A58 ANDERSON, GERALD H. Studies in Philippine church history. Ithaca, Cornell UP, 1969.

A62 ANDERSON, JAMES NORMAN DALRYMPLE. Family law in Asia and Africa. London, George Allen and Unwin, 1968.

A77 Asian newspapers' reluctant revolution. Edited by John A. Lent. Ames, Iowa State UP, 1971.

B13 BAGUIO RELIGIOUS ACCULTURATION CONFERENCE. Acculturation in the Philippines, selection of essays on changing societies, papers presented at the Baguio Religious Acculturation Conferences from 1958 to 1968. Quezon City, New Day, 1971.

B18 Bali; studies in life, thought and ritual. The Hague, W. van Hoeve, 1960.

B19 Bali; further studies in life, thought and ritual. The Hague, W. van Hoeve, 1969.

B38 BASTIN, JOHN. Malayan and Indonesian studies, essay presented to Sir Richard Winstedt on his eighty-fifth birthday, edited by John Bastin and R. Roolvink. Oxford, Clarendon Pr., 1964.

B41 BAZELL, CHARLES ERNEST. In memory of J. R. Firth. London, Longmans, Green, 1966.

B42 BELLAH, ROBERT NEELLY. Religion and progress in modern Asia. New York, Free Pr., 1965.

B43 BELO, JANE. Traditional Balinese culture. New York, Columbia UP, 1970.

B72 BRAIBANTI, RALPH J. D. Asian bureaucratic systems emergent from the British imperial tradition. Durham, Duke UP, 1966.

B85 Buiten de grenzen. Sociologische opstellen aangeboden aan Prof. Dr. W. F. Wertheim, 25 jaar Amsterdams Hoogleraar, 1946-1971. Meppel, Boom, 1971.

B91 BURMA RESEARCH SOCIETY. Fiftieth anniversary publications. Vol. I. Rangoon, 1961.

B92 _____. _____. Vol. II. Rangoon, 1960.

C21 CHANDRASEKHAR, SRIPATI. Asia's population problems, with a discussion of population and immigration in Australia. London, Allen and Unwin, 1967.

C24 Change and persistence in Thai society, essays in honor of Lauriston Sharp. Edited by G. William Skinner and A. Thomas Kirsch. Ithaca, Cornell UP, 1975.

C28 CHESNEAUX, JEAN. Tradition et revolution au Vietnam. Paris, Editions Anthropos, 1971.

C31 Compadre colonialism, studies on the Philippines under American rule. Edited by Norman G. Owen. Ann Arbor, Center for South and Southeast Asian Studies, Univ. of Michigan, 1971.

C35 CONFERENCE ON AMERICAN TRADE WITH ASIA AND THE FAR EAST, MARQUETTE UNIVERSITY, 1958. American trade with Asia and the Far East. Milwaukee, Marquette UP, 1959.

C39 CONFERENCE ON FAMILY LAW AND CUSTOMARY LAW IN ASIA, SINGAPORE, 1964. Family law and customary law, a contemporary legal perspective. The Hague, Nijhoff, 1968.

C43 CONFERENCE ON LINGUISTIC PROBLEMS OF THE INDO-PACIFIC AREA, SCHOOL OF ORIENTAL AND AFRICAN STUDIES, UNIVERSITY OF LONDON, 1965. Indo-Pacific linguistic studies. Vol. I. Amsterdam, North-Holland Publishing Co., 1965.

C44 _____. _____. Vol. II.

C47 CONFERENCE ON POPULATION, 1ST, UNIVERSITY OF THE PHILIPPINES. First conference on population, 1965. Quezon City, Univ. of the Philippines Pr., 1966.

C58 CONFERENCE ON SOCIAL DEVELOPMENT AND WELFARE IN VIETNAM, NEW YORK, 1959. Problems of freedom, South Vietnam since independence, edited by Wesley R. Fishel. New York, Free Press of Glencoe, 1961.

C66 CONFERENCE ON THERAVADA BUDDHISM, UNIVERSITY OF CHICAGO, 1962. Anthropological studies in Theravada Buddhism, by Manning Nash et al. New Haven, Yale University, 1966.

C87 COWAN, CHARLES DONALD. Economic development of South-East Asia, studies in economic history and political economy. London, George Allen and Unwin, 1964.

D25 Danses sacres. Paris, Editions du Seuil, 1963.

D44 De l'independance politique a la liberte economique et a l'egalite social en Asie du Sud-Est. Colloque tenu a Bruxelles, les 25, 26 et 27 Novembre 1964. Brussels, Institute of Sociology, Universite Libre de Bruxelles, 1966.

D49 Development administration in Asia. Edited by Edward W. Weidner. Durham, Duke UP, 1970.

D67 Dr. H. Otley Beyer, Dean of Philippine anthropology, edited by Rudolf Rahmann. Cebu City, Univ. of San Carlos, 1968.

D92 The city as a centre of change in Asia. Edited by Denis J. Dwyer. Hong Kong, Hong Kong UP, 1972.

E36 Economic interdepedence in Southeast Asia, proceedings of a conference held at Bangkok, 1967.

Edited by Theodore Morgan and Nyle Spoelstra. Madison, Univ. of Wisconsin Pr., 1968.

E78 ESPIRITU, SOCORRO C. Social foundations of community development, readings on the Philippines. Manila, Garcia, 1964.

E92 Essays offered to G. H. Luce by his colleagues and friends in honor of his seventy-fifth birthday. Ascona, Artibus Asiae, 1966. Vol. I.

E93 ______. Vol. II.

F38 Felicitation volumes of Southeast Asian studies presented to His Highness Prince Dhaninivat Kromamun Bidyalabh Bridhyakorn on the occasion of his eightieth birthday. Bangkok, Siam Society, 1965.

F56 Focus on Southeast Asia, edited by Alice Taylor. New York, Praeger, 1972.

G52 GLASSBURNER, BRUCE. Economy of Indonesia, selected readings. Ithaca, Cornell UP, 1971.

G73 GOROSPE, VITALIANO R. Responsible parenthood in the Philippines. Manila, Ateneo Publications, 1970.

G79 GRANT, JONATHAN S. Cambodia: the widening war in Indochina. New York, Washington Square Pr., 1971.

G83 GRISWOLD, A. B. Felicitation volume presented to Professor George Coedes on the occasion of his seventy fifth birthday, edited by A. B. Griswold and J. Boisselier. Ascona, Artibus Asiae, 1961.

G93 GUZMAN, RAUL P. DE. Patterns in decision making, case studies in Philippine public administration. Manila, Graduate School of Public Administration, Univ. of the Philippines, 1963.

H18 HALL, DANIEL GEORGE EDWARD. Historians of South-East Asia. London, Oxford UP, 1961.

H24 HAWKINS, EVERETT DAY. Entrepreneurship and labour skills in Indonesian economic development: a symposium. New Haven, Southeast Asia Studies, Yale Univ., 1961.

H35 HENDERSON, WILLIAM. Southeast Asia: problems of United States policy. Cambridge, MIT Pr., 1963.

H39 Hiranyagarbha, a series of articles on the archaeological work and studies of Prof. Dr. F. D. K. Bosch, to which is added the address delivered by him at his retirement from the Univ. of Leiden. Published on the occasion of the 50th anniversary of his doctorate on 14th July 1964. The Hague, Mouton, 1964.

H42 Historical interaction of China and Vietnam: institutional and cultural themes. Edgar Wickberg, compiler. Lawrence, Center for East Asian Studies, Univ. of Kansas, 1969.

H52 HOLT, CLAIRE. Culture and politics in Indonesia. Ithaca, Cornell UP, 1972.

H57 Science and scientists in the Netherlands Indies, edited by Pieter Honig and Frans Verdoorn. New York, Board for the Netherlands Indies, Surinam and Curicao, 1945.

H75 HSUEH, SHOU SHENG. Public administration in South and Southeast Asia. Brussels, International Institute of Administrative Sciences, 1962.

H84 HUGHES, HELEN. Foreign investment and industrialisation in Singapore, edited by Helen Hughes and You Poh Seng. Madison, Univ. of Wisconsin Pr., 1969.

J28 Indochina in conflict, a political assessment. Edited by Joseph J.

M52　Modernization in South-East Asia. Edited by Hans-Dieter Evers. Singapore, Oxford UP, 1973.

M57　Mon-Khmer studies. I. Saigon, Linguistic Circle of Saigon, 1964.

M58　_____. II. Saigon, Linguistic Circle of Saigon, 1966.

M59　_____. III. Saigon, Linguistic Circle of Saigon, 1969.

M61　_____. IV. Carbondale, Center for Vietnamese Studies, Southern Illinois Univ., 1973.

M77　MORTIMER, REX. Showcase state, the illusion of Indonesia's accelerated modernisation. Cremorne Junction, N.S.W., Angus and Robertson, 1973.

M95　MURDOCK, GEORGE PETER. Social structure in Southeast Asia. Chicago, Quadrangle Books, 1960.

N15　National liberation; revolution in the third world. New York, Free Pr., 1971.

N18　Nationalism, revolution and evolution in South-East Asia. Zug, Switzerland, Inter-Documentation Co., 1970.

P15　OOSTERS GENOOTSCHAP IN NEDERLAND. Acta orientalia neerlandica: proceedings of the congress of the Dutch Oriental Society held in Leiden on the occasion of its 50th anniversary, 8-9th May 1970. Leiden, Brill, 1971.

P47　Philippine institutions. Manila, Solidaridad, 1970.

R25　Religion and change in contemporary Asia. Edited by Robert F. Spencer. Minneapolis, Univ. of Minnesota Pr., 1971.

R64　ROSE, SAUL. Politics in Southern Asia. London, Macmillan, 1963.

S21　SEBEOK, THOMAS ALBERT. Current trends in linguistics. Vol. II. The Hague, Mouton, 1967.

S22　_____. _____. Vol. VIII. The Hague, Mouton, 1971.

S32　SEMINAR ON INDIA AND SOUTHEAST ASIA, DELHI, 1966. India and Southeast Asia, proceedings, edited by Bidyut Sarkar. Delhi, Indian Council for Cultural Relations, 1968.

S42　SHAND, RICHARD TREGURTHA. Agricultural development in Asia. Berkeley, Univ. of California Pr., 1969.

S44　SIAM SOCIETY. Selected articles from the Siam Society Journal. Bangkok, 1954-
Note: The numbers following the decimal points refer to the volumes within this set, except for .9 which is volume 10. Volume 9 never published?

S47　SILCOCK, THOMAS HENRY. Political economy of independent Malaya, by T. H. Silcock and E. K. Fisk. Berkeley, Univ. of California Pr., 1963.

S48　SILCOCK, THOMAS HENRY. Readings in Malayan economics. Singapore, Donald Moore, 1961.

S49　SILCOCK, THOMAS HENRY. Thailand, social and economic studies in development. Canberra, Australian National UP, 1967.

S51　SINHA, KRISHNA KISHORE. Problems of defense of South and East Asia. Bombay, Manaktalas, 1969.

S53　Six perspectives on the Philippines. Edited by George M. Guthrie. Manila, Bookmark, 1968.

S58 SKINNER, GEORGE WILLIAM. Local, ethnic and national loyalties in village Indonesia, a symposium. New Haven, Yale Univ., Southeast Asia Studies, 1959.

Soc DS 503.4 Y31 no. 8

S59 Social organization and the applications of anthropology, essays in honor of Lauriston Sharp, edited by Robert J. Smith. Ithaca, Cornell UP, 1974.

Soc GN 490 S62

S61 SUDJATMOKO. Introduction to Indonesian historiography. Ithaca, Cornell UP, 1965.

Soc DS 633.8 S8

S63 Southeast Asia's economy in the 1970's. New York, Praeger, 1971.

Soc HC 412 S596

S84 STEWARD, JULIAN HAYNES. Contemporary change in traditional societies. Vol. II. Asian rural societies. Urbana, Univ. of Illinois Pr., 1967.

Soc HN 15 S835

S87 ASIAN HISTORY CONGRESS, DELHI, 1961. Studies in Asian history, proceedings. London, Indian Council for Cultural Relations, 1969.

Uar. DS 15 A8 1961b

S89 Studies in the social history of China and Southeast Asia, essays in memory of Victor Purcell. Edited by Jerome Chen and Nicholas Tarling. Cambridge, Cambridge UP, 1970.

Soc DS 703.4 S8

S90 Studies on Asia. Lincoln, Univ. of Nebraska Pr., 1960-67. *Note:* The numbers following the decimal points refer to the volumes within this series.

Soc DS 2 S8

S91 Sulu studies, I. Jolo, Notre Dame of Jolo College, 1972.

S92 Sulu studies, II. Jolo, Notre Dame of Jolo College, 1973. *Note:* Point 1 is for volume III, 1974.

S93 SYMPOSIUM ON HISTORICAL, ARCHAEOLOGICAL AND LINGUISTIC STUDIES ON SOUTHERN CHINA, SOUTH-EAST ASIA AND

THE HONG KONG REGION, UNIV. OF HONG KONG, 1961. Symposium on historical, archaeological and linguistic studies on Southern China, South-East Asia and the Hong Kong region: papers presented at meetings held in September 1961 as part of the Golden Jubilee Congress of the Univ. of Hong Kong, edited by F. S. Drake. Hong Kong, Hong Kong UP, 1967.

S96 SUN WICHAI CHAO KHAO. Tribesmen and peasants in north Thailand. Chiangmai, Tribal Research Centre, 1969.

S98 SYMPOSIUM ON THE VIETNAM WAR, EAST CAROLINA UNIVERSITY, 1968. Essays on the Vietnam war. Greenville, East Carolina Univ. Publications, 1970.

T33 In memoriam, Phya Anuman Rajadhon, contributions in memory of the late president of the Siam Society, edited by Tej Bunnag and Michael Smithies. Bangkok, Siam Society, 1970.

T45 TILMAN, ROBERT OLIVER. Man, state and society in contemporary Southeast Asia. New York, Praeger, 1969.

Uar. DS 503.4 T5 (1966 only)

T77 Translation of culture: essays to E. E. Evans-Pritchard. London, Tavistock, 1971.

Soc GN 325 T7

U77 Urbanization and national development, edited by Leo Jakobson and Ved Prakash. Beverly Hills, Sage Foundation, 1971.

Soc KT 395 A8 U7

V27 VAN NIEL, ROBERT. Economic factors in Southeast Asian social change. Honolulu, Asian Studies Program, Univ. of Hawaii, 1968.

V43 VELLA, WALTER F. Aspects of Vietnamese history. Honolulu, Univ. Pr. of Hawaii, 1973.

DS 503.4 A83 no. 8

V52 Vietnam and the Sino-Soviet dispute, edited by Robert A. Rupen and Robert Farrell. New York, Praeger, 1967.

Articles

A.S.E.A.N.

13 SOLIDUM, ESTRELLA D. An explanation of the methodology used in a dissertation entitled "The nature of cooperation among ASEAN states as perceived through elite attitudes, a factor for regionalism." AST 10 (1972) 1-5.

14 TAN, AUGUSTINE H. H. ASEAN in perspective and the role of Singapore. Y52 pp. 370-385.

15 UDOM KERDPIBULE. The prospects for manufacturing exports of ASEAN countries, an exploratory study. MER 19 pt. 2 (1974) 21-46.

16 VAN DER KROEF, JUSTUS M. ASEAN's security needs and policies. PA 47 (1974) 154-170.

A.S.P.A.C.

17 CHOI, CHONG-KI. Problems related to economic integration in the ASPAC region. AQ (1974) 83-104.

18 HUNSBERGER, WARREN S. Economic cooperation/integration in the ASPAC and ASEAN areas. AQ (1974) 121-146.

ABADILLA, ALEJANDRO G.

19 RICARTE, PEDRO L. Alejandro G. Abadilla. PS 18 (1970) 323-349.

ABBREVIATIONS - BURMESE

20 HLA PE. Abbreviations, cryptograms and chronograms in Burmese. JBRS 47 (Dec. 1964) 385-396.

ABBREVIATIONS - INDONESIA

21 VRIES, J. W. DE. Indonesian abbreviations and acronyms. BIJ 126 (1970) 338-346.

ABUEVA, N. VELOSO

22 MORENO, VIRGINIA R. Poet's celebration of N. Veloso Abueva's *Play things and house of things*. GEJ 4 (1962) 81-84.

Academic exercises *See* DISSERTATIONS, ACADEMIC

ACCOUNTING - PHILIPPINES

23 GAROY, GABINO L. Problems that beset the accountancy practice in Baguio. SLURJ 5 (1974) 392-417.

ACHEH

24 BOXER, C. R. Achinese attack on Malacca in 1629, as described in contemporary Portuguese sources. B38 pp. 105-121.

25 BOXER, C. R. Note on Portuguese reactions to the revival of the Red Sea spice trade and the rise of Atjeh, 1540-1600. JSAH 10 (1969) 415-428.

26 COWAN, H. K. J. La legende de Samudra. AR 5 (1973) 253-286.

27 DREWES, G. W. J. Atjehse douanetarieven in het begin van de vorige eeuw. BIJ 119 (1963) 406-411.

28 DREWES, G. W. J. Nur al-Din al-Raniri's *Hujjat al-Siddiq Li-Daf al-Zindiq* reexamined. JMBRAS 47 pt. 2 (1974) 83-104.

29   ECHOLS, JOHN M. Notes on materials for the study of Atjeh in the Cornell University Library. IND 1 (1966) 124-130.

30   KATHIRITHAMBY-WELLS, J. Achehnese control over west Sumatra up to the treaty of Painan, 1663. JSAH 10 (1969) 453-479.

31   LEE KAM HING. Foreigners in the' Achehnese court, 1760-1819. JMBRAS 43 pt. 1 (1970) 64-86.

32   PENTH, HANS. Zum Verhaltnis Sayam-Atjeh im 17. Jahrhundert. JSS 57 (1969) 355-359.

33   PUVANARAJAH, T. Acheh treaty of 1819. JSAH 2 (Oct. 1961) 36-46.

34   REID, ANTHONY. The French in Sumatra and the Malay world, 1760-1890. BIJ 129 (1973) 195-238.

35   REID, ANTHONY. Habib Abdur-Rahman az-Zahir, 1833-1896. IND 13 (1972) 36-59.

36   REID, ANTHONY. Indonesian diplomacy, a documentary study of Atjehnese foreign policy in the reign of Sultan Mahmud, 1870-4. JMBRAS 42 pt. 2 (1969) 74-114.

37   SIEGEL, JAMES. Prayer and play in Atjeh, a comment on two photographs. IND 1 (1966) 1-21.

ACHINESE LANGUAGE

38   COLLINS, VAUGHN. Position of Atjehnese among Southeast Asian languages. M59 pp. 48-59.

39   COWAN, H. K. J. Atjehs Bhu, Buga. BIJ 119 (1963) 401-405.

40   DREWES, G. W. J. De invloed van de Atjehse omgeving op het Maleise spraeck ende woordboek van Frederick de Houtman. BIJ 128 (1972) 447-457.

ACRONYMS - INDONESIAN

41   VRIES, J. W. DE. Indonesian abbreviations and acronyms. BIJ 126 (1970) 338-346.

ADAT LAW - BRUNEI

42   IBRAHIM BIN MOHD. JAHFAR. Brunei adat. BMJ 1 (1969) 5-9.

ADAT LAW - INDONESIA

43   ALISJAHBANA, S. TAKDIR. Customary law and modernization in Indonesia. C39 pp. 3-16.

44   DJOJODIGOENO, M. M. Naar aanleiding van ter Haar's dies-rede van 1937. BIJ 128 (1972) 235-256.

45   KOESNOE, MOH. Receptie van de Radjam straf in de adat Sasak van Bajan. BIJ 126 (1970) 203-214.

46   STEENHOVEN, G. VAN DEN. Research on adat law in Indonesia. P15 pp. 162-165.

47   TANNER, NANCY. Disputing and dispute settlement among the Minangkabau of Indonesia. IND 8 (1969) 21-67.

48   TAUFIK ABDULLAH. Adat and Islam, an examination of conflict in Minangkabau. IND 2 (1966) 1-24.

69 ACHUTEGUI, PEDRO S. DE. Brent, Herzog, Morayta and Aglipay, by Pedro S. de Achutegui and Miguel A. Bernad. PS 8 (1960) 568-583.

70 CHANDLEE, H. ELLSWORTH. Liturgy of the Philippine Church. A58 pp. 256-276.

71 CLIFFORD, MARY DORITA. Iglesia Filipina Independiente, the revolutionary church. A58 pp. 223-255.

72 CRUZ, ROMEO V. Founding of the Aglipayan Church, an appraisal. PSSHR 26 (1961) 187-212.

73 POETHIG, RICHARD P. Philippine Independent Church, the agony of Philippine nationalism. SJ 14 (1967) 27-54.

74 SCOTT, WILLIAM HENRY. The Philippine Independent Church in history. SJ 10 (1963) 298-310.

75 VACAS, FELIX. Aglipayanism unmasked. UN 34 (1961) 227-263.

76 VICTORIANO, ENRIQUE L. What Aglipayans believe. PS 8 (1960) 292-299.

AGRICULTURAL RITES

77 JOSSELIN DE JONG, P. E. DE. Interpretation of agricultural rites in Southeast Asia, with a demonstration of use of data from both continental and insular areas. JAS 24 (1964-5) 283-291.
Comment: CONDOMINAS, GEORGES. Commentaires sur l'etude du Professor P. E. de Josselin de Jong. JAS 24 (1964-5) 291-293.
Comment: GEERTZ, HILDRED. Comment. JAS 24 (1964-5) 294-297.
Author's reply: JAS 24 (1964-5) 297-8.

AGRICULTURAL RITES - BRUNEI

78 SHARIFFUDDIN, P. M. Makan tahun, the annual feast of the Kedayans. BMJ 2 pt. 1 (1970) 61-66.

AGRICULTURAL RITES - CAMBODIA

79 CHANDLER, DAVID P. Royally sponsored human sacrifices in nineteenth century Cambodia, the cult of Nak ta Me Sa (Mahisasuramardini) at Ba Phnom. JSS 62 pt. 2 (1974) 207-222.

AGRICULTURAL RITES - INDONESIA

80 GRADER, C. J. Balang Tamak. B19 pp. 175-188.

AGRICULTURAL RITES - LAOS

81 ARCHAIMBAULT, C. Les rites pour l'obtention de la pluie a Luong Prabeng, observes en juillet 1954. SEIB 43 (1968) 200-217.

AGRICULTURAL RITES - MALAYSIA - SARAWAK

82 GALVIN, A. D. Kenyah farming year. SMJ 19 (1971) 185-235.

83 GILL, SARAH. Style and the demonic image in Dayak masks. JMBRAS 40 pt. 1 (1967) 78-92.

84 MAPING MADANG. Adat Suen, Sebob graded rites, by Maping Madang and A. D. Galvin. SMJ 13 (1966) 305-320.

85 MULOK KEDIT, PETER. Gawai Ngemali Umai, or Iban rite for padi protection. SMJ 18 (1970) 165-168.

Agricultural rites - Malaysia - Sarawak

86 NYANDOH, R. Gawai Birantu, a ceremony to remove pests from the padi field. SMJ 16 (1968) 199-208.

87 SANDIN, BENEDICT. Gawai Batu, the Iban whetstone feast. SMJ 11 (1962) 392-408.

AGRICULTURAL RITES - THAILAND

88 ANUMAN RAJADHON. Fertility rites in Thailand. JSS 48 pt. 2 (1960) 37-42.

AGRICULTURAL RITES - VIETNAM

89 LEGAY, ROGER. Prierer Lac accompagnant les rites agraires, par Roger Legay et K'Mloi Da Got. SEIB 46 (1971) 111-213.

AGRICULTURE *See also* IRRIGATION, PEASANTRY, CASSAVA, COCONUT, CORN, JUTE, OIL PALM INDUSTRY, PEANUTS, PEPPER, RICE, RUBBER INDUSTRY, SUGAR INDUSTRY, SWEET POTATOES, SWINE, TOBACCO

90 BELL, PETER F. Markets, middlemen and technology, agricultural supply response in the dualistic economies of Southeast Asia, by Peter F. Bell and Janet Tai. MER 14 pt. 1 (1969) 29-47.

91 DENEVAN, W. M. Forms, functions and associations of raised fields in the old world tropics, by W. M. Denevan and B. L. Turner. JTG 39 (1974) 24-33.

92 HARRIS, MARVIN. How green the revolution? JCA 2 (1972) 446-448.

93 JACOBY, ERICH H. Effects of the green revolution in South and South-East Asia. MAS 6 (1972) 63-69.

94 KLATT, W. Reflections on agricultural modernisation in Asia. PA 46 (1973) 534-547.

95 MALENBAUM, WILFRED. Progress through the rich or poor farmer, case studies in Asia. AS 8 (1968) 149-156.

96 RIEMENS, HENDRIK. Hot Springs conference and agriculture in Southeast Asia. H57 pp. 283-285.

97 SATO, TAKASHI. Problems in field crop production. AS 8 (1968) 829-835.

98 SHAND, R. T. Perspectives on Asia. S42 pp. 313-325.

99 WALTERS, HARRY. Green revolution in Southeast Asia in the 1970's, by Harry Walters and Joseph Willett. S63 pp. 108-183.

100 WATABE, TADAYO. Increasing the rice yield in South and Southeast Asia, by Tadayo Watabe and Keizaburo Kawaguchi. AS 8 (1968) 820-828.

AGRICULTURE - BRUNEI

101 CRAIN, JAY B. Mengalong Lun Dayeh agricultural organisation. BMJ 3 pt. 1 (1973) 1-25.

102 LIM, J. S. Short account of sago production in Kuala Balai, Belait. BMJ 3 pt. 2 (1974) 144-155.

AGRICULTURE - BURMA

103 FURNIVALL, JOHN SYDENHAM. Industrial agriculture. JBRS 48 (June 1965) 87-97.

104 LUBEIGT, G. L'introduction d'une nouvelle culture dans un etate socialiste, la cas du jute en Birmanie. SA 3 (1974) 842-879.

105 RICHTER, H. V. State agricultural credit in postwar Burma. MER 13 pt. 1 (1968) 101-117.

106 RICHTER, H. V. Union of Burma. S42 pp. 140-180.

107 SAW WIN. Statistical analysis of farm size and current expenditures. JBRS 48 (June 1965) 57-76.

108 STARGARDT, JANICE. Government and irrigation in Burma, a comparative survey. AST 6 (1968) 358-371.

AGRICULTURE - CAMBODIA

109 GARRY, ROBERT J. Changing fortunes and future of pepper growing in Cambodia. JTG 17 (1963) 133-142.

110 VIDAL, J. E. Notes ethnobotaniques sur quelques plantes en usage au Cambodge, par J. E. Vidal, G. Martel, et S. Lewitz. BEF 55 (1969) 171-232.

AGRICULTURE - INDONESIA

111 BAKKER, S. On livestock and the veterinary service in the Netherlands Indies. H57 pp. 1-4.

112 BRAND, W. Some statistical data on Indonesia. BIJ 125 (1969) 305-327.

113 FRANKE, RICHARD W. Miracle seeds and shattered dreams in Java. JCA 4 (1974) 381-388.

114 FRICKERS, J. On veterinary science and practice in the Netherlands Indies, by J. Frickers, C. H. Haasjes, and H. Preston Hoskin. H57 pp. 123-126.

115 FRUIN, TH. A. Over population and the emancipation of the village. J32 pp. 331-343.

116 HANSEN, GARY E. Indonesia's green revolution, the abandonment of a non-market strategy toward change. AS 12 (1972) 932-946.

117 HANSEN, GARY E. Rural administration and agricultural development in Indonesia. PA 44 (1971) 390-400.

118 HONIG, PIETER. Agriculture in the Netherlands Indies. H57 pp. 175-180.

119 MACKIE, J. A. C. Indonesia's government estates and their masters. PA 34 (1961) 337-360.

120 MEARS, LEON A. Suggestions for agricultural strategy. J37 pp. 37-52.

121 MILES, DOUGLAS. Note on shifting cultivation and settlement. JSS 55 (1967) 93-99.

122 PELZER, KARL J. The agricultural foundation. G52 pp. 128-161.

123 PENNY, DAVID H. Agro-economic survey of Indonesia, an appreciation. IND 11 (1971) 111-130.

124 PENNY, DAVID H. Indonesia. S42 pp. 251-279.

125 RIEFFEL, ALEXIS. Bimas program for self-sufficiency in rice production. IND 8 (1969) 103-133.

Agriculture - Indonesia

126 THOMAS, KENNETH D. Shifting cultivation and smallholder rubber production in a south Sumatran village. MER 10 pt. 1 (1965) 100-115.

127 TOJIB HADIWIDJAJA. New trends in agricultural development programs in Indonesia. J37 pp. 19-27. *Comment:* ALLEE, RALPH H. Comments. J37 pp. 28-32.

128 VAN NIEL, ROBERT. Function of landrent under the cultivation system in Java. JAS 23 (1963-4) 357-375.

129 VERDOORN, FRANS. Card index of war-time literature on tropical agriculture of interest to the Netherlands Indies. H57 p. 465.

AGRICULTURE - LAOS

130 COWARD, E. WALTER. Agrarian modernization and village leadership: irrigation leaders in Laos. AF 3 (1971) 158-163.

AGRICULTURE - MALAYSIA

131 AGARWAL, M. C. Account of the Tanjong Karang project. MER 9 pt. 2 (1964) 64-74.

132 BHATI, U. N. Farmers' technical knowledge and income, a case study of padi farmers of west Malaysia. MER 18 pt. 1 (1973) 36-47.

133 FISK, E. K. Establishment costs of small rice farms, an analytical model of returns to capital. MER 7 pt. 2 (1962) 45-63.

134 FISK, E. K. Malaysia. S42 pp. 181-214.

135 FISK, E. K. Mechanisation of agricultural smallholdings in underdeveloped areas. MER 6 pt. 2 (1961) 53-60.

136 HILL, R. D. Pepper growing in Johore. JTG 28 (1969) 32-39.

137 HO, ROBERT. Evolution of agriculture and land ownership in Saiong Mukim. MER 13 pt. 2 (1968) 81-102.

138 HO, ROBERT. Mixed farming and multiple cropping in Malaya. JTG 16 (1962) 1-17.

139 JACKSON, JAMES C. Chinese agricultural pioneering in Singapore and Johore, 1800-1917. JMBRAS 38 pt. 1 (1965) 77-105.

140 PURCAL, J. Labour utilization among men in a padi village in Province Wellesley. MER 10 pt. 2 (1965) 49-60.

141 TREGONNING, K. G. Early land administration and agricultural development of Penang. JMBRAS 39 pt. 2 (1966) 34-49.

142 WEE, Y. C. Development of pineapple cultivation in west Malaysia. JTG 30 (1970) 68-75.

AGRICULTURE - MALAYSIA - SARAWAK

143 DUNSMORE, J. R. Review of agricultural research in Sarawak. SMJ 16 (1968) 309-339.

144 HOWES, PETER. Why some of the best people aren't Christian. SMJ 9 (1960) 488-495.

145 LEE, Y. L. Agriculture in Sarawak. JTG 21 (1965) 21-29.

146 MORRIS, H. S. In the wake of mechanization, sago and society in Sarawak. S58 pp. 273-301.

147 SANDIN, BENEDICT. Simpulang or Pulang Gana, the founder of Dayak agriculture. SMJ 15 (1967) 245-406.

AGRICULTURE - PHILIPPINES

148 An analysis of the programming behavior of vegetable farmers in the Province of Benguet, by Fernando D. Bahatan, Henry Bahingawan, Peter M. Cosalan and Alberto R. Tejano. SLURJ 1 (1970) 503-580.

149 BARNETT, MILTON L. Subsistence and transition of agricultural development among the Ibaloi. Z16 pp. 299-323.

150 BERAN, GEORGE. Diseases common to animals and man, a general review with emphasis on the Philippine situation. SJ 12 (1965) 4-93.

151 BUEN, FLORENCIO. The green revolution school for farmers, a proposal. SLURJ 4 (1973) 351-366.

152 CASTILLO, GELIA T. Education for agriculture. MER 16 pt. 2 (1971) 172-193.

153 COVAR, PROSPERO. Masagana/Margate system of planting rice, a study of an agricultural innovation. E78 pp. 613-621.

154 FONOLLERA, RAYMUNDO E. Labor intensity in Philippine agriculture. C47 pp. 493-496.

155 FUJIMOTO, ISAO. Some considerations on a cultural majority, the Filipino farmer and agricultural development. Z16 pp. 343-365.

156 GARILAO, ERNESTO. AECD on rural and agricultural development. PS 19 (1971) 27-33.
Comment: FLAVIER, JUAN. Comments. PS 19 (1971) 33-4.
Comment: TANCO, ARTURO. Comments. PS 19 (1971) 34-36.

157 GUTIERREZ, JOSE S. Agricultural productivity and population increase, the Philippine case. C47 pp. 469-492.

158 HERBOLARIO, ALFRED JOSE J. Investing in rabbitry, a sound financial decision. SLURJ 2 (1971) 41-51.

159 HOOLEY, RICHARD. The Philippines, by Richard Hooley and Vernon W. Ruttan. S42 pp. 215-250.

160 KELLMAN, M. C. Some environmental components of shifting cultivation in upland Mindanao. JTG 28 (1969) 40-56.

161 New rice technology and labor absorption in Philippine agriculture. MER 16 pt. 2 (1971) 117-158.

162 ONG, MARIA LUISA. Proximate chemical composition and nitrogen partition of soya bean seeds from several strains of plants grown in the Philippines. UN 33 (1960) 285-339.

163 OPPENFELD, HORST. Labor force and utilization, by Horst and Judith Oppenfeld. E78 pp. 44-53.

164 ORACION, TIMOTEO S. Kaingin agriculture among the Bukidnons of southeastern Negros, central Philippines. E78 pp. 233-249.

165 ORACION, TIMOTEO S. Kaingin agriculture among the Bukidnons of

Agriculture - Philippines

south-eastern Negros, Philippines. JTG 17 (1963) 213-224.

166 PAL, AGATON P. Extension processes. E78 pp. 505-518.

167 SALAMANCA, BONIFACIO S. Background and early beginnings of the encomienda in the Philippines. PSSHR 26 (1961) 67-86.

168 SUTER, DWAYNE. Technological problems of the Cagayan Valley and their possible solution. SJ 11 (1964) 76-83.

169 SYCIP, FELICIDAD C. Factors related to acceptance or rejection of innovations. E78 pp. 593-611.

170 VANDERMEER, CANUTE. Corn cultivation on Cebu, an example of an advanced stage of migratory farming. JTG 17 (1963) 172-177.

AGRICULTURE - SINGAPORE

171 JACKSON, JAMES C. Chinese agricultural pioneering in Singapore and Johore, 1800-1917. JMBRAS 38 pt. 1 (1965) 77-105.

AGRICULTURE - THAILAND

172 BEHRMAN, JERE R. Significance of intracountry variations for Asian agricultural prospects, central and northern Thailand. AS 8 (1968) 157-173.

173 BERTRAND, TRENT J. Rural taxation in Thailand. PA 42 (1969) 178-188.

174 JUDD, LAURENCE C. Agricultural economy of the hills and adjacent areas: the hill Thai. S96 pp. 87-92.

175 MILES, DOUGLAS. Shifting cultivation, threats and prospects. S96 pp. 93-99.

176 MIZUNO, KOICHI. Multihousehold compounds in northeast Thailand. AS 8 (1968) 842-852.

177 SILCOCK, T. H. The rice premium and agricultural diversification. S49 pp. 231-257.

178 SILCOCK, T. H. Thailand. S42 pp. 103-139.

179 SMITH, HELEN L. Suan Sema, an illustration of changes and trends in Thai vegetable production. JSS 57 (1969) 339-348.

180 WIJEYEWARDENE, GEHAN. Note on irrigation and agriculture in a north Thai village. F38 pp. 255-259.

AGRICULTURE - VIETNAM

181 DUMONT, RENE. Problems agricoles au nord-Vietnam. FA 20 (1965) 41-60.

182 DUMONT, RENE. Problems agricoles en Republique Democratique du Vietnam. C28 pp. 385-412.

183 GORDON, ALEC. Green revolution in north Vietnam. JCA 4 (1974) 128-133.

184 LOGAN, WILLIAM J. C. How deep is the green revolution in south Vietnam, the story of the agricultural turn around in south Vietnam. AS 11 (1971) 321-330.

185 NGUYEN KHAC NHAN. Policy of key rural aggrovilles. AC 3 (July 1961) 29-49.

186 NGUYEN KHAC VIEN. L'eau, le riz, les hommes. C28 pp. 413-459.

187 TEULIERES, ROGER. L'arachide au sud Vietnam. SEIB 37 (1962) 435-463.

188 TEULIERES, ROGER. Une culture nourriciere importante au Viet-Nam, la patote douce, par Roger Teulieres et Vinh Dao. SEIB 39 (1964) 307-320.

189 TEULIERES, ROGER. Economie du manioc au sud Vietnam. SEIB 38 (1963) 559-579.

190 TEULIERES, ROGER. Les plantations de cocotiers au sud Vietnam. SEIB 39 (1964) 19-50.

191 TEULIERES, ROGER. Le riz au Viet-Nam. SEIB 41 (1966) 121-147.

192 TEULIERES, ROGER. Le tabac au Viet-Nam du sud. SEIB 40 (1965) 319-336.

193 THAI CONG TUNG. Ouvrages sur l'agriculture. SEIB 46 (1971) 396-7.

AGUILAR, FAUSTINO

194 GLORIOSO, PABLO R. Si Faustino Aguilar sa tradisyon ng nobelang Tagalog. PS 19 (1971) 307-320.

AGUINALDO, EMILIO

195 EPISTOLA, S. V. Hong Kong junta. PSSHR 26 (1961) 3-65.

196 JESUS, EDILBERTO C. DE. Aguinaldo and the American consuls. PHR 1 pt. 2 (1966) 125-167.

AGUSAN

197 FRANCISCO, JUAN R. Golden image of Agusan, a new identification. AST 1 (1963) 31-38.

198 FRANCISCO, JUAN R. Note on the golden image of Agusan. PS 11 (1963) 390-400.

199 FRANCISCO, JUAN R. Notes on the Indo-Philippine images. Z16 pp. 117-127.

200 MEULEN, W. J. VAN DER. Agusan image. PS 12 (1964) 347.

AHMAD SHAH IBN ISKANDAR

201 KATHIRITHAMBY-WELLS, J. Ahmad Shah ibn Iskandar and the late 17th century holy war in Indonesia. JMBRAS 43 pt. 1 (1970) 48-63.

AICHELE, WALTHER

202 In memoriam Walther Aichele, 27 Januari 1889-1 Mei 1971. BIJ 128 (1972) 209-213.

AIKMAN, GORDON

203 Obituary, Gordon Aikman. SMJ 11 (1962) xv-xvi.

AIMOL

204 NEEDHAM, RODNEY. Structural analysis of Aimol society. BIJ 116 (1960) 81-108.

Airlines - Philippines

222 SINGARAVELU, S. Note on the possible relationship of King Rama Khamhaeng's Sukhodaya script of Thailand to the Grantha script of south India. JSS 57 (1969) 1-28.

ALZINA, FRANCISCO IGNACIO DE

223 HESTER, EVETT D. Alzina's *Historia de Visayas*, a bibliographical note. PS 10 (1962) 331-365.

224 LIETZ, PAUL S. More about Alzina's *Historia de Visayas*. PS 10 (1962) 366-375.

225 RIXHON, GERALD. Parte natural of Alzina's manuscript of 1668, a source of anthropological data. AST 6 (1968) 183-197.

AMIR HAMZAH

226 JOHNS, A. H. Amir Hamzah, Malay prince, Indonesian poet. B38 pp. 303-319.

AMBOYNA MASSACRE

227 BASSETT, D. K. The Amboyna massacre of 1623. JSAH 1 (Sept. 1960) 1-19.

Ancestry *See* GENEALOGY

ANDERSON, CHARLES MARTIN

228 Obituary, Mr. Charles Martin Anderson. JSS 49 pt. 2 (1961) 190.

ANDERSON, JOHN

229 BASTIN, JOHN. Introduction. JMBRAS 35 pt. 4 (1965) 1-10.

ANGELES, CARLOS A.

230 ABAD, GEMINO H. Two poems in Carlos A. Angeles, *An experiment toward a poetics of the lyric poem*. AST 10 (1972) 344-360.

ANGKOR *See also* TEMPLES - CAMBODIA

231 CHANDLER, DAVID P. Eighteenth century inscription from Angkor Wat. JSS 59 pt. 2 (1971) 151-159.

232 DELVERT, JEAN. Recherches sur l'erosion des gres des monuments d'Angkor. BEF 51 (1963) 453-534.

233 DUMARCAY, J. Le Prasat Prei pres d'Angkor Vat. BEF 59 (1972) 189-192.

234 GROSLIER, BERNARD PHILIPPE. Danse et musique sous les rois d'Angkor. F38 pp. 283-292.

235 LEWITZ, SAVEROS. Inscriptions modernes d'Angkor, 1, 8, et 9. BEF 59 (1972) 101-121.

236 LEWITZ, SAVEROS. Inscriptions modernes d'Angkor, 4, 5, 6, et 7. BEF 58 (1971) 105-123.

237 LEWITZ, SAVEROS. Inscriptions modernes d'Angkor, 10, 11, 12, 13, 14, 15, 16a, 16b, et 16c. BEF 59 (1972) 221-249.

238 LEWITZ, SAVEROS. Inscriptions modernes d'Angkor, 17, 18, 19, 20, 21, 22, 23, 24, et 25. BEF 60 (1973) 163-203.

239 LEWITZ, SAVEROS. Inscriptions modernes d'Angkor, 26, 27, 28, 29, 30, 31, 32, 33. BEF 60 (1973) 205-242.

Angkor

240 MALLERET, LOUIS. Histoire abregee de l'archeologie indochinoise jusqu'a a 1950. AP 12 (1969) 43-68.

241 MALLERET, LOUIS. Maurice Glaize, 1886-1964. BEF 53 (1966) 311-330.

242 MALLERET, LOUIS. Note sur la paillote qui fut le premier immeuble de la conservation d'Angkor. SEIB 40 (1965) 203-4.

243 MARCHAL, HENRI. Notes au sujet de la ville d'Angkor Thom et de la place centrale devant le palais du roi. SEIB 36 (1961) 691-698.

244 MUS, PAUL. Angkor vu du Japon. FA 18 (1962) 521-538.

245 MUS, PAUL. Le sourire d'Angkor, art, foi et politique bouddhiques sous Jayavarman VII. G83 pp. 363-381.

ANIMISM **

246 JOSSELIN DE JONG, P. E. DE. Interpretation of agricultural rites in Southeast Asia, with a demonstration of use of data from both continental and insular areas. JAS 24 (1964-5) 283-291.
Comment: CONDOMINAS, GEORGE. Commentaires sur l'etude du Professor P. E. de Josselin de Jong. JAS 24 (1964-5) 291-293.
Comment: GEERTZ, HILDRED. Comment. JAS 24 (1964-5) 294-297.
Author's reply: JAS 24 (1964-5) 297-8.

ANIMISM - BURMA

247 BA HAN. Spiritism in Burma. JBRS 47 (1964) 3-9.

248 BROHM, JOHN. Buddhism and animism in a Burmese village. JAS 22 (1962-3) 155-167.

249 NASH, JUNE C. Living with nats, an analysis of animism in Burman village social relations. C66 pp. 117-136.

250 SHORTO, H. L. Dewatau Sotopan, a Mon prototype of the 37 nats. SOAS 30 (1967) 127-141.

ANIMISM - LAOS

251 ARCHAIMBAULT, CHARLES. Le liang du Ho Devata Luong a Luong Prabang. SEIB 46 (1971) 215-285.

252 CONDOMINAS, GEORGES. Phiban cults in rural Laos. C24 pp. 252-273.

253 MORECHAND, GUY. Le chamanisme des Hmong. BEF 54 (1968) 53-294.

ANIMISM - MALAYSIA - SABAH

254 NYANDOH, R. Origin of the Guna-Ba-ak Laba wild boar charm. SMJ 17 (1969) 153-4.

ANIMISM - MALAYSIA - SARAWAK

255 JENSEN, ERIK. Iban world, an introduction to the Iban religious view of life and the place of writing therein. SMJ 13 (1966) 1-31.

256 NYANDOH, R. King of Stone, a Land Dayak God of Sarawak and Kalimantan. SMJ 11 (1962) 390-1.

257 SHARIFFUDDIN, P. M. Melanau spirit figures. BMJ 2 pt. 1 (1970) 104-113.

ARTICLES

ANIMISM - PHILIPPINES **

258 BULATAO, JAIME C. Case study of a Quezon City poltergeist. PS 16 (1968) 178-188.

259 DEMETRIO, FRANCISCO. Engkanto belief, an essay in interpretation. PS 17 (1969) 586-596.

260 HISLOP, STEPHEN K. Anitism, a survey of religious beliefs native to the Philippines. AST 9 (1971) 144-156.

261 SCOTT, WILLIAM HENRY. Some religious terms in Sagada Igorot. Z16 pp. 480-493.

ANIMISM - THAILAND

262 ANUMAN RAJADHON. Khwan and its ceremonies. JSS 50 (1962) 119-164.

263 ANUMAN RAJADHON. Some Siamese superstitions about trees and plants. JSS 49 pt. 2 (1961) 57-63.

264 ANUMAN RAJADHON. Thai charms and amulets. JSS 52 (1964) 171-197.

265 PIKER, STEVEN. Relationship of belief systems to behavior in rural Thai society. AS 8 (1968) 384-399.

266 SANGUAN CHOTISUKHARAT. Supernatural beliefs and practices in Chiengmai. JSS 59 pt. 1 (1971) 211-231.

267 VELDER, CHRISTIAN. Chao Luang Muak Kham, the royal master with the golden crown, report on the forest spirit of Ban Saliem. JSS 51 (1963) 85-92.

ANIMISM - VIETNAM

268 BOULBET, JEAN. Borde au rendez-vous des genies (tac nang yo bon borde), un sacrifice de buffles dans un village Montagnard du Haut Donnai, tribu des Ma. SEIB 35 (1960) 627-650.

269 MORECHAND, GUY. Le chamanisme des Hmong. BEF 54 (1968) 53-294.

ANIRUDDHA, KING OF BURMA

270 LUCE, G. H. Foreign relations of King Aniruddha. S87 pp. 260-276.

ANTHROPOLOGY *See also* VILLAGE STUDIES

ANTHROPOLOGY - INDONESIA

271 KOENTJARANINGRAT. Use of anthropological methods in Indonesian historiography. S61 pp. 299-325.

ANTHROPOLOGY - PHILIPPINES

272 ANG, GERTRUDES R. Dr. H. Otley Beyer, pioneer in Philippine anthropology. D67 pp. 5-11.

273 ANTONIO, CELIA M. Anthropology in the Philippines, a directory. GEJ 12 (1966) 303-311.

274 BAILEN, JEROME B. Studies in physical anthropology of the Philippines. Z16 pp. 527-558.

275 EGGAN, FRED. Applied anthropology in the Mountain Province, Philippines. S58 pp. 196-209.

276 HOLLNSTEINER, MARY RACELIS. The study of society, a perspective from sociology and anthropology. PS 21 (1973) 455-462.

Anuman Rajadhon

ARAKANESE LANGUAGE

292 BERNOT, DENISE. Vowel systems of
     Arakanese and Tavoyan. C44 pp.
     463–474.

293 SPRIGG, R. K. Comparison of Ara-
     kanese and Burmese based on phono-
     logical formulae. L55 pp. 109–
     132.

ARAKANESE LITERATURE

294 COLLIS, M. S. Arakanese poem of
     the 16th century. B92 pp. 35–42.

ARCHAEOLOGY *See also* GLASS, GOLD,
  INSCRIPTIONS, MEGALITHIC MONUMENTS,
  PALEOGRAPHY, POTTERY

295 CHRISTIE, A. H. Some writings on
     South East Asian prehistory. H18
     pp. 107–120.

296 DUFF, ROGER. Neolithic adzes with
     differentiated butt in South Chi-
     na, South-East Asia and Polynesia.
     S93 pp. 1–14.

297 GLOVER, I. C. London colloquy on
     early South East Asia. AR 7
     (1974) 15–18.

298 HARRISSON, TOM. Puzzling waisted
     stones, from Borneo to Easter
     Island? SMJ 18 (1970) 79–88.

299 JANSE, O. Notes on some complex
     problems raised by excavations in
     South-East Asia. S93 pp. 26–28.

300 JANSE, O. Prehistory and proto-
     history of eastern India and Indo-
     china. FA 17 (1960) 2215–2217.

301 KAHLKE, H. D. Review of the pleis-
     tocene history of the Orang-Utan
     (Pongo Lacepede, 1799). AP 15
     (1972) 5–14.

302 KANEKO, ERIKA. Robert von Heine-
     Geldern, 1885–1968. AP 13 (1970)
     1–10.

303 LAMB, ALASTAIR. Some observations
     on stone and glass beads in early
     Southeast Asia. JMBRAS 38 pt. 2
     (1965) 87–124.

304 LOOFS, H. H. E. Funanese cultural
     elements in the lower Menam basin.
     JOSA 8 (1971) 5–8.

305 MALLERET, LOUIS. Notes archeo-
     logiques. BEF 51 (1963) 99–
     124.

306 MATTHEWS, J. M. Review of the
     Hoabinhian in Indo-China. AP 9
     (1966) 86–95.

307 PERICOURT, M. Observations ar-
     chaeologiques aeriennes. BEF 50
     (1960) 519–527.

308 SOLHEIM, WILHELM G. Eastern Asia
     and Oceania. AP 8 (1964) 1–9.

309 SOLHEIM, WILHELM G. Formosan re-
     lationships with Southeast Asia.
     AP 7 (1963) 251–260.

310 SOLHEIM, WILHELM G. New look of
     Southeast Asian prehistory. JSS
     60 pt. 1 (1972) 1–20.

311 SOLHEIM, WILHELM G. Northern
     Thailand, Southeast Asia, and
     world prehistory. AP 13 (1970)
     145–162.

312 SOLHEIM, WILHELM G. Prehistoric
     archaeology in eastern mainland
     Southeast Asia and the Philip-
     pines. AP 13 (1970) 47–58.

313 SOLHEIM, WILHELM G. Southeast
     Asia. AP 4 (1960) 55.

Archaeology

314   SOLHEIM, WILHELM G.   Southeast
      Asia.   AP 6 (1962) 21-31.

315   SOLHEIM, WILHELM G.   Southeast
      Asia.   AP 9 (1966) 27-31.

316   SOLHEIM, WILHELM G.   Southeast
      Asian regional organization in
      archaeology.   AP 17 (1974) 5-24.

317   TREISTMAN, JUDITH M.   Problems in
      contemporary Asian archeology.
      JAS 29 (1969-70) 363-371.

ARCHAEOLOGY - BRUNEI

318   HARRISSON, BARBARA.   Classifica-
      tion of archaeological trade ce-
      ramics from Kota Batu, Brunei.
      BMJ 2 pt. 1 (1970) 114-188.

319   HARRISSON, TOM.   Carbon-14 dates
      from Kota Batu, Brunei, Borneo.
      AP 16 (1973) 197-199.

320   HARRISSON, TOM.   Deep level carbon
      dates from Kota Batu, Brunei. BMJ
      2 pt. 3 (1971) 96-107.

321   HARRISSON, TOM.   East Malaysia and
      Brunei.   AP 10 (1967) 85-92.

322   HARRISSON, TOM.   First radio car-
      bon test dates from Kota Batu,
      Brunei and associated dating prob-
      lems in Borneo.   BMJ 2 pt. 1
      (1970) 189-197.

323   HARRISSON, TOM.   Further radio
      carbon (C-14) dates from Kota
      Batu, Brunei, back to 12,500 B.C.
      BMJ 2 pt. 4 (1972) 209-218.

324   HARRISSON, TOM.   Golden hoard of
      Limbang.   BMJ 1 (1969) 57-71.

325   HARRISSON, TOM.   Missing Brunei
      stone age.   BMJ 2 pt. 3 (1971)
      81-88.

326   HARRISSON, TOM.   Palaeolithic,
      stone age, studies in Borneo and
      adjacent islands, a new review.
      BMJ 3 pt. 2 (1974) 235-252.

327   HARRISSON, TOM.   Prehistoric glass
      analyses for Brunei.   BMJ 3 pt. 2
      (1974) 232-234.

328   HARRISSON, TOM.   Radio carbon,
      C-14, dates from Kota Batu, Brunei
      back to 12,500 B.C.   JMBRAS 45 pt.
      1 (1972) 111-115.

329   HARRISSON, TOM.   Radio-carbon
      dates for Sabah and Brunei, re-
      lated to Sarawak.   SMJ 19 (1971)
      363-366.

330   HARRISSON, TOM.   Recent archaeo-
      logical discoveries in Malaysia,
      1965, east Malaysia and Brunei.
      JMBRAS 39 pt. 1 (1966) 191-197.

331   HARRISSON, TOM.   Recent archaeo-
      logical discoveries in east
      Malaysia and Brunei.   JMBRAS 40
      pt. 1 (1967) 140-148.

332   HARRISSON, TOM.   Recent archaeo-
      logical discoveries in Malaysia,
      1967, east Malaysia and Brunei.
      JMBRAS 41 pt. 1 (1968) 180-182.

333   TATE, R. B.   Radiocarbon ages from
      quaternary terraces, prehistory in
      Brunei.   BMJ 2 pt. 3 (1971) 108-
      123.

ARCHAEOLOGY - BURMA

334   AUNG THAW.   Neolithic culture of
      the Padah-Lin caves.   AP 14 (1971)
      123-133.

335   AUNG THAW.   Neolithic culture of
      the Padah-Lin caves.   JBRS 52
      (June 1969) 9-23.

336   AUNG THAW. Union of Burma. AP 5 (1961) 58-60.

337   AUNG THAW. Union of Burma. AP 7 (1963) 22-26.

338   MYINT AUNG. Excavations at Halin. JBRS 53 (Dec. 1970) 55-64.

339   PEACOCK, B. A. V. Union of Burma. AP 4 (1960) 71-75.

ARCHAEOLOGY - CAMBODIA

340   AUBOYER, JEANNINE. Recent archae-ological work in Cambodia by the Ecole Francaise d'Extreme-Orient. FA 18 (1962) 178-182.

341   DUMARCAY, J. Le Prasat Prei pres d'Angkor Vat. BEF 59 (1972) 189-192.

342   MALLERET, LOUIS. Histoire abregee de l'archeologie indochinoise jusqu'a a 1950. AP 12 (1969) 43-68.

343   MALLERET, LOUIS. Maurice Glaize, 1886-1964. BEF 53 (1966) 311-330.

344   MALLERET, LOUIS. Vingtieme anni-versaire de la mort de Victor Goloubew, 1878-1945. BEF 53 (1966) 331-373.

345   MOURER, CECILE. Prehistoric re-search in Cambodia during the last ten years, by Cecile and Roland Mourer   AP 14 (1971) 35-42.

346   SAURIN, E. Cambodge, Laos, Viet-nam. AP 9 (1966) 32-35.

347   SAURIN, E. Paleolithique du Cam-bodge oriental. AP 9 (1966) 96-110.

348   SAURIN, E. Les recherches pre-historiques au Cambodge, Laos, et Vietnam, 1877-1966. AP 12 (1969) 27-41.

ARCHAEOLOGY - INDONESIA

349   BERNET KEMPERS, A. J. Bosch and the archaeological service of Indonesia. H39 pp. 32-40.

350   BOSCH, F. D. K. The future of Indonesian archaeological re-search. H39 pp. 13-24.

351   DAMAIS, LOUIS-CHARLES. Biblio-graphie indonesienne, publica-tions du service archeologique de l'Indonesie. BEF 51 (1963) 535-582.

352   DAMAIS, LOUIS-CHARLES. Les pub-lications epigraphiques du ser-vice archeologique de l'Indonesie. BEF 54 (1968) 295-521.

353   GALESTIN, TH. P. Bosch studies on the Jalatunda monument. H39 pp. 71-78.

354   GALIS, K. W. Nieuwe Brons-Vond-sten in het Sentani District. BIJ 116 (1960) 270-277.

355   GALIS, K. W. Recent oudheid kun-dig nieuws uit Westellijk Nieuw-Guinea. BIJ 120 (1964) 245-274.

356   HARRISSON, TOM. Six specialised stone tools from upland and south west Borneo. SMJ 12 (1965) 133-142.

357   HEINE-GELDERN, ROBERT VON. Drum named Makalamau. J41 pp. 167-179.

358   HEINE-GELDERN, ROBERT VON. Pre-historic research in the Nether-lands Indies. H57 pp. 129-167.

Archaeology - Indonesia

359 MEDWAY, LORD. Kelingkang range,
an archaeological reconnaissance,
Sarawak-Kalimantan border. SMJ 9
(1960) 648-651.

360 MULVANEY, D. J. Australian-Indonesian archaeological expedition
to Sulawesi, by D. J. Mulvaney and
R. P. Soejono. AP 13 (1970) 163-
177.

361 RESINK, TH. A. Belahan or a myth
dispelled. IND 6 (1968) 2-37.

362 SOEJONO, R. P. History of prehistoric research in Indonesia to
1950. AP 12 (1969) 69-91.

363 SOEJONO, R. P. Indonesia. AP 6
(1962) 34-43.

364 SOEJONO, R. P. Preliminary notes
on new finds of lower palaeolithic implements from Indonesia. AP
5 (1961) 217-232.

365 SOEJONO, R. P. Retrospect and
prospect of archaeology in Indonesia. JOSA 6 (1968) 114-121.

366 SOEJONO, R. P. The study of prehistory in Indonesia, retrospect
and prospect. AP 13 (1970) 11-15.

367 SOEKMONO, R. Archaeological research in Indonesia, a historical
survey. AP 12 (1969) 93-96.

368 SOEKMONO, R. Archaeology and Indonesian history. S61 pp. 36-46.

369 SOEKMONO, R. Geographical recon-
struction of northeastern central
Java and the location of Medang.
IND 4 (1967) 2-7.

370 SRI KUSUMOBROTO. Preliminary
note on Tjandi Sambisari, a recently discovered temple in central Java. IND 7 (1969) 1-4.

371 SUKARTO K. ATMODJO, M. M. Second
colophon of the *Nagarakrtagama*.
BIJ 129 (1973) 277-286.

372 TUGBY, DONALD J. Stone artifact
from lower Mandailing, Sumatra, by
Donald J. and Elise Tugby. AP 8
(1964) 166-170.

373 WEIDENREICH, FRANZ. Puzzle of
Pithecanthropus. H57 pp. 380-390.

374 WORSLEY, P. J. Study of Indonesian archaeology and ancient history. P15 pp. 155-161.

ARCHAEOLOGY - LAOS

375 SAURIN, E. Cambodge, Laos, Vietnam. AP 9 (1966) 32-35.

376 SAURIN, E. Le mobilier prehistorique de l'abri-sous-roche de
Tam Pong Haut Laos. SEIB 41
(1966) 107-118.

377 SAURIN, E. Les recherches prehistoriques au Cambodge, Laos, et
Vietnam, 1877-1966. AP 12 (1969)
27-41.

ARCHAEOLOGY - MALAYSIA

378 DUNN, FREDERICK L. Annotated bibliography of Malayan (west Malaysian) archaeology, 1962-1969, by
F. L. Dunn and B. A. V. Peacock.
AP 14 (1971) 43-48.

379 DUNN, FREDERICK L. Excavations at
Gua Kechil, Pahang. JMBRAS 37 pt.
2 (1964) 87-124.

380 JACK-HINTON, COLIN. On two archaeological field reconnaissances
in coastal Pahang relative to
Borneo. SMJ 12 (1965) 128-132.

381 LAMB, ALASTAIR. Mahayana Buddhist votive tablets in Perlis. JMBRAS 37 pt. 2 (1964) 47-59.

382 LAMB, ALASTAIR. Malaya. AP 4 (1960) 77-8.

383 LAMB, ALASTAIR. Malaya. AP 5 (1961) 61-2.

384 LAMB, ALASTAIR. Miscellaneous archaeological discoveries. JMBRAS 37 pt. 1 (1964) 166-168.

385 LAMB, ALASTAIR. Notes on beads from Johor Lama and Kota Tinggi. JMBRAS 37 pt. 1 (1964) 88-98.

386 MATTHEWS, JOHN. Results of excavations in Malaya. AP 5 (1961) 237-242.

387 MEDWAY, LORD. Excavations at Gua Kechil, Pahang. JMBRAS 42 pt. 2 (1969) 197-205.

388 PEACOCK, B. A. V. Malaysian prehistory, some current problems. A41 pp. 40-55.

389 PEACOCK, B. A. V. Pillar base architecture in ancient Kedah. JMBRAS 47 pt. 1 (1974) 66-86.

390 PEACOCK, B. A. V. Recent archaeological discoveries in Malaysia, 1962-63. JMBRAS 37 pt. 2 (1964) 201-206.

391 PEACOCK, B. A. V. Recent archaeological discoveries in Malaysia, 1964. JMBRAS 38 pt. 1 (1965) 248-255.

392 PEACOCK, B. A. V. Recent archaeological discoveries in Malaysia, 1965. JMBRAS 39 pt. 1 (1966) 198-201.

393 PEACOCK, B. A. V. Recent archaeological discoveries in Malaysia, 1967, west Malaysia, by B. A. V. Peacock and F. L. Dunn. JMBRAS 41 pt. 1 (1968) 171-179.

394 PIRIYA KRAIRKSH. Note on the Makara balastrade at Malacca. JMBRAS 47 pt. 1 (1974) 96-103.

395 TRELOAR, F. E. Chemical analysis of some metal objects from Chandi Bukit Batu Bahat, Kedah, suggested origin and date. JMBRAS 41 pt. 1 (1968) 193-198.

396 WALES, H. G. QUARITCH. Malayan archaeology of the Hindu period, some reconsiderations. JMBRAS 43 pt. 1 (1970) 1-34.

397 WALES, H. G. QUARITCH. Origin of the tulang mawas. JMBRAS 47 pt. 1 (1974) 110-1.

398 WALL, LINDSAY. Prehistoric earthenwares, pottery common to Sarawak and Malaya. SMJ 11 (1962) 417-427.

ARCHAEOLOGY - MALAYSIA - SABAH

399 CHONG, MICHAEL. Fine trapezoidal gouge and associated items from North Borneo. JMBRAS 39 pt. 2 (1966) 172-3.

400 HARRISSON, BARBARA. British Borneo. AP 4 (1960) 79-84.

401 HARRISSON, BARBARA. Tapadong, 700 years of cave history in Sabah, by Barbara Harrisson and Bambi bin Ungap. SMJ 11 (1964) 655-665.

402 HARRISSON, TOM. Bronze adze casts from interior Sarawak and Sabah. SMJ 16 (1968) 101-2.

Archaeology - Malaysia - Sabah

403 HARRISSON, TOM. East Malaysia and Brunei. AP 10 (1967) 85-92.

404 HARRISSON, TOM. Newly discovered prehistoric rock carvings, Ulu Tomani, Sabah. JMBRAS 46 pt. 1 (1973) 141-143.

405 HARRISON, TOM. Radio-carbon dates for Sabah and Brunei, related to Sarawak. SMJ 19 (1971) 363-366.

406 HARRISSON, TOM. Recent archaeological discoveries in Malaysia, 1965, east Malaysia and Brunei. JMBRAS 39 pt. 1 (1966) 191-197.

407 HARRISSON, TOM. Recent archaeological discoveries in east Malaysia and Brunei. JMBRAS 40 pt. 1 (1967) 140-148.

408 HARRISSON, TOM. Recent archaeological discoveries in Malaysia, 1967, east Malaysia and Brunei. JMBRAS 41 pt. 1 (1968) 180-182.

409 HARRISSON, TOM. Stone and bronze tool cave in Sabah. AP 8 (1964) 171-180.

410 HARRISSON, TOM. Turtleware from Borneo caves. AP 9 (1966) 134-139.

411 WILLIAMS, THOMAS RHYS. Archaeological research in North Borneo. AP 6 (1962) 230-1.

ARCHAEOLOGY - MALAYSIA - SARAWAK

412 HARRISSON, BARBARA. British Borneo. AP 4 (1960) 79-84.

413 HARRISSON, BARBARA. British Borneo. AP 5 (1961) 63-66.

414 HARRISSON, BARBARA. Malaysian Borneo. AP 7 (1963) 45-51.

415 HARRISSON, BARBARA. Malaysian Borneo. AP 8 (1964) 92-97.

416 HARRISSON, BARBARA. Recent archaeological discoveries in Malaysia, 1962-63. JMBRAS 37 pt. 2 (1964) 192-200.

417 HARRISSON, TOM. Borneo stone age, in the light of recent research. SMJ 20 (1972) 385-412.

418 HARRISSON, TOM. Bronze adze casts from interior Sarawak and Sabah. SMJ 16 (1968) 101-2.

419 HARRISSON, TOM. East Malaysia and Brunei. AP 10 (1967) 85-92.

420 HARRISSON, TOM. First C-14 date for an open site in Borneo, by Tom Harrisson and Stanley J. O'Connor. AP 15 (1972) 89-92.

421 HARRISSON, TOM. Gold in west Borneo, by Tom Harrisson and Stanley J. O'Connor. SMJ 17 (1969) 1-66.

422 HARRISSON, TOM. Palaeolithic stone age, studies in Borneo and adjacent islands, a new review. BMJ 3 pt. 2 (1974) 235-252.

423 HARRISSON, TOM. Prehistoric iron industry in the Sarawak River delta, evidence by association, by Tom Harrisson and S. J. O'Connor. SMJ 16 (1968) 1-54.

424 HARRISSON, TOM. Prehistory of Borneo. AP 13 (1970) 17-45.

425 HARRISSON, TOM. Recent archaeological discoveries in Malaysia, 1964. JMBRAS 38 pt. 1 (1965) 244-247.

Archaeology - Malaysia - Sarawak - Niah
Caves

426 HARRISSON, TOM. Recent archaeo-
     logical discoveries in Malaysia,
     1965, east Malaysia and Brunei.
     JMBRAS 39 pt. 1 (1966) 191-197.

427 HARRISSON, TOM. Recent **archaeolog-**
     ical discoveries in east Malaysia
     and Brunei. JMBRAS 40 pt. 1
     (1967) 140-148.

428 HARRISSON, TOM. Recent archaeo-
     logical discoveries in Malaysia,
     1967, east Malaysia and Brunei.
     JMBRAS 41 pt. 1 (1968) 180-182.

429 HARRISSON, TOM. Sarang caves of
     Sarawak, by Tom Harrisson and J.
     L. Reavis. SMJ 14 (1966) 249-268.

430 HARRISSON, TOM. Six specialised
     stone tools from upland and south
     west Borneo. SMJ 12 (1965) 133-
     142.

431 HARRISSON, TOM. Stone artifacts
     from Borneo paralleled in Polyne-
     sia and elsewhere. AP 16 (1973)
     195-6.

432 HARRISSON, TOM. Tanjong Tegok, a
     prehistoric cemetery on the South
     China Sea. SMJ 16 (1968) 55-63.

433 HARRISSON, TOM. Tantric shrine
     excavated at Santubong, by Tom
     Harrisson and Stanley J.
     O'Connor. SMJ 15 (1967) 201-222.

434 HARRISSON, TOM. Turtleware and
     phallic tops from Borneo, Fiji and
     elsewhere. SMJ 17 (1969) 96-98.

435 MEDWAY, LORD. Antiquity of domes-
     ticated pigs in Sarawak. JMBRAS
     46 pt. 2 (1973) 169-178.

436 MEDWAY, LORD. Kelingkang range,
     an archaeological reconnaissance,
     Sarawak-Kalimantan border. SMJ 9
     (1960) 648-651.

437 MEDWAY, LORD. Stegolophodon
     lydekkeri Osborn, a reassessment.
     SMJ 20 (1972) 339-350.

438 NYANDOH, R. Progress report on
     archaeological work at Gedong,
     1967-1969, by R. Nyandoh and Lucas
     Chin. SMJ 17 (1969) 80-88.

439 REAVIS, J. L. Caves of the Ulu
     Kakus, interior Sarawak. SMJ 14
     (1966) 269-275.

440 SOLHEIM, WILHELM G. Prehistoric
     earthenware pottery of Tanjong
     Kubor, Santubong. SMJ 12 (1965)
     1-62.

441 WALL, LINDSAY. Prehistoric
     earthenwares, pottery common to
     Sarawak and Malaya. SMJ 11
     (1962) 417-427.

442 YIM KHAI SUN. Semporna jaw. SMJ
     11 (1963) 177-8.

ARCHAEOLOGY - MALAYSIA - SARAWAK - NIAH
  CAVES **

443 ALDRIDGE, PATRICIA M. Deep bat
     remains from Niah cave expeditions
     1954-61, by Patricia M. Aldridge
     and the Earl of Cranbrook. SMJ 11
     (1963) 201-213.

444 BROOKS, SHEILAGH T. Arm position
     as correlated with sex determina-
     tion in the Niah cave extended
     burial series, Sarawak, Malaysia,
     by Sheilagh T. and Richard H.
     Brooks. SMJ 16 (1968) 67-74.

445 BROOKS, SHEILAGH T. Preliminary
     report on the palaeoserology of
     the Niah cave burials, by Sheilagh
     T. Brooks and Rodger Heglar. AP
     15 (1972) 87-8.

Archaeology - Malaysia - Sarawak - Niah
Caves

446 CRANBROOK, EARL OF. Bat remains
from Niah cave excavations, 1964.
SMJ 14 (1966) 224-228.

447 CRANBROOK, EARL OF. Niah cave
bone. VII. Crocidura (shrews).
SMJ 11 (1963) 192-195.

448 HARRISSON, BARBARA. Classification of stone age burials from
Niah Great Cave, Sarawak. SMJ 15
(1967) 126-200.

449 HARRISSON, BARBARA. Niah stone
age jar-burial, C-14 dated. SMJ
16 (1968) 64-66.

450 HARRISSON, BARBARA. Upiusing, a
late burial cave at Niah. SMJ 12
(1965) 83-116.

451 HARRISSON, TOM. Catfish (Leio-
cassis?) in Niah Great Cave de-
posit. SMJ 16 (1968) 75-6.

452 HARRISSON, TOM. Dating methods
and related deductions in the Niah
great caves. AP 5 (1961) 205-6.

453 HARRISSON, TOM. First classification of prehistoric bone and tooth
artifacts based on material from
Niah Great Cave, by Tom Harrisson
and Lord Medway. AP 6 (1962) 219-
229.

454 HARRISSON, TOM. First classification of prehistoric bone and tooth
artifacts based on material from
Niah Great Cave, by Tom Harrisson
and Lord Medway. SMJ 11 (1962)
335-362.

455 HARRISSON, TOM. Lobang Angus, a
frequentation cave at Niah. SMJ
14 (1966) 217-223.

456 HARRISSON, TOM. Magala, a series
of neolithic and metal age burial
grottos at Sekaloh, Niah, Sarawak,
by Tom and Barbara Harrisson.
JMBRAS 41 pt. 2 (1968) 148-175.

457 HARRISSON, TOM. Niah cave double
spouted vessels. SMJ 19 (1971)
367-373.

458 HARRISSON, TOM. Niah cave oyster
shell, a note. SMJ 9 (1960) 380-
388.

459 HARRISSON, TOM. Niah caves, progress report to 1967. SMJ 15
(1967) 95-6.

460 HARRISSON, TOM. Niah excavations,
1957-61. AP 5 (1961) 233.

461 HARRISSON, TOM. Niah's gorge
cave, at the limit of human reach?
SMJ 10 (1961) 326-332.

462 HARRISSON, TOM. Prehistoric
double spouted vessels excavated
from Niah caves, Borneo. JMBRAS
44 pt. 2 (1971) 35-78.

463 HARRISSON, TOM. Turtleware from
Borneo caves. AP 9 (1966) 134-
139.

464 HOOIJER, D. A. Further hell mammals from Niah. SMJ 11 (1963)
196-200.

465 HOOIJER, D. A. Giant extinct
panoglin, manis palaeojavanica
Dubois, from Niah. SMJ 9 (1960)
350-355.

466 HOOIJER, D. A. Orang-utan in Niah
cave prehistory. SMJ 9 (1960)
408-421.

467 HOOIJER, D. A. Prehistoric bone,
the gibbons and monkeys of Niah
Great Cave. SMJ 11 (1962) 428-
449.

468 KING, WAYNE. Palaeolithic reptile and amphibian remains from Niah Great Cave. SMJ 11 (1962) 450-452.

469 MEDWAY, LORD. Animal remains from Lobang Angus, Niah. SMJ 14 (1966) 185-216.

470 MEDWAY, LORD. Malay tapir in late quaternary Borneo. SMJ 9 (1960) 356-363.

471 MEDWAY, LORD. Niah cave animal bone. VI. New records. SMJ 11 (1963) 188-191.

472 MEDWAY, LORD. Niah cave animal bone. VIII. Rhinoceros in late quaternary Borneo. SMJ 12 (1965) 77-82.

473 MEDWAY, LORD. Niah cave bone. IV. Shrew, crocidura sp. SMJ 9 (1960) 364-367.

474 MEDWAY, LORD. Niah cave bone. Size changes in the teeth of two rats, rattus sabanus Thomas and rattus Muelleri Jintink. SMJ 11 (1964) 616-623.

475 MEDWAY, LORD. Niah shells, 1954-58, a preliminary report. SMJ 9 (1960) 368-379.

476 SOLHEIM, WILHELM G. Niah three colour ware and related prehistoric pottery, by Wilhelm G. Solheim, Barbara Harrisson and Lindsay Wall. SMJ 10 (1961) 227-237.

477 WELLS, CALVIN. Two neolithic burials from Lobang Jeragan, a cliff cave at Niah. SMJ 11 (1963) 214-219.

478 YIM KHAI SUN. Some Gan Kira human remains, Niah. SMJ 11 (1963) 179-187.

ARCHAEOLOGY - PHILIPPINES

479 EVANGELISTA, ALFREDO E. H. O. Beyer's Philippine neolithic in the context of postwar discoveries in local archaeology. Z16 pp. 63-87.

480 EVANGELISTA, ALFREDO E. Identifying some intrusive archaeological materials found in Philippine proto-historic sites. AST 3 (1965) 86-102.

481 EVANGELISTA, ALFREDO E. Philippines. AP 4 (1960) 85-88.

482 EVANGELISTA, ALFREDO E. Philippines. AP 5 (1961) 67-70.

483 EVANGELISTA, ALFREDO E. Philippines. AP 6 (1962) 46-7.

484 EVANGELISTA, ALFREDO E. Philippines. AP 7 (1963) 52-56.

485 EVANGELISTA, ALFREDO E. The Philippines, archaeology in the Philippines to 1950. AP 12 (1969) 97-104.

486 FOX, ROBERT B. Archaeological record of Chinese influences in the Philippines. PS 15 (1967) 41-62.

487 FOX, ROBERT B. Excavations in the Tabon caves and some problems in Philippine chronology. Z16 pp. 88-116.

488 FRANCISCO, JUAN R. Buddhist image from Karitunan site, Batangas Province. AST 1 (1963) 13-18.

Archaeology - Philippines

489 FRANCISCO, JUAN R. Note on the golden image of Agusan. PS 11 (1963) 390-400.

490 JOCANO, F. LANDA. Beginnings of Filipino society and culture. PS 15 (1967) 9-40.

491 KAMER AGA-OGLU. Ming porcelain from sites in the Philippines. AP 5 (1961) 243-252.

492 KURJACK, EDWARD B. Archaeology of Seminoho cave in Lebak, Cotabato, by Edward B. Kurjack and Craig T. Sheldon. SJ 17 (1970) 5-18.

493 KURJACK, EDWARD B. Urn burial caves of southern Cotabato, Mindanao, Philippines, by Edward B. Kurjack, Craig T. Sheldon and Maria E. Keller. SJ 18 (1971) 127-153.

494 LEGASPI, AVELINO M. Cave archaeology and environmental spirits. AP 17 (1974) 25-27.

495 MACEDA, MARCELINO N. Preliminary report on the Fenefe cave excavation, Kulaman plateau, Mindanao. Z16 pp. 265-272.

496 MAHER, ROBERT F. Archaeological investigations in central Ifugao. AP 16 (1973) 39-70.

497 SCHEANS, D. J. Newly discovered blade tool industry from the central Philippines, by D. J. Scheans, K. L. Hutterer and R. L. Cherry. AP 13 (1970) 179-181.

498 SIBLEY, WILLIS E. Discovery report, the Bongol San Miguel burial site, Guimbal, Iloilo. Z16 pp. 273-298.

499 SOLHEIM, WILHELM G. Philippine notes. AP 7 (1963) 138-143.

500 SOLHEIM, WILHELM G. Prehistoric archaeology in eastern mainland Southeast Asia and the Philippines. AP 13 (1970) 47-58.

501 SPOEHR, ALEXANDER. Archaeological approach to ethnic diversity in Zamboanga and Sulu. S92 pp. 95-101.

502 SPOEHR, ALEXANDER. Archaeological survey of southern Zamboanga and the Sulu Archipelago. AP 11 (1968) 177-185.

503 TENAZAS, ROSA C. P. Preliminary report on the salvage excavation project in Cebu City, by Rosa C. P. Tenazas and Karl Hutterer. D67 pp. 43-54.

504 VALDEPENAS, VICENTE B. Philippine prehistoric economy, by Vicente B. Valdepenas and Germelino M. Bautista. PS 22 (1974) 280-296.

505 WINTERS, NORTON J. Application of dental anthropological analysis to the human dentition of two early metal age sites, Palawan, Philippines. AP 17 (1974) 28-35.

ARCHAEOLOGY - THAILAND

506 BAYARD, DONN T. Excavation at Non Nok Tha, northeastern Thailand, 1968, an interim report. AP 13 (1970) 109-143.

507 BOELES, J. J. Note on archaeological survey and excavations in north-eastern Thailand in 1959. JSS 48 pt. 2 (1960) 85-90.

508 BRONSON, BENNET. Excavations at Chansen, Thailand, 1968 and 1969, a preliminary report, by Bennet Bronson and George F. Dales. AP 15 (1972) 15-46.

509 CHIN YOU DI. Thailand. AP 5 (1961) 54-57.

510 COEDES, G. Excavations at P'ong Tuk and their importance for the history of Siam. S44.1 pp. 204-238.

511 GORMAN, CHESTER F. Excavations at spirit cave, north Thailand, some interim interpretations. AP 13 (1970) 79-107.

512 GRISWOLD, A. B. Thoughts on a centenary. JSS 52 (1964) 21-54.

513 HARRISSON, TOM. Incised figures from the top of a lid found on Samui Island, Thailand. AP 9 (1966) 111-2.

514 HEEKEREN, H. R. VAN. Brief survey of the Sai-Yok excavations, 1961-62 season of the Thai-Danish prehistoric expedition. JSS 50 (1962) 15-18.

515 HEEKEREN, H. R. VAN. Preliminary note on the excavation of the Sai-Yok rock shelter. JSS 49 pt. 2 (1961) 99-108.

516 HEEKEREN, H. R. VAN. Thai-Danish prehistoric expedition 1960-1962. Some notes on the bronze age of Thailand and the excavation of the sawmill site at Wang Pho. JSS 51 (1963) 79-81.

517 KNUTH, EIGIL. Further report on the Sai-Yok excavations and on the work at Thai picture cave. JSS 50 (1962) 19-21.

518 KOCH, K. E. Some newly discovered prehistoric sites in northern Thailand, by K. E. Koch and M. Siebenhuner. JSS 57 (1969) 260-320.

519 LAMB, ALASTAIR. Notes on Satingphra. JMBRAS 37 pt. 1 (1964) 74-87.

520 LAMB, ALASTAIR. Stone casket from Satingpra, some further observations. JSS 53 (1965) 191-195.

521 LOOFS, H. E. E. Thai-British archaeological expedition, a preliminary report on the work of the second season, 1967, by H. E. E. Loofs and William Watson. JSS 58 pt. 2 (1970) 67-78.

522 NIELSEN, EIGIL. Thai-Danish prehistoric expedition 1960-1962, preliminary expedition 1960-61. JSS 49 pt. 1 (1961) 47-55.

523 NIELSEN, EIGIL. Thai Danish prehistoric expedition 1960-1962. JSS 50 (1962) 7-14.

524 O'CONNOR, STANLEY J. Satingphra, an expanded chronology. JMBRAS 39 pt. 1 (1966) 137-144.

525 O'CONNOR, STANLEY J. Si Chon, an early settlement in peninsular Thailand. JSS 56 (1968) 1-18.

526 PENTH, HANS GEORG. Steinwerkzeuge aus Phrao. JSS 56 (1968) 251-267.

527 PIETRUSEWSKY, MICHAEL. Palaeodemography of a prehistoric Thai population, Non Nok Tha. AP 17 (1974) 125-140.

528 SARASIN, FRITZ. Prehistorical researches in Siam. S44.3 pp. 101-132.

529 SHARP, RUTH. Some archaeological sites in north Thailand, by Ruth and Lauriston Sharp. JSS 52 (1964) 223-239.

Archaeology - Thailand

ARCHAEOLOGY - VIETNAM **

551 MALLERET, LOUIS. Les dodecaedres d'or du site D'oc-Eo. G83 pp. 343–350.

552 MALLERET, LOUIS. Histoire abregee de l'archeologie indochinoise jusqu'a a 1950. AP 12 (1969) 43–68.

553 MATTHEWS, J. M. Review of the Hoabinhian in Indo-China. AP 9 (1966) 86–95.

554 PATTE, ETIENNE. Les Ossements du Kjokkenmodding de Da But, province de Thanh Hoa. SEIB 40 (1965) 7–197.

555 SAURIN, EDMOND. Cambodge, Laos, Vietnam. AP 9 (1966) 32–35.

556 SAURIN, EDMOND. Nouveaux vestiges prehistoriques a Con-Son (Poulo-Condore). SEIB 39 (1964) 7–13.

557 SAURIN, EDMOND. Nouvelles observations prehistoriques a l'est de Saigon. SEIB 43 (1968) 1–17.

558 SAURIN, EDMOND. Le paleolithique des environs de Xuan-Loc. SEIB 46 (1971) 49–70.

559 SAURIN, EDMOND. Les recherches prehistoriques au Cambodge, Laos, et Vietnam, 1877–1966. AP 12 (1969) 27–41.

560 SAURIN, EDMOND. Station prehistorique de Hang Gon pres Xuan-Loc, Vietnam. AP 6 (1962) 163–168.

561 SMITH, JOHN. Art and archaeology of Viet-Nam in Washington. FA 17 (1960) 1789–1793.

562 SOLHEIM, WILHELM G. Eastern Asia and Oceania. AP 5 (1961) 5–13.

563 SOLHEIM, WILHELM G. Southeast Asia. AP 6 (1962) 21–31.

564 SOLHEIM, WILHELM G. Vietnam. AP 4 (1960) 63–4.

ARCHITECTURE *See also* ART, HOUSING, TEMPLES

565 DUMARCAY, J. Les charpentes rayonnantes sur plan Barlong ou carre de l'Asie meridionale. BEF 60 (1973) 85–104.

ARCHITECTURE – INDONESIA

566 DUMARCAY, J. Elements pour une histoire architecture du Borobudur. BEF 60 (1973) 105–115.

567 GRAAF, H. J. DE. Origin of the Javanese mosque. JSAH 4 (Mar. 1963) 1–5.

568 PITONO, R. Notes on the development of temple architecture in east Java. JOSA 8 (1971) 68–75.

ARCHITECTURE – MALAYSIA

569 PEACOCK, B. A. V. Pillar base architecture in ancient Kedah. JMBRAS 47 pt. 1 (1974) 66–86.

ARCHITECTURE – PHILIPPINES

570 AHLBORN, RICHARD. Spanish churches of central Luzon. PS 8 (1960) 802–813.

571 AHLBORN, RICHARD. Spanish churches of central Luzon, the provinces near Manila. PS 11 (1963) 283–300.

Architecture - Philippines

572   LEGARDA Y FERNANDEZ, BENITO.
Colonial churches of Ilocos. PS
8 (1960) 121-158.

ARCHIVES *See also* HISTORIOGRAPHY AND
HISTORICAL SOURCES, LIBRARY RESOURCES
ON . . ., MANUSCRIPTS

573   Constitution of the Southeast
Asian Regional Branch of the In-
ternational Council on Archives.
SAA 1 (1968) 33-43.

574   Proposal for a Southeast Asian
regional branch of the International Council of Archives, Malaysia. SAA 1 (1968) 8-13.

575   Proposals on organization and
collaboration, Republic of Vietnam. SAA 1 (1968) 15-6.

576   Regional cooperation in archives,
Malaysia. SAA 1 (1968) 17-8.

577   Value and importance of the establishment of a Southeast Asian
regional branch of the International Council on Archives,
Philippines. SAA 1 (1968) 19-22.

ARCHIVES - FRANCE

578   BREAZEALE, KENNON. Inventaire
des documents sur le Siam conserves aux archives de Paris.
JSS 62 pt. 2 (1974) 149-206.

579   EYMERET, JOEL. Les archives
francaises au service des etudes
indonesiennes, Java sous Daendels, 1808-1811. AR 4 (1972)
151-168.

ARCHIVES - GREAT BRITAIN

580   McCUTCHEON, JAMES. Missionary
archives in England for East and
Southeast Asia, 1968, a report.
JAS 28 (1968-9) 601-2.

581   MOIR, MARTIN I. Archival materi-
als in the London records of the
East India Company and of the
India Office relating to Southeast
Asia. SAA 2 (1969) 68-81.

ARCHIVES - INDIA

582   KESWANI, D. G. Archival sources
of Southeast Asian history in the
National Archives of India. SAA
2 (1969) 3-10.

ARCHIVES - MALAYSIA

583   Proposal for a Southeast Asian re-
gional branch of the International
Council of Archives, Malaysia.
SAA 1 (1968) 8-13.

584   Regional cooperation in archives,
Malaysia. SAA 1 (1968) 17-8.

585   VERHOEVEN, F. R. J. Lost archives
of Dutch Malacca, 1641-1824.
JMBRAS 37 pt. 2 (1964) 11-27.

586   VERHOEVEN, F. R. J. Lost archives
of Dutch Malacca, 1641-1824. PHR
1 pt. 2 (1966) 183-200.

587   VERHOEVEN, F. R. J. National archives of Malaysia. JSAH 7 (Mar.
1966) 122-130.

ARCHIVES - NETHERLANDS

589   MEILINK-ROELOFZ, M. A. P. Sources
in the General State Archives in
the Hague relating to the history

of East Asia between c.1600 and
c.1800.   F38 pp. 167-184.

590   ROESSINGH, M. P. H.   Dutch relations with the Philippines, a
survey of sources in the General
State Archives, The Hague, Netherlands.   AST 5 (1967) 377-407.

591   ROESSINGH, M. P. H.   Dutch relations with the Philippines, c.
1600-1850, a survey of sources in
the General State Archives, The
Hague, Netherlands.   SAA 2 (1969)
88-103.

ARCHIVES - PHILIPPINES

592   ARCILLA, JOSE S.   Random listing
of manuscripts in the Dominican
archives.   PS 20 (1972) 176-187.

593   QUIRINO, CARLOS.   Checklist of
documents on Gomburza from the
archdiocesan archives of Manila.
PS 21 (1973) 19-84.

594   Value and importance of the establishment of a Southeast Asian regional branch of the International
Council on Archives, Philippines.
SAA 1 (1968) 19-22.

ARCHIVES - SPAIN

595   DIAZ-TRECHUELO, MARIA LOURDES.
Primary sources of the history of
the Philippines in archives and
libraries of Spain.   SAA 2 (1969)
108-118.

596   DIAZ-TRECHUELO, MARIA LOURDES.
Primary sources on the history of
the Philippines in archives and
libraries in Spain.   PHR 2 (1969)
1-247.

ARCHIVES - UNION OF SOVIET SOCIALIST REPUBLICS

597   UZIANOV, A.   Importance of Russian archives for studies into the
history of freedom wars and popular movements in South-East Asia
in the XIX-early XX centuries.
SAA 2 (1969) 82-87.

ARCHIVES - VATICAN

598   CARRETTO, P.   Vatican papers of
the XVII century.   S44.7 pp. 177-
193.

ARCHIVES - VIETNAM

599   CHEN CHING HO.   Imperial archives
of the Nguyen Dynasty, 1802-1945.
JSAH 3 (Sept. 1962) 111-128.

600   NGUYEN HUNG CUONG.   Etat des
documents d'archives en langue
francaise au Viet-Nam.   SAA 2
(1969) 139-147.

601   NGUYEN HUNG CUONG.   Etat des
documents d'archives en langue
francaise dans la Republique du
Viet-Nam.   SEIB 44 (1969) 109-121.

ARGUNIAN

602   POUWER, J.   Structure and flexi-
bility in a New Guinea society.
BIJ 122 (1966) 158-169.

ARMAMENTS

603   BOXER, C. R.   Asian potentates and
European artillery in the 16th-
18th centuries, a footnote to
Gibson-Hill.   JMBRAS 38 pt. 2
(1965) 156-172.

Armaments

604 HARRISSON, TOM. Papuan stone-adze in central Borneo. SMJ 11 (1962) 560-562.

ARMAMENTS - BRUNEI

605 HARRISSON, TOM. Brunei cannon, their role in Southeast Asia, 1400-1900 A.D. BMJ 1 (1969) 94-118.

606 SHARIFFUDDIN, P. M. Brunei cannon. BMJ 1 (1969) 72-93.

ARMAMENTS - PHILIPPINES

607 AQUINO, MELCHOR P. Missiles and national survival. PS 8 (1960) 608-616.

ARMAMENTS - THAILAND

608 PENTH, HANS. Note on Pun. JSS 59 pt. 1 (1971) 209-210.

ARNEDO, SALVADOR MARTIN

609 ARCILLA, JOSE S. Exile of a liberal in 1870, or Father Arnedo's case. PS 19 (1971) 373-419.

ARNOLD, JOSEPH

610 BASTIN, JOHN. Further note on Dr. Joseph Arnold. JMBRAS 47 pt. 2 (1974) 149.

ART *See also* ARCHITECTURE, POTTERY, TEMPLES

611 HOLT, CLAIRE. In memoriam Robert Heine-Geldern. IND 6 (1968) 188-192.

612 KANEKO, ERIKA. Robert von Heine-Geldern, 1885-1968. AP 13 (1970) 1-10.

613 MUKERJEE, RADHAKAMAL. March of Tantrika art over the Pacific. S87 pp. 289-296.

614 SOLHEIM, WILHELM G. The antiquities problem. AP 16 (1973) 113-124.

615 Travaux de M. George Coedes, essai de bibliographie. G83 pp. 155-186.

ART - CAMBODIA

616 BENISTI, MIREILLE. Notes d'iconographie khmere. I. Deux scenes nautiques. BEF 51 (1963) 95-98.

617 BENISTI, MIREILLE. Notes d'iconographie khmere. II. Une scene d'offrande. BEF 52 (1964) 547-550.

618 BENISTI, MIREILLE. Notes d'iconographie khmere. III. Au sujet d'un linteau de Sambor Prei Kuk. BEF 53 (1966) 71-75.

619 BENISTI, MIREILLE. Notes d'iconographie khmere. IV. Au sujet d'un linteau de Vat Beset. BEF 53 (1966) 513-516.

620 BENISTI, MIREILLE. Notes d'iconographie khmere. V. Krsna et Kesin. BEF 54 (1968) 47-52.

621 BENISTI, MIREILLE. Notes d'iconographie khmere. VI. Le linteau bouddhique de Prasat Crap. BEF 55 (1969) 153-158.

622 BENISTI, MIREILLE. Notes d'iconographie khmere. VII. Karaikkalam-maiyar. BEF 55 (1969) 159-161.

Art - Indonesia

623 BENISTI, MIREILLE. Notes d'icono-
     graphie khmere. VIII. Le linteau
     de Vat Preah Theat. BEF 58 (1971)
     125-130.

624 BENISTI, MIREILLE. Notes d'icono-
     graphie khmere. IX. Le fronton
     de Yeai Pu. BEF 60 (1973) 79-83.

625 BENISTI, MIREILLE. Notes d'icono-
     graphie khmere. X. Premieres rep-
     resentations de Sri Laksmi. BEF
     61 (1974) 349-354.

626 BHATTACHARYA, KAMALESWAR. Linga-
     kosa. E93 pp. 6-13.

627 BOELES, J. J. Buddhist tutelary
     couple Hariti and Pancika, pro-
     tectors of children, from a relief
     at the Khmer sanctuary in Pimai.
     JSS 56 (1968) 187-205.

628 BOELES, J. J. Ramayana relief
     from the Khmer sanctuary at Pimai
     in north-east Thailand. JSS 57
     (1969) 163-169.

629 BOISSELIER, JEAN. Note sur quel-
     ques bronzes khmers d'aspect in-
     solite. E93 pp. 30-36.

630 BROWN, ROXANNA. A Khmer kiln
     site, Surin Province, by Roxanna
     Brown, Vance Childress and Michael
     Gluckman. JSS 62 pt. 2 (1974)
     239-252.

631 DAGENS, BRUNO. Les linteaux de-
     coratifs du Prasat Cha Chouk. BEF
     57 (1970) 91-97.

632 MALLERET, LOUIS. Une nouvelle
     statue Preangkorienne de Surya
     dans le Bas-Mekong. E93 pp. 109-
     120.

633 MARCHAL, HENRI. Banteay Srei.
     SEIB 40 (1965) 283-290.

634 MARCHAL, HENRI. Iconographie
     bouddhique au Cambodge, en Thai-
     lande et au Laos. FA 24 (1970)
     163-179.

635 ZIGMUND-CERBU, A. A propos d'un
     Vajra khmer. G83 pp. 425-431.

ART - INDONESIA

636 BOSCH, F. D. K. De asvin-goden en
     de epische tweelingen in de Oud-
     javaanse kunst en literature. BIJ
     123 (1967) 427-441.

637 BOSCH, F. D. K. Old Javanese
     bathing place, by F. D. K. Bosch
     and B. de Haan. BIJ 121 (1965)
     189-232.

638 BOSCH, F. D. K. A remarkable an-
     cient Javanese sculpture. G83 pp.
     232-240.

639 DAMAIS, LOUIS-CHARLES. A propos
     des couleurs symboliques des
     points cardinaux. BEF 56 (1969)
     75-118.

640 DUMARCAY, J. Les charpentes fig-
     ures de Prambanan. AR 7 (1974)
     139-150.

641 GALIS, K. W. Eerste rotsgrave-
     ringen in Nederlands Nieuw-Guinea
     ontdekt. BIJ 117 (1961) 464-474.

642 GALIS, K. W. Nieuwe Brons-Vondsten
     in het Sentani District. BIJ 116
     (1960) 270-277.

643 HARRISSON, TOM. Stone sculptures
     from south west Borneo, Kalimantan
     Barat. JMBRAS 46 pt. 2 (1973)
     179-184.

644 HEINE-GELDERN, ROBERT. Survivance
     de motifs de l'ancien art bouddhi-
     que de l'Inde dans l'ile de Nias.
     G83 pp. 299-306.

Art - Indonesia

645 HOLT, CLAIRE. In memoriam, Trisno Sumardjo, December 6, 1916-April 21, 1969. IND 8 (1969) 213-216.

646 HOLT, CLAIRE. Indonesia revisited. IND 9 (1970) 163-188.

647 JAINI, PADMANABH S. Story of Sudhana and Manohra, an analysis of the texts and the Borobudur reliefs. SOAS 29 (1966) 533-558.

648 LOHUIZEN-DE LEEUW, J. E. VAN. Bosch' contributions to Indian iconography and history of art. H39 pp. 59-63.

649 LOHUIZEN-DE LEEUW, J. E. VAN. Dhyani-Buddhas of Barabudur. BIJ 121 (1965) 389-416.

650 PANNENBORG-STUTTERHEIM, LOUISE J. F. M. Treasures or meditation? J41 pp. 257-263.

651 PIJPER, G. F. Minaret in Java. J41 pp. 274-283.

652 PITONO, R. Belahan problem. JOSA 8 (1971) 86-95.

653 RESINK, TH. A. Belahan or a myth dispelled. IND 6 (1968) 2-37.

654 RESINK, TH. A. De onverk laarde tempelreliefs op het hoofdgebouw van Tjandi Kedaton. BIJ 121 (1965) 438-466.

655 ROCAMORA, NANCY F. Indigenization of Indonesian art. AST 11 (1973) 98-111.

656 SOEKMONO, R. Une nouvelle interpretation de la signification du Candi. AR 7 (1974) 121-126.

657 STEINMANN, ALFRED. De afbeeldingen van planten op de spuiers van Djalatoenda. BIJ 117 (1961) 359-362.

658 TERWEN-DE LOOS, J. De Pandjireliefs van oudheid LXV op de Gunung Bekel Penanggungan. BIJ 127 (1971) 321-330.

ART - INDONESIA - BALI

659 ABEL, THEODORA M. Free designs of limited scope as a personality index, a comparison of schizophrentics with normal, subnormal, and primitive culture groups. B43 pp. 371-383.

660 BELO, JANE. Balinese children's drawing. B43 pp. 240-259.

661 DAMAIS, LOUIS-CHARLES. Etudes balinaises. La date de la sepulture royale du Gunung Kawi. BEF 50 (1960) 133-159.

662 DAMAIS, LOUIS-CHARLES. Quelques toiles balinaises de style traditionnel. G83 pp. 263-274.

663 GALESTIN, TH. P. Illustrations from the Pausyaparvan. J41 pp. 131-135.

664 HOOYKAAS, C. Pamurtian in Balinese art. IND 12 (1971) 1-20.

665 MEAD, MARGARET. Arts in Bali. B43 pp. 331-340.

666 SUKARTO K. ATMODJO, M. M. La representation phallique de la Pura Pusering Jagat a Pejeng. AR 7 (1974) 127-132.

667 VAN AKKEREN, PHILIP. Art applied to the calendar of Bali. JOSA 8 (1971) 76-85.

668 WORSLEY, P. J. Missing piece of
a Balinese painting of the Siwaratrikalpa. BIJ 126 (1970) 347-351.

ART - LAOS

669 MARCHAL, HENRI. Iconographie
bouddhique au Cambodge, en Thailande et au Laos. FA 24 (1970)
163-179.

ART - MALAYSIA - SABAH

670 HARRISSON, TOM. Curious kettle-
drum from Sabah. JMBRAS 39 pt. 2
(1966) 169-171.

671 SATHER, CLIFFORD. Note on Bajau
gravemarkers from the Semporna
district of Sabah. SMJ 16 (1968)
103-110.

ART - MALAYSIA - SARAWAK

672 CHIN, LUCAS. Trade and preservation of antiquities and other
cultural objects in Sarawak. SMJ
20 (1972) 413-419.

673 GILL, SARAH. Style and the demonic image in Dayak masks.
JMBRAS 40 pt. 1 (1967) 78-92.

674 GRISWOLD, A. B. Santubong Buddha
and its context. SMJ 11 (1962)
363-371.

675 HARRISSON, TOM. Bronze turtles in
central Borneo. JMBRAS 38 pt. 1
(1965) 256-259.

676 HARRISSON, TOM. Golden keris handle from Balingian, Sarawak.
JMBRAS 39 pt. 1 (1966) 175-181.

677 HARRISSON, TOM. Handsome bronze
jar from inland Borneo. SMJ 14
(1966) 151-155.

678 HARRISSON, TOM. Incised figures
from the top of a lid found on
Samui Island, Thailand. AP 9
(1966) 111-2.

679 KOENIGSWALD, G. H. R. VON. Papuan
stone adzes in Borneo and Dayak
art in Papua. SMJ 11 (1964) 556-
557.

680 O'CONNOR, STANLEY J. Western
peninsular Thailand and west Sarawak, ceramic and statuary comparisons, by S. J. O'Connor and Tom
Harrisson. SMJ 11 (1964) 562-566.

ART - PHILIPPINES **

681 BARADAS, DAVID B. Some implications of the Okir motif in Lanao
and Sulu art. AST 6 (1968) 129-
168.

682 BERNAD, MIGUEL A. Case of the
misnamed virgin. PS 16 (1968)
563-576.

683 CASINO, ERIC. Ethnographic art in
the Philippines, an anthropological approach. GEJ 12 (1966) 230-
267.

684 DACANAY, JULIAN E. Okil in Muslim
art, a view from the drawing
board. M24 pp. 149-162.

685 DEMETILLO, RICAREDO. Image of man
in contemporary art and literature. GEJ 4 (1962) 8-13.

686 FRANCISCO, JUAN R. Buddhist image
from Karitunan site Batangas Province. AST 1 (1963) 13-18.

687 FRANCISCO, JUAN R. Golden image
of Agusan, a new identification.
AST 1 (1963) 31-38.

Art - Philippines

688 IMAO, ABDULMARI A. Okkil. GEJ 4 (1962) 105-108.

689 JOSE, F. SIONIL. Art and revolution. SJ 17 (1970) 357-366.

690 KAMER AGA-OGLU. Ming porcelain from sites in the Philippines. AP 5 (1961) 243-252.

691 MANUUD, ANTONIO. Arts, 1960. PS 8 (1960) 814-822.

692 MANUUD, ANTONIO. The arts, January to June. PS 9 (1961) 505-519.

693 MANUUD, ANTONIO. Philippine contemporary art, a fait accompli. M24 pp. 184-194.

694 MORENO, VIRGINIA R. Poet's celebration of N. Veloso Abueva's *Play things and house of things.* GEJ 4 (1962) 81-84.

695 PARAS-PEREZ, ROD. Philippine modern international cross-currents in art. GEJ 4 (1962) 51-55.

696 Perspectives on the cultural center. DR 18 (1970) 341-358.

697 QUIRINO, CARLOS. Damian Domingo, Filipino painter. PS 9 (1961) 78-96.

698 QUIRINO, CARLOS. Manila's school of painting. PS 15 (1967) 348-353.

699 ROCES, ALFREDO R. Genre sculpture of Graciano Nepomuceno. PS 8 (1960) 483-490.

700 ROCES, ALFREDO R. Mask of Longinus. PS 9 (1961) 255-261.

701 ROCES, ALFREDO R. Philippine art, Spanish period. M24 pp. 163-183.

702 RODRIGUEZ, MANUEL. Plastic arts. UN 36 (1963) 378-381.

703 SZANTON, DAVID. Art in Sulu, a survey. PS 11 (1963) 463-502.

704 SZANTON, DAVID. Art in Sulu, a survey. S92 pp. 3-69.

705 TORRES, EMMANUEL. Arts in the Philippines, painting. PS 10 (1962) 127-133.

706 TORRES, EMMANUEL. Because it is there, the Philippines at the 32nd Venice biennale, a close look. PS 13 (1965) 330-349.

ART - THAILAND

707 BOELES, J. J. Four stone images of the Jina Buddha in the precincts of the chapel royal of the Emerald Buddha. F38 pp. 185-198.

708 BOELES, J. J. Two aspects of Buddhist iconography in Thailand. JSS 48 pt. 1 (1960) 69-79.

709 BOELES, J. J. Two yoginis of Hevajra from Thailand. E93 pp. 14-29.

710 BOISSELIER, JEAN. Les peintures murales de Wat Ko Keo Suttharam. F38 pp. 339-345.

711 BORIBAL BURIBHAND. Sculpture of peninsular Siam in the Ayuthya period, by Boribal Buribhand and A. B. Griswold. S44.2 pp. 205-279.

712 COEDES, G. Siamese votive tablets. S44.1 pp. 150-187.

713 DAMRONG RAJANUBHAB. Wat Benchamabopit and its collection of images of the Buddha. S44.1 pp. 239-281.

714 DE CASPARIS, J. G. Date of the Grahi Buddha. JSS 55 (1967) 31-40.

715 DHANINIVAT, PRINCE. Gilt lacquer screen in the audience hall of Dusit. G83 pp. 275-282.

716 DHANINIVAT, PRINCE. Hide figures of the Ramakien at the Leder-museum in Offenbach, Germany. JSS 53 (1965) 61-66.

717 FEROCI, C. Traditional Thai painting. S44.2 pp. 280-300.

718 GRISWOLD, A. B. The Buddha Si-hinga. BIJ 60 (1973) 225-6.

719 GRISWOLD, A. B. Devices and ex-pedients, Vat Pa Mok, 1727 A.D., by A. B. Griswold and Prasert na Nagara. T33 pp. 147-220.

720 GRISWOLD, A. B. Imported images and the nature of copying in the art of Siam. E93 pp. 37-73.

721 GRISWOLD, A. B. Notes on the art of Siam. V. The conversion of Jambupati. G83 pp. 295-298.

722 HEEKEREN, H. R. VAN. Metal ket-tle drum recently discovered in northwestern Thailand. BIJ 126 (1970) 455-458.

723 HUTCHINSON, E. W. Sacred images in Chiengmai. S44.2 pp. 54-73.

724 KRAISRI NIMMANAHAEMINDA. A Chiengmai image inscribed in Bur-mese and Thai. JBRS 43 (June 1960) 63-66.

725 KRAISRI NIMMANAHAEMINDA. Ham Yon, the magic testicles. E93 pp. 133-148.

726 LeMAY, REGINALD. Arts of Thai-land, a review. G83 pp. 311-313.

727 LINGAT, ROBERT. Le Wat Rajapra-tistha. G83 pp. 314-323.

728 LOHUIZEN-DE LEEUW, J. E. VAN. The stone Buddha of Chiengmai and its inscription. G83 pp. 324-329.

729 LYONS, ELIZABETH. Two Dvaravati figurines. JSS 61 pt. 1 (1973) 193-201.

730 MALLERET, LOUIS. A propos d'une sculpture du Musee National de Bangkok. F38 pp. 107-118.

731 MARCHAL, HENRI. Iconographie bouddhique au Cambodge, en Thai-lande et au Laos. FA 24 (1970) 163-179.

732 NANDAKIC, K. Inscribed model vi-hara from Chieng Sen. E93 pp. 121-132.

733 O'CONNOR, STANLEY J. Early Brah-manical sculpture at Songkhla. JSS 52 (1964) 163-169.

734 O'CONNOR, STANLEY J. Ekamukha-linga from peninsular Siam. JSS 54 (1966) 43-53.

735 O'CONNOR, STANLEY J. Satingphra, an expanded chronology. JMBRAS 39 pt. 1 (1966) 137-144.

736 O'CONNOR, STANLEY J. Si Chon, an early settlement in peninsular Thailand. JSS 56 (1968) 1-18.

737 O'CONNOR, STANLEY J. Western pen-insular Thailand and west Sarawak, ceramic and statuary comparisons, by S. J. O'Connor and Tom Harris-son. SMJ 11 (1964) 562-566.

Art - Thailand

738 PENTH, HANS. Note on old Tak. JSS 61 pt. 1 (1973) 183-186.

739 ROSENFIELD, CLARE S. Mythical animal statues at the Prasat Phra-thepphabidon. T33 pp. 273-300.

740 SMAN VARDHANABHUTI. Note on celadon ware of Sukhothai. JSS 57 (1969) 333-4.

741 SOLHEIM, WILHELM G. Thailand. AP 4 (1960) 67-69.

742 SUBHADRADIS DISKUL. Dated crowned Buddha image from Thailand. G83 pp. 409-416.

743 SUBHADRADIS DISKUL. Pierre Dupont, l'archeologie mone de Dvaravati. E93 pp. 166-174.

744 SULLIVAN, MICHAEL. Pra Sila of Chiengmai and its replicas. E93 pp. 175-178.

745 WALES, H. G. QUARITCH. Stone brackets from the Rua, Nakhon Si Thammarat. JMBRAS 47 pt. 2 (1974) 148.

746 WOODWARD, HIRAM W. Buddha's radiance. JSS 61 pt. 1 (1973) 187-191.

ART - VIETNAM

747 BARNOUIN, R. P. Les bas-reliefs des urnes dynastiques de Hue. SEIB 49 (1974) 425-583.

748 BEZACIER, LOUIS. Attitude inhabituelle commune aux arts Cam et Vietnamien du dragon-makara et du lion. G83 pp. 207-218.

749 LE THI NGOC ANH. Etude de quelques monuments representatifs de l'art francais a Saigon dans les annees 1877-1908. SEIB 48 (1973) 577-605.

750 SMITH, JOHN. Art and archaeology of Viet-Nam in Washington. FA 17 (1960) 1789-1793.

751 TRAN VAN TOAN. Le temple Hue-Nam a Hue. SEIB 44 (1969) 245-276.

752 TRAN VAN TOT. Introduction a l'art ancien du Viet-Nam. SEIB 44 (1969) 5-104.

ART, BUDDHIST *Entered here are general works not confined to one country*

753 LIM, K. W. Studies in later Buddhist iconography. BIJ 120 (1964) 327-341.

ART, CHAM

754 BROCHEUX, MICHELE. Notes sur deux bronzes Chams inedits du Musee National de Saigon. SEIB 41 (1966) 101-104.

755 DOURNES, JACQUES. De seins et d'oreilles, notes a cote de la civilisation Cam. SEIB 46 (1971) 353-359.

ART, CHINESE

756 ADDIS, J. M. Dating of Chinese porcelain found in the Philippines, a historical retrospect. PS 16 (1968) 371-380.

757 HARRISSON, TOM. Ceramic crayfish and related vessels in central Borneo, the Philippines and Sweden. SMJ 15 (1967) 1-9.

758 KAMER AGA-OGLU. Ming porcelain from sites in the Philippines. AP 5 (1961) 243-252.

759 TUTON KABOY. Ceramics and their uses among the coastal Melanus, by Tuton Kaboy and Eine Moore. SMJ 15 (1967) 10-29.

760 ZAINIE, CARLA. Early Chinese stonewares excavated in Sarawak, 1947-67, a suggested first basic classification. SMJ 15 (1967) 30-90.

ART, MON

761 BOELES, J. J. King of Sri Dvaravati and his regalia. JSS 52 (1964) 99-114.

ART EDUCATION - PHILIPPINES

762 ATABUG, ALEJANDRA C. Design for an interdisciplinary music and visual arts course in Philippine liberal arts colleges. PS 21 (1973) 268-292.

763 OCAMPO, GALO B. Fundamental direction in the philosophy and teaching of art in our educational system. UN 35 (1962) 103-112.

ARUNG SINGKANG

764 NOORDUYN, J. Arung Singkang, 1700-1765, how the victory of Wadjo began. IND 13 (1972) 61-68.

ASIA FOUNDATION

765 PIERSON, HARRY H. The Asia Foundation's programming for tribal and minority peoples in Southeast Asia. K86 pp. 847-864.

ASIA, SOUTHEAST

766 BROEK, JAN O. M. Diversity and unity in Southeast Asia. H57 pp. 36-48.

767 FISHER, CHARLES A. View of Southeast Asia. SA 1 (1971) 4-40.

768 LEVI, WERNER. The future of Southeast Asia. AS 10 (1970) 348-357.

769 Neutralisation of Southeast Asia. JCA 2 (1972) 122-3.

770 SINGH, VISHAL. Social development in Southeast Asia. S32 pp. 52-3.

771 Social development, discussion rapporteur's report. S32 pp. 61-62.

ASIA, SOUTHEAST - BIBLIOGRAPHIES

772 METAYE, ROGER. Articles recents sur l'Asie du sud-est. SEIB 46 (1971) 398-409.

773 METAYE, ROGER. Articles recents sur l'Asie du sud-est. SEIB 47 (1972) 112-147.

774 METAYE, ROGER. Articles recents sur l'Asie du sud-est. SEIB 47 (1972) 331-344.

775 METAYE, ROGER. Articles recents sur l'Asie du sud-est. SEIB 47 (1972) 539-552.

776 METAYE, ROGER. Articles recents sur l'Asie du sud-est. SEIB 47 (1972) 753-759.

777 METAYE, ROGER. Articles recents sur l'Asie du sud-est. SEIB 48 (1973) 125-134.

Asia, Southeast - Bibliographies

778 METAYE, ROGER. Articles recents sur l'Asie du sud-est. SEIB 48 (1973) 521-535.

779 METAYE, ROGER. Articles recents sur l'Asie du sud-est. SEIB 48 (1973) 625-630.

780 METAYE, ROGER. Articles recents sur l'Asie du sud-est. SEIB 49 (1974) 149-154.

781 METAYE, ROGER. Articles recents sur l'Asie du sud-est. SEIB 49 (1974) 339-347.

782 METAYE, ROGER. Articles recents sur l'Asie du sud-est. SEIB 49 (1974) 587-596.

ASIA, SOUTHEAST - DEFENCE

783 ADIE, W. A. C. Possibilities for regional defence in the post Vietnam era. RSA (1970) 139-149.

784 GOLDSMITH, R. F. K. Security of South-East Asia, a British assessment. S51 pp. 392-408.

785 MUHAMMED GHAZALI BIN SHAFIE. Defence pattern for South East Asia. S51 pp. 241-246.

786 RAKWIJIT, S. Regional cooperation and defence in the Far East, a Thai view. S51 pp. 409-428.

787 WRIGHT, L. R. Basis for a collective security organization in South and Southeast Asia. S51 pp. 442-457.

ASIA, SOUTHEAST - DESCRIPTION AND TRAVEL

788 COLLESS, BRIAN E. Giovanni de Marignolli, an Italian prelate at the court of the South East Asian Queen of Sheba. JSAH 9 (1968) 325-341.

789 FRANKE, WOLFGANG. Some remarks on Chinese historical sources on Southeast Asia with particular consideration of the Ming period, 1368-1644. SAA 2 (1968) 11-20.

790 HUARD, P. Les enquetes scientifiques francaises et l'exploration du monde exotique aux XVIIe et XVIIIe siecles, par P. Huard et M. Wong. BEF 52 (1964) 143-155.

791 JACK-HINTON, COLIN. Marco Polo in South-East Asia. JSAH 5 (Sept. 1964) 43-103.

792 JACK-HINTON, COLIN. Political and cosmographical background to the Spanish incursion into the Pacific in the sixteenth century. JMBRAS 37 pt. 2 (1964) 125-161.

793 LUCE, G. H. Fu-kan-tu-lu. B92 pp. 191-199.

794 NICHOLL, ROBERT. Odoric of Pordenone, a fourteenth century visitor to Borneo. BMJ 3 pt. 1 (1973) 62-65.

795 ROBERTSON, J. F. Using Pigafetta's journal. BMJ 3 pt. 1 (1973) 100-104.

796 SU CHUNG JEN. Places in South East Asia, the Middle East and Africa visited by Cheng Ho and his companions, A.D. 1405-1433. S93 pp. 198-211.

ASIA, SOUTHEAST - ECONOMIC CONDITIONS

797 ARASARATNAM, S. Introduction. JSAH 10 (1969) 391-394.

798 BUU HOAN. Futuristic look at the transfer of resources and technology to Southeast Asia. AF 2 (1970) 224-235.

799 COWAN, C. D. Introduction. C87 pp. 9-19.

800 Economic survey of Asia and the Far East, 1960. FA 17 (1960) 2119-2129.

801 Economic survey of Asia and the Far East, 1962. FA 19 (1963) 814-834.

802 EMERY, ROBERT F. Economic trends in Asia in 1966. AS 7 (1967) 807-823.

803 FIRTH, R. W. Money, work and social change in Indo-Pacific economic systems. S48 pp. 7-20.

804 HLA MYINT. Overall report. S63 pp. 2-105.

805 KIM, KWAN S. Economic impact of the Vietnam war in Southeast and East Asia with special references to balance of payments effects. AF 2 (1970) 22-31.

806 MALENBAUM, WILFRED. Progress through the rich or poor farmer, case studies in Asia. AS 8 (1968) 149-156.

807 NGUYEN CAO HACH. Western economic policies and Asian trade development. AS 1 (Dec. 1961) 11-18.

808 PAAUW, DOUGLAS S. Economic progress in Southeast Asia. T45 pp. 556-584.

809 SINKIN, C. G. F. New Zealand's economic interests in Southeast Asia. JSAS 2 (1971) 66-70.

Asia, Southeast - Foreign relations - Australia

810 TREGONNING, K. G. Failure of economic development and political democracy in Southeast Asia. AST 5 (1967) 323-331.

ASIA, SOUTHEAST - FOREIGN RELATIONS **

811 KOJIMA, KIYOSHI. Foreign economic relations, by Kiyoshi Kojima, Saburo Okita and Peter Drysdale. S63 pp. 254-368.

812 LEVI, WERNER. Elitist nature of new Asia's foreign policy. AS 7 (1967) 762-775.

813 LITTAUA, FERDINAND Z. Southeast Asia and the scramble of the major powers for influence in the Indian Ocean. AST 8 (1970) 374-377.

814 NUECHTERLEIN, DONALD E. Prospects for regional security in Southeast Asia. AS 8 (1968) 806-816.

815 VON DER MEHDEN, FRED R. Southeast Asian relations with Africa. AS 5 (1965) 341-349.

816 WURFEL, DAVID. Pattern of Southeast Asian response to international politics. H35 pp. 71-107.

ASIA, SOUTHEAST - FOREIGN RELATIONS - AUSTRALIA

817 CATLEY, R. Prelude to Vietnam. JSAS 2 (1971) 38-48.

818 CATLEY, R. Prospects for revolution in South-East Asia in the next decade, the role of Australia, by Bob Catley and Bruce McFarlane. JCA 4 (1974) 308-323.

819 EVANS, DAVID. Australia and developing countries, contradictions

Asia, Southeast - Foreign relations -
Australia

of capitalism. JCA 2 (1972) 131-162.

820 MARTIN, JAMES. Australia and Southeast Asia. SA 3 (1974) 752-776.

821 MILLAR, T. B. Australian policies towards Asia. AQ (1971) 305-318.

822 MILLAR, T. B. Trends in Australian defence policy. JSAS 2 (1971) 49-55.

823 MILLER, J. D. B. Australia and Southeast Asia, national interests in the 1970's. JSAS 2 (1971) 32-37.

824 PATRIDGE, SHANE. Australian defence. S51 pp. 310-323.

825 VAN DER KROEF, JUSTUS M. The Gordon manner, Australia, Southeast Asia, and the United States. PA 42 (1969) 311-333.

ASIA, SOUTHEAST - FOREIGN RELATIONS -
CANADA

826 ANDREW, ARTHUR. Canada and Asia, the shifting power balance. PA 45 (1972) 403-408.

ASIA, SOUTHEAST - FOREIGN RELATIONS -
CHINA

827 CHIU LING-YEONG. Chinese maritime expansion, 1368-1644. JOSA 3 pt. 1 (1965) 27-47.

828 GURTOV, MELVIN. Sino-Soviet relations and Southeast Asia, recent developments and future possibilities. PA 43 (1970) 491-505.

829 KALLGREN, JOYCE K. Nationalist Chinese military strength, its

use in South-East Asia. S51 pp. 297-309.

830 LUCE, G. H. Fu-kan-tu-lu. B92 pp. 191-199.

831 MAHAJANI, USHA. U.S.-Chinese detente and prospects for China's rehabilitation in Southeast Asia. SA 3 (1974) 712-739.

832 MUTHIRAM, T. G. China's policy in South East Asia. JCA 3 (1973) 335-346.

833 PETACH, L. Early relations of China with South-Eastern Asia. S87 pp. 186-190.

834 TRETIAK, DANIEL. Is China preparing to turn out, changes in Chinese levels of attention to the international environment. AS 11 (1971) 219-237.

835 WANG GUNGWU. China and South-East Asia, 1402-1424. S89 pp. 375-401.

836 WEISS, UDO. China's aid to and trade with the developing countries of the third world. AQ (1974) 203-213.

837 WEISS, UDO. China's aid to and trade with the developing countries of the third world. AQ (1974) 263-309.

838 WU CHEN-TSAI. Role of the Republic of China in collective defense. S51 pp. 294-296.

ASIA, SOUTHEAST - FOREIGN RELATIONS -
FRANCE

839 KENNEDY, B. E. Anglo-French rivalry in Southeast Asia, 1763-93, some repercussions. JSAS 4 (1973) 199-215.

ASIA, SOUTHEAST - FOREIGN RELATIONS -
GREAT BRITAIN

842   ALLEN, RICHARD. Britain's colonial aftermath in South East Asia.
AS 3 (1963) 403-414.

843   KENNEDY, B. E. Anglo-French rivalry in Southeast Asia, 1763-93,
some repercussions. JSAS 4 (1973)
199-215.

844   TARLING, NICHOLAS. British policy
in Malayan waters in the nineteenth century. J45 pp. 73-88.

ASIA, SOUTHEAST - FOREIGN RELATIONS -
INDIA

845   MAJUMDAR, R. C. Overseas expeditions of King Rajendra Cola. G83
pp. 338-342.

846   VASIL, R. K. India and South-
East Asia. S51 pp. 207-218.

ASIA, SOUTHEAST - FOREIGN RELATIONS -
JAPAN

847   FIFIELD, RUSSELL. Japan and post-
war Southeast Asia. AST 3 (1965)
370-376.

848   HOWELL, LLEWELLYN D. Great power
influence among Southeast Asian
states, a quantitative measurement. AST 9 (1971) 243-273.

849   KAHN, HERMAN. Japan and Pacific
Asia in the 1970's, by Herman

Asia, Southeast - Foreign relations -
Union of Soviet Socialist Republics

Kahn and Max Singer. AS 11 (1971)
399-412.

850   KAKIZAWA, KOJI. Quelques reflexions sur les relations economiques entre le Japon et les pays
d'Asie. RSA (1970) 249-261.

851   MENDEL, DOUGLAS H. Limits of
Japanese aid to South and Southeast Asia. AF 6 pt. 2 (1974) 1-
11.

852   ONISHI, AKIRA. Japanese interests
in Southeast Asia, a Japanese
view. AS 11 (1971) 413-421.

853   PLUVIER, JAN M. Anti-Japans ver-
zet in Zuid-Oost-Azie-enkele
notities. B85 pp. 175-187.

854   Presence et politique economiques
japonaises en Asie du sud-est. FA
(1974 pt. 2) 19-33.

ASIA, SOUTHEAST - FOREIGN RELATIONS -
NEW ZEALAND

855   SINKIN, C. G. F. New Zealand's
economic interests in Southeast
Asia. JSAS 2 (1971) 66-70.

ASIA, SOUTHEAST - FOREIGN RELATIONS -
UNION OF SOVIET SOCIALIST REPUBLICS

856   GURTOV, MELVIN. Sino-Soviet relations and Southeast Asia, recent
developments and future possibilities. PA 43 (1970) 491-505.

857   QUESTED, R. Russian interest in
Southeast Asia, outlines and
sources, 1803-1970. JSAS 1 pt. 2
(1970) 48-60.

858   WU, YUAN-LI. The Soviet economic
offensive in Asia and its effect
on United States-Asian trade. C35
pp. 291-317.

---

840   KERVEN, DANIEL. Esquisse sur la
politique asiatique de la France.
FA 20 (1965) 283-297.

841   KERVEN, DANIEL. On French policy
in Asia. FA 20 (1965) 298-302.

Asia, Southeast - Foreign relations -
  United States

<u>ASIA, SOUTHEAST - FOREIGN RELATIONS -
  UNITED STATES</u>

859 ALLISON, JOHN M. United States
     diplomacy in Southeast Asia, the
     limits of policy. H35 pp. 165-189.

860 CADY, JOHN F. Historical back-
     ground of United States policy in
     Southeast Asia. H35 pp. 1-26.

861 DARLING, FRANK C. United States
     policy in Southeast Asia, perma-
     nency and change. AS 14 (1974)
     608-626.

862 DEVILLERS, PHILIPPE. Strategies
     et tactiques americaines en Asie
     orientale. FA 24 (1970) 219-250.

863 GEERTZ, CLIFFORD. Social-cultural
     context of policy in Southeast
     Asia. H35 pp. 45-70.

864 GORALSKI, ROBERT S. Radio broad-
     casting in Asia and the "Voice of
     America." S90.1 pp. 88-97.

865 GOULD, JAMES W. American imperi-
     alism in Southeast Asia before
     1898. JSAS 3 (1972) 306-314.

866 HENDERSON, WILLIAM. Some reflec-
     tions on United States policy in
     Southeast Asia. H35 pp. 249-263.

867 HOWELL, LLEWELLYN D. Great power
     influence among Southeast Asian
     states, a quantitative measure-
     ment. AST 9 (1971) 243-273.

868 JOHNSON, ROBERT H. Nixon doctrine
     and the new policy environment.
     J28 pp. 175-200.

869 JORDAN, AMOS A. United States
     foreign assistance in Southeast
     Asia. H35 pp. 212-226.

870 LINEBARGER, PAUL M. A. Psycho-
     logical instruments of policy in
     Southeast Asia, by Paul M. A. and
     Genevieve C. Linebarger. H35 pp.
     227-248.

871 NUECHTERLEIN, DONALD E. U.S.
     national interests in Southeast
     Asia, a reappraisal. AS 11 (1971)
     1054-1070.

872 QUAH SIEW TIEN, JON. Assessment
     of United States' technical
     assistance programs in public ad-
     ministration in Southeast Asia.
     RSAS 2 (1972) 37-48.

873 SIMON, SHELDON W. The Nixon doc-
     trine and prospects for Asian re-
     gional security cooperation. AF
     5 pt. 1 (1973) 1-16.

874 SMITH, ROGER M. Some Southeast
     Asian views of American foreign
     policy. H35 pp. 108-133.

875 SOWARD, F. H. Great debate over
     American policy in Southeast Asia.
     PA 40 (1967) 341-346.

876 SPECTOR, RONALD. American image
     of Southeast Asia, 1790-1865, a
     preliminary assessment. JSAS 3
     (1972) 299-305.

877 TRAGER, FRANK N. American foreign
     policy in Southeast Asia. S90.6
     pp. 17-59.

878 TRAGER, FRANK N. Never negotiate
     freedom, the case of Laos and
     Vietnam. AS 1 (Jan. 1962) 3-11.

879 VAN DER KROEF, JUSTUS M. The
     Gordon manner, Australia, South-
     east Asia, and the United States.
     PA 42 (1969) 311-333.

880 WOLF, CHARLES. Some aspects of the value of Southeast Asia to the United States. H35 pp. 27-44.

881 WU, YUAN-LI. The Soviet economic offensive in Asia and its effect on United States-Asian trade. C35 pp. 291-317.

882 YOUNG, KENNETH T. Implications for United States policy. AS 11 (1971) 422-427.

883 ZABLOCKI, CLEMENT J. The political climate of America's trade with Asia. C35 pp. 1-10.

ASIA, SOUTHEAST - HISTORY **

884 ALATAS, SYED HUSSEIN. Theoretical aspects of Southeast Asian history, John Bastin and the study of Southeast Asian history. AST 2 (1964) 247-260.

885 ARASARATNAM, S. Introduction. JSAH 10 (1969) 391-394.

886 ARASARATNAM, S. Use of Dutch material for Southeast Asian historical writing. JSAH 3 (Mar. 1962) 95-105.

887 BASSETT, D. K. European influence in South East Asia, c.1500-1630. JSAH 4 (Sept. 1963) 134-165.

888 BENDA, HARRY J. Peasant movements in colonial Southeast Asia. AST 3 (1965) 420-434.

889 BENDA, HARRY J. The structure of Southeast Asian history, some preliminary observations. JSAH 3 (Mar. 1962) 106-138.

890 BENDA, HARRY J. The structure of Southeast Asian history, some preliminary observations. T45 pp. 23-44.

891 BOXER, C. R. Portuguese and Spanish projects for the conquest of Southeast Asia, 1580-1600. JAH 3 (1969) 118-136.

892 COEDES, GEORGE. L'annee du lievre, 1219 A.D. J41 pp. 83-88.

893 COEDES, GEORGE. Le XIe siecle dans la peninsule indochinoise. FA 18 (1962) 247-253.

894 COEDES, GEORGE. Some problems in the ancient history of the Hinduized states of South-East Asia. JSAH 5 (Sept. 1964) 1-14.

895 COLLANTES, LOURDES Y. Bibliography of materials available in the library system of the University of the Philippines on the modern history of Southeast Asia, by Lourdes Y. Collantes and J. A. Larkin. AST 2 (1964) 261-285.

896 Current research in South-East Asian history. JSAH 2 (Oct. 1961) 83-90.

897 HALL, D. G. E. International conflicts in South-East Asia, a historical survey. JOSA 3 pt. 2 (1965) 27-38.

898 HALL, D. G. E. Looking at Southeast Asian history. JAS 19 (1959-60) 243-253.

899 HALL, D. G. E. On the study of Southeast Asian history. PA 33 (1960) 268-281.

900 HALL, D. G. E. Recent tendencies in the study of the early history of South-East Asia. PA 39 (1966) 339-348.

Asia, Southeast - History

901 L'histoire de l'Asie du sud-est. SEIB 40 (1965) 349-352.

902 JACK-HINTON, C. Ophirian conjecture, Hispano-Lusitanian optimism in South-East Asia and the Pacific in the sixteenth century. PHR 1 pt. 1 (1965) 194-224.
Comment: RODRIGUEZ, ISACIO R. Literary value of the Ophirian conjecture in the Spanish writings and enterprises of the 16th century. PHR 1 pt. 1 (1965) 224-228.

903 KELLY, G. M. Teaching of Southeast Asian history. JSAH 7 (Mar. 1966) 86-96.

904 KENNEDY, B. E. Anglo-French rivalry in Southeast Asia, 1763-93, some repercussions. JSAS 4 (1973) 199-215.

905 LY TIO FANE, MADELEINE. Pierre Poivre et l'expansion francaise dans l'Indo-Pacifique. BEF 53 (1966) 453-510.

906 MACGREGOR, I. A. Some aspects of Portuguese historical writing of the sixteenth and seventeenth centuries on Southeast Asia. H18 pp. 172-199.

907 MEILINK-ROELOFSZ, M. A. P. European influence in Southeast Asia, 1500-1630. JSAH 5 (Sept. 1964) 184-197.

908 TARLING, NICHOLAS. Superintendence of British interests in Southeast Asia in the nineteenth century. JSAH 7 (Mar. 1966) 97-110.

909 WERTHEIM, W. F. Asian history and the western historian, rejoinder to Professor Bastin. BIJ 119 (1963) 149-160.

ASIA, SOUTHEAST - LAWS, STATUTES, ETC.

910 KHETARPAL, S. P. Codification of Hindu law. C39 pp. 202-233.

ASIA, SOUTHEAST - MINORITIES

911 DOEKER, GUNTHER. Federalism, human rights and the protection of minorities in South and South East Asia. D44 pp. 49-62.

912 KUNSTADTER, PETER. Introduction. K86 pp. 3-72.

913 PIERSON, HARRY H. The Asia Foundation's programming for tribal and minority peoples in Southeast Asia. K86 pp. 847-864.

ASIA, SOUTHEAST - POLITICS AND GOVERNMENT

914 CARNELL, FRANCIS. Political ideas and ideologies in South and South-East Asia. R64 pp. 261-302.

915 CHATTERJEE, B. R. Guided democracy at work in South-East Asia. S87 pp. 415-418.

916 CORPUZ, ONOFRE D. Political evolution of South and Southeast Asia since independence, a survey. AST 2 (1964) 67-70.

917 EMERSON, RUPERT. Erosion of democracy. JAS 20 (1960-1) 1-8.

918 GIRLING, J. L. S. Regional security in Southeast Asia. JSAS 2 (1971) 56-65.

919 JACOBY, ERICH H. Revolution and intervention. JCA 1 pt. 1 (1970) 15-19.

920 KATTENBURG, PAUL M. Obstacles to political community, Southeast Asia in comparative perspective. SA 2 (1972-3) 192-209.

921 KITAGAWA, JOSEPH M. Buddhism and Asian politics. AS 2 (July 1962) 1-11.

922 LACOUTURE, JEAN. Notes sur les Cesars du tiers-monde. FA 18 (1962) 9-15.

923 LEDESMA, LILIA S. Concept of sovereignty in pre-modern Asia, its socio-political implications. AST 9 (1971) 89-106.

924 LOVELL, JOHN P. Military and political change in Asia, by John P. Lovell and C. I. Eugene Kim. PA 40 (1967) 113-123.

925 MILNE, R. S. Political modernization and development, a review article. PA 39 (1966) 135-144.

926 MUS, PAUL. Cosmodrames et politique en Asie du sud-est. D44 pp. 75-98.

927 PAUKER, GUY J. Political doctrines and practical politics in Southeast Asia. PA 35 (1962) 3-10.

928 ROSE, SAUL. Political institutions. R64 pp. 303-343.

929 ROSE, SAUL. Political modernisation in Asia. FA 22 (1968) 31-45.

930 ROUCEK, JOSEPH S. Geopolitics of Southeast Asia. FA 19 (1964) 1078-1094.

931 SHEN YU DAI. Asian unity and disunity, impressions and reflections, 1964-65. AST 4 (1966) 135-148.

932 SHILS, EDWARD. The military in the political development of the new states. J52 pp. 7-67.

933 THOMSON, GEORGE C. Emergence of political leadership in the change from colonialism to nationalism. L23 pp. 17-38.

934 TREGONNING, K. G. Failure of economic development and political democracy in Southeast Asia. AST 5 (1967) 323-331.

935 ZINKIN, MAURICE. Operative forces. R64 pp. 344-378.

ASIA, SOUTHEAST - POPULATION

936 CHANDRASEKHAR, S. Asia's population problems and solutions. C21 pp. 11-47.

937 FISHER, CHARLES A. Some comments on population growth in South-East Asia, with special reference to the period since 1830. C87 pp. 48-71.

938 OEI JIN BEE. Teaching about the demographic problems of Southeast Asia, by Oei Jin Bee, Teo Siew Eng and Tan Lee Wah. RSAS 3 pts. 1-2 (1973) 15-26.

939 PAW U, RICHARD. Population problems in Asia. UN 38 (1965) 587-598.

940 STUART, FRANCIS H. Patterns of population and society in Southeast Asia. SJ 15 (1968) 546-554.

941 YOU POH SENG. Aspects of population growth and population policy, by You Poh Seng and Stephen Yeh. S63 pp. 448-580.

Asia, Southeast - Religion

early Indonesian novel. MAS 7
(1973) 179–192.

ATENEO DE MANILA UNIVERSITY

958 BERNAD, MIGUEL A. The Ateneo is
like malaria or insanity or almost like baptism. PS 21 (1973)
207–212.

959 FERRIOLS, ROQUE J. Memoir of six
years. PS 22 (1974) 338–345.

Atjeh *See* ACHEH

ATONI

960 CUNNINGHAM, CLARK E. Atoni kin
categories and conventional behavior. BIJ 123 (1967) 53–70.

961 CUNNINGHAM, CLARK E. Order in
the Atoni house. BIJ 120 (1964)
34–68.

962 CUNNINGHAM, CLARK E. Soba, an
Atoni village of west Timor. K52
pp. 63–89.

963 MIDDELKOOP, P. De betekenis van
de Timorese term Atoni Amaf. BIJ
127 (1971) 393–396.

ATTITUDES

964 CATAPUSAN, BENICIO T. New approaches to ethnic understanding.
PSSHR 30 (1965) 329–342.

965 HOWELL, LLEWELLYN. Attitudinal
distance in Southeast Asia, social
and political ingredients in integration. SA 3 (1974–5) 577–605.

966 TAMNEY, JOSEPH B. Economic satisfaction and political loyalty in

Southeast Asia. SAJSS 1 pt. 2
(1973) 35–42.

ATTITUDES – BURMA

967 THEODORSON, GEORGE A. Attitudes
of Burmese men and women to male
dominance in the family. JBRS 51
(1968) 17–21.

968 THEODORSON, GEORGE A. Burmese attitudes towards children. JBRS
45 (1962) 205–208.

ATTITUDES – INDONESIA

969 KUNTOWIDJOJO. Economic and religious attitudes of entrepreneurs
in a village industry, notes on
the community of Batur. IND 12
(1971) 47–55.

970 LAIYA, BAMBOWO. Attitude of Nias
towards Christianity. SJ 21
(1974) 100–115.

971 THOMAS, R. MURRAY. Attitudes
toward birth control in Bandung,
Indonesia. IND 4 (1967) 74–87.

ATTITUDES – PHILIPPINES **

972 GOMEZ, HILARIO M. Studying attitudes of Muslims in the Philippines. SJ 19 (1972) 425–443.

973 GREEN, JUSTIN J. Social backgrounds, attitudes and political
behavior, a study of a Philippine
elite. SA 2 (1972–3) 300–336.

974 PORMENTO, ZENAIDA G. Attitudes of
teachers towards student activism
in the Philippines. SLURJ 1
(1970) 643–668.

Attitudes - Philippines

975 REYNOLDS, HARRIET R. Continuity and change as shown by attitudes of two generations of Chinese in the Ilocos provinces, Philippines. SJ 13 (1966) 12-21.

976 VALDES, M. TRINITAS. Parental attitudes and their effects on exceptional children. SLURJ 1 (1970) 631-642.

977 WEIGHTMAN, GEORGE HENRY. Study of prejudice in a personalistic society, an analysis of an attitude survey of college students, University of the Philippines. AST 2 (1964) 87-101.

978 YOUNGBLOOD, ROBERT L. Family strictness, social class and political attitudes among Manila high school students. AS 13 (1973) 761-771.

ATTITUDES - VIETNAM

979 MARR, DAVID. Political attitudes and activities of young urban intellectuals in South Viet-Nam. AS 6 (1966) 249-263.

AUSTRONESIAN LANGUAGES

980 ANCEAUX, J. C. Austronesian linguistics and intra-subgroup comparison. C43 pp. 309-314.

981 CHRETIEN, C. DOUGLAS. Statistical structure of the proto-Austronesian morph. C43 pp. 243-270.

982 DYEN, ISIDORE. Austronesian languages and proto-Austronesian. S22 pp. 5-54.

983 HAUDRICOURT, ANDRE G. Problems of Austronesian comparative philology. C43 pp. 315-329.

984 HOLMER, NILS M. Types of consonant alternation in Austronesian, especially Melanesian. C44 pp. 475-494.

985 KAHLER, H. Contribution to a consideration of the present state of knowledge in the field of Austronesian languages. L55 pp. 156-159.

986 MILKE, WILHELM. Comparative notes on the Austronesian languages of New Guinea. C43 pp. 330-348.

987 POU, SAVEROS. Proto-Indonesian and Mon-Khmer, by Saveros Pou and Philip N. Jenner. AP 17 (1974) 112-124.

988 ROSARIO, GONSALO DEL. Modernization-standardization plan for the Austronesian derived national languages of Southeast Asia. AST 6 (1968) 1-18.

989 UHLENBECK, E. M. Comparative study of the Austronesian languages. L55 pp. 24-27.

AUTOMATION - PHILIPPINES

990 ABINOJA, JOSE B. Design of a system to process current student data for Saint Louis University on the IBM 1130 computer. SLURJ 2 (1971) 75-170.

991 FRONDA, PAUL E. Problems encountered in the processing of current academic data by the IBM electronic data processing department of Saint Louis University. SLURJ 4 (1973) 149-193.

AYUDHYA

992   BOELES, J. J.   Note on an eye wit-
      ness account in Dutch of the de-
      struction of Ayudhya in 1767.   JSS
      56 (1968) 101-111.

993   DAMRONG, PRINCE.   The foundation
      of Ayuthia.   S44.3 pp. 199-202.

994   DHANI NIVAT, PRINCE.   The city of
      Thawarawadi Sri Ayudhya.   S44.3
      pp. 229-235.

995   FRANKFURTER, O.   Events in Ayud-
      dhya from Chulasakaraj 686-966.
      S44.1 pp. 38-64.

996   GRISWOLD, A. B.   Epigraphic and
      historical studies.   IV. Law prom-
      ulgated by the king of Ayudhya
      in 1397 A.D.   JSS 57 (1969) 109-
      148.

997   HA WAT, KHUN LUANG.   Statement.
      S44.6 pp. 185-228.

998   MOSEL, JAMES N.   Recently dis-
      covered account of a Spanish em-
      bassy to Ayudhya in 1718.   F38
      pp. 123-128.

999   STERNSTEIN, LARRY.   Krung Kao,
      the old capital of Ayutthaya.   JSS
      53 (1965) 83-121.

1000 STERNSTEIN, LARRY.   Notes on
      Krung Kao.   JSS 54 (1966) 211-220.

1001 SUMET, JUMSAI.   Reconstruction of
      the city plan of Ayudhya.   T33
      pp. 301-314.

1002 WYATT, DAVID K.   Abridged royal
      chronicle of Ayudhya of Prince
      Paramanuchitchinorot.   JSS 61 pt.
      1 (1973) 25-50.

BA HAN

1003 Ba Han, an obituary.   JBRS 52
      (June 1969) 25-6.

BA LWIN

1004 Obituary note, Maha Tharay Sithu U
      Ba Lwin.   JBRS 51 (1968) 189.

BA SHIN

1005 NAI PAN HLA.   Bohmu Ba Shin, an
      obituary.   JBRS 55 (1972) 101.

BAC LIEU PROVINCE

1006 NGUYEN HUY.   Les marais salants de
      la Province de Bac-Lieu, par
      Nguyen Huy et Huynh Tu.   SEIB 49
      (1974) 285-305.

BAGOBO

1007 RAATS, P. J.   On a spirit of the
      Bagobo.   D67 pp. 86-100.

BAGOBO LITERATURE

1008 MANUEL, E. ARSENIO.   Upland Bagobo
      narratives, recorded with the help
      of Bagobo friends.   PSSHR 26
      (1961) 431-552.

BAGUIO

1009 BUEN, FLORENCIO.   A year-round
      school program for the Baguio city
      high school.   SLURJ 5 (1974) 188-
      198.

1010 GAROY, GABINO L.   Problems that
      beset the accountancy practice in
      Baguio.   SLURJ 5 (1974) 392-417.

Baguio

1011 MULATA, JOSE GAVILANGOSO. Pro-
      duction and distribution problems
      encountered in the management of
      the water supply system of Baguio
      City. SLURJ 2 (1971) 177-241.

1012 TORRENTO, CARIDAD J. Establishing
      norms for the Philippine non-
      verbal intelligence test in Baguio
      City's public elementary schools
      and the study of children's cate-
      gorization responses, by Caridad
      J. Torrento and Juan Ngalob.
      SLURJ 2 (1971) 540-614.

1013 TRINIDAD, CARIDAD E. A study of
      the academic preparation and
      assignment of teachers in the
      Catholic secondary schools of
      Baguio City and the mountain prov-
      inces for the school year 1971-
      1972. SLURJ 4 (1973) 240-304.

BAGUIO RELIGIOUS ACCULTURATION CONFER-
      ENCE

1014 NACPIL, EMERITO P. Theologians
      response to the BRAC 1967 Filipino
      family survey. SLQ 6 (1968) 426-
      427.

1015 POETHIG, RICHARD P. BRAC in pros-
      pect. SJ 19 (1972) 217-8.

1016 REYNOLDS, HUBERT. BRAC 1971,
      retrospect and prospect. SJ 19
      (1972) 209-216.

BAHNAR

1017 BANKER, JOHN E. Bahnar religion.
      SA 2 (1972-3) 88-124.

1018 GUILLEMINET, P. Languages spe-
      ciaux utilises dans la tribu Bah-
      nar du Kontum, sud Viet-nam, Indo-
      chine. BEF 50 (1960) 117-132.

BAHNAR LANGUAGE

1019 BANKER, ELIZABETH M. Bahnar af-
      fixation. M57 pp. 99-117.

1020 BANKER, ELIZABETH M. Bahnar re-
      duplication. M57 pp. 119-134.

1021 BANKER, JOHN E. Transformational
      paradigms of Bahnar clauses. M57
      pp. 7-39.

1022 SMITH, KENNETH D. Eastern north
      Bahnaric: Cua and Kotua. M61 pp.
      113-118.

BAJAU

1023 ALMAN, JOHN H. Bajau pottery.
      SMJ 9 (1960) 583-602.

1024 ALMAN, JOHN H. Bajau weaving,
      Tempasuk plain. SMJ 9 (1960) 603-
      637.

1025 CABRERA, AGUSTIN A. Badjaus,
      cultural identity and education.
      UN 42 (1969) 107-142.

1026 KIEFER, THOMAS M. Gravemarkers
      and the repression of sexual sym-
      bolism, the case of two Philip-
      pine-Borneo Moslem societies, by
      Thomas M. Kiefer and Clifford
      Sather. BIJ 126 (1970) 75-90.

1027 NIMMO, H. ARLO. Bajau of Sulu,
      fiction and fact. PS 16 (1968)
      771-776.

1028 NIMMO, H. ARLO. Reflections on
      Bajau history. PS 16 (1968) 32-
      59.

1029 NIMMO, H. ARLO. You will remember
      us because we have sung for you.
      PS 20 (1972) 299-322.

1030 SATHER, CLIFFORD. Note on Bajau gravermarkers from the Semporna District of Sabah. SMJ 16 (1968) 103-110.

BAJAU LITERATURE

1031 SATHER, CLIFFORD. Bajau riddles. SMJ 12 (1965) 162.

BAKETANS

1032 SANDIN, BENEDICT. Baketans. SMJ 15 (1967) 228-242.

1033 SANDIN, BENEDICT. Baketans. SMJ 16 (1968) 111-121.

BAKO NATIONAL PARK

1034 BROWNE, F. G. Borer beetles from Bako National Park. SMJ 10 (1961) 300-318.

1035 START, ANTHONY N. Some bats of Bako National Park, Sarawak. SMJ 20 (1972) 371-376.

BALAGTAS, FRANCISCO

1036 SAN JUAN, E. What is Balagtas' *To Cecilia* all about, an experiment in interpretation. GEJ 7 (1964) 48-62.

BALANGAO LANGUAGE

1037 SHETLER, JO. Balangao nonverbal clause nuclei. AST 6 (1968) 208-222.

BALESTIER, JOSEPH B.

1038 SHAROM AHMAT. Joseph B. Balestier, the first American Consul in Singapore, 1833-1852. JMBRAS 39 pt. 2 (1966) 108-122.

BALFAS, M.

1039 BALFAS, M. Child of the revolution, *Anak revolusi*. IND 17 (1974) 43-50.

BALI

1040 BIRKELBACH, AUBREY W. Subak association. IND 16 (1973) 153-169.

1041 CHINKAK. Statement of Chinkak on Bali, translated by Charnvit Kaset-siri. IND 7 (1969) 83-122.

1042 DAMAIS, LOUIS-CHARLES. Etudes balinaises. BEF 51 (1963) 125-131.

1043 Les etudes balinaises en Indonesie. AR 7 (1974) 171-174.

1044 GARDNER, ESTELLE. Island strife and L. V. Helms. SMJ 14 (1966) 396-421.

1045 GRADER, C. J. Irrigation system in the region of Jembrana. B18 pp. 267-288.

1046 GRAVES, ELIZABETH. Nineteenth century Siamese account of Bali, with introduction and notes by Elizabeth Graves and Charnvit Kaset-siri. IND 7 (1969) 77-81.

1047 GUENOT, HENRI. Pages d'exotisme. III. Le planteur de Java, 1860. AR 3 (1972) 106-112.

Bali

BALINESE

BALINESE LANGUAGE

BALINESE LITERATURE

1072 HOOYKAAS, C. Balinese folktale.
      J41 pp. 185-192.

1073 HOOYKAAS, C. Balinese Sengguhu
      priest, a shaman, but not a sufi,
      a Saiva and a **Vaisnava**. B38 pp.
      267-281.

1074 HOOYKAAS, C. Books made in Bali.
      BIJ 119 (1963) 371-386.

1075 HOOYKAAS, C. Exorcistic litany
      from Bali. BIJ 125 (1969) 356-
      370.

1076 HOOYKAAS, JACOBA. Balinese folk-
      tale on the origin of mice. BIJ
      117 **(1961)** 279-281.

1077 HOOYKAAS, JACOBA. Changeling in
      Balinese folklore and religion.
      BIJ 116 (1960) 424-436.

1078 SUKARTO K. ATMODJO, M. M. Pre-
      liminary report on the copper
      plate inscription of Asahduren.
      BIJ 126 (1970) 215-227.

1079 SUKARTO K. ATMODJO, M. M. Second
      colophon of the *Nagarakrtagama*.
      BIJ 129 (1973) 277-286.

1080 SUPOMO, S. Lord of the mountains,
      in the fourteenth century kakawin.
      BIJ 128 (1972) 281-297.

BALTAZAR, FRANCISCO

1081 LUMBERA, BIENVENIDO. *Florante at
      Laura* and the formalization of
      tradition in Tagalog poetry. PS
      15 (1967) 545-575.

BALUGYUN ISLAND

1082 THET LWIN. Balugyun sample sur-
      vey, 1962. JBRS 48 (June 1965)
      43-56.

BALUY RIVER

1083 ROUSSEAU, JEROME. Baluy area.
      SMJ 22 (1974) 17-27.

BAMBANG KUSNOHADI

1084 GUNAWAN, ANDREW H. Honor to a
      friend, Bambang Kusnohadi. IND
      16 (1973) 148-152.

BANDUNG CONFERENCE

1085 PAUKER, GUY J. Rise and fall of
      Afro-Asian solidarity. AS 5
      (1965) 425-432.

1086 WEINSTEIN, FRANKLIN B. Second
      Asian-African conference, pre-
      liminary bouts. AS 5 (1965) 359-
      373.

BANG CHAN

1087 HANKS, JANE RICHARDSON. Rural
      Thai village's view of human
      character. F38 pp. 77-84.

1088 HANKS, LUCIEN M. Bang Chan and
      Bangkok, five perspectives on the
      relation of local to national his-
      tory. JSAH 8 (1967) 250-256.

BANGKOK

1089 FRYER, D. W. The million city in
      Southeast Asia. T45 pp. 72-87.

1090 HANKS, LUCIEN M. Bang Chan and
      Bangkok, five perspectives on the
      relation of local to national his-
      tory. JSAH 8 (1967) 250-256.

1091 SMITHIES, MICHAEL. Village Mons
      of Bangkok. JSS 60 pt. 1 (1972)
      307-332.

Bangkok

1092 STERNSTEIN, LARRY. Bangkok at mid-nineteenth century. F38 pp. 17-23.

1093 STERNSTEIN, LARRY. Bangkok at the turn of the century, Mongkut and Chulalongkorn entertain the west. JSS 54 (1966) 55-71.

1094 STERNSTEIN, LARRY. Planning the future of Bangkok. D92 pp. 243-254.

BANJARMASIN

1095 NICHOLL, ROBERT. Mission of Father Antonino Ventimiglia to Borneo. BMJ 2 pt. 4 (1972) 183-205.

1096 SUNTHARALINGAM, R. British in Banjarmasin, an abortive attempt at settlement, 1700-1707. JSAH 4 (Sept. 1963) 33-50.

BANKS AND BANKING *See also* ASIAN DEVELOPMENT BANK, FINANCE, MONEY

1097 LEIGHTON-BOYCE, J. British eastern exchange banks, an outline of the main factors affecting their business up to 1914. C87 pp. 20-26.

BANKS AND BANKING - BURMA

1098 MAUNG MAUNG HLA. Some aspects of central banking in Burma. B91 pp. 147-155.

BANKS AND BANKING - INDONESIA

1099 ARNDT, H. W. Banking in hyper-inflation and stabilization. G52 pp. 359-395.

1100 WARDHANA, ALI. The Indonesian banking system, the central bank. G52 pp. 338-358.

BANKS AND BANKING - MALAYSIA

1101 ISMAIL ALI BIN MOHAMED ALI. Role of central banking in industrialization. MER 8 pt. 1 (1963) 14-19.

1102 LEE, SHENG YI. Banking and financial development of Singapore and Malaysia since 1958. SAJSS 1 pt. 1 (1973) 1-16.

1103 LEE, SHENG YI. Development of commercial banking in Singapore and the states of Malaya. MER 11 pt. 1 (1966) 84-100.

1104 LEE, SHENG YI. Liquidity and growth, the case of a local bank, by Lee Sheng Yi and Kenny Wee. SAJSS 2 (1974) 1-27.

1105 SHORT, BROCK K. Indigenous banking in an early period of development, the Straits Settlements, 1914-1940. MER 16 pt. 1 (1971) 57-75.

1106 SIEW NIM CHEE. Federation central bank. S48 pp. 480-486.

1107 SILCOCK, T. H. Merdeka in the money market. S48 pp. 487-493.

1108 TAN EE LEONG. Chinese banks incorporated in Singapore and the Federation of Malaya. JMBRAS 42 pt. 1 (1969) 256-281.

1109 TAN EE LEONG. Chinese banks incorporated in Singapore and the Federation of Malaya. S48 pp. 454-479.

BANKS AND BANKING - PHILIPPINES

1110 CUADERNO, MIGUEL. The central bank and economic planning. M38 pp. 92-108.

1111 LICAROS, GREGORIO S. The banking system and economic planning. M38 pp. 109-122.

BANKS AND BANKING - SINGAPORE

1112 LEE, SHENG YI. Banking and financial development of Singapore and Malaysia since 1958. SAJSS 1 pt. 1 (1973) 1-16.

1113 LEE, SHENG YI. Development of commercial banking in Singapore and the states of Malaya. MER 11 pt. 1 (1966) 84-100.

1114 LEE, SHENG YI. Liquidity and growth, the case of a local bank, by Lee Sheng Yi and Kenny Wee. SAJSS 2 (1974) 1-27.

1115 LEE, SHENG YI. Note on banking and currency in Singapore. MER 12 pt. 2 (1967) 122-126.

1116 LIM CHONG YAH. Monetary system and bank structure, by Lim Chong Yah and Doreen Phua. Y52 pp. 127-159.

1117 SHORT, BROCK K. Indigenous banking in an early period of development, the Straits Settlements, 1914-1940. MER 16 pt. 1 (1971) 57-75.

1118 TAN EE LEONG. Chinese banks incorporated in Singapore and the Federation of Malaya. JMBRAS 42 pt. 1 (1969) 256-281.

1119 TAN EE LEONG. Chinese banks incorporated in Singapore and the Federation of Malaya. S48 pp. 454-479.

BANKS AND BANKING - THAILAND

1120 SILCOCK, T. H. Money and banking. S49 pp. 170-205.

BANKS AND BANKING - VIETNAM

1121 SCHIFF, FRANK W. Monetary reorganization and the emergence of central banking. L52 pp. 259-287.

1122 SLUSSER, H. ROBERT. Early steps toward an industrial development bank. L52 pp. 245-254. *Comment:* NGUYEN DUY XUAN. Commentary. L52 pp. 255-6.

Basel Mission *See* CHRISTIANITY - MALAYSIA

BASILAN ISLAND

1123 MOLONY, CAROL H. It's still genocide even if they die by starvation. JCA 3 (1973) 491-496.

1124 SPOEHR, ALEXANDER. Spanish remains in Basilan and Sulu. S93 pp. 105-112.

BASKETS - MALAYSIA - SARAWAK

1125 SANDIN, BENEDICT. Garong baskets. SMJ 11 (1963) 321-326.

BASSETT, D. K.

1126 MEILINK-ROELOFSZ, M. A. P. European influence in Southeast Asia, 1500-1630. JSAH 5 (Sept. 1964) 184-197.

Bastin, John

BASTIN, JOHN

1127 ALATAS, SYED HUSSEIN. Theoretical aspects of Southeast Asian history, John **Bastin and the study of** Southeast Asian history. AST 2 (1964) 247-260.

1128 WERTHEIM, W. F. Asian history and the western historian, rejoinder to Professor Bastin. BIJ 119 (1963) 149-160.

BATAAN

1129 Bataan. UN 34 (Dec. 1961) 91-103.

BATAKS

1130 BRUNNER, EDWARD M. Toba Batak village. S58 pp. 52-64.

1131 HOLT, CLAIRE. Batak dances, notes by Claire Holt. IND 12 (1971) 65-84.

1132 MASRI SINGARIMBUN. Kutagamber, a village of the Karo. K52 pp. 115-128.

1133 SAMSON, JOSE A. Bataks of Sumurod and Kalakuasan. UN 40 (1967) 194-206.

1134 SIAGAN, TOENGGOEL P. Bibliography on the Batak peoples. IND 2 (1966) 161-184.

1135 VOORHOEVE, P. Sanskrit maandnamen in het Bataks. BIJ 128 (1972) 494-496.

BATAN LANGUAGE

1136 HOOKER, BETTY. Cohesion in Ivatan. AST 10 (1972) 33-43.

1137 YAMADA, YUKIHIRO. Fishing economy of the Itbayat, Batanes, Philippines with special reference to its vocabulary. AST 5 (1967) 137-219.

1138 YAMADA, YUKIHARO. Speech disguise in Itbayaten numerals. AST 10 (1972) 44-49.

BATANGAS PROVINCE

1139 EINSIEDEL, LUZ A. Success and failure in selected community development projects in Batangas. E78 pp. 624-633.

BATS - MALAYSIA - SARAWAK

1140 FOGDEN, M. P. L. Bats in Ulu Kakus and Sarang caves. SMJ 14 (1966) 247-8.

1141 HARRISSON, TOM. Bats netted in and round Niah Great Cave, 1965-6. SMJ 14 (1966) 229-233.

1142 HILL, J. E. Collection of bats from Sarawak. SMJ 14 (1966) 237-246.

1143 LIM BOO LIAT. Notes on the food habit of bats from the Fourth Division, Sarawak with special reference to a new record of Bornean bat, by Lim Boo Liat, Choi Koh Shin and Illar Muul. SMJ 20 (1972) 351-357.

1144 MEDWAY, LORD. Reproductive cycle of lesser bent-winged bat, **Miniopterus australis,** at Niah. SMJ 18 (1970) 401-409.

1145 PIRLOT, PAUL. Report on a collection of bats from Sarawak. SMJ 16 (1968) 253-256.

1146 START, ANTHONY N. Notes on Dya-
copterus spadiceus from Sarawak.
SMJ 20 (1972) 367–369.

1147 START, ANTHONY N. Some bats of
Bako National Park, Sarawak. SMJ
20 (1972) 371–376.

BAUTISTA, CIRILO F.

1148 CANILAO, CARLOS M. The reordered
reality in *The cave and other
poems*. SLURJ 3 (1972) 472–554.

BAWEAN

1149 VREDENBREGT, JACOB. Bawean migrations, some preliminary notes.
BIJ 120 (1964) 109–139.

BAYFIELD, G. T.

1150 HALL, D. G. E. British writers of
Burmese history from Dalrymple to
Bayfield. H18 pp. 255–266.

BEA, AUGUSTIN CARDINAL

1151 QUASHA, WILLIAM H. Tribute to
Augustin Cardinal Bea. PS 18
(1970) 645–653.

BEACHES - MALAYSIA

1152 NOSSIN, J. J. Beach ridges on
the east coast of Malaya. JTG 18
(1964) 111–117.

1153 SWAN, S. B. ST. C. Raised beach
at Kahang, Johor, peninsular Malaysia. JTG 38 (1974) 55–60.

BEACHES - SINGAPORE

1154 SWAN, S. B. ST. C. Coastal geomorphology in a humid tropical low
energy environment, the islands of
Singapore. JTG 33 (1971) 43–61.

1155 WONG, P. P. Beach formation between breakwaters, southeast
coast, Singapore. JTG 37 (1973)
68–73.

BELAHAN

1156 PITONO, R. Belahan problem. JOSA
8 (1971) 86–95.

1157 RESINK, TH. A. Belahan, of een
mythe ontluisterd. BIJ 123
(1967) 250–266.

1158 RESINK, TH. A. Belahan or a myth
dispelled. IND 6 (1968) 2–37.

BENDA, HARRY J.

1159 KAHIN, GEORGE McT. In memoriam,
Harry J. Benda. IND 13 (1972)
211–215.

1160 LEGGE, J. D. In memoriam, Harry
Jindrich Benda, 1919–1971. JSAS 3
(1972) 169–170.

1161 McVEY, RUTH T. Harry J. Benda.
JAS 31 (1971–2) 589–590.

1162 SARTONO KARTODIRDJO. In memoriam,
Harry Jindrich Benda, 1919–1971.
JSAS 3 (1972) 171–174.

1163 WERTHEIM, W. F. Harry J. Benda,
1919–1971. BIJ 128 (1972) 214–
218.

Benguet Province

BIDAYUH LITERATURE

1183 RUBENSTEIN, CAROL. Poems of in-
      digenous peoples of Sarawak: some
      of the songs and chants. Pt. 1.
      Iban, Bidayuh, Melanau. SMJ 21
      (1973) 1-722.

BIKOL

1184 LYNCH, FRANK. Social class in a
      Bikol town. E78 pp. 164-169.

1185 OWEN, NORMAN G. The *Principalia*
      in Philippine history, Kabikolan
      1790-1898. PS 22 (1974) 297-324.

BIKOL LITERATURE **

1186 CALLEJA-REYES, JOSE. Ibalon, an
      ancient Bicol epic. PS 16 (1968)
      318-347.

1187 DATO, LUIS G. Life of Christ, a
      free version of the Bikol passion.
      DR 11 (1963) 91-125.

1188 ESPINAS, MERITO B. Critical study
      of Ibalong, the Bikol folk epic
      fragment. UN 41 (1968) 173-250.

1189 ESPINAS, MERITO B. Sarung banggi,
      Bikol's regional song. UN 41
      (1968) 257-260.

BILAAN

1190 CABRERA, SANTIAGO B. Origin,
      folkways and customs of the
      Bilaans of southern Cotabato. UN
      40 (1967) 182-193.

1191 GENOTIVA, LORENZO C. Bilaan re-
      ligious beliefs and practices.
      SJ 13 (1966) 56-74.

BILAAN LANGUAGE

1192 McLACHLIN, BETTY. Verbal clauses
      of Sarangani Bilaan, by Betty
      McLachlin and Barbara Blackburn.
      AST 6 (1968) 108-128.

BINUKID LANGUAGE

1193 POST, URSULA R. Morphophonemic
      alterations in Binukid. PSSHR 30
      (1965) 52-56.

BIRDS - BORNEO

1194 FOGDEN, M. P. L. Borneo bird
      notes, 1963-65. SMJ 12 (1965)
      395-414.

1195 FOGDEN, M. P. L. Borneo bird
      notes, 1965-66. SMJ 14 (1966)
      308-319.

1196 HARRISSON, TOM. Sarawak status of
      the tree sparrow (Passer montanus)
      and moorhen (Gallinula chloropus)
      in Borneo. SMJ 19 (1971) 355-358.

1197 MEES, G. F. Crypsirina temia
      (Daudin), a forgotten member of
      the Borneo avifauna. SMJ 12
      (1965) 386-392.

BIRDS - BRUNEI

1198 DEAKIN, GEORGE. Year's observa-
      tion of Brunei birds. BMJ 1
      (1969) 218-222.

1199 HARRISSON, TOM. Birds from the
      Brunei rest house verandah. BMJ 3
      pt. 2 (1974) 265-270.

1200 HARRISSON, TOM. Birds from the
      Brunei rest house verandah, II.
      BMJ 2 pt. 3 (1971) 142-146.

Birds - Brunei

BIRDS - MALAYSIA

BIRDS - MALAYSIA - SABAH

BIRDS - MALAYSIA - SARAWAK

BIRDS - PHILIPPINES

1222 CARUMBANA, ESTHER E. Ecological study of certain game birds in southern Negros Oriental, Philippines, by Esther E. Carumbana and A. C. Alcala. SJ 21 (1974) 139-173.

1223 GONZALES, RODOLFO B. Foraging deployment of velvet-fronted nuthatches and elegant titmice, by Rodolfo B. Gonzales and Angel C. Alcala. SJ 16 (1969) 402-408.

1224 GONZALES, RODOLFO B. Observations of the postnatal development of the Philippine grass owl. SJ 15 (1968) 343-352.

1225 GONZALES, RODOLFO B. Study of the breeding biology and ecology of the monkey eating eagle. SJ 15 (1968) 461-500.

BIRDS NESTS - MALAYSIA - SABAH

1226 OROLFO, P. Discovery of birds' nest caves in North Borneo. SMJ 10 (1961) 270-273.

Birth *See* CHILDBIRTH

BIRTH CONTROL - INDONESIA

1227 POSTMA, PETRONELLA A. Djakarta and family planning. RSAS 1 pt. 3 (1971) 24-44.

1228 THOMAS, R. MURRAY. Attitudes toward birth control in Bandung, Indonesia. IND 4 (1967) 74-87.

BIRTH CONTROL - PHILIPPINES

1229 CONCEPCION, MERCEDES B. Factors associated with married women's ideal family size and approval of family planning, by Mercedes B. Concepcion and Gerry E. Hendershot. SLQ 6 (1968) 355-374.

1230 DEATS, RICHARD L. Statements of other churches on responsible parenthood. G73 pp. 222-231.

1231 Discussion. C47 pp. 138-148.

1232 GOROSPE, VITALIANO R. Catholic hierarchy and the population problem. G73 pp. 157-163.

1233 GOROSPE, VITALIANO R. Catholic hierarchy and the population problem. PS 17 (1969) 806-810.

1234 GOROSPE, VITALIANO R. Responsible parenthood in the Philippines today. PS 14 (1966) 470-481.

1235 GUTHRIE, GEORGE M. Psychological factors and preferred family size. SLQ 6 (1968) 391-398.

1236 HEALY, GERALD W. After *Humanae Vitae*, contraception and abortion. PS 22 (1974) 263-279.

1237 HOLLNSTEINER, MARY R. Modernization and family planning. G73 pp. 45-52.

1238 LAING, JOHN E. Progress report on the Silliman family planning project. SLQ 6 (1968) 415-422.

1239 MANALILI, ALFREDO LUIS CURA. Family planning movement and the Protestant's view. UN 39 (1966) 383-399.

1240 MASLOG, CRISPIN C. Problem of language in family planning terminology. SJ 21 (1974) 344-349.

1241 NACPIL, EMERITO P. Theologians response to the BRAC 1967 Filipino family survey. SLQ 6 (1968) 426-7.

Birth control - Philippines

1242 PAL, AGATON P. Family planning
     project at Silliman University,
     experiences and insights. SJ 15
     (1968) 371-384.

1243 PATRON, JOSEFINA S. Perspective
     for a program in family planning.
     SJ 20 (1973) 357-372.

1244 Philippine society and population
     problems: questions addressed to
     Philippine theologians. G73 pp.
     261-266.

1245 PHILIPPINES. COMMISSION ON POPULA-
     TION. Statement on **population**
     policy and program. G73 pp. 253-
     257.

1246 Responsible parenthood and family
     planning, the experience of Fili-
     pino couples. G73 pp. 235-250.

1247 ROSALES, VICENTE J. A. Control of
     population growth in the Philip-
     pines. UN 39 (1966) 460-467.

1248 SANVICTORES, LOURDES L. Is there
     an economical need for family
     limitation in the Philippines?
     UN 38 (1965) 439.

1249 VALENCIA, LUZVIMINDA. Broadway
     project, an exploratory KAP study.
     GEJ 21 (1971) 59-72.

BIRTH CONTROL - SINGAPORE

1250 CHANG, CHEN-TUNG. A study of
     Singapore's national family plan-
     ning programme, by Chang Chen-Tung
     and Stephen Yeh. MER 17 pt. 1
     (1972) 51-77.

1251 CHEN, PETER S. J. Family planning
     program and policy in Singapore.
     RSAS 2 (1972) 49-56.

BISAYAN **

1252 BEWSHER, R. A. The word Bisaya
     and Brunei. SMJ 11 (1962) 559.

1253 CARROLL, JOHN. The word Bisaya in
     the Philippines and Borneo. SMJ
     9 (1960) 499-541.

1254 DAVIS, G. C. Borneo Bisaya music
     in western ears. SMJ 9 (1960)
     496-498.

1255 DEMETRIO, FRANCISCO. Toward a
     classification of Bisayan folk be-
     liefs and customs. PS 16 (1968)
     663-689.

1256 DEMETRIO, FRANCISCO. Toward a
     classification of Bisayan folk be-
     liefs and customs. PS 17 (1969)
     3-39.

1257 HART, DONN V. Buhawi of the Bi-
     sayas, the revitalization process
     and legend making in the Philip-
     pines. Z16 pp. 366-396.

1258 HESTER, EVETT D. Alzina's *His-
     toria de Visayas*, a bibliographi-
     cal note. PS 10 (1962) 331-365.

1259 JOCANO, F. LANDA. Notes on **Phil-
     ippine divinities**. AST 6 (1968)
     169-182.

1260 LIETZ, PAUL S. More about Al-
     zina's *Historia de Visayas*. PS 10
     (1962) 366-375.

1261 RIXHON, GERALD. Parte natural of
     Alzina's manuscript of 1668, a
     source of anthropological data.
     AST 6 (1968) 183-197.

1262 SANDIN, BENEDICT. Bisayan and in-
     digenous peoples of Limbang. SMJ
     20 (1972) 41-51.

1263 SANTAMARIA, ALBERTO. Visaya el Victorioso, notas para la historia de Filipinas. UN 33 (1960) 343-365.

1264 SONZA, DEMY P. Bisaya of Borneo and the Philippines, a new look at the Maragtas. SMJ 20 (1972) 31-40.

1265 YENGOYAN, A. A. Baptism and Bisayanization among the Mandaya of eastern Mindanao, Philippines. AST 4 (1966) 324-327.

BISAYAN LANGUAGE

1266 ARANETA, F. Bisayans of Borneo and the Tagalogs and Visayans of the Philippines. SMJ 9 (1960) 542-564.

1267 MASLOG, CRISPIN C. Problem of language in family planning terminology. SJ 21 (1974) 344-349.

1268 TROSDAL, MIMI. Foreign influences on **Cebuano-Bisaya**. D67 pp. 63-70.

1269 VERSTRAELEN, EUGENE. Analysis of language. SLQ 1 (1963) 335-382.

1270 VERSTRAELEN, EUGENE. Analysis of language. SLQ 2 (1964) **51-76**.

1271 VERSTRAELEN, EUGENE. Essays towards a historical description of Tagalog and Cebuano Bisaya. PS 8 (1960) 491-514.

1272 VERSTRAELEN, EUGENE. Some further remarks about the L-feature. PS 9 (1961) 72-77.

BLACK TAI

1273 FIPPINGER, DOROTHY CRAWFORD. **Kinship terms of the Black Tai people.** JSS 59 pt. 1 (1971) 65-82.

1274 FIPPINGER, JAY. Black Tai government. SA 2 (1972-3) 71-76.

BLAS, ANGEL DE

1275 ESPINOSA, JOSE F. Friar Angel de Blas, the man, the scholar, the psychologist, by Jose F. Espinosa and Jose A. Samson. UN 35 (1962) 3-11.

BLIUNS

1276 TUTON KABOY. Bliun people. SMJ 17 (1969) 155-162.

BLOOD

1277 FLATZ, GEBHARD. Hemoglobin E in Southeast Asia. F38 pp. 91-106.

BOATS - BRUNEI

1278 HARRISSON, TOM. Kedayan rafts. BMJ 2 pt. 1 (1970) 52-60.

1279 HARRISSON, TOM. **Survival of** Kedayan rafts. BMJ 2 pt. 4 (1972) 168-172.

BOATS - INDONESIA

1280 PALM, C. H. M. Vaartuigen en visvangst van Anjar Lor, Bantam, West-Java. BIJ 118 (1962) 217-270.

1296 Bibliographical list of books and articles published by Dr. F. D. K. Bosch. H39 pp. 95-106.

1297 Biographical note. H39 pp. 9-11.

1298 COEDES, GEORGE. Les recherches de Bosch sur l'epoque des Sailendra, le probleme de l'expansion indienne dans l'archipel. H39 pp. 42-47.

1299 DAMAIS, L. C. Bosch et l'epigraphie indonesienne. H39 pp. 49-58.

1300 FONTEIN, J. Bosch and the Barabudur studies. H39 pp. 64-70.

1301 GALESTIN, TH. P. Bosch studies on the Jalatunda monument. H39 pp. 71-78.

1302 LIM, K. W. Bosch and Balinese culture. H39 pp. 80-87.

1303 LOHUIZEN-DE LEEUW, J. E. VAN. Bosch' contributions to Indian iconography and history of art. H39 pp. 59-63.

1304 POTT, P. H. Bosch' contribution to the study of Indian symbolism. H39 pp. 88-94.

1305 POTT, P. H. In memoriam, F. D. K. Bosch, 17 June 1887-20 July 1967. BIJ 123 (1967) 409-426.

BOT BIN RAJA JUMAAT, RAJA

1306 MOHAMAD AMIN HASSAN. Raja Bot bin Raja Jumaat. JMBRAS 40 pt. 2 (1967) 68-93.

BOUROTTE, BERNARD

1307 VUONG HONG SEN. Hommage a Bernard Bourotte, 1896-1968. SEIB 48 (1973) 553-557.

BOWRING, JOHN

1308 TARLING, NICHOLAS. Mission of Sir John Bowring to Siam. JSS 50 pt. 2 (1962) 91-118.

BRADDELL, ROLAND ST. JOHN

1309 RAMANI, R. In memoriam, Dato Sir Roland St. John Braddell, 20/12/1880-15/11/1966. JMBRAS 41 pt. 1 (1968) 1-10.

BRENT, CHARLES HENRY *See also* CAVITE MUTINY

1310 ACHUTEGUI, PEDRO S. DE. Brent, Herzog, Morayta and Aglipay, by Pedro S. de Achutegui and Miguel A. Bernad. PS 8 (1960) 568-583.

1311 OGILBY, LYMAN C. Bishop Brent and the vision at Edinburgh. SJ 9 (1962) 340-347.

BRILLANTES, GREGORIO

1312 BERNAD, MIGUEL A. **Tarlac** and **Andromeda**, the stories of Gregorio Brillantes. PS 9 (1961) 166-172.

1313 LOCSIN, MARIA CECILIA V. Exiles, a reading of Gregorio Brillantes' *The distance to Andromeda*. PS 15 (1967) 407-424.

British Museum

Brunei - Foreign relations - Philippines

BROWNELL, HERBERT

British recognition.   PHR 1 pt. 1
(1965) 365-385.

1334   PATERNO, ROBERTO.   American military bases in the Philippines,
the Brownell opinion.   PS 12
(1964) 391-423.

BRU

1335   MILLER, JOHN D.   Bru kinship.   SA
2 (1972-3) 62-70.

BRU LANGUAGE

1336   MILLER, CAROLYN P.   Substantive
phrase in Brou.   M57 pp. 63-80.

1337   MILLER, JOHN D.   Word clauses in
Brou.   M57 pp. 41-62.

1338   PIAT, MARTINE.   Quelques corre-
spondences entre le Khmer et le
Bru, langue montagnarde du centre
Vietnam.   SEIB 37 (1962) 312-323.

BRUNEI - BIBLIOGRAPHY

1339   HARRISSON, TOM.   Brunei in
JMBRAS XLI, 1968, 2. BMJ 1 (1969)
190-1.

1340   HARRISSON, TOM.   Brunei in the
Sarawak Museum Journal.   BMJ 1
(1969) 180-189.

1341   MAXWELL, ALLEN R.   Brunei bibliography in the JSBRAS and JMBRAS.
BMJ 2 pt. 1 (1970) 264-268.

BRUNEI - DESCRIPTION AND TRAVEL

1342   BROWN, CARRIE C.   Early account of
Brunei by Sung Lien.   BMJ 2 pt. 4
(1972) 219-231.

1343   HARRISSON, TOM.   Rennell manuscript in the Brunei Museum.   BMJ
1 (1969) 157-165.

1344   HARRISSON, TOM.   Unpublished
Rennell ms., a Borneo-Philippine
journey, 1762-63.   JMBRAS 39 pt. 1
(1966) 92-136.

1345   PIGAFETTA, ANTONIO.   Account of
Brunei in 1521.   BMJ 3 pt. 2
(1974) 171-179.

1346   Spanish accounts of their expeditions against Brunei in 1578-79.
BMJ 3 pt. 2 (1974) 180-221.

BRUNEI - FOREIGN RELATIONS - GREAT BRITAIN

1347   BROWN, D. E.   Two Colonial Office
memoranda on the history of Brunei
by Sir Reginald Edward Stubbs.
JMBRAS 41 pt. 2 (1968) 83-116.

BRUNEI - FOREIGN RELATIONS - MALAYSIA

1348   CRISSWELL, C. N.   Origins of the
Limbang claim.   JSAS 2 (1971) 218-
229.

BRUNEI - FOREIGN RELATIONS - PHILIPPINES

1349   ANGELES, F. DELOR.   Brunei and the
Moro wars.   BMJ 1 (1969) 119-132.

1350   SHORT, BROCK K.   Brunei, Sulu and
Sabah.   BMJ 1 (1969) 133-146.

BRUNEI - SOCIAL CONDITIONS

1369 BROWN, D. E. Ampuan in Brunei.
      BMJ 2 pt. 4 (1972) 207-8.

1370 BROWN, D. E. Inter-hierarchical
      commissions in a Bornean plural
      society. SAJSS 1 pt. 1 (1973)
      97-116.

1371 BROWN, D. E. Social structure of
      nineteenth century Brunei. BMJ 1
      (1969) 166-179.

BRUNEI MUSEUM

1372 HARRISSON, BARBARA. European
      trade ceramics in the Brunei
      Museum. BMJ 3 pt. 1 (1973) 66-87.

1373 HARRISSON, TOM. The Brunei
      Museum. JMBRAS 45 pt. 1 (1972)
      119-120.

1374 HARRISSON, TOM. Rennell manu-
      script in the Brunei Museum. BMJ
      1 (1969) 157-165.

1375 HARRISSON, TOM. Unpublished
      Rennell ms, a Borneo-Philippine
      journey, 1762-63. JMBRAS 39 pt. 1
      (1966) 92-136.

1376 SHARIFFUDDIN, P. M. Museum de-
      velopment in Brunei, Borneo, 1953-
      1973. BMJ 3 pt. 1 (1973) 51-61.

1377 SHARIFFUDDIN, P. M. Some problems
      of getting materials for the
      Brunei Museum. BMJ 2 pt. 1 (1970)
      1-16.

BUDDHISM

1378 ANUMAN RAJADHON. Thet Mahachat.
      B91 pp. 1-8.

1379 CHAN HTOON. Presidential address.
      FA 18 (1962) 29-35.

1380 CHI HSIEN LIN. Language problem
      of primitive Buddhism. JBRS 43
      (June 1960) 9-15.

1381 DRISCOLL, JOHN P. Concepts of
      reality in Buddhist thought. AST
      4 (1966) 236-239.

1382 DUTT, S. Migrations of Buddhism
      over Asia. S87 pp. 40-44.

1383 FILLIOZAT, J. Emigration of In-
      dian Buddhists to Indo-China, c.
      A.D. 1200. S87 pp. 45-48.

1384 KITAGAWA, JOSEPH M. Buddhism and
      Asian politics. AS 2 (July 1962)
      1-11.

1385 MARTINI, GINETTE. Brapamsukula-
      nisamsam. BEF 60 (1973) 55-78.

1386 MARTINI, GINETTE. Un Jataka con-
      cernant le dernier repas de
      Buddha. BEF 59 (1972) 251-255.

1387 MARTINI, GINETTE. Les titres des
      Jataka dans les manuscrits Pali de
      la Bibliotheque Nationale de
      Paris. BEF 51 (1963) 79-93.

1388 MARTINI, GINETTE. Valukacetiya.
      BEF 57 (1970) 155-168.

1389 MIYAMOTO, SHOSON. Time and eter-
      nity in Buddhism. AC 3 (Apr.
      1961) 63-78.

1390 MUKERJEE, RADHAKAMAL. March of
      Tantrika art over the Pacific.
      S87 pp. 289-296.

1391 MUS, PAUL. Cosmodrames et politi-
      ques en Asie du sud-est. D44 pp.
      75-98.

Buddhism

1392 NASH, MANNING. Introduction. C66 pp. vii-xi.

1393 ROXAS-LIM, AURORA. Buddhism in early Southeast Asia, a contribution to the study of culture change. AST 11 (1973) 75-97.

1394 SARKISYANZ, M. Religious influences on national emancipation and socialist movements in South-East Asia. D44 pp. 63-74.

1395 SIHANOUK, NORODOM. Inaugural address, 6th Conference of the World Fellowship of Buddhists, Phnom-Penh, November 14-22,1961. FA 18 (1962) 25-28.

1396 SONI, R. L. Sixth Conference of the World Fellowship of Buddhists. FA 18 (1962) 41-46.

1397 THICH MINH CHAU. Cultural co-operation through Buddhist culture. S32 pp. 109-110.

1398 TRAGER, FRANK N. Reflections on Buddhism and the social order in Southern Asia. B91 pp. 529-543.

1399 TRAN QUANG THUAN. Notion of salvation in Buddhist philosophy. AC 3 (Apr. 1961) 79-90.

BUDDHISM - BURMA **

1400 AUNG THAN. Relation between the Samgha and state and laity. JBRS 48 (June 1965) 1-7.

1401 BA HAN. Burmese cosmogony and cosmology. JBRS 48 (June 1965) 9-16.

1402 BA HAN. *Shin Uttamagyaw and his Tawla,* a nature poem. B92 pp. 7-16.

1403 BA SHIN. Buddha images of Tai Yuan types found in Burma. E93 pp. 1-5.

1404 BECHERT, HEINZ. Theravada Buddhist Sangha, some general observations on historical and political factors in its development. JAS 29 (1969-70) 761-778.

1405 BROHM, JOHN. Buddhism and animism in a Burmese village. JAS 22 (1962-3) 155-167.

1406 GODAKUMBURA, C. E. Chapada and Chapada Saddhammajotipala. JBRS 52 (June 1969) 1-7.

1407 GODAKUMBURA, C. E. Relations between Burma and Ceylon. JBRS 49 (Dec. 1966) 145-162.

1408 GUYOT, DOROTHY. Uses of Buddhism in wartime Burma. AST 7 (1969) 50-80.

1409 HLA AUNG. Some aspects of marriage under Burmese Buddhist law and Malayan Muslim law. JBRS 48 (Dec. 1965) 1-15.

1410 KHIN ZAW. Folk-song collector's letter from the Mon country in Lower Burma, 1941. E92 pp. 164-166.

1411 KING, WINSTON L. Buddhism and political power in Burma. S90.3 pp. 9-19.

1412 LU PE WIN. Jatakas in Burma. E93 pp. 94-108.

1413 LUCE, G. H. A Chieng Mai Mahathera visits Pagan, 1393 A.D., by G. H. Luce and Ba Shin. G83 pp. 330-337.

1414 MENDELSON, E. MICHAEL. Messianic Buddhist association in Upper

1415 MYA MAUNG. Cultural value and economic change in Burma. AS 4 (1964) 757-764.

1416 NASH, MANNING. Buddhist revitalization in the nation state, the Burmese experience. R25 pp. 105-122.

1417 NASH, MANNING. Burmese Buddhism in everyday life. T45 pp. 103-114.

1418 NASH, MANNING. Ritual and ceremonial cycle in Upper Burma. C66 pp. 97-115.

1419 PARPAN, ALFREDO G. Modernization and the secular state in Southeast Asia. AST 10 (1972) 245-255.

1420 PE MAUNG TIN. Buddhism in the inscriptions of Pagan. B92 pp. 423-441.

1421 PERRIN, JEAN. A propos d'un Buddha date du pays Mon. E93 pp. 149-155.

1422 PFANNER, DAVID E. Buddhist monk in rural Burmese society. C66 pp. 77-96.

1423 PFANNER, DAVID E. Theravada Buddhism and village economic behavior, a Burmese and Thai comparison, by David E. Pfanner and Jasper Ingersoll. JAS 21 (1961-2) 341-361.

1424 SARKISYANZ, E. Buddhist background of Burmese socialism before 1962. AQ (1971) 373-390.

1425 SARKISYANZ, MANUEL. On the place of U Nu's Buddhist socialism in Burma's history of ideas. S90.2 pp. 53-62.

1426 VON DER MEHDEN, FRED R. Burma's religious campaign against communism. PA 33 (1960) 290-299.

1427 VON DER MEHDEN, FRED R. Changing pattern of religion and politics in Burma. S90.2 pp. 63-73.

1428 VON DER MEHDEN, FRED R. Rise and fall of the religious state in Burma. SA 1 (1971) 74-88.

1429 World Institute of Buddhist Culture. FA 17 (1960) 2837-2841.

BUDDHISM - CAMBODIA

1430 BAREAU, ANDRE. Quelques ermitages et centres de meditation bouddhiques au Cambodge. BEF 56 (1969) 11-28.

1431 BOELES, J. J. Buddhist tutelary couple Hariti and Pancika, protectors of children, from a relief at the Khmer sanctuary in Pimai. JSS 56 (1968) 187-205.

1432 CHOAN. Les travaux de construction a la Pagode de Tep-Pranam, par Choan et Sarin. BEF 57 (1970) 129-133.

1433 CHOAN. Le Venerable Chef de la Pagode de Tep-Pranam, par Choan et Sarin. BEF 57 (1970) 127-8.

1434 EBIHARA, MAY. Interrelations between Buddhism and social systems in Cambodian peasant culture. C66 pp. 175-196.

1435 JAINI, PADMANABH S. Mahadibbamanta, a paritta manuscript from Cambodia. SOAS 28 (1965) 61-80.

1436 Le monastere bouddhique de Tep Pranam a Oudong. BEF 56 (1969) 29-56.

Buddhism - Cambodia

1437 MUS, PAUL. Le sourire d'Angkor, art, foi et politique bouddhiques sous Jayavarman VII. G83 pp. 363-381.

1438 SARIN. Les moines et novices que etudient a Vat Tep-Pranam, par Sarin et Choan. BEF 57 (1970) 134-154.

BUDDHISM - INDONESIA

1439 HOOYKAAS, C. Buddhism in Bali. F38 pp. 25-33.

1440 JAINI, PADMANABH S. Story of Sudhana and Manohra, an analysis of the texts and the Borobudur reliefs. SOAS 29 (1966) 533-558.

1441 MULDER, NIELS. Saminism and Buddhism, a note on a field visit to a Samin community. AQ (1974) 253-258.

BUDDHISM - LAOS

1442 ARCHAIMBAULT, CHARLES. La fete du T'at a Luong Prabang. E92 pp. 5-47.

1443 VONGSAVANH BOUTSAVATH. Lao popular Buddhism and community development, by Vongsavanh Boutsavath and Georges Chapelier. JSS 61 pt. 2 (1973) 1-38.

BUDDHISM - MALAYSIA

1444 GRISWOLD, A. B. Santubong Buddha and its context. SMJ 11 (1962) 363-371.

1445 LAMB, ALASTAIR. Mahayana Buddhist votive tablets in Perlis. JMBRAS 37 pt. 2 (1964) 47-59.

BUDDHISM - PHILIPPINES

1446 FRANCISCO, JUAN R. Buddhist image from Karitunan site, Batangas Province. AST 1 (1963) 13-18.

1447 FRANCISCO, JUAN R. Notes on the Indo-Philippine images. Z16 pp. 117-127.

BUDDHISM - THAILAND

1448 AYABE, TSUNEO. Dek Wat and Thai education, the case of Tambon Ban Khem. JSS 61 pt. 2 (1973) 39-52.

1449 BIDYALANKARANA, PRINCE. Buddha's footprints. S44.2 pp. 37-53.

1450 BOELES, J. J. Two aspects of Buddhist iconography in Thailand. JSS 48 pt. 1 (1960) 69-79.

1451 BUNNAG, JANE. Monk layman interaction in central Thai society. T33 pp. 88-106.

1452 BURR, ANGELA. Religious institutional diversity, social, structural, and conceptional unity: Islam and Buddhism in a southern Thai coastal fishing village. JSS 60 pt. 2 (1972) 183-215.

1453 COEDES, G. Siamese votive tablets. S44.1 pp. 150-187.

1454 DENIS, EUGENE. L'origine cingalaise du P'rah Malay. F38 pp. 329-338.

1455 DHANINIVAT. Sonkrant of Mon as recorded in the inscriptions of Wat Pra Jetupon in Bangkok. E92 pp. 117-119.

1456 GRISWOLD, A. B. Devices and expedients, Vat Pa Mok, 1727 A.D., by A. B. Griswold and Prasert na Nagara. T33 pp. 147-220.

1457 GRISWOLD, A. B. Notes on the art of Siam. V. The conversion of Jambupati. G83 pp. 295-298.

1458 INGERSOLL, JASPER. Merit and identity in village Thailand. C24 pp. 219-251.

1459 INGERSOLL, JASPER. Priest role in central village Thailand. C66 pp. 61-76.

1460 ISHII, YONEO. Church and state in Thailand. AS 8 (1968) 864-871.

1461 ISHII, YONEO. Note on contemporary Thai Buddhism. EACS 13 (1974) 32-35.
Comment: KIYOMI, MORIDKA. Comments. EACS 13 (1974) 35-6.

1462 JAINI, PADMANABH S. Mahadibbamanta, a paritta manuscript from Cambodia. SOAS 28 (1965) 61-80.

1463 KEYES, CHARLES F. Buddhism and national integration in Thailand. JAS 30 (1970-1) 551-567.

1464 KIRSCH, A. THOMAS. Economy, polity, and religion in Thailand. C24 pp. 172-196.

1465 KLAUSNER, WILLIAM. Hua Paw tales, by William and Kampan Klausner. T33 pp. 107-109.

1466 KRAISRI NIMMANHAEMINDA. A Chiengmai image inscribed in Burmese and Thai. JBRS 43 (June 1960) 63-66.

1467 LAMB, ALASTAIR. Mahayana Buddhist votive tablets in Perlis. JMBRAS 37 pt. 2 (1964) 47-59.

1468 LUCE, G. H. A Chieng Mai Mahathera visits Pagan, 1393 A.D., by G. H. Luce and Ba Shin. G83 pp. 330-337.

1469 MARTINI, GINETTE. Pancabuddhabyakarana. BEF 55 (1969) 125-144.

1470 MOERMAN, MICHAEL. Ban Ping's temple, the center of a loosely structured society. C66 pp. 137-174.

1471 MORELL, DAVID. The impermanence of society, Marxism, Buddhism and the political philosophy of Thailand's Pridi Panomyong, by David and Susan Morell. SA 2 (1972) 396-424.

1472 MULDER, J. A. N. Sociology and religion in Thailand, a critique. JSS 55 (1967) 101-111.

1473 PFANNER, DAVID E. Theravada Buddhism and village economic behavior, a Burmese and Thai comparison, by David E. Pfanner and Jasper Ingersoll. JAS 21 (1961-2) 341-361.

1474 PRASERT YAMKLINFUNG. Family, religion and socio-economic change in Thailand. EACS 13 (1974) 20-31.

1475 TAMBIAH, S. J. Buddhism and this worldly activity. MAS 7 (1973) 1-20.

1476 TERWIEL, B. M. Five percepts and ritual in rural Thailand. JSS 60 pt. 1 (1972) 333-343.

BUDDHISM - VIETNAM

1477 JOINER, CHARLES A. South Vietnam's Buddhist crisis, organization for charity, dissidence, and unity. AS 4 (1964) 915-928.

1478 MUS, PAUL. Le bouddhisme dans l'histoire et la societe vietnamiennes. C28 pp. 58-73.

Buddhism - Vietnam

1479 NARADA MAHA THERA. My visits to Viet-Nam. FA 17 (1960) 1741-1745.

1480 SARGENT, G. E. Intellectual atmosphere in Lingnan at the time of the introduction of Buddhism. S93 pp. 161-171.

1481 SCIGLIANO, ROBERT. Vietnam, politics and religion. AS 4 (1964) 666-673.

1482 WOODSIDE, ALEXANDER. Vietnamese Buddhism, the Vietnamese court and China in the 1800's. H42 pp. 11-24.

BUDGET - PHILIPPINES

1483 LAPENA, NICOLAS D. A p27 million budget for the DCI. G93 pp. 401-447.

1484 LAURETA, AMANCIA G. Legislative authorization of the budget. A28 pp. 282-292.

BUDGET - SINGAPORE

1485 ABRAHAM, W. I. Note on the growth and changing composition of gross domestic expenditure in Singapore, by W. I. Abraham and Peter C. K. Tan. MER 15 pt. 2 (1970) 42-48.

BUDGET - VIETNAM

1486 SCIGLIANO, ROBERT G. Budget process in south Vietnam. PA 33 (1960) 48-60.

BUGINESE

1487 CENSE, A. A. Old Buginese and Macassarese diaries. BIJ 122 (1966) 416-428.

1488 CHABOT, HENDRIK T. Bontoramba, a village of Goa, south Sulawesi. K52 pp. 189-209.

1489 KRATZ, U. Pro- und antibuginesische Texte zur Geschichte Johors im 18. Jahrhundert, ein Beitrag zur Quellenlage. BIJ 130 (1974) 289-296.

1490 NOORDUYN, J. Arung Singkang, 1700-1765, how the victory of Wadjo began. IND 13 (1972) 61-68.

BUGINESE LITERATURE

1491 ANDI ZAINAL ABIDIN. The I La Galigo epic cycle of south Celebes and its diffusion. IND 17 (1974) 160-169.

1492 KERN, R. A. Een episode uit het La Galigo Epos. BIJ 117 (1961) 363-383.

BUHAWI

1493 HART, DONN V. Buhawi of the Bisayas, the revitalization process and legend making in the Philippines. Z16 pp. 366-396.

BUI QUANG CHIEN

1494 SMITH, R. B. Bui Quang Chien and the Constitutionalist Party in French Cochinchina, 1917-30. MAS 3 (1969) 131-150.

BUKIDNONS

1495 LYNCH, FRANK. Bukidnon of north-central Mindanao in 1889. PS 15 (1967) 464-482.

1496　ORACION, TIMOTEO S.　Bukidnons of southeastern Negros, Philippines. SJ 8 (1961) 205-210.

1497　ORACION, TIMOTEO S.　Kaingin agriculture among the Bukidnons of south-eastern Negros, Philippines. JTG 17 (1963) 213-224.

1498　ORACION, TIMOTEO S.　Preliminary report on some cultural aspects of the Bukidnons on southeastern Negros Island, Philippines.　UN 40 (1967) 156-181.

BULOSAN, CARLOS

1499　BULOSAN, CARLOS.　Sound of falling light, letters in exile.　DR 8 (1960) 185-277.

1500　DAROY, PETRONILO BN.　Carlos Bulosan, the politics of literature. SLQ 6 (1968) 193-206.

1501　FRANCISCO, JUAN R.　On the sources of Bulosan's *My father goes to court*.　GEJ 11 (1966) 28-34.

1502　SAN JUAN, E.　An introduction to Carlos Bulosan.　DR 20 (1972) 1-13.

1503　SAN JUAN, E.　Note to Bulosan's *The story of a letter*.　DR 20 (1972) 17-24.

BUNA

1504　FRIEDBERG, CLAUDINE.　Reperage et decoupage du temps chez les Bunaq du centre de Timor.　AR 6 (1973) 119-144.

BUNA LANGUAGE

1505　COWAN, H. K. J.　Le Buna de Timor, une langue Ouest-Papoue.　BIJ 119 (1963) 387-400.

Bureaucracy　*See*　CIVIL SERVICE

BURGOS, JOSE　*See also*　CAVITE MUTINY

1506　QUIRINO, CARLOS.　Checklist of documents on Gomburza from the archdiocesan archives of Manila. PS 21 (1973) 19-84.

1507　QUIRINO, CARLOS.　More documents on Burgos.　PS 18 (1970) 161-177.

1508　SCHUMACHER, JOHN N.　Authenticity of the writings attributed to Father Jose Burgos.　PS 18 (1970) 3-51.

1509　SCHUMACHER, JOHN N.　Documents relating to Jose Burgos and the Cavite Mutiny of 1872, by John N. Schumacher and Nicholas P. Cushner.　PS 17 (1969) 457-529.

BURMA

1510　L'annee 1966 en Asie, Birmanie. FA 22 (1968) 107-109.

1511　BADGLEY, JOHN.　Burma, the army vows legitimacy.　AS 12 (1972) 177-181.

1512　BUTWELL, RICHARD.　Ne Win's Burma, at the end of the first decade. AS 12 (1972) 901-912.

1513　FLEISCHMANN, KLAUS.　Problems of contemporary Burma.　AQ (1973) 71-89.

Burma

ARTICLES

1534 SILVERSTEIN, JOSEF. Problems in Burma: economic, political and diplomatic. AS 7 (1967) 117-125.

1535 SOE MYINT. Financing the deficit since independence. JBRS 44 (1961) 183-195.

1536 STIFEL, LAURENCE D. Burmese socialism, economic problems of the first decade. PA 45 (1972) 60-74.

1537 STIFEL, LAWRENCE D. Economics of the Burmese way to socialism. AS 11 (1971) 803-817.

1538 THET TUN. Critique of a new preface to J. S. Furnivall's *An introduction to the political economy of Burma*. JBRS 47 (1964) 379-383.

1539 TRAGER, FRANK N. Burma, 1967, a better ending than beginning. AS 8 (1968) 110-119.

BURMA - FOREIGN RELATIONS

1540 LUCE, G. H. Countries neighbouring Burma. B92 pp. 239-306.

1541 LUCE, G. H. Foreign relations of King Aniruddha. S87 pp. 260-276.

BURMA - FOREIGN RELATIONS - CHINA

1542 BADGLEY, JOHN H. Burma's China crisis, the choices ahead. AS 7 (1967) 753-761.

1543 HOADLEY, J. STEPHEN. China-Burma border settlement, a retrospective evaluation. AF 2 (1970) 104-116.

1544 HOLMES, ROBERT A. Burma's foreign policy toward China since 1962. PA 45 (1972) 240-254.

Burma - Foreign relations - Great Britain

1545 HOLMES, ROBERT A. China-Burma relations since the rift. AS 12 (1972) 686-700.

1546 JADOUL, IVAN. Relations Sino-Birmanes et la revolution culturelle. RSA (1968) 249-272. *Comment:* Discussion. RSA (1968) 273-281.

1547 LUCE, G. H. The Tan (A.D. 97-132) and the Ngai-Lao. B92 pp. 201-238.

1548 SEVERINO, RODOLFO. Pressures on Burma's foreign policy, a case study. PS 16 (1968) 460-486.

1549 TRAGER, FRANK. Burma and China. JSAH 5 (Mar. 1964) 29-61.

BURMA - FOREIGN RELATIONS - DENMARK

1550 CHRISTIAN, J. L. Denmark's interest in Burma and the Nicobar Islands, 1620-1883. B92 pp. 17-34.

BURMA - FOREIGN RELATIONS - FRANCE

1551 PRESCHEZ, PHILIPPE. Les relations entre la France et la Birmanie au XVIIIe et au XIXe siecles. FA 21 (1966) 277-425.

BURMA - FOREIGN RELATIONS - GREAT BRITAIN

1552 BLACKMORE, THAUNG. British quest for China trade by the routes across Burma, 1826-1876. S93 pp. 180-190.

1553 SHEIN. Provincial contract system of British Indian Empire, in relation to Burma, a case of fiscal exploitation, by Shein, Myint Myint Thant and Tin Tin Sein. JBRS 52 (Dec. 1969) 1-26.

BURMA - FOREIGN RELATIONS - INDIA

1554   PEARN, B. R.   King Bering. B92
       pp. 443-473.

BURMA - FOREIGN RELATIONS - INDONESIA

1555   HALL, D. G. E.   The Daghregister
       of Batavia and Dutch trade with
       Burma in the 17th century. B92
       pp. 99-116.

BURMA - FOREIGN RELATIONS - ITALY

1556   BA, VIVIEN.   The Burmese embassy
       to Italy in 1872. JBRS 53 pt. 2
       (1970) 65-76.

1557   BA, VIVIEN.   Diplomatic documents
       relating to the Burmese-Italian
       treaty of 1871. JBRS 53 pt. 2
       (1970) 15-54.

BURMA - FOREIGN RELATIONS - NETHERLANDS

1558   HALL, D. G. E.   Studies in Dutch
       relations with Arakan. I. Dutch
       relations with King Thirithudhamma
       of Arakan, 1622-38. B92 pp. 67-
       77.

1559   HALL, D. G. E.   Studies in Dutch
       relations with Arakan. II. Dutch
       trade with Arakan in the first
       half of the 17th century. B92 pp.
       77-88.

1560   HALL, D. G. E.   Studies in Dutch
       relations with Arakan. III. Shah
       Shuja and the Dutch withdrawal of
       1665. B92 pp. 88-97.

BURMA - FOREIGN RELATIONS - PORTUGAL

1561   FURNIVALL, J. S.   Europeans in
       Burma, the early Portuguese. B92
       pp. 61-66.

BURMA - FOREIGN RELATIONS - SRI LANKA

1562   GODAKUMBURA, C. E.   Relations be-
       tween Burma and Ceylon. JBRS 49
       (1966) 145-162.

1563   MON BOKAY.   Relations between Cey-
       lon and Burma in the 11th century
       A.D. E92 pp. 93-95.

BURMA - FOREIGN RELATIONS - THAILAND

1564   Burmese invasions of Siam, trans-
       lated from the Hmannan Yazawin
       Dawgyi. S44.5 pp. 3-83.

1565   Intercourse between Burma and Siam
       as recorded in Hmannan Yazawindaw-
       gyi. S44.5 pp. 85-207.

1566   Intercourse between Burma and Siam
       as recorded in Hmannan Yazawindaw-
       gyi. S44.6 pp. 1-183.

BURMA - FOREIGN RELATIONS - VATICAN

1567   BA, VIVIAN.   Some papal corre-
       spondence with the kings of Burma.
       JBRS 50 (1967) 11-19.

BURMA - FOREIGN RELATIONS - VIETNAM

1568   BA, VIVIAN.   Extracts from the
       collection of laws and customs of
       the Great South (Kingdom of Viet-
       nam) and the true history of the
       Great South, additional data from
       French, Vietnamese and other
       sources on the Burmese embassy to
       Vietnam in 1823-4. JBRS 49 (1966)
       35-50.

1569 PEARN, B. R. Burmese embassy to Vietnam, 1823–24. JBRS 47 (1964) 149–172.

BURMA – FRONTIER TROUBLES

1570 HOADLEY, J. STEPHEN. China–Burma border settlement, a retrospective evaluation. AF 2 (1970) 104–116.

1571 MAUNG MAUNG. Burma–China boundary settlement. AS 1 (Mar. 1961) 38–43.

1572 WHITTAM, DAPHNE E. Sino–Burmese boundary treaty. PA 34 (1961) 174–183.

BURMA – HISTORY

1573 BA HAN. Emergence of the Burmese nation. JBRS 48 (Dec. 1965) 25–38.

1574 CHEW, ERNEST. Withdrawal of the last British residency from Upper Burma in 1879. JSAH 10 (1969) 253–278.

1575 HALL, D. G. E. British writers of Burmese history from Dalrymple to Bayfield. H18 pp. 255–266.

1576 KEYES, CHARLES F. New evidence on northern Thai frontier history. T33 pp. 221–249.

1577 LU PE WIN. Old Burma, early Pagan. JBRS 54 (1971) 1–30.

1578 LUCE, GORDON H. Aspects of Pagan history, later period. T33 pp. 129–146.

1579 LUCE, GORDON H. Burma down to the fall of Pagan, an outline, part I,

by G. H. Luce and Pe Maung Tin. B92 pp. 385–403.

1580 LUCE, GORDON H. Some old references to the south of Burma and Ceylon. F38 pp. 269–282.

1581 PRESCHEZ, PHILIPPE. Les relations entre la France et la Birmanie au XVIIIe et au XIXe siecles. FA 21 (1966) 277–425.

1582 SHORTO, H. L. 32 myos in the medieval Mon kingdom. SOAS 26 (1963) 572–591.

1583 SIDHU, JAGJIT SINGH. Historical background to Burma's acceptance of western culture. EACS 6 (1967) 41–54.

1584 SIMMONDS, E. H. S. Thalang letters, 1773–94, political aspects and the trade in arms. SOAS 26 (1963) 592–619.

1585 THAN TUN. Administration under King Thalun, 1629–48. JBRS 51 (1968) 173–188.

1586 THAN TUN. An estimation of articles on Burmese history published in the JBRS, 1910–70. JBRS 53 (June 1970) 53–66.

1587 TINKER, HUGH. Arthur Phayre and Henry Yule, two soldier-administrator historians. H18 pp. 267–278.

BURMA – LAWS, STATUTES, ETC.

1588 HLA AUNG. Burmese concept of law. JBRS 52 (Dec. 1969) 27–41.

1589 HLA AUNG. Code versus custom in the development of Burmese law. JBRS 49 (1966) 163–172.

Burma - Laws, statutes, etc.

1590 HLA AUNG. Effect of Anglo-Indian legislation on Burmese customary law. C39 pp. 67-88.

1591 MAUNG KYIN SWI. Origin and development of the Dhammathats. JBRS 49 (1966) 173-205.

BURMA - MINORITIES *See also* AIMOL, INDIANS, KACHIN, KARENS, KAYAN, MON, PANTHAYS, PURUM, PYU, SHANS, TAY, YAO

1592 BRANT, CHARLES S. Missionaries among the hill tribes of Burma, by Charles S. Brant and Mi Mi Khaing. AS 1 (Mar. 1961) 44-51.

1593 LEHMAN, F. K. Ethnic categories in Burma and the theory of social systems. K86 pp. 93-124.

1594 KUNSTADTER, PETER. Burma, introduction. K86 pp. 75-91.

1595 THEODORSON, GEORGE A. Minority peoples in the Union of Burma. JSAH 5 (Mar. 1964) 1-16.

BURMA - POLITICS AND GOVERNMENT

1596 BLACKMORE, THAUNG. Dilemma of the British representative to the Burmese court after the outbreak of a palace revolution in 1866. JSAH 10 (1969) 236-252.

1597 BUTWELL, RICHARD. Burmese political development, impact of a nationalist heritage. N18 pp. 124-147.

1598 BUTWELL, RICHARD. Civilians and soldiers in Burma. S90.2 pp. 74-85.

1599 BUTWELL, RICHARD. Four failures of U Nu's second premiership. AS 2 (Mar. 1962) 3-11.

1600 FIC, VICTOR M. Political leadership in Burma. L23 pp. 227-250.

1601 GUYOT, JAMES F. Bureaucratic transformation in Burma. B72 pp. 354-443.

1602 KING, WINSTON L. Buddhism and political power in Burma. S90.3 pp. 9-19.

1603 KYAN. King Mindon's councillors. JBRS 44 (June 1961) 43-60.

1604 LEHMAN, F. K. Ethnic categories in Burma and the theory of social systems. K86 pp. 93-124.

1605 McLENNAN, BARBARA. Evolution of concepts of representation in Burma. JSAH 8 (1967) 268-284.

1606 NASH, MANNING. Party building in Upper Burma. AS 3 (1963) 197-202.

1607 PARPAN, ALFREDO G. Modernization and the secular state in Southeast Asia. AST 10 (1972) 245-255.

1608 PYE, LUCIAN. The army in Burmese politics. J52 pp. 231-251.

1609 ROUCEK, JOSEPH S. Burma in geopolitics. RSA (1968) 47-82.

1610 SILVERSTEIN, JOSEF. Burma. K17 pp. 73-179.

1611 SOLOMON, ROBERT L. Saya San and the Burmese rebellion. MAS 3 (1969) 209-223.

1612 TINKER, HUGH. The politics of Burma. R64 pp. 105-118.

1613 TINKER, HUGH. Structure of the British imperial heritage. B72 pp. 23-86.

1614 VON DER MEHDEN, FRED R.   Changing
pattern of religion and politics
in Burma.   S90.2 pp. 63-73.

1615 VON DER MEHDEN, FRED R.   Rise and
fall of the religious state in
Burma.   SA 1 (1971) 74-88.

1616 WALINSKY, LOUIS J.   Rise and fall
of U Nu.   PA 38 (1965) 269-281.

1617 YI YI.   Life at the Burmese court
under the Konbaung kings.   JBRS 44
(June 1961) 85-129.

BURMA - POLITICS AND GOVERNMENT - 1962-

1618 BADGLEY, JOHN H.   Burma, the nexus
of socialism and two political
traditions.   AS 3 (1963) 89-95.

1619 BADGLEY, JOHN H.   Burma's military
government, a political analysis.
AS 2 (Aug. 1962) 24-31.

1620 BADGLEY, JOHN H.   Burma's zealot
Wungyis, Maoists or St. Simonists?
AS 5 (1965) 55-62.

1621 BADGLEY, JOHN H.   Union of Burma,
age twenty two.   AS 11 (1971)
149-158.

1622 BUTWELL, RICHARD.   U Nu's second
comeback try.   AS 9 (1969) 868-
876.

1623 CADY, JOHN F.   Burma's military
dictatorship.   AST 3 (1965) 490-
516.

1624 CHANG, DAVID W.   The military and
nation building in Korea, Burma
and Pakistan.   AS 9 (1969) 818-
830.

1625 CHANG, DAVID W.   The military and
nation building in Korea, Burma
and Pakistan.   AST 8 (1970) 1-24.

1626 HOLMES, ROBERT A.   Burmese domestic policy, the politics of Bur-
manization.   AS 7 (1967) 188-197.

1627 SILVERSTEIN, JOSEF.   Burma, Ne
Win's revolution considered.   AS 6
(1966) 95-102.

1628 SILVERSTEIN, JOSEF.   First steps
on the Burmese way to socialism.
AS 4 (1964) 716-722.

1629 SILVERSTEIN, JOSEF.   Problems in
Burma: economic, political and
diplomatic.   AS 7 (1967) 117-125.

1630 TRAGER, FRANK N.   Burma, 1968, a
new beginning?   AS 9 (1969) 104-
114.

1631 VON DER MEHDEN, FRED.   Burmese way
to socialism.   AS 3 (1963) 129-
135.

1632 WIANT, JON A.   Burma, loosening up
on the tiger's tail.   AS 13 (1973)
179-186.

Burma - **Religion** *See* BUDDHISM - BURMA
HINDUISM - BURMA

BURMA - SOCIAL CONDITIONS

1633 BA HAN.   Aspects of Burmese rural
life of old.   JBRS 51 (1968) 9-16.

1634 BA HAN.   Piquant splendors of the
Burmese life of old.   JBRS 50
(1967) 21-31.

1635 KYAW YIN.   Problem of crime and
the criminal and its solution in
socialist Burma.   JBRS 47 (1964)
205-224.

1636 LISSAK, MOSHE.   Class structure of
Burma, continuity and change.
JSAS 1 pt. 1 (1970) 60-73.

Burma - Social conditions

1637 NASH, MANNING. Southeast Asian
society: dual or multiple? JAS
23 (1963-4) 417-423.

1638 THEODORSON, GEORGE A. Burmese attitudes towards children. JBRS
45 (Dec. 1962) 205-208.

BURMA - TREATIES - CHINA

1639 MAUNG MAUNG. Burma-China boundary
settlement. AS 1 (Mar. 1961) 38-
43.

1640 WHITTAM, DAPHNE E. Sino-Burmese
boundary treaty. PA 34 (1961)
174-183.

BURMA - TREATIES - ITALY

1641 BA, VIVIEN. Diplomatic documents
relating to the Burmese-Italian
treaty of 1871. JBRS 53 pt. 2
(1970) 15-54.

BURMA RESEARCH SOCIETY

1642 CHIT THOUNG. Inaugural address of
the fiftieth anniversary celebration of the Burma Research Society
28 Dec. 1959. JBRS 43 (June 1960)
25-31.

1643 FURNIVALL, J. S. Inaugural address. JBRS 43 (June 1960) 41-50.

1644 Journal of Burma Research Society.
JBRS 47 (1964) 1-2.

1645 MAY OUNG. Inaugural address.
B92 pp. 1-6.

1646 PE MAUNG TIN. Text publication
sub-committee of the Burma Research Society. JBRS 47 (1964)
367-378.

1647 THAN TUN. An estimation of articles on Burmese history published
in the JBRS, 1910-70. JBRS 53
(June 1970) 53-66.

BURMESE LANGUAGE

1648 ALLOTT, ANNA I. Categories for
the description of the verbal
syntagma in Burmese. C44 pp. 283-
309.

1649 BA HAN. Some of the problems of a
lexicographer. JBRS 45 (June
1962) 1-5.

1650 CORNYN, WILLIAM S. Burma. S21
pp. 777-781.

1651 FORBES, KATHLEEN. Compound nouns
in Burmese. JBRS 50 (1967) 195-
221.

1652 FORBES, KATHLEEN. Neologisms in
English and Burmese. JBRS 50
(1967) 47-69.

1653 FORBES, KATHLEEN. Parts of speech
in Burmese and the Burmese quali-
fiers. JBRS 52 (Dec. 1969) 43-65.

1654 FORBES, KATHLEEN. Some examples
of depletion of meaning in Burmese. JBRS 51 (1968) 23-28.

1655 HLA PE. Abbreviations, cryptograms and chronograms in Burmese.
JBRS 47 (1964) 385-396.

1656 HLA PE. Re-examination of Burmese
classifiers. C44 pp. 163-185.

1657 HLA PE. Re-examination of Burmese
classifiers. JBRS 50 (1967) 177-
193.

1658 HLA PE. Some adapted Pali loan
words in Burmese. B91 pp. 71-99.

Burmese literature

1659 HLA PE. Some cognate words in Burmese and other Tibeto-Burman languages. 1. Maru. JBRS 53 (June 1970) 1-24.

1660 HLA PE. Tentative list of Mon loan words in Burmese. JBRS 50 (1967) 71-94.

1661 LA RAW MARAN. Note on the development of tonal systems in Tibeto Burman. L27 pp. 1-24.

1662 LEHMAN, F. K. Some diachronic rules of Burmese phonology, the problem of the final palatals. L27 pp. 1-34.

1663 LU PE WIN. Multiplicity of malapropism in my mother tongue. JBRS 48 (1965) 17-42.
Comment: HLA PE. Malapropism and U Lu Pe Win. JBRS 49 (1966) 19-28.
Author's reply: Malapropism, my reply to Dr. Hla Pe. JBRS 50 (1967) 33-46.

1664 OKELL, JOHN. **Nissaya Burmese, a** case of systematic adaptation to a foreign grammar and syntax. C44 pp. 186-227.

1665 OKELL, JOHN. **Nissaya Burmese, a** case of systematic adaptation to a foreign grammar and syntax. JBRS 50 (1967) 95-123.

1666 SPRIGG, R. K. Burmese orthography and the tonal classification of Burmese lexical items. JBRS 47 (1964) 415-440.

1667 SPRIGG, R. K. Comparison of Arakanese and Burmese based on phonological formulae. L55 pp. 109-132.

1668 SPRIGG, R. K. Prosodic analysis and Burmese syllable-initial features. JBRS 50 (1967) 263-284.

1669 SPRIGG, R. K. Prosodic analysis and phonological formulae, in Tibeto-Burman linguistic comparison. L55 pp. 79-108.

1670 TIN LWIN. Pali-Burmese Nissaya. JBRS 46 (June 1963) 43-51.

BURMESE LITERATURE

1671 BA HAN. *Shin Uttamagyaw and his Tawla,* a nature poem. B92 pp. 7-16.

1672 BADGLEY, JOHN H. Intellectuals and the national vision, the Burmese case. AS 9 (1969) 598-613.

1673 HLA PE. Burmese poetry, 1300-1971. JBRS 54 (1971) 59-114.

1674 HLA PE. Rise of popular literature in Burma. JBRS 51 (1968) 125-144.

1675 HLA PE. Three immortal Burmese songs, by Hla Pe, Anna J. Allott and John Okell. SOAS 26 (1963) 559-571.

1676 KHIN ZAW. New translation of Letwethondara's famous Ratu. B92 pp. 149-156.

1677 LU PE WIN. Jatakas in Burma. E93 pp. 94-108.

1678 PE MAUNG TIN. The Burmese novel. B92 pp. 405-410.

1679 PE MAUNG TIN. Text publication sub-committee of the Burma Research Society. JBRS 47 (1964) 367-378.

1680 STERNBACH, LUDWIK. Pali Lokaniti and the Burmese Niti Kyan and their sources. SOAS 26 (1963) 329-345.

Burmese literature

1681 STEWART, J. A.   Roselle buds.
B92 pp. 545-6.

1682 TET HTOOT.   Nature of the Burmese
chronicles.   H18 pp. 50-62.

1683 THEIN HAN.   Study of the rise of
the Burmese novel.   JBRS 51 (1968)
1-7.

1684 Translation of three shield dance
songs attributed to the Lord of
Myinzaing.   E92 pp. 240-1.

1685 WUN.   Pagan and Velu.   E92 pp.
viii-ix.

BURNEY, HENRY

1686 HALL, D. G. E.   British writers of
Burmese history from Dalrymple to
Bayfield.   H18 pp. 255-266.

BUWAYA

1687 DeRAEDT, JULES.   Some notes on
Buwaya society.   SLQ 7 (1969) 7-
112.

CAGAYON DE ORO

1688 MADIGAN, FRANCIS C.   Early history
of Cagayan de Oro.   PS 11 (1963)
76-130.

CALENDARS - BURMA

1689 LU PE WIN.   Burmese calendar.
JBRS 50 (1967) 223-244.

1690 NASH, MANNING.   Ritual and ceremonial cycle in Upper Burma.   C66
pp. 97-115.

CALENDARS - CAMBODIA

1691 POREE-MASPERO, EVELINE.   Le cycle
des douze animaux dans le vie des
Cambodgiens.   BEF 50 (1960) 311-
365.

CALENDARS - INDONESIA

1692 GORIS, R.   Holidays and holy days.
B18 pp. 113-129.

1693 VAN AKKEREN, PHILIP.   Art applied
to the calendar of Bali.   JOSA 8
(1971) 76-85.

1694 VOORHOEVE, P.   Sanskrit maandnamen
in het Bataks.   BIJ 128 (1972)
494-496.

CALENDARS - VIETNAM

1695 HIEU CHAN.   Buffalo talk.   AC 3
(Jan. 1961) 105-108.

CAMACHO Y AVILA, DIEGO

1696 GANZON, ANGELITA F.   Diego Camacho
y Avila, archbishop of Manila.
PHR 1 pt. 2 (1966) 63-91.

CAMBODIA

1697 L'annee 1966 en Asie, Cambodia.
FA 22 (1968) 98-101.

1698 GORDON, BERNARD K.   Cambodia, following the leader, by Bernard K.
Gordon and Kathryn Young.   AS 10
(1970) 169-176.

1699 IENG SARY.   Cambodia 1972.   JCA 2
(1972) 212-216.

1700 KIRK, DONALD.   Cambodia 1973, year
of the bomb halt.   AS 14 (1974)
89-100.

Cambodia - Foreign relations - Thailand

1701 List of microfilms deposited in the Centre for East Asian Cultural Studies, pt. 3, Cambodia, reels 1 to 71. EACS 8 (1969) 53-74.

1702 POOLE, PETER A. Cambodia, the cost of survival. AS 12 (1972) 148-155.

1703 POOLE, PETER A. Cambodia, will Vietnam truce halt drift to civil war? AS 13 (1973) 76-82.

1704 WITHINGTON, WILLIAM A. Cambodia. F56 pp. 100-118.

1705 YOUNG, KENNETH RAY. Asia-Pacific conference on Cambodia. AF 3 (1971) 104-110.

CAMBODIA - ECONOMIC CONDITIONS

1706 KIRK, DONALD. Cambodia's economic crisis. AS 11 (1971) 238-255.

CAMBODIA - FOREIGN RELATIONS

1707 GORDON, BERNARD K. Cambodia, where foreign policy counts. AS 5 (1965) 433-448.

1708 GORDON, BERNARD K. Cambodia's foreign relations, Sihanouk and after. J28 pp. 155-173.

1709 LEIFER, MICHAEL. Cambodia and her neighbors. PA 34 (1961) 361-374.

CAMBODIA - FOREIGN RELATIONS - CHINA

1710 KAO KAN. L'evolution des relations sino-cambodgiennes, 1963-1970. FA pt. 1 (1974) 79-95.

1711 MARSOT, ALAIN-GERARD. China's aid to Cambodia. PA 42 (1969) 189-198.

1712 UNGER, JONATHAN. Mao's Indochina tactic. G79 pp. 139-149.

CAMBODIA - FOREIGN RELATIONS - FRANCE

1713 DeGAULLE, C. Discours a Phnom Penh. FA 20 (1965) 510-513.

1714 GUPTA, H. R. Early phase of the freedom struggle in Indochina. S87 pp. 477-484.

CAMBODIA - FOREIGN RELATIONS - GREAT BRITAIN

1715 TARLING, NICHOLAS. British policy towards Siam, Cambodia, and Vietnam, 1842-1858. AST 4 (1966) 240-258.

CAMBODIA - FOREIGN RELATIONS - PHILIPPINES

1716 QUIRINO, CARLOS. First Philippine expedition to Indo-China. JSAH 10 (1969) 491-500.

CAMBODIA - FOREIGN RELATIONS - THAILAND

1717 CHANDLER, DAVID P. Cambodia's relations with Siam in the early Bangkok period, the politics of a tributary state. JSS 60 pt. 1 (1972) 153-169.

1718 SINGH, L. P. Thai-Cambodian temple dispute. AS 2 (Oct. 1962) 23-26.

Cambodia - Foreign relations - United
  States

CAMBODIA - FOREIGN RELATIONS - UNITED
  STATES

1719 FALK, RICHARD A. The Cambodian
      operation and international law.
      G79 pp. 150-171.

1720 Most important facts about U.S.
      intervention in Cambodia. JCA 1
      pt. 3 (1971) 111-116.

1721 SCHURMANN, FRANZ. Nixon's trap.
      G79 pp. 217-229.

CAMBODIA - FOREIGN RELATIONS - VIETNAM

1722 CHANDLER, DAVID P. Cambodia's re-
      lations with Siam in the early
      Bangkok period, the politics of a
      tributary state. JSS 60 pt. 1
      (1972) 153-169.

1723 GURTOV, MELVIN. Indochina in
      north Vietnamese strategy. J28
      pp. 137-154.

CAMBODIA - HISTORY

1724 CHANDLER, DAVID P. Royally spon-
      sored human sacrifices in nine-
      teenth century Cambodia, the cult
      of Nak ta Me Sa (Mahisasuramar-
      dini) at Ba Phnom. JSS 62 pt. 2
      (1974) 207-222.

1725 FABRICIUS, PIERRE. Prolegomenes
      a l'histoire khmere. FA 17 (1960)
      1451-1472.

1726 GRISON, PIERRE. Le Cambodge en
      quete de ses origines. FA 17
      (1960) 1963-1967.

1727 HIRSHFIELD, CLAIRE. Struggle for
      the Mekong banks, 1892-1896. JSAH
      9 (1968) 25-52.

1728 OSBORNE, MILTON. Abridged Cambo-
      dian chronicle, a Thai version of
      Cambodian history, by Milton Os-
      borne and David K. Wyatt. FA 22
      (1968) 189-203.

1729 OSBORNE, MILTON. History and
      kingship in contemporary Cambodia.
      JSAH 7 (Mar. 1966) 1-14.

1730 OSBORNE, MILTON. Notes on early
      Cambodian provincial history,
      Isanapura and Sambhupura. FA 20
      (1965) 433-449.

1731 PIAT, MARTINE. Chroniques royales
      khmer. SEIB 49 (1974) 35-140.

1732 PIAT, MARTINE. Note sur la pre-
      miere apparition du Cambodge dans
      la cartographie europeenne. SEIB
      48 (1973) 119-120.

1733 SMITH, ROGER M. Khmer empire,
      French rule, and the path to in-
      dependence. G79 pp. 55-68.

1734 SVAY MUOY. Histoire de Keo Preah
      Phleung d'apres les annales des
      rois khmers. SEIB 47 (1972) 375-
      394.

1735 WOLTERS, O. W. North-western Cam-
      bodia in the seventh century.
      SOAS 37 (1974) 355-384.

CAMBODIA - MINORITIES *See also* CHAMS,
  CHINESE - CAMBODIA, KHMER, VIETNAMESE
  - CAMBODIA

1736 TURTON, ANDREW. National minority
      peoples in Indo-China. JCA 4
      (1974) 336-343.

CAMBODIA - POLITICS AND GOVERNMENT

1737 BUCHANAN, KEITH. Cambodian royal
      socialism. L23 pp. 251-269.

Cambodia - Politics and government -
1970-

1738 DEVILLERS, PHILIPPE. Dynamics of
power in Cambodia. R64 pp. 143-
163.

1739 DOLEZAL, IVAN. Policy of neutrality and the international position
of Cambodia. AAS 4 (1968) 57-79.

1740 FALL, BERNARD. Problemes politiques des etats poly-ethniques en
Indochine. FA 18 (1962) 129-152.

1741 GORDON, BERNARD K. Cambodia,
shadow over Angkor. AS 9 (1969)
58-68.

1742 LANCASTER, DONALD. The decline of
Prince Sihanouk's regime. J28 pp.
47-55.

1743 LEIFER, MICHAEL. Cambodia and her
neighbors. PA 34 (1961) 361-374.

1744 LEIFER, MICHAEL. Cambodia, in
search of neutrality. AS 3 (1963)
55-60.

1745 LEIFER, MICHAEL. Cambodia, the
limits of diplomacy. AS 7 (1967)
69-73.

1746 LEIFER, MICHAEL. Cambodia, the
politics of accommodation. AS 4
(1964) 674-679.

1747 LEIFER, MICHAEL. Cambodian opposition. AS 2 (Apr. 1962) 11-15.

1748 LEIFER, MICHAEL. Failure of political institutionalization in
Cambodia. MAS 2 (1968) 125-140.

1749 LEIFER, MICHAEL. Peace and war in
Cambodia. SA 1 (1971) 58-73.

1750 LEIFER, MICHAEL. Problems of
authority and political succession in Cambodia. N18 pp. 148-
174.

1751 OSBORNE, MILTON E. History and
kingship in contemporary Cambodia.
JSAH 7 (Mar. 1966) 1-14.

1752 OSBORNE, MILTON E. King making in
Cambodia, from Sisowath to Sihanouk. JSAS 4 (1973) 169-185.

1753 PENH, P. N. Une synthese de la
crise cambodgienne. SA 1 (1971)
222-240.

1754 ROSOFF, WILLIAM. Dissension in
the kingdom. G79 pp. 81-94.

1755 ROUCEK, JOSEPH S. Cambodia in
geopolitics. RSA (1970) 197-223.

1756 SIMON, JEAN-PIERRE. Cambodia,
pursuit of crisis. AS 5 (1965)
49-54.

1757 SMITH, ROGER M. Cambodia. K17
pp. 593-675.

1758 SMITH, ROGER M. Cambodia, between
Scylla and Charybdis. AS 8 (1968)
72-79.

1759 SMITH, ROGER M. Cambodia's neutrality and the Laotian crisis.
AS 1 (July 1961) 17-24.

CAMBODIA - POLITICS AND GOVERNMENT -
  1970-

1760 ALLMAN, T. D. Anatomy of a coup.
G79 pp. 97-104.

1761 Cambodia, before the end of the
dry season. JCA 4 (1974) 241-246.

1762 GARRETT, BANNING. National United
Front of Cambodia. G79 pp. 130-
138.

1763 GIRLING, J. L. S. Resistance in
Cambodia. AS 12 (1972) 549-563.

Cambodia - Politics and government -
  1970-

1764 GORDON, BERNARD K. The Khmer Re-
     public that was the Cambodia that
     was, by Bernard K. Gordon and
     Kathryn Young. AS 11 (1971) 26-
     40.

1765 GRANT, JONATHAN S. Regime of Lon
     Nol. G79 pp. 113-129.

1766 IENG SARY. Report from the lib-
     erated zone of Cambodia. JCA 2
     (1972) 120-122.

1767 OSBORNE, MILTON. Effacing the
     God-King, internal developments in
     Cambodia since March 1970. J28
     pp. 57-80.

1768 Reality of the NUFC and its armed
     forces in Cambodia. JCA 1 pt. 3
     (1971) 123-127.

1769 SIHANOUK, NORODOM. 43rd message
     to the Khmer nation. JCA 3 (1973)
     387-8.

1770 Statement of the Royal Government
     of National Union of Cambodia at
     the end of the national congress.
     JCA 3 (1973) 487-491.

1771 THIOUNN PRASITH. The situation in
     Cambodia reviewed. JCA 4 (1974)
     113-123.

Cambodia - Religion *See* BUDDHISM -
  CAMBODIA, HINDUISM - CAMBODIA

Cambodian language *See* KHMER LANGUAGE

CAMIGUIN

1772 ELIO Y SANCHEZ, VICENTE. History
     of Camiguin. PS 20 (1972) 106-
     146.

CANNIBALISM - INDONESIA

1773 KOCH, KLAUS-FRIEDRICH. Warfare
     and anthropophagy in Jale society.
     BIJ 126 (1970) 37-58.

CANO, FLAVIO ZARAGOZA

1774 AGRAVA, LEONOR. Flavio Zaragoza
     Cano. GEJ 6 (1963) 38-41.

CAODAISM

1775 NGUYEN TRAN HUAN. Histoire d'une
     secte religigeuse au Vietnam: le
     Caodaisme. C28 pp. 189-214.

1776 SMITH, R. B. Introduction to
     Caodaism. I. Origins and early
     history. SOAS 33 (1970) 335-349.

1777 SMITH, R. B. Introduction to
     Caodaism. II. Beliefs and organi-
     zation. SOAS 33 (1970) 573-589.

CAPISNON LITERATURE

1778 CLAVEL, LEOTHINY S. Folklore and
     communication. AST 8 (1970) 218-
     247.

CARITA PARAHYANGAN

1779 NOORDUYN J. Het Begingedeelte van
     de Carita Parahyangan, tekst, ver-
     taling, commentaar. BIJ 118
     (1962) 405-432.

1780 NOORDUYN, J. Enige nadere gegevens
     over tekst en inhoud van de Carita
     Parahyangan. BIJ 122 (1966) 366-
     374.

1781 NOORDUYN, J. Over het eerste ge-
     deelte van de Oud-Soendase Carita
     Parahyangan. BIJ 118 (1962) 374-
     383.

CASPER, LINDA **

1782 HIDALGO, PERLA R. The art of *The peninsulars* by Linda Casper. SLURJ 2 (1971) 267-292.

CASWELL, JESSE

1783 BRADLEY, WILLIAM L. Prince Mongkut and Jesse Caswell. JSS 54 (1966) 29-41.

CATHOLIC CHURCH

1784 American Catholic bishops on Vietnam and peace. FA 21 (1966) 237-240.

1785 McCARTHY, CHARLES. First expedition of Jesuits from the Philippines to China. PS 18 (1970) 634-644.

CATHOLIC CHURCH - PHILIPPINES **

1786 ABELLA, DOMINGO. Bishops of Caceres and Jaro. PS 11 (1963) 548-556.

1787 ABELLA, DOMINGO. Bishops of Nueva Segobia. PS 10 (1962) 577-585.

1788 ABELLA, DOMINGO. Succession of bishops of Cebu. PS 8 (1960) 535-543.

1789 ANTONISSEN, A. Carlos Cuarteron. JMBRAS 39 pt. 1 (1966) 168-171.

1790 BAUTISTA, PURIFICACION G. Cursillo movement, its impact on Philippine society. AST 10 (1972) 232-244.

1791 BERNAD, MIGUEL A. Case of the misnamed virgin. PS 16 (1968) 563-576.

1792 BLANCO, JOSE C. Aggiornamento and works of liberation. PS 20 (1972) 439-448.

1793 BRUNNER, PAUL. Bishops' directives on participation in the mass. PS 9 (1961) 557-570.

1794 COSTA, H. DE LA. Religious renewal, an Asian view. PS 20 (1972) 93-105.

1795 CULLUM, LEO A. Diocesan seminaries in the Philippines. PS 20 (1972) 65-92.

1796 CULLUM, LEO A. San Carlos Seminary and the Jesuits. PS 18 (1970) 479-545.

1797 CUMMINS, JAMES S. Archbishop Felipe Pardo's last will. A58 pp. 105-112.

1798 CUSHNER, NICHOLAS P. Meysapan, the formation and social effects of a landed estate in the Philippines. JAH 7 (1973) 30-53.

1799 DEINER, PAUL W. Participation of Philippine bishops in Vatican II. SJ 17 (1970) 231-247.

1800 GIORDANO, PASQUALE. Challenge of faith today. PS 22 (1974) 3-18.

1801 GOROSPE, VITALIANO R. Catholic hierarchy and the population problem. PS 17 (1969) 806-810.

1802 GOWING, PETER G. Christianity in the Philippines, yesterday and today. SJ 12 (1965) 109-151.

1803 HEALY, GERALD. Theology for sisters. PS 8 (1960) 833-836.

Catholic Church - Philippines

1804   JOCANO, F. LANDA. Filipino Catholicism, a case study in religious change. AST 5 (1967) 42-64.

1805   MANALIGOD, AMBROSIO. Role of the foreign missionary in the Philippine church today, 1971. SJ 19 (1972) 153-161.

1806   Pax Romana conferences in Manila. PS 8 (1960) 362-388.

1807   QUASHA, WILLIAM H. Tribute to Augustin Cardinal Bea. PS 18 (1970) 645-653.

1808   ROCES, ALFREDO R. Mask of Longinus. PS 9 (1961) 255-261.

1809   ROSAL, NICOLAS LL. Unjust position of the Church in the Philippine constitution. UN 33 (1960) 682-739.

1810   ROSAL, NICOLAS LL. Unjust position of the Church in the Philippine constitution. UN 34 (1961) 46-94.

1811   WILEY, SAMUEL R. Our ecumenical task in the Philippine situation. PS 14 (1966) 293-298.

CATHOLIC CHURCH - PHILIPPINES - HISTORY

1812   ARAGON, J. GAYO. Controversy over justification of Spanish rule in the Philippines. A58 pp. 3-21.

1813   ARCILLA, JOSE S. Christianization of Davao Oriental, excerpts from Jesuit missionary letters. PS 19 (1971) 639-724.

1814   BOXER, C. R. Three unpublished Jesuit letters on Philippine and Mariana missions, 1681-1689. PS 10 (1962) 434-442.

1815   COSTA, HORACIO DE LA. Development of the native clergy in the Philippines. A58 pp. 65-104.

1816   COSTA, HORACIO DE LA. Episcopal jurisdiction in the Philippines during the Spanish regime. A58 pp. 44-64.

1817   CUSHNER, NICHOLAS P. Abandonment of Tamontaka Reduction, 1898-1899. PS 12 (1964) 288-296.

1818   EVANGELISTA, OSCAR L. Religious problems in the Philippines and the American Catholic Church, 1898-1907. AST 6 (1968) 248-262.

1819   GANZON, ANGELITA F. Diego Camacho y Avila, archbishop of Manila. PHR 1 pt. 2 (1966) 63-91.

1820   GEEROMS, HENRY. Former Spanish missions in the Cordillera, northern Luzon. SLQ 3 (1965) 17-56.

1821   GEEROMS, HENRY. Former Spanish missions in the Cordillera, northern Luzon. SLQ 3 (1965) 437-480.

1822   GEEROMS, HENRY. Former Spanish missions in the Cordillera, northern Luzon. SLQ 4 (1966) 373-436.

1823   GOWING, PETER G. Disentanglement of church and state early in the American regime in the Philippines. A58 pp. 203-222.

1824   HARTENDORP, A. V. H. Two stories of the Japanese occupation. PHR 1 pt. 2 (1966) 92-124.

1825   LUCENA, JEPHITE. Mons. Domingo de Salazar, O.P., 1512-1594, first bishop of the Philippines. UN 34 (Dec. 1961) 86-90.

ARTICLES

1826 MAJUL, CESAR ADIB. Anticleri-
calism during the reform movement
and the Philippine revolution.
A58 pp. 152-171.

1827 ORTIZ, JUSTINO C. Christianity
in the Philippines. UN 36 (1963)
352-356.

1828 PHELAN, JOHN LEDDY. Prebaptismal
instruction and the administration of baptism in the Philippines during the sixteenth century. A58 pp. 22-43.

1829 SCOTT, WILLIAM HENRY. Birth and
death of a mission, a chapter in
Philippine church history. PS 13
(1965) 801-821.

1830 VICENTE, VITORIANO. Apuntes para
la historia de la teologia en
Filipinas. UN 37 (1964) 523-535.

1831 VICENTE, VITORIANO. Apuntes para
la historia de la teologia en
Filipinas. UN 38 (1965) 102-114.

1832 VICENTE, VITORIANO. Apuntes para
la historia de la teologia en
Filipinas. UN 38 (1965) 233-247.

1833 VICENTE, VITORIANO. Apuntes para
la historia de la teologia en
Filipinas. UN 38 (1965) 387-394.

CATHOLIC CHURCH - VIETNAM

1834 CLEMENTIN, JEAN-RAOUL. Le com-
portement politique des institutions Catholiques au Vietnam. C28
pp. 108-134.

1835 IRVING, R. E. M.   M.R.P. and
French policy in Indochina, 1945-
1954, with special reference to
the influence of Catholicism. FA
23 (1969) 257-269.

1836 LABRUSSE, S. DE. A l'occasion du
tricentenaire d'Alexandre de
Rhodes. SEIB 35 (1960) 682.

1837 NGUYEN T. Les Catholiques vietnamiens et les perspectives de
paix au Vietnam. FA 22 (1968)
221-232.

1838 VO LONG TE. Contribution a
l'etude d'un des premiers poemes
narratifs d'inspiration Catholique
en langue vietnamienne romanisee,
Ine tu dao van ou *Le martyre
d'Agnes*. SEIB 42 (1967) 307-336.

CATHOLIC EDUCATIONAL ASSOCIATION OF THE PHILIPPINES

1839 CEAP convention of 1960. PS 8
(1960) 689-716.

CAVITE MUTINY

1840 QUIRINO, CARLOS. More documents
on Burgos. PS 18 (1970) 161-177.

1841 SCHUMACHER, JOHN N. Authenticity
of the writings attributed to
Father Jose Burgos. PS 18 (1970)
3-51.

1842 SCHUMACHER, JOHN N. The Cavite
Mutiny, an essay on the published
sources. PS 20 (1972) 603-632.

1843 SCHUMACHER, JOHN N. Documents relating to Jose Burgos and the
Cavite Mutiny of 1872, by John N.
Schumacher and Nicholas P. Cushner. PS 17 (1969) 457-529.

CEBU

1844 CALBRECHT, JOSEPH. Finding and
origin of the Santo Nino of Cebu.
SLQ 3 (1965) 7-16.

Cebu

1845 LIU, WILLIAM T. Fertility patterns in Cebu. B13 pp. 167-205.

CELEBES

1846 CENSE, A. A. Old Buginese and Macassarese diaries. BIJ 122 (1966) 416-428.

1847 DOEPPERS, DANIEL F. Incident in the PRRI/Permesta rebellion of 1958. IND 14 (1972) 182-195.

1848 Les fouilles et l'histoire a Celebes sud. AR 3 (1972) 205-212.

1849 LOMBARD-SALMON, CL. Communaute chinoise de Makasar, vie collective et organisations. FA 23 (1969) 159-193.

1850 NAWAWI, MOHD. A. Tradition, mobilization and development in Indonesia. M52 pp. 19-35.

1851 NOORDUYN, J. Origins of south Celebes historical writing. S61 pp. 137-155.

1852 PELRAS, CHRISTIAN. Hierarchie et pouvoir traditionnels en pays Wadjo. AR 1 (1970) 169-191.

1853 PELRAS, CHRISTIAN. Hierarchie et pouvoir traditionnels en pays Wadjo. AR 2 (1971) 197-223.

1854 WALLACE, ALFRED RUSSEL. Explorations in Celebes. H57 pp. 362-380.

CEMENT INDUSTRY - SINGAPORE

1855 LIM POH TIN, EILEEN. Study of the cement industry of Singapore. MER 15 pt. 2 (1970) 104-113.

CENSORSHIP - INDONESIA

1856 SIAGIAN, GAJUS. La censure cinematographique. AR 5 (1973) 183-190.

CENSORSHIP - MALAYSIA

1857 STEVENSON, REX. Cinemas and censorship in colonial Malaya. JSAS 5 (1974) 209-224.

CENSUS *See also the subdivision POPULATION under individual countries*

CENSUS - BURMA - 1953-54

1858 SAW WIN. Statistical analysis of farm size and current expenditures. JBRS 48 (1965) 57-76.

CENSUS - MALAYSIA - SARAWAK - 1960

1859 SAW SWEE HOOK. Labour force of Sarawak in 1960, by Saw Swee Hook and Cheng Siok Hwa. AST 8 (1970) 135-142.

CENSUS - PHILIPPINES - 1960

1860 ACHUTEGUI, PEDRO S. DE. Aglipayan churches and the census of 1960. PS 12 (1964) 446-459.

CENSUS - PHILIPPINES - 1970

1861 The Philippine 1970 census on population and housing, an interpretation for the northern Luzon provinces, by Paul Beghin, Raf van Hellemont, Juan Ngalob, and Emiel Roekaerts. SLURJ 3 (1972) 327-356.

Chao Phya River

CENTRE FOR EAST ASIAN CULTURAL STUDIES

1862 Activities of the Centre for East
      Asian Cultural Studies, 1965-1966.
      EACS 5 (1966) 29-37.

1863 Activities of the Centre for East
      Asian Cultural Studies, 1966-1968.
      EACS 7 (1968) 59-75.

1864 Activities of the Centre for East
      Asian Cultural Studies, 1968-1970.
      EACS 10 (1971) 33-52.

1865 Centre for East Asian Cultural
      Studies. EACS 1 (1962) 59-72.

1866 Centre for East Asian Cultural
      Studies. FA 19 (1963) 710-712.

1867 List of microfilms deposited in
      the Centre for East Asian Cultural
      Studies. EACS 9 (1970) 57-107.

1868 List of microfilms deposited in
      the Centre for East Asian Cultural
      Studies, part 1, Malaysia, reels
      4001-4152. EACS 7 (1968) 77-98.

1869 List of microfilms deposited in
      the Centre for East Asian Cultural
      Studies, part 2, Malaysia, reels
      1 to 216. EACS 8 (1969) 41-52.

1870 List of microfilms deposited in
      the Centre for East Asian Cultural
      Studies, part 3, Cambodia, reels
      1 to 71. EACS 8 (1969) 53-74.

1871 Review of activities of the Centre
      for East Asian Cultural Studies.
      EACS 5 (1966) 16-24.

Chairil Anwar *See* ANWAR, CHAIRIL

CHAM

1872 DOURNES, JACQUES. Recherches sur
      le haut Champa. FA 24 (1970) 143-
      162.

1873 LAFONT, P. B. Contribution a
      l'etude des structures sociales des
      Cham du Viet-nam. BEF 52 (1964)
      157-171.

1874 MOUSSAY, GERARD. Coup d'oeil sur
      les Cam d'aujourd'hui. SEIB 46
      (1971) 361-373.

CHAM LANGUAGE

1875 BLOOD, DORIS. Women's speech
      characteristics in Cham. AC 3
      (July 1961) 139-143.

1876 HAUDRICOURT, ANDRE G. Limits and
      connections of Austroasiatic in
      the northeast. Z52 pp. 44-56.

CHAM THONGKHAMWAN

1877 WYATT, DAVID K. Maha Cham Thong-
      khamwan. JSS 60 pt. 1 (1972) 467-
      469.

CHANG PI-SHIH

1878 GODLEY, MICHAEL R. Chang Pi-shih
      and Nanyang Chinese involvement in
      south China's railroads, 1896-
      1911. JSAS 4 (1973) 16-30.

CHAO PHYA RIVER

1879 SMALL, LESLIE E. Historical de-
      velopment of the greater Chao Phya
      water control project, an economic
      perspective. JSS 61 pt. 1 (1973)
      1-24.

CHILDREN - BURMA

1896   BA HAN.   Burmese complex, its
       roots.   JBRS 46 (June 1963) 1-10.

1897   THEODORSON, GEORGE A.   Burmese
       attitudes towards children.   JBRS
       45 (1962) 205-208.

CHILDREN - INDONESIA

1898   ROSE, CATHARINE S.   Malnutrition
       in children in Indonesia, by
       Catharine S. Rose and Paul Gyorgy.
       J37 pp. 143-164.

CHILDREN - INDONESIA - BALI

1899   BELO, JANE.   Balinese children's
       drawing.   B43 pp. 240-259.

1900   BELO, JANE.   Study of customs
       pertaining to twins in Bali.   B43
       pp. 3-56.

1901   CUISINIER, JEANNE.   Le ritual
       familial a Bali.   BEF 52 (1964)
       415-428.

1902   McPHEE, COLIN.   Children and music
       in Bali.   B43 pp. 212-239.

1903   MEAD, MARGARET.   Children and
       ritual in Bali.   B43 pp. 198-211.

CHILDREN - MALAYSIA

1904   NEEDHAM, RODNEY.   Temer names.
       JMBRAS 37 pt. 1 (1964) 121-125.

CHILDREN - MALAYSIA - SARAWAK

1905   GALVIN, A. D.   Naming ceremonies
       among the Baram Kenyahs.   BMJ 3
       pt. 1 (1973) 34-40.

1906   GARMAN, M. A.   Murut (Lun Bawang)
       prepositions and noun particles in
       children's speech, by M. A. Garman,
       P. D. Griffiths, and R. J. Wales.
       SMJ 18 (1970) 353-376.

1907   METCALF, PETER.   Berawan adoption
       practices.   SMJ 22 (1974) 275-286.

1908   WADSWORTH, G. R.   Heights and
       weights of Sarawak children.   SMJ
       11 (1963) 307-320.

1909   WARREN, GEORGE LEWIS.   Heights and
       weights of school children in the
       Kapit District, Sarawak, by George
       Lewis Warren, Carolyn Kocher War-
       ren and Norvin Dean Schuman.   SMJ
       12 (1965) 351-359.

CHILDREN - PHILIPPINES

1910   BERAN, JANICE.   Characteristics of
       children's play and games in the
       southern Philippines.   SJ 20
       (1973) 100-113.

1911   BERAN, JANICE.   Some elements of
       power in Filipino children's
       play.   SJ 20 (1973) 194-207.

1912   HOFILENA, FERNANDO P.   Child in
       the Fil-American setting.   UN 38
       (1965) 505-510.

1913   HOFILENA, FERNANDO P.   Periods of
       crisis in childhood.   UN 37 (1964)
       119-122.

1914   HOFILENA, FERNANDO P.   Role of the
       special Child Study Center in Men-
       tal Hygiene in the Philippines.
       UN 37 (1964) 584-589.

1915   JOCANO, F. LANDA.   Maternal and
       child care among the Tagalogs in
       Bay, Laguna, Philippines.   AST 8
       (1970) 277-300.

Children - Philippines

1916 MASLOG, FLORITA S. Health profile of school children in Dumaguete City. SJ 20 (1973) 208-216.

1917 PANIZO, ALFREDO. Infanticide and population. UN 38 (1965) 599-610.

1918 PORTER, LUZ S. Role of physical-physiological activity in infants growth and development. SJ 18 (1971) 343-356.

1919 QUISUMBING, LOURDES R. Introduction to the study of child-rearing practices in the rural environs of Cebu City. D67 pp. 78-85.

1920 SAMSON, JOSE A. Schizophrenia among Filipino children. UN 38 (1965) 298-310.

1921 TEMPORAL, ALMA M. Some Filipino child rearing practices and personality development. SJ 15 (1968) 385-398.

1922 TORRENTO, CARIDAD J. Establishing norms for the Philippine non-verbal intelligence test in Baguio City's public elementary schools and the study of children's categorization responses, by Caridad J. Torrento and Juan Ngalob. SLURJ 2 (1971) 540-614.

1923 VALDES, M. TRINITAS. Parental attitudes and their effects on exceptional children. SLURJ 1 (1970) 631-642.

CHILDREN - THAILAND

1924 AYABE, TSUNEO. Dek Wat and Thai education, the case of Tambon Ban Khem. JSS 61 pt. 2 (1973) 39-52.

CHILDREN - VIETNAM

1925 KERMARREC, R. P. JEAN. Les enfants tigres. SEIB 47 (1972) 163-194.

CHIN LANGUAGE

1926 HENDERSON, EUGENIE J. A. Notes on Teizang, a northern Chin dialect. SOAS 26 (1963) 551-558.

CHINDWIN RIVER

1927 SARIN, DEV D. Textural characteristics of channel sediments of the Chindwin River. JBRS 47 (1964) 325-365.

CHINESE **

1928 CHANG, DAVID W. Current status of Chinese minorities in Southeast Asia. AS 13 (1973) 587-603.

1929 CHIU LING-YEONG. Chinese maritime expansion, 1368-1644. JOSA 3 pt. 1 (1965) 27-47.

1930 FREEDMAN, MAURICE. The Chinese in Southeast Asia, a longer view. T45 pp. 431-449.

1931 FREEDMAN, MAURICE. Epicycle of Cathay, or the southward expansion of the Sinologists. S58 pp. 302-332.

1932 FREEDMAN, MAURICE. Handling of money, a note on the background of the economic sophistication of overseas Chinese. S48 pp. 38-42.

1933 GO GIEN TJWAN. De historische wortels van de Baperki-beweging. B85 pp. 47-68.

1934 GO GIEN TJWAN. Role of the overseas Chinese in the Southeast
Asian revolutions and their adjustments to new states. N18 pp.
59-73.

1935 GODLEY, MICHAEL R. Chang Pi-shih
and Nanyang Chinese involvement in
south China's railroads, 1896-
1911. JSAS 4 (1973) 16-30.

1936 GOLFIN, R. P. Influence de la
Chine populaire sur les peuples
de l'Asie du sud-est. AST 3
(1965) 571-584.

1937 HARRISSON, TOM. Nanhai trade, Dr.
Wang, Poli, Brunei, West and East.
AP 4 (1960) 56-58.
Comment: WANG GUNGWU. Mr.
Harrisson and the western bias of
the Nanhai trade. AP 4 (1960)
59-61.

1938 HOWELL, LLEWELLYN D. The Chinese
in Southeast Asia, China commit-
ments and local assimilation.
AST 11 pt. 3 (1973) 37-53.

1939 LIU, WILLIAM T. Achievement
motivation among Chinese youth in
Southeast Asia. AS 5 (1965) 186-
196.

1940 MILLS, J. V. Arab and Chinese
navigators in Malaysian waters
in about A.D. 1500. JMBRAS 47
pt. 2 (1974) 1-82.

1941 NGGAWA, DARIUS W. Chinese diffusion in Southeast Asia. UN 37
(1964) 196-251.

1942 OLIVIER, GOERGES. Les Chinois du
sud et la race sua-mongole, par
Georges Olivier et Jacques Ruffie.
BEF 53 (1966) 227-271.

1943 PETACH, L. Early relations of
China with South-Eastern Asia.
S87 pp. 186-190.

1944 SKINNER, G. WILLIAM. Overseas
Chinese leadership, paradigm for a
paradox. L23 pp. 191-207.

1945 SUYAMA, TAKU. Pang societies and
the economy of Chinese immigrants
in Southeast Asia. J45 pp. 193-
213.

1946 THE SIAUW GIAP. Religion and
overseas Chinese assimilation in
Southeast Asian countries. RSA
(1965) 67-83.

1947 WILLETTS, WILLIAM. Maritime adventures of Grand Eunuch Ho. JSAH
5 (Sept. 1964) 25-42.

1948 WILLMOTT, WILLIAM E. Overseas
Chinese today and tomorrow. PA
42 (1969) 206-214.

1949 WOLTERS, O. W. The Po-Ssu pine
trees. SOAS 23 (1960) 323-350.

CHINESE - BRUNEI

1950 FRANKE, WOLFGANG. Chinese tomb
inscription of A.D. 1264, discovered recently in Brunei, a preliminary report, by Wolfgang
Franke and Chen Tieh-fan. BMJ 3
pt. 1 (1973) 91-99.

1951 HARRISSON, TOM. Nanhai trade, Dr.
Wang, Poli, Brunei, West and East.
AP 4 (1960) 56-58.
Comment: WANG GUNGWU. Mr.
Harrisson and the western bias of
the Nanhai trade. AP 4 (1960) 59-
61.

1952 LEE, Y. L. Chinese in Sarawak and
Brunei. SMJ 11 (1964) 516-532.

CHINESE - BURMA

1953   CHEN YI-SEIN. Chinese in Rangoon
        during the 18th and 19th centu-
        ries. E92 pp. 107-111.

1954   THEODORSON, GEORGE A. Minority
        peoples of the Union of Burma.
        JSAH 5 (Mar. 1964) 1-16.

1955   YEGAR, MOSHE. Panthay (Chinese
        Muslims) of Burma and Yunnan.
        JSAH 7 (Mar. 1966) 73-85.

CHINESE - CAMBODIA

1956   WILLMOTT, W. E. History and
        sociology of the Chinese in Cam-
        bodia prior to the French pro-
        tectorate. JSAH 7 (Mar. 1966)
        15-38.

CHINESE - INDONESIA

1957   BAKS, C. Chinese communities in
        eastern Java, a few remarks. AST
        8 (1970) 248-259.

1958   LOMBARD-SALMON, CLAUDINE. Un
        Chinois a Java, 1729-1736. BEF
        59 (1972) 279-318.

1959   LOMBARD-SALMON, CLAUDINE. Com-
        munaute chinoise de Makasar, vie
        collective et organisations. FA
        23 (1969) 159-193.

1960   LOMBARD-SALMON, CLAUDINE. Le
        Sjair de l'Association Chinoise
        de Batavia, 1905. AR 2 (1971)
        55-100.

1961   MOZINGO, DAVID. Sino-Indonesian
        dual nationality treaty. AS 1
        (Dec. 1961) 25-31.

1962   PALMIER, LESLIE H. Batik manu-
        facture in a Chinese community in
        Java. H24 pp. 75-97.

1963   PANGLAYKIM, J. Study of entre-
        preneurship in developing coun-
        tries, the development of one
        Chinese concern in Indonesia, by
        J. Panglaykim and I. Parmer. JSAS
        1 pt. 1 (1970) 85-95.

1964   REID, ANTHONY. Early Chinese
        migration into north Sumatra. S89
        pp. 289-320.

1965   SURYADINATA, LEO. Indonesian
        Chinese education, past and pres-
        ent. IND 14 (1972) 49-71.

1966   SURYADINATA, LEO. Pre-war Indo-
        nesian nationalism and the Pera-
        nakan Chinese. IND 11 (1971) 83-
        94.

1967   THE SIAUW GIAP. Group conflict in
        a plural society. RSA (1966) 1-
        31.

1968   THE SIAUW GIAP. Group conflict in
        a plural society, anti-Chinese
        riots in Indonesia. RSA (1966)
        185-217.

1969   WELDON, PETER D. Indonesian and
        Chinese status and language dif-
        ferences in urban Java. JSAS 5
        (1974) 37-54.

1970   WILLIAMS, LEA E. Ethical program
        and the Chinese of Indonesia.
        JSAH 2 (July 1961) 35-42.

CHINESE - LAOS

1971   HALPERN, JOEL. Role of the
        Chinese in Lao society. JSS 49
        pt. 1 (1961) 21-46.

CHINESE – MALAYSIA

1972 AKASHI, YOJI. Japanese policy
      towards the Malayan Chinese, 1941-
      1945. JSAS 1 pt. 2 (1970) 61-89.

1973 ALATAS, SYED HUSSEIN. Religion
      and modernization in South-East
      Asia. M52 pp. 153-169.

1974 BUXBAUM, DAVID C. Chinese family
      law in a common law setting. A
      note on the institutional environ-
      ment and the substantive family
      law of the Chinese in Singapore
      and Malaysia. C39 pp. 146-177.

1975 CHENG SIOK HWA. Government leg-
      islation for Chinese secret so-
      cieties in the Straits Settlements
      in the late 19th century. AST 10
      (1972) 262-271.

1976 COLLETTA, N. J. Education of
      Chinese workers' children on
      Malaysia's plantation frontier,
      myths and realities, by N. J.
      Colletta and Wong Ah Sung. AS 14
      (1974) 827-844.

1977 COMBER, LEON. Chinese education,
      perennial Malayan problem. AS 1
      (Oct. 1961) 30-35.

1978 EBERHARD, WOLFRAM. Cultural bag-
      gage of Chinese emigrants, stories
      and novels read by Chinese stu-
      dents in Malaya. AS 11 (1971)
      445-462.

1979 FRANKE, WOLFGANG. Some problems
      of Chinese schools and education
      in Southeast Asia, in particular
      Malaysia and Singapore. RSA
      (1968) 115-121.

1980 GOSLING, L. A. P. Migration and
      assimilation of rural Chinese in
      Trengganu. B38 pp. 203-221.

1981 HEIDHUES, MARY F. SOMERS. Peking
      and the overseas Chinese, the
      Malaysian dispute. AS 6 (1966)
      276-287.

1982 JACKSON, JAMES C. Chinese agri-
      cultural pioneering in Singapore
      and Johore, 1800-1917. JMBRAS 38
      pt. 1 (1965) 77-105.

1983 KERSHAW, ROGER. The Chinese in
      Kelantan, west Malaysia, as medi-
      ators of political integration to
      the Kelantan Thais. RSAS 3 pts.
      3-4 (1973) 1-10.

1984 KHOO, S. H. Spatial aspects of
      Foochow settlement in west Malay-
      sia, with special reference to
      Sitiawan, Perak, since 1902, by
      S. H. Khoo, G. Cho and K. E. Chan.
      AST 10 (1972) 77-94.

1985 KUCHLER, JOHANNES. Penang's
      Chinese population, a preliminary
      account of its origin and social
      geographic pattern. AST 3 (1965)
      435-458.

1986 LEE, Y. L. Kukup, a Chinese
      fishing village in south west Ma-
      laya. JTG 16 (1962) 131-148.

1987 NEWELL, WILLIAM H. Chinese place
      names in Province Wellesley. JTG
      19 (1964) 58-61.

1988 PARMER, J. NORMAN. Chinese estate
      workers' strikes in Malaya in
      March 1937. C87 pp. 154-173.

1989 PNG POH SENG. Kuomintang in Ma-
      laya. J45 pp. 214-225.

1990 PNG POH SENG. Kuomintang in Ma-
      laya, 1912-1941. JSAH 2 (Mar.
      1961) 1-41.

1991 POUVATCHY, JOSEPH. Les minorites
      etrangeres in Malaisie. FA
      (1974 pt. 2) 57-70.

Chinese - Malaysia

1992 RABUSHKA, ALVIN. Racial stereo-
      types in Malaya. AS 11 (1971)
      709-716.

1993 SANDHU, KERNIAL SINGH. Chinese
      colonization of Malacca, a study
      in population change 1500-1957
      A.D. JTG 15 (1961) 1-26.

1994 SMITH, T. E. Immigration and
      permanent settlement of Chinese
      and Indians in Malaya, and the
      future growth of the Malay and
      Chinese communities. C87 pp. 174-
      185.

1995 SOH ENG LIM. Tan Cheng Lock, his
      leadership of the Malayan Chinese.
      JSAH 1 (Mar. 1960) 34-61.

1996 TILMAN, ROBERT O. Socialization
      of the Chinese into Malaysian
      politics, some preliminary obser-
      vations. S90.7 pp. 107-120.

1997 WANG GUNGWU. Traditional leader-
      ship in a new nation, the Chinese
      in Malaya and Singapore. A41 pp.
      170-187.

1998 WANG GUNGWU. Traditional leader-
      ship in a new nation, the Chinese
      in Malaya and Singapore. L23 pp.
      208-222.

1999 YEN CHING HWANG. Ch'ing's sale of
      honours and the Chinese leadership
      in Singapore and Malaya, 1877-
      1912. JSAS 1 pt. 2 (1970) 20-32.

CHINESE - MALAYSIA - SABAH

2000 GLICK, HENRY ROBERT. The Chinese
      community in Sabah and the 1963
      election. AS 5 (1965) 144-151.

2001 LEE, EDWIN. Emergence of Towkay
      leaders in party politics in
      Sabah. JSAH 9 (1968) 306-324.

2002 MILNE, R. S. Patrons, clients and
      ethnicity, the case of Sarawak and
      Sabah in Malaysia. AS 13 (1973)
      891-907.

2003 TARLING, NICHOLAS. The entrepot
      at Labuan and the Chinese. S89
      pp. 355-373.

CHINESE - MALAYSIA - SARAWAK

2004 FIDLER, RICHARD C. Population
      diversity in a Sarawak bazaar
      town. SMJ 20 (1972) 195-233.

2005 HIPKINS, JAMES R. History of the
      Chinese in Borneo. SMJ 19 (1971)
      109-153.

2006 LEE, Y. L. Chinese in Sarawak and
      Brunei. SMJ 11 (1964) 516-532.

2007 LO HSIANG LIN. Chinese presiden-
      tial system in Kalimantan. SMJ 9
      (1960) 670-674.

2008 LOCKARD, CRAIG A. Charles Brooke
      and the foundations of the modern
      Chinese community in Sarawak,
      1863-1917. SMJ 19 (1971) 77-108.

2009 LOCKARD, CRAIG A. Leadership and
      power within the Chinese community
      of Sarawak, a historical survey.
      JSAS 2 (1971) 195-217.

2010 MILNE, R. S. Patrons, clients and
      ethnicity, the case of Sarawak and
      Sabah in Malaysia. AS 13 (1973)
      891-907.

2011 TAYLOR, BRIAN. The Chinese re-
      volt. SMJ 17 (1969) 290-293.

2012 VAN DER KROEF, JUSTUS M. Chinese minority aspirations and problems in Sarawak. PA 39 (1966) 64-82.

CHINESE - PHILIPPINES

2013 APPLETON, SHELDON. Overseas Chinese and economic nationalization in the Philippines. JAS 19 (1959-60) 151-161.

2014 ARENSMEYER, ELLIOTT C. Foreign accounts of the Chinese in the Philippines, 18th-19th centuries. PS 18 (1970) 83-102.

2015 BLAKER, JAMES ROLAND. The Chinese newspaper in the Philippines, toward the definition of a tool. AST 3 (1965) 243-261.

2016 CARMEN, ROLANDO V. DEL. The Chinese in the Philippines, integration revisited. AF 6 pt. 2 (1974) 43-53.

2017 CATAPUSAN, BENICIO T. Ethnic and racial distance. PSSHR 30 (1965) 87-108.

2018 FONACIER, THOMAS S. Chinese in the Philippines during the American regime, 1898-1946. S87 pp. 117-134.

2019 FOX, ROBERT B. Archaeological record of Chinese influences in the Philippines. PS 15 (1967) 41-62.

2020 GINSBERG, PHILIP. Chinese in the Philippine revolution. AST 8 (1970) 143-159.

2021 JAZMINES, ALAN. Chinatown impressions. DR 13 (1965) 355-358.

2022 McCARTHY, CHARLES J. Slaughter of Sangleys in 1639. PS 18 (1970) 659-667.

2023 McPHELIN, MICHAEL. Chinese question. PS 9 (1961) 333-338.

2024 REYNOLDS, HARRIET R. Continuity and change as shown by attitudes of two generations of Chinese in the Ilocos provinces, Philippines. SJ 13 (1966) 12-21.

2025 REYNOLDS, HUBERT. Overseas Chinese college students in the Philippines, a case study, abstract. SJ 17 (1970) 345-6.

2026 REYNOLDS, HUBERT. Why Chinese traders approached the Philippines late, and from the south. Z16 pp. 463-479.

2027 TAN, ALLEN L. Inter-ethnic images between Filipinos and Chinese in the Philippines, by Allen L. Tan and Grace E. de Vera. AST 7 (1969) 125-133.

2028 TAN, ALLEN L. Survey of studies on anti-Sinoism in the Philippines. AST 6 (1968) 198-207.

2029 TAN, ANTONIO S. Chinese in the Philippines and the Chinese revolution of 1911. AST 8 (1970) 160-185.

2030 TAN, ANTONIO S. Methods in cross cultural research, the case of Chinese and Filipinos. GEJ 12 (1966) 215-224.

2031 WANG TEH MING. Sino-Filipino historico-cultural relations. PSSHR 29 (1964) 277-471.

2032 WEIGHTMAN, GEORGE H. Anti-Sinicism in the Philippines. AST 5 (1967) 220-231.

2033 WEIGHTMAN, GEORGE H. Philippine-Chinese image of the Filipino. PA 40 (1967) 315-323.

Chinese - Philippines

2034 WICKBERG, EDGAR. Chinese mestizo in Philippine history. JSAH 5 (Mar. 1964) 62-100.

2035 WICKBERG, EDGAR. Early Chinese economic influence in the Philippines, 1850-1898. PA 35 (1962) 275-285.

CHINESE - SINGAPORE

2036 BRADDELL, ROLAND. Lung Ya Men and Tan Ma Hsi. JMBRAS 42 pt. 1 (1969) 10-24.

2037 BUXBAUM, DAVID C. Chinese family law in a common law setting. A note on the institutional environment and the substantive family law of the Chinese in Singapore and Malaysia. C39 pp. 146-177.

2038 CHENG SIOK HWA. Government legislation for Chinese secret societies in the Straits Settlements in the late 19th century. AST 10 (1972) 262-271.

2039 EE, JOYCE. Chinese migration to Singapore, 1896-1941. JSAH 2 (Mar. 1961) 42-62.

2040 FRANKE, WOLFGANG, Some problems of Chinese schools and education in Southeast Asia, in particular Malaysia and Singapore. RSA (1968) 115-121.

2041 FREEDMAN, MAURICE. Chinese family law in Singapore, the rout of custom. A62 pp. 49-72.

2042 FREEDMAN, MAURICE. Chinese kinship and marriage in Singapore. JSAH 3 (Sept. 1962) 65-73.

2043 FREEDMAN, MAURICE. Religion and social realignment among the Chinese in Singapore, by Maurice Freedman and Marjorie Topley. JAS 21 (1961-2) 3-23.

2044 GAMBA, CHARLES. Chinese associations in Singapore. JMBRAS 39 pt. 2 (1966) 123-168.

2045 JACKSON, JAMES C. Chinese agricultural pioneering in Singapore and Johore, 1800-1917. JMBRAS 38 pt. 1 (1965) 77-105.

2046 JACKSON, R. N. Grasping the nettle, first successes in the struggle to govern the Chinese in Malaya. JMBRAS 40 pt. 1 (1967) 130-139.

2047 NG SIEW YOONG. Chinese protectorate in Singapore, 1877-1900. JSAH 2 (Mar. 1961) 89-116.

2048 PANG WING SENG. The double seventh incident, 1937, Singapore Chinese response to the outbreak of the Sino-Japanese war. JSAS 4 (1973) 269-299.

2049 PNG POH SENG. Straits Chinese in Singapore, a case of local identity and socio-cultural accommodation. JSAH 10 (1969) 95-114.

2050 WANG GUNGWU. Traditional leadership in a new nation, the Chinese in Malaya and Singapore. A41 pp. 170-187.

2051 WANG GUNGWU. Traditional leadership in a new nation, the Chinese in Malaya and Singapore. L23 pp. 208-222.

2052 WILLIAMS, LEA E. Chinese leadership in early British Singapore. AST 2 (1964) 170-179.

2053 YEN CHING HWANG. Ch'ing's sale of honours and the Chinese leadership in Singapore and Malaya, 1877-1912. JSAS 1 pt. 2 (1970) 20-32.

2054 YONG CHING FATT. Preliminary
      study of Chinese leadership in
      Singapore, 1900-1941. JSAH 9
      (1968) 258-285.

CHINESE - THAILAND

2055 AYAL, ELIEZIER B. Private enter-
      prise and economic progress in
      Thailand. JAS 26 (1966-7) 5-14.

2056 JIANG, JOSEPH P. L. Chinese in
      Thailand, past and present. JSAH
      7 (Mar. 1966) 39-65.

2057 MOTE, F. W. Rural Haw (Yunnanese
      Chinese) of northern Thailand.
      K86 pp. 487-524.

CHINESE - VIETNAM

2058 BROCHEUX, P. Vietnamiens et mi-
      norites en Cochinchine pendant la
      periode coloniale. MAS 6 (1972)
      443-457.

2059 BUTTINGER, JOSEPH. Ethnic minor-
      ities in the Republic of Vietnam.
      C58 pp. 99-121.

2060 CHAN, HOK LAM. Chinese refugees
      in Annam and Champa at the end of
      the Sung dynasty. JSAH 7 (Sept.
      1966) 1-10.

2061 DE JAEGHER, RAYMOND J. Chinese in
      Vietnam. L52 pp. 107-111.
      Comment: FALL, BERNARD B. Com-
      mentary. L52 pp. 111-117.

2062 MARSOT, ALAIN GERARD. Anti-Manchu
      Chinese revolutionaries and the
      French authorities in Indochina.
      SA 2 (1972) 474-486.

2063 MURAKAMI, HIDEO. Viet Nam and the
      question of Chinese aggression.
      JSAH 7 (Sept. 1966) 11-26.

2064 TSUNG TO WAY. Survey of Chinese
      occupations. L52 pp. 118-125.

CHINESE LANGUAGE

2065 HAUDRICOURT, ANDRE G. Note sur
      les dialectes de la region de
      Moncay. BEF 50 (1960) 161-177.

CHINESE LITERATURE

2066 EBERHARD, WOLFRAM. Cultural bag-
      gage of Chinese emigrants, stories
      and novels read by Chinese stu-
      dents in Malaya. AS 11 (1971)
      445-462.

2067 HO KUANG CHUNG. Chinese litera-
      ture in South-East Asia. S93 pp.
      300-305.

2068 LOMBARD-SALMON, CLAUDINE. Le
      sjair de l'Association Chinoise de
      Batavia, 1905. AR 2 (1971) 55-
      100.

2069 LUCE, G. H. Countries neighbour-
      ing Burma. B92 pp. 239-306.

2070 LUCE, G. H. Fu-kan-tu-lu. B92
      pp. 191-199.

2071 LUCE, G. H. The Tan (A.D. 97-132)
      and the Ngai-lao. B92 pp. 201-
      238.

2072 TJAN TJOE SOM. Chinese historical
      sources and historiography. S61
      pp. 194-205.

2090 VARNEY, PETER D. Some early Iban leaders in the Anglican Church in Sarawak. SMJ 17 (1969) 273-289.

CHRISTIANITY - PHILIPPINES *See also* AGLIPAYAN CHURCH, CATHOLIC CHURCH - PHILIPPINES, IGLESIA NI CRISTO

2091 ALBERTO, TEOPISTO V. Formal signing of the agreement on baptism between the Lutheran Church in the Philippines and the Roman Catholic Church in the Philippines. PS 20 (1972) 147-160.

2092 ANDERSON, GERALD H. Providence and politics behind Protestant missionary beginnings in the Philippines. A58 pp. 279-300.

2093 ARCILLA, JOSE S. Christianization of Davao Oriental, excerpts from Jesuit missionary letters. PS 19 (1971) 639-724.

2094 ARICHEA, DANIEL C. Effective communication of the Christian message in the Philippines. SJ 18 (1971) 298-311.

2095 BOXER, C. R. Three unpublished Jesuit letters on Philippine and Mariana missions, 1681-1689. PS 10 (1962) 434-442.

2096 BULATAO, JAIME. Split-level Christianity. M24 pp. 16-33.

2097 CARROLL, JOHN J. Magic and religion. P47 pp. 40-74.

2098 CUERQUIS, FLORENCIO R. Baptismal rites in Protestant churches in the Philippines. PS 16 (1968) 169-177.

2099 DATO, LUIS G. Life of Christ, a free version of the Bikol passion. DR 11 (1963) 91-125.

2100 DEATS, RICHARD L. Nationalism and the churches in the Philippines. SJ 12 (1965) 152-167.

2101 DEATS, RICHARD L. Statements of other churches on responsible parenthood. G73 pp. 222-231.

2102 DEMETRIO, FRANCISCO R. On Orasyones, or magical power and living Christianity. SJ 19 (1972) 355-363.

2103 ELWOOD, DOUGLAS J. Popular Filipino concepts of Christ, report of an exploratory study. SJ 18 (1971) 154-163.

2104 ELWOOD, DOUGLAS J. Varieties of Christianity in the Philippines. A58 pp. 366-386.

2105 FERNANDEZ, PERFECTO V. Legal status of the churches in the Philippines. DR 8 (1960) 23-120.

2106 FORONDA, MARCELINO. National churches. UN 36 (1963) 357-365.

2107 FOX, ROBERT B. Function of religion in society, the Christian worker and social change. B13 pp. 1-8.

2108 GONZALES, ENRIQUE. Baptismal rites in Filipino Christian churches. PS 16 (1968) 160-168.

2109 GOROSPE, VITALIANO R. **Christian** koinonia and some Philippine cultural influences. PS 18 (1970) 52-82.

2110 GOROSPE, VITALIANO R. Christian renewal of Filipino values. PS 14 (1966) 191-227.

2111 GOWING, PETER G. Christianity in the Philippines, yesterday and today. SJ 12 (1965) 109-151.

Christianity - Philippines

2133 SITOY, T. VALENTINO. Coming of Protestant missions to the Philippines. SJ 14 (1967) 1-26.

2134 SITOY, T. VALENTINO. Search for unity among non-Roman Christians in the Philippines. SJ 12 (1965) 196-210.

2135 YENGOYAN, A. A. Baptism and Bisayanization among the Mandaya of eastern Mindanao, Philippines. AST 4 (1966) 324-327.

CHRISTIANITY - THAILAND

2136 BRADLEY, WILLIAM L. Prince Mongkut and Jesse Caswell. JSS 54 (1966) 29-41.

2137 GIBLIN, R. W. Abbe de Choisy. S44.8 pp. 1-16.

Christianity - Vietnam *See* CATHOLIC CHURCH - VIETNAM

CHRONOLOGY - BURMA

2138 Burmese invasions of Siam, translated from the Hmannan Yazawin Dawgyi. S44.5 pp. 3-83.

2139 HARVEY, G. E. Bayinnaung's living descendant, the Magh Bohmong. JBRS 44 (1961) 35-42.

2140 Intercourse between Burma and Siam as recorded in Hmannan Yazawindawgyi. S44.5 pp. 85-207.

2141 Intercourse between Burma and Siam as recorded in Hmannan Yazawindawgyi. S44.6 pp. 1-183.

2142 TET HTOOT. Nature of the Burmese chronicles. H18 pp. 50-62.

2143 TIN OHN. Modern historical writing in Burmese, 1724-1942, a brief study of the Burmese chronicles of the eighteenth and nineteenth centuries and their influence upon historical writing. H18 pp. 85-93.

CHRONOLOGY - CAMBODIA

2144 OSBORNE, MILTON. Abridged Cambodian chronicle, a Thai version of Cambodian history, by Milton Osborne and David Wyatt. FA 22 (1968) 189-203.

2145 PIAT, MARTINE. Chroniques royales khmer. SEIB 49 (1974) 35-140.

2146 SVAY MUOY. Histoire de Keo Preah Phleung d'apres les annales des rois khmers. SEIB 47 (1972) 375-394.

CHRONOLOGY - LAOS

2147 ARCHAIMBAULT, CHARLES. Annales de l'ancien royaume de Sieng Khwang. BEF 53 (1966) 557-673.

CHRONOLOGY - MALAYSIA

2148 WINSTEDT, RICHARD. Malay chronicles from Sumatra and Malaya. H18 pp. 24-28.

2149 WYATT, DAVID K. Nineteenth century Kelantan, a Thai view. K33 pp. 1-21.

CHRONOLOGY - THAILAND

2150 HA WAT, KHUN LUANG. Statement. S44.6 pp. 185-228.

2168 SCHULZ, LAWRENCE E. Bureaucracy and modernization, the impact of development administration in Indonesia. AF 6 pt. 1 (1974) 19-31.

CIVIL SERVICE - PHILIPPINES

2169 ABUEVA, JOSE VELOSO. Administrative culture and behavior and middle civil servants in the Philippines. D49 pp. 132-186.

2170 ESTRADA, SALVADOR. How the government may improve the civil service. UN 38 (1965) 611-623.

2171 FRANCISCO, GREGORIO A. Career development of Filipino higher civil servants. A28 pp. 390-408.

2172 FRANCISCO, GREGORIO A. 50-50 agreement, by Gregorio A. Francisco and Raul P. de Guzman. G93 pp. 105-135.

2173 JENISTA, FRANK L. Problems of the colonial civil service, an illustration from the career of Manuel L. Quezon. SA 3 (1974) 808-829.

2174 JORGE, LIGAYA. The 1956 general clerical examination announcement. G93 pp. 315-336.

2175 OCAMPO, ROMEO B. Disputed directorship, by Romeo B. Ocampo, Simeon M. Agustin and Elpidio Valencia. G93 pp. 277-314.

2176 PANGILINAN, ROBERTO M. Civil service system. A28 pp. 383-390.

CIVIL SERVICE - SINGAPORE

2177 SEAH CHEE MEOW. Public relations in the Singapore bureaucracy, a neglected aspect in administration. SAJSS 1 pt. 2 (1973) 53-62.

CIVIL SERVICE - THAILAND

2178 EVERS, HANS-DIETER. Formation of a social class structure, urbanization, bureaucratization and social mobility in Thailand. JSAH 7 (Sept. 1966) 100-115.

CIVIL SERVICE - VIETNAM

2179 JOINER, CHARLES A. Organizing bureaucrats, south Vietnam's National Revolutionary Civil Servants League, by Charles A. Joiner and Roy Jumper. AS 3 (1963) 203-215.

CLEMENTI, CECIL

2180 TARLING, NICHOLAS. Sir Cecil Clementi and the Federation of British Borneo. JMBRAS 44 pt. 2 (1971) 1-34.

CLIFFORD, HUGH

2181 ALLEN, J. DE V. Two imperialists, a study of Sir Frank Swettenham and Sir Hugh Clifford. JMBRAS 37 pt. 1 (1964) 41-73.

2182 KHOO KAY KIM. Introduction. JMBRAS 34 pt. 1 (1961) xi-xviii.

CLOTHING AND DRESS - THAILAND

2183 HINTON, E. M. Dress of the Pwo Karen of north Thailand. JSS 62 pt. 1 (1974) 27-34.

Clothing and dress - Thailand

2184 SEIDENFADEN, ERIK. Siam's tribal dresses. S44.2 pp. 84-94.

COCONUTS - INDONESIA

2185 LABYS, WALTER C. A lauric oil exports model based on capital stock supply adjustment. MER 18 pt. 1 (1973) 1-10.

COCONUTS - PHILIPPINES

2186 LABYS, WALTER C. A lauric oil exports model based on capital stock supply adjustment. MER 18 pt. 1 (1973) 1-10.

COCONUTS - VIETNAM

2187 TEULIERES, ROGER. Les plantations de cocotiers au sud-Vietnam. SEIB 39 (1964) 19-50.

COEDES, GEORGE

2188 FILLIOZAT, JEAN. Notice sur la vie et les travaux de M. George Coedes. BEF 57 (1970) 1-24.

2189 OSBORNE, MILTON. Professor George Coedes, 1886-1969, a memoir. JSAS 1 pt. 1 (1970) 1-2.

2190 PIAT, MARTINE. La vie et l'oeuvre de George Coedes, 1886-1969. SEIB 46 (1971) 301-321.

2191 POTT, P. H. In memoriam George Coedes, 10 Augustus 1886-2 Oktober 1969. BIJ 127 (1971) 209-214.

2192 Professor George Coedes, an appreciation. JSS 58 pt. 1 (1970) 170-1.

2193 STERN, PHILIPPE. Dedicace d'un prochain ouvrage. G83 pp. 407-8.

2194 Travaux de M. George Coedes, essai de bibliographie. G83 pp. 155-186.

COEN, JAN PIETERZOON

2195 COOLHAAS, W. PH. Wie was de Schrijver van de Tegenwerpinge tegen Coen's Kolonisatieplannen? BIJ 130 (1974) 297-305.

COFRADIA DE SAN JOSE

2196 LEE, DAVID C. Some reflections about the Cofradia de San Jose as a Philippine religious uprising. AST 9 (1971) 126-143.

2197 SWEET, DAVID. Proto-political peasant movement in the Spanish Philippines, the Cofradia de San Jose and the Tayabas rebellion of 1841. AST 8 (1970) 94-119.

COINS

2198 THORNTON-PETT, PETER. Sarawak Museum numismatic collection. SMJ 12 (1965) 148-160.

COINS - MALAYSIA

2199 SIM EWE EONG. Ringgit. JMBRAS 47 pt. 1 (1974) 58-65.

COINS - THAILAND

2200 BOELES, J. J. Note on the ancient city called Lavapura. JSS 55 (1967) 113-4.

2201 CAMPOS, J. DE. Origin of the tical. S44.2 pp. 95-111.

2202 GUEHLER, ULRICH. Essay on the symbols and marks of old Siamese coins. S44.9 pp. 124-148.

2203 GUEHLER, ULRICH. Further studies of old Thai coins. S44.9 pp. 29-69.

2204 GUEHLER, ULRICH. Notes on old Siamese coins. S44.9 pp. 90-123.

2205 GUEHLER, ULRICH. Some investigations on the evolution of the pre Bangkok coinage. S44.9 pp. 70-89.

2206 KNEEDLER, W. HARDING. Coins of north Siam. S44.9 pp. 3-28.

COLOMBO PLAN

2207 Japan's aid to South and South-East Asia under the Colombo Plan. FA 17 (1960) 1920-1924.

COLORUM UPRISINGS

2208 GUERRERO, MILAGROS C. Colorum uprisings, 1924-1931. AST 5 (1967) 65-78.

COMMERCE *See also* RETAIL TRADE **

2209 ARASARATNAM, S. Some notes on the Dutch in Malacca and the Indo-Malayan trade, 1641-1670. JSAH 10 (1969) 480-490.

2210 Asian highway, from caravan routes to modern roads. FA 17 (1960) 1909-1919.

2211 BARR, ROBERT J. Significance of Asian trade to the United States. C35 pp. 215-225.

2212 BASSETT, D. K. British commercial and strategic interest in the Malay peninsula during the late eighteenth century. B38 pp. 122-140.

2213 BELL, PETER F. Markets, middlemen and technology, agricultural supply response in the dualistic economies of Southeast Asia, by Peter F. Bell and Janet Tai. MER 14 pt. 1 (1969) 29-47.

2214 BRAND, W. Observations on trade, aid and development with special reference to Southeast Asia. D44 pp. 123-136.

2215 BUI QUANG TUNG. Un rescape russe sur le sol vietnamien au XIXe siecle. S93 pp. 295-299.

2216 CHAN CHEUNG. Smuggling trade between China and Southeast Asia during the Ming dynasty. S93 pp. 223-227.

2217 CHOU, K. R. Hong Kong's changing pattern of trade and economic interdependence in Southeast Asia. E36 pp. 155-177.
Comment: LAMPMAN, ROBERT J. Comment. E36 pp. 179-180.
Comment: PAAUW, DOUGLAS S. Comment. E36 pp. 277-282.

2218 COPPOCK, JOSEPH D. Instability of export earnings for Asia and the Far East after World War II. AF 5 pt. 3 (1973) 93-105.

2219 COWAN, C. D. Continuity and change in the international history of maritime South East Asia. JSAH 9 (1968) 1-11.

2220 Export instability in the primary exporting countries. S48 pp. 106-170.

Commerce

2221 GORDON, WILLIAM E. Economic
growth and foreign trade of Asia.
C35 pp. 247-289.

2222 GRIFFING, ROBERT P. Trade porce-
lain and stoneware in Southeast
Asia, a report of a symposium.
AP 5 (1961) 235-6.

2223 HALL, D. G. E. From Mergui to
Singapore, 1686-1819, a neglected
chapter in the naval history of
the Indian Ocean. S44.8 pp. 253-
270.

2224 HARRISSON, TOM. Nanhai trade, Dr.
Wang, Poli, Brunei, West and East.
AP 4 (1960) 56-58.
Comment: WANG GUNGWU. Mr.
Harrisson and the western bias of
the Nanhai trade. AP 4 (1960)
59-61.

2225 HYDE, FRANCIS E. British shipping
companies and East and South-East
Asia, 1860-1939. C87 pp. 27-47.

2226 LAKDAWALA, D. T. Prospects of
India's trade with ECAFE countries
by D. T. Lakdawala and R. H.
Patil. E36 pp. 241-273.
Comment: PAAUW, DOUGLAS S. Com-
ment. E36 pp. 277-282.
Comment: SICAT, GERARDO P. Com-
ment. E36 pp. 275-6.

2227 LAMB, ALASTAIR. Takuapa, the
probable site of a pre-Malaccan
entrepot in the Malay peninsula.
B38 pp. 76-86.

2228 LAMB, ALASTAIR. Visit to Siraf,
an ancient port on the Persian
Gulf. JMBRAS 37 pt. 1 (1964) 1-
19.

2229 LASH, NICHOLAS A. Asian exports,
the evidence reconsidered. AF 6
pt. 2 (1974) 12-27.

2230 LUEY, PAUL. On discrepancies in
trade statistics of trading partners. MER 16 pt. 1 (1971) 13-23.
Comment: Comment. MER 16 pt. 1
(1971) 24-28.
Author's reply: MER 16 pt. 1
(1971) 29-32.
Comment: COLOSI, JOSEPH. Discrepancies in trade statistics, a
comment on Paul Luey's note, by
Joseph Colosi, Seiji Naya, and
Theodore Morgan. MER 17 pt. 1
(1972) 130-1.

2231 MILLS, J. V. Arab and Chinese
navigators in Malaysian waters in
about A.D. 1500. JMBRAS 47 pt. 2
(1974) 1-82.

2232 PEARSON, M. N. Spain and Spanish
trade in Southeast Asia. JAH 2
(1968) 109-129.

2233 SAKAMAKI, SHUNZO. Ryukyu and
Southeast Asia. JAS 23 (1963-4)
383-389.

2234 Les services commerciaux francais
en Asie meriodionale et orientale.
FA 20 (1965) 520-522.

2235 SHERK, DONALD R. New international trade models and their relevance for developing Asia. MER
14 pt. 2 (1969) 1-17.

2236 SICAT, GERARDO P. Intercountry
trade, the effects of bilateral-
ism, development, and regional ad-
vantage. MER 14 pt. 2 (1969) 94-
112.

2237 SUBHAN, MALCOLM. Southeast Asia
at the United Nations conference
on trade and development. D44 pp.
137-150.

2238   Summary and conclusions.   E36 pp. 389-417.

2239   TOUSSAINT, A.   Notes on trade relations between Mauritius (Ile de France) and the Far East, 1773-1810.   PHR 1 pt. 1 (1965) 320-333.

2240   UDOM KERDPIBULE.   The prospects for manufacturing exports of ASEAN countries, an exploratory study.   MER 19 pt. 2 (1974) 21-46.

2241   UKA TJANDRASAMITA.   Sea trade of the Moslems to the eastern countries and the rise of Islam in Indonesia.   S87 pp. 92-97.

2242   Viewpoints from the Bangkok conference.   E36 pp. 375-387.

2243   WEISS, UDO.   China's aid to and trade with the developing countries of the third world.   AQ (1974) 203-213.

2244   WEISS, UDO.   China's aid to and trade with the developing countries of the third world.   AQ (1974) 263-309.

2245   WOLTERS, O. W.   The Po-Ssu pine trees.   SOAS 23 (1960) 323-350.

2246   WU, YUAN-LI.   The Soviet economic offensive in Asia and its effect on United States-Asian trade.   C35 pp. 291-317.

2247   ZABLOCKI, CLEMENT J.   The political climate of America's trade with Asia.   C35 pp. 1-10.

COMMERCE - BRUNEI

2248   HARRISSON, BARBARA.   Classification of archaeological trade ceramics from Kota Batu, Brunei.   BMJ 2 pt. 1 (1970) 114-188.

COMMERCE - BURMA

2249   BLACKMORE, THAUNG.   British quest for China trade by the routes across Burma, 1826-1876.   S93 pp. 180-190.

2250   HALL, D. G. E.   The Daghregister of Batavia and Dutch trade with Burma in the 17th century.   B92 pp. 99-116.

2251   HALL, D. G. E.   Studies in Dutch relations with Arakan.   II. Dutch trade with Arakan in the first half of the 17th century.   B92 pp. 77-88.

COMMERCE - INDONESIA

2252   BASSETT, D. K.   British trade and policy in Indonesia, 1760-1772.   BIJ 120 (1964) 197-223.

2253   BOXER, C. R.   Note on Portuguese reactions to the revival of the Red Sea spice trade and the rise of Atjeh, 1540-1600.   JSAH 10 (1969) 415-428.

2254   CALDWELL, J. A. M.   Indonesian export and production from the decline of the culture system to the first world war.   C87 pp. 72-101.

2255   DREWES, G. W. J.   Atjehse douanetarieven in het begin van de vorige eeuw.   BIJ 119 (1963) 406-411.

2256   HALL, D. G. E.   The Daghregister of Batavia and Dutch trade with Burma in the 17th century.   B92 pp. 99-116.

2257   JACOLIN, HENRY.   Le commerce exterieur indonesien de 1963 a 1969/70.   AR 4 (1972) 179-222.

2277 CHEONG WENG EANG. Changing the rules of the game, the India-Manila trade, 1785-1809. JSAS 1 pt. 2 (1970) 1-19.

2278 CHEONG, WENG EANG. Decline of Manila as the Spanish entrepot in the Far East, 1785-1826, its impact on the pattern of Southeast Asian trade. JSAS 2 (1971) 142-158.

2279 Chinese oil and Philippine sugar. JCA 4 (1974) 562-564.

2280 CUSHNER, NICHOLAS P. Manila-Andalusia trade rivalry in the early Bourbon period. PS 8 (1960) 544-556.

2281 GALVIN, JOHN. Supplies from Manila for the California missions, 1781-1783. PS 12 (1964) 494-510.

2282 GOODMAN, GRANT K. Japan and Philippine beer, the 1930's. JSAS 1 pt. 1 (1970) 54-59.

2283 HEDINGER, H. KING. Toward greater Philippine exports. PS 11 (1963) 151-157.

2284 IRVINE, REED J. American trade with the Philippines. C35 pp. 173-183.

2285 McPHELIN, MICHAEL. Philippines, international trade and problems of modernization. PS 14 (1966) 553-574.

2286 MEDINA, ISAGANI R. American logbooks and journals in Salem, Massachusetts on the Philippines, 1796-1894. AST 11 (1973) 177-198.

2287 QUIASON, SERAFIN D. Early contacts of the English East India Company with Mindanao. PSSHR 26 (1961) 175-186.

2288 QUIASON, SERAFIN D. Early trade of the English East India Company with Manila. PHR 1 pt. 1 (1965) 272-297.

2289 QUIASON, SERAFIN D. English country trade with Manila prior to 1708. AST 1 (1963) 64-83.

2290 QUIASON, SERAFIN D. Synopsis of early English country trade with the Philippines. GEJ 5 (1963) 26-34.

2291 RAMOS, E. M. Foreign trade, the balance of strengths. SJ 13 (1966) 1-11.

2292 REYNOLDS, HUBERT. Why Chinese traders approached the Philippines late, and from the south. Z16 pp. 463-479.

2293 RIVERA, CORNELIO T. Mariveles free trade zone, potential and opportunity. PS 19 (1971) 733-738.

2294 SANIEL, JOSEFA M. Japan and the Philippines, 1868-1898. PSSHR 27 (1962) 1-409.

2295 SARTE, CONCORDIO MA. Smuggling, an offense against justice. UN 36 (1963) 494-555.

2296 ZAVALA, SILVIO. Asia and America. PS 12 (1964) 516-519.

COMMERCE - SINGAPORE

2297 ABRAHAMSSON, B. J. Recent developments in international shipping with reference to Singapore. MER

Commerce – Singapore

14 pt. 2 (1969) 26–39.
Comment: KHOO CHENG LOCK, ERIC. Comment. MER 14 pt. 2 (1969) 40–43.

2298 BLAKE, D. J. Patterns of Singapore's trade, 1961–1966. MER 13 pt. 1 (1968) 39–69.

2299 BOGAARS, GEORGE. Effect of the opening of the Suez Canal on the trade and development of Singapore. JMBRAS 42 pt. 1 (1969) 208–251.

2300 CHIANG HAI DING. Early shipping conference of Singapore, 1897–1911. JSAH 10 (1969) 50–68.

2301 CHIANG HAI DING. Statistics of the Straits Settlements foreign trade, 1870–1915. MER 10 pt. 1 (1965) 73–83.

2302 CHUA, JOON ENG. The accuracy and external consistency of Singapore's trade statistics, by Chua Joon Eng and Theodore Morgan. MER 17 pt. 1 (1972) 8–24.

2303 HOLMES, WARREN J. Oceania's place in United States foreign trade. C35 pp. 11–15.

2304 KING, FRANK H. Progress in Commonwealth East Asia and American trade prospects. C35 pp. 29–48.

2305 KOH FOONG YIN. Business activity index for Singapore, 1960–68, by Koh Foong Yin and G. W. Betz. MER 13 pt. 2 (1968) 64–80.

2306 LEWIS, DIANNE. Growth of the country trade to the Straits of Malacca, 1760–1777. JMBRAS 43 pt. 2 (1970) 114–129.

2307 LOCKWOOD, WILLIAM W. Employment, technology and education in Asia, concluding summary statement, conference on manpower problems in East and Southeast Asia, University of Singapore, May 22–28, 1971. MER 16 pt. 2 (1971) 6–24.

2308 McCLELLAN, JOE. Entrepot trade. Y52 pp. 180–188.

2309 MORGAN, THEODORE. Terms of trade for Singapore's entrepot economy, by Theodore Morgan and Chua Joon Eng. MER 15 pt. 2 (1970) 64–78.

2310 NG HEAN WENG. External trade, trend, composition and direction. Y52 pp. 160–179.

2311 RICHTER, H. V. Indonesia's share in the entrepot trade of the states of Malaya and Singapore prior to confrontation. MER 11 pt. 2 (1966) 28–45.

2312 SHAROM AHMAT. American trade with Singapore, 1819–65. JMBRAS 38 pt. 2 (1965) 241–257.

2313 TARLING, NICHOLAS. Prince of merchants and the lion city. JMBRAS 37 pt. 1 (1964) 20–40.

2314 TREGONNING, K. G. Origin of the Straits Steamship Company in 1890. JMBRAS 38 pt. 2 (1965) 274–289.

2315 TURNBULL, C. M. European mercantile community in Singapore, 1819–1867. JSAH 10 (1969) 12–35.

2316 WONG LIN KEN. Trade of Singapore, 1819–69. JMBRAS 33 pt. 4 (1960) 5–315.

2317 YEUNG, PATRICK. Analysis of the potential gains and contributions of the entrepot trade. MER 13 pt. 1 (1968) 1–10.

COMMERCE - THAILAND

2318 CORDEN, W. M. The exchange rate system and the taxation of trade. S49 pp. 151-169.

2319 CORDEN, W. M. Trade and the balance of payments, by W. M. Corden and H. V. Richter. S49 pp. 128-150.

2320 DHANI NIVAT, PRINCE. Early trade relations between Denmark and Siam, by Prince Dhani Nivat and Erik Seidenfaden. S44.8 pp. 271-288.

2321 An early British merchant in Bangkok. S44.8 pp. 232-251.

2322 HAFNER, JAMES A. Riverine commerce in Thailand, tradition in decline. JSS 62 pt. 2 (1974) 7-24.

2323 INGRAM, JAMES C. Thailand's rice trade and the allocation of resources. C87 pp. 102-126.

2324 MOERMAN, MICHAEL. Chiangkham's trade in the old days. C24 pp. 151-171.

2325 NUNN, W. Some notes upon the development of the commerce of Siam. S44.3 pp. 203-227.

2326 RENAUD, BERTRAND M. The effect of the rice export tax on the domestic rice price level in Thailand. MER 16 pt. 1 (1971) 84-107.

2327 SPINKS, CHARLES NELSON. Siam and the pottery trade of Asia. S44.3 pp. 247-315.

2328 SUPARB YOSSUNDARA. Some salient aspects of Thailand's trade, 1955-64, by Suparb Yossundara and Yune Huntrakoon. E36 pp. 127-150.

2329 THANAT KHOMAN. Trade and investment possibilities in Thailand. C35 pp. 205-214.

2330 USHER, DAN. Thai rice trade. S49 pp. 206-230.

COMMUNICATIONS *See also* NEWSPAPERS, PERIODICALS, RADIO BROADCASTING

2331 SARKAR, CHANCHAL. Communication in Southeast Asia. S32 pp. 47-51.

2332 WITTERMANS, TAMME. Language in its social context, by Tamme and Elizabeth Wittermans. AST 6 (1968) 26-36.

COMMUNICATIONS - BURMA

2333 MAUNG KYI. Process of communication in modernisation of rural society, a survey report on two Burmese villages. MER 18 pt. 1 (1973) 55-73.

COMMUNICATIONS - INDONESIA

2334 ANDERSON, BENEDICT R. O'G. Notes on contemporary Indonesian political communication. IND 16 (1973) 39-80.

2335 BONNEFF, MARCEL. Les bandes dessinees en Indonesie, diffusion et public. AR 4 (1972) 169-178.

COMMUNICATIONS - MALAYSIA

2336 HARRISSON, TOM. Three secret communication systems among Borneo nomads and their dogs. JMBRAS 38 pt. 2 (1965) 67-86.

2337 LANGLEY, G. A. Telecommunications in Malaya. JTG 17 (1963) 79-91.

Communications - Philippines

COMMUNICATIONS - PHILIPPINES

2338 ARNALDO, CARLOS. Electronic information media in the second decade of development. PS 19 (1971) 420-433.

2339 ARNALDO, CARLOS. Mass media, prospects for development. P47 pp. 105-135.

2340 CLAVEL, LEOTHINY S. Agrarian reform communication, concepts and methods. AST 10 (1972) 390-406.

2341 CLAVEL, LEOTHINY S. Folklore and communication. AST 8 (1970) 218-247.

2342 DeYOUNG, JOHN E. Communication channels and functional literacy in the Philippine barrio, by John E. DeYoung and Chester L. Hunt. E78 pp. 251-266.

2343 DeYOUNG, JOHN E. Communication channels and functional literacy in the Philippine barrio, by John E. DeYoung and Chester L. Hunt. JAS 22 (1962-3) 67-77.

2344 EBARLE, SOLOMON L. Effective government publicity and interpretation. SJ 8 (1961) 3-17.

2345 FELICIANO, GLORIA D. Toward an effective medium of communication for the Filipino masses. AST 8 (1970) 196-202.

2346 LENT, JOHN A. Philippine mass communications bibliography. First cumulation of sources on areas of advertising, journalism, newspaper, magazine, public relations, radio, television, movies. SJ 12 (1965) 291-392.

2347 LENT, JOHN A. Philippine provincial press. SJ 16 (1969) 273-290.

2348 McHALE, THOMAS R. The Philippines in transition. JAS 20 (1960-1) 331-341.

2349 MARSELLA, JOY A. Some contributions of the Philippine magazine to the development of Philippine culture. PS 17 (1969) 297-331.

2350 MASLOG, CRISPIN. Images and the mass media. SJ 17 (1970) 47-58.

2351 MASLOG, CRISPIN. Journalism and communications program at Silliman University, an overview. SJ 14 (1967) 395-402.

2352 MASLOG, CRISPIN. Philippine mass media. SJ 19 (1972) 495-523.

2353 MASLOG, CRISPIN. Problems of Filipino communication with Americans. SJ 18 (1971) 321-330.

2354 PASCASIO, EMY M. Communication breakdowns. SJ 18 (1971) 312-320.

2355 PATRON, JOSEFINA S. Mass communications teaching and training in the Philippines. SJ 20 (1973) 49-74.

2356 PATRON, JOSEFINA S. Mass media, Philippine style. SJ 21 (1974) 29-59.

2357 PIA, JUAN. The minister and radio, by Juan Pia and Filomena V. Magdamo. SJ 16 (1969) 149-159.

2358 ROSENBERG, DAVID A. Civil liberties and the mass media under martial law in the Philippines. PA 47 (1974) 472-484.

2359 SANTUICO, NATIVIDAD V. Ang sikolohiya ng komunikasyon. GEJ 25 (1973-4) 149-153.

COMMUNICATIONS - VIETNAM

2360 PHAM THI NGOAN. Introduction au
Nam-Phong, 1917-1934. SEIB 48
(1973) 167-501.

COMMUNISM

2361 BENDA, HARRY J. Reflections on
Asian communism. T45 pp. 259-269.

2362 DOUGHERTY, JOHN M. Communism
seminar in Cebu. PS 8 (1960) 840-
845.

2363 RAY, HEMEN. Communist influence
on the social and political developments in Southeast Asia. D44
pp. 25-47.

2364 SINGHAL, D. P. Nationalism and
communism in Southeast Asia, a
brief survey. JSAH 3 (Mar. 1962)
56-66.

2365 TRAGER, FRANK N. Communist challenge in Southeast Asia. H35 pp.
134-164.

2366 TRAGER, FRANK N. Never negotiate
freedom, the case of Laos and
Vietnam. AS 1 (Jan. 1962) 3-11.

2367 WERTHEIM, W. F. Communist views
of state capitalism, with special
reference to South and Southeast
Asia. N18 pp. 107-123.

COMMUNISM - BURMA

2368 VON DER MEHDEN, FRED. Burma's
religious campaign against communism. PA 33 (1960) 290-299.

COMMUNISM - CAMBODIA

2369 BROWN, DAVID E. Exporting insurgency, the communists in Cambodia.
J28 pp. 125-135.

COMMUNISM - INDONESIA *See also* PARTAI
KOMUNIS INDONESIA

2370 AARSSE, ROBERT. Sneevliet et le
debut du communisme en Indonesie.
FA 24 (1970) 267-282.

2371 HINDLEY, DONALD. Indonesian communists and the CPSU twenty-second
congress. AS 2 (Mar. 1962) 20-27.

2372 MORTIMER, REX. Class, social
cleavage and Indonesian communism.
IND 8 (1969) 1-20.

2373 PAUKER, GUY J. Current communist
tactics in Indonesia. AS 1 (May
1961) 26-35.

2374 SEMAUN. Early account of the independence movement, translated
and commented on by Ruth McVey.
IND 1 (1966) 46-75.

2375 STROMQUIST, SHELTON. Communist
uprisings of 1926-27 in Indonesia,
a re-interpretation. JSAH 8
(1967) 189-200.

2376 VAN DER KROEF, JUSTUS. Dilemmas
of Indonesian communism. PA 35
(1962) 141-159.

2377 VAN DER KROEF, JUSTUS. Indonesian
communism and the changing balance
of power. PA 37 (1964) 357-383.

2378 VAN DER KROEF, JUSTUS. Indonesian
communism since the 1965 coup. PA
43 (1970) 34-60.

2379 VAN DER KROEF, JUSTUS. Indonesian
communism's revolutionary
gymnastics. AS 5 (1965) 217-232.

Communism - Indonesia

2380   VAN DER KROEF, JUSTUS. Peasant
        and land reform in Indonesian com-
        munism. JSAH 4 (Mar. 1963) 30-61.

2381   VAN DER KROEF, JUSTUS. Sarawak-
        Indonesian border insurgency. MAS
        2 (1968) 245-265.

Communism - Laos *See* PATHET LAO

COMMUNISM - MALAYSIA

2382   On the recent surrender of guer-
        rillas in Sarawak. JCA 4 (1974)
        233-235.

2383   SHORT, ANTHONY. Communism, race
        and politics in Malaysia. AS 10
        (1970) 1081-1089.

2384   VAN DER KROEF, JUSTUS. Communism
        in Sarawak today. AS 6 (1966)
        568-579.

2385   VAN DER KROEF, JUSTUS. Communism
        in Singapore and Malaysia. AST 4
        (1966) 549-571.

2386   VAN DER KROEF, JUSTUS. Sarawak-
        Indonesian border insurgency. MAS
        2 (1968) 245-265.

COMMUNISM - PHILIPPINES

2387   CONSTANTINO, JOSEFINA D. Outlaw-
        ing communism. UN 40 (1967) 434-
        447.

2388   SAULO, ALFREDO B. Challenge of
        communism to our Christian socie-
        ty. SJ 16 (1969) 263-272.

2389   SOLIMAN, MARCOS G. Local commun-
        ist movement today. A28 pp. 519-
        524.

2390   VAN DER KROEF, JUSTUS M. Commun-
        ism and reform in the Philippines.
        PA 46 (1973) 29-58.

COMMUNISM - SINGAPORE

2391   VAN DER KROEF, JUSTUS. Communism
        in Singapore and Malaysia. AST 4
        (1966) 549-571.

COMMUNISM - THAILAND

2392   ESPOSITO, BRUCE J. Can a single
        spark ignite a paddyfield, the
        case of Thai insurgency. AST 8
        (1970) 318-325.

2393   MORELL, DAVID. The impermanence
        of society, Marxism, Buddhism and
        the political philosophy of Thai-
        land's Pridi Panomyong, by David
        and Susan Morell. SA 2 (1972)
        396-424.

COMMUNISM - VIETNAM

2394   L'agression communiste au Vietnam.
        FA 20 (1965) 481-496.

2395   CHESNEAUX, JEAN. Les fondements
        historiques du communisme viet-
        namien. C28 pp. 215-237.

2396   CONLEY, MICHAEL CHARLES. Commun-
        ist thought and Viet Cong tactics.
        AS 8 (1968) 206-222.

2397   DUIKER, WILLIAM J. Hanoi scruti-
        nizes the past, the Marxist evalu-
        ation of Phan Boi Chau and Phan
        Chu Trinh. SA 1 (1971) 242-254.

2398   DUIKER, WILLIAM J. Red Soviets of
        Nghe-Tinh, an early communist re-
        bellion in Vietnam. JSAS 4 (1973)
        186-198.

Community development - Philippines

2399 HEYMANN, HANS. Imposing communism on the economy of south Vietnam, a conjectural view. AS 11 (1971) 376-384.

2400 MAU, MICHAEL P. Training of cadres in the Lao Dong Party of north Vietnam, 1960-1967. AS 9 (1969) 281-296.

2401 NGUYEN KHAC VIEN. Confucianisme et Marxisme au Vietnam. C28 pp. 21-57.

2402 NGUYEN VIET KHAI. Who has no family? Who has no fatherland? JCA 2 (1972) 125-127.

2403 ROLPH, HAMMOND. Vietnamese communism and the protracted war. AS 12 (1972) 783-792.

2404 SELDEN, MARK. Revolution and third world development. N15 pp. 214-248.

2405 SMITH, RALPH. Antecedents of the Viet Cong. N18 pp. 1-15.

2406 SOLA POOL, ITHIEL DE. Political alternatives to the Viet Cong. AS 7 (1967) 555-566.

2407 THORNTON, THOMAS PERRY. Foreign relations of the Asian communist satellites. PA 35 (1962) 341-352.

2408 TURLEY, WILLIAM S. Civil-military relations in north Vietnam. AS 9 (1969) 879-899.

2409 TURLEY, WILLIAM S. Women in the communist revolution in Vietnam. AS 12 (1972) 793-805.

COMMUNITY DEVELOPMENT - INDONESIA

2410 HANSEN, GARY. Episodes in rural modernization, problems in the Bimas program. IND 11 (1971) 63-81.

2411 HUIZER, GERRIT. Betting on the weak, from counterpoint towards revolution. B85 pp. 104-129.

COMMUNITY DEVELOPMENT - LAOS

2412 VONGSAVANH BOUTSAVATH. Lao popular Buddhism and community development, by Vongsavanh Boutsavath and Georges Chapelier. JSS 61 pt. 2 (1973) 1-38.

COMMUNITY DEVELOPMENT - PHILIPPINES

2413 ABUEVA, JOSE V. Interrelation between local governments and community developments. E78 pp. 431-438.

2414 ABUEVA, JOSE V. Local government, community development, and political stability. A28 pp. 468-475.

2415 BARNETT, MILTON L. Anthropology, home economics and rural development. GEJ 12 (1966) 150-161.

2416 CARSON, ARTHUR L. Progress and the common people. SJ 21 (1974) 229-236.

2417 Community development program. A28 pp. 465-468.

2418 Community development project. E78 pp. 500-503.

2419 DAVIDSON, CARTER. Self-help: Jimmy Yen's proven aid for developing nations. E78 pp. 440-446.

2420 Development program in action, a progress report on a Philippine case, by Gelia Tagumpay-Castillo, Conrado M. Dimoano, Jesus C.

Community development - Philippines

Calleja, and Shirley F. Parcon. AST 2 (1964) 37-66.

2421 EINSIEDEL, LUZ A. Success and failure in selected community development projects in Batangas. E78 pp. 624-633.

2422 GARCIA, MARIANO J. Philippine community development program. UN 40 (1967) 494-526.

2423 McMILLAN, ROBERT T. Use of surveys in community development. E78 pp. 635-641.

2424 New aspects of the social question, Mater et Magistra. E78 pp. 119-128.

2425 OPPENFELD, HORST VON. Farm development, an approach in rural improvement. E78 pp. 113-118.

2426 OREN, PAUL. Myth of painless metamorphosis, community development. E78 pp. 129-139.
Comment: SMYTHE, LEWIS S. C. Comment. E78 pp. 139-142.

2427 POLSON, ROBERT A. Community development in the Philippines, observations and comments. E78 pp. 86-95.

2428 REYNOLDS, HUBERT. Importance of measuring and comparing development projects in process. SJ 16 (1969) 431-435.

2429 SMYTHE, LEWIS S. C. Eight approaches to rural community development. E78 pp. 100-113.

2430 SYCIP, FELICIDAD C. Factors related to acceptance or rejection of innovations. E78 pp. 593-611.

2431 Three workers. E78 pp. 475-499.

2432 VILLANUEVA, BUENAVENTURA M. Community development program of the Philippine government. E78 pp. 520-534.

2433 ZAMORA, MARIO D. Toward a science of social man, community development and anthropology. GEJ 12 (1966) 172-188.

COMMUNITY DEVELOPMENT - THAILAND

2434 BERTHOLET, C. J. L. Community development in the Land of the Free, an appraisal of the first decade of community development. D44 pp. 173-191.

CONFUCIUS AND CONFUCIANISM - INDONESIA

2435 SURYADINATA, LEO. Confucianism in Indonesia, past and present. SA 3 (1974) 880-903.

CONFUCIUS AND CONFUCIANISM - VIETNAM

2436 NGUYEN KHAC VIEN. Confucianisme et Marxisme au Vietnam. C28 pp. 21-57.

2437 NGUYEN VAN PHONG. La diffusion du Confucianisme au Vietnam. FA 21 (1966) 179-196.

CONGRESSES AND CONVENTIONS *See also* A.E.C.D., AFRO-ASIAN CONFERENCE, BAGUIO RELIGIOUS ACCULTURATION CONFERENCE, BANDUNG CONFERENCE, INTERNATIONAL CONGRESS OF ORIENTALISTS, UNITED NATIONS CONFERENCE ON TRADE AND DEVELOPMENT, WORLD FELLOWSHIP OF BUDDHISTS **

2438 CONSTANTINO, RENATO. New Asia. JCA 2 (1972) 439-442.

2439 HARRISSON, TOM. Primate special symposium no. 2 of the 1966 Pacific Science Congress. AP 10 (1967) 19-21.

2440 KRUPA, VIKTOR. Sektion Australien und Ozeanien auf dem VII Internationalen Kongress der Anthropologischen und Ethnographischen Wissenschaften in Moskau, 3/8-10/8/1964. AAS 2 (1966) 137-139.

2441 Liste des communications presentees ou Congres de Culture Malaise, Puntjak, avril, 1971. AR 1 (1970) 55.

2442 LOCKWOOD, WILLIAM W. Employment, technology and education in Asia, concluding summary statement, Conference on Manpower Problems in East and Southeast Asia, University of Singapore, May 22-28, 1971. MER 16 pt. 2 (1971) 6-24.

2443 Pour une Indochine nouvelle, un discours de S. A. R. Norodom Sihanouk. FA 20 (1965) 97-113.

CONRAD, JOSEPH

2444 ORDONEZ, ELMER A. Early Joseph Conrad, revisions and style. PSSHR 33 (1968) 1-192.

2445 RESINK, G. J. Conrad's hudigs. BIJ 128 (1972) 358-363.

2446 RESINK, G. J. Geur van Makassar. BIJ 128 (1972) 364-5.

2447 RESINK, G. J. Jozef Korzeniowski's voornaamste lectuur betreffende Indonesie. BIJ 117 (1961) 209-237.

COOLIDGE FOUNDATION

2448 Coolidge Foundation. H57 p. 482.

COOPERATIVE SOCIETIES *See also* SOCIETIES

COOPERATIVE SOCIETIES - INDONESIA

2449 BIRKELBACH, AUBREY W. Subak association. IND 16 (1973) 153-169.

2450 DAM, H. TEN. Cooperation and social structure in the village of Chibodas. J32 pp. 345-382.

COOPERATIVE SOCIETIES - LAOS

2451 TABLENTE, NATHANIEL B. Economic and technical feasibility study of cooperatives and credit in Laos. AST 5 (1967) 524-542.

COOPERATIVE SOCIETIES - MALAYSIA

2452 DRAKE, P. J. Financial aspects of the cooperative movement in Malaya. MER 11 pt. 1 (1966) 57-83.

2453 FREDERICKS, L. J. Impact of the cooperative movement in colonial Malaya, 1922-40. JMBRAS 46 pt. 2 (1973) 151-168.

COOPERATIVE SOCIETIES - PHILIPPINES

2454 MATURAN, EULALIO G. Failure of a Philippine barrio credit union. SJ 15 (1968) 228-242.

2455 MATURAN, EULALIO G. Successful experiment in grassroots cooperation. SJ 15 (1968) 501-527.

Cooperative societies - Vietnam

COOPERATIVE SOCIETIES - VIETNAM

2456 KAUFMAN, HOWARD K. Culao, a Vietnamese fishing cooperative and its problems. S58 pp. 235-272.

2457 TRAN NGOC LIEN. Growth of agricultural credit and cooperatives in Vietnam. C58 pp. 177-189.

2458 WOODSIDE, ALEXANDER. Decolonization and agricultural reform in northern Vietnam. AS 10 (1970) 705-723.

CORN - PHILIPPINES

2459 BOKINGO, BENJAMIN. Effect of DDT-Rice bran mixture on corn borer, by Benjamin Bokingo and Ireneo R. Esmera. SJ 7 (1960) 153-162.

2460 VANDERMEER, CANUTE. Corn cultivation on Cebu, an example of an advanced stage of migratory farming. JTG 17 (1963) 172-177.

CORPORATIONS - PHILIPPINES

2461 HOLLNSTEINER, MARY R. Note to management on traditional Filipino values in business enterprises, the Lumber Company as a case study. PS 13 (1965) 350-354.

2462 McPHELIN, MICHAEL. Purchase of Meralco. PS 9 (1961) 525-528.

2463 MILNE, R. S. Role of government corporations in the Philippines. PA 34 (1961) 257-270.

2464 MORANTTE, P. C. PAL story. G93 pp. 151-196.

2465 PAPA, JOSE L. Critique of foreign corporations doing business in the Philippines. UN 36 (1963) 184-227.

2466 SAMONTE, ABELARDO G. Sale of the Maria Cristina Fertilizer Plant, by Abelardo G. Samonte and Ledivina C. Vidallon. G93 pp. 69-104.

2467 SCAFF, ALVIN H. Class stratification in the EDCOR communities. E78 pp. 193-199.

2468 TADENA, ROMUALDO B. Appointing a PTA chairman-general manager. G93 pp. 241-275.

CORREGIDOR

2469 Corregidor. DR 11 (1963) 343-380.

CORRUPTION

2470 SCOTT, JAMES C. Essay on the political functions of corruption. AST 5 (1967) 501-523.

CORRUPTION - INDONESIA

2471 SMITH, THEODORE M. Corruption, tradition and change. IND 11 (1971) 21-40.

CORRUPTION - MALAYSIA

2472 MILNE, R. S. Patrons, clients and ethnicity, the case of Sarawak and Sabah in Malaysia. AS 13 (1973) 891-907.

CORRUPTION - PHILIPPINES

2473 GARCIA, GUMERSINDO. National moral bankruptcy. DR 12 (1964) 253-265.

2474   IGLESIAS, GABRIEL U. Passage of the anti-graft law. G93 pp. 15-68.

2475   KIUNISALA, E. R. Illegal spending and partisanship in elections. A28 pp. 75-79.

2476   PAGUIO, BERNABE B. Vote buying. A28 pp. 80-1.

2477   ROCES, JOAQUIN P. Rule of the underworld. A28 pp. 85-6.

COTABATO PROVINCE

2478   HUNT, CHESTER L. Ethnic stratification and integration in Cotabato. E78 pp. 202-231.

COTTAGE INDUSTRIES

2479   FRYER, DONALD W. Development of cottage and small scale industries in Malaya and in Southeast Asia. JTG 17 (1963) 92-98.

COTTAGE INDUSTRIES - INDONESIA

2480   HAWKINS, EVERETT D. Batik industry, the role of the Javanese entrepreneur. H24 pp. 39-74.

2481   KUNTOWIDJOJO. Economic and religious attitudes of entrepreneurs in a village industry, notes on the community of Batur. IND 12 (1971) 47-55.

2482   LASKER, BRUNO. Small industries in Indonesia. H57 pp. 468-9.

2483   PALMIER, LESLIE H. Batik manufacture in a Chinese community in Java. H24 pp. 75-97.

COUNSELING - PHILIPPINES

2484   McCARTHY, MAUREEN. Provincial receptivity to guidance and counseling. PS 18 (1970) 769-773.

COURTS - BURMA

2485   YI YI. Judicial system of King Mindon. JBRS 45 (1962) 7-27.

COURTS - INDONESIA

2486   LEV, DANIEL S. Judicial unification in post-colonial Indonesia. IND 16 (1973) 1-37.

2487   QUIKO, EDO. Political trial of Raden Subandrio in Indonesia. AF 4 pt. 2 (1972) 49-60.

COURTS - PHILIPPINES

2488   BAUTISTA, FELIX ANGELO. Administration of justice. A28 pp. 353-356.

2489   CARMEN, ROLANDO V. DEL. Constitutionalism and the supreme court in a changing Philippine polity. AS 13 (1973) 1050-1061.

2490   Documents, the academic freedom issue of 1961, or, the ordeal of a man of academe. PSSHR 29 (1964) 151-276.

2491   LIWAG, JUAN R. Critique of the supreme court. A28 pp. 364-370.

2492   RAMA, NAPOLEON G. Supreme court in action. A28 pp. 357-364.

2493   SANCHEZ, CONRADO V. Role of judges. A28 pp. 370-375.

Courts - Philippines

2494   SANTOS, IGNACIO P. Ventaja del castellano en nuestros tribunales. GEJ 6 (1963) 29-32.

2495   TATE, C. NEAL. Political development and the Philippine judiciary. AF 6 pt. 1 (1974) 32-44.

2496   TOLENTINO, ARTURO M. For a strong and independent judiciary. A28 pp. 375-6.

COURTS AND COURTIERS - BRUNEI

2497   BROWN, D. E. Coronation of Sultan Muhammad Jamalul Alam, 1918. BMJ 2 pt. 3 (1971) 74-80.

2498   MOHAMMAD ZAIN BIN HAJI SERUDIN, HAJI. Selayang pandang mengenai adat istiadat Brunei. BMJ 2 pt. 3 (1971) 1-10.

2499   SHARIFFUDDIN, P. M. Batu Tarsilah, the genealogical tablet of the Sultans of Brunei, by P. M. Shariffuddin and Abd. Latif Hj. Ibrahim. JMBRAS 47 pt. 1 (1974) 87-95.
        Comment: SWEENEY, AMIN. Batu Tarsilah, a short comment. JMBRAS 47 pt. 2 (1974) 151-2.

COURTS AND COURTIERS - BURMA

2500   KYAN. Twan: San: Wan Maha Cansu U: Rhwai. JBRS 45 (1962) 29-39.

2501   YI YI. Life at the Burmese court under the Konbaung kings. JBRS 44 (1961) 85-129.

2502   YI YI. Thrones of the Burmese kings. JBRS 43 (Dec. 1960) 97-123.

COURTS AND COURTIERS - CAMBODIA

2503   PRASIDH SILAPABANLENG. Thai music at the court of Cambodia, a personal souvenir of Luang Pradit Phairoh's visit in 1930. JSS 58 pt. 1 (1970) 121-124.

COURTS AND COURTIERS - INDONESIA

2504   ANDERSON, BEN R. O'G. Diachronic fieldnotes on the coronation anniversary at the kraton Surakarta held on December 18, 1963. IND 3 (1967) 63-71.

2505   BONNEFF, MARCEL. Le renouveau d'un rituel royal, les garebeg a Yogyakarta. AR 8 (1974) 119-146.

2506   GRAAF, H. J. DE. Sadjarah Pangiwa lan panengen, de Stamboom ter linker- en ter rechterzijde, 1733-1743. BIJ 126 (1970) 332-337.

2507   LEE KAM HING. Foreigners in the Achehnese court, 1760-1819. JMBRAS 43 pt. 1 (1970) 64-86.

2508   MINATTUR, JOSEPH. Note on temenggong. RSA (1970) 113-115.

2509   NAERSSEN, F. H. VAN. Some aspects of the Hindu-Javanese kraton. JOSA 2 pt. 1 (1963) 14-19.

2510   Note sur le culte rendu a la Roro Kidul par les ramasseurs de nids d'hirondelles. AR 3 (1972) 131-2.

2511   TERWEN-DE LOOS, J. De gouden koets van de sultan. BIJ 123 (1967) 366-372.

COURTS AND COURTIERS - MALAYSIA

2512   ANDAYA, BARBARA WATSON. Installation of the first sultan of

Selangor in 1766. JMBRAS 47 pt. 1
(1974) 41-57.

2513 MINATTUR, JOSEPH. Note on temenggong. RSA (1970) 113-115.

2514 YEO KIM WAH. Selangor succession
dispute, 1933-38. JSAS 2 (1971)
169-184.

COURTS AND COURTIERS - THAILAND

2515 BRADLEY, WILLIAM L. Notes on the
accession of King Mongkut. JSS
57 (1969) 149-162.

2516 BRODBECK, JEAN-CLAUDE. L'intron-
isation du Prince Heritier de
Thailande, 28-12-1972. SEIB 48
(1973) 559-575.

2517 DHANI. Note, protocol of the
royal family. JSS 48 pt. 2
(1960) 91-2.

COURTS AND COURTIERS - VIETNAM

2518 NGUYEN DINH HOA. Vietnamese names
and titles. AC 2 (Apr. 1960) 117-
131.

CRAWFURD, JOHN

2519 HARRISON, B.   English historians
of the Indian archipelago, Crawfurd and St. John. H18 pp. 245-
254.

CRIME AND CRIMINALS

2520 SOLHEIM, WILHELM G. The antiquities problem. AP 16 (1973) 113-
124.

2521 Statement on political prisoners
in South East Asia. JCA 3 (1973)
370-1.

CRIME AND CRIMINALS - BURMA

2522 KYAW YIN. Problem of crime and
the criminal and its solution in
socialist Burma. JBRS 47 (1964)
205-224.

CRIME AND CRIMINALS - INDONESIA

2523 BUDIARDJO, CARMEL. Three years as
a political prisoner in Indonesia.
JCA 3 (1973) 371-374.

2524 Indonesia: the biggest number of
political prisoners in the world.
JCA 2 (1972) 112-120.

CRIME AND CRIMINALS - MALAYSIA

2525 Law of preventive detention in
Malaya. JCA 4 (1974) 375-381.

2526 TURNBULL, C. M. Internal security
in the Straits Settlements, 1826-
1867. JSAS 1 pt. 1 (1970) 37-53.

CRIME AND CRIMINALS - PHILIPPINES

2527 ASHBURN, FRANKLIN G. Some recent
inquiries into the structure-
function of conflict gangs in the
Manila city jail. AST 3 (1965)
126-144.

2528 CARROLL, JOHN J. Sociological aspects of crime control. PS 17
(1969) 799-805.

2529 Philippines, humane martial law,
the first twenty four hours in an
ISAFP safehouse. JCA 4 (1974)
259-261.

Crime and criminals - Philippines

2530 Political repression in the Philippines. JCA 1 pt. 4 (1970) 86-88.

2531 RICE, DELBERT. Punishment for crime, influence on personality. SJ 17 (1970) 170-194.

2532 VIBAR, ELISEO A. Understanding the Filipino character and the prevention of crimes. UN 38 (1965) 559-569.

2533 VILLEGAS, ANTONIO J. Criminality, government and the citizenry. A28 pp. 87-90.

CRIME AND CRIMINALS - SINGAPORE

2534 Appeal from Singapore. JCA 3 (1973) 237-239.

2535 Ill treatment of political prisoners by the PAP regime. JCA 4 (1974) 564-566.

2536 Joint press statement of Singapore Polytechnic Student's Union and University of Singapore Student's Union. JCA 4 (1974) 370-372.

2537 Letter to Waldheim on the situation in Singapore. JCA 3 (1973) 377-379.

2538 LIM HOCK SIEW. From Singapore prison. JCA 2 (1972) 330-334.

2539 Political detainees in Singapore. JCA 1 pt. 3 (1971) 117-8.

2540 Resolutely uphold the correct stand, forever be loyal and never yield. JCA 3 (1973) 374-376.

2541 TURNBULL, C. M. Convicts in the Straits Settlements. JMBRAS 43 pt. 1 (1970) 87-103.

2542 TURNBULL, C. M. Internal security in the Straits Settlements, 1826-1867. JSAS 1 pt. 1 (1970) 37-53.

CRIME AND CRIMINALS - VIETNAM

2543 NGUYEN KHAC VIEN. With the survivors of the prisons of Saigon. JCA 4 (1974) 77-82.

CRISOLOGO, MENA PECSON

2544 HUFANA, ALEJANDRINO G. Mena Pecson Crisologo and Iloko drama. DR 10 (1962) 1-204.

CRUZ, ANDRES CRISTOBAL

2545 GARCIA, LUISA E. Thought and technique in *White wall, selected Tondo stories*. SLURJ 1 (1970) 329-402.

CUA LANGUAGE

2546 BURTON, EVA. Brief sketch of Cua clause structure. M59 pp. 5-8.

2547 MAIER, JACQUELINE G. Cua phonemes. M59 pp. 9-19.

CUARTERON, CARLOS

2548 ANTONISSEN, A. Carlos Cuarteron. JMBRAS 39 pt. 1 (1966) 168-171.

CUISINIER, JEANNE

2549 BERTHE, LOUIS. Bibliographie. BEF 53 (1966) 5-6.

2549a FILLIOZAT, JEAN. Jeanne Cuisinier, 1890-1964. BEF 53 (1966) 1-3.

2550 VREEDE-DE STUERS, CORA. In memoriam, Jeanne Cuisinier. BIJ 120 (1964) 389-392.

CULTURE

2551 ABDUL RASHID IBRAHIM. Cultural background of the ECAFE region and the challenge of economic development. JSS 50 pt. 1 (1962) 35-49.

2552 ALISJAHBANA, S. TAKDIR. Confluence and conflict of culture in Malaysia in world perspective. A41 pp. 20-39.

2553 BAPAT, P. V. Cultural migration from India to countries in South-East Asia. S87 pp. 177-185.

2554 CHOU, K. R. Some elementary ideas on the strengthening of cultural links between India and Southeast Asia. S32 pp. 83-85.

2555 COREMANS, PAUL. La degradation du patrimoine culturel dans le sud-est asiatique. RSA (1963) 215-228.

2556 DESAI, SANTOSH N. Ramayana, an instrument of historical contact and cultural transmission between India and Asia. JAS 30 (1970-1) 5-20.

2557 FURNIVALL, J. S. Inaugural address. JBRS 43 (June 1960) 41-50.

2558 HARRISSON, TOM. Changing contexts of South East Asia, 21,950 B.C. to 1950 A.D., some patterns in human change. SMJ 11 (1962) 453-467.

2559 NAYAGAM, XAVIER S. THANI. Ideals and values common to South and Southeast Asian cultures. A41 pp. 80-89.

2560 RAY, NIHARRANJAN. Nature and character of cultural development in India and Southeast Asia. S32 pp. 102-108.

2561 SHARP, LAURISTON. Cultural continuities and discontinuities in Southeast Asia. JAS 22 (1962-3) 3-11.

2562 SHARP, LAURISTON. Cultural continuities and discontinuities in Southeast Asia. T45 pp. 45-54.

2563 SINGARAVELU, S. Comparative study of the Sanskrit, Tamil, Thai and Malay versions of the story of Rama with special reference to the process of acculturation in the Southeast Asian versions. JSS 56 (1968) 137-185.

2564 SIRCAR, D. C. Karnata contribution to the spread of Indianism in South-East Asia. S87 pp. 286-288.

2565 TAIB OSMAN, MOHD. The aims, approaches and problems in the study of folk literature or oral tradition, with particular reference to Malay culture. BMJ 2 pt. 4 (1972) 159-164.

2566 THAM SEONG CHEE. Cultural diversity and national identity. RSAS 1 pt. 3 (1971) 3-19.

2567 THAM SEONG CHEE. The culture process in Southeast Asia. RSAS 4 pts. 1-2 (1974) 11-22.

2568 YABES, LEOPOLDO Y. Mutual appreciation of eastern and western cultural values. DR 8 (1960) 567-585.

CULTURE - BURMA

2569 BA HAN. Aspects of Burmese rural life of old. JBRS 51 (1968) 9-16.

2570 BA HAN. Burmese complex, its roots. JBRS 46 (June 1963) 1-10.

2571 CADY, JOHN F. Modernization versus traditionalism in Burma. B91 pp. 17-25.

2572 MYA MAUNG. Cultural value and economic change in Burma. AS 4 (1964) 757-764.

2573 SEIN TU. Psychodynamics of Burmese personality. JBRS 47 (1964) 263-285.

2574 SIDHU, JAGJIT SINGH. Historical background to Burma's acceptance of western culture. EACS 6 (1967) 41-54.

CULTURE - CAMBODIA

2575 GROSLIER, BERNARD PHILIPPE. Our knowledge of Khmer civilization, a re-appraisal. JSS 48 pt. 1 (1960) 1-28.

2576 LUCE, GORDON H. Rice and religion, a study of old Mon-Khmer evolution and culture. JSS 53 (1965) 139-152.

CULTURE - INDONESIA

2577 ANDERSON, BENEDICT R. O'G. The idea of power in Javanese culture. H52 pp. 1-69.

2578 CUISINIER, JEANNE. Indonesians and nature. FA 18 (1962) 219-223.

2579 DOUGLAS, STEPHEN A. Science and technology and the political culture. J37 pp. 238-258.

2580 GEERTZ, CLIFFORD. Afterword, the politics of meaning. H52 pp. 319-335.

2581 JOHNS, ANTHONY H. Role of structural organisation and myth in Javanese historiography. JAS 24 (1964-5) 91-99.
Comment: BERG, C. C. Commentary. JAS 24 (1964-5) 100-103.

2582 LIEBERMAN, FREDRIC. Relationships of musical and cultural contrasts in Java and Bali. AST 5 (1967) 274-281.

2583 LOCHER, G. W. Cultuurgeschiedenis, planning en voorspelbaarheid. BIJ 127 (1971) 146-164.

2584 LOCHER, G. W. Nieuwe perspectieven in de Studie van de acculturatie. BIJ 119 (1963) 122-139.

2585 MILCENT, BENEDICTE. Ki Hadjar Dewantara et l'Association des Civilisations. AR 1 (1970) 67-87.

2586 MINATTUR, JOSEPH. South Indian culture contacts in Nusantara. RSA (1969) 105-114.

2587 MULDER, J. A. NIELS. Aliran Kebatinan as an expression of the Javanese worldview. JSAS 1 pt. 2 (1970) 105-114.

2588 NGHIEM-THAM. Persistance culturelle du substrat indonesien chez les vietnamiens actuels. S93 pp. 23-25.

2589 NUSJIRWAN TIRTAAMIDJAJA. A Bedaja ketawang dance performance at the court of Surakarta. IND 3 (1967) 31-61.

2590 ROBSON, S. O. The wajang and the study of Javanese cultural history. JOSA 3 pt. 2 (1965) 16-26.

2591 SUTJIPTO WIRJOSUPARTO. Historical aspects of Indonesia's acceptance of western culture. EACS 6 (1967) 82-109.

2592 ZOETMULDER, P. J. Significance of the study of culture and religion for Indonesian historiography. S61 pp. 326-343.

CULTURE - INDONESIA - BALI

2593 BATESON, GREGORY. Bali, the value system of a steady state. B43 pp. 384-401.

2594 CUISINIER, JEANNE. Le ritual familial a Bali. BEF 52 (1964) 415-428.

2595 LIEBERMAN, FREDRIC. Relationships of musical and cultural contrasts in Java and Bali. AST 5 (1967) 274-281.

2596 LIM, K. W. Bosch and Balinese culture. H39 pp. 80-87.

2597 SWELLENGREBEL, J. L. Balinese history and the elements of Balinese culture. B18 pp. 16-35.

2598 SWELLENGREBEL, J. L. Patterns of the cosmic order. B18 pp. 36-53.

CULTURE - LAOS

2599 MORECHAND, GUY. The many languages and cultures of Laos. L18 pp. 28-34.

CULTURE - MALAYSIA

2600 ALISJAHBANA, S. TAKDIR. Acculturation and modernization in Malaysia and the arising world culture. A41 pp. 235-252.

2601 ARASARATNAM, S. Aspects of society and cultural life of Indians in Malaysia. A41 pp. 101-107.

2602 al-ATTAS, SYED MUHAMMAD NAGUIB. L'Islam et la culture malaise. AR 4 (1972) 132-150.

2603 HAILE, N. S. Myths of the town dweller. SMJ 9 (1960) 675-678.

2604 McGEE, T. G. Cultural role of cities, a case study of Kuala Lumpur. JTG 17 (1963) 178-196.

2605 MINATTUR, JOSEPH. Dravidian elements in Malay culture. RSA (1968) 99-105.

2606 MINATTUR, JOSEPH. Some characteristics of Indian culture in Malaysia. A41 pp. 90-100.

2607 PLUVIER, JAN M. Cultural aspects of the colonial period of Malayan history. A41 pp. 220-234.

2608 La premier conference UNESCO sur la "culture malaise," Kuala Lumpur, janvier 1972. AR 4 (1972) 27-30.

2609 Ruthless suppression of culture and art by the Malaysian government. JCA 4 (1974) 255-258.

2610 SANDHU, KERNIAL SINGH. Communalism, the primary threat to Malayan unity. AS 2 (Aug. 1962) 32-37.

2611 SANDIN, BENEDICT. Punan La'ong, two notes. SMJ 12 (1965) 185-187.

2612 TAIB BIN OSMAN, MOHD. Patterns of supernatural premises underlying the institution of the bomoh in Malay culture. BIJ 128 (1972) 219-234.

2613 TREGONNING, K. G. Historical aspects of Malaysia's acceptance of

Culture - Malaysia

western culture. EACS 6 (1967) 164-175.

2614 WOLFF, ROBERT J. Modern medicine and traditional culture, confrontation on the Malay peninsula. T45 pp. 132-144.

CULTURE - PHILIPPINES

2615 ALZONA, ENCARNACION. Cultural nationalism in the Philippines. DR 9 (1961) 433-448.

2616 ARANETA, FRANCISCO. Problem of cultural diversity. PS 12 (1964) 232-243.

2617 ARJONA, ADORACION. Ningas Kugon and Manana habit. UN 38 (1965) 546-551.

2618 BATESON, MARY CATHERINE. Insight in a bicultural context. PS 16 (1968) 605-621.

2619 BERNAD, MIGUEL A. Philippine culture and social values. PS 22 (1974) 363-373.

2620 BERNAD, MIGUEL A. Philippine culture and the Filipino identity. PS 19 (1971) 573-592.

2621 BULATAO, JAIME C. Hiya. PS 12 (1964) 424-438.

2622 BULATAO, JAIME C. Philippine values, the Manileno's mainsprings. PS 10 (1962) 45-81.

2623 BULATAO, JAIME C. Split-level Christianity. M24 pp. 16-33.

2624 CARROLL, JOHN J. Filipino heritage. P47 pp. 1-9.

2625 CESPEDES, CAROL H. The new middle class in the Philippines, a case

study in cultural change, by Carol H. Cespedes and Eugene Gibbs. AS 12 (1972) 879-886.

2626 CLAVEL, LEOTHINY S. Folklore and communication. AST 8 (1970) 218-247.

2627 CORPUZ, O. D. Cultural foundations. A28 pp. 6-18.

2628 CORPUZ, O. D. Cultural foundations of Philippine politics. E78 pp. 407-425.

2629 COSTA, HORACIO DE LA. History and Philippine culture. PS 9 (1961) 346-354.

2630 ESTRADA, JOSEFA. Hospitality and loyalty of the Filipinos. UN 38 (1965) 552-558.

2631 FURER-HAIMENDORF, CHRISTOPH VON. Culture change and the conduct of conflicts among Filipino tribesmen. MAS 4 (1970) 193-209.

2632 GOROSPE, VITALIANO R. Christian renewal of Filipino values. PS 14 (1966) 191-227.

2633 GUTHRIE, GEORGE M. Philippine temperament. G53 pp. 49-83.

2634 JOCANO, F. LANDA. Beyer's theory on Filipino prehistory and culture, an alternative approach to the problem. Z16 pp. 128-150.

2635 JOCANO, F. LANDA. Child training and adult behavior, a case study in Filipino socialization. GEJ 14 (1967) 34-47.

2636 JOCANO, F. LANDA. Cultural idiom and the problem of planned change, a case study from a Philippine municipality. AST 10 (1972) 157-178.

2637 JOCANO, F. LANDA. Philippines at Spanish contact, an essay in ethnohistory. M24 pp. 49-89.

2638 LAWLESS, ROBERT. Foundation for culture-and-personality research in the Philippines. AST 5 (1967) 101-136.

2639 LYNCH, FRANK. Philippine values, social acceptance. PS 10 (1962) 82-99.

2640 McCARRON, JOHN. Some notes on language in culture. M24 pp. 207-224.

2641 MANGLAPUS, RAUL S. Philippine culture and modernization. B42 pp. 30-42.

2642 MANIS, JEROME G. Philippine culture in transition. E78 pp. 2-25.

2643 MARSELLA, JOY A. Some contributions of the Philippine magazine to the development of Philippine culture. PS 17 (1969) 297-331.

2644 MERCADO, LEONARDO N. Notes on the Filipino philosophy of work and leisure. PS 22 (1974) 71-80.

2645 MOLINA, ANTONIO M. Filipino culture. UN 36 (1963) 346-351.

2646 MORALES, ALFREDO T. Anthropology and education change in the Philippines. GEJ 12 (1966) 268-295.

2647 ORACION, TIMOTEO S. Notes on the culture of Negritos on Negros Island. SJ 7 (1960) 201-218.

2648 PAL, AGATON PALEN. Philippine barrio, a study of social organization in relation to planned cultural change. E78 pp. 62-73.

2649 REYES, RAMON C. Secularization and religious acculturation. PS 20 (1972) 40-48.

2650 REYES, RAMON C. Secularization and religious acculturation. SJ 19 (1972) 162-169.

2651 REYES, RAMON C. Sources of Filipino thought. PS 21 (1973) 429-437.

2652 REYNOLDS, HUBERT. Concepts of acculturation. B13 pp. 21-32.

2653 SAMSON, JOSE A. Peculiar patterns of behavior in Filipino setting. UN 38 (1965) 524-536.

2654 SAN JUAN, E. Reactionary ideology in Philippine culture. JCA 3 (1973) 414-426.

2655 SANTOS, R. JOEL DE LOS. How Christian-Muslim relations affect acculturation and development. SJ 20 (1973) 252-257.

2656 SISON, MITOS. Geography and its influence on culture. M24 pp. 838-843.

2657 STAPLETON, ARCHIE C. Modern educational concepts and traditional Philippine culture. SLQ 5 (1967) 141-152.

2658 TAN, ANTONIO L. Methods in cross cultural research, the case of Chinese and Filipinos. GEJ 12 (1966) 215-224.

2659 VAN DER KROEF, JUSTUS. Patterns of cultural conflict in Philippine life. PA 39 (1966) 326-338.

2660 ZAMORA, MARIO D. Introduction to anthropology, by Mario D. Zamora and Robert Lawless. GEJ 12 (1966) 1-16.

CULTURE - PHILIPPINES - FOREIGN INFLU-
  ENCES

2661 ABELLA, DOMINGO. Brief introduction to the study of western cultural penetration in the Philippines. EACS 6 (1967) 176-189.

2662 AGONCILLO, TEODORO A. Cultural
aspect of the Japanese occupation.
PSSHR 28 (1963) 351-394.

2663 AGONCILLO, TEODORO A. Oriental
heritage of the Philippines. S87
pp. 191-200.

2664 BULATAO, JAIME. Changing social
values. PS 10 (1962) 206-214.

2665 FRANCISCO, JUAN R. On the date of
the coming of Indian influence in
the Philippines. PHR 1 pt. 1
(1965) 136-152.

2666 MACEDA, JOSE. Latin qualities in
Brazil and the Philippines. AST
2 (1964) 223-230.

2667 MAJUL, CESAR ADIB. Islamic and
Arab cultural influences in the
south of the Philippines. JSAH
7 (Sept. 1966) 61-73.

2668 MANIS, JEROME G. Philippine culture in transition. SJ 7 (1960)
105-133.

2669 MERINO, JESUS. Eastern culture in
the Philippines. UN 36 (1963)
329-336.

2670 QUIRINO, CARLOS. Cultural relations between India and the Philippines. S32 pp. 96-98.

2671 ROSALES, VICENTE. Influence of
Spanish culture on the psychology
of the Filipino. UN 38 (1965)
498-504.

2672 SAN JUAN, E. Radicalism in contemporary Philippine culture. DR
17 (1969) 324-342.

2673 TEJON, GUILLERMO. Western culture
in the Philippines. UN 36 (1963)
337-345.

2674 WANG TEH MING. Sino-Filipino
historico cultural relations.
PSSHR 29 (1964) 277-471.

CULTURE - THAILAND

2675 ANUMAN RAJADHON. Khwan and its
ceremonies. JSS 50 pt. 2 (1962)
119-164.

2676 ANUMAN RAJADHON. Luck measurement
in Thailand. E92 pp. 1-4.

2677 ANUMAN RAJADHON. Notes on the
thread-square in Thailand. JSS 55
(1967) 161-182.

2678 ANUMAN RAJADHON. Thai traditional
salutation. JSS 49 pt. 2 (1961)
159-169.

2679 AYAL, ELIEZER B. Value systems
and economic development in Japan
and Thailand. T45 pp. 535-549.

2680 BRADLEY, WILLIAM L. What a Christian has learned from the Buddhists. T33 pp. 359-369.

2681 DAMRONG RAJANUBHAB. Introduction
of western culture in Siam. S44.7
pp. 1-12.

2682 DHANI NIVAT, PRINCE. Reconstruction of Rama I of the Chakri dynasty. S44.4 pp. 238-265.

2683 MOERMAN, MICHAEL. Western culture
and the Thai way of life. T45 pp.
145-161.

2684 PHILLIPS, HERBERT P. Culture of Siamese intellectuals. C24 pp. 324-357.

2685 TITIMA PHITAKSPRAIWAN. Acceptance of western culture in Thailand. EACS 6 (1967) 190-200.

2686 VIET HUNG. How the Thais celebrate their lunar new year. AC 3 (Jan. 1961) 109-120.

CULTURE - VIETNAM

2687 Bibliography on the acceptance of western cultures in Vietnam from the XVIth century to the XXth century. EACS 6 (1967) 228-249.

2688 CHRISTIE, A. H. Ancient cultures of Indo-China. AC 2 (Apr. 1960) 51-69.

2689 DANG THAI MAI. Place of Vietnamese language in the building of a new culture of the Vietnamese people. JBRS 43 (1960) 33-36.

2690 FAIRBANKS, HENRY GEORGE. Integrate or perish. AC 2 (Jan. 1960) 49-57.

2691 GRISON, PIERRE. Approches de l'ame vietnamienne. FA 17 (1960) 2367-2373.

2692 JANSE, O. Viet-Nam carrefour de peuples et de civilisations. FA 17 (1960) 1645-1670.

2693 NGHIEM-THAM. Persistance culturelle du substrat indonesien chez les vietnamiens actuels. S93 pp. 23-25.

2694 NGUYEN DANG THUC. Vietnamese synthesis in culture. B91 pp. 419-425.

2695 NGUYEN KHAC KHAM. Acceptance of western cultures in Vietnam from the XVIth century to the XXth century. EACS 6 (1967) 201-227.

2696 NGUYEN KHAC VIEN. Culture and revolution in Vietnam, by Nguyen Khac Vien and Ly Van Sau. JCA 3 (1973) 473-482.

2697 NGUYEN VAN PHONG. La diffusion du Confucianisme au Vietnam. FA 21 (1966) 179-196.

2698 THAI VAN KIEM. Meanings and old customs of the Tet, a Vietnamese new year festival. AC 3 (Jan. 1961) 49-54.

2699 TRAN QUANG THUAN. Some aspects of the Vietnamese society. AC 2 (July 1960) 47-67.

CURSILLO DE CRISTIANIDAD

2700 BAUTISTA, PURIFICACION G. Cursillo movement, its impact on Philippine society. AST 10 (1972) 232-244.

DAENDELS, HERMAN WILLEM

2701 EYMERET, JOEL. Les archives francaises au service des etudes indonesiennes, Java sous Daendels, 1808-1811. AR 4 (1972) 151-168.

DALRYMPLE, ALEXANDER

2702 HALL, D. G. E. British writers of Burmese history from Dalrymple to Bayfield. H18 pp. 255-266.

Damais, Louis Charles

2722 HOLT, CLAIRE. Form and function
of the dance in Bali, by Claire
Holt and Gregory Bateson. B43 pp.
322-330.

2723 HUDSON, JUDITH M. Some observations on dance in Kalimantan. IND
12 (1971) 132-150.

2724 McPHEE, COLIN. Dance in Bali.
B43 pp. 290-321.

2725 NUSJIRWAN TIRTAAMIDJAJA. A Bedaja
ketawang dance performance at the
court of Surakarta. IND 3 (1967)
31-61.

2726 ZOETE, BERYL DE. Dance and drama
in Bali, by Beryl de Zoete and
Walter Spies. B43 pp. 260-289.

DANCE - MALAYSIA

2727 GALVIN, A. D. Dressing up for the
dance, by A. D. Galvin and F.
Baartmans. SMJ 12 (1965) 171-2.

2728 HARRISSON, TOM. Dancing out the
journey of the dead. SMJ 20
(1972) 173-178.

2729 SEELER, JOAN. Some notes on traditional dances of Sarawak. SMJ
17 (1969) 163-201.

2730 SHEPPARD, MUBIN. Joget gamalan
Trengganu. JMBRAS 40 pt. 1 (1967)
149-152.

2731 SHEPPARD, MUBIN. Manora in Kelantan. JMBRAS 46 pt. 1 (1973) 160-
170.

DANCE - PHILIPPINES

2732 CASINO, ERIC. Lunsay, song dance
of the Jama Mapun of Sulu. AST 4
(1966) 316-323.

2733 MacTAVISH, SHONA. Tribal dance in
Mindanao. SJ 20 (1973) 217-225.

2734 MANUUD, ANTONIO G. The arts,
January to June. PS 9 (1961) 505-
519.

2735 MANUUD, ANTONIO G. Arts, 1960.
PS 8 (1960) 814-822.

DANI

2736 PLOEG, A. Some comparative re-
marks about the Dani of the Baliem
Valley and the Dani at Bokondini.
BIJ 122 (1966) 255-273.

DANTE ALIGHIERI

2737 SANTILLAN-CASTRENCE, PURA. Dante
and the Filipino. DR 13 (1965)
268-282.

DAUDIN, PIERRE

2738 LANGLET, PHILIPPE. Hommage a
Pierre Daudin, 1900-1973. SEIB 49
(1974) 175-183.

Dayaks *See* DYAK

DEATH CUSTOMS AND RITES *See also*
  MEGALITHIC MONUMENTS

2739 MALLERET, LOUIS. Notes archeologiques. BEF 51 (1963) 99-124.

DEATH CUSTOMS AND RITES - BRUNEI

2740 GALVIN, A. D. A Sebob dirge, sung
on the occasion of the death of
Tama Jangan Jau by Belawing Lupa.
BMJ 2 pt. 4 (1972) 1-158.

2761 SATHER, CLIFFORD. Note on Bajau
gravemarkers from the Semporna
District of Sabah. SMJ 16 (1968)
103-110.

DEATH CUSTOMS AND RITES – MALAYSIA –
SARAWAK

2762 BROOKS, SHEILAGH T. Arm position
as correlated with sex determination in the Niah cave extended
burial series, Sarawak, Malaysia,
by Sheilagh T. and Richard H.
Brooks. SMJ 16 (1968) 67-74.

2763 BROOKS, SHEILAGH T. Preliminary
report on the palaeoserology of
the Niah cave burials, by Sheilagh
T. Brooks and Rodger Heglar. AP
15 (1972) 87-8.

2764 GALVIN, A. D. Headhunting, fact
or fiction. BMJ 3 pt. 2 (1974)
16-104.

2765 GALVIN, A. D. Mamat ceremonies,
Long Moh, Upper Baram, Sarawak,
commemorative ceremony for the
dead. BMJ 2 pt. 1 (1970) 17-29.

2766 HADDON, A. C. Some Baram (Sarawak) coffin burials before 1900.
SMJ 11 (1964) 553-555.

2767 HARRISSON, BARBARA. Classification of stone age burials from
Niah Great Cave, Sarawak. SMJ 15
(1967) 126-200.

2768 HARRISSON, TOM. After life for
Kayan infants in Kalimantan. SMJ
10 (1961) 214-5.

2769 HARRISSON, TOM. Borneo death.
BIJ 118 (1962) 1-41.

2770 HARRISSON, TOM. Borneo writing.
BIJ 121 (1965) 1-57.

Death customs and rites – Malaysia –
Sarawak

2771 HARRISSON, TOM. Dancing out the
journey of the dead. SMJ 20
(1972) 173-178.

2772 HARRISSON, TOM. Early jar burials
in Borneo and elsewhere. AP 17
(1974) 141-144.

2773 HARRISSON, TOM. Magala, a series
of neolithic and metal age burial
grottos at Sekaloh, Niah, Sarawak,
by Tom and Barbara Harrisson.
JMBRAS 41 pt. 2 (1968) 148-175.

2774 HARRISSON, TOM. Maloh coffin designs. SMJ 14 (1966) 146-150.

2775 HARRISSON, TOM. Miniature burial
pot from Niah Great Cave. SMJ 15
(1967) 91-2.

2776 HARRISSON, TOM. Sarawak Kenyah
journey through death. SMJ 10
(1961) 191-213.

2777 HARRISSON, TOM. Sarawak Museum's
Punan salong and Puso's jar. SMJ
11 (1963) 327-339.

2778 HARRISSON, TOM. Translucent glass
rings from Borneo. AP 6 (1962)
236-238.

2779 MORGAN, STEPHANIE. An Iban funeral near Saratok, 1969, by Stephanie Morgan and Paul Beavitt. SMJ
19 (1971) 277-311.

2780 NEEDHAM, RODNEY. Death names and
solidarity in Penan society. BIJ
121 (1965) 58-76.

2781 O'CONNOR, STANLEY J. Gold foil
burial amulets in Bali, Philippines and Borneo, by Stanley J.
O'Connor and Tom Harrisson. JMBRAS
44 pt. 1 (1971) 71-77.

2782 RICHARDS, A. J. N. Tibang, Tebang
Tilong and Mandai. SMJ 10 (1962)
409-411.

Death customs and rites - Malaysia -
  Sarawak

2783 SANDIN, BENEDICT. Garong baskets.
      SMJ 11 (1963) 321-326.

2784 SANDIN, BENEDICT. Gawai Antu, Sea
      Dayak feast of the departed spir-
      its. SMJ 10 (1961) 170-190.

2785 SANDIN, BENEDICT. Saribas Iban
      death dirge. SMJ 14 (1966) 15-80.

2786 SANDIN, BENEDICT. Two origins of
      Iban burial custom. SMJ 17
      (1969) 113-119.

2787 THOMAS, SHARON. Burial customs of
      the Kejamans. SMJ 19 (1971) 313-
      316.

2788 WELLS, CALVIN. Two neolithic
      burials from Lobang Jeragan, a
      cliff cave at Niah. SMJ 11 (1963)
      214-219.

2789 YAP YOON KEONG. Punan corpse that
      smells of durian. SMJ 11 (1963)
      94-98.

DEATH CUSTOMS AND RITES - PHILIPPINES

2790 ABUEVA, N. VELOSO. A grave pro-
      posal. GEJ 4 (1962) 103-4.

2791 DEMETRIO, FRANCISCO. Death, its
      origin and related beliefs among
      early Filipinos. PS 14 (1966)
      355-395.

2792 JOCANO, F. LANDA. Notes on the
      Sulod concept of death, the soul,
      and the region of the dead. PS
      12 (1964) 51-62.

2793 KASMAN, EDWARD SALKIYA. Birth and
      death rituals among the Tausugs of
      Siasi. UN 35 (1962) 291-340.

2794 KIEFER, THOMAS M. Gravemarkers
      and the repression of sexual sym-
      bolism, the case of two Philippine-
      Borneo Moslem societies, by Thomas
      M. Kiefer and Clifford Sather.
      BIJ 126 (1970) 75-90.

2795 KIEFER, THOMAS M. Parrang Sabbil,
      ritual suicide among the Tausug of
      Jolo. BIJ 129 (1973) 108-123.

2796 O'CONNOR, STANLEY J. Gold foil
      burial amulets in Bali, Philip-
      pines and Borneo, by Stanley J.
      O'Connor and Tom Harrisson. JMBRAS
      44 pt. 1 (1971) 71-77.

2797 PACYAYA, ALFREDO G. Religious ac-
      culturation in Sagada. B13 pp.
      128-139.

2798 VISTA, SALVADOR B. Notes on a
      Subanon ritual. SJ 21 (1974) 279-
      283.

DEATH CUSTOMS AND RITES - THAILAND

2799 KICKERT, ROBERT. Funeral in Yang
      Terng, Changwat Ubol, northeast
      Thailand. JSS 48 pt. 2 (1960) 73-
      83.

2800 LINGAT, R. Les suicides religieux
      au Siam. F38 pp. 71-75.

2801 SORENSEN, PER. Shaman grave. F38
      pp. 303-318.

DEATH CUSTOMS AND RITES - VIETNAM

2802 BARNOUIN, R. P. Les bas-reliefs
      des urnes dynastiques de Hue.
      SEIB 49 (1974) 425-583.

2803 COSTELLO, NANCY A. Socially ap-
      proved homicide among the Katu.
      SA 2 (1972-3) 77-87.

2804 FONTAINE, HENRI. Nouveau champ
      de jarres dans la Province de
      Long Khanh. SEIB 47 (1972) 397-
      485.

2805 FONTAINE, HENRI. Renseignements
      nouveaux sur la ceramique du champ
      de jarres funeraires de Dau-Giay.
      SEIB 46 (1971) 323-337.

2806 SAUL, JANICE E. Nung funerals.
      SA 2 (1972-3) 130-135.

2807 TRAN VAN PHUOC. Chronique:
      funerailles d'une baleine, Thuan-
      an (Thua-thien) 8-12 fevrier 1973.
      SEIB 49 (1974) 271-283.

DE CHOISY, ABBE

2808 GIBLIN, R. W. Abbe de Choisy.
      S44.8 pp. 1-16.

Dekker, Eduard Douwes *See* MUTATULI

DELANEY, JOHN PATRICK

2809 GOUGH, RAYMOND V. John Patrick
      Delaney, S.J., 1906-1956, I. the
      early years. PS 14 (1966) 3-24.

DEN

2810 LE VAN HAO. Introduction a
      l'ethnologie du Den et du Chua,
      Viet-Nam septentrional. RSA
      (1963) 79-114.

2811 LE VAN HAO. Introduction a
      l'ethnologie du Den et du Chua
      Viet-Nam septentrional. RSA
      (1964) 27-68.

DEWAN BAHASA DAN PUSTAKA, BRUNEI

2812 Note sur le Dewan Bahasa dan Pus-
      taka de Brunei. AR 3 (1972) 20-
      22.

DEWAN BAHASA DAN PUSTAKA, KUALA LUMPUR

2813 METZGER, LAURENT. L'Institut
      malaysien de langue et de littera-
      ture. AR 2 (1971) 23-28.

DHAMMATHATS

2814 MAUNG KYIN SWI. Origin and devel-
      opment of the Dhammathats. JBRS
      49 (1966) 173-205.

DHANINIVAT KROMAMUN BIDYALABH BRIDHYA-
      KORN, PRINCE

2815 Works of Prince Dhaninivat, a
      bibliography. F38 pp. v-ix.

DIET - BURMA

2816 WITTFOGEL, H. Grading commercial
      values of shrimp paste (hmyin
      ngapi) in Burma and detecting
      adulterations with fish and shrimp
      peels in it. JBRS 44 (1961) 237-
      246.

DIET - INDONESIA

2817 Pages d'exotisme, 4. Exotisme et
      cuisine. AR 4 (1972) 128-130.

2818 ROSE, CATHARINE S. Malnutrition
      in children in Indonesia, by
      Catharine S. Rose and Paul Gyorgy.
      J37 pp. 143-164.

Diet – Malaysia

2835 GIESER, RUTH. Natural clusters in Kalinga disease terms, by Ruth Gieser and Joseph E. Grimes. AST 10 (1972) 24-32.

2836 VILLANUEVA, GAUDENCIO. Factors guiding the population growth in the Philippines, malaria eradication in the Philippines. UN 39 (1966) 350-356.

DISSERTATIONS, ACADEMIC - PHILIPPINES

2837 Abstracts of M.A. theses at Silliman University. SJ 17 (1970) 211-229.

2838 Abstracts of M.A. theses at Silliman University. SJ 18 (1971) 97-123.

2839 Abstracts of M.A. theses at Silliman University. SJ 18 (1971) 217-239.

2840 Abstracts of M.A. theses at Silliman University. SJ 18 (1971) 441-452.

2841 Abstracts of M.A. theses at Silliman University. SJ 19 (1972) 112-121.

2842 Abstracts of M.A. theses at Silliman University. SJ 19 (1972) 230-247.

2843 List of theses, 1962. SLQ 1 (1963) 237-246.

2844 List of theses, 1962. SLQ 1 (1963) 565-575.

2845 List of theses submitted to the Bureau of Private Schools, from January to December 1963. SLQ 3 (1965) 117-126.

2846 List of theses, 1963. SLQ 3 (1965) 279-292.

2847 List of theses accessioned by the Bureau of Private Schools Library from January to December 1964. SLQ 3 (1965) 609-642.

2848 List of theses accessioned by the Bureau of Private Schools Library from January to December 1965. SLQ 4 (1966) 89-102.

2849 List of theses accessioned by the Bureau of Private Schools Library from January to December 1966. SLQ 4 (1966) 571-596.

2850 List of theses accessioned by the Bureau of Private Schools Library from January to December 1967. SLQ 6 (1968) 443-480.

2851 M.A. theses completed at Silliman University 1937-68. SJ 16 (1969) 445-452.

2852 M.A. theses completed at Silliman University 1968-69. SJ 16 (1969) 114-5.

2853 Thesis abstracts. SLURJ 3 (1972) 640.

2854 University thesis abstracts. UN 33 (1960) 419-448.

DISSERTATIONS, ACADEMIC - SINGAPORE

2855 CHIA SIOW YUE. Survey of academic exercises submitted to the Economics Department, University of Singapore for the academic session 1967/68. MER 13 pt. 1 (1968) 118-127.

DOUGLAS, BLOOMFIELD

2874 JACKSON, JAMES C. Kuala Lumpur in the 1880's, the contribution of Bloomfield Douglas. JSAH 4 (Sept. 1963) 117-127.

DRABBE, PETRUS

2875 ANCEAUX, J. C. Lijst van ge-schriften van P. Drabbe. BIJ 126 (1970) 461-2.

2876 GONDA, J. Pater Petrus Drabbe, M.S.C. BIJ 126 (1970) 459-461.

DRAMA *See also* DANCE, MUSIC

2877 JACQUOT, JEAN. Theatres d'Asie. J49 pp. 285-293.

2878 SINGARAVELU, S. Invocations to Nataraja in the Southeast Asian shadow plays, with special reference to the Kelantan shadow play. JSS 58 pt. 2 (1970) 45-54.

DRAMA - BURMA

2879 BA HAN. Evolution of Burmese dramatic performances and festal occasions. JBRS 49 (1966) 1-18.

2880 STEWART, J. A. Burmese drama. B92 pp. 517-522.

DRAMA - CAMBODIA

2881 SHEPPARD, MUBIN. Khmer shadow play and its links with ancient India. A possible source of the Malay shadow play of Kelantan and Trengganu. JMBRAS 41 pt. 1 (1968) 199-204.

DRAMA - INDONESIA

2882 AVELING, HARRY G. Analysis of Utuy Tatang Sontani's *Suling*. BIJ 125 (1969) 328-343.

2883 BONNEFF, MARCEL. L'histoire du condor et du mastodonte. AR 7 (1974) 9-13.

2884 BRANDON, JAMES R. Play production in the Indonesian professional theater. AC 2 (Jan. 1960) 73-87.

2885 CUISINIER, JEANNE. Le theatre en Indonesie. J49 pp. 223-241.

2886 HEINS, E. L. Cueing the gamalan in Javanese wayang performance. IND 9 (1970) 101-127.

2887 HOOYKAAS, C. Note on the Mahabha-rata in Malaysia and Indonesia, Sabha-Parva found in Bali. JMBRAS 38 pt. 2 (1965) 125-128.

2888 McPHEE, COLIN. Balinese wayang kulit and its music. B43 pp. 146-197.

2889 MEAD, MARGARET. Community drama, Bali and America. B43 pp. 341-349.

2890 MEAD, MARGARET. Strolling players in the mountains of Bali. B43 pp. 137-145.

2891 ONGHOKHAM. Wayang Topeng world of Malang. IND 14 (1972) 110-124.

2892 PEACOCK, JAMES L. Anti-Dutch, anti-Muslim drama among Surabaja proletarians, a description of performances and responses. IND 4 (1967) 44-73.

2893 ROBSON, S. O. The wajang and the study of Javanese cultural history. JOSA 3 pt. 2 (1965) 16-26.

Drama - Indonesia

2915 MANUUD, ANTONIO G. Arts, 1960.
PS 8 (1960) 814-822.

2916 MUNOZ, MA. TERESA. Notes on theater, pre-Hispanic Philippines,
religion, myth, religious ritual.
M24 pp. 648-667.

2917 PANIZO, ALFREDO. Introduction to
the Pampango theatre, by Alfredo
Panizo and Rodolfo V. Cortez. UN
41 (1968) 124-137.

2918 RAMAS, WILHELMINA Q. Sugbuanon
drama, a preliminary list of plays
acquired by the university. AST
11 pt. 3 (1973) 153-172.

2919 Reflections through a red star.
DR 18 (1970) 380-386.

2920 Review of the performing arts,
April to June, 1962. UN 35 (1962)
435-439.

2921 Survey of the performing arts,
July to September, 1961. UN 34
(Dec. 1961) 123-129.

2922 Survey of the performing arts,
October to December, 1961. UN 35
(1962) 139-144.

2923 Survey of the performing arts,
January to March, 1962. UN 35
(1962) 278-282.

2924 TINIO, ROLANDO S. Arts in the
Philippines, a theatre misunderstood. PS 10 (1962) 133-137.

2925 TINIO, ROLANDO S. Retracing old
grounds, the paradox of Philippine
theater. M24 pp. 689-701.

2926 TUKAY-GOMEZ, CONSUELO. Pablo
Mejia as a dramatist, with special
reference to his *Say silib na
tobunbolo*. DR 11 (1963) 456-495.

DRAMA - THAILAND

2927 COEDES, GEORGE. Origine et evolution des diverses formes du theatre traditionnel en Thailande.
SEIB 38 (1963) 491-506.

2928 DHANINIVAT, PRINCE. Hide figures
of the Ramakien at the Ledermuseum
in Offenbach, Germany. JSS 53
(1965) 61-66.

2929 DHANINIVAT, PRINCE. The shadow
play as a possible origin of the
masked play. S44.2 pp. 177-184.

2930 GINSBURG, HENRY D. Manora dance
drama, an introduction. JSS 60
pt. 2 (1972) 169-181.

2931 MAHAVAJIRAVUDH. Notes on the
Siamese theatre. JSS 55 (1967)
1-30.

2932 SIMMONDS, E. H. S. Mahorasop in a
Thai Manora manuscript. SOAS 30
(1967) 391-403.

2933 SIMMONDS, E. H. S. New evidence
on Thai shadow play invocations.
SOAS 24 (1961) 542-559.

2934 SMITHIES, MICHAEL. Likay, a note
on the origin, form and future of
Siamese folk opera. JSS 59 pt. 1
(1971) 33-64.

2935 SMITHIES, MICHAEL. Nang Talung,
the shadow theatre of southern
Thailand, by Michael Smithies and
Euayporn Kerdchouay. JSS 60 pt. 1
(1972) 379-390.

2936 SMITHIES, MICHAEL. Wai Kru cere-
mony of the Nang Yai, by Michael
Smithies and Euayporn Kerdchouay.
JSS 62 pt. 1 (1974) 143-147.

DRAMA - VIETNAM

2937 TRAN VAN KHE. Le theatre vietnamien. J49 pp. 203-219.

DREAMS - MALAYSIA - SARAWAK

2938 SANDIN, BENEDICT. Iban hero
dreams and apparitions. SMJ 14
(1966) 91-123.

DRUGS *See also* POISONS

2939 SANTOS, CONCEPCION B. Pharma-
cognostical study of eucalyptus
Deglupto Blume together with a
chemical study of its volatile
oil. UN 33 (1960) 740-806.

2940 WOLTERS, O. W. The Po-Ssu pine
trees. SOAS 23 (1960) 323-350.

DRUGS - BURMA

2941 Phytochemical studies of Holar-
rhena Antidysenterica grown in
Burma. JBRS 48 (June 1965) 77-84.

DRUGS - LAOS

2942 FEINGOLD, DAVID. Opium and
politics in Laos. L18 pp. 322-
339.

DRUGS - SINGAPORE

2943 CHENG U WEN. Opium in the Straits
Settlements, 1867-1910. JSAH 2
(Mar. 1961) 63-88a.

DUAL NATIONALITY

2944 MOZINGO, DAVID. Sino-Indonesian
dual nationality treaty. AS 1
(Dec. 1961) 25-31.

2945 YOUNG, KENNETH RAY. Sino-Indonesian dual nationality treaty, an
evaluation. AF 2 (1970) 172-182.

DUCOS, JOSE

2946 BERNAD, MIGUEL A. Father Ducos
and the Muslim wars, 1752-1759.
PS 16 (1968) 690-728.

DUMAGUETE CITY

2947 CHANG SHUB ROH. Looc, Dumaguete
City, a study of an urban slum
community. SJ 17 (1970) 248-285.

2948 MASLOG, FLORITA S. Health profile
of school children in Dumaguete
City. SJ 20 (1973) 208-216.

2949 POTTER, DAVID LEIGH. Compadrazgo
in Dumaguete, the strategy of
selection. SJ 21 (1974) 1-28.

DURAND, MAURICE

2950 HUARD, P. Maurice Durand, 1914-
1966. SEIB 41 (1966) 151-154.

2951 Maurice Durand, 1914-1966. BEF
55 (1969) 19-22.

2952 TA TRONG HIEP. In memoriam, Maurice Durand, 1914-1966. FA 20
(1965) 517-519.

DUSUN

2953 ABDUL LATIF HAJI IBRAHIM. Dusun
tribal dances (Alai). BMJ 1
(1969) 10-14.

2954 ALMAN, JOHN H. Dusun pottery,
Tuaran area. SMJ 9 (1960) 565-582.

2955　APPELL, GEORGE N.　Death of Serip Usman in Rungus tradition.　SMJ 12 (1965) 228-9.

2956　APPELL, GEORGE N.　Ethnographic profiles of the Dusun speaking peoples of Sabah, Malaysia. JMBRAS 41 pt. 2 (1968) 131-147.

2957　APPELL, GEORGE N.　Long-house apartment of the Rungus Dusun. SMJ 11 (1964) 570-573.

2958　APPELL, GEORGE N.　Social anthropological census for cognatic societies and its application among the Rungus of northern Borneo.　BIJ 125 (1969) 80-93.

2959　APPELL, GEORGE N.　Social groupings among the Rungus, a cognatic society of northern Borneo. JMBRAS 41 pt. 2 (1968) 193-202.

2960　ERCHAK, GERALD M.　Dusun social and symbolic orders.　SMJ 20 (1972) 301-313.

2961　HARRISSON, TOM.　Dusun jars, from Mayfair and Friesland through Cairo to Sabah.　SMJ 12 (1965) 69-74.

DUSUN LANGUAGE

2962　CLAYRE, B. M.　Focus, a preliminary survey of some languages of eastern Malaysia.　SMJ 18 (1970) 193-219.

2963　LEES, SHIRLEY P.　Apparent and real differences in Dusun linguistics.　SMJ 11 (1964) 574-577.

DUSUN LITERATURE

2964　WILLIAMS, THOMAS RHYS.　Tambunan Dusun origin myth.　JMBRAS 33 pt. 1 (1960) 95-103.

Dutch East India Company　*See* VEREENIGTE OOST-INDISCHE COMPAGNIE

DUY-TAN, EMPEROR OF ANNAM

2965　THEBAULT, E. P.　Le tragique destin d'un emperor d'Annam, Prince Vinh-San, 1900-1945, Empereur Duy-Tan, 1907-1916.　FA 24 (1970) 3-40.

DVARAVATI

2966　BOELES, J. J.　King of Sri Dvaravati and his regalia.　JSS 52 (1964) 99-114.

2967　BOISSELIER, JEAN.　Recentes recherches a Nakhon Pathom.　JSS 58 pt. 2 (1970) 55-65.

2968　COEDES, GEORGE.　Les Mons de Dvaravati.　E92 pp. 112-116.

2969　LUCE, GORDON H.　Dvaravati and old Burma.　JSS 53 (1965) 9-25.

2970　LYONS, ELIZABETH.　Two Dvaravati figurines.　JSS 61 pt. 1 (1973) 193-201.

2971　SUBHADRADIS DISKUL.　Pierre Dupont, l'archeologie mone de Dvaravati.　E93 pp. 166-174.

2972　WALES, H. G. QUARITCH.　Muang Bon, a town of northern Dvaravati.　JSS 53 (1965) 1-7.

DYAK

2973　COURT, CHRISTOPHER.　Kinship terms of reference of the Mentu Land Dayaks in phonemic notation.　BIJ 126 (1970) 436-465.

Dyak

2974 DANANDJAJA, JAMES. Comparative analysis of kinship in central Kalimantan and Nias. SMJ 19 (1971) 237-252.

2975 GEDDES, W. R. Countryside and the jungle. T45 pp. 88-97.

2976 GILL, SARAH. Style and the demonic image in Dayak masks. JMBRAS 40 pt. 1 (1967) 78-92.

2977 HOWES, PETER. Why some of the best people aren't Christian. SMJ 9 (1960) 488-495.

2978 HUDSON, ALFRED B. Padju Epat Ma'anjan Dajak in historical perspective. IND 4 (1967) 8-42.

2979 HUDSON, JUDITH M. Some observations on dance in Kalimantan. IND 12 (1971) 132-150.

2980 MARTINOIR, NINANE DE. Unity of Dayak mythology. A41 pp. 56-64.

2981 MEDWAY, LORD. Batu sep, a modern stone artifact. SMJ 15 (1967) 93-4.

2982 SIDAWAY, DAVID. Influence of Christianity on Biatah speaking Land Dayaks. SMJ 17 (1969) 139-152.

2983 TUTON KABOY. Dayaks of Lundu District, by Tuton Kaboy and Benedict Sandin. SMJ 16 (1968) 122-140.

DYAK LANGUAGE

2984 COURT, CHRISTOPHER. Pointing and asking, a note on deixis in Mentu Land Dayak. BIJ 123 (1967) 520-1.

DYAK LITERATURE

2985 HEWITT, JOHN. First land Dayaks. SMJ 10 (1961) 112-117.

2986 INGAI, JOSEPH. Pancha and Padong origins. SMJ 16 (1968) 195-198.

2987 JUDKINS, RUSSELL A. Silanting Kuning's transformation, liminality in a Land Dayak myth. An analysis of *Nine Dayak nights*. SMJ 17 (1969) 123-138.

2988 SANDIN, BENEDICT. Simpulang or Pulang Gana, the founder of Dayak agriculture. SMJ 15 (1967) 245-406.

E.C.A.F.E.

2989 For Asia's future, the role of ECAFE. FA 17 (1960) 1523-1527.

2990 Economic development in Asia, a report on the Economic Commission for Asia and the Far East (ECAFE) activities in 1965. FA 20 (1965) 349-361.

EARL, GEORGE SAMUEL WINDSOR

2991 JONES, RUSSELL. Earl, Logan and Indonesia. AR 6 (1973) 93-118.

EARTHQUAKES - INDONESIA

2992 KEMPEN, C. P. BREST VAN. Earthquakes in the Netherlands Indies. H57 pp. 35-6.

2993 TJIA, H. D. Nature of displacements along the Semangko fault zone, Sumatra. JTG 30 (1970) 63-67.

EARTHQUAKES - MALAYSIA - SABAH

2994 MILNE, JOHN. Earthquakes and re-
     lated phenomena in north and west
     Borneo. SMJ 14 (1966) 1-5.

EAST INDIA COMPANY

2995 MOIR, MARTIN I. Archival materi-
     als in the London records of the
     East India Company and of the
     India Office relating to Southeast
     Asia. SAA 2 (1969) 68-81.

2996 NISH, IAN. British mercantile
     cooperation in the India-China
     trade from the end of the East
     India Company's trading monopoly.
     JSAH 3 (Sept. 1962) 74-91.

2997 QUIASON, SERAFIN D. Early con-
     tacts of the English East India
     Company with Mindanao. PSSHR 26
     (1961) 175-186.

2998 QUAISON, SERAFIN D. Early trade
     of the English East India Company
     with Manila. PHR 1 pt. 1 (1965)
     272-297.

2999 QUIASON, SERAFIN D. East India
     Company in Manila, 1762-1764.
     PSSHR 28 (1963) 424-444.

3000 QUIASON, SERAFIN D. Synopsis of
     early English country trade with
     the Philippines. GEJ 5 (1963)
     26-34.

ECOLE FRANCAISE D'EXTREME-ORIENT

3001 AUBOYER, JEANNINE. Recent archae-
     ological work in Cambodia by the
     Ecole Francaise d'Extreme-Orient.
     FA 18 (1962) 178-182.

ECOLOGY - MALAYSIA

3002 AIKEN, S. ROBERT. Images of na-
     ture in Swettenham's early writ-
     ings, prolegomenon to a historical
     perspective on peninsular Malay-
     sia's ecological problems. AST
     11 pt. 3 (1973) 135-152.

ECOLOGY - PHILIPPINES

3003 CASINO, ERIC S. Jama Mapun ethno-
     ecology, economic and symbolic
     (of grains, winds and stars). AST
     5 (1967) 1-32.

ECOLOGY - THAILAND

3004 HAFNER, JAMES L. Man and environ-
     ment in rural Thailand. JSS 61
     pt. 2 (1973) 129-138.

Economic Commission on Asia and the Far
   East *See* E.C.A.F.E.

ECONOMIC DEVELOPMENT

3005 ABDUL RASHID IBRAHIM. Cultural
     background of the ECAFE region and
     the challenge of economic develop-
     ment. JSS 50 pt. 1 (1962) 35-49.

3006 BANIK, SUNIL. Regional economic
     cooperation and integration move-
     ments and the Asian Development
     Bank, hope of the less developed.
     AST 6 (1968) 395-420.

3007 BELL, PETER F. Contradictions of
     post-war development in Southeast
     Asia, by Peter F. Bell and Stephen
     A. Resnick. JCA 1 pt. 1 (1970)
     37-49.

3008 BERRY, BRIAN J. L. City size and
     economic development, conceptual

Economic development

synthesis and policy problems,
with special reference to South
and Southeast Asia. U77 pp. 111-
155.

3009 BRAND, W. Observations on trade,
aid and development with special
reference to Southeast Asia. D44
pp. 123-136.

3010 CASTILLO, GELIA T. Quest for
development and the discovery of
Asia by Asians. AST 10 (1972)
321-335.

3011 CLERCK, MARCEL DE. L'education
des adultes en vue du developpement rural. RSA (1963) 1-50.

3012 Economic development in Asia, a
report on the Economic Commission
for Asia and the Far East (ECAFE)
activities in 1965. FA 20 (1965)
349-361.

3013 GOH KENG SWEE. Economic development and modernization in South-
East Asia. M52 pp. 81-93.

3014 GORDON, BERNARD K. Economic im-
pediments to regionalism in Southeast Asia. AS 3 (1963) 235-244.

3015 GORDON, WILLIAM E. Economic
growth and foreign trade of Asia.
C35 pp. 247-289.

3016 HLA MYINT. Inward and outward
looking countries of Southeast
Asia. MER 12 pt. 1 (1967) 1-13.

3017 HOSELITZ, BERT F. Urbanization
and economic growth. D92 pp. 3-
15.

3018 IRVINE, REED J. Some lessons of
the development decade. AS 10
(1970) 552-562.

3019 Japan's aid to South and Southeast
Asia under the Colombo Plan. FA
17 (1960) 1920-1924.

3020 JORDAN, AMOS A. United States
foreign assistance in Southeast
Asia. H35 pp. 212-226.

3021 LE THANH KHOI. Education et
developpement en Asie orientale.
D44 pp. 165-172.

3022 OSHIMA, HARRY T. Income inequal-
ity and economic growth, the post-
war experience of Asian countries.
MER 15 pt. 2 (1970) 7-41.
Comment: MANGAHAS, MAHAR. Note
on "Income inequity and economic
growth, the postwar experience of
Asian countries." MER 18 pt. 1
(1973) 11-14.

3023 PAAUW, DOUGLAS S. Economic progress in Southeast Asia. JAS 23
(1963-4) 69-92.

3024 PAAUW, DOUGLAS S. Economic progress in Southeast Asia. T45 pp.
556-584.

3025 RAMANA, D. V. Towards an appraisal and a strategy of development
for the ECAFE region countries.
MER 18 pt. 2 (1973) 16-36.

3026 ROTH, DAVID F. Towards a multidi-
mensional approach to rural policy
optimalization, the case of rural
change strategies in Asia. JSAS 3
(1972) 123-141.

3027 SHAND, R. T. Perspectives on
Asia. S42 pp. 313-325.

3028 TRAN VAN DINH. Territorial planning and equipping in Asia. AC 3
(Apr. 1961) 13-30.

3029 UDOM KERDPIBULE. The prospects
for manufacturing exports of ASEAN

countries, an exploratory study.
MER 19 pt. 2 (1974) 21-46.

2030   VU QUOC THUC. Economic development in Southeast Asian countries.
AC 2 (Jan. 1960) 1-31.

3031   WALTERS, HARRY. Green revolution
in Southeast Asia in the 1970's,
by Harry Walters and Joseph Willett. S63 pp. 108-183.

3032   WEILLER, JEAN. Liens entre les
plans ou programmes de developpement et les conditions de participation aux echanges interna-
tionaux. D44 pp. 151-163.

3033   WERTHEIM, W. F. Evolution, involution and revolution in
Southern Asia. D44 pp. 109-121.

3034   WERTHEIM, W. F. Resistance to
change, from whom? M52 pp. 97-
107.

3035   WHEATON, WILLIAM L. C. Urban
housing in economic development,
by William L. C. and Margaret F.
Wheaton. D92 pp. 141-151.

3036   ZWAENEPOEL, PAUL P. Possibilities
for human progress in a changing
world. SLURJ 3 (1972) 292-326.

ECONOMIC DEVELOPMENT - BRUNEI

3037   LEE, Y. L. Development of resources in British Borneo and its
impact on settlement. SMJ 11
(1962) 563-589.

ECONOMIC DEVELOPMENT - BURMA

3038   AYE HLAING. Observations on some
patterns of economic development.
B91 pp. 9-16.

3039   KHIN MAUNG KYI. Western enterprise and economic development in
Burma. JBRS 53 (June 1970) 25-51.

3040   MYA MAUNG. Cultural value and
economic change in Burma. T45 pp.
527-534.

3041   RICHTER, H. V. Union of Burma.
S42 pp. 140-180.

ECONOMIC DEVELOPMENT - INDONESIA

3042   BLAKE, D. J. Estates and economic
development in northeast Sumatra.
MER 8 pt. 1 (1963) 98-110.

3043   CORDEN, W. M. Development of the
Indonesian exchange rate system,
by W. M. Corden and J. A. C.
Mackie. MER 7 pt. 1 (1962) 37-60.

3044   FRANKE, RICHARD W. Limited good
and cargo cult in Indonesian economic development. JCA 2 (1972)
366-381.

3045   HIGGINS, BENJAMIN H. Introduction. H24 pp. 1-38.

3046   HONG LAN OEI. Implications of
Indonesia's new foreign investment
policy for economic development.
IND 7 (1969) 33-66.

3047   MORTIMER, REX. Indonesia, growth
or development? M77 pp. 51-66.

3048   PANGLAYKIM, J. Study of entrepreneurship in developing countries,
the development of one Chinese
concern in Indonesia, by J. Panglaykim and I. Parmer. JSAS 1 pt.
1 (1970) 85-95.

3049   PAUKER, GUY J. Political consequences of rural development programs in Indonesia. PA 41 (1968)
386-402.

Economic development - Indonesia

3050 PENNY, DAVID H. Economics and
Indonesian agricultural develop-
ment, by David H. Penny and J.
Price Gittinger. G52 pp. 162-178.

3051 PENNY, DAVID H. Economics and
Indonesian agricultural develop-
ment, by David H. Penny and J.
Price Gittinger. J37 pp. 259-273.

3052 PENNY, DAVID H. Indonesia. S42
pp. 251-279.

3053 POND, D. H. Development investment in Indonesia, 1956-1963. MER
9 pt. 2 (1964) 92-105.

3054 POND, D. H. Foreign economic
assistance to Indonesia, 1956-
1963. MER 10 pt. 1 (1965) 84-99.

ECONOMIC DEVELOPMENT - MALAYSIA **

3055 ABRAHAM, W. I. New measures of
economic growth and structural
change of the Malaysian economy
in the post-1960 period. MER 14
pt. 1 (1969) 65-79.

3056 BHATI, U. N. Farmers' technical
knowledge and income, a case study
of padi farmers of west Malaysia.
MER 18 pt. 1 (1973) 36-47.

3057 BILAS, RICHARD A. Growth of
physical output in the Federation
of Malaya, 1930-1960. MER 8 pt.
2 (1963) 81-90.

3058 DRABBLE, J. H. Some thoughts on
the economic development of Malaya
under British administration.
JSAS 5 (1974) 199-208.

3059 FISK, E. K. Malaysia. S42 pp.
181-214.

3060 FISK, E. K. Productivity and income from rubber in an established
Malay reservation. MER 6 pt. 1
(1961) 13-22.

3061 FISK, E. K. Rural development
policy. S47 pp. 174-194.

3062 FRYER, DONALD W. Some aspects of
the Malaysian rural development
program. V27 pp. 71-90.

3063 LEE, Y. L. Development of resources in British Borneo and its
impact on settlement. SMJ 11
(1962) 563-589.

3064 LEONARD, PATRICK L. Farm planning
and land development schemes. MER
14 pt. 1 (1969) 80-96.

3065 LIM, DAVID. Export instability
and economic development in west
Malaysia, 1947-1968. MER 17 pt. 2
(1972) 99-113.

3066 McHALE, THOMAS R. Natural rubber
and Malaysian economic development. MER 10 pt. 1 (1965) 16-43.

3067 McKENNA, DON. Financial developments since independence. S47 pp.
195-209.

3068 McTAGGART, W. D. The May 1969
disturbances in Malaysia, impact
of a conflict on development pattern. AF 3 (1971) 219-236.

3069 McTAGGART, W. D. Strategy of regional development in Perlis, west
Malaysia. JTG 29 (1969) 39-48.

3070 RAO, V. V. BHANOJI. Inter-sector-
al relationship and structural
change in west Malaysia, 1960-67.
MER 17 pt. 2 (1972) 40-65.

3071 SHAMSUL BAHRIN, TUNKU. Preliminary study of the fringe alienation
schemes in west Malaysia. JTG 28
(1969) 75-83.

3072 SILCOCK, T. H. Economics of population policy in the Federation of Malaya. S48 pp. 85-93.

3073 SILCOCK, T. H. Some problems of economic growth in the British territories in South-East Asia. S48 pp. 43-62.

3074 SNODGRASS, DONALD R. Capital stock and Malayan economic growth, a preliminary analysis. MER 11 pt. 2 (1966) 63-85.

3075 SWIFT, M. G. Accumulation of capital in a peasant economy. S48 pp. 21-37.

3076 WHEELWRIGHT, E. L. Reflections on some problems of industrial development in Malaya. MER 8 pt. 1 (1963) 66-80.

3077 WITTON, RON. Malaysia, changing masters. JCA 2 (1972) 192-198.

3078 WONG, LESLIE G. J. Foreword, papers presented at the symposium on the role of management in industrialization in Malaysia. MER 8 pt. 1 (1963) 1-3.

ECONOMIC DEVELOPMENT - PHILIPPINES

3079 CARROLL, EARL. Management of national growth. SJ 10 (1963) 43-48.

3080 CARROLL, JOHN J. Philippine social organization and national development. PS 14 (1966) 575-590.

3081 CARROLL, JOHN J. Twin revolution. PS 11 (1963) 573-579.

3082 CONCEPCION, MERCEDES B. Demographic factors in Philippine development. C47 pp. 80-84.

Comment: Discussion. C47 pp. 89-103.

3083 DeRAEDT, JULES. Development and land reform. SLURJ 2 (1971) 19-28.

3084 DeRAEDT, JULES. Modernization, the local instance of a global process. SLURJ 5 (1974) 303-344.

3085 FLOR, DIOSDADO. Factors guiding the population growth in the Philippines, economic development and population pressure in the Philippines. UN 39 (1966) 357-367.

3086 HOOLEY, RICHARD. The Philippines, by Richard Hooley and Vernon W. Ruttan. S42 pp. 215-250.

3087 HOUSTON, C. O. Political and social aspects of Philippine economic development. E78 pp. 74-84.

3088 MARTIN, LAURENCE P. Introduction of PERT/CPM method of planning at Benguet Consolidated, Inc. SLURJ 1 (1970) 180-214.

3089 MILNE, R. S. New administration and the new economic program in the Philippines. AS 2 (Sept. 1962) 36-42.

3090 OWEN, NORMAN G. Philippine economic development and American policy, a reappraisal. C31 pp. 103-128.

3091 RESNICK, STEPHEN A. Second path to capitalism, a model of international development. JCA 3 (1973) 133-148.

3092 RIVERA, CORNELIO T. Mariveles free trade zone, potential and opportunity. PS 19 (1971) 733-738.

Economic development - Philippines

3093 ROTH, DAVID F. Philippine rural development, the case study of an incremental policy strategy. AF 5 pt. 3 (1973) 43-73.

3094 ROXAS, SIXTO K. Discovering economic imperatives for national growth. PS 15 (1967) 221-240.

3095 ROXAS, SIXTO K. Organizing the next wave of development. PS 15 (1967) 576-591.

3096 ROXAS, SIXTO K. Public administration and economic development. A28 pp. 524-531.

3097 SICAT, GERARDO P. Output, capital, labor and population, projections from the supply side, by Gerardo P. Sicat and Rosa Linda P. Tidalgo. C47 pp. 354-388.

3098 STORER, JAMES A. Philippine economic planning and progress, 1945-1960, by James A. Storer and Teresita L. de Guzman. M38 pp. 5-37.

3099 TRINIDAD, NORMA C. Production of tall oil from Benguet pine trees. SLURJ 1 (1970) 259-294.

3100 TUPAS, ISABELO. Rural development and the Philippine community school. E78 pp. 558-561.

3101 VALDEPENAS, VICENTE B. Private initiatives in national development. PS 21 (1973) 321-327.

3102 VILLANUEVA, PATROCINIO S. Some socio-economic effects of rural roads. E78 pp. 287-291.

3103 VILLEGAS, EDUARDO L. Health, population growth and development. PS 19 (1971) 37-42.
Comment: BENGZON, ALFREDO R. Comments. PS 19 (1971) 44-48.

Comment: CONCEPCION, MERCEDES B. Comments. PS 19 (1971) 43-4.

3104 ZENOFF, DAVID. New look at economic nationalism. PS 10 (1962) 215-233.

ECONOMIC DEVELOPMENT - SINGAPORE

3105 BOTTOMLEY, ANTHONY. Role of foreign branch plants in the industrialization of Singapore. MER 7 pt. 1 (1962) 26-36.

3106 CHEN, PETER S. J. Growth and income distribution in Singapore. SAJSS 2 (1974) 119-130.

3107 FONTAINE, JEAN-PIERRE. Le miracle de Singapour. AQ (1974) 339-345.

3108 HUGHES, HELEN. From entrepot trade to manufacturing. H84 pp. 1-45.

3109 LIM CHONG YAH. Economic development of Singapore in the sixties and beyond. Y52 pp. 1-42.

3110 OSHIMA, HARRY T. Growth and unemployment in Singapore. MER 12 pt. 2 (1967) 32-58.

3111 WHEELWRIGHT, E. L. Reflections on some problems of industrial development in Malaya. MER 8 pt. 1 (1963) 66-80.

ECONOMIC DEVELOPMENT - THAILAND

3112 AYAL, ELIEZER B. Some crucial issues in Thailand's economic development. PA 34 (1961) 157-164.

3113 AYAL, ELIEZER B. Value systems and economic development in Japan and Thailand. T45 pp. 535-549.

3114 CHALMERS, JAMES A. On linking
      supply and demand in macro models
      of developing countries, with an
      illustration involving Thailand.
      MER 17 pt. 2 (1972) 121-142.

3115 CHATTHIP NARTSUPHA. Services led
      growth in Thailand, 1956-1970.
      SAJSS 1 pt. 1 (1973) 75-79.

3116 FEENY, DAVID. Some comments on
      Thai development planning. AS 12
      (1972) 317-326.

3117 HOUGH, RICHARD LEE. Development
      and security in Thailand, lessons
      from other Asian countries. AS 9
      (1969) 178-187.

3118 HUFF, LEE W. Thai Mobile Develop-
      ment Unit program. K86 pp. 425-
      486.

3119 KIRSCH, A. THOMAS. Economy, pol-
      ity, and religion in Thailand.
      C24 pp. 172-196.

3120 MORELL, DAVID. Legislative inter-
      vention in Thailand's development
      process, a case study. AS 12
      (1972) 627-646.

3121 MUSCAT, ROBERT J. Growth and the
      free market, a case study in
      Thailand. MER 11 pt. 1 (1966)
      114-125.

3122 SILCOCK, T. H. Outline of eco-
      nomic development, 1945-65. S49
      pp. 1-26.

3123 SILCOCK, T. H. Thailand. S42 pp.
      103-139.

3124 VICHITVONG N. POMBHEJARA. Second
      phase of Thailand's six year eco-
      nomic development plan, 1964-66.
      AS 5 (1965) 161-168.

3125 VIKSNINS, GEORGE J. United States
      military spending and the economy
      of Thailand, 1967-1972. AS 13
      (1973) 441-457.

3126 WITTON, RONALD A. Ideology and
      utopia in development. JCA 1 pt.
      2 (1970) 36-49.

ECONOMIC DEVELOPMENT - VIETNAM

3127 CASEY, R. G. Summary of Viet-
      Nam's political and economic prog-
      ress. L52 pp. 333-339.
      Comment: HENDERSON, WILLIAM.
      Commentary. L52 pp. 342-3.
      Comment: PRICE, HOYT. Commen-
      tary. L52 pp. 339-341.
      Author's reply: L52 pp. 343-4.
      Comment: HENDERSON, WILLIAM.
      Commentary. L52 pp. 344-5.

3128 HENDRY, JAMES B. Economic devel-
      opment under conditions of guer-
      rilla warfare, the case of Viet-
      nam. AS 2 (June 1962) 1-12.

3129 MORRISON, LAWRENCE. Industrial
      development efforts. L52 pp. 214-
      231.
      Comment: HUNTER, JOHN M. Com-
      mentary. L52 pp. 231-234.
      Comment: LINDHOLM, R. W. Com-
      mentary. L52 pp. 234-5.
      Author's reply: L52 pp. 235-240.

3130 NGUYEN PHUC SA. General report on
      industrial development. L52 pp.
      241-244.

3131 ROSEBERY, FRANK D. Experiment in
      planning economic and social de-
      velopment, 1956-57. L52 pp. 193-
      199.

3132 TAYLOR, MILTON C. South Viet-Nam,
      lavish aid, limited progress. PA
      34 (1961) 242-256.

Economic development - Vietnam

ECONOMIC DEVELOPMENT FOUNDATION

ECONOMIC HISTORY

ECONOMIC HISTORY - BURMA

ECONOMIC HISTORY - INDONESIA

introductory survey, 1815-1930.
JBRS 48 (Dec. 1965) 41-64.

3152 Introduction. J32 pp. 1-64.

3153 LEWIS, DIANNE. Growth of the
country trade to the Straits of
Malacca, 1760-1777. JMBRAS 43 pt.
2 (1970) 114-129.

3154 NOORDUYN, J. Further topographical notes on the ferry charter of
1358, with appendices on Djipang
and Bodjanegara. BIJ 124 (1968)
460-481.

3155 PELZER, KARL J. The Spanish tobacco monopoly in the Philippines,
1782-1883, and the Dutch forced
cultivation system in Indonesia,
1834-1870. AR 8 (1974) 147-153.

3156 SHAROM AHMAT. Some problems of
the Rhode Island traders in Java,
1799-1836. JSAH 6 (Mar. 1965) 94-
106.

3157 TARLING, NICHOLAS. The Palmer
loans. BIJ 119 (1963) 161-188.

3158 VAN NIEL, ROBERT. Function of
landrent under the cultivation
system in Java. JAS 23 (1963-4)
357-375.

3159 VAN NIEL, ROBERT. Measurement of
change under the cultivation
system in Java, 1837-1851. IND
14 (1972) 89-109.

3160 VAN NIEL, ROBERT. Regulation of
sugar production in Java, 1830-
1840. V27 pp. 91-108.

ECONOMIC HISTORY - MALAYSIA

3161 ANDERSON, JOHN. Political and
commercial considerations relative
to the Malayan peninsula and the

British settlements in the Straits
of Malacca. JMBRAS 35 pt. 4
(1965) i-xv, 1-204, i-lxviii.

3162 BASTIN, JOHN. Introduction.
JMBRAS 35 pt. 4 (1965) 1-10.

3163 CHANDRAN, J. Private enterprise
and British policy in the Malay
peninsula, the case of the Malay
Railway and Works Construction
Company, 1893-1895. JMBRAS 37 pt.
2 (1964) 28-46.

3164 CHIANG HAI DING. Origins of the
Malaysian currency system, 1867-
1906. JMBRAS 39 pt. 1 (1966) 1-
18.

3165 DRABBLE, J. H. Some thoughts on
the economic development of Malaya
under the British administration.
JSAS 5 (1974) 199-208.

3166 IRWIN, GRAHAM W. The Dutch and the
tin trade of Malaya in the seventeenth century. S89 pp. 267-287.

3167 LAMB, ALASTAIR. Takuapa, the
probable site of a pre-Malaccan
entrepot in the Malay peninsula.
B38 pp. 76-86.

3168 LEWIS, DIANNE. Growth of the
country trade to the Straits of
Malacca, 1760-1777. JMBRAS 43 pt.
2 (1970) 114-129.

3169 LOCKARD, CRAIG A. Charles Brooke
and the foundations of the modern
Chinese community in Sarawak,
1863-1917. SMJ 19 (1971) 77-108.

3170 MOY-THOMAS, A. H. Economic development under the second rajah,
1870-1917. SMJ 10 (1961) 50-58.

3171 RAWLINS, J. S. D. French enterprise in Malaya. JMBRAS 39 pt. 2
(1966) 50-94.

Economic history - Malaysia

3172 ROBERT, LESLIE RATNASINGAM. Duff syndicate in Kelantan, 1900-1902. JMBRAS 45 pt. 1 (1972) 81-110.

3173 SHAROM AHMAT. Structure of the economy of Kedah, 1879-1905. JMBRAS 43 pt. 2 (1970) 1-24.

3174 SINCLAIR, KEITH. Hobson and Lenin in Johore, Colonial Office policy towards British concessionaires and investors, 1878-1907. MAS 1 (1967) 335-352.

3175 TARLING, NICHOLAS. The entrepot at Labuan and the Chinese. S89 pp. 355-373.

3176 YUEN CHOY LENG. Japanese rubber and iron investments in Malaya, 1900-1941. JSAS 5 (1974) 18-36.

ECONOMIC HISTORY - PHILIPPINES **

3177 BAUZON, LESLIE E. Encomienda system as a Spanish colonial institution in the Philippines, 1571-1604. SJ 14 (1967) 197-241.

3178 CHEONG WENG EANG. Changing the rules of the game, the India-Manila trade, 1785-1809. JSAS 1 pt. 2 (1970) 1-19.

3179 CHEONG, WENG EANG. Decline of Manila as the Spanish entrepot in the Far East, 1785-1826, its impact on the pattern of Southeast Asian trade. JSAS 2 (1971) 142-158.

3180 CUMMINS, JAMES S. Labor in the colonial Philippines, the *Discurso Parenetico* of Gomez de Espinosa, by James S. Cummins and Nicholas P. Cushner. PS 22 (1974) 117-203.

3181 CUSHNER, NICHOLAS P. Manila-Andalusia trade rivalry in the early Bourbon period. PS 8 (1960) 544-556.

3182 CUSHNER, NICHOLAS P. Meysapan, the formation and social effects of a landed estate in the Philippines. JAH 7 (1973) 30-53.

3183 DIAZ-TRECHUELO, MARIA LOURDES. Economic development of the Philippines in the second half of the eighteenth century. PS 11 (1963) 195-231.

3184 DIAZ-TRECHUELO, MARIA LOURDES. Eighteenth century Philippine economy: agriculture. PS 14 (1966) 65-126.

3185 DIAZ-TRECHUELO, MARIA LOURDES. Eighteenth century Philippine economy: commerce. PS 14 (1966) 253-279.

3186 DIAZ-TRECHUELO, MARIA LOURDES. Eighteenth century Philippine economy: mining. PS 13 (1965) 763-800.

3187 DIAZ-TRECHUELO, MARIA LOURDES. Philippine economic development plans, 1746-1779. PS 12 (1964) 203-231.

3188 LARKIN, JOHN A. Causes of an involuted society, a theoretical approach to rural Southeast Asian history. JAS 30 (1970-1) 783-795.

3189 MOLINA, ANTONIO M. Word on forced labor in the Philippines. UN 34 (Dec. 1961) 6-12.

3190 PELZER, KARL J. The Spanish tobacco monopoly in the Philippines, 1782-1883, and the Dutch forced cultivation system in Indonesia, 1834-1870. AR 8 (1974) 147-153.

3191 ROTH, DENNIS. Casas de reservas in the Philippines. JSAS 5 (1974) 115-124.

3192 SALAMANCA, BONIFACIO S. Background and early beginnings of the encomienda in the Philippines. PSSHR 26 (1961) 67-86.

3193 TARLING, NICHOLAS. Consul Farren and the Philippines. JMBRAS 38 pt. 2 (1965) 258-273.

3194 VALDEPENAS, VICENTE B. Philippine prehistoric economy, by Vicente B. Valdepenas and Germelino M. Bautista. PS 22 (1974) 280-296.

3195 WICKBERG, EDGAR. Early Chinese economic influence in the Philippines, 1850-1898. PA 35 (1962) 275-285.

ECONOMIC HISTORY - SINGAPORE

3196 CHIANG, HAI DING. Sino-British mercantile relations in Singapore's entrepot trade, 1870-1915. S89 pp. 247-266.

3197 HUGHES, HELEN. From entrepot trade to manufacturing. H84 pp. 1-45.

3198 TREGONNING, K. G. Origin of the Straits Steamship Company in 1890. JMBRAS 38 pt. 2 (1965) 274-289.

3199 TURNBULL, C. M. European mercantile community in Singapore, 1819-1867. JSAH 10 (1969) 12-35.

3200 WONG LIN KEN. Trade of Singapore, 1819-69. JMBRAS 33 pt. 4 (1960) 5-315.

ECONOMIC HISTORY - VIETNAM

3201 CHESNEAUX, JEAN. L'implantation geographique des interets coloniaux au Vietnam et ses rapports avec l'economie traditionnelle. C28 pp. 74-88.

3202 LANOUE, HENRI. L'emprise economique des Etats-Unis sur l'Indochine avant 1950. C28 pp. 292-328.

3203 MUSOLF, LLOYD D. Public enterprise and development perspectives in south Vietnam. AS 3 (1963) 357-371.

3204 NGUYEN THE ANH. Quelques aspects economiques et sociaux du problem du riz au Vietnam dans la premiere moitie du XIXe siecle. SEIB 42 (1967) 7-22.

ECONOMIC POLICY

3205 GOH KENG SWEE. Social, political and institutional aspects of development planning. MER 10 pt. 1 (1965) 1-15.

3206 SINGER, H. W. Development plans in Asia. C35 pp. 163-171.

3207 USHER, DAN. Government ownership of industry in Asia. MER 6 pt. 2 (1961) 61-67.

ECONOMIC POLICY - BURMA

3208 MALI, K. S. Public expenditures and inflationary impact in Burma, 1951-59. JBRS 45 (1962) 49-78.

3209 SOE MYINT. Financing the deficit since independence. JBRS 44 (1961) 183-195.

Economic policy - Burma

3210 THET TUN. Organization of planning machinery, lessons from Burmese experience. JBRS 46 (June 1963) 27-34.

3211 THET TUN. Review of economic planning in Burma. B91 pp. 485-527.

3212 WALINSKY, LOUIS J. Role of the military in development planning, Burma. T45 pp. 340-350.

ECONOMIC POLICY - INDONESIA

3213 GLASSBURNER, BRUCE. Economic policy making in Indonesia, 1950-1957. G52 pp. 70-98.

3214 GLASSBURNER, BRUCE. Swing of the hoe, retooling begins in the Indonesian economy, by Bruce Glassburner and Kenneth D. Thomas. AS 1 (June 1961) 3-12.

3215 HANSEN, GARY E. Indonesia's green revolution, the abandonment of a non-market strategy toward change. AS 12 (1972) 932-946.

3216 HINDLEY, DONALD. Foreign aid to Indonesia and its political implications. PA 36 (1963) 107-119.

3217 HONG LAN OEI. Implications of Indonesia's new foreign investment policy for economic development. IND 7 (1969) 33-66.

3218 HONG LAN OEI. Indonesia's economic stabilization and rehabilitation program, an evaluation. IND 5 (1968) 135-174.

3219 HUMPHREY, DON D. Indonesia's national plan for economic development. AS 2 (Dec. 1962) 12-21.

3220 OWEN, WYN F. Structural planning in densely populated countries, an introduction with applications to Indonesia. MER 14 pt. 1 (1969) 97-114.

3221 PANGLAYKIM, J. New order and the economy. IND 3 (1967) 73-120.

3222 PAUKER, GUY J. Indonesia's eight year development plan. PA 34 (1961) 115-130.

3223 POND, D. H. Foreign economic assistance to Indonesia, 1956-1963. MER 10 pt. 1 (1965) 84-99.

3224 RICE, ROBERT. Sumitro's role in foreign trade policy. IND 8 (1969) 183-211.

3225 THOMAS, K. D. Indonesia's development cabinet, background to current problems and the five year plan. AS 9 (1969) 223-238.

3226 TINKER, IRENE. Planning for regional development in Indonesia, by Irene Tinker and Millidge Walker. AS 13 (1973) 1102-1120.

ECONOMIC POLICY - MALAYSIA

3227 SILCOCK, T. H. General review of economic policy. S47 pp. 242-275.

ECONOMIC POLICY - PHILIPPINES

3228 ARANETA, SALVADOR. The planning, the approval and implementation of economic policy. M38 pp. 132-146.

3229 AYTONA, DOMINADOR R. Budget commission, finance and economic planning. M38 pp. 83-91.

3230 LOCSIN, JOSE C. The National Economic Council and economic planning. M38 pp. 147-160.

3231 McPHELIN, MICHAEL. Economic nationalism and planned stagnation.
PS 18 (1970) 147-160.

3232 PERALTA, VICENTE L. Congress and
economic planning. M38 pp. 76-82.

3233 PUYAT, GIL J. Congress and economic planning. M38 pp. 62-75.

3234 VALDEPENAS, VICENTE B. Should
the government buy into Filoil?
PS 19 (1971) 604-615.

3235 VIRATA, LEONIDES S. Private
enterprise and economic planning.
M38 pp. 123-131.

ECONOMIC POLICY - SINGAPORE

3236 LEE SOO ANN. Role of the government in the economy. Y52 pp. 81-
100.

3237 NG KIAT CHONG. Evaluation of the
policy of tariff protection on
wire rods in Singapore. MER 17
pt. 1 (1972) 78-98.

ECONOMIC POLICY - THAILAND

3238 AYAL, ELIEZER B. Thailand's six
year national economic development
plan. AS 1 (Jan. 1962) 33-42.

3239 HARING, JOSEPH E. Financial policy in postwar Thailand, external
equilibrium and domestic development, by Joseph E. Haring and
Larry E. Westphal. AS 8 (1968)
364-377.

3240 SILCOCK, T. H. Promotion of industry and the planning process.
S49 pp. 258-288.

ECONOMIC POLICY - VIETNAM

3241 VU QUOC THUC. National planning
in Vietnam. AS 1 (Sept. 1961) 3-
9.

EDUCATION *See also* LITERACY, STUDENTS

3242 BEGHIN, PAUL. Asian education
drama, an appraisal of Gunnar
Myrdal's views on education in
South Asia. SLURJ 3 (1972) 359-
372.

3243 CLERCK, MARCEL DE. L'education
des adultes en vue du developpement rural. RSA (1963) 1-50.

3244 DART, FRANCIS E. Science education in developing countries. J37
pp. 180-197.

3245 HART, DONN V. Southeast Asia and
education: a bibliographical introduction. SJ 10 (1963) 240-271.

3246 LARKIN, LEO H. Instructional
television in Southeast Asia. PS
14 (1966) 460-470.

3247 LE THANH KHOI. Education et developpement in Asie orientale.
D44 pp. 165-172.

3248 ORATA, PEDRO T. Are literacy
campaigns becoming obsolete? E78
pp. 584-589.

3249 ROBINSON, KENNETH. Revolution in
education. S89 pp. 321-333.

3250 SHUKLA, S. Some problems of educational development in India and
Southeast Asia. S32 pp. 54-60.

3251 SINCO, VICENTE G. Rizal and education. DR 9 (1961) 297-310.

Education

3252 SUNDRUM, R. M. Manpower and educational development in East and Southeast Asia, a summary of conference proceedings. MER 16 pt. 2 (1971) 78-90.

3253 Third international conference on educational research in Asia and the southern Pacific, 1968. SLQ 6 (1968) 496-509.

3254 TJONG TIAT LIEM. Education and development in Southeast Asia. SJ 17 (1970) 420-443.

EDUCATION - BURMA

3255 BA, VIVIAN. Beginnings of western education in Burma, the Catholic effort. JBRS 47 (1964) 287-323.

3256 CUNG GIU NGUYEN. Education in Burma. AC 3 (Jan. 1961) 97-103.

3257 GUYOT, JAMES F. The clerk mentality in Burmese education. T45 pp. 212-227.

3258 KAUNG. The beginnings of Christian missionary education in Burma, 1600-1824. B92 pp. 117-133.

3259 KAUNG. 1824-53 Roman Catholic and American Baptist mission schools. B92 pp. 135-147.

3260 KAUNG. Survey of the history of education in Burma before the British conquest and after. JBRS 46 (Dec. 1963) 5-124.

EDUCATION - INDONESIA

3261 CASTLES, LANCE. Notes on the Islamic school at Gontor. IND 1 (1966) 30-45.

3262 DREWES, G. W. J. Study of Arabic grammar in Indonesia. P15 pp. 61-70.

3263 HADJAR DEWANTARA, KI. Some aspects of national education and the Taman Siswa Institute of Jogjakarta. IND 4 (1967) 150-168.

3264 KARTINI, RADEN AJENG. Educate the Javanese. IND 17 (1974) 83-98.

3265 LANDHEER, B. Education in the Netherlands Indies, a symposium. H57 pp. 474-5.

3266 McVEY, RUTH T. Taman Siswa and the Indonesian national awakening. IND 4 (1967) 128-149.

3267 MULWANTO, F. X. Educational system in Indonesia, the Pantjasila national education. UN 39 (1966) 56-65.

3268 SURYADINATA, LEO. Indonesian Chinese education, past and present. IND 14 (1972) 49-71.

3269 THOMAS, R. MURRAY. Educational remnants of military occupation, the Japanese in Indonesia. AS 6 (1966) 630-642.

3270 THOMAS, R. MURRAY. Effects of Indonesian population growth on educational development, 1940-1968. AS 9 (1969) 498-514.

3271 THOMAS, R. MURRAY. Indonesian science education and national development. J37 pp. 198-221.

3272 WAART, A. DE. Medical education in the Netherlands Indies. H57 pp. 359-362.

EDUCATION - MALAYSIA

3273 BEER, BRIGITTE DE. L'Institut de Technologie MARA de Kuala Lumpur. AR 1 (1970) 45-50.

3274 CASTILLO, GELIA T. Education for agriculture. MER 16 pt. 2 (1971) 172-193.

3275 COLLETTA, N. J. Education of Chinese workers' children on Malaysia's plantation frontier, myths and realities, by N. J. Colletta and Wong Ah Sung. AS 14 (1974) 827-844.

3276 COMBER, LEON. Chinese education, perennial Malayan problem. AS 1 (Oct. 1961) 30-35.

3277 DHAT, KHARAK SINGH. Education and problems of Malaysian nationhood. UN 39 (1966) 49-55.

3278 FRANKE, WOLFGANG. Some problems of Chinese schools and education in Southeast Asia, in particular Malaysia and Singapore. RSA (1968) 115-121.

3279 HAMDAN BIN SHEIKH TAHIR, HAJI. Development of the Malay language as a medium of instruction in schools. A43 pp. 146-160.

3280 LOH FOOK-SENG, PHILIP. Review of the educational developments in the Federated Malay States to 1939. JSAS 5 (1974) 225-238.

3281 NASH, MANNING. Ethnicity, centrality and education in Pasir Mas. K33 pp. 243-258.

3282 SEYMOUR, J. M. Objectives of primary education in Sarawak, from a rural perspective. SMJ 19 (1971) 167-183.

3283 STEVENSON, REX. Selangor Raja School. JMBRAS 41 pt. 1 (1968) 183-192.

3284 TILMAN, ROBERT O. Education and political development in Malaysia. T45 pp. 228-242.

3285 WARREN, GEORGE LEWIS. Heights and weights of school children in the Kapit District, Sarawak, by George Lewis Warren, Carolyn Kocher Warren and Norvin Dean Schuman. SMJ 12 (1965) 351-359.

EDUCATION - PHILIPPINES

3286 APPLETON, FREDERIC G. Humaneness in Philippine schools. SJ 20 (1973) 40-48.

3287 ARANETA, FRANCISCO. Some problems of Philippine education. PS 9 (1961) 205-219.

3288 ARCILLA, JOSE S. Philippine education, some observations from history. PS 20 (1972) 273-286.

3289 ARQUIZA, LINO Q. Use of a sociometric device in guidance and counseling, by Lino Q. and Ensebia C. Arquiza. SJ 7 (1960) 52-71.

3290 BANGAOET, DAMASO M. Republic Act 4670, its effects on teachers and the teaching profession. SLURJ 1 (1970) 621-630.

3291 BENNETT, D. C. Aspects of literacy and educational attainment in the Philippines. PS 17 (1969) 597-604.

3292 BERAN, JANICE ANN. Growth and development of physical education for women in the Philippines. SJ 15 (1968) 427-438.

Education - Philippines

3293 BERNARDINO, VITALIANO. Philippine community school. E78 pp. 555-557.

3294 BERNAS, JOAQUIN G. Dr. Salcedo and the liberty of education. PS 9 (1961) 520-525.

3295 BUEN, FLORENCIO. A resource approach to educational planning in the Philippines, a proposal. SLURJ 3 (1972) 411-426.

3296 BUEN, FLORENCIO. A year-round school program for the Baguio city high school. SLURJ 5 (1974) 188-198.

3297 C.E.A.P. convention of 1960. PS 8 (1960) 689-716.

3298 CAPIZ, PASCUAL. Politics and the English language in the Philippines. DR 8 (1960) 307-319.

3299 CLIFFORD, MARY DORITA. Religion and the public schools in the Philippines, 1899-1906. A58 pp. 301-324.

3300 CONSTANTINO, RENATO. Mis-education of the Filipino. JCA 1 pt. 1 (1970) 20-36.

3301 CORPUZ, ONOFRE D. Education and socio-economic change in the Philippines, 1870-1960's. PSSHR 32 (1967) 193-268.

3302 CORPUZ, ONOFRE D. Philippine education on trial. SJ 19 (1972) 123-129.

3303 ESTOLLOSO, DELFIN D. Moral leadership in education. SJ 9 (1962) 133-142.

3304 ESTOLLOSO, PRISCILLA SOLIS. Teaching is a moral responsibility. SJ 7 (1960) 18-22.

3305 FIRMALINO, TITO C. District supervisor's dilemma. G93 pp. 549-587.

3306 FLEEGE, URBAN H. First impressions of the community schools. E78 pp. 577-581.

3307 FLEEGE, URBAN H. Some thoughts on the present needs of the community schools. E78 pp. 581-584.

3308 FLORES, PEDRO V. Accountability and the classroom teacher. SJ 20 (1973) 1-14.

3309 FLORES, PEDRO V. Student achievement as index of teaching effectiveness. SJ 20 (1973) 15-39.

3310 FOX, HENRY FREDERICK. Primary education in the Philippines, 1565-1863. PS 13 (1965) 207-231.

3311 FOX, HENRY FREDERICK. Some notes on education in Cebu Province, 1820-1898, by Frederick Fox and Juan Mercader. PS 9 (1961) 20-46.

3312 GALANG, RICARDO C. Textbook publishing in the Philippines. UN 34 (Dec. 1961) 13-39.

3313 GREGORIO, HERMAN C. Recent trend in school administration and supervision. SJ 8 (1961) 198-204.

3314 HILA, ANTONIO C. Laurelian education and the task of nation building. DR 17 (1969) 377-382.

3315 JUNTADO, LORETO. Special problems in the teaching of English to Filipino students. SJ 14 (1967) 315-324.

3316 KEANE, JOHN T. Education, strengths and weaknesses. P47 pp. 75-104.

3317 LAZARO, GUILLERMO R. Behavioral sciences and Philippine education. GEJ 14 (1967) 60-74.

3318 LENERT, THOMAS. Critical appraisal of the Philippine philosophy of education. UN 36 (1963) 25-69.

3319 LENERT, THOMAS. Critical appraisal of the Philippine philosophy of education. UN 36 (1963) 228-279.

3320 LLAMZON, TEODORO A. On the medium of instruction, English or Piliino. PS 18 (1970) 683-694.

3321 LORENZO, ROMAN F. Laguna approach to community education. E78 pp. 561-568.

3322 LYNCH, FRANK. Philippine influentials on education. SJ 20 (1973) 271-282.

3323 McCARTHY, MAUREEN. Provincial receptivity to guidance and counseling. PS 18 (1970) 769-773.

3324 McHALE, THOMAS R. The Philippines in transition. JAS 20 (1960-1) 331-341.

3325 MAJUL, CESAR ADIB. Education during the reform movement and the Philippine revolution. DR 15 (1967) 185-257.

3326 MANUEL, JUAN L. Philippine educational problems. SJ 9 (1962) 52-64.

3327 MARTIN, DALMACIO. Language, education and literacy. SJ 15 (1968) 414-426.

3328 MEANY, JAMES J. Sinco report. PS 10 (1962) 32-44.

3329 MUNN, MERTON D. Some thoughts concerning education. SJ 12 (1965) 412-426.

3330 OCAMPO, GALO B. Fundamental direction in the philosophy and teaching of art in our educational system. UN 35 (1962) 103-112.

3331 ORIAN, ANUNCIACION D. Should Pilipino supplant English as the medium of instruction in Philippine schools? SLURJ 1 (1970) 444-472.

3332 PAL, AGATON P. Extension process. SJ 7 (1960) 285-297.

3333 PAL, AGATON P. Extension processes. E78 pp. 505-518.

3334 PERDICES, MA. CONSUELO. On nutrition. UN 33 (1960) 545-563.

3335 PRATT, WILLIAM F. Illustrative projections of school enrollment. C47 pp. 389-422.

3336 PRATT, WILLIAM F. Summary of background paper on population projects. C47 pp. 104-111. Comment: Discussion. C47 pp. 116-127.

3337 PRUDENTE, NEMESIO. Education for nationalism. DR 17 (1969) 59-67.

3338 RAMOS, NORBERTO DE. Administrative planning, lay teacher cooperation. UN 33 (1960) 373-379.

3339 RAMOS, NORBERTO DE. Admissions and promotions. UN 33 (1960) 595-609.

3340 RECTO-FAMA, CLEOPATRA. Philippine community schools. UN 40 (1967) 464-493.

Education - Philippines

3341 Relation of schooling to size of family. C47 pp. 502-507.

3342 Religious instruction in public schools: HB 13043, or Cuenco Bill. PSSHR 30 (1965) 365-426.

3343 REYES, RAMON C. Report on the workshop on education. PS 19 (1971) 111-115.
Comment: ARQUIZA, LINO Q. Comments. PS 19 (1971) 115-117.
Comment: PIA, JUAN. Comments. PS 19 (1971) 117-119.

3344 ROCES, ALEJANDRO R. Mabini's thoughts on education. GEJ 2 (1961) 1-6.

3345 ROSARIO, FLORANGEL Z. Instruction by television in secondary schools. PS 12 (1964) 723-726.

3346 Selected data on Philippine schools, 1964-65. SLQ 6 (1968) 241-257.

3347 SIBAYAN, BONIFACIO P. Language policy, language engineering and literacy, the Philippines. S22 pp. 1038-1062.

3348 SIEGA, GORGONIO D. Philippine education, prospect and retrospect. SJ 20 (1973) 114-128.

3349 SINCO, VICENTE G. Education and national self-realization. DR 8 (1960) 5-16.

3350 SISON, BIENVENIDO. Bridging the gap between the standards of the curriculum and the level of instruction to students. UN 34 (Dec. 1961) 77-85.

3351 STAPLETON, ARCHIE C. Modern educational concepts and traditional Philippine culture. SLQ 5 (1967) 141-152.

3352 TORRES, FELIPE T. Vocational/ technical education and the changing Philippine society, a value approach. SLURJ 4 (1973) 227-239.

3353 TUPAS, ISABELO. Rural development and the Philippine community school. E78 pp. 558-561.

3354 YABES, LEOPOLDO Y. Language problem and the future of English in Philippine education. GEJ 17 (1969) 131-147.

EDUCATION - PHILIPPINES - MINORITY EDUCATION

3355 CABRERA, AGUSTIN A. Badjaus, cultural identity and education. UN 42 (1969) 107-142.

3356 DESMET, CARLOS. Schools of Tagudin. PS 12 (1964) 113-117.

3357 FRANCISCO, JUAN R. Intercultural encounter in a frontier area, the case of the public school teacher and an ethnic minority. GEJ 14 (1967) 16-33.

3358 SCOTT, WILLIAM HENRY. Boyhood in Sagada. SJ 10 (1963) 387-399.

3359 SCOTT, WILLIAM HENRY. Educational work with a cultural minority. B13 pp. 140-148.

3360 SCOTT, WILLIAM HENRY. Educational work with a cultural minority. SJ 11 (1964) 39-48.

3361 SORIANO, LICERIA B. Our Moro problem and the community school in Mindanao. E78 pp. 569-577.

EDUCATION - PHILIPPINES - PRIVATE
  SCHOOLS

3362   ARABIA, ARSENIO BRIONES. Educa-
       tion through private initiative
       in the Philippines. UN 39 (1966)
       127-136.

3363   CARBONELL, GUADALUPE A. Evalua-
       tion of the supervisory activi-
       ties of the Catholic elementary
       schools of the mountain provinces.
       SLURJ 4 (1973) 414-479.

3364   CARBONELL, GUADALUPE A. Evalua-
       tion of supervisory activities of
       the Catholic elementary schools
       of the mountain provinces. SLURJ
       4 (1973) 548-657.

3365   CORPUZ, ONOFRE D. Challenges
       ahead for private education. SJ
       13 (1966) 469-474.

3366   FLORES, PEDRO V. Relationship
       between goals of ambition and
       vocational preferences of students
       in the Silliman University high
       school. SJ 8 (1961) 107-117.

3367   LINSSEN, GERARD. Catholic sec-
       ondary education: objectives and
       aims and their realization in the
       Mt. Province. SJ 11 (1964) 35-38.

3368   MUNN, MERTON D. Association of
       Christian Schools and Colleges
       and accreditation in the Philip-
       pines. SJ 9 (1962) 24-31.

3369   Philippine private schools, 1963-
       1964. SLQ 3 (1965) 490-496.

3370   Statistics on Philippine private
       schools, 1962-63. SLQ 2 (1964)
       353-355.

3371   TRINIDAD, CARIDAD E. A study of
       the academic preparation and as-
       signment of teachers in the

Catholic secondary schools of
Baguio City and the mountain provinces for the school year, 1971-
1972. SLURJ 4 (1973) 240-304.

3372   YGNALAGA, EMILIANO C. Study of
       the status of Silliman University
       high school graduates. SJ 7
       (1960) 72-84.

3373   ZWAENEPOEL, PAUL P. Administrator
       teacher relations in the Philip-
       pine context. SLURJ 1 (1970) 409-
       443.

EDUCATION - SINGAPORE

3374   CLARK, DAVID H. Manpower planning
       in Singapore. MER 16 pt. 2 (1971)
       194-211.

3375   CLARK, DAVID H. Returns to
       schooling and training in Singa-
       pore, by David H. Clark and Pang
       Eng Fong. MER 15 pt. 2 (1970) 79-
       103.

3376   FRANKE, WOLFGANG. Some problems
       of Chinese schools and education
       in Southeast Asia, in particular
       Malaysia and Singapore. RSA
       (1968) 115-121.

3377   GWEE YEE HEAN. Education and the
       multiracial society. M49 pp. 208-
       215.

3378   HOUGH, G. G. Notes on the educa-
       tional policy of Sir Stamford
       Raffles. JMBRAS 42 pt. 1 (1969)
       155-160.

EDUCATION - THAILAND

3379   AYABE, TSUNEO. Dek Wat and Thai
       education: the case of Tambon Ban
       Khem. JSS 61 pt. 2 (1973) 39-52.

Education - Thailand

3380 SANAN INTRAPRASERT. Problems and education system in Thailand. UN 39 (1966) 88-97.

3381 SOEN, DAN. Education in the northern region of Thailand, an attempt at analysis, by Dan Soen and M. Tamir. AQ (1973) 313-328.

3382 TONGSOOK KATEROJNA. Boyhood and young manhood of a Thai teacher. DR 9 (1961) 265-292.

3383 WYATT, DAVID K. Almost forgotten, Ban Phraya Nana School. T33 pp. 1-8.

3384 WYATT, DAVID K. Education and the modernization of Thai society. C24 pp. 125-149.

3385 WYATT, DAVID K. Samuel McFarland and early educational moderniza- tion in Thailand, 1877-1895. F38 pp. 1-16.

EDUCATION - VIETNAM

3386 EATON, DAVID C. Education as an aspect of development, Vietnam. SA 1 (1971) 256-274.

3387 HILDRETH, ELON E. Challenge in education. L52 pp. 143-161.

3388 LE XUAN KHOA. Traditional human- ism and Vietnamese educational concepts. AC 2 (July 1960) 79-88.

3389 NGHIEM, DANG. National Institute of Administration. L52 pp. 162- 166.
      Comment: FOX, GUY H. Commentary. L52 pp. 166-172.

3390 PATT, JACK M. Backwardness of Vietnamese education. RSA (1970) 105-111.

3391 PIKE, EDGAR N. Problems of educa- tion in Vietnam. C58 pp. 75-97.

3392 PIKE, EDGAR N. Public and private education in Vietnam. AC 2 (Apr. 1960) 79-116.

3393 VU DUC BANG. Dong Kinh Free School movement, 1907-1908. V43 pp. 30-95.

EDUCATION, HIGHER

3394 L'Asie et l'enseignement univer- sitaire a Paris, annee 1966-67. FA 21 (1966) 247-254.

3395 COQUIA, JORGE R. First Asian con- ference on legal education. PS 11 (1963) 150-1.

3396 FISCHER, JOSEPH. Universities and the political process in Southeast Asia. PA 36 (1963) 3-15.

3397 FISHER, MARGUERITE J. Higher edu- cation of women and national de- velopment in Asia. AS 8 (1968) 263-269.

3398 HLA MYINT. Universities of South- east Asia and economic develop- ment. PA 35 (1962) 116-127.

3399 NARVASA, ANDRES R. Report on the ASAIHL convention in Kuala Lumpur and Singapore, January 29 to Feb- ruary 10, 1966. UN 39 (1966) 152- 157.

3400 NGUYEN KHAC HOACH. Higher educa- tion and national needs in South- east Asia. S32 pp. 30-33.

3401 PACHECO, ESTHER M. Association of Southeast Asian Institutions of Higher Learning (ASAIHL) seventh general conference. SLQ 7 (1969) 143-148.

3402 WU TEH YAO. Asian patterns of higher education. SJ 7 (1960) 3-12.

EDUCATION, HIGHER - BURMA

3403 NYI NYI. Development of university education in Burma. JBRS 47 (1964) 11-72.

3404 SILVERSTEIN, JOSEF. University students and politics in Burma, by Josef Silverstein and Julian Wohl. PA 37 (1964) 50-65.

EDUCATION, HIGHER - INDONESIA

3405 BONNEFF, MARCEL. GAMA, portrait d'une universite. AR 2 (1971) 29-53.

3406 DeIONGH, R. C. Some educational problems in Indonesia. JOSA 4 pt. 1 (1966) 35-49.

3407 LYMAN, PRINCETON N. Students and politics in Indonesia and Korea. PA 38 (1965) 282-293.

3408 RESINK, G. J. Rechtschoogeschool, jongereneed, "Stuw" en gestuwden. BIJ 130 (1974) 428-449.

EDUCATION, HIGHER - PHILIPPINES *See also* ATENEO DE MANILA UNIVERSITY; MANILA. UNIVERSITY OF SANTO TOMAS; QUEZON, PHILIPPINES. UNIVERSITY OF THE PHILIPPINES; ST. LOUIS UNIVERSITY, BAGUIO; SILLIMAN UNIVERSITY

3409 ABELLA, DOMINGO. State of higher education in the Philippines to 1863, a historical reappraisal. PHR 1 pt. 1 (1965) 1-46.

3410 ALBARRACIN, NARCISCO. Problems of Philippine universities. SLQ 1 (1963) 489-512.

3411 ALBARRACIN, NARCISCO. Status of graduate education in the Philippines. SLQ 1 (1963) 199-222.

3412 ANTONIO, ANTOLINA T. Teaching Spanish as a second language to Filipino college students. GEJ 6 (1963) 61-79.

3413 ARQUIZA, LINO Q. Problems in the measurement and evaluation of student teaching effectiveness. SJ 12 (1965) 436-445.

3414 ATABUG, ALEJANDRA C. Design for an interdisciplinary music and visual arts course in Philippine liberal arts colleges. PS 21 (1973) 268-292.

3415 BACALA, J. C. First nursing school in the Philippines. UN 33 (1960) 180-185.

3416 BALCRUZ, EMMANUEL MA. R. The accreditation movement in the Philippines as a catalyst for improving higher education. SLURJ 2 (1971) 242-266.

3417 BONIFACIO, ARMANDO F. Pilipino as medium of instruction at the university level. DR 17 (1969) 105-130.

3418 BOWLER, FRANCIS L. Problem of autonomy in higher education. SJ 13 (1966) 485-493.

3419 CALDERON, CICERO D. Case for Christian higher education in Asia. SJ 18 (1971) 72-74.

3420 CALDERON, CICERO D. Our stake in higher education. SJ 9 (1962) 299-304.

Education, higher - Philippines

3421 CARBONELL, GUADALUPE A. Functional relationships of Filipino cultural values and methods of college teaching. SLURJ 3 (1972) 26-39.

3422 CAVANNA, ANTONIO MA. El porvenir del espanol en nuestras universidades. GEJ 6 (1963) 9-14.

3423 DIAZ, JESUS. Goals of university education and means of achieving them. SJ 13 (1966) 475-484.

3424 Documents, the academic freedom issue of 1961, or, the ordeal of a man of academe. PSSHR 29 (1964) 151-276.

3425 DOHERTY, JOHN F. Graduate school consortium in faculty and other resources. UN 39 (1966) 250-255.

3426 DWYER, D. J. Case for more geography in Philippine universities, by D. J. Dwyer, T. W. Luna and D. C. Salita. PS 9 (1961) 601-610.

3427 ESTACIO, CEFERINA I. C. Harvard literacy project in Israel and its implication for the Philippines. UN 40 (1967) 563-578.

3428 FLORES, PEDRO V. Challenge of change in a Christian university. SJ 18 (1971) 63-71.

3429 GABILA, ANTONIO S. University in a Philippine setting. SJ 9 (1962) 208.

3430 GOODMAN, GRANT K. Philippine-Japanese professorial exchanges in the 1930's. JSAH 9 (1968) 229-240.

3431 ISIDRO, ANTONIO N. New frontier in educational objectives. SJ 9 (1962) 241-246.

3432 JAMIAS, CRISTINO. Presentation. PSSHR 28 (1963) 491-493.

3434 LAVA, JOSEFA C. There was one man: on the teaching of humanities. GEJ 4 (1962) 1-7.

3435 LOPEZ, SALVADOR P. Filipino university and the challenge of nation building. SJ 18 (1971) 337-342.

3436 LOPEZ, SALVADOR P. University as social critic and agent of change. DR 17 (1969) 97-104.

3437 LORENZO, ROMAN F. Public school system and the university. SJ 12 (1965) 427-435.

3438 MASLOG, CRISPIN. Communication and journalism education in the Philippines. SJ 18 (1971) 357-374.

3439 MENDOZA, GABINO A. Business curriculum and the faculty for the 1970's. PS 17 (1969) 436-456.

3440 MORALES, ALFREDO T. Excellence above democratic and cultural dualisms. SJ 9 (1962) 233-240.

3441 MUNN, MERTON D. The Association of Christian Schools and Colleges and accreditation in the Philippines. SJ 9 (1962) 24-31.

3442 NGALOB, JUAN. Reasons of undergraduate students for enrolling in summer classes. SLURJ 1 (1970) 677-693.

3443 OCAMPO, FELICISIMO. Academic freedom and freedom from subversion. DR 9 (1961) 37-50.

3444 ORDONEZ, ELMER A. Case for English studies. GEJ 17 (1969) 148-152.

3445 PATRON, JOSEFINA S. Mass communications teaching and training in the Philippines. SJ 20 (1973) 49-74.

3446 PERPINAN, JESUS E. Horizons in administration and finance. SJ 9 (1962) 247-254.

3447 POETHIG, RICHARD P. Occupational mobility among Philippine Protestant seminary graduates. SLQ 5 (1967) 117-140.

3448 PUENTEVELLA, RENATO L. Teaching of freshman English to the honors section. SJ 14 (1967) 287-297.

3449 QUIRKE, NEIL J. Problem of promoting inter-university cooperation. SJ 13 (1966) 494-498.

3450 RICO, GORGONIA S. College students perception of teacher effectiveness along five postulated dimensions. SLURJ 2 (1971) 363-438.

3451 ROMULO, CARLOS P. Closing remarks. PSSHR 28 (1963) 494-5.

3452 SANDERS, ALBERT J. What is the mission of a Christian university in the Philippines today? SJ 10 (1963) 127-134.

3453 SINCO, VICENTE G. Plan for concentrated guided study. GEJ 1 (1961) 3-29.

3454 SINCO, VICENTE G. Two statements on academic freedom. DR 9 (1961) 8-22.

3455 TAYKO, PERLA RIZALINA MATURAN. Survey of teacher education in the natural sciences in the Visayas. SJ 20 (1973) 75-90.

3456 TIEMPO, EDILBERTO K. Graduate school and the university. SJ 18 (1971) 56-62.

3457 VASQUEZ, NOEL D. Proposed practicum course, towards university participation in direct social development. PS 21 (1973) 450-454.

3458 VICENTE, VICTORIANO. El P. Alonso Sandin segun el libro de grados de la universidad. UN 39 (1966) 269-280.

3459 ZWAENEPOEL, PAUL P. Summary, evaluation and recommendations (tertiary education in the Philippines, a systems analysis, an area study as a contribution to comparative education). SLURJ 5 (1974) 518-604.

3460 ZWAENEPOEL, PAUL P. Universities in the Philippines at the dawn of the 70's. SLURJ 2 (1971) 64-74.

EDUCATION, HIGHER - SINGAPORE *See also* NANYANG UNIVERSITY; SINGAPORE. UNIVERSITY

3461 LEE, Y. K. Medical education in the Straits, 1876-1971. JMBRAS 46 pt. 1 (1973) 101-122.

3462 LIM CHONG YAH. Teaching and research in the social sciences in Singapore. RSAS 1 pt. 1 (1971) 30-33.

3463 WILSON, H. E. Abortive plan for an Anglo Chinese college in Singapore. JMBRAS 45 pt. 2 (1972) 97-109.

ELECTIONS - MALAYSIA - 1963

3481   GLICK, HENRY ROBERT. The Chinese community in Sabah and the 1963 election. AS 5 (1965) 144-151.

3482   TILMAN, ROBERT O. Elections in Sarawak. AS 3 (1963) 507-518.

ELECTIONS - MALAYSIA - 1967

3483   MILNE, R. S. Patterns and peculiarities of voting in Sabah, 1967, by R. S. Milne and K. J. Ratnam. AS 9 (1969) 373-381.

ELECTIONS - MALAYSIA - 1969

3484   DRUMMOND, STUART. Malaysian elections of 1969, an analysis of the campaign and the results, by Stuart Drummond and David Hawkins. AS 10 (1970) 320-335.

3485   RATNAM, K. J. The 1969 parliamentary election in west Malaysia, by K. J. Ratnam and R. S. Milne. PA 43 (1970) 203-226.

3486   RUDNER, MARTIN. Malaysian general election of 1969, a political analysis. MAS 4 (1970) 1-21.

3487   SNIDER, NANCY L. Race, leitmotiv of the Malayan election drama. AS 10 (1970) 1070-1080.

ELECTIONS - MALAYSIA - 1970

3488   MILNE, R. S. The Sarawak elections of 1970, an analysis of the vote, by R. S. Milne and K. J. Ratnam. JSAS 3 (1972) 111-122.

ELECTIONS - MALAYSIA - 1973 **

3489   LIM KIT SIANG. Repression in Malaysia. JCA 4 (1974) 137.

ELECTIONS - PHILIPPINES

3490   ABUEVA, JOSE V. The Philippines, political tradition and change. AS 10 (1970) 56-64.

3491   KIUNISALA, E. R. Illegal spending and partisanship in elections. A28 pp. 75-79.

3492   LIM, PILAR HIDALGO. Women's suffrage since 1937. UN 40 (1967) 414-422.

3493   PAGUIO, BERNABE B. Vote buying. A28 pp. 80-1.

3494   TUTAY, FILEMON V. Violence and terrorism in elections. A28 pp. 81-84.

3495   VILLANUEVA, A. B. Philippine Congress and the barrio electoral process. JSAS 2 (1971) 115-125.

ELECTIONS - PHILIPPINES - 1953

3496   MARQUETTE, JESSE F. Charismatic authority and Philippine political behavior, the election of 1953. AST 10 (1972) 50-63.

ELECTIONS - PHILIPPINES - 1959

3497   ABUEVA, JOSE V. Citizens League and the 1959 local elections. G93 pp. 505-547.

Elections - Philippines - 1961

ELECTIONS - PHILIPPINES - 1961

3498 CONCEPCION, RODOLFO F. Operation quick count. PS 10 (1962) 145-150.

3499 MEADOWS, MARTIN. Philippine political parties and the 1961 election. PA 35 (1962) 261-274.

3500 SOLIVEN, MAXIMO V. Elections, 1961. PS 10 (1962) 3-31.

3501 STARNER, FRANCES L. Philippine economic development and the two party system. AS 2 (July 1962) 17-23.

3502 VILLANUEVA, BUENAVENTURA M. Party struggle and the peoples mandate, by Buenaventura M. Villanueva and Gelia T. Castillo. A28 pp. 119-128.

3503 WURFEL, DAVID. Philippine elections, support for democracy. AS 2 (May 1962) 25-37.

ELECTIONS - PHILIPPINES - 1964

3504 ABLETEZ, JOSE P. Election of barrio capitanes. A28 pp. 142-145.

ELECTIONS - PHILIPPINES - 1965

3505 MEADOWS, MARTIN. Implications of the 1965 Philippine election, the view from America. AST 4 (1966) 381-391.

3506 Philippine presidential election. FA 20 (1965) 87-96.

ELECTIONS - SINGAPORE

3507 YEO KIM WAH. Study of two early elections in Singapore. JMBRAS 45 pt. 1 (1972) 57-80.

ELECTIONS - SINGAPORE - 1972

3508 The coming general election in Singapore, will it be the last one? JCA 2 (1972) 270-273.

ELECTIONS - THAILAND - 1969

3509 NEHER, CLARK D. Constitutionalism and elections in Thailand. PA 43 (1970) 240-257.

3510 NEHER, CLARK D. Thailand, the politics of continuity. AS 10 (1970) 161-167.

ELECTIONS - VIETNAM

3511 SILVERMAN, JERRY MARK. Political presence and electoral support in South Vietnam. AS 14 (1974) 397-417.

3512 SILVERMAN, JERRY MARK. South Vietnam, the symbolic nature of election campaign appeals. JSAS 3 (1972) 44-62.

ELECTIONS - VIETNAM - 1959

3513 NGUYEN TUYET MAI. Electioneering Vietnamese style. AS 2 (Nov. 1962) 11-18.

ELECTIONS - VIETNAM - 1967

3514 JOINER, CHARLES A. South Vietnam, political, military and constitutional arenas in nation building. AS 8 (1968) 58-71.

3515 TAILLEFER, JEAN. Les elections au
      sud-Vietnam. FA 21 (1966) 447-
      457.

ELECTIONS - VIETNAM - 1971

3516 KIRK, DONALD. The Thieu presi-
      dential campaign, background and
      consequences of the single-
      candidacy phenomenon. AS 12
      (1972) 609-624.

ELECTRICITY - BURMA

3517 MAUNG MAUNG KHA. Survey of some
      energy sources for Burma. JBRS
      50 (1967) 1-9.

ELEPHANTS - BURMA

3518 MYA MAUNG. Elephant catching co-
      operative society of Burma, a
      case study on the effect of
      planned socio-economic change.
      AS 6 (1966) 327-337.

ELEPHANTS - THAILAND

3519 GILES, FRANCIS H. Adversaria of
      elephant hunting (together with an
      account of all the rites, obser-
      vances and acts of worship to be
      performed in connection therewith,
      as well as notes on vocabularies
      of spirit language, fake or taboo
      language and elephant command
      words). S44.2 pp. 1-36.

ELITES *See also* INTELLECTUALS

3520 SIMBULAN, DANTE C. On models and
      reality, some notes on the ap-
      proaches to the study of elites

in developing societies. AST 6
(1968) 421-430.

3521 SOLIDUM, ESTRELLA D. An explana-
      tion of the methodology used in a
      dissertation entitled "The nature
      of cooperation among ASEAN states
      as perceived through elite atti-
      tudes - a factor for regionalism."
      AST 10 (1972) 1-5.

ELITES - INDONESIA

3522 Current data on the Indonesian
      military elite. IND 18 (1974)
      153-167.

3523 SLUIMERS, L. Nieuwe orde op Java,
      de Japanse bezettingspolitiek en
      de Indonesische elites, 1942-1943.
      BIJ 124 (1968) 336-367.

3524 SUTHERLAND, HEATHER. Notes on
      Java's regent families. IND 16
      (1973) 112-147.

3525 SUTHERLAND, HEATHER. Notes on
      Java's regent families, pt. II.
      IND 17 (1974) 1-42.

3526 WEINSTEIN, FRANKLIN B. Indonesian
      elite's view of the world and the
      foreign policy of development.
      IND 12 (1971) 97-131.

ELITES - LAOS

3527 HALPERN, JOEL M. Observations on
      the social structure of the Lao
      elite. AS 1 (July 1961) 25-32.

ELITES - PHILIPPINES

3528 ABUEVA, JOSE V. The elite and the
      people. A28 pp. 23-28.

English language

East and Southeast Asia, University of Singapore, May 22-28, 1971. MER 16 pt. 2 (1971) 6-24.

3547 OSHIMA, HARRY T. Labor absorption in East and Southeast Asia, a summary with interpretation of postwar experience. MER 16 pt. 2 (1971) 55-77.

EMPLOYMENT - INDONESIA

3548 HAWKINS, EVERETT D. Job inflation in Indonesia. AS 6 (1966) 264-275.

EMPLOYMENT - MALAYSIA

3549 JACKSON, R. N. Changing patterns of employment in Malayan tin mining. JSAH 4 (Sept. 1963) 105-116.

3550 JONES, GAVIN W. Employment characteristics of small towns in Malaya. MER 10 pt. 1 (1965) 44-72.

3551 PURCAL, J. Labour utilization among men in a padi village in Province Wellesley. MER 10 pt. 2 (1965) 49-60.

EMPLOYMENT - PHILIPPINES

3552 New rice technology and labor absorption in Philippine agriculture. MER 16 pt. 2 (1971) 117-158.

EMPLOYMENT - SINGAPORE

3553 CLARK, D. H. Manpower planning in Singapore. MER 16 pt. 2 (1971) 194-211.

3554 OSHIMA, HARRY T. Growth and unemployment in Singapore. MER 12 pt. 2 (1967) 32-58.

ENDEH

3555 NEEDHAM, RODNEY. Endeh, terminology, alliance and analysis. BIJ 124 (1968) 305-335.

3556 NEEDHAM, RODNEY. Endeh II, test and confirmation. BIJ 126 (1970) 246-258.

ENGLISH LANGUAGE

3557 BERGER, KENNETH W. Common articulatory errors of English-speaking Filipinos. SJ 16 (1969) 424-426.

3558 BOWEN, J. DONALD. Freshman English in college. UN 40 (1967) 622-630.

3559 CAPIZ, PASCUAL. Politics and the English language in the Philippines. DR 8 (1960) 307-319.

3560 DADUFALZA, CONCEPCION D. English in the general education program. GEJ 1 (1961) 50-55.

3561 HIDALGO, CESAR A. Linguistics: its development and its contribution to English teaching. GEJ 17 (1969) 3-24.

3562 JUNTADO, LORETO. Special problems in the teaching of English to Filipino students. SJ 14 (1967) 315-324.

3563 New syllabus of English 5. GEJ 17 (1969) 51-58.

3564 ORDONEZ, ELMER A. Case for English studies. GEJ 17 (1969) 148-152.

English language

3565 ORDONEZ, ELMER A. Future of English in the university. GEJ 17 (1969) 47-50.

3566 PASCUAL, INEZ VILLA-REAL. Problems of a language teacher. UN 40 (1967) 709-715.

3567 PATERNO, ADELAIDA. Testing pronunciation of English as a foreign language, twenty questions. UN 40 (1967) 681-695.

3568 PUENTEVELLA, RENATO L. Teaching of freshman English to the honors section. SJ 14 (1967) 287-297.

3569 RAMOS, MAXIMO. Can English last much longer here? UN 40 (1967) 671-680.

3570 SASO, MICHAEL R. Teaching English in cultural context. PS 10 (1962) 475-477.

3571 TAN, ARSENIA B. Contrastive analysis of the English and Tagalog consonant systems, by Arsenia B. Tan and Antonia F. Villanueva. UN 40 (1967) 631-639.

3572 WILSON, ROBERT D. Contrastive analysis of segments of transformational grammars of English and Tagalog. UN 40 (1967) 640-646.

3573 YABES, LEOPOLDO Y. Language problem and the future of English in Philippine education. GEJ 17 (1969) 131-147.

3574 YABES, LEOPOLDO Y. Teaching of English in college and universities. DR 12 (1964) 284-296.

EPISTOLA, NIEVES BENITO

3575 EPISTOLA, NIEVES BENITO. Three poems. DR 18 (1970) 54-61.

ESPINO, FEDERICO LICSI

3576 ESPINO, FEDERICO LICSI. Ritual for saints and lovers. DR 18 (1970) 48-53.

ESSER, S. J.

3577 Mededelingen uit de verslagen van Dr. S. J. Esser, Taalambtenaar voor Celebes, 1928-1944. BIJ 119 (1963) 329-370.

EURASIANS - INDONESIA

3578 VAN DER VEUR, PAUL W. Cultural aspects of the Eurasian community in Indonesian colonial society. IND 6 (1968) 38-53.

3579 VAN DER VEUR, PAUL W. Eurasian dilemma in Indonesia. JAS 20 (1960-1) 45-60.

3580 VAN DER VEUR, PAUL W. Eurasians of Indonesia, a problem and challenge in colonial history. JSAH 9 (1968) 191-207.

3581 VAN DER VEUR, PAUL W. Race and color in colonial society, biographical sketches by a Eurasian woman concerning pre-World War II Indonesia, translated and edited by Paul W. van der Veur. IND 8 (1969) 69-79.

EURASIANS - MALAYSIA

3582 CHAN KOK ENG. Population growth and migration of the Eurasians in

Malacca since 1871. JTG 35 (1972)
17-25.

EVANS, IVOR HUGH NORMAN

3583 TWEEDIE, M. W. F. Ivor Hugh Norman Evans. JMBRAS 33 pt. 1 (1960)
109-110.

FALL, BERNARD B.

3584 DEVILLERS, PHILIPPE. Bernard
Fall. FA 21 (1966) 147-160.

FAMILY

3585 MADGE, CHARLES. Relevance of
family patterns in the process of
modernization in East Asia. S58
pp. 161-195.

FAMILY - BURMA

3586 THEODORSON, GEORGE A. Attitudes
of Burmese men and women to male
dominance in the family. JBRS 51
(1968) 17-21.

FAMILY - INDONESIA

3587 KOENTJARANINGRAT. Family and religion in Indonesia. EACS 13
(1974) 59-68.
Comment: TEIGO, YOSHIDA. Comments. EACS 13 (1974) 69-71.

FAMILY - INDONESIA - BALI

3588 BELO, JANE. A study of a Balinese
family. B43 pp. 350-370.

3589 SWELLENGREBEL, J. L. Nonconformity in the Balinese family. B19
pp. 199-212.

3590 SWELLENGREBEL, J. L. Religious
practices of the family and the
individual. B18 pp. 54-67.

FAMILY - MALAYSIA

3591 BUXBAUM, DAVID C. Chinese family
law in a common law setting. A
note on the institutional environment and the substantive family
law of the Chinese in Singapore
and Malaysia. C39 pp. 146-177.

3592 METCALF, PETER. Berawan adoption
practices. SMJ 22 (1974) 275-286.

3593 MOHAMED DIN BIN ALI. Malay customary law and the family. C39
pp. 181-201.

3594 MOKHZANI, B. A. R. The Malay
family and religion. EACS 13
(1974) 37-48.
Comment: SHIN, ANZAI. Comments.
EACS 13 (1974) 49-50.

FAMILY - PHILIPPINES

3595 ALMANZOR, ANGELINA. Values and
problems of the Filipino family.
SLQ 6 (1968) 430-432.

3596 CARROLL, JOHN J. The family in a
time of change. P47 pp. 10-16.

3597 FLORES, BIENVENIDO V. Analysis of
Philippine family studies, 1952-
1971: a preliminary report of an
effort at inventorization and
evaluation of family theory and
research in the Philippines.
SLURJ 5 (1974) 45-97.

3598 FLORES, BIENVENIDO V. Analysis of
Philippine family studies, 1952-
1971: a preliminary report of an
effort at inventorization and
evaluation of family theory and

Family - Philippines

research in the Philippines.
SLURJ 5 (1974) 199-240.

3599 FLORES, BIENVENIDO V. Analysis of
Philippine family studies, 1952-
1971: a preliminary report of an
effort at inventorization and
evaluation of family theory and
research in the Philippines.
SLURJ 5 (1974) 345-391.

3600 HOLLNSTEINER, MARY R. The Filipino family confronts the modern
world. G73 pp. 19-44.

3601 LYNCH, FRANK. The BRAC 1967
Filipino family survey, by Frank
Lynch and Perla Q. Makil. B13
pp. 206-221.

3602 LYNCH, FRANK. The BRAC 1967
Filipino family survey, by Frank
Lynch and Perla Q. Makil. G73
pp. 53-71.

3603 LYNCH, FRANK. The BRAC 1967
Filipino family survey, by Frank
Lynch and Perla Q. Makil. SLQ 6
(1968) 293-330.

3604 LYNCH, FRANK. Summary and conclusions of the eleventh Baguio
Religious Acculturation Conference. SLQ 6 (1968) 437-442.

3605 POETHIG, RICHARD P. Philippine
urban family. B13 pp. 222-234.

3606 POETHIG, RICHARD P. Philippine
urban family. SLQ 6 (1968) 375-
390.

3607 RAMIREZ, MINA. Phenomenology of
the Filipino family. SLQ 6 (1968)
339-354.

3608 REYES, VIRGILIO A. Lack of dialogue within the Filipino family.
GEJ 25 (1973-4) 127-135.

3609 SANTOS-CUYUGAN, RUBEN. Socio-
cultural change and the Filipino
family. E78 pp. 363-374.

3610 SENDEN, FRANCIS. Some remarks of
a phenomenologist on the BRAC 1967
Filipino family survey. SLQ 6
(1968) 331-338.

FAMILY - SINGAPORE

3611 BUXBAUM, DAVID. Chinese family
law in a common law setting. A
note on the institutional environment and the substantive family
law of the Chinese in Singapore
and Malaysia. C39 pp. 146-177.

3612 FREEDMAN, MAURICE. Chinese family
law in Singapore, the rout of
custom. A62 pp. 49-72.

FAMILY - THAILAND

3613 ADUL WICHIENCHAROEN. Some main
features of modernization of ancient family law in Thailand, by
Adul Wichiencharoen and Luang
Chamroon Netisastra. C39 pp. 89-
106.

3614 PRASERT YAMKLINFUNG. Family, religion and socio-economic change
in Thailand. EACS 13 (1974) 20-31.

FAMILY - VIETNAM

3615 MUCKA, JAN. Kinship system and
terminology in Vietnam. AAS 7
(1971) 33-39.

3616 NGUYEN KHAC-KHAM. Some similari-
ties and dissimilarities between
Japanese and Vietnamese households.
EACS 13 (1974) 16-18.

Family histories *See* GENEALOGY

Family planning *See* BIRTH CONTROL

FARREN, J. W.

3617 TARLING, NICHOLAS. Consul Farren
      and the Philippines. JMBRAS 38
      pt. 2 (1965) 258-273.

FAUNA *See also* BATS, BIRDS, DOGS,
   ELEPHANTS, FISHES, ORANGUTANS, SNAKES,
   TURTLES

3618 BARLOW, H. S. John Waterstradt,
      1869-1944. JMBRAS 42 pt. 2 (1969)
      115-129.

3619 HARRISSON, TOM. Primate special
      symposium no. 2 of the 1966
      Pacific Science Congress. AP 10
      (1967) 19-21.

3620 JOHNSON, D. S. Land crabs.
      JMBRAS 38 pt. 2 (1965) 43-66.

3621 THAI VAN KIEM. Le culte de la
      baleine. SEIB 47 (1972) 309-329.

FAUNA - BRUNEI

3622 BIRKENMEIER, ERIKA. Notes on the
      order mantodea, with reference to
      Brunei. BMJ 1 (1969) 225-233.

3623 BIRKENMEIER, ERIKA. Observations
      on Amantis Reticulata (Haan) in
      Brunei (Dictyoptera-Mantidae).
      BMJ 2 pt. 3 (1971) 147-159.

3624 HO KIAM FUI. Distribution of re-
      cent Benthonic Foraminifera in
      the inner Brunei Bay. BMJ 2 pt.
      3 (1971) 124-137.

3625 MAHMOOD, D. N. P. Scanning elec-
      tron microscope studies of se-
      lected foraminifera from the seria
      formation, Penanjong, Brunei.
      BMJ 3 pt. 2 (1974) 271-284.

FAUNA - BURMA

3626 GATES, G. E. Earthworms of Burma.
      B91 pp. 51-58.

3627 THA MYINT. Some of the animals of
      Maungmagan and adjoining shores.
      JBRS 44 (1961) 197-224.

FAUNA - INDONESIA

3628 DAMMERMAN, K. W. Tjiboas Biologi-
      cal Station and Forest Reserve,
      the fauna of Tjiboas. H57 pp.
      404-409.

3629 DOTY, MAXWELL S. Development of
      marine resources in Indonesia, by
      Maxwell S. Doty and Aprilany
      Soegiarto. J37 pp. 70-89.

3630 LIEFTINCK, M. A. Development of
      the zoological museum at Buiten-
      zorg. H57 pp. 226-231.

3631 MAYR, ERNST. Wallace's line in
      the light of recent zoogeographic
      studies. H57 pp. 241-250.

3632 WENT, F. W. Tjiboas Biological
      Station and Forest Reserve, a
      naturalists paradise. H57 p. 403.

3633 WESTERMANN, J. H. Wild life con-
      servation in the Netherlands em-
      pire, its national and interna-
      tional aspects. H57 pp. 417-424.

Fauna - Malaysia

FAUNA - MALAYSIA

3634 HARRISON, J. L. Numbers of mammals on the Malaysian islands. JMBRAS 38 pt. 2 (1965) 26-42.

FAUNA - MALAYSIA - EAST MALAYSIA

3635 BEST, A. E. G. List of butterflies caught around Kuching, Sarawak, December 1968. SMJ 17 (1969) 385-390.

3636 BROWNE, F. G. Borer beetles from Bako National Park. SMJ 10 (1961) 300-318.

3637 CHIN, LUCAS. Protected animals in Sarawak. SMJ 19 (1971) 359-361.

3638 GUAN ANAK SURENG. Pukoh of North Borneo, a missing missing link? SMJ 10 (1961) 333-4.

3639 HARRISSON, BARBARA. Lanthanotus borneensis, habits and observations. SMJ 10 (1961) 286-292.

3640 HARRISSON, BARBARA. Tree shrew (tupaia tana), a twin birth and consequences. SMJ 11 (1963) 262-265.

3641 HARRISSON, TOM. Cold blooded vertebrates of the Niah cave area. SMJ 14 (1966) 276-286.

3642 HARRISSON, TOM. Flying foxes (pteropus) over Niah cave area, 1965-66, by Tom and Barbara Harrisson. SMJ 14 (1966) 234-236.

3643 HARRISSON, TOM. Lanthanotus borneensis, the first 30 live ones. SMJ 11 (1963) 299-301.

3644 HARRISSON, TOM. Niah's new cave dwelling gecko, habits. SMJ 10 (1961) 277-282.

3645 HARRISSON, TOM. Notes on robber wasps (sphex diabolicus) in Niah caves. SMJ 14 (1966) 287-290.

3646 HARRISSON, TOM. Record-size Lanthanotus alive (1966), casual notes. SMJ 14 (1966) 323-334.

3647 HARRISSON, TOM. To scale a pangolin, by Tom Harrisson and Loh Chee Yin. SMJ 12 (1965) 415-418.

3648 ILLAR MUUL. Habitat distribution and ectoparasites of small mammals in Sarawak, by Illar Muul and Lim Boo Liat. SMJ 20 (1972) 359-366.

3649 INGER, ROBERT F. New cave dwelling lizard of the genus Cyrtodactylus from Niah, by Robert F. Inger and Wayne King. SMJ 10 (1961) 274-276.

3650 KING, WAYNE. Palaeolithic reptile and amphibian remains from Niah Great Cave. SMJ 11 (1962) 450-452.

3651 LIM BOO LIAT. Collection of small mammals from Tuaran and the southwest face of Mt. Kinabalu, Sabah, by Lim Boo Liat and D. Heyneman. SMJ 16 (1968) 257-276.

3652 LIM BOO LIAT. Food and weights of small animals from the First Division, Sarawak. SMJ 12 (1965) 360-372.

3653 MEDWAY, LORD. Mammals of Borneo, field keys and an annotated checklist. JMBRAS 36 pt. 3 (1963) 1-193.

3654 MEDWAY, LORD. Stegolophodon lydekkeri Osborn, a reassessment. SMJ 20 (1972) 339-350.

Fauna - Philippines

3655 MERTENS, ROBERT. Keeping of Borneo earless monitors (Lanthanotus borneensis). SMJ 14 (1966) 320-322.

3656 MERTENS, ROBERT. Lanthanotus, an important lizard in evolution. SMJ 10 (1961) 283-285.

3657 NIEMITZ, CARSTEN. Puzzle about Tarsius. SMJ 20 (1972) 329-337.

3658 SPRACKLAND, ROBERT G. Further notes on Lanthanotus. SMJ 18 (1970) 412-3.

3659 SPRACKLAND, ROBERT G. Summary of observations of the earless monitor, Lanthanotus borneensis. SMJ 20 (1972) 323-327.

3660 TAN KONG BENG. Stomach contents of some Borneo mammals. SMJ 12 (1965) 373-385.

3661 WAN, M. T. K. Bionomics and control of the diamondback moth, Plutella xylostella L. (P. maculipennis Curt.) (Lep. Plutellidae) in Sarawak, Malaysian Borneo. SMJ 18 (1970) 377-398.

3662 WAN, M. T. K. Some observations on the black rice shield bug Scotinophara coarctata F. (Hemiptera: Pentatomidae) in Sarawak, Malaysian Borneo. SMJ 19 (1971) 347-354.

FAUNA - PHILIPPINES

3663 ALCALA, ANGEL C. Notes on the birds and mammals of Boracay, Caluya, Carabao, Semirara and Sibay Islands, Philippines, by A. C. Alcala and Pedro Alvida. SJ 17 (1970) 444-454.

3664 ALCALA, ANGEL C. Notes on the food habits of three Philippine wild mammals, by Angel C. Alcala and Walter C. Brown. SJ 16 (1969) 91-94.

3665 ALCALA, ANGEL C. Sponge crab Dromidiopsis Dormia as predator of the Crown of Thorns starfish. SJ 21 (1974) 174-177.

3666 BERAN, BRUCE D. Observations on the Crown of Thorns starfish in Dumaguete Bay. SJ 19 (1972) 381-386.

3667 CROOK, PHILIP G. Endoparasites of Philippine land vertebrates, a preliminary survey of southern Negros, by Philip G. Crook and Angel C. Alcala. SJ 15 (1968) 323-342.

3668 GONZALES, RODOLFO B. Behavioral notes on captive sail-tailed lizards (Hydrosaurus pustulosus: Agamidae). SJ 21 (1974) 129-138.

3669 GONZALES, RODOLFO B. Patterns of display and social structure of the flying lizards (Draco volans: Agamidae). SJ 19 (1972) 364-380.

3670 GREGORIO, SAMUEL B. Mosquitos in Dumaguete City and their public health importance, a preliminary survey, by Samuel B. Gregorio and George W. Beran. SJ 15 (1968) 365-370.

3671 GUERRERO, R. D. Notes on the small mammal populations of Dumaguete City. SJ 18 (1971) 430-435.

3672 GUIDOTE-GARCIA, ROSALINDA. Philippine schistosomiasis, a critical study of the snail vector (Oncomelania Quadrasi) and the search for effective molluscicides. UN 33 (1960) 5-79.

Fauna - Philippines

3673 LAVINA, EINSTEIN M. Ecological studies on Philippine Siganid fishes in southern Negros, Philippines, by Einstein M. Lavina and A. C. Alcala. SJ 21 (1974) 191-210.

3674 LAVINA, EINSTEIN M. Endoparasites of certain Philippine land vertebrates, by Einstein M. Lavina and Angel C. Alcala. SJ 16 (1969) 137-148.

3675 RABOR, DIOSCORO S. List of the land vertebrates of Negros Island, Philippines, by D. S. Rabor, A. C. Alcala, and R. B. Gonzales. SJ 17 (1970) 297-316.

3676 RABOR, DIOSCORO S. Report on the zoological expeditions in the Philippines for the period 1961-1966. SJ 13 (1966) 605-616.

3677 REYES, ALFREDO Y. Food habits of Brachymeles Gracilis Taylori Brown. SJ 17 (1970) 67-72.

3678 REYES, ALFREDO Y. Food habits of Draco volans Linnaeus. SJ 15 (1968) 353-356.

3679 REYES, ALFREDO Y. Food habits of Mabuya multifasciata Kuhl. SJ 7 (1960) 313-323.

FAUNA - SINGAPORE

3680 MURPHY, D. H. Tullbergia (Stenaphorura) Gibsoni n. sp., (Collembola, Onychiuridae) from the grasslands in Singapore. JMBRAS 38 pt. 2 (1965) 22-25.

FAUNA - VIETNAM

3681 NGUYEN DINH HUNG. Present conception of marine sciences, the role of the Nhatrang Institute of Oceanography. AC 3 (Jan. 1961) 1-12.

FEDERACION INTERNACIONAL DE ABOGADAS

3682 COQUIA, JORGE R. FIDA resolution. PS 8 (1960) 837-840.

FESTIVALS

3683 TARYO, OHBAYASHI. Merit-making and feasts of merit in tribal religions of Southeast Asia. EACS 13 (1974) 72-74.

FESTIVALS - BURMA

3684 BA HAN. Evolution of Burmese dramatic performances and festal occasions. JBRS 49 (1966) 1-18.

FESTIVALS - INDONESIA - BALI

3685 FRANKEN, H. J. Festival of Jayaprana at Kalianget. B18 pp. 233-265.

3686 GORIS, R. Decennial festival in the village of Selat. B19 pp. 105-129.

3687 GORIS, R. Holidays and holy days. B18 pp. 113-129.

FESTIVALS - LAOS

3688 ARCHAIMBAULT, CHARLES. La fete du T'at a Luong Prabang. E92 pp. 5-47.

3689 ARCHAIMBAULT, CHARLES. La fete du T'at a Sieng Khwang (Laos), contribution a l'etude du Ti Ki. G83 pp. 187-200.

FESTIVALS – MALAYSIA – SARAWAK

3690 GALVIN, A. D. Headhunting, fact
      or fiction? BMJ 3 pt. 2 (1974)
      16-104.

3691 GALVIN, A. D. Mamat, Leppo Tau,
      Long Moh. SMJ 13 (1966) 296-304.

3692 HARRISSON, TOM. Kalimantan
      writing board and the Mamat fes-
      tival. SMJ 13 (1966) 287-295.

3693 SANDIN, BENEDICT. Gawai Antu, Sea
      Dayak feast of the departed spir-
      its. SMJ 10 (1961) 170-190.

3694 SANDIN, BENEDICT. Gawai Batu, the
      Iban whetstone feast. SMJ 11
      (1962) 392-408.

FESTIVALS – PHILIPPINES

3695 WULFF, INGER. Yakan Maulud
      celebration. Z16 pp. 494-502.

FESTIVALS – THAILAND

3696 ANUMAN RAJADHON. Fertility rites
      in Thailand. JSS 48 pt. 2 (1960)
      37-42.

3697 ANUMAN RAJADHON. Loi krathong.
      S44.2 pp. 197-204.

3698 VIET HUNG. How the Thais cele-
      brate their lunar new year. AC 3
      (Jan. 1961) 109-120.

3699 WALKER, ANTHONY R. La Hu Nyi
      (Red La Hu) new year celebrations.
      JSS 58 pt. 1 (1970) 1-44.

3700 WALKER, ANTHONY R. Lahu Nyi (Red
      Lahu) new year texts, 1. JSS 62
      pt. 1 (1974) 1-26.

FESTIVALS – VIETNAM

3701 THAI VAN KIEM. Les fetes tradi-
      tionnelles vietnamiennes. SEIB 36
      (1961) 53-67.

3702 THAI VAN KIEM. Meanings and old
      customs of the Tet, a Vietnamese
      new year festival. AC 3 (Jan.
      1961) 49-54.

FIELDING, W. G. A.

3703 SKINNER, C. Eye witness account
      of the invasion of Java in 1811,
      the diary of Lt. W. G. A. Field-
      ing. JMBRAS 44 pt. 1 (1971) 1-
      51.

FINANCE *See also* BANKS AND BANKING,
  MONEY, TAXATION

3704 MENON, P. K. Financing the lower
      Mekong River basin development PA
      44 (1971) 566-579.

3705 STIKKER, DIRK U. Impact of for-
      eign private investment, by Dirk
      U. Stikker and Ryokichi Hirono.
      S63 pp. 370-445.

FINANCE – BURMA

3706 ADAS, MICHAEL. Immigrant Asians
      and the economic impact of Euro-
      pean imperialism, the role of the
      south Indian chettiars in British
      Burma. JAS 33 (1973-4) 385-401.

3707 KHIN THAN KYWE. Financing the
      small manufacturing establishments
      of Burma. B91 pp. 107-142.

3708 RICHTER, H. V. State agricultural
      credit in postwar Burma. MER 13
      pt. 1 (1968) 101-117.

Finance - Burma

3709 SHEIN. Provincial contract system of British Indian empire, in relation to Burma, a case of fiscal exploitation, by Shein, Myint Myint Thant and Tin Tin Sein. JBRS 52 (Dec. 1969) 1-26.

FINANCE - INDONESIA

3710 POND, D. H. Development investment in Indonesia, 1956-1963. MER 9 pt. 2 (1964) 92-105.

3711 SMITH, R. S. Political economy of regional and urban revenue policy in Indonesia. AS 11 (1971) 761-786.

3712 TARLING, NICHOLAS. The Palmer loans. BIJ 119 (1963) 161-188.

3713 WHITE, LAWRENCE J. Problems and prospects of the Indonesian foreign exchange system. IND 14 (1972) 125-156.

FINANCE - MALAYSIA

3714 ABRAHAM, W. I. Growth and composition of Malaysia's capital stock. MER 14 pt. 2 (1969) 44-54.

3715 CORDEN, W. M. Malayan balance of payments problem. S47 pp. 112-130.

3716 DAVIES, W. E. Flow-of-funds social accounting, a Malayan example, by W. E. Davies and P. J. Drake. MER 9 pt. 2 (1964) 49-63.

3717 DRAKE, P. J. Financial aspects of the cooperative movement in Malaya. MER 11 pt. 1 (1966) 57-83.

3718 ISMAIL ALI BIN MOHAMED ALI. Role of central banking in industrialization. MER 8 pt. 1 (1963) 14-19.

3719 ISMAIL BIN DATO ABDUL RAHMAN. A new government looks at American investment. C35 pp. 71-78.

3720 LEE, SHENG YI. Banking and financial development of Singapore and Malaysia since 1958. SAJSS 1 pt. 1 (1973) 1-16.

3721 LEE, SHENG YI. Recent trends in the balance of payments of Malaysia and Singapore. MER 19 pt. 2 (1974) 72-85.

3722 LEE SOO ANN. Financial planning of investment in Malaysia. MER 14 pt. 1 (1969) 48-64.

3723 LEE SOO ANN. Fiscal policy and political transition, the case of Malaya, 1948-1960. JSAS 5 (1974) 102-114.

3724 McKENNA, DON. Financial developments since independence. S47 pp. 195-209.

3725 MORGAN, D. J. International compensatory financing applied to the Federation of Malaya and Singapore. MER 7 pt. 2 (1962) 64-76.

3726 SHORT, BROCK K. Relation between money and spending in west Malaysia and Singapore, 1951-1966. MER 17 pt. 2 (1972) 25-39.

3727 SILCOCK, T. H. Merdeka in the money market. S48 pp. 487-493.

3728 ZENOFF, DAVID. New look at economic nationalism. PS 10 (1962) 215-233.

FINANCE - PHILIPPINES

3729 CRUZ, AVELINO E. Portfolio management for the individual investor. SLURJ 1 (1970) 238-258.

3730 CUADERNO, MIGUEL. The central bank and economic planning. M38 pp. 92-108.

3731 MARIANO, LEONARDO C. Local government finance. A28 pp. 453-465.

3732 PEEK, PETER. Household savings and demographic change in the Philippines. MER 19 pt. 2 (1974) 86-104.

3733 SOBERANO, JOSE D. Fiscal policy controversy. G93 pp. 337-400.

FINANCE - SINGAPORE

3734 DAVIES, GETHYN. United Kingdom investment. H84 pp. 46-61.

3735 HICKS, URSULA K. Finance of the city state. MER 5 pt. 2 (1960) 1-9.

3736 HIRONO, RYOKICHI. Japanese investment. H84 pp. 86-111.

3737 HUGHES, HELEN. Australian investment. H84 pp. 62-85.

3738 HUGHES, HELEN. Conclusions. H84 pp. 177-210.

3739 KAPUR, BASANT K. Tentative flow of funds account for Singapore. MER 15 pt. 2 (1970) 49-63.

3740 LEE, SHENG YI. Asian dollar market in Singapore. MER 16 pt. 1 (1971) 46-56.

3741 LEE, SHENG YI. Banking and financial development of Singapore and Malaysia since 1958. SAJSS 1 pt. 1 (1973) 1-16.

3742 LEE, SHENG YI. Financial and credit institutions. M49 pp. 147-160.

3743 LEE, SHENG YI. Public finance. Y52 pp. 101-126.

3744 LEE, SHENG YI. Recent trends in the balance of payments of Malaysia and Singapore. MER 19 pt. 2 (1974) 72-85.

3745 LINDERT, PETER H. United States investment. H84 pp. 154-176.

3746 LUEY, PAUL. Hong Kong investment. H84 pp. 112-139.

3747 LUEY, PAUL. Taiwan investment, by Paul Luey and Ung Gim Sei. H84 pp. 140-153.

3748 MA, RONALD. Public sector accounts of Singapore, 1966, by Ronald Ma and Peter C. K. Tan. MER 15 pt. 1 (1970) 17-65.

3749 MORGAN, D. J. International compensatory financing applied to the Federation of Malaya and Singapore. MER 7 pt. 2 (1962) 64-76.

3750 PARK, YOON-SHIK. Asia-dollar market, its structure and potential. AF 5 pt. 1 (1973) 73-81.

3751 SHORT, BROCK K. Relation between money and spending in west Malaysia and Singapore, 1951-1966. MER 17 pt. 2 (1972) 25-39.

FINANCE – VIETNAM

3752 LINDHOLM, RICHARD W. American aid
      and its financial impact. L52 pp.
      317–323.
      Comment: HOTHAM, DAVID. Com-
      mentary. L52 pp. 323–325.
      Comment: HUNTER, JOHN M. Com-
      mentary. L52 pp. 327–330.
      Comment: TRAN VAN KIEN. Com-
      mentary. L52 pp. 325–327.

3753 SCHIFF, FRANK W. Monetary re-
      organization and the emergence of
      central banking. L52 pp. 259–287.

3754 SLUSSER, H. ROBERT. Early steps
      toward an industrial development
      bank. L52 pp. 245–254.
      Comment: NGUYEN DUY XUAN. Com-
      mentary. L52 pp. 255–6.

FISHES – BRUNEI

3755 ALFRED, ERIC R. Occurrence of the
      pentacerotid fish Histiopterus
      typus, Temminck and Schlegel off
      the Brunei coast. BMJ 2 pt. 1
      (1970) 318–9.

3756 BIRKENMEIER, ELMAR. Notes on
      some coral fishes in Brunei
      waters. BMJ 2 pt. 1 (1970) 294–
      317.

FISHES – BURMA

3757 KHIN THANT. Silurus Burmanensis,
      a new species of fish from the
      Inle Lake, southern Shan State,
      Burma. JBRS 49 (1966) 219–221.

FISHES – INDONESIA

3758 HERRE, ALBERT W. C. T. Research
      on fish and fisheries in the Indo-
      Australian archipelago. H57 pp.
      167–175.

FISHES – VIETNAM

3759 NGUYEN CHAU. La peche aux crevettes
      au centre Viet-Nam, par Nguyen
      Chau et Tran De. SEIB 39 (1964)
      487–507.

3760 NGUYEN CHAU. To trinh khao sat ve
      tom tai trung phan, [by] Nguyen
      Chau [and] Tran De. SEIB 39
      (1964) 513–530.

3761 NGUYEN THI LAU. Le poisson dans
      l'alimentation du vietnamien, par
      Nguyen Thi Lau et C. Richard.
      SEIB 35 (1960) 527–543.

3762 Le poisson dans l'alimentation du
      Vietnam, 2e partie, conserves ap-
      pertisees, farines et saucisses de
      poisson, par C. Richard, Nguyen
      Nhu Nghi, Nguyen Thi Lau, et F.
      Litalien. SEIB 36 (1961) 89–106.

3763 TRAN NGOC LOI. Ca co gia-tri
      thuong mai tai Viet Nam [by] Tran
      Ngoc Loi [and] Nguyen Chau. SEIB
      39 (1964) 365–422.

3764 TRAN NGOC LOI. Les poissons
      d'importance commerciale au Viet-
      Nam, par Tran Ngoc Loi et Nguyen
      Chau. SEIB 39 (1964) 325–362.

FISHING – BRUNEI

3765 BIRKENMEIER, ELMAR. Fisheries
      development in Brunei. BMJ 1
      (1969) 192–196.

FISHING – INDONESIA

3766 BARNES, R. H. Lamalerap, a
      whaling village in eastern Indone-
      sia. IND 17 (1974) 136–159.

3767 HERRE, ALBERT W. C. T. Research on fish and fisheries in the Indo-Australian archipelago. H57 pp. 167-175.

3768 International aspects of the protection of coastal fisheries. H57 pp. 475-477.

3769 MYERS, EARL H. Fisheries program for the Netherlands East Indies. H57 pp. 483-4.

3770 PALM, C. H. M. Vaartuigen en visvangst van Anjar Lor, Bantam, west-Java. BIJ 118 (1962) 217-270.

FISHING - MALAYSIA

3771 ALFRED, ERIC R. Annotated bibliography of Malayan fresh water fisheries. JMBRAS 39 pt. 1 (1966) 145-165.

3772 HARRISSON, TOM. Some Malay fishing cycles, a second note, by Tom Harrisson and A. K. Marican Salleh. SMJ 9 (1960) 652-654.

3773 LEE, Y. L. Kukup, a Chinese fishing village in south west Malaya. JTG 16 (1962) 131-148.

FISHING - PHILIPPINES

3774 CANTERO-PASTRANO, CECILIA L. Report on a Visayan fishing barrio. E78 pp. 30-41.

3775 JULIANO, ROGELIO O. Fisheries education and research in the Philippines. GEJ 7 (1964) 117-126.

3776 LAWLESS, ROBERT. Hunting and fishing among the southern Kalinga. AST 11 pt. 3 (1973) 83-109.

3777 YAMADA, YUKIHARO. Fishing economy of the Itbayat, Batanes, Philippines with special reference to its vocabulary. AST 5 (1967) 137-219.

FISHING - SINGAPORE

3778 TAN LEE WAH. Carp culture in Singapore, a case study. JTG 35 (1972) 67-74.

FISHING - VIETNAM

3779 KAUFMAN, HOWARD K. Culao, a Vietnamese fishing cooperative and its problems. S58 pp. 235-272.

3780 NGUYEN CHAU. Danh ca bang chat no, [by] Nguyen Chau [and] Phan Hay. SEIB 37 (1962) 277-284.

3781 NGUYEN CHAU. La peche aux matieres explosives, par Nguyen Chau et Phan Hay. SEIB 37 (1962) 267-274.

3782 NGUYEN THUY ANH. Luoi Dang ou madrague vietnamienne dans la region de Khanh-Hoa, Nha Trang. SEIB 41 (1966) 167-290.

FLOODS - MALAYSIA

3783 CHARLTON, F. G. Standard catchments in the estimation of flood flows. JTG 18 (1964) 43-53.

FLOODS - SINGAPORE

3784 CHIA LIN SIEN. Record floods of 10th December 1969 in Singapore, by Chia Lin Sien and Chang Kin Koon. JTG 33 (1971) 9-19.

Flora

FLORA

3785 BARLOW, H. S. John Waterstradt, 1869–1944. JMBRAS 42 pt. 2 (1969) 115–129.

3786 MULLER, J. Pollen from the South China Sea, a correction. SMJ 10 (1961) 325.

3787 THAN TUN. Effect of concentration of salts on their rate of absorption by plants in water culture and the role of aeration. JBRS 44 (1961) 225–235.

3788 WHYTE, ROBERT ORR. The Gramineae, wild and cultivated, of monsoonal and equatorial Asia. I. Southeast Asia. AP 15 (1972) 127–151.

FLORA - BRUNEI

3789 CORNER, E. J. H. Tropical botanist's introduction to Borneo. SMJ 10 (1961) 1–16.

3790 PEREGRINE, W. T. H. Common edible mushroom (Agaricus sp.) in Brunei, by W. T. H. Peregrine and Kassim bin Ahmad. BMJ 3 pt. 1 (1973) 146–149.

3791 TENG SENG KEH. Preliminary report on the species of planktonic marine diatoms found in Brunei waters. BMJ 2 pt. 1 (1970) 279–293.

FLORA - BURMA

3792 NATH, DEWAN MOHINDER. Botanical survey of the southern Shan states with a note on the vegetation of the Inle Lake. B91 pp. 161–418.

FLORA - CAMBODIA

3793 LEWITZ, S. Lexique des noms d'arbes et d'arbustes du Cambodge, par S. Lewitz et B. Rollet. BEF 60 (1973) 117–162.

3794 VIDAL, J. E. Notes ethnobotaniques sur quelques plantes en usage au Cambodge, par J. E. Vidal, G. Martel, et S. Lewitz. BEF 55 (1969) 171–232.

FLORA - INDONESIA

3795 BERNARD, CHARLES J. Le jardin botanique de Buitenzorg et les institutions de botanique appliquee aux Indes Neerlandaises. H57 pp. 10–15.

3796 DOTY, MAXWELL S. Development of marine resources in Indonesia, by Maxwell S. Doty and Aprilany Soegiarto. J37 pp. 70–89.

3797 FAIRCHILD, DAVID G. American plant hunter in the Netherlands Indies. H57 pp. 79–99.

3798 LEEUWEN, W. M. DOCTERS VAN. Tjiboas Biological Station and Forest Reserve, the flora of Tjiboas. H57 pp. 410–413.

3799 MASSART, JEAN. Notes javanaises. H57 pp. 231–240.

3800 SOEMARWOTO, OTTO. Development of the National Biological Institute. J37 pp. 53–69.

3801 STEENIS, C. G. G. J. VAN. Botanical exploration trip in south Sumatra. H57 pp. 335–343.

3802 STEINMANN, ALFRED. De afbeeldingen van planten op de spuiers van Djalatoenda. BIJ 117 (1961) 359–362.

3803 WENT, F. A. F. C. Short history
of general botany in the Netherlands Indies. H57 pp. 390-402.

3804 WENT, F. W. Tjiboas Biological
Station and Forest Reserve, a
naturalists paradise. H57 p. 403.

FLORA - MALAYSIA

3805 CORNER, E. J. H. Tropical botanist's introduction to Borneo.
SMJ 10 (1961) 1-16.

3806 GILLILAND, H. B. Geographical
distribution of Malayan grasses.
JTG 17 (1963) 20-23.

3807 KENG, HSUAN. Size and affinities
of the flora of the Malay peninsula. JTG 31 (1970) 43-56.

3808 KERN, J. H. Viburnum amplificatum
Kern, an endemic wayfaring tree
from Borneo. SMJ 9 (1960) 679-
681.

3809 WYATT-SMITH, J. Preliminary
vegetation map of Malaya with
descriptions of the vegetation
types. JTG 18 (1964) 193-213.

FLORA - PHILIPPINES

3810 LYNCH, FRANK. Today's native is
yesterday's visitor. PS 11
(1963) 431-433.

3811 MUD, PAULO. Eucalyptus trees.
PS 9 (1961) 528-531.

3812 ONG, MARIA LUISA. Proximate
chemical composition and nitrogen
partition of soya bean seeds from
several strains of plants grown
in the Philippines. UN 33 (1960)
285-339.

3813 ORTEGA, E. P. Algal association
in Caulerpa communities in southern Negros, Philippines, by E. P.
Ortega, A. C. Alcala and A. Y.
Reyes. SJ 21 (1974) 178-190.

3814 PAKILIT, ARNOVIO M. Ecological
notes on Eucheuma. SJ 17 (1970)
317-327.

3815 RODRIGUEZ, LORENZO. Botanical
garden of Manila and Sebastian
Vidal y Soler. UN 35 (1962) 258-
277.

3816 SANTOS, CONCEPCION B. Pharmacog-
nostical study of eucalyptus
Deglupta Blume together with a
chemical study of its volatile
oil. UN 33 (1960) 740-806.

FLORA - THAILAND

3817 LARSEN, KAI. Costus Dhaninivatii,
a new species from S. E. Thailand.
F38 pp. 149-152.

3818 SEIDENFADEN, GUNNAR. Bulbophyllum
Dhaninivatii, a new orchid from
Thailand. F38 pp. 153-155.

FLORA - VIETNAM

3819 BOULBET, JEAN. Description de la
vegetation en pays Ma, Boucle et
plateau du Haut Donnai, Vietnam
sud. SEIB 35 (1960) 545-574.

3820 Introduction a l'etude des sables
littoraux du sud-Vietnam. Note
no. 6. La vegetation du littoral
entre Da-Nang (Tourone), et Hue,
par J. P. Barry, Le Cong Kiet,
Pham Hoang Ho, et Nguyen Van Thuy.
SEIB 38 (1963) 509-529.

3821 LY VAN HOI. Guide botanique de la
ville de Saigon. SEIB 43 (1968)

Flora - Vietnam

3822 NGO VINH LONG. Leaf abscission.
      G79 pp. 201-213.

3823 NGUYEN DING HUNG. Present con-
      ception of marine sciences, the
      role of the Nhatrang Institute of
      Oceanography. AC 3 (Jan. 1961)
      1-12.

3824 NGUYEN VAN THON. Enrichissement
      des forets de coniferes par intro-
      duction d'essences resineuses
      exotiques sur les hauts-plateaux
      du Langbian. SEIB 47 (1972) 197-
      215.

3825 THAI CONG TUNG. Les principales
      formations vegetales de la plaine
      de Phan-Rang (Ninh-Thuan). SEIB
      45 pt. 4 (1970) 39-79.

3826 VIDAL, J. E. Bibliographie bo-
      tanique indochinoise. SEIB 47
      (1972) 655-749.

FOLK LITERATURE

3827 DOMINGO, ROLANDO T. Selected
      observations. DR 13 (1965) 79-80.

3828 TAIB OSMAN, MOHD. The aims, ap-
      proaches and problems in the
      study of folk literature or oral
      tradition with particular refer-
      ence to Malay culture. BMJ 2 pt.
      4 (1972) 159-164.

FOLK LITERATURE - BURMA

3829 BERNOT, D. Etes-vous fachee,
      belle-mere?, conte Marma. E92
      pp. 59-66.

3830 KHIN ZAW. Folk-song collector's
      letter from the Mon country in
      Lower Burma, 1941. E92 pp.
      164-166.

3831 LU GALE. Paddy planting songs.
      B92 pp. 157-167.

3832 OHN. Face, butterfly and two
      songs, a prologue to a study of
      the elements of myth and magic in
      Burmese politics. JBRS 46 (June
      1963) 11-25.

3833 PO BYU. Burmese proverbs and
      sayings. B92 pp. 477-483.

3834 SAO SAIMONG. Shan folk tales.
      JBRS 43 (1960) 83-90.

3835 STERNBACH, LUDWIK. Pali Lokaniti
      and the Burmese Niti Kyan and
      their sources. SOAS 26 (1963)
      329-345.

3836 STEWART, J. A. Some songs and a
      riddle. B92 pp. 523-525.

FOLK LITERATURE - CAMBODIA

3837 POREE-MASPERO, EVELINE. Tradi-
      tions orales de Pursat et de
      Kampot. G83 pp. 394-398.

FOLK LITERATURE - INDONESIA

3838 ADAMS, M. J. Myths and self image
      among the Kapunduk people of
      Sumba. IND 10 (1970) 80-106.

3839 ANDI ZAINAL ABIDIN. The I La
      Galigo epic cycle of south Celebes
      and its diffusion. IND 17 (1974)
      160-169.

3840 HOOYKAAS, C. Balinese folktale.
      J41 pp. 185-192.

3841 HOOYKAAS, JACOBA. Changeling in
      Balinese folklore and religion.
      BIJ 116 (1960) 424-436.

Folk literature - Malaysia - Sarawak

3842 JAMUH, GEORGE. Pelandok, the villain-hero in Sarawak and interior Kalimantan, south Borneo, by George Jamuh, T. Harrisson and Benedict Sandin. SMJ 11 (1962) 524-534.

3843 MIDDELKOOP, P. Nai tirans en nai besis in kosmische huwelijksrelatie met de krokodil. BIJ 127 (1971) 434-451.

3844 WATUSEKE, F. S. Tondanose raadsels. BIJ 128 (1972) 330-336.

FOLK LITERATURE - LAOS

3845 LAFONT, PIERRE-BERNARD. Contes P'u Tai. SEIB 46 (1971) 21-48.

FOLK LITERATURE - MALAYSIA

3846 SWEENEY, AMIN. Professional Malay story telling. Part I. Some questions of style and presentation. JMBRAS 46 pt. 2 (1973) 1-53.

FOLK LITERATURE - MALAYSIA - SABAH

3847 ARANETA, F. Bisayans of Borneo and the Tagalogs and Visayans of the Philippines. SMJ 9 (1960) 542-564.

3848 FRANCISCO, JUAN R. Some Philippine tales compared with parallels in North Borneo. GEJ 5 (1963) 62-77.

3849 FRANCISCO, JUAN R. Some Philippine tales compared with parallels in North Borneo. SMJ 11 (1962) 511-523.

3850 HARRISSON, BARBARA. Stories from Kinabatangan caves, Sabah, by Barbara Harrisson and Michael Chong. SMJ 12 (1965) 117-127.

3851 SATHER, CLIFFORD. Bajau riddles. SMJ 12 (1965) 162.

FOLK LITERATURE - MALAYSIA - SARAWAK

3852 ARANETA, F. Bisayans of Borneo and the Tagalogs and Visayans of the Philippines. SMJ 9 (1960) 542-564.

3853 DANANDJAJA, JAMES. Some Kahayan legends. SMJ 19 (1971) 265-276.

3854 DEEGAN, JAMES. Some Lun Bawang spirit chants. SMJ 18 (1970) 264-280.

3855 DEEGAN, JAMES. Upai Kasan, a Lun Bawang folktale, by James Deegan and Robin Usad. SMJ 20 (1972) 107-144.

3856 GALLIH BALANG. Origin of poison inside Borneo. SMJ 12 (1965) 235.

3857 GALVIN, A. D. Bilian limanjong, a Morik song. SMJ 12 (1965) 163-165.

3858 GALVIN, A. D. Child of Padan Sigau, a Sebob saga. SMJ 12 (1965) 166-170.

3859 GALVIN, A. D. How Balan Nyaring ventured to Alo Malau, a Kenyah epic story. SMJ 18 (1970) 220-263.

3860 GALVIN, A. D. Kenyah farming year. SMJ 19 (1971) 185-235.

3861 GALVIN, A. D. Marriage of Senan and Aping. BMJ 2 pt. 3 (1971) 11-16.

Folk literature – Malaysia – Sarawak

3862 GALVIN, A. D. Suket, a Kenyah song from Long Je'eh, Baram. BMJ 3 pt. 1 (1973) 41-50.

3863 HADDON, A. C. Tortoise and the mouse deer, Kenyah. SMJ 11 (1962) 535-6.

3864 HARRISSON, TOM. Gibbon in west Borneo folklore and augury. SMJ 14 (1966) 132-145.

3865 HARRISSON, TOM. Iban and Ngaju, a significant bird folklore parallel, by Tom and Barbara Harrisson. SMJ 16 (1968) 186-194.

3866 HARRISSON, TOM. Sea going cuckoo and other themes significant in the Saribas story. SMJ 11 (1964) 537-540.

3867 HARRISSON, TOM. Tevau Naa, a central Borneo folk cycle in part. JMBRAS 37 pt. 2 (1964) 60-86.

3868 INA ANAK KALOM. Selako folktale, Ne' Dibo and the Lundu Sebuyau, by Ina Anak Kalom and A. B. Hudson. SMJ 19 (1971) 317-323.

3869 INA ANAK KALOM. Selako traditional history, a story on the origins of Kampong Pueh, by Ina Anak Kalom and A. B. Hudson. SMJ 18 (1970) 281-300.

3870 INGAI, JOSEPH. Pancha and Padong origins. SMJ 16 (1968) 195-198.

3871 JAMUH, GEORGE. Melanau population destroyed by poisonous snake. SMJ 12 (1965) 230-234.

3872 JAMUH, GEORGE. Pelandok, the villain-hero in Sarawak and interior Kalimantan, south Borneo, by George Jamuh, T. Harrisson and Benedict Sandin. SMJ 11 (1962) 524-534.

3873 MARTINOIR, NINANE DE. Unity of Dayak mythology. A41 pp. 56-64.

3874 MEDWAY, LORD. Niah ballad. SMJ 9 (1960) 393-407.

3875 NAEN ANAK JERAMAN. Invisible bird and the roaming head, a Land Dayak transformation. SMJ 11 (1963) 108-113.

3876 NYANDOH, R. Man weds sow, three versions. SMJ 14 (1966) 124-131.

3877 NYANDOH, R. Manjah, the magic stone of Niah. SMJ 9 (1960) 389-392.

3878 NYANDOH, R. Seven Land Dayak stories of Sarawak and Kalimantan. SMJ 11 (1963) 114-131.

3879 RUBENSTEIN, CAROL. Poems of indigenous peoples of Sarawak: some of the songs and chants. Pt. I. Iban, Bidayuh, Melanau. SMJ 21 (1973) 1-722.

3880 SANDIN, BENEDICT. Apai Salui sleeps with a corpse, an Iban folk story. SMJ 15 (1967) 223-227.

3881 SANDIN, BENEDICT. History of the people in Balingian subdistrict, Mukah, Sarawak. SMJ 19 (1971) 37-45.

3882 SANDIN, BENEDICT. History of the people of Bangkit, Paku, Saribas. SMJ 19 (1971) 21-36.

3883 SANDIN, BENEDICT. Owl marries the moon, a Saribas story. SMJ 11 (1964) 534-536.

3884 SANDIN, BENEDICT. Simpulang, or Pulang Gana, the founder of Dayak agriculture. SMJ 15 (1967) 245-406.

3885 SANDIN, BENEDICT. Tatau people of the Kakus and Anap Rivers, Fourth Division, Sarawak. SMJ 18 (1970) 162-168.

3886 SANDIN, BENEDICT. Tragi-comic tales of Apai Salui, Iban. SMJ 9 (1960) 638-647.

3887 SIBAT ANAK MUJAH. Tanggok jadi enggau bulan (Iban text). SMJ 11 (1964) 541-543.

3888 TUTON KABOY. Some stories about the Siteng people. SMJ 19 (1971) 47-51.

FOLK LITERATURE - PHILIPPINES **

3889 ARANETA, F. Bisayans of Borneo and the Tagalogs and Visayans of the Philippines. SMJ 9 (1960) 542-564.

3890 CLAVEL, LEOTHINY S. Folklore and communication. AST 8 (1970) 218-247.

3891 CORONEL, MARIA DELIA. Ifugao stories. UN 39 (1966) 591-612.

3892 CORONEL, MARIA DELIA. Kalinga-Bontoc stories. UN 39 (1966) 615-629.

3893 CORONEL, MARIA DELIA. Mindanao stories. UN 39 (1966) 523-543.

3894 CORONEL, MARIA DELIA. Tagalog and Ilocano stories. UN 39 (1966) 579-588.

3895 CORONEL, MARIA DELIA. Taosug-Samal stories. UN 39 (1966) 503-519.

3896 CORONEL, MARIA DELIA. Visayan stories. UN 39 (1966) 547-576.

3897 DEMETRIO, FRANCISCO R. Themes in Philippine folk tales. AST 10 (1972) 6-17.

3898 DEMETRIO, FRANCISCO R. Towards a systematic analysis of Philippine folktales. SJ 17 (1970) 111-143.

3899 ESPINAS, MERITO B. Critical study of Ibalong, the Bikol folk epic fragment. UN 41 (1968) 173-250.

3900 ESPINAS, MERITO B. Sarung banggi, Bikol's regional song. UN 41 (1968) 257-260.

3901 EUGENIO, DAMIANA L. Philippine proverb lore. PSSHR 31 (1966) 231-421.

3902 FERNANDEZ, DOREEN G. Ten Hiligaynon poems, translations and an introduction. PS 21 (1973) 187-205.

3903 FRANCISCO, JUAN R. Indian influences in the Philippines, with special reference to language and literature. PSSHR 28 (1963) 1-310.

3904 FRANCISCO, JUAN R. Some Philippine tales compared with parallels in North Borneo. GEJ 5 (1963) 62-77.

3905 FRANCISCO, JUAN R. Some Philippine tales compared with parallels in North Borneo. SMJ 11 (1962) 511-523.

3906 FREI, ERNEST J. Laurence Lee Wilson, recorder of Mountain Province folklore. SLQ 5 (1967) 41-66.

3907 HART, DONN V. Buhawi of the Bisayas, the revitalization process and legend making in the Philippines. Z16 pp. 366-396.

Folk literature - Philippines

3908   HUFANA, ALEJANDRINO G.   Sources
       of retrieval in Philippine ver-
       nacular literature.   GEJ 17 (1969)
       125-130.

3909   JOCANO, F. LANDA.   Epic of Labaw
       Donggon.   PSSHR 29 (1964) 1-103.

3910   JOCANO, F. LANDA.   Twenty-three
       place name legends from Antique
       Province, Philippines.   AST 3
       (1965) 16-40.

3911   LAMBRECHT, FRANCIS.   Hudhud of
       Dinulawan and Bugan at Gonhadan.
       SLQ 5 (1967) 267-713.

3912   LAMBRECHT, FRANCIS.   Ifugaw Hudhud
       literature.   M24 pp. 816-837.

3913   LOPEZ, ROGELIO M.   Earth-diver
       myth, towards a theory of its
       diffusion in Asia.   AST 10 (1972)
       429-448.

3914   MACDONALD, CHARLES.   Mythe de
       creation Palawan.   AR 8 (1974)
       91-118.

3915   MANUEL, E. ARSENIO.   Agyu, the
       Ilianon epic of Mindanao.   UN 42
       (1969) 5-104.

3916   MANUEL, E. ARSENIO.   On the study
       of Philippine folklore.   M24 pp.
       253-286.

3917   NUNES, EVELYN H.   Some epic laws
       of the Donggon, a study in struc-
       ture.   PS 20 (1972) 563-576.

3918   NURGE, ETHEL D.   Nature of the
       supernatural in four myths from
       Guinhangdan, Leyte, Philippines.
       SJ 8 (1961) 78-97.

3919   NURGE, ETHEL D.   Third myth from
       Guinhangdan.   SJ 7 (1960) 219-235.

3920   PEREZ, ALEJANDRINO Q.   Pampango
       folklore, proverbs, riddles, folk-
       songs.   UN 41 (1968) 67-123.

3921   RAHMANN, RUDOLF.   Animal horns
       and similar motifs in Filipino,
       Eurasian and Amerindian folklore,
       by Rudolf Rahmann and Jose Kuizon.
       AST 3 (1965) 403-419.

3922   RIXHON, GERARD.   Cooperative ven-
       ture in folk-literature collection
       and translation.   S91 pp. 163-171.

3923   RIXHON, GERARD.   Mullung, a Tausug
       storyteller.   S91 pp. 172-189.

3924   SONZA, DEMY P.   Bisaya of Borneo
       and the Philippines, a new look at
       the Maragtas.   SMJ 20 (1972) 31-
       40.

FOLK LITERATURE - THAILAND

3925   ANUMAN RAJADHON.   King U-Thong of
       Thai folk tale.   F38 pp. 35-40.

3926   ANUMAN RAJADHON.   Study on Thai
       folk tale.   JSS 53 (1965) 133-137.

3927   KLAUSNER, WILLIAM J.   Hua Paw
       tales, by William J. and Kampan
       Klausner.   T33 pp. 107-109.

3928   KLAUSNER, WILLIAM J.   In-law tales,
       a note on northeastern Thai ethnog-
       raphy.   JSS 61 pt. 2 (1973) 143-
       148.

FOLK LITERATURE - VIETNAM **

3929   BUI QUANG TUNG.   Le soulevement
       soeurs Trung, a travers les textes
       et le folklore vietnamien.   SEIB
       36 (1961) 70-85.

3930   NGUYEN CONG HUAN.   Le crapaud est
       l'oncle du dieu du ciel, conte

vietnamien. FA 17 (1960) 2610-2612.

3931 NGUYEN CONG HUAN. Dictons et chansons populaires relatifs aux conditions atmospheriques et a l'agriculture au Vietnam. SEIB 48 (1973) 7-22.

3932 THAI VAN KIEM. Curiosities toponymiques et folkloriques du sud-Vietnam. SEIB 35 (1960) 505-526.

3933 THAI VAN KIEM. La sagesse vietnamienne a travers les proverbes et dictons populaires. SEIB 48 (1973) 25-49.

FONACIER, TOMAS S.

3934 Curriculum vitae, Tomas S. Fonacier. AST 2 (1964) 139-141.

3935 Curriculum vitae, Tomas S. Fonacier. PSSHR 28 (1963) 496-498.

3936 JAMIAS, CRISTINO. Presentation. PSSHR 28 (1963) 491-493.

3937 ROMULO, CARLOS P. Closing remarks. PSSHR 28 (1963) 494-5.

Food *See* DIET

FOOD SUPPLY - MALAYSIA - SARAWAK

3938 HARRISSON, TOM. Nuts and Malays on Tanjong Datu. SMJ 9 (1960) 655-669.

3939 MEDWAY, LORD. Antiquity of domesticated pigs in Sarawak. JMBRAS 46 pt. 2 (1973) 169-178.

FOOD SUPPLY - PHILIPPINES

3940 PAKILIT, ARNOVIO M. Ecological notes on Eucheuma. SJ 17 (1970) 317-327.

3941 TABLANTE, NATHANIEL B. Food and population problems in the Philippines. AST 4 (1966) 374-380.

FORBES, W. CAMERON

3942 SPECTOR, ROBERT M. W. Cameron Forbes in the Philippines, a study in proconsular power. JSAH 7 (Sept. 1966) 74-92.

FORESTS AND FORESTRY

3943 POORE, M. E. D. Problems in the classification of tropical rain forest. JTG 17 (1963) 12-19.

FORESTS AND FORESTRY - BURMA

3944 MAI AUNG. Comparative study of conventional chipped bamboo versus shredded bamboo produced by the Ubari shredder for making pulp by soda process, by Mai Aung, J. E. Fleury and Freddy Ba Hli. B91 pp. 143-146.

FORESTS AND FORESTRY - INDONESIA

3945 KOPPEL, C. VAN DE. Forestry in the outer provinces of the Netherlands Indies. H57 pp. 217-221.

3946 MOON, D. G. Development of naval stores and pulpwood supplied from the pinus mercusii of northern Sumatra. H57 pp. 263-265.

FORESTS AND FORESTRY - MALAYSIA - SABAH

3947   FOX, J. E. D.   Soils and forest on ultrabasic hill north east of Ranau, Sabah, by J. E. D. Fox and Tan Teong Hing.   JTG 32 (1971) 38-48.

3948   JOHN, DAVID W.   The timber industry and forest administration in Sabah under Chartered Company rule.   JSAS 5 (1974) 55-81.

FORESTS AND FORESTRY - PHILIPPINES

3949   HOLLNSTEINER, MARY R.   Note to management on traditional Filipino values in business enterprises, the Lumber Company as a case study.   PS 13 (1965) 350-354.

3950   TRINIDAD, NORMA C.   Production of tall oil from Benguet pine trees. SLURJ 1 (1970) 259-294.

FORESTS AND FORESTRY - VIETNAM

3951   MAURAND, PAUL.   Politique forestiere a envisager au Viet-Nam dans l'apres-guerre.   SEIB 43 (1968) 267-309.

FORREST, THOMAS

3952   BASSETT, D. K.   Thomas Forrest, an eighteenth century mariner. JMBRAS 34 pt. 2 (1961) 106-122.

FRANCE. ARCHIVES NATIONALES

3953   BREAZEALE, KENNON.   Inventaire des documents sur le Siam conserves aux archives de Paris.   JSS 62 pt. 2 (1974) 149-206.

FRANCE. MIN. DES AFFAIRES ETRANGERES

3954   BA, VIVIAN.   King Mindon and the world fair of 1867 held in Paris, from documents in the French Foreign Office.   JBRS 48 (Dec. 1965) 17-23.

FRANCISCO, LAZARO

3955   SIKAT, ROGELIO R.   Ang sining ni Lazaro Francisco.   PS 18 (1970) 252-272.

Freedom movements *See* INDEPENDENCE MOVEMENTS

FREEMASONS - PHILIPPINES

3956   SCHUMACHER, JOHN N.   Filipino masonry in Madrid, 1889-1896.   PHR 1 pt. 2 (1966) 168-182.

3957   SCHUMACHER, JOHN N.   Philippine masonry to 1890.   AST 4 (1966) 328-341.

FUNAN

3958   COLLESS, BRIAN E.   Ancient Bnam empire, Funan and Ponan.   JOSA 9 (1972) 21-31.

3960   LOOFS, H. H. E.   Funanese cultural elements in the lower Menam basin. JOSA 8 (1971) 5-8.

FURNIVALL, JOHN SYDENHAM

3961   THET TUN.   Critique of a new preface to J. S. Furnivall's *An introduction to the political economy of Burma*.   JBRS 47 (1964) 379-383.

FUTURISM - PHILIPPINES

3962　KEILING, HANNS P.　Global barrio
ethics.　SJ 17 (1970) 367-386.

GADDANG

3963　LAMBRECHT, GODFREY.　Aintu rites
among the Gaddang.　PS 8 (1960)
584-602.

GADDANG LANGUAGE

3964　TROYER, LESTER O.　Gaddang af-
firmatives and negatives.　AST 6
(1968) 99-101.

3965　TROYER, LESTER O.　Linguistics as
a window into man's mind, Gaddang
time segmentation.　GEJ 12 (1966)
109-118.

GAJAH MADA

3966　MINATTUR, JOSEPH.　Gaja Mada's
Palapa.　JMBRAS 39 pt. 1 (1966)
185-187.

3967　MINATTUR, JOSEPH.　Gaja Mada's
Palapa.　RSA (1966) 237-239.

GAJAH MADA UNIVERSITY

3968　BONNEFF, MARCEL.　GAMA, portrait
d'une universite.　AR 2 (1971)
29-53.

GALIGO EPOS

3969　KERN, R. A.　Een episode uit het
la Galigo Epos.　BIJ 117 (1961)
363-383.

GALVEY, GUILLERMO

3970　Expedition of Comandante Guillermo
Galvey to Baguio in 1829.　UN 35
(1962) 128-138.

GAMBLING - THAILAND

3971　CARTWRIGHT, B. O.　The Huey lot-
tery.　S44.1 pp. 131-149.

GAYET, GEORGE

3972　Necrologie.　SEIB 37 (1962) 255.

GEDDES, W. R.

3973　JUDKINS, RUSSELL A.　Silanting
Kuning's transformation, liminality in a Land Dayak myth.　An
analysis of *Nine Dayak nights*.
SMJ 17 (1969) 123-138.

GEELMUYDEN, NICOLOI

3974　Geelmuyden, Nicoloi.　JSS 52
(1964) 255.

GEERTZ, CLIFFORD

3975　CRUIKSHANK, ROBERT B.　Abangan,
Santri and Prijaji, a critique.
JSAS 3 (1972) 39-43.

GENEALOGY　*See also*　CHRONOLOGY

GENEALOGY - BRUNEI

3976　SHARIFFUDDIN, P. M.　Genealogical
tablet (Batu Tarsilah) of the sultans of Brunei, by P. M. Shariffuddin and Abd. Latif Hj. Ibrahim.
BMJ 3 pt. 2 (1974) 253-264.

GENEALOGY - BURMA

3977 SHORTO, H. L. Mon genealogy of kings, observations on the Nidana Arambhakatha. H18 pp. 63-72.

GENEALOGY - INDONESIA **

3978 GALVIN, A. D. Leppo Tau genealogies. SMJ 12 (1965) 173-175.

GENEALOGY - MALAYSIA - SARAWAK

3979 RICHARDS, ANTHONY. Descent of some Saribas Malays. SMJ 11 (1963) 99-107.

3980 SANDIN, BENEDICT. Descent of some Saribas Malays and Ibans. SMJ 11 (1964) 512-515.

GENEALOGY - THAILAND

3981 HANKS, JANE R. Recitation of patrilineages among the Akha. S58 pp. 114-127.

GENEVA AGREEMENT, 1962

3982 CZYZAK, JOHN J. International conference on Laos and the Geneva agreement of 1962, by John J. Czyzak and Carl F. Salans. JSAH 7 (Sept. 1966) 27-47.

3983 DOLEZAL, IVAN. Two attempts at the neutralization of Laos, 1954-1962. AAS 2 (1966) 68-102.

3984 LAM NGUYEN ANH. Geneva agreement and the Sisyhean war. AC 2 (July 1960) 29-36.

GENEVA CONFERENCE, 1954

3985 DOLEZAL, IVAN. Two attempts at the neutralization of Laos, 1954-1962. AAS 2 (1966) 68-102.

3986 LEE, CHAE JIN. Communist China and the Geneva conference on Laos, a reappraisal. AS 9 (1969) 522-539.

3987 THEE, MAREK. Background notes on the 1954 Geneva agreements on Laos and the Vientiane agreements of 1956-1957. L18 pp. 121-138.

GEOGRAPHY *See also* GEOLOGY

3988 FISHER, CHARLES A. Southeast Asia, the Balkans of the Orient? A study in continuity and change. T45 pp. 55-71.

3989 MEULEN, W. J. VAN DER. Suvarnadvipa and the Chryse Chersonesos. IND 18 (1974) 1-40.

3990 OOI JIN BEE. Human geography. AP 4 (1960) 137-140.

3991 OOI JIN BEE. Human geography. AP 5 (1961) 109-112.

3992 OOI JIN BEE. Human geography. AP 7 (1963) 101-104.

3993 OOI JIN BEE. Human geography, 1963. AP 8 (1964) 126-128.

GEOGRAPHY - INDONESIA

3994 PELZER, KARL J. Geographical literature on Indonesia. J37 pp. 90-116.

GEOGRAPHY - MALAYSIA

3995   OLOFIN, E. A. Classification of
       slope angles for land planning
       purposes. JTG 39 (1974) 72-77.

GEOGRAPHY - PHILIPPINES

3996   DWYER, D. J. Case for more geog-
       raphy in Philippine universities,
       by D. J. Dwyer, T. W. Luna and D.
       C. Salita. PS 9 (1961) 601-610.

GEOLOGY *See also* BEACHES, EARTHQUAKES,
   GEOGRAPHY, SOILS, VOLCANOES

3997   DUDAL, R. Major soils of South-
       east Asia, their characteristics,
       distribution, use and agricul-
       tural potential, by R. Dudal and
       F. R. Moormann. JTG 18 (1964)
       54-80.

3998   KOENIGSWALD, G. H. R. VON.
       Tektites in Borneo and elsewhere.
       SMJ 10 (1961) 319-324.

GEOLOGY - BRUNEI

3999   ANDERSON, J. A. R. Structure and
       development of the peat swamps of
       Sarawak and Brunei. JTG 18 (1964)
       7-16.

4000   ECKERT, H. R. Planktonic fora-
       minifera and time stratigraphy in
       well Ampa2. BMJ 2 pt. 1 (1970)
       320-327.

4001   TATE, R. B. Longshore drift and
       its effect on the new Muara Port.
       BMJ 2 pt. 1 (1970) 238-252.

4002   TATE, R. B. Paleo-environmental
       studies in Brunei. BMJ 3 pt. 2
       (1974) 285-305.

4003   TATE, R. B. Tektites in Brunei.
       BMJ 2 pt. 1 (1970) 253-263.

4004   WILFORD, G. E. Effects of late
       tertiary and quaternary tectonic
       movements on the geomorphological
       evolution of Brunei and adjacent
       parts of Sarawak. JTG 24 (1967)
       50-56.

GEOLOGY - BURMA

4005   BA THAN HAQ. Geology and economic
       possibilities of the area between
       the Pawn Chaung and Salween River,
       southeast of Loikaw, Kayah State,
       by Ba Than Haq and D. L. Searle.
       JBRS 44 (1961) 13-23.

4006   SARIN, DEV D. Petrography and
       origin of Taungtha formation ex-
       posed at Taungtha, Myingyan Dis-
       trict. JBRS 47 (1964) 183-204.

4007   SARIN, DEV D. Textural character-
       istics of channel sediments of the
       Chindwin River. JBRS 47 (1964)
       325-365.

4008   THA HLA. Petrography of the rocks
       of the Kyaukse Hill, Upper Burma,
       by Tha Hla and Ba Than. B91 pp.
       441-472.

GEOLOGY - INDONESIA

4009   MYERS, EARL H. Recent studies of
       sediments in the Java Sea and
       their significance in relation to
       stratigraphic and petroleum geol-
       ogy. H57 pp. 265-269.

4010   POSTHUMUS, O. Paleobotanical re-
       search in the Netherlands Indies,
       its past and its future. H57 pp.
       279-283.

Geology - Indonesia

4011 STAUFFER, H. Geology of the Netherlands Indies. H57 pp. 320-335.

4012 TJIA, H. D. Nature of displacements along the Semangko fault zone, Sumatra. JTG 30 (1970) 63-67.

4013 VERSTAPPEN, H. TH. Geomorphology of Sumatra. JTG 18 (1964) 184-191.

4014 VERSTAPPEN, H. TH. Some observations on Karst development in the Malay archipelago. JTG 14 (1960) 1-10.

GEOLOGY - MALAYSIA

4015 BURTON, C. K. Older alluvium of Johore and Singapore. JTG 18 (1964) 30-42.

4016 CHARLTON, F. G. Standard catchments in the estimation of flood flows. JTG 18 (1964) 43-53.

4017 DOUGLAS, IAN. Erosion in the Sungei Gombak catchment, Selangor, Malaysia. JTG 26 (1968) 1-16.

4018 EYLES, R. J. Depth of dissection of the west Malaysian landscape. JTG 28 (1969) 23-31.

4019 EYLES, R. J. Laterite at Kerdau, Pahang, Malaya. JTG 25 (1967) 18-23.

4020 HILL, R. D. Changes in beach form at Sri Pantai, northeast Johore, Malaysia. JTG 23 (1966) 19-27.

4021 JOSEPH, K. T. Sedentary soils of Kedah and their suggested utilization. JTG 18 (1964) 101-110.

4022 JOSEPH, K. T. Toposequence on limestone parent material in north Kedah, Malaya. JTG 27 (1968) 19-22.

4023 KOOPMANS, B. N. Geomorphological and historical data of the lower course of the Perak River (Dindings). JMBRAS 37 pt. 2 (1964) 175-191.

4024 NOSSIN, J. J. Beach ridges on the east coast of Malaya. JTG 18 (1964) 111-117.

4025 NOSSIN, J. J. Geomorphic history of the northern Pahang delta. JTG 20 (1965) 54-64.

4026 PANTON, W. P. The 1962 soil map of Malaya. JTG 18 (1964) 118-124.

4027 PATON, J. R. Origin of the limestone hills of Malaya. JTG 18 (1964) 134-147.

4028 SWAN, S. B. ST. C. Maps of two indices of terrain, Johor, Malaya. JTG 25 (1967) 48-57.

4029 TAY, T. H. Distribution, characteristics, uses and potential of peat in west Malaysia. JTG 29 (1969) 58-63.

4030 TJIA, H. D. Lineament pattern on Penang Island, west Malaysia. JTG 32 (1971) 56-61.

GEOLOGY - MALAYSIA - EAST MALAYSIA

4031 ANDERSON, J. A. R. Structure and development of the peat swamps of Sarawak and Brunei. JTG 18 (1964) 7-16.

4032 COLLENETTE, P. Physiographic classification of North Borneo. JTG 17 (1963) 28-33.

4033 HAILE, N. S. Quaternary geomor-
      phological history of north Sara-
      wak, discussion. SMJ 16 (1968)
      277-281.

4034 MILNE, JOHN. Earthquakes and re-
      lated phenomenia in north and
      west Borneo. SMJ 14 (1966) 1-5.

4035 WALL, J. R. D. Quaternary geo-
      morphological history of north
      Sarawak with special reference to
      the Subis Karst, Niah. SMJ 15
      (1967) 97-125.

4036 WALL, J. R. D. Topography-soil
      relationships in lowland Sarawak.
      JTG 18 (1964) 192-199.

4037 WILFORD, G. E. Effects of late
      tertiary and quaternary tectonic
      movements on the geomorphological
      evolution of Brunei and adjacent
      parts of Sarawak. JTG 24 (1967)
      50-56.

4038 WILFORD, G. E. Karst topography
      in Sarawak, by G. E. Wilford and
      J. R. D. Wall. JTG 21 (1965) 44-
      70.

GEOLOGY - PHILIPPINES

4039 BARRERA, ALFREDO. Classification
      and utilization of some Philippine
      soils. JTG 18 (1964) 17-29.

4040 ESPINAS, MERITO B. Eruptions of
      Mayon. UN 41 (1968) 251-256.

4041 LUNA, TELESFORO W. Land and
      natural resources of the Philip-
      pines. C47 pp. 161-184.

4042 SAMSON, JOSE A. Tarow caves of
      Dakuton. UN 40 (1967) 542-547.

GEOLOGY - SINGAPORE

4043 BURTON, C. K. Older alluvium of
      Johore and Singapore. JTG 18
      (1964) 30-42.

4044 WONG POH POH. Changing landscapes
      of Singapore Island. M49 pp. 20-
      51.

4045 WONG POH POH. Surface configura-
      tion of Singapore Island, a quan-
      titative description. JTG 29
      (1969) 64-74.

GEOLOGY - VIETNAM

4046 FONTAINE, HENRI. Publications du
      Service Geologique de la Direction
      des Ressources Naturelles, Minis-
      tere de l'Economie, Republique
      du Vietnam. SEIB 47 (1972) 523-
      537.

4047 HOANG THI THAN. Le Service Geo-
      logique de l'Indochine, 1898-1953.
      Le Service Geologique de la Re-
      publique du Vietnam, depuis 1953.
      SEIB 48 (1973) 607-617.

4048 Introduction a l'etude des sables
      littoraux du sud-Vietnam. Note
      no. 6. La vegetation du littoral
      entre Da-Nang (Tourone) et Hue,
      par J. P. Barry, Le Cong Kiet,
      Pham Hoang Ho, et Nguyen Van Thuy.
      SEIB 38 (1963) 509-529.

4049 NGUYEN HUY. Les formations
      lateritiques a Binh-Duong. SEIB
      43 (1968) 29-49.

GHIL, RENE

4050 GHIL, RENE. L'odeur d'Ilang-
      ilang. AR 1 (1970) 103-4.

Gibson-Hill, Carl Alexander

4068 LOMBARD, DENYS. Un expert Saxon dans les mines d'or de Sumatra au XVIIeme s. AR 2 (1971) 225-242.

4069 O'CONNOR, STANLEY J. Gold-foil burial amulets in Bali, Philippines and Borneo, by Stanley J. O'Connor and Tom Harrisson. JMBRAS 44 pt. 1 (1971) 71-77.

GOLD - LAOS

4070 KAUFMAN, RICHARD H. Asian gold trade. AS 5 (1965) 233-244.

GOLD - MALAYSIA - SARAWAK

4071 HARRISSON, TOM. Gold in west Borneo, by Tom Harrisson and Stanley J. O'Connor. SMJ 17 (1969) 1-66.

4072 HARRISSON, TOM. Gold, west Borneo and Philippine crafts compared. SMJ 16 (1968) 77-84.

4073 HARRISSON, TOM. Golden keris handle from Balingian, Sarawak. JMBRAS 39 pt. 1 (1966) 175-181.

4074 O'CONNOR, STANLEY J. Gold-foil burial amulets in Bali, Philippines and Borneo, by Stanley J. O'Connor and Tom Harrisson. JMBRAS 44 pt. 1 (1971) 71-77.

GOLD - PHILIPPINES

4075 FRANCISCO, JUAN R. Golden image of Agusan, a new identification. AST 1 (1963) 31-38.

4076 FRANCISCO, JUAN R. Note on the golden image of Agusan. PS 11 (1963) 390-400.

4077 HARRISSON, TOM. Gold, west Borneo and Philippine crafts compared. SMJ 16 (1968) 77-84.

4078 MEULEN, W. J. VAN DER. Agusan image. PS 12 (1964) 347.

4079 O'CONNOR, STANLEY J. Gold-foil burial amulets in Bali, Philippines and Borneo, by Stanley J. O'Connor and Tom Harrisson. JMBRAS 44 pt. 1 (1971) 71-77.

GOLD - SINGAPORE

4080 WINSTEDT, RICHARD O. Gold ornaments dug up at Fort Canning, Singapore. JMBRAS 42 pt. 1 (1969) 49-52.

GOLD - THAILAND

4081 KAUFMAN, RICHARD H. Asian gold trade. AS 5 (1965) 233-244.

GOLD - VIETNAM

4082 MALLERET, LOUIS. Les dodecaedres d'or du site D'oc-Eo. G83 pp. 343-350.

GOLOUBEW, VICTOR

4083 MALLERET, LOUIS. Un oublie, Victor Goloubew, membre de l'Ecole Francaise d'Extreme-Orient, 1878-1945. SEIB 39 (1964) 433-448.

4084 MALLERET, LOUIS. Vingtieme anniversaire de la mort de Victor Goloubew, 1878-1945. BEF 53 (1966) 331-373.

Gomes, Mariano

GROOT VAN KRAAIJENBURG, JOHAN PIETER
 CORNETS DE

4099 REINSMA, R. Uit de Aantekeningen
      van een oud-Indisch ambtenaar,
      Jhr. Johan Pieter Cornets de
      Groot van Kraaijenburg. BIJ 122
      (1966) 229-254.

GUARDIA DE HONOR DE MARIA

4100 STURTEVANT, DAVID R. Guardia de
      Honor, revitalization within the
      revolution. AST 4 (1966) 342-
      352.

GUERRERO, WILFREDO MA.

4101 GARCIA, ANGELINA M. Critique on
      Wilfredo Ma. Guerrero's play
      Close-up. DR 20 (1972) 137-143.

GUERRILLA WARFARE

4102 EQBAL AHMAD. Revolutionary war-
      fare and counterinsurgency. N15
      pp. 137-213.

4103 ROUCEK, JOSEPH S. Role of com-
      munist guerrillas in Far East and
      South-East Asia. AQ (1972) 157-
      166.

4104 STUPAK, RONALD J. Guerrilla war-
      fare, a strategic analysis in the
      superpower context, by Ronald J.
      Stupak and Donald C. Booher. RSA
      (1970) 181-196.

GUERRILLA WARFARE - PHILIPPINES

4105 HART, DONN V. Bibliographical
      essay, guerrilla warfare and the
      Filipino resistance on Negros
      Island in the Bisayas, 1942-1945.
      JSAH 5 (Mar. 1964) 101-125.

4106 LEAR, ELMER N. Western Leyte
      guerrilla warfare forces, a case
      study in the non-legitimation of
      a guerrilla organization. JSAH 9
      (1968) 69-94.

4107 LENT, JOHN A. Guerrilla presses
      of the Philippines, 1941-45. AST
      8 (1970) 260-274.

GUERRILLA WARFARE - THAILAND

4108 ESPOSITO, BRUCE J. Can a single
      spark ignite a paddyfield, the
      case of Thai insurgency. AST 8
      (1970) 318-325.

GUERRILLA WARFARE - VIETNAM *See also*
 VIETNAM WAR

4109 FOURNIAU, CHARLES. Les traditions
      de la lutte nationale au Vietnam,
      l'insurrection des lettres, 1885-
      1895. C28 pp. 89-107.

4110 HENDRY, JAMES B. Economic devel-
      opment under conditions of guer-
      rilla warfare, the case of Viet-
      nam. AS 2 (June 1962) 1-12.

4111 JOHNSON, CHALMERS. Third genera-
      tion of guerrilla warfare. AS 8
      (1968) 435-447.

GUILLEMINET, PAUL

4112 MALLERET, LOUIS. Paul Guilleminet,
      1888-1966. BEF 54 (1968) 1-8.

GUILLERMO, GELACIO Y.

4113 HOSILLOS, LUCILA. A poet takes on
      the dragon. DR 18 (1970) 284-292.

Habib Abdur Rahman

HARVARD UNIVERSITY

4131 APPELL, G. N. Penis pin at Pea-
      body Museum, Harvard University.
      JMBRAS 41 pt. 2 (1968) 203-205.

4132 ESTACIO, CEFERINA I. C. Harvard
      literacy project in Israel and its
      implication for the Philippines.
      UN 40 (1967) 563-578.

HAVILAND, C. D.

4133 HARRISSON, TOM. Second to none,
      our first curator, and others.
      SMJ 10 (1961) 17-29.

HAW

4134 MOTE, F. W. Rural Haw (Yunnanese
      Chinese) of northern Thailand.
      K86 pp. 487-524.

HAWAII. UNIVERSITY. EAST-WEST CENTER

4135 WITTERMANS, T. Enkele aanteken-
      ingen over het East West Center te
      Honolulu. BIJ 120 (1964) 461-465.

HAWKINS, EVERETT D.

4136 In memoriam, Everett D. Hawkins.
      SA 1 (1971) 2-3.

HAYDEN, JOSEPH RALSTON

4137 EDGERTON, RONALD K. Joseph
      Ralston Hayden, the education of
      a colonialist. C31 pp. 195-226.

HEINE-GELDERN, ROBERT VON

4138 HOLT, CLAIRE. In memoriam Robert
      Heine-Geldern. IND 6 (1968) 188-
      192.

4139 KANEKO, ERIKA. Robert von Heine-
      Geldern, 1885-1968. AP 13 (1970)
      1-10.

HELMS, LUDVIG VERNER

4140 GARDNER, ESTELLE. Footnote to
      Sarawak, 1859. SMJ 11 (1963) 32-
      59.

4141 GARDNER, ESTELLE. Island strife
      and L. V. Helms. SMJ 14 (1966)
      396-421.

HERNANDEZ, AMADO V.

4142 Amado V. Hernandez. PS 18 (1970)
      227-8.

4143 CRUZ, ANDRES CRISTOBAL. Ka Amado,
      Bartolina at Barikada. PS 19
      (1971) 255-286.

4144 MALAY, ROSARIO R. *Mga Ibong Man-
      daragit* and the second propaganda
      movement. GEJ 17 (1969) 107-117.

4145 MELENDREZ, PATRICIA M. Monomythic
      reading of Amado V. Hernandez's
      Mga Ibong Mandaragit. GEJ 7
      (1964) 39-47.

HERZOG, BISHOP

4146 ACHUTEGUI, PEDRO S. DE. Brent,
      Herzog, Morayta and Aglipay, by
      Pedro S. de Achutegui and Miguel
      A. Bernad. PS 8 (1960) 568-583.

HIKAYAT ABDULLAH

4147 MUNSHI ABDULLAH. Hikayat Abdullah.
      JMBRAS 42 pt. 1 (1969) 85-106.

Hikayat Acheh

HIKAYAT ACHEH

4148 ISKANDAR, T. Three Malay historical writings in the first half of
the 17th century. JMBRAS 40 pt. 2
(1967) 38-53.

4149 PENTH, HANS GEORG. Account in the
Hikajat Atjeh on relations between
Siam and Atjeh. F38 pp. 55-69.

4150 PENTH, HANS GEORG. Zur Siam
episode in der Hikajat Atjeh.
JSS 55 (1967) 287-290.

HIKAYAT BACHTIAR

4151 VOORHOEVE, P. De grote Hikajat
Bachtiar. BIJ 125 (1969) 374-5.

HIKAYAT HANG TUAH

4152 ISKANDAR, T. Some historical
sources used by the author of
Hikayat Hang Tuah. JMBRAS 43 pt.
1 (1970) 35-47.

HIKAYAT MUHAMMAD MUKABIL

4153 DREWES, G. W. J. Hikayat Muhammad
Mukabil, the story of the Kadi and
the learned brigand. BIJ 126
(1970) 309-331.

HIKAYAT PATANI

4154 WYATT, DAVID. Thai version of
Newbold's Hikayat Patani. JMBRAS
40 pt. 2 (1967) 16-37.

HIKAYAT RAJA-RAJA PASAI

4155 Hikayat Raja-Raja Pasai, a revised romanised version of Raffles MS 67, together with an

English translation by A. H. Hill.
JMBRAS 33 pt. 2 (1960) 7-215.

4156 SWEENEY, P. L. AMIN. Connection
between the Hikayat Raja2 Pasai
and the Sejarah Melayu. JMBRAS
40 pt. 2 (1967) 94-105.

4157 TEEUW, A. Hikayat Raja-Raja Pasai
and Sejarah Melayu. B38 pp. 222-
234.

HILARIO, VICENTO

4158 On Professor Vicento Hilario. DR
14 (1966) 200-202.

HILIGAYNON LITERATURE

4159 *Barter of Panay*, a drama adapted
from R. Demetillo's *Barter in
Panay* and the Hiligaynon epic
Maragtas. DR 14 (1966) 109-126.

4160 FERNANDEZ, DOREEN G. Ten Hiligaynon poems, translations and an
introduction. PS 21 (1973) 187-205.
205.

HINDUISM

4161 BOELES, J. J. Migration of the
magic syllable Om. J41 pp. 40-56.

4162 COEDES, GEORGE. Some problems in
the ancient history of the Hinduized states of South-East Asia.
JSAH 5 (Sept. 1964) 1-14.

4163 MUS, PAUL. Cosmodrames et politique en Asie du sud-est. D44 pp.
75-98.

4164 THAO NHOUY ABHAY. Sur l'histoire
des etats compris entre l'Inde et
la Chine. JBRS 43 (1960) 91-93.

HINDUISM - BURMA

4165 GUHA, DEVAPRASAD. Ghoramanta,
      alias Goravinda, a Burmese god.
      JBRS 43 (1960) 51-55.

HINDUISM - CAMBODIA

4166 BENISTI, MIREILLE. Notes d'icon-
      ographie khmere. VIII. Le lin-
      teau de Vat Preah Theat. BEF 58
      (1971) 125-130.

4167 BENISTI, MIREILLE. Notes d'icon-
      ographie khmere. X. Premieres
      representations de Sri Laksmi.
      BEF 61 (1974) 349-354.

4168 THIERRY, SOLANGE. Les danses
      sacrees au Cambodge. D25 pp. 343-
      374.

HINDUISM - INDONESIA **

4169 COEDES, GEORGE. Les recherches de
      Bosch sur l'epoque des Sailendra,
      le probleme de l'expansion indi-
      enne dans l'archipel. H39 pp. 42-
      47.

4170 DAMAIS, LOUIS-CHARLES. Etudes
      javanaises. Le nom de la diete
      tantrique de 1214 Saka. BEF 50
      (1960) 407-416.

4171 HOOYKAAS, C. Saiva-Siddhanta in
      Java and Bali, some remarks on its
      recent study. BIJ 118 (1962) 309-
      327.

4172 HOOYKAAS, JACOBA. Myth of the
      young cowherd and the little girl.
      BIJ 117 (1961) 267-278.

4173 KANWAR, H. I. S. Indian culture
      in Indonesia. FA 17 (1960) 1819-
      1823.

4174 MINATTUR, JOSEPH. Gaja Mada's
      Palapa. JMBRAS 39 pt. 1 (1966)
      185-187.

4175 MINATTUR, JOSEPH. Gaja Mada's
      Palapa. RSA (1966) 237-239.

4176 POTT, P. H. Bosch' contribution
      to the study of Indian symbolism.
      H39 pp. 88-94.

4177 SARKAR, HIMANSU BHUSAN. South
      India in old Javanese and Sanskrit
      inscriptions. BIJ 125 (1969) 193-
      206.

HINDUISM - INDONESIA - BALI **

4178 BATESON, GREGORY. Old temple and
      a new myth. B43 pp. 111-136.

4179 BOON, JAMES A. Progress of the
      ancestors in a Balinese temple
      group, pre 1906-1972. JAS 34
      (1974-5) 7-25.

4180 CUISINIER, JEANNE. Les danses
      sacrees a Bali et a Java. D25 pp.
      375-410.

4181 GEERTZ, CLIFFORD. Internal con-
      version in contemporary Bali. B38
      pp. 282-302.

4182 GORIS, R. Holidays and holy days.
      B18 pp. 113-129.

4183 GORIS, R. Temple system. B18 pp.
      100-111.

4184 GRADER, C. J. Balang Tamak. B19
      pp. 175-188.

4185 GRADER, C. J. Pemayun temple of
      the Banjar of Tegal. B18 pp. 187-
      231.

4185a GRADER, C. J. Pura Meduwe Karang
      at Kubutambahan. B19 pp. 131-174.

Hinduism - Indonesia - Bali

4186 GRADER, C. J. State temples of
Mengwi. B18 pp. 155-186.

4187 HOOYKAAS, C. Balinese Sengguhu
priest, a shaman, but not a sufi,
a Saiva and a Vaisnava. B38 pp.
267-281.

4188 HOOYKAAS, C. Bauddha brahmins in
Bali. SOAS 26 (1963) 544-550.

4189 HOOYKAAS, C. Exorcistic litany
from Bali. BIJ 125 (1969) 356-
370.

4190 HOOYKAAS, C. Saiva-Siddhanta in
Java and Bali, some remarks on its
recent study. BIJ 118 (1962) 309-
327.

4191 HOOYKAAS, JACOBA. Balinese folktale on the origin of mice. BIJ
117 (1961) 279-281.

4192 I GUSTI NGURAH BAGUS. Karya Taur
Agung Ekadasa Rudra, rite centenaire de purification au temple
de Besakih, Bali. AR 8 (1974)
59-66.

4193 KORN, V. E. Consecration of a
priest. B18 pp. 131-153.

4194 MEAD, MARGARET. Children and
ritual in Bali. B43 pp. 198-211.

4195 SWELLENGREBEL, J. L. Religious
practices of the family and the
individual. B18 pp. 54-67.

4196 SWELLENGREBEL, J. L. Some religious problems of today. B18 pp.
68-76.

4197 TAN, ROGER Y. D. Domestic
architecture of south Bali. BIJ
123 (1967) 442-475.

HINDUISM - MALAYSIA

4198 WALES, H. G. QUARITCH. Malayan
archaeology of the Hindu period,
some reconsiderations. JMBRAS 43
pt. 1 (1970) 1-34.

HINDUISM - SINGAPORE

4199 BABB, LAWRENCE A. Hindu medium-
ship in Singapore. SAJSS 2 (1974)
29-43.

HINDUISM - THAILAND

4200 FILLIOZAT, JEAN. Kailasaparampara. F38 pp. 241-247.

4201 GRISWOLD, A. B. Epigraphic and
historical studies. No. 14. Inscription of the Siva of Kamben
Bejra, by A. B. Griswold and Prasert na Nagara. JSS 62 pt. 2
(1974) 223-238.

4202 O'CONNOR, STANLEY J. Early Brah-
manical sculpture at Songkhla.
JSS 52 (1964) 163-169.

4203 O'CONNOR, STANLEY J. Ekamukha-
linga from peninsular Siam. JSS
54 (1966) 43-53.

4204 O'CONNOR, STANLEY J. Takuapa
Visnu, a further note. JMBRAS 41
pt. 1 (1968) 205-207.

4205 SIMMONDS, E. H. S. New evidence
on Thai shadow play invocations.
SOAS 24 (1961) 542-559.

4206 WALES, H. G. QUARITCH. Note on
the Takuapa Visnu. JMBRAS 40 pt.
1 (1967) 153-4.

HISTORIANS – INDONESIA

4207   DE CASPARIS, J. G. Historical writing on Indonesia, early period. H18 pp. 121-163.

4208   HARRISON, B. English historians of the Indian archipelago, Crawfurd and St. John. H18 pp. 245-254.

4209   PLUVIER, J. M. Recent Dutch contributions to modern Indonesian history. JSAH 8 (1967) 201-225.

4210   SARTONO KARTODIRDJO. Historical study and historians in Indonesia today. JSAH 4 (Mar. 1963) 22-29.

4211   SOEDJATMOKO. The Indonesian historian and his time. S61 pp. 404-415.

HISTORIANS – PHILIPPINES

4212   CARROLL, JOHN. Contemporary Philippine historians and Philippine history. JSAH 2 (Oct. 1961) 23-35.

HISTORIOGRAPHY AND HISTORICAL SOURCES
See also ARCHIVES, CHRONOLOGY, LIBRARY RESOURCES ON . . ., MANUSCRIPTS

4213   CHIU LING YEONG. Ming Shih-lu, new studies on South-East Asia. S93 pp. 212-3.

4214   FRANKE, WOLFGANG. Some remarks on Chinese historical sources on Southeast Asia, with particular consideration of the Ming period, 1368-1644. SAA 2 (1968) 11-20.

4215   GRAAF, H. J. DE. Aspects of Dutch historical writings on colonial activities in South East Asia, with special reference to the indigenous peoples during the sixteenth and seventeenth centuries. H18 pp. 213-224.

4216   HALL, D. G. E. Integrity of Southeast Asian history. JSAS 4 (1973) 159-168.

4217   HALL, D. G. E. On the study of Southeast Asian history. PA 33 (1960) 268-281.

4218   KESWANI, D. G. Archival sources of Southeast Asian history in the National Archives of India. SAA 2 (1969) 3-10.

4219   MACDONALD, A. W. Application of a South East Asia centric conception of history to mainland South East Asia. H18 pp. 326-335.

4220   MACGREGOR, I. A. Some aspects of Portuguese historical writing of the sixteenth and seventeenth centuries on Southeast Asia. H18 pp. 172-199.

4221   MACHIN, G. I. T. Colonial post-mortem, a survey of the historical controversy. JSAH 3 (Sept. 1962) 129-138.

4222   MEILINK-ROELOFSZ, M. A. P. Private papers of Artus Gijsels as a source for the history of East Asia. JSAH 10 (1969) 540-559.

4223   MEILINK-ROELOFSZ, M. A. P. Sources in the General State Archives in the Hague relating to the history of East Asia between c.1600 and c.1800. F38 pp. 167-184.

4224   MILLS, L. A. American historical writing on South East Asia. H18 pp. 286-300.

Historiography and historical sources

4225 MOIR, MARTIN I. Archival materials in the London records of the East India Company and of the India Office relating to Southeast Asia. SAA 2 (1969) 68-81.

4226 PEARSON, JAMES D. Manuscripts and documents in the British Isles relating to South-East Asia, the Wainwright-Matthews guide. SAA 2 (1969) 65-67.

4227 ROMEIN, J. M. Significance of the comparative approach in Asian historiography. S61 pp. 380-394.

4228 SMAIL, JOHN R. W. On the possibility of an autonomous history of modern Southeast Asia. JSAH 2 (July 1961) 72-102.

HISTORIOGRAPHY AND HISTORICAL SOURCES - BRUNEI

4229 BROWN, D. E. Sultan Mumins will and related documents. BMJ 3 pt. 2 (1974) 156-170.

4230 Spanish accounts of their expeditions against Brunei in 1578-79. BMJ 3 pt. 2 (1974) 180-221.

HISTORIOGRAPHY AND HISTORICAL SOURCES - BURMA

4231 ADAS, MICHAEL. Imperialist rhetoric and modern historiography, the case of Lower Burma before and after conquest. JSAS 3 (1972) 175-192.

4232 BA, VIVIAN. Extracts from the collection of laws and customs of the Great South (Kingdom of Vietnam) and the true history of the Great South, additional data from French, Vietnamese and other sources on the Burmese embassy to Vietnam in 1823-24. JBRS 49 (1966) 35-50.

4233 BA, VIVIAN. King Mindon and the world fair of 1867 held in Paris, from documents in the French Foreign Office. JBRS 48 (Dec. 1965) 17-23.

4234 BA, VIVIAN. One century recalls another. JBRS 46 (June 1963) 65-79.

4235 BLACKMORE, THAUNG. Burmese historical literature and native and foreign scholarship, a few observations. S93 pp. 310-319.

4236 SHORTO, H. L. Mon genealogy of kings, observations on the Nidana Arambhakatha. H18 pp. 63-72.

4237 TET HTOOT. Nature of the Burmese chronicles. H18 pp. 50-62.

4238 TIN OHN. Modern historical writing in Burmese, 1724-1942, a brief study of the Burmese chronicles of the eighteenth and nineteenth centuries and their influence upon historical writing. H18 pp. 85-93.

4239 TINKER, HUGH. Burma. W43 pp. 448-459.

4240 YI YI. Additional Burmese historiographical sources, 1752-78. SAA 2 (1969) 119-138.

4241 YI YI. Burmese sources for the history of the Konbaung period, 1752-1885. JSAH 6 (Mar. 1965) 48-66.

HISTORIOGRAPHY AND HISTORICAL SOURCES - CAMBODIA

4242 MALLERET, L. Position of historical studies in the countries of

Historiography and historical sources –
Indonesia

former French Indo-China in 1956.
H18 pp. 301-312.

HISTORIOGRAPHY AND HISTORICAL SOURCES –
INDONESIA **

4243 ANDI ZAINAL ABIDIN. Notes on the
lontara as historical sources.
IND 12 (1971) 159-172.

4244 BAMBANG OETOMO. Some remarks on
modern Indonesian historiography.
H18 pp. 73-84.

4245 BASTIN, JOHN. English sources for
the modern period of Indonesian
history. S61 pp. 252-271.

4246 BERG, C. C. Javanese historiography, a synopsis of its evolution. H18 pp. 13-23.

4247 BERG, C. C. Work of Professor
Krom. H18 pp. 164-171.

4248 BOTTOMS, J. C. Some Malay historical sources, a bibliographical
note. S61 pp. 156-193.

4249 BOXER, C. R. Some Portuguese
sources for Indonesian historiography. S61 pp. 217-233.

4250 COOLHAAS, W. PH. Dutch contributions to the historiography of
colonial activity in the eighteenth and nineteenth centuries.
H18 pp. 225-234.

4251 DAMAIS, L. CH. Preseventeenth
century Indonesian history,
sources and directions. S61 pp.
24-35.

4252 DE CASPARIS, J. G. Historical
writing on Indonesia, early period. H18 pp. 121-163.

4253 DJAJADININGRAT, HOESEIN. Local
traditions and the study of Indonesian history. S61 pp. 74-85.

4254 DREWES, G. W. J. New light on the
coming of Islam to Indonesia? BIJ
124 (1968) 433-459.

4255 GRAAF, H. J. DE. Later Javanese
sources and historiography. S61
pp. 118-136.

4256 HOOYKAAS, C. Critical stage in
the study of Indonesia's past.
H18 pp. 313-325.

4257 IRWIN, GRAHAM. Dutch historical
sources. S61 pp. 234-251.

4258 JOHNS, ANTHONY H. Muslim mystics
and historical writing. H18 pp.
37-49.

4259 JOHNS, ANTHONY H. Role of struc-
tural organisation and myth in
Javanese historiography. JAS 24
(1964-5) 91-99.
Comment: BERG, C. C. Commentary.
JAS 24 (1964-5) 100-103.

4260 KISHI, KOICHI. Recent Japanese
sources for Indonesian historiography. S61 pp. 206-216.

4261 KOENTJARANINGRAT. Use of anthropological methods in Indonesian
historiography. S61 pp. 299-325.

4262 LOMBARD, DENYS. Deuxieme semi-
naire d'histoire nationale, Djog-
djakarta, 26-29 aout 1970. Les
Indonesiens font le point sur
l'histoire de leur pays. BEF 58
(1971) 281-298.

4263 McVEY, RUTH T. Soviet sources for
Indonesian history. S61 pp. 272-
298.

Historiography and historical sources –
  Indonesia

4264 MOHAMMAD ALI. Historiographical
      problems. S61 pp. 1-23.

4265 NOORDUYN, J. Origins of south
      Celebes historical writing. S61
      pp. 137-155.

4266 NOORDUYN, J. Some aspects of
      Macassar-Buginese historiography.
      H18 pp. 29-36.

4267 NUGROHO NOTOSUSANTO. Problems in
      the study and teaching of national
      history in Indonesia. JSAH 6
      (Mar. 1965) 1-16.

4268 SARTONO KARTODIRDJO. Historical
      study and historians in Indonesia
      today. JSAH 4 (Mar. 1963) 22-29.

4269 Selected documents relating to the
      September 30th movement and its
      epilogue. IND 1 (1966) 131-204.

4270 SOETJIPTO WIRJOSOEPARTO. Signif-
      icance of the chronograms
      (Tjandra-Sengkala) for the inter-
      pretation of the history of Indo-
      nesia. JOSA 8 (1971) 96-112.

4271 TAN, F. J. E. Aspects of an In-
      donesian economic historiography.
      S61 pp. 395-403.

4272 VAN NIEL, ROBERT. Nineteenth cen-
      tury Java, an analysis of his-
      torical sources and method. AST
      4 (1966) 201-212.

4273 ZOETMULDER, P. J. Significance of
      the study of culture and religion
      for Indonesian historiography.
      S61 pp. 326-343.

HISTORIOGRAPHY AND HISTORICAL SOURCES –
  LAOS

4274 MALLERET, L. Position of histori-
      cal studies in the countries of

former French Indo-China in 1956.
H18 pp. 301-312.

HISTORIOGRAPHY AND HISTORICAL SOURCES –
  MALAYSIA

4275 BASTIN, JOHN. Problems of per-
      sonality in the reinterpretation
      of modern Malayan history. B38
      pp. 141-155.

4276 BOTTOMS, J. C. Some Malay his-
      torical sources, a bibliographical
      note. S61 pp. 156-193.

4277 KACHORN SUKHABANIJ. Siamese docu-
      ments concerning Captain Francis
      Light. J45 pp. 1-9.

4278 SNEDDON, J. N. A problem in the
      sources of Malaya's history. JOSA
      5 (1967) 152-157.

4279 TURNBULL, C. MARY. Malaysia. W43
      pp. 460-492.

HISTORIOGRAPHY AND HISTORICAL SOURCES –
  PHILIPPINES

4280 BOXER, C. R. Preliminary report
      on a collection of documents
      looted at Manila in 1762-64, and
      now in the Lilly Library, Indiana
      University. SAA 2 (1969) 104-107.

4281 BOXER, C. R. Some aspects of
      Spanish historical writing on the
      Philippines. H18 pp. 200-212.

4282 DIAZ-TRECHUELO, MARIA LOURDES.
      Primary sources on the history of
      the Philippines in archives and
      libraries of Spain. PHR 2 (1969)
      1-247.

4283 DIAZ-TRECHUELO, MARIA LOURDES.
      Primary sources on the history of
      the Philippines in archives and

libraries in Spain.   SAA 2 (1969)
108-118.

4284   FAST, JONATHAN.   Philippine historiography and the de-mystifica-
tion of imperialism, a review
essay, by Jonathan Fast and Luzviminda Francisco.   JCA 4 (1974)
344-358.

4285   HART, DONN V.   Central Philippines University's World War II
manuscript collection.   JAS 25
(1965-6) 123.

4286   HART, DONN V.   Central Philippines University's World War II
manuscript collection.   JSAH 6
(Sept. 1965) 129-130.

4287   LARKIN, JOHN A.   Place of local
history in Philippine historiography.   JSAH 8 (1967) 306-317.

4288   Philippine historical documents in
the National Archives of Mexico.
AST 4 (1966) 149-197.

4289   SCHUMACHER, JOHN N.   The Cavite
Mutiny, an essay on the published
sources.   PS 20 (1972) 603-632.

4290   SCOTT, WILLIAM HENRY.   Critical
study of the prehispanic source
materials for the study of Philippine history.   UN 42 (1968)
275-440.

4291   SCOTT, WILLIAM HENRY.   Proper use
of documents.   PS 11 (1963) 328-
335.
Comment: ACHUTEGUI, PEDRO S. DE.
Reply to Mr. Scott, by Pedro S.
de Achutegui and Miguel A. Bernad.
PS 11 (1963) 335-341.

HISTORIOGRAPHY AND HISTORICAL SOURCES – THAILAND

4292   BREAZEALE, KENNON.   Transition in
historical writing, the works of
Prince Damrong Rachanuphap.   JSS
59 pt. 2 (1971) 25-49.

4293   DAMRONG, PRINCE.   The story of the
records of Siamese history.   S44.1
pp. 79-98.

4294   GRIMM, T.   Thailand in the light
of official Chinese historiography,
a chapter in the history of the
Ming dynasty.   JSS 49 pt. 1 (1961)
1-20.

4295   KACHORN SUKHABANIJ.   Siamese documents concerning Captain Francis
Light.   J45 pp. 1-9.

4296   REYNOLDS, CRAIG J.   Case of K. S.
R. Kulap, a challenge to royal
historical writing in late nineteenth century Thailand.   JSS 61
pt. 2 (1973) 63-90.

4297   WYATT, DAVID K.   Thai historical
materials in Bangkok, by David K.
Wyatt and Constance M. Wilson.
JAS 25 (1965-6) 105-118.

HISTORIOGRAPHY AND HISTORICAL SOURCES – VIETNAM **

4298   CHESNEAUX, JEAN.   French historiography and the evolution of colonial Vietnam.   H18 pp. 235-244.

4299   HONEY, P. J.   Modern Vietnamese
historiography.   H18 pp. 94-104.

4300   KIMURA, SOKICHI.   Annotated translation of *Dai-nam Chinh-bien Liet-
truyen So-tap, Nam-chuong-truyen*
(description of Luang Prabang).
SA 1 (1971) 153-163.

Historiography and historical sources –
  Vietnam

4301 MALLERET, L. Position of histori-
      cal studies in the countries of
      former French Indo-China in 1956.
      H18 pp. 301-312.

4302 NGUYEN THE ANH. Les publications
      de documents historiques dans la
      Republique du Vietnam depuis 1955.
      SEIB 43 (1968) 53-60.

4303 OSBORNE, MILTON E. Truong Vinh
      Ky and Phan Thanh Gian, the prob-
      lem of a nationalist interpreta-
      tion of 19th century Vietnamese
      history. JAS 30 (1970-1) 81-93.

4304 SMITH, R. B. Sino-Vietnamese
      sources for the Nguyen period, an
      introduction. SOAS 30 (1967)
      600-621.

4305 WHITMORE, JOHN K. Note on the
      location of source materials for
      early Vietnamese history. JAS 29
      (1969-70) 657-662.

4306 WHITMORE, JOHN K. Vietnamese
      historical sources for the reign
      of Le Thanh-tong, 1460-1497. JAS
      29 (1969-70) 373-394.

HMONG

4307 MORECHAND, GUY. Le chamanisme des
      Hmong. BEF 54 (1968) 53-294.

HO CHI MINH

4308 FALL, BERNARD B. Ho Chi Minh,
      like it or not. T45 pp. 412-425.

4309 Ho Chi Minh, an appreciation by
      the U.S. Office of Strategic
      Services. FA 23 (1969) 304.

4310 UTRECHT, ERNST. Interview with
      Ho Chi Minh. JCA 3 (1973) 219-
      223.

HO LING

4311 DAMAIS, LOUIS-CHARLES. Etudes
      sino-indonesiennes. III. La
      transcription chinoise Ho Ling
      comme designation de Java. BEF
      52 (1964) 93-141.

HOLT, CLAIRE

4312 ANDERSON, BENEDICT. In memoriam,
      Claire Holt. IND 10 (1970) 190-
      193.

HOOP, A. N. J. TH. A. TH. VAN DER

4313 BERNET KEMPERS, A. J. In memoriam
      Dr. A. N. J. Th. a Th. van der
      Hoop, 9 Maart 1893-2 Februari
      1969. BIJ 125 (1969) 401-428.

HOUGRON, JEAN

4314 BOAK, DENIS. Jean Hougron and *La
      nuit indochinoise*. FA 18 (1962)
      489-501.

HOUSING

4315 DWYER, D. J. Attitudes towards
      spontaneous settlement in third
      world cities. D92 pp. 166-178.

4316 WHEATON, WILLIAM L. C. Urban
      housing in economic development,
      by William L. C. and Margaret F.
      Wheaton. D92 pp. 141-151.

HOUSING – INDONESIA

4317 TAN, ROGER Y. D. Domestic archi-
      tecture of south Bali. BIJ 123
      (1967) 442-475.

HOUSING - MALAYSIA

4318 APPELL, GEORGE N. Long-house apartment of the Rungus Dusun. SMJ 11 (1964) 570-573.

4319 CRAIN, JAY B. Mengalong Lun Dayeh longhouse. SMJ 18 (1970) 169-185.

4320 GALVIN, A. D. Headhunting, fact or fiction? BMJ 3 pt. 2 (1974) 16-104.

4321 SHEPPARD, MUBIN. Traditional Malay house forms in Trengganu and Kelantan. JMBRAS 42 pt. 2 (1969) 1-9.

HOUSING - PHILIPPINES **

4322 BELLO, MOISES C. Some notes on house styles in a Kankanai village. AST 3 (1965) 41-54.

4323 BENNETT, D. C. Some rural and urban housing differences in the Philippines. PS 18 (1970) 654-658.

4324 ENDRIGA, DOLORES A. Housing aspirations of three groups of U.P. campus residents. GEJ 21 (1971) 103-4.

4325 JAINAL, TUWAN IKLALI. House-building among the Tausug, by Tuwan Iklali Jainal, Gerard Rixhon and David Ruppert. S91 pp. 81-121.

4326 PACYAYA, ALFREDO G. Acculturation and culture change in Sagada. SJ 11 (1964) 14-25.

4327 The Philippine 1970 census on population and housing, an interpretation for the northern Luzon provinces, by Paul Beghin, Raf van Hellemont, Juan Ngalob and Emiel Roekaerts. SLURJ 3 (1972) 327-356.

4328 REYNOLDS, HUBERT. Multi-level house of the Manobo in Salangsang and its inter-relations with other aspects of culture. SJ 13 (1966) 581-593.

HOUSING - SINGAPORE

4329 GOH CHUI MUAH. Note on housing finance in Singapore. MER 18 pt. 2 (1973) 37-42.

4330 GREENWOOD, PETER G. Buildings and climate in Singapore, by Peter G. Greenwood and R. D. Hill. JTG 26 (1968) 37-47.

4331 TEH CHEANG WAN. Public housing. M49 pp. 171-180.

4332 WEE, ANN. Some social implications of rehousing programmes in Singapore. D92 pp. 216-230.

4333 YEH, STEPHEN H. K. Housing conditions and housing needs in Singapore. MER 19 pt. 2 (1974) 47-71.

4334 YEH, STEPHEN H. K. Housing conditions in Singapore, by Stephen H. K. Yeh and Lee Yoke San. MER 13 pt. 1 (1968) 11-38.

4335 YEH, STEPHEN H. K. Size and structure of households in Singapore, 1957-1966. MER 12 pt. 2 (1967) 97-115.

4336 YEUNG, YUE MAN. Commercial patterns in Singapore's public housing estates, by Yeung Yue Man and Stephen H. K. Yeh. JTG 33 (1971) 73-86.

Housing - Singapore

4337 YEUNG, YUE MAN. Comparative per-
spectives on public housing in
Singapore and Hong Kong, by Yeung
Yue Man and D. W. Drakakis-Smith.
AS 14 (1974) 763-775.

4338 YOU POH SENG. Sample household
survey of Singapore, 1966, by You
Poh Seng and Stephen H. K. Yeh.
MER 12 pt. 1 (1967) 47-63.

HOUSING - THAILAND

4339 KRAISRI NIMMANAHAEMINDA. Ham
Yon, the magic testicles. E93 pp.
133-148.

HOUSING - VIETNAM

4340 TEULIERES, ROGER. La maison rurale
vietnamienne et les circonstances
de son evolution dans la region
sud-orientale du Viet-Nam. SEIB
36 (1961) 661-679.

HOUTMAN, FREDERICK DE

4341 DREWES, G. W. J. De invloed van
de Atjehse omgeving op het
Maleise spraeck ende woordboek van
Frederick de Houtman. BIJ 128
(1972) 447-457.

HRE LANGUAGE

4342 PHILLIPS, RICHARD L. Vowel distribution in Hre. M61 pp. 63-68.

HUE

4343 BARNOUIN, R. P. Les arenes de
Hue. SEIB 49 (1974) 385-421.

HUKBALAHAP MOVEMENT

4344 CONSTANTINO, JOSEFINA D. Outlaw-
ing communism. UN 40 (1967) 434-
447.

4345 HOUGH, RICHARD LEE. Development
and security in Thailand, lessons
from other Asian countries. AS 9
(1969) 178-187.

4346 KERKVLIET, BEN J. Peasant society
and unrest prior to the Huk revolution in the Philippines. AST
9 (1971) 164-213.

4347 ZIMMERMAN, SHIRLEY. Hukbalahap
movement, 1946-1954. SJ 15 (1968)
555-584.

HULL UNIVERSITY. CENTRE FOR SOUTH EAST
ASIAN STUDIES

4348 CAYRAC-BLANCHARD, FRANCOISE. Un
colloque sur l'Indonesie apres les
elections de 1971. AR 3 (1972)
17-19.

HURGRONJE, CH. SNOUCK

4349 KRACKOVSKY, I. J. To the memory
of Ch. Snouck Hurgronje, honorary
member of the Academy of Sciences
of the U.S.S.R., 8-2-1857 to
26-6-1936. BIJ 122 (1966) 375-378.

HUTCHINSON, EDWARD WALTER

4350 Edward Walter Hutchinson. JSS 60
pt. 2 (1972) 394.

IBALOI

4351 BARNETT, MILTON L. Subsistence
and transition of agricultural
development among the Ibaloi. Z16
pp. 299-323.

4352 RESURRECCION, ABELARDO S. A study of a conflict of interest in the use of land in the Ambuklao-Binga watershed, a land economic approach. SLURJ 2 (1971) 630-680.

IBAN

4353 AUSTIN, ROBERT F. The Iban of Sarawak. SA 3 (1974) 905-921.

4354 BEAVITT, PAUL. Ngayap, changes in the pattern of premarital relations of the Iban. SMJ 15 (1967) 407-413.

4355 BLACK, I. D. Dayaks in North Borneo, the Chartered Company and the Sea Dayaks of Sarawak. SMJ 17 (1969) 245-272.

4356 FREEMAN, J. D. Iban augury. BIJ 117 (1961) 141-167.

4357 FREEMAN, J. D. Iban of western Borneo. M95 pp. 65-87.

4358 HARRISSON, TOM. Iban and Ngaju, a significant bird folklore parallel, by Tom and Barbara Harrisson. SMJ 16 (1968) 186-194.

4359 JAMUH, GEORGE. Bornean cooking: Malay, Melanau, Sea Dayak. SMJ 14 (1966) 158-182.

4360 JAMUH, GEORGE. Bornean cooking, II. SMJ 17 (1969) 202-230.

4361 JENSEN, ERIK. Iban world, an introduction to the Iban religious view of life and the place of writing therein. SMJ 13 (1966) 1-31.

4362 KEDIT, PETER MULOK. Gawai betambah-bulu. SMJ 17 (1969) 120-122.

4363 LEE, Y. L. Dayaks of Sarawak. JTG 23 (1966) 28-39.

4364 MACEDA, JOSE. Field recording Sea Dayak music. SMJ 11 (1962) 486-500.

4365 MARGIT ILONA KOMANYI. Iban woman's role, a brief summary of observations at Samu on the Paku River. SMJ 19 (1971) 253-256.

4366 MARTINOIR, NINANE DE. Unity of Dayak mythology. A41 pp. 56-64.

4367 MORGAN, STEPHANIE. Iban aggressive expansion, some background factors. SMJ 16 (1968) 141-185.

4368 MORGAN, STEPHANIE. An Iban funeral near Saratok, 1969, by Stephanie Morgan and Paul Beavitt. SMJ 19 (1971) 277-311.

4369 MULOK KEDIT, PETER. Gawai Ngemali Umai, or Iban rite for padi protection. SMJ 18 (1970) 165-168.

4370 PRINGLE, ROBERT. Asun's rebellion, the political growing pains of a tribal society in Brooke Sarawak, 1929-1940. SMJ 16 (1968) 346-376.

4371 RICHARDS, ANTHONY J. N. Iban augury. SMJ 20 (1972) 63-81.

4372 RICHARDS, ANTHONY J. N. Tibang, Tebang, Tilong and Mandai. SMJ 11 (1962) 409-411.

4373 SANDIN, BENEDICT. Garong baskets. SMJ 11 (1963) 321-326.

4374 SANDIN, BENEDICT. Gawai Antu, Sea Dayak feast of the departed spirits. SMJ 10 (1961) 170-190.

4375 SANDIN, BENEDICT. Gawai Batu, the Iban whetstone feast. SMJ 11 (1962) 392-408.

Iban

IBAN LITERATURE

4376 SANDIN, BENEDICT. History of the people of Bangkit, Paku, Saribas. SMJ 19 (1971) 21-36.

4377 SANDIN, BENEDICT. Iban hero dreams and apparitions. SMJ 14 (1966) 91-123.

4378 SANDIN, BENEDICT. Iban leaders. SMJ 18 (1970) 89-161.

4379 SANDIN, BENEDICT. Saribas Iban death dirge. SMJ 14 (1966) 15-80.

4380 SANDIN, BENEDICT. Some Iban (Sea Dayak) customary law in Sarawak. C39 pp. 40-44.

4381 SANDIN, BENEDICT. Two origins of Iban burial custom. SMJ 17 (1969) 113-119.

4382 VARNEY, PETER D. Some early Iban leaders in the Anglican Church in Sarawak. SMJ 17 (1969) 273-289.

4383 WARD, A. B. Some Sea Dayak customs and fines, 1909-15. SMJ 10 (1961) 82-102.

IBAN LANGUAGE

4384 BAUGHMAN, BURR. Spelling of Iban. SMJ 11 (1963) 132-137.

4385 HOWELL, W. Supplement to Howell and Bailey's *Sea Dayak dictionary.* SMJ 10 (1961) 127-169.

4386 JENSEN, ERIK. Towards an Iban fowler, the language of the Iban. SMJ 11 (1964) 544-552.

4387 BADILLO, VICTOR L. Color of a lunar eclipse. PS 19 (1971) 731-732.

4388 HARRISSON, TOM. Borneo writing. BIJ 121 (1965) 1-57.

4389 HARRISSON, TOM. Borneo writing boards, by Tom Harrisson and Benedict Sandin. SMJ 13 (1966) 32-286.

4390 JENSEN, ERIK. Towards an Iban fowler, the language of the Iban. SMJ 11 (1964) 544-552.

4391 RUBENSTEIN, CAROL. Poems of indigenous peoples of Sarawak: some of the songs and chants. Pt. I. Iban, Bidayuh, Melanau. SMJ 21 (1973) 1-722.

4392 SANDIN, BENEDICT. Apai Salui sleeps with a corpse, an Iban folk story. SMJ 15 (1967) 223-227.

4393 SANDIN, BENEDICT. Five mythological stories of the Iban. SMJ 17 (1969) 99-112.

4394 SIBAT ANAK MUJAH. Tanggok jadi enggau bulan (Iban text). SMJ 11 (1964) 541-543.

IFUGAO **

4395 CLAVEL, LEOTHINY S. National integration, a content analysis of magazine articles on the Ifugaos. DR 17 (1969) 390-416.

4396 CONKLIN, HAROLD C. Ifugao ethnobotany, 1905-1965, the 1911 Beyer-Merrill report in perspective. Z16 pp. 204-262.

4397 DeRAEDT, JULES. Religious representations in northern Luzon. SLQ 2 (1964) 245-348.

4398 DULAWAN, LOURDES S. Ifugaos. UN 40 (1967) 4-52.

4399 LAMBRECHT, FRANCIS. Adoption of Ifugao local customs in Christianity. B13 pp. 90-111.
Comment: REID, LAWRENCE. Comments. B13 pp. 112-115.

4400 LAMBRECHT, FRANCIS. Adoption of Ifugao local customs in Christianity. SLQ 1 (1963) 5-30.

4401 LAMBRECHT, FRANCIS. Adoption of Ifugao local customs in Christianity. SLQ 2 (1964) 129-146.

4402 LAMBRECHT, FRANCIS. Family and kinship perspectives in Ifugaw communities. SLQ 6 (1968) 399-414.

4403 LAMBRECHT, FRANCIS. Ifugao custom and the moral law. PS 10 (1962) 275-299.
Comment: SCOTT, WILLIAM HENRY. Comment on Ifugao custom and the moral law. PS 10 (1962) 300-303.

4404 LAMBRECHT, FRANCIS. Kalinga and Ifugaw concepts of the universe. SJ 19 (1972) 195-208.

4405 LAMBRECHT, FRANCIS. Main factors of resistance to culture change in Ifugaoland. B13 pp. 83-89.

4406 LAMBRECHT, FRANCIS. Property laws of custom among the Ifugaos. SJ 11 (1964) 57-70.

4407 LORRIN-BONA DE SANTOS, ROSARIO. Un Ifugao face a la guerre. AR 3 (1972) 29-53.

4408 REYES, RAMON C. Secularization and religious acculturation. PS 20 (1972) 40-48.

4409 REYES, RAMON C. Secularization and religious acculturation. SJ 19 (1972) 162-169.

4410 SCOTT, WILLIAM HENRY. The Ifugaos a hundred years ago. UN 40 (1967) 53-65.

IFUGAO LITERATURE **

4411 LAMBRECHT, FRANCIS. Hudhud of Dinulawan and Bugan at Gonhadan. SLQ 5 (1967) 267-713.

4412 LAMBRECHT, FRANCIS. Ifugaw Hudhud literature. M24 pp. 816-837.

4413 LAMBRECHT, FRANCIS. Ifugaw Hudhud literature. SLQ 3 (1965) 191-214.

4414 LORRIN-BONA DE SANTOS, ROSARIO. Un Ifugao face a la guerre. AR 3 (1972) 29-53.

IGLESIA NI CRISTO

4415 ANDO, HIROFUMI. Study of the Iglesia ni Cristo, a political-religious sect in the Philippines. PA 42 (1969) 334-345.

4416 FORONDA, MARCELINO. National churches. UN 36 (1963) 357-365.

4417 KAVANAGH, JOSEPH J. Voice of the Iglesia ni Cristo, 1951-1961. PS 9 (1961) 651-665.

4418 SANDERS, ALBERT J. Appraisal of the Iglesia ni Cristo. A58 pp. 350-365.

Igorot

IGOROT

4419 BACDAYAN, ALBERT S. Religious conversion and social reintegration in a western Bontoc village complex. SLQ 5 (1967) 27-40.

4420 CAWED-OTEYZA, CARMENCITA. Culture of the Bontoc Igorots. UN 38 (1965) 317-377.

4421 CLAERHOUDT, ALFONSO. Songs of a people, Igorot customs in eastern Benguet. SLQ 4 (1966) 163-278.

4422 DeRAEDT, JULES. Religious representations in northern Luzon. SLQ 2 (1964) 245-348.

4423 EGGAN, FRED. Sagada Igorots of northern Luzon. M95 pp. 24-50.

4424 PACYAYA, ALFREDO G. Acculturation and culture change in Sagada. SJ 11 (1964) 14-25.

4425 SCOTT, WILLIAM HENRY. Boyhood in Sagada. SJ 10 (1963) 387-399.

4426 SCOTT, WILLIAM HENRY. Igorot responses to Spanish aims, 1576-1896. PS 18 (1970) 695-717.

IGOROT LANGUAGE

4427 SCOTT, WILLIAM HENRY. Some religious terms in Sagada Igorot. Z16 pp. 480-493.

4428 SCOTT, WILLIAM HENRY. Word Igorot. PS 10 (1962) 234-248.

IGOROT LITERATURE

4429 CORONEL, MARIA DELIA. Kalinga-Bontoc stories. UN 39 (1966) 615-629.

IGOROT STUDY CENTER

4430 HAKCHOLNA, WILLIAM. Catalogue of works on Cordillera ethnography in the Igorot Study Center, Sagada, Mountain Province. SLQ 7 (1969) 113-142.

ILIANON LITERATURE

4431 MANUEL, E. ARSENIO. Agyu, the Ilianon epic of Mindanao. UN 42 (1969) 5-104.

Ilocano language *See* ILOKO LANGUAGE

ILOKO LANGUAGE

4432 CONSTANTINO, ERNESTO. Ilukano pluralizers. PSSHR 28 (1963) 408-415.

4433 CONSTANTINO, ERNESTO. Personal pronouns of Tagalog, Ilukano, Isinai and Kapampangan. Z16 pp. 567-596.

ILOKO LITERATURE

4434 BAUZON, KENNETH ESPANA. Lam-ang in transition. DR 22 (1974) 277-302.

4435 CORONEL, MARIA DELIA. Tagalog and Ilocano stories. UN 39 (1966) 579-588.

4436 HUFANA, ALEJANDRINO G. Mena Pecson Crisologo and Iloko drama. DR 10 (Jan. 1962) 1-204.

4437 HUFANA, ALEJANDRINO G. Songs in available Iloko plays. GEJ 11 (1966) 8-18.

INAS

4438   LEWIS, DIANE. Inas, a study of
        local history. JMBRAS 33 pt. 1
        (1960) 65-94.

INCOME - MALAYSIA

4439   SILCOCK, T. H. Approximate racial
        division of national income. S47
        pp. 276-281.

INCOME - SINGAPORE

4440   CHEN, PETER S. J. Growth and in-
        come distribution in Singapore.
        SAJSS 2 (1974) 119-130.

INDEPENDENCE MOVEMENTS

4441   TINKER, HUGH. Approaches towards
        independence of countries in
        Southeast Asia. D44 pp. 15-24.

4442   UZIANOV, A. Importance of Russian
        archives for studies into the his-
        tory of freedom wars and popular
        movements in South-East Asia in
        the XIX-early XX centuries. SAA 2
        (1969) 82-87.

INDEPENDENCE MOVEMENTS - INDONESIA

4443   KAHIN, AUDREY. Some preliminary
        observations on west Sumatra
        during the revolution. IND 18
        (1974) 76-117.

4444   PLUVIER, JAN. Dutch war crimes in
        Indonesia. JCA 2 (1972) 199-202.

4445   SEMAUN. Early account of the in-
        dependence movement, translated
        and commented on by Ruth McVey.
        IND 1 (1966) 46-75.

4446   VAN DER VEUR, PAUL W. Eurasian
        dilemma in Indonesia. JAS 20
        (1960-1) 45-60.

INDEPENDENCE MOVEMENTS - LAOS

4447   ADAMS, NINA S. Patrons, clients
        and revolutionaries, the Lao
        search for independence, 1945-
        1954. L18 pp. 100-120.

INDEPENDENCE MOVEMENTS - PHILIPPINES

4448   AGONCILLO, TEODORO A. Malolos,
        the crisis of the republic.
        PSSHR 25 (1960) 1-831.

4449   CUSHNER, NICHOLAS P. British
        consular dispatches and the
        Philippine independence movement,
        1872-1901. PS 16 (1968) 501-534.

4450   FRIEND, THEODORE. Philippine
        sugar industry and the politics of
        independence, 1929-1935. JAS 22
        (1962-3) 179-192.

INDEPENDENCE MOVEMENTS - VIETNAM

4451   CHESNEAUX, JEAN. Les revolution-
        naires vietnamiens face au Kim Van
        Kieu. C28 pp. 356-384.

4452   LACOUTURE, JEAN. Dialogues avec
        les revolutionnaires vietnamiens,
        par Jean Lacouture, Philippe De-
        villers, et Bernard Dranber. C28
        pp. 238-264.

India Office *See* GREAT BRITAIN. INDIA
OFFICE

Indians

INDIANS

4453 HATLEY, R. The overseas Indian in Southeast Asia: Burma, Malaysia and Singapore. T45 pp. 450-466.

INDIANS - BURMA

4454 ADAS, MICHAEL. Immigrant Asians and the economic impact of European imperialism: the role of the south Indian chettiars in British Burma. JAS 33 (1973-4) 385-401.

INDIANS - MALAYSIA

4455 ARASARATNAM, S. Aspects of society and cultural life of Indians in Malaysia. A41 pp. 101-107.

4456 ARASARATNAM, S. Social reform and reformist pressure groups among the Indians of Malaya and Singapore, 1930-1955. JMBRAS 40 pt. 2 (1967) 54-67.

4457 FEE. Kampong Padre, a Tamil settlement near Bagan Serai, Perak. JMBRAS 36 pt. 1 (1963) 153-181.

4458 JAIN, RAVINDRA K. Leadership and authority in a plantation, a case study of Indians in Malaya, c. 1900-42. L23 pp. 163-173.

4459 MINATTUR, JOSEPH. Malaya, what's in the name? JSS 54 (1966) 19-28.

4460 MINATTUR, JOSEPH. Malaya, what's in the name? RSA (1965) 159-168.

4461 MINATTUR, JOSEPH. Some characteristics of Indian culture in Malaysia. A41 pp. 90-100.

4462 POUVATCHY, JOSEPH. Les minorites etrangeres in Malaisie. FA (1974 pt. 2) 57-70.

4463 RABUSHKA, ALVIN. Racial stereotypes in Malaya. AS 11 (1971) 709-716.

4464 SANDHU, KERNIAL SINGH. Sikh immigration into Malaya during the period of British rule. S89 pp. 335-354.

4465 SANDHU, KERNIAL SINGH. Some preliminary observations of the origins and characteristics of Indian migration to Malaya, 1786-1957. J45 pp. 40-72.

4466 SMITH, T. E. Immigration and permanent settlement of Chinese and Indians in Malaya, and the future growth of the Malay and Chinese communities. C87 pp. 174-185.

INDIANS - SINGAPORE

4467 ARASARATNAM, S. Social reform and reformist pressure groups among the Indians of Malaya and Singapore, 1930-1955. JMBRAS 40 pt. 2 (1967) 54-67.

4468 SANDHU, KERNIAL SINGH. Some aspects of Indian settlement in Singapore, 1819-1969. JSAH 10 (1969) 193-201.

4469 SANDHU, KERNIAL SINGH. Some preliminary observations of the origins and characteristics of Indian migration to Malaya, 1786-1957. J45 pp. 40-72.

4470 TURNBULL, C. M. Convicts in the Straits Settlements. JMBRAS 43 pt. 1 (1970) 87-103.

INDONESIA

4471 ALLISON, JOHN M. Indonesia, the end of the beginning? AS 10 (1970) 143-151.

4472 L'annee 1966 en Asie, Indonesie. FA 22 (1968) 114-117.

4473 BENDA, HARRY J. Le probleme de la decolonisation en Indonesie, elements de continuite et de changement. D44 pp. 193-212.

4474 CAYRAC, FRANCOISE. Chronique d'Indonesie, 1973. AR 8 (1964) 3-20.

4475 GENEST, JULES. 1970 en Indonesie. AR 1 (1970) 7-26.

4476 GENEST, JULES. Chronique d'Indonesie, janvier-juillet, 1971. AR 2 (1971) 3-14.

4477 GENEST, JULES. Chronique d'Indonesie, juillet-decembre, 1971. AR 3 (1972) 3-16.

4478 GENEST, JULES. Chronique d'Indonesie, janvier-juin, 1972. AR 4 (1972) 3-11.

4479 GENEST, JULES. Chronique d'Indonesie, second semestre, 1972. AR 5 (1973) 3-16.

4480 JONES, RUSSELL. Earl, Logan and Indonesia. AR 6 (1973) 93-118.

4481 MOHAMMED A. NAWAWI. Stagnation as a basis of regionalism, a lesson from Indonesia. AS 9 (1969) 934-945.

4482 Pour une documentation sur l'actualite, Indonesian current affairs translation service. AR 4 (1972) 12-20.

4483 SAMSON, ALLAN A. Indonesia 1973, a climate of concern. AS 14 (1974) 157-165.

4484 WITHINGTON, WILLIAM A. Indonesia. F56 pp. 185-201.

INDONESIA - ARMY

4485 BRITTON, PETER. The Indonesian army, stabiliser and dynamiser. M77 pp. 83-98.

4486 CROUCH, HAROLD. The army, the parties and elections. IND 11 (1971) 177-191.

4487 Current data on the Indonesian army elite. IND 7 (1969) 195-201.

4488 Current data on the Indonesian military elite. IND 15 (1973) 187-197.

4489 Current data on the Indonesian military elite. IND 18 (1974) 153-167.

4490 Current data on the Indonesian military elite after the reorganization of 1969-1970. IND 10 (1970) 194-208.

4491 Data on the current military elite. IND 3 (1967) 205-216.

4492 FEDERSPIEL, HOWARD M. The military and Islam in Sukarno's Indonesia. PA 46 (1973) 407-420.

4493 LEV, DANIEL S. Political role of the army in Indonesia. PA 36 (1963) 349-364.

4494 LEV, DANIEL S. Political role of the army in Indonesia. T45 pp. 287-302.

4495 McVEY, RUTH. Post revolutionary transformation of the Indonesian army. IND 11 (1971) 131-176.

Indonesia - Army

4496 McVEY, RUTH. Post revolutionary transformation of the Indonesian army. IND 13 (1972) 147-181.

4497 PAGET, ROGER K. The military in Indonesian politics, the burden of power. PA 40 (1967) 294-314.

4498 PAUKER, GUY J. Indonesia, the year of transition. AS 7 (1967) 138-150.

4499 PAUKER, GUY J. Role of the military in Indonesia. J52 pp. 185-230.

4500 POLOMKA, PETER. Indonesian army and foreign policy, a reappraisal. AQ (1972) 363-382.

4501 ROCAMORA, J. E. Recent changes in army commands. IND 4 (1967) 227-229.

4502 SAMSON, ALLAN A. Army and Islam in Indonesia. PA 44 (1971) 545-565.

4503 SMAIL, JOHN R. W. Military politics of north Sumatra, December 1956-October 1957. IND 6 (1968) 128-187.

4504 SUNDHAUSSEN, ULF. The fashioning of unity in the Indonesian army. AQ (1971) 181-212.

4505 SUNDHAUSSEN, ULF. The military in research on Indonesian politics. JAS 31 (1971-2) 355-365.

4506 TRAN BUU KHANH. Le cheminement de l'armee indonesienne vers le pouvoir. RSA (1967) 217-235.

4507 UTRECHT, ERNST. The Indonesian army as an instrument of repression. JCA 2 (1972) 56-67.

4508 UTRECHT, ERNST. Recent conflicts inside the Indonesian army. JCA 4 (1974) 324-335.

INDONESIA - BIBLIOGRAPHY

4509 Bibliographie sommaire [of works on moving pictures]. AR 5 (1973) 135-137.

4510 ECHOLS, JOHN M. In memoriam, G. F. Ockeloen, 1904-1966. IND 2 (1966) 157-159.

4511 PELZER, KARL J. Geographical literature on Indonesia. J37 pp. 90-116.

4512 Recent bibliographies on the Netherlands East Indies. H57 pp. 465-467.

4513 Some recent publications on Indonesia. IND 10 (1970) 209-217.

INDONESIA - CONSTITUTION

4514 PALMIER, LESLIE H. Centralization in Indonesia. PA 33 (1960) 169-180.

INDONESIA - DEFENSES

4515 SAJIDIMAN SURJOHADIPRODJO. Defence of Indonesia. S51 pp. 219-240.

INDONESIA - DESCRIPTION AND TRAVEL

4516 DAMAIS, LOUIS-CHARLES. Etudes sino-indonesiennes. BEF 50 (1960) 1-35.

4517 FORBES, HENRY O. Through Bantam and the Preanger Regencies in the eighties. H57 pp. 104-122.

4518 HOLT, CLAIRE. Indonesia revisited. IND 9 (1970) 163-188.

4519 JACOBS, HUBERT. Admiraal Wybrant Warwyck **schrift aan de Sultan van** Ternate. BIJ 125 (1969) 344-355.

4520 LEK, L. Snellius expedition. H57 pp. 473-4.

4521 LOMBARD, DENYS. Voyageurs francais dans l'archipel insulinden XVIIeme, XVIIIeme et XIXeme s. AR 1 (1970) 141-168.

4522 RESINK, G. J. Jozef Korzeniowski's voornaamste lectuur betreffende Indonesie. BIJ 117 (1961) 209-237.

4523 RUSLAN ABDULGANI. My childhood world. IND 17 (1974) 112-135.

4524 SIRK, M. J. Rumphius, the blind seer of Amboina. H57 pp. 295-308.

INDONESIA - ECONOMIC CONDITIONS

4525 ANDERSON, BEN. The problem of rice, stenographic notes on the fourth session of Sanyo Kaigi, January 8, 2605, 10:00 a.m., translated with an introduction by Ben Anderson. IND 2 (1966) 77-123.

4526 BOEKE, J. H. Social and economic needs. J32 pp. 69-74.

4527 BURGER, D. H. Government's native economic policy. J32 pp. 317-329.

4528 CHESNEL, GERARD. Statistiques economiques indonesiennes 1970. AR 1 (1970) 27-33.

4529 Economy and economic policy, general and historical. G52 pp. 1-15.

4530 FISHER, CHARLES A. Economic myth and geographical reality in Indonesia. MAS 1 (1967) 155-189.

4531 GELDEREN, J. VAN. Economics of the tropical colony. J32 pp. 111-164.

4532 GLASSBURNER, BRUCE. Indonesian economic policy after Sukarno. G52 pp. 426-443.

4533 GLASSBURNER, BRUCE. Swing of the hoe, retooling begins in the Indonesian economy, by Bruce Glassburner and Kenneth D. Thomas. AS 1 (June 1961) 3-12.

4534 GONGGRIJP, G. Colonial economics and theoretical economics. J32 pp. 75-91.

4535 GONGGRIJP, G. Value curves and the lowest level of the Indies economy. J32 pp. 93-109.

4536 HAWKINS, EVERETT D. Job inflation in Indonesia. AS 6 (1966) 264-275.

4537 HONG LAN OEI. Indonesia's economic stabilization and rehabilitation program, an evaluation. IND 5 (1968) 135-174.

4538 KOLFF, G. H. VAN DER. Brown and white economy, unity in diversity. J32 pp. 215-250.

4539 KUSUMOWIDAGDO, SUWITO. Land, man and his determination to work. J37 pp. 9-16.

4540 MACKIE, J. A. C. The Indonesian economy, 1950-1963. G52 pp. 16-69.

Indonesia - Economic conditions

4541 MACKIE, J. A. C. Indonesia's government estates and their masters. PA 34 (1961) 337-360.

4542 MUBYARTO. Rice price, marketing and food policy in Indonesia. MER 13 pt. 2 (1968) 103-114.

4543 PANGLAYKIM, J. New order and the economy. IND 3 (1967) 73-120.

4544 PANGLAYKIM, J. Road to Amsterdam and beyond, aspects of Indonesia's stabilization program, by J. Panglaykim and K. D. Thomas. AS 7 (1967) 689-702.

4545 PAUKER, GUY J. Indonesia, the age of reason? AS 8 (1968) 133-147.

4546 PENNY, DAVID H. Agro-economic survey of Indonesia, an appreciation. IND 11 (1971) 111-130.

4547 RICE, ROBERT. Sumitro's role in foreign trade policy. IND 8 (1969) 183-211.

4548 SCOTT, SUMMER. Challenge to American corporate investment in Indonesia. AS 12 (1972) 399-415.

4549 SIREGAR, ARIFIN M. Indonesian entrepreneurs. AS 9 (1969) 343-358.

4550 WELLENSTEIN, E. P. Remarks on dualistic economics. J32 pp. 193-213.

4551 WITHINGTON, W. A. Problems and potentialities of development of western Indonesia, Sumatra as an example of third world characteristics. RSA (1969) 79-103.

INDONESIA - FOREIGN RELATIONS

4552 BUNNELL, FREDERICK P. An administrator's view of Indonesian foreign policy. IND 18 (1974) 71-75.

4553 BUNNELL, FREDERICK P. Guided democracy foreign policy, 1960-1965, President Sukarno moves from non-alignment to confrontation. IND 2 (1966) 37-76.

4554 HINDLEY, DONALD. Foreign aid to Indonesia and its political implications. PA 36 (1963) 107-119.

4555 HORN, ROBERT C. Indonesia's response to changing big power alignments. PA 46 (1973) 515-533.

4556 KWA CHONG GUAN. Historical roots of Indonesian irredentism. AST 8 (1970) 38-52.

4557 POLOMKA, PETER. Indonesian army and foreign policy, a reappraisal. AQ (1972) 363-382.

4558 PURNADI PURBATJARAKA. Shahbandars in the archipelago. JSAH 2 (July 1961) 1-9.

4559 REID, ANTHONY. Indonesian diplomacy, a documentary study of Atjehnese foreign policy in the reign of Sultan Mahmud, 1870-4. JMBRAS 42 pt. 2 (1969) 74-114.

4560 SILLIMAN, G. SIDNEY. Indonesian foreign policy in flux, a study of the Republic of Indonesia in relation to the giants of the cold war. SJ 13 (1966) 22-55.

4561 SINGH, LALITA P. Indonesian foreign policy, the linkage between domestic power balance and foreign policy behavior. SA 1 (1971) 378-394.

4562 WEINSTEIN, FRANKLIN B. Indonesian
elite's view of the world and the
foreign policy of development.
IND 12 (1971) 97-113.

INDONESIA - FOREIGN RELATIONS -
  AUSTRALIA

4563 CAPELL, A. Early Indonesian contacts with north Australia. JOSA
3 pt. 1 (1965) 67-75.

4564 HUDSON, W. J. Australia and Indonesian independence. JSAH 8
(1967) 226-239.

4565 LOCKWOOD, RUPERT. Indonesian
exiles in Australia, 1942-47.
IND 10 (1970) 37-56.

INDONESIA - FOREIGN RELATIONS - BURMA

4566 HALL, D. G. E. The Daghregister
of Batavia and Dutch trade with
Burma in the 17th century. B92
pp. 99-116.

INDONESIA - FOREIGN RELATIONS - CHINA

4567 CHIU LING YEONG. Sino-Javanese
relations in the early Ming period. S93 pp. 214-222.

4568 HEIDHUES, MARY F. SOMERS. Peking
and the overseas Chinese, the
Malaysian dispute. AS 6 (1966)
276-287.

4569 MOZINGO, DAVID. Sino-Indonesian
dual nationality treaty. AS 1
(Dec. 1961) 25-31.

4570 TJAN TJOE SOM. Chinese historical
sources and historiography. S61
pp. 194-205.

4571 VAN DER KROEF, JUSTUS M. Before
the thaw, recent Indonesian attitudes toward people's China. AS
13 (1973) 513-530.

4572 YOUNG, KENNETH RAY. Sino-Indonesian dual nationality treaty, an
evaluation. AF 2 (1970) 172-182.

INDONESIA - FOREIGN RELATIONS - FRANCE

4573 BELLAMAL, A. Pour une politique
francaise dans le monde malayo-
indonesien. FA (1974 pt. 2) 35-
44.

4574 LOMBARD, DENYS. Voyageurs francais dans l'archipel insulinden
XVIIeme, XVIIIeme et XIXeme s. AR
1 (1970) 141-168.

4575 MILCENT, BENEDICTE. L'Indonesie a
Paris, 1974. AR 8 (1974) 35-44.

4576 REID, A. The French in Sumatra
and the Malay world, 1760-1890.
BIJ 129 (1973) 195-238.

INDONESIA - FOREIGN RELATIONS - GREAT
  BRITAIN

4577 BASSETT, D. K. British trade and
policy in Indonesia, 1760-1772.
BIJ 120 (1964) 197-223.

4578 KATHIRITHAMBY-WELLS, J. Survey of
the effects of British influence
on indigenous authority in south-
west Sumatra, 1685-1824. BIJ 129
(1973) 239-268.

INDONESIA - FOREIGN RELATIONS - INDIA

4579 DUTT, NITISH K. Indonesia-India
relations, 1955-67. AST 10 (1972)
196-220.

Indonesia - Foreign relations - India

4580 LOHUIZEN-DE LEEUW, J. E. VAN.
Early 16th century link between
Gujarat and Java. E93 pp. 89-93.

4581 SINGH, L. P. Dynamics of Indian-
Indonesian relations. AS 7 (1967)
655-666.

INDONESIA - FOREIGN RELATIONS - JAPAN

4582 KESAVAN, K. V. Attitude of Indonesia towards the Japanese peace
treaty. AST 10 (1972) 407-415.

INDONESIA - FOREIGN RELATIONS -
MALAYSIA

4583 GORDON, BERNARD K. Potential for
Indonesian expansion. PA 36
(1963) 378-393.

4584 GREEN, L. C. Indonesia, the
United Nations and Malaysia. JSAH
6 (Sept. 1965) 71-86.

4585 GROSSHOLTZ, JEAN. Rise and demise
of konfrontasi, impact on politics
in Malaysia. AST 6 (1968) 325-
339.

4586 HINDLEY, DONALD. Indonesia's
confrontation with Malaysia, a
search for motives. AS 4 (1964)
904-913.

4587 KAHIN, GEORGE McT. Malaysia and
Indonesia. PA 37 (1964) 253-270.

4588 ROUCEK, JOSEPH S. Geopolitical
aspects of the Indonesian-
Malaysian dispute. RSA (1965)
275-303.

4589 SINGH, L. P. Malaysia and
Australian-Indonesian relations.
RSA (1964) 277-293.

4590 SUTTER, JOHN O. Two faces of konfrontasi: crush Malaysia, and the
gestapu. AS 6 (1966) 523-546.

4591 VAN DER KROEF, JUSTUS M. Indonesia, Malaya and the North Borneo
crisis. AS 3 (1963) 173-181.

4592 VAN DER KROEF, JUSTUS M. Sarawak-
Indonesian border insurgency. MAS
2 (1968) 245-265.

INDONESIA - FOREIGN RELATIONS -
NETHERLANDS

4593 BURGER, D. H. Government's native
economic policy. J32 pp. 317-329.

4594 LIJPHART, AREND. Indonesian image
of West Irian. AS 1 (July 1961)
9-16.

4595 PALMIER, LESLIE H. Indonesian-
Dutch relations. JSAH 2 (July
1961) 24-34.

4596 RESINK, G. J. Inlandsche staten
in den Oosterschen archipel, 1873-
1915. BIJ 116 (1960) 313-349.
Comment: VAN DER KROEF, JUSTUS M.
On the sovereignty of Indonesian
states, a rejoinder. BIJ 117
(1961) 238-266.

4597 WERTHEIM, W. F. De geest van het
Oostindisch gouvernement, honderd
jaar geleden. BIJ 117 (1961) 305-
343.

4598 WERTHEIM, W. F. De geest van het
Oostindisch gouvernement, honderd
jaar geleden, II. BIJ 117 (1961)
436-463.

INDONESIA - FOREIGN RELATIONS -
PAKISTAN

4599   SAYEED, K. B.   Southeast Asia in
       Pakistan's foreign policy.   PA 41
       (1968) 230-244.

INDONESIA - FOREIGN RELATIONS -
PHILIPPINES

4600   FRANCISCO, JUAN R.   Sri Vijaya and
       the Philippines, a review.   PSSHR
       26 (1961) 87-109.

4601   KUSNO UTOMO.   Imperatives of
       Philippine-Indonesian relations.
       SJ 18 (1971) 198-205.

4602   MEADOWS, MARTIN.   Theories of
       external-internal political rela-
       tionships, a case study of Indo-
       nesia and the Philippines.   AST 6
       (1968) 297-324.

INDONESIA - FOREIGN RELATIONS -
PORTUGAL

4603   WEATHERBEE, DONALD E.   Portuguese
       Timor, an Indonesian dilemma.   AS
       6 (1966) 683-695.

INDONESIA - FOREIGN RELATIONS - SRI
LANKA

4604   DeCASPARIS, J. G.   New evidence
       on cultural relations between Java
       and Ceylon in ancient times.   G83
       pp. 241-248.

4605   PARANAVITANA, S.   Ceylon and Sri
       Vijaya.   E92 pp. 205-212.

INDONESIA - FOREIGN RELATIONS - THAILAND

4606   PENTH, HANS GEORG.   Account in the
       Hikajat Atjeh on relations between
       Siam and Atjeh.   F38 pp. 55-69.

4607   PENTH, HANS GEORG.   Zum Verhaltnis
       Sayam-Atjeh im 17 Jahrhundert.
       JSS 57 (1969) 355-359.

INDONESIA - FOREIGN RELATIONS - TURKEY

4608   REID, ANTHONY.   Sixteenth century
       Turkish influence in western Indo-
       nesia.   JSAH 10 (1969) 395-414.

INDONESIA - FOREIGN RELATIONS - UNION OF
SOVIET SOCIALIST REPUBLICS

4609   DERKACH, NADIA.   Soviet policy
       towards Indonesia in the West
       Irian and the Malaysian disputes.
       AS 5 (1965) 566-571.

4610   PAUKER, GUY J.   General Nasution's
       mission to Moscow.   AS 1 (Mar.
       1961) 13-22.

INDONESIA - FOREIGN RELATIONS - UNITED
STATES

4611   DOEPPERS, DANIEL F.   Incident in
       the PRRI/Permesta rebellion of
       1958.   IND 14 (1972) 182-195.

4612   PAAUW, DOUGLAS S.   Prospects for
       American trade with Indonesia.
       C35 pp. 185-204.

4613   SCOTT, SUMMER.   Challenge to
       American corporate investment in
       Indonesia.   AS 12 (1972) 399-415.

INDONESIA - HISTORY

4614   AVELING, H. G.   Seventeenth cen-
       tury Bandanese society in fact and
       fiction, Tambera assessed.   BIJ
       123 (1967) 347-365.

Indonesia - History

4615 BASSETT, D. K.   The Amboyna massacre of 1623.   JSAH 1 (Sept. 1960) 1-19.

4616 COOLHAAS, W. PH.   Reael, Coen, de Carpentier en Specx.   BIJ 129 (1973) 269-276.

4617 COOLHAAS, W. PH.   Wie was de Schrijver van de Tegenwerpinge tegen Coen's Kolonisatieplannen?   BIJ 130 (1974) 297-305.

4618 COWAN, C. D.   Continuity and change in the international history of maritime South East Asia.   JSAH 9 (1968) 1-11.

4619 GRAAF, H. J. DE.   Sadjarah Pangiwa lan panengen, de Stamboom ter linker- en ter rechterzijde, 1733-1743.   BIJ 126 (1970) 332-337.

4620 HOFFMAN, J. E.   Early policies in the Malacca jurisdiction of the United East India Company, the Malay peninsula and Netherlands East Indies attachment.   JSAS 3 (1972) 1-38.

4621 KATHIRITHAMBY-WELLS, J.   Ahmad Shah Ibn Iskandar and the late 17th century holy war in Indonesia.   JMBRAS 43 pt. 1 (1970) 48-63.

4622 NAERSSEN, F. H. VAN.   Cailendra interregnum.   J41 pp. 249-253.

4623 NOORDUYN, J.   Further topographical notes on the ferry charter of 1358, with appendices on Djipang and Bodjanegara.   BIJ 124 (1968) 460-481.

4624 NOORDUYN, J.   Names of Hayam Wuruk's sisters.   BIJ 124 (1968) 542-544.

4625 RAUSA-GOMEZ, LOURDES.   Sri Vijaya and Madjapahit.   PS 15 (1967) 63-107.

4626 SARTONO KARTODIRDJO.   Agrarian radicalism in Java, its setting and development.   H52 pp. 70-125.

4627 SUNTHARALINGAM, R.   British in Banjarmasin, an abortive attempt at settlement, 1700-1707.   JSAH 4 (Sept. 1963) 33-50.

4628 SUTJIPTO WIRJOSUPARTO.   Historical aspects of Indonesia's acceptance of western culture.   EACS 6 (1967) 82-109.

4629 VAN DER KROEF, JUSTUS M.   National and international dimensions of Indonesian history.   JSAH 6 (Mar. 1965) 17-32.

4630 WERTHEIM, W. F.   The past revived, reply to G. W. Locher.   BIJ 118 (1962) 183-192.

4631 WESTENDORP BOERMA, J. J.   Een muts met honderd keelbandjes.   BIJ 125 (1969) 487-495.

4632 YAMIN, H. MUHAMMAD.   Legal and historical review of Indonesia's sovereignty over the ages.   DR 9 (1961) 175-221.

INDONESIA - HISTORY - 19TH AND 20TH CENTURIES

4633 BENDA, HARRY J.   Samin movement, by Harry J. Benda and Lance Castles.   BIJ 125 (1969) 207-240.

4634 PLUVIER, J. M.   Dutch-Indonesian relations, 1940-1941.   JSAH 6 (Mar. 1965) 33-47.

4635 PUVANARAJAH, T.   Acheh treaty of 1819, by T. Puvanarajah and R.

Suntharalingam. JSAH 2 (Oct. 1961) 36-46.

4636 REINSMA, R. Uit de Aantekeningen van een Oud-Indisch ambtenaar, Jhr. Johan Pieter Cornets de Groot van Kraaijenburg. BIJ 122 (1966) 229-254.

4637 SARTONO KARTODIRDJO. Bureaucracy and aristocracy, the Indonesian experience in the XIXth century. AR 7 (1974) 151-168.

4638 THE SIAUW GAP. Samin and Samat movements in Java, two examples of peasant resistance. RSA (1967) 303-310.

4639 WERTHEIM, W. F. De geest van het Oostindisch gouvernement, honderd jaar geleden. BIJ 117 (1961) 305-343.

4640 WERTHEIM, W. F. De geest van het Oostindisch gouvernement, honderd jaar geleden, II. BIJ 117 (1961) 436-463.

4641 WERTHEIM, W. F. De perkaras van 100 jaar geleden. BIJ 119 (1963) 412-414.
Comment: NIEUWENHUYS, R. Tot de Hoofd-Zaak van Lebak, een antwoord aan Prof. Wertheim. BIJ 118 (1962) 271-276.

INDONESIA – LAWS, STATUTES, ETC. *See also* ADAT LAW – INDONESIA

4642 HOADLEY, MASON C. Continuity and change in Javanese legal tradition, the evidence of Jayapattra. IND 11 (1971) 95-109.

4643 HOLLEMAN, J. F. Het Belang van de adviezen van het dorpshoofd en de dorpsjustitie voor de nationale rechter in Indonesie. BIJ 127 (1971) 492-496.

4644 LEV, DANIEL S. Judicial institutions and legal culture in Indonesia. H52 pp. 246-318.

4645 RESINK, G. J. Significance of the history of international law in Indonesia. S61 pp. 359-379.

4646 VREEDE-DE STUERS, CORA. A propos du R. U. U., histoire d'une legislation matrimoniale. AR 8 (1974) 21-30.

INDONESIA – MINORITIES *See also* ATONI, ARGUNIANS, BALINESE, BATAKS, BAWEAN, BUGINESE, BUNA, CHINESE, DANI, ENDEH, EURASIANS, JALE, JAVANESE, KAPUNDUK, KAYAN, KODI, MA'ANJAN, MALOHS, MINANG-KABAU, PADJU EPAT, PUNAN, REDJANG, ROTINESE, SANGIRESE, SIMALUNGUN, SUKU, SUMBA, SUMBAWA, SUNDANESE, TORADJA, WADJO

4647 LIDDLE, R. WILLIAM. Ethnicity and political organization, three east Sumatran cases. H52 pp. 126-178.

4648 PELRAS, CHRISTIAN. Notes sur quelques populations aquatiques de l'archipel nusantarien. AR 3 (1972) 133-168.

INDONESIA – POLITICS AND GOVERNMENT

4649 ABEYASEKERE, SUSAN. The Soetardjo petition. IND 15 (1973) 80-107.

4650 BENDA, HARRY J. Pattern of administrative reforms in the closing years of Dutch rule in Indonesia. JAS 25 (1965-6) 589-605.

4651 CHOI, YEARN H. Political style and the democratic process in Indonesia and the Philippines. AST 9 (1971) 214-228.

Indonesia - Politics and government

INDONESIA - POLITICS AND GOVERNMENT -
  1949-1965

Indonesia - Politics and government -
1965-

4674 FEITH, HERBERT. President Soekarno, the army and the communists, the triangle changes shape.
AS 4 (1964) 969-980.

4675 GOH CHENG TEIK. Why Indonesia's
attempt at democracy in the mid-
1950's failed. MAS 6 (1972) 225-
244.

4676 GUNAWAN, B. Political mobilization in Indonesia, nationalists
against communists. MAS 7 (1973)
707-715.

4677 HARDOJO, R. A. S. Foundation of
Indonesia's nation building. GEJ
5 (1963) 146-157.

4678 HAUSWEDELL, PETER CHRISTIAN. Sukarno, radical or conservative,
Indonesian politics, 1964-5. IND
15 (1973) 108-143.

4679 HINDLEY, DONALD. Political power
and the October 1965 coup in Indonesia. JAS 26 (1966-7) 237-249.

4680 KAHIN, GEORGE McTURNAN. Indonesia. K18 pp. 533-700.

4681 LEV, DANIEL S. Indonesia 1965,
the year of the coup. AS 6 (1966)
103-110.

4682 LEV, DANIEL S. Political role of
the army in Indonesia. PA 36
(1963) 349-364.

4683 PALMIER, LESLIE H. Centralization
in Indonesia. PA 33 (1960) 169-
180.

4684 PALMIER, LESLIE H. The 30 September movement in Indonesia.
MAS 5 (1971) 1-20.

4685 PAUKER, EWA T. Ganefo I, sports
and politics in Djakarta. AS 5
(1965) 171-185.

4686 PAUKER, GUY J. Indonesia in 1963,
the year of wasted opportunities.
AS 4 (1964) 687-694.

4687 PAUKER, GUY J. Indonesia in 1964,
towards a people's democracy? AS 5
(1965) 88-97.

4688 PAUKER, GUY J. Indonesia, internal development or external expansion? AS 3 (1963) 69-75.

4689 PLUVIER, JAN. Indonesia before
the holocaust. JCA 1 pt. 2 (1970)
9-21.

4690 SMAIL, JOHN R. W. Military politics of north Sumatra, December
1956-October 1957. IND 6 (1968)
128-187.

4691 SOEJATNO. Revolution and social
tensions in Surakarta, 1945-1950.
IND 17 (1974) 99-111.

4692 VAN DER KROEF, JUSTUS M. Indonesia's national philosophy. FA 18
(1962) 1-8.

4693 VAN DER KROEF, JUSTUS M. Origins
of the 1965 coup in Indonesia,
probabilities and alternatives.
JSAS 3 (1972) 277-298.

4694 WERTHEIM, W. F. Indonesia before
and after the Untung coup. PA 39
(1966) 115-127.

INDONESIA - POLITICS AND GOVERNMENT -
1965-

4695 ALLISON, JOHN M. Indonesia, year
of pragmatists. AS 9 (1969) 130-
137.

4696 ANDERSON, BEN. In memoriam, Soe
Hok Gie. IND 9 (1970) 225-227.

Indonesia - Politics and government -
  1965-

4697 Bangkok-Jakarta connection. JCA
      4 (1974) 238-241.

4698 Continuity and change, four Indo-
      nesian cabinets since October 1,
      1965, with scattered data on their
      members organizational and ethnic
      affiliations, age and place of
      birth. IND 2 (1966) 185-222.

4699 CROUCH, HAROLD. Military politics
      under Indonesia's new order. PA
      45 (1972) 206-219.

4700 Current data on the Indonesian
      army elite. IND 7 (1969) 195-201.

4701 Current data on the Indonesian
      military elite. IND 15 (1973)
      187-197.

4702 Current data on the Indonesian
      military elite after the reorgani-
      zation of 1969-1970. IND 10
      (1970) 194-208.

4703 Data on the current military
      elite. IND 3 (1967) 205-216.

4704 DeIONGH, R. C. Indonesia, a new
      era of pragmatism? JOSA 6 (1968)
      50-58.

4705 DELIAR NOER. Indonesia's contem-
      porary political problems. AST 8
      (1970) 366-373.

4706 Development cabinet, June 6,
      1968. IND 6 (1968) 193.

4707 FEITH, HERBERT. Suharto's search
      for a political format. IND 6
      (1968) 88-105.

4708 HINDLEY, DONALD. Alirans and the
      fall of the old order. IND 9
      (1970) 23-66.

4709 HINDLEY, DONALD. Indonesia 1970,
      the workings of Pantjasila democ-
      racy. AS 11 (1971) 111-120.

4710 HINDLEY, DONALD. Indonesia 1971,
      Pantjasila democracy and the sec-
      ond parliamentary elections. AS
      12 (1972) 56-68.

4711 LIDDLE, R. WILLIAM. Evolution
      from above, national leadership
      and local development in Indone-
      sia. JAS 32 (1972-3) 287-309.

4712 PAGET, ROGER K. The military in
      Indonesian politics, the burden of
      power. PA 40 (1967) 294-314.

4713 PAUKER, GUY J. Gestapu affair of
      1965, reflections on the politics
      of instability in Indonesia. SA 1
      (1971) 42-56.

4714 PAUKER, GUY J. Indonesia, the age
      of reason? AS 8 (1968) 133-147.

4715 PAUKER, GUY J. Indonesia, the
      year of transition. AS 7 (1967)
      138-150.

4716 RO, KWANG H. Indonesia, Sukarno
      and afterwards. AF 1 pt. 3 (1969)
      1-10.

4717 ROOSMAN, S. Indonesia, aftermath
      of a shock. AQ (1972) 321-340.

4718 SAMSON, ALLAN A. Indonesia 1972,
      the solidification of military
      control. AS 13 (1973) 127-139.

4719 SAMSON, ALLAN A. Islam in Indone-
      sian politics. AS 8 (1968) 1001-
      1017.

4720 SCHMEITS, ERIC. September 30th
      affair in Indonesia, as seen
      through the world press. FA 20
      (1965) 209-238.

4721 Selected documents relating to the
      September 30th movement and its
      epilogue. IND 1 (1966) 131-204.

4722 SIHOMBING, O. DAULAT P. Indonesia since September 30, 1965. SJ 18 (1971) 206-216.

4723 SUHARTO. October dawns in Djakarta. FA 20 (1965) 497-509.

4724 THOMAS, K. D. Indonesia's development cabinet, background to current problems and the five year plan, by K. D. Thomas and J. Panglaykim. AS 9 (1969) 223-238.

4725 USAMAH. War and humanity, notes on personal experience. IND 9 (1970) 89-99.

4726 VAN DER KROEF, JUSTUS M. Gestapu in Indonesia. T45 pp. 303-325.

4727 VAN DER KROEF, JUSTUS M. Interpretations of the 1965 Indonesian coup, a review of the literature. PA 43 (1970) 557-577.

4728 WARD, KEN. Indonesia's modernisation, ideology and practice. M77 pp. 67-82.

4729 WERTHEIM, W. F. Suharto and the Untung coup, the missing link. JCA 1 pt. 2 (1970) 50-57.

INDONESIA - POPULATION

4730 FRUIN, TH. A. Overpopulation and the emancipation of the village. J32 pp. 331-343.

4731 HAWKINS, EVERETT D. Indonesia's population problem. C21 pp. 119-145.

4732 HUNTER, ALEX. Notes on Indonesian population. G52 pp. 183-195.

4733 KEYFITZ, NATHAN. Indonesian population and the European industrial revolution. AS 5 (1965) 503-514.

4734 MOHR, E. C. J. Relation between soil and population density in the Netherlands Indies. H57 pp. 254-262.

4735 THOMAS, R. MURRAY. Effects of Indonesian population growth on educational development, 1940-1968. AS 9 (1969) 498-514.

4736 WITHINGTON, WILLIAM A. Distribution of population in Sumatra, Indonesia, 1961. JTG 17 (1963) 203-212.

4737 WITHINGTON, WILLIAM A. Problems and potentialities of development of western Indonesia, Sumatra as an example of third world characteristics. RSA (1969) 79-103.

INDONESIA - RELIGION *See also* BUDDHISM, HINDUISM, ISLAM

4738 BOLAND, B. J. Religion as a subject of inquiry in present day Indonesia. P15 pp. 149-154.

4739 COOLEY, FRANK L. Altar and throne in central Moluccan societies. IND 2 (1966) 135-156.

4740 INDRAKUSUMA, J. Pangestu, suatu pandangan hidup Djawa. AR 4 (1972) 32-48.

4741 MONTEIL, VINCENT. Relationship between religions in Indonesia. AR 1 (1970) 35-44.

4742 SOEBARDI. Santri religious elements as reflected in the *Book of Tjentini*. BIJ 127 (1971) 331-349.

Indonesia - Religion

4743 VANAKKEREN, PHILIP. A contemporary Indonesian messiah, a profile. JOSA 7 (1970) 134-146.

4744 VREDENBREGT, J. Dabus in west Java. BIJ 129 (1973) 302-320.

4745 ZOETMULDER, P. J. Significance of the study of culture and religion for Indonesian historiography. S61 pp. 326-343.

INDONESIA - SOCIAL CONDITIONS

4746 BOEKE, J. H. Social and economic needs. J32 pp. 69-74.

4747 BREMAN, J. Over oude en nieuwe afhankelijkheids-relaties, de maatschappelijke context van patronage en makelaardij. B85 pp. 31-46.

4748 CUNNINGHAM, CLARK E. Characterizing a social system, the loose-tight dichotomy. L62 pp. 106-114.

4749 GUNAWAN, BASUKI. Aliran en sociale structuur. B85 pp. 69-85.

4750 LEVINE, DAVID. History and social structure in the study of contemporary Indonesia. IND 7 (1969) 5-19.

4751 MORTIMER, REX. Class, social cleavage and Indonesian communism. IND 8 (1969) 1-20.

4752 SELO SOEMARDJAN. Social stratification and social mobility in Indonesia. EACS 4 (1965) 52-73.

4753 SOEPOMO POEDJOSOEDARMO. Javanese speech levels. IND 6 (1968) 54-81.

4754 TANNER, NANCY. Disputing and dispute settlement among the Minang-kabau of Indonesia. IND 8 (1969) 21-67.

4755 UTRECHT, ERNST. American sociologists on Indonesia. JCA 3 (1973) 39-45.
      Comment: WITTON, RON. Comment. JCA 3 (1973) 467-469.
      Author's reply: JCA 3 (1973) 470.

4756 VREDENBREGT, J. Dabus in west Java. BIJ 129 (1973) 302-320.

INDONESIA - STATISTICS

4757 BRAND, W. Some statistical data on Indonesia. BIJ 125 (1969) 305-327.

INDONESIA - TREATIES

4758 YOUNG, KENNETH RAY. Sino-Indonesian dual nationality treaty, an evaluation. AF 2 (1970) 172-182.

INDONESIAN LANGUAGE See also MALAY LANGUAGE

4759 ALISJAHBANA, S. TAKDIR. Language policy, language engineering and literacy, Indonesia and Malaysia. S22 pp. 1087-1109.

4760 ALISJAHBANA, S. TAKDIR. Modernization of the Indonesian-Malay language in the 19th and 20th century. A43 pp. 181-210.

4761 ALISJAHBANA, S. TAKDIR. Writing of normative grammar for Indonesian language. A43 pp. 246-254.

4762 ALTMANN, GABRIEL. Structure of Indonesian morphemes. AAS 3 (1967) 23-36.

4763 ANCEAUX, J. C. Linguistic theories about the Austronesian homeland. BIJ 121 (1965) 417-432.

4764 ANDERSON, BEN. Languages of Indonesian politics. IND 1 (1966) 89-116.

4765 ASMAH HAJI OMAR. Toward the standardization of Bahasa Melayu and Bahasa Indonesia. A43 pp. 170-180.

4766 ECHOLS, JOHN M. In memoriam, W. J. S. Purwadarminta, 1904-1968. IND 8 (1969) 217.

4767 HARIMURTI KRIDALAKSANA. Towards a standardization of phonologic and morphologic borrowed elements in Bahasa Indonesia. A43 pp. 211-232.

4768 HOED, BENNY H. La politique linguistic et ses problems dans une Indonesie en developpement. AR 5 (1973) 17-37.

4769 LABROUSSE, PIERRE. L'elaboration d'apres corpus d'un dictionnaire de 1'Indonesien contemporain. AR 4 (1972) 21-26.

4770 MATTULADA. Modernization of Indonesian and the promotion of friendship and understanding among nations. A43 pp. 233-245.

4771 PANGANIBAN, JOSE VILLA. Studies in word relationships among Philippine languages, Malay and Bahasa Indonesia. UN 36 (1963) 131-143.

4772 PARNICKEL, B. Austronesian philology in the Soviet Union. BIJ 121 (1965) 245-258.

4773 ROSARIO, GONSALO DEL. Modernization-standardization plan for the Austronesian derived national languages of Southeast Asia. AST 6 (1968) 1-18.

4774 RUZUI, SEPTY. Survey of relations between Indonesian, Malay and the main languages of the Philippines. UN 35 (1962) 22-80.

4775 SPITZBARDT, HARRY. Algorithm for syntactic permutations in Indonesian. AAS 3 (1967) 13-22.

4776 SPITZBARDT, HARRY. Lexical and morphological impact of Sanskrit on modern Indonesian. AAS 9 (1973) 97-113.

4777 STEVENS, ALAN M. Pseudo transitive verbs in Indonesian. IND 9 (1970) 67-72.

4778 UHLENBECK, E. M. Indonesia and Malaysia. S21 pp. 847-898.

4779 UHLENBECK, E. M. Indonesia and Malaysia. S22 pp. 55-111.

4780 UKUN SURJAMAN. Problem of personal pronouns in Bahasa Indonesia and the representation of the words nia and ia. AST 6 (1968) 90-98.

4781 VRIES, J. W. DE. Indonesian abbreviations and acronyms. BIJ 126 (1970) 338-346.

INDONESIAN LITERATURE *See also* MALAY LITERATURE, FOLK LITERATURE - INDONESIA, AND THE NAMES OF INDIVIDUAL AUTHORS **

4782 BALFAS, M. Child of the revolution (Anak revolusi). IND 17 (1974) 43-50.

4783 CHAMBERT-LOIR, HENRI. La sauvegarde des litteratures regionales

Indonesian literature

indonesiennes. AR 7 (1974) 175-198.

4784 MOCHTAR LUBIS. La veritable histoire du suicide de Hadji Djala. AR 4 (1972) 74-80.

4785 ROSIDI, AJIP. Among the family. IND 1 (1966) 117-123.

4786 ROSIDI, AJIP. Le bouc. AR 2 (1971) 129-138.

4787 ROSIDI, AJIP. A Japanese, translated by William Frederick. IND 6 (1968) 82-87.

4788 ROSIDI, AJIP. Perdjalanan di Malaysia, quatre poemes originaux. AR 2 (1971) 120-122.

4789 ROSIDI, AJIP. Perdjalanan penganten. AR 2 (1971) 139-152.

4790 RUSLAN ABDULGANI. My childhood world. IND 17 (1974) 112-135.

4791 SOL TAS. Souvenirs of sjahir, translated by Ruth McVey. IND 8 (1969) 135-154.

4792 TOER, PRAMOEDYA ANANTA. It's not an all night fair, bukan pasar malam, translated with an introduction by William Watson. IND 15 (1973) 21-79.

4793 ZULIDAHLAN. Totale est maintenant ma douleur en ce monde. AR 6 (1973) 81-85.

INDONESIAN LITERATURE - CRITICISM **

4794 ALTMANN, GABRIEL. Binomial index of euphony for Indonesian poetry. AAS 2 (1966) 62-67.

4795 AVELING, HARRY. Alternative reading of Sanusi Pane's *Sadjak*.

4796 AVELING, HARRY G. Analysis of Utuy Tatang Sontani's *Suling*. BIJ 125 (1969) 328-343.

4797 AVELING, HARRY G. Indonesian wasteland, the verse of Rivai Apin. BIJ 127 (1971) 350-374.

4798 AVELING, HARRY G. Seventeenth century Bandanese society in fact and fiction, Tambera assessed. BIJ 123 (1967) 347-365.

4799 AVELING, HARRY G. Sitti Nurbaja, some reconsiderations. BIJ 126 (1970) 228-245.

4800 AVELING, HARRY G. Some conventions of prewar Indonesian verse. BIJ 128 (1972) 417-429.

4801 AVELING, HARRY G. Thorny rose, the avoidance of passion in modern Indonesian literature. IND 7 (1969) 67-76.

4802 BALFAS, M. Wrong upbringing, characterization in an early Indonesian novel. JOSA 6 (1968) 5-15.

4803 BUDIMAN, ARIEF. Quelques problemes de la litterature indonesienne moderne. AR 7 (1974) 3-8.

4804 CHAMBERT-LOIR, HENRI. Angkatan 66, une nouvelle vogue? AR 1 (1970) 89-95.

4805 CHAMBERT-LOIR, HENRI. La documentation litteraire de H. B. Jassin. AR 7 (1974) 93-114.

4806 CHAMBERT-LOIR, HENRI. Horison, six annees d'une revue litteraire indonesienne. AR 4 (1972) 81-89.

4807 CHAMBERT-LOIR, HENRI. Lantaran Ajip Rosidi. AR 2 (1971) 123-128.

4808 COWAN, H. K. J. La legende de Samudra. AR 5 (1973) 253-286.

4809 DJAMIN, NASJAH. Les derniers moments de Chairil Anwar. AR 4 (1972) 49-73.

4810 DREWES, G. W. J. Hikajat Muhammad Mukabil, the story of the Kadi and the learned brigand. BIJ 126 (1970) 309-331.

4811 FOULCHER, KEITH R. Survey of events surrounding Manikebu, the struggle for cultural and intellectual freedom in Indonesian literature. BIJ 125 (1969) 429-465.

4812 HOLT, CLAIRE. In memoriam, Trisno Sumardjo, December 6, 1916-April 21, 1969. IND 8 (1969) 213-216.

4813 JOHNS, A. H. Amir Hamzah, Malay prince, Indonesian poet. B38 pp. 303-319.

4814 JOHNS, A. H. Chairil Anwar, an interpretation. BIJ 120 (1964) 393-408.

4815 JOHNS, A. H. Sufism as a category in Indonesian literature and history. JSAH 2 (July 1961) 10-23.

4816 LABROUSSE, PIERRE. Entretien avec Ajip. AR 2 (1971) 116-119.

4817 LABROUSSE, PIERRE. Retour a Djatiwangi. AR 2 (1971) 153-166.

4818 LOMBARD-SALMON, CLAUDINE. Le sjair de l'Association Chinoise de Batavia, 1905. AR 2 (1971) 55-100.

4819 LOMBARD-SALMON, CLAUDINE. Societe peranakan et utopie, deux romans sino-malais, 1934-1939. AR 3 (1972) 169-195.

4820 NEEDHAM, RODNEY. Jataka, Pancatantra and Kodi fables. BIJ 116 (1960) 232-262.

4821 RAS, J. J. Panji romance and W. H. Rassers' analysis of its theme. BIJ 129 (1973) 411-456.

4822 RICKLEFS, M. C. Note on Professor Johns's *Gift addressed to the spirit of the prophet*. BIJ 129 (1973) 347-349.

4823 SOEBARDI. Raden Ngabehi Jasadipura I, court poet of Surakarta, his life and works. IND 8 (1969) 81-102.

4824 SOEWITO SANTOSO. Islamization of Indonesian/Malay literature in its early period. JOSA 8 (1971) 9-27.

4825 SUTHERLAND, HEATHER. Pudjangga baru, aspects of Indonesian intellectual life in the 1930's. IND 6 (1968) 106-127.

4826 TEEUW, A. Impact of Balai Pustaka on modern Indonesian literature. SOAS 35 (1972) 111-127.

4827 TEEUW, A. Modern Indonesian literature abroad. BIJ 127 (1971) 256-263.

4828 VOORHOEVE, P. Author of the *Sjair Radin Menteri*. BIJ 126 (1970) 259-260.

4829 WATSON, C. W. Salah Asuhan and the romantic tradition in the early Indonesian novel. MAS 7 (1973) 179-192.

Indonesian literature - Criticism

4830 WATSON, C. W. Some preliminary
     remarks on the antecedents of
     modern Indonesian literature.
     BIJ 127 (1971) 417-433.

4831 WING KARDJO. Ajip Rosidi dalam
     potret diri. AR 2 (1971) 111-115.

INDUSTRIALIZATION

4832 HUGHES, HELEN. Manufacturing
     industry sector. S63 pp. 186-251.

INDUSTRIALIZATION - BURMA

4833 KHIN THAN KYWE. Financing the
     small manufacturing establish-
     ments of Burma. B91 pp. 107-142.

INDUSTRIALIZATION - INDONESIA

4834 KING, DWIGHT Y. Social develop-
     ment in Indonesia, a macro anal-
     ysis. AS 14 (1974) 918-935.

4835 PANGLAYKIM. Indonesian state
     enterprises and worker-management
     councils (Dewan Perusahaan). AS
     3 (1963) 285-288.

4836 WILLNER, RUTH ANN. Adaptation of
     peasants to conditions of factory
     labor, a case study in Java. AS
     3 (1963) 560-571.

4837 WILLNER, RUTH ANN. Problems of
     management and authority in a
     transitional society, a case
     study of a Javanese factory. T45
     pp. 162-178.

INDUSTRIALIZATION - MALAYSIA

4838 ISMAIL ALI BIN MOHAMED ALI. Role
     of central banking in industriali-
     zation. MER 8 pt. 1 (1963) 14-19.

4839 WHEELWRIGHT, E. L. Industrializa-
     tion in Malaya. S47 pp. 210-241.

4840 WHEELWRIGHT, E. L. Reflections on
     some problems of industrial devel-
     opment in Malaya. MER 8 pt. 1
     (1963) 66-80.

4841 WITHELL, GORDON W. Management of
     change in industry. MER 8 pt. 1
     (1963) 25-28.

4842 WONG, LESLIE G. J. Foreword,
     papers presented at the symposium
     on the role of management in in-
     dustrialization in Malaysia. MER
     8 pt. 1 (1963) 1-3.

INDUSTRIALIZATION - SINGAPORE

4843 CHALMERS, W. E. Industrial rela-
     tions, by W. E. Chalmers and Pang
     Eng Fong. M49 pp. 109-126.

4844 CHIA SIOW YUE. Growth and pattern
     of industrialization. Y52 pp.
     189-223.

4845 CHUA, WEE MENG. Inter-industry
     analysis of the Singapore economy,
     1967. MER 17 pt. 1 (1972) 25-49.

4846 GOH CHOK TONG. Industrial growth,
     1959-66. M49 pp. 127-146.

4847 HUAN, S. H. Measures to promote
     industrialization. Y52 pp. 224-
     245.

4848 HUGHES, HELEN. Conclusions. H84
     pp. 177-210.

4849 HUGHES, HELEN. From entrepot
     trade to manufacturing. H84 pp.
     1-45.

4850 LIM POH TIN, EILEEN. Study of the
     cement industry of Singapore. MER
     15 pt. 2 (1970) 104-113.

4851 NG KIAT CHONG. Evaluation of the policy of tariff protection on wire rods in Singapore. MER 17 pt. 1 (1972) 78-98.

4852 WHEELWRIGHT, E. L. Reflections on some problems of industrial development in Malaya. MER 8 pt. 1 (1963) 66-80.

4853 WONG, AMY. On the variation of wages, proprietary income and output in selected small-scale manufacturing industries in Singapore. MER 19 pt. 1 (1974) 65-83.

INDUSTRIALIZATION - THAILAND **

4854 Modernization and industrialization of Thai society, a sociological analysis, by Kenichi Tominaga, Hiroshi Komai, Hideo Okamoto and Michiko Ise. EACS 9 (1970) 1-56.

4855 SILCOCK, T. H. Promotion of industry and the planning process. S49 pp. 258-288.

INDUSTRIALIZATION - VIETNAM

4856 NGUYEN PHUC SA. General report on industrial development. L52 pp. 241-244.

INFLATION - BURMA

4857 MALI, K. S. Public expenditures and inflationary impact in Burma, 1951-59. JBRS 45 (1962) 49-78.

INFLATION - INDONESIA

4858 HAWKINS, EVERETT D. Job inflation in Indonesia. AS 6 (1966) 264-275.

INLE LAKE

4859 NATH, DEWAN MOHINDER. Botanical survey of the southern Shan states with a note on the vegetation of the Inle Lake. B91 pp. 161-418.

INSCRIPTIONS

4860 BROWN, CARRIE C. Two Ming texts concerning King Ma-Na-Je-Chia-Na of P'o-Ni. BMJ 3 pt. 2 (1974) 222-229.

4861 DAMAIS, LOUIS-CHARLES. L'epigraphie musulmane dans le sud-est asiatique. BEF 54 (1968) 567-604.

4862 LOMBARD-SALMON, CL. Recentes etudes sur l'epigraphie chinoise en Asie du sud-est. AR 8 (1974) 213-223.

4863 TAN YEOK SEONG. Sri Vijayan inscription of Canton, A.D. 1079. JSAH 5 (Sept. 1964) 17-24.

INSCRIPTIONS - BRUNEI

4864 FRANKE, WOLFGANG. Chinese tomb inscription of A.D. 1264, discovered recently in Brunei, a preliminary report, by Wolfgang Franke and Chen Tieh-fan. BMJ 3 pt. 1 (1973) 91-99.

4865 SHARIFFUDDIN, P. M. Genealogical tablet (Batu Tarsilah) of the sultans of Brunei, by P. M. Shariffuddin and Abd. Latif Hj. Ibrahim. BMJ 3 pt. 2 (1974) 253-264.

INSCRIPTIONS - BURMA

4866 CHAM TONGKAMWAN. Tai inscription in the museum at Pagan, Burma. G83 pp. 249-252.

Inscriptions - Burma

4867 COEDES, GEORGE. Documents epigraphiques provenant de Tenasserim. F38 pp. 203-209.

4868 LUCE, G. H. Shwegugyi Pagoda inscription, by G. H. Luce and Pe Maung Tin. B92 pp. 377-384.

4869 NAI PAN HLA. Mon copper plate in the National Library, Bangkok, by Nai Pan Hla and E. Guillon. JBRS 55 (1972) 9-18.

4870 PE MAUNG TIN. Buddhism in the inscriptions of Pagan. B92 pp. 423-441.

4871 PE MAUNG TIN. Women in the inscriptions of Pagan. B92 pp. 411-421.

4872 VICKERY, MICHAEL. Khmer inscriptions of Tennasserim, a reinterpretation. JSS 61 pt. 1 (1973) 51-70.

INSCRIPTIONS - CAMBODIA

4873 BHATTACHARYA, KAMALESWAR. Recherches sur le vocabulaire des inscriptions sanskrites du Cambodge. BEF 52 (1964) 1-72.

4874 BHATTACHARYA, KAMALESWAR. Supplement aux recherches sur le vocabulaire des inscriptions sanskrites du Cambodge. BEF 53 (1966) 273-277.

4875 BHATTACHARYA, KAMALESWAR. Supplement aux recherches sur le vocabulaire des inscriptions sanskrites du Cambodge. BEF 55 (1969) 145-151.

4876 CHANDLER, DAVID P. Eighteenth century inscription from Angkor Wat. JSS 59 pt. 2 (1971) 151-159.

4877 JACQUES, CLAUDE. Etudes d'epigraphie cambodgienne. I. La stele du Phnom Sres. BEF 54 (1968) 605-622.

4878 JACQUES, CLAUDE. Etudes d'epigraphie cambodgienne. IV. Deux inscriptions du Phnom Bakhen, K. 464 et K. 558. V. La stele du Prasat Cha Chuk, K. 1034. BEF 57 (1970) 57-89.

4879 JACQUES, CLAUDE. Etudes d'epigraphie cambodgienne. VI. Sur les donnees chronologiques de la stele de Tuol Ta Pec, K. 834. BEF 58 (1971) 163-176.

4880 JACQUES, CLAUDE. Etudes d'epigraphie cambodgienne. VII. Sur l'emplacement du royaume d'Aninditapura. VIII. La carriere de Jayavarman. BEF 59 (1972) 193-220.

4881 JACQUES, CLAUDE. Supplement au tome VIII des inscriptions du Cambodge. BEF 58 (1971) 177-195.

4882 JACQUES, CLAUDE. Inscriptions diverses recemment decouvertes en Thailande. BEF 56 (1969) 57-73.

4883 LEWITZ, SAVEROS. L'inscription de Phimeanakas, K. 484, etude linguistique. BEF 58 (1971) 91-103.

4884 LEWITZ, SAVEROS. Inscriptions modernes d'Angkor, 1, 8, et 9. BEF 59 (1972) 101-121.

4885 LEWITZ, SAVEROS. Inscriptions modernes d'Angkor, 2 et 3. Textes en Kmer moyen. BEF 57 (1970) 99-126.

4886 LEWITZ, SAVEROS. Inscriptions modernes d'Angkor, 4, 5, 6, et 7. BEF 58 (1971) 105-123.

4887 LEWITZ, SAVEROS. Inscriptions modernes d'Angkor, 10, 11, 12, 13, 14, 15, 16a, 16b, et 16c. BEF 59 (1972) 221-249.

4888 LEWITZ, SAVEROS. Inscriptions modernes d'Angkor, 17, 18, 19, 20, 21, 22, 23, 24, et 25. BEF 60 (1973) 163-203.

4889 LEWITZ, SAVEROS. Inscriptions modernes d'Angkor, 26, 27, 28, 29, 30, 31, 32, 33. BEF 60 (1973) 205-242.

4890 POU, SAVEROS. Inscriptions modernes d'Angkor, 35, 36, 37, et 39 (1). BEF 61 (1974) 301-337.

4891 RICKLEFS, M. C. Land and the law in the epigraphy of tenth century Cambodia. JAS 26 (1966-7) 411-420.

INSCRIPTIONS - INDONESIA

4892 BUCHARI. Epigraphy and Indonesian historiography. S61 pp. 47-73.

4893 COEDES, G. Possible interpretation of the inscription at Kedukan Bukit, Palembang. B38 pp. 24-32.

4894 COWAN, H. K. J. Een interessant getuigenis betreffende de vroegste Islam in Noord-Sumatra. BIJ 117 (1961) 410-416.

4895 DAMAIS, LOUIS-CHARLES. Bosch et l'epigraphie indonesienne. H39 pp. 49-58.

4896 DAMAIS, LOUIS-CHARLES. Etudes soumatranaises, la date de l'inscription de Hujung Langit. BEF 50 (1960) 275-288.

4897 DAMAIS, LOUIS-CHARLES. Etudes soumatranaises, l'inscription de Ulu Belu, Soumatra meridional. BEF 50 (1960) 289-310.

4898 DAMAIS, LOUIS-CHARLES. La langue B, des inscriptions de Sri Wijaya. BEF 54 (1968) 523-566.

4899 DAMAIS, LOUIS-CHARLES. Les publications epigraphiques du service archeologique de l'Indonesie. BEF 54 (1968) 295-521.

4900 DeCASPARIS, J. G. New evidence on cultural relations between Java and Ceylon in ancient times. G83 pp. 241-248.

4901 GALIS, K. W. Eerste rotsgraveringen in Nederlands Nieuw-Guinea ontdekt. BIJ 117 (1961) 464-474.

4902 HOADLEY, MASON C. Continuity and change in Javanese legal tradition, the evidence of Jayapattra. IND 11 (1971) 95-109.

4903 MINATTUR, JOSEPH. Note on the King Kundungga of the east Borneo inscriptions. JSAH 5 (Sept. 1964) 181-183.

4904 NOORDUYN, J. Purnavarman's river works near Tugu, by J. Noorduyn and H. Th. Verstappen. BIJ 128 (1972) 298-307.

4905 SARKAR, HIMANSU BHUSAN. South India in old Javanese and Sanskrit inscriptions. BIJ 125 (1969) 193-206.

4906 SUKARTO K. ATMODJO, M. M. Preliminary report on the copper plate inscription of Asahduren. BIJ 126 (1970) 215-227.

Inscriptions - Laos

INSCRIPTIONS - LAOS

4907 GUILLON, E. Recherches sur quelques inscriptions Mon. BEF 61 (1974) 339-348.

INSCRIPTIONS - THAILAND

4908 BOELES, J. J. Note on Tamil relations with south Thailand and the identification of Ptolemy's Tacola. JSS 54 (1966) 221-230.

4909 BOELES, J. J. Note on the ancient city called Lavapura. JSS 55 (1967) 113-4.

4910 BOISSELIER, JEAN. Un fragment inscrit de roue de la loi de Lopburi. G83 pp. 225-231.

4911 CHAND CHIRAYU RAJANI. Review article, A. B. Griswold and Prasert na Nagara, Epigraphic and historical studies, nos. 1-8. JSS 61 pt. 1 (1973) 261-301.

4912 CHAND CHIRAYU RAJANI. Review article, A. B. Griswold and Prasert na Nagara, Epigraphic and historical studies, no. 9 and no. 10. JSS 61 pt. 2 (1973) 167-182.

4913 CHHABRA, B. CH. Bangkok museum stone inscription of Mahendravarman. JSS 49 pt. 2 (1961) 109-111.

4914 COEDES, G. L'annee du lievre, 1219 A.D. J41 pp. 83-88.

4915 DeCASPARIS, J. G. Date of the Grahi Buddha. JSS 55 (1967) 31-40.

4916 DHANINIVAT, PRINCE. Inscriptions of Wat Phra Jetubon. S44.4 pp. 143-184.

4917 DHANINIVAT, PRINCE. Sonkrant of Mon as recorded in the inscriptions of Wat Pra Jetupon in Bangkok. E92 pp. 117-119.

4918 GRISWOLD, A. B. Epigraphic and historical studies. I. Declaration of independence and its consequences. JSS 56 (1968) 207-249.

4919 GRISWOLD, A. B. Epigraphic and historical studies. II. Asokarama inscription of 1399 A.D., by A. B. Griswold and Prasert na Nagara. JSS 57 (1969) 29-56.

4920 GRISWOLD, A. B. Epigraphic and historical studies. III. Pact between Sukhodaya and Nan, by A. B. Griswold and Prasert na Nagara. JSS 57 (1969) 57-107.

4921 GRISWOLD, A. B. Epigraphic and historical studies. IV. Law promulgated by the king of Ayudhya in 1397 A.D. JSS 57 (1969) 109-148.

4922 GRISWOLD, A. B. Epigraphic and historical studies. V. Pact between uncle and nephew, by A. B. Griswold and Prasert na Nagara. JSS 58 pt. 1 (1970) 89-113.

4923 GRISWOLD, A. B. Epigraphic and historical studies. VI. Inscription in old Mon from Wieng Mano in Ching Mai Province, by A. B. Griswold and Prasert na Nagara. JSS 59 pt. 1 (1971) 153-156.

4924 GRISWOLD, A. B. Epigraphic and historical studies. VII. Inscription of Vat Traban Jan Phoak, face I, 1380 A.D., by A. B. Griswold and Prasert na Nagara. JSS 59 pt. 1 (1971) 157-188.

4925 GRISWOLD, A. B. Epigraphic and historical studies. VIII. Inscription of Vat Jan Lom, 1384 A.D., by A. B. Griswold and Prasert na Nagara. JSS 59 pt. 1 (1971) 189-208.

4926 GRISWOLD, A. B. Epigraphic and historical studies. IX. Inscription of King Rama Kamhen of Sukhodaya, 1292 A.D., by A. B. Griswold and Prasert na Nagara. JSS 59 pt. 2 (1971) 179-228.

4927 GRISWOLD, A. B. Epigraphic and historical studies. X. King Lodaiya of Sukhodaya and his contemporaries, by A. B. Griswold and Prasert na Nagara. JSS 60 pt. 1 (1972) 21-152.

4928 GRISWOLD, A. B. Addendum to epigraphic and historical studies, no. X, by A. B. Griswold and Prasert na Nagara. JSS 61 pt. 1 (1973) 179-181.

4929 GRISWOLD, A. B. Epigraphic and historical studies. XI pt. 1. Epigraphy of Mahadharmaraja I of Sukhodaya, by A. B. Griswold and Prasert na Nagara. JSS 61 pt. 1 (1973) 71-178.
Comment: VICKERY, MICHAEL. Note on the date of the Traibhumikatha. JSS 62 pt. 2 (1974) 275-284.

4930 GRISWOLD, A. B. Epigraphic and historical studies. XI pt. 2. Epigraphy of Mahadharmaraja I of Sukhodaya, by A. B. Griswold and Prasert na Nagara. JSS 61 pt. 2 (1973) 91-128.

4931 GRISWOLD, A. B. Epigraphic and historical studies. XII. Inscription 9, by A. B. Griswold and Prasert na Nagara. JSS 62 pt. 1 (1974) 89-121.

4932 GRISWOLD, A. B. Epigraphic and historical studies. XIII. The inscription of Wat Pra Yun, by A. B. Griswold and Prasert na Nagara. JSS 62 pt. 1 (1974) 123-141.

4933 GRISWOLD, A. B. Epigraphic and historical studies. XIV. Inscription of the Siva of Kamben Bejra, by A. B. Griswold and Prasert na Nagara. JSS 62 pt. 2 (1974) 223-238.

4934 JACQUES, CLAUDE. Inscriptions diverses recemment decourvertes en Thailande. BEF 56 (1969) 57-73.

4935 KRAISRI NIMMANAHAEMINDA. Inscribed silver plate grant to the Lawa of Boh Luang. F38 pp. 233-238.
Comment: SANIDH RANGSIT, M. C. Additional note on the silver plate grant from Boh Luang. F38 pp. 239-240.

4936 LOHUIZEN-DE LEEUW, J. E. VAN. The stone Buddha of Chiengmai and its inscription. G83 pp. 324-329.

4937 PENTH, HANS. Stone inscription from Wat Dong Bunnak (Phan). JSS 59 pt. 2 (1971) 175-178.

4938 SINGARAVELU, S. Note on the possible relationship of King Rama Khamhaeng's Sukhodaya script of Thailand to the Grantha script of south India. JSS 57 (1969) 1-28.

INSCRIPTIONS - VIETNAM

4939 BHATTACHARYA, KAMALESWAR. Precisions sur la paleographie de l'inscriptions dite de Vo-Canh. G83 pp. 218-224.

4940 FILLIOZAT, JEAN. L'inscription dite de Vo-Canh. BEF 55 (1969) 107-116.

Inscriptions - Vietnam

INSTITUTE OF ASIAN ECONOMIC AFFAIRS

INSTITUTE OF PACIFIC RELATIONS

INSURANCE - MALAYSIA

INTELLECTUALS

INTELLECTUALS - BURMA

INTELLECTUALS - INDONESIA

INTELLECTUALS - PHILIPPINES

4961   YABES, LEOPOLDO Y.   Rizal and the
       liberal intellectual tradition.
       DR 11 (1963) 159-167.

4962   YABES, LEOPOLDO Y.   Two intellec-
       tual traditions.   AST 1 (1963) 84-
       104.

4963   YABES, LEOPOLDO Y.   Two intellec-
       tual traditions.   DR 11 (1963)
       391-423.

INTELLECTUALS - THAILAND

4964   PHILLIPS, HERBERT P.   Culture of
       Siamese intellectuals.   C24 pp.
       324-357.

INTELLECTUALS - VIETNAM

4965   MARR, DAVID.   Political attitudes
       and activities of young urban
       intellectuals in south Viet-Nam.
       AS 6 (1966) 249-263.

4966   PHAN BOI CHAU.   Memoires.   FA 22
       (1968) 263-470.

4967   SARGENT, G. E.   Intellectual at-
       mosphere in Lingnan at the time
       of the introduction of Buddhism.
       S93 pp. 161-171.

4968   VUONG VAN BAC.   Why did the Viet-
       namese intelligentsia fail in its
       leadership responsibility toward
       the nation?   AC 3 (July 1961) 13-
       28.

INTERNATIONAL CONGRESS OF ORIENTALISTS,
   27TH, ANN ARBOR

4969   SORENSEN, PER.   Brief account of
       the twenty-seventh International
       Congress of Orientalists, Ann

Arbor, Michigan, U.S.A., 13-19
August 1967.   AP 10 (1967) 13-4.

INTERNATIONAL CONGRESS OF ORIENTALISTS,
   28TH, CANBERRA

4970   Liste des communications concern-
       ant le monde insulindien presente
       au 28eme Congres International des
       Orientalistes, Canberra, janvier
       1971.   AR 1 (1970) 51-54.

INTERNATIONAL CONGRESS OF ORIENTALISTS,
   29TH, PARIS

4971   Les etudes malaises au XIXe Con-
       gres des Orientalistes, Paris, 16-
       22 juillet 1973.   AR 6 (1973) 3-
       11.

4972   LANGLET, MADAME.   Notes sur les
       changements du milieu humain dans
       la Republique du Vietnam, communi-
       cation faite au 29e Congres des
       Orientalistes, Paris, 17 juillet
       1973, par Madame Langlet et Quach
       Thanh Tam.   SEIB 49 (1974) 1-30.

INTERNATIONAL VOLUNTARY SERVICES

4973   LEWALLEN, JOHN.   Reluctant coun-
       terinsurgents, International
       Voluntary Services in Laos.   L18
       pp. 357-371.

4974   WILSON, T. HUNTER.   An IVS volun-
       teer writes from Laos.   L18 pp.
       372-376.

IRRIGATION - BURMA

4975   STARGARDT, JANICE.   Government and
       irrigation in Burma, a comparative
       survey.   AST 6 (1968) 358-371.

IRRIGATION - INDONESIA

4976 BIRKELBACH, AUBREY W. Subak association. IND 16 (1973) 153-169.

4977 GRADER, C. J. Irrigation system in the region of Jembrana. B18 pp. 267-288.

4978 LIEFRINCK, F. A. Rice cultivation in northern Bali. B19 pp. 1-73.

4979 NOORDUYN, J. Purnavarman's river works near Tugu, by J. Noorduyn and H. Th. Verstappen. BIJ 128 (1972) 298-307.

IRRIGATION - MALAYSIA

4980 SHORT, D. E. Origins of an irrigation policy in Malaya, a review of developments prior to the establishment of the Drainage and Irrigation Department, by D. E. Short and James C. Jackson. JMBRAS 44 pt. 1 (1971) 78-103.

IRRIGATION - THAILAND

4981 SMALL, LESLIE E. Historical development of the greater Chao Phya water control project, an economic perspective. JSS 61 pt. 1 (1973) 1-24.

4982 SMALL, LESLIE E. Water control and development in the central plain of Thailand. SA 3 (1974) 678-697.

4983 SMITH, HELEN L. Suan Sema, an illustration of changes and trends in Thai vegetable production. JSS 57 (1969) 339-348.

4984 WIJEYEWARDENE, GEHAN. Note on irrigation and agriculture in a north Thai village. F38 pp. 255-259.

ISINAI LANGUAGE

4985 CONSTANTINO, ERNESTO. Personal pronouns of Tagalog, Ilukano, Isinai and Kapampangan. Z16 pp. 567-596.

4986 PAZ, CONSUELO J. -ad in Isinai. AST 3 (1965) 114-125.

ISLAM

4987 ALATAS, SYED HUSSEIN. Religion and modernization in South-East Asia. M52 pp. 153-169.

4988 BROWN, CARRIE C. Some Ming regulations on the provisions for tributary delegations. BMJ 3 pt. 2 (1974) 230-1.

4989 DAMAIS, LOUIS-CHARLES. L'epigraphie musulmane dans le sud-est asiatique. BEF 54 (1968) 567-604.

4990 EVANGELISTA, OSCAR L. Some aspects of the history of Islam in Southeast Asia. SJ 18 (1971) 180-189.

4991 FRANCISCO, JUAN R. Rama story in the post-Muslim Malay literature of Southeast Asia. SMJ 11 (1962) 468-485.

4992 TAMNEY, JOSEPH B. Scarcity of identity, the relation between religious identity add national identity. M52 pp. 175-198.

4993 YUSOF A. TALIB. Les Hadramis et le monde malais, essai de bibliographie critique des ouvrages europeens sur l'emigration hadramite aux XIXe et XXe siecles. AR 7 (1974) 41-68.

ISLAM - BRUNEI

4994   HARRISSON, TOM. Advent of Islam
to west and north Borneo, an attempted reconstruction of some
possible sequences. JMBRAS 45 pt.
1 (1972) 10-20.

ISLAM - BURMA

4995   BA SHIN. Coming of Islam to
Burma, down to A.D. 1700. S87 pp.
98-110.

4996   THAUNG. Panthay interlude in
Yunnan, a study in vicissitudes
through the Burmese kaleidoscope.
B91 pp. 473-483.

4997   YEGAR, MOSHE. Panthay (Chinese
Muslims) of Burma and Yunnan.
JSAH 7 (Mar. 1966) 73-85.

ISLAM - INDONESIA **

4998   al-ATTAS, SYED NAGUIB. New light
on the life of Hamzah Fansuri.
JMBRAS 40 pt. 1 (1967) 42-51.

4999   COWAN, H. K. J. Een interessant
getuigenis betreffende de vroegste
Islam in Noord-Sumatra. BIJ 117
(1961) 410-416.

5000   DOBBIN, CHRISTINE. Islamic re-
vivalism in Minangkabau at the
turn of the nineteenth century.
MAS 8 (1974) 319-356.

5001   DREWES, G. W. J. New light on the
coming of Islam to Indonesia? BIJ
124 (1968) 433-459.

5002   DREWES, G. W. J. Struggle between
Javanism and Islam as illustrated

by the Serat Dermagandul. BIJ 122
(1966) 309-365.

5003   FEDERSPIEL, HOWARD M. The military and Islam in Sukarno's Indonesia. PA 46 (1973) 407-420.

5004   FEDERSPIEL, HOWARD M. Muhammadi-
jah, a study of an orthodox Islamic movement in Indonesia. IND
10 (1970) 57-79.

5005   GEERTZ, CLIFFORD. Modernization
in a Muslim society, the Indonesian case. B42 pp. 93-108.

5006   GEERTZ, CLIFFORD. Modernization
in a Muslim society, the Indonesian case. T45 pp. 201-211.

5007   GOWING, PETER G. Non Islamic
elements in Indonesian Islam. SJ
15 (1968) 528-545.

5008   GRAAF, H. J. DE. Origin of the
Javanese mosque. JSAH 4 (Mar.
1963) 1-5.

5009   HILL, A. H. The coming of Islam
to north Sumatra. JSAH 4 (Mar.
1963) 6-21.

5010   JAY, ROBERT R. History and personal experience, religious and
political conflict in Java. R25
pp. 143-164.

5011   JOHNS, A. H. Muslim mystics and
historical writing. H18 pp. 37-
49.

5012   JOHNS, A. H. Sufism as a category
in Indonesian literature and history. JSAH 2 (July 1961) 10-23.

5013   KATHIRITHAMBY-WELLS, J. Ahmad
Shah Ibn Iskandar and the late
17th century holy war in Indonesia. JMBRAS 43 pt. 1 (1970) 48-63.

Islam - Indonesia

ISLAM - MALAYSIA **

5036 al-ATTAS, SYED MUHAMMAD NAGUIB. L'Islam et la culture malaise. AR 4 (1972) 132-150.

5037 al-ATTAS, SYED MUHAMMAD NAGUIB. Islamic culture in Malaysia. A41 pp. 123-130.

5038 COLLESS, BRIAN E. Persian merchants and missionaries in medieval Malaya. JMBRAS 42 pt. 2 (1969) 10-47.

5039 HARRISSON, TOM. Advent of Islam to west and north Borneo, an attempted reconstruction of some possible sequences. JMBRAS 45 pt. 1 (1972) 10-20.

5040 HLA AUNG. Some aspects of marriage under Burmese Buddhist law and Malayan Muslim law. JBRS 48 (Dec. 1965) 1-15.

5041 HOOKER, M. B. Adat and Islam in Malaya. BIJ 130 (1974) 69-90.

5042 JOSSELIN DE JONG, P. E. DE. Islam versus adat in Negri Sembilan, Malaya. BIJ 116 (1960) 158-203.

5043 KESSLER, CLIVE S. Muslim identity and political behaviour in Kelantan. K33 pp. 272-313.

5044 MACKEEN, A. M. M. Islamic constitutional document in Malaya. A41 pp. 131-138.

5045 MAJUL, CESAR ADIB. Theories on the introduction and expansion of Islam in Malaysia. SJ 11 (1964) 335-398.

5046 MOKHZANI, B. A. R. The Malay family and religion. EACS 13 (1974) 37-48.
Comment: SHIN, ANZAI. Comments. EACS 13 (1974) 49-50.

5047 MUHAMMAD SALLEH B. WAN MUSA. Theological debates, Wan Musa b. Haji Abdul Samad and his family, by Muhammad Salleh b. Wan Musa and S. Othman Kelantan. K33 pp. 153-169.

5048 RATNAM, K. J. Religion and politics in Malaya. T45 pp. 351-361.

5049 REID, ANTHONY. Nineteenth century pan-Islam in Indonesia and Malaysia. JAS 26 (1966-7) 267-283.

5050 ROFF, WILLIAM R. Islam as an agent of modernization, an episode in Kelantan history. M52 pp. 170-174.

5051 ROFF, WILLIAM R. Origin and early years of the Majlis Ugama. K33 pp. 101-152.

5052 SOEWITO SANTOSO. Islamization of Indonesian/Malay literature in its early period. JOSA 8 (1971) 9-27.

5053 THAM SEONG CHEE. Sociological aspects of religious reform in Malaya. RSAS 1 pt. 2 (1971) 29-41.

5054 VON DER MEHDEN, FRED R. Religion and politics in Malaya. AS 3 (1963) 609-615.

5055 WAKE, CHRISTOPHER H. Malacca's early kings and the reception of Islam. JSAH 5 (Sept. 1964) 104-132.

5056 WILDER, WILLIAM. Islam, other factors and Malay backwardness, comments on an argument. MAS 2 (1968) 155-164.

5057 WINZELER, ROBERT L. Social organization of Islam in Kelantan. K33 pp. 259-271.

ISLAM - PHILIPPINES

5058 ANGELES, F. DELOR. Brunei and the
Moro wars. BMJ 1 (1969) 119-132.

5059 ARCE, WILFREDO F. Social organization of the Muslim peoples of
Sulu. PS 11 (1963) 242-263.
Comment: ESLAO, NENA B. Comment
on social organization of the
Muslim peoples of Sulu. PS 11
(1963) 264-266.
Comment: STONE, RICHARD L. Comment on social organization of the
Muslim peoples of Sulu. PS 11
(1963) 263-4.

5060 ASIRI J. ABUBAKAR. Muslim Philippines, with reference to the Sulus,
Muslim-Christian contradictions
and the Mindanao crisis. AST 11
(1973) 112-128.

5061 BERNAD, MIGUEL A. Father Ducos
and the Muslim wars, 1752-1759.
PS 16 (1968) 690-728.

5062 BILLMAN, CUTHBERT. Islam in
Sulu. PS 8 (1960) 51-57.

5063 GOMEZ, HILARIO M. Studying attitudes of Muslims in the Philippines. SJ 19 (1972) 425-443.

5064 GONZALEZ, MARY A. Religious
minorities in the Philippines. UN
36 (1963) 366-372.

5065 GOWING, PETER G. Islam, the contemporary scene. PS 12 (1964)
639-647.

5066 GOWING, PETER G. Muslim-American
relations in the Philippines,
1899-1920. AST 6 (1968) 372-382.

5067 GOWING, PETER G. Muslim Filipinos, present condition and future
prospects. SJ 9 (1962) 305-316.

5068 KIEFER, THOMAS M. Gravemarkers
and the repression of sexual symbolism, the case of two Philippine-Borneo Moslem societies, by
Thomas M. Kiefer and Clifford
Sather. BIJ 126 (1970) 75-90.

5069 MAJUL, CESAR ADIB. Cultural and
religious responses to development
and social change. DR 18 (1970)
1-21.

5070 MAJUL, CESAR ADIB. Islamic and
Arab cultural influences in the
south of the Philippines. JSAH 7
(Sept. 1966) 61-73.

5071 MAJUL, CESAR ADIB. Political and
historical notes on the old Sulu
sultanate. JMBRAS 38 pt. 1 (1965)
23-42.

5072 MAJUL, CESAR ADIB. Role of Islam
in the history of the Filipino
people. AST 4 (1966) 303-315.

5073 MAQUISO, ELENA G. Langkat, its
relationship to the Ulahingan. SJ
17 (1970) 407-419.

5074 MOLONY, CAROL H. It's still genocide even if they die by starvation. JCA 3 (1973) 491-496.

5075 MUNDO, LIGAYA DEL. Marawi in
retrospect. JCA 4 (1974) 124-126.

5076 O'SHAUGHNESSY, THOMAS J. Islam,
surrender to God. PS 15 (1967)
108-129.

5077 OSORIO, EMMANUEL L. Christian-
Muslim integration. SJ 20 (1973)
258-270.

5078 SANTOS, R. JOEL DE LOS. How
Christian-Muslim relations affect
acculturation and development. SJ
20 (1973) 252-257.

5079 SORIANO, LICERIA B. Our Moro problem and the community school in Mindanao. E78 pp. 569-577.

5080 STONE, RICHARD L. Some aspects of Muslim social organization. M24 pp. 90-133.

5081 TAN, SAMUEL K. Unity and disunity in the Muslim struggle. AST 11 pt. 3 (1973) 110-134.

5082 THOMAS, RALPH B. Asia for Asiatics? Muslim Filipino responses to Japanese occupation and propaganda during World War II. AF 4 pt. 3 (1972) 43-60.

5083 WULFF, INGER. Yakan Maulud celebration. Z16 pp. 494-502.

5084 WULFF, INGER. Yakan of Basilan. SJ 18 (1971) 436-440.

ISLAM - THAILAND

5085 BURR, ANGELA. Religious institutional diversity, social, structural, and conceptional unity: Islam and Buddhism in a southern Thai coastal fishing village. JSS 60 pt. 2 (1972) 183-215.

5086 SUHRKE, ASTRI. Thai Muslims, some aspects of minority integration. PA 43 (1970) 531-547.

5087 THOMAS, M. LADD. Bureaucratic attitudes and behavior as obstacles to political integration of Thai Muslims. SA 3 (1974-5) 545-566.

5088 THOMAS, M. LADD. Political socialization of the Thai-Islam. S90.7 pp. 89-105.

ISNEG

5089 DeRAEDT, JULES. Religious representations in northern Luzon. SLQ 2 (1964) 245-348.

5090 SMART, JOHN E. Manolay cult, the genesis and dissolution of millenarian sentiments among the Isneg of northern Luzon. AST 8 (1970) 53-93.

Itayat language *See* BATAN LANGUAGE

Ivatan language *See* BATAN LANGUAGE

JACKSON, PHILLIP

5091 PEARSON, H. F. Lt. Jackson's plan of Singapore. JMBRAS 42 pt. 1 (1969) 161-165.

5092 PEARSON, H. F. Singapore from the sea, June 1823, notes on a recently discovered sketch attributed to Lt. Phillip Jackson. JMBRAS 42 pt. 1 (1969) 133-144.

JALATUNDA

5093 BOSCH, F. D. K. Old Javanese bathing place, Jalatunda, by F. D. K. Bosch and B. de Haan. BIJ 121 (1965) 189-232.

JALE

5094 KOCH, KLAUS-FRIEDRICH. Semantics of kinship terms, the Jale case. BIJ 128 (1972) 81-98.

5095 KOCH, KLAUS-FRIEDRICH. Warfare and anthropophagy in Jale society. BIJ 126 (1970) 37-58.

Jama Mapun

JAMA MAPUN

5096 CASINO, ERIC S. Jama Mapun ethnoecology, economic and symbolic (of grains, winds and stars). AST 5 (1967) 1-32.

5097 CASINO, ERIC S. Lunsay, song dance of the Jama Mapun of Sulu. AST 4 (1966) 316-323.

JAMUH, GEORGE

5098 HARRISSON, TOM. George Jamuh, M. B. E., a personal tribute. SMJ 11 (1963) xix-xxi.

JAPANESE - PHILIPPINES

5099 GOODMAN, GRANT K. A flood of immigration, patterns and problems of Japanese migration to the Philippines during the first four decades of the twentieth century. PHR 1 pt. 1 (1965) 170-193.

5100 SANIEL, JOSEFA M. Japanese minority in the Philippines before Pearl Harbor, social organization in Davao. AST 4 (1966) 103-126.

JARAI

5101 DOURNES, JACQUES. Orphelin transforme, jalons mythologiques. AR 2 (1971) 168-196.

5102 VOTH, DONALD E. Translation from *Nghiem Tham* (Seeking to understand the highland people, the tribal kingdoms of the Vietnamese court in the past, the King of Fire and the King of Waters). SA 1 (1971) 335-363.

JASADIPURA I, RADEN NGABEHI

5103 SOEBARDI. Raden Ngabehi Jasadipura I, court poet of Surakarta, his life and works. IND 8 (1969) 81-102.

JASSIN, H. B.

5104 CHAMBERT-LOIR, HENRI. La documentation litteraire de H. B. Jassin. AR 7 (1974) 93-114.

JATAKA TALES **

5105 MARTINI, GINETTE. Les titres des Jataka dans les manuscrits Pali de la Bibliotheque Nationale de Paris. BEF 51 (1963) 79-93.

5106 NEEDHAM, RODNEY. Jataka, Pancatantra and Kodi fables. BIJ 116 (1960) 232-262.

JAVA

5107 ARNOLD, JOSEPH. Java journal of Dr. Joseph Arnold, edited with an introduction by John Bastin. JMBRAS 46 pt. 1 (1973) 1-92.

5108 BASTIN, JOHN. Further note on Dr. Joseph Arnold. JMBRAS 47 pt. 2 (1974) 149.

5109 BERG, C. C. Javanese picture of the past. S61 pp. 86-117.

5110 BOECHARI. Preliminary note on the study of the old Javanese civil administration. S87 pp. 356-360.

5111 COLLESS, BRIAN E. Walaing and the Sailendras of Java. JOSA 7 (1970) 15-22.

5112 CRUIKSHANK, ROBERT B. Abangan, Santri and Prijaji, a critique. JSAS 3 (1972) 39-43.

5113 DAMAIS, LOUIS-CHARLES. Etudes sino-indonesiennes. III. La transcription chinoise Ho Ling comme designation de Java. BEF 52 (1964) 93-141.

5114 EYMERET, JOEL. Les archives francaises au service des etudes indonesiennes, Java sous Daendels, 1808-1811. AR 4 (1972) 151-168.

5115 JAY, ROBERT R. History and personal experience, religious and political conflict in Java. R25 pp. 143-164.

5116 LOMBARD-SALMON, CLAUDINE. Un chinois a Java, 1729-1736. BEF 59 (1972) 279-318.

5117 NAERSSEN, F. H. VAN. Some aspects of the Hindu-Javanese kraton. JOSA 2 pt. 1 (1963) 14-19.

5118 Pages d'exotisme. V. Un roman d'amour a Java. AR 6 (1973) 87-90.

5119 Pages d'exotisme. VII. La Java des Polars. AR 8 (1974) 83-88.

5120 PIGEAUD, THEODORE. Erucakra-Vairocana. J41 pp. 270-273.

5121 SKINNER, C. Eyewitness account of the invasion of Java in 1811, the diary of Lt. W. G. A. Fielding. JMBRAS 44 pt. 1 (1971) 1-51.

5122 SLUIMERS, L. E. L. Enige theoretische beschouwingen over de Japanse bezettingsperiod op Java. B85 pp. 240-266.

5123 SOEBARDI. Prince Mangku Nagara IV, a ruler and a poet of 19th century Java. JOSA 8 (1971) 28-58.

5124 UTRECHT, ERNST. Class struggle and politics in Java. JCA 2 (1972) 274-282.

5125 VAN NIEL, ROBERT. Measurement of change under the cultivation system in Java, 1837-1851. IND 14 (1972) 89-109.

5126 WELDON, PETER D. Indonesian and Chinese status and language differences in urban Java. JSAS 5 (1974) 37-54.

5127 WERTHEIM, W. F. Social change in Java, 1900-1930, by W. F. Wertheim and The Siauw Gap. PA 35 (1962) 223-247.

JAVANESE

5128 ANDERSON, BENEDICT R. O'G. The idea of power in Javanese culture. H52 pp. 1-69.

5129 CHAILLEY-BERT, J. Pages d'exotisme. II. La societe javanaise selon J. Chailley-Bert, 1900. AR 2 (1971) 107-8.

5130 DAMAIS, LOUIS-CHARLES. Etudes javanaises. Le nom de la diete tantrique de 1214 Saka. BEF 50 (1960) 407-416.

5131 GEERTZ, CLIFFORD. Javanese village. S58 pp. 34-41.

5132 HAWKINS, EVERETT D. Batik industry, the role of the Javanese entrepreneur. H24 pp. 39-74.

5133 HOADLEY, MASON C. Continuity and change in Javanese legal tradition, the evidence of Jayapattra. IND 11 (1971) 95-109.

Javanese

5134 KAMPTO UTOMO. Villages of unplanned resettlers in the sub-
district Kaliredjo, central Lampung. K52 pp. 281-298.

5135 KOENTJARANINGRAT, R. M. Javanese
of south central of Java. M95
pp. 88-115.

5136 KOENTJARANINGRAT, R. M. Tjelapar,
a village in south central Java.
K52 pp. 244-280.

5137 KUMAR, ANN. Dipanagara, 1787?-
1855. IND 13 (1972) 69-118.

5138 LOCKARD, CRAIG A. Javanese as
emigrant, observations on the
development of Javanese settlements overseas. IND 11 (1971) 41-
62.

5139 MULDER, J. A. NIELS. Aliran
Kebatinan as an expression of the
Javanese worldview. JSAS 1 pt. 2
(1970) 105-114.

5140 MULDER, J. A. NIELS. Comparative
note on the Thai and the Javanese
worldview as expressed by religious practice and belief. JSS
58 pt. 2 (1970) 79-85.

5141 ROBSON, S. O. The wajang and the
study of Javanese cultural history. JOSA 3 pt. 2 (1965) 16-26.

5142 WENGEN, G. D. VAN. Tajoeb, een
Prestige-Feest bij de Javanen in
Suriname. BIJ 119 (1963) 106-121.

JAVANESE LANGUAGE

5143 BERG, C. C. Iets over de Javaanse
worden Tekwan en Tekon. BIJ 130
(1974) 313-323.

5144 BRAKEL, L. F. Note on the importance of the Ngoko-Krama distinc-

tion for the determination of
Javanese language structure. BIJ
125 (1969) 263-266.

5145 DE CASPARIS, J. G. L'importance
de la disyllabie en javanais. J41
pp. 63-76.

5146 RAS, J. J. Lange consonanten in
enige Indonesische talen. BIJ 126
(1970) 429-447.

5147 SOEPOMO POEDJOSOEDARMO. Javanese
speech levels. IND 6 (1968) 54-
81.

5148 SOEPOMO POEDJOSOEDARMO. Word list
of Javanese non-Ngoko vocabularies. IND 7 (1969) 165-190.

5149 UHLENBECK, E. M. Some preliminary
remarks on Javanese syntax. C44
pp. 53-70.

JAVANESE LITERATURE

5150 AICHELE, W. Fragmente, kleine
beitrage zur Interpretation alt-
javanischer Dichtung. BIJ 123
(1967) 217-249.

5151 BERG, C. C. Javanese picture of
the past. S61 pp. 86-117.

5152 BOSCH, F. D. K. De asvin-goden en
de epische tweelingen in de Oud-
javaanse kunst en literature. BIJ
123 (1967) 427-441.

5153 CAREY, P. B. R. Javanese histories of Dipanagara, the *Buku Kedhun
Kebo*, its authorship and historical importance. BIJ 130 (1974)
259-288.

5154 DREWES, G. W. J. Javanese poems
dealing with or attributed to the
saint of Bonan. BIJ 124 (1968)
209-240.

5155 DREWES, G. W. J. De ontdekking van Poerbatjaraka. BIJ 129 (1973) 482-492.

5156 DREWES, G. W. J. Struggle between Javanism and Islam as illustrated by the *Serat Dermagandul*. BIJ 122 (1966) 309-365.

5157 ENSINK, J. Sutasoma's teaching to Gajavaktra, the snake and the tigress. BIJ 130 (1974) 195-226.

5158 GHIL, RENE. L'odeur d'Ilang-ilang. AR 1 (1970) 103-4.

5159 GRAAF, H. J. DE. Later Javanese sources and historiography. S61 pp. 118-136.

5160 HOOYKAAS, JACOBA. Myth of the young cowherd and the little girl. BIJ 117 (1961) 267-278.

5161 JOHNS, ANTHONY H. On translating the *Nagarakrtagama*. C44 pp. 531-563.

5162 JOHNS, ANTHONY H. Role of structural organisation and myth in Javanese historiography. JAS 24 (1964-5) 91-99.
Comment: BERG, C. C. Commentary. JAS 24 (1964-5) 100-103.

5163 RICKLEFS, M. C. Consideration of three versions of the *Babad tanah Djawi*, with excerpts on the fall of Madjapahit. SOAS 35 (1972) 285-315.

5164 RICKLEFS, M. C. On the authorship of Leiden Cod. or. 2191, *Babad Mangkubumi*. BIJ 127 (1971) 264-273.

5165 ROBSON, S. O. Kawi classics in Bali. BIJ 128 (1972) 308-329.

5166 SARKAR, HIMANSU BHUSAN. South India in old Javanese and Sanskrit inscriptions. BIJ 125 (1969) 193-206.

5167 SOEBARDI. Santri religious elements as reflected in the *Book of Tjentini*. BIJ 127 (1971) 331-349.

5168 SOEPOMO POEDJOSOEDARMO. Establishment of Surakarta, a translation from the *Babad Gianti*, by Soepomo Poedjosoedarmo and M. C. Ricklefs. IND 4 (1967) 88-108.

5169 SOEWITO SANTOSO. Samaya of Bharadah and Kuturan. IND 17 (1974) 51-66.

5170 SUKARTO K. ATMODJO, M. M. Charter of Dayankayu. BIJ 128 (1972) 257-280.

5171 SUPOMO, S. Dating of the old Javanese Uttarakanda. JOSA 8 (1971) 59-67.

5172 SURANTO ATMOSAPUTRO. *Serat Wedatama*, a translation by Suranto Atmosaputro and Martin F. Hatch. IND 14 (1972) 157-181.

5173 VENKATASUBBIAH, A. Some Sanskrit stanzas in the Javanese *Tantri Kamandaka*. BIJ 121 (1965) 350-359.

JAYAVARMAN VII

5174 MUS, PAUL. Le sourire d'Angkor, art, foi et politique Bouddhiques sous Jayavarman VII. G83 pp. 363-381.

JEH

5175 GRADIN, DWIGHT. Rites of passage among the Jeh. SA 2 (1972-3) 53-61.

Jeh language

Josselin de Jong, Jan Petrus Benjamin de

JOAQUIN, NICK

5193 CRUZ, EDGARDO DELA. Things loved, things remembered, Joaquin's *Portrait* and William's *Menagerie*. PS 14 (1966) 242-252.

5194 GARCIA, REGINA T. Reading of Nick Joaquin's *The woman who had two navels*. PS 15 (1967) 288-306.

5195 HOSILLOS, LUCILA V. Cleaving vision, an approach to Nick Joaquin through dialects. PSSHR 30 (1965) 295-324.

5196 LACABA, EMMANUEL A. F. Winter after summer solstice, the later Joaquin. PS 16 (1968) 381-390.

5197 LLORCA, RAYMOND L. Nick Joaquin without tears, impressions on his fiction so far. SJ 16 (1969) 1-58.

5198 MELENDREZ, PATRICIA M. Archetype in Nick Joaquin's *The woman who had two navels*. SLQ 6 (1968) 171-192.

5199 OLOROSO, LAURA S. Nick Joaquin and his brightly burning prose works. M24 pp. 765-792.

5200 Two students on Nick Joaquin's art. GEJ 11 (1966) 45-64.

JOGJAKARTA

5201 KUMAR, ANN. Dipanagara, 1787?-1855. IND 13 (1972) 69-118.

JOHORE **

5202 ALLEN, J. DE V. Johore, 1901-1914, the railway concession, the Johore Advisory Board, Swettenham's resignation and the first general advisor. JMBRAS 45 pt. 2 (1972) 1-28.

5203 ANDAYA, LEONARD Y. Raja Kechil and the Minangkabau conquest of Johore in 1718. JMBRAS 45 pt. 2 (1972) 51-75.

5204 GUYOT, DOROTHY. Politics of land, comparative development in two states of Malaysia. PA 44 (1971) 368-389.

5205 KRATZ, U. Pro- und antibuginesische Texte zur Geschichte Johors im 18. Jahrhundert, ein Beitrag zur Quellenlage. BIJ 130 (1974) 289-296.

5206 SINCLAIR, KEITH. British advance in Johore, 1885-1914. JMBRAS 40 pt. 1 (1967) 93-110.

5207 SWAN, S. B. ST. C. Land surface mapping, Johor, west Malaysia. JTG 31 (1970) 91-103.

5208 THIO, EUNICE. British policy towards Johore, from advice to control. JMBRAS 40 pt. 1 (1967) 1-41.

Jorai *See* JARAI

JOSSELIN DE JONG, JAN PETRUS BENJAMIN DE

5209 BAAL, J. VAN. Jan Petrus Benjamin de Josselin de Jong, 13 Maart 1886-15 November 1964. BIJ 121 (1965) 293-302.

JOURNALISM - PHILIPPINES

5210 MASLOG, CRISPIN. Communication and journalism education in the Philippines. SJ 18 (1971) 357-374.

5211 MASLOG, CRISPIN. Journalism and communications program at Silliman University, an overview. SJ 14 (1967) 395-402.

JOURNALISM - SINGAPORE

5212 ROFF, WILLIAM R. Malayo-Muslim world of Singapore at the close of the nineteenth century. JAS 24 (1964-5) 75-90.

JUNGHUHN, FRANZ

5213 LEERSUM, P. VAN. History of cinchona, Junghuhn and cinchona cultivation. H57 pp. 190-196.

JUTE - BURMA

5214 LUBEIGT, G. L'introduction d'une nouvelle culture dans un etate socialiste, le cas du jute en Birmanie. SA 3 (1974) 842-879.

KACHIN

5215 MARAN LA RAW. Toward a basis for understanding the minorities in Burma, the Kachin example. K86 pp. 125-146.

5216 MORSE, ROBERT. Oral tradition and Rawang migration routes, by Robert and Betty Morse. E92 pp. 195-204.

KADAZANS

5217 ROFF, MARGARET. Rise and demise of Kadazan nationalism. JSAH 10 (1969) 326-343.

KAHAYANS

5218 DANANDJAJA, JAMES. Some Kahayan legends. SMJ 19 (1971) 265-276.

KAINGINS

5219 ORACION, TIMOTEO S. Kaingin agriculture among the Bukidnons of southeastern Negros, central Philippines. E78 pp. 233-249.

KAJANG

5220 MARTINOIR, BRIAN L. DE. Notes on the Kajang. SMJ 22 (1974) 265-273.

KALAH

5221 FATIMI, S. Q. In quest of Kalah. JSAH 1 (Sept. 1960) 65-109.

5222 LAMB, ALASTAIR. Visit to Siraf, an ancient port on the Persian Gulf. JMBRAS 37 pt. 1 (1964) 1-19.

KALAHANS

5223 RICE, DELBERT. Developing indigenous church music in the Kalahan society. SJ 16 (1969) 339-359.

5224 RICE, DELBERT. Punishment for crime, influence on personality. SJ 17 (1970) 170-194.

KALIMANTAN

5225   NICHOLL, ROBERT. Mission of
Father Antonino Ventimiglia to
Borneo. BMJ 2 pt. 4 (1972) 183-
205.

5226   People's army in north Kalimantan
gets stronger daily. JCA 3 (1973)
109-111.

KALINGA

5227   DeRAEDT, JULES. Religious representations in northern Luzon.
SLQ 2 (1964) 245-348.

5228   DeRAEDT, JULES. Some notes on
Buwaya society. SLQ 7 (1969) 7-
112.

5229   FURER-HAIMENDORF, CHRISTOPH VON.
Culture change and the conduct of
conflicts among Filipino tribesmen. MAS 4 (1970) 193-209.

5230   LAMBRECHT, FRANCISCO. Kalinga
and Ifugaw concepts of the universe. SJ 19 (1972) 195-208.

5231   LAWLESS, ROBERT. Hunting and
fishing among the southern Kalinga.
Kalinga. AST 11 pt. 3 (1973) 83-
109.

5232   MAGANNON, ESTEBAN T. Trends in
religious acculturation among the
Lubo Kalinga. SJ 19 (1972) 170-
191.

5233   SUGGUIYAO, MIGUEL. Kalinga primitive culture, by Miguel and
Rosario Sugguiyao. SLQ 1 (1963)
289-304.

5234   SUGGUIYAO, MIGUEL. Kalinga primitive culture, by Miguel and
Rosario Sugguiyao. SLQ 2 (1964)
181-200.

KALINGA LANGUAGE

5235   GIESER, RUTH. Natural clusters in
Kalinga disease terms, by Ruth
Gieser and Joseph E. Grimes. AST
10 (1972) 24-32.

KALINGA LITERATURE

5236   CORONEL, MARIA DELIA. Kalinga-
Bontoc stories. UN 39 (1966) 615-
629.

KAN-T'O-LI

5237   BOELES, J. J. Note on the toponymy of the ancient Kantoli in
peninsular Thailand. JSS 55
(1967) 291-297.

KANARAY-A LANGUAGE

5238   DIAZ, MOISES S. Analysis of the
Kinaray-A pronoun system, its
morpho-semantic components. UN 35
(1962) 524-528.

KANKANAY

5239   BELLO, MOISES C. Some notes on
house styles in a Kankanai village. AST 3 (1965) 41-54.

5240   BELLO, MOISES C. Some observations
on beliefs and rituals of the
Bakun-Kankanay. Z16 pp. 324-342.

5241   DeRAEDT, JULES. Religious representations in northern Luzon. SLQ
2 (1964) 245-348.

5242   ENCARNACION, VICENTE. Leadership
in a Benguet village. PS 9 (1961)
571-580.
Comment: LEANO, ISABEL. Comment
on leadership in a Benguet village.
PS 9 (1961) 580-583.

Kankanay language

KATU

5260 COSTELLO, NANCY A. Socially approved homicide among the Katu.
SA 2 (1972-3) 77-87.

KATU LANGUAGE

5261 COSTELLO, NANCY A. The Katu noun phrase. M59 pp. 21-35.

5262 WALLACE, JUDITH M. Katu personal pronouns. M58 pp. 55-86.

5263 WALLACE, JUDITH M. Katu pilgrimage. M59 pp. 64-73.

KAW

5264 CHOB KACHA ANANDA. Akha swinging ceremony. JSS 59 pt. 1 (1971) 119-128.

5265 HANKS, JANE R. Recitation of patrilineages among the Akha.
S58 pp. 114-127.

5265 KICKERT, ROBERT W. Akha village structure. S96 pp. 35-40.

KAW LANGUAGE

5266 DELLINGER, D. Some comments on Akha, its relationships and structure, and a proposal for a writing system. S96 pp. 108-112.

5267 WYSS, P. Thai orthography for Akha. S96 pp. 113-116.

KAYAH

5268 LEHMAN, F. K. Burma, Kayah society as a function of the Shan-Burma-Karen context. S84 pp. 1-104.

KAYAN

5269 HARRISSON, TOM. After life for Kayan infants in Kalimantan. SMJ 10 (1961) 214-5.

5270 METCALF, PETER. The Baram District: a survey of Kenyah, Kayan and Penan peoples. SMJ 22 (1974) 29-40.

5271 PRATTIS, IAN. Kayan-Kenyah Bungan cult in Sarawak. SMJ 11 (1963) 64-87.

5272 WHITTIER, HERBERT L. Apo Kayan area of east Kalimantan, by Herbert L. and Patricia R. Whittier.
SMJ 22 (1974) 5-15.

5273 WHITTIER, PATRICIA R. Some Apo Kayan megaliths, by Patricia R. and Herbert L. Whittier. SMJ 22 (1974) 369-381.

KAYAN LANGUAGE

5274 CLAYRE, B. Outline of Kayan grammar, by B. Clayre and L. Cubit.
SMJ 22 (1974) 43-91.

5274a CUBIT, L. E. Kayan phonemics.
BIJ 120 (1964) 409-423.

5275 ROUSSEAU, JEROME. Vocabulary of Baluy Kayan. SMJ 22 (1974) 93-152.

5276 URQUHART, I. A. N. Vocabulary comparisons, 1911-1961. SMJ 10 (1961) 120-124.

KAYAN LITERATURE

5277 RUBENSTEIN, CAROL. Poems of indigenous peoples of Sarawak: some of the songs and chants. SMJ 21 (1973) 723-1389.

Kayon

KAYON

5278　KERMARREC, R. P. JEAN. Les enfants tigres. SEIB 47 (1972) 163-
194.

KECHIL, RAJA

5279　ANDAYA, LEONARD Y. Raja Kechil
and the Minangkabau conquest of
Johore in 1718. JMBRAS 45 pt. 2
(1972) 51-75.

KEDAH

5280　ALLEN, J. DE VERE. Elephant and
mousedeer, a new version: Anglo-
Kedah relations, 1905-1915.
JMBRAS 41 pt. 1 (1968) 54-94.

5281　CAREY, ISKANDAR. Kensiu negritos
of Baling, Kedah. JMBRAS 43 pt. 1
(1970) 143-154.

5282　JOSEPH, K. T. Sedentary soils of
Kedah and their suggested utilization. JTG 18 (1964) 101-110.

5283　PEACOCK, B. A. V. Pillar base
architecture in ancient Kedah.
JMBRAS 47 pt. 1 (1974) 66-86.

5284　SHAROM AHMAT. Kedah-Siam relations, 1821-1905. JSS 59 pt. 1
(1971) 97-117.

5285　SHAROM AHMAT. Political structure
of the state of Kedah, 1879-1905.
JSAS 1 pt. 2 (1970) 115-128.

5286　SHAROM AHMAT. Structure of the
economy of Kedah, 1879-1905.
JMBRAS 43 pt. 2 (1970) 1-24.

5287　SKINNER, C. Kedah letter of 1839.
B38 pp. 156-165.

5288　ZAHARAH MAHMUD. Population of
Kedah in the nineteenth century.
JSAS 3 (1972) 193-209.

KEDAYAN

5289　HARRISSON, TOM. Kedayan rafts.
BMJ 2 pt. 1 (1970) 52-60.

5290　HARRISSON, TOM. Survival of
Kedayan rafts. BMJ 2 pt. 4 (1972)
168-172.

5291　MAXWELL, ALLEN R. On the various
spellings of the word Kadayan.
BMJ 2 pt. 1 (1970) 87-103.

5292　SATHER, CLIFFORD A. Kampong Selanyau, social and economic organization of a Kedayan rice growing
village in Sarawak, by Clifford A.
Sather and Hatta Solhee. SMJ 22
(1974) 249-266.

5293　SHARIFFUDDIN, P. M. Kedayans.
BMJ 1 (1969) 15-23.

5294　SHARIFFUDDIN, P. M. Makan tahun,
the annual feast of the Kedayans.
BMJ 2 pt. 1 (1970) 61-66.

KEDAYAN LANGUAGE

5295　MAXWELL, A. R. Kedayan ethno-
ornithology, a preliminary report.
BMJ 1 (1969) 197-217.

KEJAMANS

5296　THOMAS, SHARON. Burial customs of
the Kejamans. SMJ 19 (1971) 313-
316.

KELABIT

5297 HARRISSON, TOM. Ceramic crayfish
and related vessels in central
Borneo, the Philippines and Sweden. SMJ 15 (1967) 1-9.

5298 HARRISSON, TOM. Miniature burial
pot from Niah Great Cave. SMJ 15
(1967) 91-2.

KELABIT LANGUAGE

5299 HARRISSON, TOM. Douglas' 1911
vocabulary in practise. SMJ 10
(1961) 125-6.

5300 URQUHART, I. A. N. Vocabulary
comparisons, 1911-1961. SMJ 10
(1961) 120-124.

KELABIT LITERATURE

5301 LABANG, LIAN. Married megaliths
in upland Kalimantan. SMJ 11
(1962) 383-385.

5302 RUBENSTEIN, CAROL. Poems of indigenous peoples of Sarawak: some
of the songs and chants. SMJ 21
(1973) 723-1389.

KELANTAN **

5303 al-AHMADI, ABDUL RAHMAN. Notes
towards a history of Malay periodicals in Kelantan. K33 pp. 170-
189.

5304 ALLEN, J. DE V. Kelantan rising
of 1915, some thoughts on the concept of resistance in British
Malayan history. JSAH 9 (1968)
241-257.

5305 Bibliography of Kelantan. K33 pp.
319-350.

5306 CHAN SU MING. Kelantan and Trengganu, 1909-1939. JMBRAS 38 pt. 1
(1965) 159-198.

5307 CLIFFORD, HUGH. Report on the
expedition recently led into
Trengganu and Kelantan on the east
coast of the Malay peninsula.
JMBRAS 34 pt. 1 (1961) 1-162.

5308 DOWNS, R. E. A rural community in
Kelantan Malaya, a brief account
of its socio-economic organization
and regional setting. S90.1 pp.
51-62.

5309 DOWNS, RICHARD. A Kelantanese
village of Malaya. S84 pp. 105-
186.

5310 FIRTH, RAYMOND. Faith and scepti-
cism in Kelantan village magic.
K33 pp. 190-224.

5311 FIRTH, RAYMOND. Relations between
personal kin (waris) among Kelantan Malays. S58 pp. 23-61.

5312 IBRAHIM NIK MAHMOOD. To' Janggut
rebellion of 1915. K33 pp. 62-86.

5313 KERSHAW, ROGER. The Chinese in
Kelantan, west Malaysia, as medi-
ators of political integration to
the Kelantan Thais. RSAS 3 pts.
3-4 (1973) 1-10.

5314 KESSLER, CLIVE S. Muslim identity
and political behaviour in Kelantan. K33 pp. 272-313.

5315 KHOO KAY KIM. Introduction.
JMBRAS 34 pt. 1 (1961) xi-xviii.

5316 MOHAMED B. NIK MOHD. SALLEH. Kelantan in transition, 1891-1910.
K33 pp. 22-61.

5317 MOHAMMAD TAIB USMAN. Note on Abdullah's account of the Kelantan

Kelantan

civil war in his *Kesah Pelayaran Abdullah*. BIJ 120 (1964) 342-349.

5318 NASH, MANNING. Ethnicity, centrality and education in Pasir Mas. K33 pp. 243-258.

5319 RAYBECK, DOUGLAS A. Social stress and social structure in Kelantan village life. K33 pp. 225-242.

5320 ROBERT, LESLIE RATNASINGAM. Duff syndicate in Kelantan, 1900-1902. JMBRAS 45 pt. 1 (1972) 81-110.

5321 ROFF, WILLIAM R. Islam as an agent of modernization, an episode in Kelantan history. M52 pp. 170-174.

5322 ROFF, WILLIAM R. Origin and early years of the Majlis Ugama. K33 pp. 101-152.

5323 SHEPPARD, MUBIN. Manora in Kelantan. JMBRAS 46 pt. 1 (1973) 160-170.

5324 SHEPPARD, MUBIN. Traditional Malay house forms in Trengganu and Kelantan. JMBRAS 42 pt. 2 (1969) 1-9.

5325 SKINNER, C. Dating of the civil war in Kelantan referred to in the *Kesah Pelayaran Abdullah*. BIJ 121 (1965) 433-437.

5326 SWEENEY, AMIN. Shadow play of Kelantan, report on a period of field research. JMBRAS 43 pt. 2 (1970) 53-80.

5327 WINZELER, ROBERT L. Social organization of Islam in Kelantan. K33 pp. 259-271.

5328 WYATT, DAVID K. Nineteenth century Kelantan, a Thai view. K33 pp. 1-21.

KELABIT LITERATURE

5329 RUBENSTEIN, CAROL. Poems of indigenous peoples of Sarawak: some of the songs and chants. SMJ 21 (1973) 723-1389.

KEMPEN, C. P. BREST VAN

5330 WATUSEKE, F. S. C. P. Brest van Kempen, resident van Manado? BIJ 129 (1973) 350-1.
Comment: Naschrift. BIJ 129 (1973) 351-2.

KENNEDY, RAYMOND

5331 HOEBEL, E. ADAMSON. Contribution of Professor Raymond Kennedy to Indonesian ethnology. H57 pp. 472-3.

KENYAH

5332 BAARTMANS, FRANCIS. Marriage among the Lepo Tau Kenyah, Long Moh, Baram, Sarawak. BMJ 2 pt. 3 (1971) 17-30.

5333 CONLEY, WILLIAM W. Kenyah cultural themes and their interrelationships. SMJ 22 (1974) 303-309.

5334 CONLEY, WILLIAM W. Kenyah receptivity and response to Christianity. SMJ 22 (1974) 311-324.

5335 GALVIN, A. D. Faith healing rites among the Kenyahs. BMJ 3 pt. 2 (1974) 13-15.

5336 GALVIN, A. D. Headhunting, fact or fiction? BMJ 3 pt. 2 (1974) 16-104.

5337 GALVIN, A. D. Kenyah farming year. SMJ 19 (1971) 185-235.

5338   GALVIN, A. D. Kenyah omen birds
       and beasts. SMJ 20 (1972) 53-62.

5339   GALVIN, A. D. Long Kiput Kenyahs.
       BMJ 3 pt. 2 (1974) 9-12.

5340   GALVIN, A. D. Mamat ceremonies,
       Long Moh, Upper Baram, Sarawak,
       commemorative ceremony for the
       dead. BMJ 2 pt. 1 (1970) 17-29.

5341   GALVIN, A. D. Naming ceremonies
       among the Baram Kenyahs. BMJ 3
       pt. 1 (1973) 34-40.

5342   GALVIN, A. D. A Sebob dirge, sung
       on the occasion of the death of
       Tama Jangan Jau by Belawing Lupa.
       BMJ 2 pt. 4 (1972) 1-158.

5343   HARRISSON, TOM. Sarawak Kenyah
       journey through death. SMJ 10
       (1961) 191-213.

5344   MAPING MADANG. Adat Suen, Sebob
       graded rites, by Maping Madang and
       A. D. Galvin. SMJ 13 (1966) 305-
       320.

5345   METCALF, PETER. The Baram Dis-
       trict: a survey of Kenyah, Kayan
       and Penan peoples. SMJ 22 (1974)
       29-40.

5346   PRATTIS, IAN. Kayan-Kenyah Bungan
       cult in Sarawak. SMJ 11 (1963)
       64-87.

5347   WHITTIER, HERBERT L. Apo Kayan
       area of east Kalimantan, by Her-
       bert L. and Patricia R. Whittier.
       SMJ 22 (1974) 5-15.

KENYAH LANGUAGE

5348   GALVIN, A. D. Kenyah figures of
       speech. SMJ 14 (1966) 183-4.

5349   URQUHART, I. A. N. Vocabulary
       comparisons, 1911-1961. SMJ 10
       (1961) 120-124.

KENYAH LITERATURE

5350   BELAWING TINGANG. Story of the
       Long Kiput Kenyah. SMJ 22 (1974)
       349-352.

5351   GALVIN, A. D. Five sorts of Sara-
       wak and Kalimantan Kenyah song.
       SMJ 11 (1962) 501-510.

5352   GALVIN, A. D. How Balan Nyaring
       ventured to Alo Malau, a Kenyah
       epic story. SMJ 18 (1970) 220-
       263.

5353   GALVIN, A. D. Kenyah astronaut.
       BMJ 2 pt. 1 (1970) 30-38.

5354   GALVIN, A. D. Kenyah omen birds
       and beasts. SMJ 20 (1972) 53-62.

5355   GALVIN, A. D. Marriage of Senan
       and Aping. BMJ 2 pt. 3 (1971) 11-
       16.

5356   GALVIN, A. D. A Sebob dirge, sung
       on the occasion of the death of
       Tama Jangan Jau by Belawing Lupa.
       BMJ 2 pt. 4 (1972) 1-158.

5357   GALVIN, A. D. Some Baram Kenyah
       songs. SMJ 14 (1966) 6-14.

5358   GALVIN, A. D. Suket, a Kenyah
       song from Long Je'eh, Baram. BMJ
       3 pt. 1 (1973) 41-50.

5359   HADDON, A. C. Tortoise and the
       mouse deer, Kenyah. SMJ 11 (1962)
       535-6.

5360   RUBENSTEIN, CAROL. Poems of indig-
       enous peoples of Sarawak: some
       of the songs and chants. SMJ 21
       (1973) 723-1389.

Kenyah literature

5361 TAMA INO BALAN. Prayers for the erection of a new house among the Lepo Tau Kenyah. SMJ 22 (1974) 353-368.

KERINTJI LITERATURE

5362 VOORHOEVE, P. Kerintji documents. BIJ 126 (1970) 369-399.

KEUNING, J.

5363 LOCHER, G. W. In memoriam, J. Keuning, 12 Juli 1911-13 Augustus 1965. BIJ 123 (1967) 1-9.

KHMER

5364 CHATTERJI, B. R. Current tradition among the Kambojs of north India relating to the Khmers of Cambodia. G83 pp. 253-4.

5365 COEDES, GEORGE. L'avenir des etudes khmeres. SEIB 40 (1965) 207-213.

5366 MABBETT, I. W. Devaraja. JSAH 10 (1969) 202-223.

KHMER LANGUAGE

5367 JACOB, JUDITH M. Linguistics in Cambodia and on Cambodian. S21 pp. 899-919.

5368 JACOB, JUDITH M. Notes on the numerals and numeral coefficients in old, middle and modern Khmer. C44 pp. 143-162.

5369 JACOB, JUDITH M. Prefixation and infixation in old Mon, old Khmer, and modern Khmer. L55 pp. 62-70.

5370 JACOB, JUDITH M. Some features of Khmer versification. B41 pp. 227-241.

5371 JACOB, JUDITH M. Structure of the word in old Khmer. SOAS 23 (1960) 351-368.

5372 JACQUES, CLAUDE. Etudes d'epigraphie cambodgienne. IV. Deux inscriptions du Phnom Bakhen, K. 464 et K. 558. V. La stele du Prasat Cha Chuk, K. 1034. BEF 57 (1970) 57-89.

5373 JACQUES, CLAUDE. Etudes d'epigraphie cambodgienne. VI. Sur les donnees chronologiques de la stele de Tuol Ta Pec, K. 834. BEF 58 (1971) 163-176.

5374 JACQUES, CLAUDE. Etudes d'epigraphie cambodgienne. VII. Sur l'emplacement du royaume d'Aninditapura. VIII. La carriere de Jayavarman. BEF 59 (1972) 193-222.

5375 JACQUES, CLAUDE. Supplement au tome VIII des inscriptions du Cambodge. BEF 58 (1971) 177-195.

5376 LEWITZ, SAVEROS. L'inscription de Phimeanakas, K. 484, etude linguistique. BEF 58 (1971) 91-103.

5377 LEWITZ, SAVEROS. Inscriptions modernes d'Angkor, 1, 8 et 9. BEF 59 (1972) 101-121.

5378 LEWITZ, SAVEROS. Inscriptions modernes d'Angkor, 2 et 3, textes en Kmer moyen. BEF 57 (1970) 99-126.

5379 LEWITZ, SAVEROS. Inscriptions modernes d'Angkor, 4, 5, 6, et 7. BEF 58 (1971) 105-123.

5380 LEWITZ, SAVEROS. Inscriptions modernes d'Angkor, 10, 11, 12, 13,

14, 15, 16a, 16b, et 16c. BEF 59
(1972) 221-249.

5381 LEWITZ, SAVEROS. Inscriptions
modernes d'Angkor, 17, 18, 19, 20,
21, 22, 23, 24, et 25. BEF 60
(1973) 163-203.

5382 LEWITZ, SAVEROS. Inscriptions
modernes d'Angkor, 26, 27, 28, 29,
30, 31, 32, 33. BEF 60 (1973)
205-242.

5383 LEWITZ, SAVEROS. Note sur la
translitteration du cambodgien.
BEF 55 (1969) 163-169.

5384 LEWITZ, SAVEROS. La toponymie
khmere. BEF 53 (1966) 375-450.

5385 NOSS, RICHARD B. Paired adjec-
tives in Cambodian. JSS 58 pt. 1
(1970) 115-120.

5386 NOSS, RICHARD B. Treatment of
*/R/ in two modern Khmer dialects.
Z52 pp. 89-95.

5387 POU, SAVEROS. Inscriptions
modernes d'Angkor, 35, 36, 37 et
39 (1). BEF 61 (1974) 301-337.

5388 URAISI VARASARIN. Une tentative
d'interpretation du mot "Pangat"
en vieux-khmer. JSS 61 pt. 2
(1973) 139-142.

5389 VICKERY, MICHAEL. Khmer inscriptions of Tennasserim, a reinterpretation. JSS 61 pt. 1 (1973)
51-70.

KHMER LITERATURE

5390 AU CHHIENG. Sanscrit "Jour de
Yama" et vieux khmer "Dixieme jour
lunaire." G83 pp. 201-206.

5391 PIAT, MARTINE. Chroniques royales
khmer. SEIB 49 (1974) 35-140.

5392 SVAY MUOY. Histoire de Keo Preah
Phleung, d'apres des *Annales des
rois khmers*. SEIB 47 (1972) 375-
394.

KHMU

5393 LeBAR, FRANK M. Observations on
the movement of Khmu into north
Thailand. JSS 55 (1967) 61-79.

5394 SMALLEY, WILLIAM A. Cian, Khmu
culture hero. F38 pp. 41-54.

KHMU LANGUAGE

5395 SMALLEY, WILLIAM A. Bibliography
of Khmu. M61 pp. 23-32.

KHON PA

5396 BOELES, J. J. Second expedition
to the Mrabri (Khon Pa) of north
Thailand. JSS 51 (1963) 133-160.

5397 FLATZ, GEBHARD. Mrabri, anthropo-
metric, genetic and medical exami-
nations. JSS 51 (1963) 161-177.

5398 KRAISRI NIMMANAHAEMINDA. Expedition to the Khon Pa (or Phi Tong
Luang?), by Kraisri Nimmanahaeminda and Julian Hartland-Swann. JSS
50 (1962) 165-186.

5399 VELDER, CHRISTIAN. Description of
the Mrabri camp. JSS 51 (1963)
185-188.

KHWAN

5400 ANUMAN RAJADHON. Khwan and its
ceremonies. JSS 50 (1962) 119-164.

Kim Van Kieu

KIM VAN KIEU

5401   CHESNEAUX, JEAN. Les revolution-
naires vietnamiens face au Kim Van
Kieu. C28 pp. 356-384.

KINIRAYA LITERATURE

5402   JOCANO, F. LANDA. Epic of Labaw
Donggon. PSSHR 29 (1964) 1-103.

5403   NUNES, EVELYN H. Some epic laws
of the Donggon, a study in structure. PS 20 (1972) 563-576.

KODI

5404   NEEDHAM, RODNEY. Age, category
and descent, to Professor Raymond
Firth. BIJ 122 (1966) 1-35.

KODI LITERATURE

5405   NEEDHAM, RODNEY. Jataka, Pancatantra and Kodi fables. BIJ 116
(1960) 232-262.

KONBAUNG DYNASTY

5406   YI YI. Burmese sources for the
history of the Konbaung period,
1752-1885. JSAH 6 (Mar. 1965) 48-
66.

5407   YI YI. Life at the Burmese court
under the Konbaung kings. JBRS
44 (1961) 85-129.

KONFRONTASI

5408   BUNNELL, FREDERICK P. Guided
democracy foreign policy, 1960-
1965, President Sukarno moves from
non-alignment to confrontation.
IND 2 (1966) 37-76.

5409   DERKACH, NADIA. Soviet policy towards Indonesia in the West Irian
and the Malaysian disputes. AS 5
(1965) 566-571.

5410   GORDON, BERNARD K. Potential for
Indonesian expansion. PA 36
(1963) 378-393.

5411   GROSSHOLTZ, JEAN. Rise and demise
of Konfrontasi, impact on politics
in Malaysia. AST 6 (1968) 325-339.

5412   HINDLEY, DONALD. Indonesia's confrontation with Malaysia, a search
for motives. AS 4 (1964) 904-913.

5413   KAHIN, GEORGE McT. Malaysia and
Indonesia. PA 37 (1964) 253-270.

5414   MEADOWS, MARTIN. Theories of ex-
ternal-internal political relationships, a case study of Indonesia and the Philippines. AST 6
(1968) 297-324.

5415   RICHTER, H. V. Indonesia's share
in the entrepot trade of the
states of Malaya and Singapore
prior to confrontation. MER 11
pt. 2 (1966) 28-45.

5416   SUTTER, JOHN O. Two faces of Konfrontasi: crush Malaysia and the
gestapu. AS 6 (1966) 523-546.

5417   VAN DER KROEF, JUSTUS M. Indonesia, Malaya and the North Borneo
crisis. AS 3 (1963) 173-181.

KORN, VICTOR EMANUEL

5418   PRINS. In memoriam, Victor
Emanuel Korn. BIJ 126 (1970) 193-
202.

KOXINGA **

5419 McCARTHY, CHARLES J. On the
      Koxinga threat of 1662. PS 18
      (1970) 187-196.

KROM, N. J.

5420 BERG, C. C. Work of Professor
      Krom. H18 pp. 164-171.

KUALA LUMPUR

5421 JACKSON, JAMES C. Kuala Lumpur in
      the 1880's, the contribution of
      Bloomfield Douglas. JSAH 4 (Sept.
      1963) 117-127.

5422 McGEE, T. G. Cultural role of
      cities, a case study of Kuala
      Lumpur. JTG 17 (1963) 178-196.

5423 McTAGGART, W. D. Kampong Pandan,
      a study of a Malay kampong in
      Kuala Lumpur, by W. D. McTaggart
      and R. McEachern. D92 pp. 125-
      138.

5424 SHAM SANI. Observations on the
      effect of a city's form and func-
      tions on temperature patterns, a
      case of Kuala Lumpur. JTG 36
      (1973) 60-65.

KUI LANGUAGE

5425 JOHNSTON, RICHARD. Kuy basic word
      list. M59 pp. 1-4.

KULAP, K. S. R.

5426 REYNOLDS, CRAIG J. Case of K. S.
      R. Kulap, a challenge to royal
      historical writing in late nine-
      teenth century Thailand. JSS 61
      pt. 2 (1973) 63-90.

KUNDUNGGA, KING

5427 MINATTUR, JOSEPH. Note on the
      King Kundungga of the east Borneo
      inscriptions. JSAH 5 (Sept. 1964)
      181-183.

KUNLUN

5428 KACHORN SUKHABANIJ. Two Thai mss
      on the K'unlun kingdom. S93 pp.
      70-74.

KUOMINTANG - MALAYSIA

5429 PNG POH SENG. Kuomintang in Ma-
      laya. J45 pp. 214-225.

5430 PNG POH SENG. Kuomintang in Ma-
      laya, 1912-1941. JSAH 2 (Mar.
      1961) 1-41.

KYOTO UNIV. CENTER FOR SOUTHEAST ASIAN
STUDIES

5431 Center of South East Asian Studies
      Kyoto University. EACS 3 (1964)
      54-57.

5432 IWAMURA, SHINOBU. Research at the
      Center for Southeast Asian Studies
      Kyoto University. AS 8 (1968)
      819.

5433 Program for Southeast Asian
      Studies at Kyoto University. FA
      19 (1963) 941-947.

LABOR AND LABORING CLASSES *See also*
PEASANTRY

5434 HAUSER, PHILIP M. Measurement of
      labour utilization. MER 19 pt. 1
      (1974) 1-15.

Labor and laboring classes

5435 OSHIMA, HARRY T. Labor absorption in East and Southeast Asia, a summary with interpretation of postwar experience. MER 16 pt. 2 (1971) 55-77.

5436 SUNDRUM, R. M. Manpower and educational development in East and Southeast Asia, a summary of conference proceedings. MER 16 pt. 2 (1971) 78-90.

5437 YEH, STEPHEN. Labour force supply in Southeast Asia, by Stephen Yeh and You Poh Seng. MER 16 pt. 2 (1971) 25-54.

LABOR AND LABORING CLASSES - INDONESIA

5438 BLAKE, DONALD J. Labour shortage and unemployment in northeast Sumatra. MER 7 pt. 2 (1962) 106-118.

5439 GUTHRIE, HAROLD W. Development of a skilled labor force in Indonesia. H24 pp. 98-140.

5440 HAWKINS, E. D. Labor in developing countries: Indonesia. G52 pp. 196-250.

LABOR AND LABORING CLASSES - MALAYSIA

5441 ALATAS, SYED HUSSEIN. Grading of occupational prestige amongst the Malays in Malaysia. JMBRAS 41 pt. 1 (1968) 146-156.

5442 JONES, G. W. Female participation in the labour force in a plural economy, the Malayan example. MER 10 pt. 2 (1965) 61-82.

5443 PARMER, J. NORMAN. Chinese estate workers' strikes in Malaya in March 1937. C87 pp. 154-173.

5444 SAW SWEE HOCK. Future trends in the population and labour force of west Malaysia. RSAS 3 pts. 1-2 (1973) 27-44.

5445 SAW SWEE HOCK. Labour force of Sarawak in 1960, by Saw Swee Hock and Cheng Siok Hwa. AST 8 (1970) 135-142.

5446 SAW SWEE HOCK. Postwar labour force of Sabah. RSAS 1 pt. 2 (1971) 42-47.

5447 SIEW NIM CHEE. Labour and tin mining in Malaya. S48 pp. 404-439.

LABOR AND LABORING CLASSES - PHILIPPINES

5448 CARROLL, JOHN J. Philippine labor unions. PS 9 (1961) 220-254.

5449 CATER, SONYA DIANE. Philippine Federation of Free Farmers, a case study in mass agrarian organizations. E78 pp. 449-473.

5450 CUMMINS, JAMES S. Labor in the colonial Philippines, the *Discurso Parenetico* of Gomez de Espinosa, by James S. Cummins and Nicholas P. Cushner. PS 22 (1974) 117-203.

5451 MENDOZA, EDMUND E. Employment problems in Philippine economy. SLURJ 4 (1973) 305-329.

5452 MOLINA, ANTONIO M. Word on forced labor in the Philippines. UN 34 (Dec. 1961) 6-12.

5453 The 1961 labor manifesto. DR 9 (1961) 545-554.

5454 OPPENFELD, HORST. Labor force and utilization, by Horst and Judith Oppenfeld. E78 pp. 44-53.

5455 ROTH, DENNIS. Casas de Reservas
in the Philippines. JSAS 5 (1974)
115-124.

5456 TIDALGO, ROSA LINDA. Output,
capital, labor and population,
projections from the supply side.
C47 pp. 85-88.
Comment: Discussion. C47 pp.
89-103.

5457 Trend of the labor force. C47
pp. 497-502.

LABOR AND LABORING CLASSES - SINGAPORE

5458 BLAKE, D. J. Statistical note,
deflator for earnings of workmen,
1953-1965. MER 12 pt. 2 (1967)
127-132.

5459 CHEW, DAVID C. E. Investment in
human capital. Y52 pp. 292-306.

5460 CHEW, DAVID C. E. Population and
manpower, by David C. E. Chew and
Amina H. Degani. M49 pp. 85-108.

5461 CLARK, DAVID H. Labour market
and industrial relations. Y52 pp.
307-327.

5462 CLARK, DAVID H. Manpower in
larger manufacturing firms in
Singapore. MER 16 pt. 1 (1971)
33-45.

5463 KLEINSORGE, PAUL L. Labor arbi-
tration systems: Australia, the
United States, and Singapore.
MER 8 pt. 2 (1963) 69-80.

5464 PANG ENG FONG. Note on labour
underutilization in Singapore.
MER 18 pt. 1 (1973) 15-23.

5465 PARMER, N. Attempts at labor
organization by Chinese workers in
certain industries in Singapore in
the 1930's. J45 pp. 239-255.

5466 WONG, AMY. On the variation of
wages, proprietory income and output in selected small-scale manufacturing industries in Singapore.
MER 19 pt. 1 (1974) 65-83.

LABOR AND LABORING CLASSES - VIETNAM

5467 HENDRY, JAMES B. Some social and
economic characteristics of the
work force in Saigon. C58 pp.
191-218.

LABRADOR, JUAN

5468 Rev. Fr. Juan Labrador, 1894-1967.
UN 40 (1967) 548-550.

LABUAN

5469 TARLING, NICHOLAS. The entrepot
at Labuan and the Chinese. S89
pp. 355-373.

LAC

5470 LEGAY, ROGER. Prierer Lac accom-
pagnant les rites agraires, par
Roger Legay et K'Mloi Da Got.
SEIB 46 (1971) 111-213.

LAHU

5471 WALKER, ANTHONY R. Blessing
feasts and ancestor propitiation
among the Lahu Nyi (Red Lahu).
JSS 60 pt. 1 (1972) 345-373.

5472 WALKER, ANTHONY R. Divisions of
the Lahu people. JSS 62 pt. 2
(1974) 253-268.

Lahu

5473 WALKER, ANTHONY R. La Hu Nyi (Red La Hu) new year celebrations. JSS 58 pt. 1 (1970) 1-44.

5474 WALKER, ANTHONY R. Messianic movements among the Lahu of the Yunnan-Indochina borderlands. SA 3 (1974) 698-711.

5475 WALKER, ANTHONY R. Red Lahu village society, an introductory survey. S96 pp. 41-52.

LAHU LANGUAGE

5476 BURLING, ROBBINS. A problem in the phonology of Lahu. E92 pp. 97-101.

LAHU LITERATURE

5477 SPIELMANN, HANS J. Note on the literature of the Lahu Shehleh and Lahu Na of northern Thailand. JSS 57 (1969) 321-332.

5478 WALKER, ANTHONY R. Lahu Nyi (Red Lahu) new year texts, 1. JSS 62 pt. 1 (1974) 1-26.

LAN ONG

5479 NGUYEN TRAN HUAN. La personnalite et l'ethique de Lan Ong. SEIB 48 (1973) 503-511.

LAND

5480 PELZER, KARL J. Man's role in changing the landscape of Southeast Asia. JAS 27 (1967-8) 269-279.

5481 PRAKASH, VED. Land policies for urban development. U77 pp. 205-224.

5482 TROLL, C. Landscape ecology and land development, with special reference to the tropics. JTG 17 (1963) 1-11.

LAND - BURMA

5483 HUKE, ROBERT E. Mayan-Lajung, changing land use and capital investment. JBRS 45 (1962) 193-203.

5484 STAMP, L. DUDLEY. Basic land resources of Burma. B91 pp. 435-439.

LAND - INDONESIA

5485 SHAMSUL BAHRIN, TUNKU. Policies on land settlement in insular Southeast Asia, a comparative study. MAS 5 (1971) 21-34.

LAND - MALAYSIA

5486 ALEXANDER, J. B. Evolution of land suitability maps in the Federation of Malaya. JTG 18 (1964) 1-6.

5487 DEGANI, AMINA H. Land development authority, an economic necessity? MER 9 pt. 2 (1964) 75-82. *Comment:* HILL, R. D. Comments on the land development authority, an economic necessity? MER 10 pt. 1 (1965) 116-121.

5488 GUYOT, DOROTHY. Politics of land, comparative development in two states of Malaysia. PA 44 (1971) 368-389.

5489 HILL, R. D. Agricultural land tenure in west Malaysia. MER 12 pt. 1 (1967) 99-116.

5490 HO, ROBERT. Land settlement projects in Malaya, an assessment of the role of the Federal Land Development Authority. JTG 20 (1965) 1-15.

5491 KUCHIBA, MAUO. Cooperation patterns in a Malay village, by Mauo Kuchiba and Yoshihiro Tsubouchi. AS 8 (1968) 836-841.

5492 LEE, Y. L. Land use in Sarawak. SMJ 16 (1968) 282-308.

5493 LEE, Y. L. Some factors in the development and planning of land use in British Borneo. JTG 15 (1961) 66-81.

5494 LEONARD, PATRICK L. Farm planning and land development schemes. MER 14 pt. 1 (1969) 80-96.

5495 Peasant's appeal, an appeal to all friends in the city from the peasants of Telok Gong. JCA 3 (1973) 120-1.

5496 SHAMSUL BAHRIN, TUNKU. Policies on land settlement in insular Southeast Asia, a comparative study. MAS 5 (1971) 21-34.

5497 SHAMSUL BAHRIN, TUNKU. Preliminary study of the fringe alienation schemes in west Malaysia. JTG 28 (1969) 75-83.

5498 SINGH, S. Evaluation of three land development schemes in Malaysia. MER 13 pt. 1 (1968) 89-100.

5499 TREGONNING, K. G. Early land administration and agricultural development of Penang. JMBRAS 39 pt. 2 (1966) 34-49.

5500 UNGKU AZIZ. Subdivision of estates in Malaya, 1951-1960, author's reply. MER 11 pt. 2 (1966) 46-62.

LAND - PHILIPPINES

5501 KAUT, CHARLES. Process and social structure in a Philippine lowland settlement. S90.1 pp. 35-50.

5502 KRINKS, PETER. Old wine in a new bottle, land settlement and agrarian problems in the Philippines. JSAS 5 (1974) 1-17.

5503 MUIJZENBERG, OTTO D. VAN DEN. Involutie of evolutie in centraal Luzon? B85 pp. 151-174.

5504 RESURRECCION, ABELARDO S. A study of a conflict of interest in the use of land in the Ambuklao-Binga watershed, a land economic approach. SLURJ 2 (1971) 630-680.

5505 SHAMSUL BAHRIN, TUNKU. Land conflicts in the Tanay resettlement project, Rizal, Philippines. JTG 27 (1968) 50-58.

5506 SHAMSUL BAHRIN, TUNKU. Policies on land settlement in insular Southeast Asia, a comparative study. MAS 5 (1971) 21-34.

LAND - THAILAND

5507 NG, RONALD C. Y. Some land-use problems of north-east Thailand. MAS 4 (1970) 23-42.

LAND - VIETNAM

5508 ADAMS, JOHN. Land and economy in traditional Vietnam, by John Adams and Nancy Hancock. JSAS 1 pt. 2 (1970) 90-98.

5509 HENDERSON, WILLIAM. Opening of new lands and villages, the Republic of Vietnam land development program. C58 pp. 123-137.

Land – Vietnam

5510 SALKIN, JAY S. Land size and patterns of resource productivity in south Vietnamese rice production. SA 1 (1971) 116-127.

Land Dayaks *See* DYAK

LAND TENURE

5511 RUTTAN, VERNON W. Equity and productivity issues in modern agrarian reform legislation. PS 14 (1966) 52-64.

LAND TENURE – BURMA

5512 CHENG SIOK HWA. Land tenure problems in Burma, 1852 to 1940. JMBRAS 38 pt. 1 (1965) 106-134.

LAND TENURE – CAMBODIA

5513 RICKLEFS, M. C. Land and the law in the epigraphy of tenth century Cambodia. JAS 26 (1966-7) 411-420.

LAND TENURE – INDONESIA

5514 BASTIN, JOHN. Working of the early land rent system in west Java. BIJ 116 (1960) 301-312.

5515 GLASSBURNER, BRUCE. Swing of the hoe: retooling begins in the Indonesian economy, by Bruce Glassburner and Kenneth D. Thomas. AS 1 (June 1961) 3-12.

5516 MACKIE, J. A. C. Indonesia's government estates and their masters. PA 34 (1961) 337-360.

5517 SOEMARDJAN, SELO. Land reform in Indonesia. AS 1 (Feb. 1962) 23-30.

5518 UTRECHT, ERNST. Land reform and Bimas in Indonesia. JCA 3 (1973) 149-164.

5519 VAN DER KROEF, JUSTUS M. Peasant and land reform in Indonesian communism. JSAH 4 (Mar. 1963) 30-61.

LAND TENURE – MALAYSIA

5520 HO, ROBERT. Evolution of agriculture and land ownership in Saiong Mukim. MER 13 pt. 2 (1968) 81-102.

5521 HO, ROBERT. Land ownership and economic prospects of Malayan peasants. MAS 4 (1970) 83-92.

LAND TENURE – PHILIPPINES

5522 ANDERSON, JAMES N. Land and society in a Pangasinan community. E78 pp. 171-192.

5523 BAUZON, LESLIE E. Encomienda system as a Spanish colonial institution in the Philippines, 1571-1604. SJ 14 (1967) 197-241.

5524 DeRAEDT, JULES. Development and land reform. SLURJ 2 (1971) 19-28.

5525 KERKVLIET, BENEDICT J. Land reform in the Philippines since the Marcos coup. PA 47 (1974) 286-304.

5526 KRINKS, PETER. Old wine in a new bottle, land settlement and agrarian problems in the Philippines. JSAS 5 (1974) 1-17.

5527 McCOY, ALFRED W. U.S. foreign policy and the tenant farmers of Asia. FA 24 (1970) 41-77.

5528 McLENNAN, MARSHALL S. Land and tenancy in the central Luzon plain. PS 17 (1969) 651-682.

5529 Philippine land reform, trick or treat? JCA 4 (1974) 390-397.

5530 SALAMANCA, BONIFACIO S. Background and early beginnings of the encomienda in the Philippines. PSSHR 26 (1961) 67-86.

5531 SALITA, DOMINGO C. Land ownership, tenancy and reform. UN 40 (1967) 527-541.

5532 STARNER, FRANCES L. Landed interests and the enactment of Land Reform Bill of 1955. A28 pp. 230-234.

LAND TENURE - THAILAND

5533 DIXON, H. DEMAINE. Land tenure patterns and agricultural development in N. E. Thailand, a case study of the Lam Pao irrigation area in Changwat Kalasin, by H. Demaine and C. J. Dixon. JSS 60 pt. 2 (1972) 45-60.

5534 STERNSTEIN, LARRY. Aspects of agricultural land tenure in Thailand. JTG 24 (1967) 22-29.

5535 WIJEYEWARDENE, G. Some aspects of rural life in Thailand. S49 pp. 65-83.

5536 YANO, TORU. Land tenure in Thailand. AS 8 (1968) 853-863.

LAND TENURE - VIETNAM

5537 BREDO, WILLIAM. Agrarian reform in Vietnam, Vietcong and government of Vietnam strategies in conflict. AS 10 (1970) 738-750.

5538 BROCHEUX, PIERRE. Les grands Dien Chu de la Cochinchine occidentale pendant la periode coloniale. C28 pp. 147-163.

5539 GITTINGER, J. PRICE. Agrarian reform. L52 pp. 200-208.
Comment: Commentary, a Vietnamese official on Gittinger. L52 pp. 212-3.
Comment: LINDHOLM, R. W. Commentary. L52 pp. 211-2.
Comment: WURFEL, DAVID. Commentary. L52 pp. 209-211.

5540 GITTINGER, J. PRICE. Note on the economic impact of totalitarian land tenure change, the Vietnamese experience. MER 5 pt. 2 (1960) 81-84.

5541 LADEJINSKY, WOLF. Agrarian reform in the Republic of Vietnam. C58 pp. 153-175.

5542 McCOY, ALFRED W. U.S. foreign policy and the tenant farmers of Asia. FA 24 (1970) 41-77.

5543 MITCHELL, EDWARD J. Significance of land tenure in the Vietnamese insurgency. AS 7 (1967) 577-580.

5544 PROSTERMAN, ROY L. Land to the tiller in south Vietnam, the tables turn. AS 10 (1970) 751-764.

5545 SALTER, MacDONALD. The broadening base of land reform in south Vietnam. AS 10 (1970) 724-737.

LANGUAGE PROBLEMS - MALAYSIA

5546 DOOLEY, F. JAMES. Language problem in Malaya. UN 35 (1962) 198-207.

LANGUAGE PROBLEMS – PHILIPPINES

5547 ASUNCION–LANDE, NOBLEZA. Multi-
lingualism, politics and Filipinism. AS 11 (1971) 677–692.

5548 PANGANIBAN, JOSE V. Language
nationalism, and internationalism.
UN 34 (Dec. 1961) 57–63.

5549 PANIZO, ALFREDO. Linguistic problems, corruption vs. purity. UN
34 (Sept. 1961) 30–38.

5550 RAMOS, MAXIMO. Can English last
much longer here? UN 40 (1967)
671–680.

5551 SAMONTE, AURORA L. Language problem in the Philippines. UN 40
(1967) 555–562.

LANGUAGE STUDY AND TEACHING – PHILIP-
PINES

5552 BARCELONA, HERMINIA M. Language
laboratory and foreign language
learning. UN 40 (1967) 579–598.

5553 BOWEN, J. DONALD. Freshman English in college. UN 40 (1967)
622–630.

5554 HIDALGO, CESAR A. Linguistics:
its development and its contribution to English teaching. GEJ 17
(1969) 3–24.

5555 JAMIAS, CRISTINO. Response. DR
12 (1964) 120–131.

5556 JOCANO, F. LANDA. Language learning as part of fieldwork technique, some problems in communication. AST 8 (1970) 203–217.

5557 PASCUAL, INEZ VILLA-REAL. Problems of a language teacher. UN
40 (1967) 709–715.

5558 PATERNO, ADELAIDA. Testing pronunciation of English as a foreign
language, twenty questions. UN 40
(1967) 681–695.

5559 RUSTIA, ERLINDA F. The teacher
of composition asks, traditional
grammar or structural linguistics?
UN 40 (1967) 696–700.

LANGUAGES *See also* AUSTRONESIAN LAN-
GUAGES, MON-KHMER LANGUAGES

5560 ABDUL RAHMAN, TUNKU. Opening address by the Prime Minister of Malaysia. A43 pp. 1–5.

5561 ALISJAHBANA, S. TAKDIR. Modernization of languages in Asia in
historical and socio-cultural perspective. A43 pp. 6–23.

5562 ALISJAHBANA, S. TAKDIR. New national languages, a problem modern
linguistics has failed to solve.
C44 pp. 515–530.

5563 ASMAH HAJI OMAR. Comparative linguistics in Southeast Asia, its
scope and method of approach. BMJ
2 pt. 4 (1972) 165–167.

5564 BARKER, MILTON E. Linguistics.
AP 4 (1960) 133–135.

5565 BARKER, MILTON E. Linguistics.
AP 5 (1961) 107–8.

5566 BARKER, MILTON E. Linguistics.
AP 6 (1962) 65–73.

5567 BARKER, MILTON E. Linguistics.
AP 7 (1963) 86–100.

5568 BARKER, MILTON E. Linguistics.
AP 8 (1964) 115–125.

5569 COLLINS, VAUGHN. Position of Atjehnese among Southeast Asian
languages. M59 pp. 48–59.

5570 DYEN, ISIDORE. Position of the Malayopolynesian languages of Formosa. AP 7 (1963) 261-271.

5571 FISCHER, J. L. Style contrasts in Pacific languages. S22 pp. 1129-1162.

5572 GONDA, J. Influence of Indian languages. S22 pp. 955-968.

5573 GREENBERG, JOSEPH H. Indo-Pacific hypothesis. S22 pp. 807-871.

5574 HAUDRICOURT, ANDRE G. Limits and connections of Austroasiatic in the northeast. Z52 pp. 44-56.

5575 HEIDT, KARL M. Modernization or westernization. A43 pp. 24-39.

5576 HENDERSON, EUGENIE J. A. Topography of certain phonetic and morphological characteristics of South East Asian languages. C44 pp. 400-434.

5577 HOLMER, NILS M. Morphological structure of the Austroasiatic languages. L55 pp. 17-23.

5578 Institute for the study of the languages and cultures of Asia and Africa, Tokyo. EACS 5 (1966) 44-49.

5579 KRUPA, VIKTOR. Conference on linguistic problems of the Indo-Pacific area, London 5-8 January 1965. AAS 2 (1966) 139-141.

5580 LAYCOCK, D. C. Intrusive languages, English and other Germanic languages. S22 pp. 877-902.

5581 NEMENZO, CATALINA A. Southeast Asian languages and literature in English, an annotated bibliography. PSSHR 34 (1969) 1-984.

5582 O'GRADY, GEOFFREY N. Checklist of Oceanic language and dialect names, by Geoffrey N. O'Grady and Charles A. Zisa. S22 pp. 1189-1278.

5583 THOMAS, DAVID D. Checking vowel contrasts by rhyming. M58 pp. 99-102.

5584 WITTERMANS, ELIZABETH P. Concept of situation in sociolinguistic analysis. A43 pp. 40-46.

5585 WURM, S. A. Pidgins, creoles and lingue franche. S22 pp. 999-1021.

Languages – Brunei *See* KEDAYAN LANGUAGE, MALAY LANGUAGE

LANGUAGES – BURMA *See also the following languages:* ARAKANESE, BURMESE, CHIN, DANAW, JINGHPAW, KAREN, LEPCHA, MON, PALAUNG, PRAOK, RAWANG, RIANGLAN, RONG, SHAN, TAVOYAN

5586 Dictionaries of the national races of the Union of Burma. JBRS 50 (1967) 125-6.

5587 LUCE, G. H. Burma languages. JBRS 51 (1968) 29-34.

LANGUAGES – CAMBODIA *See also* KHMER LANGUAGE

5588 DYEN, ISIDORE. Chamic languages. S22 pp. 200-210.

LANGUAGES – INDONESIA *See also the following languages:* ASMAT, ACHENESE, BALINESE, BUNA, INDONESIAN, JAVANESE, KAPAUKU, LEPU TAU, MALAY, OIRATA, PANTAR, ROTINESE, SENTANI, SUNDANESE, TIMORESE

Languages - Indonesia

5589 KAHLER, HANS. Dialect and language, investigated with some examples from Indonesian languages. C44 pp. 497-514.

5590 Mededelingen uit de verslagen van Dr. S. J. Esser, Taalambtenaar voor Celebes, 1928-1944. BIJ 119 (1963) 329-370.

5591 MILKE, WILHELM. Comparative notes on the Austronesian languages of New Guinea. C43 pp. 330-348.

5592 RAS, J. J. Lange consonanten in enige Indonesische talen, dubbel geschreven mediale Consonanten. BIJ 124 (1968) 521-541.

5593 UHLENBECK, E. M. Indonesia and Malaysia. S21 pp. 847-898.

5594 UHLENBECK, E. M. Indonesia and Malaysia. S22 pp. 55-111.

5595 UHLENBECK, E. M. Languages of Indonesia, past, present and future. SA 1 (1971) 208-221.

5596 WELDON, PETER D. Indonesian and Chinese status and language differences in urban Java. JSAS 5 (1974) 37-54.

5597 WURM, S. A. Language policy, language engineering and literacy, New Guinea and Australia. S22 pp. 1025-1038.

LANGUAGES - LAOS *See also the following languages:* LAO, NGEQ, NYAHEUN, TA-OI, THAI

5598 MORECHAND, GUY. The many languages and cultures of Laos. L18 pp. 28-34.

LANGUAGES - MALAYSIA *See also the following languages:* DUSUN, DYAK, IBAN, KAYAN, KELABIT, KENYAH, LEPU TAU, LUN BAWANG, MALAY, MANDAILING, MELANAU, MURIK, MURUT, NGAJU, PUNAN, SABAN, SELAKO, SULUK

5599 ASMAH HAJI OMAR. Malaysian mosaic of languages. A41 pp. 188-202.

5600 CLAYRE, B. M. Focus, a preliminary survey of some languages of eastern Malaysia. SMJ 18 (1970) 193-219.

5601 HANCOCK, IAN F. Some Dutch derived items in Papia Kristang. BIJ 126 (1970) 352-356.

5602 HUDSON, A. B. Note on Selako, Malayic Dayak and Land Dayak languages in western Borneo. SMJ 18 (1970) 301-318.

LANGUAGES - PHILIPPINES *See also the following languages:* AKLAN, BALANGAO, BATAN, BILAAN, BINUKID, BISAYAN, DIBABAWON, GADDANG, IGOROT, ILOKO, ISINAI, KALINGA, KANARAY-A, KANKANAY, KAPAMPANGAN, MAHARADIA, MAMANWA, MANOBO, PILIPINO, SANGIRESE, SPANISH, TAGALOG, TAGBANUA, TAOSUG **

5603 BERGER, KENNETH W. Linguistic study in the Philippines, a brief bibliographic history. SJ 18 (1971) 164-179.

5604 BOWEN, J. DONALD. Hispanic languages and influence in Oceania. S22 pp. 938-952.

5605 CONSTANTINO, ERNESTO. Personal pronouns of Tagalog, Ilukano, Isinai and Kapampangan. Z16 pp. 567-596.

5606 CONSTANTINO, ERNESTO. Sentence patterns of the ten major Philippine languages. AST 2 (1964) 29-36.

5607 CONSTANTINO, ERNESTO. Sentence patterns of twenty-six Philippine languages. C44 pp. 71-124.

5608 CONSTANTINO, ERNESTO. Some problems in Philippine linguistics. AST 1 (1963) 23-30.

5609 CONSTANTINO, ERNESTO. Tagalog and other major languages of the Philippines. S22 pp. 112-154.

5610 FOX, ROBERT B. Preliminary glotto chronology for northern Luzon, by Robert B. Fox, Willis E. Sibley and Fred Eggan. AST 3 (1965) 103-113.

5611 FRANCISCO, JUAN R. Indian influences in the Philippines, with special reference to language and literature. PSSHR 28 (1963) 1-310.

5612 FRANCISCO, JUAN R. Maharadia Lawana. AST 7 (1969) 186-249.

5613 HEMPHILL, RODERICK J. Philippine language scene. B13 pp. 157-166.

5614 HIDALGO, ARACELI C. Two mental processes, focusing and emphasizing, and their linguistic manifestations. DR 17 (1969) 252-264.

5615 LOPEZ, CECILIO. Contributions to a comparative Philippine syntax. C44 pp. 3-16.

5616 LOPEZ, CECILIO. Origins of the Philippine languages. PS 15 (1967) 130-166.

5617 LOPEZ, CECILIO. Response. AST 1 (1963) 6-9.

5618 McKAUGHAN, HOWARD. Minor languages of the Philippines. S22 pp. 155-167.

5619 McLACHLIN, BETTY. Verbal clauses of Sarangani Bilaan, by Betty McLachlin and Barbara Blackburn. AST 6 (1968) 108-128.

5620 MARYOTT, KENNETH R. Phonology and morphophonemics of Tabukang Sangir. PSSHR 26 (1961) 111-126.

5621 MERCADO, LEONARDO N. Filipino thought. PS 20 (1972) 207-272.

5622 MERCADO, LEONARDO N. Reflections on Buut-Loob-Nakem. PS 20 (1972) 577-601.

5623 MOHRING, HANS. Concerning the word Suluk. SMJ 15 (1967) 243-4.

5624 PANGANIBAN, JOSE VILLA. Studies in word relationships among Philippine languages, Malay and Bahasa Indonesia. UN 36 (1963) 131-143.

5625 PASCASIO, EMY M. Language situation in the Philippines from the Spanish era to the present. M24 pp. 225-252.

5626 RUCH, ED. Substantive marking particles in Kalamian Tagbanwa. PSSHR 26 (1961) 213-218.

5627 VERSTRAELEN, EUGENE. Analysis of language. SLQ 1 (1963) 335-382.

5628 VERSTRAELEN, EUGENE. Analysis of language. SLQ 2 (1964) 51-76.

5629 WATERMAN, G. HENRY. Translation of theological terms into major Philippine dialects. B13 pp. 33-42.

Languages - Philippines

5630 WILLIAMS, J. DAVID. Speech and
language in the Philippines. DR
18 (1970) 248-258.

LANGUAGES - THAILAND *See also the following languages:* KHMU, LAHU, MIAO,
MON, MRABRI, MUONG, SEAK, THAI, YAO

5631 GEDNEY, WILLIAM J. Thailand and
Laos. S21 pp. 782-814.

5632 ROOP, DeLAGNEL H. Problem of
linguistic diversity in Thailand,
an approach to a solution. S96
pp. 100-107.

LANGUAGES - VIETNAM *See also the fol-
lowing languages:* BAHNAR, BRU, CHAM,
CHRAU, HALANG, HRE, JEH, KATU, LOLO,
MNONG, MUONG, NGEQ, NYAHEUN, PACOH,
SEDANG, THAI, TODRAH, VIETNAMESE, YAO

5633 DYEN, ISIDORE. Chamic languages.
S22 pp. 200-210.

5634 HAUDRICOURT, ANDRE G. Note sur
les dialects de la region de Moncay. BEF 50 (1960) 161-177.

5635 THOMAS, DAVID. Mon-Khmer in north
Vietnam. M59 pp. 74-5.

5636 THOMAS, DAVID D. Mon-Khmer sub-
groupings in Vietnam. Z52 pp.
194-202.

LANSDOWNE, LORD

5637 CHANDRAN, JESHURAN. Lord Lansdowne and the anti-German clique
at the Foreign Office, their role
in the making of the Anglo-Siamese
agreement of 1902. JSAS 3 (1972)
229-246.

LAO

5638 CONDOMINAS, GEORGES. The Lao.
L18 pp. 9-27.

5639 HALPERN, JOEL M. Observations on
the social structure of the Lao
elite. AS 1 (July 1961) 25-32.

5640 KEYES, CHARLES F. Kin groups in a
Thai-Lao community. C24 pp. 274-
297.

LAO DONG *See also* POLITICAL PARTIES -
VIETNAM

5641 HONEY, P. J. North Vietnam's
Workers' Party and south Vietnam's
Peoples Revolutionary Party. PA
35 (1962) 375-383.

5642 NORMAND, MARJORIE WEINER. Party
system in north Vietnam. JSAH 8
(1967) 68-82.

LAO LANGUAGE

5643 GEDNEY, WILLIAM J. Thailand and
Laos. S21 pp. 782-814.

LAO LITERATURE

5644 ARCHAIMBAULT, CHARLES. Le cycle
de Nang Oua-Nang Malong, et son
substrat sociologique. FA 17
(1960) 2581-2604.

LA'ONG

5645 SANDIN, BENEDICT. Punan La'ong,
two notes. SMJ 12 (1965) 185-187.

LAOS

5646 L'annee 1966 en Asie, Laos. FA 22 (1968) 101-104.

5647 BROWN, MacALISTER. Laos 1973, wary steps towards peace, by MacAlister Brown and Joseph J. Zasloff. AS 14 (1974) 166-174.

5648 DODD, THOMAS J. Laos and the Southeast Asian crisis, a congressional speech by Senator Thomas J. Dodd, May 21, 1962. L18 pp. 398-400.

5649 HALPERN, JOEL M. Laos, future prospects and their limitations. AS 6 (1966) 59-65.

5650 HAWKINS, RICHARD S. D. Contours, cultures, and conflict. L18 pp. 3-8.

5651 Laos, one year of brilliant achievement in all fields. JCA 3 (1973) 105-107.

5652 ROUCEK, JOSEPH S. Laos in contemporary world politics, an American view. RSA (1965) 85-100.

5653 UNGER, LEONARD. Laos. F56 pp. 119-130.

5654 ZASLOFF, JOSEPH J. Laos 1972, the war, politics and peace negotiations. AS 13 (1973) 60-75.

5655 ZASLOFF, JOSEPH J. Laos, the forgotten war widens. AS 10 (1970) 65-72.

LAOS - ARMY

5656 TRAN VAN DINH. Birth of the Pathet Lao Army. L18 pp. 424-438.

LAOS - DESCRIPTION AND TRAVEL

5657 DECORNOY, JACQUES. Life in the Pathet Lao liberated zone. L18 pp. 411-423.

5658 Nationalist awakening, by a young Lao official. T45 pp. 277-286.

LAOS - ECONOMIC CONDITIONS

5659 JOEL, CLARK. Foreign exchange operations fund for Laos, an interesting experiment in monetary stabilization. AS 6 (1966) 134-149.

5660 TABLENTE, NATHANIEL B. Economic and technical feasibility study of cooperatives and credit in Laos. AST 5 (1967) 524-542.

LAOS - FOREIGN RELATIONS

5661 SIMMONDS, E. H. S. Evolution of foreign policy in Laos since independence. MAS 2 (1968) 1-30.

LAOS - FOREIGN RELATIONS - FRANCE

5662 McCOY, ALFRED W. French colonialism in Laos, 1893-1945. L18 pp. 67-99.

5663 La visite a Paris du roi du Laos. FA 20 (1965) 514-516.

LAOS - FOREIGN RELATIONS - THAILAND

5664 WILSON, DAVID A. Bangkok's dim view to the east. AS 1 (June 1961) 13-17.

5665 WYATT, DAVID K. Siam and Laos, 1767-1827. JSAH 4 (Sept. 1963) 13-32.

Laos – Politics and government

5687 MURDOCH, JOHN B. The 1901–1902 holy man's rebellion. JSS 62 pt. 1 (1974) 47–66.

5688 WHITMORE, JOHN K. Thai-Vietnamese struggle for Laos in the nineteenth century. L18 pp. 52–66.

LAOS – LAWS, STATUTES, ETC.

5689 CONDOMINAS, GEORGES. Notes sur le droit foncier Lao en milieu rural dans la plaine de Vientiane. G83 pp. 255–262.

5690 WESTERMEYER, JOSEPH J. Traditional and constitutional law, a study of change in Laos. AS 11 (1971) 562–569.

LAOS – MINORITIES *See also* KHMU, MEO, MNONG, THAI, YAO

5691 HALPERN, JOEL. Laos, introduction, by Joel Halpern and Peter Kunstadter. K86 pp. 233–258.

5692 OSBORN, G. M. T. Government and the hill tribes of Laos. K86 pp. 259–270.

5693 TURTON, ANDREW. National minority peoples in Indo-China. JCA 4 (1974) 336–343.

5694 WARD, JAMES THOMAS. U.S. aid to hill tribe refugees in Laos. K86 pp. 295–303.

LAOS – POLITICS AND GOVERNMENT

5695 Agreement on restoring peace and achieving national accord in Laos. JCA 3 (1973) 249–253.

5696 CZYZAK, JOHN J. International conference on Laos and the Geneva agreement of 1962, by John J. Czyzak and Carl F. Salans. JSAH 7 (Sept. 1966) 27–47.

5697 DEVILLERS, PHILIPPE. The Laotian conflict in perspective. L18 pp. 37–51.

5698 DOLEZAL, IVAN. Two attempts at the neutralization of Laos, 1954–1962. AAS 2 (1966) 68–102.

5699 DOMMEN, ARTHUR J. Lao politics under Prince Souvanna Phouma. J28 pp. 81–97.

5700 DOMMEN, ARTHUR J. Laos, the troubled neutral. AS 7 (1967) 74–80.

5701 DOMMEN, ARTHUR J. Laos, the year of the Ho Chi Minh trail. AS 12 (1972) 138–147.

5702 DOMMEN, ARTHUR J. Toward negotiations in Laos. AS 11 (1971) 41–50.

5703 FALL, BERNARD. Problems politiques des etats poly-ethniques en Indochine. FA 18 (1962) 129–152.

5704 GIRLING, J. L. S. Laos, falling domino? PA 43 (1970) 370–383.

5705 HILL, KENNETH L. Laos, the Vientiane agreement. JSAH 8 (Sept. 1967) 257–267.

5706 HOANG NGUYEN. Vientiane agreement. JCA 3 (1973) 482–486.

5707 KOMMADAM, SIMON. Breaking the backbone of the Nixon doctrine in Laos. JCA 2 (1972) 208–212.

5708 LANGER, PAUL F. Laos, preparing for a settlement in Vietnam. AS 9 (1969) 69–74.

Laos - Politics and Government

5709 LANGER, PAUL F. Laos, search for peace in the midst of war. AS 8 (1968) 80-86.

5710 LEE, CHAE JIN. Communist China and the Geneva conference on Laos, a reappraisal. AS 9 (1969) 522-539.

5711 PORTER, D. GARETH. After Geneva, subverting Laotian neutrality. L18 pp. 179-212.

5712 SIMMONDS, STUART. Independence and political rivalry in Laos, 1945-61. R64 pp. 164-199.

5713 SIMMONDS, STUART. Laos, a renewal of crisis. AS 4 (1964) 680-685.

5714 SINGH, L. P. Laos and Vietnam since Dien Bien Phu. RSA (1965) 145-158.

5715 SITHON KOMMADAM. Great victories, heavy but glorious tasks. JCA 4 (1974) 262-267.

5716 SMITH, ROGER M. Laos. K17 pp. 525-592.

5717 SMITH, ROGER M. Laos in perspective. AS 3 (1963) 61-68.

5718 SOUVANNA PHOUMA. Le Laos, avant garde du monde libre. FA 17 (1960) 1427-1434.

5719 SOUVANNA PHOUMA. Laos le fond du probleme. FA 17 (1960) 1824-1826.

5720 THEE, MAREK. Background notes on the 1954 Geneva agreements on Laos and the Vientiane agreements of 1956-1957. L18 pp. 121-138.

5721 ZASLOFF, JOSEPH J. Leadership and organization of the Pathet Lao. J28 pp. 113-123.

LAOS - RELIGION *See also* BUDDHISM - LAOS

5722 ARCHAIMBAULT, C. Religious structures in Laos. JSS 52 (1964) 57-74.

5723 SMALLEY, WILLIAM A. Cian, Khmu culture hero. F38 pp. 41-54.

LAOS - SOCIAL CONDITIONS

5724 CHAPELIER, GEORGES. Plain of Jars, social changes under five years of Pathet-Lao administration, by Georges Chapelier and Josyane van Malderghem. AQ (1971) 61-89.

5725 COWARD, E. WALTER. Differentiation of synaptic leadership in rural Laos. JAS 30 (1970-1) 135.

5726 HALPERN, JOEL M. Observations on the social structure of the Lao elite. AS 1 (July 1961) 25-32.

5727 SANG SEUNSOM. Quelques indications elementaires et generales sur les differenciations sociales peu accentuees existant parmi les populations du Laos rural et sur les modifications moderees et peu frequentes intervenant dans cette gradation sociale faiblement differenciee caracterisant les habitants des communautes villageoises Lao. EACS 4 (1965) 133-137.

LATAH

5728 GEERTZ, HILDRED. Latah in Java, a theoretical paradox. IND 5 (1968) 93-104.

LAUREL, JOSE PACIANO

5729 AGPALO, REMIGIO E. Pro Deo et
patria, the political philosophy
of Jose P. Laurel. AST 3 (1965)
163-192.

5730 ESPINO, FEDERICO LICSI. Wounds of
war, in memoriam, Jose P. Laurel,
Sr. DR 17 (1969) 351-357.

5731 GOROSPE, VITALIANO R. Laurel's
political and moral philosophy.
PS 11 (1963) 419-428.

5732 HILA, ANTONIO C. Laurelian education and the task of nation building. DR 17 (1969) 377-382.

5733 STEINBERG, DAVID. Jose P. Laurel:
a collaborator misunderstood. JAS
24 (1964-5) 651-665.

LAUREL-LANGLEY AGREEMENT

5734 FLORES, PEDRO V. Economic expectations and results under the
Laurel-Langley agreement, 1956-
1965. SJ 14 (1967) 55-66.

LAWA

5735 FLATZ, GEBHARD. Khalo or Mae Rim
Lawa, a remnant of the Lawa population of northern Thailand. JSS
58 pt. 2 (1970) 87-104.

5736 KAUFFMANN, H. E. Some social and
religious institutions of the
Lawa, N.W. Thailand. JSS 60 pt. 1
(1972) 237-306.

5737 KAUFFMANN, H. E. Stone memorials
of the Lawa, northwest Thailand.
JSS 59 pt. 1 (1971) 129-151.

5738 KRAISRI NIMMANAHAEMINDA. Inscribed silver plate grant to the
Lawa of Boh Luang. F38 pp. 233-
238.

5739 OBAYASHI, TARYO. Lawa and Sgau
Karen in northwestern Thailand.
JSS 52 (1964) 199-216.

5740 SANIDH RANGSIT, M. C. Additional
note on the silver plate grant
from Boh Luang. F38 pp. 239-240.

LAYA, JUAN C.

5741 SAN JUAN, E. Juan C. Laya's *His
native soil*, and the limits of
bourgeois/liberal individualism.
DR 18 (1970) 187-231.

LE THANH-TONG

5742 WHITMORE, JOHN K. Vietnamese historical sources for the reign of
Le Thanh-tong, 1460-1497. JAS 29
(1969-70) 373-394.

LEBAK

5743 WERTHEIM, W. F. De perkaras van
100 jaar geleden. BIJ 119 (1963)
412-414.
Comment: NIEUWENHUYS, R. Tot de
Hoofd-Zaak van Lebak, een antwoord
aan Prof. Wertheim. BIJ 118 (1962)
271-276.

LEGAZPI, MIGUEL LOPEZ DE

5744 CUSHNER, NICHOLAS P. Legazpi,
1564-1572. PS 13 (1965) 163-206.

5745 RODRIGUEZ, ISACIO R. Bibliography
on Legazpi and Urdaneta and their
joint expedition. PS 13 (1965)
287-329.

Le May, Reginald

LE MAY, REGINALD

5746 Reginald Le May. JSS 60 pt. 2
(1972) 395-6.

LEPCHA LANGUAGE

5747 FORREST, R. A. D. Linguistic
position of Rong (Lepcha). JBRS
45 (1962) 41-47.

LEPPO TAU

5748 GALVIN, A. D. Leppo Tau genealogies. SMJ 12 (1965) 173-175.

5749 GALVIN, A. D. Mamat chants and
ceremonies, Long Moh, upper Baram.
SMJ 16 (1968) 235-248.

5750 GALVIN, A. D. Mamat, Leppo Tau,
Long Moh. SMJ 13 (1966) 296-304.

5751 HARRISSON, TOM. Kalimantan writing board and the Mamat festival.
SMJ 13 (1966) 287-295.

5752 PABIT ENJOK. Three Leppo Tau
punishment stories. SMJ 12 (1965)
176-178.

LEPPO TAU LANGUAGE

5753 LEES, SHIRLEY P. Introduction to
the sound system of Lepu Tau. SMJ
12 (1965) 179-184.

LET-WE-THON-DARA

5754 KHIN ZAW. New translation of
Letwethondara's famous Ratu. B92
pp. 149-156.

LEYTE

5755 LEAR, ELMER N. Western Leyte
guerrilla warfare forces, a case
study in the non-legitimation of a
guerrilla organization. JSAH 9
(1968) 69-94.

LIBRARIES - INDONESIA

5756 SOEMADIKARTA, LILY K. Development
of library services in Indonesia.
J37 pp. 222-232.

LIBRARIES - PHILIPPINES

5757 DIMAYA, P. D. Circulation, resources, financial support and
librarian qualifications of Philippine public libraries. SJ 7
(1960) 298-312.

5758 GARCIA, RAMON M. Abolition of the
circulating division, by Ramon M.
Garcia and Francisco Nemenzo. G93
pp. 137-150.

LIBRARIES - VIETNAM

5759 VO LONG TE. Chronique culturelle,
la Bibliotheque Nationale de la
Republique du Vietnam. SEIB 47
(1972) 505-511.

LIBRARY RESOURCES *See also* ARCHIVES, HISTORIOGRAPHY AND HISTORICAL SOURCES, MANUSCRIPTS

LIBRARY RESOURCES - BURMA

5760 Catalogue of books in the library
of the Burma Research Society,
corrected up to 31st December 1964.
JBRS 47 (1964) 445-556.

LIBRARY RESOURCES – FRANCE

5761 MARTINI, GINETTE. Les titres des Jataka dan les manuscrits Pali de la Bibliotheque Nationale de Paris. BEF 51 (1963) 79-93.

LIBRARY RESOURCES – GERMANY

5762 MEILINK-ROELOFSZ, M. A. P. Private papers of Artus Gijsels as source for the history of East Asia. JSAH 10 (1969) 540-550.

LIBRARY RESOURCES – INDONESIA

5763 BONNEFF, MARCEL. Les bandes dessinees en Indonesie, diffusion et public. AR 4 (1972) 169-178.

5764 CHAMBERT-LOIR, HENRI. La documentation litteraire de H. B. Jassin. AR 7 (1974) 93-114.

LIBRARY RESOURCES – JAPAN

5765 Index to microfilms deposited in the Centre for East Asian Cultural Studies. EACS 8 (1969) 75-91.

5766 Toyo Bunko (The Oriental Library) and its latest activities. FA 19 (1963) 707-709.

LIBRARY RESOURCES – MALAYSIA

5767 LOH CHIN YIN. A. R. Wallace collection in the Sarawak Museum reference library. SMJ 15 (1967) 446-455.

LIBRARY RESOURCES – PHILIPPINES

5768 COLLANTES, LOURDES Y. Bibliography of materials available in the library system of the University of the Philippines on the modern history of Southeast Asia, by Lourdes Y. Collantes and J. A. Larkin. AST 2 (1964) 261-285.

5769 Recent acquisitions of the Silliman University library system. SJ 21 (1974) 291-314.

5770 SEGUERRA, MARTHA B. Bibliography of materials available in the Institute of Asian Studies Library on South and East Asia, as of June 1964. AST 2 (1964) 421-463.

LIBRARY RESOURCES – THAILAND

5771 Accessions to the library from July to December 1959. JSS 48 pt. 1 (1960) 111-117.

5772 Accessions to the Siam Society Library from January to June 1960. JSS 48 pt. 2 (1960) 135-146.

5773 Accessions to the Siam Society Library from July to December 1960. JSS 49 pt. 1 (1961) 87-98.

5774 Accessions to the Siam Society Library from January 1961 to June 1961. JSS 49 pt. 2 (1961) 183-189.

5775 Accessions to the Siam Society's library from July to December 1961. JSS 50 (1962) 73-79.

5776 Accessions to the Siam Society's library from January to December 1962. JSS 50 (1962) 193-206.

5777 Accessions to the Siam Society's library from January to April 1963. JSS 51 (1963) 101-123.

5778 Accessions to the Siam Society's library from May to December 1963. JSS 52 (1964) 133-149.

Library resources - Thailand

5779　Accessions to the Siam Society's library from January to June 1964. JSS 52 (1964) 257-272.

5780　Accessions to the Siam Society's library from July to December 1964. JSS 53 (1965) 215-235.

5781　Accessions to the Siam Society's library, January to December 1965. JSS 54 (1966) 93-109.

5782　Accessions to the Siam Society's library from January to August 1966. JSS 55 (1967) 143-160.

5783　NAI PAN HLA. Mon copper plate in the National Library, Bangkok, by Nai Pan Hla and E. Guillon. JBRS 55 (1972) 9-18.

5784　PREM PURACHATRA, PRINCE. New library and research centre of the Siam Society. JSS 50 (1962) 1-5.

LIBRARY RESOURCES - VIETNAM

5785　Liste des ouvrages entres a la bibliotheque pendant l'annee 1963. SEIB 39 (1964) 141-145.

5786　Liste des ouvrages recus a la bibliotheque en 1964-1965. SEIB 40 (1965) 359-366.

5787　Note sur quelques revues d'interet general acquises recemment par la Bibliotheque de la Societe des Etudes Indochinoises. SEIB 35 (1960) 703-711.

LIBRARY RESOURCES - UNITED STATES

5788　ANDERSON, GERALD H. Research libraries in New York City spe-cializing in Christian missions. JAS 25 (1965-6) 733-736.

LIBRARY RESOURCES ON CAMBODIA - JAPAN

5789　List of microfilms deposited in the Centre for East Asian Cultural Studies, pt. 3, Cambodia, reels 1 to 71. EACS 8 (1969) 53-74.

LIBRARY RESOURCES ON INDONESIA - GREAT BRITAIN

5790　RICKLEFS, M. C. Inventory of the Javanese manuscript collection in the British Museum. BIJ 125 (1969) 241-262.

LIBRARY RESOURCES ON INDONESIA - IRELAND

5791　VOORHOEVE, P. Additional Indone-sian manuscripts in the Chester Beatty Library, a supplement to the Batak collection. BIJ 124 (1968) 368-385.

LIBRARY RESOURCES ON INDONESIA - UNITED STATES

5792　COOLHAAS, W. PH. Alfred Reed papers. BIJ 120 (1964) 376-7.

5793　ECHOLS, JOHN M. Notes on materi-als for the study of Atjeh in the Cornell University Library. IND 1 (1966) 124-130.

5794　HONIG, PIETER. Central depository library for the Netherlands Indies in New York City by Pieter Honig and Frans Verdoorn. H57 pp. 462-465.

5795　LANDHEER, B. Netherlands studies unit at the Library of Congress. H57 pp. 481-2.

5796 VAN NIEL, ROBERT. The Alfred A.
Reed papers and other materials
pertaining to the East Indies in
the state of Rhode Island, U.S.A.
BIJ 120 (1964) 224-230.

LIBRARY RESOURCES ON LAOS - LAOS

5797 LAFONT, PIERRE-BERNARD. Inventaire des manuscrits des pagodes
du Laos. BEF 52 (1964) 429-545.

LIBRARY RESOURCES ON MALAYSIA - JAPAN

5798 List of microfilms deposited in
the Centre for East Asian Cultural
Studies. Part 1, Malaysia, reels
4001 to 4152. EACS 7 (1968) 77-
98.

5799 List of microfilms deposited in
the Centre for East Asian Cultural
Studies. Part 2, Malaysia, reels 1
to 216. EACS 8 (1969) 41-52.

5800 WILLIAMS, LEA E. Some Japanese
sources on Malayan history. JSAH
4 (Sept. 1963) 101-104.

LIBRARY RESOURCES ON MALAYSIA - SINGA-PORE

5801 TURNBULL, C. M. Bibliography of
writings in English on British
Malaya, 1786-1867. JMBRAS 33 pt.
3 (1960) 327-424.

LIBRARY RESOURCES ON MALAYSIA - UNITED STATES

5802 ROFF, WILLIAM R. Malaysian state
council minutes in New York.
JMBRAS 42 pt. 2 (1969) 213-219.

5803 TEEUW, A. Malay manuscripts in
the Library of Congress. BIJ 123
(1967) 517-520.

LIBRARY RESOURCES ON THAILAND - THAILAND

5804 STERNSTEIN, LARRY. Catalogue of
maps of Thailand in the museum of
the Royal Thai Survey Department,
Bangkok. JSS 56 (1968) 47-99.

5805 WYATT, DAVID K. Thai historical
materials in Bangkok, by David K.
Wyatt and Constance M. Wilson.
JAS 25 (1965-6) 105-118.

LIBRARY RESOURCES ON THE PHILIPPINES - MEXICO

5806 Philippine historical documents in
the National Archives of Mexico.
AST 4 (1966) 149-197.

5807 QUIRINO, CARLOS. Philippine documents in Mexico. AST 3 (1965)
585-619.

LIBRARY RESOURCES ON THE PHILIPPINES - JAPAN

5808 List of microfilms deposited in the
Centre for East Asian Cultural
Studies. EACS 9 (1970) 57-107.

LIBRARY RESOURCES ON THE PHILIPPINES - PHILIPPINES

5809 HAKCHOLNA, WILLIAM. Catalogue of
works on Cordillera ethnography in
the Igorot Study Center, Sagada,
Mountain Province. SLQ 7 (1969)
113-142.

5810 HART, DONN V. Central Philippine
University's World War II manuscript collection. JAS 25 (1965-
1966) 123.

Library resources on the Philippines –
  Philippines

5810 HART, DONN V. Central Philippines
      University's World War II manu-
      script collection. JSAH 6 (Sept.
      1965) 129-130.

5811 NIEMEYER, E. VICTOR. American
      historical collection of Fili-
      piniana. PS 9 (1961) 414-422.

LIBRARY RESOURCES ON THE PHILIPPINES –
  SPAIN

5812 CUESTA, MARIA. Graino collection.
      PS 9 (1961) 355-357.

5813 DIAZ-TRECHUELO, MARIA LOURDES.
      Primary sources of the history of
      the Philippines in archives and
      libraries in Spain. SAA 2 (1969)
      108-118.

5814 DIAZ-TRECHUELO, MARIA LOURDES.
      Primary sources on the history of
      the Philippines in archives and
      libraries of Spain. PHR 2 (1969)
      1-247.

5815 MYRICK, CONRAD. Golden store of
      history. AST 4 (1966) 213-225.

LIBRARY RESOURCES ON THE PHILIPPINES –
  UNITED STATES

5816 BOXER, C. R. Preliminary report
      on a collection of documents
      looted at Manila in 1762-64, and
      now in the Lilly Library, Indiana
      University. SAA 2 (1969) 104-107.

LIBRARY RESOURCES ON VIETNAM

5817 WHITMORE, JOHN K. Note on the
      location of source materials for
      early Vietnamese history. JAS 29
      (1969-70) 657-662.

LIGHT, FRANCIS

5818 BONNEY, R. Francis Light and
      Penang. JMBRAS 38 pt. 1 (1965)
      135-158.

5819 KACHORN SUKHABANIJ. Siamese docu-
      ments concerning Captain Francis
      Light. J45 pp. 1-9.

5820 SIMMONDS, E. H. S. An 18th cen-
      tury travel document in Thai. F38
      pp. 157-165.

5821 SIMMONDS, E. H. S. Francis Light
      and the ladies of Thalang. JMBRAS
      38 pt. 2 (1965) 213-228.

5822 SIMMONDS, E. H. S. Thalang let-
      ters, 1773-94, political aspects
      and the trade in arms. SOAS 26
      (1963) 592-619.

LIMBANG RIVER

5823 CRISSWELL, C. N. Origins of the
      Limbang claim. JSAS 2 (1971) 218-
      229.

LISU

5824 DESSAINT, ALAIN Y. Lisu settle-
      ment patterns. JSS 60 pt. 1 (1972)
      (1972) 195-204.

5825 DURRENBERGER, PAUL. Regional con-
      text of the economy of a Lisu vil-
      lage in northern Thailand. SA 3
      (1974-5) 569-575.

LITERACY *See also* EDUCATION

5826 ORATA, PEDRO T. Are literacy
      campaigns becoming obsolete? E78
      pp. 584-589.

LITERACY - PHILIPPINES

5827 BENNETT, D. C. Aspects of literacy and educational attainment in the Philippines. PS 17 (1969) 597-604.

5828 DeYOUNG, JOHN E. Communication channels and functional literacy in the Philippine barrio, by John E. DeYoung and Chester L. Hunt. E78 pp. 251-266.

5829 DeYOUNG, JOHN E. Communication channels and functional literacy in the Philippine barrio, by John E. DeYoung and Chester L. Hunt. JAS 22 (1962-3) 67-77.

5830 ESTACIO, CEFERINA I. C. Harvard literacy project in Israel and its implication for the Philippines. UN 40 (1967) 563-578.

5831 MARTIN, DALMACIO. Language, education and literacy. SJ 15 (1968) 414-426.

LITERARY PRIZES - PHILIPPINES

5832 CONSTANTINO, JOSEFINA D. First reconnaissance awards. DR 14 (1966) 135-138.

LITERATURE *See also the following literatures:* CHINESE, FOLK, PALI, SANSKRIT

5833 FRANCISCO, JUAN R. Indian literature in Southeast Asia. SJ 17 (1970) 144-161.

5834 GONZALEZ, N. V. M. Asian literature, some figures in the landscape. AST 2 (1964) 76-81.

5835 NEMENZO, CATALINA A. Southeast Asian languages and literature in English, an annotated bibliography. PSSHR 34 (1969) 1-984.

5836 SINGARAVELU, S. Legends of the Naga-Princess in south India and Southeast Asia. T33 pp. 9-15.

5837 TIEMPO, EDITH L. Southeast Asian poetry, tension for unity. SJ 17 (1970) 93-110.

5838 WOODCOCK, GEORGE. A distant and a deadly shore, notes on the literature of the sahibs. PA 46 (1973) 94-110.

Literature - Burma *See the following literatures:* BURMESE, MARMA, MON

Literature - Cambodia *See* KHMER LITERATURE

Literature - Indonesia *See the following literatures:* BALINESE, BUGINESE, INDONESIAN, JAVANESE, KERINTJI, KODI, MINANGKABAU, SUNDANESE, TONDA

Literature - Laos *See* LAO LITERATURE

Literature - Malaysia *See the following literatures:* BAJAU, DUSUN, DYAK, IBAN, KELABIT, KENYAH, MALAY, MELANAU, MORIK, MURUT, NIAH, SARIBAS, SEBOB, SELAKO

Literature - Philippines *See the following literatures:* BAGOBO, BIKOL, CAPISNON, HILIGAYNON, IFUGAO, ILIANON, ILOKO, KINIRAYA, MANGYAN, MANOBO, MARANAO, PAMPANGA, PILIPINO, SPANISH, TAGALOG, TAOSUG

Literature - Thailand

Literature - Thailand *See the following literatures:* LAHU, MON, THAI

Literature - Vietnam *See* VIETNAMESE LITERATURE

LOCAL GOVERNMENT - INDONESIA

5839 LOGSDON, MARTHA GAY. Neighborhood organization in Jakarta. IND 18 (1974) 53-70.

5840 PARSUDI SUPARLAN. Gelandangan of Jakarta, politics among the poorest people in the capital of Indonesia. IND 18 (1974) 41-52.

LOCAL GOVERNMENT - LAOS

5841 KERR, ALLEN D. Municipal government in Laos. AS 12 (1972) 510-517.

LOCAL GOVERNMENT - MALAYSIA

5842 TENNANT, PAUL. Abolition of elective local government in Penang. JSAS 4 (1973) 72-87.

5843 TENNANT, PAUL. Decline of elective local government in Malaysia. AS 13 (1973) 347-365.

LOCAL GOVERNMENT - PHILIPPINES

5844 HOLLNSTEINER, MARY R. Dynamics of power in a Philippine municipality. E78 pp. 293-307.

5845 HOLLNSTEINER, MARY R. Dynamics of power in a Philippine municipality. E78 pp. 652-654.

5846 MACHADO, K. G. Changing aspects of factionalism in Philippine local politics. AS 11 (1971) 1182-1199.

5847 MACHADO, K. G. From tradition faction to machine, changing patterns of political leadership and organization in the rural Philippines. JAS 33 (1973-4) 523-547.

5848 OCAMPO, ROMEO B. Formal structure and functions of Philippine local governments. A28 pp. 437-446.

5849 SANTOS, ARLYNE G. DE LOS. Local government as perceived by barrio residents of Tadiangan, Tuba, Benguet. GEJ 21 (1971) 73-81.

5850 SIBLEY, WILLIS E. Leadership in a Philippine barrio. E78 pp. 308-315.

5851 SILVESTRE, REYNALDO. The presidency, congress, and local government administration. DR 20 (1972) 82-103.

5852 THOMAS, M. LADD. Centralism in the Philippines, past and present causes. A28 pp. 420-431.

5853 ZAMORA, MARIO D. Political history, autonomy and change, the case of the barrio charter. AST 5 (1967) 79-100.

LOCAL GOVERNMENT - THAILAND

5854 RUBIN, HERBERT J. Effects of institutional change upon a dependency culture, the commune council 275 in rural Thailand, by Herbert J. and Irene S. Rubin. AS 13 (1973) 270-287.

5855 RUBIN, HERBERT J. Will and awe, illustrations of Thai villager dependency upon officials. JAS 32 (1972-3) 425-444.

LOCAL GOVERNMENT - VIETNAM

5856 SILVERMAN, JERRY M. Local government and national integration in
south Vietnam. PA 47 (1974) 305-
325.

LOGAN, JAMES RICHARDSON

5857 JONES, RUSSELL. Earl, Logan and
Indonesia. AR 6 (1973) 93-118.

LOLO LANGUAGE

5858 MATISOFF, JAMES A. Tonal split in
Loloish checked syllables. L27
pp. 1-44.

LOMBOK

5859 GARDNER, ESTELLE. Island strife
and L. V. Helms. SMJ 14 (1966)
396-421.

5860 GNEWOESJEWA, E. I. De levensge-
schiedenis van W. P. Mamalyga
(Malygin), rust verstoorder in
Nederlands-Indie. BIJ 121 (1965)
303-349.

LON NOL

5861 Protagonists: Norodom Sihanouk
and Lon Nol. G79 pp. 105-112.

LONDON UNIV. SCHOOL OF ORIENTAL AND
AFRICAN STUDIES

5862 GLOVER, I. C. London colloquy on
early South East Asia. AR 7
(1974) 15-18.

LOPBURI

5863 DAMRONG, PRINCE. Historical
sketch of Lopburi. S44.4 pp. 111-
131.

5864 HUTCHINSON, E. W. Phaulkon's
house at Lopburi. S44.4 pp. 132-
142.

LOPEZ, CECILIO

5865 Cecilio Lopez, curriculum vitae.
AST 1 (1963) 107-111.

5866 ROMULO, CARLOS P. Farewell to a
scholar. AST 1 (1963) 1-5.

LOW, HUGH

5867 BROWN, D. E. Hugh Low on the history of Brunei. BMJ 1 (1969) 147-
156.

LUA

5868 KUNSTADTER, PETER. Lua' and Skaw
Karen of Maehongson Province,
northwestern Thailand. K86 pp.
639-674.

LUCE, HORDON H.

5869 BA SHIN. Works of Mr. G. H. Luce,
compiled by Ba Shin and A. B.
Griswold. E92 pp. xi-xvi.

LUKBAN

5870 RUSTIA, ERLINDA F. Lukban, summer
capital of Quezon Province. UN 36
(1963) 589-593.

Lun Bawang

5888 MAJUL, CESAR ADIB. Mabini, archi-
      tect of the Philippine revolution.
      GEJ 2 (1961) 47-51.

5889 MAJUL, CESAR ADIB. Relevance of
      Mabini's social ideas to our
      times. AST 11 (1973) 28-36.

5890 MAJUL, CESAR ADIB. Rizal and
      Mabini in relation to our national
      community. GEJ 2 (1961) 14-17.

5891 ROCES, ALEJANDRO R. Mabini's
      thoughts on education. GEJ 2
      (1961) 1-6.

5892 ROMULO, CARLOS P. Jefferson and
      Mabini. GEJ 2 (1961) 7-13.

5893 VILLANUEVA, HONESTO A. Apolinario
      Mabini, his exile to Guam. GEJ 2
      (1961) 32-39.

5894 VILLARROEL, FIDEL. Apolinario
      Mabini, his birthdate and student
      years. UN 37 (1964) 162-195.

MACAPAGAL, DIOSDADO

5895 President elect Diosdado Macapa-
      gal's academic background and
      political leadership. UN 34
      (Dec. 1961) 1-5.

5896 STARNER, FRANCES. The Philip-
      pines, politics of the new era.
      AS 3 (1963) 41-47.

MACASSAR

5897 RESINK, G. J. Geur van Makassar.
      BIJ 128 (1972) 364-5.

McDOUGALL, FRANCIS THOMAS

5898 BERWICK, JOE. Bishop Francis
      Thomas McDougall. SMJ 18 (1970)
      423-4.

McFARLAND, SAMUEL

5899 WYATT, DAVID K. Samuel McFarland
      and early educational moderniza-
      tion in Thailand, 1877-1895. F38
      pp. 1-16.

MACGREGOR, IAN ALISTAIR

5900 TREGONNING, K. G. Ian Alistair
      Macgregor. JMBRAS 33 pt. 1 (1960)
      110-1.

MAEANDER (H. M. S. SHIP)

5901 COWAN, C. D. New harbour, Singa-
      pore, and the cruise of HMS
      Maeander 1848-49. JMBRAS 38 pt. 2
      (1965) 229-240.

MAGIC - BURMA

5902 OHN. Face, butterfly and two
      songs, a prologue to a study of
      the elements of myth and magic in
      Burmese politics. JBRS 46 (June
      1963) 11-25.

5903 STEWART, J. A. Spinning magic.
      B92 pp. 527-544.

MAGIC - MALAYSIA

5904 FIRTH, RAYMOND. Faith and scepti-
      cism in Kelantan village magic.
      K33 pp. 190-224.

5905 JAMUH, GEORGE. Love and hate
      charms. SMJ 9 (1960) 468-487.

5906 NYANDOH, R. Manjoh, the magic
      stone of Niah. SMJ 9 (1960) 389-
      392.

MAGIC - PHILIPPINES

5907 DEMETRIO, FRANCISCO R. On Orasyones, or magical power and living Christianity. SJ 19 (1972) 355-363.

5908 SAMSON, JOSE A. Occultism among early Filipinos. UN 33 (1960) 380-393.

MAGSAYSAY, RAMON

5909 RAMSAY, ANSIL. Ramon Magsaysay and the Philippine peasantry. PSSHR 30 (1965) 65-86.

MAH MERI

5910 CAREY, ISKANDAR. Brief account of the Mah Meri. JMBRAS 46 pt. 2 (1973) 185-194.

MAHABHARATA

5911 BOSCH, F. D. K. Bhimastava. J41 pp. 57-62.

5912 HOOYKAAS, C. Note on the Mahabharata in Malaysia and Indonesia, Sabha-Parva found in Bali. JMBRAS 38 pt. 2 (1965) 125-128.

MAHENDRAVARMAN

5913 CHHABRA, B. CH. Bangkok museum stone inscription of Mahendravarman. JSS 49 pt. 2 (1961) 109-111.

MAHMUD, SULTAN OF ACHEH

5914 REID, ANTHONY. Indonesian diplomacy, a documentary study of Atjehnese foreign policy in the reign of Sultan Mahmud, 1870-4. JMBRAS 42 pt. 2 (1969) 74-114.

MAHMUD, SULTAN OF RIAU AND LINGGA

5915 MATHESON, VIRGINIA. Mahmud, Sultan of Riau and Lingga, 1823-1864. IND 13 (1972) 119-146.

Maize *See* CORN

MAJAPAHIT

5916 NOORDUYN, J. Names of Hayam Wuruk's sisters. BIJ 124 (1968) 542-544.

5917 RAUSA-GOMEZ, LOURDES. Sri Vijaya and Madjapahit. PS 15 (1967) 63-107.

5918 RICKLEFS, M. C. Consideration of three versions of the *Babad Tanah Djawi*, with excerpts on the fall of Madjapahit. SOAS 35 (1972) 285-315.

MALACCA

5919 ARASARATNAM, S. Some notes on the Dutch in Malacca and the Indo-Malayan trade, 1641-1670. JSAH 10 (1969) 480-490.

5920 al-ATTAS, SYED NAGUIB. Note on the opening of relations between China and Malacca, 1403-05. JMBRAS 38 pt. 1 (1965) 260-264.

5921 BASSETT, D. K. European influence in South East Asia, c.1500-1630. JSAH 4 (Sept. 1963) 134-165.

5922 BASSETT, D. K. Surrender of Dutch Malacca, 1795. BIJ 117 (1961) 344-358.

5923 BOXER, C. R. Achinese attack on Malacca in 1629, as described in contemporary Portuguese sources. B38 pp. 105-121.

5924 CHAN KOK ENG. Population growth and migration of the Eurasians in Malacca since 1871. JTG 35 (1972) 17-25.

5925 COOLHAAS, W. PH. Malacca under Jan van Riebeeck. JMBRAS 38 pt. 2 (1965) 173-182.

5926 EMANUELS, H. W. Undang-undang Malaka. JOSA 2 pt. 2 (1964) 82-89.

5927 HOFFMAN, J. E. Early policies in the Malacca jurisdiction of the United East India Company, the Malay peninsula and Netherlands East Indies attachment. JSAS 3 (1972) 1-38.

5928 JACK-HINTON, COLIN. Malacca and Goa and the question of race relations in the Portuguese overseas provinces. JSAH 10 (1969) 513-539.

5930 JOSSELIN DE JONG, P. E. DE. The Malacca sultanate, an account from a hitherto untranslated Portuguese source. JSAH 1 (Sept. 1960) 20-30.

5931 SANDHU, KERNIAL SINGH. Chinese colonization of Malacca, a study in population change 1500-1957 A.D. JTG 15 (1961) 1-26.

5932 SAR DESAI, D. R. Portuguese administration in Malacca, 1511-1641. JSAH 10 (1969) 501-512.

5933 STEIN CALLENFELS, P. V. VAN. Founder of Malacca. JMBRAS 42 pt. 1 (1969) 63-70.

5934 TIEN TSE CHANG. Malacca and the failure of the first Portuguese embassy to Peking. JSAH 3 (Sept. 1962) 45-64.

5935 WAKE, CHRISTOPHER H. Malacca's early kings and the reception of Islam. JSAH 5 (Sept. 1964) 104-132.

5936 WANG, GUNGWU. First three rulers of Malacca. JMBRAS 41 pt. 1 (1968) 11-22.

5937 WANG, GUNGWU. Opening of relations between China and Malacca, 1403-5. B38 pp. 87-104.

5938 WYATT, DAVID K. Thai Kata Mandiarapala and Malacca. JSS 55 (1967) 279-286.

MALARIA - PHILIPPINES

5939 VILLANUEVA, GAUDENCIO. Factors guiding the population growth in the Philippines, malaria eradication in the Philippines. UN 39 (1966) 350-356.

MALAY LANGUAGE *See also* INDONESIAN LANGUAGE

5940 ALISJAHBANA, S. TAKDIR. Language policy, language engineering and literacy, Indonesia and Malaysia. S22 pp. 1087-1109.

5941 ALISJAHBANA, S. TAKDIR. Modernization of the Indonesian-Malay language in the 19th and 20th century. A43 pp. 181-210.

5942 ASMAH BINTE HAJI OMAR. Interplay of structural and socio-cultural factors in the development of the Malay languages. AST 6 (1968) 19-25.

Malay language

5943 ASMAH BINTE HAJI OMAR. Role of dialects in the modernization of language. A43 pp. 161-169.

5944 ASMAH BINTE HAJI OMAR. Toward the standardization of Bahasa Melayu and Bahasa Indonesia. A43 pp. 170-180.

5945 Brunei and the modernization of the Malay language. A43 pp. 140-145.

5946 DREWES, G. W. J. De invloed van de Atjehse omgeving op het Maleise spraeck ende woordboek van Frederick de Houtman. BIJ 128 (1972) 447-457.

5947 HAMDAN BIN SHEIKH TAHIR, HAJI. Development of the Malay language as a medium of instruction in schools. A43 pp. 146-160.

5948 ISMAIL HUSSEIN. Malay philology, possible contribution from Malaysia. RSAS 1 pt. 3 (1971) 20-23.

5949 JONES, RUSSELL. Harimau. BIJ 126 (1970) 260-262.

5950 JOSSELIN DE JONG, P. E. DE. Character of the Malay annals. B38 pp. 235-241.

5951 KIMBALL, LINDA AMY. First phrases of a Brunei child. BMJ 2 pt. 4 (1972) 173-182.

5952 KIMBALL, LINDA AMY. First words of a Brunei child. BMJ 2 pt. 1 (1970) 67-86.

5953 KIMBALL, LINDA AMY. More first phrases of a Brunei child. BMJ 3 pt. 2 (1974) 1-8.

5954 KIMBALL, LINDA AMY. More first words of a Brunei child. BMJ 2 pt. 3 (1971) 39-55.

5955 MAHMUD BAKY. Brunei and the official language issue. A43 pp. 134-139.

5956 MILNER, G. B. Liquid consonants and the relationship of Polynesian to Austronesian languages. SOAS 26 (1963) 620-631.

5957 MINATTUR, JOSEPH. Note on berita. JMBRAS 39 pt. 1 (1966) 188-190.

5958 MINATTUR, JOSEPH. Note on berita. RSA (1967) 99-101.

5959 PANGANIBAN, JOSE VILLA. Studies in word relationships among Philippine languages, Malay and Bahasa Indonesia. UN 36 (1963) 131-143.

5960 PHILLIPS, N. G. Topic clauses in Malay. SOAS 33 (1970) 560-572.

5961 ROFF, MARGARET. Politics of language in Malaya. AS 7 (1967) 316-328.

5962 ROOLVINK, R. Passive-active per-/berber-//per-memper- correspondence in Malay. C44 pp. 310-337.

5963 ROSARIO, GONSALO DEL. Modernization-standardization plan for the Austronesian derived national languages of Southeast Asia. AST 6 (1968) 1-18.

5964 RUZUI, SEPTY. Survey of relations between Indonesia, Malaya and the main languages of the Philippines. UN 35 (1962) 22-80.

5965 UHLENBECK, E. M. Indonesia and Malaysia. S21 pp. 847-898.

5966 UHLENBECK, E. M. Indonesia and Malaysia. S22 pp. 55-111.

MALAY LITERATURE *See also* INDONESIAN LITERATURE

5967 ABDULLAH B. ABDUL KADIR. Shaer kampong gelam terbakar, edited with notes by C. Skinner. JMBRAS 45 pt. 1 (1972) 21-56.

5968 ALTMANN, GABRIEL. Climax in Malay pantun, by Gabriel Altmann and Robert Stukovsky. AAS 1 (1965) 13-20.

5969 ALTMANN, GABRIEL. Some phonic features of Malay shaer. AAS 4 (1968) 9-16.

5970 BARRETT, E. C. G. Further light on Sir Richard Winstedt's undescribed Malay version of the Ramayana. SOAS 26 (1963) 531-543.

5971 BOTTOMS, J. C. Some Malay historical sources, a bibliographical note. S61 pp. 156-193.

5972 CHAMBERT-LOIR, HENRI. Trois traductions anglais du malais. BEF 60 (1973) 401-410.

5973 FRANCISCO, JUAN R. Rama story in the post-Muslim Malay literature of Southeast Asia. SMJ 11 (1962) 468-485.

5974 ISKANDAR, T. Some historical sources used by the author of *Hikayat Hang Tuah*. JMBRAS 43 pt. 1 (1970) 35-47.

5975 ISKANDAR, T. Three Malay historical writings in the first half of the 17th century. JMBRAS 40 pt. 2 (1967) 38-53.

5976 ISMAIL HUSSEIN. Study of traditional Malay literature. AST 6 (1968) 66-89.

5977 ISMAIL HUSSEIN. Study of traditional Malay literature. JMBRAS 39 pt. 2 (1966) 1-22.

5978 JONES, RUSSELL. Dating of Ms. Maxwell 93 in the Royal Asiatic Society Library. JMBRAS 45 pt. 1 (1972) 116-118.

5979 JOSSELIN DE JONG, P. E. DE. Rise and decline of a national hero. JMBRAS 38 pt. 2 (1965) 140-155.

5980 Malay annals, chapter III. JMBRAS 42 pt. 1 (1969) 25-33.

5981 MATHESON, VIRGINIA. *Tuhfat al-Nafis*, structure and sources. BIJ 127 (1971) 375-392.

5982 METZGER, LAURENT. Hari sastra, trois journees litteraires a Kota Baharu, 1-3 aout 1972. AR 5 (1973) 39-46.

5983 MOHAMMAD TAIB USMAN. Note on Abdullah's account of the Kelantan civil war in his *Kesah Pelayaran Abdullah*. BIJ 120 (1964) 342-349.

5984 MUNSHI ABDULLAH. *Hikayat Abdullah*. JMBRAS 42 pt. 1 (1969) 85-106.

5985 NYANDOH, R. Young princess who married a wild boar, a Malay version. SMJ 19 (1971) 325-330.

5986 PENTH, HANS GEORG. Account in the *Hikajat Atjeh* on relations between Siam and Atjeh. F38 pp. 55-69.

5987 PENTH, HANS GEORG. Zur Siam episode in der *Hikajat Atjeh*. JSS 55 (1967) 287-290.

Malay literature

5988 ROFF, WILLIAM R. The mystery of the first Malay novel, and who was Rokambul? BIJ 130 (1974) 450-464.

5989 ROOLVINK, R. Answer of Pasai. JMBRAS 38 pt. 2 (1965) 129-139.

5990 ROOLVINK, R. Five line songs in the *Sejarah Melayu*? BIJ 122 (1966) 455-457.

5991 ROOLVINK, R. Two new old Malay manuscripts. B38 pp. 242-255.

5992 ROOLVINK, R. Variant versions of the Malay annals. BIJ 123 (1967) 301-324.

5993 SINGARAVELU, S. Comparative study of the Sanskrit, Tamil, Thai and Malay versions of the story of Rama with special reference to the process of acculturation in the Southeast Asian versions. JSS 56 (1968) 137-185.

5994 SKINNER, C. Dating of the civil war in Kelantan referred to in the *Kesah Pelayaran Abdullah*. BIJ 121 (1965) 433-437.

5995 SOEWITO SANTOSO. Islamization of Indonesian/Malay literature in its early period. JOSA 8 (1971) 9-27.

5996 SWEENEY, P. L. AMIN. Connection between the *Hikayat Raja2 Pasai* and the *Sejarah Melayu*. JMBRAS 40 pt. 2 (1967) 94-105.

5997 SWEENEY, P. L. AMIN. Peran Hutan, a Malay wayang drama. JMBRAS 44 pt. 2 (1971) 79-107.

5998 SWEENEY, P. L. AMIN. Professional Malay story telling. Part I. Some questions of style and presentation. JMBRAS 46 pt. 2 (1973) 1-53.

5999 SWEENEY, P. L. AMIN. *Silsilah Raja-Raja Berunai*. JMBRAS 41 pt. 2 (1968) 1-82.

6000 SWEENEY, P. L. AMIN. *Silsilah Raja-Raja Berunai*, errata and a short note. JMBRAS 42 pt. 2 (1969) 222-224.

6001 SWEENEY, P. L. AMIN. Some observations on the Malay shair. JMBRAS 44 pt. 1 (1971) 52-70.

6003 TEEUW, A. *Hikayat Raja-Raja Pasai* and *Sejarah Melayu*. B38 pp. 222-234.

6004 TEEUW, A. Malay shair, problems of origin and tradition. BIJ 122 (1966) 429-446.

6005 THAM SEONG CHEE. Negativism, conservatism and ritualism in modern Malay literature. RSAS 3 pts. 3-4 (1973) 11-37.

6006 VOORHOEVE, P. De grote *Hikajat Bachtiar*. BIJ 125 (1969) 374-5.

6007 VOORHOEVE, P. Malay scriptorium. B38 pp. 256-266.

6008 VOORHOEVE, P. Origin of the Malay sjair. BIJ 124 (1968) 277-8.

6009 WINSTEDT, RICHARD. Malay chronicles from Sumatra and Malaya. H18 pp. 24-28.

6010 ZAINAL ABIDIN BIN ABDUL WAHID. *Sejarah Melayu*. AST 4 (1966) 445-451.

MALAY RAILWAY AND WORKS CONSTRUCTION CO.

6011 CHANDRAN, J. Private enterprise and British policy in the Malay peninsula, the case of the Malay Railway and Works Construction

Company, 1893–1895. JMBRAS 37 pt. 2 (1964) 28–46.

MALAYAN EMERGENCY

6012 HAMZAH SENDUT. Rasah, a resettlement village in Malaya. AS 1 (Nov. 1961) 21–26.

6013 RENICK, RHODERICK DHU. Emergency regulations of Malaya, causes and effect. JSAH 6 (Sept. 1965) 1–39.

6014 SANDHU, KERNIAL SINGH. Emergency resettlement in Malaya. JTG 18 (1964) 157–183.

6015 SANDHU, KERNIAL SINGH. Saga of the squatter in Malaya, a preliminary survey of the causes, characteristics and consequences of the resettlement of rural dwellers during the emergency between 1948 and 1960. JSAH 5 (Mar. 1964) 143–177.

6016 SHORT, ANTHONY H. Nationalism and the emergency in Malaya. N18 pp. 43–58.

6017 TILMAN, ROBERT O. Non-lessons of the Malayan emergency. AS 6 (1966) 407–419.

MALAYS

6018 ALATAS, SYED HUSSEIN. Grading of occupational prestige amongst the Malays in Malaysia. JMBRAS 41 pt. 1 (1968) 146–156.

6019 ALATAS, SYED HUSSEIN. Religion and modernization in South-East Asia. M52 pp. 153–169.

6020 BANKS, DAVID J. Malay kinship terms and Morgan's Malayan terminology, the complexity of simplicity. BIJ 130 (1974) 44–68.

6021 FIRTH, RAYMOND. Relations between personal kin (waris) among Kelantan Malays. S58 pp. 23–61.

6022 HARRISSON, TOM. Malays of southwest Sarawak before Malaysia. SMJ 11 (1964) 341–511.

6023 HUSIN ALI, S. Note on Malay society and culture. A41 pp. 65–74.

6024 HUSIN ALI, S. Patterns of rural leadership in Malaya. JMBRAS 41 pt. 1 (1968) 95–145.

6025 JAMUH, GEORGE. Bornean cooking: Malay, Melanau, Sea Dayak. SMJ 14 (1966) 158–182.

6026 JAMUH, GEORGE. Bornean cooking, II. SMJ 17 (1969) 202–230.

6027 KAHAR BADOR, A. Social rank, status-honour and social class consciousness amongst the Malays. M52 pp. 132–149.

6028 KHOO KAY KIM. Malay society, 1874–1920's. JSAS 5 (1974) 179–198.

6029 McGEE, T. G. Rural-urban migration in a plural society, a case study of Malays in west Malaysia. D92 pp. 108–124.

6030 McTAGGART, W. D. Kampong Pandan, a study of a Malay kampong in Kuala Lumpur, by W. D. McTaggart and R. McEachern. D92 pp. 125–138.

6031 NAGATA, JUDITH A. Adat in the city, some perceptions and practices among urban Malays. BIJ 130 (1974) 91–109.

Malays

6032 ONG BOON GEOK. Social structure of the resettled Malay community in Geylang Seral, Singapore. RSAS 4 pts. 1-2 (1974) 44-63.

6033 PARKINSON, BRIEN K. Non-economic factors in the economic retardation of the rural Malays. MAS 1 (1967) 31-46.
Comment: WILDER, WILLIAM. Islam, other factors and Malay backwardness, comments on an argument. MAS 2 (1968) 155-164.
Author's reply: Economic retardation of the Malays, a rejoinder. MAS 2 (1968) 267-272.

6034 RAMSAY, A. B. Mengambil tanda. JMBRAS 47 pt. 2 (1974) 150.

6035 REBUSHKA, ALVIN. Racial stereotypes in Malaya. AS 11 (1971) 709-716.

6036 ROFF, WILLIAM R. Kaum muda-kaum tua, innovation and reaction amongst the Malays, 1900-1941. J45 pp. 162-192.

6037 ROFF, WILLIAM R. Malayo-Muslim world of Singapore at the close of the nineteenth century. JAS 24 (1964-5) 75-90.

6038 SANDIN, BENEDICT. Origin of the Saribas Malays. SMJ 17 (1969) 231-244.

6039 SHAHRUM BIN YUB. Collections of Malay artifacts, a brief general survey. A41 pp. 75-79.

6040 THAM SEONG CHEE. Ideology, politics and economic modernization, the case of the Malays in Malaysia. SAJSS 1 pt. 1 (1973) 41-59.

6041 THAM SEONG CHEE. Tradition, values and society among the Malays. RSAS 1 pt. 4 (1971) 10-20.

6042 WINZELER, ROBERT L. Ethnic complexity and ethnic relations in an east coast Malay town. SAJSS 2 (1974) 45-61.

MALAYSIA

6043 L'annee 1966 en Asie, Malaisie. FA 22 (1968) 109-112.

6044 CHEE, STEPHEN. Malaysia and Singapore, separate identities, different priorities. AS 13 (1973) 151-161.

6045 CHEE, STEPHEN. Malaysia and Singapore, the political economy of multiracial development. AS 14 (1974) 183-191.

6046 FISHER, CHARLES A. Geographical setting of the proposed Malaysian federation, some preliminary considerations. JTG 17 (1963) 99-115.

6047 HSU YUN TSIAO. Notes on the studies of ancient Malaya. S93 pp. 172-176.

6048 List of microfilms deposited in the Centre for East Asian Cultural Studies. Part 1. Malaysia, reels 4001-4152. EACS 7 (1968) 77-98.

6049 List of microfilms deposited in the Centre for East Asian Cultural Studies. Part 2. Malaysia, reels 1 to 216. EACS 8 (1969) 41-52.

6050 MINATTUR, JOSEPH. Malaya, what's in the name? JSS 54 (1966) 19-28.

6051 MINATTUR, JOSEPH. Malaya, what's in the name? RSA (1965) 159-168.

6052 Pages d'exotisme. VI. Une utopie en insulinde. Les lettres de Malasie de Paul Adam, 1898. AR 7 (1974) 115-118.

6053   ROGERS, MARVIN L. Malaysia and
       Singapore, 1971 developments. AS
       12 (1972) 168-176.

6054   THOMPSON, KENNETH. Malaysia.
       F56 pp. 152-165.

MALAYSIA - ARMY

6055   DOL RAMLI. History of the Malay
       regiment, 1933-1942. JMBRAS 38
       pt. 1 (1965) 199-243.

MALAYSIA - BIBLIOGRAPHY

6056   ALFRED, ERIC R. Annotated bibli-
       ography of Malayan fresh water
       fisheries. JMBRAS 39 pt. 1
       (1966) 145-165.

6057   DUNN, F. L. Annotated bibliogra-
       phy of Malayan (west Malaysian)
       archaeology, 1962-1969, by F. L.
       Dunn and B. A. V. Peacock. AP 14
       (1971) 43-48.

6058   LIM, BEDA. Malaya, a background
       bibliography. JMBRAS 35 pts. 2-3
       (1962) 1-199.

6059   LIM, HUCK TEE. Index Malaysiana,
       an index to the *Journal of the
       Straits Branch, Royal Asiatic
       Society* and the *Journal of the
       Malayan Branch, Royal Asiatic
       Society*, 1878-1963, by Lim Huck
       Tee and D. E. K. Wijasuriya.
       JMBRAS 36 pt. 4 (1963) 1-395.

6060   TURNBULL, C. M. Bibliography of
       writings in English on British
       Malaya, 1786-1867. JMBRAS 33 pt.
       3 (1960) 327-424.

MALAYSIA - BIOGRAPHICAL DIRECTORIES

6061   JOSSELIN DE JONG, P. E. DE. Who's
       who in the Malay annals. JMBRAS
       34 pt. 2 (1961) 1-89.

6062   JOSSELIN DE JONG, P. E. DE. Who's
       who in the Malay annals. JMBRAS
       42 pt. 1 (1969) 34-41.

MALAYSIA - CONSTITUTION

6063   GROVES, H. Notes on the constitu-
       tion of the Federation of Malaya.
       J45 pp. 268-273.

MALAYSIA - DESCRIPTION AND TRAVEL

6064   ANDERSON, JOHN. Political and
       commercial considerations relative
       to the Malayan peninsula and the
       British settlements in the Straits
       of Malacca. JMBRAS 35 pt. 4
       (1965) i-xv, 1-204, i-lxviii.

6065   COLLESS, BRIAN E. Early western
       ports of the Malay peninsula.
       JTG 29 (1969) 1-9.

MALAYSIA - ECONOMIC CONDITIONS

6066   CHENG U WEN. Opium in the Straits
       Settlements, 1867-1910. JSAH 2
       (Mar. 1961) 63-88a.

6067   CORDEN, W. M. Malayan balance of
       payments problem. S47 pp. 112-
       130.

6068   DAVIS, H. CRAIG. Input-output
       forecasts, a comparison of west
       Malaysia with the Netherlands, by
       H. Craig Davis and Geoffrey B.
       Hainsworth. MER 19 pt. 1 (1974)
       84-93.

Malaysia - Economic conditions

6069 DODD, JOSEPH W. Colonial economy, 1967, the case of Malaysia. AS 9 (1969) 438-446.

6070 FISK, E. K. Features of the rural economy. S47 pp. 163-173.

6071 HARVIE, C. H. Export multipliers and the stability of the Federation of Malaya's economy. MER 9 pt. 1 (1964) 80-89.

6072 KEESING, DONALD B. Thailand and Malaysia, a case for a common market? MER 10 pt. 2 (1965) 102-113.

6073 McDONALD, DANIEL. Responsibility for published financial statements. MER 8 pt. 1 (1963) 40-44.

6074 McHALE, T. R. Introduction to econocological theory. MER 5 pt. 1 (1960) 7-12.

6075 Malaya and British Borneo. S48 pp. 171-184.

6076 Malaysian myths. JCA 2 (1972) 217-8.

6077 SILCOCK, T. H. Economic potential of Malaya. S48 pp. 94-100.

6078 WHARTON, C. R. Marketing, merchandising and money lending: a note on middleman monopsony in Malaya. MER 7 pt. 2 (1962) 24-44.

MALAYSIA - FOREIGN RELATIONS

6079 BOYCE, PETER. Policy without authority, Singapore's external affairs power. JSAH 6 (Sept. 1965) 87-103.

6080 OTT, MARVIN C. Foreign policy formation in Malaysia. AS 12 (1972) 225-241.

6081 PARMER, J. NORMAN. Malaysia, changing a little to keep face. AS 7 (1967) 131-137.

6082 VELLUT, JEAN-LUC. Le monde Afro-Asiatique et l'affaire de Malaysia, une illustration du probleme des mediations internationales. RSA (1965) 37-53.

MALAYSIA - FOREIGN RELATIONS - AUSTRALIA

6083 BOYCE, PETER J. Bonds of culture and commonwealth in Southeast Asia. JSAS 2 (1971) 71-77.

6084 BOYCE, PETER J. Twenty-one years of Australian diplomacy in Malaya. JSAH 4 (Sept. 1963) 65-100.

6085 McDOUGALL, DEREK. Evolution of Australia's defence policy in relation to Malaysia-Singapore, 1964-1971. JSAS 3 (1972) 97-110.

6086 SINGH, L. P. Malaysia and Australian-Indonesian relations. RSA (1964) 277-293.

MALAYSIA - FOREIGN RELATIONS - BRUNEI

6087 CRISSWELL, C. N. Origins of the Limbang claim. JSAS 2 (1971) 218-229.

MALAYSIA - FOREIGN RELATIONS - CHINA

6088 China's new relations with Malaysia. JCA 4 (1974) 388-390.

6089 VAN DER KROEF, JUSTUS M. The Malaysian formula model for future Sino-Southeast Asian relations? AQ (1974) 311-337.

6090 WANG GUNGWU. Opening of relations between China and Malacca, 1403-5. B38 pp. 87-104.

MALAYSIA - FOREIGN RELATIONS - FRANCE

6091   BELLAMAL, A. Pour une politique francaise dans le monde malayo-indonesien. FA (1974 pt. 2) 35-44.

6092   DUNMORE, JOHN. French visitors to Trengganu in the eighteenth century. JMBRAS 46 pt. 1 (1973) 144-159.

6093   RAWLINS, J. S. D. French enterprise in Malaya. JMBRAS 39 pt. 2 (1966) 50-94.

6094   REID, A. The French in Sumatra and the Malay world, 1760-1890. BIJ 129 (1973) 195-238.

MALAYSIA - FOREIGN RELATIONS - GREAT BRITAIN

6095   ALLEN, J. DE VERE. Ancien regime in Trengganu, 1909-1919. JMBRAS 41 pt. 1 (1968) 23-53.

6096   ALLEN, J. DE VERE. Colonial Office and the Malay states, 1867-73. JMBRAS 36 pt. 1 (1963) 1-36.

6097   ALLEN, J. DE VERE. Elephant and mousedeer, a new version: Anglo-Kedah relations, 1905-1915. JMBRAS 41 pt. 1 (1968) 54-94.

6098   BASSETT, D. K. Anglo-Malay relations, 1786-1795. JMBRAS 38 pt. 2 (1965) 183-212.

6099   HAWKINS, DAVID C. Britain and Malaysia, another view, was the decision to withdraw entirely voluntary or was Britain pushed a little? AS 9 (1969) 546-562.

6100   KHOO KAY KIM. Origin of British administration in Malaya. JMBRAS 39 pt. 1 (1966) 52-91.

6101   KHOO KAY KIM. Pangkor engagement of 1874. JMBRAS 47 pt. 1 (1974) 1-12.

6102   LEIFER, MICHAEL. Astride the straits of Johore, the British presence and Commonwealth rivalry in Southeast Asia. MAS 1 (1967) 283-296.

6103   McDOUGALL, DEREK. The Wilson government and the British defence commitment in Malaysia-Singapore. JSAS 4 (1973) 229-240.

6104   SADKA, EMILY. Colonial Office and the protected Malay states. B38 pp. 184-202.

6105   SINCLAIR, KEITH. British advance in Johore, 1885-1914. JMBRAS 40 pt. 1 (1967) 93-110.

6106   THIO, EUNICE. British forward movement in the Malay peninsula, 1880-1889. J45 pp. 120-134.

6107   THIO, EUNICE. British policy towards Johore, from advice to control. JMBRAS 40 pt. 1 (1967) 1-41.

6108   THIO, EUNICE. Some aspects of the federation of the Malay states, 1896-1910. JMBRAS 40 pt. 2 (1967) 3-15.

6109   TURNBULL, C. M. British planning for post-war Malaya. JSAS 5 (1974) 239-254.

6110   TURNBULL, C. M. Origins of British control in the Malay states before colonial rule. B38 pp. 166-183.

Malaysia - Foreign relations - Indonesia

MALAYSIA - FOREIGN RELATIONS - INDONESIA

6111 GORDON, BERNARD K. Potential for Indonesian expansion. PA 36 (1963) 378-393.

6112 GREEN, L. C. Indonesia, the United Nations and Malaysia. JSAH 6 (Sept. 1965) 71-86.

6113 GROSSHOLTZ, JEAN. Rise and demise of konfrontasi, impact on politics in Malaysia. AST 6 (1968) 325-339.

6114 HEIDHUES, MARY F. SOMERS. Peking and the overseas Chinese, the Malaysian dispute. AS 6 (1966) 276-287.

6115 HINDLEY, DONALD. Indonesia's confrontation with Malaysia, a search for motives. AS 4 (1964) 904-913.

6116 KAHIN, GEORGE McT. Malaysia and Indonesia. PA 37 (1964) 253-270.

6117 ROUCEK, JOSEPH S. Geopolitical aspects of the Indonesian-Malaysian dispute. RSA (1965) 275-303.

6118 SINGH, L. P. Malaysia and Australian-Indonesian relations. RSA (1964) 277-293.

6119 SUTTER, JOHN O. Two faces of konfrontasi: crush Malaysia and the gestapu. AS 6 (1966) 523-546.

6120 VAN DER KROEF, JUSTUS M. Indonesia, Malaya and the North Borneo crisis. AS 3 (1963) 173-181.

6121 VAN DER KROEF, JUSTUS M. Sarawak-Indonesian border insurgency. MAS 2 (1968) 245-265.

MALAYSIA - FOREIGN RELATIONS - JAPAN

6122 AKASHI, YOJI. Japanese policy towards the Malayan Chinese, 1941-1945. JSAS 1 pt. 2 (1970) 61-89.

6123 ITAGAKI, YOICHI. Some aspects of the Japanese policy for Malaya under the occupation, with special reference to nationalism. J45 pp. 256-267.

6124 YUEN CHOY LENG. Japanese rubber and iron investments in Malaya, 1900-1941. JSAS 5 (1974) 18-36.

MALAYSIA - FOREIGN RELATIONS - NETHER-
LANDS

6125 IRWIN, GRAHAM W. The Dutch and the tin trade of Malaya in the seventeenth century. S89 pp. 267-287.

MALAYSIA - FOREIGN RELATIONS - NEW
ZEALAND

6126 JACKSON, KEITH. Because it's there . . . , a consideration of the decision to commit New Zealand troops to Malaysia beyond 1971. JSAS 2 (1971) 22-31.

MALAYSIA - FOREIGN RELATIONS - PAKISTAN

6127 SAYEED, K. B. Southeast Asia in Pakistan's foreign policy. PA 41 (1968) 230-244.

MALAYSIA - FOREIGN RELATIONS - PHILIP-
PINES

6128 FERNANDEZ, ALEJANDRO M. Secretary General's role in the Malaysia conflict. DR 12 (1964) 160-171.

6129   NOBLE, LELA GARNER. National in-
       terest and national image, Philip-
       pine policy in Asia. AS 13 (1973)
       560-576.

6130   ORTIZ, PACIFICO A. Legal aspects
       of the North Borneo question. PS
       11 (1963) 18-64.

6131   TREGONNING, K. G. Philippine
       claim to Sabah. JMBRAS 43 pt. 1
       (1970) 161-170.

6132   VILLADOLID, ALICE C. Sociological
       ties binding the Philippines and
       North Borneo. UN 35 (1962) 515-
       523.

6133   WRIGHT, LEIGH R. Historical notes
       on the North Borneo dispute. JAS
       25 (1965-6) 471-484.

MALAYSIA – FOREIGN RELATIONS – SINGAPORE

6134   BOTTOMLEY, ANTHONY. Some economic
       implications of the proposed
       Malaysia federation from the point
       of view of Singapore. MER 7 pt.
       2 (1962) 95-105.

6135   LAU TEIK SOON. Malaysia-Singapore
       relations, crisis of adjustment,
       1965-68. JSAH 10 (1969) 155-176.

MALAYSIA – FOREIGN RELATIONS – THAILAND

6136   SHAROM AHMAT. Kedah-Siam rela-
       tions, 1821-1905. JSS 59 pt. 1
       (1971) 97-117.

6137   THAMSOOK NUMNONDA. Negotiations
       regarding the cession of Siamese
       Malay states, 1907-1909. JSS 55
       (1967) 227-235.

MALAYSIA – FOREIGN RELATIONS – UNITED
STATES

6138   HOLMES, WARREN J. Oceania's place
       in United States foreign trade.
       C35 pp. 11-15.

6139   ISMAIL BIN DATO ABDUL RAHMAN. A
       new government looks at American
       investment. C35 pp. 71-78.

6140   KING, FRANK H. H. Progress in
       Commonwealth East Asia and Ameri-
       can trade prospects. C35 pp. 29-
       48.

MALAYSIA – HISTORY

6141   ALLEN, J. DE VERE. Colonial Of-
       fice and the Malay states, 1867-
       73. JMBRAS 36 pt. 1 (1963) 1-36.

6142   ALLEN, J. DE VERE. The Kelantan
       rising of 1915, some thoughts on
       the concept of resistance in Brit-
       ish Malayan history. JSAH 9
       (1968) 241-257.

6143   BASSETT, D. K. Anglo-Malay rela-
       tions, 1786-1795. JMBRAS 38 pt. 2
       (1965) 183-212.

6144   BASSETT, D. K. British commercial
       and strategic interest in the Ma-
       lay peninsula during the late
       eighteenth century. B38 pp. 122-
       140.

6145   BASTIN, JOHN. Problems of person-
       ality in the reinterpretation of
       modern Malayan history. B38 pp.
       141-155.

6145a BOXER, C. R. Achinese attack on
       Malacca in 1629, as described in
       contemporary Portuguese sources.
       B38 pp. 105-121.

Malaysia - History

6146 CANT, R. G. Pahang in 1888, the eve of British administration. JTG 19 (1964) 4-19.

6147 CHANDRAN, JESHURUN. British Foreign Office and the Siamese Malay states, 1890-97. MAS 5 (1971) 143-159.

6148 CHEW, ERNEST. First state council in the protected Malay states. JMBRAS 39 pt. 1 (1966) 182-184.

6149 CHEW, ERNEST. Reasons for British intervention in Malaya, review and reconsideration. JSAH 6 (Mar. 1965) 81-93.

6150 CHEW, ERNEST. Sir Frank Swettenham and the federation of the Malay states. MAS 2 (1968) 51-69.

6151 CHEW, ERNEST. Swettenham and British rule in west Malaya. JSAS 5 (1974) 166-178.

6152 COLLESS, BRIAN E. Early western ports of the Malay peninsula. JTG 29 (1969) 1-9.

6153 KHOO KAY KIM. Origin of British administration in Malaya. JMBRAS 39 pt. 1 (1966) 52-91.

6154 KHOO KAY KIM. Pangkor engagement of 1874. JMBRAS 47 pt. 1 (1974) 1-12.

6155 KLEIN, IRA. British expansion in Malaya, 1897-1902. JSAH 9 (1968) 53-68.

6156 LEWIS, DIANE. Inas, a study of local history. JMBRAS 33 pt. 1 (1960) 65-94.

6157 MacINTYRE, D. Britain's intervention in Malaya, the origin of Lord Kimberley's instructions to Sir Andrew Clark in 1873. JSAH 2 (Oct. 1961) 47-69.

6158 MILLS, L. A. British Malaya, 1824-67. JMBRAS 33 pt. 3 (1960) 9-326.

6159 SADKA, EMILY. Colonial Office and the protected Malay states. B38 pp. 184-202.

6160 SKINNER, C. Abdullah's voyage to the east coast seen through contemporary eyes. JMBRAS 39 pt. 2 (1966) 23-33.

6161 TARLING, NICHOLAS. Borneo and British intervention in Malaya. JSAS 5 (1974) 159-165.

6162 TARLING, NICHOLAS. Intervention and non-intervention in Malaya. JAS 21 (1961-2) 523-527.

6163 TARLING, NICHOLAS. The Kim Eng Seng. JSAH 4 (Mar. 1963) 103-114.

6164 THIO, EUNICE. Britains search for security in north Malaya, 1886-1897. JSAH 10 (1969) 279-303.

6165 THIO, EUNICE. Some aspects of the federation of the Malay states, 1896-1910. JMBRAS 40 pt. 2 (1967) 3-15.

6166 TREGONNING, K. G. Historical aspects of Malaysia's acceptance of western culture. EACS 6 (1967) 164-175.

6167 TREGONNING, K. G. How Germany made Malaya British. AST 2 (1964) 180-187.

6168 TURNBULL, C. M. Bibliography of writings in English on British Malaya, 1786-1867. JMBRAS 33 pt. 3 (1960) 327-424.

6169 TURNBULL, C. M. Origins of British control in the Malay states before colonial rule. B38 pp. 166-183.

6170 WANG GUNGWU. Opening of relations between China and Malacca, 1403-5. B38 pp. 87-104.

6171 WHEATLEY, PAUL. Desultory remarks on the ancient history of the Malay peninsula. B38 pp. 33-75.

6172 WILLIAMS, LEA E. Some Japanese sources on Malayan history. JSAH 4 (Sept. 1963) 101-104.

MALAYSIA - LAWS, STATUTES, ETC. *See also* ADAT LAW - MALAYSIA

6173 CHENG SIOK HWA. Government legislation for Chinese secret societies in the Straits Settlements in the late 19th century. AST 10 (1972) 262-271.

6174 CHIN, LUCAS. Trade and preservation of antiquities and other cultural objects in Sarawak. SMJ 20 (1972) 413-419.

6175 EMANUELS, H. W. Undang-undang Malaka. JOSA 2 pt. 2 (1964) 82-89.

6176 HOOKER, M. B. Note on the Malayan legal digests. JMBRAS 41 pt. 1 (1968) 157-170.

6177 HOOKER, M. B. Relationship between Chinese law and common law in Malaysia, Singapore and Hong Kong. JAS 28 (1968-9) 723-742.

6178 Law of preventive detention in Malaya. JCA 4 (1974) 375-381.

6179 RENICK, RHODERICK DHU. Emergency regulations of Malaya, causes and effect. JSAH 6 (Sept. 1965) 1-39.

6180 SANDIN, BENEDICT. Some Iban (Sea Dayak) customary law in Sarawak. C39 pp. 40-44.

MALAYSIA - MINORITIES *See also* BAJAU, BAKETAN, BERAWAN, BISAYAH, BLIUN, CHINESE, DUSUN, DYAK, EURASIANS, IBAN, INDIANS, KADAZANS, KAHAYAN, KAJANG, KAYAN, KEJAMAN, KELABIT, KENYAH, LEPPO TAU, LUN BAWANG, MAH MERI, MALOH, MURUT, NEGRITOS, NGAJU, PENAN, PERSIANS, PUNAN, SAKAI, SEBOB, SELAKO, SEMAI, SEMELAI, SITENG, SIWANG, SRE, TEMIAR

6181 BABCOCK, TIM G. Indigenous ethnicity in Sarawak. SMJ 22 (1974) 191-202.

6182 CAREY, ISKANDAR. Religious problem among the orang asli. JMBRAS 43 pt. 1 (1970) 155-160.

6183 FEE. Kampong Padre, a Tamil settlement near Bagan Serai, Perak. JMBRAS 36 pt. 1 (1963) 153-181.

6184 HARRISSON, TOM. Tribes, minorities, and the central government in Sarawak, Malaysia. K86 pp. 317-352.

6185 JONES, ALUN. Orang asli, an outline of their progress in modern Malaya. JSAH 9 (1968) 286-305.

6186 McTAGGART, W. D. Distribution of ethnic groups in Malaya, 1947-57. JTG 26 (1968) 69-81.

6187 NEEDHAM, RODNEY. Age, category and descent, to Professor Raymond Firth. BIJ 122 (1966) 1-35.

6188 PELRAS, CHRISTIAN. Notes sur quelques populations aquatiques de l'archipel nusantarien. AR 3 (1972) 133-168.

Malaysia - Minorities

MALAYSIA - POLITICS AND GOVERNMENT

Malaysia – Politics and government –
1963-1965

6211 ROFF, WILLIAM R. Malaysian state
council minutes in New York.
JMBRAS 42 pt. 2 (1969) 213-219.

6212 ROGERS, MARVIN L. Politicization
and political development in a
rural Malay community. AS 9
(1969) 919-933.

6213 RUDNER, MARTIN. Draft development
plan of the Federation of Malaya,
1950-55. JSAS 3 (1972) 63-96.

6214 RUDNER, MARTIN. Organization of
the British military administration in Malaya, 1946-48. JSAH 9
(1968) 95-106.

6215 RUDNER, MARTIN. Political structure of the Malayan Union. JMBRAS
43 pt. 1 (1970) 116-128.

6216 SADKA, EMMA. Malaysia, the political background. S47 pp. 28-58.

6217 SADKA, EMMA. Singapore and the
Federation, problems of merger.
AS 1 (Jan. 1962) 17-25.

6218 SILCOCK, T. H. Communal and party
structure. S47 pp. 1-27.

6219 SINGHAL, D. P. United states of
Malaysia. AS 1 (Oct. 1961) 16-22.

6220 SOH ENG LIM. Tan Cheng Lock,
his leadership of the Malayan
Chinese. JSAH 1 (Mar. 1960) 34-
61.

6221 SOENARNO, RADIN. Malay nationalism, 1896-1941. JSAH 1 (Mar.
1960) 1-33.

6222 STARNER, FRANCES L. Malaysia and
the North Borneo territories. AS
3 (1963) 519-534.

6223 STEVENSON, M. R. Malayan Union
and the historians. JSAH 10
(1969) 344-354.

6224 TENNANT, PAUL. Decline of elective local government in Malaysia.
AS 13 (1973) 347-365.

6225 TILMAN, ROBERT O. Bureaucratic
development in Malaya. B72 pp.
550-604.

6226 TILMAN, ROBERT O. Socialization
of the Chinese into Malaysian
politics, some preliminary observations. S90.7 pp. 107-120.

6227 TINKER, HUGH. Structure of the
British imperial heritage. B72
pp. 23-86.

6228 VON DER MEHDEN, FRED R. Some aspects of political ideology in
Malaysia. S90.5 pp. 95-104.

6229 YEO KIM WAH. Anti-federation
movement in Malaya, 1946-48. JSAS
4 (1973) 31-51.

<u>MALAYSIA – POLITICS AND GOVERNMENT –
1963-1965</u>

6230 GROSSHOLTZ, JEAN. Exploration of
Malaysian meanings. AS 6 (1966)
227-240.

6231 LEIFER, MICHAEL. Communal violence in Singapore. AS 4 (1964)
1115-1121.

6232 LEIFER, MICHAEL. Singapore in Malaysia, the politics of federation. JSAH 6 (Sept. 1965) 54-70.

6233 MEANS, GORDON P. Malaysia, a new
federation in Southeast Asia. PA
36 (1963) 138-159.

6234 MILNE, R. S. Malaysia. AS 4
(1964) 695-701.

6258 SMITH, T. E. Immigration and per-
      manent settlement of Chinese and
      Indians in Malaya, and the future
      growth of the Malay and Chinese
      communities. C87 pp. 174-185.

6259 ZAHARAH MAHMUD. Population of
      Kedah in the nineteenth century.
      JSAS 3 (1972) 193-209.

MALAYSIA - RELIGION *See also* BUD-
      DHISM - MALAYSIA, CHRISTIANITY - MA-
      LAYSIA, HINDUISM - MALAYSIA, ISLAM -
      MALAYSIA

6260 CAREY, ISKANDAR. Religious prob-
      lem among the orang asli. JMBRAS
      43 pt. 1 (1970) 155-160.

MALAYSIA - SOCIAL CONDITIONS

6261 FREEDMAN, MAURICE. Growth of a
      plural society in Malaya. PA
      33 (1960) 158-168.

6262 LABI, MARIA L. C. Re-analysis of
      Negri Sembilan socio-political
      organization. JMBRAS 42 pt. 2
      (1969) 145-154.

6263 McTAGGART, W. DONALD. Grading of
      social areas in Georgetown, Pe-
      nang. JTG 23 (1966) 40-46.

6264 MOKHZANI, B. A. R. Study of so-
      cial stratification and social
      mobility in Malaya. EACS 4 (1965)
      138-162.

6265 RIAZ HASSAN. Some aspects of oc-
      cupational and class structure in
      west Malaysia. SAJSS 1 pt. 1
      (1973) 17-40.

6266 SINGH, JASBIR SARJIT. Social
      stratification in Petaling Jaya,
      Malaysia. SAJSS 2 (1974) 75-92.

6267 THAM SEONG CHEE. Sociological as-
      pects of religious reform in Ma-
      laya. RSAS 1 pt. 2 (1971) 29-41.

MALAYSIA - STATISTICS

6268 KUNSTADTER, PETER. Malaysia, in-
      troduction. K86 pp. 307-316.

MALLERET, LOUIS

6269 FILLIOZAT, JEAN. Louis Malleret,
      1901-1970. BEF 58 (1971) 1-15.

6270 SAURIN, EDMOND. La vie et
      l'oeuvre de Louis Malleret, 1901-
      1970. SEIB 46 (1971) 7-20.

MALOHS

6271 HARRISSON, TOM. Maloh coffin de-
      signs. SMJ 14 (1966) 146-150.

6272 HARRISSON, TOM. Malohs of Kali-
      mantan, ethnological notes. SMJ
      12 (1965) 236-350.

6273 KING, VICTOR. Additional notes on
      the Malohs and related peoples of
      Kalimantan Barat, the value of
      Dutch ethnography. SMJ 20 (1972)
      83-105.

6274 KING, VICTOR T. Maloh social
      structure. SMJ 22 (1974) 203-227.

MALOLOS

6275 AGONCILLO, TEODORO A. Malolos,
      the crisis of the republic. PSSHR
      25 (1960) 1-831.

6276 ARUEGO, JOSE M. Malolos constitu-
      tion. A28 pp. 43-4.

Mamalyga, W. P.

MAMALYGA, W. P.

6277 GNEWOESJEWA, E. I. De levensge-
schiedenis van W. P. Mamalyga
(Malygin), rustverstoorder in
Nederlands-Indie. BIJ 121 (1965)
303-349.

MAMANWA LANGUAGE

6278 MILLER, JEANNE. Mamanwa phonemes
and orthography. PSSHR 30 (1965)
343-347.

MANDAILING LANGUAGE

6279 TUGBY, DONALD. The persistence of
the Mandailing language in west
Malaysia, by Donald Tugby and
Brian Embury. SAJSS 1 pt. 2
(1973) 29-33.

MANDALAY

6280 MAUNG MAUNG TIN. Mindon Min's
development plan for the Mandalay
area, by Maung Maung Tin and
Thomas Owen Morris. JBRS 49
(1966) 29-34.

MANDAYA

6281 YENGOYAN, A. A. Baptism and
Bisayanization among the Mandaya
of eastern Mindanao, Philippines.
AST 4 (1966) 324-327.

MANGKU NAGARA, PRINCE

6282 SOEBARDI. Prince Mangku Nagara
IV, a ruler and a poet of 19th
century Java. JOSA 8 (1971) 28-
58.

MANGYAN

6283 MACEDA, MARCELINO N. Brief report
on some Mangyans in northern
Oriental Mindoro. UN 40 (1967)
102-155.

6284 PAZ, EMERTERIO DE LA. Survey of
the Hanunoo Mangyan culture and
barriers to change. UN 41 (1968)
3-63.

MANGYAN LITERATURE

6285 POSTMA, ANTONIO. Ambahan, a
Mangyan-Hanunoo poetic form. AST
3 (1965) 71-85.

MANILA

6286 ARCINAS, FE R. Adjustment of migrants in an urban enclave, Pobres
Purok. GEJ 21 (1971) 1-29.

6287 ASHBURN, FRANKLIN G. Some recent
inquiries into the structure-
function of conflict gangs in the
Manila city jail. AST 3 (1965)
126-144.

6288 CHEONG, W. E. Canton and Manila
in the eighteenth century. S89
pp. 227-246.

6289 COSTA, HORACIO DE LA. Siege and
capture of Manila by the British,
September-October 1762. PS 10
(1962) 607-650.

6290 DWYER, D. J. Problem of in-migration and squatter settlement in
Asian cities: two case studies,
Manila and Victoria-Kowloon. AST
2 (1964) 145-169.

6291 FRYER, D. W. The million city in
Southeast Asia. T45 pp. 72-87.

6292 GALANG, MA. FELICITAS D. Over a
cup of coffee and the changing
face of the city. SLURJ 1 (1970)
745-775.

6293 HOLLNSTEINER, MARY R. Becoming
an urbanite, the neighbourhood as
a learning environment. D92 pp.
29-40.

6294 HOLLNSTEINER, MARY R. Inner Tondo
as a way of life. B13 pp. 235-245.

6295 HOLLNSTEINER, MARY R. Inner Tondo
as a way of life. SLQ 5 (1967)
13-26.

6296 JAZMINES, ALAN. Chinatown impressions. DR 13 (1965) 355-358.

6297 McPHELIN, MICHAEL. Manila, the
primate city. PS 17 (1969) 781-
789.

6298 MYRICK, CONRAD. Some aspects of
the British occupation of Manila.
A58 pp. 113-130.

6299 PRATT, WILLIAM F. Family size
and expectations in Manila. SLQ
5 (1967) 153-184.

6300 QUIASON, SERAFIN D. East India
Company in Manila, 1762-1764.
PSSHR 28 (1963) 424-444.

6301 REED, ROBERT R. Colonial origins
of Manila and Batavia, desultory
notes on nascent metropolitan
primacy and urban systems in
Southeast Asia. AST 5 (1967) 543-
562.

6302 ROXAS-LIM, AURORA. Memory needs
an address. GEJ 4 (1962) 38-46.

6303 SAMSON, JOSE A. Data on the
cause of youth problems in the
city of Manila. UN 35 (1962)
469-474.

6304 TUBANGUI, HELEN R. Manila area
study. PHR 1 pt. 1 (1965) 334-
364.

6305 VILORIA, LEANDRO A. Manilenos,
significant elites in urban development and nation building in the
Philippines. D92 pp. 16-28.

6306 WENGERT, EGBERT S. Aviles-
Legarda-Mendiola traffic experiment, by Egbert S. Wengert and
Primitivo R. de Leon. G93 pp.
475-503.

MANILA. OBSERVATORY

6307 HENNESSEY, JAMES J. Manila Observatory. PS 8 (1960) 99-120.

6308 HIDALGO, ANGEL. Miguel Selga,
1879-1956, priest and scientist.
PS 15 (1967) 307-347.

6309 SCHUMACHER, JOHN N. One hundred
years of Jesuit scientists, the
Manila Observatory, 1865-1965. PS
13 (1965) 258-286.

MANILA. UNIVERSITY OF SANTO TOMAS

6310 AQUINO, ROSARIO. Medical social
service department, U.S.T. hospital. UN 38 (1965) 463-471.

6311 University thesis abstracts. UN
33 (1960) 419-448.

MANOBO

6312 MACEDA, MARCELINO. Manobo society,
selected patterns and possible
change. D67 pp. 21-30.

6313 REYNOLDS, HUBERT. Multi-level
house of the Manobo in Salangsang
and its inter-relations with other

Manobo

aspects of culture. SJ 13 (1966) 581-593.

MANOBO LANGUAGE

6314 BARNARD, MYRA L. Dibabawon non-verbal clauses. Z16 pp. 559-566.

MANOBO LITERATURE

6315 LANGKAN. Visit of Lagabaan to Nelendangan, an episode of the Manobo epic Ulahingan, chanted by Langkan and Santiago Abod. SJ 17 (1970) 19-46.

6316 MAQUISO, ELENA G. Langkat, its relationship to the Ulahingan. SJ 17 (1970) 407-419.

6317 MAQUISO, ELENA G. Ulahingan, a Manobo epic. SJ 16 (1969) 227-238.

6318 MAQUISO, ELENA G. Ulahingan episodes, the creativity of the Manobos. SJ 16 (1969) 360-374.

6319 Visit of Lagabaan to Nelendangan, an episode of the Manobo epic Ulahingan. SJ 20 (1973) 136-162.

MANOLAY CULT

6320 SMART, JOHN E. Manolay cult, the genesis and dissolution of millenarian sentiments among the Isneg of northern Luzon. AST 8 (1970) 53-93.

MANUSCRIPTS

6321 JONES, RUSSELL. More light on Malay manuscripts. AR 8 (1974) 45-58.

6322 VOORHOEVE, P. Malay scriptorium. B38 pp. 256-266.

MANUSCRIPTS - BRUNEI

6323 HARRISSON, TOM. Rennell manuscript in the Brunei Museum. BMJ 1 (1969) 157-165.

6324 HARRISSON, TOM. Unpublished Rennell Ms., a Borneo-Philippine journey, 1762-63. JMBRAS 39 pt. 1 (1966) 92-136.

MANUSCRIPTS - CAMBODIA

6325 JAINI, PADMANABH S. Mahadibbamanta, a paritta manuscript from Cambodia. SOAS 28 (1965) 61-80.

MANUSCRIPTS - FRANCE

6326 HUTCHINSON, E. W. Four French state manuscripts relating to embassies between France and Siam in the XVIIth century. S44.8 pp. 95-157.

6327 MARTINI, GINETTE. Les titres des Jataka dans les manuscrits Pali de la Bibliotheque Nationale de Paris. BEF 51 (1963) 79-93.

6328 VOORHOEVE, P. Les manuscrits malais de la Bibliotheque Nationale de Paris. AR 6 (1973) 42-80.

MANUSCRIPTS - GERMANY

6329 WENK, KLAUS. Zu einer Landkarte Sued-und Ostasiens. F38 pp. 119-122.

MANUSCRIPTS – GREAT BRITAIN

6330 PEARSON, JAMES D. Manuscripts and documents in the British Isles relating to South-East Asia, the Wainwright-Matthews guide. SAA 2 (1969) 65-67.

6331 RICKLEFS, M. C. Consideration of three versions of the *Babad Tanah Djawi,* with excerpts on the fall of Madjapahit. SOAS 35 (1972) 285-315.

6332 RICKLEFS, M. C. Inventory of the Javanese manuscript collection in the British Museum. BIJ 125 (1969) 241-262.

MANUSCRIPTS – INDONESIA

6333 ANDI ZAINAL ABIDIN. Notes on the lontara as historical sources. IND 12 (1971) 159-172.

6334 DAMAIS, LOUIS-CHARLES. Quelques nouvelles dates de manuscrits balinais. BEF 51 (1963) 132-142.

6335 HOOYKAAS, C. Books made in Bali. BIJ 119 (1963) 371-386.

6336 HOOYKAAS, C. La conservation des manuscrits et de la parole parlee en Indonesie. AR 6 (1973) 33-41.

6337 NOORDUYN, J. Traces of an old Sundanese Ramayana tradition. IND 12 (1971) 151-157.

6338 SUKARTO K. ATMODJO, M. M. Second colophon of the *Nagarakrtagama.* BIJ 129 (1973) 277-286.

6339 VOORHOEVE, P. Kerintji documents. BIJ 126 (1970) 369-399.

MANUSCRIPTS – IRELAND

6340 VOORHOEVE, P. Additional Indonesian manuscripts in the Chester Beatty Library, a supplement to the Batak collection. BIJ 124 (1968) 368-385.

MANUSCRIPTS – ITALY

6341 BA, VIVIAN. 110th anniversary of the Gallo manuscript, 1859-1969. JBRS 54 (1971) 115-117.

MANUSCRIPTS – LAOS

6342 LAFONT, PIERRE-BERNARD. Inventaire des manuscrits des pagodes du Laos. BEF 52 (1964) 429-545.

MANUSCRIPTS – MALAYSIA

6343 *Hikayat Raja-Raja Pasai,* a revised romanised version of Raffles Ms 67, together with an English translation by A. H. Hill. JMBRAS 33 pt. 2 (1960) 7-215.

6344 ROOLVINK, R. Two new old Malay manuscripts. B38 pp. 242-255.

6345 VOORHOEVE, P. Notes on some manuscripts in the library of the Dewan Bahasa dan Pustaka, Kuala Lumpur. BIJ 125 (1969) 371-373.

MANUSCRIPTS – NETHERLANDS

6346 RICKLEFS, M. C. On the authorship of Leiden Cod. or. 2191, *Babad Mangkubumi.* BIJ 127 (1971) 264-273.

Manuscripts - Philippines

MANUSCRIPTS - PHILIPPINES

6347 ARCILLA, JOSE S. Random listing
of manuscripts in the Dominican
archives. PS 20 (1972) 176-187.

6348 EGGAN, FRED. Povedano manuscript
of 1572, by Fred Eggan and E. D.
Hester. PS 8 (1960) 526-534.

6349 ELIO Y SANCHEZ, VICENTE. History
of Camiguin. PS 20 (1972) 106-
146.

6350 HART, DONN V. Central Philippines
University's World War II manuscript collection. JAS 25 (1965-
66) 123.

6351 HART, DONN V. Central Philippines
University's World War II manuscript collection. JSAH 6 (Sept.
1965) 129-130.

6352 RIXHON, GERALD. Parte natural of
Alzina's manuscript of 1668, a
source of anthropological data.
AST 6 (1968) 183-197.

MANUSCRIPTS - SINGAPORE

6353 JONES, RUSSELL. Dating of Ms.
Maxwell 93 in the Royal Asiatic
Society Library. JMBRAS 45 pt. 1
(1972) 116-118.

MANUSCRIPTS - THAILAND

6354 JAINI, PADMANABH S. Mahadibbamanta, a paritta manuscript from
Cambodia. SOAS 28 (1965) 61-80.

6355 KACHORN SUKHABANIJ. Two Thai mss.
on the K'unlun kingdom. S93 pp.
70-74.

6356 KEYES, CHARLES F. New evidence
on northern Thai frontier history.
T33 pp. 221-249.

6357 MARR, J. R. Some manuscripts in
Grantha script in Bangkok. SOAS 32
(1969) 281-322.

6358 MARR, J. R. Some manuscripts in
Grantha script in Bangkok, II. JSS
60 pt. 2 (1972) 61-86.

6359 MARTINI, GINETTE. Brapamsukulanisamsam. BEF 60 (1973) 55-78.

6360 MARTINI, GINETTE. Un Jataka concernant le dernier repas de Buddha. BEF 59 (1972) 251-255.

6361 SIMMONDS, E. H. S. Mahorasop in a
Thai Manora manuscript. SOAS 30
(1967) 391-403.

6362 SIMMONDS, E. H. S. Mahorasop II,
the Thai National Library manuscript. SOAS 34 (1971) 119-131.

MANUSCRIPTS - UNITED STATES

6363 TEEUW, A. Malay manuscripts in
the Library of Congress. BIJ 123
(1967) 517-520.

MAPHILINDO *See also* REGIONALISM

6364 BUTWELL, RICHARD. Malaysia and
its impact on the international
relations of Southeast Asia. AS 4
(1964) 940-946.

6365 SHEN YU DAI. Asian unity and disunity, impressions and reflections
1964-65. AST 4 (1966) 135-148.

MAPS

6366 BLAKISTON, N. Maps, plans and
charts of Southeast Asia in the
Public Record Office. SAA 2
(1969) 21-64.

6367 STERNSTEIN, LARRY. Note on three
Polo maps, by Larry Sternstein
and John Black. F38 pp. 347-349.

MAPS - BORNEO

6368 BROEK, JAN O. M. Borneo on maps
of the 16th and 17th centuries.
SMJ 11 (1964) 649-654.

MAPS - BRUNEI

6369 BROWN, D. E. Maps and the history
of Brunei. BMJ 3 pt. 1 (1973) 88-
90.

MAPS - CAMBODIA

6370 PIAT, MARTINE. Note sur la
premiere apparition du Cambodge
dans la cartographie europeenne.
SEIB 48 (1973) 119-120.

MAPS - INDONESIA

6371 VALKENBURG, S. VAN. Topographical
service of the Netherlands Indies.
H57 pp. 471-2.

MAPS - MALAYSIA

6372 ALEXANDER, J. B. Evolution of
land suitability maps in the Federation of Malaya. JTG 18 (1964)
1-6.

6373 EYLES, R. J. Stream representation on Malayan maps. JTG 22
(1966) 1-9.

6374 KOOPMANS, B. N. Structural map of
north and central Pahang. JTG 22
(1966) 23-29.

6375 PANTON, W. P. The 1962 soil map
of Malaya. JTG 18 (1964) 118-124.

6376 SWAN, S. B. ST. C. Land surface
mapping, Johor, west Malaysia.
JTG 31 (1970) 91-103.

6377 SWAN, S. B. ST. C. Maps of two
indices of terrain, Johor, Malaya.
JTG 25 (1967) 48-57.

6378 WYATT-SMITH, J. Preliminary
vegetation map of Malaya with descriptions of the vegetation
types. JTG 18 (1964) 193-213.

MAPS - PHILIPPINES

6379 MUROGA, NOBUO. The Philippines in
old Chinese maps. PHR 2 (1969)
265-268.

MAPS - THAILAND

6380 KENNEDY, VICTOR. Indigenous early
nineteenth century map of central
and northeast Thailand. T33 pp.
315-348.

6381 SALWIDHANNIDHES, PHYA. Study of
early cartography of Thailand.
JSS 50 (1962) 81-89.

6382 STERNSTEIN, LARRY. Catalogue of
maps of Thailand in the museum of
the Royal Thai Survey Department,
Bangkok. JSS 56 (1968) 47-99.

6383 STERNSTEIN, LARRY. Historical
atlas of Thailand. JSS 52 (1964)
7-20.

6384 STERNSTEIN, LARRY. Krung Kao, the
old capital of Ayutthaya. JSS 53
(1965) 83-121.

6385 WENK, KALUS. Zu einer Landkarte
Sued-und Ostasiens. F38 pp. 119-
122.

<u>MAPS - VIETNAM</u>

6386 Haut Nghe-an et Tran-ninh, d'apres
      la geographie manuscrite de Dong-
      Khanh, 1886. SEIB 46 (1971) 86-7.

<u>MARAGTAS</u>

6387 ARANETA, F. Bisayans of Borneo
      and the Tagalogs and Visayans of
      the Philippines. SMJ 9 (1960)
      542-564.

<u>MARAH RUSLI</u>

6388 AVELING, H. G. *Sitti Nurbaja*,
      some reconsiderations. BIJ 126
      (1970) 228-245.

<u>MARANAO</u>

6389 BARADAS, DAVID B. Some implica-
      tions of the Okir motif in Lanao
      and Sulu art. AST 6 (1968) 129-
      168.

6390 Concept of Maranaw culture change.
      DR 18 (1970) 318-325.

<u>MARANAO LITERATURE</u>

6391 FRANCISCO, JUAN R. Maharadia
      Lawana. AST 7 (1969) 186-249.

<u>MARCHAL, HENRI</u>

6392 BOISSELIER, JEAN. Le vie et
      l'oeuvre d'Henri Marchal, 1876-
      1970. SEIB 47 (1972) 7-36.

<u>MARCOS, FERDINAND E.</u>

6393 ROMULO, CARLOS P. Ferdinand E.
      Marcos and Philippine leadership,
      a profile. DR 14 (1966) 223-226.

<u>MARIANO, PATRICIO</u>

6394 ESCASA, NENITA O. Si Patricio
      Mariano at ang kasiningan ng
      kanyang mga dula. PS 19 (1971)
      321-340.

<u>MARIGNOLLI, GIOVANNI DE</u>

6395 COLLESS, BRIAN E. Giovanni de
      Marignolli, an Italian prelate at
      the court of the South East Asian
      Queen of Sheba. JSAH 9 (1968)
      325-341.

<u>MARIVELES, PHILIPPINES</u>

6396 RIVERA, CORNELIO T. Mariveles
      free trade zone, potential and
      opportunity. PS 19 (1971) 733-
      738.

<u>MARMA LITERATURE</u>

6397 BERNOT, D. Etes-vous fachee,
      belle-mere, conte Marma. E92 pp.
      59-66.

<u>MARRIAGE CUSTOMS AND RITES</u>

6398 BERTING, J. Solidarity, stratifi-
      cation and sentiments, the uni-
      lateral cross-cousin marriage ac-
      cording to the theories of Levi-
      Strauss, Leach, and Homans and
      Schneider, by J. Berting and H.
      Philipsen. BIJ 116 (1960) 55-80.

Marriage customs and rites - Malaysia

6399 JOSSELIN DE JONG, P. E. DE.
Circulerend connubium en het
dubbel-unilineale principe. BIJ
120 (1964) 181-194.

6400 KLOOS, P. Duolineaire afstamming
en het Matrilaterale cross-
cousin huwelijk, repliek. BIJ
119 (1964) 368-375.

6401 NEEDHAM, RODNEY. Notes on the
analysis of asymmetric alliance.
BIJ 117 (1961) 93-117.
Comment: BERTING, J. Unilateral
cross-cousin marriage, a reply to
Needham, by J. Berting and H.
Philipsen. BIJ 118 (1962) 155-
159.
Author's reply: Notes on comparative method and prescriptive
alliance. BIJ 118 (1962) 160-182.

6402 NEEDHAM, RODNEY. Symmetry and
asymmetry in prescriptive alliance:
further comments on an alleged
fallacy. BIJ 119 (1963) 267-283.

6403 SHAPIRO, WARREN. Asymmetric
marriage in Australia and Southeast Asia. BIJ 125 (1969) 71-79.

MARRIAGE CUSTOMS AND RITES - BRUNEI

6404 SHARIFFUDDIN, P. M. Royal wedding.
BMJ 1 (1969) 1-4.

MARRIAGE CUSTOMS AND RITES - BURMA

6405 GLEDHILL, ALAN. Community of
property in the marriage law of
Burma. A62 pp. 205-217.

6406 HLA AUNG. Some aspects of marriage under Burmese Buddhist law
and Malayan Muslim law. JBRS 48
(Dec. 1965) 1-15.

MARRIAGE CUSTOMS AND RITES - CAMBODIA

6407 NOU, KER. Kpuon Abah-bibah ou le
livre de mariage des khmers, par
Ker et Nhiek Nou. BEF 60 (1973)
243-328.

MARRIAGE CUSTOMS AND RITES - INDONESIA

6408 BALANG SIRAN, PENGHULU. Murut
wedding in Kalimantan, by Penghulu Balang Siran and Benedict
Sandin. SMJ 11 (1963) 88-93.

6409 DJOJODIGOENO, M. M. Bloedverwantschap en clangemeenschap onder de
Minangkabauers. BIJ 124 (1968)
262-272.

6410 KLOOS, P. Duolineaire afstamming
en het matrilaterale cross-cousin
huwelijk. BIJ 119 (1963) 287-299.

6411 MARETIN, J. V. Disappearance of
matriclan survivals in Minangkabau
family and marriage relations.
BIJ 117 (1961) 168-195.

6412 MASRI SINGARIMBUN. Marriage and
divorce in Mojolama, by Masri
Singarimbun and Chris Manning.
IND 17 (1974) 67-82.

6413 NEEDHAM, RODNEY. Endeh II, test
and confirmation. BIJ 126 (1970)
246-258.

6414 VREEDE-DE STUERS, CORA. A propos
du R.U.U., histoire d'une legislation matrimoniale. AR 8 (1974)
21-30.

MARRIAGE CUSTOMS AND RITES - MALAYSIA

6415 AHMAD IBRAHIM. Muslims in Malaysia and Singapore, the law of
matrimonial property. A62 pp.
182-204.

Marriage customs and rites - Malaysia

6416 BAARTMANS, FRANCIS. Marriage among the Lepo Tau Kenyah, Long Moh, Baram, Sarawak. BMJ 2 pt. 3 (1971) 17-30.

6417 HLA AUNG. Some aspects of marriage under Burmese Buddhist law and Malayan Muslim law. JBRS 48 (Dec. 1965) 1-15.

6418 RABUSHKA, ALVIN. Intermarriage in Malaya, some notes on the persistence of the race factor. AQ (1971) 103-108.

MARRIAGE CUSTOMS AND RITES - PHILIPPINES

6419 INDAH ANNURA. Didactic ballad on marriage as sung by Indah Annura. S92.1 pp. 131-150.

6420 PALLESEN, KEMP. Reciprocity in Samal marriage. S91 pp. 122-142.

6421 TAN, BELEN. Changing marriage patterns among slum dwellers, by Belen Tan and Gatue Medina. GEJ 21 (1971) 31-58.

MARRIAGE CUSTOMS AND RITES - SINGAPORE

6422 AHMAD IBRAHIM. Muslims in Malaysia and Singapore, the law of matrimonial property. A62 pp. 182-204.

6423 FREEDMAN, MAURICE. Chinese kinship and marriage in Singapore. JSAH 3 (Sept. 1962) 65-73.

6424 YEH, STEPHEN H. K. Chinese marriage patterns in Singapore. MER 9 pt. 1 (1964) 102-112.

MARRIAGE CUSTOMS AND RITES - THAILAND

6425 KEMP, JEREMY H. Initial marriage residence in rural Thailand. T33 pp. 73-85.

MARU LANGUAGE

6426 HLA PE. Some cognate words in Burmese and other Tibeto-Burman languages. 1. Maru. JBRS 53 (June 1970) 1-24.

MARX, KARL

6427 ROSALES, RODULFO S. Karl Marx in juristic thought, some views on the Philippine legal order. SLURJ 2 (1971) 681-694.

Masons *See* FREEMASONS

MATHEMATICS STUDY AND TEACHING - PHILIPPINES

6428 MAPA, FELINA G. For greater mathematical literacy. GEJ 9 (1965) 30-35.

6429 MAPA, FELINA G. Mathematics 1 in the general education program. GEJ 1 (1961) 75-83.

6430 NEBRES, BIENVENIDO F. Mathematics and mathematicians in the Philippines. PS 21 (1973) 409-423.

6431 SIOSON, F. M. Mathematical research in the Philippines. PS 15 (1967) 241-258.

MAUNGMAGAN

6432 THA MYINT. Some of the animals of Maungmagan and adjoining shores. JBRS 44 (1961) 197-224.

MAURAND, PAUL

6433　THAI CONG TUNG. Paul Maurand.
　　　SEIB 45 pt. 1 (1970) 117.

MEDANG

6434　SOEKMONO, R. Geographical recon-
　　　struction of northeastern central
　　　Java and the location of Medang.
　　　IND 4 (1967) 2-7.

MEDICAL CARE - CAMBODIA

6435　HUARD, PIERRE. Le medecine
　　　cambodgienne traditionnelle. FA
　　　19 (1963) 676-686.

6436　PIAT, MARTINE. Medecine populaire
　　　au Cambodge. SEIB 40 (1965) 301-
　　　315.

MEDICAL CARE - INDONESIA

6437　BOAK, RUTH A. Needs as seen by
　　　a visiting professor. J37 pp.
　　　174-179.

6438　BRANDEWIE, ERNEST. New Guinea
　　　sickness and values, their dis-
　　　covery and integration. D67 pp.
　　　101-122.

6439　GORKOM, K. W. VAN. History of
　　　cinchona, cinchona cultivation
　　　after Junghuhn's death. H57 pp.
　　　196-203.

6440　GORKOM, K. W. VAN. History of
　　　cinchona, the introduction of
　　　cinchona into Java. H57 pp. 182-
　　　190.

6441　GROOT, K. P. Missionary physicians
　　　and hospitals in the Netherlands
　　　Indies. H57 pp. 126-128.

6442　HONIG, PIETER. History of cin-
　　　chona, a short introductory re-
　　　view. H57 pp. 181-2.

6443　LEERSUM, P. VAN. History of cin-
　　　chona, Junghuhn and cinchona cul-
　　　tivation. H57 pp. 190-196.

6444　TAYLOR, NORMAN. History of cin-
　　　chona, modern developments. H57
　　　pp. 203-207.

6445　WELLINGTON, JOHN S. Medical
　　　science and technology. J37 pp.
　　　165-173.

MEDICAL CARE - MALAYSIA

6446　BAARTMANS, F. Kakus Punan mud
　　　healing rites. SMJ 14 (1966) 81-
　　　86.

6447　BARNES, G. T. Melanau curing
　　　ceremony (Payun) at Mukah. SMJ 14
　　　(1966) 87-90.

6448　GALVIN, A. D. Faith healing rites
　　　among the Kenyahs. BMJ 3 pt. 2
　　　(1974) 13-15.

6449　HARRISSON, TOM. To scale a pango-
　　　lin, by Tom Harrisson and Loh Chee
　　　Yin. SMJ 12 (1965) 415-418.

6450　TAIB BIN OSMAN, MOHD. Patterns of
　　　supernatural premises underlying
　　　the institution of the bomoh in
　　　Malay culture. BIJ 128 (1972)
　　　219-234.

6451　WOLFF, ROBERT J. Modern medicine
　　　and traditional culture, confron-
　　　tation on the Malay peninsula.
　　　T45 pp. 132-144.

Medical care - Philippines

MEDICAL CARE - PHILIPPINES

6452 ALIMURUNG, MARIANO M. Catholic medical press in the Philippines. UN 34 (Sept. 1961) 103-105.

6453 ALIMURUNG, MARIANO M. Hardships and partnerships in medical research in the Philippines. UN 35 (1962) 244-248.

6454 AQUINO, ROSARIO. Medical social service department, U.S.T. hospital. UN 38 (1965) 463-471.

6455 BACALA, J. C. First nursing school in the Philippines. UN 33 (1960) 180-185.

6456 CHENG, CHARLES L. Problems of highland medical practice. B13 pp. 149-155.

6457 GLASSER, PAUL H. Role of the behavioral sciences in medicine. GEJ 14 (1967) 89-97.

6458 LAMBRECHT, GODFREY. Anitu rites among the Gaddang. PS 8 (1960) 584-602.

6459 PONTENILA, MARIA. Sorcery in the framework of folk medicine on Siquijor Island, by Maria Ponte-nila and Hubert Reynolds. SJ 18 (1971) 75-96.

6460 PRATT, WILLIAM F. Summary of background paper on population projects. C47 pp. 104-111. *Comment:* Discussion. C47 pp. 116-127.

6461 REYES, WILFREDO L. Philippine population growth and health development. C47 pp. 423-468.

6462 REYES, WILFREDO L. Summary of background paper, Philippine population growth and health develop-ment. C47 pp. 112-115. *Comment:* Discussion. C47 pp. 116-127.

6463 RODRIGUEZ, LORENZO. Catholic Pharmacists Guild of the Philippines looks at the International Federation of Catholic Pharmacists. UN 34 (Mar. 1961) 135-139.

MEDICAL CARE - SINGAPORE

6464 CHEW, DAVID C. E. Manpower survey of the dental profession in Singapore. MER 11 pt. 2 (1966) 86-109.

6465 CHEW, DAVID C. E. Manpower survey of the pharmaceutical profession in Singapore. MER 12 pt. 1 (1967) 64-78.

6466 KNIGHT, ARTHUR. Tan Tock Seng's Hospital, Singapore. JMBRAS 42 pt. 1 (1969) 252-255.

6467 LEE, Y. K. Medical education in the Straits, 1786-1871. JMBRAS 46 pt. 1 (1973) 101-122.

MEDICAL CARE - THAILAND

6468 BRYANT, JOHN. Health needs of rural Thailand, a challenge to traditional university structure and function. JSS 58 pt. 1 (1970) 45-66.

6469 GRISWOLD, A. B. Rishis of Wat Po. F38 pp. 319-328.

6470 UDOM POSHAKRISHNA. Geschichte der Chirurgie in Thailand, 1828-1922. JSS 51 (1963) 59-78.

6471 WALKER, ANTHONY R. Blessing feasts and ancestor propitiation among the Lahu Nyi (Red Lahu). JSS 60 pt. 1 (1972) 345-373.

MEDICAL CARE - VIETNAM

6472 ANG DVAN NGU. Role of the masses
in raising the standard of welfare. JBRS 43 (1960) 37-40.

6473 BAIN, CHESTER A. Persistence of
tradition in modern Vietnamese
medicine. SA 3 (1974-5) 607-619.

6474 HUARD, PIERRE. Le President
Nguyen Xuan Chu, 1898-1967. BEF
58 (1971) 271-280.

6475 LICHTENWALNER, CRAIG S. Health
progress in Vietnam. C58 pp. 219-
228.

6476 NGUYEN TRAN HUAN. La personnalite
et l'ethique de Lan Ong. SEIB 48
(1973) 503-511.

6477 PHAM DINH HO. La medecine vietnamienne au XVIIIe siecle. Texte
original de Pham Dinh Ho, extrait
du Vu Trung Tuy But, traduit par
Nguyen Tran Huan. BEF 60 (1973)
375-384.

MEGALITHIC MONUMENTS *See also* DEATH
CUSTOMS AND RITES

MEGALITHIC MONUMENTS - INDONESIA

6478 KOENIGSWALD, G. H. R. VON. Remarkable megalith and gold ear
ring from Java, with Borneo affinities. SMJ 11 (1962) 372-375.

6479 LABANG, LIAN. Married megaliths
in upland Kalimantan. SMJ 11
(1962) 383-385.

MEGALITHIC MONUMENTS - MALAYSIA

6480 CHANDRAN, J. Cultural significance of the Pengkalan Kempas
megaliths. JMBRAS 46 pt. 1 (1973)
93-100.

6481 HARRISSON, TOM. Dying megalithic
of North Borneo. SMJ 10 (1962)
386-389.

6482 HARRISSON, TOM. Megalithic evi-
dences in east Malaysia, an introductory summary. JMBRAS 46 pt. 1
(1973) 123-139.

6483 HARRISSON, TOM. The megalithic in
east Malaysia. II. Stone urns
from the Kelabit Highlands, Sarawak. JMBRAS 47 pt. 1 (1974) 105-
109.

6484 HARRISSON, TOM. Megaliths of central Borneo and western Malaya
compared. SMJ 11 (1962) 376-382.

6485 WHITTIER, PATRICIA R. Some Apo
Kayan megaliths, by Patricia R.
and Herbert L. Whittier. SMJ 22
(1974) 369-381.

MEGALITHIC MONUMENTS - PHILIPPINES

6486 LOOFS, H. H. E. Some remarks on
Philippine megaliths. AST 3 (1965)
393-402.

MEGALITHIC MONUMENTS - THAILAND

6487 HUTCHINSON, E. W. Megaliths in
Bayab. S44.2 pp. 78-83.

6488 KAUFFMANN, H. E. Stone memorials
of the Lawa, northwest Thailand.
JSS 59 pt. 1 (1971) 129-151.

MEINESZ, FELIX ALEXANDER VENING

6489 FIELD, RICHARD M. Felix Alexander
Vening Meinesz, exponent of international cooperation through geoscience. H57 pp. 99-104.

Mejia, Pablo

MEJIA, PABLO

6490 TUKAY-GOMEZ, CONSUELO. Pablo
Mejia as a dramatist, with special
reference to his *Say silib na
tobunbolo*. DR 11 (1963) 456-495.

MEKONG RIVER

6491 COHEN, LOUIS A. International
cooperation for development, the
Mekong project. F56 pp. 13-30.

6492 GOMANE, JEANNE-PIERRE. L'amenage-
ment du bassin du Mekong. RSA
(1967) 237-258.

6493 HIRSHFIELD, CLAIRE. Struggle for
the Mekong banks, 1892-1896.
JSAH 9 (1968) 25-52.

6494 JENKINS, DAVID. Lower Mekong
scheme. AS 8 (1968) 456-464.

6495 MENON, P. K. Financing the lower
Mekong River basin development.
PA 44 (1971) 566-579.

6496 PHILIP, NICHOLAS. The Mekong, a
resource for south Vietnam. AS
11 (1971) 371-375.

6497 Project for the Mekong, international action for the future. FA
17 (1960) 2494-2501.

6498 SEWELL, W. R. DERRICK. Mekong
scheme, guideline for a solution
to strife in Southeast Asia. AS
8 (1968) 448-455.

6499 SOLHEIM, WILHELM G. Importance
of anthropological research to the
Mekong Valley Project, by Wilhelm
G. Solheim and Robert A. Hackenberg. FA 17 (1960) 2459-2474.

6500 ZANOBETTI, DINO. Un modele
mathematique du bassin du Bas-
Mekong. FA 19 (1963) 1000-1003.

MELANAU

6501 BARNES, G. T. Melanau curing
ceremony (Payun) at Mukah. SMJ 14
(1966) 87-90.

6502 HARRISSON, TOM. Golden keris handle from Balingian, Sarawak.
JMBRAS 39 pt. 1 (1966) 175-181.

6503 JAMUH, GEORGE. Bornean cooking:
Malay, Melanau, Sea Dayak. SMJ 14
(1966) 158-182.

6504 JAMUH, GEORGE. Bornean cooking
II. SMJ 17 (1969) 202-230.

6505 JAMUH, GEORGE. Melanau population
destroyed by poisonous snake. SMJ
12 (1965) 230-234.

6506 NEWINGTON, P. C. B. Melanau
memories. SMJ 10 (1961) 103-107.

6507 SANDIN, BENEDICT. History of the
people in Balingian subdistrict,
Mukah, Sarawak. SMJ 19 (1971) 37-
45.

6508 SHARIFFUDDIN, P. M. Melanau
spirit figures. BMJ 2 pt. 1
(1970) 104-113.

MELANAU LANGUAGE

6509 CLAYRE, I. F. C. S. Spelling of
Melanau (nee Milano). SMJ 18
(1970) 330-352.

MELANAU LITERATURE

6510 RUBENSTEIN, CAROL. Poems of indigenous peoples of Sarawak: some
of the songs and chants. Pt. 1.
Iban, Bidayuh, Melanau. SMJ 21
(1973) 1-722.

MENTAL ILLNESS – INDONESIA

6511 ABEL, THEODORA M. Free designs of limited scope as a personality index, a comparison of schizophrentics with normal, subnormal, and primitive culture groups. B43 pp. 371-383.

6512 GEERTZ, HILDRED. Latch in Java, a theoretical paradox. IND 5 (1968) 93-104.

6513 MITCHELL, ISTUTIAH GUNAWAN. Socio-cultural environment and mental disturbance, three Minangkabau case histories. IND 7 (1969) 123-137.

MENTAL ILLNESS – MALAYSIA

6514 DENTAN, R. K. Semai response to mental aberration. BIJ 124 (1968) 135-158.

MENTAL ILLNESS – PHILIPPINES

6515 CULLIGAN, JAMES F. National mental health conference. PS 10 (1962) 153-155.

6516 DALTON, J. ALBERT. Trends in Philippine mental health promotion, clinical pastoral training. SLQ 5 (1967) 89-98.

MENTAL ILLNESS – SINGAPORE

6517 RIAZ HASSAN. Urban environment and mental health, with special reference to Singapore and other developing countries. RSAS 1 pt. 2 (1971) 48-65.

MENTAL TESTS – PHILIPPINES

6518 NERI-RABAGO, EMPERATRIZ. Role of psychometrics in guidance. UN 37 (1964) 329-337.

6519 SAMSON, EMMANUEL VIT. Applicability of the Minnesota Multiphasic Personality Inventory to Filipino subjects, by Emmanuel Vit. and Jose A. Samson. UN 33 (1960) 610-620.

6520 SAMSON, JOSE A. Rorschach technique applied to Filipinos. UN 33 (1960) 878-894.

6521 TORRENTO, CARIDAD J. Establishing norms for the Philippine non-verbal intelligence test in Baguio City's public elementary schools and the study of children's categorization responses. SLURJ 2 (1971) 540-614.

Meo *See* MIAO

METEOROLOGY

6522 NIEUWOLT, S. Uniformity and variation in an equatorial climate. JTG 27 (1968) 23-39.

METEOROLOGY – INDONESIA

6523 BRAAK, C. On the climate of and meteorological research in the Netherlands Indies. H57 pp. 15-22.

6524 MOHR, E. C. J. Climate and soil in the Netherlands Indies. H57 pp. 250-254.

METEOROLOGY - MALAYSIA

6525 CHIA LIN SIEN. Analysis of rainfall patterns in Selangor. JTG 27 (1968) 1-18.

6526 CHIA LIN SIEN. Reliability of west Malaysian rainfall records, an objective evaluation. JTG 36 (1973) 1-7.

6527 DALE, W. L. Rainfall of Malaya. JTG 14 (1960) 11-28.

6528 DALE, W. L. Sunshine in Malaya. JTG 19 (1964) 20-26.

6529 DALE, W. L. Surface temperatures in Malaya. JTG 17 (1963) 57-71.

6530 NIEUWOLT, S. Evaporation and water balances in Malaya. JTG 20 (1965) 34-53.

6531 PETERSEN, ROBERT M. Wurm II climate at Niah cave. SMJ 17 (1969) 67-79.

6532 RAMAGE, C. S. Diurnal variation of summer rainfall of Malaya. JTG 19 (1964) 62-68.

6533 SHAM SANI. Observations on the effect of a city's form and functions on temperature patterns, a case of Kuala Lumpur. JTG 36 (1973) 60-65.

METEOROLOGY - PHILIPPINES

6534 HIDALGO, ANGEL. Miguel Selga, 1879-1956, priest and scientist. PS 15 (1967) 307-347.

6535 SELGA, MIGUEL. Catalogue of Philippine typhoons, 414-1703. PS 20 (1972) 12-39.

METEOROLOGY - SINGAPORE

6536 GREENWOOD, PETER G. Buildings and climate in Singapore, by Peter G. Greenwood and R. D. Hill. JTG 26 (1968) 37-47.

6537 NIEUWOLT, S. Urban microclimate of Singapore. JTG 22 (1966) 30-37.

MIANG

6538 VAN ROY, EDWARD. Interpretation of northern Thai peasant economy. JAS 26 (1966-7) 421-432.

MIAO *See also* YAO

6539 BARNEY, G. LINWOOD. Meo of Xieng Khouang Province, Laos. K86 pp. 271-294.

6540 MARKS, THOMAS A. Meo hill tribe problem in north Thailand. AS 13 (1973) 929-944.

6541 RUEY YIH FU. Study of the Miao people. S93 pp. 49-58.

6542 WARD, JAMES THOMAS. U.S. aid to hill tribe refugees in Laos. K86 pp. 295-303.

MIAO LANGUAGE

6543 DOWNER, G. B. Chinese, Thai, and Miao-Yao. L55 pp. 133-139.

6544 DOWNER, G. B. Tone change and tone shift in White Miao. SOAS 30 (1967) 589-599.

6545 HAUDRICOURT, ANDRE G. Limits and connections of Austroasiatic in the northeast. Z52 pp. 44-56.

MIGRATIONS

6546 FILLIOZAT, J. Emigration of In-
      dian Buddhists to Indo-China,
      c.A.D. 1200. S87 pp. 45-48.

6547 SILCOCK, T. H. Migration problems
      of the Far East. S48 pp. 63-84.

6548 YUSOF A. TALIB. Les Hadramis et
      le monde malais, essai de bibli-
      ographie critique des ouvrages
      europeens sur l'emigration hadra-
      mite aux XIXe et XXe siecles. AR
      7 (1974) 41-68.

MIGRATIONS - BURMA

6549 ADAS, MICHAEL. Immigrant Asians
      and the economic impact of Euro-
      pean imperialism, the role of the
      south Indian chettiars in British
      Burma. JAS 33 (1973-4) 385-401.

6550 MORSE, ROBERT. Oral tradition
      and Rawang migration routes, by
      Robert and Betty Morse. E92 pp.
      195-204.

MIGRATIONS - INDONESIA

6551 REID, ANTHONY. Early Chinese
      migration into north Sumatra.
      S89 pp. 289-320.

MIGRATIONS - MALAYSIA

6552 KHOO, S. H. Spatial aspects of
      Foochow settlement in west Malay-
      sia, with special reference to
      Sitiawan, Perak, since 1902, by
      S. H. Khoo, G. Cho and K. E. Chan.
      AST 10 (1972) 77-94.

6553 LOCKARD, CRAIG A. Javanese as
      emigrant, observations on the de-
      velopment of Javanese settlements
      overseas. IND 11 (1971) 41-62.

6554 SANDHU, KERNIAL SINGH. Sikh im-
      migration into Malaya during the
      period of British rule. S89 pp.
      335-354.

6555 SAW SWEE HOCK. Migration policies
      in Malaysia and Singapore, by Saw
      Swee Hock and Cheng Siok Hwa.
      RSAS 1 pt. 3 (1971) 45-61.

6556 SHAMSUL BAHRIN, TUNKU. Growth and
      distribution of the Indonesian
      population in Malaya. BIJ 123
      (1967) 267-286.

6557 SHAMSUL BAHRIN, TUNKU. Pattern of
      Indonesian migration and settle-
      ment in Malaya. AST 5 (1967) 233-
      257.

6558 SMITH, T. E. Immigration and per-
      manent settlement of Chinese and
      Indians in Malaya, and the future
      growth of the Malay and Chinese
      communities. C87 pp. 174-185.

6559 TUGBY, DONALD. The persistence of
      the Mandailing language in west
      Malaysia, by Donald Tugby and
      Brian Embury. SAJSS 1 pt. 2
      (1973) 29-33.

MIGRATIONS - PHILIPPINES

6560 FRANCISCO, JUAN R. Reflexions on
      the migration theory vis-a-vis the
      coming of Indian influences in the
      Philippines. AST 9 (1971) 307-
      314.

6561 GOODMAN, GRANT K. A flood of im-
      migration, patterns and problems
      of Japanese migration to the
      Philippines during the first four
      decades of the twentieth century.
      PHR 1 pt. 1 (1965) 170-193.

Migrations - Philippines

6562 SANIEL, JOSEFA M. Japanese
      minority in the Philippines before
      Pearl Harbor, social organization
      in Davao. AST 4 (1966) 103-126.

MIGRATIONS - SINGAPORE

6563 EE, JOYCE. Chinese migration to
      Singapore, 1896-1941. JSAH 2
      (Mar. 1961) 42-62.

6564 SANDHU, KERNIAL SINGH. Some as-
      pects of Indian settlement in
      Singapore, 1819-1969. JSAH 10
      (1969) 193-201.

6565 SAW SWEE HOCK. Migration policies
      in Malaysia and Singapore, by Saw
      Swee Hock and Cheng Siok Hwa.
      RSAS 1 pt. 3 (1971) 45-61.

6566 VREDENBREGT, JACOB. Bawean migra-
      tions, some preliminary notes.
      BIJ 120 (1964) 109-139.

MIGRATIONS - THAILAND

6567 DHANINIVAT, PRINCE. Thai migra-
      tions. S93 pp. 43-48.

6568 HALLIDAY, F. Immigration of the
      Mons into Siam. S44.1 pp. 65-77.

6569 LeBAR, FRANK M. Observations on
      the movement of Khmu into north
      Thailand. JSS 55 (1967) 61-79.

MIGRATIONS, INTERNAL *See also* URBANI-
      ZATION

MIGRATIONS, INTERNAL - INDONESIA

6570 McNICOLL, GEOFFREY. Internal mi-
      gration in Indonesia, descriptive
      notes. IND 5 (1968) 29-92.

6571 SHAMSUL BAHRIN, TUNKU. Policies
      on land settlement in insular
      Southeast Asia, a comparative
      study. MAS 5 (1971) 21-34.

MIGRATIONS, INTERNAL - MALAYSIA

6572 HAMZAH-SENDUT. Rasah, a resettle-
      ment village in Malaya. AS 1
      (Nov. 1961) 21-26.

6573 McGEE, T. G. Rural-urban migra-
      tion in a plural society, a case
      study of Malays in west Malaysia.
      D92 pp. 108-124.

6574 Plight of Federal Land Development
      Authority settlers in Malaya. JCA
      3 (1973) 367-370.

6575 PRYOR, ROBIN J. Analysis of the
      streams of interstate migrants in
      peninsular Malaysia. SAJSS 2
      (1974) 63-73.

6576 SANDHU, KERNIAL SINGH. Emergency
      resettlement in Malaya. JTG 18
      (1964) 157-183.

6577 SANDHU, KERNIAL SINGH. Saga of
      the squatter in Malaya, a prelim-
      inary survey of the causes, char-
      acteristics and consequences of
      the resettlement of rural dwellers
      during the emergency between 1948
      and 1960. JSAH 5 (Mar. 1964) 143-
      177.

6578 SHAMSUL BAHRIN, TUNKU. Policies
      on land settlement in insular
      Southeast Asia, a comparative
      study. MAS 5 (1971) 21-34.

6579 ZAHARAH BINTI HJ. MAHMUD. Period
      and the nature of traditional set-
      tlement in the Malay peninsula.
      JMBRAS 43 pt. 2 (1970) 81-113.

MIGRATIONS, INTERNAL - PHILIPPINES

6580   ARCINAS, FE R.   Adjustment of
       migrants in an urban enclave,
       Pobres Purok.   GEJ 21 (1971) 1-29.

6581   DWYER, D. J.   Problem of in-migra-
       tion and squatter settlement in
       Asian cities: two case studies,
       Manila and Victoria-Kowloon.   AST
       2 (1964) 145-169.

6582   KRINKS, P. A.   Peasant coloniza-
       tion in Mindanao.   JTG 30 (1970)
       38-47.

6583   McHALE, THOMAS R.   The Philippines
       in transition.   JAS 20 (1960-1)
       331-341.

6584   PASCUAL, ELVIRA M.   Internal mi-
       gration in the Philippines.   C47
       pp. 315-353.

6585   PASCUAL, ELVIRA M.   Population
       redistribution in the Philippines.
       UN 39 (1966) 453-459.

6586   RUBIO, CLARISSA A.   Exploration
       into settler's adjustment in a
       resettlement community.   GEJ 21
       (1971) 83-90.

6587   SHAMSUL BAHRIN, TUNKU.   Policies
       on land settlement in insular
       Southeast Asia, a comparative
       study.   MAS 5 (1971) 21-34.

6588   SIMKINS, PAUL D.   Growth and in-
       ternal migrations of the Philip-
       pine population, 1948 to 1960, by
       Paul D. Simkins and Frederick L.
       Wernstedt.   JTG 17 (1963) 197-202.

6589   VERA, FE V. VITO DE.   Internal
       migration as a temporary solution
       to the population problems of the
       Philippines, by Fe V. Vito de
       Vera and Elfren Micor.   UN 39
       (1966) 440-452.

6590   WERNSTEDT, FREDERICK L.   Migra-
       tions and the settlement of Min-
       danao, by Frederick L. Wernstedt
       and Paul D. Simkins.   JAS 25
       (1965-6) 83-103.

MIGRATIONS, INTERNAL - THAILAND

6591   NG, RONALD.   A study of recent in-
       ternal migration in Thailand.   JTG
       31 (1970) 65-78.

MIGRATIONS, INTERNAL - VIETNAM

6592   BUI VAN LUONG.   Role of friendly
       nations.   L52 pp. 48-53.
       Comment: FALL, BERNARD B.   Com-
       mentary.   L52 pp. 54-58.
       Author's reply: L52 pp. 58-61.
       Comment: FALL, BERNARD B.   Com-
       mentary.   L52 pp. 61-2.

6593   HARNETT, JOSEPH J.   Work of the
       Roman Catholic groups.   L52 pp.
       77-82.

6594   Role of the United States Navy,
       chronology of events.   L52 pp. 63-
       76.

MIIR

6595   BOULBET, JEAN.   Le Miir, culture
       itinerante avec jachere forestiere
       en pays Maa, region de Blao, bas-
       sin du fleuve Daa Dong (Dong Nai).
       BEF 53 (1966) 77-98.

MINANGKABAU

6596   ANDAYA, LEONARD Y.   Raja Kechil
       and the Minangkabau conquest of
       Johore in 1718.   JMBRAS 45 pt. 2
       (1972) 51-75.

Minangkabau

agrarian problems in the Philippines. JSAS 5 (1974) 1-17.

6618 KRINKS, P. A. Peasant colonization in Mindanao. JTG 30 (1970) 38-47.

6619 MacTAVISH, SHONA. Tribal dance in Mindanao. SJ 20 (1973) 217-235.

6620 MADIGAN, FRANCIS C. Early history of Cagayan de Oro. PS 11 (1963) 76-130.

6621 MUNDO, LIGAYA DEL. Marawi in retrospect. JCA 4 (1974) 124-126.

6622 QUIASON, SERAFIN D. Early contacts of the English East India Company with Mindanao. PSSHR 26 (1961) 175-186.

6623 SANIEL, JOSEFA M. Japanese minority in the Philippines before Pearl Harbor, social organization in Davao. AST 4 (1966) 103-126.

6624 SMYTHE, DONALD. Pershing and the Mount Bagsak campaign of 1913. PS 12 (1964) 3-31.

6625 WERNSTEDT, FREDERICK L. Migrations and the settlement of Mindanao, by Frederick L. Wernstedt and Paul D. Simkins. JAS 25 (1965-6) 83-103.

6626 YENGOYAN, A. A. Baptism and Bisayanization among the Mandaya of eastern Mindanao, Philippines. AST 4 (1966) 324-327.

MINDON MIN, KING OF BURMA

6627 BA, VIVIAN. King Mindon and the world fair of 1867 held in Paris, from documents in the French Foreign Office. JBRS 48 (Dec. 1965) 17-23.

6628 DESAI, W. S. King Mindon's funeral. B91 pp. 27-31.

6629 KYAN. King Mindon's councillors. JBRS 44 (1961) 43-60.

6630 MAUNG MAUNG TIN. Mindon Min's development plan for the Mandalay area, by Maung Maung Tin and Thomas Owen Morris. JBRS 49 (1966) 29-34.

6631 YI YI. Judicial system of King Mindon. JBRS 45 (1962) 7-27.

MINDORO

6632 AGPALO, REMIGIO E. Political modernization in the Philippines, the politics and the political elite of Occidental Mindoro. M52 pp. 36-62.

MINES AND MINING *See also* GOLD, PETROLEUM, TIN INDUSTRY

MINES AND MINING - BURMA

6633 AUNG KHIN. Natural soda of Burma. JBRS 44 (1961) 1-11.

6634 TIN TUN. Flotation of Monywa copper ore. JBRS 48 (June 1965) 99-112.

MINES AND MINING - INDONESIA

6635 BEMMELEN, R. W. VAN. On the mineral resources of the Netherlands Indies and their industrial possibilities. H57 pp. 5-10.

6636 KOESOEMADINATA, R. P. Mineral resources in Indonesian development, by R. P. Koesoemadinata and V. E. Nelson. J37 pp. 117-139.

MOLUCCAS

6654   COOLEY, FRANK L. Altar and throne
        in central Moluccan societies.
        IND 2 (1966) 135-156.

MON

6655   COEDES, GEORGE. Les Mons de
        Dvaravati. E92 pp. 112-116.

6656   DHANINIVAT. Sonkrant of Mon as
        recorded in the inscriptions of
        Wat Pra Jetupon in Bangkok. E92
        pp. 117-119.

6657   FOSTER, BRIAN L. Ethnic identity
        of the Mons in Thailand. JSS 61
        pt. 1 (1973) 203-226.

6658   HALLIDAY, F. Immigration of the
        Mons into Siam. S44.1 pp. 65-77.

6659   KHIN ZAW. Folk-song collector's
        letter from the Mon country in
        Lower Burma, 1941. E92 pp. 164-
        166.

6660   PERRIN, JEAN. A propos d'un Bud-
        dha date du pays Mon. E93 pp.
        149-155.

6661   SHORTO, H. L. Dewatan Sotopan, a
        Mon prototype of the 37 nats.
        SOAS 30 (1967) 127-141.

6662   SHORTO, H. L. 32 myos in the
        medieval Mon kingdom. SOAS 26
        (1963) 572-591.

6663   SMITHIES, MICHAEL. Village Mons
        of Bangkok. JSS 60 pt. 1 (1972)
        307-332.

MON KHMER LANGUAGES *See also the fol-
    lowing languages:* BAHNAR, BRU, CHRAU,
    CUA, DANAW, HALANG, KATU, KUI, PACOH,
    SEDANG, STIENG, TODRAH

6664   HAUDRICOURT, A. G. Notes de
        geographie linguistique Austro-
        asiatique. E92 pp. 131-138.

6665   PINNOW, H. J. Personal pronouns
        in the Austroasiatic languages, a
        historical study. C43 pp. 3-42.

6666   POU, SAVEROS. Proto-Indonesian
        and Mon-Khmer, by Saveros Pou and
        Philip N. Jenner. AP 17 (1974)
        112-124.

6667   REIJN, E. O. VAN. Some remarks on
        the dialects of north Kerintji, a
        link with the Mon-Khmer languages.
        JMBRAS 47 pt. 2 (1974) 130-138.

6668   SHORTO, H. L. Structural patterns
        of northern Mon-Khmer languages.
        L55 pp. 45-61.

6669   SHORTO, H. L. Three Mon-Khmer
        word families. SOAS 36 (1973)
        374-381.

6670   THOMAS, DAVID. Mon-Khmer in north
        Vietnam. M59 pp. 74-5.

6671   THOMAS, DAVID. Note on the
        branches of Mon-Khmer. M61 pp.
        139-141.

6672   THOMAS, DAVID. Survey of Austro-
        asiatic and Mon-Khmer comparative
        studies. M57 pp. 149-163.

6673   WATSON, RICHARD. Note on Ta-oi,
        Nge and Nyaheun. M59 p. 130.

6673a   WILSON, RUTH S. Comparison of
        Mu'o'ng with some Mon-Khmer lan-
        guages. Z52 pp. 203-213.

Mon language

MON LANGUAGE

6674 GRISWOLD, A. B. Epigraphic and historical studies. VI. Inscription in old Mon from Wieng Mano in Chieng Mai Province, by A. B. Griswold and Prasert na Nagara. JSS 59 pt. 1 (1971) 153-156.

6675 GUILLON, E. Recherches sur quelques inscriptions Mon. BEF 61 (1974) 339-348.

6676 HLA PE. Tentative list of Mon loan words in Burmese. JBRS 50 (1967) 71-94.

6677 JACOB, JUDITH M. Prefixation and infixation in old Mon, old Khmer, and modern Khmer. L55 pp. 62-70.

6678 LUCE, GORDON H. Rice and religion, a study of old Mon-Khmer evolution and culture. JSS 53 (1965) 139-152.

6679 SHORTO, H. L. Interpretation of archaic writing systems. C43 pp. 88-97.

6680 SHORTO, H. L. Mon labial clusters. SOAS 32 (1969) 104-114.

6681 SHORTO, H. L. Mon vowel systems, a problem in phonological statement. B41 pp. 398-409.

MON LITERATURE

6682 SHORTO, H. L. Mon genealogy of kings, observations on the Nidana Arambhakatha. H18 pp. 63-72.

MONEY *See also* BANKS AND BANKING, FINANCE

6683 CHIANG, HAI DING. Silver dollars in Southeast Asia. AST 3 (1965) 459-469.

6684 FREEDMAN, MAURICE. Handling of money, a note on the background of the economic sophistication of overseas Chinese. S48 pp. 38-42.

MONEY - INDONESIA

6685 CORDEN, W. M. Development of the Indonesian exchange rate system, by W. M. Corden and J. A. C. Mackie. MER 7 pt. 1 (1962) 37-60.

6686 GLASSBURNER, BRUCE. Pricing of foreign exchange in Indonesia, 1966-1967. G52 pp. 396-422.

MONEY - LAOS

6687 JOEL, CLARK. Foreign exchange operations fund for Laos, an interesting experiment in monetary stabilization. AS 6 (1966) 134-149.

MONEY - MALAYSIA

6688 ABRAHAM, W. I. Growth and composition of Malaysia's capital stock. MER 14 pt. 2 (1969) 44-54.

6689 CAINE, SYDNEY. Monetary systems of the colonies, Malaya. S48 pp. 446-453.

6690 CHIANG HAI DING. Origins of the Malaysian currency system, 1867-1906. JMBRAS 39 pt. 1 (1966) 1-18.

6691 CHUNG, N. H. PAUL. Currency reform of the Straits Settlements and Malay states, misunderstood intention, by N. H. Paul Chung and Chong Fei Wan. MER 18 pt. 1 (1973) 48-54.

6692 DAVIES, W. E. Flow-of-funds social accounting, a Malayan example, by W. E. Davies and P. J. Drake. MER 9 pt. 2 (1964) 49–63.

6693 ISMAIL ALI BIN MOHAMED ALI. Role of central banking in industrialization. MER 8 pt. 1 (1963) 14–19.

6694 LEE SHENG YI. The floating of sterling, the impending international monetary reform and the repercussions on Singapore and Malaysia. RSAS 2 (1972) 1–13.

6695 SWIFT, M. G. Accumulation of capital in a peasant economy. S48 pp. 21–37.

MONEY – PHILIPPINES

6696 DAVID, FERNANDO S. Monetary policy and the treasury. PS 11 (1963) 581–586.

6697 EMERY, ROBERT F. Successful Philippine decontrol and devaluation. AS 3 (1963) 274–284.

6698 McHALE, THOMAS R. The Philippines in transition. JAS 20 (1960–1) 331–341.

6699 PAYER, CHERYL ANN. Exchange controls and national capitalism, the Philippines experience. JCA 3 (1973) 54–69.

6700 ROXAS, SIXTO K. Exchange decontrol in the Philippines. PS 10 (1962) 183–205.

MONEY – SINGAPORE

6701 BETZ, GEORGE W. Note on the money supply in Singapore, 1957–1966. MER 12 pt. 2 (1967) 116–121.

6702 CHUNG, N. H. PAUL. Currency reform of the Straits Settlements and the Malay states, misunderstood intention, by N. H. Paul Chung and Chong Fei Wan. MER 18 pt. 1 (1973) 48–54.

6703 LEE SHENG YI. The floating of sterling, the impending international monetary reform and the repercussions on Singapore and Malaysia. RSAS 2 (1972) 1–13.

6704 LEE SHENG YI. Note on banking and currency in Singapore. MER 12 pt. 2 (1967) 122–126.

6705 LIM CHONG YAH. Monetary system and bank structure, by Lim Chong Yah and Doreen Phua. Y52 pp. 127–159.

6706 WONG, K. P. Monthly model of Singapore's monetary sector. MER 19 pt. 1 (1974) 46–64.

MONEY – THAILAND

6707 BROWN, IAN G. Paper currency, the government note issues in the reign of King Chulalongkorn. JSS 60 pt. 2 (1972) 23–44.

6708 SILCOCK, T. H. Money and banking. S49 pp. 170–205.

MONEY – VIETNAM

6709 HUYN VAN LANG. Foreign exchange policy of Viet-Nam. L52 pp. 288–301.
Comment: HUNT, PIERRE. Commentary. L52 pp. 303–306.
Comment: HUNTER, JOHN M. Commentary. L52 pp. 301–303.
Author's reply: L52 pp. 306–7.
Comment: HUNT, PIERRE. Commentary. L52 pp. 307–8.

MONGKUT, KING OF SIAM

6710 BRADLEY, WILLIAM L. Notes on the accession of King Mongkut. JSS 57 (1969) 149-162.

6711 FRANKFURTER, O. King Mongkut. S44.1 pp. 1-17.

6712 GRISWOLD, A. B. King Mongkut in perspective. S44.4 pp. 266-306.

6713 LINGAT, R. La vie religieuse du roi Mongkut. S44.1 pp. 18-37.

6714 SENI PRAMOJ. King Mongkut as a legislator. S44.4 pp. 203-237.

MONKEYS

6715 HARRISSON, TOM. Gibbon in west Borneo folklore and augury. SMJ 14 (1966) 132-145.

6716 HOOIJER, D. A. Prehistoric bone, the gibbons and monkeys of Niah Great Cave. SMJ 11 (1962) 428-449.

6717 POURNELLE, GEORGE H. Observations on captive proboscis monkeys, nasalis larvatus. SMJ 9 (1960) 458-460.

MONTAGNARDS

6718 BUTTINGER, JOSEPH. Ethnic minorities in the Republic of Vietnam. C58 pp. 99-121.

6719 CONDOMINAS, GEORGE. Vietnamiens et Montagnards du centre et sud-Vietnam. C28 pp. 135-146.

6720 JACKSON, LARRY R. Vietnamese revolution and the Montagnards. AS 9 (1969) 313-330.

6721 LEGAY, ROGER. Essai de bibliographie pratique sur les populations Montagnardes du sud-Vietnam, 1935-1966, par Roger Legay et Tran Van Tot. SEIB 42 (1967) 258-299.

6722 PORTET, M. Facteurs economiques et evolution sociale des Montagnards du nord-Indochine. FA 17 (1960) 1925-1933.

MORAYTA, MIGUEL

6723 ACHUTEGUI, PEDRO S. DE. Brent, Herzog, Morayta and Aglipay, by Pedro S. de Achutegui and Miguel A. Bernad. PS 8 (1960) 568-583.

MORGA, ANTONIO DE

6724 CUMMINS, J. S. Antonio de Morga and his *Sucesos de las Islas Filipinas*. JSAH 10 (1969) 560-581.

MORGAN, LEWIS HENRY

6725 BANKS, DAVID J. Malay kinship terms and Morgan's Malayan terminology, the complexity of simplicity. BIJ 130 (1974) 44-68.

MORIK LITERATURE

6726 GALVIN, A. D. Bilian limanjong, a Morik song. SMJ 12 (1965) 163-165.

MOTIVATION

6727 LIU, WILLIAM T. Achievement motivation among Chinese youth in Southeast Asia. AS 5 (1965) 186-196.

MOTIVATION – PHILIPPINES

6728 ORIAN, ANUNCIACION D. Motivations of Saint Louis University graduate students. SLURJ 2 (1971) 317–327.

MOTTE, PIERRE LAMBERT DE LA

6729 CHORIN, L. A. C. From Paris to Ayutha three hundred years ago, June 18th 1660 to August 22nd 1662. JSS 50 (1962) 23–33.

MOUHOT, HENRI

6730 MALLERET, LOUIS. Le centenaire de la mort d'Henri Mouhot, 1826–1861. SEIB 36 (1961) 683–687.

MOUNT CANLAON

6731 BERNAD, MIGUEL A. Ascent of Mount Canlaon. PS 9 (1961) 469–487.

MOUNT MAYON

6732 ESPINAS, MERITO B. Eruptions of Mayon. UN 41 (1968) 251–256.

MOUNT OPHIR

6733 JACK-HINTON, C. Ophirian conjecture, Hispano-Lusitanian optimism in South-East Asia and the Pacific in the sixteenth century. PHR 1 pt. 1 (1965) 194–224.
Comment: RODRIGUEZ, ISACIO R. Literary value of the Ophirian conjecture in the Spanish writings and enterprises of the 16th century. PHR 1 pt. 1 (1965) 224–228.

MOUNTAIN PROVINCE

6734 EGGAN, FRED. Applied anthropology in the Mountain Province, Philippines. S58 pp. 196–209.

MOVING PICTURES – INDONESIA

6735 Bibliographie sommaire. AR 5 (1973) 135–137.

6736 BIRAN, MISBACH JUSA. Les vedettes du cinema indonesien, par Misbach Jusa Biran et K. H. Ramadhan. AR 5 (1973) 165–174.

6737 BONNEFF, MARCEL. Deux images pour un reve, la bande dessinee et le cinema indonesiens. AR 5 (1973) 197–208.

6738 Budget d'un film. AR 5 (1973) 195–6.

6739 LABROUSSE, PIERRE. Drames sociaux et ordre contemporain. AR 5 (1973) 139–163.

6740 LABROUSSE, PIERRE. Entretien avec Fifi Young. AR 5 (1973) 175–177.

6741 LOMBARD, DENYS. De la signification du film silat. AR 5 (1973) 213–229.

6742 LOMBARD, DENYS. Entretien avec Djadug Djajakusuma. AR 5 (1973) 178–182.

6743 LOMBARD, DENYS. Images des cinemas indonesien et malaysien. AR 5 (1973) 103–134.

6744 Points de repere. AR 5 (1973) 54–102.

6745 SIAGIAN, GAJUS. La censure cinematographique. AR 5 (1973) 183–190.

Moving pictures - Indonesia

MULTATULI *(Pseud. of Eduard Douwes Dek-*
ker)

6766 BRAKEL, L. F. Wawelaar en van
      Davelaar. BIJ 128 (1972) 493-4.

6767 CHAMBERT-LOIR, HENRI. Multatuli.
      FA 23 (1969) 305-324.

6768 ENKLAAR, I. H. Wawelaar en van
      Davelaar. BIJ 129 (1973) 493-4.

6769 NIEUWENHUYS, R. Rouffaer en
      Multatuli. BIJ 116 (1960) 408-
      423.

6770 ROELANDT, L. Multatuli et la
      liberte du travail aux Indes
      Neerlandaises. AR 3 (1972) 81-96.

MUMIN, SULTAN OF BRUNEI

6771 BROWN, D. E. Sultan Mumin's will
      and related documents. BMJ 3 pt.
      2 (1974) 156-170.

MUNSHI ABDULLAH

6772 GIBSON-HILL, CARL ALEXANDER. Date
      of Munshi Abdullah's first visit
      to Singapore. JMBRAS 42 pt. 1
      (1969) 107-111.

6773 MOHAMMAD TAIB USMAN. Note on
      Abdullah's account of the Kelantan
      civil war in his *Kesah Pelayaran*
      Abdullah. BIJ 120 (1964) 342-349.

6774 SKINNER, C. Abdullah's voyage to
      the east coast seen through con-
      temporary eyes. JMBRAS 39 pt. 2
      (1966) 23-33.

6775 SKINNER, C. Dating the civil war
      in Kelantan referred to in the
      Kesah Pelayaran Abdullah. BIJ 121
      (1965) 433-437.

MUONG LANGUAGE

6776 BARKER, MILTON E. Vietnamese-
      Muong tone correspondences. Z52
      pp. 9-27.

6777 WILSON, RUTH S. Comparison of
      Mu'o'ng with some Mon-Khmer lan-
      guages. Z52 pp. 203-213.

MURIK LANGUAGE

6778 BLUST, ROBERT A. A Murik vocabu-
      lary, with a note on the linguis-
      tic position of Murik. SMJ 22
      (1974) 153-189.

MURRAY, ERSKINE

6779 PEARN, B. R. Erskine Murray's
      fatal adventure in Borneo, 1843-
      44. IND 7 (1969) 21-32.

MURUT

6780 BALANG SIRAN, PENGHULU. Murut
      wedding in Kalimantan, by Penghulu
      Balang Siran and Benedict Sandin.
      SMJ 11 (1963) 88-93.

6781 CRAIN, JAY B. Domestic family and
      long house among the Mengalong Lun
      Dayeh. SMJ 18 (1970) 186-192.

6782 CRAIN, JAY B. Mengalong Lun Dayeh
      longhouse. SMJ 18 (1970) 169-185.

6783 CRAIN, JAY B. Murut depopulation
      and the Sipitang Lun Dayeh.
      JMBRAS 45 pt. 2 (1972) 110-121.

6784 DEEGAN, JAMES. Community frag-
      mentation among the Lun Bawang.
      SMJ 22 (1974) 229-247.

6785 DEEGAN, JAMES. Some Lun Bawang
      spirit chants. SMJ 18 (1970) 264-
      280.

Murut

6786 HARRISSON, TOM. Ethnological notes on the Muruts of the Sepulut River, Sabah. JMBRAS 40 pt. 1 (1967) 111-129.

6787 LeBAR, FRANK M. Legend, culture history, and geomorphology in the Kelabit-Kerayan highland of north central Borneo. JMBRAS 43 pt. 1 (1970) 183-185.

6788 LEY, C. H. Muruts of Sabah, North Borneo. K86 pp. 353-365.

MURUT LANGUAGE

6789 CLAYRE, B. Preliminary comparative study of the Lun Bawang (Murut) and Sa'ban languages of Sarawak. SMJ 20 (1972) 145-171.

6790 GARMAN, M. A. Murut (Lun Bawang) prepositions and noun particles in children's speech, by M. A. Garman, P. D. Griffiths and R. J. Wales. SMJ 18 (1970) 353-376.

MURUT LITERATURE

6791 DEEGAN, JAMES. Upai Kasan, a Lun Bawang folktale, by James Deegan and Robin Usad. SMJ 20 (1972) 107-144.

6792 JAMUH, GEORGE. Penghulu Lasong Piri speaks from Kalimantan. SMJ 11 (1962) 554-558.

MUS, PAUL

6793 LACOUTURE, JEAN. Paul Mus vivant. FA 23 (1969) 325-329.

6794 MORECHAND, GUY. Paul Mus, 1902-1969. BEF 57 (1970) 25-42.

MUSEUMS - BRUNEI

6795 HARRISSON, TOM. The Brunei Museum. JMBRAS 45 pt. 1 (1972) 119-120.

6796 SHARIFFUDDIN, P. M. Museum development in Brunei, Borneo, 1953-1973. BMJ 3 pt. 1 (1973) 51-61.

6797 SHARIFFUDDIN, P. M. Some problems of getting materials for the Brunei Museum. BMJ 2 pt. 1 (1970) 1-16.

MUSEUMS - MALAYSIA

6798 HARRISSON, TOM. Second to none, our first curator, and others. SMJ 10 (1961) 17-29.

6799 MACASKIE, C. F. North Borneo museums of the past. SMJ 10 (1961) 118-9.

6800 SHAHRUM BIN YUB. Collections of Malay artifacts, a brief general survey. A41 pp. 75-79.

MUSEUMS - PHILIPPINES

6801 ZAMORA, MARIO D. The U.P.-National Museum memorandum of agreement, a historic context. AST 3 (1965) 155-160.

MUSIC See also DANCE, DRAMA

MUSIC - BURMA

6802 BA HAN. Evolution of Burmese dramatic performances and festal occasions. JBRS 49 (1966) 1-18.

6803 MAUNG MAUNG KHA. Acoustical analysis of the vibrations of bamboo bars used in Pattalars. JBRS 46 (June 1963) 53-64.

MUSIC - CAMBODIA

6804 GROSLIER, BERNARD PHILIPPE. Danse
      et musique sous les rois d'Angkor.
      F38 pp. 283-292.

MUSIC - INDONESIA

6805 FARIDA SOEMARGONO. Les chansons
      de Benjamin, un corpus du Jakar-
      tanais? AR 7 (1974) 69-92.

6806 GALVIN, A. D. Five sorts of
      Sarawak and Kalimantan Kenyah
      song. SMJ 11 (1962) 501-510.

6807 HEINS, ERNST L. Cueing the gama-
      lan in Javanese wayang perfor-
      mance. IND 9 (1970) 101-127.

6808 HEINS, ERNST L. Music of the
      Serimpi Anglir Mendung, some
      musicological observations on
      central Javanese ceremonial court
      dances. IND 3 (1967) 135-151.

6809 HEINS, ERNST L. Supplemental
      note on a recent Javanese gamelan
      record. IND 1 (1966) 22-29.

6810 LIEBERMAN, FREDRIC. Relationships
      of musical and cultural contrasts
      in Java and Bali. AST 5 (1967)
      274-281.

6811 McPHEE, COLIN. Balinese wayang
      kulit and its music. B43 pp. 146-
      197.

6812 McPHEE, COLIN. Children and music
      in Bali. B43 pp. 212-239.

6813 SCHREINER, LOTHAR. Gondang-Musik
      als uberlieferungsgestalt altvolk-
      ischer Lebensordnung. BIJ 126
      (1970) 400-428.

MUSIC - MALAYSIA

6814 BASTIN, JOHN. Brass kettledrums
      in Sabah. SOAS 34 (1971) 132-138.

6815 DAVIS, G. C. Borneo Bisaya music
      in western ears. SMJ 9 (1960)
      496-498.

6816 GALVIN, A. D. Five sorts of Sara-
      wak and Kalimantan Kenyah song.
      SMJ 11 (1962) 501-510.

6817 MACEDA, JOSE. Field-recording
      Sea Dayak music. SMJ 11 (1962)
      486-500.

6818 SHEPPARD, MUBIN. Joget gamalan
      Trengganu. JMBRAS 40 pt. 1 (1967)
      149-152.

MUSIC - PHILIPPINES

6819 ATABUG, ALEJANDRA C. Design for
      an interdisciplinary music and
      visual arts course in Philippine
      liberal arts colleges. PS 21
      (1973) 268-292.

6820 ESPINAS, MERITO B. Sarung banggi,
      Bikol's regional song. UN 41
      (1968) 257-260.

6821 KASILAG, LUCRECIA R. Evaluating
      the authenticity of folk songs.
      SJ 8 (1961) 29-33.

6822 KATIGBAK, AIDA. State of music in
      the Philippines. UN 36 (1963)
      373-377.

6823 LEON, FELIPE PADILLA DE. Poetry,
      music and social consciousness.
      PS 17 (1969) 266-282.

6824 MACEDA, JOSE. Magindanao music.
      PS 9 (1961) 666-671.

Music - Philippines

6825 MACEDA, JOSE. Music research at the University of the Philippines. SJ 17 (1970) 395-397.

6826 MACEDA, JOSE. Place of Asian music in Philippine contemporary society. AST 2 (1964) 71-75.

6827 MADRID, ESTHER SAMONTE. Prelude and testament, an anatomy of the art of sound. GEJ 4 (1962) 19-30.

6828 MANGAHAS, RUBY K. State of music research in the Philippines. SJ 17 (1970) 387-390.

6829 MANUUD, ANTONIO G. Arts, 1960. PS 8 (1960) 814-822.

6830 MANUUD, ANTONIO G. The arts, January to June. PS 9 (1961) 505-519.

6831 MAQUISO, ELENA G. Characteristics of indigenous Filipino music. SJ 15 (1968) 92-110.

6832 MARTIN, DALMACIO. Evolution of the national anthem. SJ 15 (1968) 1-6.

6833 MOLINA, ANTONIO J. Philippine music and poetry. M24 pp. 195-206.

6834 NIMMO, H. ARLO. You will remember us because we have sung for you. PS 20 (1972) 299-322.

6835 ORACION, TIMOTEO S. Philippine folk songs according to their origin. SJ 8 (1961) 42-48.

6836 PALMORE, MIRIAM G. Problems of music research in the Philippines. SJ 17 (1970) 391-395.

6837 PANGANIBAN, BIENVENIDO S. P. Jeunesses musicales, its role in the Philippines. UN 35 (1962) 559-562.

6838 RAYMUNDO, GRACIANA, SISTER. Sacred music in the Philippines. SJ 17 (1970) 397-401.

6839 RAYMUNDO, LUZ J. Classification of folk songs according to grade levels. SJ 8 (1961) 49-54.

6840 Review of the performing arts, April to June, 1962. UN 35 (1962) 435-439.

6841 RICE, DELBERT. Developing indigenous church music in the Kalahan society. SJ 16 (1969) 339-359.

6842 ROSARIO, ALEJANDRO DEL. Collection of folk songs. SJ 8 (1961) 25-28.

6843 Survey of the performing arts, July to September, 1961. UN 34 (Dec. 1961) 123-129.

6844 Survey of the performing arts, October to December, 1961. UN 35 (1962) 139-144.

6845 Survey of the performing arts, January to March, 1962. UN 35 (1962) 278-282.

6846 TIEMPO, EDITH L. When music sings in the hearts of the people. SJ 8 (1961) 20-24.

6847 TRIMILLOS, RICARDO D. Setting of vocal music among the Tausug. S91 pp. 65-80.

6848 VERSTRAELEN, EUGENE. Some remarks about Tinguian music. D67 pp. 55-62.

MUSIC - THAILAND

6849 MORTON, DAVID. Thai traditional
music, hothouse plant or sturdy
stock? JSS 58 pt. 2 (1970) 1-44.

6850 PRASIDH SILAPABANLENG. Thai music
at the court of Cambodia, a personal souvenir of Luang Pradit
Phairoh's visit in 1930. JSS 58
pt. 1 (1970) 121-124.

MUSIC - VIETNAM

6851 ADDISS, STEPHEN. Theater music of
Vietnam. SA 1 (1971) 128-152.

6852 DO TRONG HUE. Le chant a cli-
quettes. SEIB 37 (1962) 393-405.

6853 JANSE, OLOV R. T. On the origins
of traditional Vietnamese music.
AP 6 (1962) 145-162.

6854 NGUYEN HUU BA. Towards a renais-
sance of Vietnam's traditional
music. AC 3 (Jan. 1961) 13-16.

6855 NGUYEN HUU TAN. La femme vietnamienne d'autrefois a travers
les chansons populaires. SEIB 45
pt. 1 (1970) 1-113.

6856 THAI VAN KIEM. Panorama de la
musique classique vietnamienne
des origines a nos jours. SEIB 39
(1964) 55-102.

6857 TRAN VAN KHE. Principes de base
dans les musiques de l'Extreme-
Orient. FA 18 (1962) 387-413.

6858 TRAN VAN KHE. Problems of Far
Eastern musical tradition today.
FA 17 (1960) 2261-2266.

6859 TRAN VAN KHE. Le public de con-
cert en Orient devant les changements d'ordre sociologique. FA 21
(1966) 549-562.

MUSICAL INSTRUMENTS - INDONESIA

6860 KUNST, JAAP. Origin of the keman-
ak. BIJ 116 (1960) 263-269.

MUSICAL INSTRUMENTS - MALAYSIA

6861 BASTIN, JOHN. Brass kettledrums
in Sabah. SOAS 34 (1971) 132-138.

6862 HARRISSON, TOM. Curious kettle-
drum from Sabah. JMBRAS 39 pt. 2
(1966) 169-171.

MUSICAL INSTRUMENTS - PHILIPPINES

6863 FRANCISCO, JUAN R. Note on the
Pa'gang, a Tagbanuwa bamboo
musical instrument. AST 5 (1967)
33-41.

MYNGOON, PRINCE

6864 BA, VIVIAN. Prince Myngoon's
odyssey. JBRS 54 (1971) 31-58.

MYRDAL, GUNNAR

6865 BEGHIN, PAUL. Asian education
drama, an appraisal of Gunnar
Myrdal's views on education in
South Asia. SLURJ 3 (1972) 359-
372.

Mythology *See* FOLK LITERATURE

NABALOI

6866 DeRAEDT, JULES. Religious representations in northern Luzon. SLQ
2 (1964) 245-348.

Naerssen, F. H. van

NAERSSEN, F. H. VAN

6867   Professor F. H. van Naerssen.
JOSA 6 (1968) 2-4.

NAKAMURA, ABE-NO

6868   DAUDIN, PIERRE.   Un Japonais a la
cour des Tang, Gouverneur du
Protectorat d'Annam, Abe-No Nakamura, alias Tchao Heng, 698-770.
SEIB 40 (1965) 217-280.

NAM-PHONG

6869   PHAM THI NGOAN.   Introduction au
Nam-Phong, 1917-1934.   SEIB 48
(1973) 167-501.

NAMES - CAMBODIA

6870   LEWITZ, S.   Lexique des noms
d'arbes et d'arbustes du Cambodge,
par S. Lewitz et B. Rollet.   BEF
60 (1973) 117-162.

NAMES - INDONESIA

6871   KOHAR RONY, A.   Indonesian names,
a guide to bibliographic listing.
IND 10 (1970) 27-36.

NAMES - MALAYSIA

6872   BENJAMIN, GEOFFREY.   Temiar personal names.   BIJ 124 (1968) 99-
134.

6873   GALVIN, A. D.   Naming ceremonies
among the Baram Kenyahs.   BMJ 3
pt. 1 (1973) 34-40.

6874   HODGSON, GEOFFREY.   Malay conventional sib-names.   JMBRAS 40 pt.
2 (1967) 106-121.

NAMES - PENAN

6875   NEEDHAM, RODNEY.   Penan friendship
names.   T77 pp. 203-230.

NAMES - VIETNAM

6876   NGUYEN DINH HOA.   Vietnamese names
and titles.   AC 2 (Apr. 1960) 117-
131.

6877   WATSON, RICHARD L.   Pacoh names.
M59 pp. 77-89.

NAMES, GEOGRAPHICAL

6878   JAO TSUNG I.   Some place names in
the south seas in the *Yung-lo Ta-
tien*.   S93 pp. 191-197.

NAMES, GEOGRAPHICAL - BRUNEI

6879   ABDUL LATIF HAJI IBRAHIM.   Variations and changes in the names and
locations of the wards of Brunei's
Kampong Ayer over the last century.   BMJ 2 pt. 3 (1971) 56-73.

NAMES, GEOGRAPHICAL - BURMA

6880   RISPAUD, JEAN.   Contribution a la
geographie historique de la haute
Birmanie.   E92 pp. 213-223.

NAMES, GEOGRAPHICAL - INDONESIA

6881   NOORDUYN, J.   Apa-apa als Java-
anese plaatsnaam.   BIJ 127 (1971)
278-9.

NAMES, GEOGRAPHICAL - MALAYSIA

6882   CHAN, K. E.   Place names in the
Sitiawan area, Perak, by K. E.
Chan, C. H. Cho and S. H. Khoo.
JSAS 2 (1971) 185-194.

NAMES, GEOGRAPHICAL - THAILAND

6883 DHANINIVAT, PRINCE. Wat Sijum, Sriraja and Lavo. JSS 53 (1965) 67-8.

NAN

6884 GRISWOLD, A. B. Epigraphic and historical studies. III. Pact between Sukhodaya and Nan, by A. B. Griswold and Prasert na Nagara. JSS 57 (1969) 57-107.

NANYANG UNIVERSITY

6885 FIC, VICTOR M. Nanyang University, Singapore, plans for research. JSAH 6 (Sept. 1965) 125-128.

NASUTION, A. H.

6886 PAUKER, GUY J. General Nasution's mission to Moscow. AS 1 (Mar. 1961) 13-22.

6887 VAN DER KROEF, JUSTUS M. Nasution, Sukarno and the west New Guinea dispute. AS 1 (Aug. 1961) 20-24.

NATIONALISM

6888 ALISJAHBANA, S. TAKDIR. New national languages, a problem modern linguistics has failed to solve. C44 pp. 515-530.

6889 CALDWELL, MALCOLM. Subversion or social revolution in South-East Asia. N18 pp. 74-106.

6890 EMERSON, RUPERT. Paradoxes of Asian nationalism. T45 pp. 247-258.

6891 EMERSON, RUPERT. Post-independence nationalism in South and Southeast Asia, a reconsideration. PA 44 (1971) 173-192.

6892 GALLAGHER, JOHN. Imperialism and nationalism in Asia. S87 pp. 393-398.

6893 GO GIEN-TJWAN. Role of the overseas Chinese in the Southeast Asian revolutions and their adjustments to new states. N18 pp. 59-73.

6894 GREGORIO, SAMUEL B. Rizal, apostle of Asian nationalism, a review of the 1967 Knights of Rizal seminar-institute. SJ 15 (1968) 16-28.

6895 LLAMZON, TEODORO A. Integrative function of language, do we need a national language to unite us? PS 21 (1973) 259-267.

6896 SINGHAL, D. P. Nationalism and communism in Southeast Asia, a brief survey. JSAH 3 (Mar. 1962) 56-66.

6897 TAMNEY, JOSEPH B. Scarcity of identity, the relation between religious identity and national identity. M52 pp. 175-198.

6898 THAM SEONG CHEE. Cultural diversity and national identity. RSAS 1 pt. 3 (1971) 3-19.

NATIONALISM - BURMA

6899 BUTWELL, RICHARD. Burmese political development, impact of a nationalist heritage. N18 pp. 124-147.

6900 SATHYAMURTHY, T. V. Some aspects of Burmese nationalism. N18 pp. 16-42.

Nationalism - Burma

6901   TIN HTWAY. Role of literature in nation building. JBRS 55 (1972) 19-46.

NATIONALISM - INDONESIA

6902   ABEYASEKERE, SUSAN. Partai Indonesia Raja, 1936-42, a study in cooperative nationalism. JSAS 3 (1972) 262-276.

6903   ABEYASEKERE, SUSAN. The Soetardjo petition. IND 15 (1973) 80-107.

6904   KARTODIRDJO, SARTONO. Some problems on the genesis of nationalism in Indonesia. JSAH 3 (Mar. 1962) 67-94.

6905   McVEY, RUTH T. Taman Siswa and the Indonesian national awakening. IND 4 (1967) 128-149.

6906   NAWAWI, MOHD. A. Punitive colonialism, the Dutch and the Indonesian national integration. JSAS 2 (1971) 159-168.

6907   SUKARNO. Birth of Pantja Sila. T45 pp. 270-276.

6908   SURYADINATA, LEO. Pre-war Indonesian nationalism and the Peranakan Chinese. IND 11 (1971) 83-94.

6909   TJONG TIAT LIEM. Indonesian youth and nationalism in historical perspective. SJ 18 (1971) 190-197.

6910   VAN DER KROEF, JUSTUS M. Indonesian nationalism reconsidered. PA 45 (1972) 42-59.

6911   VAN DER KROEF, JUSTUS M. Nationalism and politics in west New Guinea. PA 34 (1961) 38-53.

NATIONALISM - MALAYSIA

6912   ISHAK BIN TADIN. Dato Onn and Malay nationalism, 1946-1951. JSAH 1 (Mar. 1960) 62-99.

6913   ITAGAKI, YOICHI. Some aspects of the Japanese policy for Malaya under the occupation, with special reference to nationalism. J45 pp. 256-267.

6914   ONGKILI, JAMES P. The British and Malayan nationalism, 1946-1957. JSAS 5 (1974) 255-277.

6915   ROFF, MARGARET. Rise and demise of Kadazan nationalism. JSAH 10 (1969) 326-343.

6916   SHORT, ANTHONY H. Nationalism and the emergency in Malaya. N18 pp. 43-58.

6917   SOENARDNO, RADIN. Malay nationalism, 1896-1941. JSAH 1 (Mar. 1960) 1-33.

NATIONALISM - PHILIPPINES

6918   ALZONA, ENCARNACION. Cultural nationalism in the Philippines. DR 9 (1961) 433-448.

6919   APPLETON, SHELDON. Overseas Chinese and economic nationalization in the Philippines. JAS 19 (1959-60) 151-161.

6920   ARCILLA, JOSE S. Leadership and nationalism, a historian's view. PS 19 (1971) 725-730.

6921   CORPUZ, ONOFRE DIZON. Western colonization and the Filipino response. DR 9 (1961) 139-174.

6922 CRUZ, ROMEO V. Nationalism of Marcelo H. del Pilar. GEJ 5 (1963) 13–25.

6923 Cultural nationalism and world traditions. DR 18 (1970) 306–317.

6924 DEATS, RICHARD L. Nationalism and the churches in the Philippines. SJ 12 (1965) 152–167.

6925 DEATS, RICHARD L. Nicolas Zamora, religious nationalist. A58 pp. 325–336.

6926 ESPIRITU, AUGUSTO CAESAR A. Economic nationalism should effectuate just relationships in society. SJ 14 (1967) 389–394.

6927 GOLAY, FRANK H. Nature of Filipino nationalism. A28 pp. 511–517.

6928 HARRISSON, TOM. Background to Philippine nationalism, the complex impacts of past influences from Brunei Bay and elsewhere. BMJ 2 pt. 1 (1970) 209–237.

6929 HIDALGO, CESAR A. Responsible nationalism through linguistics. DR 18 (1970) 232–247.

6930 HUNT, CHESTER L. Sociology and national integration. SJ 8 (1961) 189–197.

6931 MAHAJANI, USHA. Development of Philippine Asianism. AST 3 (1965) 221–242.

6932 MAJUL, CESAR ADIB. Mabini, architect of the Philippine revolution. GEJ 2 (1961) 47–51.

6933 MAJUL, CESAR ADIB. National identity and the Philippine university. AST 11 pt. 2 (1973) 41–46.

6934 MAJUL, CESAR ADIB. Rizal and Mabini in relation to our national community. GEJ 2 (1961) 14–17.

6935 MARASIGAN, VICENTE. Planetization problems. PS 21 (1973) 311–320.

6936 MARTIN, DALMACIO. Evolution of the national anthem. SJ 15 (1968) 1–6.

6937 MEADOWS, MARTIN. Colonialism, social structure and nationalism, the Philippine case. PA 44 (1971) 337–352.

6938 MERINO, JESUS. Religiosity and nationalism among the Filipinos. UN 38 (1965) 537–545.

6939 MILNE, R. S. Uniqueness of Philippine nationalism. JSAH 4 (Mar. 1963) 75–87.

6940 PANGANIBAN, JOSE V. Language nationalism, and internationalism. UN 34 (Dec. 1961) 57–63.

6941 POETHIG, RICHARD P. Philippine Independent Church, the agony of Philippine nationalism. SJ 14 (1967) 27–54.

6942 PRUDENTE, NEMESIO. Education for nationalism. DR 17 (1969) 59–67.

6943 ROMULO, CARLOS P. Nationalism and the arts and sciences. DR 13 (1965) 127–139.

6944 ROMULO, CARLOS P. Nationalism in Filipinism. A28 pp. 517–519.

6945 ROMULO, CARLOS P. Our national identity. GEJ 5 (1963) 3–12.

6946 SILVESTRE, REYNALDO. Imperialism and Filipino nationalism. PS 21 (1973) 293–310.

Nationalism - Philippines

6947   YABES, LEOPOLDO Y.   Problems of cultural nationalism.   DR 9 (1961) 94-104.

NATIONALISM - SINGAPORE

6948   ALATAS, SYED HUSSEIN.   Modernization and national consciousness. M49 pp. 216-232.

NATIONALISM - THAILAND

6949   GREENE, STEPHEN.   King Wachirawut's policy of nationalism.   T33 pp. 251-259.

NATIONALISM - VIETNAM

6950   DUIKER, WILLIAM J.   Phan Boi Chau, Asian revolutionary in a changing world.   JAS 31 (1971-2) 77-88.

6951   HAMMER, ELLEN J.   Nationalism vs. colonialism and communism.   L52 pp. 3-8.

6952   WOODSIDE, ALEXANDER.   Ideology and integration in post-colonial Vietnamese nationalism.   PA 44 (1971) 487-510.

NATS

6953   NASH, JUNE C.   Living with nats, an analysis of animism in Burman village social relations.   C66 pp. 117-136.

NATURAL RESOURCES - PHILIPPINES

6954   RABOR, DIOSCORO S.   Conservation in the Philippines.   SJ 13 (1966) 594-604.

NE WIN

6955   CADY, JOHN F.   Burma's military dictatorship.   AST 3 (1965) 490-516.

NEGRI SEMBILAN

6956   HAMZAH-SENDUT.   Rasah, a resettlement village in Malaya.   AS 1 (Nov. 1961) 21-26.

6957   HOOKER, M. B.   Early adat constitution of Negri Sembilan, 1773-1824.   JMBRAS 44 pt. 1 (1971) 104-116.

6958   HOOKER, M. B.   Relationship between the adat and state constitutions of Negri Sembilan.   JMBRAS 42 pt. 2 (1969) 155-172.

6959   LABI, MARIA L. C.   Re-analysis of Negri Sembilan socio-political organization.   JMBRAS 42 pt. 2 (1969) 145-154.

6960   LEWIS, DIANE.   Inas, a study of local history.   JMBRAS 33 pt. 1 (1960) 65-94.

NEGRITOS - MALAYSIA

6961   CAREY, ISKANDAR.   Kensiu Negritos of Baling, Kedah.   JMBRAS 43 pt. 1 (1970) 143-154.

NEGRITOS - PHILIPPINES

6962   ORACION, TIMOTEO S.   Bais forest preserve Negritos, some notes on their rituals and ceremonials. Z16 pp. 419-442.

6963   ORACION, TIMOTEO S.   Notes on the culture of Negritos on Negros Island.   SJ 7 (1960) 201-218.

6964 PANIZO, ALFREDO. Negritos or Aetas. UN 40 (1967) 66-101.

6965 PARKER, LUTHER. Report on work among the Negritos of Pampanga during the period from April 5th to May 31st 1908. AST 2 (1964) 105-130.

6966 SCHEBESTA, PAUL. H. Otley Beyer and the research on the Negritos of the Philippines. D67 pp. 12-20.

NEGRITOS - THAILAND

6967 BRANDT, JOHN H. The Negrito of peninsular Thailand. JSS 49 pt. 2 (1961) 123-158.

6968 BRANDT, JOHN H. Southeast Asian Negrito, further notes on the Negrito of south Thailand. JSS 53 (1965) 27-43.

NEGROS ISLAND

6969 CARUMBANA, ESTHER E. Ecological study of certain game birds in southern Negros Oriental, Philippines, by Esther E. Carumbana and A. C. Alcala. SJ 21 (1974) 139-173.

6970 HART, DONN V. Bibliographical essay, guerrilla warfare and the Filipino resistance on Negros Island in the Bisayas, 1942-1945. JSAH 5 (Mar. 1964) 101-125.

6971 LAVINA, EINSTEIN M. Ecological study on Philippine Siganid fishes in southern Negros, Philippines, by Einstein M. Lavina and A. C. Alcala. SJ 21 (1974) 191-210.

6972 Negros 1899-1900, testimony by the American military commander. SJ 19 (1972) 389-424.

6973 ORACION, TIMOTEO S. Notes on the culture of Negritos on Negros Island. SJ 7 (1960) 201-218.

6974 ORTEGA, E. P. Algal association in Caulerpa communities in southern Negros, Philippines, by E. P. Ortega, A. C. Alcala and A. Y. Reyes. SJ 21 (1974) 178-190.

6975 RABOR, D. S. List of the land vertebrates of Negros Island, Philippines, by D. S. Rabor, A. C. Alcala and R. B. Gonzales. SJ 17 (1970) 297-316.

NEPOMUECENO, GRACIANO

6976 ROCES, ALFREDO R. Genre sculpture of Graciano Nepomuceno. PS 8 (1960) 483-490.

NETHERLANDS. RIJKSARCHIEF

6977 MEILINK-ROELOFZ, M. A. P. Sources in the General State Archives in the Hague relating to the history of East Asia between c.1600 and c. 1800. F38 pp. 167-184.

6978 ROESSINGH, M. P. H. Dutch relations with the Philippines, c. 1600-1850, a survey of sources in the General State Archives, The Hague, Netherlands. SAA 2 (1969) 88-103.

NEW YORK PUBLIC LIBRARY

6979 HONIG, PIETER. Central depository library for the Netherlands Indies in New York City, by Pieter Honig and Frans Verdoorn. H57 pp. 462-465.

Newbold, T. J.

face of the city. SLURJ 1 (1970) 745-775.

7000 GUILLERMO, ARTEMIO R. A readership survey of *Taliba*, a Philippine newspaper. SJ 21 (1974) 356-366.

7001 GUILLERMO, ARTEMIO R. Tagalog press of the Philippines. SJ 19 (1972) 524-549.

7002 Indispensable *Collegian*. DR 18 (1970) 371-374.

7003 KALAW, TEODORO M. *El Renacimiento* libel suit. DR 11 (1963) 285-298.

7004 LENT, JOHN A. Philippine provincial press. SJ 16 (1969) 273-290.

7005 LENT, JOHN A. The Philippines. A77 pp. 191-209.

7006 LENT, JOHN A. Press of the Philippines, its history and problems. SJ 14 (1967) 67-90.

7007 MALAY, CAROLINA. Anatomie de la presse philippine. FA 24 (1970) 283-324.

7008 MASLOG, CRISPIN. *Bohol Chronicle*, case study of a successful community paper. SJ 17 (1970) 195-210.

7009 OWEN, THEODORE. Daily press. UN 36 (1963) 426-432.

7010 YABES, LEOPOLDO Y. The Philippine press and its democratic tradition. DR 8 (1960) 495-510.

NEWSPAPERS - SINGAPORE

7011 BIRCH, E. W. Vernacular press in the Straits. JMBRAS 42 pt. 1 (1969) 192-195.

7012 BURE, JEAN-REMY. La presse chinoise quotidienne de Singapour. AR 6 (1973) 185-204.

7013 GIBSON-HILL, CARL ALEXANDER. *Singapore Chronicle*, 1824-37. JMBRAS 42 pt. 1 (1969) 166-191.

7014 HILL, R. D. Materials for historical geography and economic history of Southeast Asia in nineteenth century Malayan newspapers. JMBRAS 44 pt. 2 (1971) 151-198.

7015 LIM PUI HUEN, PATRICIA. Newspapers published in the Malaysian area, with a union list of local holdings. SAA 2 (1969) 157-198.

7016 TAMNEY, JOSEPH B. The *Singapore Herald* affair. AST 10 (1972) 256-261.

7017 TAN PENG SIEW. Malaysia and Singapore. A77 pp. 179-190.

NEWSPAPERS - THAILAND

7018 MITCHELL, JOHN D. Thailand. A77 pp. 210-233.

NEWSPAPERS - VIETNAM

7019 NGUYEN THAI. South Vietnam. A77 pp. 234-254.

NGAJU

7020 HARRISSON, TOM. Iban and Ngaju, a significant bird folklore parallel, by Tom and Barbara Harrisson. SMJ 16 (1968) 186-194.

Ngaju language

NGAJU LANGUAGE

7021   MOHRING, H. Why did the Ngaju
       Dayak call the Malays Olo Masi?
       SMJ 20 (1972) 315-322.

NGEQ LANGUAGE

7022   SMITH, RONALD L. Ngeq phonemes.
       M61 pp. 77-84.

7023   SMITH, RONALD L. Reduplication
       in Ngeq. M61 pp. 85-111.

NGO DINH DIEM

7024   HAMMER, ELLEN J. Political back-
       ground of Ngo Dinh Diem. L52 pp.
       37-41.
       Comment: BUTTINGER, JOSEPH.
       Commentary. L52 pp. 42-44.

7025   SCIGLIANO, ROBERT. Vietnam,
       politics and religion. AS 4
       (1964) 666-673.

NGUYEN DINH CHIEU

7026   VO LONG TE. Chronique culturelle,
       presence du poete, Nguyen Dinh
       Chieu, 1822-1888. SEIB 46 (1971)
       375-385.

NGUYEN DU

7027   BARUCH, JACQUES. *Le Kim Van Kieu,*
       poeme national vietnamien de
       Nguyen Du. RSA (1963) 185-213.

NGUYEN DYNASTY

7028   CHEN CHING HO. Imperial archives
       of the Nguyen Dynasty, 1802-1945.
       JSAH 3 (Sept. 1962) 111-128.

NGUYEN TRUONG TO

7029   THAI VAN KIEM. Nguyen Truong To,
       patriote, reformiste, poete et
       homme d'action. SEIB 47 (1972)
       489-502.

Nguyen Tuong Tam *See* NHAT LINH

NGUYEN XUAN CHU

7030   HUARD, PIERRE. Le president
       Nguyen Xuan Chu, 1898-1967. BEF
       58 (1971) 271-280.

NHAT LINH

7031   O'HARROW, STEPHEN. Some back-
       ground notes on Nhat Linh (Nguyen
       Tuong Tam), 1906-1963. FA 22
       (1968) 205-220.

NIAH CAVES *See also* ARCHAEOLOGY -
MALAYSIA - SARAWAK - NIAH CAVES

7032   HARRISSON, BARBARA. Aide-memoire
       in Niah cave guano. SMJ 13 (1966)
       321-2.

7033   HARRISSON, TOM. Bats netted in
       and round Niah Great Cave, 1965-6.
       SMJ 14 (1966) 229-233.

7034   HARRISSON, TOM. Cold blooded
       vertebrates of the Niah cave area.
       SMJ 14 (1966) 276-286.

7035   HARRISSON, TOM. Collocalia
       breeding, July 1961 at Niah. SMJ
       10 (1961) 269.

7036   HARRISSON, TOM. Flying foxes
       (Pteropus) over Niah cave area,
       1965-66, by Tom and Barbara Har-
       risson. SMJ 14 (1966) 234-236.

7037 HARRISSON, TOM. Incised figures
      from the top of a lid found on
      Samui Island, Thailand. AP 9
      (1966) 111-2.

7038 HARRISSON, TOM. Miniature burial
      pot from Niah Great Cave. SMJ 15
      (1967) 91-2.

7039 HARRISSON, TOM. Niah's new cave
      dwelling gecko, habits. SMJ 10
      (1961) 277-282.

7040 HARRISSON, TOM. Notes on robber
      wasps (Sphex diabolicus) in Niah
      caves. SMJ 14 (1966) 287-290.

7041 INGER, ROBERT F. New cave dwell-
      ing lizard of the genus Cyrto-
      dactylus from Niah, by Robert F.
      Inger and Wayne King. SMJ 10
      (1961) 274-276.

7042 MEDWAY, LORD. Batu sep, a modern
      stone artifact. SMJ 15 (1967)
      93-4.

7043 MEDWAY, LORD. Reproductive cycle
      of lesser bent-winged bat, Miniop-
      terus australis at Niah. SMJ
      18 (1970) 401-409.

7044 PETERSEN, ROBERT M. Wurm II
      climate at Niah cave. SMJ 17
      (1969) 67-79.

7045 WALL, J. R. D. Quaternary geo-
      morphological history of north
      Sarawak with special reference to
      the Subis Karst, Niah. SMJ 15
      (1967) 97-125.

NIAH LITERATURE

7046 MEDWAY, LORD. Niah ballad. SMJ
      9 (1960) 393-407.

NIAS

7047 DANANDJAJA, JAMES. Comparative
      analysis of kinship in central
      Kalimantan and Nias. SMJ 19
      (1971) 237-252.

7048 HEINE-GELDERN, ROBERT. Survivance
      de motifs de l'ancien art Boud-
      dhique de l'Inde dans l'Ile de
      Nias. G83 pp. 299-306.

7049 HOLT, CLAIRE. Dances of Sumatra
      and Nias, notes by Claire Holt.
      IND 11 (1971) 1-20.

7050 LAIYA, BAMBOWO. Attitude of Nias
      towards Christianity. SJ 21
      (1974) 100-115.

North Borneo Company *See* BRITISH
  NORTH BORNEO CHARTERED COMPANY

NOZALEDA Y VILLA, BERNARDINO

7051 GUERRERO, LEON MA. Nozaleda and
      Pons, two Spanish friars in exo-
      dus. A58 pp. 172-202.

NU, U

7052 BUTWELL, RICHARD. Four failures
      of U Nu's second premiership. AS
      2 (1962) 3-11.

7053 BUTWELL, RICHARD. U Nu's second
      comeback try. AS 9 (1969) 868-
      876.

7054 NU, U. Speech before the Overseas
      Press Club, New York, on 10th
      Sept. 1969. JCA 1 pt. 2 (1970)
      86-90.

7055 WALINSKY, LOUIS J. Rise and fall
      of U Nu. PA 38 (1965) 269-281.

Nung

NUNG

7056 SAUL, JANICE E. Nung funerals.
      SA 2 (1972-3) 130-135.

Nutrition *See* DIET

NYAHEUN LANGUAGE

7057 DAVIS, JOHN J. Notes on Nyaheun
      grammar. M61 pp. 69-75.

OBITUARIES *The people listed in this
  section have obituaries cited under
  their names*

        Aichele, Walther
        Aikman, Gordon
        Anderson, Charles Martin
        Anuman Rajadhon
        Ba Han
        Ba Lwin
        Ba Shin
        Bambang Kusnohadi
        Benda, Harry J.
        Berthe, Louis
        Beyer, H. Otley
        Bezacier, Louis
        Blas, Angel de
        Bosch, F. D. K.
        Bourotte, Bernard
        Braddell, Roland St. John
        Castanon, Jesus
        Cham Thongkhamwan
        Chorin, L. A. C.
        Chula Chakrabongse, Elisabeth
        Coedes, George
        Cuisinier, Jeanne
        Damais, Louis-Charles
        Daudin, Pierre
        Djajadiningrat, Pangeran Ario
          Hoesein
        Doan Quan Tan
        Drabbe, Petrus
        Durand, Maurice
        Evans, Ivor Hugh Norman
        Fall, Bernard

        Gayet, George
        Geelmuyden, Nicoloi
        Gibson-Hill, Carl Alexander
        Glaize, Maurice
        Goloubew, Victor
        Goris, Roelof
        Guilleminet, Paul
        Hart, G. H. C.
        Hawkins, Everett D.
        Heine-Geldern, Robert von
        Holt, Claire
        Hoop, A. N. J. Th. a Th. van der
        Hutchinson, Edward Walter
        Jamuh, George
        Josselin de Jong, Jan Petrus
          Benjamin de
        Keuning, J.
        Korn, Victor Emanuel
        Labrador, Juan
        Le May, Reginald
        Macgreggor, Ian Alistair
        Malleret, Louis
        Marchal, Henri
        Maurand, Paul
        Mus, Paul
        Ockeloen, Gijsbertus Franciscus
        Poerbatjaraka
        Purwadarminta, W. J. S.
        Rassers, Willem Huibert
        Recto, Claro M.
        Ridley, Henry Nicholas
        Rouffaer, G. P.
        Sartono, R. M.
        Sithiporn Kridakara
        Sitsen, P. H.
        Soe Hok Gie
        Soetjipto Wirjosoeparto
        Sumardjo, Trisno
        Sumonajat Svastikul, Momrajawongs
        Tran Ham Tan
        Verschueren, Jan
        Vilallonga, Joaquin
        Winstedt, Richard O.

OCKELOEN, GIJSBERTUS FRANCISCUS

7058 ECHOLS, JOHN M. In memoriam, G.
      F. Ockeloen, 1904-1966. IND 2
      (1966) 157-159.

ODORIC OF PORDENONE

7059   NICHOLL, ROBERT. Odoric of Porde-
       none, a fourteenth century visitor
       to Borneo. BMJ 3 pt. 1 (1973)
       62-65.

OGER, HENRI-JOSEPH

7060   HUARD, PIERRE. Le pionnier de la
       technologie vietnamienne, Henri
       Oger, 1885-1936. BEF 57 (1970)
       215-217.

Oil   *See*   PETROLEUM

OIL PALM INDUSTRY - MALAYSIA

7061   GRAY, B. S. Potential of the oil
       palm in Malaya. JTG 17 (1963)
       127-132.

7062   ROSENQUIST, E. A. Soils and the
       fertilization of rubber and oil
       palm. JTG 18 (1964) 148-156.

OIRATA LANGUAGE

7063   COWAN, H. K. J. Oirata language.
       C43 pp. 360-370.

ONN, DATO

7064   ISHAK BIN TADIN. Dato Onn and
       Malay nationalism, 1946-1951.
       JSAH 1 (Mar. 1960) 62-99.

ORANG LAUT

7065   GIBSON-HILL, CARL ALEXANDER.
       Orang Laut of Singapore River and
       the Sampan Panjang. JMBRAS 42 pt.
       1 (1969) 118-132.

7066   RIDLEY, H. N. Orang Laut of
       Singapore. JMBRAS 42 pt. 1 (1969)
       117.

7067   SKEAT, W. K. Orang Laut of Singa-
       pore, by W. K. Skeat and H. N.
       Ridley. JMBRAS 42 pt. 1 (1969)
       114-116.

ORANGUTANS - MALAYSIA

7068   CHIN, LUCAS. Notes on orangutan
       and marine turtles. SMJ 18 (1970)
       414-5.

7069   CHIN, LUCAS. Notes on orangutans,
       bird ringing project and turtles.
       SMJ 16 (1968) 249-252.

7070   CHIN, LUCAS. Notes on turtles and
       orangutans, 1969. SMJ 17 (1969)
       403-4.

7071   GUAN ANAK SURENG. Orangutan on
       Mt. Kinabalu, 1961. SMJ 10 (1961)
       262-3.

7072   GUAN ANAK SURENG. Six orang
       stories. SMJ 9 (1960) 452-457.

7073   HAILE, N. S. Orang-human co-
       existence in North Borneo. SMJ 11
       (1963) 259-261.

7074   HARRISSON, BARBARA. Nesting be-
       haviour of semi-wild juvenile
       orangutans. SMJ 17 (1969) 336-
       384.

7075   HARRISSON, BARBARA. Orangutan,
       what chances of survival? SMJ 10
       (1961) 238-261.

7076   HARRISSON, BARBARA. Study of
       orangutan behaviour in semi-wild
       state, 1956-1960. SMJ 9 (1960)
       422-447.

Orangutans - Malaysia

Pahang.   JMBRAS 47 pt. 2 (1974) 123-129.

7098   VOON PHIN KEONG.   Size aspects of rubber smallholdings in west Malaysia, a case study of Bentong, Pahang.   JTG 34 (1972) 65-76.

PAKIL

7099   Our historical heritage, Pakil. UN 34 (1961) 71-80.

PALAUNG LANGUAGE

7100   SHORTO, H. L.   Structural patterns of northern Mon-Khmer languages. L55 pp. 45-61.

7101   SHORTO, H. L.   Word and syllable patterns in Palaung.   SOAS 23 (1960) 544-557.

PALAWAN

7102   KIKUCHI, YASUSHI.   Preliminary notes on the social structure of the Palawan, Palawan Island, Philippines.   AST 9 (1971) 315-327.

PALE LANGUAGE

7103   JANZEN, HERMANN.   Grammar analysis of Pale clauses and phrases, by Hermann and Margarete Janzen. JBRS 55 (1972) 47-100.

PALEOGRAPHY - MALAYSIA

7104   HARRISSON, TOM.   Kalimantan writing board and the Mamat festival. SMJ 13 (1966) 287-295.

7105   HARRISSON, TOM.   Unexplained Kalimantan Murut-Kelabit boards and burial rites, by Tom Harrisson and Penghulu Balang Siran.   SMJ 13 (1966) 335-340.

7106   MAPING MADANG.   Adat Suen, Sebob graded rites, by Maping Madang and A. D. Galvin.   SMJ 13 (1966) 305-320.

PALEOGRAPHY - PHILIPPINES

7107   FRANCISCO, JUAN R.   Palaeographic studies in the Philippines.   SMJ 13 (1966) 417-426.

PALI LANGUAGE

7108   BAPAT, P. V.   Anacchariya, anascarya, anvascarya.   F38 pp. 227-232.

7109   CHI HSIEN LIN.   Language problem of primitive Buddhism.   JBRS 43 (1960) 9-15.

PALI LANGUAGE - BURMA

7110   HLA PE.   Some adapted Pali loan words in Burmese.   B91 pp. 71-99.

7111   TIN LWIN.   Pali-Burmese Nissaya. JBRS 46 (June 1963) 43-51.

PALI LITERATURE

7112   MARTINI, GINETTE.   Brapamsukulanisamsam.   BEF 60 (1973) 55-78.

7113   MARTINI, GINETTE.   Un Jataka concernant le dernier repas de Buddha.   BEF 59 (1972) 251-255.

Palmer, John

PALMER, JOHN

7114 TARLING, NICHOLAS. The Palmer loans. BIJ 119 (1963) 161-188.

7115 TARLING, NICHOLAS. Prince of merchants and the lion city. JMBRAS 37 pt. 1 (1964) 20-40.

PAMPANGA

7116 LARKIN, JOHN A. Causes of an involuted society, a theoretical approach to rural Southeast Asian history. JAS 30 (1970-1) 783-795.

7117 PARKER, LUTHER. Report on work among the Negritos of Pampanga during the period from April 5th to May 31st 1908. AST 2 (1964) 105-130.

7118 SANTICO, REALIDAD Q. Research in a Pampanga village. AST 7 (1969) 264-269.

PAMPANGA LITERATURE

7119 AGUAS, JUAN S. Juan Crisostomo Soto and Pampangan drama. DR 10 (July 1962) 1-138.

7120 PANIZO, ALFREDO. Introduction to the Pampango theatre, by Alfredo Panizo and Rodolfo V. Cortez. UN 41 (1968) 124-137.

7121 PEREZ, ALEJANDRINO Q. Pampango folklore, proverbs, riddles, folksongs. UN 41 (1968) 67-123.

PANGANIBAN, CIRIO H.

7122 MEDINA, B. S. Panganiban, tradisyon at modernismo. PS 19 (1971) 287-306.

PANGASINAN

7123 ANDERSON, JAMES N. Land and society in a Pangasinan community. E78 pp. 171-192.

PANJI

7124 DHANI NIVAT, PRINCE. Siamese versions of the Panji romance. J41 pp. 95-101.

7125 RAS, J. J. Panji romance and W. H. Rassers' analysis of its theme. BIJ 129 (1973) 411-456.

7126 TERWEN-DE LOOS, J. De Pandji-reliefs van oudheid LXV op de Gunung Bekel Penanggungan. BIJ 127 (1971) 321-330.

PANTAR LANGUAGE

7127 WATUSEKE, F. S. Gegevens over de taal van Pantar-een Irian taal. BIJ 129 (1973) 340-345.
Comment: ANCEAUX, J. C. Comment. BIJ 129 (1973) 345-6.

PANTHAYS

7128 THAUNG. Panthay interlude in Yunnan, a study in vicissitudes through the Burmese kaleidoscope. B91 pp. 473-483.

7129 YEGAR, MOSHE. Panthay (Chinese Muslims) of Burma and Yunnan. JSAH 7 (Mar. 1966) 73-85.

PAPIA KRISTANG

7130 HANCOCK, IAN F. Some Dutch derived items in Papia Kristang. BIJ 126 (1970) 352-356.

Partai Komunis Indonesia

PARAMANUCHITCHINOROT, PRINCE

7131 WYATT, DAVID K. Abridged royal
chronicle of Ayudhya of Prince
Paramanuchitchinorot. JSS 61 pt.
1 (1973) 25-50.

PARDO, FELIPE

7132 CUMMINS, JAMES S. Archbishop
Felipe Pardo's last will. A58
pp. 105-112.

PARDO DE TAVERA, T. H.

7133 FRANCISCO, JUAN R. Further notes
on Pardo de Tavera's *El Sanscrito
en la lengua Tagalog*. AST 6
(1968) 223-234.
Comment: SALAZAR, Z. A. Footnote
to Dr. Francisco's notes on Tavera. AST 6 (1968) 431-444.

7134 ONORATO, MICHAEL P. Five statements. PS 17 (1969) 756-780.

PARIS. BIBLIOTHEQUE NATIONALE

7135 MARTINI, GINETTE. Les titres des
Jataka dan les manuscrits Pali de
la Bibliotheque Nationale de
Paris. BEF 51 (1963) 79-93.

PARNASSIA

7136 CHIEN CHO PO. Notes on the distribution of Chinese parnassia.
JBRS 43 (1960) 17-23.

PARTAI KOMUNIS INDONESIA

7137 BASS, JEROME. The PKI and the
attempted coup. JSAS 1 pt. 1
(1970) 96-105.

7138 FEITH, HERBERT. President Soekarno, the army and the Communists,
the triangle changes shape. AS 4
(1964) 969-980.

7139 HINDLEY, DONALD. Indonesian communists and the CPSU twenty second congress. AS 2 (Mar. 1962)
20-27.

7140 HINDLEY, DONALD. Political power
and the October 1965 coup in Indonesia. JAS 26 (1966-7) 237-249.

7141 MORTIMER, REX. Class, social
cleavage and Indonesian communism.
IND 8 (1969) 1-20.

7142 PAUKER, EWA T. Has the Sukarno
regime weakened the PKI? AS 4
(1964) 1058-1070.

7143 PAUKER, GUY J. Current communist
tactics in Indonesia. AS 1 (May
1961) 26-35.

7144 Statement by the Central Committee
of the Communist Party of Indonesia. JCA 1 pt. 2 (1970) 91-94.

7145 Statement of the Central Committee
of the Communist Party of Indonesia. JCA 2 (1972) 335-337.

7146 VAN DER KROEF, JUSTUS M. Dilemmas
of Indonesian communism. PA 35
(1962) 141-159.

7147 VAN DER KROEF, JUSTUS M. Indonesian communism and the changing
balance of power. PA 37 (1964)
357-383.

7148 VAN DER KROEF, JUSTUS M. Indonesian communism's revolutionary
gymnastics. AS 5 (1965) 217-232.

7149 VAN DER KROEF, JUSTUS M. Indonesian communist policy and the
sixth party congress. PA 33
(1960) 227-249.

Partai Komunis Indonesia

7167 LYNCH, FRANK. Philippines Peace Corps survey. SLQ 5 (1967) 67-76.

7168 McCARRON, JOHN W. Peace Corps. PS 10 (1962) 150-1.

7169 MAHAJANI, USHA. American people to people democracy, the Peace Corps in the Philippines. AS 4 (1964) 777-787.

PEASANTRY

7170 BENDA, HARRY J. Peasant movements in colonial Southeast Asia. AST 3 (1965) 420-434.

7171 CALDWELL, MALCOLM. Role of the peasantry in the revolution. JCA 1 pt. 1 (1970) 50-64.

7172 HINDLEY, DONALD. Political conflict potential, politicization, and the peasantry in the underdeveloped countries. AST 3 (1965) 470-489.

7173 SCOTT, JAMES. Politics of survival, peasant response to progress in Southeast Asia, by James Scott and Ben Kerkvliet. JSAS 4 (1973) 241-268.

PEASANTRY - INDONESIA

7174 BENDA, HARRY J. Samin movement, by Harry J. Benda and Lance Castles. BIJ 125 (1969) 207-240.

7175 KING, VICTOR T. Some observations on the Samin movement of north central Java, suggestions for the theoretical analysis of the dynamics of rural unrest. BIJ 129 (1973) 457-481.

7176 MULDER, NIELS. Saminism and Buddhism, a note on a field visit to a Samin community. AQ (1974) 253-258.

7177 THE SIAUW GIAP. Samin and Samat movements in Java, two examples of peasant resistance. RSA (1967) 303-310.

7178 THE SIAUW GIAP. Samin and Samat movements in Java, two examples of peasant resistance. RSA (1968) 107-113.

7179 THE SIAUW GIAP. Samin movement in Java, complementary remarks. RSA (1969) 63-77.

PEASANTRY - MALAYSIA

7180 Peasants' appeal, an appeal to all friends in the city from the peasants of Telok Gong. JCA 3 (1973) 120-1.

7181 Plight of Federal Land Development Authority settlers in Malaya. JCA 3 (1973) 367-370.

PEASANTRY - PHILIPPINES

7182 DAVIS, WILLIAM G. Economic limitations and social relationships in a Philippine marketplace, capital accumulation in a peasant economy. V27 pp. 1-28.

7183 FUJIMOTO, ISAO. Some considerations on a cultural majority, the Filipino farmer and agricultural development. Z16 pp. 343-365.

7184 KERKVLIET, BEN J. Peasant society and unrest prior to the Huk revolution in the Philippines. AST 9 (1971) 164-213.

7185 LEE, DAVID C. Some reflections about the Cofradia de San Jose as

Peasantry - Philippines

7205 TAE YUL NAM. Singapore's one party system, its relationship to democracy and political stability. PA 42 (1969) 465-480.

PEPPER - CAMBODIA

7206 GARRY, ROBERT J. Changing fortunes and future of pepper growing in Cambodia. JTG 17 (1963) 133-142.

PEPPER - MALAYSIA

7207 HILL, R. D. Pepper growing in Johore. JTG 28 (1969) 32-39.

PERAK

7208 CHAN, K. E. Place names in the Sitiawan area, Perak, by K. E. Chan, C. H. Cho and S. H. Khoo. JSAS 2 (1971) 185-194.

7209 FEE. Kampong Padre, a Tamil settlement near Bagan Serai, Perak. JMBRAS 36 pt. 1 (1963) 153-181.

7210 KHOO, S. H. Spatial aspects of Foochow settlement in west Malaysia, with special reference to Sitiawan, Perak, since 1902, by S. H. Khoo, G. Cho and K. E. Chan. AST 10 (1972) 77-94.

7211 SADKA, EMILY. State councils in Perak and Selangor, 1877-1895. J45 pp. 89-119.

PERIODICALS - BURMA

7212 *Journal of Burma Research Society.* JBRS 47 (1964) 1-2.

PERIODICALS - INDONESIA

7213 CHAMBERT-LOIR, HENRI. *Horison,* six annees d'une revue litteraire indonesienne. AR 4 (1972) 81-89.

7214 DAMAIS, LOUIS-CHARLES. Bibliographie indonesienne, compte rendu de *Bahasa dan Budaja.* BEF 50 (1960) 417-518.

7215 DAMAIS, LOUIS-CHARLES. Compte rendu de *Bahasa dan Budaja.* BEF 51 (1963) 583-594.

7216 DAMAIS, LOUIS-CHARLES. Compte rendu de *Bahasa dan Budaja.* BEF 52 (1964) 204-240.

PERIODICALS - MALAYSIA

7217 LIM HUCK TEE. *Index Malaysiana, an index to the Journal of the Straits Branch, Royal Asiatic Society and the Journal of the Malayan Branch, Royal Asiatic Society, 1878-1963,* by Lim Huck Tee and D. E. K. Wijasuriya. JMBRAS 36 pt. 4 (1963) 1-395.

PERIODICALS - PHILIPPINES

7218 CARUNUNGAN, CELSO AL. Filipino magazines. UN 36 (1963) 419-425.

7219 MARSELLA, JOY A. Some contributions of the Philippine magazine to the development of Philippine culture. PS 17 (1969) 297-331.

7220 Retrospection of *Unitas'* forty years of fruitful service to the university. UN 34 (Sept. 1961) 1-4.

7221 Twenty years of *Philippine Studies.* PS 20 (1972) 3-11.

Periodicals - Philippines - Indexes

PERIODICALS - PHILIPPINES - INDEXES

7222   BANAS, ELISEO P. Decennial index
       to the *Silliman journal*, 1954-
       1963. SJ 10 (1963) 486-526.

7223   BANAS, ELISEO P. Selected Philip-
       pine periodical index. SJ 7
       (1960) 238-253.

7224   BANAS, ELISEO P. Selected Philip-
       pine periodical index. SJ 7
       (1960) 328-343.

7225   BANAS, ELISEO P. Selected Philip-
       pine periodical index, January-
       March, 1961. SJ 8 (1961) 59-66.

7226   BANAS, ELISEO P. Selected Philip-
       pine periodical index, April-June,
       1961. SJ 8 (1961) 122-155.

7227   BANAS, ELISEO P. Selected Philip-
       pine periodical index, July-
       September, 1961. SJ 8 (1961)
       216-245.

7228   BANAS, ELISEO P. Selected Philip-
       pine periodical index, October-
       December, 1961. SJ 8 (1961) 335-
       362.

7229   SIEGA, GORGONIO D. Selected Phil-
       ippine periodical index, January-
       March, 1962, by Gorgonio D. Siega
       and Eliseo P. Banas. SJ 9 (1962)
       69-97.

7230   SIEGA, GORGONIO D. Selected Phil-
       ippine periodical index, April-
       June, 1962, by Gorgonio D. Siega
       and Eliseo P. Banas. SJ 9 (1962)
       169-202.

7231   SIEGA, GORGONIO D. Selected Phil-
       ippine periodical index, July-
       September 1962, by Gorgonio D.
       Siega and Eliseo P. Banas. SJ 9
       (1962) 257-292.

7232   SIEGA, GORGONIO D. Selected Phil-
       ippine periodical index, October-
       December, 1962, by Gorgonio D.
       Siega and Eliseo P. Banas. SJ 9
       (1962) 360-410.

7233   SIEGA, GORGONIO D. Selected Phil-
       ippine periodical index, January-
       March, 1963, by Gorgonio D. Siega
       and Eliseo P. Banas. SJ 10 (1963)
       60-110.

7234   SIEGA, GORGONIO D. Selected Phil-
       ippine periodical index, April-
       June, 1963, by Gorgonio D. Siega
       and Eliseo P. Banas. SJ 10 (1963)
       163-234.

7235   SIEGA, GORGONIO D. Selected Phil-
       ippine periodical index, July-
       September, 1963, by Gorgonio D.
       Siega and Eliseo P. Banas. SJ 10
       (1963) 319-368.

7236   SIEGA, GORGONIO D. Selected Phil-
       ippine periodical index, October-
       December, 1963, by Gorgonio D.
       Siega and Eliseo P. Banas. SJ 10
       (1963) 426-483.

7237   SIEGA, GORGONIO D. Selected Phil-
       ippine periodical index, by
       Gorgonio D. Siega and Eliseo P.
       Banas. SJ 11 (1964) 96-185.

7238   SIEGA, GORGONIO D. Selected Phil-
       ippine periodical index, October-
       December, 1964, by Gorgonio D.
       Siega and Eliseo P. Banas. SJ 11
       (1964) 406-486.

7239   SIEGA, GORGONIO D. Selected peri-
       odical index, January-April, 1965,
       by Gorgonio D. Siega and Eliseo P.
       Banas. SJ 12 (1965) 461-572.

7240   SIEGA, GORGONIO D. Selected Phil-
       ippine periodical index, second
       quarter, 1965, by Gorgonio D.
       Siega and Eliseo P. Banas. SJ 13
       (1966) 85-242.

7241 SIEGA, GORGONIO D. Selected Philippine periodical index, third quarter, 1965, by Gorgonio D. Siega and Eliseo P. Banas. SJ 13 (1966) 303-468.

7242 SIEGA, GORGONIO D. Selected Philippine periodical index, fourth quarter, 1965, by Gorgonio D. Siega and Eliseo P. Banas. SJ 13 (1966) 501-579.

7243 SIEGA, GORGONIO D. Selected Philippine periodical index, first quarter, 1966, by Gorgonio D. Siega and Eliseo P. Banas. SJ 13 (1966) 649-750.

7244 SIEGA, GORGONIO D. Selected Philippine periodical index, first quarter, 1967, by Gorgonio D. Siega and Eliseo P. Banas. SJ 14 (1967) 97-196.

7245 SIEGA, GORGONIO D. Selected Philippine periodical index, second quarter, 1967. SJ 14 (1967) 279-385.

7246 SIEGA, GORGONIO D. Selected Philippine periodical index, by Gorgonio D. Siega and Eliseo P. Banas. SJ 16 (1969 supp.) 1-98.

PERIODICALS - SINGAPORE

7247 LIM HUCK TEE. *Index Malaysiana, an index to the Journal of the Straits Branch, Royal Asiatic Society and the Journal of the Malayan Branch, Royal Asiatic Society, 1878-1963,* by Lim Huck Tee and D. E. K. Wijasuriya. JMBRAS 36 pt. 4 (1963) 1-395.

PERIODICALS - VIETNAM

7248 METAYE, ROGER. Tables du *Bulletin de la Societe des Etudes Indochinoises, 1883-1971.* SEIB 46 (1971) 435-603.

PERLIS

7249 HUSSAIN BABA BIN MOHAMAD. Sejarah negeri dan raja2 Perlis. JMBRAS 42 pt. 2 (1969) 173-196.

7250 McTAGGART, W. D. Strategy of regional development in Perlis, west Malaysia. JTG 29 (1969) 39-48.

PERSHING, JOHN J.

7251 SMYTHE, DONALD. Pershing and the Mount Bagsak campaign of 1913. PS 12 (1964) 3-31.

PERSIANS - MALAYSIA

7252 COLLESS, BRIAN E. Persian merchants and missionaries in medieval Malaya. JMBRAS 42 pt. 2 (1969) 10-47.

PETALING JAYA

7253 SINGH, JASBIR SARJIT. Social stratification in Petaling Jaya, Malaysia. SAJSS 2 (1974) 75-92.

PETROLEUM

7254 CALDWELL, MALCOLM. Oil and imperialism in East Asia. JCA 1 pt. 3 (1971) 5-35.

Petroleum - Indonesia

PETROLEUM - INDONESIA

7255   HUNTER, ALEX. Indonesian oil in-
       dustry. G52 pp. 254-314.

7256   MYERS, EARL H. Recent studies of
       sediments in the Java Sea and
       their significance in relation to
       stratigraphic and petroleum geol-
       ogy. H57 pp. 265-269.

7257   PALMER, INGRID. Oil prices and
       the Indonesian economy. JCA 4
       (1974) 180-185.

PETROLEUM - MALAYSIA

7258   HARPER, G. C. Miri field, 1910-
       1972. SMJ 20 (1972) 21-30.

PETROLEUM - PHILIPPINES

7259   VALDEPENAS, VICENTE B. Should the
       government buy into Filoil? PS
       19 (1971) 604-615.

PHAN BOI CHAU

7260   BOUDAREL, GEORGES. Bibliographie
       des oeuvres relatives a Phan Boi
       Chau editees en Quoc Ngu a Hanoi
       depuis 1954. BEF 56 (1969) 151-
       176.

7261   DUIKER, WILLIAM J. Hanoi scruti-
       nizes the past, the Marxist eval-
       uation of Phan Boi Chau and Phan
       Chu Trinh. SA 1 (1971) 242-254.

7262   DUIKER, WILLIAM J. Phan Boi Chau,
       Asian revolutionary in a changing
       world. JAS 31 (1971-2) 77-88.

7263   PHAN BOI CHAU. Memoires. FA 22
       (1968) 263-470.

PHAN CHU TRINH

7264   DUIKER, WILLIAM J. Hanoi scruti-
       nizes the past, the Marxist eval-
       uation of Phan Boi Chau and Phan
       Chu Trinh. SA 1 (1971) 242-254.

PHAN THAN GIAN

7265   OSBORNE, MILTON E. Truong Vinh Ky
       and Phan Thanh Gian, the problem
       of a nationalist interpretation of
       19th century Vietnamese history.
       JAS 30 (1970-1) 81-93.

PHAULKON, CONSTANTINE

7266   HUTCHINSON, E. W. The French
       foreign mission in Siam during the
       XVIIth century. S44.8 pp. 17-90.

7267   HUTCHINSON, E. W. Phaulkon's
       house at Lopburi. S44.4 pp. 132-
       142.

PHAYRE, ARTHUR

7268   TINKER, HUGH. Arthur Phayre and
       Henry Yule, two soldier-adminis-
       trator historians. H18 pp. 267-
       278.

PHILIPPINE FEDERATION OF FREE FARMERS

7269   CATER, SONYA DIANE. Philippine
       Federation of Free Farmers, a case
       study in mass agrarian organiza-
       tions. E78 pp. 449-473.

Philippine Independent Church *See*
   AGLIPAYAN CHURCH

PHILIPPINE LITERATURE *See also individual authors and the following literatures:* BAGOBO, BIKOL, BISAYAN, CAPISNON, HILIGAYNON, IFUGAO, IGOROT, ILIANON, ILOKO, KALINGA, KINIRAYA, MANGYAN, MANOBO, MARANAO, PAMPANGA, PILIPINO, SPANISH, TAGALOG, TAOSUG

7270 ABELLA, DOMINGO. Some notes on the historical background of Philippine literature. M24 pp. 34-48.

7271 AGONCILLO, TEODORO A. Cultural aspect of the Japanese occupation. PSSHR 28 (1963) 351-394.

7272 AGRAVA, LEONOR. Flavio Zaragoza Cano. GEJ 6 (1963) 38-41.

7273 ALINEA, ESTANISLAO. Philippine literature in Spanish from the literature of protest to efflorescence. M24 pp. 508-517.

7274 ARCELLANA, FRANCISCO. Bienvenido N. Santos. M24 pp. 714-721.

7275 BERNAD, MIGUEL A. Church and Philippine literature in the Spanish era. M24 pp. 518-526.

7276 BERNAD, MIGUEL A. Future of Philippine literature. M24 pp. 793-798.

7277 BULAONG, GRACE F. Satire in Philippine literature. GEJ 11 (1966) 56-80.

7278 CASPER, LEONARD. Elitism, the hazards of being a vernacular writer. PS 17 (1969) 283-296.

7279 CASTRENCE, PURA S. Philippine literature. DR 13 (1965) 359-365.

7280 CORONEL, MARIA DELIA. Introduction. UN 39 (1966) 489-499.

7281 DAROY, PETRONILO BN. Aspects of Philippine writing in English. PS 17 (1969) 248-265.

7282 DEMETILLO, RICAREDO S. Image of man in contemporary art and literature. GEJ 4 (1962) 8-13.

7283 DEMETILLO, RICAREDO S. State of Philippine criticism. M24 pp. 702-713.

7284 ECHOLS, JOHN M. The background of literatures in Southeast Asia and the Philippines. G53 pp. 133-164.

7285 FERNANDO, FELIPE D. Aurelio Tolentino, playwright, poet, and patriot. PS 12 (1964) 83-92.

7286 Filipino criticism for Philippine literature. DR 18 (1970) 375-379.

7287 FRANCISCO, JUAN R. Indian influences in the Philippines, with special reference to language and literature. PSSHR 28 (1963) 1-310.

7288 GONZALEZ, N. V. M. Difficulties with Filipiniana. M24 pp. 539-545.

7289 HOSILLOS, LUCILA V. American reception of Philippine literature, 1898-1941. GEJ 11 (1966) 81-117.

7290 HOSILLOS, LUCILA V. Emergence of Filipino literature toward national identity. AST 4 (1966) 430-444.

7291 JOCANO, F. LANDA. Some aspects of Filipino vernacular literature. M24 pp. 287-307.

7292 MALAY, ROSARIO R. *Mga Ibong Mandaragit* and the second propaganda movement. GEJ 17 (1969) 107-117.

Philippine literature

PHILIPPINE LITERATURE - BIBLIOGRAPHY

of the Philippines, 1859-1897.
AST 8 (1970) 386-393.

7318 VELASCO, ADORACION TORIO. The
contemporary Filipino short story
in English. PSSHR 37 (1972) 1-
263.

PHILIPPINE LITERATURE - POETRY

7319 ABAD, GEMINO H. *Fugitive emphasis*. DR 21 (1973) 95-251.

7320 AFABLE, FERNANDO. Two poems. PS
13 (1965) 111-2.

7321 AFUANG, BENJAMIN V. Poems. SLQ
6 (1968) 217-8.

7322 AYALA, TITA LACAMBRA. Two poems.
PS 13 (1965) 109-110.

7323 BAUTISTA, CIRILO F. Poems. SLQ
6 (1968) 219-222.

7324 BULOSAN, CARLOS. *If you want to
know what we are*. DR 20 (1972)
14-16.

7325 CUADRA, JOLICO. Two poems. PS
13 (1965) 81-2.

7326 DAUZ, FLORENTINO S. *Notes for
a Filipino poet-scholar abroad*.
GEJ 7 (1964) 1-2.

7327 DAVID, F. G. Poems. DR 13
(1965) 343-347.

7328 DEMETILLO, RICAREDO. *The city and
the thread of light* and other
poems. DR 22 (1974) 1-84.

7329 DEMETILLO, RICAREDO. Five poems.
DR 12 (1964) 233-240.

7330 DEMETILLO, RICAREDO. Golden
jubilee ode libretto. DR 9 (1961)
513-528.

7331 DEMETILLO, RICAREDO. *Picasso as a
harlequin*. GEJ 4 (1962) 85.

7332 DEMETILLO, RICAREDO. Poems. SLQ
6 (1968) 223-4.

7333 DEMETILLO, RICAREDO. *Rizal*. DR 9
(1961) 396-399.

7334 DEMETILLO, RICAREDO. *The scarecrow Christ*. DR 21 (1973) 1-90.

7335 EPISTOLA, NIEVES B. *Collage, a
questionable sonnet*. DR 20 (1972)
45.

7336 EPISTOLA, NIEVES B. *Three and
free tropical truth tables*. DR 20
(1972) 41-44.

7337 EPISTOLA, NIEVES BENITO. Three
poems. DR 18 (1970) 54-61.

7338 ESPINO, FEDERICO LICSI. *Attic attitudes*, three poems. DR 17
(1969) 130-132.

7339 ESPINO, FEDERICO LICSI. *Connois-
seur du mal*. DR 14 (1966) 59.

7340 ESPINO, FEDERICO LICSI. *Images of
isolation*. DR 17 (1969) 265-6.

7341 ESPINO, FEDERICO LICSI. Poems.
SLQ 6 (1968) 225.

7342 ESPINO, FEDERICO LICSI. *Wounds of
war, in memoriam, Jose P. Laurel,
Sr*. DR 17 (1969) 351-357.

7343 FORONDA, MARCELINO A. Poems. SLQ
6 (1968) 226-7.

7344 FRANCISCO, JUAN R. Poem. DR 12
(1964) 241.

7345 GUILLERMO, GELACIO Y. *Let all
ways that lead to you*. GEJ 4
(1962) 77.

Philippine literature - Poetry

PHILIPPINE LITERATURE - POETRY - CRITI-
CISM

7375 BERNAD, MIGUEL A. Poets of the Philippine revolution. PS 22 (1974) 81-92.

7376 CANILAO, CARLOS M. The reordered reality in *The cave* and other poems. SLURJ 3 (1972) 472-554.

7377 Escapee to universality, portrait of a Filipino poet as escapee to the non-existent kingdom of universalism. DR 18 (1970) 329-340.

7378 ESTANISLAO, ROSARIO C. Notas breves sobre Manuel Bernabe, poeta laureado en espanol. GEJ 6 (1963) 33-37.

7379 GONZALEZ, N. V. M. Poetic myth in Philippine literature. DR 13 (1965) 157-176.

7380 GUILLERMO, GELACIO Y. Closed or open: Philippine poetry in English. GEJ 17 (1969) 99-106.

7381 HERNANDEZ, JOSE MA. Rizal's poetry and drama. UN 34 (Sept. 1961) 55.

7382 HOSILLOS, LUCILA. A poet takes on the dragon. DR 18 (1970) 284-292.

7383 HUFANA, ALEJANDRINO G. Impressions on Filipino verses and verse making in English. GEJ 5 (1963) 35-61.

7384 HUFANA, ALEJANDRINO G. Notes on poetry, with integrated critique and verse compilation. DR 20 (1972) 145-520.

7385 LEON, FELIPE PADILLA DE. Poetry, music and social consciousness. PS 17 (1969) 266-282.

7386 MANUUD, ANTONIO G. Toward a theory concerning the development of Filipino poetry in Spanish. M24 pp. 457-482.

7387 MOLINA, ANTONIO J. Philippine music and poetry. M24 pp. 195-206.

7388 TIEMPO, EDITH L. Philippine poetry in English. SJ 13 (1966) 617-621.

7389 TINIO, ROLANDO S. Period of awareness, the poets. M24 pp. 618-633.

7390 TINIO, ROLANDO S. Villa's values, or, the poet you cannot always make out, or succeed in liking once you are able to. M24 pp. 722-738.

7391 VIRAY, MANUEL A. Racial heritage. G53 pp. 165-198.

PHILIPPINE LITERATURE - PROSE

7392 ALFON, ESTRELLA D. *Mama.* PS 13 (1965) 32-37.

7393 ARAGO, JORGE. *Escapade.* GEJ 4 (1962) 65-71.

7394 AYALA, JOSE V. *And the dancer, dancing.* PS 13 (1965) 64-75.

7395 BALOY, CLEOTILDE. *Mother and son.* DR 13 (1965) 348-354.

7396 BAYOT, ANTONIO O. *Rigodon, or the dance of life,* a full length play in three parts. DR 8 (1960) 321-469.

7397 BULOSAN, CARLOS. *Sound of falling light, letters in exile.* DR 8 (1960) 185-277.

7398 CACNIO, LEOPOLDO N. *March of the lovers.* PS 13 (1965) 113-157.

Philippine literature - Prose

7399 CRISTOBAL, ADRIAN. *I, Suliman.*
      GEJ 4 (1962) 56-64.

7400 DACANAY, JULIAN E. *Badjao.* PS
      13 (1965) 43-60.

7401 ESPINO, FEDERICO LICSI. *Ritual
      for saints and lovers.* DR 18
      (1970) 48-53.

7402 GOMEZ, GUILLERMO. *Cruel prince,
      a fairy tale for adults.* DR 11
      (1963) 25-35.

7403 GONZALEZ, N. V. M. *Bed of sores.*
      SLQ 6 (1968) 207-216.

7404 GONZALEZ, N. V. M. *Notes on a
      method and a culture.* GEJ 4
      (1962) 87-94.

7405 JESUS, ORTUOSTE DE. *Naked songs.*
      PS 13 (1965) 1-22.

7406 NOLLEDO, WILFRIDO D. *For Alonzo,
      among the alfalfa.* PS 13 (1965)
      83-94.

7407 PUCAY, ALFRED. *Tomorrow, a simple
      heartache.* DR 14 (1966) 43-58.

7408 SANTOS, BIENVENIDO N. *Moonlight
      laundry.* PS 13 (1965) 100-108.

7409 SICAT, GERARDO P. *Fable for our
      times, a tale of two countries.*
      DR 17 (1969) 358-376.

7410 TALEON, JORSHINELLE L. *Step,
      step.* DR 14 (1966) 101-108.

7411 VEYRA, JAIME C. DE. Selections
      from *Hispanidad en Filipinas.*
      M24 pp. 799-815.

7412 ZUIDEMA, NANCY. *The club.* DR 14
      (1966) 127-137.

7413 ZUIDEMA, NANCY. *Puddles.* DR 14
      (1966) 40-42.

PHILIPPINE LITERATURE - PROSE - CRITI-
CISM

7414 ABDUL MAJID BIN NABI BAKSH. The
      Filipino novel in English, a
      critical history. PSSHR 35 (1970)
      1-193.

7415 ARCELLANA, FRANCISCO. Period of
      emergence, the short story. M24
      pp. 603-617.

7416 ARCELLANA, FRANCISCO. Pride of
      fiction. GEJ 17 (1969) 118-124.

7417 ARENSMEYER, ELLIOTT C. Little
      mansions, some aspects of Jose
      Rizal as a novelist. PS 18 (1970)
      740-752.

7418 BAUTISTA, ABRAHAM R. Hope in more
      than conquerors. SLURJ 2 (1971)
      535-539.

7419 BERNAD, MIGUEL A. Hand of the
      enemy, the stories of Kerima Polo-
      tan. PS 17 (1969) 40-59.

7420 BERNAD, MIGUEL A. Some aspects of
      Rizal's novels. M24 pp. 527-538.

7421 CASPER, LEONARD. Desire and doom
      in Kerima Polotan. PS 17 (1969)
      60-71.

7422 CENIZA, RIORITA E. Sequential and
      non-sequential signals in short
      story openings. SJ 14 (1967) 325-
      351.

7423 CONSTANTINO, JOSEFINA D. *The
      peninsulars.* DR 13 (1965) 66-71.

7424 CRUZ, EDGARDO DELA. Things loved,
      things remembered, Joaquin's *Por-
      trait* and William's *Menagerie.* PS
      14 (1966) 242-252.

7425 CRUZ, ISAGANI R. Illusion and the
      inner cell, a critical analysis of

the later stories of Arturo B. Rotor. PS 18 (1970) 753-768.

7426 DAROY, PETRONILO BN. Ideas of European liberalism in the fiction of Rizal. PSSHR 30 (1965) 109-183.

7427 DAROY, PETRONILO BN. Love in Filipino fiction. DR 12 (1964) 224-232.

7428 DAROY, PETRONILO BN. The novel in the Philippines. AST 7 (1969) 180-185.

7429 GARCIA, LUISA E. Thought and technique in *White wall, selected Tondo stories*. SLURJ 1 (1970) 329-402.

7430 HERNANDEZ-CHUNG, LILIA. Introduction to peninsular prose fiction of the Philippines, 1859-1897. AST 8 (1970) 386-393.

7431 HIDALGO, PERLA R. The art of *The peninsulars* by Linda Casper. SLURJ 2 (1971) 267-292.

7432 HIGHLEY, MONA P. Inigo Ed. Regalado, eclectic novelist. DR 18 (1970) 293-297.

7433 JESUS, EDILBERTO DE. On this soil, in this climate, growth in the novels of N. V. M. Gonzalez. M24 pp. 739-764.

7434 MARTIN, DALMACIO. *Hamlet* and its possible influence on Rizal's novels. SJ 13 (1966) 635-640.

7435 MORALES, CONSUELO B. Pio Baroja en paradox, Rey. GEJ 6 (1963) 42-45.

7436 OLOROSO, LAURA S. Nick Joaquin and his brightly burning prose works. M24 pp. 765-792.

7437 RAMOS, MAXIMO B. The Rizal story in Philippine fiction. DR 9 (1961) 383-395.

7438 REYES, SOLEDAD. Theme in the stories of Macario Pineda. PS 19 (1971) 456-489.

7439 SAN JUAN, E. Juan C. Laya's *His native soil*, and the limits of bourgeois/liberal individualism. DR 18 (1970) 187-231.

7440 SANIEL, JOSEFA M. Jose Rizal and Suehiro Tetcho, Filipino and Japanese political novelists. AST 2 (1964) 353-371.

7441 SANTOS, BIENVENIDO. Filipino novel in English. M24 pp. 634-647.

7442 SCHNEIDER, HERBERT. Period of emergence of Philippine letters, 1930-1944. M24 pp. 575-588.

7443 SCHUMACHER, JOHN N. Authenticity of the writings attributed to Father Jose Burgos. PS 18 (1970) 3-51.

7444 VELASCO, ADORACION TORIO. The contemporary Filipino short story in English. PSSHR 37 (1972) 1-263.

7445 YABES, LEOPOLDO Y. Pioneering in the Filipino short story in English, 1925-1940. GEJ 11 (1966) 118-134.

7446 YABES, LEOPOLDO Y. Rizal's novels. DR 11 (1963) 82-90.

PHILIPPINE MEDICAL ASSOCIATION

7447 STAUFFER, ROBERT B. Philippine interest groups, an index of political development. AST 3 (1965) 193-220.

Philippine Medical Association

7448 STAUFFER, ROBERT B. Philippine
Medical Association, a case study
in interest group development.
A28 pp. 238-244.

PHILIPPINES

7449 ADKINS, JOHN H. Philippines 1971,
events of a year, trends of the
future. AS 12 (1972) 78-85.

7450 ADKINS, JOHN H. Philippines 1972,
we'll wait and see. AS 13 (1973)
140-150.

7451 L'annee 1966 en Asie, Philippines.
FA 22 (1968) 117-8.

7452 CORPUZ, O. D. Our search for
ideology. E78 pp. 426-429.

7453 CUTSHALL, ALDEN. The Philippines.
F56 pp. 202-220.

7454 FERNANDEZ, JOSE B. New patriot-
ism in our times. SJ 21 (1974)
60-65.

7455 Greatness begins with our leaders.
A28 pp. 547-8.

7456 GROSSHOLTZ, JEAN. Philippines
1973, whither Marcos? AS 14
(1974) 101-112.

7457 HEADY, FERREL. Six ecological
factors. A28 pp. 19-22.

7458 LYNCH, FRANK. Philippines, bridge
to Southeast Asia. PS 15 (1967)
167-176.

7459 NARDIN, DENIS. Philippines 1969.
FA 23 (1969) 243-256.

7460 President's state of the nation
address. SLQ 7 (1969) 152-156.

7461 WILEY, SAMUEL R. State of the nation, a challenge to Christian
scholarship. PS 14 (1966) 25-37.

PHILIPPINES - BIBLIOGRAPHY

7462 ANDERSON, GERALD H. Missionary
readings on the Philippines, a
guide. SJ 12 (1965) 211-227.

7463 BERGER, KENNETH W. Linguistic
study in the Philippines, a brief
bibliographic history. SJ 18
(1971) 164-179.

7464 FORONDA, MARCELINO A. Bibliography of Father Vanoverbergh's
works. UN 42 (1969) ii-iv.

7465 HAKCHOLNA, WILLIAM. Catalogue of
works on Cordillera ethnography in
the Igorot Study Center, Sagada,
Mountain Province. SLQ 7 (1969)
113-142.

7466 List of microfilms deposited in
the Centre for East Asian Cultural
Studies. EACS 9 (1970) 57-107.

7467 MANUEL, E. ARSENIO. Scope and
nature of Philippine bibliography
making. GEJ 12 (1966) 207-214.

7468 OWEN, NORMAN G. Select bibliography, by Norman G. Owen and Michael
Cullinane. C31 pp. 227-252.

7469 RIXHON, GERARD. Selected list of
recent works on Sulu. S91 pp.
143-162.

7470 RODRIGUEZ, ISACIO R. Bibliography
on Legazpi and Urdaneta and their
joint expedition. PS 13 (1965)
287-329.

7471 SCHUMACHER, JOHN N. Bibliographical survey of Philippine church
history, by John N. Schumacher and

Gerald H. Anderson. A58 pp. 389-412.

7472 SCHUMACHER, JOHN N. Wenceslao E. Retana, an historiographical study. PS 10 (1962) 550-576.

PHILIPPINES - CONSTITUTION

7473 ARANETA, SALVADOR. Our constitutional heritage. A28 pp. 52-55.

7474 ARUEGO, JOSE M. Malolos constitution. A28 pp. 43-4.

7475 CALDERON, CICERO D. Should bill of rights include economic and social rights? SJ 16 (1969) 427-430.

7476 CARMEN, ROLANDO V. DEL. Constitutionalism and the Supreme Court in a changing Philippine polity. AS 13 (1973) 1050-1061.

7477 CONCEPCION, ROBERTO. Amendments to our constitution. SLQ 1 (1963) 171-178.

7478 GONZALEZ, ANDREW. The 1973 constitution and the bilingual education policy of the Department of Education and Culture. PS 22 (1974) 325-337.

7479 GOROSPE, VITALIANO R. Some basic values in the 1971 constitutional convention, a Christian perspective. PS 20 (1972) 166-175.

7480 LOPEZ, SALVADOR P. Rizal and the Philippine constitution. DR 17 (1969) 317-323.

7481 OCAMPO, FELICISIMO. Academic freedom and freedom from subversion. DR 9 (1961) 37-50.

7482 RAMOS, NORBERTO DE. Constitutional amendments, a summary. UN 35 (1962) 459-468.

7483 RECTO, CLARO M. Our future under the constitution. A28 pp. 56-60.

7484 ROSAL, NICOLAS LL. Unjust position of the Church in the Philippine constitution. UN 33 (1960) 682-739.

7485 ROSAL, NICOLAS LL. Unjust position of the Church in the Philippine constitution. UN 34 (Mar. 1961) 46-94.

7486 SINCO, VICENTE G. Two statements on academic freedom. DR 9 (1961) 8-22.

7487 YABES, LEOPOLDO Y. Let's study the new constitution, the language provision. PSSHR 38 (1973) 1-173.

PHILIPPINES - DESCRIPTION AND TRAVEL

7488 BLUMBERG, ARNOLD. A Belgian view of the Philippines: 1899. AST 11 pt. 2 (1973) 123-127.

7489 BOXER, C. R. Three unpublished Jesuit letters on Philippine and Mariana missions, 1681-1689. PS 10 (1962) 434-442.

7490 Expedition of Comandante Guillermo Galvey to Baguio in 1829. UN 35 (1962) 128-138.

7491 HARRISSON, TOM. Rennell manuscript in the Brunei Museum. BMJ 1 (1969) 157-165.

7492 HARRISSON, TOM. Unpublished Rennell ms., a Borneo-Philippine journey, 1762-63. JMBRAS 39 pt. 1 (1966) 92-136.

Philippines - Description and travel

7493   SCOTT, WILLIAM HENRY. Birth and
       death of a mission, a chapter in
       Philippine church history. PS 13
       (1965) 801-821.

PHILIPPINES - ECONOMIC CONDITIONS

7494   ANDERSON, JAMES N. Buy and sell
       and economic personalism, founda-
       tions for Philippine entrepre-
       neurship. AS 9 (1969) 641-668.

7495   CARROLL, JOHN J. The economy,
       rising expectations, limited
       fulfillment. P47 pp. 17-39.

7496   CARROLL, JOHN J. Filipino entre-
       preneurship in manufacturing. PS
       10 (1962) 100-126.

7497   EMERY, ROBERT F. Successful Phil-
       ippine decontrol and devaluation.
       AS 3 (1963) 274-284.

7498   Farm life resources and income.
       E78 pp. 41-43.

7499   GOLAY, FRANK H. The Philippine
       economy. G53 pp. 199-279.

7500   GUERRERO, MILAGROS C. Survey of
       Japanese trade and investments in
       the Philippines, with special
       references to Philippine-American
       reactions 1900-1941. PSSHR 31
       (1966) 1-129.

7501   McPHELIN, MICHAEL. Filipino first
       policy and economic growth. PS 8
       (1960) 270-291.

7502   McPHELIN, MICHAEL. Financial
       achievement of 1960. PS 9 (1961)
       140-144.

7503   MILNE, R. S. Role of government
       corporations in the Philippines.
       PA 34 (1961) 257-270.

7504   MONTEMAYOR, JEREMIAS. The Philip-
       pine socio-economic situation. SJ
       19 (1972) 42-58.

7505   PAPA, JOSE L. Critique of foreign
       corporations doing business in the
       Philippines. UN 36 (1963) 184-
       227.

7506   Political transmission 15, an
       analysis. PS 8 (1960) 3-50.

7507   STARNER, FRANCES L. Philippine
       economic development and the two
       party system. AS 2 (July 1962)
       17-23.

7508   VALDEPENAS, VICENTE B. Economic
       challenge in the Philippines. PS
       16 (1968) 278-296.

7509   VALDEPENAS, VICENTE B. Economics
       in human development. PS 21
       (1973) 443-449.

7510   VALDEPENAS, VICENTE B. Foreign
       operators in the Philippine econ-
       omy. PS 18 (1970) 546-557.

7511   VALDEPENAS, VICENTE B. Japan in
       postwar Philippine economy. PS 18
       (1970) 718-739.

7512   VENTURA, MAMERTO S. Post-war eco-
       nomic difficulties facing the
       young republic. PSSHR 31 (1966)
       169-197.

PHILIPPINES - FOREIGN RELATIONS

7513   MARCOS, FERDINAND E. Our foreign
       policy. A28 pp. 486-494.

7514   PELAEZ, EMMANUEL. Philippine
       foreign policy, the whole and its
       parts. A28 pp. 480-486.

7515   RAMOS, NORBERTO DE. International
       projection. UN 36 (1963) 452-458.

7516 SALONGA, JOVITA. Myths and realities in Philippine foreign
policy. A28 pp. 496-506.

7517 VELLUT, J. L. Foreign relations
of the second republic of the
Philippines, 1943-1945. JSAH 5
(Mar. 1964) 126-142.

7518 VELLUT, J. L. From Baguio to
Bandung, foreign policy debates
in the Philippines, 1950-1955.
RSA (1963) 229-246.

PHILIPPINES - FOREIGN RELATIONS -
BELGIUM

7519 BLUMBERG, ARNOLD. Belgium and a
Philippine protectorate, a still-
born plan. AST 10 (1972) 336-343.

PHILIPPINES - FOREIGN RELATIONS -
BRUNEI

7520 ANGELES, F. DELOR. Brunei and
the Moro wars. BMJ 1 (1969) 119-
132.

7521 SHORT, BROCK K. Brunei, Sulu and
Sabah. BMJ 1 (1969) 133-146.

PHILIPPINES - FOREIGN RELATIONS -
CAMBODIA

7523 QUIRINO, CARLOS. First Philippine
expedition to Indo-China. JSAH 10
(1969) 491-500.

PHILIPPINES - FOREIGN RELATIONS - CHINA

7524 ABELLA, DOMINGO. Koxinga nearly
ended Spanish rule in the Philippines in 1662. PHR 2 (1969) 295-
350.

Philippines - Foreign relations - Great
Britain

7525 McCARTHY, CHARLES. First expedition of Jesuits from the Philippines to China. PS 18 (1970) 634-
644.

7526 TAN, ANTONIO S. Chinese in the
Philippines and the Chinese revolution of 1911. AST 8 (1970) 160-
185.

7527 Vice premier Li Hsien Nien gives
banquet in name of Premier Chou
En Lai for Madame Marcos. JCA 4
(1974) 560-562.

PHILIPPINES - FOREIGN RELATIONS -
FRANCE

7528 BELLAMAL, A. Pour une politique
francaise dans le monde malayo-
indonesien. FA (1974 pt. 2) 35-
44.

7529 COSTA, HORACIO DE LA. Early
French contacts with the Philippines. PS 11 (1963) 401-418.

PHILIPPINES - FOREIGN RELATIONS -
GERMANY

7530 GUERRERO, LEON MA. Kaiser and the
Philippines. PS 9 (1961) 584-600.

PHILIPPINES - FOREIGN RELATIONS - GREAT
BRITAIN

7531 COSTA, HORACIO DE LA. Siege and
capture of Manila by the British,
September-October 1762. PS 10
(1962) 607-650.

7532 CUSHNER, NICHOLAS P. British con-
sular dispatches and the Philippine independence movement, 1872-
1901. PS 16 (1968) 501-534.

Philippines - Foreign relations - Great
  Britain

7533 MYRICK, CONRAD. Some aspects of
      the British occupation of Manila.
      A58 pp. 113-130.

7534 PILCHER, JOHN. Great Britain and
      the Philippines. PS 8 (1960)
      603-608.

7535 QUIASON, SERAFIN D. Synopsis of
      early English country trade with
      the Philippines. GEJ 5 (1963)
      26-34.

7536 QUIRINO, CARLOS. Aftermath of
      the British invasion of the Phil-
      ippines. PS 16 (1968) 540-544.

7537 TARLING, NICHOLAS. Consul Farren
      and the Philippines. JMBRAS 38
      pt. 2 (1965) 258-273.

PHILIPPINES - FOREIGN RELATIONS - INDIA

7538 CHEONG, W. E. Anglo-Spanish-
      Portuguese clandestine trade be-
      tween the ports of British India
      and Manila, 1785-1790. PHR 1 pt.
      1 (1965) 80-94.

7539 FRANCISCO, JUAN R. On the date of
      the coming of Indian influence in
      the Philippines. PHR 1 pt. 1
      (1965) 136-152.

7540 FRANCISCO, JUAN R. Reflexions on
      the migration theory vis-a-vis
      the coming of Indian influences
      in the Philippines. AST 9 (1971)
      307-314.

7541 QUIRINO, CARLOS. Cultural rela-
      tions between India and the Phil-
      ippines. S32 pp. 96-98.

7542 RYE, AJIT SINGH. Survey of
      Philippine-India relations in the
      post-independence period. AST 6
      (1968) 271-285.

PHILIPPINES - FOREIGN RELATIONS -
  INDONESIA

7543 FRANCISCO, JUAN R. Sri Vijaya and
      the Philippines, a review. PSSHR
      26 (1961) 87-109.

7544 KUSNO UTOMO. Imperatives of
      Philippine-Indonesian relations.
      SJ 18 (1971) 198-205.

7545 MEADOWS, MARTIN. Theories of
      external-internal political rela-
      tionships, a case study of Indo-
      nesia and the Philippines. AST 6
      (1968) 297-324.

PHILIPPINES - FOREIGN RELATIONS - JAPAN

7546 GOODMAN, GRANT K. Davaokuo?
      Japan in Philippine politics,
      1931-1941. S90.3 pp. 185-196.

7547 GOODMAN, GRANT K. A flood of im-
      migration, patterns and problems
      of Japanese migration to the
      Philippines during the first four
      decades of the twentieth century.
      PHR 1 pt. 1 (1965) 170-193.

7548 GOODMAN, GRANT K. General Artemio
      Ricarte and Japan. JSAH 7 (Sept.
      1966) 48-60.

7549 GOODMAN, GRANT K. Japan and Phil-
      ippine beer, the 1930's. JSAS 1
      pt. 1 (1970) 54-59.

7550 GOODMAN, GRANT K. Japanese Pan-
      Asianism in the Philippines, the
      Hirippin Dai Ajia Kyokai. S90.7
      pp. 133-143.

7551 GOODMAN, GRANT K. Philippine-
      Japanese professorial exchanges in
      the 1930's. JSAH 9 (1968) 229-
      240.

7552 GOODMAN, GRANT K. Problem of Philippine independence and Japan, the first three decades of American colonial rule. SA 1 (1971) 164-190.

7553 GUERRERO, MILAGROS C. Survey of Japanese trade and investments in the Philippines with special references to Philippine-American reactions 1900-1941. PSSHR 31 (1966) 1-129.

7554 SANIEL, JOSEFA M. Four Japanese, their plans for the expansion of Japan to the Philippines. AST 1 (1963) 52-63.

7555 SANIEL, JOSEFA M. Four Japanese, their plans for the expansion of Japan to the Philippines. JSAH 4 (Sept. 1963) 1-12.

7556 SANIEL, JOSEFA M. Japan and the Philippines, 1868-1898. PSSHR 27 (1962) 1-409.

7557 SANIEL, JOSEFA M. Okuma Shigenobu and the 1898 Philippine problem. PHR 1 pt. 1 (1965) 298-319.

7558 VALDEPENAS, VICENTE B. Japan in postwar Philippine economy. PS 18 (1970) 718-739.

PHILIPPINES - FOREIGN RELATIONS - MALAYSIA

7559 FERNANDEZ, ALEJANDRO M. Secretary General's role in the Malaysia conflict. DR 12 (1964) 160-171.

7560 JACOBINI, H. B. Fundamentals of Philippine policy toward Malaysia. AS 4 (1964) 1144-1151.

7561 NOBLE, LELA GARNER. National interest and national image, Philippine policy in Asia. AS 13 (1973) 560-576.

Philippines - Foreign relations - Netherlands

7562 ORTIZ, PACIFICO A. Legal aspects of the North Borneo question. PS 11 (1963) 18-64.

7563 SHORT, BROCK K. Brunei, Sulu and Sabah. BMJ 1 (1969) 133-146.

7564 TREGONNING, K. G. Philippine claim to Sabah. JMBRAS 43 pt. 1 (1970) 161-170.

7565 VILLADOLID, ALICE C. Sociological ties binding the Philippines and North Borneo. UN 35 (1962) 515-523.

7566 WRIGHT, LEIGH R. Historical notes on the North Borneo dispute. JAS 25 (1965-6) 471-484.

PHILIPPINES - FOREIGN RELATIONS - MEXICO

7567 BERNAL, RAFAEL. Mexican heritage in the Philippines. UN 37 (1964) 292-300.

7568 GARCIA, FRANCISCO E. La historia comun de Filipinas y Mexico. GEJ 7 (1964) 209-211.

PHILIPPINES - FOREIGN RELATIONS - NETHERLANDS

7569 CHANG, TIEN TSE. Spanish-Dutch naval battle of 1617 outside Manila Bay. JSAH 7 (Mar. 1966) 111-121.

7570 CHANG, TIEN TSE. Spanish-Dutch naval battle of 1617 outside Manila Bay. PHR 1 pt. 1 (1965) 68-79.

7571 ROESSINGH, M. P. H. Dutch relations with the Philippines, c. 1600-1850, a survey of sources in

Philippines - Foreign relations -
Netherlands

the General State Archives, The
Hague, Netherlands. SAA 2 (1969)
88-103.

7572 ROESSINGH, M. P. H. Nederlandse
betrekkingen met de Philippijnen,
1600-1800. BIJ 124 (1968) 482-
504.

PHILIPPINES - FOREIGN RELATIONS - SPAIN

7573 AGONCILLO, TEODORO A. Malolos,
the crisis of the republic.
PSSHR 25 (1960) 1-831.

7574 ARAGON, J. GAYO. Controversy over
justification of Spanish rule in
the Philippines. A58 pp. 3-21.

7575 CASTIELLA, FERNANDO. Spain and
the Philippines. UN 38 (1965)
248-260.

7576 CHANG, TIEN TSE. Spanish-Dutch
naval battle of 1617 outside
Manila Bay. JSAH 7 (Mar. 1966)
111-121.

7577 CHANG, TIEN TSE. Spanish-Dutch
naval battle of 1617 outside
Manila Bay. PHR 1 pt. 1 (1965)
68-79.

7578 MOLINA, ANTONIO M. Genesis of
Philippine separatism. UN 36
(1963) 433-445.

7579 MOLINA, ANTONIO M. Myth of Carlos
Maria de la Torre. UN 36 (1963)
152-157.

7580 VEYRA, JAIME C. DE. Selections
from *Hispanidad en Filipinas*.
M24 pp. 799-815.

PHILIPPINES - FOREIGN RELATIONS - UNION
SOVIET SOCIALIST REPUBLICS

7581 BARYSHNIKOVA, O. Ang Pag-aaral
hinggil sa Pilipinas sa USSR, [by]
O. Baryshnikova, G. Levinson [and]
Yu. Levtonova. AST 11 pt. 2
(1973) 75-83.

PHILIPPINES - FOREIGN RELATIONS - UNITED
STATES

7582 AQUINO, RAMON C. Legal landmarks
of American colonial rule. A28
pp. 44-48.

7583 Better use could be made of U.S.
assistance and other support to
the Philippines. JCA 4 (1974)
126-128.

7584 BLUMBERG, ARNOLD. Belgium and a
Philippine protectorate, a still-
born plan. AST 10 (1972) 336-343.

7585 CRUZ, ROMEO V. America's colonial
desk and the Philippines, 1898-
1934. PSSHR 37 (1972) 267-514.

7586 FLORES, PEDRO V. Economic expectations and results under the
Laurel-Langley agreement, 1956-
1965. SJ 14 (1967) 55-66.

7587 FRIEND, THEODORE W. Philippine
independence and the last lame
duck congress. PS 12 (1964) 260-
276.

7588 FRIEND, THEODORE W. Veto and repassage of the Hare-Hawes-Cutting
Act, a catalogue of motives. PS
12 (1964) 666-680.

7589 GATES, JOHN M. The Philippines
and Vietnam, another false anal-
ogy. AST 10 (1972) 64-76.

7590 GUERRERO, MILAGROS C. Survey of Japanese trade and investments in the Philippines, with special references to Philippine-American reactions 1900-1941. PSSHR 31 (1966) 1-129.

7591 IRVINE, REED J. American trade with the Philippines. C35 pp. 173-183.

7592 JESUS, EDILBERTO C. DE. Aguinaldo and the American consuls. PHR 1 pt. 2 (1966) 125-167.

7593 KOLKO, GABRIEL. The United States and the Philippines, the beginning of another Vietnam? JCA 3 (1973) 70-84.

7594 LOPEZ, SALVADOR P. New basis for Philippine-American relations. DR 11 (1963) 17-24.

7595 LOPEZ, SALVADOR P. Philippine-American relations in the decade of the seventies. DR 17 (1969) 343-350.

7596 McHALE, THOMAS R. Development of American policy towards the Philippines. PS 9 (1961) 47-71.

7597 MEADOWS, MARTIN. Recent developments in Philippine-American relations, a case study in emergent nationalism. AS 5 (1965) 305-318.

7598 MEDINA, ISAGANI R. American logbooks and journals in Salem, Massachusetts on the Philippines, 1796-1894. AST 11 (1973) 177-198.

7599 Negros 1899-1900, testimony by the American military commander. SJ 19 (1972) 389-424.

7600 PATERNO, ROBERTO. American military bases in the Philippines, the Brownell opinion. PS 12 (1964) 391-423.

7601 TAN, SAMUEL K. Sulu under American military rule, 1899-1913. PSSHR 32 (1967) 1-187.

7602 THOMAS, IVOR B. American imperialism in the Philippines. SJ 20 (1973) 373-403.

PHILIPPINES - FOREIGN RELATIONS - VIETNAM

7603 ABELLA, DOMINGO. When Filipino colonial troops fought in Viet-Nam in 1858. PHR 1 pt. 2 (1966) 1-16.

7604 ARELLANO, OSCAR J. How operation brotherhood got to Viet Nam. PS 14 (1966) 396-409.

7605 BERNAD, MIGUEL A. First year of the PHILCAG in Viet Nam. PS 16 (1968) 131-154.

7606 INGLES, JOSE D. Philippine position on the Vietnam question. PS 14 (1966) 633-652.

PHILIPPINES - HISTORY

7607 ABAYA, HERNANDO J. Correcting the wrongs of the past. DR 8 (1960) 151-183.

7608 ABELLA, DOMINGO. Brief introduction to the study of western cultural penetration in the Philippines. EACS 6 (1967) 176-189.

7609 AGONCILLO, TEODORO A. Imagination in history. DR 13 (1965) 10-21.

7610 AGONCILLO, TEODORO A. Philippine history and institutions in the general education program. GEJ 1 (1961) 93-101.

Philippines - History

7611 CORPUZ, ONOFRE DIZON. Western colonisation and the Filipino response. JSAH 3 (Mar. 1962) 1-23.

7612 CULLUM, LEO A. Notes on the revolution in Surigao. PS 9 (1961) 488-494.

7613 JESUS, EDILBERTO C. DE. Controversy over Zamboanga. PHR 2 (1969) 275-294.

7614 JOCANO, F. LANDA. Beyer's theory on Filipino prehistory and culture, an alternative approach to the problem. Z16 pp. 128-150.

7615 JOCANO, F. LANDA. Ideology and radical movements in the Philippines, a preliminary view. M52 pp. 199-222.

7616 JOSE, VIVENCIO R. Rise and fall of Antonio Luna. PSSHR 36 (1971) 1-511.

7617 MADIGAN, FRANCIS C. Problems of growth, the future population of the Philippines. PS 16 (1968) 3-31.

7618 MAJUL, CESAR ADIB. Political and historical notes on the old Sulu sultanate. PHR 1 pt. 1 (1965) 229-251.

7619 MARTIN, DALMACIO. June twelfth, a historical critique. SJ 14 (1967) 242-253.

7620 MOLINA, ANTONIO M. Genesis of Philippine separatism. UN 36 (1963) 433-445.

7621 RICE, DELBERT. Ancient Philippine democracy, pre-Hispanic social structures and their modern implications. SJ 19 (1972) 249-312.

7622 SCHUMACHER, JOHN N. Recent historical writing on the Philippines abroad. PS 9 (1961) 97-127.

7623 SCHUMACHER, JOHN N. Recent historical writing on the Philippines abroad. PS 11 (1963) 557-572.

7624 SCOTT, WILLIAM HENRY. Critical study of the prehispanic source materials for the study of Philippine history. UN 41 (1968) 275-440.

7625 ZAVALA, SILVIO. New world contacts with Asia. AST 2 (1964) 213-222.

PHILIPPINES - HISTORY - 1500-1898

7626 ABBOTT, WILLIAM. Spanish conquerors of the Philippines from Magellan to Dasmarinas. PHR 2 (1969) 248-264.

7627 ABELLA, DOMINGO. Koxinga nearly ended Spanish rule in the Philippines in 1662. PHR 2 (1969) 295-350.

7628 AGONCILLO, TEODORO A. Malolos, the crisis of the republic. PSSHR 25 (1960) 1-831.

7629 ARAGON, J. GAYO. Controversy over justification of Spanish rule in the Philippines. A58 pp. 3-21.

7630 ARCILLA, JOSE S. Slavery, flogging and other moral cases in 17th century Philippines. PS 20 (1972) 399-416.

7631 BERNAD, MIGUEL A. Father Ducos and the Muslim wars, 1752-1759. PS 16 (1968) 690-728.

7632 BERNAL, RAFAEL. La experiencia Mexicana en Filipinas. UN 37 (1964) 52-67.

7633 CALBRECHT, JOSEPH. Finding and origin of the Santo Nino of Cebu. SLQ 3 (1965) 7-16.

7634 CHANG, TIEN TSE. Spanish-Dutch naval battle of 1617 outside Manila Bay. JSAH 7 (Mar. 1966) 111-121.

7635 CHANG, TIEN TSE. Spanish-Dutch naval battle of 1617 outside Manila Bay. PHR 1 pt. 1 (1965) 68-79.

7636 COSTA, HORACIO DE LA. Siege and capture of Manila by the British, September-October 1762. PS 10 (1962) 607-650.

7637 CUMMINS, J. S. Antonio de Morga and his *Sucesos de las Islas Filipinas*. JSAH 10 (1969) 560-581.

7638 CUSHNER, NICHOLAS P. Legazpi, 1564-1572. PS 13 (1965) 163-206.

7639 EPISTOLA, S. V. Hong Kong junta. PSSHR 26 (1961) 3-65.

7640 FORBES-GANZON, GUADALUPE. *La Solidaridad, Quincenario Democratico*, vol. I number 4, 31 March 1889. The original text with English version. PSSHR 26 (1961) 233-290.

7641 FORBES-GANZON, GUADALUPE. *La Solidaridad, Quincenario Democratico*, vol. numbers 5 and 6, April 15 and 30, 1889. The original text with English version. PSSHR 26 (1961) 319-425.

7642 LEE, DAVID C. Some reflections about the Cofradia de San Jose as a Philippine religious uprising. AST 9 (1971) 126-143.

7643 McCARTHY, CHARLES J. On the Koxinga threat of 1662. PS 18 (1970) 187-196.

7644 MAJUL, CESAR ADIB. Social background of the revolution. AST 9 (1971) 1-23.

7645 QUIRINO, CARLOS. Aftermath of the British invasion of the Philippines. PS 16 (1968) 540-544.

7646 RODRIGUEZ, ISACIO R. Bibliography on Legazpi and Urdaneta and their joint expedition. PS 13 (1965) 287-329.

7647 SCHUMACHER, JOHN N. Documents relating to Jose Burgos and the Cavite Mutiny of 1872, by John N. Schumacher and Nicholas P. Cushner. PS 17 (1969) 457-529.

7648 SWEET, DAVID. Proto-political peasant movement in the Spanish Philippines, the Cofradia de San Jose and the Tayabas rebellion of 1841. AST 8 (1970) 94-119.

7649 VALENZUELA, PIO. Memoirs of the K. K. K. and the Philippine revolution. DR 11 (1963) 498-518.

7650 VEYRA, JAIME C. DE. Selections from *Hispanidad en Filipinas*. M24 pp. 799-815.

PHILIPPINES - HISTORY - 1898-1946

7651 GOWING, PETER G. American mood and the Philippines, 1898-1899. SJ 16 (1969) 59-75.

7652 HART, DONN V. Central Philippines University's World War II manuscript collection. JAS 25 (1965-66) 123.

Philippines - History - 1898-1946

PHILIPPINES - LAWS, STATUTES, ETC.

PHILIPPINES - MINORITIES *See also* BAJAU, BASILAN, BATAK, BISAYAN, BUKIDNON, CHINESE, JAMA MAPUN, KAINGIN, MANGYAN, NEGRITOS, PALAWAN, SAMAL, SAMARAN, SULOD, SULU, TAGBANUA, TAOSUG, TASADAY, TINGUIANES, YAKAN

Filipino cultural minorities. A28
pp. 30-34.

7674 RAHMANN, RUDOLF. Our responsi-
bilities toward the cultural minorities. Z16 pp. 443-462.

7675 RESURRECCION, ABELARDO S. A
study of a conflict of interest
in the use of land in the Ambuklao-Binga Watershed, a land economic approach. SLURJ 2 (1971)
630-680.

7676 RICH, JOHN. Conferences on cultural minorities. PS 15 (1967)
177-182.

7677 WHITE, WILLIAM LAWRENCE. Challenge of the national minorities.
SJ 15 (1968) 87-91.

PHILIPPINES - MINORITIES - LUZON *See
also* BIKOL, BUWAYA, GADDANG, IBALOI,
IFUGAO, IGOROT, ISNEG, KALAHAN,
KALINGA, KANKANAY, NABALOI, PAMPANGA,
PANGASINAN, TAGALOG, TINGUINES

7678 EGGAN, FRED. Some aspects of bilateral social systems in the
northern Philippines. Z16 pp.
186-203.

7679 HAKCHOLNA, WILLIAM. Catalogue of
works on Cordillera ethnography
in the Igorot Study Center, Sagada,
Mountain Province. SLQ 7 (1969)
113-142.

7680 PACYAYA, ALFRED G. Acculturation and culture change in Sagada.
SJ 11 (1964) 14-25.

7681 SCOTT, WILLIAM HENRY. Boyhood in
Sagada. SJ 10 (1963) 387-399.

7682 SCOTT, WILLIAM HENRY. Educational
work with a cultural minority.
B13 pp. 140-148.

7683 SCOTT, WILLIAM HENRY. Educational
work with a cultural minority. SJ
11 (1964) 39-48.

PHILIPPINES - MINORITIES - MINDANAO *See
also* BAGOBO, BILAN, BUKIDNON, MAN-
DAYA, MANOBO, MARANAO, SUBANUN,
TIRURAI

7684 SANIEL, JOSEFA M. Japanese minority in the Philippines before
Pearl Harbor, social organization
in Davao. AST 4 (1966) 103-126.

PHILIPPINES - POLITICS AND GOVERNMENT

7685 ABUEVA, JOSE V. Functional development of the political system.
A28 pp. 60-63.

7686 ABUEVA, JOSE V. Political stability, development and welfare. A28
pp. 533-537.

7687 AGPALO, REMIGIO E. Pandaggo-sa-
ilaw, the politics of Occidental
Mindoro. PSSHR 28 (1963) 445-488.

7688 AGPALO, REMIGIO E. The Philippine
political system in the perspective of history. SJ 19 (1972) 1-
27.

7689 AGPALO, REMIGIO E. Regulation of
lobbying in the Philippines. A28
pp. 234-238.

7690 ALFONSO, CARIDAD S. Executive-
legislative relations. A28 pp.
343-346.

7691 ARANETA, FRANCISCO. Politics and
government. P47 pp. 136-154.

7692 ARCELLANA, EMERENCIANA Y. Indigenous political institutions.
A28 pp. 38-42.

Philippines - Politics and government

7693 ARCILLA, JOSE S. Exile of a
liberal in 1870, or Father Arnedo's case. PS 19 (1971) 373-419.

7694 ASPIRAS, JOSE D. Greatness, a
quality of leaders and men. A28
pp. 548-550.

7695 BERNAS, J. G. Democracy at the
grass roots. PS 8 (1960) 177-
180.

7696 CANOY, REUBEN R. Politics is
everybody's concern. SJ 16
(1969) 291-298.

7697 CAPIZ, PASCUAL. Religion of
politics. DR 17 (1969) 417-429.

7698 CHOI, YEARN H. Political style
and the democratic process in
Indonesia and the Philippines.
AST 9 (1971) 214-228.

7699 CORPUZ, O. D. Cultural foundations of Philippine politics.
E78 pp. 407-425.

7700 DARLING, FRANK C. Political development in Thailand and the
Philippines, a comparative analysis. SA 1 (1971) 90-115.

7701 FISCHER, GEORGES. The political
evolution of the Philippines.
R64 pp. 250-260.

7702 FRANTZICH, STEVE. Party switching
in the Philippine context. PS 16
(1968) 750-768.

7703 IGLESIAS, GABRIEL U. Our political and civil rights. A28 pp.
68-75.

7704 JESUS, EDILBERTO C. DE. Aguinaldo
and the American consuls. PHR 1
pt. 2 (1966) 125-167.

7705 LANDE, CARL H. Parties and politics in the Philippines. AS 8
(1968) 725-747.

7706 LANDE, CARL H. Political attitudes and behavior. A28 pp. 95-
114.

7707 LANDE, CARL H. Politics in the
Philippines. T45 pp. 362-381.

7708 LAURETA, AMANCIA G. Legislative
authorization of the budget. A28
pp. 282-292.

7709 MANGLAPUS, RAUL S. The case for
decentralization. A28 pp. 432-3.

7710 MANGLAPUS, RAUL S. State of Filipino democracy. A28 pp. 538-546.

7711 MILNE, R. S. Political finance in
Southeast Asia with particular
reference to the Philippines and
Malaysia. PA 41 (1968) 491-510.

7712 OBEN, RAMON T. On national affairs. UN 36 (1963) 446-451.

7713 PATANNE, EUFEMIO P. Political
opinion. A28 pp. 114-118.

7714 Political transmission 15, an
analysis. PS 8 (1960) 3-50.

7715 ROMANI, JOHN. Balance between
centralization and decentralization. A28 pp. 434-437.

7716 SILVESTRE, REYNALDO. The presidency, congress, and local government administration. DR 20 (1972)
82-103.

7717 SUHRKE, ASTRI. Political rituals
in developing nations, the case of
the Philippines. JSAS 2 (1971)
126-141.

7718 THOMAS, M. LADD. Centralism in the Philippines, past and present causes. A28 pp. 420-431.

7719 THOMAS, M. LADD. Historical origins of Philippine centralism. JSAH 4 (Sept. 1963) 51-64.

7720 WURFEL, DAVID. Individuals and groups in the Philippine policy process. A28 pp. 208-223.

7721 WURFEL, DAVID. The Philippines. K17 pp. 677-769.

PHILIPPINES - POLITICS AND GOVERNMENT - 1898-1946

7722 ALFONSO, OSCAR M. Taft's views on the Philippines for the Filipinos. AST 6 (1968) 237-247.

7723 ALIP, EUFRONIO M. First Filipino cabinet. UN 40 (1967) 395-405.

7724 BEADLES, JOHN A. Debate in the United States concerning Philippine independence, 1912-1916. PS 16 (1968) 421-441.

7725 CASAMBRE, NAPOLEON J. Response to Harrison's administration in the Philippines, 1913-1921. AST 7 (1969) 156-170.

7726 CRUZ, ROMEO V. America's colonial desk and the Philippines, 1898-1934. PSSHR 37 (1972) 267-514.

7727 CULLINANE, MICHAEL. Implementing the new order, the structure and supervision of local government during the Taft era. C31 pp. 13-75.

7728 FERNANDEZ, ALEJANDRO M. The 1898 republic and statehood. AST 4 (1966) 572-596.

Philippines - Politics and government - 1898-1946

7729 FRIEND, THEODORE A. American interests and Philippine independence, 1929-1933. PS 11 (1963) 505-523.

7730 FRIEND, THEODORE A. Manuel Quezon, charismatic conservative. PHR 1 pt. 1 (1965) 153-169.

7731 FRIEND, THEODORE A. Philippine independence and the last lame duck congress. PS 12 (1964) 260-276.

7732 FRIEND, THEODORE A. Philippine interests and the mission for independence, 1929-1932. PS 12 (1964) 63-82.

7733 FRIEND, THEODORE A. Philippine sugar industry and the politics of independence, 1929-1935. JAS 22 (1962-3) 179-192.

7734 FRIEND, THEODORE A. Veto and repassage of the Hare-Hawes-Cutting Act, a catalogue of motives. PS 12 (1964) 666-680.

7735 GOODMAN, GRANT K. Problem of Philippine independence and Japan, the first three decades of American colonial rule. SA 1 (1971) 164-190.

7736 GOSIENGFIAO, VICTOR. Japanese occupation, the cultural campaign. PS 14 (1966) 228-242.

7737 GOWING, PETER. Muslim-American relations in the Philippines, 1899-1920. AST 6 (1968) 372-382.

7738 GUERRERO, MILAGROS C. Colorum uprisings, 1924-1931. AST 5 (1967) 65-78.

7739 HOLLI, MELVIN G. View of the American campaign against Filipino insurgents, 1900. PS 17 (1969) 97-111.

Philippines - Politics and government -
1898-1946

7762 WHEELER, GERALD E. Manuel L. Quezon and the American presidents. AST 2 (1964) 231-246.

PHILIPPINES - POLITICS AND GOVERNMENT - 1946-1965

7763 BUTWELL, RICHARD. The Philippines, changing of the guard. AS 6 (1966) 43-48.

7764 BUTWELL, RICHARD. The Philippines, prelude to elections. AS 5 (1965) 43-48.

7765 A day with the president. A28 pp. 329-334.

7766 DRILON, REX D. Does democracy work in the Philippines? DR 9 (1961) 85-93.

7767 GAMBOA, MA. ELENA. Problem of reapportionment in the lower house, by Ma. Elena Gamboa and Raul P. de Guzman. A28 pp. 260-264.

7768 IGLESIAS, GABRIEL U. Structure and functions of congress, by Gabriel U. Iglesias and Abelardo Tolentino. A28 pp. 249-256.

7769 LOCSIN, TEODORO M. So called two party system in the Philippines. AST 2 (1964) 82-86.

7770 MEADOWS, MARTIN. Challenge to the new era in Philippine politics. PA 37 (1964) 296-306.

7771 NGUYEN CAO HACH. U.S. policy of hesitancy on the problem of colony. AC 3 (July 1961) 67-102.

7772 PAREJA, INOCENIO. Organizing congress. A28 pp. 257-260.

Philippines - Politics and government - 1965-

7773 RECTO, CLARO M. Evil of religious test in our democracy. DR 9 (1961) 65-84.

7774 SCHMITT, WILLIAM J. Suspension of congressman Osmena. PS 9 (1961) 144-153.

7775 STARNER, FRANCES. The Philippines, politics of the new era. AS 3 (1963) 41-47.

7776 WURFEL, DAVID. Changing Philippines. AS 4 (1964) 702-710.

PHILIPPINES - POLITICS AND GOVERNMENT - 1965-

7777 CARMEN, ROLANDO V. DEL. Constitutionalism and the Supreme Court in a changing Philippine polity. AS 13 (1973) 1050-1061.

7778 GROSSHOLTZ, JEAN. The Philippines, midterm doldrums for Marcos. AS 8 (1968) 52-57.

7779 GROSSHOLTZ, JEAN. The Philippines, new adventures with old problems. AS 9 (1969) 50-57.

7780 MACAHIYA, ERNESTO R. Footnote to revolution and social change, the Philippine case. AST 7 (1969) 142-155.

7781 MELCHOR, ALEJANDRO. Asian solution to an Asian problem. SJ 20 (1973) 129-135.

7782 OVERHOLT, WILLIAM. Martial law, revolution and democracy in the Philippines. SA 2 (1972-3) 158-190.

7783 Political repression in the Philippines. JCA 1 pt. 4 (1970) 86-88.

Philippines - Politics and government -
  1965-

7784 ROTH, DAVID F. Deterioration and reconstruction of national political parameters, the Philippines during the 1970's. AS 13 (1973) 812-825.

7785 Three documents from the Philippines. JCA 2 (1972) 454-460.

7786 TILMAN, ROBERT O. The Philippines in 1970, a difficult decade begins. AS 11 (1971) 139-148.

7787 Unity against repression. JCA 2 (1972) 123-125.

7788 VAN DER KROEF, JUSTUS M. Communism and reform in the Philippines. PA 46 (1973) 29-58.

7789 WURFEL, DAVID. The Philippines, intensified dialogue. AS 7 (1967) 47-52.

PHILIPPINES - POPULATION

7790 BALITON, JESUS Q. The effects of population growth in the production and distribution of palay in the province of Nueva Vizcaya. SLURJ 5 (1974) 418-462.

7791 BALITON, JESUS Q. The effects of population growth in the production and distribution of palay in the province of Nueva Vizcaya. SLURJ 5 (1974) 469-517.

7792 CONCEPCION, MERCEDES B. Philippine population crisis, fact or fancy? UN 39 (1960) 332-340.

7793 CONCEPCION, MERCEDES B. The Philippine population problem. G73 pp. 1-18.

7794 CONCEPCION, MERCEDES B. Population of the Philippines. C47 pp. 185-199.

7795 FLOR, DIOSDADO. Factors guiding the population growth in the Philippines, economic development and population pressure in the Philippines. UN 39 (1966) 357-367.

7796 GOROSPE, VITALIANO R. Catholic hierarchy and the population problem. PS 17 (1969) 806-810.

7797 GUTIERREZ, JOSE S. Agricultural productivity and population increase, the Philippine case. C47 pp. 469-492.

7798 HILARIO, ELVIRA A. Factors guiding the population growth in the Philippines, socio-economic factors, by Elvira A. Hilario and Grace S. David. UN 39 (1966) 341-349.

7799 HUNT, CHESTER L. Ethnic stratification and integration in Cotabato. E78 pp. 202-231.

7800 LIU, WILLIAM T. Fertility patterns in Cebu. B13 pp. 167-205.

7801 LORIMER, FRANK W. Analysis and projections of the population of the Philippines. C47 pp. 200-314.

7802 LUNA, TELESFORO W. Geographic distribution of population. UN 39 (1966) 424-439.

7803 PANIZO, ALFREDO. Population, here is a problem. UN 39 (1966) 322-331.

7804 PASCUAL, ELVIRA M. Population redistribtuion in the Philippines. UN 39 (1966) 453-459.

7805 PEEK, PETER. Household savings and demographic change in the Philippines. MER 19 pt. 2 (1974) 86-104.

7806 Relation of schooling to size of family. C47 pp. 502-507.

7807 Republic of the Philippines population reaches 27 million. SLQ 1 (1963) 247-8.

7808 REYES, WILFREDO L. Philippine population growth and health development. C47 pp. 423-468.

7809 SALCEDO, JUAN. Closing address, trends and prospects of population growth. C47 pp. 149-159.

7810 SIMKINS, PAUL D. Growth and internal migrations of the Philippine population, 1948 to 1960, by Paul D. Simkins and Frederick L. Wernstedt. JTG 17 (1963) 197-202.

7811 TABLANTE, NATHANIEL B. Food and population problems in the Philippines. AST 4 (1966) 374-380.

7812 VERA, FE V. VITO DE. Internal migration as a temporary solution to the population problems of the Philippines, by Fe V. Vito de Vera and Elfren Micor. UN 39 (1966) 440-452.

7813 YENGOYAN, ARAM A. Initial populating of the Philippines, some problems and interpretations. Z16 pp. 175-185.

7814 ZUMEL-LOPEZ, MARIA LUISA. Aging population in the Philippines, an economic and social asset or liability? UN 39 (1966) 468-474.

PHILIPPINES - RELIGION *See also*
  BUDDHISM - PHILIPPINES, CHRISTIANITY - PHILIPPINES, CATHOLIC CHURCH, AGLIPAYAN CHURCH, IGLESIA NI CRISTO

7815 ARENS, RICHARD. Religious rituals and their socio-economic implications in Philippine society. E78 pp. 377-389.

7816 BELLO, MOISES. Some observations on beliefs and rituals of the Bakun-Kinkanay. Z16 pp. 324-342.

7817 BOSTROM, LYNN C. Filipino Bahala Na and American fatalism. SJ 15 (1968) 399-413.

7818 DeRAEDT, JULES. Religious representations in northern Luzon. SLQ 2 (1964) 245-348.

7819 FERNANDEZ, RENATO C. Supernatural beliefs related to the disaster, July-August 1972. SLURJ 4 (1973) 122-148.

7820 GONZALEZ, MARY A. Religious minorities in the Philippines. UN 36 (1963) 366-372.

7821 HISLOP, STEPHEN K. Anitism, a survey of religious beliefs native to the Philippines. AST 9 (1971) 144-156.

7822 JOCANO, F. LANDA. Filipino Catholicism, a case study in religious change. AST 5 (1967) 42-64.

7823 JOCANO, F. LANDA. Notes on Philippine divinities. AST 6 (1968) 169-182.

7824 JOCANO, F. LANDA. Philippine mythology and general education. GEJ 12 (1966) 143-149.

7825 MAQUISO, ELENA G. Langkat, its relationship to the Ulahingan. SJ 17 (1970) 407-419.

7826 MUNOZ, MA. TERESA. Notes on theater, pre-Hispanic Philippines, religion, myth, religious ritual. M24 pp. 648-667.

Philippines - Religion

7827 ORACION, TIMOTEO S. Anthropology of religion and general education. GEJ 12 (1966) 189-206.

7828 PACYAYA, ALFREDO G. Religious acculturation in Sagada. B13 pp. 128-139.

7829 PAL, AGATON P. People's conception of the world. E78 pp. 390-398.

7830 ROCES, ALFREDO R. Mask of Longinus. PS 9 (1961) 255-261.

7831 SCOTT, WILLIAM HENRY. Apo-Dios concept in northern Luzon. B13 pp. 116-127.

7832 SCOTT, WILLIAM HENRY. Apo-Dios concept in northern Luzon. PS 8 (1960) 772-788.

7833 SCOTT, WILLIAM HENRY. Some religious terms in Sagada Igorot. Z16 pp. 480-493.

7834 SMART, JOHN E. Manolay cult, the genesis and dissolution of millenarian sentiments among the Isneg of northern Luzon. AST 8 (1970) 53-93.

7835 SYCIP, FELICIDAD C. Factors related to acceptance or rejection of innovations. E78 pp. 399-403.

PHILIPPINES - SOCIAL CONDITIONS

7836 ARCILLA, JOSE S. Slavery, flogging and other moral cases in 17th century Philippines. PS 20 (1972) 399-416.

7837 ARENS, RICHARD. Religious rituals and their socio-economic implications in Philippine society. E78 pp. 377-389.

7838 BARTOLOME, C. C. Problem of aging among Filipinos. PSSHR 26 (1961) 219-232.

7839 CARROLL, JOHN J. Philippine social organization and national development. PS 14 (1966) 575-590.

7840 CARROLL, JOHN J. Traditional Philippine social structure. SJ 19 (1972) 80-88.

7841 CASINO, ERIC S. Jama Mapun ethnoecology, economic and symbolic (of grains, winds and stars). AST 5 (1967) 1-32.

7842 CASTILLO, GELIA T. Mirror, mirror on the wall, an analysis of changing social images in a developing society. AST 9 (1971) 24-36.

7843 CASTILLO, GELIA T. Study of occupational evaluation in the Philippines. PSSHR 26 (1961) 129-165.

7844 CATAPUSAN, BENICIO T. Ethnic and racial distance. PSSHR 30 (1965) 87-108.

7845 COLLER, RICHARD W. Analysis of the social effects of donated radios on barrio life. E78 pp. 268-285.

7846 COLLER, RICHARD W. Barrio Gacao, a study of village ecology and the schistosomiasis problem. E78 pp. 536-549.

7847 COLLER, RICHARD W. Barrio Gacao, a study of village ecology and the schistosomiasis problem. E78 pp. 642-652.

7848 EGGAN, FRED. Philippine social structure. G53 pp. 1-48.

7849 EGGAN, FRED. Some aspects of bilateral social systems in the

northern Philippines. Z16 pp.
186-203.

7850 FLIEGER, WILHELM. The Philippines in transition. SJ 19
(1972) 33-41.

7851 FOX, ROBERT B. Filipino concept
of self esteem. E78 pp. 356-362.

7852 HARRISSON, TOM. Palang, its his-
tory and protohistory in west
Borneo and the Philippines.
JMBRAS 37 pt. 2 (1964) 162-174.

7853 HART, DONN V. Christian Filipino
society approaching the 21st century. SJ 18 (1971) 21-55.

7854 HENDRICKX, HERMAN. Old testament
view of social justice and Philippine society. SJ 18 (1971) 258-
269.

7855 HOLLNSTEINER, MARY R. Reciprocity
in the lowland Philippines. E78
pp. 335-355.

7856 HOLLNSTEINER, MARY R. Reciprocity
in the lowland Philippines. PS 9
(1961) 387-413.

7857 HUNT, CHESTER L. Changing social
patterns in the Philippines. SJ
9 (1962) 32-43.

7858 INFANTE, TERESITA R. Woman in
early Philippines, and among the
cultural minorities. UN 42 (1969)
4-196.

7859 ISRAEL, CAROLYN CRISPINO. Gapang,
the practice of sleepcrawling in a
Tagalog community. AST 9 (1971)
157-163.

7860 JOCANO, FELIPE LANDA. Filipino
social structure and value system.
SJ 19 (1972) 59-79.

7861 JOSE, F. SIONIL. Art and revolution. SJ 17 (1970) 357-366.

7862 LYNCH, FRANK. Philippine values
II, social acceptance. E78 pp.
318-332.

7863 LYNCH, FRANK. Social class in a
Bikol town. E78 pp. 164-169.

7864 LYNCH, FRANK. Trends report of
studies in social stratification
and social mobility in the Philippines. EACS 4 (1965) 163-191.

7865 MAGDALENA, FEDERICO V. Cumulative
scales to measure level of living
of two Philippine communities.
GEJ 21 (1971) 99-101.

7866 MATURAV, EULALIO G. Social dimensions of rural development. SJ 19
(1972) 130-145.

7867 MONTEMAYOR, JEREMIAS. The Philippine socio-economic situation. SJ
19 (1972) 42-58.

7868 ORIAN, ANUNCIACION D. Observations on Philippine status symbols,
regional characteristics, and social stratification. SLURJ 2
(1971) 52-63.

7869 OWEN, NORMAN G. Introduction,
Philippine society and American
colonialism. C31 pp. 1-12.

7870 PACANA, HONESTO CH. Notes on a
Filipino rule of conduct: non-
interference. E78 pp. 332-334.

7871 RICE, DELBERT. Ancient Philippine
democracy, pre-Hispanic social
structures and their modern implications. SJ 19 (1972) 249-312.

7872 SCAFF, ALVIN H. Class stratification in the EDCOR communities.
E78 pp. 193-199.

Philippines - Social conditions

7873 Social class. E78 pp. 144-163.

7874 STONE, RICHARD L. Some aspects of Muslim social organization. M24 pp. 90-133.

PHILIPPINES - TREATIES

7875 JOHNSON, STEPHEN F. Philippine treaty patterns, 1946-1965. AF 4 pt. 3 (1972) 11-29.

PHILIPPINES. CONGRESS

7876 ABUEVA, JOSE V. Social backgrounds and recruitment of legislators and administrators. A28 pp. 264-282.

7877 FRANCISCO, GREGORIO A. Congress and patronage, by Gregorio A. Francisco and Raul P. de Guzman. A28 pp. 299-305.

7878 FRANCISCO, GREGORIO A. 50-50 agreement, by Gregorio A. Francisco and Raul P. de Guzman. G93 pp. 105-135.

7879 GAMBOA, MA. ELENA. Problem of reapportionment in the lower house, by Ma. Elena Gamboa and Raul P. de Guzman. A28 pp. 260-264.

7880 IGLESIAS, GABRIEL U. Structure and functions of congress, by Gabriel U. Iglesias and Abelardo Tolentino. A28 pp. 249-256.

7881 JENISTA, FRANK. Conflict in the Philippine legislature: the Commission and the Assembly from 1907-1913. C31 pp. 77-101.

7882 PAREJA, INOCENIO. Organizing congress. A28 pp. 257-260.

7883 ROCES, JOAQUIN R. Congressional power of investigation. A28 pp. 293-299.

PHILIPPINES. DEPT. OF EDUCATION AND CULTURE

7884 GONZALEZ, ANDREW. The 1973 constitution and the bilingual education policy of the Department of Education and Culture. PS 22 (1974) 325-337.

PHILIPPINES. NATIONAL ECONOMIC COUNCIL

7885 ARANETA, SALVADOR. The planning, the approval and implementation of economic policy. M38 pp. 132-146.

7886 LOCSIN, JOSE C. The National Economic Council and economic planning. M38 pp. 147-160.

7887 MILNE, R. S. The National Economic Council and its relation to other government agencies. M38 pp. 184-203.

7888 PERALTA, VICENTE L. Congress and economic planning. M38 pp. 76-82.

7889 PUYAT, GIL J. Congress and economic planning. M38 pp. 62-75.

7890 REYES, HERMENEGILDO B. National Economic Council, planning and private enterprise. M38 pp. 48-61.

7891 RODRIGUEZ, FILEMON C. National Economic Council, past and present. M38 pp. 38-47.

PHILIPPINES. PRESIDENT

7892 A day with the president. A28 pp. 329-334.

7893 GARCIA, CARLOS P. On the powers of the president. SJ 19 (1972) 28-32.

7894 JACOBINI, H. B. Observations on the Philippine vice presidency. A28 pp. 334-342.

7895 ROMANI, JOHN H. Observations on the Philippine presidency. A28 pp. 311-321.

7896 SISON, JESUS C. Power and functions of the president. A28 pp. 322-329.

PHILOSOPHY - PHILIPPINES

7897 MERCADO, LEONARDO N. Filipino thought. PS 20 (1972) 207-272.

PHILOSOPHY - VIETNAM

7898 NGUYEN DANG THUC. Eastern philosophy and national tradition. AC 3 (July 1961) 133-137.

7899 NGUYEN DANG THUC. Oriental philosophical thought. AC 3 (Apr. 1961) 1-11.

PHRAO, THAILAND

7900 PENTH, HANS. Old Phrao. JSS 60 pt. 1 (1972) 375-378.

PHU THAI

7901 KIRSCH, A. THOMAS. Development and mobility among the Phu Thai of northeast Thailand. AS 6 (1966) 370-378.

PHUKET ISLAND

7902 GERINI, G. E. Historical retrospect of Junkceylon Island. S44.4 pp. 3-109.

PIGAFETTA, ANTONIO

7903 ROBERTSON, J. F. Using Pigafetta's journal. BMJ 3 pt. 1 (1973) 100-104.

PILAR, MARCELO H. DEL

7904 CRUZ, ROMEO V. Nationalism of Marcelo H. del Pilar. GEJ 5 (1963) 13-25.

7905 YABES, LEOPOLDO Y. Plaridel as intellectual and writer. DR 11 (1963) 299-310.

7906 ZAPANTA, LEA S. Marcelo H. del Pilar, the political thinker. PSSHR 31 (1966) 133-168.

7907 ZAPANTA, LEA S. Political ideas of Marcelo H. del Pilar. DR 15 (1967) 1-182.

PILIPINO LANGUAGE *See also* TAGALOG LANGUAGE

7908 ASPILLERA, PARALUMAN S. Filling a gap in the modernization of Pilipino. A43 pp. 91-111.

7909 BERGER, KENNETH W. Most frequently found words in printed Pilipino. DR 17 (1969) 133-162.

7910 BERGER, KENNETH W. Proposal for a Pilipino dictionary listing adopted English words. SJ 21 (1974) 367-444.

Pilipino language

7911 BERNAL, RAFAEL. Mexican influence in Filipino language. UN 36 (1963) 312-315.

7912 BONIFACIO, ARMANDO F. Pilipino as medium of instruction at the university level. DR 17 (1969) 105-130.

7913 FERRIOLS, ROQUE J. Memoir of six years. PS 22 (1974) 338-345.

7914 GONZALEZ, ANDREW. The 1973 constitution and the bilingual education policy of the Department of Education and Culture. PS 22 (1974) 325-337.

7915 HIDALGO, CESAR A. Responsible nationalism through linguistics. DR 18 (1970) 232-247.

7916 ISIDIRO, ANTONIO. Modernization of the Philippine national language, Pilipino. A43 pp. 112-119.

7917 ORDONEZ, ELMER A. Case for English studies. GEJ 17 (1969) 148-152.

7918 ORIAN, ANUNCIACION D. Should Pilipino supplant English as the medium of instruction in Philippine schools? SLURJ 1 (1970) 444-472.

7919 PAGUIO, MA. ELENA A. Filipino as a medium of instruction in speech. GEJ 25 (1973-4) 69-74.

7920 PANGANIBAN, JOSE VILLA. Background of the Filipino language. UN 34 (Sept. 1961) 110-1.

7921 PANGANIBAN, JOSE VILLA. Present situation of Pilipino. UN 39 (1966) 301-306.

7922 Prospects for Pilipino. PS 9 (1961) 301-310.

7923 UKUN SURJAMAN. Pilipino numerals, a discourse on language integration. AST 7 (1969) 171-179.

7924 VICENCIO, MA. NENITA C. Descriptive study of nonfluencies occurring in English and Pilipino impromptu speeches of forty Speech 1 students. GEJ 25 (1973-4) 95-102.

7925 VILLANUEVA, ANTONIA F. Origin, growth and future of Pilipino. UN 39 (1966) 288-300.

7926 YABES, LEOPOLDO Y. Let's study the new constitution, the language provision. PSSHR 38 (1973) 1-173.

PILIPINO LITERATURE *See also* TAGALOG LITERATURE

7927 ABUEG, EFREN R. Panitikang Pilipino, pakikilahok, 1946-1968. PS 17 (1969) 220-248.

PINEDA, MACARIO

7928 DIZON, ANACLETO I. Macario Pineda. PS 18 (1970) 350-363.

7929 REYES, SOLEDAD. Theme in the stories of Macario Pineda. PS 19 (1971) 456-489.

PINTO, FERNAO MENDEZ

7930 WOOD, W. A. R. Fernao Mendez Pinto's account of events in Siam. S44.7 pp. 195-209.

Place names *See* NAMES, GEOGRAPHICAL

POERBATJARAKA

7931 DREWES, G. W. J. De ontdekking
      van Poerbatjaraka. BIJ 129 (1973)
      482-492.

7932 PIGEAUD, TH. In memoriam, Profes-
      sor Poerbatjaraka. BIJ 122 (1966)
      405-412.

POISONS

7933 ANUMAN RAJADHON. Data on condi-
      tioned poison, a folklore study.
      JSS 53 (1965) 69-82.

7934 GALLIH BALANG. Origin of poison
      inside Borneo. SMJ 12 (1965) 235.

7935 JAMUH, GEORGE. Ideas about
      poisoning. SMJ 9 (1960) 461-467.

7936 JAMUH, GEORGE. Melanau population
      destroyed by poisonous snake. SMJ
      12 (1965) 230-234.

POIVRE, PIERRE

7937 LY TIO FANE, MADELEINE. Pierre
      Poivre et l'expansion francaise
      dans l'Indo-Pacifique. BEF 53
      (1966) 453-510.

POLICE - MALAYSIA

7938 MORRAH, PATRICK. History of the
      Malayan police. JMBRAS 36 pt. 2
      (1963) 5-172.

7939 TURNBULL, C. M. Internal security
      in the Straits Settlements, 1826-
      1867. JSAS 1 pt. 1 (1970) 37-53.

POLICE - SINGAPORE

7940 TURNBULL, C. M. Internal security
      in the Straits Settlements, 1826-
      1867. JSAS 1 pt. 1 (1970) 37-53.

POLITICAL PARTIES

7941 GAMER, ROBERT E. Southeast Asia's
      political systems, an overview.
      JSAH 8 (1967) 139-185.

7942 McLENNAN, BARBARA N. Political
      parties and economic development
      in developing states, by Barbara
      N. McLennan and Robert D. Cantor.
      AQ (1973) 177-192.

7943 SATHYAMURTHY, T. V. Introduction.
      JSAH 8 (1967) 2-7.

POLITICAL PARTIES - BURMA

7944 NASH, MANNING. Party building in
      Upper Burma. AS 3 (1963) 197-202.

7945 SILVERSTEIN, JOSEF. Burma Social-
      ist Program Party and its rivals,
      a one plus party system. JSAH 8
      (1967) 8-18.

POLITICAL PARTIES - CAMBODIA

7946 Cambodia, country without parties.
      JSAH 8 (1967) 40-51.

7947 Joint communique of the delegation
      of the FUNK and the GRUNC and the
      delegation of the Lao Patriotic
      Front. JCA 4 (1974) 367-370.

7948 Political programme of the Nation-
      al United Front of Kampuchea
      (FUNK). JCA 1 pt. 2 (1970) 80-85.

POLITICAL PARTIES - PHILIPPINES

7970 HOLLNSTEINER, MARY R. Development of political parties in a town. A28 pp. 158-180.

7971 LAMBINO, ANTONIO B. Party responsibility in legislation. PS 12 (1964) 511-516.

7972 LANDE, CARL H. Brief history of political parties. A28 pp. 151-157.

7973 LANDE, CARL H. Parties and politics in the Philippines. AS 8 (1968) 725-747.

7974 LANDE, CARL H. Party politics in the Philippines. G53 pp. 85-131.

7975 LANDE, CARL H. Philippine political party system. JSAH 8 (1967) 19-39.

7976 LOCSIN, TEODORO M. Two party system and democracy. A28 pp. 200-203.

7977 MEADOWS, MARTIN. Philippine political parties and the 1961 election. PA 35 (1962) 261-274.

7978 MEADOWS, MARTIN. Political parties and presidential politics. A28 pp. 188-200.

7979 MILNE, R. S. Filipino party system. A28 pp. 181-187.

7980 ONORATO, MICHAEL PAUL. Democrata Party. PS 12 (1964) 342-347.

7981 Three documents from the Philippines. JCA 2 (1972) 454-460.

POLITICAL PARTIES - SINGAPORE *See also* PEOPLES ACTION PARTY

7982 BELLOWS, THOMAS J. Singapore party system. JSAH 8 (1967) 122-138.

7983 GAMER, ROBERT E. Parties and pressure groups. M49 pp. 197-207.

7984 YEO KIM WAH. Study of three early political parties in Singapore, 1945-1955. JSAH 10 (1969) 115-141.

POLITICAL PARTIES - THAILAND

7985 DARLING, FRANK C. Political parties in Thailand. PA 44 (1971) 228-241.

POLITICAL PARTIES - VIETNAM

7986 GOODMAN, ALLAN E. South Vietnam, neither war nor peace. AS 10 (1970) 107-132.

7987 HONEY, P. J. North Vietnam's Workers' Party and south Vietnam's Peoples Revolutionary Party. PA 35 (1962) 375-383.

7988 IRVING, R. E. M. M. R. P. and French policy in Indochina, 1945-1954, with special reference to the influence of Catholicism. FA 23 (1969) 257-269.

7989 JOINER, CHARLES A. Patterns of political party behavior in south Vietnam. JSAH 8 (1967) 83-98.

7990 MAU, MICHAEL P. Training of cadres in the Lao Dong Party of north Vietnam, 1960-1967. AS 9 (1969) 281-296.

7991 NORMAND, MARJORIE WEINER. Party system in north Vietnam. JSAH 8 (1967) 68-82.

Political parties - Vietnam

7992　PHAN THIEN CHAU. Leadership in the Viet Nam Workers Party, the process of transition. AS 12 (1972) 772-782.

7993　SCIGLIANO, ROBERT G. Political parties in south Vietnam under the republic. PA 33 (1960) 327-346.

7994　SMITH, R. B. Bui Quang Chien and the Constitutionalist Party in French Cochinchina, 1917-30. MAS 3 (1969) 131-150.

POLITICAL SCIENCE

7995　VAN DER KROEF, JUSTUS M. Indonesian ideological lexicon. AS 2 (July 1962) 24-30.

7996　WU TEH YAO. Teaching political science in South-East Asia today. JSAS 5 (1974) 125-133.

7997　WU TEH YAO. Teaching political science in Southeast Asia today. RSAS 3 pts. 1-2 (1973) 1-14.

POLO, MARCO

7998　JACK-HINTON, COLIN. Marco Polo in South-East Asia. JSAH 5 (Sept. 1964) 43-103.

7999　STERNSTEIN, LARRY. Note on three Polo maps, by Larry Sternstein and John Black. F38 pp. 347-349.

POLOTAN, KERIMA

8000　BERNAD, MIGUEL A. Hand of the enemy, the stories of Kerima Polotan. PS 17 (1969) 40-59.

8001　CASPER, LEONARD. Desire and doom in Kerima Polotan. PS 17 (1969) 60-71.

PONS Y TORRES, SALVADOR

8002　GUERRERO, LEON MA. Nozaleda and Pons, two Spanish friars in exodus. A58 pp. 172-202.

Population　*See this subdivision under individual countries*

Population control　*See*　BIRTH CONTROL

PORTS - MALAYSIA

8003　COLLESS, BRIAN E. Early western ports of the Malay peninsula. JTG 29 (1969) 1-9.

PORTUGUESE TIMOR

8004　CLAMAGIRAND, BRIGITTE. Le travail du coton chez les Ema de Timor portugais. AR 3 (1972) 55-80.

8005　WEATHERBEE, DONALD E. Portuguese Timor, an Indonesian dilemma. AS 6 (1966) 683-695.

POTTERY　*See also*　ARCHAEOLOGY

8006　GRIFFING, ROBERT P. Trade porcelain and stoneware in Southeast Asia, a report of a symposium. AP 5 (1961) 235-6.

8007　HARRISSON, BARBARA. Stonewares, Marco Polo ware in Southeast Asia. SMJ 11 (1962) 412-416.

8008　HARRISSON, TOM. Trade porcelain and stoneware in South East Asia,

including Borneo. SMJ 10 (1961)
222-226.

8009   SOLHEIM, WILHELM G. Further relationships of the Sa-Huynh-
Kalanay pottery tradition. AP 8
(1964) 196-211.

8010   SOLHEIM, WILHELM G. Sa-Huynh-
Kalanay pottery tradition, past
and future research. Z16 pp.
151-174.

8011   SOLHEIM, WILHELM G. Two pottery
traditions of late prehistoric
times in South-East Asia. S93
pp. 15-22.

POTTERY – BRUNEI

8012   HARRISSON, BARBARA. Classification of archaeological trade
ceramics from Kota Batu, Brunei.
BMJ 2 pt. 1 (1970) 114-188.

8013   HARRISSON, BARBARA. European
trade ceramics in the Brunei
Museum. BMJ 3 pt. 1 (1973) 66-87.

8014   HARRISSON, BARBARA. Sungai Lumut,
a 15th century burial ground, by
Barbara Harrisson and P. M.
Shariffuddin. BMJ 1 (1969) 24-56.

8015   HARRISSON, TOM. Siege of Pulau
Chermin. BMJ 2 pt. 1 (1970) 198-
208.

POTTERY – CAMBODIA

8016   BROWN, ROXANNA. A Khmer kiln
site, Surin Province, by Roxanna
Brown, Vance Childress and Michael
Gluckman. JSS 62 pt. 2 (1974)
239-252.

POTTERY – INDONESIA

8017   SUKARTO K. A., M. M. Notes on pottery manufacture near Raba, east
Sumbawa. AP 16 (1973) 71-74.

POTTERY – LAOS

8018   SOLHEIM, WILHELM G. Notes on pottery manufacture near Luang Prabang, Laos. JSS 55 (1967) 81-84.

8019   VELDER, CHRISTIAN. La poterie du
Wat Si Satthanak, Vientiane, Laos.
F38 pp. 199-201.

POTTERY – MALAYSIA

8020   HARRISSON, TOM. Double spouted
vessels. II. In west Malaysia and
Singapore from prehistory to the
present day. JMBRAS 47 pt. 2
(1974) 139-147.

8021   MATTHEWS, JOHN. Kerubong hoard.
PS 10 (1962) 386-433.

8022   MATTHEWS, JOHN. Results of excavations in Malaya. AP 5 (1961)
237-242.

8023   WALL, LINDSAY. Prehistoric
earthenwares pottery common to
Sarawak and Malaya. SMJ 11 (1962)
417-427.

POTTERY – MALAYSIA – SABAH

8024   ALMAN, JOHN H. Bajau pottery.
SMJ 9 (1960) 583-602.

8025   ALMAN, JOHN H. Dusun pottery,
Tuaran area. SMJ 9 (1960) 565-
582.

8026   HARRISSON, TOM. Small Dusun type
jar in the Sarawak Museum. SMJ 14
(1966) 156-7.

8050 TRELOAR, F. E. Stoneware bottles in the Sarawak Museum, vessels for mercury trade? SMJ 20
(1972) 377-384.

8051 TUTON KABOY. Ceramics and their
uses among the coastal Melanus,
by Tuton Kaboy and Eine Moore.
SMJ 15 (1967) 10-29.

8052 WALL, LINDSAY. Prehistoric
earthenwares, pottery common to
Sarawak and Malaya. SMJ 11 (1962)
417-427.

8053 ZAINIE, CARLA. Early Chinese
stonewares excavated in Sarawak,
1947-67, a suggested first basic
classification. SMJ 15 (1967)
30-90.

POTTERY - PHILIPPINES

8054 ABAYA, CONSUELO. On collecting
pottery. GEJ 4 (1962) 98-102.

8055 ADDIS, J. M. Dating of Chinese
porcelain found in the Philippines, a historical retrospect.
PS 16 (1968) 371-380.

8056 AUROY, ISABELITA R. Pottery
heirlooms from Mindanao. PS 11
(1963) 164-167.

8057 AYALA, FERNANDO ZOBEL DE. First
Philippine porcelain. PS 9
(1961) 17-19.

8058 ERDBERG-CONSTEN, ELEANOR. Manila
trade pottery seminar. PS 16
(1968) 545-557.

8059 HARRISSON, TOM. Ceramic crayfish
and related vessels in central
Borneo, the Philippines and Sweden. SMJ 15 (1967) 1-9.

8060 KAMER AGA OGLU. Ming porcelain
from sites in the Philippines.
AP 5 (1961) 243-252.

POTTERY - SINGAPORE

8061 HARRISSON, TOM. Double spouted
vessels. II. In west Malaysia and
Singapore from prehistory to the
present day. JMBRAS 47 pt. 2
(1974) 139-147.

POTTERY - THAILAND

8062 GRAHAM, W. A. Pottery in Siam.
S44.1 pp. 99-130.

8063 HARRISSON, TOM. Incised figures
from the top of a lid found on
Sanui Island, Thailand. AP 9
(1966) 111-2.

8064 O'CONNOR, S. J. Western peninsular Thailand and west Sarawak,
ceramic and statuary comparisons,
by S. J. O'Connor and Tom Harrisson. SMJ 11 (1964) 562-566.

8065 SMAN VARDHANABHUTI. Note on
celadon ware of Sukhothai. JSS
57 (1969) 333-4.

8066 SOLHEIM, WILHELM G. Pottery manufacture in Sting Mor and Ban Nong
Sua Kin Ma, Thailand. JSS 52
(1964) 151-161.

8067 SOLHEIM, WILHELM G. Preliminary
report on a new pottery complex in
northeastern Thailand. F38 pp.
249-254.

8068 SPINKS, CHARLES NELSON. Covered
bowls of the Sawankhalok kilns.
T33 pp. 261-272.

8069 SPINKS, CHARLES NELSON. Early
Thai pottery. SMJ 10 (1961) 216-
221.

Pottery - Thailand

8070 SPINKS, CHARLES NELSON. Siam and the pottery trade of Asia. S44.3 pp. 247-315.

8071 VAN ESTERIK, PENELOPE. Preliminary analysis of Ban Chaing painted pottery, northeast Thailand. AP 16 (1973) 174-194.

POTTERY - VIETNAM

8072 FONTAINE, HENRI. Nouveau champ de jarres dans la province de Long Khanh. SEIB 47 (1972) 397-485.

8073 FONTAINE, HENRI. Renseignements nouveaux sur la ceramique du champ de jarres funeraires de Dau-Giay. SEIB 46 (1971) 323-337.

8074 SAURIN, EDMOND. Le champ de jarres de Hang Gon pres Xuan Loc (sud Viet-Nam). BEF 60 (1973) 329-357.

8075 SAURIN, EDMOND. Station prehistorique a Hang-Gon pres Xuan-Loc, sud-Viet Nam. BEF 51 (1963) 433-452.

PRAOK LANGUAGE

8076 SHORTO, H. L. Structural patterns of northern Mon-Khmer languages. L55 pp. 45-61.

PRIDI PANOMYONG

8077 MORELL, DAVID. The impermanence of society, Marxism, Buddhism and the political philosophy of Thailand's Pridi Panomyong, by David and Susan Morell. SA 2 (1972) 396-424.

Printing *See* PUBLISHERS AND PUBLISHING

Prisoners *See* CRIME AND CRIMINALS

Psychological tests *See* MENTAL TESTS

PSYCHOLOGY - PHILIPPINES

8078 ESTRADA, JOSEFA. Inferiority complex, a Filipino trait? UN 38 (1965) 517-523.

8079 MERINO, JESUS M. Oriental traits and the psychology of the Filipinos. UN 38 (1965) 488-497.

8080 ROQUE, DATIVA C. Study of the Zeigarnik phenomenon in Philippine setting. SLURJ 2 (1971) 29-40.

8081 ROSALES, VICENTE. Influence of Spanish culture on the psychology of the Filipino. UN 38 (1965) 498-504.

8082 SAMSON, EMMANUEL V. Typologies and the Filipino temperament. UN 38 (1965) 511-516.

8083 SAMSON, JOSE A. Is there a Filipino psychology? UN 38 (1965) 477-487.

8084 SECHREST, LEE. Occurrence of a nervous mannerism in two cultures. AST 9 (1971) 55-63.

PUBLIC ADMINISTRATION

8085 CHAPEL, YVES. Quelques experiences de gestion centralisee de la fonction publique dans le sud-est asiatique. RSA (1967) 71-84.

8086 HSUEH, S. S. Eastern regional co-operation in public administration. H75 pp. 241-249.

8087 HSUEH, S. S. Technical cooperation in development administration in South and Southeast Asia. D49 pp. 339-365.

8088 QUAH SIEW TIEN, JON. Assessment of United States technical assistance programs in public administration in Southeast Asia. RSAS 2 (1972) 37-48.

PUBLIC ADMINISTRATION - BURMA

8089 KYAN. King Mindon's councillors. JBRS 44 (1961) 43-60.

8090 KYAN. Village administration in Upper Burma during 1886-87. JBRS 52 (Dec. 1969) 67-80.

8091 THAN TUN. Administration under King Thalun, 1629-48. JBRS 51 (1968) 173-188.

8092 THAUNG. Public administration in Burma. H75 pp. 11-27.

PUBLIC ADMINISTRATION - CAMBODIA

8093 TIM KENN. Public administration in Cambodia. H75 pp. 29-41.

PUBLIC ADMINISTRATION - INDONESIA

8094 BENDA, HARRY J. Pattern of administrative reforms in the closing years of Dutch rule in Indonesia. JAS 25 (1965-6) 589-605.

8095 PRAJUDI ATMOSUDIRDJO. Some notes on public administration in Indonesia. H75 pp. 43-50.

8096 PURBATJARAKA, PURNADI. Shahbandars in the archipelago. JSAH 2 (July 1961) 1-9.

PUBLIC ADMINISTRATION - MALAYSIA

8097 GROVES, HARRY E. Public administration in the Federation of Malaya. H75 pp. 77-92.

8098 KHOO KAY KIM. Origin of British administration in Malaya. JMBRAS 39 pt. 1 (1966) 52-91.

8099 NESS, GAYL D. Modernization and indigenous control of the bureaucracy in Malaysia. AS 5 (1965) 467-473.

8100 RUDNER, MARTIN. Organization of the British military administration in Malaya, 1946-48. JSAH 9 (1968) 95-106.

8101 TILMAN, ROBERT O. Public Service Commissions in the Federation of Malaya. JAS 20 (1960-1) 181-196.

PUBLIC ADMINISTRATION - PHILIPPINES

8102 CORPUZ, ONOFRE D. Evolution of the bureaucracy in the Philippines. A28 pp. 381-2.

8103 ESQUELA, ESTER. Controversial pipes, by Ester Esquela and Leandro A. Viloria. G93 pp. 197-240.

8104 FIRMALINO, TITO C. District supervisor's dilemma. G93 pp. 549-587.

8105 GUZMAN, RAUL P. DE. Change order no. 1, by Raul P. de Guzman and Frank Landers. G93 pp. 449-474.

Public administration - Philippines

PUBLISHERS AND PUBLISHING - BRUNEI

8123 Note sur le Dewan Bahasa dan Pustaka de Brunei. AR 3 (1972) 20-22.

PUBLISHERS AND PUBLISHING - BURMA

8124 BA, VIVIAN. Beginnings of western education in Burma, the Catholic effort. JBRS 47 (1964) 287-323.

8125 BA, VIVIAN. Odyssey of the first Burmese types. JBRS 45 (1962) 209-213.

8126 PEARN, B. R. Burmese printed books before Judson. B92 pp. 475-6.

PUBLISHERS AND PUBLISHING - INDONESIA

8127 CHAMBERT-LOIR, HENRI. Les editions Nusa Indah. AR 8 (1974) 31-34.

8128 DAMAIS, LOUIS-CHARLES. Bibliographie indonesienne, publications du service archeologique de l'Indonesie. BEF 51 (1963) 535-582.

8129 DAMAIS, LOUIS-CHARLES. Les publications epigraphiques du service archeologique de l'Indonesie. BEF 54 (1968) 295-521.

8130 DREWES, G. W. J. D. A. Rinkes, a note on his life and work. BIJ 117 (1961) 417-435.

8131 GALIS, K. W. Nieuw Guinea journalistiek. BIJ 119 (1963) 189-200.

8132 HOOYKAAS, C. Books made in Bali. BIJ 119 (1963) 371-386.

8133 Une nouvelle maison d'edition a Djakarta, Pustaka Jaya. AR 3 (1972) 24-27.

8134 TAYLOR, CARL. Indonesian views of China. AS 3 (1963) 165-172.

8135 TEEUW, A. Impact of Balai Pustaka on modern Indonesian literature. SOAS 35 (1972) 111-127.

PUBLISHERS AND PUBLISHING - MALAYSIA

8136 al-AHMADI, ABDUL RAHMAN. Notes towards a history of Malay periodicals in Kelantan. K33 pp. 170-189.

8137 METZGER, LAURENT. L'Institut malaysien de langue et de litterature. AR 2 (1971) 23-28.

8138 TREGONNING, K. G. Acquisition of Malaysian source material. JSAH 6 (Sept. 1965) 118-124.

PUBLISHERS AND PUBLISHING - PHILIPPINES

8139 ALIMURUNG, MARIANO M. Catholic medical press in the Philippines. UN 34 (Sept. 1961) 103-105.

8140 BERNAD, MIGUEL A. Episode in Philippine bibliographical history, the discovery of the earliest books printed in the Philippines. F38 pp. 293-302.

8141 CULLUM, LEO A. Philippine copyrighted material, 1959-1960. PS 9 (1961) 128-139.

8142 GALANG, RICARDO C. Textbook publishing in the Philippines. UN 34 (Dec. 1961) 13-39.

8143 HART, DONN V. Philippine publications, available materials and sources of acquisition. JSAH 8 (1967) 285-305.

Publishers and publishing - Philippines

8144   LENT, JOHN A. Book publishing in the Philippines. UN 41 (1968) 261-275.

8145   LENT, JOHN A. Guerrilla presses of the Philippines, 1941-45. AST 8 (1970) 260-274.

8146   LENT, JOHN A. Philippine provincial press. SJ 16 (1969) 273-290.

8147   PO, JOAQUIN. Bookselling in Manila. PS 8 (1960) 389-393.

8148   QUIRINO, CARLOS. Rare Manila imprint. PHR 1 pt. 2 (1966) 201-203.

8149   STA. MARIA, FELIXBERTO C. Scholarly publishing in the Philippines: a review and assessment. PS 21 (1973) 3-18.

PUBLISHERS AND PUBLISHING - SINGAPORE

8150   BIRCH, E. W. Vernacular press in the Straits. JMBRAS 42 pt. 1 (1969) 192-195.

8151   TAN, PETER C. Statistical materials on Singapore. Y52 pp. 386-417.

PUBLISHERS AND PUBLISHING - THAILAND

8152   CHUN PRABHAVI VADHANA. Special publications for free distribution. JSS 61 pt. 1 (1973) 227-260.

PUBLISHERS AND PUBLISHING - VIETNAM

8153   BOUDAREL, GEORGES. Bibliographie des oeuvres relatives a Phan Boi Chau editees en Quoc Ngu a Hanoi depuis 1954. BEF 56 (1969) 151-176.

PUNAN

8154   BAARTMANS, F. Kakus Punan mud healing rites. SMJ 14 (1966) 81-86.

8155   ELLIS, D. B. Study of the Punan Busang. SMJ 20 (1972) 235-299.

8156   HARRISSON, TOM. Sarawak Museum's Punan salong and Puso's jar. SMJ 11 (1963) 327-339.

8157   HARRISSON, TOM. Three secret communication systems among Borneo nomads and their dogs. JMBRAS 38 pt. 2 (1965) 67-86.

8158   LANGUB, JAYL. Adaptation to a settled life by the Punan of the Belaga sub-district. SMJ 22 (1974) 295-301.

8159   WHITTIER, HERBERT L. Apo Kayan area of east Kalimantan, by Herbert L. and Patricia R. Whittier. SMJ 22 (1974) 5-15.

PUNAN LANGUAGE

8160   HARRISSON, TOM. Punan Busang bird names. SMJ 12 (1965) 201-206.

8161   TUTON KABOY. Punan vocabularies. SMJ 12 (1965) 188-200.

PURCELL, VICTOR WILLIAM WILLIAMS SAUNDERS

8162   SPRENKEL, SYBILLE VAN DER. V. W. W. S. Purcell, a memoir. S89 pp. 3-20.

8163   Writings by the late Dr. Victor Purcell. S89 pp. 403-405.

PURUM

8164   NEEDHAM, RODNEY. Notes on the analysis of asymmetric alliance. BIJ 117 (1961) 93-117.
Comment: BERTING, J. Unilateral cross-cousin marriage, a reply to Needham, by J. Berting and H. Philipsen. BIJ 118 (1962) 155-159. *Author's reply:* Notes on comparative method and prescriptive alliance. BIJ 118 (1962) 160-182.

PURWADARMINTA, W. J. S.

8165   ECHOLS, JOHN M. In memoriam, W. J. S. Purwadarminta, 1904-1968. IND 8 (1969) 217.

PURWOKO

8166   VAN AKKEREN, PHILIP. A contemporary Indonesian messiah, a profile. JOSA 7 (1970) 134-146.

PYU

8167   LUCE, G. H. Ancient Pyu. B92 pp. 307-321.

QUEZON, MANUEL LUIS

8168   FRIEND, THEODORE. Manuel Quezon, charismatic conservative. PHR 1 pt. 1 (1965) 153-169.

8169   HUTCHINSON, JOSEPH F. Quezon's role in Philippine independence. C31 pp. 157-194.

8170   JENISTA, FRANK L. Problems of the colonial civil service, an illustration from the career of Manuel L. Quezon. SA 3 (1974) 808-829.

Quezon, Philippines. University of the Philippines

8171   LOPEZ, SALVADOR P. Quezon and student activism. DR 17 (1969) 15-23.

8172   ONORATO, MICHAEL P. Manuel Luis Quezon and his modus operandi. AF 5 pt. 3 (1973) 75-83.

8173   WHEELER, GERALD E. Manuel L. Quezon and the American presidents. AST 2 (1964) 231-246.

QUEZON, PHILIPPINES. UNIVERSITY OF THE PHILIPPINES

8174   AGPALO, REMIGIO E. Crisis of authority, the political scientist in the University of the Philippines. DR 20 (1972) 104-126.

8175   BENGZON, CESAR. U.P. and the courts, a parallel. DR 11 (1963) 385-390.

8176   COVAR, PROSPERO R. Farm and home development program of the College of Agriculture, University of the Philippines. SJ 11 (1964) 71-83.

8177   DEMETILLO, RICAREDO. Golden jubilee ode libretto. DR 9 (1961) 513-528.

8178   Department of Speech and Drama, 1959-1974. GEJ 25 (1973-4) 163-165.

8179   Indispensable *Collegian.* DR 18 (1970) 371-374.

8180   JAMIAS, CRISTINO. Response. DR 12 (1964) 120-131.

8181   JAMIAS, CRISTINO. University of the Philippines, the first half century. DR 10 special supp. (1962) 1-275.

Quezon, Philippines. University of the
  Philippines

8182 LOPEZ, SALVADOR P. Student acti-
      vism in the University of the
      Philippines. DR 17 (1969) 37-40.

8183 MACAPAGAL, DIOSDADO. Freedom at
      the University of the Philippines.
      DR 12 (1964) 135-137.

8184 MACEDA, JOSE. Music research at
      the University of the Philippines.
      SJ 17 (1970) 395-397.

8185 MAJUL, CESAR ADIB. Assault on the
      academic freedom of the University
      of the Philippines. DR 9 (1961)
      51-64.

8186 MAJUL, CESAR ADIB. Nature and
      rise of the secular university.
      DR 12 (1964) 138-159.

8187 MAPA, FELINA G. For greater
      mathematical literacy. GEJ 9
      (1965) 30-35.

8188 MELENDEZ, PEDRO. U.P. Department
      of Anthropology, 1914-1965, by
      Pedro Melendez and Josephine
      Caccam. Z16 pp. 6-22.

8189 MIRANDA, B. T. Basic natural
      sciences in the University of the
      Philippines. GEJ 7 (1964) 127-133.

8190 New syllabus of English 5. GEJ
      17 (1969) 51-58.

8191 ORDONEZ, ELMER A. Future of Eng-
      lish in the university. GEJ 17
      (1969) 47-50.

8192 ROMULO, CARLOS P. Toward the best
      university for the Filipino. DR
      11 (1963) 131-158.

8193 ROMULO, CARLOS P. U.P., its con-
      stant values, and student activism.
      DR 17 (1969) 24-36.

8194 TANADA, LORENZO M. The University
      of the Philippines and the conven-
      tional wisdom. DR 9 (1961) 415-
      422.

8195 WEIGHTMAN, GEORGE HENRY. Study of
      prejudice in a personalistic soci-
      ety, an analysis of an attitude
      survey of college students, Uni-
      versity of the Philippines. AST 2
      (1964) 87-101.

8196 YABES, LEOPOLDO Y. Anti-intel-
      lectual and obscurantist attack on
      the university. DR 9 (1961) 243-
      249.

8197 YABES, LEOPOLDO Y. Continuing
      growth and vitality of the uni-
      versity. DR 8 (1960) 589-590.

8198 YABES, LEOPOLDO Y. Higher educa-
      tion in the humanities. DR 8
      (1960) 600-612.

8199 YABES, LEOPOLDO Y. Independence
      and integrity of the university.
      DR 8 (1960) 586-588.

8200 ZAMORA, MARIO D. The U.P.-
      National Museum memorandum of
      agreement, a historic context.
      AST 3 (1965) 155-160.

QUEZON, PHILIPPINES. UNIV. OF THE PHI-
  LIPPINES. GENERAL EDUCATION PROGRAM

8201 AGONCILLO, TEODORO A. Philippine
      history and institutions in the
      general education program. GEJ 1
      (1961) 93-101.

8202 ASIS, CONSUELO V. Natural science
      II in the general education pro-
      gram. GEJ 1 (1961) 89-92.

8203 BENITEZ, LOURDES ABAD SANTOS.
      Speech I in the general education
      program. GEJ 1 (1961) 56-61.

Quezon, Philippines. Univ. of the Philippines. Libraries

8204 BONIFACIO, ARMANDO F. Critical thinking and general education. GEJ 1 (1961) 159-171.

8205 BONIFACIO, ARMANDO F. Hard look at the U.P. general education program. GEJ 17 (1969) 153-177.

8206 BONIFACIO, ARMANDO F. Hard look at the U.P. general education program, or does the U.P. general education program rest on a mistake? DR 17 (1969) 283-306.

8207 CORPUZ, O. D. Social science II in the general education program. GEJ 1 (1961) 111-127.

8208 DADUFALZA, CONCEPCION D. English in the general education program. GEJ 1 (1961) 50-55.

8209 EPISTOLA, S. V. Asian studies in general education. GEJ 1 (1961) 102-110.

8210 GUEVARA-FERNANDEZ, PACITA. Humanities I in the general education program. GEJ 1 (1961) 128-137.

8211 JOCANO, F. LANDA. Philippine mythology and general education. GEJ 12 (1966) 143-149.

8212 LAUREL, LILIA H. Spanish in the general education program, by Lilia H. Laurel and Antolina T. Antonio. GEJ 1 (1961) 62-74.

8213 MAGNO, MELECIO S. Natural science I in the general education program. GEJ 1 (1961) 84-88.

8214 MAJUL, CESAR ADIB. Role of a general education program in an engineering curriculum. GEJ 9 (1965) 1-13.

8215 MAPA, FELINA G. Mathematics I in the general education program. GEJ 1 (1961) 75-83.

8216 ORACION, TIMOTEO S. Anthropology of religion and general education. GEJ 12 (1966) 189-206.

8217 PASCUAL, RICARDO R. Humanities II in the general education program. GEJ 1 (1961) 138-158.

8218 TENMATAY, AUGUSTO L. General education in the University of the Philippines. GEJ 1 (1961) 30-49.

8219 VIRATA, ENRIQUE T. College of liberal arts and general education. DR 8 (1960) 17-22.

8220 YABES, LEOPOLDO Y. Idea of general education. DR 8 (1960) 591-599.

QUEZON, PHILIPPINES. UNIV. OF THE PHILIPPINES. LIBRARIES

8221 COLLANTES, LOURDES Y. Bibliography of materials available in the library system of the University of the Philippines on the modern history of Southeast Asia, by Lourdes Y. Collantes and J. A. Larkin. AST 2 (1964) 261-285.

8222 RAMAS, WILHELMINA Q. Sugbuanon drama, a preliminary list of plays acquired by the University. AST 11 pt. 3 (1973) 153-172.

8223 SEGUERRA, MARTHA B. Bibliography of materials available in the Institute of Asian Studies Library on South and East Asia, as of June 1964. AST 2 (1964) 421-463.

8224 VERZOSA, NATIVIDAD P. Gabriel A. Bernardo, a memoir. PS 11 (1963) 524-535.

Quoc Ngu

RAMAYANA

8242 BARRETT, E. C. G. Further light
      on Sir Richard Winstedt's unde-
      scribed Malay version of the Rama-
      yana. SOAS 26 (1963) 531-543.

8243 BOELES, J. J. Ramayana relief
      from the Khmer sanctuary at Pimai
      in north-east Thailand. JSS 57
      (1969) 163-169.

8244 DESAI, SANTOSH N. Ramayana, an
      instrument of historical contact
      and cultural transmission between
      India and Asia. JAS 30 (1970-1)
      5-20.

8245 FRANCISCO, JUAN R. Rama story in
      the post-Muslim Malay literature
      of Southeast Asia. SMJ 11 (1962)
      468-485.

8246 NAYAGAM, XAVIER S. THANI. Clas-
      sical love poetry in Tamil. F38
      pp. 261-268.

8247 SINGARAVELU, S. Comparative study
      of the Sanskrit, Tamil, Thai and
      Malay versions of the story of
      Rama with special reference to the
      process of acculturation in the
      Southeast Asian versions. JSS 56
      (1968) 137-185.

RAMAYANA - CAMBODIA

8248 MARTINI, FRANCOIS. Quelques notes
      sur le Ramker. G83 pp. 351-362.

RAMAYANA - INDONESIA

8249 AICHELE, W. Zu Ramas Begegnung
      mit Parasurama. BIJ 128 (1972)
      351-353.

8250 HEYTING, L. C. Rama's sandalen op
      Bali. BIJ 123 (1967) 373-378.

8251 HOOYKAAS, C. Interpolated or
      genuine? BIJ 116 (1960) 278-9.

8252 NOORDUYN, J. Traces of an old
      Sundanese Ramayana tradition. IND
      12 (1971) 151-157.

RAMAYANA - THAILAND

8253 DHANINIVAT, PRINCE. Hide figures
      of the Ramakien at the Ledermuseum
      in Offenbach, Germany. JSS 53
      (1965) 61-66.

8254 DHANINIVAT, PRINCE. The Ramakien,
      a Siamese version of the story of
      Rama. B91 pp. 33-45.

8255 VELDER, CHRISTIAN. Notes on the
      saga of Rama in Thailand. JSS 56
      (1968) 33-46.

RANGOON

8256 CHEN YI-SEIN. Chinese in Rangoon
      during the 18th and 19th centu-
      ries. E92 pp. 107-111.

al-RANIRI

8257 DREWES, G. W. J. Nur al-Din al-
      Raniri's *Hujjat al-Siddiq Li-Daf
      al-Zindiq* reexamined. JMBRAS 47
      pt. 2 (1974) 83-104.

RASSERS, WILLEM HUIBERT

8258 LOCHER, G. W. Willem Huibert Ras-
      sers, Roosendaal 16 September
      1877-Leiden 15 May 1973. BIJ 130
      (1974) 1-15.

8259 RAS, J. J. Panji romance and W.
      H. Rassers' analysis of its theme.
      BIJ 129 (1973) 411-456.

Rawang language

RAWANG LANGUAGE

RECONNAISSANCE AWARDS

RECTO, C. M.

REDJANG

REED, ALFRED A.

REFUGEES - LAOS

REFUGEES - VIETNAM

REGALADO, INIGO ED.

REGIONALISM *See also* A.S.A., A.S.E.A.N., MAPHILINDO

8274 BUTWELL, RICHARD. Malaysia and
      its impact on the international
      relations of Southeast Asia. AS
      4 (1964) 940-946.

8275 BUTWELL, RICHARD. Patterns of
      regional relations in Southeast
      Asia. S90.4 pp. 171-184.

8276 BUU HOAN. Regionalism, limita-
      tions and possibilities. MER 14
      pt. 2 (1969) 18-25.

8277 CHOI, CHONG-KI. Problems related
      to economic integration in the
      ASPAC region. AQ (1974) 83-104.

8278 COHEN, LOUIS A. International
      cooperation for development, the
      Mekong project. F56 pp. 13-30.

8279 EMERSON, RUPERT. South and South-
      East Asia as a political region.
      R64 pp. 1-7.
      Comment: ZINKIN, MAURICE. Com-
      ment. R64 pp. 7-8.

8280 GINSBURG, NORTON S. The politi-
      cal dimension, regionalism and
      extraregional relations. F56 pp.
      3-12.

8281 GORDON, BERNARD K. Regionalism
      in Southeast Asia. T45 pp. 506-
      522.

8282 HORELICK, ARNOLD L. The Soviet
      Union's Asian collective security
      proposal, a club in search of
      members. PA 47 (1974) 269-285.

8283 HOWELL, LLEWELLYN D. Southeast
      Asian foreign policy behavior in
      an integration context, by Llewel-
      lyn D. Howell and Charles W.
      Kegley. AF 6 pt. 3 (1974) 27-44.

8284 HSUEH, S. S. Eastern regional co-
      operation in public administra-
      tion. H75 pp. 241-249.

8285 HUNSBERGER, WARREN S. Economic
      cooperation/integration in the
      ASPAC and ASEAN areas. AQ (1974)
      121-146.

8286 KEESING, DONALD B. Thailand and
      Malaysia, a case for a common
      market? MER 10 pt. 2 (1965) 102-
      113.

8287 KITAMURA, HIROSHI. Aspects of re-
      gional harmonization of national
      development plans, by Hiroshi
      Kitamura and A. N. Bhagat. E36
      pp. 39-56.
      Comment: NURUL ISLAM. Comment.
      E36 pp. 59-61.
      Comment: TANG, ANTHONY. Comment.
      E36 pp. 57-8.

8288 LEIFER, MICHAEL. Trends in re-
      gional association in South East
      Asia. AST 2 (1964) 188-198.

8289 LOKANATHAN, P. S. Note on eco-
      nomic cooperation between India
      and Southeast Asian countries.
      S32 pp. 13-15.
      Comment: Economic development,
      rapporteur's report on session I.
      S32 pp. 22-24.

8290 McHALE, THOMAS R. The Philippines
      in the economy of Southeast Asia.
      SJ 17 (1970) 162-169.

8291 McINTYRE, ANGUS. The greater
      Indonesia idea of nationalism in
      Malaya and Indonesia. MAS 7
      (1973) 75-83.

8292 POLLARD, VINCENT K. ASA and ASEAN,
      1961-1967, Southeast Asian re-
      gionalism. AS 10 (1970) 244-255.

Regionalism

8293 POLLARD, VINCENT K. Southeast Asian regionalism. JCA 1 pt. 4 (1971) 45-54.

8294 RAKWIJIT, S. Regional cooperation and defence in the Far East, a Thai view. S51 pp. 409-428.

8295 RAMANA, D. V. Towards an appraisal and a strategy of development for the ECAFE region countries. MER 18 pt. 2 (1973) 16-36.

8296 SOLIDUM, ESTRELLA D. An explanation of the methodology used in a dissertation entitled "The nature of cooperation among ASEAN states as perceived through elite attitudes - a factor for regionalism." AST 10 (1972) 1-5.

8297 Summary and conclusions. E36 pp. 389-417.

8298 TRAN VIET SON. Is it possible to create an Asian bloc? AC 2 (Jan. 1960) 59-72.

8299 VAN DER KROEF, JUSTUS M. ASEAN's security needs and policies. PA 47 (1974) 154-170.

8300 Viewpoints from the Bangkok conference. E36 pp. 375-387.

8301 WILCOX, CLAIR. Regional cooperation in Southeast Asia. MER 9 pt. 2 (1964) 106-114.

8302 WRIGHT, L. R. Basis for a collective security organization in South and Southeast Asia. S51 pp. 442-457.

8303 WU TA YEH. Problems and prospects of economic cooperation in Southeast Asia. E36 pp. 15-36.
Comment: LIM CHONG YAH. Comment. E36 pp. 37-8.
Comment: NURUL ISLAM. Comment.

EL RENACIMIENTO

8304 KALAW, TEODORO M. *El Renacimiento* libel suit. DR 11 (1963) 285-298.

RENDRA, W. S.

8305 BONNEFF, MARCEL. L'histoire du condor et du mastodonte. AR 7 (1974) 9-13.

RENNELL, JAMES

8306 HARRISSON, TOM. Rennell manuscript in the Brunei Museum. BMJ 1 (1969) 157-165.

8307 HARRISSON, TOM. Unpublished Rennell ms., a Borneo-Philippine journey, 1762-63. JMBRAS 39 pt. 1 (1966) 92-136.

RESEARCH *See also* DISSERTATIONS, ACADEMIC

8308 Current research in South-East Asian history. JSAH 2 (Oct. 1961) 83-90.

8309 ENOKI, KAZUO. Some impressions of Southeast Asian trip from October 28 to November 21, 1962. EACS 3 (1964) 1-7.

8310 Les etudes malaises au XIXe Congres des Orientalistes, Paris, 16-22 juillet 1973. AR 6 (1973) 3-11. 11.

8311 GLOVER, I. C. London colloquy on early South East Asia. AR 7 (1974) 15-18.

8312 HUARD, P. Les enquetes scientifiques francaises et l'exploration
du monde exotique aux XVIIe et
XVIIIe siecles, par P. Huard et M.
Wong. BEF 52 (1964) 143-155.

8313 KAHLER, H. Contribution to a consideration of the present state of
knowledge in the field of Austronesian languages. L55 pp. 156-159.

8314 KRUPA, VIKTOR. Sektion Australien
und Ozeanien auf dem VII Internationalen Kongress der Anthropologischen und Ethnographischen
Wissenschaften in Moskau, 3/8-
10/8/1964. AAS 2 (1966) 137-139.

8315 MOHAMMAD TAIB OSMAN. The aims,
approaches and problems in the
study of folk literature or oral
tradition, with particular reference to Malay culture. BMJ 2 pt.
4 (1972) 159-164.

8316 MORTIMER, REX. From Ball to
Arndt, the liberal impasse in
Australian scholarship on Southeast
Asia. M77 pp. 101-130.

8317 NAKANE, CHIE. Report of the Southeast Asia trip. EACS 2 pt. 3
(1963) 17-37.

8318 PANIZO, ALFREDO. New knowledge
through research in humanities.
UN 39 (1966) 30-38.

8319 PIERSON, HARRY H. The Asia Foundation's programming for tribal and
minority peoples in Southeast Asia.
K86 pp. 847-864.

8320 SOLHEIM, WILHELM G. International
congresses and symposia. AP 10
(1967) 1-8.

8321 SORENSEN, PER. Brief account of
the twenty-seventh International
Congress of Orientalists, Ann

Arbor, Michigan, U.S.A., 13-19
August 1967. AP 10 (1967) 13-4.

8322 Third international conference on
educational research in Asia and
the southern Pacific, 1968. SLQ
6 (1968) 496-509.

8323 TINKER, HUGH. Political studies
and new Asia. PA 33 (1960) 300-
304.

8324 UHLENBECK, E. M. Perspectief der
Nederlandse Orientalistiek. BIJ
123 (1967) 205-216.

8325 ZAMORA, MARIO D. Filipino in an
Indian village, problems in field
research. AST 3 (1965) 145-152.

RESEARCH - BURMA

8326 BA HLI, F. Some trends in scientific research. JBRS 55 (1972) 1-
8.

RESEARCH - CAMBODIA

8327 DUCH PHAN. [Discussion minutes on
Asian studies in Cambodia.] EACS
1 (1962) 31-2.

RESEARCH - INDONESIA

8328 BACHTIAR, HARSJA. Research in Indonesia by Dutch scholars. P15
pp. 141-148.

8329 Les etudes balinaises en Indonesie. AR 7 (1974) 171-174.

8330 HOOYKAAS, C. Saiva-Siddhanta in
Java and Bali, some remarks on its
recent study. BIJ 118 (1962) 309-
327.

Research - Indonesia

8331 KISHI, KOICHI. Recent Japanese sources for Indonesian historiography. S61 pp. 206-216.

8332 KOOLHAAS, D. R. History of chemistry in the Netherlands Indies, half a century of phytochemical research. H57 pp. 207-215.

8333 LOMBARD, DENYS. Trois recentes etudes sovietiques concernant Indonesie. AR 7 (1974) 169-171.

8334 POUWER, J. New Guinea as a field for ethnological study, a preliminary analysis. BIJ 117 (1961) 1-24.

8335 POUWER, J. Structural and functional approach in cultural anthropology, theoretical reflections with reference to research in western New Guinea. BIJ 122 (1966) 129-144.

8336 UTRECHT, ERNST. American sociologists on Indonesia. JCA 3 (1973) 39-45.
Comment: WITTON, RON. Comment. JCA 3 (1973) 467-469.
Author's reply: 470.

RESEARCH - MALAYSIA

8337 APPELL, GEORGE N. Social anthropological census for cognatic societies and its application among the Rungus of northern Borneo. BIJ 125 (1969) 80-93.

8338 DUNSMORE, J. R. Review of agricultural research in Sarawak. SMJ 16 (1968) 309-339.

RESEARCH - PHILIPPINES

8339 ALIMURUNG, MARIANO M. Hardships and partnerships in medical research in the Philippines. UN 35 (1962) 244-248.

8340 BAILEN, JEROME B. Studies in physical anthropology of the Philippines. Z16 pp. 527-558.

8341 BARIA-VALENCIA, LUZVIMINDA. Teaching and research in the rural social sciences in the Philippines, by Luzviminda Baria-Valencia and Manuel Flores-Bonifacio. GEJ 21 (1971) 105-121.

8342 FLORES, BIENVENIDO V. Analysis of Philippine family studies, 1952-1971: a preliminary report of an effort at inventorization and evaluation of family theory and research in the Philippines. SLURJ 5 (1974) 45-97.

8343 FLORES, BIENVENIDO V. Analysis of Philippine family studies, 1952-1971: a preliminary report of an effort at inventorization and evaluation of family theory and research in the Philippines. SLURJ 5 (1974) 199-240.

8344 FLORES, BIENVENIDO V. Analysis of Philippine family studies, 1952-1971: a preliminary report of an effort at inventorization and evaluation of family theory and research in the Philippines. SLURJ 5 (1974) 345-391.

8345 ISRAEL, CAROLYN C. Kinship and socialization in a suburban community. AST 7 (1969) 270-275.

8346 JOCANO, F. LANDA. Language learning as part of fieldwork technique, some problems in communication. AST 8 (1970) 203-217.

8347 KAUT, CHARLES. Researcher and research, a personal approach. SJ 11 (1964) 84-88.

8348 List of research projects in Silliman University, compiled by the University Research Center, second semester, 1969-70. SJ 17 (1970) 82-85.

8349 LYNCH, FRANK. Ateneo expedition to Sulu. PS 10 (1962) 314-316.

8350 MACEDA, JOSE. Music research at the University of the Philippines. SJ 17 (1970) 395-397.

8351 MANGAHAS, RUBY K. State of music research in the Philippines. SJ 17 (1970) 387-390.

8352 MARANON, JOAQUIN. On scientific research. UN 33 (1960) 809-822.

8353 MORALES, ALFREDO T. Anthropology and education change in the Philippines. GEJ 12 (1966) 268-295.

8354 On going projects of SU Research Council. SJ 21 (1974) 125-127.

8355 PALMORE, MIRIAM G. Problems of music research in the Philippines. SJ 17 (1970) 391-395.

8356 Partial list of faculty and staff publications, Silliman University, 1968-69. SJ 17 (1970) 86-89.

8357 Partial list of faculty and staff publications, Silliman University, 1969-70. SJ 17 (1970) 354-356.

8358 Problems and hazards of fieldwork, the case of the Filipina researcher, introductory note. AST 7 (1969) 253-4.

8359 PROVINSE, JOHN H. Western research techniques and non-western values. E78 pp. 655-668.

8360 RABOR, DIOSCORO S. Report on the zoological expeditions in the Philippines for the period 1961-1966. SJ 13 (1966) 605-616.

8361 RIXHON, GERARD. Ten years of research in Sulu, 1961-1971. S91 pp. 1-18.

8362 RODRIGUEZ, LORENZO. On the progress of Philippine botanical research. UN 34 (Dec. 1961) 64-76.

8363 SANTICO, REALIDAD Q. Research in a Pampanga village. AST 7 (1969) 264-269.

8364 SIOSON, F. M. Mathematical research in the Philippines. PS 15 (1967) 241-258.

8365 TAMANIO, MARIALITA M. Research in a cockpit. AST 7 (1969) 255-263.

8366 VALENZUELA, PATROCINIO. Natural sciences, 1956-1959. PS 8 (1960) 515-525.

8367 YABES, LEOPOLDO Y. Observations on some aspects of Philippine scholarship and H. Otley Beyer. Z16 pp. 48-60.

8368 YABES, LEOPOLDO Y. Present situation and problems of the organization of research in East Asian studies. DR 9 (1961) 529-544.

RESEARCH – SINGAPORE

8369 CHAN KAI YAU. Aspects of educational research in Singapore. RSAS 1 pt. 1 (1971) 54-5.

8370 CHEN, PETER S. J. Teaching and research in the social sciences in Singapore. RSAS 1 pt. 1 (1971) 45-51.

8371 CHIA SIOW YUE. Survey of academic exercises submitted to the eco-

Research - Singapore

nomics department, University of
Singapore for the academic session
1967/68. MER 13 pt. 1 (1968) 118-
127.

8372 FIC, VICTOR M. Nanyang University,
Singapore, plans for research.
JSAH 6 (Sept. 1965) 125-128.

8373 LIM CHONG YAH. Teaching and research in the social sciences in
Singapore. RSAS 1 pt. 1 (1971)
30-33.

8374 OOI JIN BEE. Relevance in social
science research in Singapore.
RSAS 1 pt. 1 (1971) 34-36.

8375 RIAZ HASSAN. Sociology and sociological research in Singapore.
RSAS 1 pt. 1 (1971) 22-24.

8376 TAN, T. K. Constitution of a
National Research Consultancy
Centre in Singapore. RSAS 1 pt. 1
(1971) 37-39.

8377 WELDON, PETER D. Research in the
social sciences at the University
of Singapore. RSAS 1 pt. 1 (1971)
40-44.

RESEARCH - THAILAND

8378 JACOBS, MILTON. Alliance of
anthropological and sociological
concepts and methodologies in
field research in Thailand. JSS
62 pt. 1 (1974) 35-46.

8379 PRACHOOM CHOMCHAI. Research in
Asian studies in Thailand. EACS
1 (1962) 114-122.

RESEARCH - VIETNAM

8380 NGUYEN DINH HUNG. Present conception of marine sciences, the

role of the Nhatrang Institute of
Oceanography. AC 3 (Jan. 1961)
1-12.

RESEARCH CENTERS ON SOUTHEAST ASIA -
AUSTRALIA

8381 TARLING, NICHOLAS. Southeast Asia
in Australasian universities.
JSAS 2 (1971) 78-85.

RESEARCH CENTERS ON SOUTHEAST ASIA -
CZECHOSLOVAKIA

8382 L'Institute Oriental de Prague.
FA 22 (1968) 500-505.

RESEARCH CENTERS ON SOUTHEAST ASIA -
FRANCE

8383 Varietes internationales. SEIB 35
(1960) 696-702.

RESEARCH CENTERS ON SOUTHEAST ASIA -
GREAT BRITAIN

8384 PHILIPS, C. H. Modern Asian
studies in the universities of the
United Kingdom. MAS 1 (1967) 1-
14.

RESEARCH CENTERS ON SOUTHEAST ASIA -
HONG KONG

8385 DRAKE, F. S. Institute of Oriental Studies, University of Hong
Kong. EACS 1 (1962) 74-85.

RESEARCH CENTERS ON SOUTHEAST ASIA -
INDIA

8386 Research Council for Cultural
Studies, programme of activities
for 1965-1966. EACS 5 (1966) 38-
43.

RESEARCH CENTERS ON SOUTHEAST ASIA – INDONESIA

8387 COSTER, CH. Work of the West Java Research Institute in Buitenzorg. H57 pp. 55-59.

8388 KOOLHAAS, D. R. History of chemistry in the Netherlands Indies, researches by visitors from abroad at Buitenzorg, 1884-1934. H57 pp. 215-217.

RESEARCH CENTERS ON SOUTHEAST ASIA – JAPAN

8389 Activities of the Centre for East Asian Cultural Studies, 1965-1966. EACS 5 (1966) 29-37.

8390 Activities of the Centre for East Asian Cultural Studies, 1966-1968. EACS 7 (1968) 59-75.

8391 Activities of the Centre for East Asian Cultural Studies, 1968-1970. EACS 10 (1971) 33-52.

8392 Center for East Asian Cultural Studies. EACS 1 (1962) 59-72.

8393 Center for East Asian Cultural Studies. FA 19 (1963) 710-712.

8394 Center of South East Asian Studies, Kyoto University. EACS 3 (1964) 54-57.

8395 Institute for the Study of the Languages and Cultures of Asia and Africa, Tokyo. EACS 5 (1966) 44-49.

8396 Institute of Asian Economic Affairs research program for 1961-62. EACS 2 pt. 1 (1963) 38-49.

8397 IWAMURA, SHINOBU. Research at the Center for Southeast Asian Studies, Kyoto University. AS 8 (1968) 819.

8398 Present situation of Asian studies in Japan. EACS 1 (1962) 86-96.

8399 Program for Southeast Asian studies at Kyoto University. FA 19 (1963) 941-947.

8400 Review of activities of the Centre for East Asian Cultural Studies. EACS 5 (1966) 16-24.

RESEARCH CENTERS ON SOUTHEAST ASIA – NETHERLANDS

8401 ENGERS, JAMES F. Board for the Netherlands Indies, Surinam and Curacao. H57 pp. 461-2.

8402 VERDOORN, FRANS. Scientific institutions, societies and research workers in the Netherlands, by Frans and J. G. Verdoorn. H57 pp. 426-460.

RESEARCH CENTERS ON SOUTHEAST ASIA – PHILIPPINES

8403 ROMULO, CARLOS P. New ideopolis in Asia. DR 13 (1965) 240-251.

8404 VESLOT, JEAN-LOUIS. Universites et revues de sciences humaines aux Philippines. AR 1 (1970) 59-65.

8405 YABES, LEOPOLDO Y. Report from the Philippines on the present situation and problems of the organization or research in East Asian studies. EACS 1 (1962) 105-113.

Research centers on Southeast Asia -
Singapore

RESEARCH CENTERS ON SOUTHEAST ASIA -
SINGAPORE

8406   Centre for South-East Asian Stud-
       ies, University of Singapore.
       EACS 5 (1966) 50-52.

8407   MANGUIN, PIERRE-YVES. La recherche
       sur l'Asie du sud-est a Singapour
       institutions et ressources. AR 6
       (1973) 13-23.

RESEARCH CENTERS ON SOUTHEAST ASIA -
THAILAND

8408   GEDDES, WILLIAM R. Tribal Research
       Centre, Thailand, an account of
       plans and activities. K86 pp. 553-
       581.

RESEARCH CENTERS ON SOUTHEAST ASIA -
UNION OF SOVIET SOCIALIST REPUBLICS

8409   LECLERC, JACQUES. Les etudes in-
       donesiennes a l'Institut d'Orient
       de l'Academie des Sciences de
       l'URSS. AR 6 (1973) 25-30.

RESEARCH CENTERS ON SOUTHEAST ASIA -
UNITED STATES

8410   BELSHAW, HORACE. Institute of
       Pacific Relations. H57 pp. 478-9.

8411   Coolidge Foundation. H57 p. 482.

8412   ENGERS, JAMES F. Netherlands and
       Netherlands Indies Council of the
       Institute of Pacific Relations.
       H57 pp. 479-480.

8413   GURNEY, NATALIE. Southeast Asia
       Institute and its activities.
       H57 pp. 480-1.

8414   MANTELL, C. L. Activities of the
       Netherlands Indies Laboratories.
       H57 pp. 482-3.

8415   ROMULO, CARLOS P. New ideopolis
       in Asia. DR 13 (1965) 240-251.

8416   VAN NIEL, ROBERT. Southeast Asian
       studies in the U.S.A. JSAH 5
       (Mar. 1964) 188-194.

8417   WITTERMANS, T. Enkele aanteken-
       ingen over het East West Center te
       Honolulu. BIJ 120 (1964) 461-465.

RESEARCH CENTERS ON SOUTHEAST ASIA -
VIETNAM

8418   Varietes au Vietnam. SEIB 35
       (1960) 691-695.

RETAIL TRADE *See also* COMMERCE

RETAIL TRADE - BRUNEI

8419   ABDUL LATIF HAJI IBRAHIM. Padian,
       its market and the women vendors.
       BMJ 2 pt. 1 (1970) 39-51.

RETAIL TRADE - PHILIPPINES

8420   AGPALO, REMIGIO E. Pressure
       groups and the nationalization of
       retail trade. A28 pp. 223-229.

8421   APPLETON, SHELDON. Overseas Chi-
       nese and economic nationalization
       in the Philippines. JAS 19 (1959-
       60) 151-161.

8422   BENJAMIN, J. The Filipino family
       owned business, a matriarchal
       model, by J. Benjamin, C. Alvarez
       and Patricia M. Alvarez. PS 20
       (1972) 547-561.

8423   FORONDA, CONRADO FLORES. Observa-
       tions on some buying habits of the

Filipino housewife. SLURJ 2 (1971)
453–462.

RETAIL TRADE – SINGAPORE

8424 BELLETT, J. Singapore's central
area retail pattern in transition.
JTG 28 (1969) 1–16.

RETANA Y GAMBOA, WENCESLAO E.

8425 SCHUMACHER, JOHN N. Wenceslao E.
Retana, an historiographical study.
PS 10 (1962) 550–576.

REYES, ISABELO DE LOS

8426 ACHUTEGUI, PEDRO S. DE. Bishop
Isabelo de los Reyes, Jr., an
ecumenical tribute. PS 19 (1971)
557–572.

RHODES, ALEXANDER DE

8427 LABRUSSE, S. DE. A l'occasion du
tricentenaire d'Alexandre de
Rhodes. SEIB 35 (1960) 682.

8428 TORRALBA, EDUARDO. La date de
naissance du Pere de Rhodes, 15
mars 1591, est-elle exacte? SEIB
35 (1960) 683–689.

RIANG–LANG LANGUAGE

8429 SHORTO, H. L. Structural patterns
of northern Mon–Khmer languages.
L55 pp. 45–61.

RICARTE Y GARCIA, ARTEMIO

8430 GOODMAN, GRANT K. General Artemio
Ricarte and Japan. JSAH 7 (Sept.
1966) 48–60.

8431 LUNA, MARIA PILAR S. General
Artemio Ricarte y Garcia, a Filipino nationalist. AST 9 (1971)
229–241.

RICE

8432 BUEN, FLORENCIO. The green revolution school for farmers, a proposal. SLURJ 4 (1973) 351–366.

8433 LUCE, GORDON H. Rice and religion, a study of old Mon–Khmer
evolution and culture. JSS 53
(1965) 139–152.

8434 OWEN, NORMAN G. Rice industry of
mainland Southeast Asia, 1850–
1914. JSS 59 pt. 2 (1971) 75–143.

8435 WATABE, TADAYO. Increasing the
rice yield in South and Southeast
Asia, by Tadayo Watabe and Keizaburo Kawaguchi. AS 8 (1968) 820–
828.

RICE – BRUNEI

8436 CRAIN, JAY B. Mengalong Lun
Dayeh agricultural organisation.
BMJ 3 pt. 1 (1973) 1–25.

8437 HEWITT, B. R. Rice varieties in
the state of Brunei. BMJ 2 pt. 4
(1972) 241–243.

8438 HEWITT, B. R. Rice varieties in
the Temburong District of the
state of Brunei, by B. R. Hewitt
and Muhamad bin Yasin. BMJ 2 pt.
3 (1971) 138–141.

RICE – BURMA

8439 BA HLI, FREDDY. Problems of high
acid rice bran oils in Burma and
their solutions, by Freddy Ba Hli,

Rice - Burma

Thein Nyun and Kyaw Thaung. JBRS 46 (June 1963) 35-41.

8440 CHENG SIOK HWA. Development of the Burmese rice industry in the late nineteenth century. JSAH 6 (Mar. 1965) 67-80.

8441 LU GALE. Paddy planting songs. B92 pp. 157-167.

RICE - INDONESIA

8442 ANDERSON, BEN. The problem of rice, stenographic notes on the fourth session of Sanyo Kaigi, January 8, 2605, 10:00 a.m., translated with an introduction by Ben Anderson. IND 2 (1966) 77-123.

8443 HANSEN, GARY E. Indonesia's green revolution, the abandonment of a non-market strategy toward change. AS 12 (1972) 932-946.

8444 LIEFRINCK, F. A. Rice cultivation in northern Bali. B19 pp. 1-73.

8445 MUBYARTO. Rice price, marketing and food policy in Indonesia. MER 13 pt. 2 (1968) 103-114.

8446 RIEFFEL, ALEXIS. Bimas program for self sufficiency in rice production. IND 8 (1969) 103-133.

8447 UTRECHT, ERNST. Land reform and Bimas in Indonesia. JCA 3 (1973) 149-164.

RICE - MALAYSIA

8448 AGARWAL, M. C. Account of the Tanjong Karang project. MER 9 pt. 2 (1964) 64-74.

8449 BHATI, U. N. Farmers technical knowledge and income, a case study of padi farmers of west Malaysia. MER 18 pt. 1 (1973) 36-47.

8450 CHENG SIOK HWA. Rice industry of Malaya, a historical survey. JMBRAS 42 pt. 2 (1969) 130-144.

8451 FISK, E. K. Establishment costs of small rice farms, an analytical model of returns to capital. MER 7 pt. 2 (1962) 45-63.

8452 HO, ROBERT. Rice production in Malaya, a review of problems and prospects. JTG 29 (1969) 21-32.

8453 HUANG, YUKON. Some reflections on padi double cropping in west Malaysia. MER 17 pt. 1 (1972) 119-129.

8454 JACKSON, JAMES C. Rice cultivation in west Malaysia, relationships between culture history, customary practices and recent developments. JMBRAS 45 pt. 2 (1972) 76-96.

8455 PURCAL, J. Labour utilization among men in a padi village in Province Wellesley. MER 10 pt. 2 (1965) 49-60.

8456 SATHER, CLIFFORD A. Kampong Selanyau, social and economic organization of a Kedayan rice growing village in Sarawak, by Clifford A. Sather and Hatta Solhee. SMJ 22 (1974) 249-266.

8457 VIRACH ARROMDEE. Can west Malaysia become self sufficient in rice by 1975? MER 14 pt. 2 (1969) 79-93.

8458 ZAHARAH BINTI HJ. MAHMUD. Period and the nature of traditional settlement in the Malay peninsula. JMBRAS 43 pt. 2 (1970) 81-113.

Richardson, David Lester

RICE - PHILIPPINES

8459   BALITON, JESUS Q. The effects of population growth in the production and distribution of palay in the province of Nueva Vizcaya. SLURJ 5 (1974) 418-462.

8460   BALITON, JESUS Q. The effects of population growth in the production and distribution of palay in the province of Nueva Vizcaya. SLURJ 5 (1974) 469-517.

8461   COVAR, PROSPERO. Masagana/Margate system of planting rice, a study of an agricultural innovation. E78 pp. 613-621.

8462   LOPEZ, ROGELIO M. Origin of the rice terraces in Luzon and their presence in the island of Cebu, Philippines, a brief review of hypotheses. D67 pp. 31-42.

8463   New rice technology and labor absorption in Philippine agriculture. MER 16 pt. 2 (1971) 117-158.

8464   PACYAYA, ALFRED G. Acculturation and culture change in Sagada. SJ 11 (1964) 14-25.

8465   WOLTERS, W. G. Waar is de rijst gebleven? B85 pp. 317-332.

RICE - THAILAND

8466   HAFNER, JAMES A. Spatial dynamics of rice milling and commodity flow in central Thailand. JTG 37 (1973) 30-38.

8467   INGRAM, JAMES C. Thailand's rice trade and the allocation of resources. C87 pp. 102-126.

8468   RENAUD, BERTRAND M. The effect of the rice export tax on the domestic rice price level in Thailand. MER 16 pt. 1 (1971) 84-107.

8469   SILCOCK, T. H. The rice premium and agricultural diversification. S49 pp. 231-257.

8470   USHER, DAN. Thai rice trade. S49 pp. 206-230.

8471   VAN ROY, EDWARD. Malthusian squeeze on Thailand's rice economy. AS 7 (1967) 469-481.

RICE - VIETNAM

8472   NGUYEN THE ANH. Quelques aspects economiques et sociaux du problem du riz au Vietnam dans la premiere moitie du XIXe siecle. SEIB 42 (1967) 7-22.

8473   SALKIN, JAY S. Land size and patterns of resource productivity in South Vietnamese rice production. SA 1 (1971) 116-127.

8474   SALKIN, JAY S. Optimal level of production in generalized production functions, an application to south Vietnamese rice production. MER 18 pt. 2 (1973) 60-67.

8475   SALKIN, JAY S. Technological and environmental factors in rice production in south Vietnam. MER 15 pt. 1 (1970) 106-119.

8476   TEULIERES, ROGER. Le riz au Viet-Nam. SEIB 41 (1966) 121-147.

RICHARDSON, DAVID LESTER

8477   LANGHAM-CARTER, R. R. David Lester Richardson, diplomat and explorer. JBRS 49 (1966) 207-218.

Ridley, Henry Nicholas

8497 CONSTANTINO, RENATO. Veneration
      without understanding. DR 18
      (1970) 22-47.

8498 CONSTANTINO, RENATO. Veneration
      without understanding. JCA 1 pt.
      4 (1971) 3-18.

8499 CULLUM, LEO A. Rizal and the old
      Dipolog Church. PS 10 (1962) 156.

8500 CULLUM, LEO A. Traces of Rizal.
      PS 9 (1961) 531-2.

8501 DAROY, PETRONILO BN. Ideas of
      European liberalism in the fiction
      of Rizal. PSSHR 30 (1965) 109-183.

8502 DEMETILLO, RICAREDO. Rizal. DR 9
      (1961) 396-399.

8503 FISHER, MARGUERITE J. Jose Rizal
      centennial, by Marguerite J.
      Fisher and Luis Montilla. JAS 21
      (1961-2) 441-443.

8504 FISHER, MARGUERITE J. Jose Rizal,
      first Asian exponent of liberal
      democracy. DR 9 (1961) 467-484.

8505 FRANCISCO, JUAN R. Preliminary
      notes on Rizal's *Ultimo adios* in
      Sanskrit. DR 9 (1961) 377-382.

8506 GREGORIO, SAMUEL B. Rizal,
      apostle of Asian nationalism. A
      review of the 1967 Knights of Rizal
      seminar-institute. SJ 15 (1968)
      16-28.

8507 HERNANDEZ, JOSE MA. Rizal's
      poetry and drama. UN 34 (Sept.
      1961) 55.

8508 HESSEL, EUGENE A. Rizal's retrac-
      tion, a note on the debate. A58
      pp. 133-151.

8509 HESSEL, EUGENE A. Rizal's retrac-
      tion, a note on the debate. SJ 12
      (1965) 168-183.

8510 International congress on Rizal,
      commission reports. DR 12 (1964)
      172-193.

8511 LOPEZ, SALVADOR P. Rizal and the
      Philippine constitution. DR 17
      (1969) 317-323.

8512 MAJUL, CESAR ADIB. Education
      during the reform movement and the
      Philippine revolution. DR 15
      (1967) 185-257.

8513 MAJUL, CESAR ADIB. Maria Clara's
      locket, a significance. GEJ 11
      (1966) 19-27.

8514 MAJUL, CESAR ADIB. Reflections on
      Rizal's concept of national senti-
      ment. DR 9 (1961) 449-466.

8515 MAJUL, CESAR ADIB. Rizal and
      Mabini in relation to our national
      community. GEJ 2 (1961) 14-17.

8516 MARTIN, DALMACIO. *Hamlet* and its
      possible influence on Rizal's
      novels. SJ 13 (1966) 635-640.

8517 MOLINA, ANTONIO M. Rizal,
      Hispanista. UN 33 (1960) 366-372.

8518 MORALES, ALFREDO T. Children of
      the storm, Rizal's artistic
      imagery. DR 9 (1961) 311-326.

8519 NEVINS, ALLAN. Three American
      patriots needed to match Rizal.
      DR 9 (1961) 364-367.

8520 OCAMPO, ESTABAN A. DE. Dr. Jose
      Rizal, father of Filipino nation-
      alism. JSAH 3 (Mar. 1962) 44-55.

Rizal y Alonso, Jose

8521 ORARA, E. DE GUZMAN. Notes on preliminary notes on Rizal's *Ultimo adios* in Sanskrit. DR 13 (1965) 140-156.

8522 PADILLA, BENITO N. S. Rizal's ideological basis of a revolution. DR 9 (1961) 327-353.

8523 PAOLI, ENRIQUE. A Rizal. GEJ 6 (1963) 50.

8524 PASCUAL, RICARDO R. Institutional interpretation of Rizal's novels. GEJ 5 (1963) 78-85.

8525 RAMOS, MAXIMO B. The Rizal story in Philippine fiction. DR 9 (1961) 383-395.

8526 RUBIO, HILARION F. Rizal as a musician. SJ 17 (1970) 401-406.

8527 SALAVERIA, RODOLFO A. This day marks the hundredth year. DR 12 (1964) 297-8.

8528 SAN JUAN, E. Rizal and the human condition, some preliminary notes. GEJ 7 (1964) 135-154.

8529 SANIEL, JOSEFA M. Jose Rizal and Suehiro Tetcho, Filipino and Japanese political novelists. AST 2 (1964) 353-371.

8530 SCHUMACHER, JOHN N. Some notes on Rizal in Dapitan. PS 11 (1963) 301-313.

8531 SINCO, VICENTE G. Rizal and education. DR 9 (1961) 297-310.

8532 YABES, LEOPOLDO Y. Great sage, teacher, and benefactor of humanity. DR 8 (1960) 511-566.

8533 YABES, LEOPOLDO Y. Rizal and the liberal intellectual tradition. DR 11 (1963) 159-167.

8534 YABES, LEOPOLDO Y. Rizal and the life of the mind. DR 9 (1961) 368-376.

8535 YABES, LEOPOLDO Y. Rizal's novels. DR 11 (1963) 82-90.

ROBERTS, J. W.

8536 NGUYEN THE ANH. L'Angleterre et le Viet-Nam en 1803, la mission de J. W. Roberts. SEIB 40 (1965) 339-347.

ROGLAI

8537 COBBEY, VURNELL. Some northern Roglai beliefs about the supernatural. SA 2 (1972-3) 125-129.

8538 LEE, LOIS. Pregnancy and childbirth practices of the northern Roglai. SA 2 (1972-3) 26-52.

ROLIN-JAEQUEMYNS, GUSTAVE

8539 SAINT-HUBERT, CHRISTIAN DE. Rolin-Jaequemyns (Chao Phya Aphay Raja) and the Belgian legal advisors in Siam at the turn of the century. JSS 53 (1965) 181-190.

Rong language   *See*   LEPCHA LANGUAGE

ROORDA VAN EYSINGA, P. P.

8540 WERTHEIM, W. F. Doopceel van de dichter van de vloekzang, drie telgen van het geslacht Roorda van Eysinga. BIJ 116 (1960) 437-480.

ROSARIO, DEOGRACIAS A.

8541   MATUTE, GENOVEVA EDROZA.   Deogra-
       cias A. Rosario, ama ng maikling
       kathang Tagalog.   PS 19 (1971)
       341-372.

ROSIDI, AJIP

8542   CHAMBERT-LOIR, HENRI.   Lantaran
       Ajip Rosidi.   AR 2 (1971) 123-128.

8543   LABROUSSE, PIERRE.   Entretien avec
       Ajip.   AR 2 (1971) 116-119.

8544   LABROUSSE, PIERRE.   Retour a
       Djatiwangi.   AR 2 (1971) 153-166.

8545   WING KARDJO.   Ajip Rosidi dalam
       potret diri.   AR 2 (1971) 111-115.

ROTINESE

8546   FOX, JAMES J.   Rotinese dynastic
       genealogy, structure and event.
       T77 pp. 37-77.

ROTINESE LANGUAGE

8547   FOX, JAMES J.   Semantic parallelism
       in Rotinese ritual language.   BIJ
       127 (1971) 215-255.

ROTOR, ARTURO B.

8548   CRUZ, ISAGINI R.   Illusion and the
       inner cell, a critical analysis of
       the later stories of Arturo B.
       Rotor.   PS 18 (1970) 753-768.

ROUFFAER, G. P.

8549   GRAAF, H. J. DE.   Herdenking G. P.
       Rouffaer, op 9 Juli 1960.   BIJ 116
       (1960) 397-407.

8550   NIEUWENHUYS, R.   Rouffaer en
       Multatuli.   BIJ 116 (1960) 408-
       423.

ROYAL ASIATIC SOCIETY OF GREAT BRITAIN
AND IRELAND, MALAYAN BRANCH. JOURNAL

8551   COWAN, C. D.   Ideas of history in
       the *Journal of the Malayan
       (Straits) Branch of the Royal
       Asiatic Society*, 1878-1941.   H18
       pp. 279-285.

8552   LIM HUCK TEE.   *Index Malaysiana,
       an index to the Journal of the
       Straits Branch, Royal Asiatic
       Society and the Journal of the
       Malayan Branch, Royal Asiatic
       Society, 1878-1963.*   JMBRAS 36 pt.
       4 (1963) 1-395.

8553   MAXWELL, ALLEN R.   Brunei bibli-
       ography in the JSBRAS and JMBRAS.
       BMJ 2 pt. 1 (1970) 264-268.

ROYAL ASIATIC SOCIETY OF GREAT BRITAIN
AND IRELAND, MALAYSIAN BRANCH. LIBRARY

8554   JONES, RUSSELL.   Dating of Ms.
       Maxwell 93 in the Royal Asiatic
       Society Library.   JMBRAS 45 pt. 1
       (1972) 116-118.

Royal Asiatic Society of Great Britain
and Ireland, Straits Branch. Journal
See   ROYAL ASIATIC SOCIETY OF GREAT
BRITAIN AND IRELAND, MALAYAN BRANCH.
JOURNAL

RUBBER INDUSTRY

8555   AHMAD MAHZAN AYOB.   United States
       import demand and prices of nat-
       ural rubber, by Ahmad Mahzan Ayob
       and Anthony Prato.   MER 18 pt. 1
       (1973) 24-35.

Rubber industry

8556 BENHAM, F. C. Rubber industry. S48 pp. 284-299.

8557 COOMBS, G. E. The organization devised by the International Rubber Regulation Committee for the conduct of research and propaganda, under the 1934 agreement between the governments of France, the United Kingdom, India, the Netherlands, and Siam to regulate the production and export of rubber. H57 pp. 48-54.

8558 McHALE, T. R. Changing technology and shifts in the supply and demands for rubber, an analytical history. MER 9 pt. 2 (1964) 24-48.

8559 McHALE, T. R. Competition between synthetic and natural rubber. MER 6 pt. 1 (1961) 23-31.

RUBBER INDUSTRY - BRUNEI

8560 JANARDANAN, E. C. Brunei Malay rubber beginnings. SMJ 11 (1962) 598-9.

RUBBER INDUSTRY - BURMA

8561 TIN HTOO. District by district account of the rubber industry of Burma. JBRS 45 (1962) 181-192.

8562 TIN HTOO. Overall view of the rubber industry of Burma. JBRS 45 (1962) 91-107.

8563 VOON PHIN KEONG. Rubber industry of Burma, 1876-1964. JSAS 4 (1973) 216-228.

RUBBER INDUSTRY - INDONESIA

8564 TENGWALL, T. A. History of rubber cultivation and research in the Netherlands Indies. H57 pp. 344-351.

8565 THOMAS, KENNETH D. Shifting cultivation and smallholder rubber production in a south Sumatran village. MER 10 pt. 1 (1965) 100-115.

RUBBER INDUSTRY - MALAYSIA

8566 BAUER, P. T. Economics of planting density in rubber growing. S48 pp. 236-241.

8567 BAUER, P. T. Malayan rubber policy. S48 pp. 300-314.

8568 BAUER, P. T. Some aspects of the Malayan rubber slump, 1929-33. S48 pp. 185-200.

8569 BAUER, P. T. Working of rubber regulation. S48 pp. 242-267. *Comment:* SILCOCK, T. H. Note on the working of rubber regulation. S48 pp. 268-275. *Author's reply:* Rejoinder. S48 pp. 276-283.

8570 CORDEN, W. M. Prospects for Malayan exports. S47 pp. 93-111.

8571 DRABBLE, J. H. Investment in the rubber industry in Malaya, c. 1900-1922. JSAS 3 (1972) 247-261.

8572 DRABBLE, J. H. Plantation rubber industry in Malaya up to 1922. JMBRAS 40 pt. 1 (1967) 52-77.

8573 FISK, E. K. Productivity and income from rubber in an established Malay reservation. MER 6 pt. 1 (1961) 13-22.

8574 GREENWOOD, J. M. F. Rubber smallholdings in the Federation of Malaya. JTG 18 (1964) 81-100.

8575 HALIM ISMAIL, A. Some considerations regarding the optimum ages for replanting rubber trees on smallholdings in Malaya. MER 14 pt. 2 (1969) 55–78.

8576 HO, ROBERT. Labour inputs of rubber producing smallholders in Malaya. MER 12 pt. 1 (1967) 79–89.

8577 LEE, GEORGE. Commodity production and reproduction amongst the Malayan peasantry. JCA 3 (1973) 441–456.

8578 LIM CHONG YAH. Export taxes on rubber in Malaya, a survey of post-war development. MER 5 pt. 2 (1960) 46–58.

8579 LIM CHONG YAH. Malayan rubber replanting taxes. MER 6 pt. 2 (1961) 43–52.

8580 LIM TECK GHEE. Malayan peasant smallholders and the Stevenson restriction scheme, 1922–28. JMBRAS 47 pt. 2 (1974) 105–122.

8581 McHALE, THOMAS R. Malayan economy and stereo-regular rubbers. AS 1 (June 1961) 25–28.

8582 McHALE, THOMAS R. Natural rubber and Malaysian economic development. MER 10 pt. 1 (1965) 16–43.

8583 McHALE, THOMAS R. Rubber smallholdings in Malaya, their changing nature, role and prospects. MER 10 pt. 2 (1965) 35–48.

8584 Malaya and British Borneo. S48 pp. 171–184.

8585 OOI JIN BEE. Rubber industry of the Federation of Malaya. JTG 15 (1961) 46–65.

8586 PARMER, J. NORMAN. Chinese estate workers' strikes in Malaya in March 1937. C87 pp.

8587 ROSENQUIST, E. A. Soils and fertilization of rubber and oil palm. JTG 18 (1964) 148–156.

8588 RUDNER, MARTIN. Rubber strategy for post-war Malaya, 1945–48. JSAS 1 pt. 1 (1970) 23–36. *Comment:* BAUER, P. T. Post-war Malayan rubber policy, a comment. JSAS 4 (1973) 133–138. *Author's reply:* JSAS 4 (1973) 300–304.

8589 TAN, A. H. H. Incidence of export taxes on small producers. MER 12 pt. 1 (1967) 90–98.

8590 VOON PHIN KEONG. Rubber small holdings industry in Selangor, 1895–1920. JTG 24 (1967) 43–49.

8591 VOON PHIN KEONG. Size aspects of rubber smallholdings in west Malaysia, a case study of Bentong, Pahang. JTG 34 (1972) 65–76.

8592 WAH, FRANCIS CHAN KWONG. Preliminary study of the supply response of Malayan rubber estates between 1948 and 1959. MER 7 pt. 2 (1962) 77–94.

8593 WATSON, G. A. Rubber cultivation in a diversified agriculture, notes on its relegation to the poorer soils of Malaya, North Borneo and Sarawak. SMJ 11 (1962) 590–597.

8594 WHARTON, CLIFTON R. Rubber supply conditions, some policy implications. S47 pp. 131–162.

8595 WYCHERLEY, P. R. Variation in the performance of Hevea in Malaya. JTG 17 (1963) 143–171.

Rubber industry - Malaysia

8596 YUEN CHOY LENG. Japanese rubber and iron investments in Malaya, 1900-1941. JSAS 5 (1974) 18-36.

RUBBER INDUSTRY - THAILAND

8597 STIFEL, LAURENCE D. Growth of the rubber economy of southern Thailand. JSAS 4 (1973) 107-132.

8598 STIFEL, LAURENCE D. Rubber and the economy of southern Thailand. JSS 59 pt. 2 (1971) 3-23.

RUMPHIUS, GEORG EVERHARD

8599 SIRK, M. J. Rumphius, the blind seer of Amboina. H57 pp. 295-308.

S.E.A.T.O.

8600 BUTWELL, RICHARD. Institutional growth of the Southeast Asian Treaty Organization, circumstances of the changes. AST 3 (1965) 377-390.

8601 FIFIELD, RUSSELL H. Another look at SEATO. H35 pp. 190-211.

8602 KENNEDY, D. E. Scope for collective security in Southern Asia. S51 pp. 197-206.

8603 NAIRN, RONALD C. SEATO, a critique. PA 41 (1968) 5-18.

8604 NUECHTERLEIN, DONALD E. Thailand and SEATO: a ten year appraisal. AS 4 (1964) 1174-1181.

SABAH

8605 APPELL, GEORGE N. Death of Serip Usman in Rungus tradition. SMJ 12 (1965) 228-9.

8606 APPELL, GEORGE N. Ethnographic profiles of the Dusun speaking peoples of Sabah, Malaysia. JMBRAS 41 pt. 2 (1968) 131-147.

8607 BLACK, I. D. Ending of Brunei rule in Sabah, 1878-1902. JMBRAS 41 pt. 2 (1968) 176-192.

8608 COATES, AUSTIN. Philippines national hero, Rizal, in Sandakan. SMJ 11 (1962) 537-553.

8609 JOHN, DAVID W. The tobacco industry of North Borneo, a distinctive form of plantation agriculture, by David W. John and James C. Jackson. JSAS 4 (1973) 88-106.

8610 LEE, EDWIN. Emergence of Towkay leaders in party politics in Sabah. JSAH 9 (1968) 306-324.

8611 LEE YONG LENG. Population changes in Sabah, 1951-60. JTG 26 (1968) 55-68.

8612 MEANS, GORDON P. Eastern Malaysia, the politics of federalism. AS 8 (1968) 289-308.

8613 OROLFO. Discovery of birds' nest caves in North Borneo. SMJ 10 (1961) 270-273.

8614 ROBERTSON, J. F. Fertility in the urban kampongs of Kota Kinabalu, Sabah, Malaysia. SMJ 19 (1971) 257-263.

8615 ROBERTSON, J. F. Very young brides. BMJ 2 pt. 3 (1971) 31-38.

8616 ROFF, MARGARET. Rise and demise of Kadazan nationalism. JSAH 10 (1969) 326-343.

8617 TARLING, NICHOLAS. Sir Cecil Clementi and the Federation of British Borneo. JMBRAS 44 pt. 2 (1971) 1-34.

St. John, Horace

SABAH DISPUTE

8618 FERNANDEZ, ALEJANDRO M. Secretary General's role in the Malaysia conflict. DR 12 (1964) 160-171.

8619 ORTIZ, PACIFICO A. Legal aspects of the North Borneo question. PS 11 (1963) 18-64.

8620 SHORT, BROCK K. Brunei, Sulu and Sabah. BMJ 1 (1969) 133-146.

8621 TREGONNING, K. G. Philippine claim to Sabah. JMBRAS 43 pt. 1 (1970) 161-170.

8622 VILLADOLID, ALICE C. Sociological ties binding the Philippines and North Borneo. UN 35 (1962) 515-523.

8623 WRIGHT, LEIGH R. Historical notes on the North Borneo dispute. JAS 25 (1965-6) 471-484.

SA'BAN LANGUAGE

8624 CLAYRE, B. Preliminary comparative study of the Lun Bawang (Murut) and Sa'ban languages of Sarawak. SMJ 20 (1972) 145-171.

8625 CLAYRE, I. F. C. S. Sa'bans revisited, a sequel to Bolang and Harrisson, 1949. SMJ 18 (1970) 319-329.

SAI-YOK

8626 HEEKEREN, H. R. VAN. Brief survey of the Sai-Yok excavations, 1961-62 season of the Thai-Danish prehistoric expedition. JSS 50 (1962) 15-18.

8627 HEEKEREN, H. R. VAN. Preliminary note on the excavation of the Sai-Yok rock shelter. JSS 49 pt. 2 (1961) 99-108.

8628 KNUTH, EIGIL. Further report on the Sai-Yok excavations and on the work at Thai picture cave. JSS 50 (1962) 19-21.

8629 NIELSEN, EIGIL. Thai Danish prehistoric expedition, 1960-1962. JSS 50 (1962) 7-14.

SAIGON

8630 FRYER, D. W. The million city in Southeast Asia. T45 pp. 72-87.

8631 LE THI NGOC ANH. Etude de quelques monuments representatifs de l'art francais a Saigon dans les annees 1877-1908. SEIB 48 (1973) 577-605.

8632 MOSS, LAURENCE A. G. War and urbanization in Indochina, by Laurence A. G. Moss and Zmarak M. Shalizi. G79 pp. 175-200.

8633 THAI VAN KIEM. Interpretation d'une carte ancienne de Saigon. SEIB 37 (1962) 409-431.

SAIGON. MUSEE NATIONAL

8634 BROCHEUX, MICHELE. Notes sur deux bronzes chams inedits du Musee National de Saigon. SEIB 41 (1966) 101-104.

ST. JOHN, HORACE

8635 HARRISON, B. English historians of the Indian archipelago, Crawfurd and St. John. H18 pp. 245-254.

Saint Louis University, Baguio, Philippines

SAMIN MOVEMENT

8652 BENDA, HARRY J. Peasant movements in colonial Southeast Asia. AST 3 (1965) 420-434.

8653 BENDA, HARRY J. Samin movement, by Harry J. Benda and Lance Castles. BIJ 125 (1969) 207-240.

8654 KING, VICTOR T. Some observations on the Samin movement of north central Java, suggestions for the theoretical analysis of the dynamics of rural unrest. BIJ 129 (1973) 457-481.

8655 MULDER, NIELS. Saminism and Buddhism, a note on a field visit to a Samin community. AQ (1974) 253-258.

8656 THE SIAUW GIAP. Samin and Samat movements in Java, two examples of peasant resistance. RSA (1967) 303-310.

8657 THE SIAUW GIAP. Samin and Samat movements in Java, two examples of peasant resistance. RSA (1968) 107-113.

8658 THE SIAUW GIAP. Samin movement in Java, complementary remarks. RSA (1969) 63-77.

SAMPLING - BURMA

8659 THET LWIN. Balugyun sample survey, 1962. JBRS 48 (June 1965) 43-56.

SAN CARLOS SEMINARY, MANILA

8660 CULLUM, LEO A. San Carlos Seminary and the Jesuits. PS 18 (1970) 479-545.

SANCHEZ, FRANCISCO DE PAULA MIGUEL

8661 CULLUM, LEO A. Francisco de Paula Sanchez, 1849-1928. PS 8 (1960) 334-361.

SANDIN, P. ALONSO

8662 VICENTE, VICTORIANO. El P. Alonso Sandin segun el libro de grados de la universidad. UN 39 (1966) 269-280.

SANG NILA UTAMA

8663 WINSTEDT, RICHARD O. Founder of old Singapore. JMBRAS 42 pt. 1 (1969) 42.

SANGIRESE

8664 CHABOT, H. TH. Processes of change in Siau, 1890-1950. BIJ 125 (1969) 94-102.

SANGIRESE LANGUAGE

8665 MARYOTT, KENNETH R. Phonology and morphophonemics of Tabukang Sangir. PSSHR 26 (1961) 111-126.

SANSKRIT LANGUAGE

8666 BHATTACHARYA, KAMALESWAR. Recherches sur le vocabulaire des inscriptions sanskrites du Cambodge. BEF 52 (1964) 1-72.

8667 BHATTACHARYA, KAMALESWAR. Supplement aux recherches sur le vocabulaire des inscriptions sanskrites du Cambodge. BEF 53 (1966) 273-277.

Sanskrit language

8668 BHATTACHARYA, KAMALESWAR. Supplement aux recherches sur le vocabulaire des inscriptions sanskrites du Cambodge. BEF 55 (1969) 145-151.

8669 CHI HSIEN LIN. Language problem of primitive Buddhism. JBRS 43 (1960) 9-15.

8670 FRANCISCO, JUAN R. Further notes on Pardo de Tavera's *El Sanscrito en la lengua Tagalog*. AST 6 (1968) 223-234.
Comment: SALAZAR, Z. A. Footnote to Dr. Francisco's notes on Tavera. AST 6 (1968) 431-444.

8671 JACQUES, CLAUDE. Etudes d'epigraphie cambodgienne. IV. Deux inscriptions du Phnom Bakhen, K. 464 et K. 558. V. La stele du Prasat Cha Chuk, K. 1034. BEF 57 (1970) 57-89.

8672 MINATTUR, JOSEPH. Note on berita. JMBRAS 39 pt. 1 (1966) 188-190.

8673 SPITZBARDT, HARRY. Lexical and morphological impact of Sanskrit on modern Indonesian. AAS 9 (1973) 97-113.

8674 VOORHOEVE, P. Sanskrit maandnamen in het Bataks. BIJ 128 (1972) 494-496.

SANSKRIT LITERATURE *See also* MAHABHARATA, RAMAYANA

8675 AU CHHIENG. Sanscrit "jour de Yama" et vieux khmer "dixieme jour lunaire." G83 pp. 201-206.

8676 BOELES, J. J. Migration of the magic syllable Om. J41 pp. 40-56.

8677 FILLIOZAT, JEAN. Kailasaparampara. F38 pp. 241-247.

8678 FRANCISCO, JUAN R. Preliminary notes on Rizal's *Ultimo adios* in Sanskrit. DR 9 (1961) 377-382.

8679 HOOYKAAS, C. Saiva-Siddhanta in Java and Bali, some remarks on its recent study. BIJ 118 (1962) 309-327.

8680 HOOYKAAS, JACOBA. Myth of the young cowherd and the little girl. BIJ 117 (1961) 267-278.

8681 JONG, J. W. DE. Notes on the sources and the text of the *Sang Hyang Kamahayanan Mantranaya*. BIJ 130 (1974) 465-482.

8682 MARR, J. R. Some manuscripts in Grantha script in Bangkok. SOAS 32 (1969) 281-322.

8683 MARR, J. R. Some manuscripts in Grantha script in Bangkok, II. JSS 60 pt. 2 (1972) 61-86.

8684 NEEDHAM, RODNEY. Jataka, Pancatantra and Kodi fables. BIJ 116 (1960) 232-262.

8685 ORARA, E. DE GUZMAN. Notes on preliminary notes on Rizal's *Ultimo adios* in Sanskrit. DR 13 (1965) 140-156.

8686 SARKAR, HIMANSU BHUSAN. South India in old Javanese and Sanskrit inscriptions. BIJ 125 (1969) 193-206.

8687 VENKATASUBBIAH, A. Some Sanskrit stanzas in the Javanese *Tantri Kamandaka*. BIJ 121 (1965) 350-359.

8688 VOGEL, J. PH. Bosch' thesis on the legend of Jimutavahana. H39 pp. 25-31.

Santo Tomas University *See* MANILA.
  UNIVERSITY OF SANTO TOMAS

SANTOS, BIENVENIDO N.

8689 ARCELLANA, FRANCISCO. Bienvenido
N. Santos. M24 pp. 714-721.

SANTRI, KJAHI RADEN

8690 ROBSON, S. O. Kjahi Raden Santri.
BIJ 121 (1965) 259-264.

SANUSI PANE

8691 AVELING, HARRY. Alternative reading of Sanusi Pane's *Sadjak*. BIJ
128 (1972) 491-493.

SARAWAK - BIBLIOGRAPHY

8692 LOH CHEE YIN. Some important publications omitted from Cotter's
bibliography, prior to 1965. SMJ
14 (1966) 354-375.

SARAWAK - DESCRIPTION AND TRAVEL

8693 APPELL, G. N. Early American adventurers in Borneo, a brief note
and request for information.
JMBRAS 42 pt. 2 (1969) 220-1.

8694 CHRISTIE, ELLA. First tourist,
astana guest, Kuching, 1904. SMJ
10 (1961) 43-49.

8695 GARDNER, ESTELLE. Footnote to
Sarawak, 1859. SMJ 11 (1963) 32-
59.

8696 HOSE, ERNEST. Notes from the old
days. SMJ 10 (1961) 108-111.

8697 WILDER, JAMES AUSTIN. Journal of
James Austin Wilder during his
visit to Sarawak in 1896, edited
by G. N. Appell. SMJ 16 (1968)
407-434.

8698 WILDER, JAMES AUSTIN. Journal of
James Austin Wilder during his
visit to Sarawak in 1896, II,
edited by G. N. Appell. SMJ 17
(1969) 315-335.

SARAWAK - ECONOMIC CONDITIONS

8699 HARRISSON, TOM. Nuts and Malays
on Tanjong Datu. SMJ 9 (1960)
655-669.

SARAWAK - FOREIGN RELATIONS

8700 HARRISSON, TOM. Papuan shield,
Tibetan beads, etc. inside Borneo.
SMJ 11 (1964) 558-561.

SARAWAK - FOREIGN RELATIONS - GREAT
  BRITAIN

8701 TARLING, NICHOLAS. Britain and
Sarawak in the twentieth century,
Raja Charles, Raja Vyner and the
Colonial Office. JMBRAS 43 pt. 2
(1970) 25-52.

8702 WRIGHT, L. R. Sarawak's relations
with Britain, 1858 to 1870. SMJ
11 (1964) 628-648.

8703 WRIGHT, L. R. Status of Sarawak
under Raja James Brooke and British recognition. PHR 1 pt. 1
(1965) 365-385.

SARAWAK - HISTORY

8704 HARRISSON, TOM. Backwash to
piracy, a rajah's royal rages and

the *Straits Times* editor of 1851.
SMJ 11 (1963) 13-31.

8705 HARRISSON, TOM. Malays of South-
west Sarawak before Malaysia. SMJ
11 (1964) 341-511.

8706 HARRISSON, TOM. What ailed Miss
Poncelet in 1895? SMJ 11 (1963)
60-63.

8707 PRINGLE, ROBERT M. Asun's rebellion, the political growing pains
of a tribal society in Brooke
Sarawak, 1929-1940. SMJ 16 (1968)
346-376.

8708 PRINGLE, ROBERT M. The Brookes of
Sarawak, reformers in spite of
themselves. SMJ 19 (1971) 53-76.

8709 PRINGLE, ROBERT M. Murder of Fox
and Steele, Masahor's version.
SMJ 12 (1965) 215-227.

8710 SANDIN, BENEDICT. Origin of the
Saribas Malays. SMJ 17 (1969)
231-244.

8711 SAUNDERS, G. E. James Brooke's
visit to Brunei in 1844, a reappraisal. SMJ 17 (1969) 294-314.

8712 TARLING, NICHOLAS. Sir Cecil Clementi and the Federation of British
Borneo. JMBRAS 44 pt. 2 (1971) 1-
34.

8713 TARLING, NICHOLAS. Sir James
Brooke and Brunei. SMJ 11 (1963)
1-12.

8714 TAYLOR, BRIAN. The Chinese revolt.
SMJ 17 (1969) 290-293.

8715 TUTON KABOY. The murder of Steele
and Fox, two versions. SMJ 12
(1965) 207-214.

SARAWAK - MINORITIES *A list of the
minorities of Sarawak is included in:*
MALAYSIA - MINORITIES

8716 HARRISSON, TOM. Three secret communication systems among Borneo
nomads and their dogs. JMBRAS 38
pt. 2 (1965) 67-86.

SARAWAK - POLITICS AND GOVERNMENT

8717 BUCK, W. S. B. Brookes in exile,
1941-. SMJ 10 (1961) 59-81.

8718 DOERING, OTTO C. Government in
Sarawak under Charles Brooke.
JMBRAS 39 pt. 2 (1966) 95-107.

8719 MEANS, GORDON P. Eastern Malaysia, the politics of federalism.
AS 8 (1968) 289-308.

8720 REINHARDT, JON M. Administrative
policy and practice in Sarawak,
continuity and change under the
Brookes. JAS 29 (1969-70) 851-
862.

8721 RUNCIMAN, STEVEN. No independent
prince, 1861. SMJ 10 (1961) 30-1.

8722 SANDIN, BENEDICT. Iban leaders.
SMJ 18 (1970) 89-161.

8723 SAUNDERS, GRAHAM. James Brooke
and Asian government. BMJ 3 pt. 1
(1973) 105-117.

8724 TILMAN, ROBERT O. Sarawak political scene. PA 37 (1964) 412-425.

8725 VAN DER KROEF, JUSTUS M. Communism in Sarawak today. AS 6 (1966)
568-579.

SARAWAK – POPULATION

8726 FIDLER, RICHARD C. Population diversity in a Sarawak bazaar town. SMJ 20 (1972) 195–233.

8727 LEE, Y. L. Dayaks of Sarawak. JTG 23 (1966) 28–39.

8728 SAW SWEE HOOK. Labour force of Sarawak in 1960, by Saw Swee Hook and Cheng Siok Hwa. AST 8 (1970) 135–142.

SARAWAK – RELIGION *See also* CHRISTIANITY – MALAYSIA – EAST MALAYSIA

8729 PRATTIS, IAN. Kayan-Kenyah Bungan cult in Sarawak. SMJ 11 (1963) 64–87.

8730 TAMA INO BALAN. Prayers for the erection of a new house among the Lepo Tau Kenyah. SMJ 22 (1974) 353–368.

SARAWAK – SOCIAL CONDITIONS

8731 COURT, CHRISTOPHER. Kinship terms of reference of the Mentu Land Dayaks in phonemic notation. BIJ 126 (1970) 463–465.

8732 HARRISSON, TOM. Palang, its history and proto-history in west Borneo and the Philippines. JMBRAS 37 pt. 2 (1964) 162–174.

8733 HARRISSON, TOM. Palang, three further notes. JMBRAS 39 pt. 1 (1966) 172–174.

8734 SANDIN, BENEDICT. Punan La'ong, two notes. SMJ 12 (1965) 185–187.

8735 THOMAS, SHARON. Women's tattoos of the upper Rajang. SMJ 16 (1968) 209–234.

SARAWAK MUSEUM

8736 HARRISSON, TOM. Kelabit duck ewer in the Sarawak Museum. SMJ 16 (1968) 100.

8737 HARRISSON, TOM. Sarawak Museum's Punan salong and Puso's jar. SMJ 11 (1963) 327–339.

8738 HARRISSON, TOM. Second to none, our first curator, and others. SMJ 10 (1961) 17–29.

8739 HARRISSON, TOM. Small Dusun type jar in the Sarawak Museum. SMJ 14 (1966) 156–7.

8740 LOH CHIN YIN. A. R. Wallace collection in the Sarawak Museum reference library. SMJ 15 (1967) 446–455.

8741 TRELOAR, F. E. Stoneware bottles in the Sarawak Museum, vessels for mercury trade? SMJ 20 (1972) 377–384.

SARIBAS LITERATURE

8742 HARRISSON, TOM. Sea going cuckoo and other themes significant in the Saribas story. SMJ 11 (1964) 537–540.

8743 SANDIN, BENEDICT. Owl marries the moon, a Saribas story. SMJ 11 (1964) 534–536.

SARTONO, R. M.

8744 LEV, DANIEL S. In memoriam, R. M. Sartono. IND 7 (1969) 191–193.

Sather, Clifford

SATHER, CLIFFORD

8745 WILLIAMS, THOMAS R. Comment on the social anthropology of Sabah, response to Appell, Sather and Goethals. SMJ 16 (1968) 440-452.

SATINGPHRA

8746 LAMB, ALASTAIR. Notes on Satingphra. JMBRAS 37 pt. 1 (1964) 74-87.

8747 LAMB, ALASTAIR. Stone casket from Satingpra, some further observations. JSS 53 (1965) 191-195.

SAYA SAN

8748 SOLOMON, ROBERT L. Saya San and the Burmese rebellion. MAS 3 (1969) 209-223.

SCIENCE - INDONESIA

8749 FIELD, RICHARD M. Felix Alexander Vening Meinesz, exponent of international cooperation through geoscience. H57 pp. 99-104.

8750 Scientific development, discussion rapporteur's report. S32 pp. 76-79.

8751 VERDOORN, FRANS. Scientific institutions, societies and research workers in the Netherlands, by Frans and J. G. Verdoorn. H57 pp. 426-460.

SCIENCE - PHILIPPINES

8752 APRIETO, PACIFICO N. What is science writing? GEJ 9 (1965) 14-21.

8753 BANTUG, J. P. Rizal and the progress of the natural sciences. PS 9 (1961) 3-16.

8754 GONZALEZ, SALVADOR R. Exact sciences. UN 36 (1963) 395-402.

8755 KAPAUAN, AMANDO. Science courses and the Filipino student. PS 21 (1973) 424-428.

8756 LLENADO, ESTELA F. Applied science in the Philippines. UN 36 (1963) 403-407.

8757 MAGNO, MELECIO S. Natural science 1 in the general education program. GEJ 1 (1961) 84-88.

8758 MANUEL, CANUTO G. Problems of science and technological development in Southeast Asia and ways and means of regional collaboration. S32 pp. 67-73.

8759 MARANON, JOAQUIN. On scientific research. UN 33 (1960) 809-822.

8760 MARANON, JOAQUIN. Trends in the biological sciences in the Philippines, then and now. UN 36 (1963) 387-394.

8761 MIRANDA, B. T. Basic natural sciences in the University of the Philippines. GEJ 7 (1964) 127-133.

8762 RODRIGUEZ, LORENZO. On the progress of Philippine botanical research. UN 34 (Dec. 1961) 64-76.

8763 SALCEDO, JUAN. Role of natural sciences in modern Philippines. SJ 12 (1965) 239-244.

8764 SCHUMACHER, JOHN N. One hundred years of Jesuit scientists, the Manila Observatory, 1865-1965. PS 13 (1965) 258-286.

8765 TAYKO, PERLA RIZALINA MATURAN. Survey of teacher education in the natural sciences in the Visayas. SJ 20 (1973) 75-90.

8766 VALENZUELA, PATROCINIO. Natural sciences, 1956-1959. PS 8 (1960) 515-525.

SCIENCE - VIETNAM

8767 HUARD, PIERRE. Le pionnier de la technologie vietnamienne, Henri Oger, 1885-1936. BEF 57 (1970) 215-217.

8768 HUARD, PIERRE. La science au Vietnam, par P. Huard et M. M. Durand. SEIB 38 (1967) 533-555.

Sea Dayaks *See* IBAN

SEBOB

8769 GOCKEL, GUIDO. The Long Pekun Sebob. SMJ 22 (1974) 325-328.

8770 MAPING MADANG. Adat Suen, Sebob graded rites. SMJ 13 (1966) 305-320.

8771 SELING SAWING. Flight from the Usun Apau to the headwaters of the Tinjar. SMJ 22 (1974) 331-348.

SEBOB LITERATURE

8772 GALVIN, A. D. Child of Padan Sigau, a Sebob saga. SMJ 12 (1965) 166-170.

SEDANG LANGUAGE

8773 SMITH, KENNETH D. Denasolaryngealization in Sedang folk-linguistics. M61 pp. 53-62.

8774 SMITH, KENNETH D. More on Sedang ethnodialects. M61 pp. 43-51.

8775 SMITH, KENNETH D. Sedang affixation. M59 pp. 108-129.

8776 SMITH, KENNETH D. Sedang dialects. SEIB 42 (1967) 195-255.

SEJARAH MELAYU

8777 ISKANDAR, T. Three Malay historical writings in the first half of the 17th century. JMBRAS 40 pt. 2 (1967) 38-53.

8778 JOSSELIN DE JONG, P. E. DE. Character of the Malay annals. B38 pp. 235-241.

8779 JOSSELIN DE JONG, P. E. DE. Rise and decline of a national hero. JMBRAS 38 pt. 2 (1965) 140-155.

8780 JOSSELIN DE JONG, P. E. DE. Who's who in the Malay annals. JMBRAS 34 pt. 2 (1961) 1-89.

8781 JOSSELIN DE JONG, P. E. DE. Who's who in the Malay annals. JMBRAS 42 pt. 1 (1969) 34-41.

8782 LINEHAN, W. Kings of 14th century Singapore. JMBRAS 42 pt. 1 (1969) 53-62.

8783 Malay annals, chapter III. JMBRAS 42 pt. 1 (1969) 25-33.

8784 ROOLVINK, R. Answer of Pasai. JMBRAS 38 pt. 2 (1965) 129-139.

8785 ROOLVINK, R. Five line songs in the Sejarah Melayu? BIJ 122 (1966) 455-457.

Sejarah Melayu

8786 ROOLVINK, R. Variant versions of the Malay annals. BIJ 123 (1967) 301-324.

8787 SWEENEY, P. L. AMIN. Connection between the Hikayat Raja2 Pasai and the Sejarah Melayu. JMBRAS 40 pt. 2 (1967) 94-105.

8788 TEEUW, A. Hikayat Raja-Raja Pasai and Sejarah Melayu. B38 pp. 222-234.

8789 ZAINAL ABIDIN BIN ABDUL WAHID. Sejarah Melayu. AST 4 (1966) 445-451.

SELAKO LANGUAGE

8790 HUDSON, A. B. Note on Selako, Malayic Dayak and Land Dayak languages in western Borneo. SMJ 18 (1970) 301-318.

SELAKO LITERATURE

8791 INA ANAK KALOM. Selako folktale, Ne' Dibo and the Lundu Sebuyau, by Ina Anak Kalom and A. B. Hudson. SMJ 19 (1971) 317-323.

8792 INA ANAK KALOM. Selako traditional history, a story on the origins of Kampong Pueh, by Ina Anak Kalom and A. B. Hudson. SMJ 18 (1970) 281-300.

SELANGOR

8793 ANDAYA, BARBARA WATSON. Installation of the first sultan of Selangor in 1766. JMBRAS 47 pt. 1 (1974) 41-57.

8794 JACKSON, JAMES C. Population changes in Selangor state, 1850-1891. JTG 19 (1964) 42-57.

8795 LOW KWAI SIM. Water balance of five catchments in Selangor, west Malaysia, by Low Kwai Sim and Goh Kim Chuan. JTG 35 (1972) 60-66.

8796 MOHAMAD AMIN HASSAN. Raja Bot bin Raja Jumaat. JMBRAS 40 pt. 2 (1967) 68-93.

8797 RADCLIFFE, DAVID. Peopling of Ulu Langat. IND 8 (1969) 155-182.

8798 SADKA, EMILY. State councils in Perak and Selangor, 1877-1895. J45 pp. 89-119.

8799 VOON PHIN KEONG. Rubber smallholdings industry in Selangor, 1895-1920. JTG 24 (1967) 43-49.

8800 YEO KIM WAH. Selangor succession dispute, 1933-38. JSAS 2 (1971) 169-184.

SELGA, MIGUEL

8801 HIDALGO, ANGEL. Miguel Selga, 1879-1956, priest and scientist. PS 15 (1967) 307-347.

SEMARANG

8802 COBBAN, JAMES L. Uncontrolled urban settlement, the kampong question in Semarang, 1905-1940. BIJ 130 (1974) 403-427.

SEMELAI

8803 NEEDHAM, RODNEY. Some ethnographic notes on Semelai in northern Pahang. JMBRAS 47 pt. 2 (1974) 123-129.

Senoi *See* SAKAI

SENTANI LANGUAGE

8804 VOORHOEVE, C. L. Some notes on the linguistic relations between the Sentani and Asmat languages of New Guinea. BIJ 125 (1969) 466-486.

SEX CUSTOMS - MALAYSIA

8805 APPELL, G. N. Penis pin at Peabody Museum, Harvard University. JMBRAS 41 pt. 2 (1968) 203-205.

8806 BEAVITT, PAUL. Ngayap, changes in the pattern of premarital relations of the Iban. SMJ 15 (1967) 407-413.

8807 HARRISSON, TOM. Palang, its history and proto-history in west Borneo and the Philippines. JMBRAS 37 pt. 2 (1964) 162-174.

8808 HARRISSON, TOM. Palang, three further notes. JMBRAS 39 pt. 1 (1966) 172-174.

SEX CUSTOMS - PHILIPPINES

8809 HARRISSON, TOM. Palang, its history and proto-history in west Borneo and the Philippines. JMBRAS 37 pt. 2 (1964) 162-174.

8810 HARRISSON, TOM. Palang, three further notes. JMBRAS 39 pt. 1 (1966) 172-174.

8811 ROEKAERTS, EMIEL. The sexual behavior of junior and senior college students. SLURJ 3 (1972) 113-291.

8812 VELASCO, MARIA THERESA L. Why wait until marriage? Premarital intercourse vs. premarital chastity. SLURJ 3 (1972) 11-25.

SEX CUSTOMS - THAILAND

8813 SMITH, HAROLD E. Polygyny and marriage registration in Thailand. SA 2 (1972-3) 290-299.

SHAHBANDARS

8814 PURNADI PURBATJARAKA. Shahbandars in the archipelago. JSAH 2 (July 1961) 1-9.

SHAN

8815 COCHRANE, W. W. Les Chan septentrionaux. FA 17 (1960) 1859-1879.

8816 LEHMAN, F. K. Burma, Kayah society as a function of the Shan-Burma-Karen context. S84 pp. 1-104.

SHAN LANGUAGE

8817 EGEROD, SOREN. Romanization of Shan. B91 pp. 47-49.

SHAN LITERATURE

8818 SAO SAIMONG. Shan folk tales. JBRS 43 (1960) 83-90.

SHARP, LAURISTON

8819 SKINNER, G. WILLIAM. Introduction, by G. William Skinner and A. Thomas Kirsch. C24 pp. 9-24.

8820 SMITH, ROBERT J. Introduction. S58 pp. 7-19.

Shingenobu, Okuma

SHIGENOBU, OKUMA

8821 SANIEL, JOSEFA M. Okuma Shigenobu
and the 1898 Philippine problem.
PHR 1 pt. 1 (1965) 298-319.

Ships *See* BOATS

SIAM SOCIETY. JOURNAL

8822 DHANINIVAT, KROMAMUN BIDYALABH.
Transcription of Siamese, yet
another experiment which I used
for some twenty years in the
Journal of the Siam Society. T33
pp. 69-72.

SIAM SOCIETY. LIBRARY

8823 Accessions to the library from
July to December 1959. JSS 48 pt.
1 (1960) 111-117.

8824 Accessions to the Siam Society
Library from January to June 1960.
JSS 48 pt. 2 (1960) 135-146.

8825 Accessions to the Siam Society
Library from July to December 1960.
JSS 49 pt. 1 (1961) 87-98.

8826 Accessions to the Siam Society
Library from January 1961 to June
1961. JSS 49 pt. 2 (1961) 183-189.

8827 Accessions to the Siam Society's
Library from July to December 1961.
JSS 50 (1962) 73-79.

8828 Accessions to the Siam Society's
Library from January to December
1962. JSS 50 (1962) 193-206.

8829 Accessions to the Siam Society's
Library from January to April 1963.
JSS 51 (1963) 101-123.

8830 Accessions to the Siam Society's
Library, from May to December
1963. JSS 52 (1964) 133-149.

8831 Accessions to the Siam Society's
Library from January to June 1964.
JSS 52 (1964) 257-272.

8832 Accessions to the Siam Society's
Library from July to December
1964. JSS 53 (1965) 215-235.

8833 Accessions to the Siam Society's
Library, January to December 1965.
JSS 54 (1966) 93-109.

8834 Accessions to the Siam Society's
Library from January to August
1966. JSS 55 (1967) 143-160.

SIENG KHWANG

8835 ARCHAIMBAULT, CHARLES. Annales de
l'ancien royaume de Sieng Khwang.
BEF 53 (1966) 557-673.

SIHANOUK, NORODOM

8836 BENDIX, REINHARD. Reflections on
charismatic leadership. AS 7
(1967) 341-352.

8837 HAN SUYIN. Portraits of the
prince, by Han Suyin and Robert
Shaplen. G79 pp. 74-80.

8838 Pour une Indochine nouvelle, un
discours de S. A. R. Norodom
Sihanouk. FA 20 (1965) 97-113.

8839 Protagonists: Norodom Sihanouk
and Lon Nol. G79 pp. 105-112.

8840 SIHANOUK, NORODOM. Third message
to the nation, April 20, 1970.
JCA 1 pt. 1 (1970) 83-89.

8841 SMITH, ROGER M. The politics of Sihanouk. G79 pp. 69-73.

8842 SMITH, ROGER M. Prince Norodom Sihanouk of Cambodia. AS 7 (1967) 353-362.

8843 SMITH, ROGER M. Prince Norodom Sihanouk of Cambodia. T45 pp. 393-402.

Silk *See* TEXTILES

SILLIMAN JOURNAL

8844 BANAS, ELISEO P. Decennial index to the *Silliman journal*, 1954-1963. SJ 10 (1963) 486-526.

SILLIMAN UNIVERSITY

8845 ARQUIZA, LINO Q. Educational work from a Protestant perspective. SJ 11 (1964) 26-33.
Comment: ELWOOD, DOUGLAS J. Additional comments. SJ 11 (1964) 33-4.

8846 ARQUIZA, LINO Q. Use of a socio-metric device in guidance and counseling, by Lino Q. and Eusebia C. Arquiza. SJ 7 (1960) 52-71.

8847 CALDERON, CICERO D. Case for Christian higher education in Asia. SJ 18 (1971) 72-74.

8848 CALDERON, CICERO D. Redefining a university's objectives. SJ 16 (1969) 299-306.

8849 CALDERON, CICERO D. Silliman University and its mission. SJ 9 (1962) 209-217.

8850 DEINER, PAUL W. Is Silliman a Christian university? SJ 17 (1970) 59-66.

8851 FLORES, EDUARDO. National relevance and involvement for the Law School. SJ 20 (1973) 91-99.

8852 FLORES, PEDRO V. Student achievement as index of teaching effectiveness. SJ 20 (1973) 15-39.

8853 GABILA, ANTONIO S. University in a Philippine setting. SJ 9 (1962) 208.

8854 JACINTO, JOSE S. A look at our program, is Silliman University fulfilling its mission as a Christian university? SJ 10 (1963) 135-146.

8855 LAING, JOHN E. Progress report on the Silliman family planning project. SLQ 6 (1968) 415-422.

8856 List of research projects in Silliman University, compiled by the University Research Center, second semester, 1969-70. SJ 17 (1970) 82-85.

8857 MASLOG, CRISPIN. Journalism and communications program at Silliman University, an overview. SJ 14 (1967) 395-402.

8858 MUNN, MERTON D. Counseling program at Silliman University. SJ 10 (1963) 147-153.

8859 MUNN, MERTON D. New frontiers for Silliman. SJ 9 (1962) 105-119.

8860 MUNN, MERTON D. Quality education at Silliman University. SJ 7 (1960) 257-284.

8861 On going projects of SU Research Council. SJ 21 (1974) 125-127.

Silliman University

8862 PAL, AGATON P. Ideal patterns and
value judgments in development
program planning. SJ 7 (1960)
134-152.

8863 Partial list of faculty and staff
publications, Silliman University,
1968-69. SJ 17 (1970) 86-89.

8864 Partial list of faculty and staff
publications, Silliman University,
1969-70. SJ 17 (1970) 354-356.

8865 SINCO, VICENTE G. The university
and national issues. SJ 9 (1962)
5-14.

8866 VILLAREAL, CORNELIO T. Nation
building, the continuing challenge.
SJ 10 (1963) 38-41.

8867 WICKLER, HOWARD. Philosophy of
vocational education. SJ 7 (1960)
23-35.

SILLIMAN UNIVERSITY. LIBRARY

8868 SIEGA, GORGONIO D. Looking back-
ward, the first fifty-five years
of Silliman University Library.
SJ 12 (1965) 262-278.

SILVA, JUAN DE

8869 QUIRINO, CARLOS. Rare Manila imprint. PHR 1 pt. 2 (1966) 201-203.

SINCO, VICENTE G.

8870 MEANY, JAMES J. Sinco report. PS
10 (1962) 32-44.

8871 SINCO, VICENTE G. Plan for concentrated guided study. GEJ 1
(1961) 3-29.

SINGAPORE

8872 L'annee 1966 en Asie, Singapour.
FA 22 (1968) 113-4.

8873 CHEE, STEPHEN. Malaysia and
Singapore, separate identities,
different priorities. AS 13
(1973) 151-161.

8874 CHEE, STEPHEN. Malaysia and
Singapore, the political economy
of multiracial development. AS 14
(1974) 183-191.

8875 FRYER, D. W. The million city in
Southeast Asia. T45 pp. 72-87.

8876 HSU YUN TSIAO. Singapore in the
remote past. JMBRAS 45 pt. 1
(1972) 1-9.

8877 OOI JIN-BEE. Singapore, the
balance sheet. M49 pp. 1-13.

8878 ROGERS, MARVIN L. Malaysia and
Singapore, 1971 developments. AS
12 (1972) 168-176.

8879 THIO, EUNICE. Introduction.
JMBRAS 42 pt. 1 (1969) 1-4.

8880 WIKKRAMATILEKE, R. Focus on
Singapore, 1964. JTG 20 (1965)
73-83.

8881 YEUNG, YUE-MAN. Singapore. F56
pp. 166-184.

SINGAPORE - BIBLIOGRAPHY

8882 LIM HUCK TEE. *Index Malaysiana,
an index to the Journal of the
Straits Branch, Royal Asiatic
Society and the Journal of the
Malayan Branch, Royal Asiatic
Society, 1878-1963,* by Lim Huck
Tee and D. E. K. Wijasuriya.
JMBRAS 36 pt. 4 (1963) 1-395.

8883   WANG CHEN HSIU CHIN. Select bibliography, by Wang Chen Hsiu Chin and Manijeh Namazie. M49 pp. 233-277.

SINGAPORE - CONSTITUTION

8884   TURNBULL, C. M. Constitutional development, 1819-1968. M49 pp. 181-196.

SINGAPORE - DEFENSES

8885   McINTYRE, W. DAVID. Strategic significance of Singapore, 1917-1942, the naval base and the Commonwealth. JSAH 10 (1969) 69-94.

8886   THOMSON, G. G. Strategy of a sovereign Singapore. S51 pp. 265-293.

SINGAPORE - DESCRIPTION AND TRAVEL

8887   ABDULLAH BIN ABDUL KADIR. Shaer kampong gelam terbakar, edited with notes by C. Skinner. JMBRAS 45 pt. 1 (1972) 21-56.

8888   BRADDELL, ROLAND. Lung Ya Men and Tan Ma Hsi. JMBRAS 42 pt. 1 (1969) 10-24.

8889   HAUGHTON, H. T. Native names of streets in Singapore. JMBRAS 42 pt. 1 (1969) 196-207.

8890   PEARSON, H. F. Lt. Jackson's plan of Singapore. JMBRAS 42 pt. 1 (1969) 161-165.

8891   PEARSON, H. F. Singapore from the sea, June 1823, notes on a recently discovered sketch attributed to Lt. Phillip Jackson. JMBRAS 42 pt. 1 (1969) 133-144.

SINGAPORE - ECONOMIC CONDITIONS

8892   BAKER, M. Economic, social and cultural problems of Singapore. S32 pp. 16-21.

8893   BHANOJI RAO, V. V. Progress in primary production. Y52 pp. 246-262.

8894   CHIANG HAI DING. Early shipping conference of Singapore, 1897-1911. JSAH 10 (1969) 50-68.

8895   CHUA, WEE MENG. Inter-industry analysis of the Singapore economy, 1967. MER 17 pt. 1 (1972) 25-49.

8896   LIM CHONG YAH. The Singapore economy and the Vietnam war, by Lim Chong Yah and Ow Chwee Huay. Y52 pp. 352-369.

8897   LIM CHONG YAH. Singapore's position in the world economy. RSAS pt. 4 (1971) 3-9.

8898   McDONALD, DANIEL. Responsibility for published financial statements. MER 8 pt. 1 (1963) 40-44.

8899   WONG, K. P. Macroeconomic model of Singapore, 1960-69. MER 19 pt. 1 (1974) 35-45.

8900   YEUNG, PATRICK. Analysis of the potential gains and contributions of the entrepot trade. MER 13 pt. 1 (1968) 1-10.

SINGAPORE - FOREIGN RELATIONS

8901   BOYCE, PETER. Policy without authority, Singapore's external affairs power. JSAH 6 (Sept. 1965) 87-103.

8902   CHAN HENG CHEE. Singapore's foreign policy, 1965-1968. JSAH 10 (1969) 177-191.

8920 CHIANG HAI DING. Early shipping conference of Singapore, 1897-1911. JSAH 10 (1969) 50-68.

8921 COLLESS, BRIAN E. Ancient history of Singapore. JSAH 10 (1969) 1-11.

8922 COWAN, C. D. New harbour, Singapore, and the cruise of H. M. S. Maeander, 1848-49. JMBRAS 38 pt. 2 (1965) 229-240.

8923 GIBSON-HILL, C. A. Master attendants at Singapore, 1819-1867. JMBRAS 33 pt. 1 (1960) 1-64.

8924 HSU YUN TSIAO. Notes on the historical position of Singapore. J45 pp. 226-238.

8925 JACKSON, R. N. Grasping the nettle, first successes in the struggle to govern the Chinese in Malaya. JMBRAS 40 pt. 1 (1967) 130-139.

8926 Landing of Raffles in Singapore. JMBRAS 42 pt. 1 (1969) 78-9.

8927 MAXWELL, W. E. Founding of Singapore. JMBRAS 42 pt. 1 (1969) 81-84.

8928 MILLS, L. A. British Malaya, 1824-67. JMBRAS 33 pt. 3 (1960) 9-326.

8929 NG SIEW YOONG. Chinese protectorate in Singapore, 1877-1900. JSAH 2 (Mar. 1961) 89-116.

8930 RAFFLES, THOMAS S. Founding of Singapore. JMBRAS 42 pt. 1 (1969) 71-77.

8931 READ, W. H. Landing of Raffles in Singapore. JMBRAS 42 pt. 1 (1969) 80.

8932 ROFF, WILLIAM R. Malayo-Muslim world of Singapore at the close of the nineteenth century. JAS 24 (1964-5) 75-90.

8933 TARLING, NICHOLAS. Prince of merchants and the lion city. JMBRAS 37 pt. 1 (1964) 20-40.

8934 TAY, J. S. Attempts of Raffles to establish a British base in South-East Asia, 1818-1819. JSAH 1 (Sept. 1960) 31-49.

8935 TREGONNING, K. G. Historical background. M49 pp. 14-19.

8936 TURNBULL, C. M. Bibliography of writings in English on British Malaya, 1786-1867. JMBRAS 33 pt. 3 (1960) 327-424.

8937 WILKINSON, R. J. Old Singapore. JMBRAS 42 pt. 1 (1969) 43-48.

8938 WILLIAMS, LEA E. Chinese leadership in early British Singapore. AST 2 (1964) 170-179.

8939 WINSTEDT, RICHARD O. Founder of Singapore. JMBRAS 42 pt. 1 (1969) 42.

8940 WINSTEDT, RICHARD O. Note on the founding of Singapore. JSAH 5 (Sept. 1964) 15-6.

8941 WINSTEDT, RICHARD O. Tumasik or old Singapore. JMBRAS 42 pt. 1 (1969) 5-9.

SINGAPORE - LAWS, STATUTES, ETC.

8942 CHENG SIOK HWA. Government legislation for Chinese secret societies in the Straits Settlements in the late 19th century. AST 10 (1972) 262-271.

Singapore - Laws, statutes, etc.

8943 HOOKER, M. B. Relationship between Chinese law and common law in Malaysia, Singapore, and Hong Kong. JAS 28 (1968-9) 723-742.

Singapore - Minorities *See* CHINESE, INDIANS, MALAYS, ORANG LAUT

SINGAPORE - POLITICS AND GOVERNMENT

8944 GIBBONS, D. S. Political tutelage in rural Singapore, the measurement and analysis of the cognitive political culture of some Chinese farmers, by D. S. Gibbons and Chan Heng Chee. JSAS 2 (1971) 100-114.

8945 KATHIRITHAMBY-WELLS, J. Early Singapore and the inception of a British administrative tradition in the Straits Settlements, 1819-1832. JMBRAS 42 pt. 2 (1969) 48-73.

8946 LEE, Y. K. Grand jury in early Singapore, 1819-1873. JMBRAS 46 pt. 2 (1973) 55-150.

8947 LEIFER, MICHAEL. Communal violence in Singapore. AS 4 (1964) 1115-1121.

8948 MARSHALL, DAVID. Singapore's struggle for nationhood, 1945-1959. JSAS 1 pt. 2 (1970) 99-104.

8949 PANG CHENG LIAN. Peoples Action Party, 1954-1963. JSAH 10 (1969) 142-154.

8950 SADKA, EMMA. Singapore and the Federation, problems of merger. AS 1 (Jan. 1962) 17-25.

8951 SEAH CHEE MEOW. Singapore politics, 1945-63, the myth of the leftward drift. RSAS 1 pt. 4 (1971) 21-32.

8952 TINKER, HUGH. Structure of the British imperial heritage. B72 pp. 23-86.

8953 YEO KIM WAH. Study of three early political parties in Singapore, 1945-1955. JSAH 10 (1969) 115-141.

SINGAPORE - POLITICS AND GOVERNMENT - 1965-

8954 BASS, JEROME R. Malaysia and Singapore, moving apart? AS 9 (1969) 122-129.

8955 CHANG, DAVID W. Nation building in Singapore. AS 8 (1968) 761-773.

8956 GROSSHOLTZ, JEAN. Exploration of Malaysian meanings. AS 6 (1966) 227-240.

8957 MILNE, R. S. Singapore's exit from Malaysia, the consequences of ambiguity. AS 6 (1966) 175-184.

8958 ROGERS, MARVIN. Malaysia/Singapore, problems and challenges of the seventies. AS 11 (1971) 121-130.

8959 TAE YUL NAM. Singapore's one party system, its relationship to democracy and political stability. PA 42 (1969) 465-480.

8960 TILMAN, ROBERT O. Malaysia and Singapore, the failure of a federation. T45 pp. 490-505.

SINGAPORE - POPULATION

8961 BARTLEY, W. Population of Singapore in 1819. JMBRAS 42 pt. 1 (1969) 112-3.

8962 BHANOJI RAO, V. V. Brief study of age specific birth proportions, Japan and Singapore, by V. V. Bhanoji Rao and G. Shantakumar. MER 17 pt. 2 (1972) 16-24.

8963 CHANG, CHEN TUNG. Factors influencing the declining birth rate in Singapore. MER 15 pt. 1 (1970) 83-100.

8964 CHENG SIOK HWA. Non citizen population of Singapore, 1970. RSAS 3 pts. 3-4 (1973) 38-57.

8965 CHEW, DAVID C. E. Population and manpower, by David C. E. Chew and Amina H. Degani. M49 pp. 85-108.

8966 NEVILLE, R. J. W. Areal distribution of population in Singapore. JTG 20 (1965) 16-25.

8967 NEVILLE, WARWICK. Demographic structure and its economic and social implications. M49 pp. 69-84.

8968 NEVILLE, WARWICK. Distribution of population in the post-war period. M49 pp. 52-68.

8969 NEVILLE, WARWICK. Population dynamics and contemporary Singapore. D92 pp. 96-107.

8970 RODRIGUEZ, CARIDAD A. Singapore's plural society and its social, physical, economic and political implications. SJ 21 (1974) 246-257.

8971 SAW SWEE HOCK. Changing population structure in Singapore during 1824-1962. MER 9 pt. 1 (1964) 90-101.

8972 SAW SWEE HOCK. Economic characteristics of the population of Singapore, 1957, by Saw Swee Hock and Ronald Ma. MER 5 pt. 1 (1960) 31-51.

8973 SAW SWEE HOCK. Estimation of Singapore's population by quinary age group for 1962 and 1967. MER 15 pt. 1 (1970) 101-105.

8974 SAW SWEE HOCK. Population trends in Singapore, 1819-1967. JSAH 10 (1969) 36-49.

8975 SHANTAKUMAR, G. Note on the recent increase in fertility in Singapore. MER 18 pt. 2 (1973) 43-49.

8976 YOU POH SENG. Population growth and population characteristics, by You Poh Seng, V. V. Bhanoji Rao and G. Shantakumar. Y52 pp. 43-80.

8977 YOU POH SENG. Population of Singapore, 1966, demographic structure, social and economic characteristics. MER 12 pt. 2 (1967) 59-96.

8978 YOU POH SENG. Sample household survey of Singapore, 1966, by You Poh Seng and Stephen H. K. Yeh. MER 12 pt. 1 (1967) 47-63.

SINGAPORE - RELIGION

8979 FREEDMAN, MAURICE. Religion and social realignment among the Chinese in Singapore, by Maurice Freedman and Marjorie Topley. JAS 21 (1961-2) 3-23.

SINGAPORE - SOCIAL CONDITIONS

8980 BAKER, M. Economic, social and cultural problems of Singapore. S32 pp. 16-21.

Singapore – Social conditions

8981 FREEDMAN, MAURICE. Chinese kinship and marriage in Singapore.
JSAH 3 (Sept. 1962) 65-73.

8982 FREEDMAN, MAURICE. Religion and
social realignment among the Chinese in Singapore, by Maurice
Freedman and Marjorie Topley.
JAS 21 (1961-2) 3-23.

8983 ONG BOON GEOK. Social structure
of the resettled Malay community
in Geylang Seral, Singapore. RSAS
4 pts. 1-2 (1974) 44-63.

8984 PNG POH SENG. Straits Chinese in
Singapore, a case of local identity
and socio-cultural accommodation.
JSAH 10 (1969) 95-114.

8985 WELDON, PETER D. Socio-economic
status as a planning variable, the
case of Singapore, by Peter D.
Weldon and Tan Tsu Haung. SAJSS
1 pt. 1 (1973) 61-73.

8986 YEH, STEPHEN H. K. Trends and
issues in social development. Y52
pp. 263-291.

SINGAPORE - STATISTICS

8987 TAN, PETER C. Statistical materials on Singapore. Y52 pp. 386-417.

SINGAPORE. BOTANICAL GARDEN

8988 HANITSCH, R. Letters of Nathaniel
Wallich relating to the establishment of Botanical Garden in Singapore. JMBRAS 42 pt. 1 (1969) 145-
154.

SINGAPORE. UNIVERSITY

8989 BURE, JEAN-REMY. Les etudiants de
l'Universite de Singapour. FA 24
(1970) 181-188.

8990 Centre for South-East Asian Studies, University of Singapore.
EACS 5 (1966) 50-52.

8991 CHIA SIOW YUE. Survey of academic
exercises submitted to the economics department, University of
Singapore for the academic session
1967-68. MER 13 pt. 1 (1968) 118-
127.

8992 WELDON, PETER D. Research in the
social sciences at the University
of Singapore. RSAS 1 pt. 1 (1971)
40-44.

SINGAPORE CHRONICLE

8993 GIBSON-HILL, CARL ALEXANDER.
Singapore Chronicle, 1824-37.
JMBRAS 42 pt. 1 (1969) 166-191.

SINGAPORE HERALD

8994 TAMNEY, JOSEPH B. The *Singapore
Herald* affair. AST 10 (1972) 256-
261.

SITENG

8995 TUTON KABOY. Some stories about
the Siteng people. SMJ 19 (1971)
47-51.

SITHIPORN KRIDAKARA

8996 His serene highness Prince Sithiporn Kridakara. JSS 60 pt. 1
(1972) 470-473.

SITSEN, P. H.

8997 VEEN, ADRIAAN VAN DER. In memoriam
      P. H. Sitsen. H57 pp. 469-470.

SITTANG VALLEY, BURMA

8998 KHIN MA LAY. Urban study of the
      Sittang Valley. JBRS 45 (1962)
      163-180.

SITTI NURBAJA

8999 AVELING, H. G. Sitti Nurbaja,
      some reconsiderations. BIJ 126
      (1970) 228-245.

SIWANG

9000 NEEDHAM, RODNEY. Age, category
      and descent, to Professor Raymond
      Firth. BIJ 122 (1966) 1-35.

SMUGGLING – PHILIPPINES

9001 SARTE, CONCORDIO MA. Smuggling,
      an offense against justice. UN 36
      (1963) 494-555.

SNAKES – MALAYSIA

9002 HAILE, NEVILLE S. Snake bites
      man, two recent Borneo cases. SMJ
      11 (1963) 291-298.

9003 JAMUH, GEORGE. Melanau population
      destroyed by poisonous snake. SMJ
      12 (1965) 230-234.

9004 LIM, B. L. Genus of snakes
      (Oreocalamus) new to Malaya. SMJ
      18 (1970) 410-1.

SNAKES – PHILIPPINES

9005 ALCALA, A. C. Some facts and
      fancies about Philippine snakes.
      SJ 16 (1969) 257-262.

9006 LEVITON, ALAN E. Keys to the
      dangerously venomous terrestrial
      snakes of the Philippine Islands.
      SJ 8 (1961) 98-106.

SNEEVLIET, HENDRICUS J. F. M.

9007 AARSSE, ROBERT. Sneevliet et le
      debut du communisme en Indonesie.
      FA 24 (1970) 267-282.

SNELLIUS EXPEDITION

9008 LEK, L. Snellius expedition. H57
      pp. 473-4.

SOCIAL SCIENCES

9009 LIEW PAK CHOONG. A plea for a
      relevant, involved and critical
      social science. RSAS 1 pt. 1
      (1971) 28-9.

SOCIAL SCIENCES – INDONESIA

9010 PENNY, D. H. Teaching social
      science research methods in Indo-
      nesia and Australia. RSAS 1 pt. 4
      (1971) 33-46.

SOCIAL SCIENCES – PHILIPPINES

9011 BARIA-VALENCIA, LUZVIMINDA.
      Teaching and research in the rural
      social sciences in the Philip-
      pines, by Luzviminda Baria-
      Valencia and Manuel Flores-
      Bonifacio. GEJ 21 (1971) 105-121.

SOCIAL SCIENCES - SINGAPORE

9012 CHEN, PETER S. J. Teaching and
research in the social sciences in
Singapore. RSAS 1 pt. 1 (1971)
45-51.

9013 LIM CHONG YAH. Teaching and research in the social sciences in
Singapore. RSAS 1 pt. 1 (1971)
30-33.

9014 OOI JIN BEE. Relevance in social
science research in Singapore.
RSAS 1 pt. 1 (1971) 34-36.

9015 RAYNER, MARY. Social sciences in
Singapore, nature, role and problems. RSAS 1 pt. 1 (1971) 25-27.

9016 THAM SEONG CHEE. The social sciences and modernisation in Singapore. RSAS 1 pt. 1 (1971) 11-17.
Comment: SHAW, K. E. Comment.
RSAS 1 pt. 1 (1971) 18-9.

9017 WELDON, PETER D. Research in the
social sciences at the University
of Singapore. RSAS 1 pt. 1 (1970)
40-44.

SOCIETE DES ETUDES INDOCHINOISES

9018 La Societe des Etudes Indochinoises
a 90 ans. SEIB 48 (1973) 513-519.

SOCIETE DES ETUDES INDOCHINOISES.
BULLETIN

9019 METAYE, ROGER. Tables du *Bulletin
de la Societe des Etudes Indochinoises,* 1883-1971. SEIB 46
(1971) 435-603.

SOCIETE DES ETUDES INDOCHINOISES.
LIBRARY

9020 Liste des ouvrages entres a la
bibliotheque pendant l'annee 1963.
SEIB 39 (1964) 141-145.

9021 Liste des ouvrages recus a la
bibliotheque en 1964-1965. SEIB
40 (1965) 359-366.

9022 Note sur quelques revues d'interet
general acquises recemment par la
Bibliotheque de la Societe des
Etudes Indochinoises. SEIB 35
(1960) 703-711.

SOCIETIES

9023 NASH, MANNING. Southeast Asian
society: dual or multiple. JAS
23 (1963-4) 417-423.
Comment: HIGGINS, BENJAMIN.
Southeast Asian society: dual or
multiple, comments. JAS 23 (1963-
64) 425-427.
Comment: PYE, LUCIAN W. Perspective requires two points of vision, comments. JAS 23 (1963-4)
429-431.

SOCIOLOGY

9024 WERTHEIM, W. F. The sociological
approach. S61 pp. 344-358.

SOCIOLOGY - PHILIPPINES

9025 HOLLNSTEINER, MARY RACELIS. The
study of society, a perspective
from sociology and anthropology.
PS 21 (1973) 455-462.

SOCIOLOGY - SINGAPORE

9026 RIAZ HASSAN. Sociology and socio-
      logical research in Singapore.
      RSAS 1 pt. 1 (1971) 22-24.

SOE HOK GIE

9027 ANDERSON, BEN. In memoriam, Soe
      Hok Gie. IND 9 (1970) 225-227.

SOETARDJO KARTOHADIKOESOEMO

9028 ABEYASEKERE, SUSAN. The Soetardjo
      petition. IND 15 (1973) 80-107.

SOETJIPTO WIRJOSOEPARTO

9029 LOOFS, H. H. E. Raden Mas Soetjip-
      to Wirjosoeparto, 1915-1971. JOSA
      8 (1971) 3-4.

SOILS

9030 DUDAL, R. Major soils of Southeast
      Asia, their characteristics, dis-
      tribution, use and agricultural
      potential, by R. Dudal and F. R.
      Moormann. JTG 18 (1964) 54-80.

SOILS - INDONESIA

9031 MOHR, E. C. J. Climate and soil
      in the Netherlands Indies. H57
      pp. 250-254.

9032 MOHR, E. C. J. Relation between
      soil and population density in the
      Netherlands Indies. H57 pp. 254-
      262.

SOILS - MALAYSIA

9033 EYLES, R. J. Laterite at Kerdau,
      Pahang, Malaya. JTG 25 (1967) 18-
      23.

9034 EYLES, R. J. Soil creep on a
      humid tropical slope, by R. J.
      Eyles and R. Ho. JTG 31 (1970)
      40-42.

9035 FOX, J. E. D. Soils and forest on
      ultrabasic hill north east of
      Ranau Sabah, by J. E. D. Fox and
      Tan Teong Hing. JTG 32 (1971)
      38-48.

9036 JOSEPH, K. T. Sedentary soils of
      Kedah and their suggested utiliza-
      tion. JTG 18 (1964) 101-110.

9037 PANTON, W. P. The 1962 soil map
      of Malaya. JTG 18 (1964) 118-124.

9038 PARBERY, D. B. Chemical analysis
      of south Malayan peat soil, by D.
      B. Parbery and R. M. Venkatacha-
      lam. JTG 18 (1964) 125-133.

9039 WALL, J. R. D. Topography-soil
      relationships in lowland Sarawak.
      JTG 18 (1964) 192-199.

SOILS - PHILIPPINES

9040 BARRERA, ALFREDO. Classification
      and utilization of some Philippine
      soils. JTG 18 (1964) 17-29.

LA SOLIDARIDAD

9041 FORBES-GANZON, GUADALUPE. *La
      Solidaridad, Quincenario Demo-
      cratico*, vol. I, number 4, 31
      March 1889. The original text
      with English version. PSSHR 26
      (1961) 233-290.

SPICES

9058 BOXER, C. R. Note on Portuguese reactions to the revival of the Red Sea spice trade and the rise of Atjeh, 1540-1600. JSAH 10 (1969) 415-428.

9059 RAY, G. F. Economy of Asian spices. MER 8 pt. 1 (1963) 45-65.

SPORTS

9060 PAUKER, EWA T. Ganefo I, sports and politics in Djakarta. AS 5 (1965) 171-185.

SPORTS - INDONESIA

9061 SIEGEL, JAMES. Prayer and play in Atjeh, a comment on two photographs. IND 1 (1966) 1-21.

SPORTS - MALAYSIA

9062 FIDLER, RICHARD C. Some games in Kanowit bazaar. SMJ 19 (1971) 331-346.

9063 MOHAMMAD TAIB OSMAN. Text on the rules of the Kelantan bullfight. JMBRAS 37 pt. 2 (1964) 1-10.

SPORTS - PHILIPPINES

9064 BERAN, JANICE ANN V. Characteristics of children's play and games in the southern Philippines. SJ 20 (1973) 100-113.

9065 BERAN, JANICE ANN V. Some elements of power in Filipino children's play. SJ 20 (1973) 194-207.

9066 TAMANIO, MARIALITA M. Research in a cockpit. AST 7 (1969) 255-263.

SPORTS - THAILAND

9067 SCHWEISGUTH, P. Note sur les jeux de cerf volants en Thailande. S44.2 pp. 112-144.

9068 SIMMONDS, E. H. S. Mahorasop II, the Thai National Library manuscript. SOAS 34 (1971) 119-131.

SPORTS - VIETNAM

9069 BARNOUIN, R. P. Les arenes de Hue. SEIB 49 (1974) 385-421.

SRE

9070 DOURNES, JACQUES. Orphelin transforme, jalons mythologiques. AR 2 (1971) 168-196.

SRIVIJAYA

9071 CHAND CHIRAYU RAJANI. Review article, background to the Sri Vijaya story. JSS 62 pt. 2 (1974) 285-324.

9072 COEDES, G. Empire of the south seas, Srivijaya from the VIIth to the XIIIth centuries. S44.2 pp. 145-159.

9073 DAMAIS, LOUIS-CHARLES. La langue B, des inscriptions de Sri Wijaya. BEF 54 (1968) 523-566.

9074 FRANCISCO, JUAN R. Sri Vijaya and the Philippines, a review. PSSHR 26 (1961) 87-109.

9075 NAERSSEN, F. H. VAN. Cailendra interregnum. J41 pp. 249-253.

9076 PARANAVITANA, S. Ceylon and Sri Vijaya. E92 pp. 205-212.

Srivijaya

9077 RAUSA-GOMEZ, LOURDES. Sri Vijaya and Madjapahit. PS 15 (1967) 63-107.

9078 TAN YEOK SEONG. Sri Vijayan inscription of Canton, A.D. 1079. JSAH 5 (Sept. 1964) 17-24.

9079 WOLTERS, O. W. Note on the capital of Srivijaya during the eleventh century. E92 pp. 225-239.

9080 WOLTERS, O. W. Srivijayan expansion in the seventh century. G83 pp. 417-424.

STAMPS - BRUNEI

9081 CAVE, BRIAN J. Postage stamps of Brunei, 1895-1941, a philatelic outline. BMJ 3 pt. 1 (1973) 127-145.

STAMPS - INDONESIA

9082 LECLERC, JACQUES. Iconologie politique du timbre-poste indonesien. AR 6 (1973) 145-183.

STAMPS - THAILAND

9083 LINDENBERG, PAUL P. Early postal history of Thailand. S44.4 pp. 185-202.

STAUNTON, JOHN

9084 SCOTT, WILLIAM HENRY. Engineers dream, John Staunton and the mission of St. Mary the Virgin, Sagada. A58 pp. 337-349.

STIENG LANGUAGE

9085 HAUPERS, RALPH. Stieng phonemes. M59 pp. 131-137.

STRAITS STEAMSHIP COMPANY

9086 TREGONNING, K. G. Origin of the Straits Steamship Company in 1890. JMBRAS 38 pt. 2 (1965) 274-289.

STRAITS TRADING COMPANY, LTD.

9087 TREGONNING, K. G. Straits tin, a brief account of the first seventy five years of the Straits Trading Company, Limited. JMBRAS 36 pt. 1 (1963) 79-152.

STUBBS, REGINALD EDWARD

9088 BROWN, D. E. Two Colonial Office memoranda on the history of Brunei by Sir Reginald Edward Stubbs. JMBRAS 41 pt. 2 (1968) 83-116.

STUDENTS

9089 ALTBACH, PHILIP G. Student movements in historical perspective, the Asian case. JSAS 1 pt. 1 (1970) 74-84.

9090 FISCHER, JOSEPH. The university student in South and Southeast Asia. T45 pp. 187-200.

9091 ROUCEK, J. S. Politics of Asia's students and intellectuals. RSA (1969) 159-173.

9092 TAMNEY, JOSEPH B. Economic satisfaction and political loyalty in Southeast Asia. SAJSS 1 pt. 2 (1973) 35-42.

STUDENTS - BURMA

9093　SILVERSTEIN, JOSEF.　Burmese and Malaysian student politics, a preliminary comparative inquiry. JSAS 1 pt. 1 (1970) 3-22.

9094　SILVERSTEIN, JOSEF.　University students and politics in Burma, by Josef Silverstein and Julian Wohl. PA 37 (1964) 50-65.

STUDENTS - CAMBODIA

9095　SARIN.　Les moines et novices que etudient a Vat Tep-Pranam, par Sarin et Choan.　BEF 57 (1970) 134-154.

STUDENTS - INDONESIA

9096　KULIANG, JOE.　From acquiescence to hyperactivism, the political role of non-communist university students in Indonesia, by Joe and J. K. L. Kuliang. RSA (1969) 175-189.

9097　LYMAN, PRINCETON N.　Students and politics in Indonesia and Korea. PA 38 (1965) 282-293.

9098　ROFF, WILLIAM R.　Indonesian and Malay students in Cairo in the 1920's.　IND 9 (1970) 73-87.

9099　SMITH, THEODORE M.　Indonesian university students and their career aspirations, by Theodore M. Smith and Harold F. Carpenter.　AS 14 (1974) 807-826.

9100　Student upheaval in Indonesia. JCA 4 (1974) 398-405.

STUDENTS - MALAYSIA

9101　EBERHARD, WOLFRAM.　Cultural baggage of Chinese emigrants, stories and novels read by Chinese students in Malaya.　AS 11 (1971) 445-462.

9102　ROFF, WILLIAM R.　Indonesian and Malay students in Cairo in the 1920's.　IND 9 (1970) 73-87.

9103　SILVERSTEIN, JOSEF.　Burmese and Malaysian student politics, a preliminary comparative inquiry. JSAS 1 pt. 1 (1970) 3-22.

STUDENTS - PHILIPPINES

9104　AYSON, ELMILA B.　Influences of study attitudes and habits on academic performance.　SLURJ 3 (1972) 430-471.

9105　BARICAN, FERNANDO.　Student activism.　DR 17 (1969) 77-79.

9106　BARTOLOME, ALBEN G.　Student perceptions of the counselor.　PS 20 (1972) 449-457.

9107　BODDEZ, MARTHA.　An analysis of the self concept and the impact of success and failure upon the perception of perfection of performance and upon the self concept of junior high school students. SLURJ 4 (1973) 367-413.

9108　CORPUZ, ONOFRE D.　Student power in the Philippines, a perspective. DR 17 (1969) 1-14.

9109　DAROY, PETRONILO BN.　Student activism and the faculty.　DR 17 (1969) 80-84.

9110　ELWOOD, DOUGLAS J.　Popular Filipino concepts of Christ, report of

Students - Philippines

9133 YOUNGBLOOD, ROBERT L. Family
      strictness, social class and polit-
      ical attitudes among Manila high
      school students. AS 13 (1973)
      761-771.

9134 YOUNGBLOOD, ROBERT L. Political
      transmission process among parents
      and students in Manila. AF 5 pt.
      2 (1973) 111-120.

STUDENTS - SINGAPORE

9135 BURE, JEAN-REMY. Les etudiants de
      l'Universite de Singapour. FA 24
      (1970) 181-188.

9136 Joint press statement of Singapore
      Polytechnic Student's Union and
      University of Singapore Students
      Union. JCA 4 (1974) 370-372.

STUDENTS - THAILAND

9137 DARLING, FRANK C. Student protest
      and political change in Thailand.
      PA 47 (1974) 5-19.

9138 HEINZE, RUTH-INGE. Ten days in
      October, students vs. the military,
      an account of the student uprising
      in Thailand. AS 14 (1974) 491-
      508.

9139 ZIMMERMAN, ROBERT F. Student rev-
      olution in Thailand, the end of
      the Thai bureaucratic polity? AS
      14 (1974) 509-529.

SUBANDRIO, RADEN

9140 QUIKO, EDO. Political trial of
      Raden Subandrio in Indonesia. AF
      4 pt. 2 (1972) 49-60.

SUBANUNS

9141 FRAKE, CHARLES O. Eastern Subanun
      of Mindanao. M95 pp. 51-64.

9142 VISTA, SALVADOR B. Notes on a
      Subanon ritual. SJ 21 (1974) 279-
      283.

SUGAR INDUSTRY - INDONESIA

9143 PANGLAYKIM, J. Study of entre-
      preneurship in developing coun-
      tries, the development of one Chi-
      nese concern in Indonesia, by J.
      Panglaykim and I. Parmer. JSAS 1
      pt. 1 (1970) 85-95.

9144 VAN NIEL, ROBERT. Regulation of
      sugar production in Java, 1830-
      1840. V27 pp. 91-108.

SUGAR INDUSTRY - PHILIPPINES

9145 FRIEND, THEODORE. Philippine
      sugar industry and the politics of
      independence, 1929-1935. JAS 22
      (1962-3) 179-192.

9146 SCHUL, NORMAN W. Hacienda
      magnitude and Philippine sugar
      cane production. AST 5 (1967)
      258-273.

SUGBUANON LITERATURE

9147 RAMAS, WILHELMINA Q. Sugbuanon
      drama, a preliminary list of plays
      acquired by the University. AST
      11 pt. 3 (1973) 153-172.

SUKARNO

9148 DAHM, BERNARD. Sukarno and his-
      tory. T45 pp. 403-411.

Sukarno

9149 GATOT MANGKUPRADJA, RADEN. Peta and my relations with the Japanese, a correction of Sukarno's autobiography. IND 5 (1968) 105-134.

9150 HAUSWEDELL, PETER CHRISTIAN. Sukarno, radical or conservative, Indonesian politics, 1964-5. IND 15 (1973) 108-143.

9151 HERING, B. B. Sukarnos Sturz, eine Rezension. AQ (1971) 109-119.

9152 VAN DER KROEF, JUSTUS M. Nasution, Sukarno and the West New Guinea dispute. AS 1 (Aug. 1961) 20-24.

9153 VAN DER KROEF, JUSTUS M. Sukarno the ideologue. PA 41 (1968) 245-261.
Comment: DAHM, BERNARD. Sukarno, the ideologue. PA 42 (1969) 55-57.

SUKHODAYA

9154 CHAND CHIRAYU RAJANI. Review article, A. B. Griswold and Prasert na Nagara "Epigraphic and historical studies" nos. 1-8. JSS 61 pt. 1 (1973) 261-301.

9155 CHAND CHIRAYU RAJANI. Review article, A. B. Griswold and Prasert na Nagara "Epigraphic and historical studies" no. 9 and no. 10. JSS 61 pt. 2 (1973) 167-182.

9156 FLOOD, E. THADEUS. Sukhothai-Mongol relations, a note on relevant Chinese and Thai sources, with translations. JSS 57 (1969) 201-257.

9157 GRISWOLD, A. B. Epigraphic and historical studies. III. Pact between Sukhodaya and Nan, by A. B. Griswold and Prasert na Nagara. JSS 57 (1969) 57-107.

9158 GRISWOLD, A. B. Epigraphic and historical studies. V. Pact between uncle and nephew, by A. B. Griswold and Prasert na Nagara. JSS 58 pt. 1 (1970) 89-113.

9159 GRISWOLD, A. B. Epigraphic and historical studies. IX. Inscription of King Rama Kamhen of Sukhodaya, 1292 A.D., by A. B. Griswold and Prasert na Nagara. JSS 59 pt. 2 (1971) 179-228.

9160 GRISWOLD, A. B. Epigraphic and historical studies. X. King Lodaiya of Sukhodaya and his contemporaries, by A. B. Griswold and Prasert na Nagara. JSS 60 pt. 1 (1972) 21-152.

9161 GRISWOLD, A. B. Addendum to epigraphic and historical studies, no. X, by A. B. Griswold and Prasert na Nagara. JSS 61 pt. 1 (1973) 179-181.

9162 GRISWOLD, A. B. Epigraphic and historical studies. XI pt. 1. Epigraphy of Mahadharmaraja I of Sukhodaya, by A. B. Griswold and Prasert na Nagara. JSS 61 pt. 1 (1973) 71-178.

9163 GRISWOLD, A. B. Epigraphic and historical studies. XI pt. 2. Epigraphy of Mahadharmaraja I of Sukhodaya, by A. B. Griswold and Prasert na Nagara. JSS 61 pt. 2 (1973) 91-128.

9164 GRISWOLD, A. B. On kingship and sociaty at Sukhodaya, by A. B. Griswold and Prasert na Nagara. C24 pp. 29-92.

9165 PENTH, HANS. Note on old Tak. JSS 61 pt. 1 (1973) 183-186.

SUKU SIMALUNGUN

9166 LIDDLE, R. W. Suku Simalungun, an ethnic group in search of representation. IND 3 (1967) 1-28.

Sulewesi *See* CELEBES

SULU ARCHIPELAGO

9167 ABDULMARI A. IMAO. Okkil. GEJ 4 (1962) 105-108.

9168 ASIRI J. ABUBAKAR. Muslim Philippines, with reference to the Sulus, Muslim-Christian contradictions, and the Mindanao crisis. AST 11 (1973) 112-128.

9169 BARADAS, DAVID B. Some implications of the Okir motif in Lanao and Sulu art. AST 6 (1968) 129-168.

9170 COSTA, H. DE LA. Muhammad Alimuddin I of Sulu, the early years. AST 2 (1964) 199-212.

9171 COSTA, H. DE LA. Muhammad Alimuddin I, Sultan of Sulu, 1735-1773. JMBRAS 38 pt. 1 (1965) 43-76.

9172 COSTA, H. DE LA. Muhammad Alimuddin I, Sultan of Sulu, 1735-1773. PHR 1 pt. 1 (1965) 95-135.

9173 DACANAY, JULIAN E. Okil in Muslim art, a view from the drawing board. M24 pp. 149-162.

9174 KASMAN, EDWARD SALKIYA. Birth and death rituals among the Tausugs of Siasi. UN 35 (1962) 291-340.

9175 KIEFER, THOMAS M. Tausug polity and the sultanate of Sulu, a segmentary state in the southern Philippines. S91 pp. 19-64.

9176 MAJUL, CESAR ADIB. Political and historical notes on the old Sulu sultanate. JMBRAS 38 pt. 1 (1965) 23-42.

9177 MAJUL, CESAR ADIB. Political and historical notes on the old Sulu sultanate. PHR 1 pt. 1 (1965) 229-251.

9178 MAJUL, CESAR ADIB. Succession in the old Sulu sultanate. PHR 1 pt. 1 (1965) 252-271.

9179 NIMMO, H. ARLO. Reflections on Bajau history. PS 16 (1968) 32-59.

9180 NIMMO, H. ARLO. You will remember us because we have sung for you. PS 20 (1972) 299-322.

9181 RIXHON, GERARD. Educational work in Sulu. SJ 11 (1964) 49-56.

9182 RIXHON, GERARD. Selected list of recent works on Sulu. S91 pp. 143-162.

9183 RIXHON, GERARD. Ten years of research in Sulu, 1961-1971. S91 pp. 1-18.

9184 SPOEHR, ALEXANDER. Spanish remains in Basilan and Sulu. S93 pp. 105-112.

9185 SZANTON, DAVID. Art in Sulu, a survey. PS 11 (1963) 463-502.

9186 SZANTON, DAVID. Art in Sulu, a survey. S92 pp. 3-69.

9187 TAN, SAMUEL K. Sulu under American military rule, 1899-1913. PSSHR 32 (1967) 1-187.

9188 WANG, TEH-MING. Notes on the Sulu Islands in *Chu-Fan-Chih*. AST 9 (1971) 76-78.

zone, Sumatra. JTG 30 (1970) 63–
67.

9211 WITHINGTON, WILLIAM A. Distribution of population in Sumatra, Indonesia, 1961. JTG 17 (1963) 203–
212.

9212 WITHINGTON, WILLIAM A. Problems
and potentialities of development
of western Indonesia, Sumatra as
an example of third world characteristics. RSA (1969) 79–103.

SUMBA

9213 ADAMS, MARIE JEANNE. Myths and
self image among the Kapunduk
people of Sumba. IND 10 (1970)
80–106.

9214 ADAMS, MARIE JEANNE. Symbols of
the organized community in east
Sumba, Indonesia. BIJ 130 (1974)
324–347.

9215 ADAMS, MARIE JEANNE. Work patterns
and symbolic structures in a village culture, east Sumba, Indonesia. SA 1 (1971) 320–334.

SUMBAWA

9216 GOETHALS, PETER R. Rarak, a swid-
den village of west Sumbawa. K52
pp. 30–62.

9217 GOETHALS, PETER R. Sumbawan village. S58 pp. 12–23.

9218 SUKARTO K. A., M. M. Notes on pottery manufacture near Raba, east
Sumbawa. AP 16 (1973) 71–74.

SUMITRO DJOJOHADIKUSUMO

9219 RICE, ROBERT. Sumitro's role in
foreign trade policy. IND 8
(1969) 183–211.

SUMONAJAT SVASTIKUL, MOMRAJAWONGS

9220 Sumonajat Svastikul, Momrajawongs.
JSS 52 (1964) 253.

SUNDANESE

9221 PALMER, ANDREA WILCOX. Situradja,
a village in highland Priangan.
K52 pp. 299–325.

SUNDANESE LANGUAGE

9222 ROBINS, R. H. Some typological
observations on Sundanese morphology. C44 pp. 435–450.

SUNDANESE LITERATURE

9223 NOORDUYN, J. Het Begingedeelte
van de Carita Parahyangan, tekst,
vertaling, commentaar. BIJ 118
(1962) 405–432.

9224 NOORDUYN, J. Enige nadere gegevens over tekst en inhoud van de
Carita Parahyangan. BIJ 122
(1966) 366–374.

9225 NOORDUYN, J. Over het eerste ge-
deelte van de Oud-Soendase Carita
Parahyangan. BIJ 118 (1962) 374–
383.

9226 NOORDUYN, J. Traces of an old
Sundanese Ramayana tradition. IND
12 (1971) 151–157.

9227 ROSIDI, AJIP. My experiences in
recording pantun Sunda. IND 16
(1973) 105–111.

9245 FRANCISCO, JUAN R.   Further notes
      on Pardo de Tavera's *El Sanscrito
      en la lengua Tagalog*.   AST 6 (1968)
      223-234.
      Comment: SALAZAR, Z. A.   Footnote
      to Dr. Francisco's notes on Tavera.
      AST 6 (1968) 431-444.

9246 GENZOR, JOZEF.   Spanish loanwords
      in Tagalog.   AAS 5 (1969) 17-25.

9247 GENZOR, JOZEF.   Towards a typo-
      logical characteristic of the
      Tagalog language.   AAS 6 (1970)
      51-56.

9248 JAMIAS, JUAN F.   Comprehensibility
      of modernized versus traditional
      Tagalog, by Juan F. Jamias, Cata-
      lina M. Montecillo and Jovita C.
      Gongon.   AST 8 (1970) 187-195.

9249 LLAMZON, TEODORO A.   On Tagalog as
      dominant language.   PS 16 (1968)
      729-749.

9250 LOPEZ, CECILIO.   Spanish overlay
      in Tagalog.   C43 pp. 467-504.

9251 MANUEL, E. ARSENIO.   Lexicographic
      study of Tayabas Tagalog.   DR 19
      (1971) 1-420.

9252 PANGANIBAN, JOSE VILLA.   Present
      situation of Pilipino.   UN 39
      (1966) 301-306.

9253 PARNICKEL, B.   Austronesian philol-
      ogy in the Soviet Union.   BIJ 121
      (1965) 245-258.

9254 ROSARIO, GONSALO DEL.   Moderniza-
      tion-standardization plan for the
      Austronesian derived national lan-
      guages of Southeast Asia.   AST 6
      (1968) 1-18.

9255 TAN, ARSENIA B.   Contrastive anal-
      ysis of the English and Tagalog
      consonant systems, by Arsenia B.
      Tan and Antonia F. Villanueva.   UN
      40 (1967) 631-639.

9256 TAN, ARSENIA B.   Is "ng" a prepo-
      sition or an article?   UN 40
      (1967) 700-709.

9257 TAN, ARSENIA B.   Some structural
      features of the Tagalog nouns,
      clues to the identification of the
      Tagalog nouns into subclasses.   UN
      40 (1967) 647-651.

9258 VERSTRAELEN, EUGENE.   Essays to-
      wards a historical description of
      Tagalog and Cebuano Bisaya.   PS 8
      (1960) 491-514.

9259 VERSTRAELEN, EUGENE.   Some further
      remarks about the L-feature.   PS 9
      (1961) 72-77.

9260 VESLOT, JEAN-LOUIS.   Note sur le
      Bugtong.   AR 2 (1971) 101-103.

9261 VILLANUEVA, ANTONIA F.   Origin,
      growth and future of Pilipino.   UN
      39 (1966) 288-300.

9262 WILSON, ROBERT D.   Contrastive
      analysis of segments of trans-
      formational grammars of English
      and Tagalog.   UN 40 (1967) 640-
      646.

9263 YABES, LEOPOLDO Y.   Developing a
      national language for Philippines.
      A43 pp. 120-133.

TAGALOG LITERATURE   *See also*   PILIPINO
LITERATURE

9264 AGONCILLO, TEODORO A.   Pasulyap na
      tingin sa panitikang Tagalog, 1900-
      1950.   PS 18 (1970) 229-251.

Tagalog literature

9265 ALMARIO, VIRGILIO S. Ang Romanti-
      kong imahinasyon ni Jose Corazon
      de Jesus. PS 18 (1970) 299-322.

9266 Amado V. Hernandez. PS 18 (1970)
      227-8.

9267 CORONEL, MARIA DELIA. Tagalog and
      Ilocano stories. UN 39 (1966)
      579-588.

9268 CRUZ, ANDRES CRISTOBAL. Ka Amado,
      Bartolina at Barikada. PS 19
      (1971) 255-286.

9269 DIZON, ANACLETO I. Macario Pineda.
      PS 18 (1970) 350-363.

9270 ESCASA, NENITA O. Si Patricio
      Mariano at ang kasiningan ng
      kanyang mga dula. PS 19 (1971)
      321-340.

9271 GLORIOSO, PABLO R. Si Faustino
      Aguilar sa tradisyon ng nobelang
      Tagalog. PS 19 (1971) 307-320.

9272 GONZALEZ, N. V. M. Rich man's
      house. DR 13 (1965) 72-78.

9273 GUILLERMO, ARTEMIO R. Tagalog
      press of the Philippines. SJ 19
      (1972) 524-549.

9274 LANDICHO, DOMINGO G. Paglalakbay,
      mga piling tula. DR 22 (1974)
      303-398.

9275 LUMBERA, BIENVENIDO L. Alliance
      and revolution, Tagalog writing
      during the war years. M24 pp.
      385-402.

9276 LUMBERA, BIENVENIDO L. Arts in the
      Philippines, the Tagalog film and
      the logic of irony. PS 10 (1962)
      137-144.

9277 LUMBERA, BIENVENIDO L. Assimila-
      tion and synthesis, 1700-1800,
      Tagalog poetry in the eighteenth
      century. PS 16 (1968) 622-662.

9278 LUMBERA, BIENVENIDO L. Consolida-
      tion of tradition in nineteenth
      century Tagalog poetry. PS 17
      (1969) 377-411.

9279 LUMBERA, BIENVENIDO L. *Florante
      at Laura* and the formalization of
      tradition in Tagalog poetry. PS
      15 (1967) 545-575.

9280 LUMBERA, BIENVENIDO L. Folk tra-
      dition of Tagalog poetry. M24 pp.
      331-360.

9281 LUMBERA, BIENVENIDO L. Literary
      relations of Tagalog literature.
      M24 pp. 308-330.

9282 LUMBERA, BIENVENIDO L. Philippine
      literature and the Filipino per-
      sonality. M24 pp. 1-15.

9283 LUMBERA, BIENVENIDO L. Rehabili-
      tation and new beginnings, Tagalog
      literature since the Second World
      War. M24 pp. 403-435.

9284 MANGAHAS, ROGELIO G. Ilang
      Silahis ng *Banaag at Sikat*. PS 18
      (1970) 273-298.

9285 MATUTE, GENOVEVA EDROZA. Deo-
      gracias A. Rosario, ama ng maik-
      ling kathang Tagalog. PS 19
      (1971) 341-372.

9286 MEDINA, B. S. Panganiban, tradi-
      syon at modernismo. PS 19 (1971)
      287-306.

9287 MUNDO, CLODUALDO DEL. Literary
      criticism in Tagalog. M24 pp.
      436-456.

9288 MUNDO, CLODUALDO DEL. Spanish and
      American colonial literature in
      Tagalog. M24 pp. 361-384.

9289 RICARTE, PEDRO L. Alejandro G. Abadilla. PS 18 (1970) 323-349.

9290 RUBIN-RABSON, GRACE. Talambuhay ng isang baliw, katotohanang naglaho at nagbalik. Isinalaysay kay Marguerite Sechehaye sa Wikang Pranses, Bersiyong Ingles ni Grace Rubin-Rabson. DR 22 (1974) 191-273.

9291 SALAZAR, ZEUS A. Note sur la litterature Tagale contemporaine. AST 11 (1973) 129-150.

9292 SAN JUAN, E. Panitikan, a critical introduction to Tagalog literature. AST 4 (1966) 412-429.

9293 SIKAT, ROGELIO R. Ang sining ni Lazaro Francisco. PS 18 (1970) 252-272.

9294 ZAMORA, MARCELA C. Rosauro Almario, a study. DR 13 (1965) 27-54.

TAGBANUA

9295 FOX, ROBERT B. Function of religion in society, the Christian worker and social change. B13 pp. 1-8.

TAGBANUA LANGUAGE

9296 RUCH, ED. Substantive marking particles in Kalamian Tagbanwa. PSSHR 26 (1961) 213-218.

TAGORE, RABINDRANATH

9297 NGUYEN DANG THUC. Poet Rabindranath Tagore and Vietnam. AC 2 (July 1960) 37-46.

TAMAN SISWA

9298 HADJAR DEWANTARA, KI. Some aspects of national education and the Taman Siswa Institute of Jogjakarta. IND 4 (1967) 150-168.

9299 McVEY, RUTH T. Taman Siswa and the Indonesian national awakening. IND 4 (1967) 128-149.

TAMIL LITERATURE

9300 NAYAGAM, XAVIER S. THANI. Classical love poetry in Tamil. F38 pp. 261-268.

9301 SINGARAVELU, S. Comparative study of the Sanskrit, Tamil, Thai and Malay versions of the story of Rama, with special reference to the process of acculturation in the Southeast Asian versions. JSS 56 (1968) 137-185.

TAN CHENG LOCK

9302 SOH ENG LIM. Tan Cheng Lock, his leadership of the Malayan Chinese. JSAH 1 (Mar. 1960) 34-61.

TAN MALAKA

9303 MRAZEK, RUDOLF. Tan Malaka, a political personality's structure of experience. IND 14 (1972) 1-48.

TAN TOCK SENG

9304 KNIGHT, ARTHUR. Tan Tock Seng's Hospital, Singapore. JMBRAS 42 pt. 1 (1969) 252-255.

Tanay Resettlement Project

TANAY RESETTLEMENT PROJECT

9305 SHAMSUL, BAHREIN, TUNKU. Land conflicts in the Tanay Resettlement Project, Rizal, Philippines. JTG 27 (1968) 50-58.

TANJONG KARANG

9306 AGARWAL, M. C. Account of the Tanjong Karang Project. MER 9 pt. 2 (1964) 64-74.

TAOSUG

9307 JAINAL, TUWAN IKLALI. Housebuilding among the Tausug, by Tuwan Iklali Jainal, Gerard Rixhon and David Ruppert. S91 pp. 81-121.

9308 KIEFER, THOMAS M. Gravemarkers and the repression of sexual symbolism, the case of two Philippine-Borneo Moslem societies, by Thomas M. Kiefer and Clifford Sather. BIJ 126 (1970) 75-90.

9309 KIEFER, THOMAS M. Parrang Sabbil, ritual suicide among the Tausug of Jolo. BIJ 129 (1973) 108-123.

9310 KIEFER, THOMAS M. Tausug polity and the sultanate of Sulu, a segmentary state in the southern Philippines. S91 pp. 19-64.

9311 TRIMILLOS, RICARDO D. Setting of vocal music among the Tausug. S91 pp. 65-80.

TAOSUG LANGUAGE

9312 ASHLEY, SEYMOUR. Case classification of Tausug verbs. S92 pp. 70-85.

9313 ASHLEY, SEYMOUR. Notes on Tausug orthography. S92 pp. 86-94.

9314 KIEFER, THOMAS M. Concerning the word Suluk. SMJ 16 (1968) 438-9.

TAOSUG LITERATURE

9315 CORONEL, MARIA DELIA. Taosug-Samal stories. UN 39 (1966) 503-519.

9316 Four folk narratives from Mullung, a Tausug storyteller. S91 pp. 191-271.

9317 IBBALAHIM, IMAM. Sultan Sulayman and Sumayang Galura, a story told by Imam Ibbalahim. S92.1 pp. 153-165.

9318 INDAH ANNURA. Didactic ballad on marriage as sung by Indah Annura. S92.1 pp. 131-150.

9319 INDAH ANNURA. Parang Sabil of Abdulla and Putli Isara in Spanish times, a Tausug ballad sung by Indah Annura. S92 pp. 160-191.

9320 MULLUNG. Creation of Palay, a story told by Mullung. S92.1 pp. 166-181.

9321 MULLUNG. Munabi, a story narrated by Mullung. S92.1 pp. 197-220.

9322 RIXHON, GERARD. Cooperative venture in folk-literature collection and translation. S91 pp. 163-171.

9323 RIXHON, GERARD. Mullung, a Tausug storyteller. S91 pp. 172-189.

9324 RIXHON, GERARD. Tausug literature, an overview. S92.1 pp. 1-86.

9325 SALUAN PANAY. Origin of edible fruits and animals, a story narrated by Saluan Panay. S92.1 pp. 182-195.

9326   Selected Tausug poems.   S92.1 pp. 115–129.

9327   Selection of Tausug riddles and proverbs.   S92 pp. 210–224.

TASADAY

9328   SALAZAR, ZEUS A.   Second footnote on the Tasaday.   AST 11 pt. 2 (1973) 97–113.

TATAUS

9329   SANDIN, BENEDICT.   Tatau people of the Kakus and Anap Rivers, Fourth Division, Sarawak.   SMJ 18 (1970) 162–168.

Tausug *See* TAOSUG

TAVOYAN LANGUAGE

9330   BERNOT, DENISE.   Vowel systems of Arakanese and Tavoyan.   C44 pp. 463–474.

TAXATION - BURMA

9331   FURNIVALL, J. S.   Early revenue history of Tenasserim, land revenue.   B92 pp. 49–59.

TAXATION - INDONESIA

9332   DREWES, G. W. J.   Atjehse douane-tarieven in het begin van de vorige eeuw.   BIJ 119 (1963) 406–411.

TAXATION - LAOS

9333   PIETRANTONI, E.   Note sur les classes de revenus au Laos et au Tonkin avant 1945.   SEIB 43 (1968) 181–194.

TAXATION - MALAYSIA

9334   EDWARDS, C. T.   Future role of import and excise duty taxation in the states of Malaya and Singapore.   MER 11 pt. 1 (1966) 29–56.

9335   EDWARDS, C. T.   Structure of import and excise duty taxation in the states of Malaya and Singapore.   MER 10 pt. 2 (1965) 83–101.

9336   LIM CHONG YAH.   Export taxes on rubber in Malaya, a survey of post-war development.   MER 5 pt. 2 (1960) 46–58.

9337   LIM CHONG YAH.   Malayan rubber re-planting taxes.   MER 6 pt. 2 (1961) 43–52.

9338   McLURE, CHARLES E.   Incidence of taxation in west Malaysia.   MER 17 pt. 2 (1972) 66–98.

9339   TAN, A. H. H.   Incidence of export taxes on small producers.   MER 12 pt. 1 (1967) 90–98.

TAXATION - PHILIPPINES

9340   LUTON, HARRY.   American internal revenue policy in the Philippines to 1916.   C31 pp. 129–155.

TAXATION - SINGAPORE

9341   EDWARDS, C. T.   Future role of import and excise duty taxation in the states of Malaya and Singapore.   MER 11 pt. 1 (1966) 29–56.

9342   EDWARDS, C. T.   Structure of import and excise duty taxation in

Taxation - Singapore

the states of Malaya and Singapore.
MER 10 pt. 2 (1965) 83-101.

9343 McKINNON, RONALD I. Export expansion through tax policy, the case for a value added tax in Singapore. MER 11 pt. 2 (1966) 1-27.

9344 McKINNON, RONALD I. Value added tax for Singapore, correction. MER 12 pt. 1 (1967) 36-38.
Comment: BIRD, RICHARD M. Value added tax for Singapore, comment. MER 12 pt. 1 (1967) 39-41.
Author's reply: Value added tax for Singapore, rejoinder. MER 12 pt. 1 (1967) 42-46.
Comment: EDWARDS, C. T. Value added tax? MER 13 pt. 2 (1968) 22-49.
Comment: WU TA YEH. McKinnon's value added tax and industrial development in Singapore. MER 13 pt. 2 (1968) 50-63.

TAXATION - THAILAND

9345 BERTRAND, TRENT J. Rural taxation in Thailand. PA 42 (1969) 178-188.

9346 CORDEN, W. M. The exchange rate system and the taxation of trade. S49 pp. 151-169.

9347 RENAUD, BERTRAND M. The effect of the rice export tax on the domestic rice price level in Thailand. MER 16 pt. 1 (1971) 84-107.

TAXATION - VIETNAM

9348 PIETRANTONI, E. Note sur les classes de revenus au Laos et au Tonkin avant 1945. SEIB 43 (1968) 181-194.

9349 VU THIEN VINH. Tax reforms in Viet-Nam. L52 pp. 309-311.

Comment: COLE, DAVID C. Commentary. L52 pp. 314-316.
Comment: LINDHOLM, RICHARD. Commentary. L52 pp. 312-314.

TEILHARD DE CHARDIN, PIERRE

9350 CASINO, ERIC S. Teilhard's phenomenon and the Filipino. DR 13 (1965) 81-100.

TEMPLES - BURMA

9351 LUCE, G. H. The greater temples of Pagan. B92 pp. 169-177.

9352 LUCE, G. H. Shwegugyi Pagoda inscription, by G. H. Luce and Pe Maung Tin. B92 pp. 377-384.

9353 LUCE, G. H. The smaller temples of Pagan. B92 pp. 179-189.

9354 SINCLAIR, W. B. Monasteries of Pagan. B92 pp. 505-515.

TEMPLES - CAMBODIA *See also* ANGKOR

9355 BENISTI, MIREILLE. Notes d'iconographie khmere. Au sujet d'un linteau de Sambor Prei Kuk. BEF 53 (1966) 71-75.

9356 BENISTI, MIREILLE. Notes d'iconographie khmere. Au sujet d'un linteau de Vat Beset. BEF 53 (1966) 513-516.

9357 CHOAN. Les travaux de construction a la Pagode de Tep-Pranam, par Choan et Sarin. BEF 57 (1970) 129-133.

9358 CHOAN. Le Venerable Chef de la Pagode de Tep-Pranam, par Choan et Sarin. BEF 57 (1970) 127-8.

9359 DUMARCAY, J. Le Prasat Prei pres
      d'Angkor Vat. BEF 59 (1972) 189-
      192.

9360 MARCHAL, HENRI. Banteay Srei.
      SEIB 40 (1965) 283-290.

9361 Le monastere bouddhique de Tep
      Pranam a Oudong. BEF 56 (1969)
      29-56.

9362 SARIN. Les moines et novices que
      etudient a Vat Tep-Pranam, par
      Sarin et Choan. BEF 57 (1970)
      134-154.

TEMPLES - INDONESIA *See also* BOROBUDUR

9363 DUMARCAY, J. Les charpentes
      figures de Prambanan. AR 7 (1974)
      139-150.

TEMPLES - INDONESIA - BALI

9364 GORIS, R. Pura Besakih, Bali's
      state temple. B19 pp. 75-88.

9365 GORIS, R. Pura Besakih through
      the centuries. B19 pp. 89-104.

9366 GORIS, R. Temple system. B18 pp.
      100-111.

9367 GRADER, C. J. Balang Tamak. B19
      pp. 175-188.

9368 GRADER, C. J. Pemayun temple of
      the Banjar of Tegal. B18 pp. 187-
      231.

9369 GRADER, C. J. Pura Meduwe Karang
      at Kubutambahan. B19 pp. 131-174.

9370 GRADER, C. J. State temples of
      Mengwi. B18 pp. 155-186.

9371 I GUSTI NGURAH BAGUS. Karya Taur
      Agung Ekadasa Rudra, rite cen-
      tenaire de purification au temple
      de Besakih, Bali. AR 8 (1974) 59-
      66.

TEMPLES - LAOS

9372 VELDER, CHRISTIAN. La poterie du
      Wat Si Satthanak, Vientiane, Laos.
      F38 pp. 199-201.

TEMPLES - THAILAND

9373 AYABE, TSUNEO. Dek Wat and Thai
      education, the case of Tambon Ban
      Khem. JSS 61 pt. 2 (1973) 39-52.

9374 DAMRONG RAJANUBHAB. Wat Benchama-
      bopit and its collection of images
      of the Buddha. S44.1 pp. 239-281.

9375 DHANINIVAT, PRINCE. Inscriptions
      of Wat Phra Jetubon. S44.4 pp.
      143-184.

9376 DHANINIVAT, PRINCE. Sonkrant of
      Mon as recorded in the inscrip-
      tions of Wat Pra Jetupon in Bang-
      kok. E92 pp. 117-119.

9377 GRISWOLD, A. B. Devices and ex-
      pedients, Vat Pa Mok, 1727 A.D., by
      A. B. Grisowld and Prasert na
      Nagara. T33 pp. 147-220.

9378 LINGAT, ROBERT. Le Wat Rajapra-
      tistha. G83 pp. 314-323.

9379 PENTH, HANS. Note on the history
      of Wat Umong Thera Jan, Chiengmai.
      JSS 62 pt. 2 (1974) 269-274.

TEMPLES - VIETNAM

9380 TRAN VAN TOAN. Le temple Hue-Nam
      a Hue. SEIB 44 (1969) 245-276.

Ternate

TERNATE

9381 JACOBS, HUBERT. Admiraal Wybrant
Warwyck schrift aan de Sultan van
Ternate. BIJ 125 (1969) 344-355.

TEXTILES

9382 SEN, S. P. Role of Indian textiles
in Southeast Asian trade in the
seventeenth century. JSAH 3 (Sept.
1962) 92-110.

TEXTILES - BURMA

9383 STEWART, J. A. Spinning magic.
B92 pp. 527-544.

TEXTILES - INDONESIA

9384 HARRISSON, TOM. Bark beaters from
Sabah, Sarawak and Kalimantan.
SMJ 11 (1964) 597-601.

9385 HAWKINS, EVERETT D. Batik industry, the role of the Javanese
entrepreneur. H24 pp. 39-74.

9386 PALMER, INGRID. The textile industry, by Ingrid Palmer and Lance
Castles. G52 pp. 315-336.

9387 PALMIER, LESLIE H. Batik manufacture in a Chinese community in
Java. H24 pp. 75-97.

TEXTILES - MALAYSIA

9388 ALMAN, JOHN H. Bajau weaving,
Tempasuk plain. SMJ 9 (1960) 603-
637.

9389 HARRISSON, TOM. Bark beaters from
Sabah, Sarawak and Kalimantan.
SMJ 11 (1964) 597-601.

TEXTILES - PORTUGUESE TIMOR

9390 CLAMAGIRAND, BRIGITTE. Le travail
du coton chez les Ema de Timor
portugais. AR 3 (1972) 55-80.

TEXTILES - VIETNAM

9391 BOULBET, JEAN. Modes et techniques du pays Ma. SEIB 39 (1964)
169-288.

9392 BOULBET, JEAN. Modes et techniques du pays Maa. BEF 52 (1964)
359-414.

9393 TEULIERES, ROGER. La sericulture
au sud Viet-Nam. SEIB 37 (1962)
7-36.

THAI

9394 CARTHEW, M. History of the Thai
in Yunnan, 2205 B.C.-1253 A.D.
S44.3 pp. 133-170.

9395 JUDD, LAURENCE C. Agricultural
economy of the hills and adjacent
areas: the hill Thai. S96 pp.
87-92.

9396 KERSHAW, ROGER. The Chinese in
Kelantan, west Malaysia, as medi-
ators of political integration to
the Kelantan Thais. RSAS 3 pts.
3-4 (1973) 1-10.

9397 KEYES, CHARLES F. Kin groups in a
Thai-Lao community. C24 pp. 274-
297.

9398 KINGSHILL, KONRAD. Seven themes
of Ku Daeng. S96 pp. 26-34.

9399 MARLOWE, GERTRUDE WOODRUFF. Economic variety in a north Thai village. S96 pp. 15-25.

9400 MOERMAN, MICHAEL. Kinship and commerce in a Thai-Lue village. T45 pp. 550-555.

9401 MOERMAN, MICHAEL. Minority and its government, the Thai-Lue of northern Thailand. K86 pp. 401-424.

9402 TURTON, ANDREW. Matrilineal descent groups and spirit cults of the Thai-Yuan in northern Thailand. JSS 60 pt. 2 (1972) 217-256.

THAI LANGUAGE

9403 BEE, PETER. Analysis of Thai tones, an argument. JSS 56 (1968) 273-287.

9404 BEE, PETER. Kan in modern Thai. JSS 60 pt. 2 (1972) 87-134.

9405 BOONLUA DEBYASUVARN, M. L. Delimma [sic.] of language in a developing country. A43 pp. 255-274.

9406 DHANINIVAT, KROMAMUN BIDYALABH. Transcription of Siamese, yet another experiment which I used for some twenty years in the *Journal of the Siam Society*. T33 pp. 69-72.

9407 GEDNEY, WILLIAM J. Thailand and Laos. S21 pp. 782-814.

9408 GEDNEY, WILLIAM J. Yay, a northern Tai language in north Vietnam. C43 pp. 180-193.

9409 GRISWOLD, A. B. After thoughts on the romanization of Siamese. JSS 48 pt. 1 (1960) 29-68.

9410 HAUDRICOURT, ANDRE G. Limits and connections of Austroasiatic in the northeast. Z52 pp. 44-56.

9414 HAUDRICOURT, ANDRE G. Note sur les dialectes de la region de Moncay. BEF 50 (1960) 161-177.

9415 HONEY, P. J. Thai and Vietnamese, some elements of nominal structure compared, by P. J. Honey and E. H. S. Simmonds. L55 pp. 71-78.

9416 JONES, ROBERT B. Comparative Thai studies, a critique. E92 pp. 160-163.

9417 JONES, ROBERT B. On the reconstruction of proto-Thai. C43 pp. 194-229.

9418 LI, FANG-KUEI. Relationship between tones and initials in Tai. Z52 pp. 82-88.

9419 LI, FANG-KUEI. Some dental clusters in Tai. SOAS 36 (1973) 334-339.

9420 LI, FANG-KUEI. The Tai and the Kam-Sui languages. C43 pp. 148-179.

9421 PENTH, HANS. Note on Ap nam ap tha. JSS 62 pt. 1 (1974) 148-150.

9422 SIMMONDS, E. H. S. Notes on some Tai dialects of Laos and neighbouring regions. C43 pp. 133-147.

9423 UDOM WAROTAMASIKKHADIT. Computerized alphabetization of Thai, by Udom Warotamasikkhadit and David Lande. T33 pp. 39-54.

9424 WAN WAITHAYAKON. Coining Thai words. T33 pp. 33-38.

9425 WIJEYEWARDENE, GEHAN. Language of courtship in Chiengmai. JSS 56 (1968) 21-32.

Thai literature

THAI LITERATURE

9426 CHAM TONGKAMWAN. Tai inscription in the museum at Pagan, Burma. G83 pp. 249-252.

9427 DHANINIVAT, PRINCE. The Ramakien, a Siamese version of the story of Rama. B91 pp. 33-45.

9428 DHANINIVAT, PRINCE. Siamese versions of the Panji romance. J41 pp. 95-101.

9429 MANAS CHITAKASEM. Emergence and development of the Nirat genre in Thai poetry. JSS 60 pt. 2 (1972) 135-168.

9430 MARTINI, GINETTE. Pancabuddhabya-karana. BEF 55 (1969) 125-144.

9431 SCHWEISGUTH, P. Les Nirat ou poemes d'adieu dans la litterature siamoise. S44.2 pp. 185-196.

9432 SINGARAVELU, S. Comparative study of the Sanskrit, Tamil, Thai and Malay versions of the story of Rama with special reference to the process of acculturation in the Southeast Asian versions. JSS 56 (1968) 137-185.

9433 SODEMANN, UTE. Social criticism in modern Thai narrative fiction. JSS 59 pt. 1 (1971) 25-32.

9434 SWEARER, DONALD K. Myth, legend and history in the northern Thai chronicles. JSS 62 pt. 1 (1974) 67-88.

9435 UDOM WAROTAMASIKKHADIT. Note on internal rhyme in Thai poetry. JSS 56 (1968) 269-272.

9436 VELDER, CHRISTIAN. Notes on the saga of Rama in Thailand. JSS 56 (1968) 33-46.

9437 WYATT, DAVID. Thai version of Newbold's Hikayat Patani. JMBRAS 40 pt. 2 (1967) 16-37.

THAILAND

9438 L'annee 1966 en Asie, Thailande. FA 22 (1968) 104-107.

9439 NEHER, CLARK D. Thailand, the politics of continuity. AS 10 (1970) 161-168.

9440 RACE, JEFFREY. Thailand 1973, we certainly have been ravaged by something. AS 14 (1974) 192-203.

9441 STERNSTEIN, LARRY. Distribution of Thai centres at mid-nineteenth century. JSAH 7 (Mar. 1966) 66-72.

9442 UNGER, LEONARD. Thailand. F56 pp. 82-99.

THAILAND - ARMY

9443 WILSON, DAVID A. The military in Thai politics. J52 pp. 253-275.

THAILAND - BIBLIOGRAPHY

9444 OSANKA, FRANKLIN MARK. Thailand, research resources in print in America. AF 2 (1970) 67-69.

THAILAND - DEFENSES

9445 PENTH, HANS. Fortifications of Chieng Sen. T33 pp. 349-351.

THAILAND - DESCRIPTION AND TRAVEL

9446 CAMPOS, JOAQUIM DE. Early Portuguese accounts of Thailand. S44.7 pp. 211-237.

9447 CHORIN, L. A. C. From Paris to
Ayutha three hundred years ago,
June 18th 1660 to August 22nd,
1662. JSS 50 (1962) 23-33.

9448 GERINI, G. E. Historical retrospect of Junkceylon Island. S44.4
pp. 3-109.

9449 GUEHLER, ULRICH. Travels of Ludovico di Varthema and his visit to
Siam, Banghella and Pegu A.D.
1505. S44.7 pp. 239-276.

9450 HUTCHINSON, E. Journey of Mgr.
Lambert, Bishop of Beritus, from
Tenasserim to Siam in 1662. S44.8
pp. 91-94.

9451 SIMMONDS, E. H. S. An 18th century travel document in Thai. F38
pp. 157-165.

9452 WOOD, W. A. R. Fernao Mendez
Pinto's account of events in Siam.
S44.7 pp. 195-209.

THAILAND - ECONOMIC CONDITIONS

9453 AYAL, ELIEZER B. Thailand's six
year national economic development
plan. AS 1 (Jan. 1962) 33-42.

9454 BEHRMAN, JERE R. Significance of
intracountry variations for Asian
agricultural prospects, central
and northern Thailand. AS 8 (Mar.
1968) 157-173.

9455 BELL, PETER F. Thailand's northeast, regional underdevelopment,
insurgency and official response.
PA 42 (1969) 47-54.

9456 KESSING, DONALD B. Thailand and
Malaysia, a case for a common market? MER 10 pt. 2 (1965) 102-113.

9457 LONG, MILLARD F. Economic development in northeast Thailand,
problems and prospects. AS 6
(1966) 355-361.

9458 PRACHOOM CHOMCHAI. Development
and trade, an appraisal of Thailand's recent experience. AST 4
(1966) 259-267.

9459 PROT PANITPAKDI. National accounts estimates of Thailand. S49
pp. 105-127.

9460 PUEY UNGPHAKORN. Thailand's economic prospects. JSS 58 pt. 2
(1970) 127-144.

9461 SILCOCK, T. H. Summary and assessment. S49 pp. 289-307.

9462 VAN ROY, EDWARD. Malthusian
squeeze on Thailand's rice economy. AS 7 (1967) 469-481.

9463 VICHITVONG N. POMBHEJARA. Second
phase of Thailand's six year economic development plan, 1964-66.
AS 5 (1965) 161-168.

THAILAND - FOREIGN RELATIONS

9464 ASTRI SUHRKI. Smaller nation
diplomacy, Thailand's current
dilemmas. AS 11 (1971) 429-444.

9465 McCARTHY, JAMES E. National image
and diplomacy, the case of Thailand. SA 2 (1972) 427-453.

9466 NUECHTERLEIN, DONALD E. Thailand
and SEATO: a ten year appraisal.
AS 4 (1964) 1174-1181.

9467 OBLAS, PETER B. A very small part
of world affairs, Siam's policy on
treaty revision and the Paris
Peace Conference. JSS 59 pt. 2
(1971) 51-74.

Thailand - Foreign relations

9468 SINGH, L. P. Thai foreign policy, the current phase. AS 3 (1963) 535-543.

9469 SMITH, H. B. Nineteenth century Siamese adventures in fringe diplomacy. SA 1 (1971) 288-299.

9470 TARLING, NICHOLAS. Siam and Sir James Brooke. JSS 48 pt. 2 (1960) 43-72.

THAILAND - FOREIGN RELATIONS - BELGIUM

9471 SAINT-HUBERT, CHRISTIAN DE. Rolin-Jaequemyns (Chao Phya Aphay Raja) and the Belgian legal advisors in Siam at the turn of the century. JSS 53 (1965) 181-190.

THAILAND - FOREIGN RELATIONS - BURMA

9472 Burmese invasions of Siam, translated from the Hmannan Yazawin Dawgyi. S44.5 pp. 3-83.

9473 Intercourse between Burma and Siam as recorded in Hmannan Yazawindaw-gyi. S44.5 pp. 85-207.

9474 Intercourse between Burma and Siam as recorded in Hmannan Yazawindaw-gyi. S44.6 pp. 1-183.

THAILAND - FOREIGN RELATIONS - CAMBODIA

9475 CHANDLER, DAVID P. Cambodia's relations with Siam in the early Bangkok period, the politics of a tributary state. JSS 60 pt. 1 (1972) 153-169.

9476 SINGH, L. P. Thai-Cambodian temple dispute. AS 2 (Oct. 1962) 23-26.

THAILAND - FOREIGN RELATIONS - DENMARK

9477 DHANI NIVAT, PRINCE. Early trade relations between Denmark and Siam, by Prince Dhani Nivat and Erik Seidenfaden. S44.8 pp. 271-288.

THAILAND - FOREIGN RELATIONS - FRANCE

9478 CHANDRAN, JESHURUN. Anglo-French declaration of January 1896 and the independence of Siam. JSS 58 pt. 2 (1970) 105-126.

9479 FLOOD, E. THADEUS. The 1940 Franco-Thai border dispute and Phibuun Sonkhraam's commitment to Japan. JSAH 10 (1969) 304-325.

9480 GOLDMAN, MINTON F. Franco-British rivalry over Siam, 1896-1904. JSAS 3 (1972) 210-228.

9481 HUTCHINSON, E. W. Four French state manuscripts relating to embassies between France and Siam in the XVIIth century. S44.8 pp. 95-157.

9482 HUTCHINSON, E. W. The French foreign mission in Siam during the XVIIth century. S44.8 pp. 17-90.

9483 HUTCHINSON, E. W. The French garrison at Bangkok in 1687-88. S44.8 pp. 201-217.

9484 HUTCHINSON, E. W. Retirement of the French garrison from Bangkok in the year 1688. S44.8 pp. 159-199.

9485 OSBORNE, MILTON. Abridged Cambodian chronicle, a Thai version of Cambodian history, by Milton Osborne and David K. Wyatt. FA 22 (1968) 189-203.

THAILAND – FOREIGN RELATIONS – GREAT BRITAIN

9486 BASSETT, D. K. English relations with Siam in the seventeenth century. JMBRAS 34 pt. 2 (1961) 90-105.

9487 CHANDRAN, JESHURUN. Anglo-French declaration of January 1896 and the independence of Siam. JSS 58 pt. 2 (1970) 105-126.

9488 CHANDRAN, JESHURUN. The British Foreign Office and the Siamese Malay states, 1890-97. MAS 5 (1971) 143-159.

9489 CHANDRAN, JESHURUN. British foreign policy and the extraterritorial question in Siam, 1891-1900. JMBRAS 38 pt. 2 (1965) 290-313.

9490 CHANDRAN, JESHURUN. Lord Lansdowne and the anti-German clique at the Foreign Office, their role in the making of the Anglo-Siamese agreement of 1902. JSAS 3 (1972) 229-246.

9491 DARLING, FRANK C. British and American influence in postwar Thailand. JSAH 4 (Mar. 1963) 88-102.

9492 An early British merchant in Bangkok. S44.8 pp. 232-251.

9493 FRANKFURTER, O. Sir James Brooke in Siam, 1850. SMJ 10 (1961) 32-42.

9494 GOLDMAN, MINTON F. Franco-British rivalry over Siam, 1896-1904. JSAS 3 (1972) 210-228.

9495 Mission of Sir James Brooke to Siam, September 1850. S44.8 pp. 219-231.

9496 TARLING, NICHOLAS. British policy towards Siam, Cambodia, and Vietnam, 1842-1858. AST 4 (1966) 240-258.

9497 TARLING, NICHOLAS. Harry Parkes' negotiations in Bangkok in 1856. JSS 53 (1965) 153-180.

9498 THAMSOOK NUMNONDA. Anglo-Siamese secret convention of 1897. JSS 53 (1965) 45-60.

THAILAND – FOREIGN RELATIONS – INDONESIA

9499 PENTH, HANS GEORG. Account in the Hikajat Atjeh on relations between Siam and Atjeh. F38 pp. 55-69.

9500 PENTH, HANS GEORG. Zum Verhaltnis Sayam-Atjeh im 17 Jahrhundert. JSS 57 (1969) 355-359.

THAILAND – FOREIGN RELATIONS – JAPAN

9501 FLOOD, E. THADEUS. The 1940 Franco-Thai border dispute and Phibuun Sonkhraam's commitment to Japan. JSAH 10 (1969) 304-325.

9502 ISHII, YONEO. Seventeenth century Japanese documents about Siam. JSS 59 pt. 2 (1971) 161-174.

THAILAND – FOREIGN RELATIONS – LAOS

9503 WYATT, DAVID K. Siam and Laos, 1767-1827. JSAH 4 (Sept. 1963) 13-32.

THAILAND – FOREIGN RELATIONS – MALAYSIA

9504 ANDERSON, JOHN. Political and commercial considerations relative to the Malayan peninsula and the British settlements in the Straits

Thailand - Foreign relations - Malaysia

of Malacca. JMBRAS 35 pt. 4 (1965)
i-xv, 1-204, i-lxviii.

9505 BASTIN, JOHN. Introduction.
JMBRAS 35 pt. 4 (1965) 1-10.

9506 SHAROM AHMAT. Kedah-Siam relations, 1821-1905. JSS 59 pt. 1
(1971) 97-117.

9507 THAMSOOK NUMNONDA. Negotiations
regarding the cession of Siamese
Malay states 1907-1909. JSS 55
(1967) 227-235.

THAILAND - FOREIGN RELATIONS - NETHER-
LANDS

9508 BLANKWAARDT, W. Notes upon the
relations between Holland and
Siam. S44.7 pp. 13-30.

THAILAND - FOREIGN RELATIONS - PORTUGAL

9509 MENDONCA E CUNHA, HELDER DE. The
1820 land concession to the Portuguese. JSS 59 pt. 2 (1971) 145-
149.

THAILAND - FOREIGN RELATIONS - SPAIN

9510 MOSEL, JAMES N. Recently discovered account of a Spanish embassy to Ayudhya in 1718. F38 pp.
123-128.

THAILAND - FOREIGN RELATIONS - UNION OF
SOVIET SOCIALIST REPUBLICS

9511 SHIRK, PAUL R. Thai-Soviet relations. AS 9 (1969) 682-693.

THAILAND - FOREIGN RELATIONS - UNITED
STATES

9512 DARLING, FRANK C. America and
Thailand. AS 7 (1967) 213-225.

9513 DARLING, FRANK C. British and
American influence in postwar
Thailand. JSAH 4 (Mar. 1963) 88-
102.

9514 FREEMAN, HAROLD. Working with
groups in technical assistance
programs, applied anthropology and
social psychology. GEJ 12 (1966)
73-85.

9515 MARTIN, JAMES V. Thai-American
relations in World War II. JAS 22
(1962-3) 451-467.

9516 MORROW, MICHAEL. Thailand,
bombers and bases, America's new
frontier. JCA 2 (1972) 382-402.

9517 O'NEIL, WAYNE. Thailand, America's troubled ally. JCA 1 pt. 4
(1971) 55-59.

9518 PURCELL, VICTOR. Relinquishment
by the United States of extra-
territoriality in Siam. JMBRAS 37
pt. 1 (1964) 99-120.

9519 THAMSOOK NUMNONDA. The first
American advisers in Thai history.
JSS 62 pt. 2 (1974) 121-148.

9520 THANAT KHOMAN. Trade and investment possibilities in Thailand.
C35 pp. 205-214.

9521 VIKSNINS, GEORGE J. United States
military spending and the economy
of Thailand, 1967-1972. AS 13
(1973) 441-457.

9522 WEHNER, WOLFGANG. American involvement in Thailand. JCA 3
(1973) 292-305.

THAILAND - FOREIGN RELATIONS - VATICAN

9523 CARRETTO, P. Vatican papers of the XVII century. S44.7 pp. 177-193.

THAILAND - FOREIGN RELATIONS - VIETNAM

9524 WHITMORE, JOHN K. Thai-Vietnamese struggle for Laos in the nineteenth century. L18 pp. 52-66.

THAILAND - FRONTIER TROUBLES

9525 FLOOD, E. THADEUS. The 1940 Franco-Thai border dispute and Phibuun Sonkhraam's commitment to Japan. JSAH 10 (1969) 304-325.

9526 WILSON, DAVID A. Bangkok's dim view to the east. AS 1 (June 1961) 13-17.

THAILAND - HISTORY *See also* AYUDHYA, DVARAVATI, SUKHODAYA

9527 AKIN RABIBHADANA. Clientship and class structure in the early Bangkok period. C24 pp. 93-124.

9528 BOELES, J. J. Note on an eye witness account in Dutch of the destruction of Ayudhya in 1767. JSS 56 (1968) 101-111.

9529 BOELES, J. J. Note on the toponymy of the ancient Kantoli in peninsular Thailand. JSS 55 (1967) 291-297.

9530 FLOOD, E. THADEUS. Sukhothai-Mongol relations, a note on relevant Chinese and Thai sources with translations. JSS 57 (1969) 201-257.

9531 GRISWOLD, A. B. Epigraphic and historical studies. I. Declaration of independence and its consequences. JSS 56 (1968) 207-249.

9532 GRISWOLD, A. B. Epigraphic and historical studies. V. Pact between uncle and nephew, by A. B. Griswold and Prasert na Nagara. JSS 58 pt. 1 (1970) 89-113.

9533 KAEHORN SUKHABANJ. Proposed dating of the Yonok-Chiengsaen dynasty. JBRS 43 (1960) 57-62.

9534 KEYES, CHARLES F. New evidence on northern Thai frontier history. T33 pp. 221-249.

9535 Narrative of the revolutions which took place in Siam in the year 1688. S44.3 pp. 1-35.

9536 PENTH, HANS GEORGE. Zum Siam episode in der Hikajat Atjeh. JSS 55 (1967) 287-290.

9537 RISPAUD, JEAN. Introduction a l'histoire des Tay du Yunnan et de Birmanie. FA 17 (1960) 1849-1859.

9538 SIMMONDS, E. H. S. An 18th century travel document in Thai. F38 pp. 157-165.

9539 SIMMONDS, E. H. S. Thalang letters, 1773-94, political aspects and the trade in arms. SOAS 26 (1963) 592-619.

9540 SMITH, R. B. Thailand and Vietnam, some thoughts towards a comparative historical analysis. JSS 60 pt. 2 (1972) 1-21.

9541 THONG, KING PHRA CHAO U. History of Siam in the period antecedent to the founding of Ayuddhya. S44.3 pp. 36-100.

Thailand - History

9561 GEDDES, WILLIAM R. The Tribal Research Centre, Thailand, an account of plans and activities. K86 pp. 553-581.

9562 HINTON, PETER. Introduction. S96 pp. 1-11.

9563 HOGAN, DAVID W. Men of the sea, coastal tribes of south Thailand's west coast. JSS 60 pt. 1 (1972) 205-235.

9564 HUFF, LEE W. The Thai Mobile Development Unit program. K86 pp. 425-486.

9565 KUNSTADTER, PETER. Hill and valley populations in northwestern Thailand. S96 pp. 69-85.

9566 KUNSTADTER, PETER. Thailand, introduction. K86 pp. 369-400.

9567 MANNDORFF, HANS. The hill tribe program of the Public Welfare Department, Ministry of Interior, Thailand, research and socio-economic development. K86 pp. 525-552.

9568 SEIDENFADEN, ERIK. Siam's tribal dresses. S44.2 pp. 84-94.

9569 SUWAN RUENYOTE. Development and welfare for the hill tribes in Thailand. S96 pp. 12-14.

THAILAND - POLITICS AND GOVERNMENT

9570 BATSON, BENJAMIN A. The fall of the Phibun government. JSS 62 pt. 2 (1974) 89-120.

9571 BELL, PETER F. Thailand's northeast, regional underdevelopment, insurgency and official response. PA 42 (1969) 47-54.

9572 CHARNVIT KASETSIRI. The first Phibun government and its involvement in World War II. JSS 62 pt. 2 (1974) 25-88.

9573 DARLING, FRANK C. Marshal Sarit and absolutist rule in Thailand. PA 33 (1960) 347-360.

9574 DARLING, FRANK C. Political development in Thailand and the Philippines, a comparative analysis. SA 1 (1971) 90-115.

9575 DARLING, FRANK C. Thailand, de-escalation and uncertainty. AS 9 (1969) 115-121.

9576 DARLING, FRANK C. Thailand, stability and escalation. AS 8 (1968) 120-126.

9577 DHANI, PRINCE. The old Siamese conception of the monarchy. S44.2 pp. 160-175.

9578 FISTIE, PIERRE. Thailande, resurgence du danger au nord-est. FA 21 (1966) 47-62.

9579 GIRLING, J. L. S. Thailand's new course. PA 42 (1969) 346-359.

9580 HANKS, L. M. Two visions of freedom, Thai and American. F38 pp. 85-90.

9581 HINDLEY, DONALD. Thailand, the politics of passivity. PA 41 (1968) 355-371.

9582 HUFF, LEE W. The Thai Mobile Development Unit program. K86 pp. 425-486.

9583 ISHII, YONEO. Church and state in Thailand. AS 8 (1968) 864-871.

9584 MEZEY, MICHAEL L. The 1971 coup in Thailand, understanding why the

Thailand - Politics and government

legislature fails. AS 13 (1973) 306-317.

9585 MORELL, DAVID. Legislative intervention in Thailand's development process, a case study. AS 12 (1972) 627-646.

9586 MORELL, DAVID. Thailand, if you would know how the villagers really feel, abandon intimidation. AS 13 (1973) 162-178.

9587 MORELL, DAVID. Thailand, military checkmate. AS 12 (1972) 156-167.

9588 NEHER, CLARK D. Thailand, toward fundamental change. AS 11 (1971) 131-138.

9589 NUECHTERLEIN, DONALD E. Thailand after Sarit. AS 4 (1964) 842-850.

9590 NUECHTERLEIN, DONALD E. Thailand, another Vietnam? AS 7 (1967) 126-130.

9591 NUECHTERLEIN, DONALD E. Thailand, year of danger and of hope. AS 6 (1966) 119-124.

9592 PRACHOOM CHOMCHAI. Nature and significance of Thai political philosophy. GEJ 7 (1964) 181-190.

9593 RACE, JEFFREY. The war in northern Thailand. MAS 8 (1974) 85-112.

9594 SIMMONDS, STUART. Thailand, a conservative state. R64 pp. 119-142.

9595 SRIVISARN VACHA, PHYA. Kingship in Siam. S44.3 pp. 237-246.

9596 WILSON, DAVID A. Introductory comment on politics and the northeast. AS 6 (1966) 349-352.

9597 WILSON, DAVID A. The military in Thai politics. J52 pp. 253-275.

9598 WILSON, DAVID A. The military in Thai politics. T45 pp. 326-339.

9599 WILSON, DAVID A. Thailand. K17 pp. 1-72.

9600 WILSON, DAVID A. Thailand, a new leader. AS 4 (1964) 711-715.

9601 WILSON, DAVID A. Thailand, old leaders and new directions. AS 3 (1963) 83-87.

9602 WILSON, DAVID A. Thailand, scandal and progress. AS 5 (1965) 108-112.

9603 WYATT, DAVID K. Family politics in nineteenth century Thailand. JSAH 9 (1968) 208-228.

9604 YOUNG, STEPHEN B. Northeastern Thai village, a non-participatory democracy. AS 8 (1968) 873-886.

THAILAND - POLITICS AND GOVERNMENT - 1973-

9605 DARLING, FRANK C. Student protest and political change in Thailand. PA 47 (1974) 5-19.

9606 HEINZE, RUTH-INGE. Ten days in October, students vs. the military an account of the student uprising in Thailand. AS 14 (1974) 491-508.

9607 PRUDHISAN JUMBALA. Towards a theory of group formation in Thai society and pressure groups in Thailand after the October 1973 uprising. AS 14 (1974) 530-545.

THAILAND - POPULATION

9608 CALDWELL, J. C. Demographic
structure. S49 pp. 27-64.

9609 STERNSTEIN, LARRY. Settlement patterns in Thailand. JTG 21 (1965)
30-43.

9610 VISID PRACHUABMOH. The longitudinal study of social, economic, and
demographic change in Thailand,
review of findings, by Visid Prachuabmoh and John Knodel. AS 14
(1974) 350-364.

THAILAND - RELIGION *See also* BUDDHISM,
CHRISTIANITY, HINDUISM, ISLAM

9611 KRAISRI NIMMANHAEMINDA. Lawa
guardian spirits of Chiengmai.
JSS 55 (1967) 185-225.

9612 LINGAT, R. Les suicides religieux
au Siam. F38 pp. 71-75.

9613 MULDER, J. A. NIELS. Comparative
note on the Thai and the Javanese
worldview as expressed by religious practice and belief. JSS 58
pt. 2 (1970) 79-85.

9614 MULDER, J. A. NIELS. Sociology
and religion in Thailand, a critique. JSS 55 (1967) 101-111.

THAILAND - SOCIAL CONDITIONS

9615 AKIN RABIBHADANA. Clientship and
class structure in the early Bangkok period. C24 pp. 93-124.

9616 ANUMAN RAJADHON. Khwan and its
ceremonies. JSS 50 pt. 2 (1962)
119-164.

9617 ANUMAN RAJADHON. Thai traditional
salutation. JSS 49 pt. 2 (1961)
159-169.

9618 BOONSANONG PUNYODYANA. Social
structure, social system, and two
levels of analysis, a Thai view.
L62 pp. 77-105.

9619 BUNNAG, JANE. Loose structure,
fact or fancy, Thai society reexamined. JSS 59 pt. 1 (1971) 1-
23.

9620 EMBREE, JOHN F. Thailand, a
loosely structured social system.
L62 pp. 3-15.

9621 EVERS, HANS-DIETER. Models of
social systems, loosely and tight-
ly structured. L62 pp. 115-127.

9622 GILES, FRANCIS H. About a love
philtre known to the Siamese as
Nam Man Prai, spirit oil. S44.2
pp. 74-77.

9623 HANKS, LUCIEN M. Thai social
order as entourage and circle.
C24 pp. 197-218.

9624 KIRSCH, A. THOMAS. Development
and mobility among the Phu Thai of
northeast Thailand. T45 pp. 481-
489.

9625 KIRSCH, A. THOMAS. Loose structure, theory or description. L62
pp. 39-60.

9626 KLAUSNER, WILLIAM J. In-law tales
a note on northeastern Thai ethnography. JSS 61 pt. 2 (1973) 143-
148.

9627 Modernization and industrialization of Thai society, a sociological analysis, by Kenichi Tominaga,
Hiroshi Komai, Hideo Okamoto and
Michiko Ise. EACS 8 (1969) 1-39.

9628 Modernization and industrialization of Thai society, a sociological analysis, by Kenichi Tominaga,

Thailand - Social conditions

Hiroshi Komai, Hideo Okamoto and Michiko Ise. EACS 9 (1970) 1-56.

9629 MOERMAN, MICHAEL. The study of Thai society, summary comments. L62 pp. 128-132.

9630 MULDER, J. A. NIELS. Notes on the structural analysis of Thai peasant villages, a critique and a recommendation. JSS 55 (1967) 273-277.

9631 MULDER, J. A. NIELS. Origin, development and use of the concept of loose structure in the literature about Thailand, an evaluation. L62 pp. 16-24.

9632 MULDER, J. A. NIELS. Sociology and religion in Thailand, a critique. JSS 55 (1967) 101-111.

9633 PHILLIPS, HERBERT P. Scope and limits of the loose structure concept. L62 pp. 25-38.

9634 PIKER, STEVEN. Loose structure and the analysis of Thai social organization. L62 pp. 61-76.

9635 PIKER, STEVEN. Sources of stability and instability in rural Thai society. JAS 27 (1967-8) 777-790.

9636 PRACHOOM CHOMCHAI. Development of human rights in Thailand, a historical sketch. EACS 12 (1973) 1-10.

9637 PRACHOOM CHOMCHAI. Trends report of studies in social stratification and social mobility in Thailand. EACS 4 (1965) 192-204.

9638 PUEY UNGPHAKORN. The society of Siam. JSS 62 pt. 2 (1974) 1-6.

9639 RUBIN, HERBERT J. Effects of institutional change upon a dependency culture, the commune council

275 in rural Thailand, by Herbert J. and Irene S. Rubin. AS 13 (1973) 270-287.

9640 RUBIN, HERBERT J. Framework for the analysis of villager, official contact in rural Thailand. SA 2 (1972-3) 232-262.

9641 WIJEYEWARDENE, GEHAN. Language of courtship in Chiengmai. JSS 56 (1968) 21-32.

9642 WIJEYEWARDENE, GEHAN. Note on patrons and Pau Liang. JSS 59 pt. 2 (1971) 229-233.

9643 WILLIAMS, MICHAEL C. Thailand, the demise of a traditional society. JCA 3 (1973) 427-440.

THAILAND - TREATIES

9644 OBLAS, PETER B. Treaty revision and the role of the American foreign affairs adviser, 1909-1925. JSS 60 pt. 1 (1972) 171-186.

9645 TARLING, NICHOLAS. Harry Parkes' negotiations in Bangkok in 1856. JSS 53 (1965) 153-180.

9646 TARLING, NICHOLAS. Mission of Sir John Bowring to Siam. JSS 50 pt. 2 (1962) 91-118.

THAILAND. MINISTER OF INTERIOR

9647 MANNDORFF, HANS. Hill tribe program of the Public Welfare Department, Ministry of Interior, Thailand, research and socio-economic development. K86 pp. 525-552.

THAILAND. NATIONAL LIBRARY

9648 SIMMONDS, E. H. S. Mahorasop II,
the Thai National Library manuscript. SOAS 34 (1971) 119-131.

THAILAND. NATIONAL MUSEUM

9649 MALLERET, LOUIS. A propos d'une
sculpture du Musee National de
Bangkok. F38 pp. 107-118.

THAILAND. ROYAL THAI SURVEY DEPARTMENT

9650 STERNSTEIN, LARRY. Catalogue of
maps of Thailand in the museum of
the Royal Thai Survey Department,
Bangkok. JSS 56 (1968) 47-99.

THALUN, KING OF BURMA

9651 THAN TUN. Administration under
King Thalun, 1629-48. JBRS 51
(1968) 173-188.

THANT, U

9652 TRAGER, FRANK N. U Thant of
Burma, a biographic note. AS 1
(Dec. 1961) 32-34.

Theses *See* DISSERTATIONS, ACADEMIC

THIEU TRI, EMPEROR OF VIETNAM

9653 DAUDIN, PIERRE. Poemes anacy-
cliques de l'empereur Thieu Tri.
SEIB 47 (1972) 81-104.

9654 DAUDIN, PIERRE. Poemes anacy-
cliques de l'empereur Thieu Tri.
SEIB 49 (1974) 225-251.

TIEMPO, EDILBERTO K.

9655 BAUTISTA, ABRAHAM R. Hope in more
than conquerors. SLURJ 2 (1971)
535-539.

TIMORESE LANGUAGE

9656 MIDDELKOOP, P. De betekenis van
de Timorese term Atoni amaf. BIJ
127 (1971) 393-396.

TIN INDUSTRY

9657 BROWN, C. P. Some implications of
tin price stabilisation. MER 17
pt. 1 (1972) 99-118.

9658 COURTENAY, P. P. Changing patterns in the tin mining and smelt-
ing industry of Southeast Asia.
JTG 25 (1967) 8-17.

9659 EASTHAM, J. K. Rationalization in
the tin industry. S48 pp. 320-
344.

9660 LIM CHONG YAH. Reappraisal of the
1953 international tin agreement.
MER 5 pt. 1 (1960) 13-24.

9661 LIM, DAVID. Note on supply response of tin producers, 1949-
1969. MER 18 pt. 2 (1973) 50-59.

9662 ROGERS, CHRISTOPHER D. Consumer
participation in the international
tin agreements. MER 14 pt. 2
(1969) 113-129.

TIN INDUSTRY - MALAYSIA

9663 IRWIN, GRAHAM W. The Dutch and
the tin trade of Malaya in the
seventeenth century. S89 pp. 267-
287.

9663 WENT, F. W. Tjiboas Biological
      Station and Forest Reserve, a
      naturalists paradise. H57 p. 403.

TOBACCO - INDONESIA

9664 ROELOFSEN, P. A. Recent research
      at the Deli Tobacco Research Sta-
      tion. H57 pp. 285-289.

TOBACCO - MALAYSIA

9665 JOHN, DAVID W. The tobacco indus-
      try of North Borneo, a distinctive
      form of plantation agriculture, by
      David W. John and James C. Jackson.
      JSAS 4 (1973) 88-106.

TOBACCO - PHILIPPINES

9666 PELZER, KARL J. The Spanish tobac-
      co monopoly in the Philippines,
      1782-1883 and the Dutch forced
      cultivation system in Indonesia,
      1834-1870. AR 8 (1974) 147-153.

9667 TADENA, ROMUALDO B. Appointing a
      P.T.A. chairman-general manager.
      G93 pp. 241-275.

TOBACCO - VIETNAM

9668 TEULIERES, ROGER. Le tabac au
      Viet-Nam du sud. SEIB 40 (1965)
      319-336.

TODRAH LANGUAGE

9669 GREGERSON, KENNETH J. Development
      of Todrah register. M61 pp. 143-
      184.

TOLENTINO, AURELIO

9670 FERNANDO, FELIPE D. Aurelio To-
      lentino, playwright, poet and
      patriot. PS 12 (1964) 83-92.

TONDA LITERATURE

9671 WATUSEKE, F. S. Tondanose raad-
      sels. BIJ 128 (1972) 330-336.

TORADJA

9672 CRYSTAL, ERIC. Cooking pot poli-
      tics, a Toraja village study. IND
      18 (1974) 118-151.

TORRE, CARLOS MARIA DE LA

9673 MOLINA, ANTONIO M. The myth of
      Carlos Maria de la Torre. UN 36
      (1963) 152-157.

TOYO BUNKO

9674 Toyo Bunko (The Oriental Library)
      and its latest activities. FA 19
      (1963) 707-709.

Trade *See* COMMERCE

TRADE UNIONS

9675 MUKHERJEE, AMAL. Role of trade
      unions towards economic freedom
      and social equality. D44 pp. 99-
      107.

TRADE UNIONS - MALAYSIA

9676 JACKSON, R. N. Notes on trade
      unionism amongst government em-
      ployees in the Federation of

Trade unions - Malaysia

Malaya, 1948-1957. JMBRAS 43 pt. 1 (1970) 129-142.

9677 RUDNER, MARTIN. Malayan labor in transition, labor policy and trade unionism, 1955-63. MAS 7 (1973) 21-45.

TRADE UNIONS - SINGAPORE

9678 HEYZER, NOELEEN. Ideological and attitudinal differences among Singapore trade union leaders, by Noeleen Heyzer, Peter D. Weldon and Wee Gek Sim. AST 10 (1972) 378-389.

TRAN HAM TAN

9679 Necrologie, Tran-Ham-Tan, 1887-1957. BEF 50 (1960) 179-181.

TRANSLATIONS

9680 KRUPA, VIKTOR. Some remarks on the translation process. AAS 4 (1968) 49-56.

TRANSPORTATION *See also* AIRLINES, RAILROADS

9681 Asian highway, from caravan routes to modern roads. FA 17 (1960) 1909-1919.

TRANSPORTATION - INDONESIA

9682 POND, DONALD H. Indonesian surface transport facilities and investment. V27 pp. 53-70.

TRANSPORTATION - MALAYSIA

9683 LEINBACH, THOMAS R. The spread of transportation and its impact upon the modernization of Malaya, 1887-1911. JTG 39 (1974) 54-62.

TRANSPORTATION - PHILIPPINES

9684 FLORES, JOAQUIN P. Highway construction in the Mountain Province. SLQ 1 (1963) 305-334.

9685 VILLANUEVA, PATROCINIO S. Some socio-economic effects of rural roads. E78 pp. 287-291.

9686 WENGERT, EGBERT S. Aviles-Legarda-Mendiola traffic experiment, by Egbert S. Wengert and Primitivo R. de Leon. G93 pp. 475-503.

TRANSPORTATION - SINGAPORE

9687 KOH SEOW TEE. Transportation system and problems. Y52 pp. 328-351.

TRANSPORTATION - THAILAND

9688 HAFNER, JAMES A. Riverine commerce in Thailand, tradition in decline. JSS 62 pt. 2 (1974) 7-24.

TRENGGANU

9689 ALLEN, J. DE VERE. Ancien regime in Trengganu, 1909-1919. JMBRAS 41 pt. 1 (1968) 23-53.

9690 CHAN SU MING. Kelantan and Trengganu, 1909-1939. JMBRAS 38 pt. 1 (1965) 159-198.

9691 CLIFFORD, HUGH. Report on the expedition recently led into Trengganu and Kelantan on the east coast of the Malay peninsula. JMBRAS 34 pt. 1 (1961) 1-162.

9692 DUNMORE, JOHN. French visitors to Trengganu in the eighteenth century. JMBRAS 46 pt. 1 (1973) 144-159.

9693 GOSLING, L. A. P. Migration and assimilation of rural Chinese in Trengganu. B38 pp. 203-221.

9694 GUYOT, DOROTHY. Politics of land, comparative development in two states of Malaysia. PA 44 (1971) 368-389.

9695 KHOO KAY KIM. Introduction. JMBRAS 34 pt. 1 (1961) xi-xviii.

9696 MACKEEN, A. M. M. Islamic constitutional document in Malaya. A41 pp. 131-138.

9697 SHEPPARD, MUBIN. Traditional Malay house forms in Trengganu and Kelantan. JMBRAS 42 pt. 2 (1969) 1-9.

9698 SKINNER, CYRIL. Trengganu leader of 1839. JSAH 5 (Mar. 1964) 178-187.

TRIBAL RESEARCH CENTRE

9699 GEDDES, WILLIAM R. The Tribal Research Centre, Thailand, an account of plans and activities. K86 pp. 553-581.

TUHFAT UL-NAFIS

9700 MATHESON, VIRGINIA. Mahmud, Sultan of Riau and Lingga, 1823-1864. IND 13 (1972) 119-146.

9701 MATHESON, VIRGINIA. *Tuhfat al-Nafis*, structure and sources. BIJ 127 (1971) 375-392.

9702 SWEENEY, AMIN. Sir Richard Winstedt's summary of the *Tuhfat ul-Nafis*. JMBRAS 40 pt. 1 (1967) 155-6.

TURTLES - BRUNEI

9703 BIRKENMEIER, ELMAR. Juvenile leathery turtles, Dermochelys coriacea (Linnaeus) in captivity. BMJ 2 pt. 3 (1971) 160-172.

TURTLES - MALAYSIA - SABAH

9704 HARRISSON, TOM. Notes on marine turtles, Sabah's turtle islands. SMJ 11 (1964) 624-627.

TURTLES - MALAYSIA - SARAWAK

9705 CHIN, LUCAS. Notes on orangutan and marine turtles. SMJ 18 (1970) 414-5.

9706 CHIN, LUCAS. Notes on orangutans, bird ringing project and turtles. SMJ 16 (1968) 249-252.

9707 CHIN, LUCAS. Notes on turtles and orangutans, 1969. SMJ 17 (1969) 403-4.

9708 HARRISSON, TOM. Notes on marine turtles, a report on the Sarawak turtle industry, 1966, with recommendations for the future. SMJ 15 (1967) 424-436.

9709 HARRISSON, TOM. Notes on marine turtles, albino green turtles and sacred ones. SMJ 11 (1963) 304-306.

Turtles - Malaysia - Sarawak

9710 HARRISSON, TOM. Notes on marine turtles, growth rate of the hawksbill. SMJ 11 (1963) 302-3.

9711 HARRISSON, TOM. Notes on marine turtles, Sabah and Sarawak islands compared. SMJ 14 (1966) 335-340.

9712 HARRISSON, TOM. Notes on marine turtles, some loggerhead and hawksbill comparisons with the green turtle. SMJ 12 (1965) 419-422.

9713 HARRISSON, TOM. Notes on the green turtle, chelonia mydas, monthly laying cycles. SMJ 11 (1962) 624-630.

9714 HARRISSON, TOM. Notes on the green turtle, chelonia mydas, some emergence variations. SMJ 11 (1962) 610-613.

9715 HARRISSON, TOM. Notes on the green turtle, chelonia mydas, some new hatching observations. SMJ 10 (1961) 293-299.

9716 HARRISSON, TOM. Notes on the green turtle, chelonia mydas, west Borneo numbers, the downward trend. SMJ 11 (1962) 614-623.

9717 LYONS, DANIEL D. Keys to shell bones of Bornean emydid turtles. SMJ 17 (1969) 89-95.

TURTLES - VIETNAM

9718 RICHARD, C. Les oeufs de tortue de mer, chelonia mydas, aliment traditionnel vietnamien, composition chimique et valeur alimentaire, par C. Richard et Nguyen Thi Lau. SEIB 37 (1962) 75-84.

Ty-Casper, Linda *See* CASPER, LINDA

TYPHOONS - PHILIPPINES

9719 SELGA, MIGUEL. Catalogue of Philippine typhoons, 414-1703. PS 20 (1972) 12-39.

UNITAS

9720 Retrospection of *Unitas*' forty years of fruitful service to the university. UN 34 (Sept. 1961) 1-4.

UNITED NATIONS

9721 AFRICA, BERNABE. Philippine participation in the United Nations. A28 pp. 494-496.

9722 KIM, JUNG-GUN. Reflections on recent international politics, United Nations, and the Viet-Nam war. S98 pp. 80-96.

9723 PHOUMI VONGVICHIT. Excerpt of speech at the 29 session of the United Nations General Assembly on September 25, 1974. JCA 4 (1974) 558-560.

9724 POLAK, J. J. U.N.R.R.A. H57 pp. 477-8.

9725 ROBINS, LINDA C. What ever happened to the U.N. trusteeship of Indochina? FA 23 (1969) 271-303.

9726 SABLOSKY, IRVING L. The United Nations and Southeast Asia. SJ 10 (1963) 117-126.

UNITED NATIONS CONFERENCE ON TRADE AND DEVELOPMENT

9727 SUBHAN, MALCOLM. Southeast Asia at the United Nations Conference on Trade and Development. D44 pp. 137-150.

UNITED NATIONS EDUCATIONAL, SCIENTIFIC
AND CULTURAL ORGANIZATION

9728 ECHES, RAYMOND. Activites de
l'UNESCO a Saigon, 18-26 mars 1960.
SEIB 35 (1960) 575-580.

9729 La premiere conference UNESCO sur
la culture malaise, Kuala Lumpur,
janvier 1972. AR 4 (1972) 27-30.

UNITED STATES - DESCRIPTION AND TRAVEL

9730 CALDERON, CICERO D. An Asian looks
at the United States. SJ 14 (1967)
363-371.

9731 MASLOG, CRISPIN. Filipino and Indian students' images of the United
States. SJ 16 (1969) 76-90.

UNITED STATES. LIBRARY OF CONGRESS

9732 LANDHEER, B. Netherlands studies
unit at the Library of Congress.
H57 pp. 481-2.

9733 TEEUW, A. Malay manuscripts in the
Library of Congress. BIJ 123
(1967) 517-520.

University of Santo Tomas *See* MANILA.
UNIVERSITY OF SANTO TOMAS

University of Singapore *See* SINGAPORE.
UNIVERSITY

University of the Philippines *See*
QUEZON, PHILIPPINES. UNIVERSITY OF THE
PHILIPPINES

URBANIZATION

9734 BERRY, BRIAN J. L. City size and
economic development, conceptual
synthesis and policy problems,
with special reference to South
and Southeast Asia. U77 pp. 111-
155.

9735 BOSE, ASHISH. The urbanization
process in South and Southeast
Asia. U77 pp. 81-109.

9736 DESMOND, GERALD M. Impact of
national and regional development
policies on urbanization. U77 pp.
57-79.

9737 DWYER, D. J. Attitudes towards
spontaneous settlement in third
world cities. D92 pp. 166-178.

9738 FRYER, DONALD W. The million city
in Southeast Asia. T45 pp. 72-87.

9739 FRYER, DONALD W. Primate cities
of Southeast Asia and their problems. F56 pp. 31-42.

9740 GINSBURG, NORTON. Planning the
future of the Asian city. D92 pp.
269-283.

9741 GINSBURG, NORTON S. Planning the
future of the Southeast Asian
city. F56 pp. 43-56.

9742 HAMZAH SENDUT. City size distribution of Southeast Asia. AST 4
(1966) 268-280.

9743 HOSELITZ, BERT F. Urbanization
and economic growth. D92 pp. 3-
15.

9744 LAQUIAN, APRODICIO A. The Asian
city and the political process.
D92 pp. 41-55.

Urbanization

9745 LAQUIAN, APRODICIO A. Slums and squatters in South and Southeast Asia. U77 pp. 183-203.

9746 McGEE, T. G. Catalysts or cancers, the role of cities in Asian society. U77 pp. 157-181.

9747 MOSS, LAURENCE A. G. War and urbanization in Indochina, by Laurence A. G. Moss and Zmarak M. Shalizi. G79 pp. 175-200.

9748 PRAKASH, VED. Land policies for urban development. U77 pp. 205-224.

9749 REED, ROBERT R. Colonial origins of Manila and Batavia, desultory notes on nascent metropolitan primacy and urban systems in Southeast Asia. AST 5 (1967) 543-562.

9750 REED, ROBERT R. Primate city in Southeast Asia, conceptual definitions and colonial origins. AST 10 (1972) 283-320.

9751 SINGH, TARLOK. Urban development policy and the role of governments and public authorities. U77 pp. 225-240.

9752 SUBHAN, MALCOLM. Growth of the city in Asia. RSA (1968) 83-97.

9753 WHEATON, WILLIAM L. C. Urban housing in economic development, by William L. C. and Margaret F. Wheaton. D92 pp. 141-151.

URBANIZATION - BIBLIOGRAPHY

9754 JAKOBSON, LEO. Selected bibliography, by Leo Jakobson and Ved Prakash. U77 pp. 241-310.

URBANIZATION - BURMA

9755 KHIN MY LAY. Urban study of the Sittang Valley. JBRS 45 (1962) 163-180.

URBANIZATION - INDONESIA

9756 CASTLES, LANCE. Ethnic profile of Djakarta. IND 3 (1967) 153-204.

9757 COBBAN, JAMES L. Uncontrolled urban settlement, the kampong question in Semarang, 1905-1940. BIJ 130 (1974) 403-427.

9758 DEWEY, ALICE. Restructuring roles as a strategy of urban adaptation. V27 pp. 29-52.

9759 KING, DWIGHT Y. Social development in Indonesia, a macro analysis. AS 14 (1974) 918-935.

9760 McNICOLL, GEOFFREY. Internal migration in Indonesia, descriptive notes. IND 5 (1968) 29-92.

9761 MILONE, PAULINE D. Contemporary urbanization in Indonesia. AS 4 (1964) 1000-1012.

9762 WELDON, PETER D. Indonesian and Chinese status and language differences in urban Java. JSAS 5 (1974) 37-54.

URBANIZATION - MALAYSIA

9763 HAMZAH SENDUT. Contemporary urbanization in Malaysia. AS 6 (1966) 484-491.

9764 HAMZAH SENDUT. Patterns of urbanization in Malaya. JTG 16 (1962) 114-130.

Articles

9765 HIPKINS, JAMES R. Sarawak and urbanization. SMJ 20 (1972) 179-193.

9766 McGEE, T. G. Cultural role of cities, a case study of Kuala Lumpur. JTG 17 (1963) 178-196.

9767 NAGATA, JUDITH A. Adat in the city, some perceptions and practices among urban Malays. BIJ 130 (1974) 91-109.

9768 NEVILLE, R. J. W. Urban study of Pontian Kechil, south west Malaya. JTG 16 (1962) 32-56.

9769 PRYOR, ROBIN J. Changing settlement system of west Malaysia. JTG 37 (1973) 53-67.

9770 SAW SWEE HOCK. Patterns of urbanization in west Malaysia, 1911-1970. MER 17 pt. 2 (1972) 114-120.

9771 SINGH, JASBIR SARJIT. Social stratification in Petaling Jaya, Malaysia. SAJSS 2 (1974) 75-92.

URBANIZATION - PHILIPPINES

9772 ARCINAS, FE R. Adjustment of migrants in an urban enclave, Pobres Purok. GEJ 21 (1971) 1-29.

9773 CHANG SHUB ROH. Looc, Dumaguete City, a study of an urban slum community. SJ 17 (1970) 248-285.

9774 DOEPPERS, DANIEL F. Development of Philippine cities before 1900. JAS 31 (1971-2) 769-792.

9775 DWYER, D. J. Problem of in-migration and squatter settlement in Asian cities: two case studies, Manila and Victoria-Kowloon. AST 2 (1964) 145-169.

9776 HOLLNSTEINER, MARY R. Becoming an urbanite, the neighbourhood as a learning environment. D92 pp. 29-40.

9777 HOLLNSTEINER, MARY R. Inner Tondo as a way of life. B13 pp. 235-245.

9778 IKE, NOBUTAKA. Urbanization and political opposition, the Philippines and Japan. AST 7 (1969) 134-141.

9779 McHALE, THOMAS R. The Philippines in transition. JAS 20 (1960-1) 331-341.

9780 POETHIG, RICHARD P. The Philippine urban family. B13 pp. 222-234.

9781 TAN, BELEN. Changing marriage patterns among slum dwellers, by Belen Tan and Gatue Medina. GEJ 21 (1971) 31-58.

9782 VILORIA, LEANDRO A. Manilenos, significant elites in urban development and nation building in the Philippines. D92 pp. 16-28.

URBANIZATION - SINGAPORE

9783 CHOE, ALAN F. C. Urban renewal. M49 pp. 161-170.

9784 RIAZ HASSAN. Urban environment and mental health, with special reference to Singapore and other developing countries. RSAS 1 pt. 2 (1971) 48-65.

URBANIZATION - THAILAND

9785 EVERS, HANS-DIETER. Formation of a social class structure, urbanization, bureaucratization and

Urbanization - Thailand

social mobility in Thailand. JSAH 7 (Sept. 1966) 100-115.

URBANIZATION - VIETNAM

9786 LANGLET, MADAME. Notes sur les changements du milieu humain dans la Republique du Vietnam, communication faite au 29e Congress des Orientalistes, Paris, 17 juillet 1973, par Madame Langlet et Quach Thanh Tam. SEIB 49 (1974) 1-30.

9787 RONDINELLI, DENNIS A. Postwar reconstruction in Vietnam, the case for an urbanization policy. AF 5 pt. 3 (1973) 1-15.

9788 WOODSIDE, ALEXANDER. Development of social organizations in Vietnamese cities in the late colonial period. PA 44 (1971) 39-64.

UTTAMAGYAW

9789 BA HAN. Shin Uttamagyaw and his Tawla, a nature poem. B92 pp. 7-16.

VAJIRAVUDH, KING OF THAILAND

9790 GREENE, STEPHEN. King Wachirawut's policy of nationalism. T33 pp. 251-259.

VANOVERBERGH, MORICE

9791 FORONDA, MARCELINO A. Bibliography of Father Vanoverbergh's works. UN 42 (1969) ii-iv.

VARENNE, ALEXANDRE

9792 FREDERICK, WILLIAM H. Alexandre Varenne and politics in Indochina, 1925-1926. V43 pp. 96-159.

VARTHEMA, LUDOVICO DI

9793 GUEHLER, ULRICH. Travels of Ludovico di Varthema and his visit to Siam, Banghella and Pegu, A.D. 1505. S44.7 pp. 239-276.

VENTIMIGLIA, ANTONINO

9794 NICHOLL, ROBERT. Mission of Father Antonino Ventimiglia to Borneo. BMJ 2 pt. 4 (1972) 183-205.

VEREENIGTE OOST-INDISCHE COMPAGNIE

9795 COOLHAAS, W. PH. Reael, Coen, de Carpentier en Specx. BIJ 129 (1973) 269-276.

9796 COOLHAAS, W. PH. Wie was de Schrijver van de Tegenwerpinge tegen Coen's Kolonisatieplannen? BIJ 130 (1974) 297-305.

9797 HOFFMAN, J. E. Early policies in the Malacca jurisdiction of the United East India Company, the Malay peninsula and Netherlands East Indies attachment. JSAS 3 (1972) 1-38.

VERSCHUEREN, JAN

9798 BAAL, J. VAN. In memoriam, Pater Jan Verschueren. BIJ 127 (1971) 490-1.

VIDAL Y SOLER, SEBASTIAN

9799 RODRIGUEZ, LORENZO. Botanical garden of Manila and Sebastian Vidal y Soler. UN 35 (1962) 258-277.

ARTICLES

VIET CONG

9800 SOLA POOL, ITHIEL DE. Political alternatives to the Viet Cong. AS 7 (1967) 555-566.

VIETNAM

9801 L'annee 1966 en Asie, Vietnam. FA 22 (1968) 91-98.

9802 CHERRY, BENJAMIN. Eyewitness in south Vietnam. JCA 3 (1973) 224-233.

9803 FANON, JOSIE. Vietnam, capital of the new world. JCA 2 (1972) 442-3.

9804 FISHEL, WESLEY R. Foreword. C58 pp. v-vii.

9805 GOODMAN, ALLAN E. South Vietnam, neither war nor peace. AS 10 (1970) 107-132.

9806 HUNTINGTON, SAMUEL P. Introduction, social science and Vietnam. AS 7 (1967) 503-506.

9807 LINDHOLM, RICHARD WADSWORTH. Introduction. L52 pp. ix-xi.

9808 NGUYEN VAN CHIEN. Reflections sur les problemes actuels du Viet-Nam. RSA (1965) 183-257.

9809 1972, a great year. JCA 3 (1973) 103-105.

9810 PIKE, DOUGLAS. North Vietnam in 1971. AS 12 (1972) 16-24.

9811 PIKE, DOUGLAS. North Vietnam in the year 1972. AS 13 (1973) 46-59.

9812 SILVERMAN, JERRY M. South Vietnam and the return to political struggle. AS 14 (1974) 65-77.

9813 TURLEY, WILLIAM S. The Democratic Republic of Vietnam and the third stage of the revolution. AS 14 (1974) 78-88.

9814 Vietnam. F56 pp. 131-151.

VIETNAM - BIBLIOGRAPHY

9815 FONTAINE, HENRI. Publications du Service Geologique de la Direction des Ressources Naturelles, Ministere de l'Economie, Republique du Vietnam. SEIB 47 (1972) 523-537.

9816 LANGLET, PHILIPPE. Elements bibliographiques d'histoire vietnamienne. SEIB 45 pt. 1 (1970) 119-126.

9817 LEGAY, ROGER. Essai de bibliographie pratique sur les populations montagnardes du sud-Vietnam, 1935-1966, par Roger Legay et Tran Van Tot. SEIB 42 (1967) 258-299.

9818 NGUYEN THE ANH. Presentation d'ouvrages recents sur l'histoire vietnamienne. SEIB 45 pt. 4 (1970) 83-88.

9819 NGUYEN THE ANH. Quelques livres recents sur les etudes vietnamiennes. SEIB 47 (1972) 760-762.

9820 Presentation d'ouvrages. SEIB 46 (1971) 89-95.

9821 THAI CONG TUNG. Ouvrages sur l'agriculture. SEIB 46 (1971) 396-397.

9822 VIDAL, J. E. Bibliographie botanique indochinoise. SEIB 47 (1972) 655-749.

Vietnam - Bibliography

9823 VO LONG TE. Dictionnaires viet-
      namiens. SEIB 47 (1972) 109-111.

9824 VO LONG TE. Presentation d'ouv-
      rages recents sur la litterature
      vietnamienne. SEIB 45 pt. 4 (1970)
      89-98.

9825 VO LONG TE. Traductions et etudes
      vietnamiennes recentes. SEIB 46
      (1971) 389-395.

VIETNAM - CONSTITUTION

9826 CORLEY, FRANCIS J. The president
      in the constitution of the Repub-
      lic of Viet-Nam. PA 34 (1961)
      165-174.

9827 DEVEREUX, ROBERT. South Vietnam's
      new constitutional structure. AS
      8 (1968) 627-645.

9828 FALL, BERNARD B. North Vietnam's
      constitution and government. PA
      33 (1960) 282-290.

VIETNAM - DESCRIPTION AND TRAVEL

9829 BOULBET, JEAN. Description de la
      vegetation en pays Ma, Boucle et
      plateau du Haut Donnai, Vietnam
      sud. SEIB 35 (1960) 545-574.

9830 GERARD, M. La region de Camau
      vers 1898. SEIB 43 (1968) 221-247.

9831 NARADA MAHA THERA. My visits to
      Viet-Nam. FA 17 (1960) 1741-1745.

VIETNAM - ECONOMIC CONDITIONS

9832 ANG DVAN NGU. Role of the masses
      in raising the standard of welfare.
      JBRS 43 (1960) 37-40.

9833 BENNETT, JOHN T. Political impli-
      cations of economic change, south
      Vietnam. AS 7 (1967) 581-591.

9834 BERTRAND, TRENT J. Evaluation of
      U.S. economic aid to Vietnam,
      1955-59. FA 21 (1966) 207-228.

9835 BUU HOAN. South Vietnamese econ-
      omy in the transition to peace
      and after. AS 11 (1971) 305-320.

9836 COLE, DAVID C. Economic setting.
      L52 pp. 176-190.
      Comment: LINDHOLM, R. W. Commen-
      tary. L52 pp. 190-192.

9837 HARNETT, JOSEPH J. Critique of
      the program for the economic in-
      tegration of the refugees. L52
      pp. 83-87.
      Comment: CARDINAUX, ALFRED L.
      Commentary. L52 pp. 87-92.
      Comment: CARROLL, M. J. Commen-
      tary. L52 pp. 95-6.
      Comment: FALL, BERNARD B. Commen-
      tary. L52 pp. 92-95.
      Comment: LE PICHON, JEAN. Commen-
      tary. L52 pp. 96-100.
      Author's reply: Father Harnett on
      Cardinaux, Fall, Carroll and Le
      Pichon. L52 pp. 101-103.

9838 HENDRY, JAMES B. Economic devel-
      opment under conditions of guer-
      rilla warfare, the case of Viet-
      nam. AS 2 (June 1962) 1-12.

9839 LE KHOA. Economic situation in
      Vietnam. AC 2 (Apr. 1960) 17-50.

9840 MISSOFFE, FRANCOIS. Perspectives
      economiques vietnamiennes. FA
      (1974 pt. 1) 7-18.

9841 NATHAN, ROBERT R. Consequences of
      partition. C58 pp. 1-8.

9842 NGUYEN KHAC NHAN. Policy of key
      rural aggrovilles. AC 3 (July
      1961) 29-49.

9843 NGUYEN TIEN HUNG. Note on north south trade, a possible economic approach to the Vietnam conflict. AS 11 (1971) 385-6.

9844 PHILIP, NICHOLAS. The Mekong, a resource for south Vietnam. AS 11 (1971) 371-375.

9845 SILVER, SOLOMON. Changes in the midst of war. AS 11 (1971) 331-340.

9846 STRUYK, RAYMOND J. Price determinants in the Republic of Vietnam, 1966-1970. MER 18 pt. 1 (1973) 74-80.

9847 TAYLOR, MILTON C. South Viet-Nam, lavish aid, limited progress. PA 34 (1961) 242-256.

9848 TSUNG TO WAY. Survey of Chinese occupations. L52 pp. 118-125.

9849 VU QUOC THUC. National planning in Vietnam. AS 1 (Sept. 1961) 3-9.

9850 WILLIAMS, ALBERT P. South Vietnam's development in a postwar era, a commentary on the Thuc-Lilienthal report. AS 11 (1971) 352-370.

VIETNAM - FOREIGN RELATIONS

9851 THAI VAN KIEM. Curiosites diplomatiques et protocolaires du Vietnam d'autrefois. SEIB 38 (1963) 583-610.

9852 THORNTON, THOMAS PERRY. Foreign relations of the Asian communist satellites. PA 35 (1962) 341-352.

VIETNAM - FOREIGN RELATIONS - BURMA

9853 PEARN, B. R. Burmese embassy to Vietnam, 1823-24. JBRS 47 (1964) 149-172.

VIETNAM - FOREIGN RELATIONS - CAMBODIA

9854 CHANDLER, DAVID P. Cambodia's relations with Siam in the early Bangkok period, the politics of a tributary state. JSS 60 pt. 1 (1972) 153-169.

9855 GURTOV, MELVIN. Indochina in north Vietnamese strategy. J28 pp. 137-154.

VIETNAM - FOREIGN RELATIONS - CHINA

9856 CHEN, KING C. Chinese occupation of Vietnam, 1945-46. FA 23 (1969) 3-28.

9857 CHEN, KING C. Hanoi vs. Peking, policies and relations, a survey. AS 12 (1972) 806-817.

9858 CHEN, KING C. North Vietnam in the Sino-Soviet dispute, 1962-64. AS 4 (1964) 1023-1036.

9859 COUGHLIN, M. Vietnam, in China's shadow. JSAH 8 (1967) 240-249.

9860 DAUDIN, PIERRE. Un japonais a la cour des Tang, Gouverneur du Protectorat d'Annam, Abe-No Nakamaro alias Tchao Heng, 698-770. SEIB 40 (1965) 217-280.

9861 GLAUBITZ, JOACHIM. Relations between communist China and Vietnam. V52 pp. 57-67.

9862 GROSSMAN, BERNHARD. The influence of the war in Vietnam on the economy of communist China. V52 pp. 68-73.

Vietnam - Foreign relations - China

9863 LAFFEY, ELLA. Content of the Sino-Vietnamese tributary relationship in the late 19th century. H42 pp. 25-35.

9864 MADING, KLAUS. Suzerainty over Annam, a legal discussion, China's traditional concept destroyed by French ascendency. S93 pp. 150-152.

9865 MARSOT, ALAIN GERARD. Anti-Manchu Chinese revolutionaries and the French authorities in Indochina. SA 2 (1972) 474-486.

9866 TAO, JAY. Mao's world outlook, Vietnam and the revolution in China. AS 8 (1968) 416-432.

9867 TRUONG BUU LAM. Comments and generalities on Sino-Vietnamese relations. H42 pp. 36-49.

9868 VASILJEV, IVO. China-north Vietnam relations. RSA (1968) 215-220. *Comment:* Discussion. RSA (1968) 221-227.

VIETNAM - FOREIGN RELATIONS - FRANCE

9869 Les forces politiques francaises et la guerre du Vietnam. FA 21 (1966) 124-135.

9870 La France et l'Asie, relations politiques et diplomatiques. FA 22 (1968) 119-123.

9871 GARNER, REUBEN. The French in Indochina, some impressions of the colonial inspectors, 1867-1913. SA 3 (1974) 830-840.

9872 GUPTA, H. R. Early phase of the freedom struggle in Indochina. S87 pp. 477-484.

9873 IRVING, R. E. M. M.R.P. and French policy in Indochina, 1945-1954, with special reference to the influence of Catholicism. FA 23 (1969) 257-269.

9874 MADING, KLAUS. Suzerainty over Annam, a legal discussion, China's traditional concept destroyed by French ascendency. S93 pp. 150-152.

9875 MARLE, ROBERT. La pacification du Tonkin, 1891-1896. SEIB 47 (1972) 37-80.

9876 NGUYEN XUAN THO. La penetration francaise au Vietnam, apres le traite de 1874. SA 1 (1971) 300-319.

9877 NGUYEN XUAN THO. La penetration francaise au Vietnam, l'attitude de la Chine et des puissances europeennes devant les evenements du Tonkin. SA 2 (1972-3) 264-284.

9878 NGUYEN XUAN THO. Le traite de 1874. SA 1 (1971) 192-207.

VIETNAM - FOREIGN RELATIONS - GREAT BRITAIN

9879 LAMB, ALASTAIR. British missions to Cochin China, 1778-1882. JMBRAS 34 pts. 3-4 (1961) 1-248.

9880 NGUYEN THE ANH. L'Angleterre et le Viet-Nam en 1803, la mission de J. W. Roberts. SEIB 40 (1965) 339-347.

9881 TARLING, NICHOLAS. British policy towards Siam, Cambodia, and Vietnam, 1842-1858. AST 4 (1966) 240-258.

9882   TARLING, NICHOLAS. British rela-
       tions with Vietnam, 1822–1858.
       JMBRAS 39 pt. 1 (1966) 19–51.

VIETNAM - FOREIGN RELATIONS - JAPAN

9883 MALMGREN, HAROLD B. The United
     States, the new Pacific basin era
     and Vietnam. AS 11 (1971) 387–398.

9884 STORRY, RICHARD. Repercussions in
     Japan. V52 pp. 74–82.

VIETNAM - FOREIGN RELATIONS - LAOS

9885 GURTOV, MELVIN. Indochina in north
     Vietnamese strategy. J28 pp. 137–
     154.

VIETNAM - FOREIGN RELATIONS - PHILIPPINES

9886 ABELLA, DOMINGO. When Filipino
     colonial troops fought in Viet-Nam
     in 1858. PHR 1 pt. 2 (1966) 1–16.

9887 ARELLANO, OSCAR J. How operation
     brotherhood got to Viet Nam. PS
     14 (1966) 396–409.

9888 BERNAD, MIGUEL A. First year of
     the PHILCAG in Viet Nam. PS 16
     (1968) 131–154.

9889 INGLES, JOSE D. Philippine posi-
     tion on the Vietnam question. PS
     14 (1966) 633–652.

VIETNAM - FOREIGN RELATIONS - THAILAND

9890 WHITMORE, JOHN K. Thai-Vietnamese
     struggle for Laos in the nineteenth
     century. L18 pp. 52–66.

Vietnam - Foreign relations - United
States

VIETNAM - FOREIGN RELATIONS - UNION OF
SOVIET SOCIALIST REPUBLICS

9891 BALLIS, WILLIAM B. Relations be-
     tween the USSR and Vietnam. V52
     pp. 43–56.

9892 CHEN, KING. North Vietnam in the
     Sino-Soviet dispute, 1962–64. AS
     4 (1964) 1023–1036.

9893 HALEVY, ZVI. Vietnamese and Chi-
     nese recipients of higher academic
     degrees in the USSR, 1962–1972.
     SA 2 (1972–3) 338–346.

VIETNAM - FOREIGN RELATIONS - UNITED
STATES

9894 BERTRAND, TRENT J. Evaluation of
     U.S. economic aid to Vietnam,
     1955–59. FA 21 (1966) 207–228.

9895 BUCHANAN, KEITH. American way of
     death, genocide in Indochina. JCA
     1 pt. 3 (1971) 100–105.

9896 DARLING, FRANK C. American policy
     in Vietnam, its role in the quake-
     land theory and international
     peace. AS 11 (1971) 818–839.

9897 DRACHMAN, EDWARD. Prospects of
     U.S. military disengagement from
     Southeast Asia. RSA (1970) 151–
     160.

9898 GARDINER, ARTHUR Z. Aspects of
     foreign aid. AC 2 (July 1960) 17–
     27.

9899 HOTHAM, DAVID. General considera-
     tion of American programs. L52
     pp. 346–354.
     Comment: DURDIN, PEGGY. Commen-
     tary. L52 p. 354.
     Comment: MECKLIN, JOHN M. Com-
     mentary. L52 pp. 354–358.
     Author's reply: L52 pp. 359–362.

Vietnam - Foreign relations - United
  States

9900 LINDHOLM, RICHARD W. American aid
     and its financial impact. L52 pp.
     317-323.
     Comment: HOTHAM, DAVID. Commen-
     tary. L52 pp. 323-325.
     Comment: HUNTER, JOHN M. Commen-
     tary. L52 pp. 327-330.
     Comment: TRAN VAN KIEN. Commen-
     tary. L52 pp. 325-327.

9901 MALMGREN, HAROLD B. The United
     States, the new Pacific basin era
     and Vietnam. AS 11 (1971) 387-
     398.

9902 O'DONNELL, JOHN B. Strategic ham-
     let program in Kien Hoa Province,
     south Vietnam, a case study of
     counter-insurgency. K86 pp. 703-
     744.

9903 OLSEN, EDWARD A. The Nixon doc-
     trine in East Asian perspective.
     AF 5 pt. 1 (1973) 17-28.

9904 POND, ELIZABETH. South Vietnamese
     politics and the American with-
     drawal. J28 pp. 1-24.

9905 SCHURMANN, FRANZ. Waning of the
     American empire. JCA 1 pt. 3
     (1971) 74-91.

9906 SIRACUSA, JOSEPH M. The United
     States, Viet Nam, and the cold war,
     a reappraisal. JSAS 5 (1974) 82-
     101.

9907 SPECTOR, RONALD. What the local
     Annamites are thinking, American
     views of Vietnamese in China,
     1942-1945. SA 3 (1974) 740-751.

9908 THAI VAN KIEM. Les premieres re-
     lations entre le Viet-Nam et les
     Etats-Unis d'Amerique. SEIB 37
     (1962) 286-310.

9909 YOUNG, KENNETH T. United States
     policy and Vietnamese political

viability, 1954-1967. AS 7 (1967)
507-514.

VIETNAM - HISTORY

9910 Bibliography on the acceptance of
     western cultures in Vietnam from
     the XVIth century to the XXth cen-
     tury. EACS 6 (1967) 228-249.

9911 BUI QUANG TUNG. La succession de
     Thieu-Tri. SEIB 42 (1967) 27-175.

9912 BUI QUANG TUNG. Tables synop-
     tiques de chronologie viet-
     namienne. BEF 51 (1963) 1-78.

9913 CHAN, HOK LAM. Chinese refugees
     in Annam and Champa at the end of
     the Sung dynasty. JSAH 7 (Sept.
     1966) 1-10.

9914 COTTER, MICHAEL G. Towards a so-
     cial history of the Vietnamese
     southward movement. JSAH 9 (1968)
     12-24.

9915 DAUDIN, PIERRE. Un japonais a la
     cour des Tang, Gouverneur du Pro-
     tectorate d'Annam, Abe-No Nakamaro
     alias Tchao Heng, 698-770. SEIB
     40 (1965) 217-280.

9916 DEVILLERS, PHILIPPE. Au sud-Viet-
     nam . . . il y a cent ans. FA 20
     (1965) 139-156.

9917 DEVILLERS, PHILIPPE. Au sud-Viet-
     nam . . . il y a cent ans. FA 20
     (1965) 325-347.

9918 HUYNH KIM KHANH. Vietnamese
     August revolution reinterpreted.
     JAS 30 (1970-1) 761-782.

9919 LANGLET, PHILIPPE. Elements bib-
     liographiques d'histoire viet-
     namienne. SEIB 45 pt. 1 (1970)
     119-126.

9920 LANGLET, PHILIPPE. La tradition
vietnamienne, un etat national au
sein de la civilisation chinoise.
SEIB 45 pts. 2-3 (1970) 1-52.

9921 MARLE, ROBERT. La pacification du
Tonkin, 1891-1896. SEIB 47 (1972)
37-80.

9922 MURAKAMI, HIDEO. Viet Nam and the
question of Chinese aggression.
JSAH 7 (Sept. 1966) 11-26.

9923 NGUYEN DANG THUC. Origins of the
Vietnamese people. AC 3 (Jan.
1961) 17-39.

9924 NGUYEN KHAC KHAM. Acceptance of
western cultures in Vietnam from
the XVIth century to the XXth century. EACS 6 (1967) 201-227.

9925 NGUYEN THE ANH. L'Angleterre et
le Viet-Nam en 1803, la mission de
J. W. Roberts. SEIB 40 (1965) 339-
347.

9926 NGUYEN THE ANH. Presentation
d'ouvrages recents sur l'histoire
vietnamienne. SEIB 45 pt. 4
(1970) 83-88.

9927 NGUYEN THE ANH. Les publications
de documents historiques dans la
Republique du Vietnam depuis 1955.
SEIB 43 (1968) 53-60.

9928 PHAN THANH SON. Le mouvement
ouvrier vietnamien de 1920 a 1930.
C28 pp. 164-188.

9929 PHUNG VAN DAN. La formation ter-
ritoriale du Viet Nam. RSA (1963)
247-294.

9930 SMITH, R. B. Cycle of Confucian-
ization in Vietnam. V43 pp. 1-29.

9931 SMITH, R. B. Thailand and Vietnam,
some thoughts towards a comparative

historical analysis. JSS 60 pt. 2
(1972) 1-21.

9932 TEXIER, MURIEL. Le Mandarinat au
Viet-Nam au XIXe siecle. SEIB 37
(1962) 327-376.

9933 WHITMORE, JOHN K. Vietnamese
adaptations of Chinese government
structure in the fifteenth century. H42 pp. 1-10.

VIETNAM - LAWS, STATUTES, ETC.

9934 CHEN CHING HO. On the rules and
regulations of the Duong-Thuong
Hoi-Quan at Faifo (Hoi-an), central Vietnam. SAA 2 (1969) 148-
156.

9935 GINSBURGS, GEORGE. Soviet sources
on the law of north Vietnam. AS
13 (1973) 659-676.

9936 GINSBURGS, GEORGE. Soviet sources
on the law of north Vietnam. AS
13 (1973) 980-988.

9937 NGUYEN XUAN CHANH. Widow's
statute in Vietnamese customary
law. C39 pp. 252-261.

9938 OSBORNE, MILTON E. Debate on a
legal code for colonial Cochinchina, the 1869 commission. JSAH
10 (1969) 224-235.

VIETNAM - MINORITIES *See also* BAHNAR,
BLACK TAI, BRU, CHAM, CHINESE, CHRAU,
CHUA, DEN, DINH, HMONG, JORAI, JEH,
KATU, KAYON, LAC, MAA, MIIR, MNONG,
MOI, MONTAGNARDS, NUNG, ROGLAI, SRE,
YAO

9939 GREGERSON, MARILYN J. Ethnic minorities of Vietnam. SA 2 (1972-
73) 11-17.

9962 THEBAULT, E. P. Le tragique destin d'un emperor d'Annam, Prince Vinh-San, 1900-1945, Empereur Duy-Tan, 1907-1916. FA 24 (1970) 3-40.

9963 WURFEL, DAVID. Saigon political elite, focus on four cabinets. AS 7 (1967) 527-539.

9964 YOUNG, KENNETH T. United States policy and Vietnamese political viability, 1954-1967. AS 7 (1967) 507-514.

VIETNAM - POLITICS AND GOVERNMENT - 1954-1963

9965 BUTTINGER, JOSEPH. Miracle of Viet-Nam. L52 pp. 9-31.

9966 CASEY, R. G. Summary of Viet-Nam's political and economic progress. L52 pp. 333-339.
Comment: HENDERSON, WILLIAM. Commentary. L52 pp. 342-3.
Comment: PRICE, HOYT. Commentary. L52 pp. 339-341.
Author's reply: L52 pp. 343-4.
Comment: HENDERSON, WILLIAM. Commentary. L52 pp. 344-5.

9967 CHRISTIAN, JEAN. Liberte de l'Asie. FA 18 (1962) 73-83.

9968 DONNELL, JOHN C. Personalism in Vietnam. C58 pp. 29-67.

9969 DORSEY, JOHN T. Stresses and strains in a developing administrative system. C58 pp. 139-152.

9970 FALL, BERNARD B. North Vietnam's constitution and government. PA 33 (1960) 282-290.

9971 FALL, BERNARD B. Problemes politiques des etats poly-ethniques en Indochine. FA 18 (1962) 129-152.

Vietnam - Politics and government - 1954-1963

9972 FISHEL, WESLEY R. Political realities in Vietnam. AS 1 (Apr. 1961) 15-23.

9973 FISHEL, WESLEY R. Problems of democratic growth in free Vietnam. C58 pp. 9-28.

9974 HAMMER, ELLEN J. South Viet Nam, the limits of political action. PA 35 (1962) 24-36.

9975 JOINER, CHARLES A. Organizing bureaucrats, south Vietnam's National Revolutionary Civil Servants' League, by Charles A. Joiner and Roy Jumper. AS 3 (1963) 203-215.

9976 JOINER, CHARLES A. South Vietnam's Buddhist crisis, organization for charity, dissidence, and unity. AS 4 (1964) 915-928.

9977 MANSFIELD, MIKE. Introduction. C58 pp. ix-xiv.

9978 SCIGLIANO, ROBERT G. Budget process in south Vietnam. PA 33 (1960) 48-60.

9979 SCIGLIANO, ROBERT G. Vietnam, politics and religion. AS 4 (1964) 666-673.

9980 SINGH, L. P. Laos and Vietnam since Dien Bien Phu. RSA (1965) 145-158.

9981 TRAN VAN MINH. Can Vietnam be neutralist? AC 3 (July 1961) 1-12.

9982 VUONG VAN BAC. Why did the Vietnamese intelligentsia fail in its leadership responsibility toward the nation? AC 3 (July 1961) 13-28.

Vietnam - Politics and government - 1963-

VIETNAM - POLITICS AND GOVERNMENT - 1963-

9983 BULLINGTON, JAMES R. South Vietnamese countryside, non-Communist political perceptions, by James R. Bullington and James D. Rosenthal. AS 10 (1970) 651-661.

9984 BURCHETT, WILFRED. Excerpt of an interview. JCA 3 (1973) 385-6.

9985 DEVEREUX, ROBERT. South Vietnam's new constitutional structure. AS 8 (1968) 627-645.

9986 DONNELL, JOHN C. South Vietnam, struggle politics and the bigger war, by John C. Donnell and Charles A. Joiner. AS 7 (1967) 53-68.

9987 FISHEL, WESLEY R. Eleventh hour in Vietnam. AS 5 (1965) 98-107.

9988 GOODMAN, ALLAN E. End of the war as a setting for the future development of south Vietnam. AS 11 (1971) 341-351.

9989 GOODMAN, ALLAN E. South Vietnam and the politics of self support, by Allan E. Goodman, Randolph Harris and John C. Wood. AS 11 (1971) 1-25.

9990 HOADLEY, J. STEPHEN. Coalition building in south Vietnam, a critique. AF 3 (1971) 67-8.

9991 HUYNH VAN LY. Two existing south Vietnamese administrations. JCA 4 (1974) 170-179.

9992 JOINER, CHARLES A. South Vietnam, the politics of peace. AS 9 (1969) 138-155.

9993 KING, PETER. Political balance in Saigon. PA 44 (1971) 401-420.

9994 KOLKO, GABRIEL. Dynamics of reconstruction and victory, the PRG of south Vietnam. JCA 4 (1974) 71-76.

9995 LE PHONG. Speech at a press conference held on June 5, on the occasion of the first anniversary of the P.R.G. JCA 1 pt. 1 (1970) 97-102.

9996 NGUYEN THI BINH. PRG elaborates a number of points in the 10 point overall solution. JCA 1 pt. 2 (1970) 76-79.

9997 NGUYEN THI BINH. 7 point statement by the PRG of south Vietnam. JCA 1 pt. 4 (1971) 84-86.

9998 POND, ELIZABETH. South Vietnamese politics and the American withdrawal. J28 pp. 1-24.

9999 SACKS, I. MILTON. Restructuring government in south Vietnam. AS 7 (1967) 515-526.

10000 TAI SUNG AN. Fourth national assembly of north Vietnam, significant developments. AS 12 (1972) 310-316.

10001 TURLEY, WILLIAM S. The DRV since the death of Ho Chi Minh, the politics of a revolution in transition. J28 pp. 25-45.

VIETNAM - RELIGION *See also* BUDDHISM, CAODAISM, CATHOLIC CHURCH

10002 BANKER, JOHN E. Bahnar religion. SA 2 (1972-3) 88-124.

10003 COBBEY, VURNELL. Some northern Roglai beliefs about the supernatural. SA 2 (1972-3) 125-129.

10004   TRAN VAN TOAN. La sainte reli-
        gion de l'immortelle celeste dans
        la region de Hue, centre Viet-
        Nam. RSA (1966) 77-102.

10005   TRAN VAN TOAN. La sainte reli-
        gion de l'immortelle celeste dans
        la region de Hue, centre Viet-
        Nam. RSA (1966) 241-258.

10006   TRAN VAN TOAN. La sainte reli-
        gion de l'immortelle celeste dans
        la region de Hue. RSA (1967)
        103-130.

10007   TRAN VAN TOAN. Le temple Hue-Nam
        a Hue. SEIB 44 (1969) 245-276.

VIETNAM - SOCIAL CONDITIONS

10008   LE VAN HOANG. La stratification
        et la mobilite sociale au Viet-
        Nam. EACS 4 (1965) 205-226.

10009   SORENSON, JOHN L. Social bases
        of instability in rural Southeast
        Asia. AS 9 (1969) 540-545.

10010   THAI VAN KIEM. Les fetes tradi-
        tionnelles vietnamiennes. SEIB
        36 (1961) 53-67.

10011   TRAN QUANG THUAN. Some aspects
        of the Vietnamese society. AC 2
        (July 1960) 47-67.

10012   WOODSIDE, ALEXANDER. Development
        of social organizations in Viet-
        namese cities in the late colonial
        period. PA 44 (1971) 39-64.

VIETNAM - TREATIES

10013   NGUYEN XUAN THO. La penetration
        francaise au Vietnam, apres le
        traite de 1874. SA 1 (1971) 300-
        319.

10014   NGUYEN XUAN THO. Le traite de
        1874. SA 1 (1971) 192-207.

VIETNAM. GEOLOGIC SERVICE

10015   FONTAINE, HENRI. Publications du
        Service Geologique de la Direc-
        tion des Ressources Naturelles,
        Ministere de l'Economie, Repub-
        lique du Vietnam. SEIB 47 (1972)
        523-537.

10016   HOANG THI THAN. Le Service Geo-
        logique de l'Indochine, 1898-
        1953. Le Service Geologique de la
        Republique du Vietnam, depuis
        1953. SEIB 48 (1973) 607-617.

VIETNAM WAR

10017   L'agression communiste au Viet-
        nam. FA 20 (1965) 481-496.

10018   American Catholic bishops on
        Vietnam and peace. FA 21 (1966)
        237-240.

10019   BOUDAREL, GEORGES. Essai sur la
        pensee militaire vietnamienne.
        C28 pp. 460-495.

10020   CALDWELL, MALCOLM. Origins of
        the Indo-China war. RSAS 1 pt. 2
        (1971) 1-16.

10021   DALBY, MARION C. Operations in
        Vietnam. S51 pp. 247-264.

10022   DAY, HARRY R. Speculations on
        early Vietnam protests, with
        primary focus upon a would be
        draft card burning. GEJ 14
        (1967) 1-15.

10023   Documents gouvernementaux rela-
        tifs aux crimes de guerre au
        Vietnam. FA 21 (1966) 563-574.

Vietnam war

10024 Les forces politiques francaises et la guerre du Vietnam. FA 21 (1966) 124-135.

10025 HOANG XUAN HAN. Reflections sur la treve du tet au Vietnam. FA 20 (1965) 253-256.

10026 JACOBINI, M. B. Non-nuclear footnote to Dien Bien Phu. AF 2 (1970) 168-171.

10027 Japan and the Vietnam war. FA 20 (1965) 239-251.

10028 JOHNSTONE, WILLIAM C. Politics of the Vietnam war, a look at the record. S98 pp. 21-30.

10029 JOINER, CHARLES A. Ubiquity of the administrative role in counterinsurgency. AS 7 (1967) 540-554.

10030 KIM, KWAN S. Economic impact of the Vietnam war in Southeast and East Asia, with special references to balance of payments effects. AF 2 (1970) 22-31.

10031 LAM NGUYEN ANH. Geneva agreement and the Sisyhean war. AC 2 (July 1960) 29-36.

10032 LANOUE, HENRI. Comment a debute la guerre du Vietnam, le massacre de Haiphong, 23 novembre 1946. C28 pp. 265-291.

10033 Laos' role in the Indochina war, Douglas Miles interviews a member of north Vietnam's Central Committee. L18 pp. 460-462.

10034 LIM CHONG YAH. The Singapore economy and the Vietnam war, by Lim Chong Yah and Ow Chwee Huay. Y52 pp. 352-369.

10035 McALISTER, JOHN T. Mountain minorities and the Viet Minh, a key to the Indochina war. K86 pp. 771-844.

10036 PLUVIER, JAN. The Vietnamese war of independence, 1945-54, and historical objectivity. JCA 3 (1973) 277-291.

10037 RACE, JEFFREY. Mutual self limitation in civil war, the case of Vietnam. SA 2 (1972-3) 210-230.

10038 ROLPH, HAMMOND. Vietnamese communism and the protracted war. AS 12 (1972) 783-792.

10039 SACKS, MILTON. Background to the Vietnam war, an introduction. V52 pp. 1-7.

10040 THANT, U. U Thant on Vietnam. FA 21 (1966) 115-6.

10041 TILMAN, ROBERT O. Non-lessons of the Malayan emergency. AS 6 (1966) 407-419.

10042 WAITE, JAMES L. Sweden and the Vietnam criticism. SA 2 (1972-3) 454-473.

10043 WRIGHT, QUINCY. Legal aspects of the Vietnam war. S98 pp. 31-54.

VIETNAM WAR - 1954-1963

10044 Analyse politique de la guerre actuelle au sud-Vietnam. FA 20 (1965) 363-392.

10045 CHRISTIAN, JEAN. La fin d'une guerre ou l'acceleration de l'histoire. FA 17 (1960) 1678-1688.

10046 DEVILLERS, PHILIPPE. La lutte pour la reunification du Vietnam entre 1954 et 1961. C28 pp. 329–355.

10047 LACOUTURE, JEAN. Situation de l'Indochine. FA 17 (1960) 2035–2042.

10048 NEILANDS, J. B. Vietnam, progress of the chemical war. AS 10 (1970) 209–229.

10049 NGO VINH LONG. Leaf abscission. G79 pp. 201–213.

10050 O'DONNELL, JOHN B. Strategic hamlet program in Kien Hoa Province, south Vietnam, a case study of counter-insurgency. K86 pp. 703–744.

10051 RACE, JEFFREY. Origins of the second Indochina war. AS 10 (1970) 359–382.

10052 SCIGLIANO, ROBERT. Vietnam, a country at war. AS 3 (1963) 48–54.

10053 WILLIAMS, LEA E. Military doctrines of Mao Tse Tung applied to Vietnam. JSAH 4 (Sept. 1963) 128–133.

10054 ZASLOFF, JOSEPH J. Rural resettlement in south Viet Nam, the agroville program. PA 35 (1962) 327–340.

VIETNAM WAR – 1963–

10055 Air war in Indochina. JCA 2 (1972) 99–111.

10056 Applicability of the policy of containment in Asia. V52 pp. 83–98.

10057 BENOIT, EMILE. Impacts of the end of Vietnam hostilities and the reduction of British military presence in Malaysia and Singapore. S63 pp. 582–671.

10058 BERNAD, MIGUEL A. First year of the PHILCAG in Viet Nam. PS 16 (1968) 131–154.

10059 CHAUVEL, JEAN. Vingt ans apres les accords de Geneve. FA (1974 pt. 2) 5–17.

10060 CHOMSKY, NOAM. Cambodia in conflict. G79 pp. 34–51.

10061 DEVILLERS, PHILIPPE. Vietnam, the way to an honorable peace. FA 21 (1966) 593–598.

10062 DOMMEN, ARTHUR J. Laos, the year of the Ho Chi Minh trail. AS 12 (1972) 138–147.

10063 DONNELL, JOHN C. Pacification reassessed. AS 7 (1967) 567–576.

10064 DUFF, PEGGY. The Paris accords. JCA 3 (1973) 204–211.

10065 FALK, RICHARD A. The Cambodian operation and international law. G79 pp. 150–171.

10066 FISHEL, WESLEY R. Vietnam, the broadening war. AS 6 (1966) 49–58.

10067 GALULA, DAVID. Military considerations in Vietnam. V52 pp. 29–42.

10068 GIRLING, J. L. S. Nixon's Algeria, doctrine and disengagement in Indochina. PA 44 (1971) 527–544.

10069 GOODMAN, ALLAN E. Is it too late to end the Vietnam war? SA 1 (1971) 364–377.

Vietnam war - 1963-

10070   GOODMAN, ALLAN E.   Leaving the future up for grabs, the political consequences of the Vietnam cease fire.   AQ (1973) 93-109.

10071   GOODMAN, ALLAN E.   South Vietnam and the new security.   AS 12 (1972) 121-137.

10072   HONEY, P. J.   North Vietnam's model of strategy and tactics for revolution.   V52 pp. 8-28.

10073   HOWELL, JOHN M.   The Vietnam war, intervention, and the changing concept of domestic matters.   S98 pp. 55-64.

10074   HUYNH KIM KHANH.   War in Viet Nam, the U.S. official line.   PA 42 (1969) 58-67.

10075   JADOUL, IVAN.   Les dimensions nouvelles de la guerre au Vietnam.   RSA (1970) 161-180.

10076   Joint declaration of the summit conference of the Indo-Chinese peoples, April 25, 1970.   JCA 1 pt. 1 (1970) 90-96.

10077   KELLEN, KONRAD.   1971 and beyond, the view from Hanoi.   J28 pp. 99-112.

10078   KIM, JUNG-GUN.   Reflections on recent international politics, United Nations, and the Viet-Nam war.   S98 pp. 80-96.

10079   KOLKO, GABRIEL.   Vietnam, the illusion of withdrawal.   JCA 1 pt. 4 (1971) 33-39.

10080   KOLKO, GABRIEL.   War crimes and the nature of the Vietnam war.   JCA 1 pt. 1 (1970) 5-14.

10081   LACOUTURE, JEAN.   From the Vietnam war to an Indochina war.   G79 pp. 7-19.

10082   LANGER, PAUL F.   Laos, preparing for a settlement in Vietnam.   AS 9 (1969) 69-74.

10083   LE DUC THO.   Le Duc Tho sums up cease fire accord.   JCA 3 (1973) 118-120.

10084   LE DUC THO.   Statement, May 12, 1972.   JCA 2 (1972) 318-321.

10085   Negociations de Paris et le probleme vietnamien.   FA 23 (1969) 349-352.

10086   NGUYEN KHAC VIEN.   Culture and revolution in Vietnam, by Nguyen Khac Vien and Ly Van Sau.   JCA 3 (1973) 473-482.

10087   NGUYEN T.   Les catholiques vietnamiens et les perspectives de paix au Vietnam.   FA 22 (1968) 221-232.

10088   NGUYEN VAN HIEU.   Six point proposal to two party conference.   JCA 3 (1973) 253-256.

10089   NGUYEN VAN HIEU.   Statement.   JCA 3 (1973) 379-385.

10090   POPKIN, SAMUEL L.   Pacification, politics and the village.   AS 10 (1970) 662-671.

10091   RACE, JEFFREY.   How they won.   AS 10 (1970) 628-650.

10092   RAVENAL, EARL C.   Was Vietnam a mistake?   AS 14 (1974) 589-607.

10093   REISKY DE DUBNIC, VLADIMIR.   Global realignment of forces, its impact on the Indochina question.   AQ (1974) 17-41.

10094   The revolution will win.   JCA 2 (1972) 451-454.

10095 ROUCEK, JOSEPH S. Cambodia in geopolitics. RSA (1970) 197-223.

10096 RUPEN, ROBERT A. Vietnam and the Sino-Soviet dispute, a summary. V52 pp. 99-118.

10097 SCOTT, PETER DALE. Syndrome of U.S. escalation. G79 pp. 20-33.

10098 SILVER, SOLOMON. Changes in the midst of war. AS 11 (1971) 331-340.

10099 SILVERMAN, JERRY MARK. South Vietnam and the elusive peace. AS 13 (1973) 19-45.

10100 Statement of the Government of the Democratic Republic of Vietnam on Nixon's crazy war escalation and order to mine north Vietnamese harbours. JCA 2 (1972) 227-229.

10101 TURLEY, WILLIAM S. Civil-military relations in north Vietnam. AS 9 (1969) 879-899.

10102 U.S. puppet war crimes in south Vietnam since Nixon's inauguration. JCA 1 pt. 3 (1971) 118-122.

10103 Vietnam cease fire agreement. JCA 3 (1973) 239-248.

10104 Vietnam rectors appeal. JCA 2 (1972) 449-451.

10105 WEISS, PETER. Air attacks on the Democratic Republic of Vietnam by the U.S.A. on 21 November 1970. JCA 1 pt. 2 (1970) 1-8.

10106 WOLF, CHARLES. Vietnam prospects and precepts. AS 9 (1969) 157-162.

10107 ZINN, HOWARD. Vacating the premises in Vietnam. AS 9 (1969) 862-867.

VIETNAMESE

10108 POOLE, PETER A. Notes and comment: Thailand's Vietnamese refugees, can they be assimilated? PA 40 (1967) 324.

10109 POOLE, PETER A. Thailand's Vietnamese minority. AS 7 (1967) 886-895.

10110 POOLE, PETER A. The Vietnamese in Cambodia and Thailand, their role in interstate relations. AS 14 (1974) 325-337.

VIETNAMESE LANGUAGE

10111 BARKER, MILTON E. Phonological adaptation of French loanwords in Vietnamese. M59 pp. 138-147.

10112 BARKER, MILTON E. Vietnamese-Muong tone correspondences. Z52 pp. 9-27.

10113 DANG THAI MAI. Place of Vietnamese language in the building of a new culture of the Vietnamese people. JBRS 43 (1960) 33-36.

10114 DURAND, MAURICE. Les impressifs en vietnamien, etude preliminaire. SEIB 36 (1961) 1-50.

10115 DURAND, MAURICE. Transcriptions de la langue vietnamienne et l'oeuvre des missionnaires europeens. S93 pp. 288-294.

10116 GREGERSON, KENNETH J. Study of middle Vietnamese phonology. SEIB 44 (1969) 131-193.

Vietnamese language

VIETNAMESE LITERATURE

10139 LE QUY DON. Notes des choses vues et entendues (Kien van tieu luc). SEIB 48 (1973) 51–116.

10140 LE XUAN KHOA. Philosophy of life in classical Vietnamese literature. AC 3 (Jan. 1961) 41–47.

10141 MUCKA, JAN. Quelques remarques sur le conte vietnamien de la period de 1930–1945. AAS 10 (1974) 113–123.

10142 MUCKA, JAN. Quelques remarques sur la prose realistique vietnamienne. AAS 9 (1973) 65–79.

10143 O'HARROW, STEPHEN. Some background notes on Nhat Linh (Nguyen Tuong Tam, 1906–1963). FA 22 (1968) 205–220.

10144 PHAM VIET TUYEN. Traditional humanistic ideal in Vietnamese literature. AC 2 (July 1960) 115–126.

10145 THAI VAN KIEM. Nguyen Truong To, patriote, reformiste, poete et homme d'action. SEIB 47 (1972) 489–502.

10146 VO LONG TE. Chronique culturelle: presence du poete, Nguyen Dinh Chieu, 1822–1888. SEIB 46 (1971) 375–385.

10147 VO LONG TE. Contribution a l'etude d'un des premiers poemes narratifs d'inspiration catholique en langue vietnamienne romanisee, Ine tu dao van, ou, le martyre d'Agnes. SEIB 42 (1967) 307–336.

10148 VO LONG TE. L'experience poetique et l'itineraire spirituel de Han Mac Tu. SEIB 47 (1972) 567–652.

10149 VO LONG TE. Presentation d'ouvrages recents sur la litterature vietnamienne. SEIB 45 pt. 4 (1970) 89–98.

VILALLONGA, JOAQUIN

10150 BERNAD, MIGUEL A. Father Joaquin Vilallonga, 1868–1963. PS 12 (1964) 32–50.

VILLA, JOSE GARCIA

10151 TINIO, ROLANDO S. Villa's values, or, the poet you cannot always make out, or succeed in liking once you are able to. M24 pp. 722–738.

VILLAGE STUDIES

10152 SOLHEIM, WILHELM G. Importance of anthropological research to the Mekong Valley Project, by Wilhelm G. Solheim and Robert A. Hackenberg. FA 17 (1960) 2459–2474.

10153 Traditional and modern patterns of rural leadership and authority in countries of Southern Asia. L23 pp. 83–106.

10154 ZAMORA, MARIO D. Toward a science of social man, community development and anthropology. GEJ 12 (1966) 172–188.

VILLAGE STUDIES – BURMA

10155 BROHM, JOHN. Buddhism and animism in a Burmese village. JAS 22 (1962–3) 155–167.

10156 HUKE, ROBERT E. Mayan-Lajung, changing land use and capital investment. JBRS 45 (1962) 193–203.

Village studies - Burma

10157 KYAN. Village administration in Upper Burma during 1886-87. JBRS 52 (Dec. 1969) 67-80.

10158 LEHMAN, F. K. Burma, Kayah society as a function of the Shan-Burma-Karen context. S84 pp. 1-104.

10159 MAUNG KYI. Process of communication in modernisation of rural society, a survey report on two Burmese villages. MER 18 pt. 1 (1973) 55-73.

10160 NASH, JUNE C. Living with nats, an analysis of animism in Burman village social relations. C66 pp. 117-136.

10161 NASH, MANNING. Party building in Upper Burma. AS 3 (1963) 197-202.

10162 NEEDHAM, RODNEY. Structural analysis of Aimol society. BIJ 116 (1960) 81-108.

10163 PFANNER, DAVID E. Buddhist monk in rural Burmese society. C66 pp. 77-96.

10164 PFANNER, DAVID E. Theravada Buddhism and village economic behavior, a Burmese and Thai comparison, by David E. Pfanner and Jasper Ingersoll. JAS 21 (1961-62) 341-361.

VILLAGE STUDIES - CAMBODIA

10165 EBIHARA, MAY. Interrelations between Buddhism and social systems in Cambodian peasant culture. C66 pp. 175-196.

VILLAGE STUDIES - INDONESIA

10166 ADAMS, MARIE JEANNE. Symbols of the organized community in east Sumba, Indonesia. BIJ 130 (1974) 324-347.

10167 ADAMS, MARIE JEANNE. Work patterns and symbolic structures in a village culture, east Sumba, Indonesia. SA 1 (1971) 320-334.

10168 BARNES, R. H. Lamalerap, a whaling village in eastern Indonesia. IND 17 (1974) 136-159.

10169 BOEKKE, J. H. Village reconstruction. J32 pp. 301-315.

10170 CHABOT, HENDRIK T. Bontoramba, a village of Goa, south Sulawesi. K52 pp. 189-209.

10171 COOLEY, FRANK L. Allang, a village on Ambon Island. K52 pp. 129-156.

10172 COOLEY, FRANK L. Village government in the central Moluccas. IND 7 (1969) 139-163.

10173 CRYSTAL, ERIC. Cooking pot politics, a Toraja village study. IND 18 (1974) 118-151.

10174 CUNNINGHAM, CLARK E. Order in the Atoni house. BIJ 120 (1964) 34-68.

10175 CUNNINGHAM, CLARK E. Soba, an Atoni village of west Timor. K52 pp. 63-89.

10176 DANANDJAJA, JAMES. Comparative analysis of kinship in central Kalimantan and Nias. SMJ 19 (1971) 237-252.

10177 GOETHALS, PETER R. Karang Rarak, a 1955 vignette. IND 4 (1967) 110-126.

10178 GOETHALS, PETER R. Rarak, a
       swidden village of west Sumbawa.
       K52 pp. 30-62.

10179 GOETHALS, PETER R. Sumbawan vil-
       lage. S58 pp. 12-23.

10180 KOENTJARANINGRAT. Survey of so-
       cial studies on rural Indonesia.
       K52 pp. 1-29.

10181 KOENTJARANINGRAT. The village in
       Indonesia today. K52 pp. 386-405.

10182 NEEDHAM, RODNEY. Endeh, termi-
       nology, alliance and analysis.
       BIJ 124 (1968) 305-335.

10183 OOSTERWAL, GOTTFRIED. Muremarew,
       a dual organized village on the
       Mamberamo, West Irian. K52 pp.
       157-188.

10184 POUWER, J. Structural and func-
       tional approach in cultural
       anthropology, theoretical reflec-
       tions with reference to research
       in western New Guinea. BIJ 122
       (1966) 129-144.

10185 SKINNER, G. WILLIAM. Nature of
       loyalties in rural Indonesia.
       S58 pp. 1-11.

VILLAGE STUDIES - INDONESIA - BALI

10186 BELO, JANE. A study of a Bali-
       nese family. B43 pp. 350-370.

10187 GEERTZ, CLIFFORD. Tihingan, a
       Balinese village. BIJ 120 (1964)
       1-33.

10188 GEERTZ, CLIFFORD. Tihingan, a
       Balinese village. K52 pp. 210-
       243.

10189 GEERTZ, HILDRED. Balinese vil-
       lage. S58 pp. 24-33.

10190 GORIS, R. Religious character of
       the village community. B18 pp.
       77-100.

10191 I WAYAN BHADRA. Nonconformity in
       villages of northern Bali. B19
       pp. 189-198.

10192 KORN, V. E. Village republic of
       Tenganan Pegeringsingan. B18 pp.
       301-368.

VILLAGE STUDIES - INDONESIA - JAVA

10193 DAM, H. TEN. Cooperation and so-
       cial structure in the village of
       Chibodas. J32 pp. 345-382.

10194 GEERTZ, CLIFFORD. Javanese vil-
       lage. S58 pp. 34-41.

10195 HANSEN, GARY. Episodes in rural
       modernization, problems in the
       Bimas program. IND 11 (1971) 63-
       81.

10196 KOENTJARANINGRAT. Tjelapar, a
       village in south central Java.
       K52 pp. 244-280.

10197 KUNTOWIDJOJO. Economic and reli-
       gious attitudes of entrepreneurs
       in a village industry, notes on
       the community of Batur. IND 12
       (1971) 47-55.

10198 MASRI SINGARIMBUN. Marriage and
       divorce in Mojolama, by Masri
       Singarimbun and Chris Manning.
       IND 17 (1974) 67-82.

10199 PALMER, ANDREA WILCOX. Situradja,
       a village in highland Priangan.
       K52 pp. 299-325.

Village studies - Indonesia - Java

10200 PALMER, ANDREA WILCOX. Sundanese village. S58 pp. 42-51.

10201 SOEBOER BOEDHISANTOSO. Djakarsa, a fruit producing village near Djakarta. K52 pp. 326-347.

VILLAGE STUDIES - INDONESIA - KALIMANTAN

10202 DANANDJAJA, JAMES. Comparative analysis of kinship in central Kalimantan and Nias. SMJ 19 (1971) 237-252.

10203 HUDSON, ALFRED B. Padju Epat Ma'anjan Dajak in historical perspective. IND 4 (1967) 8-42.

10204 HUDSON, ALFRED B. Telang, a Ma'anjan village of central Kalimantan, by Alfred B. and Judith M. Hudson. K52 pp. 90-114.

10205 HUDSON, JUDITH M. Letters from Kalimantan. IND 1 (1966) 76-88.

10206 HUDSON, JUDITH M. Letters from Kalimantan, II. IND 2 (1966) 25-35.

10207 HUDSON, JUDITH M. Letters from Kalimantan, III. IND 3 (1967) 121-133.

VILLAGE STUDIES - INDONESIA - SUMATRA

10208 BACHTIAR, HARSJA W. Negeri Taram, a Minangkabau village community. K52 pp. 348-385.

10209 BRUNNER, EDWARD M. Toba Batak village. S58 pp. 52-64.

10210 JASPAN, M. A. Symbols at work, aspects of kinetic and mnemonic representation in Redjang ritual. BIJ 123 (1967) 476-516.

10211 KAMPTO UTOMO. Villages of unplanned resettlers in the sub-district Kaliredjo, central Lampung. K52 pp. 281-298.

10212 MASRI SINGARIMBUN. Kutagamber, a village of the Karo. K52 pp. 115-128.

10213 THOMAS, KENNETH D. Shifting cultivation and smallholder rubber production in a south Sumatran village. MER 10 pt. 1 (1965) 100-115.

VILLAGE STUDIES - LAOS

10214 BARNEY, G. LINWOOD. Meo of Xieng Khouang Province, Laos. K86 pp. 271-294.

10215 COWARD, E. WALTER. Agrarian modernization and village leadership, irrigation leaders in Laos. AF 3 (1971) 158-163.

10216 COWARD, E. WALTER. Differentiation of synaptic leadership in rural Laos. JAS 30 (1970-1) 135.

10217 KANDRE, PETER. Autonomy and integration of social systems, the Iu Mien (Yao or Man) mountain population and their neighbors. K86 pp. 583-638.

10218 SANG SEUNSOM. Quelques indications elementaires et generales sur les differenciations sociales peu accentuees existant parmi les populations du Laos rural et sur les modifications moderees et peu frequentes intervenant dans cette gradation sociale faiblement differenciee caracterisant les habitants des communautes villageoises Lao. EACS 4 (1965) 133-137.

10219 STANTON, THOMAS H. Conflict in
       Laos, the village point of view.
       AS 8 (1968) 887-900.

VILLAGE STUDIES - MALAYSIA

10220 DOWNS, RICHARD E. A Kelantanese
       village of Malaya. S84 pp. 105-
       186.

10221 DOWNS, RICHARD E. A rural com-
       munity in Kelantan Malaya, a
       brief account of its socio-
       economic organization and regional
       setting. S90.1 pp. 51-62.

10222 FEE. Kampong Padre, a Tamil set-
       tlement near Bagan Serai, Perak.
       JMBRAS 36 pt. 1 (1963) 153-181.

10223 FIRTH, RAYMOND. Faith and scep-
       ticism in Kelantan village magic.
       K33 pp. 190-224.

10224 HARRISSON, TOM. Malohs of Kali-
       mantan, ethnological notes. SMJ
       12 (1965) 236-350.

10225 HO, ROBERT. Evolution of agri-
       culture and land ownership in
       Saiong Mukim. MER 13 pt. 2
       (1968) 81-102.

10226 HUSIN ALI, S. Patterns of rural
       leadership in Malaya. JMBRAS 41
       pt. 1 (1968) 95-145.

10227 JONES, GAVIN W. Employment
       characteristics of small towns in
       Malaya. MER 10 pt. 1 (1965) 44-
       72.

10228 KUCHIBA, MAUO. Cooperation pat-
       terns in a Malay village, by Mauo
       Kuchiba and Yoshihiro Tsubouchi.
       AS 8 (1968) 836-841.

10229 LEE, Y. L. Kukup, a Chinese
       fishing village in south west
       Malaya. JTG 16 (1962) 131-148.

10230 NASH, MANNING. Ethnicity, cen-
       trality and education in Pasir
       Mas. K33 pp. 243-258.

10231 NEVILLE, R. J. W. Urban study of
       Pontian Kechil, south west Ma-
       laya. JTG 16 (1962) 32-56.

10232 PURCAL, J. Labour utilization
       among men in a padi village in
       Province Wellesley. MER 10 pt.
       2 (1965) 49-60.

10233 RAYBECK, DOUGLAS A. Social
       stress and social structure in
       Kelantan village life. K33 pp.
       225-242.

10234 ROGERS, MARVIN L. Politicization
       and political development in a
       rural Malay community. AS 9
       (1969) 919-933.

10235 SANDIN, BENEDICT. Bisayah of
       Limbang. SMJ 19 (1971) 1-20.

10236 SANDIN, BENEDICT. Iban leaders.
       SMJ 18 (1970) 89-161.

10237 SATHER, CLIFFORD A. Kampong Se-
       lanyau, social and economic or-
       ganization of a Kedayan rice
       growing village in Sarawak, by
       Clifford A. Sather and Hatta
       Solhee. SMJ 22 (1974) 249-266.

10238 WINZELER, ROBERT L. Ethnic com-
       plexity and ethnic relations in
       an east coast Malay town. SAJSS
       2 (1974) 45-61.

VILLAGE STUDIES - PHILIPPINES

10239 The barrio in 1957. E78 pp. 26-
       28.

Village studies - Philippines

10240 Barrio profile. A28 pp. 28-9.

10241 COLLER, RICHARD. Analysis of the social effects of donated radios on barrio life. E78 pp. 268-285.

10242 DeYOUNG, JOHN E. Communication channels and functional literacy in the Philippine barrio, by John E. DeYoung and Chester L. Hunt. E78 pp. 251-266.

10243 DeYOUNG, JOHN E. Communication channels and functional literacy in the Philippine barrio, by John E. DeYoung and Chester L. Hunt. JAS 22 (1962-3) 67-77.

10244 FIRMALINO, TITO C. Political attitudes in the barrio. A28 pp. 134-142.

10245 FRANCISCO, JUAN R. Intercultural encounter in a frontier area, the case of the public school teacher and an ethnic minority. GEJ 14 (1967) 16-33.

10246 HART, DONN V. Christian Filipino society approaching the 21st century. SJ 18 (1971) 21-55.

10247 JOCANO, F. LANDA. Child training and adult behavior, a case study in Filipino socialization. GEJ 14 (1967) 34-47.

10248 JOCANO, F. LANDA. Cultural idiom and the problem of planned change, a case study from a Philippine municipality. AST 10 (1972) 157-178.

10249 LAWLESS, ROBERT. Village community studies in general education. GEJ 12 (1966) 162-171.

10250 PAL, AGATON PALEN. Philippine barrio, a study of social organization in relation to planned cultural change. E78 pp. 62-73.

10251 SIBLEY, WILLIS E. Leadership in a Philippine barrio. E78 pp. 308-315.

VILLAGE STUDIES - PHILIPPINES - INDIVID-AREAS

10252 ARCE, WILFREDO F. Social organization of the Muslim peoples of Sulu. PS 11 (1963) 242-263.
Comment: ESLAO, NENA B. Comment on social organization of the Muslim peoples of Sulu. PS 11 (1963) 264-266.
Comment: STONE, RICHARD L. Comment on social organization of the Muslim peoples of Sulu. PS 11 (1963) 263-4.

10253 ARCILLA, JOSE S. Christianization of Davao Oriental, excerpts from Jesuit missionary letters. PS 19 (1971) 639-724.

10254 CABRERA, AGUSTIN A. Badjaus, cultural identity and education. UN 42 (1969) 107-142.

10255 CABRERA, SANTIAGO B. Origin, folkways and customs of the Bilaans of southern Cotabato. UN 40 (1967) 182-193.

10256 CANTERO-PASTRANO, CECILIA L. Report on a Visayan fishing barrio. E78 pp. 30-41.

10257 CASINO, ERIC S. Jama Mapun ethnoecology, economic and symbolic (of grains, winds and stars). AST 5 (1967) 1-32.

10258 CHANG, SHUB ROH. Looc, Dumaguete City, a study of an urban slum community. SJ 17 (1970) 248-285.

Village studies – Philippines – Individual areas – Luzon

10259 COLLER, RICHARD W. Barrio Gacao, a study of village ecology and the schistosomiasis problem. E78 pp. 536-549.

10260 COLLER, RICHARD W. Barrio Gacao, a study of village ecology and the schistosomiasis problem. E78 pp. 642-652.

10261 ELIO Y SANCHEZ, VICENTE. History of Camiguin. PS 20 (1972) 106-146.

10262 HART, DONN V. Personal narrative of a Samaran Filipina. AST 3 (1965) 55-70.

10263 JOCANO, F. LANDA. Conversion and the patterning of Christian experience in Malitbog, central Panay, Philippines. B13 pp. 43-72.
Comment: BULATAO, JAIME. Comments. B13 pp. 73-75.

10264 KASMAN, EDWARD SALKIYA. Birth and death rituals among the Tausugs of Siasi. UN 35 (1962) 291-340.

10265 LYNCH, FRANK. Ateneo expedition to Sulu. PS 10 (1962) 314-316.

10266 MACEDA, MARCELINO N. Brief report on some Mangyans in northern Oriental Mindoro. UN 40 (1967) 102-155.

10267 ORACION, TIMOTEO S. Bukidnons of southeastern Negros, Philippines. SJ 8 (1961) 205-210.

10268 ORACION, TIMOTEO S. Preliminary report on some cultural aspects of the Bukidnons on southeastern Negros Island, Philippines. UN 40 (1967) 156-181.

10269 PANIZO, ALFREDO. Negritos or Aetas. UN 40 (1967) 66-101.

10270 PAZ, EMETERIO DE LA. Survey of the Hanunoo Mangyan culture and barriers to change. UN 41 (1968) 3-63.

10271 PONTENILA, MARIA. Sorcery in the framework of folk medicine on Siquijor Island, by Maria Pontenila and Hubert Reynolds. SJ 18 (1971) 75-96.

10272 SAMSON, JOSE A. Bataks of Sumurod and Kalakuasan. UN 40 (1967) 194-206.

VILLAGE STUDIES – PHILIPPINES – INDIVIDUAL AREAS – LUZON

10273 ANDERSON, JAMES N. Land and society in a Pangasinan community. E78 pp. 171-192.

10274 BACDAYAN, ALBERT S. Religious conversion and social reintegration in a western Bontoc village complex. SLQ 5 (1967) 27-40.

10275 BELLO, MOISES C. Methods of field research in a Benguet village. GEJ 12 (1966) 43-65.

10276 CASTILLO, GELIA. Local leaders, status, attitudes and behavior, by Gelia Castillo, Patrocino S. Villanueva, and Felicidad V. Cordero. A28 pp. 128-133.

10277 DAVIS, WILLIAM G. Economic limitations and social relationships in a Philippine marketplace, capital accumulation in a peasant economy. V27 pp. 1-28.

10278 DeRAEDT, JULES. Some notes on Buwaya society. SLQ 7 (1969) 7-112.

Village studies - Philippines - Individual areas - Luzon

10279 DULAWAN, LOURDES S. Ifugaos. UN
       40 (1967) 4-52.

10280 HOLLNSTEINER, MARY R. Development
       of political parties in a town.
       A28 pp. 158-180.

10281 HOLLNSTEINER, MARY R. Dynamics
       of power in a Philippine munici-
       pality. E78 pp. 293-307.

10282 HOLLNSTEINER, MARY R. Dynamics
       of power in a Philippine munici-
       pality. E78 pp. 652-654.

10283 HOLLNSTEINER, MARY R. Reciprocity
       in the lowland Philippines. E78
       pp. 335-355.

10284 KAUT, CHARLES R. Bansag and
       Apelyido, problems of comparison
       in changing Tagalog social organ-
       izations. Z16 pp. 397-418.

10285 KAUT, CHARLES. Process and social
       structure in a Philippine lowland
       settlement. S90.1 pp. 35-50.

10286 LYNCH, FRANK. Social class in a
       Bikol town. E78 pp. 164-169.

10287 McDONALD, ANGUS. Slice of Philip-
       pine normality. JCA 4 (1974) 250-
       255.

10288 MACHADO, K. G. From tradition
       faction to machine, changing pat-
       terns of political leadership and
       organization in the rural Philip-
       pines. JAS 33 (1973-4) 523-547.

10289 SANTICO, REALIDAD Q. Research in
       a Pampanga village. AST 7 (1969)
       264-269.

10290 SANTOS, ARLYNE G. DE LOS. Local
       government as perceived by barrio
       residents of Tadiangan, Tuba,
       Benguet. GEJ 21 (1971) 73-81.

10291 SUGGUIYAO, MIGUEL. Kalinga
       primitive culture, by Miguel and
       Rosario Sugguiyao. SLQ 1 (1963)
       289-304.

10292 SUGGUIYAO, MIGUEL. Kalinga
       primitive culture, by Miguel and
       Rosario Sugguiyao. SLQ 2 (1964)
       181-200.

10293 TROYER, LESTER O. Linguistics as
       a window into man's mind, Gaddang
       time segmentation. GEJ 12 (1966)
       109-118.

VILLAGE STUDIES - THAILAND

10294 BURR, ANGELA. Religious institu-
       tional diversity, social, struc-
       tural, and conceptional unity:
       Islam and Buddhism in a southern
       Thai coastal fishing village.
       JSS 60 pt. 2 (1972) 183-215.

10295 DURRENBERGER, PAUL. The regional
       context of the economy of a Lisu
       village in northern Thailand. SA
       3 (1974-5) 569-575.

10296 HANKS, JANE RICHARDSON. Rural
       Thai village's view of human
       character. F38 pp. 77-84.

10297 INGERSOLL, JASPER. Merit and
       identity in village Thailand.
       C24 pp. 219-251.

10298 INGERSOLL, JASPER. Priest role
       in a central village, Thailand.
       C66 pp. 51-76.

10299 JUDD, LAURENCE C. Social change
       in commune Baw, Thailand, 1958-
       1967. S58 pp. 210-234.

10300 KANDRE, PETER. Autonomy and in-
       tegration of social systems, the
       Iu Mien (Yao or Man) mountain
       population and their neighbors.
       K86 pp. 583-638.

10301 KEYES, CHARLES F. Ethnic identity and loyalty of villagers in northeastern Thailand. AS 6 (1966) 362-369.

10302 KEYES, CHARLES F. Kin groups in a Thai-Lao community. C24 pp. 274-297.

10303 KICKERT, ROBERT W. Akha village structure. S96 pp. 35-40.

10304 KINGSHILL, KONRAD. Seven themes of Ku Daeng. S96 pp. 26-34.

10305 KIRSCH, A. THOMAS. Development and mobility among the Phu Thai of northeast Thailand. AS 6 (1966) 370-378.

10306 KUNSTADTER, PETER. Lua' and Skaw Karen of Maehongson Province, northwestern Thailand. K86 pp. 639-674.

10307 MARLOWE, GERTRUDE WOODRUFF. Economic variety in a north Thai village. S96 pp. 15-25.

10308 MIZUNO, KOICHI. Multihousehold compounds in northeast Thailand. AS 8 (1968) 842-852.

10309 MOERMAN, MICHAEL. Ban Ping's temple, the center of a loosely structured society. C66 pp. 137-174.

10310 MOERMAN, MICHAEL. Kinship and commerce in a Thai-Lue village. T45 pp. 550-555.

10311 MOERMAN, MICHAEL. Minority and its government, the Thai-Lue of northern Thailand. K86 pp. 401-424.

10312 MOERMAN, MICHAEL. A Thai village headman as a synaptic leader. JAS 28 (1968-9) 535-549.

10313 MORELL, DAVID. Legislative intervention in Thailand's development process, a case study. AS 12 (1972) 627-646.

10314 MOTE, F. W. Rural Haw (Yunnanese Chinese) of northern Thailand. K86 pp. 487-524.

10315 MULDER, J. A. N. Notes on the structural analysis of Thai peasant villages, a critique and a recommendation. JSS 55 (1967) 273-277.

10316 OBAYASHI, TARYO. Lawa and Sgau Karen in northwestern Thailand. JSS 52 (1964) 199-216.

10317 PFANNER, DAVID E. Theravada Buddhism and village economic behavior, a Burmese and Thai comparison, by David E. Pfanner and Jasper Ingersoll. JAS 21 (1961-62) 341-361.

10318 PIKER, STEVEN. Post peasant village in central plain Thai society. C24 pp. 298-323.

10319 PIKER, STEVEN. Relationship of belief systems to behavior in rural Thai society. AS 8 (1968) 384-399.

10320 PIKER, STEVEN. Sources of stability and instability in rural Thai society. JAS 27 (1967-8) 777-790.

10321 RUBIN, HERBERT J. Will and awe, illustrations of Thai villager dependency upon officials. JAS 32 (1972-3) 425-444.

Village studies - Thailand

10322 SHARP, LAURISTON. Strategy of research in longitudinal community studies, the case of a Thai rice village, by Lauriston Sharp and Robert J. Smith. AC 2 (Apr. 1960) 133-145.

10323 SMITHIES, MICHAEL. Village Mons of Bangkok. JSS 60 pt. 1 (1972) 307-332.

10324 TURTON, ANDREW. Matrilineal descent groups and spirit cults of the Thai-Yuan in northern Thailand. JSS 60 pt. 2 (1972) 217-256.

10325 VAN ROY, EDWARD. Interpretation of northern Thai peasant economy. JAS 26 (1966-7) 421-432.

10326 WALKER, ANTHONY R. Red Lahu village society, an introductory survey. S96 pp. 41-52.

10327 WIJEYEWARDENE, GEHAN. Note on irrigation and agriculture in a north Thai village. F38 pp. 255-259.

10328 WIJEYEWARDENE, GEHAN. Some aspects of rural life in Thailand. S49 pp. 65-83.

10329 YOUNG, STEPHEN B. Northeastern Thai village, a non-participatory democracy. AS 8 (1968) 873-886.

VILLAGE STUDIES - VIETNAM

10330 BOULBET, JEAN. Modes et techniques du pays Ma. SEIB 39 (1964) 169-288.

10331 BOULBET, JEAN. Modes et techniques du pays Maa. BEF 52 (1964) 359-414.

10332 DONNELL, JOHN C. Expanding political participation, the long haul from villagism to nationalism. AS 10 (1970) 688-704.

10333 GOODMAN, ALLAN E. Political implications of rural problems in south Vietnam, creating public interests. AS 10 (1970) 672-687.

10334 HENDRY, JAMES B. American aid in Vietnam, the view from a village. PA 33 (1960) 387-391.

10335 LE VAN HAO. Introduction a l'ethnologie du Dinh. SEIB 37 (1962) 41-72.

10336 NGUYEN KHAC-KHAM. Comments on Vietnamese villages. EACS 13 (1974) 18-9.

10337 NGUYEN THUY ANH. Luoi Dang ou madraque vietnamienne dans la region de Khanh-Hoa, Nha Trang. SEIB 41 (1966) 167-290.

10338 TRUONG BUU LAM. L'autorite dans les villages vietnamiens au XIXe siecle. L23 pp. 65-73.

10339 ZASLOFF, JOSEPH J. Rural resettlement in south Viet Nam, the agroville program. PA 35 (1962) 327-340.

Visayas *See* BISAYAS

VISION

10340 ABRAHAMS, PETER H. Frequency of defective colour vision in Sarawak. SMJ 16 (1968) 340-345.

VLIET, IEREMIE VAN

10341   VLIET, IEREMIE VAN. Historical
        account of Siam in the 17th cen-
        tury. S44.7 pp. 31-90.
        Comment: GILES, FRANCIS H.
        Critical analysis of van Vliet's
        Historical account of Siam in the
        17th century. S44.7 pp. 91-176.

VOLCANOES - INDONESIA

10342   BRAAKE, ALEXANDER L. TER. Vol-
        canology in the Netherlands In-
        dies. H57 pp. 22-35.

VOLCANOES - PHILIPPINES

10343   BERNAD, MIGUEL A. Ascent of
        Mount Canlaon. PS 9 (1961) 469-
        487.

10344   ESPINAS, MERITO B. Eruptions of
        Mayon. UN 41 (1968) 251-256.

10345   PANIZO, A. Taal volcano. UN 38
        (1965) 576-586.

WADJO

10346   PELRAS, CHRISTIAN. Hierarchie et
        pouvoir traditionnels en pays
        Wadjo. AR 1 (1970) 169-191.

10347   PELRAS, CHRISTIAN. Hierarchie et
        pouvoir traditionnels en pays
        Wadjo. AR 2 (1971) 197-223.

WALLACE, ALFRED RUSSEL

10348   LOH CHIN YIN. A. R. Wallace col-
        lection in the Sarawak Museum
        reference library. SMJ 15 (1967)
        446-455.

10349   MAYR, ERNST. Wallace's line in
        the light of recent zoogeographic
        studies. H57 pp. 241-250.

WAN WAITHAYAKON

10350   UNGER, LEONARD. Dedication. JSS
        59 pt. 2 (1971) 1-2.

WARWYCK, WYBRANT

10351   JACOBS, HUBERT. Admiraal Wybrant
        Warwyck schrift aan de Sultan van
        Ternate. BIJ 125 (1969) 344-355.

WATER SUPPLY - MALAYSIA

10352   LOW KWAI SIM. Water balance of
        five catchments in Selangor, west
        Malaysia, by Low Kwai Sim and Goh
        Kim Chuan. JTG 35 (1972) 60-66.

WATER SUPPLY - PHILIPPINES

10353   ESQUELA, ESTER. Controversial
        pipes, by Ester Esquela and Le-
        andro A. Viloria. G93 pp. 197-
        240.

10354   MULATA, JOSE GAVILANGOSO. Pro-
        duction and distribution problems
        encountered in the management of
        the water supply system of Baguio
        City. SLURJ 2 (1971) 177-241.

10355   RESURRECCION, ABELARDO S. A
        study of a conflict of interest
        in the use of land in the
        Ambuklao-Binga watershed, a land
        economic approach. SLURJ 2
        (1971) 630-680.

Wayang kulit *See* DRAMA

Waterstradt, John

WATERSTRADT, JOHN

10356 BARLOW, H. S. John Waterstradt, 1869-1944. JMBRAS 42 pt. 2 (1969) 115-129.

Weaving *See* TEXTILES

WEST IRIAN

10357 BONE, ROBERT C. International status of West New Guinea until 1884. JSAH 5 (Sept. 1964) 150-180.

10358 DERKACH, NADIA. Soviet policy towards Indonesia in the West Irian and the Malaysian disputes. AS 5 (1965) 566-571.

10359 HATTA, MOHAMMAD. Colonialism and the danger of war. AS 1 (Nov. 1961) 10-14.

10360 KEUNING, J. Nederlandse straf-rechtspraak aan de Wisselmeren, centraal Nederlands Nieuw-Guinea. BIJ 117 (1961) 25-50.

10361 LEEDEN, A. C. VAN DER. Social structure in New Guinea. BIJ 116 (1960) 119-149.

10362 LIJPHART, AREND. Indonesian image of West Irian. AS 1 (July 1961) 9-16.

10363 OOSTERWAL, GOTTFRIED. West Irian, population patterns and problems. AST 4 (1966) 291-302.

10364 PLOEG, A. Some comparative re-marks about the Dani of the Baliem Valley and the Dani at Bokondini. BIJ 122 (1966) 255-273.

10365 POUWER, J. New Guinea as a field for ethnological study, a prelim-inary analysis. BIJ 117 (1961) 1-24.

10366 POUWER, J. Social structure in the western interior of Sarmi, northern Netherlands New Guinea, a response to a response. BIJ 116 (1960) 365-372.

10367 POUWER, J. Structure and flexi-bility in a New Guinea society. BIJ 122 (1966) 158-169.

10368 SIMATUPANG, T. B. Indonesian Christian view of the West Irian question. AS 2 (June 1962) 28-32.

10369 VAN DER KROEF, JUSTUS M. Nasuti-on, Sukarno and the West New Guinea dispute. AS 1 (Aug. 1961) 20-24.

10370 VAN DER KROEF, JUSTUS M. Nation-alism and politics in West New Guinea. PA 34 (1961) 38-53.

10371 VAN DER KROEF, JUSTUS M. Recent developments in West New Guinea. PA 34 (1961) 279-291.

10372 VAN DER KROEF, JUSTUS M. West New Guinea, the uncertain future. AS 8 (1968) 691-707.

10373 VAN DER VEUR, PAUL W. Political awakening in West New Guinea. PA 36 (1963) 54-73.

10374 VAN DER VEUR, PAUL W. West Irian, a new era. AS 2 (Oct. 1962) 1-8.

10375 VAN DER VEUR, PAUL W. West Irian in the Indonesian fold. AS 3 (1963) 332-337.

WILDER, JAMES AUSTIN

10376 APPELL, G. N. Early American adventurers in Borneo, a brief note and request for information. JMBRAS 42 pt. 2 (1969) 220-1.

WILSON, LAURENCE LEE

10377 FREI, ERNEST J. Laurence Lee Wilson, recorder of Mountain Province folklore. SLQ 5 (1967) 41-66.

WINSTEDT, RICHARD O.

10378 BARRETT, E. C. G. Further light on Sir Richard Winstedt's undescribed Malay version of the Ramayana. SOAS 26 (1963) 531-543.

10379 BARRETT, E. C. G. Sir Richard Winstedt. SOAS 30 (1967) 272-275.

10380 BASTIN, JOHN. Introduction, Sir Richard Winstedt and his writings. B38 pp. 1-23.

10381 BROWN, C. C. Sir Richard Winstedt. SOAS 26 (1963) 497.

10382 NIK AHMAD KAMIL. [Sir Richard Winstedt.] JMBRAS 40 pt. 2 (1967) 1-2.

10383 SWEENEY, AMIN. Sir Richard Winstedt's summary of the *Tuhfat ul-Nafis*. JMBRAS 40 pt. 1 (1967) 155-6.

10384 VOORHOEVE, P. In memoriam, Sir Richard Winstedt, 2-8-1878 to 2-6-1966. BIJ 122 (1966) 413-415.

10385 ZAINAL ABIDIN BIN AHMAD. Sumbangan Sir Richard Winstedt dalam penyelidekan pengajian Melayu. B38 pp. 320-339.

WOMEN - BRUNEI

10386 ABDUL LATIF HAJI IBRAHIM. Padian, its market and the women vendors. BMJ 2 pt. 1 (1970) 39-51.

WOMEN - BURMA

10387 PE MAUNG TIN. Women in the inscriptions of Pagan. B92 pp. 411-421.

WOMEN - MALAYSIA

10388 JONES, G. W. Female participation in the labour force in a plural economy, the Malayan example. MER 10 pt. 2 (1965) 61-82.

10389 MARGIT ILONA KOMANYI. Iban woman's role, a brief summary of observations at Samu on the Paku River. SMJ 19 (1971) 253-256.

WOMEN - PHILIPPINES

10390 BENJAMIN, J. The Filipino family owned business, a matriarchal model, by J. Benjamin, C. Alvarez and Patricia M. Alvarez. PS 20 (1972) 547-561.

WOMEN - VIETNAM

10391 NGUYEN HUU TAN. La femme vietnamienne d'autrefois a travers les chansons populaires. SEIB 45 pt. 1 (1970) 1-113.

10392 NGUYEN XUAN CHANH. Widow's statute in Vietnamese customary law. C39 pp. 252-261.

10393 TURLEY, WILLIAM S. Women in the communist revolution in Vietnam. AS 12 (1972) 793-805.

Wood, Leonard

WOOD, LEONARD

10394 ONORATO, MICHAEL P. Governor
       General Leonard Wood and his ad-
       ministration, a re-appraisal. AF
       3 (1971) 237-244.

10395 ONORATO, MICHAEL P. Leonard Wood
       as Governor General, a calendar
       of selected correspondence. PS
       12 (1964) 124-148.

10396 ONORATO, MICHAEL P. Leonard Wood
       as Governor General, a calendar
       of selected correspondence, pt. 2.
       PS 12 (1964) 296-314.

10397 ONORATO, MICHAEL P. Leonard Wood
       as Governor General, a calendar
       of selected correspondence, pt. 3.
       PS 12 (1964) 699-719.

10398 ONORATO, MICHAEL P. Leonard Wood
       as Governor General, a calendar
       of selected correspondence, pt. 4.
       PS 13 (1965) 822-849.

10399 ONORATO, MICHAEL P. Leonard Wood
       as Governor General, a calendar
       of selected correspondence, a
       postscript. PS 14 (1966) 280-292.

10400 ONORATO, MICHAEL P. Leonard Wood,
       his first year as Governor Gen-
       eral, 1921-1922. AST 4 (1966)
       353-361.

Working classes *See* LABOR AND LABORING
     CLASSES

WORLD FELLOWSHIP OF BUDDHISTS

10401 CHAN HTOON. Presidential address.
       FA 18 (1962) 29-35.

10402 SIHANOUK, NORODOM. Inaugural ad-
       dress, 6th Conference of the World
       Fellowship of Buddhists, Phnom-
       Penh, November 14-22, 1961. FA 18
       (1962) 25-28.

10403 SONI, R. L. Sixth Conference of
       the World Fellowship of Bud-
       dhists. FA 18 (1962) 41-46.

WORLD WAR II

10404 BENDA, HARRY J. Introduction.
       AST 7 (1969) 1-3.

10405 PLUVIER, JAN M. Anti-Japans
       verzet in Zuid-Oost-Azie-Enkele
       notities. B85 pp. 175-187.

10406 UHALLEY, STEPHEN. Japan's south-
       ern advance, the Indochina phase.
       AST 4 (1966) 84-102.

WORLD WAR II - BURMA

10407 GUYOT, DOROTHY. Uses of Bud-
       dhism in wartime Burma. AST 7
       (1969) 50-80.

WORLD WAR II - INDONESIA

10408 ANDERSON, BEN. The problem of
       rice, stenographic notes on the
       fourth session of Sanyo Kaigi,
       January 8, 2605, 10:00 a.m.,
       translated with an introduction
       by Ben Anderson. IND 2 (1966)
       77-123.

10409 GATOT MANGKUPRADJA, RADEN. Peta
       and my relations with the Japa-
       nese, a correction of Sukarno's
       autobiography. IND 5 (1968) 105-
       134.

10410 IDRUS. Surabaja. IND 5 (1968)
       1-28.

10411 IDRUS. Two stories of the
       Japanese occupation. Fujinkai,

and, Och . . . och . . . och.
IND 2 (1966) 125-134.

10412   KESAVAN, K. V.   Attitude of Indonesia towards the Japanese peace
treaty.   AST 10 (1972) 407-415.

10413   KISHI, KOICHI.   Recent Japanese
sources for Indonesian historiography.   S61 pp. 206-216.

10414   LOCKWOOD, RUPERT.   Indonesian
exiles in Australia, 1942-47.
IND 10 (1970) 37-56.

10415   NAKAMURA, MITSUO.   General Ima-
mura and the early period of
Japanese occupation.   IND 10
(1970) 1-26.

10416   NUGROHO NOTOSUSANTO.   Revolt of a
Peta-bettalion in Blitar, February
14, 1945.   AST 7 (1969) 111-123.

10417   REID, ANTHONY.   Birth of the republic of Sumatra.   IND 12 (1971)
21-46.

10418   SLUIMERS, L. E. L.   Enige the-
oretische beschouwingen over de
Japanse bezettingsperiod op Java.
B85 pp. 240-266.

WORLD WAR II - MALAYSIA

10419   AKASHI, YOJI.   Formation of the
Malay Military Administration and
its policies, November 1941-July
1942.   AF 3 (1971) 138-157.

10420   AKASHI, YOJI.   Japanese military
administration in Malaya, its
formation and evolution in reference to sultans, the Islamic religion, and the Moslem Malays,
1941-1945.   AST 7 (1969) 81-110.

10421   AKASHI, YOJI.   Japanese policy
towards the Malayan Chinese,

1941-1945.   JSAS 1 pt. 2 (1970)
61-89.

10422   HARRISSON, TOM.   Douglas' 1911
vocabulary in practise.   SMJ 10
(1961) 125-6.

10423   ITAGAKI, YOICHI.   Some aspects of
the Japanese policy for Malaya
under the occupation, with special reference to nationalism.
J45 pp. 256-267.

WORLD WAR II - PHILIPPINES

10424   Corregidor.   DR 11 (1963) 343-
380.

10425   HART, DONN V.   Bibliographical
essay, guerrilla warfare and the
Filipino resistance on Negros
Island in the Bisayas, 1942-1945.
JSAH 5 (Mar. 1964) 101-125.

10426   HART, DONN V.   Central Philippines University's World War II
manuscript collection.   JAS 25
(1965-6) 123.

10427   HART, DONN V.   Central Philippines University's World War II
manuscript collection.   JSAH 6
(Sept. 1965) 129-130.

10428   HARTENDORP, A. V. H.   Two stories
of the Japanese occupation.   PHR
1 pt. 2 (1966) 92-124.

10429   LEAR, ELMER N.   Western Leyte
guerrilla warfare forces, a case
study in the non-legitimation of
a guerrilla organization.   JSAH 9
(1968) 69-94.

10430   LENT, JOHN A.   Guerrilla presses
of the Philippines, 1941-45.   AST
8 (1970) 260-274.

World War II - Philippines

10431 LUMBERA, BIENVENIDO. Alliance and revolution, Tagalog writing during the war years. M24 pp. 385-402.

10432 POLLACK, JOHN A. War experiences and recollections. PS 21 (1973) 360-387.

10433 STEINBERG, DAVID JOEL. Ambiguous legacy, years at war in the Philippines. PA 45 (1972) 165-190.

10434 THOMAS, RALPH B. Asia for Asiatics? Muslim Filipino responses to Japanese occupation and propaganda during World War II. AF 4 pt. 3 (1972) 43-60.

10435 VELLUT, J. L. Foreign relations of the second republic of the Philippines, 1943-1945. JSAH 5 (Mar. 1964) 126-142.

10436 VELLUT, J. L. Japanese reparations to the Philippines. AS 3 (1963) 496-506.

WORLD WAR II - SINGAPORE

10437 PANG WING SENG. The double seventh incident, 1937, Singapore Chinese response to the outbreak of the Sino-Japanese war. JSAS 4 (1973) 269-299.

WORLD WAR II - THAILAND

10438 BATSON, BENJAMIN A. The fall of the Phibun government. JSS 62 pt. 2 (1974) 89-120.

10439 CHARNVIT KASETSIRI. The first Phibun government and its involvement in World War II. JSS 62 pt. 2 (1974) 25-88.

WORLD WAR II - VIETNAM

10440 SPECTOR, RONALD. What the local Annamites are thinking, American views of Vietnamese in China, 1942-1945. SA 3 (1974) 740-751.

10441 TRUONG BUU LAM. Japan and the disruption of the Vietnamese nationalist movement. V43 pp. 237-269.

Writing *See* ALPHABETS

YAKAN

10442 FRAKE, CHARLES O. How to enter a Yakan house. S92.1 pp. 87-104.

10443 MOLONY, CAROL H. It's still genocide even if they die by starvation. JCA 3 (1973) 491-496.

10444 WULFF, INGER. Yakan Maulud celebration. Z16 pp. 494-502.

10445 WULFF, INGER. Yakan of Basilan. SJ 18 (1971) 436-440.

YAO *See also* MIAO

10446 KANDRE, PETER K. Aspects of wealth accumulation, ancestor worship and household stability among the Iu Mien-Yao, by Peter K. Kandre and Lej Tsan Kuej. F38 pp. 129-148.

10447 KANDRE, PETER K. Autonomy and integration of social systems, the Iu Mien (Yao or Man) mountain population and their neighbors. K86 pp. 583-638.

10448 MILES, DOUGLAS. Yao bridge-exchange, matrifiliation and adoption. BIJ 128 (1972) 99-117.

YAO LANGUAGE

10449 DOWNER, G. B. Chinese, Thai and Miao-Yao. L55 pp. 133-139.

10450 DOWNER, G. B. Phonology of the word in highland Yao. SOAS 24 (1961) 531-541.

10451 HAUDRICOURT, ANDRE G. Note sur les dialectes de region de Monday. BEF 50 (1960) 161-177.

YOUTH

10452 LIU, WILLIAM T. Achievement motivation among Chinese youth in Southeast Asia. AS 5 (1965) 186-196.

YOUTH - INDONESIA

10453 DOUGLAS, STEPHEN A. Ideological problems of the Indonesian youth movement. AF 4 pt. 4 (1972) 52-61.

10454 TJONG TIAT LIEM. Indonesian youth and nationalism in historical perspective. SJ 18 (1971) 190-197.

YOUTH - PHILIPPINES

10455 ESTRADA, JOSEFA G. Problems of college students. UN 37 (1964) 392-400.

10456 GEVERS, FRANCIS. Youth and their problems. SLQ 3 (1965) 233-256.

10457 McCARTHY, MAUREEN. Assessment of the perceptions of institutional-ized Filipino youth. PS 17 (1969) 112-119.

10458 MOYLAN, MARY. Happiness values of selected Filipino adolescent and young adult students in a provincial city. SLURJ 4 (1973) 1-121.

10459 NERI-RABAGO, EMPERATRIZ. Nature and concepts of guidance. UN 37 (1964) 312-320.

10460 SAMSON, JOSE A. Data on the cause of youth problems in the city of Manila. UN 35 (1962) 469-474.

10461 SAMSON, JOSE A. Need for guidance and counseling among Filipino students. UN 37 (1964) 357-366.

10462 ZIMMERMAN, MIKE. Juvenile delinquency in the Philippines, an approach for understanding. SJ 16 (1969) 117-136.

YOUTH - SINGAPORE

10463 MAH LAU FONG. Anomie of parents and juvenile delinquency in Singapore. RSAS 3 pts. 1-2 (1973) 45-53.

YOUTH - VIETNAM

10464 HO CHI MINH. Youth of Annam. JCA 2 (1972) 361-365.

10465 MARR, DAVID. Political attitudes and activities of young urban intellectuals in south Viet-Nam. AS 6 (1966) 249-263.

Yule, Henry

542

<u>YULE, HENRY</u>

10466   TINKER, HUGH. Arthur Phayre and Henry Yule, two soldier-administrator historians. H18 pp. 267-278.

ZAMBOANGA

10467   JESUS, EDILBERTO C. DE. Controversy over Zamboanga. PHR 2 (1969) 275-294.

<u>ZAMORA, JACINTO</u>

10468   QUIRINO, CARLOS. Checklist of documents on Gomburza from the archdiocesan archives of Manila. PS 21 (1973) 19-84.

<u>ZAMORA, NICOLAS</u>

10469   DEATS, RICHARD L. Nicolas Zamora, religious nationalist. A58 pp. 325-336.

Zarzuela *See* DRAMA

Zat Pwe *See* DRAMA

Supplement to Articles

ALPHABETS - BURMA

10470 EGEROD, SOREN. Romanization of Shan. B91 pp. 47-49.

ALPHABETS - THAILAND

10471 DHANINIVAT, KROMAMUN BIDYALABH. Transcription of Siamese, yet another experiment which I used for some twenty years in the *Journal of the Siam Society*. T33 pp. 69-72.

ANIMISM

10472 LAFONT, PIERRE-BERNARD. Les genies dans la peninsula indo-chinoise. SEIB 44 (1969) 207-233.

ANIMISM - PHILIPPINES

10473 DEMETRIO, FRANCISCO R. Philippine shamanism and Southeast Asian parallels. AST 11 pt. 2 (1973) 128-154.

ARCHAEOLOGY - MALAYSIA - SARAWAK - NIAH CAVES

10474 BROTHWELL, D. R. Upper Pleistocene human skull from Niah caves, Sarawak. SMJ 9 (1960) 323-349.

ARCHAEOLOGY - VIETNAM

10475 SAURIN, E. Station prehistorique a Hang-Gou pres Xuan-Loc, Sud-Viet Nam. BEF 51 (1963) 433-452.

ART - BRUNEI

10476 HARRISSON, TOM. Interesting bronzes with some ceramic parallels from Brunei and Sarawak. SMJ 12 (1965) 143-147.

ART - BURMA

10477 Burmese line sketches. JBRS 44 (June 1961) 25-34.

10478 SHORTO, H. L. Devata plaques of the Ananda basement. E93 pp. 156-165.

ART - PHILIPPINES

10479 ROXAS-LIM, AURORA. Art in Ifugao society. AST 11 pt. 2 (1973) 47-74.

ASIA, SOUTHEAST - FOREIGN RELATIONS

10480 SANIEL, JOSEFA M. Erosion of the bi-polar power structure in the 1960's: its impact upon Asian international politics. AST 11 pt. 2 (1973) 6-40.

ASIA, SOUTHEAST - HISTORY

10481 JACK-HINTON, COLIN. Political and cosmographical background to the Spanish incursion into the Pacific in the sixteenth century. JMBRAS 37 pt. 2 (1964) 125-161.

ATTITUDES - PHILIPPINES

10482 AYSON, ELMILA B. Influences of study attitudes and habits on academic performance. SLURJ 3 (1972) 430-471.

10483 CASTILLO, GELIA. Local leaders, status, attitudes and behavior, by Gelia Castillo, Patrocino S. Villanueva and Felicidad V. Cordero. A28 pp. 128-133.

10484 FIRMALINO, TITO C. Political attitudes in the barrio. A28 pp. 134-142.

BIKOL LITERATURE

10485 REALUBIT, MARIA LILIA. Preliminary catalogue of Bikol dramas. AST 11 pt. 2 (1973) 155-161.

BISAYAH

10486 SANDIN, BENEDICT. Bisayah of Limbang. SMJ 19 (1971) 1-20.

BISAYAN LITERATURE

10487 CORONEL, MARIA DELIA. Visayan stories. UN 39 (1966) 547-576.

BUDDHISM - BURMA

10488 MYA MAUNG. Cultural value and economic change in Burma. T45 pp. 527-534.

CASPER, LINDA

10489 CONSTANTINO, JOSEFINA D. *The peninsulars*. DR 13 (1965) 66-71.

CASTANON, JESUS

10490 In memoriam, death of a good man. UN 33 (1960) 681.

CATHOLIC CHURCH - PHILIPPINES

10491 GOROSPE, VITALIANO R. Catholic hierarchy and the population problem. G73 pp. 157-163.

CHINESE

10492 NGGAWA, DARIUS W. Historico-philosophical analysis of the Chinese diffusion in Southeast Asia. UN 37 (1964) 1-51.

CHRISTIANITY - PHILIPPINES

10493 BACDAYAN, ALBERT S. Religious conversion and social reintegration in a western Bontoc village complex. SLQ 5 (1967) 27-40.

COMMERCE - MALAYSIA

10494 LEWIS, DIANNE. Growth of the country trade to the Straits of Malacca, 1760-1777. JMBRAS 43 pt. 2 (1970) 114-129.

CONGRESSES AND CONVENTIONS

10495 CAYRAC-BLANCHARD, FRANCOISE. Un colloque sur l'Indonesie apres les elections de 1971. AR 3 (1972) 17-19.

10496 COQUIA, JORGE R. First Asian conference on legal education. PS 11 (1963) 150-1.

10497 CULLIGAN, JAMES F. National mental health conference. PS 10 (1962) 153-155.

10498 ERDBERG-CONSTEN, ELEANOR. Manila
trade pottery seminar. PS 16
(1968) 545-557.

10499 GLOVER, I. C. London colloquy on
early South East Asia. AR 7
(1974) 15-18.

10500 GREGORIO, SAMUEL B. Rizal, apostle of Asian nationalism. A review of the 1967 Knights of Rizal
seminar-institute. SJ 15 (1968)
16-28.

10501 GRIFFING, ROBERT P. Trade porce-
lain and stoneware in Southeast
Asia, a report of a symposium.
AP 5 (1961) 235-6.

10502 International congress on Rizal,
commission reports. DR 12 (1964)
172-193.

10503 KRUPA, VIKTOR. Conference on linguistic problems of the Indo-
Pacific area, London 5-8 January
1965. AAS 2 (1966) 139-141.

10504 LOCKWOOD, WILLIAM W. Employment,
technology and education in Asia,
concluding summary statement,
Conference on Manpower Problems
in East and Southeast Asia, University of Singapore, May 22-28,
1971. MER 16 pt. 2 (1971) 6-24.

10505 LOMBARD, DENYS. Deuxieme semi-
naire d'histoire nationale, Djog-
jakarta, 26-29 aout 1970. Les
indonesiens font le point sur
l'histoire de leur pays. BEF 58
(1971) 281-298.

10506 NARVASA, ANDRES R. Report of the
ASAIHL convention in Kuala Lumpur
and Singapore, January 29 to February 10, 1966. UN 39 (1966)
152-157.

10507 PACHECO, ESTHER M. Association
of Southeast Asian Institutions
of Higher Learning (ASAIHL)
seventh general conference. SLQ
7 (1969) 143-148.

10508 La premier conference UNESCO sur
la culture malaise, Kuala Lumpur,
janvier, 1972. AR 4 (1972) 27-
30.

10509 RICH, JOHN. Conferences on cultural minorities. PS 15 (1967)
177-182.

10510 SOLHEIM, WILHELM G. International congresses and symposia. AP
10 (1967) 1-8.

10511 SUNDRUM, R. M. Manpower and educational development in East and
Southeast Asia, a summary of conference proceedings. MER 16 pt.
2 (1971) 78-90.

10512 Third international conference on
educational research in Asia and
the southern Pacific, 1968. SLQ
6 (1968) 496-509.

10513 Viewpoints from the Bangkok conference. E36 pp. 375-387.

10514 WONG, LESLIE G. J. Foreword,
papers presented at the symposium
on the role of management in industrialization in Malaysia. MER
8 pt. 1 (1963) 1-3.

CULTURE - BRUNEI

10515 IBRAHIM BIN MOHD. JAHFAR. Brunei
adat. BMJ 1 (1969) 5-9.

DIVORCE - INDONESIA

10516 MASRI SINGARIMBUN. Marriage and
divorce in Mojolama, by Masri
Singarimbun and Chris Manning.
IND 17 (1974) 67-82.

Drama - Philippines

DRAMA - PHILIPPINES

10517 REALUBIT, MARIA LILIA. Prelimi-
       nary catalogue of Bikol dramas.
       AST 11 pt. 2 (1973) 155-161.

ECONOMIC DEVELOPMENT - MALAYSIA

10518 THAM SEONG CHEE. Ideology, poli-
       tics and economic modernization,
       the case of the Malays in Malay-
       sia. SAJSS 1 pt. 1 (1973) 41-59.

ECONOMIC HISTORY - PHILIPPINES

10519 QUIASON, SERAFIN D. East India
       Company in Manila, 1762-1764.
       PSSHR 28 (1963) 424-444.

ELECTIONS - INDONESIA

10520 CROUCH, HAROLD. The army, the
       parties and elections. IND 11
       (1971) 177-191.

ELECTIONS - MALAYSIA - 1973

10521 NUAI CHIN. Statement. JCA 3
       (1973) 496-7.

FOLK LITERATURE - PHILIPPINES

10522 LAMBRECHT, FRANCIS. Ifugaw
       Hudhud literature. SLQ 3 (1965)
       191-214.

10523 ZIEGLER, JOHN H. A 1932 collec-
       tion of Sulu folktales. S92 pp.
       105-159.

FOLK LITERATURE - VIETNAM

10524 NGUYEN DINH HOA. Vietnamese
       riddles. AC 2 (Jan. 1960) 107-
       127.

GENEALOGY - INDONESIA

10525 FOX, JAMES J. Rotinese dynastic
       genealogy, structure and event.
       T77 pp. 37-77.

HINDUISM - INDONESIA

10526 MERSHON, KATHARANE EDSON. Five
       great elements, Pancha Maha Buta.
       B43 pp. 57-66.

HINDUISM - INDONESIA - BALI

10527 HOOYKAAS, C. Weda and Sisya,
       Rsi and Bhujangga in present day
       Bali. BIJ 120 (1964) 231-244.

HISTORIOGRAPHY AND HISTORICAL SOURCES - INDONESIA

10528 NOORDUYN, J. Origins of south
       Celebes historical writing. S61
       pp. 137-155.

HISTORIOGRAPHY AND HISTORICAL SOURCES - VIETNAM

10529 NGUYEN THE ANH. Les publications
       de documents historiques dans la
       Republique du Vietnam depuis
       1955. SEIB 43 (1968) 53-60.

HOUSING - PHILIPPINES

10530 FRAKE, CHARLES O. How to enter a
       Yakan house. S92.1 pp. 87-104.

IFUGAO

10531 MAHER, ROBERT F. Archaeological
       investigations in central Ifugao.
       AP 16 (1973) 39-70.

10532 ROXAS-LIM, AURORA. Art in Ifugao society. AST 11 pt. 2 (1973) 47-74.

IFUGAO LITERATURE

10533 CORONEL, MARIA DELIA. Ifugao stories. UN 39 (1966) 591-612.

INDONESIAN LITERATURE

10534 IDRUS. Surabaja. IND 5 (1968) 1-28.

10535 IDRUS. Two stories of the Japanese occupation. Fujinkai, and, Och . . . och . . . och. IND 2 (1966) 125-134.

INDONESIAN LITERATURE - CRITICISM

10536 LOMBARD-SALMON, CLAUDINE. Aux origines de la litterature Sino-Malaise, un sjair publicitaire de 1886. AR 8 (1974) 155-186.

INDUSTRIALIZATION - THAILAND

10537 Modernization and industrialization of Thai society, a sociological analysis, by Kenichi Tominaga, Hiroshi Komai, Hideo Okamoto and Michiko Ise. EACS 8 (1969) 1-39.

ISLAM - INDONESIA

10538 TAUFIK ABDULLAH. Adat and Islam, an examination of conflict in Minangkabau. IND 2 (1966) 1-24.

ISLAM - MALAYSIA

10539 AHMAD BIN MOHAMED IBRAHIM. Islam and customary law in the Malaysian legal context. C39 pp. 107-145.

JATAKA TALES

10540 MARTINI, GINETTE. Un Jataka concernant le dernier repas de Buddha. BEF 59 (1972) 251-255.

JOHORE

10541 NOSSIN, J. J. Relief and coastal development in north-eastern Johore, Malaya. JTG 15 (1961) 27-38.

KELANTAN

10542 WINZELER, ROBERT L. Ethnic complexity and ethnic relations in an east coast Malay town. SAJSS 2 (1974) 45-61.

KOXINGA

10543 ABELLA, DOMINGO. Koxinga nearly ended Spanish rule in the Philippines in 1662. PHR 2 (1969) 295-350.

LANGUAGES - PHILIPPINES

10544 RUZUI, SEPTY. Survey of relations between Indonesian, Malay and the main languages of the Philippines. UN 35 (1962) 22-80.

LUANG PRABANG

10545 KIMURA, SOKICHI. Annotated translation of *Dai-nam Chinh-bien Liet-truyen So-tap, Nam-chuong-truyen* (description of Luang Prabang). SA 1 (1971) 153-163.

Malacca

MALACCA

10546 IRWIN, GRAHAM. Malacca fort. JSAH 3 (Sept. 1962) 19-44.

MALAYSIA - BIBLIOGRAPHIES

10547 Bibliography of Kelantan. K33 pp. 319-350.

MALOLOS

10548 AGONCILLO, TEODORO A. Malolos, the crisis of the republic. PSSHR 25 (1960) 1-831.

MANUSCRIPTS - GREAT BRITAIN

10549 RICKLEFS, M. C. Note on Professor Johns's "Gift addressed to the spirit of the prophet." BIJ 129 (1973) 347-349.

MANUSCRIPTS - MALAYSIA

10550 VOORHOEVE, P. De grote Hikajat Bachtiar. BIJ 125 (1969) 374-5.

MANUSCRIPTS - THAILAND

10551 MARR, J. R. Some manuscripts in Grantha script in Bangkok. SOAS 32 (1969) 281-322.

10552 MARR, J. R. Some manuscripts in Grantha script in Bangkok, II. JSS 60 pt. 2 (1972) 61-86.

10553 MARTINI, GINETTE. Brapamsuku-lanisamsam. BEF 60 (1973) 55-78.

10554 MARTINI, GINETTE. Un Jataka concernant le dernier repas de Buddha. BEF 59 (1972) 251-255.

MAPS

10555 SIMMONDS, E. H. S. Mahorasop II, the Thai National Library manuscript. SOAS 34 (1971) 119-131.

10556 BLAKISTON, N. Maps, plans and charts of Southeast Asia in the Public Record Office. SAA 2 (1969) 21-64.

MAT SALLEH

10557 CRISSWELL, COLIN NEIL. Mat Salleh rebellion reconsidered. SMJ 19 (1971) 155-165.

MELANAU

10558 TUTON KABOY. Ceramics and their uses among the coastal Melanus, by Tuton Kaboy and Eine Moore. SMJ 15 (1967) 10-29.

MENTAL TESTS - BURMA

10559 SEIN TU. Burmese modification of the Bernreuter Personality Inventory. JBRS 47 (1964) 77-87.

MINANGKABAU

10560 DJOJODIGOENO, M. M. Bloedverwantschap en clangemeenschap onder de Minangkabauers. BIJ 124 (1968) 262-272.

10561 KLOOS, P. Duolineaire afstamming en het matrilaterale cross-cousin huwelijk, repliek. BIJ 119 (1964) 368-375.

MONGKUT, KING OF THAILAND

10562 BRADLEY, WILLIAM L. Prince Mongkut and Jesse Caswell. JSS 54
(1966) 29-41.

NETHERLANDS. KOLONIAAL ARCHIEF

10563 ROESSINGH, M. P. H. Dutch relations with the Philippines, a
survey of sources in the General
State Archives, The Hague, Netherlands. AST 5 (1967) 377-407.

PEOPLES ACTION PARTY

10564 BELLOWS, THOMAS J. Singapore
party system. JSAH 8 (1967) 122-
138.

PHILIPPINE LITERATURE

10565 HUFANA, ALEJANDRINO G. Sources of
retrieval in Philippine vernacular
literature. GEJ 17 (1969) 125-
130.

PHILIPPINE LITERATURE - PROSE - CRITICISM

10566 VILLANUEVA, ANTONIA F. Philippine
epics. UN 41 (1968) 143-172.

PHILIPPINES - FOREIGN RELATIONS - JAPAN

10567 GOSIENGFIAO, VICTOR. Japanese occupation, the cultural campaign.
PS 14 (1966) 228-242.

PHILIPPINES - FOREIGN RELATIONS - NETHERLANDS

10568 ROESSINGH, M. P. H. Dutch relations with the Philippines, a
survey of sources in the General
State Archives, The Hague, Netherlands. AST 5 (1967) 377-407.

PHILIPPINES - POPULATION

10569 GOROSPE, VITALIANO R. Catholic
hierarchy and the population
problem. G73 pp. 157-163.

PHILIPPINES. CONGRESS

10570 PERALTA, VICENTE L. Congress and
economic planning. M38 pp. 76-82.

10571 PUYAT, GIL J. Congress and economic planning. M38 pp. 62-75.

PILIPINO LANGUAGE

10572 MARTIN, DALMACIO. Language, education and literacy. SJ 15
(1968) 414-426.

POLITICAL PARTIES - INDONESIA

10573 CROUCH, HAROLD. The army, the
parties and elections. IND 11
(1971) 177-191.

POLITICAL PARTIES - PHILIPPINES

10574 LOCSIN, TEODORO M. So called two
party system in the Philippines.
AST 2 (1964) 82-86.

SABAH

10575 CRISSWELL, COLIN NEIL. Mat
Salleh rebellion reconsidered.
SMJ 19 (1971) 155-165.

SAEK LANGUAGE

10576 GEDNEY, WILLIAM J. Saek language
of Nakhon Phanom Province. JSS
58 pt. 1 (1970) 67-87.

SAIGON

10577 HENDRY, JAMES B. Some social and economic characteristics of the work force in Saigon. C58 pp. 191-218.

SAKAI

10578 DENTAN, R. K. Semai response to mental aberration. BIJ 124 (1968) 135-158.

SAMAL LITERATURE

10579 CORONEL, MARIA DELIA. Taosug-Samal stories. UN 39 (1966) 503-519.

SANSKRIT LITERATURE

10580 BOSCH, F. D. K. Bhimastava. J41 pp. 57-62.

10581 MINATTUR, JOSEPH. Note on berita. RSA (1967) 99-101.

SARAWAK - HISTORY

10582 ONGKILI, JAMES P. Pre-western Brunei, Sarawak and Sabah. SMJ 20 (1972) 1-20.

SARAWAK - SOCIAL CONDITIONS

10583 MORRIS, H. S. In the wake of mechanization, sago and society in Sarawak. S58 pp. 273-301.

SCIENCE - PHILIPPINES

10584 ASIS, CONSUELO V. Natural science II in the general education program. GEJ 1 (1961) 89-92.

SHAH SHUJA

10585 HALL, D. G. E. Studies in Dutch relations with Arakan. III. Shah Shuja and the Dutch withdrawal of 1665. B92 pp. 88-97.

SILLIMAN UNIVERSITY

10586 Abstracts of M.A. theses at Silliman University. SJ 17 (1970) 211-229.

10587 Abstracts of M.A. theses at Silliman University. SJ 18 (1971) 97-123.

10588 Abstracts of M.A. theses at Silliman University. SJ 18 (1971) 217-239.

10589 Abstracts of M.A. theses at Silliman University. SJ 18 (1971) 441-452.

10590 Abstracts of M.A. theses at Silliman University. SJ 19 (1972) 112-121.

10591 Abstracts of M.A. theses at Silliman University. SJ 19 (1972) 230-247.

10592 YGNALAGA, EMILIANO C. Study of the status of Silliman University High School graduates. SJ 7 (1960) 72-84.

SUHARTO

10593 FEITH, HERBERT. Suharto's search for a political format. IND 6 (1968) 88-105.

SULOD

10594 JOCANO, F. LANDA. Notes on the Sulod concept of death, the soul,

and the region of the dead. PS
12 (1964) 51-62.

SUNDANESE

10595 PALMER, ANDREA WILCOX. Sundanese
village. S58 pp. 42-51.

TAGALOG LITERATURE

10596 HERNANDEZ, AMADO. Ang mga bagong
propagandista panulatang Tagalog
sa 1900-1941. PS 17 (1969) 195-
219.

10597 LUMBERA, BIENVENIDO. Poetry of
the early Tagalogs. PS 16 (1968)
221-245.

10598 LUMBERA, BIENVENIDO. Tagalog
poetry during the seventeenth
century. PS 16 (1968) 99-130.

TAOSUG

10599 KASMAN, EDWARD SALKIYA. Birth and
death rituals among the Tausugs
of Siasi. UN 35 (1962) 291-340.

TEMPLES - CAMBODIA

10600 BENISTI, MIREILLE. Notes d'iconographie khmere. VIII. Le linteau
de Vat Preah Theat. BEF 58
(1971) 125-130.

TEMPLES - THAILAND

10601 MOERMAN, MICHAEL. Ban Ping's
temple, the center of a loosely
structured society. C66 pp. 137-
174.

THAI LANGUAGE

10602 DOWNER, G. B. Chinese, Thai and
Miao-Yao. L55 pp. 133-139.

THAI LITERATURE

10603 WYATT, DAVID K. Abridged royal
chronicle of Ayudhya of Prince
Paramanuchitchinorot. JSS 61 pt.
1 (1973) 25-50.

THAILAND

10604 GEDNEY, WILLIAM J. Some questions on the northeast. AS 6
(1966) 379-380.

THAILAND - FOREIGN RELATIONS - CHINA

10605 FLOOD, E. THADEUS. Sukhothai-
Mongol relations, a note on relevant Chinese and Thai sources
with translations. JSS 57 (1969)
201-257.

THAILAND - LAWS, STATUTES, ETC.

10606 ADUL WICHIENCHAROEN. Some main
features of modernization of
ancient family law in Thailand,
by Adul Wichiencharoen and Luang
Chamroon Netisastra. C39 pp. 89-
106.

THIRITHUDHAMMA, KING OF ARAKAN

10607 HALL, D. G. E. Studies in Dutch
relations with Arakan. I. Dutch
relations with King Thirithudhamma of Arakan, 1622-38. B92
pp. 67-77.

TRANSPORTATION - LAOS

10608 SCOTT, PETER DALE. Air America,
flying the U.S. into Laos. L18
pp. 301-321.

TRUONG VINH KY

10609 OSBORNE, MILTON E. Truong Vinh
Ky and Phan Thanh Gian, the problem of a nationalist interpretation of 19th century Vietnamese
history. JAS 30 (1970-1) 81-93.

URBANIZATION - PHILIPPINES

10610 HOLLNSTEINER, MARY R. AECD, its
implications for the Philippines
urban and industrial development.
PS 19 (1971) 13-24.
Comment: BLANCO, JOSE C. Com-
ments. PS 19 (1971) 25-6.
Comment: DOROMAL, QUINTIN S.
Comments. PS 19 (1971) 24.

10611 HOLLNSTEINER, MARY R. Inner
Tondo as a way of life. SLQ 5
(1967) 13-26.

10612 POETHIG, RICHARD P. Philippine
urban family. SLQ 6 (1968) 375-
390.

VIETNAM - ECONOMIC CONDITIONS

10613 ANG DVAN NGU. Role of the masses
in raising the standard of welfare. JBRS 43 (1960) 37-40.

VIETNAM - FOREIGN RELATIONS - FRANCE

10614 MADING, KLAUS. Suzerainty over
Annam, a legal discussion, China's traditional concept destroyed by French ascendency.
S93 pp. 150-152.

VIETNAM - MINORITIES

10615 BUTTINGER, JOSEPH. Ethnic minorities in the Republic of Vietnam.
C58 pp. 99-121.

VIETNAM - POLITICS AND GOVERNMENT - 1963-

10616 JOINER, CHARLES A. South Vietnam,
political, military and constitutional arenas in nationbuilding.
AS 8 (1968) 58-71.

VIETNAM - RELIGION

10617 McLANE, JOHN R. Archaic movements and revolution in southern
Vietnam. N15 pp. 68-101.

VIETNAM WAR

10618 SOWARD, F. H. Great debate over
American policy in Southeast
Asia. PA 40 (1967) 341-346.

VILLAGE STUDIES - MALAYSIA

10619 PRATTIS, IAN. Kayan-Kenyah
Bungan cult in Sarawak. SMJ 11
(1963) 64-87.

10620 SANDIN, BENEDICT. Baketans. SMJ
16 (1968) 111-121.

10621 SWIFT, M. G. Accumulation of
capital in a peasant economy.
S48 pp. 21-37.

10622 WILLIAMS, THOMAS R. Comment on
the social anthropology of Sabah,
response to Appell, Sather and
Goethals. SMJ 16 (1968) 440-452.

VILLAGE STUDIES - PHILIPPINES - INDIVID-
UAL AREAS

10623   ORACION, TIMOTEO S.   Kaingin agriculture among the Bukidnons of
southeastern Negros, central
Philippines.   E78 pp. 233-249.

VILLAGE STUDIES - PHILIPPINES - INDIVID-
UAL AREAS - LUZON

10624   HOLLNSTEINER, MARY R.   Reciprocity
in the lowland Philippines.   PS 9
(1961) 387-413.

VILLAGE STUDIES - THAILAND

10625   SPIELMANN, HANS J.   Note on the
literature on the Lahu Shehleh
and Lahu Na of northern Thailand.
JSS 57 (1969) 321-332.

VILLAGE STUDIES - VIETNAM

10626   LE VAN HAO.   Introduction a
l'ethnologie du Dinh.   SEIB 37
(1962) 41-72.

WALLICH, NATHANIEL

10627   HANITSCH, R.   Letters of Nathaniel Wallich relating to the
establishment of Botanical Garden
in Singapore.   JMBRAS 42 pt. 1
(1969) 145-154.

WOMEN - PHILIPPINES

10628   INFANTE, TERESITA R.   Woman in
early Philippines, and among the
cultural minorities.   UN 42
(Sept. 1969) 4-196.

10629   LIM, PILAR HIDALGO.   Women's suffrage since 1937.   UN 40 (1967)
414-422.

WORLD WAR II - INDONESIA

10630   SLUIMERS, L.   Nieuwe orde op
Java, de Japanse bezettingspoli-
tiek en de Indonesische elites,
1942-1943.   BIJ 124 (1968) 336-
367.

WORLD WAR II - PHILIPPINES

10631   AGONCILLO, TEODORO A.   Cultural
aspect of the Japanese occupation.   PSSHR 28 (1963) 351-394.

10632   GOSIENGFIAO, VICTOR.   Japanese
occupation, the cultural campaign.   PS 14 (1966) 228-242.

WORLD WAR II - THAILAND

10633   MARTIN, JAMES V.   Thai-American
relations in World War II.   JAS
22 (1962-3) 451-467.

YAO

10634   CHOB KACHA ANANDA.   Le systeme de
la famille Yao.   JSS 60 pt. 1
(1972) 187-194.

Book Reviews

* ABAD, GEMINO M. Fugitive emphasis.
Quezon City, Univ. of the Philippines Pr., 1973.
    PS 22 (1974) 204-208. (J. A.
    Galdon)

ABD ALLAH IBN ABD AL-KADIR, MUNSHI.
Hikayat Abdullah. Kuala Lumpur,
Oxford UP, 1970. (Oxford in Asia
historical reprints)
    JSAS 3 (1972) 349-350. (Slamet-
    muljana)
    SOAS 35 (1972) 442. (E. C. G.
    Barrett)

Abdul Haris Nasution *See* NASUTION,
ABDUL HARIS

Abdul Majeed Mohamed Mackeen *See*
MACKEEN, ABDUL MAJEED MOHAMED

Abdul Rahman bin Yusop *See* Collins
Malay gem dictionary

ABDUL RAHMAN, TUNKU. May 13, before
and after. Kuala Lumpur, Utusan
Melayu Pr., 1969.
    JAS 31 (1971-2) 734-736. (G. D.
    Ness)

Abdullah bin Abdul Kadir *See* ABD
ALLAH IBN ABD AL-KADIR, MUNSHI

Abdullah Majid *See* RICE, OLIVER.
Modern Malay verse

ABDURACHIM, IIH. Dasar-dasar anthro-
pologi Indonesia. Bandung, Penerbit
Widjaja, 1962.
    AAS 2 (1966) 161-2. (R. Raczynski)

Abel, Elie *See* KALB, MARVIN L.
Roots of involvement

ABRERA, JOSEFA B. Annotated bibliography of the history of the sugar
industry in Panay and Negros. Quezon City, Ateneo de Manila, 1963.
    JSAH 6 (Mar. 1966) 137-8. (D. V.
    Hart)

ABUEVA, JOSE VELOSO. Focus on the
barrio; the story behind the birth
of the Philippine Community Development Program under President Magsaysay. Manila, Institute of Public
Administration, Univ. of the Philippines, 1959. (Quezon, Philippines.
Univ. of the Philippines. Institute
of Public Administration. Studies in
public administration, no. 5)
    JAS 20 (1960-1) 124-5. (D. V.
    Hart)
    PA 34 (1961) 314. (D. V. Hart)
    PS 8 (1960) 644-648. (J. E.
    Montenegro)
    SJ 8 (1961) 213-215. (C. L. Hunt)

ABUEVA, JOSE VELOSO. Foundations and
dynamics of Filipino government and
politics, by Jose V. Abueva and R.
P. de Guzman. Manila, Bookmark,
1969.
    PA 43 (1970) 470-1. (M. Leifer)

ABUEVA, JOSE VELOSO. Handbook of
Philippine public administration, by
Jose V. Abueva and Raul P. de Guzman. Manila, Social Research Associates, 1967.
    JAS 28 (1968-9) 654-5. (F. W.
    Riggs)

ABUEVA, JOSE VELOSO. Ramon Magsaysay,
a political biography. Manila, Solidaridad, 1971.
    JAS 32 (1972-3) 758-9. (G. K.
    Goodman)
    SA 2 (1972) 529. (R. P. de Guzman)

Achutegui, Pedro S. de. Aguinaldo and

ACHUTEGUI, PEDRO S. DE. Aguinaldo and
the revolution of 1896, a documentary history, by Pedro S. de Achutegui
and Miguel A. Bernad. Manila, Ateneo
de Manila, 1972.
   PA 46 (1973) 608-9. (J. A. Larkin)

ACHUTEGUI, PEDRO S. DE. Religious
revolution in the Philippines, by
Pedro S. de Achutegui and Miguel A.
Bernad. Quezon City, Ateneo de Ma-
nila UP, 1960-71. 3v.
Volume I.
   JAS 20 (1960-1) 541-2. (D. Wurfel)
   PS 8 (1960) 868-871. (L. A. Cul-
      lum)
   SJ 8 (1961) 55-6. (E. K. Higdon)
   UN 33 (1960) 667-8.
Volume II.
   JAS 27 (1967-8) 183-4. (D. Wurfel)
   SJ 15 (1968) 304-308. (P. G.
      Gowing)
   SLQ 4 (1966) 617-619. (H. Geeroms)
Volume III.
   JAS 32 (1972-3) 223-4. (J. A.
      Larkin)
   SLURJ 2 (1971) 698-9. (F. L.
      Lorente)

ADAMS, CINDY (HELLER). My friend the
dictator. Indianapolis, Bobbs-
Merrill, 1967.
   PA 41 (1968) 610-613. (B. B.
      Hering)

ADAMS, MARIE JEANNE. System and mean-
ing of East Sumba textile design, a
study in traditional Indonesian art.
New Haven, Southeast Asia Studies,
Yale Univ., 1969. (Yale Univ.
Graduate School. Southeast Asia
Studies. Cultural report series, no.
16)
   JSAS 1 pt. 1 (1970) 117-8. (C.
      Ong)
   JSS 61 pt. 1 (1973) 379-380. (H.
      W. Woodward)

Adams, Nina S. *See* Laos: war and
revolution

ADAS, MICHAEL. The Burma delta: economic development and social change
on an Asian rice frontier, 1852-
1941. Madison, Univ. of Wisconsin
Pr., 1974.
   PA 47 (1974) 569-570. (D. G. E.
      Hall)

Adat Atjeh, reproduced in facsimile
from a manuscript in the India Office Library, with an introduction
and notes by G. W. J. Drewes and P.
Voorhoeve. The Hague, Nijhoff,
1958. (Instituut voor Taal-, Land-
en Volkenkunde, Verhandelingen, deel
24)
   SOAS 23 (1960) 179. (E. C. G.
      Barrett)

Aebersold, W. E. *See* STELLER, K. G.
F. Sangirees-Nederlands woordenboek

AGONCILLO, TEODORO A. Malolos: the
crisis of the republic. Quezon
City, Univ. of the Philippines,
1960.
   JAS 21 (1961-2) 92-3. (E. Wick-
      berg)

AGONCILLO, TEODORO A. Short history
of the Filipino people, by Teodoro
A. Agoncillo and Oscar M. Alfonso.
Quezon City, Univ. of the Philip-
pines, 1960.
   PS 10 (1962) 317-319. (C. Qui-
      rino)

* AGPALO, REMIGIO E. Political elite
and the people, a study of politics
in Occidental Mindoro. Manila, College of Public Administration, Univ.
of the Philippines, 1972.
   JAS 33 (1973-4) 503-505. (K. G.
      Machado)
   PA 47 (1974) 254-256. (R. S.
      Milne)

AGPALO, REMIGIO E. Political process
and the nationalization of the retail trade in the Philippines.

Diliman, Univ. of the Philippines,
Office of Coordinator of Research,
1962.
    JAS 23 (1963-4) 142. (F. H. Golay)
    PA 37 (1964) 474. (R. Butwell)

Agricultural revolution in Southeast
Asia, report of the SEADAG Rural De-
velopment Seminar. New York, Asia
Society, 1970. 2v.
    JAS 31 (1971-2) 452-454. (B. Glass-
        burner)

AGUNG, IDE ANAK AGUNG GDE. Twenty
years Indonesian foreign policy,
1945-1965. The Hague, Mouton, 1973.
    JCA 4 (1974) 365.
    PA 47 (1974) 576-578. (J. D. Legge)

Ahmad Hasan Dani *See* DANI, AHMAD
HASAN

Ahmad M. Ibrahim *See* IBRAHIM, AHMAD
M.

AIDA, YUJI. Prisoner of the British:
a Japanese soldier's experiences in
Burma. London, Creset Pr., 1966.
    MAS 2 (1968) 280-282. (C. A.
        Fisher)

Ailsa Zainuddin *See* ZAINUDDIN, AILSA
GWENNTH

AJIA KEIZAI KENKYUJO, TOKYO. Documentary materials in Asian countries,
report of a survey by a study group
of the Institute of Asian Economic
Affairs. Tokyo, Institute of Asian
Economic Affairs, 1963.
    JAS 21 (1961-2) 371. (Choh-Ming Li)

AKADEMIIA NAUK SSSR. INSTITUT NARODOV
AZII. Iazyki Iugo-Vostochnoi Azii,
[edited by] I. A. Gorgoniev, L. N.
Morev [and] N. V. Solntseva.
Moscow, Nauka, 1967.
    AAS 5 (1969) 109-111. V. Krupa)

AKADEMIIA NAUK SSSR. INSTITUT NARODOV
AZII. Ocherki iz istorii Iugo-

Akkeren, Philip van. Sri and Christ

Vostochnoi Azii, [by] V. A. Tjurin.
Moscow, Izdatelstvo Nauka, 1965.
    AAS 3 (1967) 182-3. (R.
        Raczynski)

Akagi, Osamu *See* ISHII, YONEO. Glossary index of the Sukhothai inscriptions

Akagi, Osamu *See* ISHII, YONEO. Selected Thai bibliography on the
reign of King Chulalongkorn

AKASHI, YOJI. Nanyang Chinese nation-
al salvation movement, 1937-41.
Lawrence, Center for East Asian
Studies, Univ. of Kansas, 1970.
(Kansas. Univ. Center for East Asian
Studies. International studies, East
Asian series, research publication,
no. 5)
    JAS 30 (1970-1) 878-9. (S. Leong)
    JSAS 3 (1972) 148-150. (Png Poh-
        seng)
    PA 44 (1971) 145-6. (L. E. Wil-
        liams)

AKIN RABIBHADANA, M. R. Organization
of Thai society in the early Bangkok
period, 1782-1873. Ithaca, Southeast Asia Program, Cornell Univ.,
1969. (Cornell Univ. Southeast Asia
Program. Data paper no. 74) (Cornell
Univ. Thailand Project. Interim reports series, no. 12)
    JAS 30 (1970-1) 728-9. (T. Bunnag)
    JSAS 2 (1971) 264-5. (J. H. Kemp)
    JSS 59 pt. 1 (1971) 233-235. (W.
        F. Vella)
    PS 20 (1972) 199-200.
    SA 2 (1972) 502-514. (K. P. Lan-
        don)

AKKEREN, PHILIP VAN. Sri and Christ,
a study of the indigenous church in
east Java. London, Butterworth,
1970. (World studies of churches in
mission)
    BIJ 129 (1973) 513-516. (E. J.
        Schoonhoven)

Alatas, Syed Hussein. Modernization

ALATAS, SYED HUSSEIN. Modernization and social change, studies in modernization, religion, social change and development in South-East Asia. Sydney, Angus and Robertson, 1972.
JOSA 9 (1972) 117-8. (K. G. Tregonning)

ALATAS, SYED HUSSEIN. Sociology of corruption; the nature, function, causes and prevention of corruption. Singapore, Donald Moore, 1968.
JSAS 1 pt. 2 (1970) 142-3. (Riaz Hassan)

ALBINSKI, HENRY STEPHEN. Politics and foreign policy in Australia; the impact of Vietnam and conscription. Durham, Duke UP, 1970.
PA 44 (1971) 150-1. (H. G. Gelber)

ALEXANDER, GARTH. Silent invasion, the Chinese in Southeast Asia. London, Macdonald, 1973.
PS 21 (1973) 480-482. (C. I. McCarthy)

ALEXANDROWICZ, CHARLES HENRY. Introduction to the history of the law of nations in the East Indies, 16th, 17th, and 18th centuries. Oxford, Clarendon Pr., 1967.
JAS 27 (1967-8) 673-4. (S. P. Sharma)
MAS 4 (1970) 178-9. (P. Lyon)
PA 40 (1967) 410-1. (I. L. Head)

ALFON, ESTRELLA D. Magnificence and other stories. Manila, Regal Printing Co., 1960.
PA 35 (1962) 82-3. (D. V. Hart)

ALFONSO, OSCAR M. Theodore Roosevelt and the Philippines, 1897-1909. Quezon City, Univ. of the Philippines Pr., 1970.
JAS 30 (1970-1) 740-1. (P. W. Stanley)
PS 20 (1972) 668-671. (J. N. Schumacher)

* ALI BIN RAJA HAJI AHMAD, RAJA HAJI. Tuhfat al-Nafis. Singapore, Malaysia Publications, 1965.
JSAH 8 (Sept. 1967) 325. (C. Skinner)

ALI HAJI AHMAD. Puisi baharu Melayu; zaman permulaan. Kuala Lumpur, Dewan Bahasa dan Pustaka, 1959.
BIJ 117 (1961) 300-302. (A. Teeuw)

ALINEA, ESTANISLAO B. Historia analitica de la literatura Filipinohispana desde 1566 hasta mediados de 1964. Quezon City, 1964.
PS 12 (1964) 743-4. (M. A. Bernad)

ALISJAHBANA, SUTAN TAKDIR. Grotta Azzurra; kisah chinta dan chita. Djakarta, Dian Rakjat, 1970.
AR 3 (1972) 236-238. (H. Chambert-Loir)

ALISJAHBANA, SUTAN TAKDIR. Indonesia: social and cultural revolution. 2d. ed. Kuala Lumpur, Oxford UP, 1966.
JAS 26 (1966-7) 756-7. (M. Walker)
JSAH 8 (Sept. 1967) 346-7. (R. Van Niel)
SOAS 30 (1967) 474. (H. Tinker)

ALISJAHBANA, SUTAN TAKDIR. Values as integrating forces in personality, society and culture. Kuala Lumpur, Univ. of Malaya Pr., 1966.
BIJ 124 (1968) 558-560. (R. F. Beerling)

Aliyeva, Natalia Fedorvna *See* Grammatika Indonezii skogo iazyka

ALLEN, JAMES DE V. Malayan Union. New Haven, Southeast Asia Studies, Yale Univ., 1967. (Yale Univ. Graduate School. Southeast Asia Studies. Monograph series, no. 10)
BIJ 124 (1968) 302-3. (M. Leifer)
MAS 3 (1969) 87-8. (J. Bastin)
PA 41 (1968) 119. (R. S. Milne)

ALLEN, RICHARD HUGH SEDLEY. Malaysia, prospect and retrospect: the impact and aftermath of colonial rule. London, Oxford UP, 1968.
  PA 41 (1968) 621-2. (L. A. Williams)

ALLEN, RICHARD HUGH SEDLEY. Short introduction to the history and politics of Southeast Asia. New York, Oxford UP, 1970.
  JAS 30 (1970-1) 500-502. (L. W. Pye)
  JSAS 2 (1971) 248-9. (C. A. Trocki)
  PA 43 (1970) 625. (K. G. Tregonning)
  SA 1 (1971) 398-400. (E. Thio)

ALMOND, GABRIEL ABRAHAM. Politics of the developing areas. Princeton, Princeton UP, 1960.
  JAS 20 (1960-1) 85-87. (L. Mair)

Alonso, Isidoro *See* Catholic Church in the Philippines today

ALTBACH, PHILIP G. Higher education in developing countries: a select bibliography. Cambridge, Center for International Affairs, Harvard Univ., 1970. (Harvard Univ. Center for International Affairs. Occasional papers in international affairs, no. 24)
  PA 44 (1971) 160. (J. Fischer)

ALVAREZ ENRIQUEZ, EMIGDIO. Devil flower. New York, Hill and Wang, 1959.
  PS 9 (1961) 172-182. (J. A. Galdon)

ALZONA, ENCARNACION. Julio Nakpil and the Philippine revolution, with the autobiography of Gregoria de Jesus. Edited and translated by Encarnacion Alzona. Manila, 1964.
  PS 12 (1964) 747-8. (H. de la Costa)

AMELSVOORT, V. F. P. M. VAN. Culture, stone age and modern medicine; the early introduction of integrated rural health in a non-literate society, a New Guinea case study in medical anthropology. Assen, Van Gorcum, 1964.
  BIJ 123 (1967) 289-292. (R. S. Wassing)

AMERICAN ASSEMBLY. Philippine-American relations, edited by Frank H. Golay. Manila, Solidaridad, 1966.
  PS 15 (1967) 735-738. (A. E. Lapitan)

AMERICAN ASSEMBLY. United States and the Philippines, edited by Frank H. Golay. Engelwood Cliffs, Prentice-Hall, 1966.
  AS 7 (1967) 594.
  JAH 2 (1968) 189-190. (M. P. Onorato)
  JAS 26 (1966-7) 356-7. (T. Friend)
  MAS 1 (1967) 303-4. (M. Leifer)
  PA 39 (1966) 415-6. (R. S. Milne)

American Friends Service Committee *See* FRIENDS, SOCIETY OF. AMERICAN FRIENDS SERVICE COMMITTEE

AMERICAN UNIVERSITIES FIELD STAFF. Select bibliography: Asia, Africa, Eastern Europe, Latin America. New York, AUFS, 1960.
  PS 9 (1961) 550-1. (R. J. Suchan)

America's Asia: dissenting essays on Asian American relations, edited by Edward Friedman and Mark Selden. New York, Pantheon, 1971.
  JCA 2 (1972) 94-5. (J. Fast)

AMIN, ENTJI. Sja'ir Perang Mengkasar (The rhymed chronicle of the Macassar war) edited and translated by C. Skinner. The Hague, Nijhoff, 1963. (Instituut voor Taal-, Land- en Volkenkunde. Verhandelingen, deel 40)

Anwar, Chairil. Selected poems.

PS 15 (1967) 515-517. (J. N. Schumacher)
SLQ 5 (1967) 235-6. (S. M. Tanedo)

Anderson, Gerald H. *See* NEILL,
STEPHEN CHARLES. Concise dictionary
of the Christian world mission

ANDERSON, GERALD H. Studies in Philip-
pine church history. Ithaca, Cor-
nell UP, 1969.
JAH 5 (1971) 178-9. (E. Wickberg)
JAS 29 (1969-70) 994-997. (D. V.
Hart)
JSAS 2 (1971) 241. (J. A. Larkin)
PA 44 (1971) 467-469. (C. O.
Houston)
PS 18 (1970) 197-204. (P. S. de
Achutegui)
SA 3 (1974-5) 649-651. (N. P.
Cushner)

ANDERSON, JOHN. Acheen and the ports
of the north and east coasts of Sumatra. Kuala Lumpur, Oxford UP,
1971. (Oxford in Asia historical
reprints)
PA 45 (1972) 325-6. (D. G. E.
Hall)

* ANDREWS, WILLIAM R. Village war,
Vietnamese Communist revolutionary
activities in Dinh Tuong Province,
1960-1964. Columbia, Univ. of Missouri Pr., 1973.
PA 47 (1974) 99-100. (Huynh Kim
Khanh)

* ANDRIEU, CHARLES. L'enseignement de
Ledi Sayadaw. Paris, Albin Michel,
1961.
FA 19 (1963) 723-729. (J. Christan)

ANGLADETTE, ANDRE. Le riz. Paris,
Presses universitaires de France,
1959. (Que sais-je? no. 305)
SEIB 35 (1960) 735.

Anniversary contributions to anthropology: twelve essays. Published on
the occasion of the 40th anniversary

of the Leiden Ethnological Society.
Leiden, Brill, 1970.
BIJ 127 (1971) 190-193. (J. Van-
sina)

Anthologie de la poesie vietnamienne.
Paris, Editeurs francais reunis,
1969.
BEF 57 (1970) 243-245. (N. Louis)

ANTHONY, EDWARD MASON. Foundations of
Thai, by Edward M. Anthony, Deborah
P. French and Udom Warotamasikkadit.
Ann Arbor, Univ. of Michigan Pr.,
1967-8. 2v.
JSS 58 pt. 1 (1970) 148-154. (R.
B. Noss)

Antler, Joyce *See* FUCHS, ELINOR.
Year one of the empire

ANTONISSEN, A. Kadazan-English and
English-Kadazan dictionary. Canber-
ra, GPO, 1958.
BIJ 120 (1964) 380-383. (J. J.
Ras)

ANUMAN RAJATHON. Essays on Thai folklore. Bangkok, Social Science Association Pr. of Thailand, 1968.
JSS 58 pt. 1 (1970) 125-6. (P. J.
S. Young)

ANUMAN RAJATHON. Life and ritual in
old Siam, three studies of Thai life
and customs, translated by William
J. Gedney. New Haven, Human Relations Area Files, 1961.
PA 35 (1962) 303-4. (R. J. Coughlin)

Anuman Rajathon *See* HART, DONN
VORHIS. Southeast Asian birth
customs

ANWAR, CHAIRIL. Selected poems. New
York, New Directions, 1963. (World
poets series)
SJ 14 (1967) 274-276. (E. L.
Tiempo)

Anwar, Chairil. Sharp gravel,

Asian PEN anthology.

Keyes)
    JSAS 3 (1972) 329-330. (M. W. Ross)
    MAS 7 (1973) 306-309. (M. Barber)

ARCILLA, JOSE S. Introduction to Phil-
    ippine history. Manila, Ateneo
    Publications, 1971.
      PS 19 (1971) 739. (M. A. Bernad)

ARENS, RICHARD. Ready made garment
    industry in Minglanilla, Cebu. Que-
    zon City, Community Development Re-
    search Council, 1960. (Quezon, Phil-
    ippines. Univ. of the Philippines.
    Community Development Research Coun-
    cil. Study series, no. 6)
      JAS 20 (1960-1) 399-403. (F. C.
      Madigan and D. V. Hart)

Ariff, M. O. *See* MOHAMED ARIFF BIN
    OTHMAN

Armengol, Pedro Ortiz *See* ORTIZ
    ARMENGOL, PEDRO

ARMSTRONG, JOHN P. Sihanouk speaks.
    New York, Walker, 1964.
      AS 5 (1965) 270.
      PA 37 (1965) 88. (W. E. Willmott)

* ARTHUR, NORMAN. Auxiliary verbs in My-
    ang of northern Thailand. Chiengmai,
    American Bible Society, 1967. (Hart-
    ford studies in linguistics, no. 22)
      JAS 29 (1969-70) 492-3. (J. A.
      Matisoff)

ARUEGO, JOSE MAMINTA. Philippine gov-
    ernment in action. Manila, Univ.
    Book Supply, 1960.
      SLQ 1 (1963) 146-148. (A. G. Gar-
      cia)

ASIA SOCIETY. American institutions
    and organizations interested in Asia:
    a reference directory. Editor:
    Ward Morehouse. 2d. ed. New York,
    Taplinger, 1961.
      JAS 21 (1961-2) 372. (R. Murphey)

ASIAN-AMERICAN ASSEMBLY, KUALA LUMPUR,
    1963. Cultural affairs and interna-
    tional understanding. Kuala Lumpur,
    Univ. of Malaya Pr., 1965.
      RSA (1966) 147-149. (M. Subhan)

ASIAN CONFERENCE ON INCOME AND WEALTH,
    1ST, HONGKONG, 1960. Asian studies
    in income and wealth, papers pre-
    sented at the first Asian Conference
    on Income and Wealth. New York,
    Asia Publishing House, 1965.
      JAS 25 (1965-6) 738-9. (E. B.
      Ayal)

* ASIAN DEVELOPMENT BANK. Economic re-
    port on Thailand, November 1969.
    n.p., n.d.
      JSS 58 pt. 2 (1970) 191-194.
      (Aswin Kongsiri)

Asian Development Bank *See* Southeast
    Asia's economy in the 1970's

ASIAN HISTORY CONGRESS, 1ST, DELHI,
    1961. Studies in Asian history.
    New York, Asia Publishing House,
    1969.
      JAS 30 (1970-1) 243. (R. A. Hut-
      tenback)

Asian newspapers' reluctant revolu-
    tion. Ames, Iowa State UP, 1971.
      JAH 6 (1972) 135-6. (C. K. Byrd)
      JOSA 8 (1972) 116-7. (B. S.
      McDougall)
      JSAS 3 (1972) 319-321. (D. Wilson)
      SA 2 (1972-3) 371-374. (T. C.
      Smythe)

* ASIAN PACIFIC COUNCIL. CULTURAL AND
    SOCIAL CENTRE. Asian Pacific short
    stories. Rutland, Tuttle, 1974.
      PA 47 (1974) 580. (G. Woodcock)

Asian PEN anthology, edited by F.
    Sionil Jose. New York, Taplinger,
    1966.
      PA 41 (1968) 651-2. (W. H. New)

Asian Peoples' Anti-Communist League

ASIAN PEOPLES' ANTI-COMMUNIST LEAGUE,
VIETNAM. Important documents. Saigon, Vietnam Chapter, 1956.
    PS 10 (1962) 717. (E. J. Keyes)

ASIAN SEMINAR ON MENTAL HEALTH AND
FAMILY LIFE. Reality and vision, a
report of the first Asian Seminar on
Mental Health and Family Life, Baguio, Philippines, 6-20 December
1958, by Tsung-yi Lin. Manila, GPO,
1960.
    PS 8 (1960) 901-2. (J. Bulatao)

Asiatic mythology; a detailed description and explanation of the mytholo-
gies of all the great nations of
Asia, by J. Hackin. New York,
Crowell, 1963.
    JAS 24 (1964-5) 146-7. (R. M. Dor-
    son)

L'Asie du sud-est. Paris, Editions
Sirey, 1970-1. 2v.
    PA 46 (1973) 164-167. (J. F. Cady)

ASPILLERA, PARALUMAN S. Basic Tagalog
for foreigners and non-Tagalogs.
Rutland, Tuttle, 1969.
    JAS 29 (1969-70) 499-501. (A. M.
    Stevens)
    SA 2 (1972) 520-522. (N. Asunsion-
    Lande)

ASPILLERA, PARALUMAN S. Lessons in
basic Tagalog. 3d. ed. Manila, Phil-
Asian Publishers, 1959.
    PS 8 (1960) 447-8. (J. A. Pollock)

ASRAF. Mekar dan Segar; bunga rampai
cherita2 pendek angkatan baru. Kuala Lumpur, Oxford UP, 1959.
    BIJ 117 (1961) 300-302. (A. Teeuw)

ASSOCIATION FOR ASIAN STUDIES ON THE
PACIFIC COAST. Filipino exclusion
movement, 1927-1935, edited by Josefa
M. Saniel. Quezon City, Univ. of the
Philippines Pr., 1967. (Quezon, Phil-
ippines. Univ. of the Philippines.

Institute of Asian Studies. Occasional papers, no. 1)
    PA 41 (1968) 445-6. (G. H. Weight-
    man)

Atlas of Southeast Asia, with an introduction by D. G. E. Hall. New
York, St. Martin's Pr., 1964.
    AP 8 (1964) 138-9. (W. G. Solheim)
    BEF 55 (1969) 260-263. (D. Lom-
    bard)
    BIJ 121 (1965) 279-280. (A.
    Peeters)
    JAS 24 (1964-5) 342-3. (K. J.
    Pelzer)
    PA 38 (1965) 198-9. (K. J. Pelzer)

al-ATTAS, MUHAMMAD NAGUIB, SYED. Mys-
ticism of Hamzah Fansuri. Kuala
Lumpur, Univ. of Malaya Pr., 1970.
    AR 4 (1972) 244-248. (V. Monteil)
    SOAS 35 (1972) 209. (N. G. Phil-
    lips)

* al-ATTAS, MUHAMMAD NAGUIB, SYED. Ra-
niri and the Wujudiyyah of 17th cen-
tury Acheh. Singapore, Malaysian
Branch, Royal Asiatic Society, 1966.
(Royal Asiatic Society of Great
Britain and Ireland, Malaysian
Branch. Monographs, no. 3)
    PA 41 (1968) 114-5. (J. M. van der
    Kroef)
    SOAS 31 (1968) 427-8. (E. C. G.
    Barrett)

AUBOYER, JEANNINE. Les arts de l'Asie
orientale et de l'Extreme-Orient.
Nouv. ed. Paris, Presses universitaires de France, 1964. (Que sais-
je? no. 77)
    SEIB 39 (1964) 535.

AUBOYER, JEANNINE. Oriental world:
India and South-East Asia, by Jeannine Auboyer and Roger Goepper.
London, Hamlyn, 1968. (Landmarks of
the world's art)
    SOAS 32 (1969) 239. (M. Medley)

Auboyer, Jeannine *See* JACQUOT, JEAN.
Les theatres d'Asie

AUDRIC, JOHN. Siam, the kingdom of
the saffron robe. London, Hale,
1969.
JSS 58 pt. 1 (1970) 146-7. (M.
Smithies)

AUNG SAN. Political legacy of Aung
San. Compiled by and with an intro-
ductory essay by Josef Silverstein.
Ithaca, Southeast Asia Program, Cor-
nell Univ., 1972. (Cornell Univ.
Southeast Asia Program. Data paper,
no. 86)
JAS 33 (1973-4) 151-2. (Michael
Aung Thwin)
JSAS 5 (1974) 140-1. (A. Raja
Segaran)
PA 46 (1973) 605-6. (F. N. Trager)

AUNG THAW. Historical sites in Burma.
Rangoon, Ministry of Union Culture,
Government of the Union of Burma,
1972.
SEIB 48 (1973) 538-9. (E. Guillon)

AUNG THAW. Report on the excavations
at Beikthano. Rangoon, Revolutionary Government of Burma, Ministry of
Union Culture, 1968.
AP 12 (1969) 142-3. (B. Bronson)

AUVADE, ROBERT. Bibliographie critique des oeuvres parus sur l'Indochine francaise; un siecle d'histoire et d'enseignement. Paris,
Maisonneuve, 1965.
BEF 53 (1966) 727. (P. Huard)
SEIB 41 (1966) 317-8. (P. Brocheux)

AVERCH, HARVEY A. Crisis of ambiguity,
political and economic development
in the Philippines, by Harvey A.
Averch, F. H. Denton and J. E. Koehler. Santa Monica, Rand Corporation,
1970.
JAS 32 (1972-3) 489-500. (B. J.
Kerkvliet)

AVERCH, HARVEY A. Matrix of policy in
the Philippines, by Harvey A. Averch
Averch, John E. Koehler and Frank H.
Denton. Princeton, Princeton UP,
1971. (Rand Corporation. Research
study)
JAS 32 (1972-3) 489-500. (B. J.
Kerkvliet)
PA 45 (1972) 465-6. (R. S. Milne)
SA 3 (1974) 935-938. (H. B. Jaco-
bini)

Aya, Roderick *See* National liberation

Ayala, Fernando Zobel de *See* ZOBEL
DE AYALA, FERNANDO

AYALA Y COMPANY. LIBRARY. Classified
list of Filipiniana holdings of the
Ayala y Compania Library as of De-
cember 1960, compiled by Juan J.
Enriquez. Makati, 1961.
JAS 21 (1961-2) 248-9. (D. V.
Hart)

AYER, MARGARET. Made in Thailand, the
story of a country's arts and
crafts. New York, Knopf, 1964.
JSS 54 pt. 1 (1966) 73. (L.
Sternstein)

AZIZ, UNGKU ABDUL. Subdivision of
estates in Malaya, 1951-1960. Kuala
Lumpur, Univ. of Malaya, Dept. of
Economics, 1962. 3v.
MER 9 pt. 1 (1964) 55-62. (G. D.
Ness)
MER 9 pt. 1 (1964) 63-79. (G. D.
Quirin)

BA MAW. Breakthrough in Burma, mem-
oirs of a revolution, 1939-1946.
New Haven, Yale UP, 1968.
JAH 3 (1969) 80-82. (F. N. Trager)
JAS 28 (1968-9) 190-1. (L. W. Pye)
JSAS 1 pt. 2 (1970) 132-3. (M.
Leifer)
PA 41 (1968) 624-5. (H. Tinker)
AS 8 (1968) 817.

Ba Shin. Essays offered to G. H. Luce

JSAS 2 (1971) 235-6. (P. J. Worsley)
SOAS 35 (1972) 209. (C. von Furer-Haimendorf)

Bali; studies in life, thought and ritual. Introduction by J. L. Swellengrebel. The Hague, W. Van Hoeve, 1960. (Selected studies on Indonesia by Dutch scholars, vol. 5)
BIJ 117 (1961) 498-502. (C. Geertz)
JAS 20 (1960-1) 391-2. (H. Geertz)
PA 34 (1961) 81-83. (C. Holt)
SOAS 25 (1962) 403-4. (C. von Furer-Haimendorf)

* BANAYO, ANGELITO T. Introduction to the science of economics, by Angelito T. Banayo and Ricardo C. Bassig. Manila, Abiva, 1972.
SLURJ 2 (1971) 701-2. (J. S. Lacsina)

Banker, Elizabeth *See* Mon-Khmer studies

Banker, John *See* Mon-Khmer studies

BARBER, NOEL. War of the running dogs, the Malayan emergency: 1948-1960. New York, Weybright and Talley, 1972.
PA 46 (1973) 173-4. (G. P. Means)
SA 3 (1974) 798-801. (K. W. Yeo)

BARNETT, A. DOAK. Communist China and Asia; challenge to American policy. New York, Harper, 1960.
JSAH 3 (Sept. 1962) 160-166. (L. C. Green)

BARNETT, A. DOAK. Communist strategies in Asia, a comparative analysis of governments and parties. New York, Praeger, 1963.
JSAH 5 (1964) 230-235. (Wang Gung-Wu)

Barr, Robert F. *See* CONFERENCE ON AMERICAN TRADE WITH ASIA AND THE FAR EAST. American trade with Asia and the Far East

Bastin, John Sturgus. British in west

BARRAU, JACQUES. Plants and migrations of Pacific peoples; a symposium. Honolulu, Bishop Museum Pr., 1963.
AP 8 (1964) 133-135. (C. D. Smart)

BARRY, JEAN. Thai students in the United States; a study in attitude change. Ithaca, Southeast Asia Program, Cornell Univ., 1967. (Cornell Univ. Southeast Asia Program. Data paper, no. 66) (Cornell Univ. Thailand project. Interim reports series, no. 11)
JAS 27 (1967-8) 674-5. (E. M. Anthony)
PS 20 (1972) 199.

BARTON, ROY FRANKLIN. Ifugao law. Berkeley, Univ. of California Pr., 1969.
PA 43 (1970) 307-8. (J. Inglis)

BASCHE, JAMES R. Thailand, land of the free. New York, Taplinger, 1971.
JAS 31 (1971-2) 462-3. (B. L. Foster)
JSS 60 pt. 1 (1972) 434-5. (M. Smithies)
PA 44 (1971) 644-5. (F. C. Darling)

Bassig, Ricardo C. *See* BANAYO, ANGELITO T. Introduction to the science of economics

BASTIN, JOHN STURGUS. British in west Sumatra (1685-1825), a selection of documents, mainly from the East India Company records preserved in the India Office Library, Commonwealth Relations Office, London. Kuala Lumpur, Univ. of Malaya Pr., 1965.
BIJ 123 (1967) 383-386. (M. A. P. Meilink-Roelofsz)
JAS 25 (1965-6) 794-5. (L. R. Wright)

State UP, 1960.
JSAH 3 (Sept. 1962) 166-170. (O. D. Corpuz)

Battle of Vietiane, 1960, with historical background leading to the battle, by Chalermnit Press correspondent. Bangkok, Nai Prayura Phisnaka, 1961.
PA 35 (1962) 427-8. (L. Gordon)

BAUMANN, ERNST. Lehrbuch der indonesischen Sprache (Bahasa Indonesia). Nebst einer Einfuhrung in die Schrift und den Briefstil der Indonesier. Wiesbaden, Harrassowitz, 1967.
JAS 27 (1967-8) 675-6. (J. U. Wolff)
SOAS 32 (1969) 203-4. (E. C. G. Barrett)

Baumier, Jean *See* LACOUTURE, JEAN. Le poids du tiers-monde

BAUSANI, ALESSANDRO. Le letterature del sud-est asiatico: birmana, siamese, laotiana, cambodgiana, vietnamita, giavanese, malese-indonesiana, filippina. Florence, Sansoni, 1970. (Le Letterature den mondo, 37)
AAS 10 (1974) 208-9. (S. Fatura)

BAUSANI, ALESSANDRO. Malesia, poesia e leggende. Milan, Nuova Accademia Editrice, 1963.
BIJ 120 (1964) 386-388. (G. W. J. Drewes)

* BAUTISTA, FILOMENO M. Bautista manuscript on the Philippine revolution in Misamis Province, 1900-1901. Cagayan de Oro, Research Institute for Mindanao Culture, Xavier Univ., 1968.
PS 16 (1968) 788-9. (M. A. Bernad)

BAYARD, DONN T. Non Nok Tha; the 1968 excavation, procedure, stratigraphy and a summary of the evidence. Dunedin, Univ. of Otago, Dept. of

Behrman, Jere R. Supply response in

Anthropology, 1971. (Studies in prehistoric anthropology, vol. 4)
JSS 60 pt. 2 (1972) 333-335. (Srisakra Vallibhotama)

BAZELL, CHARLES ERNEST. In memory of J. R. Firth. London, Longmans, Green, 1966.
SOAS 30 (1967) 757-8. (C. J. E. Ball)

Beal, Christopher W. *See* Realities of Vietnam

BEATTY, ALFRED CHESTER. Catalogue of the Batak manuscripts, including two Javanese manuscripts and a Balinese painting, by P. Voorhoeve. Dublin, Hodges Figgis, 1961.
SOAS 25 (1962) 642-3. (C. Hooykaas)

BEERS, HOWARD WAYLAND. An American experience in Indonesia: the University of Kentucky affiliation with the Agricultural University at Bogor. Lexington, UP of Kentucky, 1971.
BIJ 129 (1973) 375-381. (L. F. B. Dubbeldam)
JAS 31 (1971-2) 737. (J. L. Peacock)

Beers, Howard Wayland *See* Indonesia, resources and their technological development

BEGBIE, PETER JAMES. Malayan peninsula. Kuala Lumpur, Oxford UP, 1967.
JAS 27 (1967-8) 910-1. (D. G. E. Hall)
JSAH 9 (1968) 353-4. (C. M. Turnbull)

BEHRMAN, JERE R. Supply response in underdeveloped agriculture, a case study of four major annual crops in Thailand, 1937-1963. Amsterdam, North Holland, 1968. (Contributions to economic analysis, no. 55)

Behrman, Jere R. Supply response in

    JAS 29 (1969-70) 496-498. (E. Van
    Roy)

BEISNER, ROBERT L. Twelve against em-
    pire; the anti-imperialists, 1898-
    1900. New York, McGraw-Hill, 1968.
      PS 17 (1969) 338-340. (J. N. Schu-
      macher)

* BEJ SAL. Prajum rioen bran khmaer
    phag 8, [by] Bej Sal [and] Sdoeng
    Chur. Phnom Penh, Buddhist Insti-
    tute, 2515.
      JSS 61 pt. 2 (1973) 219-221. (D.
      P. Chandler)

BELLAH, ROBERT NEELLY. Religion and
    progress in modern Asia. New York,
    Free Pr., 1965.
      JAS 25 (1965-6) 501-2. (J. M.
      Kitagawa)

BELLO, WALDEN F. Modernization: its
    impact in the Philippines. Quezon
    City, Ateneo de Manila UP, 1967.
    (Institute of Philippine Culture.
    IPC papers, no. 6)
      PS 15 (1967) 739-742. (J. Gill)

BELLOWS, THOMAS J. People's Action
    Party of Singapore, emergence of a
    dominant party system. New Haven,
    Southeast Asia Studies, Yale Univ.,
    1970. (Yale Univ. Graduate School.
    Southeast Asia Studies. Monograph
    series, no. 14)
      BIJ 128 (1972) 389-395. (P. E. de
      Josselin de Jong)
      JAS 30 (1970-1) 739-740. (R. S.
      Milne)
      JSAS 3 (1972) 144-146. (J.
      MacDougall)
      PA 44 (1971) 456-6. (Chan Heng-
      Chee)

BELO, JANE. Traditional Balinese cul-
    ture; essays. New York, Columbia
    UP, 1970.
      JAS 31 (1971-2) 458-9. (A. G.
      Dewey)

    SOAS 34 (1971) 679-680. (M. C.
    Ricklefs)

BELO, JANE. Trance in Bali. New
    York, Columbia UP, 1960.
      BIJ 116 (1960) 373-378. (J. L.
      Swellengrebel)
      JAS 20 (1960-1) 121-123. (C. Holt)
      PA 34 (1961) 212. (L. H. Palmier)
      SOAS 26 (1963) 468-9. (E. M.
      Mendelson)

BENDA, HARRY JINDRICH. Communist up-
    risings of 1926-1927 in Indonesia:
    key documents, edited with an intro-
    duction by Harry J. Benda and Ruth
    T. McVey. Ithaca, Modern Indonesia
    Project, Southeast Asia Program,
    Cornell Univ., 1960. (Cornell Univ.
    Modern Indonesia Project. Transla-
    tion series)
      JAS 21 (1961-2) 409-411. (D. Hind-
      ley)
      PA 33 (1960) 196-198. (L. W. Pye)

BENDA, HARRY JINDRICH. Continuity and
    change in Southeast Asia, collected
    journal articles of Harry J. Benda.
    New Haven, Southeast Asia Studies,
    Yale Univ., 1972. (Yale Univ. Grad-
    uate School, Southeast Asia Studies.
    Monograph series, no. 18)
      BIJ 130 (1974) 378-9. (W. F.
      Wertheim)
      JAS 33 (1973-4) 149-151. (J. D.
      Legge)
      JSAS 5 (1974) 144-146. (A. J. S.
      Reid)

BENDA, HARRY JINDRICH. Crescent and
    the rising sun: Indonesian Islam
    under Japanese occupation, 1942-45.
    The Hague, van Hoeve, 1958.
      JAS 20 (1960-1) 238-9. (A. M.
      Halpern)

Benda, Harry Jindrich *See* BASTIN,
    JOHN STURGUS. History of modern
    Southeast Asia

Bernabe, Emma. Ilokano lessons.

BENDA, HARRY JINDRICH. Japanese military administration in Indonesia: selected documents, by Harry J. Benda, James K. Irikura, and Koichi Kishi. New Haven, Yale Univ., Southeast Asia Studies, 1965. (Yale Univ. Graduate School. Southeast Asia Studies. Translation series, no. 6)
  BIJ 123 (1967) 388-390. (D. van Velden)
  MER 11 pt. 1 (1966) 132-134. (D. J. Blake)

BENDA, HARRY JINDRICH. World of Southeast Asia, selected historical readings, by Harry J. Benda and John A. Larkin. New York, Harper and Row, 1967.
  JAS 27 (1967-8) 676-7. (D. G. E. Hall)
  MAS 4 (1970) 177-8. (R. C. Y. Ng)
  PA 42 (1969) 117. (P. Harnetty)
  SA 1 (1971) 397-8. (J. F. Cady)
  SJ 14 (1967) 480.

BENHAM, FREDERIC CHARLES. Economic aid to underdeveloped countries. London, Oxford UP, 1961.
  PA 35 (1962) 92. (J. S. Conway)

BENHAM, FREDERIC CHARLES. National income of Singapore, 1956. London, Oxford UP, 1959.
  MER 5 pt. 1 (1960) 77-79. (R. Ma)

Benitez, Conrado. Philippine progress prior to 1898 *See* COMYN, TOMAS DE. State of the Philippines in 1810

BENNETT, PAUL JEROME. Conference under the tamarind tree, three essays in Burmese history. New Haven, Southeast Asia Studies, Yale Univ., 1971. (Yale Univ. Graduate School. Southeast Asia Studies. Monograph series, no. 15)
  JAS 32 (1972-3) 378-9. (D. K. Wyatt)
  PA 43 (1973) 346-7. (J. F. Cady)
  SOAS 36 (1973) 213-4. (H. L. Shorto)

BENZ, ERNST. Buddhism or communism, which holds the future of Asia? don, George Allen and Unwin, 1966.
  JSAH 8 (1967) 319-320. (S. Arasaratnam)

BERAN, JANICE A. Physical activities for the Filipina, by Janice A. Beran and Sofia A. Ravello. Dumaguete City, Univ. Pr., 1972.
  SJ 19 (1972) 387-8. (A. R. Ferrer)

BERG, CORNELIS CHRISTIAAN. Het Rijk van de vijfvoudige Buddha. Amsterdam, Noord-Hollandsche Uitgevers Maatschappij, 1962. (Akademie van Wetenschappen, Amsterdam. Afdeeling voor de Taal-, Letter-, Geschiedkundige en Wijsgeerige Wetenschappen. Verhandelingen, nieuwe reeks, deel 69, no. 1)
  SOAS 26 (1963) 462-464. (J. G. de Casparis)

BERGH, J. D. VAN DEN. Analysis of the syntax and the system of affixes of the Bisaya language of Cebu. Surigao, Sacred Heart Missionaries, 1958.
  JAS 21 (1961-2) 247-8. (J. Wolff)
  PS 8 (1960) 648-655. (H. P. McKaughan)

BERIAULT, RAYMOND. Khmers. Montreal, Lemeac, 1959.
  FA 18 (1962) 449-453. (W. E. Willmott)

BERNABE, EMMA. Ilokano lessons, by Emma Bernabe, Virginia Lapid and Bonifacio Sibayan. Honolulu, Univ. of Hawaii Pr., 1971. (Hawaii. Univ. Honolulu. Pacific and Asian Linguistics Institute. PALI language texts)
  AAS 10 (1974) 195. (J. Genzor)

Bhattacharya, Kamaleswar. Religions

BERNOT, LUCIEN. Les Cak, contribution
a l'etude ethnographique d'une population de langue loi. Paris, Centre National de la Recherche Scientifique, 1967. (Atlas Ethno-Lin-
guistique. 2. serie: Monographies,
1)
   JSS 57 pt. 1 (1969) 179-183. (H.
   E. Kauffmann)
   SOAS 32 (1969) 412-414. (H. L.
   Shorto)

BERNOT, LUCIEN. Les paysans arakanais
du Pakistan oriental. L'histoire, le
monde vegetal et l'organisation so-
ciale des refugies Marma (Mog).
Paris, Mouton, 1967. 2v. (Le monde
d'outre-mer, passe et present. 1.
serie: Etudes, 16)
   BIJ 124 (1968) 402-409. (L. G.
   Loffler)
   JSS 56 pt. 1 (1968) 113-118. (H.
   E. Kauffmann)
   SOAS 32 (1969) 412-414. (H. L.
   Shorto)

BERTHE, LOUIS. Bei Gua, itineraire
des ancetres; mythes des Bunaq de
Timor. Paris, Editions du C.N.R.S.,
1972. (Centre de documentation sur
l'Asie du sud-est. Atlas Ethno-Lin-
guistique; recherche cooperative sur
programme no. 61: 5. serie: Documents)
   AR 7 (1974) 202-204. (D. Lombard)

BERTON, PETER ALEXANDER MENQUEZ. Soviet works on Southeast Asia; a bibliography of non-periodical literature, 1946-65, by Peter Berton and
Alvin Z. Rubinstein. Los Angeles,
Univ. of Southern California Pr.,
1967. (Los Angeles. Univ. of Southern California. School of International Relations. Far Eastern and
Russian research series, no. 3)
   JAH 5 (1971) 82.
   JAS 28 (1968-9) 643-4. (J. T.
   McAlister)

   JSAH 10 (1969) 377-8. (R. Quested)
   SOAS 32 (1969) 463-4. (H. L.
   Shorto)

BERVAL, RENE DE. Presence du Bouddh-
isme. Saigon, France-Asie, 1959.
   BEF 51 (1963) 203-208. (A. Bareau)
   PA 33 (1960) 87-8. (A. F. Wright)

BEYER, HENRY OTLEY. Philippine tektites; a contribution to the study
of the tektite problem in general,
in the light of both past and recent
discoveries. Quezon City, Univ. of
the Philippines Publications in Natural History and in the New Field
of Space Science, 1962.
   PS 11 (1963) 354-356. (J. J.
   Hennessey)

BEZACIER, LOUIS. Releves de monuments
anciens du nord Viet-Nam. Paris,
Ecole Francaise d'Extreme Orient,
1959.
   FA 17 (1960) 2001-2003. (Nguyen
   Tran Huan)
   SEIB 35 (1960) 581. (L. Malleret)

BEZE, CLAUDE DE. 1688 revolution in
Siam; the memoir of Father De Beze.
Hong Kong, Hong Kong UP, 1968.
   JAH 7 (1973) 93.
   JAS 29 (1969-70) 494-5. (D. K.
   Wyatt)
   JSS 57 pt. 2 (1969) 368-370. (Tej
   Bunnag)
   PA 42 (1969) 391. (B. Harrison)
   SA 2 (1972) 502-514. (K. P. Lan-
   don)

BHATTACHARYA, KAMALESWAR. Religions
brahmaniques dans l'ancien Cambodge,
d'apres l'epigraphie et l'iconographie. Paris, Ecole Francaise
d'Extreme Orient, 1961. (Ecole Francaise d'Extreme-Orient. Publications
vol. 49)
   FA 19 (1963) 841-845. (P. Grison)

Bibliographical Society of the

BIBLIOGRAPHICAL SOCIETY OF THE PHILIP-
PINES. Checklist of Philippine government documents 1917-1949, compiled
by Consolacion B. Rebadavia. Quezon
City, Univ. of the Philippines Library, 1960.
   JAS 20 (1960-1) 550-1. (D. V. Hart)

Biehl, Max *See* DIRECK JAYANAMA.
Thailand

* BINH, PHILIPPE. Sach So sang chep cac
   viec. Saigon, 1968.
      BEF 56 (1969) 208-9. (Nguyen Tran
      Huan)

* Biology for Philippine high schools,
   the laboratory, parts I and II, and
   the teachers guide. A joint project
   of the University of the Philippines,
   the Bureau of Public Schools and the
   Bureau of Private Schools. Manila,
   n.d.
      PS 12 (1964) 749-751.

* BIRASRI, SILPA. Origin and evolution
   of Thai murals with a catalogue of
   murals in Silpakorn Gallery, by Silpa
   Birasri and D. Yupo. Bangkok, Siva-
   porn Pr., 1959.
      JSS 48 pt. 2 (1960) 116-7.

BIRD, ISABELLA L. Golden Chersonese
   and the way thither. Kuala Lumpur,
   Oxford UP, 1967. (Oxford in Asia
   historical reprints)
      MAS 4 (1970) 93-4. (E. Chew)

BIRNBAUM, ELEAZER. Books on Asia from
   the Near East to the Far East, a
   guide for the general reader. Toronto, Univ. of Toronto Pr., 1971.
      JAH 6 (1972) 194.
      PA 45 (1972) 586-7. (G. R. Nunn)
      SOAS 36 (1973) 215. (P. M. Holt)

Bisch, Jorgen *See* BISTCH, JORGEN

BISTCH, JORGEN. Ulu, the world's end.
   London, Allen and Unwin, 1961.
      PA 37 (1964) 346. (J. E. Beltz)

BISTCH, JORGEN. Why Buddha smiles.
   London, Collins, 1964.
      JSS 54 pt. 2 (1966) 232-235. (L.
      Sternstein)

BIXLER, NORMA. Burma, a profile. New
   York, Praeger, 1971.
      AF 3 (1971) 184. (E. T. Flood)
      JAS 31 (1971-2) 716-7. (F. N.
      Trager)
      PA 44 (1971) 463-4. (J. F. Cady)

BIXLER, NORMA. Burmese journey.
   Yellow Springs, Antioch Pr., 1967.
      PA 41 (1968) 153. (J. Silverstein)

BIXLER, PAUL HOWARD. Southeast Asia;
   bibliographic directions in a complex area. Middletown, Conn.,
   Choice, 1974.
      PA 47 (1974) 584. (D. G. E. Hall)
      SJ 21 (1974) 284-286. (P. G.
      Gowing)

BLACK, EUGENE ROBERT. Alternative in
   Southeast Asia. New York, Praeger,
   1969.
      JAS 29 (1969-70) 983-4. (F. N.
      Trager)
      JSAS 1 pt. 2 (1970) 140-142. (A.
      H. H. Tan)
      PA 43 (1970) 118-9. (L. P. Singh)
      SA 2 (1972) 488-502. (V. D. Ooms)

BLANCHARD, WENDELL. Thailand: its
   people, its society, its culture.
   New Haven, Human Relations Area
   Files, 1958. (Human Relations Area
   Files, Inc. Country survey series)
      JSS 53 (1965) 125. (L. Sternstein)
      PA 33 (1960) 92-94. (K. A. Lawson)

BLOFELD, JOHN EATON CALTHORPE. People
   of the sun: encounters in Siam.
   London, Hutchinson, 1960.
      JSS 49 pt. 2 (1961) 65-6.

Blood, David L. *See* THOMAS, DAVID D.
Mon-Khmer studies

BLOODWORTH, DENNIS. An eye for the
dragon; Southeast Asia observed,
1954-1970. New York, Farrar, Strauss
and Giroux, 1970.
    PA 44 (1971) 139-140. (L. E. Wil-
        liams)
    SA 2 (1972-3) 363-371. (J. Badgley)

BLOOMFIELD, BARRY CAMBRAY. Theses on
Asia; accepted by universities in
the United Kingdom and Ireland,
1877-1964. London, Cass, 1967.
    JAH 3 (1969) 87.

BLYTHE, WILFRED. Impact of Chinese
secret societies in Malaya, a historical study. London, Oxford UP,
1969.
    MAS 4 (1970) 181-2. (R. B. Smith)
    PA 43 (1970) 313-4. (Chan Heng
        Chee)
    SA 3 (1974-5) 622-627. (Ka-che Yip)
    SOAS 34 (1971) 465.

Bock, John C. *See* TAKEI, YOSHIMITSU.
Educational sponsorship by ethnicity

BOCOBO-OLIVAR, CECILIA. History of
physical education in the Philippines. Quezon City, Univ. of the
Philippines Pr., 1972.
    PS 21 (1973) 234. (A. C. Calaug)
    SLURJ 3 (1972) 638-9. (L. C.
        Bangaoet)

BODARD, LUCIEN. La guerre d'Indochine.
t. 2. L'humiliation. Paris, Gallimard, 1963.
    FA 19 (1963) 1047-1051. (J.
        Christan)
    RSA (1966) 134-136. (I. Jadoul)

BODENSTEDT, ADOLF ANDREAS. Sprache
und Politik in Indonesien; Entwicklung und Funktionen einer neuen Na-
tionalsprache. Heidelberg, Dissertationsreihe des Sudasien-Instituts

Boisselier, Jean. Le Cambodge, Asie
der Universitat Heidelberg, 1967.
(Heidelberg. Universitat. Sudasien-
Institut. Dissertationsreihe, no. 3)
    JSAS 3 (1972) 155-6. (W. Levi)
    PA 42 (1969) 240-242. (J. van der
        Kroef)

BODROGI, TIBOR. Oceanian art. Buda-
pest, Corvina, 1959.
    BIJ 116 (1960) 393-4. (S. Kooij-
        man)

Boeke, J. H. *See* KONINKLIJK INSTI-
TUUT VOOR DE TROPEN. Indonesian
economics

* BOEN SRI OEMARJATI. Bentuk lakon dalam sastra Indonesia. Djakarta,
Gunung Agung, 1971.
    AR 3 (1972) 220-222.

* BOESCH, ERNST E. Communication between doctors and patients in Thailand. Pt. 1. Survey of the problem
and analysis of the consultations.
Saarbrucken, Socio-Psychological Research Centre on Development Planning, Univ. of the Saar, 1972.
    JSS 62 pt. 1 (1974) 244-249. (J.
        Bunnag)

Bohannan, Charles T. R. *See* VALERI-
ANO, NAPOLEON D. Counter-guerrilla
operations

BOISSELIER, JEAN. Le Cambodge, Asie
du sud-est. t. 1. Manuel d'archeologie d'Extreme-Orient, le Cambodge.
Paris, Picard, 1966.
    BEF 55 (1969) 253-260. (M.
        Benisti)
    BIJ 123 (1967) 379-381. (F. D. K.
        Bosch)
    JAH 2 (1968) 74-76. (E. Stein-
        kellner)
    JAS 27 (1967-8) 433-435. (S. J.
        O'Connor)
    SEIB 42 (1967) 362-3. (M.
        Brocheux)

Boisselier, Jean. Essays offered to

BOTTO, OSCAR.   Storia delle letterature d'Oriente.   Milan, Casa F. Vallardi, 1969. 4v.
    SOAS 35 (1972) 214. (J. Bough)

Boudarel, George S.   *See*   CHESNEAUX, JEAN.   Tradition et revolution au Vietnam

BOUDET, PAUL.   Bibliographie de l'Indochine, 1930-1935. t. 4. Matieres. Paris, Librairie d'Amerique et d'Orient Adrien-Maisonneuve, 1967.
    JAS 27 (1967-8) 677-8. (J. Musgrave)

* BOULBET, JEAN.   Modes et techniques du pays Ma'.   Blao, Centre Montagnard de Dalat, 1961.
    SEIB 36 (1961) 737.

Boumann, Jan C.   *See*   South Moluccas

* BOUN XOUAY SRI SAVATH.   Le royaume du Laos.   Bangkok, 2503 B.E.
    BEF 50 (1960) 582-3. (P. B. Lafont)

BOWDITCH, NATHANIEL.   Early American-Philippine trade: the journal of Nathaniel Bowditch in Manila, 1796. Edited with an introduction by Thomas R. and Mary C. McHale. New Haven, Yale Univ., Southeast Asia Studies, 1962.   (Yale Univ. Graduate School. Southeast Asia Studies. Monograph series, no. 2)
    JAS 22 (1962-3) 494. (R. H. Green)
    JSAH 4 (Mar. 1963) 124-126. (O. D. Corpuz)
    PA 37 (1964) 239-240. (C. O. Houston)
    PS 11 (1963) 370-372. (H. de la Costa)

Bowen, Jean Donald   *See*   PHILIPPINE CENTER FOR LANGUAGE STUDY. Intermediate readings in Tagalog

Bowie, Theodore Robert   *See*   INDIANA UNIV.   Arts of Thailand

BOWIE, THEODORE ROBERT.   Sculpture of Thailand.   New York, Asia Society, 1972.
    JAS 33 (1973-4) 733-735. (P. M. Young)
    JSS 62 pt. 1 (1974) 274-278. (H. W. Woodward)

BOWRING, JOHN.   Kingdom and people of Siam.   Kuala Lumpur, Oxford UP, 1969. 2v.   (Oxford in Asia historical reprints)
    JAS 32 (1972-3) 561-2. (C. M. Wilson)
    JSS 59 pt. 1 (1971) 236-238. (T. Bunnag)

BOXER, CHARLES RALPH.   Catalogue of Philippine manuscripts in the Lilly Library.   Bloomington, Asian Studies Institute, Univ. of Indiana, 1968. (Indiana Univ. Asian Studies Research Institute. Occasional papers, no. 2)
    PS 17 (1969) 816. (N. P. Cushner)

BOXER, CHARLES RALPH.   Four centuries of Portuguese expansion, 1415-1825, a succinct survey.   Berkeley, Univ. of California Pr., 1961.
    PA 44 (1971) 259-260. (H. Livermore)

BOXER, CHARLES RALPH.   Francisco Vieira de Figueiredo, a Portuguese merchant adventurer in South East Asia, 1624-1667.   The Hague, Nijhoff, 1967.   (Instituut voor Taal-, Land- en Volkenkunde. Verhandelingen deel 52)
    PA 41 (1968) 328-9. (H. V. Livermore)
    SOAS 31 (1968) 454. (J. Bastin)

Boxer, Charles Ralph   *See*   GOMES DE BRITO, BERNARDO.   Further selections from *The tragic history of the sea*

Boxer, Charles Ralph. Great ship from

BOXER, CHARLES RALPH. Great ship from
Amacon; annals of Macao and the old
Japan trade, 1555-1640. Lisbon,
Centro de Estudios Historicos Ultra-
marinos, 1959.
   PS 9 (1961) 533-542. (N. Cushner)

BOXER, CHARLES RALPH. Portuguese sea-
borne empire, 1415-1825. London,
Hutchinson, 1969. (History of human
society)
   JMBRAS 42 pt. 2 (1969) 229-232.
     (S. Arasaratnam)
   PA 44 (1971) 259-260. (H. Liver-
     more)
   SOAS 34 (1971) 203. (D. K. Bassett)

BRACKMAN, ARNOLD C. Communist col-
lapse in Indonesia. New York, Nor-
ton, 1969.
   AS 10 (1970) 177.
   JAS 31 (1971-2) 737-739. (R. K.
     Paget)
   JSAS 3 (1972) 348-9. (J. A. C.
     Mackie)

BRACKMAN, ARNOLD C. Indonesia, Suhar-
to's road. New York, American-Asian
Educational Exchange, 1973. (Ameri-
can-Asian Educational Exchange.
Monograph series, no. 11)
   PA 47 (1974) 576-578. (J. D. Legge)

BRACKMAN, ARNOLD C. Indonesian com-
munism: a history. New York, Prae-
ger, 1963.
   AS 4 (1964) 774.
   JAS 23 (1963-4) 141-2. (R. T.
     McVey)
   JSAH 5 (Sept. 1964) 224-227. (S.
     Rose)
   PA 36 (1963) 321-2. (J. A. C.
     Mackie)
   RSA (1965) 169-170. (L. Rocher)

BRACKMAN, ARNOLD C. Southeast Asia's
second front, the power struggle in
the Malay archipelago. New York,
Praeger, 1966.
   AS 6 (1966) 300.

   JAH 1 (1967) 97-8. (J. M. van der
     Kroef)
   JAS 27 (1967-8) 678-9. (R. O.
     Tilman)

* BRADLEY, D. B. Dictionary of the
Siamese language. Bangkok, Kuru-
sapa, 1971.
   JSS 61 pt. 1 (1973) 360-363. (Napa
     Bhongbhibhat)

BRAIBANTI, RALPH J. D. Asian bureau-
cratic systems emergent from the
British imperial tradition. Durham,
Duke UP, 1966. (Duke Univ. Common-
wealth Studies Center. Publication,
no. 28)
   JAS 27 (1967-8) 367-8. (W. J.
     Siffin)
   PA 40 (1967) 347-8. (P. Mason)

BRAISTED, WILLIAM REYNOLDS. United
States Navy in the Pacific, 1909-
1922. Austin, Univ. of Texas Pr.,
1971.
   JAS 31 (1971-2) 174-5. (R. G.
     O'Conner)
   PS 20 (1972) 342-344. (L. E.
     Bauzon)

BRAKE, BRIAN. House on the klong; the
Bangkok house and Asian art collec-
tion of James Thompson. Photos:
Brian Brake. Text: William Warren.
New York, Walker/Weatherhill, 1968.
   JSS 58 pt. 2 (1970) 198-200. (M.
     Smithies)

Brand, W. *See* KONINKLIJK INSTITUUT
VOOR DE TROPEN. Indonesian town

BRANDON, JAMES R. On thrones of gold,
three Javanese shadow plays. Cam-
bridge, Harvard UP, 1970.
   JAS 31 (1971-2) 741-2. (H. Geertz)
   MAS 6 (1972) 128. (C. J. Dunn)
   SOAS 34 (1971) 647-649. (M. C.
     Ricklefs)

Brown heritage, essays on Philippine

BRANDON, JAMES R. Theatre in Southeast Asia. Cambridge, Harvard UP,
 1967.
  JAS 27 (1967-8) 911-2. (A. L.
   Becker)
  PA 41 (1968) 442-3. (M. K. Mul-
   holland)

BRECHER, MICHAEL. New states of Asia,
 a political analysis. London, Ox-
 ford UP, 1963.
  AS 4 (1964) 774.
  JAS 24 (1964-5) 313-4. (T. W.
   Simons)
  PA 37 (1964) 464-5. (F. R. von der
   Mehden)

BREESE, GERALD WILLIAM. Modernization
 and urbanization: existing and potential relationships in the third
 world. Monticello, Ill., Council of
 Planning Librarians, 1969.
  PA 42 (1969) 577-8. (N. D. Cheru-
   kupalle)

BREESE, GERALD WILLIAM. Urban Southeast Asia, a selected bibliography
 of accessible research, reports, and
 related materials on urbanism and
 urbanization in Hong Kong, Indonesia, Malaysia, the Philippines,
 Singapore, Thailand, Vietnam. New
 York, Southeast Asia Development
 Advisory Group, 1973.
  JAS 33 (1973-4) 328. (A. Howard)

BRILLANTES, GREGORIO C. Distance to
 Andromeda and other stories. Manila,
 Benipayo Pr., 1960.
  PA 35 (1962) 82-3. (D. V. Hart)

BRIMMELL, JACK HENRY. Communism in
 Southeast Asia, a political analysis.
 London, Oxford UP, 1959.
  JSAH 2 (Mar. 1961) 134-137. (Wang
   Gung-Wu)
  PA 33 (1960) 196-198. (L. W. Pye)

BRION, MARCEL. La resurrection des
 villes mortes. Paris, Plon, 1959.

 2v.
  SEIB 36 (1961) 742.

Brockman, Henrietta York (Jull) Drake
 See DRAKE-BROCKMAN, HENRIETTA YORK
 (JULL)

BRÖTEL, DIETER. Franzosischer Imperi-
 alismus in Vietnam. Die koloniale
 Expansion und die Errichtung des
 Protektorates Annam-Tonkin, 1880-
 1885. Zurich, Atlantis Verlag,
 1971. (Beitrage zur Kolonial- und
 Ubergeschichte, Bd. 8)
  JSAS 4 (1973) 306-309. (B. Dahm)

BROMLEY, H. MYRON. Phonology of lower
 Grand Valley Dani; a comparative
 structural study of skewed phonemic
 patterns. The Hague, Nijhoff, 1961.
 (Instituut voor Taal-, Land- en
 Volkenkunde. Verhandelingen, deel
 34)
  SOAS 27 (1964) 669-670. (G. B.
   Milner)

BROWN, DONALD EDWARD. Brunei, the
 structure and history of a Bornean
 Malay sultanate. Brunei, Brunei
 Museum, 1970. (Brunei Museum Jour-
 nal. Vol. 2 no. 2)
  JAS 33 (1973-4) 161-2. (R. Harri-
   son)
  JSAS 4 (1973) 325-6. (L. R.
   Wright)

BROWN, JAMES MARVIN. From ancient
 Thai to modern dialects. Bangkok,
 Social Science Association Pr.,
 1965.
  JSS 55 pt. 1 (1967) 124-129. (W.
   A. Smalley)

BROWN, MICHAEL BARRATT. After imperialism. London, Heinemann, 1963.
  SOAS 27 (1964) 681-2. (M. Caldwell)

Brown heritage, essays on Philippine
 cultural tradition and literature.

Brown heritage, essays on Philippine

Edited by Antonio G. Manuud. Quezon City, Ateneo de Manila UP, 1967.
PS 16 (1968) 409-412. (L. Casper)

BRUCE, GEORGE LUDGATE. The Burma wars, 1824-1886. London, Hart-Davis MacGibbon, 1973.
JSAS 5 (1974) 141-143. (O. B. Pollak)

BRUNO, CAYETANO. El derecho publico de la Iglesia en Indias; estudio historico-juridico. Salamanca, Instituto San Raimundo de Penafort, 1967.
PS 16 (1968) 201-2. (J. N. Schumacher)

Bruyns, A. Morzer *See* MÖRZER BRUYNS, A.

BRYANT, JOHN. Health and the developing world. Ithaca, Cornell UP, 1969.
JSS 59 pt. 2 (1971) 270-272. (Debhanom Muangman)

BUCHAN, ALASTAIR. China and the peace of Asia. New York, Praeger, 1965.
JAS 25 (1965-6) 800. (T. Ropp)

BUCHANAN, IAIN. Singapore in Southeast Asia: an economic and political appraisal. London, Bell, 1972.
JCA 2 (1972) 96-7. (M. Caldwell)
JCA 2 (1972) 301-305. (G. Raman)
JSAS 4 (1973) 152-3. (Chan Heng Chee)
RSAS 2 (1972) 64-69. (Lim Chong Yah)
SA 2 (1972) 488-502. (V. D. Ooms)

BUCHANAN, KEITH. Southeast Asian world. London, Bell, 1967.
JSAH 9 (1968) 364-5. (D. W. Fryer)
PA 41 (1968) 441-2. (K. J. Pelzer)
SOAS 31 (1968) 184-5. (H. Tinker)

BUCKLEY, CHARLES BURTON. Anecdotal history of old times in Singapore, from the foundation of the settle-

ment under the Honourable The East India Company on February 6th, 1819 to the transfer to the Colonial Office of the colonial possessions of the crown on April 1st, 1867. Kuala Lumpur, Univ. of Malaya Pr., 1965.
JAS 26 (1966-7) 531-2. (G. P. Means)
JSAH 8 (1967) 326. (Chiang Hai Ding)

BUDDHADASA, BHIKKHU. Toward the truth. Edited by Donald K. Swearer. Philadelphia, Westminster Pr., 1971.
JSS 62 pt. 2 (1974) 358-360. (Phra Rajavaramuni)

BUELL, HAROLD G. Main streets of Southeast Asia. New York, Dodd, Mead, 1962.
PA 36 (1963) 195-6. (H. W. Robinson)

* BUI QUANG TUNG. La succession de Thieu Tri. Saigon, Societe des Etudes Indochinoises, 1967. (Societe des Etudes Indochinoises. Bulletin. Nouvelle serie, XLII no. 1-2)
BEF 56 (1969) 192-195. (N. Louis)

BUI XUAN BAO. Le roman vietnamien contemporain. Saigon, Tu Sach Nhan-Van Xa Hoi, 1972.
SEIB 48 (1973) 139-142. (Tran Thi Ngoc Quynh)

Buiten de grenzen. Sociologische opstellen aangeboden aan Prof. Dr. W. F. Wertheim, 25 jaar Amsterdams Hoogleraar, 1946-1971. Meppel, Boom, 1971.
JAS 32 (1972-3) 737-8. (W. H. Frederick)
PA 45 (1972) 620-1. (J. M. van der Kroef)

BULOSAN, CARLOS. Sound of falling light; letters in exile. Quezon City, 1961.
PS 9 (1961) 551-2. (M. A. Bernad)

* BUNCHHAN MUL. Kuk Niyobay. Phnom
   Penh, Apsara, 1971.
      JSS 60 pt. 1 (1972) 439–440. (D.
       P. Chandler)

BUNNAG, JANE. Buddhist monk, Buddhist
   layman; a study of urban monastic
   organization in central Thailand.
   Cambridge, Cambridge UP, 1973.
   (Cambridge studies in social anthropology, no. 6)
      JAS 33 (1973–4) 334–5. (A. T.
       Kirsch)
      SOAS 37 (1974) 503–506. (P. J. Bee)

BUNYE, MARIA VICTORIA R. Cebuano for
   beginners, by Maria Victoria R. Bunye and Elsa Paula Yap. Honolulu,
   Univ. of Hawaii Pr., 1971. (Hawaii.
   Univ., Honolulu. Pacific and Asian
   Linguistics Institute. PALI language
   texts: Philippines)
      AAS 10 (1974) 196–7. (J. Genzor)

BUNYE, MARIA VICTORIA R. Cebuano
   grammar notes, by Maria Victoria R.
   Bunye and Elsa Paula Yap. Honolulu,
   Univ. of Hawaii Pr., 1971. (Hawaii.
   Univ., Honolulu. Pacific and Asian
   Linguistics Institute. PALI language
   texts)
      AAS 10 (1974) 196–7. (J. Genzor)

Bunye, Maria Victoria R. *See* YAP,
   ELSA PAULA. Cebuano-Visayan dictionary

BURCHETT, WILFRED G. Furtive war, the
   United States in Vietnam and Laos.
   New York, International Publishers,
   1963.
      JAS 23 (1963–4) 630–1. (W. R.
       Fishel)

BURCHETT, WILFRED G. Mekong upstream.
   Berlin, Seven Seas Publishers, 1959.
      FA 17 (1960) 1969–1971. (B. B.
       Fall)

Burdick, Eugene. Role in Manila

      PA 34 (1961) 313–4. (B. B. Fall)
      SEIB 36 (1961) 743.

Burchett, Wilfred G. *See* NORODOM
   SIHANOUK VARMAN, KING OF CAMBODIA.
   My war with the C.I.A.

BURCHETT, WILFRED G. Second Indochina war: Cambodia and Laos. New
   York, International Publishers,
   1970.
      PA 44 (1971) 591–595. (D. J.
       Duncanson)

BURCHETT, WILFRED G. La second resistance; Vietnam, 1965. Paris,
   Gallimard, 1965.
      FA 20 (1965) 126–7.

BURCHETT, WILFRED G. Vietnam, inside
   story of the guerilla war. New
   York, International Publishers,
   1965.
      JSAH 7 (Mar. 1966) 147–149. (M. E.
       Osborne)

BURCHETT, WILFRED G. Vietnam north.
   New York, International Publishers,
   1966.
      JSAH 9 (1968) 175–6. (M. Leifer)

BURCHETT, WILFRED G. Vietnam will
   win! Why the people of South Vietnam have already defeated U.S. imperialism, and how they have done
   it, by the internationally famous
   Western correspondent whose first-
   hand dispatches from Vietnam have
   become a part of the history of our
   times. New York, Monthly Review Pr.,
   1968.
      MAS 4 (1970) 373–375. (R. B.
       Smith)
      PA 43 (1970) 128–130. (M. Osborne)

BURDICK, EUGENE. Role in Manila; fif-
   teen tales of war, post war, peace,
   and adventure. New York, New American Library, 1966.
      PA 39 (1966) 458. (D. G. Collier)

Burger, Dionijs Huibert. Structural

BURGER, DIONIJS HUIBERT. Structural changes in Javanese society: the supra-village sphere. Ithaca, Southeast Asia Program, Cornell Univ., 1956. (Cornell Univ. Southeast Asia Program. Translation series)
JAS 21 (1961-2) 413-4. (C. Geertz)
JAS 21 (1961-2) 565-567. (G. J. Pauker)

Burgess, Anthony *See* WILSON, JOHN ANTHONY BURGESS

al-BURHANPURI, MUHAMMAD IBN FADL ALLAH AL-HINDI. Gift addressed to the spirit of the Prophet, by A. H. Johns. Canberra, Australian National Univ., Centre of Oriental Studies, 1965. (Oriental monograph series, no. 1)
BIJ 122 (1966) 290-300. (G. W. J. Drewes)
SOAS 29 (1966) 646-7. (C. Hooykaas)

BURLEIGH, CHARLES. Living Mekong. Sydney, Angus and Robertson, 1971.
JSS 60 pt. 2 (1972) 336-7. (M. Smithies)

BURLEY, T. M. The Philippines, an economic and social geography. London, Bell, 1973.
JSAS 5 (1974) 143-4. (Teo Siew Eng)

BURLING, ROBBINS. Hill farms and padi fields, life in mainland Southeast Asia. Englewood Cliffs, Prentice-Hall, 1965.
JAS 25 (1965-6) 167. (R. O. Tilman)

* BURLING, ROBBINS. Proto-Karen, a re-analysis. Ann Arbor, Dept. of Linguistics, Univ. of Michigan, 1969.
JAS 30 (1970-1) 230-1. (R. B. Jones)

BURLING, ROBBINS. Proto Lolo-Burmese. Bloomington, Indiana Univ., 1967. (Indiana Univ. Research Center in Anthropology, Folklore, and Linguis-

tics. Publication, 43)
SOAS 31 (1968) 648-9. (R. K. Sprigg)

BURMA RESEARCH SOCIETY. Fiftieth anniversary publications. Rangoon, 1960-
Volume I.
JSS 50 pt. 2 (1962) 51-53. (J. Silverstein)
Volume II.
JAS 21 (1961-2) 408-9. (H. Tinker)
JSS 49 pt. 2 (1961) 171-173. (C. N. Spinks)

BURNS, PETER L. Papers on Malay subjects by R. J. Wilkinson, selected and introduced by P. L. Burns. New York, Oxford UP, 1971. (Oxford in Asia historical reprints)
JSAS 3 (1972) 350-352. (C. M. Turnbull)
PA 45 (1972) 316-7. (K. G. Tregonning)

BURRELL, ROBERT MICHAEL. The Indian Ocean: a conference report, March 18-19, 1971. Edited by Robert M. Burrell and Alvin J. Cottrell. Washington, Center for Strategic Studies and International Studies, Georgetown Univ., 1971.
JSAS 5 (1974) 155-157. (Wong Lin Ken)

* al-BUSIRI. Een 16de eeuwse Maleise vertaling van de Burda van al-Busiri, uitg. en vertaald door G. W. J. Drewes. The Hague, Nijhoff, 1955. (Instituut voor Taal-, Land- en Volkenkunde. Verhandelingen, deel 18)
JMBRAS 33 pt. 1 (1960) 122-125. (A. H. Jones)

Bustrillos, Nena Rola *See* ROLA-BUSTRILLOS, NENA.

BUTTINGER, JOSEPH. Dragon defiant, a short history of Vietnam. New York, Praeger, 1972.
JAS 32 (1972-3) 754-5. (S. Parker)

Cahen, Claude. Introduction a

BUTTINGER, JOSEPH. Vietnam, a dragon
  embattled. New York, Praeger, 1967.
  2v.
    JAS 28 (1968-9) 438-440. (D.
      Wurfel)
    PA 40 (1967) 402-3. (P. J. Honey)

BUTTINGER, JOSEPH. Vietnam, a political history. New York, Praeger,
  1968.
    JAS 28 (1968-9) 648-9. (J. K.
      Whitmore)
    PA 42 (1969) 99-100. (D. J.
      Duncanson)
    PA 42 (1969) 387-8. (G. Fairbairn)

Butwell, Richard A. *See* VANDENBOSCH,
  AMRY. Changing face of Southeast
  Asia

BUTWELL, RICHARD A. Southeast Asia
  today and tomorrow; a political
  analysis. New York, Praeger, 1961.
    PA 35 (1962) 181-183. (V. Purcell)
    PS 10 (1962) 319-320. (M. McPhelin)

BUTWELL, RICHARD A. Southeast Asia
  today and tomorrow; problems of
  political development. 2d. ed. rev.
  New York, Praeger, 1969.
    JAS 29 (1969-70) 982-3. (W. Levi)
    PA 43 (1970) 301-2. (J. L. S.
      Girling)

BUTWELL, RICHARD A. U Nu of Burma.
  Stanford, Stanford UP, 1963.
    AS 4 (1964) 774.
    JAS 23 (1963-4) 485-6. (L. J.
      Walinsky)
    JSAH 5 (Sept. 1964) 199-202. (T.
      V. Sathyamurthy)
    PA 37 (1964) 92-3. (Hla Myint)
    SOAS 27 (1964) 665-6. (E. M.
      Mendelson)

BUTWELL, RICHARD A. U Nu of Burma.
  Stanford, Stanford UP, 1969.
    JAS 30 (1969-70) 229-230. (J.
      Guyot)

Buxbaum, David C. *See* CONFERENCE ON
  FAMILY LAW AND CUSTOMARY LAW IN
  ASIA, SINGAPORE, 1964. Family law
  and customary law

BYRD, CECIL K. Early printing in the
  Straits Settlements. Singapore,
  Singapore National Library, 1970.
    JAH 6 (1972) 157-8. (C. R. Boxer)

CADET, J. M. Ramakien, the Thai epic.
  Tokyo, Kodansha, 1971.
    BEF 59 (1972) 325-6. (L. Gabaude)
    JSS 60 pt. 1 (1972) 390. (Dhanini-
      vat)

CADIERE, LEOPOLD MICHEL. Syntaxe de
  la langue vietnamienne. Paris,
  Ecole Francaise d'Extreme-Orient,
  1958. (Ecole Francaise d'Extreme-
  Orient. Publications, v. 42)
    SOAS 23 (1960) 430. (P. J. Honey)

CADY, JOHN FRANK. Southeast Asia, its
  historical development. New York,
  McGraw-Hill, 1964.
    BIJ 120 (1964) 468-472. (L.
      Sluimers)
    JAS 24 (1964-5) 343-4. (C. C.
      Hobbs)
    JSAH 6 (Sept. 1965) 140-143. (B.
      Harrison)
    PA 37 (1964) 459-460. (J. D.
      Legge)

CADY, JOHN FRANK. Thailand, Burma,
  Laos and Cambodia. Englewood
  Cliffs, Prentice-Hall, 1966.
    AS 7 (1967) 593.
    JAH 3 (1969) 80-82. (F. N. Trager)
    JAS 27 (1967-8) 181-2. (M.
      Osborne)
    PA 40 (1967) 160-162. (D. G. E.
      Hall)

Cahen, Claude *See* SAUVAGET, JEAN.
  Introduction a l'histoire de l'Orient musulman

Cairns, James Ford. Eagle and the

CAIRNS, JAMES FORD. Eagle and the
lotus, Western intervention in Vietnam, 1847-1968. Melbourne, Lansdowne Pr., 1969.
   PA 43 (1970) 467-469. (D. J.
   Duncanson)

CALDWELL, MALCOLM. Cambodia in the
Southeast Asian war, by Malcolm
Caldwell and Lek Tan. New York,
Monthly Review Pr., 1973.
   JCA 3 (1973) 212-3. (P. Duff)
   PA 46 (1973) 469-471. (M. Osborne)

CALDWELL, MALCOLM. Indonesia. Toronto, Oxford UP, 1968.
   PA 42 (1969) 268. (J. D. Legge)

CALVOCORESSI, PETER. International
politics since 1945. New York,
Praeger, 1968.
   PA 41 (1968) 652. (F. H. Soward)

CAMBODIA. MINISTERE DE L'INFORMATION.
Cambodge, Phnom Penh, GPO, 1962.
   SEIB 36 (1961) 793.

CAMBODIA. MINISTERE DU PLAN. Annuaire
statistique retrospectif du Cambodge,
1937-1957. Phnom Penh, GPO, 1958.
   BEF 50 (1960) 223-228. (B. P.
   Groslier)

Cambridge history of Islam. Vol. II.
Further Islamic lands, Islamic soci-
ety and civilization. Cambridge,
Cambridge UP, 1970.
   JSAS 3 (1972) 317-319. (L. F.
   Brakel)
   MAS 7 (1973) 128-133. (E. I. J.
   Rosenthal)
   SOAS 35 (1972) 355-358. (R. C.
   Ostle)

CAMERON, ALLAN W. Viet-Nam crisis, a
documentary history. Vol. I. 1940-
1956. Ithaca, Cornell UP, 1971.
   JCA 3 (1973) 101.
   JSAS 3 (1972) 330-332. (M. Caldwell)

PA 45 (1972) 143-4. (J. L. S.
   Girling)

CAMERON, JAMES. Here is your enemy;
complete report from North Vietnam.
New York, Holt, Rinehart and
Winston, 1966.
   PA 42 (1969) 423.

CAMERON, JOHN. Our tropical posses-
sions in Malayan India. Kuala Lum-
pur, Oxford UP, 1965.
   JAS 25 (1965-6) 793. (G. P. Means)
   MAS 1 (1967) 104-106. (C. A.
   Fisher)

CAMPBELL, RUSSELL N. Noun substitutes
in modern Thai, a study in pronomi-
nality. The Hague, Mouton, 1969.
(Janua Linguarum. Series practica,
65)
   JAS 29 (1969-70) 732-3. (T. W.
   Gething)

CAO HUY THUAN. Christianisme et co-
lonialisme au Vietnam, 1857-1914.
Paris, 1968. 2v.
   BEF 59 (1972) 333-339. (Nguyen Huu
   Dang)

Careri, Giovanni Francesco Gemelli
   See GEMELLI CARERI, GIOVANNI
FRANCESCO

CARLOS PALANCA MEMORIAL AWARDS FOR
LITERATURE. Prize stories, 1950-
1955, edited by Kerima Polotan.
Manila, La Tondena, 1957.
   PS 8 (1960) 675-6. (M. A. Bernad)

CARPIO-LAUS, REMIGIA. Coordination of
agencies in the Community Develop-
ment Program. Quezon City, 1960.
(Quezon, Philippines. Univ. of the
Philippines. Community Development
Research Council. Study series, no.
7)
   JAS 22 (1962-3) 342-345. (D. V.
   Hart)

CARR, LORRAINE. To the Philippines
with love. Los Angeles, Sherbourne
Pr., 1966.
  PA 40 (1967) 201-2. (H. E. Jacob-
    son)

CARR-SAUNDERS, ALEXANDER MORRIS. New
universities overseas. London,
Allen and Unwin, 1961.
  PA 35 (1962) 90-1. (G. C. Andrew)

Carrere d'Encausse, Helene *See*
SCHRAM, STUART R. Marxisme et
l'Asie

CARRO, ANDRES. Iloko-English diction-
ary, Andres Carro's *Vocabulario
Iloco-Espanol*. Trans. and rev. by
Morice Vanoverbergh. Baguio, Catho-
lic School Pr., 1957.
  JAS 21 (1961-2) 247-8. (J. Wolff)

CARROLL, JOHN J. Changing patterns of
social structure in the Philippines,
1896-1963. Quezon City, Ateneo de
Manila UP, 1968.
  PS 16 (1968) 789-791. (J. T. Keane)

CARROLL, JOHN J. Filipino manufactur-
ing entrepreneur, agent and product
of change. Ithaca, Cornell UP, 1965.
  PA 39 (1966) 414-5. (A. Kintanar)
  PS 14 (1966) 526-528. (A. V. Ayala)
  SOAS 29 (1966) 461. (P. I. Ayre)

CARROLL, JOHN J. Philippine institu-
tions, by John J. Carroll et al.
Manila, Solidaridad, 1970.
  JAS 31 (1971-2) 465-6. (C. L. Hunt)
  SA 2 (1972) 520. (D. J. Scheans)
  SA 3 (1974-5) 655-6. (D. J.
    Scheans)

CARSON, ARTHUR LEROY. Higher educa-
tion in the Philippines. Washington,
U.S. Dept. of Health, Education and
Welfare, Office of Education, 1961.
(U.S. Office of Education. Bulletin
1961, no. 29)
  JAS 22 (1962-3) 116-7. (D. V. Hart)
  SJ 9 (1962) 255-6. (L. Q. Arquiza)

CARSON, ARTHUR LEROY. Silliman University, 1901-1959, gateway of opportunity and of service in the
Philippines. New York, United Board
for Christian Education in Asia,
1966.
  JAS 28 (1968-9) 913-915. (D. V.
    Hart)
  SJ 14 (1967) 358-361. (T. V.
    Sitoy)

CARUNUNGAN, CELSO AL. Like a big
brave man, a novel. New York, Farrar, Strauss and Cudahy, 1960.
  PS 8 (1960) 880-882. (M. A.
    Bernad)
  UN 34 (Dec. 1961) 131-133. (A.
    Panizo)

Case, Margaret H. *See* HAY, STEPHEN
N. Southeast Asian history

CASPER, LEONARD. Modern Philippine
short stories. Albuquerque, Univ.
of New Mexico Pr., 1962.
  JAS 22 (1962-3) 229-230. (D. V.
    Hart)
  PS 12 (1964) 160-165. (B. Lumbera)

CASPER, LEONARD. New writings from
the Philippines, a critique and
anthology. Syracuse, Syracuse UP,
1966.
  JAH 2 (1968) 190-1. (J. U. Wolff)
  JAS 26 (1966-7) 354-5. (D. V.
    Hart)
  PA 40 (1967) 202. (G. Woodcock)
  PS 14 (1966) 694-5. (M. A. Bernad)

CASPER, LEONARD. Wounded diamond,
studies in modern Philippine litera-
ture. Manila, Bookmark, 1964.
  JAS 25 (1965-6) 374. (E. San Juan)
  PS 13 (1965) 382-384. (E. de
    Jesus)
  SLQ 4 (1966) 132-135. (C. F.
    Bautista)

Casper, Linda Ty. The peninsulars, a

CASPER, LINDA TY. The peninsulars, a
    novel. Manila, Bookmark, 1964.
      PS 13 (1965) 850-859. (B. Lumbera)

CASTANEDA, DOMINADOR. Art in the Phil-
    ippines. Quezon City, Univ. of the
    Philippines, Office of Research Co-
    ordination, 1964.
        PS 13 (1965) 384-387. (F. N.
      Zialcita)

Castles, Lance *See* FEITH, HERBERT.
    Indonesian political thinking

CASTLES, LANCE. Religion, politics
    and economic behavior in Java, the
    Kudus cigarette industry. New Haven,
    Southeast Asia Studies, Yale Univ.,
    1967. (Yale Univ. Graduate School.
    Southeast Asia Studies. Cultural re-
    port series, no. 15)
      FA 22 (1968) 130.
      JAS 27 (1967-8) 437-8. (P. W. van
        der Veur)
      JSAH 9 (1968) 164-166. (C. Geertz)
      PA 40 (1967) 396-398. (The Siauw
        Giap)

CATER, SONYA DIANE. Philippine Feder-
    ation of Free Farmers: a case study
    in mass agrarian organization.
    Ithaca, Southeast Asia Program, Cor-
    nell Univ., 1959. (Cornell Univ.
    Southeast Asia Program. Data paper,
    no. 35)
      PS 8 (1960) 193-197. (G. S. Santos)
      PS 8 (1960) 418-426. (J. U. Monte-
        mayor)

Catholic Church in the Philippines to-
    day, by Isidoro Alonso. Manila,
    Historical Conservation Society,
    1968. (Historical Conservation So-
    ciety. Publication, no. 13)
      JAS 28 (1968-9) 912-3. (J. Larkin)
      PA 17 (1969) 811-2. (F. Lynch)

* Catholic directory of the Philippines.
    Manila, Catholic Trade School, 1965.
      SLQ 3 (1965) 160-162.

CATROUX, GEORGES. Deux actes du drama
    indochinois; Hanoi, juin 1940; Dien
    Bien Phu, mars-mai 1954. Paris,
    Plon, 1959.
      SEIB 35 (1960) 717. (S. de
        Labrusse)

* Cav bejraj burus hlek hen rajaanacakr-
    lav toy 3349. Bangkok, 2499.
      BEF 58 (1971) 321-330. (Saveng
        Phinith)

Cawphrajaa Thiphaakorawon *See*
    THIPHAAKORAWON, CHAO-PHYA

CAYRAC-BLANCHARD, FRANCOISE. Le par-
    tai communiste indonesien. Paris,
    Armand Colin, 1973. (Travaux et re-
    cherches de science politique, 26)
      AR 8 (1974) 231-234. (J. Leclerc)
      PA 47 (1974) 390-1. (J. M. van der
        Kroef)

Cazeneuve, Jean *See* Danses sacrees

Centre d'Etude des Relations Interna-
    tionales *See* Regime interne et po-
    litique exterieure dans les pays
    d'Asie

* CENTRO ESCOLAR UNIV. GRADUATE SCHOOL
    STUDENTS ASSOCIATION. Sapphires and
    pyrites, a list of dissertations and
    theses filed in the CEU library.
    Manila, Centro Escolar Univ., n.d.
      JAS 32 (1972-3) 572-3. (D. V.
        Hart)

CHAFFARD, GEORGES. Les deux guerres
    du Vietnam, de Valluy a Westmore-
    land. Paris, La Table Ronde, 1969.
    (La Table ronde de combat. Documents
    et reportage)
      FA 24 (1970) 202-207. (P.
        Devillers)
      PA 45 (1972) 142-3. (J. L. S.
        Girling)

* CHAI-ANAN SAMUDVANIJA. Sat kan muang,
    [by] Chai-Anan Samudvanija, Setha-

Chaunu, Pierre. Les Philippines et le

porn Cusripituck [and] Sawaeng
Ratanamongkolmas. Bangkok, Thai
Watlana Panich, 1971.
JSS 62 pt. 2 (1974) 346-353. (B.
A. Batson)

CHAI HON CHAN. Development of British
Malaya, 1896-1909. Kuala Lumpur,
Oxford UP, 1964.
AAS 5 (1969) 111-113. (R. Raczyn-
ski)
JSAH 6 (Sept. 1965) 150-152. (E.
Sadka)
PA 38 (1965) 207-8. (N. Tarling)
RSA (1968) 123-127. (Tran Buu
Khanh)

Chairil Anwar *See* ANWAR, CHAIRIL

CHAKRAVARTI, NALINI RANJAN. Indian
minority in Burma, the rise and de-
cline of an immigrant community.
London, Oxford UP, 1971.
JAS 31 (1971-2) 719-722. (R. L.
Feldberg)
PA 45 (1972) 137-8. (U. Mahajani)

CHAKRIT NORANITIPADUNGKARN. Moderniz-
ing Chiengmai: a study of community
elites in urban development, by
Chakrit Noranitipadungkarn and A.
Clark Hagensick. Bangkok, National
Institute of Development Administra-
tion, 1973.
JSS 62 pt. 2 (1974) 343-345. (C.
F. Keyes)

Chalermnit Press correspondent *See*
Battle of Vietiane

CHALIAND, GERARD. Peasants of North
Vietnam, trans. by Peter Wiles. Don
Mills, Ont., Longmans Canada, 1969.
PA 43 (1970) 625-630. (A. Woodside)

CHALMERS, WILLIAM ELLISON. Crucial
issues in industrial relations in
Singapore. Singapore, Donald Moore,
1967.
MER 13 pt. 1 (1968) 132-134. (H.
Kawada)

CHAMBERLAIN, ELINOR. Far command.
New York, Ballantine Books, 1953.
SJ 12 (1965) 457-459. (D. Martin)

CHAMPASSAK, SISOUK NA. Storm over
Laos, a contemporary history. New
York, Praeger, 1961.
JAS 21 (1961-2) 239-240. (D. A.
Wilson)
PA 35 (1962) 80-82. (E. A. Blais)

CHAMPASSAK, SISOUK NA. Tempete sur le
Laos. Paris, La Table Ronde, 1961.
FA 18 (1962) 233-237. (J. Chris-
tian)
SEIB 36 (1961) 744.

CHAN HENG CHEE. Singapore, the poli-
tics of survival, 1965-1967. Singa-
pore, Oxford UP, 1971.
JAS 32 (1972-3) 749. (G. D. Ness)
JSAS 4 (1973) 323-325. (R. Vasil)
MAS 7 (1973) 757. (S. Rose)
PA 44 (1971) 648. (L. E. Williams)

CHAND, EMCEE. Thai monumental bronzes
by Emcee Chand and Khien Yimsiri.
Bangkok, 1957.
SEIB 36 (1961) 754.

CHANDLER, DAVID P. Land and people of
Cambodia. Philadelphia, Lippincott,
1972. (Portraits of the nations
series)
JAS 33 (1973-4) 335-6. (J. M.
Jacob)

CHANDRASEKHAR, SRIPATI. Asia's population problems: with a discussion
of population and immigration in
Australia. London, Allen and Unwin,
1967.
AS 7 (1967) 752.
JAS 27 (1967-8) 368-9. (M. Perl-
man)

CHAUNU, PIERRE. Les Philippines et le
Pacifique des Iberiques (XVIe, XVIIe,

CHHAK SARIN. Les frontiers du Cambodge. Paris, Dalloz, 1966. (Centre
d'Etude des Pays d'Extreme-Orient,
Asie du Sud-Est, 1)
   FA 20 (1965) 408-410. (P. Devillers)

Chiang Hai Ding *See* Modern Singapore

Chin, Phui Kong *See* INGER, ROBERT F.
Fresh water fishes of North Borneo

* CHIRA CHAROENLOET. Evolution of Thailand's economy. Bangkok, Thai Watana Panich Pr., 1971.
   JSS 62 pt. 1 (1974) 238-243. (W.
   A. McCleary)

CHIRINO, PEDRO. Relacion de las islas
Filipinas, the Philippines in 1600.
Manila, Bookmark, 1969.
   JAS 30 (1970-1) 240-1. (C. O.
   Houston)
   PA 43 (1970) 471. (E. Wickberg)
   PS 18 (1970) 438-9. (N. P. Cushner)

CHOMSKY, NOAM. At war with Asia. New
York, Pantheon, 1970.
   PA 44 (1971) 309-311. (M. E.
   Osborne)

CHULA, PRINCE. Lords of life, the
paternal monarchy of Bangkok. Lon-
don, Alvin Redman, 1960.
   JAS 20 (1960-1) 543-4. (W. F.
   Vella)
   JSS 48 pt. 2 (1960) 118-121.
   PA 34 (1961) 414-5. (R. C. Nairn)

* CHULALONGKORN, KING OF THAILAND.
Chotmaihet phraratchakit raiwan.
Bangkok, 1933-65. 24v.
   SOAS 31 (1968) 382-385. (D. K.
   Wyatt)

Churatana, Prasoet *See* SAENLUANG
RATCHASOMPHAN. Nan chronicle

CIPTA LOKA CARAKA. Kamus politik pem-
bangunan. Djakarta, Jajasan Kani-

Clubb, Oliver Edmund. United States
sius, 1970.
   AR 4 (1972) 252-3. (P. Labrousse)

The city as a centre of change in
Asia. Editor: D. J. Dwyer. Hong
Kong, Hong Kong UP, 1972. (Centre of
Asian Studies series, no. 4)
   JCA 3 (1973) 214-5. (W. Easey)
   JSAS 5 (1974) 152-154. (I.
   Buchanan)
   PA 46 (1973) 111-2. (R. Murphey)

CLARKSON, JAMES D. Cultural ecology
of a Chinese village; Cameron High-
lands Malaysia. (Chicago, Dept. of
Geography. Research paper, no. 114)
   JAS 28 (1968-9) 645-6. (A. G.
   Dewey)
   JSAH 10 (1969) 369-370. (Riaz
   Hassan)

* CLAUSTRO, FELIX B. Notes on the 1973
Philippine constitution. Quezon
City, 1974.
   SLURJ 5 (1974) 463-466. (P. B.
   Sanchez)

CLEMENA ILETO, REYNALDO. Magindanao,
1860-1888, the career of Datu Uto of
Buayan. Ithaca, Southeast Asia Pro-
gram, Cornell Univ., 1971. (Cornell
Univ. Southeast Asia Program. Data
paper, 82)
   PS 20 (1972) 661-665. (J. N.
   Schumacher)

CLIFFORD, HUGH CHARLES. Stories.
Kuala Lumpur, Oxford UP, 1966.
   JAS 26 (1966-7) 536-538. (R.
   Allen)
   PA 40 (1967) 201. (D. G. E. Hall)

CLUBB, OLIVER EDMUND. United States
and the Sino-Soviet block in South-
east Asia. Washington, Brookings
Institution, 1962.
   JAS 22 (1962-3) 491. (R. Butwell)
   JSAH 6 (Mar. 1966) 138-142. (F.
   Carnell)

Clutterbuck, Richard L. Long, long

CLUTTERBUCK, RICHARD L. Long, long
  war, counterinsurgency in Malaya and
  Vietnam. New York, Praeger, 1966.
    JAS 26 (1966-7) 337-8. (F. H.
    Tucker)

CLUTTERBUCK, RICHARD L. Riot and revolution in Singapore and Malaya,
  1945-1963. London, Faber and Faber,
  1973.
    JCA 4 (1974) 99-101. (G. Raman)

COATES, AUSTIN. Rizal, Philippine nationalist and martyr. New York,
  Oxford UP, 1968.
    PA 42 (1969) 235-6. (I. B. Powell)
    PS 18 (1970) 207-209. (N. P.
    Cushner)

* COATES, KEN. Prevent the crime of
  silence: reports from the sessions
  of the international war crimes tribunal, by Ken Coates, P. Limqueco
  and P. Weiss. London, Penguin Pr.,
  1971.
    JCA 2 (1971) 86-89. (Hakim el
    Khaled)

COCKCROFT, JOHN. The Philippines.
  Sydney, Angus and Robertson, 1968.
    AAS 8 (1972) 192. (J. Genzor)

COEDES, GEORGE. Angkor, an introduction. Hong Kong, Oxford UP, 1963.
    SOAS 27 (1964) 485-6. (A. Christie)

Coedes, George. Empire of the South
  Seas. *See* BIDYALABH, KROMANUM.
  Story of Rama

COEDES, GEORGE. Les etats hindouises
  d'Indochine et d'Indonesie. Nouv.
  ed. Paris, Boccard, 1964.
    JAS 24 (1964-5) 335-6. (P.
    Wheatley)
    SEIB 39 (1964) 298-9.
    SOAS 29 (1966) 649-650. (J. G. de
    Casparis)

COEDES, GEORGE. Indianized states of
  Southeast Asia. Honolulu, East-West
  Center Pr., 1968.
    AP 11 (1968) 192-196. (S. Ikuta)
    JAS 28 (1968-9) 433-4. (P.
    Wheatley)
    JSAH 10 (1969) 356-7. (D. K.
    Wyatt)
    PA 43 (1970) 303-4. (B. Harrison)

COEDES, GEORGE. Making of South East
  Asia. London, Routledge and Kegan
  Paul, 1966.
    JAH 2 (1968) 73-4. (J. F. Cady)
    JAS 26 (1966-7) 752-3. (W. F.
    Vella)
    PA 39 (1966) 457-8. (B. Harrison)
    PS 15 (1967) 201-203. (A. B.
    Calderon)
    SOAS 30 (1967) 254. (H. Tinker)

COEDES, GEORGE. Les peuples de la
  peninsule indochinoise, histoire-
  civilisations. Paris, Dunod, 1962.
    AAS 2 (1966) 167-170. (R. Raczyn-
    ski)
    BIJ 119 (1963) 444-447. (F. D. K.
    Bosch)
    JAS 22 (1962-3) 340. (F. H.
    Tucker)
    SEIB 39 (1964) 298.
    SEIB 41 (1966) 88.

Coedes, George *See* Recueil des inscriptions du Siam

COHEN, SAUL BERNARD. Geography and
  politics in a world divided. New
  York, Random House, 1963.
    PS 13 (1965) 876-878. (F. C.
    Darling)

COLLER, RICHARD WALTER. Analysis of
  the social effects of donated radios
  on barrio life. Quezon City, 1961.
  (Quezon, Philippines. Univ. of the
  Philippines. Community Development
  Research Council. Study series, no.
  14 [i.e. 11])
    JAS 22 (1962-3) 342-345. (D. V.
    Hart)

Compadre colonialism, studies on the

COLLER, RICHARD WALTER. Barrio Gacao:
a study of village ecology and the
schistosomiasis problem. Quezon
City, 1960. (Quezon, Philippines.
Univ. of the Philippines. Community
Development Research Council. Ab-
stract series, no. 10)
JAS 20 (1960-1) 403. (E. Nurge)

COLLINS, D. G. English Lao diction-
ary. 2d. ed. Farnborough, Eng.,
Gregg International, 1972.
JSS 61 pt. 1 (1973) 364-367. (H.
C. Purnell)

Collins Malay gem dictionary: Malay-
English, English-Malay, compiled by
Abdul Rahman bin Yusop. London,
Collins, 1964.
BIJ 120 (1964) 384-386. (R. Jones)

COLLIS, MAURICE. Journey up, reminis-
cences, 1934-1968. London, Faber,
1970.
PA 45 (1972) 136-7. (J. F. Cady)

COLLIS, MAURICE. Raffles. London,
Faber, 1966.
PA 41 (1968) 450-1. (D. G. E.
Hall)

* COLOGNE. WALLRAF-RICHARTS-MUSEUM.
Schatze aus Thailand. Katalog
einer Ausstellung im 1963. n.p.,
n.d.
BIJ 121 (1965) 373-378. (F. D. K.
Bosch)

COLUMBIA UNIVERSITY. SCHOOL OF LAW.
Public international development
financing in Thailand. New York,
1963. (Columbia Univ. School of
Law. Public international develop-
ment financing; report no. 4)
JAS 24 (1964-5) 532-3. (M. L.
Thomas)

COMBER, LEON. Chinese secret socie-
ties in Malaya, a survey of the
Triad Society from 1800 to 1900.
Locust Valley, N.Y., Augustin, 1959.
(Association for Asian Studies.
Monographs, 6)
JAS 19 (1959-60) 364-5. (L. W.
Pye)
JSAH 1 (Mar. 1960) 109-129. (Wong
Lin Ken)
SOAS 23 (1960) 415-6. (G. W.
Skinner)

COMMITTEE FOR ECONOMIC DEVELOPMENT.
Economic development issues:
Greece, Israel, Taiwan, and Thai-
land. New York, Praeger, 1968.
PA 42 (1969) 422. (G. B. Hains-
worth)
PA 45 (1972) 326. (G. B. Hains-
worth)

COMMITTEE FOR ECONOMIC DEVELOPMENT OF
AUSTRALIA. Trade and aid in South-
east Asia. I. Malaysia and Singa-
pore, by Sumitro Djojohadikusumo.
Melbourne, Cheshire, 1968.
PA 42 (1969) 236-7. (C. Wolfe)

COMMITTEE OF CONCERNED ASIA SCHOLARS.
Indochina story; a fully documented
account. New York, Bantam Books,
1970.
PA 44 (1971) 641-644. (J. L. S.
Girling)

Committee on American Policy Towards
Vietnam. Consultative council. *See*
LAWYERS COMMITTEE ON AMERICAN POLI-
CY TOWARDS VIETNAM. CONSULTATIVE
COUNCIL

Compans, Henri Ternaux *See* TERNAUX-
COMPANS, HENRI

Compadre colonialism, studies on the
Philippines under American rule,
edited by Norman G. Owen. Ann
Arbor, Center for South and Southeast Asian Studies, Univ. of Michi-

Compadre colonialism, studies on the

gan, 1971. (Michigan papers on
South and Southeast Asia, no. 3)
  JAS 32 (1972-3) 224-226. (T.
    Friend)
  PA 45 (1972) 464-5. (I. B. Powell)
  SA 3 (1974) 783-785. (G. E.
    Sheeler)

COMYN, TOMAS DE. State of the Philippines in 1810: being an historical,
  statistical and descriptive account
  of the interesting portion of the
  Indian archipelago. And, Philippine
  progress prior to 1898, by Conrado
  Benitez. Manila, Filipiniana Book
  Guild, 1969. (Filipiniana Book
  Guild. Publications, 15)
    JAS 31 (1971-2) 233-235. (C. O.
      Houston)
    PA 44 (1970) 321-2. (E. Wickberg)

Condominas, Georges *See* GAUDILLOT,
  C. Plaine de Vientiane

CONDOMINAS, GEORGES. L'exotique est
  quotidien. Paris, Plon, 1965.
    SEIB 41 (1966) 315-6. (R. Legay)

CONFERENCE ON AMERICAN TRADE WITH ASIA
  AND THE FAR EAST, MARQUETTE UNIV.,
  1958. American trade with Asia and
  the Far East. Robert F. Barr, editor.
  Milwaukee, Marquette UP, 1959. (Marquette Asian studies, 1)
    JAS 19 (1959-60) 445-6. (C. F.
      Remer)
    PA 34 (1961) 94-5. (H. J. Collar)

CONFERENCE ON FAMILY LAW AND CUSTOMARY
  LAW IN ASIA, SINGAPORE, 1964. Family law and customary law, a contemporary legal perspective. Editor,
  David C. Buxbaum. The Hague, Nijhoff, 1968.
    PA 43 (1970) 472-3. (L. C. Green)

CONFERENCE ON LINGUISTIC PROBLEMS OF
  THE INDO-PACIFIC AREA, SCHOOL OF
  ORIENTAL AND AFRICAN STUDIES, UNIV.
  OF LONDON, 1965. Indo-Pacific lin-

guistic studies, edited by G. B.
Milner and Eugenie J. A. Henderson.
Amsterdam, North-Holland Publishing
Co., 1965. 2v.
  SOAS 30 (1967) 475.

CONFERENCE ON POPULATION, 1ST., UNIV.
  OF THE PHILIPPINES. First conference on population, 1965. Quezon
  City, Univ. of the Philippines Pr.,
  1966.
    PS 16 (1968) 590-592. (F. C.
      Madigan)

CONFERENCE ON SOCIAL DEVELOPMENT AND
  WELFARE IN VIETNAM, NEW YORK, 1959.
  Problems of freedom: South Vietnam
  since independence, edited by Wesley
  R. Fishel. New York, Free Pr. of
  Glencoe, 1961.
    JAS 22 (1962-3) 224-227. (B. B.
      Fall)
    JSAH 4 (Sept. 1963) 188-9. (H.
      Tinker)
    PA 36 (1963) 97-8. (B. Crozier)

CONFERENCE ON THERAVADA BUDDHISM,
  UNIV. OF CHICAGO, 1962. Anthropological studies in Theravada Buddhism,
  by Manning Nash, et al. New Haven,
  Yale Univ., 1966. (Yale Univ. Graduate School. Southeast Asia Studies.
  Cultural report series, no. 13)
    BIJ 124 (1968) 399-400. (E. R.
      Leach)
    JAS 26 (1966-7) 529-531. (F. M.
      LeBar)
    JSAH 8 (1967) 336-7. (F. R. von
      der Mehden)

CONKLIN, HAROLD C. El estudio del
  cultivo de roza. Study of shifting
  cultivation. Washington, Union Pan-
  americana, 1963. (Pan American
  Union. Dept. of Social Affairs.
  Studies and monographs, 6)
    AP 10 (1967) 163-4. (D. E. Yen)
    BIJ 123 (1967) 179-180. (P. E. de
      Josselin de Jonge)
    PS 13 (1965) 390-1. (F. Lynch)

CONKLIN, HAROLD C. Ifugao bibliography. New Haven, Yale Univ., Southeast Asia Studies, 1968. (Yale
  Univ. Graduate School. Southeast
  Asia Studies. Bibliography series,
  no. 11)
    AP 12 (1969) 147. (M. Davidson)
    PS 17 (1969) 344. (F. Lambrecht)

Constantino, Renato *See* BORLONGAN,
  ERLINDA. Catalogue of Filipiniana
  materials.

CONSTANTINO, RENATO. Making of a Filipino, a story of Philippine colonial
  politics. Quezon City, Malaya Books,
  1969.
    JCA 1 pt. 4 (1971) 76-79. (J. Fast)
    SA 2 (1972-3) 384-387. (K. G.
    Machado)

COOKE, JOSEPH R. Pronominal reference
  in Thai, Burmese and Vietnamese.
  Berkeley, Univ. of California Pr.,
  1968. (California. Univ. Univ. of
  California publications in linguistics, v. 52)
    JAS 29 (1969-70) 733-4. (F. K.
    Lehman)

COOLEY, FRANK L. Ambonese adat, a
  general description. New Haven,
  Yale Univ., Southeast Asia Studies,
  1962. (Yale Univ. Graduate School.
  Southeast Asia Studies. Cultural report series, no. 10)
    PA 37 (1964) 469-471. (L. Palmier)

COOLHAAS, WILLEM PHILIPPUS. Critical
  survey of studies on Dutch colonial
  history. The Hague, Nijhoff, 1960.
  (Instituut voor Taal-, Land- en
  Volkenkunde. Bibliographical series,
  4)
    JAS 21 (1961-2) 99-100. (J. Bastin)

Coolhaas, Willem Philippus *See* NEDER-
  LANDSCHE OOST-INDISCHE COMPAGNIE.
  General missiven van gouverneur-
  generaal en raden aan Heren XVII der
  Verenigde Oostindische Compagnie

Cornell Univ. Libraries. Checklist of

Coolie Budget Commission *See* DUTCH
  EAST INDIES. COOLIE BUDGET COMMIS-
  SION

COOMARASWAMY, ANANDA KENTISH. History
  of Indian and Indonesian art. New
  York, Dover, 1965.
    JAH 2 (1968) 156-7. (J. Auboyer)

COOPER, CHESTER. Lost crusade, America in Vietnam. New York, Dodd,
  Mead, 1970.
    PA 44 (1971) 308-9. (J. Silverman)

CORDERO-FERNANDO, GILDA. Butcher, the
  baker, the candle stick maker; thir-
  teen stories. Manila, Benipayo Pr.,
  1962.
    PS 14 (1966) 499-504. (M. A.
    Bernad)

CORNELL UNIV. DEPT. OF SOCIOLOGY AND
  ANTHROPOLOGY. CROSS-CULTURAL METH-
  ODOLOGY PROJECT. Factors related to
  acceptance of innovation in Bang
  Chan, Thailand; analysis of a survey
  conducted by the Cornell Cross-
  Cultural Methodology Project, May
  1955, by R. K. Goldsen and M. Ral-
  lis. Ithaca, Cornell Thailand Project, Cornell Univ., 1963. (Cornell
  Univ. Southeast Asia Project. Data
  paper, no. 25)
    BIJ 120 (1964) 481-484. (L.
    Sluimers)

CORNELL UNIV. LIBRARIES. Checklist of
  the Vietnamese holdings of the Wason
  Collection, Cornell University Libraries, as of June, 1971, by Giok
  Po Oey. Ithaca, Southeast Asia Program, Cornell Univ., 1971. (Cornell
  Univ. Southeast Asia Program. Data
  paper, no. 84)
    JAS 32 (1972-3) 379-380. (K.
    Taylor)
    SEIB 47 (1972) 553. (Nguyen The
    Anh)

Cornyn, William Stewart. Beginning

CORNYN, WILLIAM STEWART. Beginning
Burmese, by William S. Cornyn and D.
Haigh Roop. New Haven, Yale UP,
1968.
    SOAS 33 (1970) 669-671. (A. J.
    Allott)

CORONEL, MARIA DELIA. Stories and
legends from Filipino folklore. Manila, Univ. of Santo Tomas Pr., 1967.
    JAS 29 (1969-70) 507-8. (D. V.
    Hart)

CORPUZ, ONOFRE D. Bureaucracy in the
Philippines. Manila, Institute of
Public Administration, Univ. of the
Philippines, 1957. (Quezon, Philip-
pines. Univ. of the Philippines. In-
stitute of Public Administration.
Studies in public administration,
no. 4)
    JAS 19 (1959-60) 365-6. (H. B.
    Jacobini)

CORPUZ, ONOFRE D. The Philippines.
Englewood Cliffs, Prentice-Hall,
1965. (Modern nations in historical
perspective, S-616)
    JAS 25 (1965-6) 793-4. (D. V.
    Hart)
    JSAH 8 (1967) 329-330. (N. Tarling)
    PA 38 (1965) 438-9. (R. S. Milne)

CORTEMÜNDE, JOHAN PETRI. Dagbog fra en
Ostindiefart, 1572-75. Kronborg,
Handels-og Sofarsmuseet, 1953.
    BIJ 116 (1960) 490-492. (H. J. de
    Graaf)

COSTA, HORACIO DE LA. Background of
nationalism and other essays. Manila, Solidaridad, 1965.
    JAS 25 (1965-6) 795-6. (D. V.
    Hart)
    JSAH 7 (Sept. 1966) 143-4. (G. S.
    Maryanov)
    PS 14 (1966) 334-336. (M. A.
    Bernad)

COSTA, HORACIO DE LA. Jesuits in the
Philippines, 1581-1768. Cambridge,
Harvard UP, 1961.
    JAS 21 (1961-2) 93-4. (E. Wick-
    berg)
    PA 34 (1961) 413-4. (D. G. E.
    Hall)

COSTA, HORACIO DE LA. Readings in
Philippine history, selected historical texts presented with a commentary. Manila, Bookmark, 1965.
    JAS 25 (1965-6) 795-6. (D. V.
    Hart)
    PA 39 (1966) 450-452. (I. B.
    Powell)
    PS 14 (1966) 336-338. (M. A.
    Foronda)

COTTER, CONRAD PATRICK. Bibliography
of English language sources on human
ecology, Eastern Malaysia and Brunei. Honolulu, Univ. of Hawaii,
Dept. of Asian Studies, 1965. 2v.
    SMJ 14 (1966) 346-349. (R. M.
    Pringle)
    SMJ 14 (1966) 350-375. (Loh Chee
    Yin)

Cottrell, Alvin J. *See* BURRELL,
ROBERT MICHAEL. The Indian Ocean

COUGHLIN, RICHARD J. Double identity:
the Chinese in modern Thailand.
Hong Kong, Hong Kong UP, 1960.
    JAS 20 (1960-1) 545-6. (J. Blo-
    feld)
    JSAH 3 (Sept. 1962) 152-154. (Ann
    Wee)
    PA 36 (1963) 320. (O. W. Wolters)
    RSA (1965) 312-314. (W. de Bel)
    SOAS 24 (1961) 386-388. (E. H. S.
    Simmonds)

Coughlin, Richard J. *See* HART, DONN
VORHIS. Southeast Asian birth customs

Countries and peoples of the Pacific
basin, summaries of articles by

Soviet scholars for the Pacific Science Congress. Moscow, Nauka, 1971.
  AAS 9 (1973) 194-5. (J. Genzor)

COURTENAY, PERCY PHILIP. Geography of trade and development in Malaya. London, Bell, 1972.
  JCA 2 (1972) 306-308. (W. P. Kinney)
  SA 2 (1972) 488-502. (V. D. Ooms)

Covar, Prospero *See* QUEZON, PHILIP-PINES. UNIV. OF THE PHILIPPINES. COMMUNITY DEVELOPMENT COUNCIL. Masagana/Margate system of planting rice

COWAN, CHARLES DONALD. Economic development of Southeast Asia, studies in economic history and political economy. London, George Allen and Unwin, 1964. (Studies on modern Asia and Africa, no. 3)
  JSAH 6 (Sept. 1965) 138-140. (T. R. McHale)
  MER 10 pt. 1 (1965) 127-8. (W. M. Corden)
  PA 38 (1965) 87-8. (F. H. Golay)
  SOAS 28 (1965) 194-196. (M. Freedman)

COWAN, CHARLES DONALD. Nineteenth century Malaya: the origins of British political control. London, Oxford UP, 1961. (London Oriental series, vol. 11)
  JAS 21 (1961-2) 238-9. (B. Harrison)
  JSAH 2 (Oct. 1961) 115-120. (E. Sadka)
  SOAS 24 (1961) 605-607. (D. G. E. Hall)

COWAN, HENDRIK KAREL JAN. Grammar of the Sentani language, with specimen texts and vocabulary. The Hague, Nijhoff, 1965. (Instituut voor Taal-, Land- en Volkenkunde. Verhandelingen, deel 47)
  SOAS 30 (1967) 734-5. (G. B. Milner)

CRABB, CECIL V. Elephants and the grass, a study of nonalignment. New York, Praeger, 1965.
  PA 38 (1965) 451-2. (J. W. Holmes)

Craig, Albert M. *See* FAIRBANK, JOHN KING. East Asia; tradition and transformation

CRANE, ROBERT I. Southern Asia. Durham, N.C., 1968.
  JAS 28 (1968-9) 868-9. (R. Murphey)

CRAWFORD, ANN CADDELL. Customs and culture of Vietnam. Rutland, Tuttle, 1966. (Books to span the East and West)
  BEF 55 (1969) 290-294. N. Louis)

CRAWFURD, JOHN. Crawfurd papers, a collection of official records relating to the mission of Dr. John Crawfurd sent to Siam by the Government of India in the year 1821. Farnborough, Gregg, 1971.
  JSAS 3 (1972) 324-5. (Cheng Siok Hwa)
  JSS 62 pt. 1 (1974) 252-255. (L. M. Gesick)

CRAWFURD, JOHN. Descriptive dictionary of the Indian islands and adjacent countries. Kuala Lumpur, Oxford UP, 1971. (Oxford in Asia historical reprints)
  JAS 32 (1972-3) 367-8. (C. S. Gray)

CREDNER, WILHELM. Siam, das Land der Tai, eine Landeskunde auf Grund eigener Reisen und Forschungen. Osnabruck, Zeller, 1966.
  JSS 53 (1965) 125-6. (L. Sternstein)

CROZIER, BRIAN. Morning after, a study of independence. London, Methuen, 1963.

JCA 4 (1974) 365.
PA 47 (1974) 248-9. (J. M. van der
Kroef)

Damo-Santiago, Corazon *See* SANTIAGO,
CORAZON DAMO-

DAMPIER, WILLIAM. New voyage round
the world. New York, Dover, 1968.
PS 18 (1970) 438-9. (N. P. Cushner)

* DAMRONG RAJANUBHAB. Monuments of the
Buddha in Siam. Bangkok, Siam Soci-
ety, 1973.
JSS 62 pt. 2 (1974) 378-9. (H. D.
Ginsburg)

DAN, NGUYEN DUC. May van de van hoc
hien thuc phe phan Viet-nam. Hanoi,
Editions des sciences sociales, 1968.
AAS 7 (1971) 204-5. (J. Mucka)

DANANDJAJA, JAMES. Annotated bibliog-
raphy of Javanese folklore. Berke-
ley, Center for South and Southeast
Asia Studies, Univ. of California,
1972. (California. Univ. Center for
South and Southeast Asia Studies.
Occasional paper, no. 9)
BIJ 130 (1974) 380-1. (J. J. Ras)

* DANG NGHIEM. Viet-Nam, politics and
public administration. Honolulu,
East-West Center Pr., 1966.
AS 8 (1968) 148.

DANG THAI MAI. Van tho cach mang
Viet-Nam dau the ky xx. Hanoi, Van
Hoa, 1960?
JAS 30 (1970-1) 733-4. (D. G. Marr)

* Danh-tu y duoc phap-viet. Hanoi, 1963.
BEF 57 (1970) 266-269. (Nguyen
Tran Huan)

DANI, AHMAD HASAN. Prehistoric and
protohistory of eastern India, with
a detailed account of the neolithic
cultures in mainland South East
Asia. Calcutta, K. L. Mukhopadhyay,
1960.

JSAH 2 (Oct. 1961) 120-122. (P.
Wheatley)
SOAS 24 (1961) 596-598. (F. R.
Allchin)

DANOESOEGONDO, POERWANTO. Bahasa In-
donesia for beginners. Sydney,
Sydney UP, 1966.
BIJ 124 (1968) 545-551. (Soebardi)
SOAS 31 (1968) 182-3. (N. G.
Phillips)

Danses sacrees, par Jean Cazeneuve et
al. Paris, Editions du Seuil, 1963.
(Sources Orientales, 6)
SOAS 27 (1964) 214-5. (S. G. F.
Brandon)

Darjowidjojo, Soenjono *See* MACDONALD,
RODERICK ROSS. A student's reference grammar of modern formal Indonesian

Darling, Ann *See* DARLING, FRANK C.
Thailand, the modern kingdom

DARLING, FRANK C. Thailand and the
United States. Washington, Public
Affairs Pr., 1965.
JAS 25 (1965-6) 172-3. (M. Moer-
man)
PA 38 (1965) 437-8. (D. G. E.
Hall)

DARLING, FRANK C. Thailand, the mod-
ern kingdom, by Frank C. and Ann
Darling. Singapore, Donald Moore,
1971.
JAS 32 (1972-3) 562-3. (J. A.
Hafner)
PA 46 (1973) 185-6. (K. P. Landon)
SA 3 (1974) 793-4. (C. Hobbs)

* Darunowat. Bangkok, Phrae Kan Chang
Pr., 1969.
JSS 58 pt. 2 (1970) 145-149. (Tej
Bunnag)

Daunicht, Hubert. Der Osten nach der

DAUNICHT, HUBERT. Der Osten nach der
Erdkarte al-Huwarizmis: Beitrage
zur historischen Geographie und Geschichte Asiens. Teil II. Die ost-
und sud-ostasiatische Inselwelt und
die Meere. Bonn, Selbstverlag des
orientalischen Seminars der Universitat, 1970. (Bonner orientalistische
Studien. Neue Serie, Bd. 19a)
    SOAS 34 (1971) 205-6. (R. B.
      Serjeant)

DAUPHIN-MEUNIER, ACHILLE. Histoire du
Cambodge. Paris, Presses universitaires de France, 1961. (Que sais
je? Le point des connaissances actuelles, no. 916)
    FA 21 (1966) 599.
    JAS 21 (1961-2) 242. (Truong Buu
      Lam)

DAVIES, DAVID M. Rice bowl of Asia.
London, Hale, 1967.
    PA 42 (1969) 117. (D. Hindley)

DAVIES, S. GETHYN. Central banking in
South and East Asia. Hong Kong,
Hong Kong UP, 1960.
    SOAS 25 (1962) 404-5. (J. A. M.
      Caldwell)

DAVIS, RICHARD. Northern Thai reader.
Bangkok, Siam Society, 1970.
    JSS 59 pt. 2 (1971) 245-248. (H.
      C. Purnell)

DAY, CLIVE. [Policy and administration of] the Dutch in Java. Kuala
Lumpur, Oxford UP, 1966.
    JAS 29 (1969-70) 489-490. (W. F.
      Vella)
    JSAH 9 (1968) 354-356. (H. J.
      Benda)
    MAS 4 (1970) 371-373. (C. A.
      Fisher)
    PA 39 (1966) 458-9. (D. G. E. Hall)

De l'independence politique a la
liberte economique et a l'egalite
sociale en Asie du Sud-Est. Colloque

tenu a Bruxelles, les 25, 26 et 27
novembre 1964. Brussels, Institute
of Sociology, Universite Libre de
Bruxelles, 1966. (Brussels, Univ.
libre. Centre d'etude du Sud-Est
astiatique. Collection, 4)
    BIJ 126 (1970) 468-9. (H. J.
      Duller)

DEAN, VERA MICHELES. West and non-
west; new perspectives, an anthology,
by Vera Micheles Dean and Harry D.
Harootunian. New York, Holt, Rinehart and Winston, 1963. (Contemporary civilizations series)
    JAS 23 (1963-4) 598-9. (G. H.
      Green)

DEANE, HUGH. War in Vietnam. New
York, Monthly Review Pr., 1963.
    JAS 23 (1963-4) 483-4. (J. C.
      Donnell)

DEATS, RICHARD LOUIS. Nationalism and
Christianity in the Philippines.
Dallas, Southern Methodist UP, 1967.
    JAS 28 (1968-9) 655-6. (D. R.
      Sturtevant)
    PA 41 (1968) 614-5. (D. J. Stein-
      berg)
    SJ 14 (1967) 480-483. (P. G.
      Gowing)

DEATS, RICHARD LOUIS. Story of Meth-
odism in the Philippines. Manila,
National Council of Churches in the
Philippines, 1964.
    JAS 24 (1964-5) 706-708. (G. H.
      Anderson)
    PS 13 (1965) 741-743. (E. Frie)
    SJ 12 (1965) 230-233. (D. D.
      Alejandro)

DECKER, GUNTER. Republik Maluku Selatan, die Republik der Sud-Molukken;
Untersuchungen und Dokumente zum
Selbstbestimmungsrecht der Ambone-
sen, zum Foderalismus und Kolonial-
ismus in Indonesien. Gottingen,
Schwartz, 1957.

PA 33 (1960) 320-1. (J. M. van der
Kroef)

Delachet, Claude *See* GUILLON, EMMAN-
UEL. Dictionnaire de base francais-
birman

Deliar Noer *See* NOER, DELIAR

DELVERT, JEAN. Paysan cambodgien.
Paris, Mouton, 1961. (Le Monde
d'Outre-Mere, passe et present. 1.
ser.: Etudes, 10)
　　FA 18 (1962) 341-345. (P. Grison)
　　FA 18 (1962) 449-453. (W. E. Will-
　　　mott)
　　PA 35 (1962) 305-6. (W. E. Will-
　　　mott)
　　SEIB 36 (1961) 743.

Demariaux, Jean Claude *See* TABOULET,
GEORGES. La vie dramatique de
Gustave Viaud

DEMETILLO, RICAREDO. Authentic voice
of poetry. Quezon City, Univ. of
the Philippines, Office of Research
Coordination, 1962.
　　PS 11 (1963) 360-365. (B. Lumbera)

DEMETILLO, RICAREDO. Barter in Panay.
Quezon City, Univ. of the Philip-
pines, Office of Research Coordina-
tion, 1961.
　　PS 10 (1962) 163-166. (Sister
　　　Marie-Laurentina)

DEMETILLO, RICAREDO. Masks and signa-
ture. Quezon City, Univ. of the
Philippines Pr., 1968.
　　PS 17 (1969) 625-6. (F. C. Sta.
　　　Maria)

* DEMETRIO Y RADAZA, FRANCISCO. Towards
a survey of Philippine folklore and
mythology. Manila, Ateneo de Manila
UP, 1968.
　　JAS 29 (1969-70) 994-997. (D. V.
　　　Hart)

De Wall Malefijt, Annemarie. Javanese

DEMETRIO Y RADAZA, FRANCISCO. The
village, early Cagayan de Oro in
legend and history. Cagayan de Oro
City, Xavier Univ., 1968. (Xavier
Univ., Cagayan de Oro City, Philippines. Museum and archives publications, no. 1)
　　JAS 29 (1969-70) 994-997. (D. V.
　　　Hart)

Denton, Frank H. *See* AVERCH, HARVEY
A. A crisis of ambiguity

Denton, Frank H. *See* AVERCH, HARVEY
A. Matrix of policy in the Philippines

De Queljoe, David H. *See* QUELJOE,
DAVID H. DE

Development administration in Asia.
Edited by Edward W. Weidner. Dur-
ham, Duke UP, 1970. (Comparative
Administration Group series)
　　PA 44 (1974) 259. (R. S. Milne)

DEVELOPMENT AND RESOURCES CORPORATION.
Export prospects for Vietnam, by
Frederick T. Moore et al. New York,
Praeger, 1971.
　　JAS 32 (1972-3) 220-222. (P. F.
　　　Bell)
　　JSAS 5 (1974) 138-9. (J. Wong)

DEVILLERS, PHILIPPE. End of a war,
Indochina, 1954, by Philippe Devil-
lers and Jean Lacouture. New York,
Praeger, 1969.
　　MAS 4 (1970) 183. (R. B. Smith)
　　PA 43 (1970) 125-127. (J. L. S.
　　　Girling)

Devillers, Philippe *See* LACOUTURE,
JEAN. La fin d'une guerre

DE WAAL MALEFIJT, ANNEMARIE. Javanese
of Surinam; segment of a plural society. Assen, Van Gorcum, 1963.
　　BIJ 122 (1966) 489-494. (G. D. van
　　　Wengen)

Dewey, Alice G. Peasant marketing in

DEWEY, ALICE G. Peasant marketing in
    Java. New York, Free Pr. of Glencoe,
    1962. (Series on contemporary Java-
    nese life, 3)
        JAS 22 (1962-3) 118-120. (G. E.
        Williams)

DHANINIVAT SONAKUL, PRINCE. Collected
    articles reprinted from the Journal
    of the Siam Society on the occasion
    of his eighty-fourth birthday. Bang-
    kok, Siam Society, 1969.
        JSS 58 pt. 2 (1970) 173-4. (D. K.
        Wyatt)

* DIAZ, ZOILO S. Memorias, autobiogra-
    fia de Zoilo S. Diaz. Quezon City,
    Phoenix Pr., 1969.
        PS 18 (1970) 436-438. (M. A.
        Bernad)

DIAZ-TRECHUELO SPINOLA, MARIA LOURDES.
    Arquitectura espanola en Filipinas,
    1565-1800. Seville, 1959. (Seville.
    Universidad. Escuela de Estudios
    Hispano-Americanos. Publicaciones,
    117)
        PS 8 (1960) 656-659. (F. Zobel de
        Ayala)

DICKSON, MORA. Season in Sarawak.
    London, Dobson, 1962.
        SMJ 11 (1964) 567-569. (R. Nicholl)

* DILIMAN REVIEW (INDEXES). Diliman re-
    view index, volumes 1-8, Jan. 1953-
    Oct. 1960, by Catalina A. Nemenzo.
    Quezon City, Univ. of the Philip-
    pines, 1961.
        JAS 23 (1963-4) 316-7. (D. V.
        Hart)

DINI, NH. Pada sebuah kapal. Jakarta,
    Pustaka Jaya, 1973.
        AR 7 (1974) 207-209. (H. Chambert-
        Loir)

DIRECK JAYANAMA. Thai kap songkhram
    lok khrang thi song. Bangkok, Prae
    Pittaya Pr., 1966. 2v.

        JAS 29 (1969-70) 988-990. (E. T.
        Flood)

DIRECK JAYANAMA. Thailand in zweiten
    Weltkrieg. Tubingen, Erdmann, 1970.
        JSAS 2 (1971) 257-8. (Sarkisyanz)
        PA 44 (1971) 148-9. (W. Levi)

DIRECK JAYANAMA. Thailand, Vortrage
    und Aufsatze von Direck Jayanama,
    Klaus Wenk und Max Biehl. Frankfurt,
    Alfred Metzner, 1960. (Institut fur
    Asienkunde. Schriften, Bd. 8)
        PA 35 (1962) 426-7. (K. J. Pelzer)

Dissenter's guide to foreign policy,
    edited by Irving Howe. New York,
    Praeger, 1968.
        PA 42 (1969) 264-5. (J. F. Melby)

DJAJADININGRAT, IDRUS NASIR. Begin-
    nings of the Indonesian-Dutch nego-
    tiations and the Hoge Veluwe talks.
    Ithaca, Modern Indonesia Project,
    Southeast Asia Program, Cornell
    Univ., 1958. (Cornell Univ. Modern
    Indonesia Project. Monograph series)
        JAS 19 (1959-60) 221-2. (R. Van
        Niel)
        PA 35 (1962) 185-6. (B. Crozier)

DJAMOUR, JUDITH. Malay kinship and
    marriage in Singapore. London,
    Athlone Pr., 1959. (London School
    of Economics. Monographs on social
    anthropology, no. 21)
        JAS 20 (1960-1) 118-9. (M. H.
        Fried)
        JSAH 1 (Mar. 1960) 101-105. (M. G.
        Swift)
        PS 8 (1960) 450-453. (T. R.
        McHale)
        SOAS 24 (1961) 178-9. (E. M.
        Mendelson)

DJAMOUR, JUDITH. Muslim matrimonial
    court in Singapore. London, Athlone
    Pr., 1966. (London School of Eco-
    nomics. Monographs on social anthro-
    pology, no. 31)

Dongen, Frans Van. Tussen

BIJ 124 (1968) 286-291. (W. R.
  Roff)
PA 40 (1967) 164-5. (S. P. Khetar-
  pal)
SOAS 31 (1968) 184. (R. B.
  Serjeant)

Djojohadikusmo, Sumitro *See* COMMITTEE
  FOR ECONOMIC DEVELOPMENT OF AUSTRA-
  LIA. Trade and aid in South-East
  Asia

* DO BANG DOAN. Nhung dai le va vu khuc
  cua vua chua Viet-nam, [by] Do Bang
  Doan [and] Do Trong Hue. Saigon,
  Ministere des Affaires Culturelles,
  1969.
    BEF 57 (1970) 239-242. (Nguyen
      Tien Lang)

* DO BANG DOAN. Viet-nam Ca-tru Bien-
  khao, [by] Do Bang Doan [and] Do
  Trong Hue. Saigon, 1962.
    BEF 52 (1964) 567-577. (Le Van Hao)

Do Mong Kuong *See* NGUYEN NGOC TINH.
  Binh thu Yeu luoc

Do Trong Hue *See* DO BANG DOAN. Nhung
  dai le va vu khuc cua vua chua Vietnam

Do Trong Hue *See* DO BANG DOAN. Vietnam Ca-tru Bien-khao

DOBBY, ERNST HENRY GEORGE. Monsoon
  Asia. Chicago, Quadrangle Books,
  1961.
    JAS 21 (1961-2) 370-1. (J. D. Eyre)
    JSS 53 (1965) 124-5. (L. Stern-
      stein)

DOBBY, ERNST HENRY GEORGE. Southeast
  Asia. 7th ed. London, Univ. of London Pr., 1960.
    JSS 53 (1965) 123-4. (L. Stern-
      stein)

DOBLE, MARION. Kapauku-Malayan-Dutch-
  English dictionary. The Hague,

Nijhoff, 1960.
  SOAS 24 (1961) 622.

Dr. H. Otley Beyer, Dean of Philippine
  anthropology. Edited by Rudolf Rahmann. Cebu City, Univ. of San
  Carlos, 1968. (San Carlos publications. Series E. Miscellaneous contributions in the humanities, no. 1)
    JAS 29 (1969-70) 742-3. (C. Kaut)

* DOHAMIDE. Dan-toc Cham luoc su, Saka-
  ray cam, [by] Dohamide [and] Dokoheim. Saigon, 1965.
    BEF 55 (1969) 265-6. (T. C.
      Leocmach)

DOHRENWEND, BARBARA SNELL. Some fac-
  tors related to autonomy and depend-
  ence in twelve Javanese villages.
  Ithaca, Modern Indonesia Project,
  Southeast Asia Program, Cornell
  Univ., 1957. (Cornell Univ. Modern
  Indonesia Project. Interim reports
  series)
    JAS 21 (1961-2) 413-4. (C. Geertz)

Dokoheim *See* DOHAMIDE. Dan-toc Cham
  luoc su

DOMMEN, ARTHUR J. Conflict in Laos:
  the politics of neutralization. New
  York, Praeger, 1964.
    JAS 24 (1964-5) 703-4. (J. M.
      Halpern)

DOMMEN, ARTHUR J. Conflict in Laos:
  the politics of neutralization. Rev.
  ed. New York, Praeger, 1971.
    JAS 32 (1971-2) 121-124. (M.
      Leifer)
    JSAS 3 (1972) 166-7. (M. Leifer)
    PA 45 (1972) 155-6. (J. L. S.
      Girling)
    SA 2 (1972-3) 347-356. (U. Maha-
      jani)

DONGEN, FRANS VAN. Tussen neutrali-
  teit en imperialisme, de Nederlands-
  Chinese betrekkingen van 1863 tot

Dongen, Frans Van. Tussen

1901. Groningen, Wolters, 1966.
PA 41 (1968) 112-114. (J. M. van
der Kroef)

DONNISON, F. S. V. Burma. New York,
Praeger, 1970. (Nations of the
modern world)
JAS 30 (1970-1) 502-3. (F. N.
Trager)
JSAS 3 (1972) 323-4. (J. F. Guyot)
PA 43 (1970) 634-5. (J. F. Cady)
SA 3 (1974-5) 651-2. (N. Nyun-Han)
SOAS 34 (1971) 183-4. (D. G. E.
Hall)

DOORN, JACOBUS ADRIANUS ANTONIUS VAN.
Ontsporing van geweld, [by] J. A. A.
van Doorn [and] W. J. Hendrix. Rotterdam, Universitaire Pers Rotterdam,
1970.
JAS 32 (1972-3) 568-570. (W. H.
Frederick)

DORN, FRANK. Walkout; with Stillwell
in Burma. New York, Crowell, 1971.
PA 46 (1973) 128-9. (E. E. Rice)

DOUGLAS, STEPHEN A. Political social-
ization and student activism in In-
donesia. Urbana, Univ. of Illinois
Pr., 1970. (Illinois. Univ. Illinois
studies in the social sciences, 57)
JAS 31 (1971-2) 739-740. (J. S.
Mintz)
PA 44 (1971) 92-96. (J. Fischer and
Juwono Sudarsono)

DOURNES, JACQUES. Coordonnees: struc-
tures Jorai familiales et sociales.
Paris, Institut d'Ethnologie, 1972.
(Paris. Universite. Institut d'Eth-
nologie. Travaux et memoires, 77)
SOAS 37 (1974) 263-265. (A. Turton)

DOURNES, JACQUES. Dieu aime les
paiens; une mission de l'Eglise sur
les plateaux du Viet-Nam. Paris,
Aubier, 1963. (Theologie; etudes
publiees sous la direction de la
Faculte de theologie S. J. de Lyon-

Fourviere, 54)
FA 21 (1966) 137-139. (J. Christian)

DOW, MAYNARD WESTON. Nation building
in Southeast Asia. Boulder, Colo.,
Pruett Pr., 1966.
JAS 26 (1966-7) 753-4. (F. W.
Riggs)
PA 39 (1966) 403-4. (R. S. Milne)

DOZIER, EDWARD P. Kalinga of northern
Luzon, Philippines. New York, Holt,
Rinehart and Winston, 1967. (Case
studies in cultural anthropology)
JAS 27 (1967-8) 912-3. (F. M.
LeBar)

DOZIER, EDWARD P. Mountain arbiters,
the changing life of a Philippine
hill people. Tucson, Univ. of Ari-
zona Pr., 1966.
JAS 27 (1967-8) 912-3. (F. M.
LeBar)
PA 40 (1967) 167-8. (H. E. Jacob-
son)
SLQ 6 (1968) 125-129. (J. de
Raedt)

DRABBE, PETER. Drie Asmat dialecten.
The Hague, Nijhoff, 1963. (Instituut voor Taal-, Land- en Volkenkunde. Verhandelingen, deel 42)
SOAS 29 (1966) 459. (G. B. Milner)

DRABBE, PETER. Kaeti en Wambon; twee
Awju-dialecten. The Hague, Nijhoff,
1959.
SOAS 24 (1961) 403. (C. Hooykaas)

DRABBLE, J. H. Rubber in Malaya,
1876-1922, the genesis of the indus-
try. Kuala Lumpur, Oxford UP, 1973.
JCA 4 (1974) 111.
JSAS 5 (1974) 283-4. (M. Rudner)
SOAS 37 (1974) 725-6. (A. J.
Stockwell)

DRACHMAN, EDWARD R. United States
policy toward Vietnam, 1940-45.

Rutherford, Fairleigh Dickinson UP,
1970.
>AS 11 (1971) 301.
>PA 44 (1971) 591-595. (D. J.
>Duncanson)

Drake, F. S. *See* SYMPOSIUM ON HIS-
TORICAL, ARCHAEOLOGICAL AND LINGUIS-
TIC STUDIES ON SOUTHERN CHINA, SOUTH-
EAST ASIA AND THE HONG KONG REGION,
UNIV. OF HONG KONG, 1961.

DRAKE, PETER JOSEPH. Financial development in Malaya and Singapore.
Canberra, Australian National UP,
1969.
>MER 15 pt. 1 (1970) 66-73. (N. H.
>P. Chung)
>PA 43 (1970) 315-6. (Tae Yul Nam)

DRAKE-BROCKMAN, HENRIETTA YORK (JULL).
Voyage to disaster, the life of
Francisco Pelsaert, covering his
Indian report to the Dutch East India Company and the wreck of the
ship Batavia in 1629 off the coast
of western Australia together with
the full text of his journals concerning the rescue voyages, the mutiny on the Abrolhos Islands and the
subsequent trials of the mutineers.
Sydney, Angus and Robertson, 1963.
>SOAS 28 (1965) 434-5. (J. Bastin)

Drewes, G. W. J. *See* Adat Atjeh

Drewes, G. W. J. *See* KITAB BONANG.
Admonitions of Seh Bari

Drewes, G. W. J. *See* NAKHODA MUDA.
De biograpfie van een Minangkabausen
peperhandelaar

Drewes, G. W. J. *See* al-BUSIRI. Een
16de eeuwse Maleise vertaling

DU BOIS, CORA ALICE. Social forces in
Southeast Asia. Cambridge, Harvard
UP, 1962.
>JSS 54 pt. 1 (1966) 74-81. (L.
>Sternstein)

Duong Dinh Khue. Les chefs d'oeuvre

DUFF, ROGER. Stone adzes of Southeast
Asia; an illustrated typology.
Christchurch, Canterbury Museum
Trust Board, 1970. (Canterbury
Museum bulletin, no. 3)
>AP 17 (1974) 71. (D. J. Scheans)

DUFFAR, JEAN. Forces politiques en
Thailande. Paris, Presses Universitaires de France, 1972. (Universite
de Paris I: Pantheon-Sorbonne. Serie
science politique, 2)
>JSS 61 pt. 2 (1973) 183-185.
>(Paturaya Dasse)

DUMAL, PAUL. Ang Puting Timamanukin.
Isang dula nina Paul Dumal at Gil
Quito. Quezon City, Ateneo de Ma-
nila UP, 1968.
>PS 17 (1969) 163-165. (N. G.
>Tiongson)

DUMONT, LOUIS. Introduction a deux
theories d'anthropologie sociale:
groupes de filiation et alliance de
mariage. Paris, Mouton, 1971.
>SOAS 36 (1973) 215. (C. von Furer-
>Haimendorf)

DUNCANSON, DENNIS J. Government and
revolution in Vietnam. London, Oxford UP, 1968.
>BEF 57 (1970) 257-266. (E. Bouche)
>JAS 28 (1968-9) 440-1. (D. G.
>Marr)
>MAS 3 (1969) 79-82. (R. Smith)

Dunselman, P. Donatus *See* Kana Sera

DUNSELMAN, P. DONATUS. Uit de litera-
tuur der Mualang-Dajaks. The Hague,
Nijhoff, 1959.
>SOAS 23 (1960) 632. (C. Hooykaas)

DUONG DINH KHUE. Les chefs d'oeuvre
de la litterature vietnamienne.
Saigon, Kim Lai An Quan, 1966.
>BEF 57 (1970) 245-247. (N. Louis)

Duong Quang Ham. Ly Van Phuc, tieu-su

DUONG QUANG HAM. Ly Van Phuc, tieu-su,
van-chuong. Saigon, Nam-son, 195-.
BEF 52 (1964) 278-287. (Ta Trong
Hiep)

DUONG THANH BINH. Tagmemic comparison
of the structure of English and
Vietnamese sentences. The Hague,
Mouton, 1971. (Janua linguarum.
Series practica, 110)
SA 2 (1972-3) 380-384. (Nguyen
Dinh Hoa)
SOAS 35 (1972) 183. (P. J. Honey)

DUPONT, JOHN ELEUTHERE. Philippine
birds. Greenville, Delaware Museum
of Natural History, 1971. (Delaware
Museum of Natural History. Monograph
series, no. 2)
PS 22 (1974) 380. (C. E. Wolf)

DURAND, MAURICE M. Introduction a la
litterature vietnamienne, par Maurice
M. Durand et Nguyen Tran Huan.
Paris, Maisonneuve et Larose, 1969.
BEF 57 (1970) 247-8. (N. Louis)

Durand, Maurice M. See Phan Tran

DUROSELLE, JEAN BAPTISTE. La communaute internationale face aux jeunes
etats, par J. B. Duroselle et J.
Meyriat. Paris, Armand Colin, 1964.
(Cahiers de la Fondation Nationale
des Sciences Politiques, 126)
RSA (1966) 269-271. (I. Jadoul)

Dutch East India Company See NEDER-
LANDSCHE OOST-INDISCHE COMPAGNIE

DUTCH EAST INDIES. COOLIE BUDGET COM-
MISSION. Living conditions of
plantation workers and peasants on
Java in 1939-40; final report.
Ithaca, Cornell Univ., Southeast
Asia Program, 1956. (Cornell Univ.
Modern Indonesia Project. Transla-
tion series)
JAS 21 (1961-2) 413-4. (C. Geertz)

Dwyer, D. J. See The city as a centre of change in Asia

ECAFE REGIONAL TECHNICAL CONFERENCE ON
WATER RESOURCES DEVELOPMENT, THIRD.
Proceedings. Manila, 1958.
PA 33 (1960) 214-5.

EARL, GEORGE WINDSOR. Eastern seas.
London, Oxford UP, 1972. (Oxford in
Asia historical reprints)
JAH 8 (1974) 173-4. (L. W. Moses)
JAS 33 (1973-4) 156-7. (R.
Provencher)

EAST, WILLIAM GORDON. Changing map of
Asia, a political geography, by W.
Gordon East, O. H. K. Spate and
Charles A. Fischer. 5th ed. London,
Methuen, 1971.
JAS 32 (1972-3) 683-4. (J. E.
Spencer)
MAS 7 (1973) 280-288. (P. Wheat-
ley)

EAST INDIA COMPANY (ENGLISH). Dawn of
British trade to the East Indies as
recorded in the Court Minutes of the
East India Company, 1599-1603,
edited by Henry Stevens. London,
Cass, 1967.
PA 42 (1969) 118. (B. Harrison)

East-West Center See HAWAII. UNIV.,
HONOLULU. Center for Cultural and
Technical Interchange between East
and West

ECHOLS, JOHN M. Indonesian-English
dictionary, by John M. Echols and
Hassan Shadily. Ithaca, Cornell UP,
1961.
BEF 52 (1964) 183-196. (L. C.
Damais)
BIJ 117 (1961) 393-396. (A. Teeuw)
JAS 20 (1960-1) 548-9. (D. Carr)
SOAS 25 (1962) 422-3.

ECHOLS, JOHN M. Indonesian writing in
translation. Ithaca, Modern Indone-

sia Project, Southeast Asia Program, Cornell Univ., 1956. (Cornell Univ. Modern Indonesia Project. Translation series)
AAS 4 (1968) 140-147. (R. Stiller)

ECHOLS, JOHN M. Preliminary checklist of Indonesian imprints (1945-49) with Cornell University holdings. Ithaca, Modern Indonesia Project, Southeast Asia Program, Cornell Univ., 1965. (Cornell Univ. Modern Indonesia Project. Bibliography series)
JAS 26 (1966-7) 339-340. (C. Hobbs)

ECK, D. VAN. Juridische aspecten van geld. Deventer, Kluwer, 1970.
BIJ 126 (1970) 265-268. (J. Valkhoff)

Economic interdependence in Southeast Asia; proceedings of a conference held at Bangkok, 1967. Edited by Theodore Morgan and Nyle Spoelstra. Madison, Univ. of Wisconsin Pr., 1969.
JAS 29 (1969-70) 984-5. (E. Van Roy)
PA 43 (1970) 302-3. (L. P. Singh)
SA 2 (1972) 488-502. (V. D. Ooms)

Economic systems of the Commonwealth, by Calvin B. Hoover, et al. Durham, Duke UP, 1962. (Duke Univ. Commonwealth Studies Center. Publication no. 16)
PA 37 (1964) 240-1. (T. Soper)

EDEN, ANTHONY. Towards peace in Indo-China. London, Oxford UP, 1966. (Chatham House essays, 14)
MAS 1 (1967) 406-7. (P. J. Honey)
PA 42 (1969) 423.

Education et developpement dans le Sud-Est de l'Asie. Brussels, Editions de l'Institut de Sociologie, Universite Libre de Bruxelles, 1967. (Brussels. Universite libre. Centre

d'etude de Sud-Est asiatique. Collection, 5)
MAS 4 (1970) 95. (M. Caldwell)

EDWARDES, MICHAEL. Asia in the balance. London, Penguin Books, 1962.
PA 36 (1963) 295-297. (R. K. Sakai)

EDWARDES, MICHAEL. Ralph Fitch, Elizabethan in the Indies. New York, Barnes and Noble Books, 1973. (Great travellers)
PA 46 (1973) 595. (F. Lehmann)

EDWARDES, MICHAEL. The West in Asia, 1850-1914, a concise survey history of imperialism and its effects. New York, Putnam, 1967.
JAS 27 (1967-8) 613-4. (O. H. Shao)

EDWARDS, CLIVE THOMAS. Public finances in Malaya and Singapore. Canberra, Australian National UP, 1970.
JAS 32 (1972-3) 213-4. (D. R. Snodgrass)
PA 44 (1971) 483. (R. S. Milne)

EECHOUD, JAN VAN. Etnografie van de Kaowerawedji, centraal Nieuw-Guinea. The Hague, Nijhoff, 1962. (Instituut voor Taal-, Land- en Volkenkunde. Verhandelingen, deel 37)
SOAS 28 (1965) 192-3. (G. B. Milner)

Egerod, Sore *See* PHROMWOHAN, PHRAYA. Poem in four songs.

EINSIDEL, LUZ A. Success and failure in selected community development projects in Batangas. Quezon City, 1960. (Quezon, Philippines. Univ. of the Philippines. Community Development Research Council. Study series, no. 3)
JAS 20 (1960-1) 399-403. (F. C. Madigan and D. V. Hart)

Elegant, Robert S.   The dragon's seed

ELEGANT, ROBERT S.   The dragon's seed;
   Peking and the overseas Chinese.
   New York, St. Martin's Pr., 1959.
      JAS 19 (1959-60) 219-220. (M.
      Feldman)
      JSAH 3 (Sept. 1962) 154-156. (Png
      Poh Seng)

ELEVAZO, AURELIO OBEDOZA.   Graduate
   education in the Philippines.   Manila, Philippine Association for
   Graduate Education, 1963.
      SLQ 2 (1964) 225-6. (B. Balweg)

ELKINS, RICHARD E.   Manobo-English
   dictionary.   Honolulu, Univ. of
   Hawaii Pr., 1968.   (Oceanic linguistics. Special publication, no. 3)
      AAS 6 (1970) 228-9. (V. Krupa)
      SOAS 32 (1969) 464-5. (R. H.
      Robins)

ELLIOTT-BATEMAN, MICHAEL.   Defeat in
   the east: the mark of Mao Tse-tung
   on war.   London, Oxford UP, 1967.
      JSAH 9 (1968) 367-8. (D. S.
      Gibbons)

ELLSBERG, DANIEL.   Papers on the war.
   New York, Simon and Schuster, 1972.
      PA 46 (1973) 601. (M. Osborne)

ELWOOD, DOUGLAS J.   Christ in Philippine context; a college textbook in
   theology and religious studies, by
   Douglas J. Elwood and Patricia Ling
   Magdamo.   Quezon City, New Day, 1971.
      SJ 19 (1972) 107-111.

ELWOOD, DOUGLAS J.   Churches and sects
   in the Philippines; a descriptive
   study of contemporary religious
   movements.   Dumaguete City, Silliman
   UP, 1968. (Silliman Univ. Monographs.
   Series A, religious studies, no. 1)
      JAS 28 (1968-9) 913-915. (D. V.
      Hart)
      PS 16 (1968) 577-586. (P. S. de
      Achutegui)
      SJ 16 (1969) 112-3. (P. W. Deiner)

ELY, PAUL.   Memoires, l'Indochine dans
   la tourmente.   Paris, Plon, 1964.
      PA 38 (1965) 433-435. (B. B. Fall)
      RSA (1965) 121-123. (I. Jadoul)

EMERSON, RUPERT.   From empire to nation; the rise to self-assertion of
   Asian and African peoples.   Cambridge, Harvard UP, 1960.
      JAS 20 (1960-1) 85-87. (L. Mair)

EMERY, ROBERT FIRESTONE.   Financial
   institutions of Southeast Asia.   New
   York, Praeger, 1970.
      JAS 31 (1971-2) 454-456. (F.
      Golay)
      PA 44 (1971) 640-1. (G. B. Hains-
      worth)
      SA 2 (1972-3) 149-152. (R. Hooley)

EMMERSON, DONALD K.   Students and politics in developing nations.   New
   York, Praeger, 1968.
      PA 42 (1969) 567-8. (P. G. Alt-
      bach)

EMPOLI, GIOVANNI DA.   Lettera di Giovanni da Empoli.   Rome, L'Instituto
   italiano per il Medio ed Estremo
   Oriente, Centro italiano di Cultura
   Djakarta, 1970.   (Relazioni di viag-
   giatori italiani in Indonesia, 1)
      AR 2 (1971) 255-6. (D. Lombard)

EMST, PETER VAN.   Panorama der Volken.
   Roermond, Romen, 1964-66. 3v.
      BIJ 122 (1966) 458-460. (J. R.
      Swart)

Encyclopedia of Buddhism. Fascicule A-
   Aca, edited by G. P. Malalasekera.
   Colombo, GPO, 1961.
      FA 18 (1962) 357-361. (J. May)
      SOAS 25 (1962) 380-1. (J. W. de Jong)

ENDICOTT, KIRK MICHAEL.   An analysis of
   Malay magic.   Oxford, Clarendon Pr.,
   1970.   (Oxford monographs on social
   anthropology)
      BIJ 128 (1972) 382-384. (E.
      Postel-Coster)

SOAS 34 (1971) 646-7. (N. G. Phillips)

Endo, Noriko *See* ISHII, YONEO. Glossary index of the Sukhothai inscriptions

ENKLAAR, IDO HENDRICUS. Joseph Kam, Apostel der Molukken. The Hague, Boekencentrum, 1963. (Bijdragen tot de Zendingswetenschap, no. 4)
BIJ 121 (1965) 265-271. (J. E. C. Geissler)

ENLOE, CYNTHIA H. Ethnic conflict and political development. Boston, Little, Brown, 1973.
PA 46 (1973) 435-444. (R. S. Milne)

ENLOE, CYNTHIA H. Multi-ethnic politics, the case of Malaysia. Berkeley, Center for South and Southeast Asian Studies, Univ. of California, 1970. (California. Univ. Center for South and Southeast Asia Studies. Research monograph, no. 2)
JSAS 2 (1971) 244-246. (J. MacDougall)
PA 44 (1971) 303-305. (R. S. Milne)
SA 2 (1972-3) 356-362. (R. K. Vasil)
SJ 17 (1970) 460-462. (P. G. Gowing)

Enriquez, Emigdio Alvarez *See* ALVAREZ ENRIQUEZ, EMIGDIO

Enriquez, Juan J. *See* AYALA Y COMPANY. LIBRARY. Classified list of Filipiniana holdings

Ensiklopedi umum. Yogyakarta, Jajasan Kanisius, 1973.
AR 7 (1974) 199-202. (Iskandarwassid)

ENSINK, J. On the old Javanese Cantakaparwa and its tale of Sutasomd. The Hague, Nijhoff, 1967. (Instituut voor Taal-, Land- en

Estrella, Conrado F. Democratic

Volkenkunde. Verhandelingen, deel 54)
SOAS 31 (1968) 421-2. (C. Hooykaas)

ESCOFFIER, JEAN. Le crepuscule des blancs; roman. Paris, Plon, 1959.
SEIB 35 (1960) 736.

ESMAN, MILTON JACOB. Administration and development in Malaysia, institution building and reform in a plural society. Ithaca, Cornell UP, 1972.
JSAS 4 (1972) 143-145. (C. M. Seah)
PA 45 (1972) 626-7. (R. S. Milne)

ESPIRITU, SOCORRO C. Social foundations of community development, readings on the Philippines, edited by Socorro C. Espiritu and Chester L. Hunt. Manila, Garcia Publishing House, 1964.
PA 38 (1965) 201-2. (R. S. Milne)

Essays offered to G. H. Luce by his colleagues and friends in honour of his seventy-fifth birthday. Editors: Ba Shin, Jean Boisselier and A. B. Griswold. Ascona, Artibus Asiae, 1966. 2v. (Artibus Asiae. Supp. 23)
AP 12 (1969) 140-1. (S. J. O'Connor)
SOAS 30 (1967) 731-2. (H. Tinker)

ESSER, SAMUEL JONATHAN. De Uma-taal (west Midden-Celebes) spraakkunstige schets en teksten. The Hague, Nijhoff, 1964. (Instituut voor Taal-, Land- en Volkenkunde. Verhandelingen, deel 43)
AAS 2 (1966) 163-4. (G. Altmann)
SOAS 29 (1966) 647-8. (G. B. Milner)

ESTRELLA, CONRADO F. Democratic answer to the Philippine agrarian problem. Manila, Solidaridad, 1969.

Estrella, Conrado F. Democratic

PA 43 (1970) 640. (K. Odawara)
SLURJ 2 (1971) 695-697. (R. M.
  Astudillo)

* Ethnographic bibliography of New
  Guinea. Canberra, Australian National UP, 1968. 3v.
    AP 15 (1972) 102. (D. B. Eyde)

Evers, Hans-Dieter *See* Loosely structured social systems

EXELL, F. K. Land and the people of
  Thailand. London, A. C. Black, 1960.
    PA 35 (1962) 304-5. (R. C. Nairn)

FAGG, WILLIAM BULLER. The Raffles
  Gamelan: a historical note. London, British Museum, 1970.
    BIJ 127 (1971) 274-278. (J. Bastin)

FAIRBAIRN, GEOFFREY. Revolutionary
  warfare and communist strategy, the
  threat to South-East Asia. London,
  Faber and Faber, 1968.
    PA 42 (1969) 386-7. (R. C. Nairn)

Fairbank, John King *See* REISCHAUER,
EDWIN OLDFATHER. East Asia, the
great tradition

FAIRBANK, JOHN KING. East Asia: tra-
  dition and transformation, by John
  K. Fairbank, Edwin O. Reischauer and
  Albert M. Craig. London, Allen and
  Unwin, 1973.
    SOAS 37 (1974) 753-4. (W. G.
    Beasley)

FALK, RICHARD A. Vietnam war and international law. Princeton, Princeton UP, 1968-72. 3v.
  Volume II.
    JAS 30 (1970-1) 507-8. (V. H. Li)
    PA 43 (1970) 467-469. (D. J.
    Duncanson)
  Volume III.
    PA 46 (1973) 170-1. (M. Leifer)

FALK, STANLEY LAWRENCE. Bataan: the
  march of death. New York, Norton,
  1962.
    JAS 22 (1962-3) 494-5. (J. W.
    Killigrew)

FALK, STANLEY LAWRENCE. Decision at
  Leyte. New York, Norton, 1966.
    JAS 26 (1966-7) 546-7. (T. Ropp)

FALL, BERNARD B. Anatomy of a crisis,
  the Laos crisis of 1960-1961. Garden City, N.Y., Doubleday, 1969.
    PA 43 (1970) 311-313. (P. F.
    Langer)

FALL, BERNARD B. Indochine, 1946-
  1962; chronique d'une guerre revolu-
  tionnaire. Paris, Robert Lafont,
  1962.
    FA 19 (1963) 853-861. (J. Chris-
    tan)
    RSA (1963) 295-6. (N. T. Huan)

Fall, Bernard B. *See* HO CHI MINH.
On revolution

FALL, BERNARD B. Street without joy;
  Indochina at war, 1946-54. Harris-
  burg, Pa., Stackpole, 1961.
    FA 18 (1962) 107. (J. Lacouture)
    FA 18 (1962) 109-111. (M. Roth)
    JAS 21 (1961-2) 97-8. (R. Butwell)
    PA 36 (1963) 443-4. (P. J. Honey)

FALL, BERNARD B. Two Vietnams. New
  York, Praeger, 1963.
    PA 37 (1964) 235-6. (P. J. Honey)
    SOAS 27 (1964) 666-7. (P. J.
    Honey)

FALL, BERNARD B. Two Vietnams, a political and military analysis. Rev.
  ed. New York, Praeger, 1964.
    AS 5 (1965) 526.
    MAS 3 (1969) 79-82. (R. Smith)

FALL, BERNARD B. Le Viet-Minh, la
  Republique Democratique du Viet-Nam,
  1945-1960. Paris, Colin, 1960.

Felix, Alfonso. Chinese in the

(Cahiers de la Fondation Nationale
des Sciences Politiques, 106)
  JAS 20 (1960-1) 544. (R. Jumper)

FALL, BERNARD B. Vietnam witness,
  1953-66. New York, Praeger, 1966.
    AS 6 (1966) 405.
    JAS 26 (1966-7) 349-353. (R.
      Scigliano)

FAN CHO. Man Shu, book of the southern
  barbarians, translated by Gordon H.
  Luce and edited by G. P. Oey. Ithaca,
  Southeast Asia Program, Cornell Univ.,
  1961. (Cornell Univ. Southeast Asia
  Program. Data paper, no. 44)
    BIJ 119 (1963) 451-453. (A. F. P.
      Hulsewe)
    PA 37 (1964) 205-207. (H. J. Wiens)

Farrell, Robert *See* Vietnam and the
Sino-Soviet dispute

FARWELL, GEORGE. Mask of Asia, the
  Philippines today. New York, Praeger,
  1967.
    AS 7 (1967) 212.
    JAH 2 (1968) 192. (T. Friend)
    JAS 27 (1967-8) 188-9. (D. Wurfel)
    JSAH 9 (1968) 359-360. (D. J. Stein-
      berg)
    PS 15 (1967) 498-507. (J. M. Juco)
    SA 3 (1974) 778-782. (M. P. Fabella)

FATIMI, S. Q. Islam comes to Malaysia.
  Singapore, Malaysian Sociological Research Institute, 1963.
    JSAH 6 (Sept. 1965) 153-4. (P. E.
      de Josselin de Jong)

FAUCONNIER, HENRI. Soul of Malaya.
  Kuala Lumpur, Oxford UP, 1965.
    MAS 4 (1970) 93-4. (E. Chew)

FEDERSPIEL, HOWARD M. Persatuan Islam,
  Islamic reform in twentieth century
  Indonesia. Ithaca, Modern Indonesia
  Project, Cornell Univ., 1970. (Cor-
  nell Univ. Modern Indonesia Project.
  Monograph series)
    PS 19 (1971) 740-1. (T. J.
      O'Shaughnessy)

FEINBERG, ABRAHAM L. Rabbi Feinberg's
  Hanoi diary. Don Mills, Ont., Longmans, 1968.
    PA 42 (1969) 421. (J. L. S.
      Girling)

FEITH, HERBERT. Decline of constitutional democracy in Indonesia.
  Ithaca, Cornell UP, 1962.
    BIJ 119 (1963) 438-444. (Logemann)
    JAS 23 (1963-4) 449-456. (H. J.
      Benda)
    Author's reply: JAS 24 (1964-5)
      305-312.
    JSAH 5 (Sept. 1964) 220-224. (F. L.
      Starner)
    PA 36 (1963) 445-447. (H. Tinker)
    RSA (1965) 128-9. (L. Rocher)

FEITH, HERBERT. Indonesian political
  thinking, 1945-1965, by Herbert
  Feith and Lance Castles. Ithaca,
  Cornell UP, 1970.
    IND 11 (1971) 193-200. (Alfian)
    JAH 6 (1972) 192-3. (F. N. Trager)
    JAS 30 (1970-1) 234-5. (S. Sloan)
    PA 43 (1970) 638-9. (J. M. van der
      Kroef)

FEITH, HERBERT. The Wilopo Cabinet,
  1952-53: turning point in post-
  revolutionary Indonesia. Ithaca,
  Modern Indonesia Project, Southeast
  Asia Program, Cornell Univ., 1958.
  (Cornell Univ. Modern Indonesia Project. Monograph series)
    BIJ 116 (1960) 292. (J. Vreden-
      bregt)
    JAS 21 (1961-2) 412-3. (R. T.
      McVey)

FELICIANO, GLORIA D. Philippine mass
  media in perspective, by Gloria D.
  Feliciano and Crispulo J. Icban.
  Quezon City, Capitol Publishing
  House, 1967.
    SJ 15 (1968) 132-134. (C. Maslog)

FELIX, ALFONSO. Chinese in the Philippines, 1570-1770. Manila,

Fisher, Charles Alfred. South-East

FILIPINIANA BOOK GUILD. Colonization
   and conquest of the Philippines by
   Spain, some contemporary source documents 1559-1577. Manila, 1965.
      JAS 26 (1966-7) 766-768. (C. O.
      Houston)

FINCH, SUSAN. Republic of Indonesia
   cabinets, 1945-65, compiled by Susan
   Finch and Daniel S. Lev. Ithaca,
   Modern Indonesia Project, Southeast
   Asia Program, Cornell Univ., 1965.
   (Cornell Univ. Modern Indonesia Proj-
   ect. Interim reports series)
      JAS 25 (1965-6) 546. (J. M. van der
      Kroef)

FIRMALINO, TITO C. Political activities of barrio citizens in Iloilo as
   they affect community development.
   Quezon City, 1960. (Quezon, Philippines. Univ. of the Philippines. Community Development Research Council.
   Study series, no. 4)
      JAS 20 (1960-1) 399-403. (F. C.
      Madigan and D. V. Hart)

FIRTH, RAYMOND WILLIAM. Malay fisher-
   men, their peasant economy. 2d. rev.
   and enl. ed. London, Routledge and
   Kegan Paul, 1966. (International library of sociology and social reconstruction)
      JAS 26 (1966-7) 532-3. (M. Nash)

FIRTH, ROSEMARY. Housekeeping among
   Malay peasants. 2d. ed. London,
   Athlone Pr., 1966. (London School of
   Economics. Monographs on social an-
   thropology, no. 7)
      BIJ 124 (1968) 283-4. (M. G. Swift)
      SOAS 29 (1966) 682.

FISCHER, GEORGES. Un case de decolonisation: Les Etats-Unis et les Philippines. Paris, Librairie generale
   de droit et de jurisprudence, 1960.
   (Bibliotheque de droit international,
   t. 9)
      JAS 22 (1962-3) 89-94. (T. Friend)

FISCHER, GEORGES. Jose Rizal, Philip-
   pin, 1861-1896, un aspect du nation-
   alisme moderne. Paris, Maspero,
   1970.
      AR 1 (1970) 203-4. (D. Lombard)

Fischer, H. Th. *See* KENNEDY, RAYMOND.
   Bibliography of Indonesian peoples
   and cultures

FISCHER, JOSEPH L. Universities in
   Southeast Asia, an essay on comparison and development. Columbus, Ohio
   State UP, 1964. (International education monographs, no. 6)
      PA 37 (1964) 461. (Hla Myint)

FISCHER, LOUIS. Story of Indonesia.
   New York, Harper, 1959.
      JAS 19 (1959-60) 469-470. (J. W.
      Gould)
      PA 35 (1962) 185-6. (B. Crozier)

Fishel, Wesley R. *See* CONFERENCE ON
   SOCIAL DEVELOPMENT AND WELFARE IN
   VIETNAM, NEW YORK, 1959. Problems of
   freedom

* FISHEL, WESLEY R. Vietnam, anatomy of
   a conflict. Itasca, Ill., Peacock,
   1968.
      JAH 3 (1969) 180-1. (C. Hobbs)
      PA 42 (1969) 238-240. (D. Wurfel)

Fisher, Charles Alfred *See* EAST,
   WILLIAM GORDON. Changing map of Asia

FISHER, CHARLES ALFRED. South-East
   Asia, a social, economic, and political geography. London, Methuen,
   1964.
      JSAH 5 (Sept. 1964) 228-230. (Ooi
      Jin Bee)
      JSS 53 (1965) 123-4. (L. Stern-
      stein)
      PA 38 (1965) 198-9. (K. J. Pelzer)
      SEIB 41 (1966) 87.

Fisher, Joseph. Foreign values and

* FISHER, JOSEPH. Foreign values and
Southeast Asian scholarship. Berkeley, Center for South and Southeast
Asia Studies, Univ. of California,
1973.
      SEIB 49 (1974) 353-356. (J.
         d'Ornano)

Fisher, Margaret *See* WITHINGTON,
WILLIAM A. Southeast Asia

FISTIE, PIERRE. L'evolution de la
Thailande contemporaine. Paris,
Colin, 1967. (Cahiers de la Fondation Nationale des Sciences Politiques, 156)
      BEF 56 (1969) 179-182. (P.-B.
         Lafont)
      JAS 27 (1967-8) 680. (D. K. Wyatt)
      SOAS 31 (1968) 429-430. (M. Leifer)

FISTIE, PIERRE. Singapour et la Malaisie. Paris, Presses Universitaires
de France, 1960. (Que sais je? Le
point des connaissances actuelles,
no. 869)
      JAS 20 (1960-1) 240-1. (V. Purcell)
      SEIB 36 (1961) 756.

FISTIE, PIERRE. Sous-developpement et
utopie au Siam, le programme de re-
formes presente en 1933 par Pridi
Phanomyong. The Hague, Mouton, 1969.
(Materiaux pour l'etude de l'Extreme-
Orient moderne et contemporain. Travaux, 5)
      BEF 57 (1970) 227-230. (P.-B.
         Lafont)
      JAS 30 (1970-1) 238-9. (Neon
         Snidvongs)
      JSAS 1 pt. 2 (1970) 131-2. (Saneh
         Chamarik)
      JSS 59 pt. 2 (1971) 249-251. (A.
         Clarac)

FITZGERALD, CHARLES PATRICK. Concise
history of East Asia. London, Heinemann, 1966.
      MAS 1 (1967) 209-210. (J. Ch'en)

FITZGERALD, CHARLES PATRICK. Southern
expansion of the Chinese people,
southern fields and southern ocean.
London, Barrie and Jenkins, 1972.
      JAH 8 (1974) 188.
      SA 3 (1974-5) 622-627. (Ka-che Yip)
      SOAS 36 (1973) 712-3. (P. J. Honey)

FITZGERALD, CHARLES PATRICK. Third
China, the Chinese communities in
South East Asia. Melbourne, Cheshire,
1965.
      JAS 25 (1965-6) 796-7. (D. A.
         Wilson)
      JSAH 7 (Sept. 1966) 123-4. (L. E.
         Williams)

FITZGERALD, FRANCES. Fire in the lake;
the Vietnamese and the Americans in
Vietnam. Boston, Little, Brown,
1972.
      JAS 32 (1972-3) 564-5. (D. G. Marr)
      JCA 4 (1974) 83-93. (Nguyen Khac
         Vien)

FITZGERALD, STEPHEN. China and the
overseas Chinese, a study of Peking's
changing policy, 1949-1970. Cambridge, Cambridge UP, 1970.
      JCA 3 (1973) 218.
      JSAS 4 (1973) 327-329. (M. Leifer)
      PS 21 (1973) 234-236. (C. J.
         McCarthy)

Flaumenhaft, Carol *See* LACH, DONALD
FREDERICK. Asia on the eve of
Europe's expansion

FLETCHER, NANCY McHENRY. Separation of
Singapore from Malaysia. Ithaca,
Southeast Asia Program, Cornell Univ.,
1969. (Cornell Univ. Southeast Asia
Program. Data paper, no. 73)
      JAS 29 (1969-70) 990-1. (J. Silver-
         stein)
      JSAS 1 pt. 1 (1970) 109-110. (Lau
         Teik Soon)
      PA 43 (1970) 314. (R. S. Milne)

Flines, E. W. Orsoy de *See* MUSEUM
PUSAT. Guide to the ceramic
collection

Fraser, Thomas M. Rusembilan: a Malay

FLORENTINO, ALBERTO S. Midcentury
guide to Philippine literature in
English. Manila, Filipiniana, 1963.
    JAS 23 (1963-4) 633-4. (L. Casper)

FLORENTINO, ALBERTO S. World is an
apple and other prize plays. Manila,
Philippine Cultural Publishers, 1959.
    PS 8 (1960) 453-458. (M. A. Bernad)

Focus on Southeast Asia, edited by
Alice Taylor. New York, Praeger,
1972.
    JAH 8 (1974) 174-5. (C. K. Byrd)
    PA 46 (1973) 168. (C. A. Fisher)

FONTAINE, HENRI P. Les madreporaires
paleozoiques du Viet-Nam, du Laos, et
du Cambodge. Saigon, 1961. (Vietnam.
Service geologique. Archives geologi-
ques du Viet-nam, no. 5)
    SEIB 36 (1961) 741.

FONTEIN, JAN. Ancient Indonesian art
of the central and eastern Javanese
periods, by Jan Fontein, R. Soekmono
and Satyawati Suleiman. New York,
Asia Society, 1971.
    AR 4 (1972) 243-4.
    JAS 32 (1972-3) 371-2. (D. K.
    Dohanian)
    JSS 61 pt. 1 (1973) 377-379.
    (Subhadradis Diskul)

FORD, DANIEL. Incident at Muc Wa.
Garden City, N.Y., Doubleday, 1967.
    PA 42 (1969) 424.

FORMAN, CHARLES W. Christianity in the
non-western world. Englewood Cliffs,
Prentice-Hall, 1967.
    PA 41 (1968) 263-4. (J. Davidson)

FORMAN, MICHAEL L. Kampampangan dictionary. Honolulu, Univ. of Hawaii
Pr., 1971. (Hawaii. Univ., Honolulu.
Pacific and Asian Linguistics Institute. PALI language texts)
    AAS 10 (1974) 197-8. (J. Genzor)

FORMAN, MICHAEL L. Kampampangan grammar notes. Honolulu, Univ. of Hawaii
Pr., 1971. (Hawaii. Univ., Honolulu.
Pacific and Asian Linguistics Institute. PALI language texts)
    AAS 10 (1974) 197-8. (J. Genzor)

FORONDA, MARCELINO A. Cults honoring
Rizal. Manila, Garcia Publishing
Co., 1961.
    UN 35 (1962) 284-5. (V. J. A.
    Rosales)

FORSTER, HAROLD. Flowering lotus, a
view of Java. London, Longmans,
Green, 1958.
    PA 33 (1960) 213.

Forster, Jannette *See* McKAUGHAN,
HOWARD. Ilocano

FOX, ROBERT B. Tabon caves; archaeological explorations and excavations on
Palawan Island, Philippines. Manila,
National Museum, 1970. (Manila. National Museum. Monograph, no. 1)
    AP 17 (1974) 77-79. (H. D. Tuggle)
    JAS 31 (1971-2) 999-1000. (W. G.
    Solheim)
    SEIB 48 (1973) 631-635. (R. P. H.
    Fontaine)

FRANCE. ARCHIVES NATIONALES. La serie
d'Extreme-Orient du fonds des Archives coloniales conserve aux Archives Nationales, par Ferreol de
Ferry. Paris, GPO, 1958.
    BEF 50 (1960) 183. (P. Huard)
    SEIB 35 (1960) 731-2. (P. Huard)

FRANCISCO, JUAN R. Lectures in honour
of Dr. Cecilio Lopez. Quezon City,
Institute of Asian Studies, Univ. of
the Philippines, 1963.
    JSAH 5 (Sept. 1964) 227-8. (W. E.
    Cheong)

FRASER, THOMAS M. Rusembilan: a Malay
fishing village in southern Thailand.
Ithaca, Cornell UP, 1960. (Cornell
studies in anthropology)

Fraser, Thomas M. Rusembilan: a

JAS 20 (1960-1) 117-8. (G. W.
Skinner)

FREEDMAN, MAURICE. Chinese family and
marriage in Singapore. London, GPO,
1957. (Great Britain. Colonial Office. Colonial research studies, no.
20)
JAS 19 (1959-60) 473-475. (G. W.
Skinner)

FREEDMAN, MAURICE. Lineage organiza-
tion in southeastern China. London,
Athlone Pr., 1958. (London School
of Economics. Monographs on social
anthropology, no. 18)
BIJ 118 (1962) 478-482. (R. E.
Downs)
JAS 19 (1959-60) 333-4. (D.
Twitchett)

FREEMAN, ROGER A. Socialism and pri-
vate enterprise in equatorial Asia,
the case of Malaysia and Indonesia.
Stanford, Hoover Institution on War,
Revolution and Peace, Stanford Univ.,
1968. (Hoover Institution studies,
20)
AS 8 (1968) 950.
JAS 28 (1968-9) 437-8. (E. Van Roy)
PS 17 (1969) 349-350. (R. E. Moran)

French, Deborah P. *See* ANTHONY,
EDWARD MASON. Foundations of Thai

Friedman, Edward *See* America's Asia

FRIEND, THEODORE. Between two empires;
the ordeal of the Philippines, 1929-
1946. New Haven, Yale UP, 1965.
(Yale historical publications.
Studies, 22)
JAS 25 (1965-6) 372-3. (D. J.
Steinberg)
JSAH 7 (Sept. 1966) 141-143. (J. M.
Saniel)
PA 39 (1966) 220-222. (I. B. Powell)
PS 13 (1965) 859-865. (M. P.
Onorato)

FRIENDS, SOCIETY OF. AMERICAN FRIENDS
SERVICE COMMITTEE. Peace in Vietnam;
a new approach in Southeast Asia; a
report prepared for the American
Friends Service Committee. New York,
Hill and Wang, 1966.
PA 42 (1969) 423.

FROEHLICH, WALTER. Land tenure, industrialization and social stability experiences and prospects in Asia.
Milwaukee, Marquette UP, 1961. (Marquette Asian studies, 2)
JAS 21 (1961-2) 531-2. (R. P. Dore)
PA 35 (1962) 423-4. (M. Zinkin)

FRY, HOWARD TYRRELL. Alexander
Dalyrmple, 1737-1808, and the expan-
sion of British trade. Toronto,
Univ. of Toronto Pr., 1970. (Royal
Commonwealth Society. Imperial
Studies, no. 29)
JAS 31 (1971-2) 988-9. (P.
Wheatley)
PA 44 (1971) 462. (K. G.
Tregonning)
PS 19 (1971) 741-743. (C. Quirino)

FRYER, DONALD W. Emerging South East
Asia, a study in growth and stagna-
tion. London, George Philip, 1970.
JSS 60 pt. 1 (1972) 441-445. (A.
Hone)
MAS 5 (1971) 85-6. (J. C. Jackson)
SA 2 (1972) 488-502. (V. D. Ooms)

FUCHS, ELINOR. Year one of the empire;
a play of American politics, war, and
protest taken from the historical
record, by Elinor Fuchs and Joyce
Antler. Boston, Houghton Mifflin,
1973.
PA 47 (1974) 399-401. (C. O.
Houston)

FUNKE, FRIEDRICH W. Dammerung uber In-
donesien; Streifzuge durch Sumatra,
Java, Bali und Celebes. Bremen, Carl
Schunemann, 1959.
BIJ 116 (1960) 395-6. (W. F.
Wertheim)

Geertz, Clifford. Agricultural

FUNKE, FRIEDRICH W. Orang Abung;
  Volkstum Sud-Sumatras im Wandel.
  Leiden, Brill, 1958-1961. 2v.
    BIJ 116 (1960) 280-285. (J. C. van
      der Straaten)
    BIJ 116 (1960) 285-287. (A. N. J.
      T. A. T. van der Hoop)
    BIJ 122 (1966) 463-466. (E.
      Postel-Coster)

FURNIVALL, JOHN SYDENHAM. Governance
  of modern Burma. New York, International Secretariat, Institute of Pacific Relations, 1958.
    PA 33 (1960) 90-1. (J. S. Thompson)

FURNIVALL, JOHN SYDENHAM. Netherlands
  India, a study of plural economy.
  Cambridge, Cambridge UP, 1967.
    MAS 4 (1970) 304.

GAGLIANO, FELIX V. Communal violence
  in Malaysia, 1969, the political
  aftermath. Athens, Ohio Univ., Center for International Studies, 1970.
  (Papers in international studies.
  Southeast Asia series, no. 13)
    PA 44 (1971) 303-305. (R. S. Milne)

GALDON, JOSEPH A. Philippine fiction:
  essays from Philippine Studies, 1953-
  1972. Quezon City, Ateneo de Manila
  UP, 1972.
    SJ 20 (1973) 297-299. (R. Llorca)

Galestin, Theodor Paul See UTRECHT.
  CENTRAAL MUSEUM. Hedendaagse kunst
  van Bali

GALLOWAY, JOHN. Gulf of Tonkin resolution. Rutherford, Fairleigh
  Dickinson UP, 1970.
    PA 44 (1971) 600-1. (F. H. Soward)

GALULA, DAVID. Counterinsurgency warfare. New York, Praeger, 1964.
    PA 37 (1964) 467-8. (R. C. Nairn)

GAMBA, CHARLES. Origins of trade
  unionism in Malaya, a study in colonial labour unrest. Singapore, Eastern Universities Pr., 1962.
    MER 8 pt. 2 (1963) 91-103. (D. J.
      Blake)

GAMER, ROBERT E. Politics of urban development in Singapore. Ithaca, Cornell UP, 1972.
    JAS 33 (1973-4) 157-8. (D. Wurfel)
    PA 46 (1973) 175-6. (G. P. Means)

Gapud, Manuel M. See MADIGAN, FRANCIS
  C. Screening for college students

GARD, RICHARD ABBOTT. Buddhism. New
  York, Braziller, 1961.
    FA 20 (1965) 129-130. (J. May)

GARVAN, JOHN M. Negritos of the Philippines. Vienna, Berger Horn, 1963.
  (Wiener Beitrage zur Kulturgeschichte
  und Linguistik. Bd. 14)
    BIJ 122 (1966) 396-398. (C. H. M.
      Nooy-Palm)
    SJ 16 (1969) 102-107. (H. Reynold)

* GAUDILLOT, C. Plaine de Vientiane.
  Esquisse d'etude socio-economique,
  par C. Gaudillot et G. Condaminas.
  Paris, 1959.
    BEF 50 (1960) 574-582. (P. B.
      Lafont)

GAULTIER, MARCEL. L'etrange adventure
  de Ham-Nghi, empereur d'Annam.
  Paris, La Nef de Paris, 1959.
    SEIB 35 (1960) 733.

Gedney, William J. See ANUMAN RAJA-
  THON. Life and ritual in old Siam

GEERTZ, CLIFFORD. Agricultural involution, the processes of ecological
  change. Berkeley, Univ. of California Pr., 1963. (Association of Asian
  Studies. Monographs and papers, 11)
    JSAH 6 (Sept. 1965) 158-161. (J. R.
      W. Smail)
    PA 37 (1964) 307-311. (W. F.
      Wertheim)

Geertz, Clifford.   Islam observed

GEERTZ, CLIFFORD.   Islam observed, religious development in Morocco and Indonesia.   New Haven, Yale UP, 1968.   (Terry lectures, Yale Univ. v.37)
   BIJ 127 (1971) 293-296. (A. F. Ros)
   JAS 28 (1968-9) 909-910. (R. Firth)
   JSAH 10 (1969) 378-381. (A. H. Johns)

GEERTZ, CLIFFORD.   Peddlers and princes; social change and economic modernization in two Indonesian towns.   Chicago, Univ. of Chicago Pr., 1963.
   AS 4 (1964) 859.
   JAS 23 (1963-4) 635-6. (R. Van Niel)
   PA 37 (1964) 307-311. (W. F. Wertheim)

GEERTZ, CLIFFORD.   Person, time and conduct in Bali, an essay in cultural analysis.   New Haven, Southeast Asia Studies, Yale Univ., 1966. (Yale Univ. Graduate School. Southeast Asia Studies. Cultural report series, no. 14)
   BIJ 124 (1968) 418-420. (C. J. Grader)
   JAS 26 (1966-7) 757-759. (F. M. LeBar)
   PA 41 (1968) 115-6. (L. Palmier)

GEERTZ, CLIFFORD.   Religion of Java.   Glencoe, Free Pr., 1960.
   JAS 21 (1961-2) 403-406. (H. J. Benda)
   PA 36 (1963) 199-201. (W. F. Wertheim)

GEERTZ, CLIFFORD.   Social history of an Indonesian town.   Cambridge, MIT Pr., 1965.
   AS 5 (1965) 572.

GEERTZ, HILDRED.   Javanese family, a study of kinship and socialization.   New York, Free Pr. of Glencoe, 1961.

   JAS 22 (1962-3) 493-4. (J. L. Landgraf)
   JSAH 5 (Mar. 1964) 200-202. (M. Freedman)

GEIGER, THEODORE.   Tales of two city states, the development progress of Hong Kong and Singapore.   Washington D.C., National Planning Assoc., 1973.   (Studies in development progress, no. 3)
   PA 47 (1974) 250-1. (T. G. McGee)

GEMELLI CARERI, GIOVANNI FRANCESCO.   Voyage to the Philippines.   Manila, Filipiniana Book Guild, 1963.
   PA 39 (1966) 450-452. (I. B. Powell)

GENESTE, MAURICE.   La table des 22; roman.   Paris, Deresse, 1958.
   SEIB 35 (1960) 735-6. (G. Taboulet)

GERASSI, JOHN.   North Vietnam, a documentary.   Indianapolis, Bobbs-Merrill, 1968.
   FA 22 (1968) 131.

GHEDDO, PIERO.   Cross and the bo tree, Catholics and Buddhists in Vietnam.   New York, Sheed and Ward, 1970.
   PA 43 (1970) 632-3. (A. Roberts)

GHOSH, MANOMOHAN.   History of Cambodia, from the earliest time to the end of the French protectorate.   Saigon, Gupta, 1960.
   JAS 20 (1960-1) 544-5. (J. F. Cady)

* Gia-dinh-thung-chi: Histoire et description de la basse Cochinchine. n.p. Gregg International, 1969.
   JOSA 7 (1970) 164.

GIGON, FERNAND.   Les Americains face au Vietcong.   Paris, Flammarion, 1965.
   FA 21 (1966) 139-140. (P. Grison)
   RSA (1966) 272-274. (I. Jadoul)

GILCHRIST, ANDREW.   Bangkok top secret: being the experiences of a British

Golay, Frank H.   The Philippines

officer in the Siam country section
of Force 136.   London, Hutchinson,
1970.
  JSS 59 pt. 1 (1971) 262-3. (T.
    Smitinand)

GINSBURG, NORTON SYDNEY.   Atlas of
economic development.   Chicago, Univ.
of Chicago Pr., 1961.
  PA 36 (1963) 465-6. (D. J. M.
    Hooson)

GINSBURG, NORTON SYDNEY.   Malaya, by
N. Ginsburg and C. F. Roberts.
Seattle, Univ. of Washington Pr.,
1958.   (American Ethnological Soci-
ety. Publications)
  MER 5 pt. 1 (1960) 25-28. (U. A.
    Aziz)

GIRLING, J. L. S.   People's war, the
conditions and consequences in China
and in South-East Asia.   London,
George Allen and Unwin, 1969.
  PA 43 (1970) 123-125. (M. B.
    Yahuda)

GITEAU, MADELEINE.   Guide du Musee
National de Phnom Penh.   Phnom Penh,
Office National du Tourisme Khmer,
1960.
  SEIB 36 (1961) 742.

GITEAU, MADELEINE.   Histoire du Cambodge.   Paris, Didier, 1957.
  BEF 50 (1960) 216-222. (B. P.
    Groslier)

GITEAU, MADELEINE.   Les Khmers; sculptures khmeres, reflets de la civilisation d'Angkor.   Paris, Bibliotheque des Arts, 1965.
  RSA (1966) 262-3. (L. Rocher)
  SEIB 41 (1966) 311-2. (M. Brocheux)

GLAMANN, KRISTOF.   Dutch-Asiatic trade,
1620-1740.   Copenhagen, Danish Science Pr., 1958.
  JSAH 1 (Mar. 1960) 106-108. (D. K.
    Bassett)
  PS 8 (1960) 205-6. (N. P. Cushner)

GLASSBURNER, BRUCE.   Economy of Indone-
sia, selected readings.   Ithaca, Cor-
nell UP, 1971.
  JAS 31 (1971-2) 456-7. (D. S.
    Paauw)
  PA 46 (1973) 609. (G. G. van Beers)
  SA 3 (1974-5) 654-5. (D. C. Cole)

Gluck und Wohlergehen; die Tet-Bilder
aus Dong-ho, zehn original Holz-
schnitte. Text: Rudolf Mayer. Dres-
den, Verlag der Kunst, 1964.
  BEF 53 (1966) 305-6. (M. M. Durand)

GO PUAN SENG.   Refuge and strength.
Englewood Cliffs, Prentice-Hall,
1970.
  AR 5 (1973) 297-301. (C. Lombard-
    Salmon)

GOETHALS, PETER R.   Aspects of local
government in a Sumbawan village
(Eastern Indonesia).   Ithaca, Southeast Asia Program, Cornell Univ.,
1961.   (Cornell Univ. Modern Indonesia Project. Monograph series)
  JAS 21 (1961-2) 413. (H. Geertz)

GOETTEL, ELINOR.   Eagle of the Philip-
pines: President Manuel Quezon. New
York, Messner, 1970.
  SA 3 (1974) 796-7. (M. P. Onorato)

GOH CHENG TIEK.   May thirteenth inci-
dent and democracy in Malaysia.
Kuala Lumpur, Oxford UP, 1971.
  BIJ 130 (1974) 374-378. (The Siauw
    Giap)
  JAS 31 (1971-2) 734-736. (G. D.
    Ness)
  JSAS 4 (1973) 153-155. (R. Vasil)
  SAJSS 1 pt. 1 (1973) 134-5. (Lau
    Teik Soon)

GOH KENG SWEE.   Economics of moderniza-
tion and other essays.   Singapore,
Asia Pacific Pr., 1972.
  PA 46 (1973) 468-9. (R. S. Milne)

GOLAY, FRANK H.   The Philippines, public policy and national economic

Golay, Frank H. The Philippines

development. Ithaca, Cornell UP,
1961.
 AS 1 (Dec. 1961) 35-38. (C. Wolf)
 JAS 22 (1962-3) 114-116. (B.
  Higgins)
 PA 34 (1961) 412-3. (R. S. Milne)
 SJ 8 (1961) 332-334. (C. L. Hunt)

Golay, Frank H. *See* AMERICAN ASSEM-
 BLY. Philippine-American relations

Golay, Frank H. *See* AMERICAN ASSEM-
 BLY. United States and the Philippines

Goldsen, Rose K. *See* CORNELL UNIV.
 DEPT. OF SOCIOLOGY AND ANTHROPOLOGY.
 CROSS-CULTURAL METHODOLOGY PROJECT.
 Factors related to acceptance of
 innovations

GOMES DE BRITO, BERNARDO. Further
 selections from *The tragic history
 of the sea, 1559-1565;* narratives of
 the shipwreck of the Portuguese East
 Indiamen Aguia and Garca (1559) Sao
 Paulo (1561) and the misadventures
 of the Brazilship Santo Antonio
 (1565). Edited by C. R. Boxer. Cambridge, Cambridge UP, 1968. (Hak-
 luyt Society. Works, 2d. ser., no.
 132)
 JAH 3 (1969) 183-4. (R. L. Kagan)

GONZALEZ, N. V. M. Bamboo dancers.
 Denver, Swallow, 1961.
 JAS 21 (1961-2) 246-7. (L. Casper)
 PS 8 (1960) 458-461. (M. A. Bernad)
 Author's reply: PS 8 (1960)
 622-628.

GONZALEZ, N. V. M. Look, stranger, on
 this island now. Manila, Benipayo
 Pr., 1963.
 PS 12 (1964) 167-171. (E. de Jesus)

GOODENOUGH, WARD HUNT. Explorations
 in cultural anthropology; essays in
 honor of George Peter Murdock. New
 York, McGraw-Hill, 1964.
 PA 38 (1965) 463-4. (C. S. Belshaw)

Goodman, Allan E. *See* Indochina in
 conflict

GOODMAN, ALLAN E. Politics in war; the
 bases of political community in South
 Vietnam. Cambridge, Harvard UP,
 1973.
 PA 47 (1974) 391-393. (C. A.
  Thayer)

GOODMAN, GRANT KOHN. Davao, a case
 study in Japanese-Philippine rela-
 tions. Lawrence, Center for East
 Asian Studies, Univ. of Kansas, 1967.
 (Kansas. Univ. Center for East Asian
 Studies. International studies, East
 Asian series, research publication
 no. 1)
 JAS 28 (1968-9) 193-4. (W. H.
  Elsbree)
 JSAH 10 (1969) 372-375. (J. M.
  Saniel)
 PA 41 (1968) 444-5. (R. S. Milne)

GOODMAN, GRANT KOHN. Experiment in
 wartime intercultural relations, Philippine students in Japan, 1943-45.
 Ithaca, Southeast Asia Program, Cornell Univ., 1962. (Cornell Univ.
 Southeast Asia Program. Data paper,
 no. 46)
 PA 36 (1963) 196-199. (F. C. Jones)

GOODMAN, GRANT KOHN. Four aspects of
 Philippine-Japanese relations, 1930-
 1940. New Haven, Southeast Asia
 Studies, Yale Univ., 1967. (Yale
 Univ. Graduate School. Southeast Asia
 Studies. Monograph series, no. 9)
 BIJ 125 (1969) 503-506. (O. D. van
  den Muijzenberg)
 FA 21 (1966) 601-2. (P. Devillers)
 JSAH 9 (1968) 357-8. (R. S. Milne)
 PA 41 (1968) 443-4. (I. B. Powell)
 PS 17 (1969) 166-170. (J. M.
  Saniel)

GOODSTEIN, MARVIN E. Pace and pattern
 of Philippine economic growth: 1938,
 1948 and 1956. Ithaca, Cornell Univ.
 Southeast Asia Program, 1962.

Gowing, Peter G.   Islands under the

(Cornell Univ. Southeast Asia Pro-
gram. Data paper, no. 48)
   JAS 22 (1962-3) 339-340.
   PA 36 (1963) 202-204. (R. S. Milne)

Goodwin, John *See* NEILL, STEPHEN
CHARLES. Concise dictionary of the
Christian world

Goody, Jack *See* GOODY, JOHN RANKINE

GOODY, JOHN RANKINE. Literacy in traditional societies. New York, Cambridge UP, 1968.
   JAS 29 (1969-70) 907-8. (W. W.
   Elmendorf)

GORDON, BERNARD K. Dimensions of con-
flict in Southeast Asia. Englewood
Cliffs, Prentice-Hall, 1966.
   AS 6 (1966) 604.
   JSAH 8 (1967) 318-9. (G. K. Good-
   man)

GORDON, BERNARD K. Toward disengage-
ment in Asia, a strategy for Ameri-
can foreign policy. Englewood
Cliffs, Prentice-Hall, 1969.
   AS 10 (1970) 438.
   JSAS 1 pt. 1 (1970) 108-9. (C. E.
   Morrison)
   SA 1 (1971) 282-287. (Somsakdi
   Xuto)

Gorgoniev, Iurii Alexandrovich *See*
AKADEMIIA NAUK SSSR. INSTITUT NARODOV
AZII. Iazyki Iugo-vostochnoi Azii

GORIS, ROELOF. Bali, atlas kebudajaan.
Bali, cults and customs. Djakarta,
GPO, 195-.
   JAS 20 (1960-1) 1201. (H. Geertz)

GOROSPE, VITALIANO R. Responsible
parenthood in the Philippines. Manila, Ateneo Publications Office,
1970. (Philippine national development series)
   JAS 32 (1972-3) 759-760. (G. D.
   Ness)

GOUDRIAAN, T. Stuti and stava (Baud-
dha, Saiva and Vaisnava) of Balinese
Brahman priests, by T. Goudriaan and
C. Hooykaas. Amsterdam, North-
Holland Publishing Co., 1971. (Aka-
demie van Wetenschappen, Amsterdam.
Afdeling Letterkunde, Verhandelingen
niewe reeks, deel 76)
   BIJ 128 (1972) 375-377. (J. L.
   Swellengrebel)
   SOAS 36 (1973) 713-4. (G. E.
   Marrison)

GOULD, JAMES W. Americans in Sumatra.
The Hague, Nijhoff, 1961.
   JAS 22 (1962-3) 228. (C. Hobbs)
   PA 36 (1963) 99-100. (J. A. M.
   Caldwell)

GOULD, JAMES W. The United States and
Malaysia. Cambridge, Harvard UP,
1969.
   JAS 29 (1969-70) 735-6. (K.
   Mulliner)

GOULLART, PETER. River of the White
Lily; life in Sarawak. London, John
Murray, 1965.
   PA 39 (1966) 222-3. (T. Harrisson)

GOUR, CLAUDE-GILLES. Institutions con-
stitutionnelles et politiques du Cambodge. Paris, Dalloz, 1965. (Paris.
Universite. Institut de droit com-
pare. Les systems de droit contemporains, 18)
   FA 20 (1965) 267-8. (B. Couret)

GOUROU, PIERRE. Lecons de geographie
tropicale; lecons donnees au College
de France de 1947 a 1970. Paris,
Mouton, 1971. (Le Savoir geographique, 1)
   PA 45 (1972) 277-8. (R. Garry)

Gowing, Peter G. *See* BAGUIO RELIGIOUS
ACCULTURATION CONFERENCE. Acculturation in the Philippines

GOWING, PETER G. Islands under the
cross; the story of the Church in the

Gowing, Peter G. Islands under the

Philippines. Manila, National Council of Churches in the Philippines, 1967.
    PS 15 (1967) 524–529. (J. N. Schumacher)

GOWING, PETER G. Mosque and Moro: a study of Muslims in the Philippines. Manila, Philippine Federation of Christian Churches, 1964.
    JAS 24 (1964–5) 173–4. (D. V. Hart)
    PS 12 (1964) 533–536. (E. S. Casino)
    UN 37 (1964) 305–307. (A. Panizo)

GRAAF, HERMANUS JOHANNES DE. Catalogus van de Handschriften in Westerse talen toebehorende aan het Koninklijk Instituut voor Taal-, Land- en Volkenkunde. The Hague, Nijhoff, 1963.
    JAS 24 (1964–5) 709–710. (R. Van Niel)
    SOAS 27 (1964) 495. (J. Bastin)

GRAAF, HERMANUS JOHANNES DE. Nederlandsch-Indie onder Japansche bezetting: gegevens en documenten over de jaren 1942–1945. Franeker, T. Wever, 1960.
    JSAH 3 (Mar. 1962) 152–156. (H. J. Benda)

GRAAF, HERMANUS JOHANNES DE. De regering van Sunan Mangku-Rat I. Tegal-Wangi, Vorst van Mataram, 1646–1677. II. Opstand en ondergang. The Hague, Nijhoff, 1962. (Instituut voor Taal-, Land- en Volkenkunde. Verhandelingen, deel 33)
    SOAS 29 (1966) 681. (J. G. de Casparis)

GRAFF, HENRY FRANKLIN. American imperialism and the Philippine insurrection; testimony taken from hearings on affairs in the Philippine Islands before the Senate Committee on the Philippines, 1902. Boston, Little, Brown, 1969.
    PS 17 (1969) 818–820. (J. N. Schumacher)

Grammatika indoneziiskogo iazyka [by] Natalia Fedorovna Aliyeva. Moscow, Izdatelstvo Nauka, 1972.
    AAS 10 (1974) 204–5. (V. Krupa)
    SOAS 37 (1974) 262–3. (N. G. Phillips)

GRANT, BRUCE. Indonesia. Melbourne, Melbourne UP, 1964.
    AAS 3 (1967) 187. (R. Raczynski)
    JAS 24 (1964–5) 528–9. (D. Hindley)

GRANT, BRUCE. Indonesia. Harmondsworth, Eng., Penguin, 1967.
    JAH 3 (1969) 84–5. (C. K. Byrd)
    JAS 27 (1967–8) 680–1. (J. S. Mintz)

GRANT, JONATHAN S. Cambodia: the widening war in Indochina, by Jonathan S. Grant, Laurence A. G. Moss and Jonathan Unger. New York, Washington Square Pr., 1971.
    JAS 32 (1972–3) 121–124. (M. Leifer)
    PA 44 (1971) 645–647. (M. Leifer)

GREENE, FRED. U.S. policy and the security of Asia. New York, McGraw-Hill, 1968. (United States and China in world affairs, vol. 8)
    AS 8 (1968) 818.

GREINDL, LEOPOLD. A la recherche d'un etat independant: Leopold II et les Philippines, 1869–1875. Brussels, Academie Royale des Sciences d'Outre-Mer, 1962. (Academie royale des sciences d'outre-mer. Classe des sciences morales et politiques. Memoires in-8º, nouv. ser. t. 26, fasc. 1)
    SLQ 4 (1966) 537–570. (M.-A. van Huyse)

GRIFFITH, SAMUEL B. Peking and people's wars: an analysis of statements by official spokesmen of the Chinese Communist Party on the subject of revolutionary strategy.

Guillon, Emmanuel. Dictionnaire de

London, Pall Mall Pr., 1966.
JAH 2 (1968) 66-7. (T. P. Bern-
stein)
MAS 2 (1968) 84-5. (P. J. Honey)
PA 42 (1969) 76-81. (H. A. Steiner)

GRISWOLD, ALEXANDER B. Art of Burma,
Korea, Tibet. New York, Crown,
1964. (Art of the world, non-
European cultures; the historical,
sociological and religious backgrounds)
PA 37 (1964) 457-8. (P. C. Swann)

Griswold, Alexander B. *See* Essays
offered to G. H. Luce

GRISWOLD, ALEXANDER B. Felicitation
volume presented to Professor George
Coedes on the occasion of his seven-
ty fifth birthday, by Alexander B.
Griswold and J. Boisselier. Ascona,
Artibus Asiae, 1961. (Artibus
Asiae. Vol. 24, nos. 3-4)
FA 18 (1962) 603-605. (G. Condo-
minas)

GRISWOLD, ALEXANDER B. King Mongkut
of Siam. New York, Asia Society,
1961.
JAS 20 (1960-1) 542-3. (H. Tinker)
SEIB 36 (1961) 754.
SOAS 24 (1961) 400. (E. H. S.
Simmonds)

GRISWOLD, ALEXANDER B. Towards a his-
tory of Sukhodaya art. Bangkok,
Fine Arts Dept., 1967.
JSS 60 pt. 2 (1972) 257-284. (M.
C. Chand Chirayu Rajni)
Author's reply: JSS 61 pt. 2
(1973) 149-166.

GROSLIER, BERNARD PHILIPPE. Angkor et
le Cambodge au XVIe siecle d'apres
les sources portugaises et espag-
noles. Paris, Presses universitaires
de France, 1958.
JAS 20 (1960-1) 239-240. (K. E.
Wells)

GROSLIER, BERNARD PHILIPPE. Indo-
china. Cleveland, World, 1966.
JAH 7 (1973) 93.
PA 40 (1967) 400-402. (S. J.
O'Connor)

GROSLIER, BERNARD PHILIPPE. Indochine, carrefour des arts. Paris,
Albin Michel, 1961. (L'art dans le
monde. Civilisations non-europeennes)
SEIB 36 (1961) 755.

GROSSHOLTZ, JEAN. Politics in the
Philippines, a country study. Bos-
ton, Little, Brown, 1964.
AS 4 (1964) 1205.
PA 38 (1965) 89-91. (R. S. Milne)
PS 13 (1965) 401. (M. P. Onorato)
PS 17 (1969) 605-616. (A. M.
Geoghegan)
RSA (1966) 142-3. (M. Subhan)
UN 39 (Mar. 1966) 144-146. (E. A.
Franco)

Groves, Harry E. *See* SHERIDAN, LIONEL
ASTOR. Constitution of Malaysia

Guber, Aleksander Andreevich *See*
Politika kapitalisticheskikh derzhav

GUERRERO, AMADO. Philippine society
and revolution. Manila, Pulang Tala
Publications, 1971.
SA 2 (1972) 529. (R. P. de Guzman)

GUERRERO NAKPIL, CARMEN. Woman enough
and other essays. Quezon City,
Vibal, 1963.
PS 12 (1964) 174-177. (M. T.
Colayco)

GUERRO, LEON MARIA. First Filipino; a
biography of Jose Rizal. Manila,
National Heros Commission, 1963.
(Philippines (Repbulic) National
Heros Commission. Publications)
PS 12 (1964) 536-539. (J. N.
Schumacher)

* GUILLON, EMMANUEL. Dictionnaire de
base francais-birman, par Emmanuel

Guillon, Emmanuel. Dictionnaire de

Guillon et Claude Delachet. Rangoon, Daily Gazette Pr., 1972.
  SEIB 48 (1973) 537-8. (D. Bernot)

GULBENKIAN MUSEUM OF ORIENTAL ART AND
ARCHAEOLOGY. Descriptive and illus-
trated catalogue of the Malcolm
MacDonald collection of Chinese
ceramics in the Gulbenkian Museum of
Oriental Art and Archaeology, School
of Oriental Studies, University of
Durham, by Ireneus Laszlo Legeza.
London, Oxford UP, 1972.
  BMJ 3 pt. 1 (1973) 152-154. (T.
  Harrisson)

GULLICK, J. M. Indigenous political
systems of western Malaya. London,
Athlone Pr., 1958. (London School
of Economics. Monographs on social
anthropology, no. 17)
  BIJ 116 (1960) 379-385. (P. E. de
  Josselin de Jong)
  JSAH 1 (Mar. 1960) 101-105. (M. G.
  Swift)

GULLICK, J. M. Malaya. London,
Ernest Benn, 1963. (Nations of the
modern world)
  AAS 2 (1966) 171-2. (R. Raczynski)
  AS 4 (1964) 859.
  JAS 24 (Nov. 1964) 171. (J. N.
  Parmer)
  JSAH 5 (Sept. 1964) 207-8. (E.
  Sadka)
  MER 8 pt. 2 (1963) 118-9. (T. R.
  McHale)
  PA 37 (1964) 95. (N. Tarling)
  SOAS 28 (1965) 216. (H. Tinker)

GULLICK, J. M. Malaysia. New York,
Praeger, 1969. (Nations of the
modern world)
  JAS 29 (1969-70) 734-5. (C. A.
  Lockard)
  PA 43 (1970) 133-4. (R. Emerson)

GULLICK, J. M. Malaysia and its
neighbours. London, Routledge and
Kegan Paul, 1967.
  JAS 27 (1967-8) 681-2. (J. C.

Scott)
  JSAS 3 (1972) 346-348. (Lau Teik
  Soon)
  MAS 4 (1970) 191.
  PA 41 (1968) 119-120. (L. E.
  Williams)

GUNAWAN, BASUKI. Kudeta, staatsgreep
in Djakarta. De achtergronden van de
30 September-beweging in Indonesie.
Meppel, Boom, 1968.
  PA 41 (1968) 610-613. (B. B.
  Hering)

GURTOV, MELVIN. China and Southeast
Asia, the politics of survival, a
study of foreign policy interaction.
Lexington, Mass., Heath Lexington
Books, 1971.
  PA 46 (1973) 342-3. (M. Osborne)
  SA 3 (1974) 927-930. (R. H.
  Detrick)

GURTOV, MELVIN. First Vietnam crisis;
Chinese communist strategy and United
States involvement, 1953-1954. New
York, Columbia UP, 1967. (Columbia
Univ. East Asian Institute. East
Asian Institute series)
  AS 7 (1967) 273.

GURTOV, MELVIN. Southeast Asia tomor-
row; problems and prospects for U.S.
policy. Baltimore, Johns Hopkins Pr.,
1970.
  JAS 30 (1970-1) 227-8. (C. E.
  Morrison)
  PA 43 (1970) 466-7. (K. G.
  Tregonning)
  SA 2 (1972-3) 363-371. (J. Badgley)

GUTHRIE, GEORGE M. Child rearing and
personality development in the Phil-
ippines, by George M. Guthrie and
Pepita Jimenez Jacobs. University
Park, Pennsylvania State UP, 1966.
  JAS 26 (1966-7) 768-9. (D. V.
  Hart)
  SJ 13 (1966) 641-646. (H. R.
  Reynolds)

GUTHRIE, GEORGE M. Filipino child and
Philippine society, research reports
and essays. Manila, Philippine Normal College Pr., 1961. (Manila.
Philippine Normal College. Monograph
series, no. 1)
    GEJ 12 (1966) 296-301. (P. S.
    Manalung)
    JAS 22 (1962-3) 117. (E. Nurge)
    SJ 9 (1962) 65-67. (C. L. Hunt)

GUTHRIE, GEORGE M. Psychology of modernization in the rural Philippines.
Quezon City, Ateneo de Manila Pr.,
1970. (Quezon, Philippines. Ateneo
de Manila, Institute of Philippine
Culture. IPC papers, no. 8)
    JAS 31 (1971-2) 745-6. (D. J.
    Scheans)

Guthrie, George M. *See* Six perspectives on the Philippines

Guthrie, Harold W. *See* HAWKINS,
EVERETT DAY. Entrepreneurship and
labor skills in Indonesian economic
development

Gutkind, Peter Claus Wolfgang *See*
JONGMANS, D. G. Anthropologists in
the field

Guzman, Raul P. de *See* ABUEVA, JOSE
VELOSO. Foundations and dynamics of
Filipino government and politics

Guzman, Raul P. de *See* ABUEVA, JOSE
V. Handbook of Philippine public
administration

GUZMAN, RAUL P. DE. Patterns in decision making, case studies in Philippine public administration. Manila,
Graduate School of Public Administration, Univ. of the Philippines, 1963.
    PA 37 (1964) 95-6. (R. S. Milne)
    SJ 10 (1963) 57-8. (S. L. Ebarle)

Haan, W. de *See* Volkenkundige
encyclopedie

Hall, Daniel George Edward. Historians

HAAS, MARY ROSAMOND. Thai-English
student's dictionary. Stanford,
Stanford UP, 1964.
    SOAS 28 (1965) 663-666. (P. J. Bee)

Habsbourg, Otto de *See* OTTO, ARCHDUKE
OF AUSTRIA

Hackin, Joseph *See* Asiatic mythology

Hagensick, A. Clarke *See* CHAKRIT
NORANITIPADUNGKARN. Modernizing
Chiengmai

HAHN, EMILY. Raffles of Singapore, a
biography. Kuala Lumpur, Univ. of
Malaya Pr., 1968.
    JAS 30 (1970-1) 231-2. (T. R.
    Fennell)
    JSAS 1 pt. 1 (1970) 110-1. (C. M.
    Turnbull)

HALBERSTAM, DAVID. The best and the
brightest. New York, Random House,
1972.
    JAS 33 (1973-4) 340-342. (T. A.
    Brindley)

* HALBERSTAM, DAVID. En plein bourbier.
Paris, Buchet, 1966.
    FA 20 (1965) 407-8.

Hall, Daniel George Edward *See* Atlas
of Southeast Asia

HALL, DANIEL GEORGE EDWARD. Early English intercourse with Burma, 1587-
1743. 2d. ed. London, Cass, 1968.
    JAH 4 (1970) 188. (Maung Htin Aung)

HALL, DANIEL GEORGE EDWARD. Historians
of South-East Asia. London, Oxford
UP, 1961. (London. Univ. School of
Oriental and African Studies. His-
torical writing on the peoples of
Asia)
    BIJ 118 (1962) 384-387. (H. J. de
    Graf)
    JAS 21 (1961-2) 402-3. (J. R. W.
    Smail)
    JSAH 2 (Oct. 1961) 114-5. (K. G.

Hall, Daniel George Edward. Historians

    Tregonning)
  PA 35 (1962) 183-4. (H. J. Benda)
  SOAS 28 (1965) 447-451. (A.
    Momigliano)

HALL, DANIEL GEORGE EDWARD. History
  of South-East Asia. 2d. ed. London,
  Macmillan, 1964.
    AP 8 (1964) 137-8. (W. G. Solheim)
    PA 38 (1965) 200-1. (B. Harrison)

HALL, GORDON LANGLEY. Golden boats
  from Burma, the life of Ann Hassel-
  time Judson. Philadelphia, Macrae
  Smith, 1961.
    PA 35 (1962) 188-190. (J. F. Cady)

HALL, MAXWELL. Kinabalu guerrillas,
  an account of the Double Tenth, 1943.
  Jesselton, Borneo Literature Bureau,
  1962.
    JSAH 5 (Mar. 1964) 226. (K. G.
    Tregonning)

HALPERN, JOEL MARTIN. Aspects of vil-
  lage life and culture change in Laos.
  New York, Council on Economic and
  Cultural Affairs, 1958.
    BEF 50 (1960) 184-190. (P.-B.
    Lafont)
    SEIB 35 (1960) 740.

HALPERN, JOEL MARTIN. Economy and so-
  ciety of Laos, a brief survey. New
  Haven, Southeast Asia Studies, Yale
  Univ., 1964. (Yale Univ. Graduate
  School. Southeast Asia Studies.
  Monograph series, no. 5)
    BEF 55 (1969) 276-279. (P. B.
    Lafont)
    JAS 25 (1965-6) 646-7. (R. P.
    Mendels)

HALPERN, JOEL MARTIN. Government,
  politics, and social structures in
  Laos, a study in tradition and inno-
  vation. New Haven, Southeast Asia
  Studies, Yale Univ., 1964. (Yale
  Univ. Graduate School. Southeast
  Asia Studies. Monograph series, no.
  4)

    BEF 55 (1969) 270-276. (P. B.
    Lafont)
    BIJ 122 (1966) 392-394. (L.
    Sluimers)

HAMMARSKJOLD FORUMS, NEW YORK, OCT. 18,
  1965. Southeast Asia crisis; background papers and proceedings of the
  eighth Hammarskjold Forum, edited by
  Lyman M. Tondel. Dobbs Ferry, Oceania, 1966.
    PA 39 (1966) 404-5. (L. P. Singh)

HAMMER, ELLEN JOY. Vietnam, yesterday
  and today. New York, Holt, Rinehart
  and Winston, 1966. (Contemporary
  civilizations series)
    JAS 26 (1966-7) 760-1. (Huynh K.
    Khanh)

HAMMER, RICHARD. One morning in the
  war, the tragedy at Son My. New
  York, Coward McCann, 1970.
    PA 43 (1970) 626-630. (A. Woodside)

Hanks, Jane Richardson *See* HANKS,
  LUCIEN MASON. Ethnographic notes on
  northern Thailand

HANKS, JANE RICHARDSON. Maternity and
  its rituals in Bang Chan. Ithaca,
  Southeast Asia Program, Cornell Univ.,
  1963. (Cornell Univ. Southeast Asia
  Program. Data paper, no. 51)
    BIJ 121 (1965) 380-383.

HANKS, LUCIEN MASON. Ethnographic
  notes on northern Thailand, by L. M.
  Hanks, Jane R. Hanks and Lauriston
  Sharp. Ithaca, Southeast Asia Program, Cornell Univ., 1965. (Cornell
  Univ. Southeast Asia Program. Data
  paper, no. 58)
    BIJ 124 (1968) 400-402. (F. M.
    LeBar)
    JSAH 9 (1968) 360-1. (J. H. Kemp)
    PA 40 (1967) 206-7. (W. E. Willmott)

HANKS, LUCIEN MASON. Rice and man,
  agricultural ecology in Southeast
  Asia. Chicago, Aldine-Atheron, 1972.

Harrisson, Thomas Harnett.   The Malays

(Worlds of man)
   JAS 32 (1972-3) 368-9. (P.
   Wheatley)
   JSS 62 pt. 1 (1974) 212-221.
   (Kobkua Suwannathat-Pian)

HANNA, WILLARD ANDERSON.   Bung Karno's
Indonesia; a collection of 25 re-
ports written for the American Uni-
versities Field Staff.   New York,
American Universities Field Staff,
1960.
   JAS 20 (1960-1) 116-7. (H. Feith)
   PA 34 (1961) 309-311. (W. F.
   Wertheim)

HANNA, WILLARD ANDERSON.   Eight nation
makers, Southeast Asia's charismatic
statesmen.   New York, St. Martin's
Pr., 1964.
   AS 5 (1965) 169.

HANNA, WILLARD ANDERSON.   Formation of
Malaysia; new factor in world poli-
tics, an analytical history and as-
sessment of the prospects of the
newest state in Southeast Asia.   New
York, American Universities Field
Staff, 1964.
   JAS 24 (1964-5) 340. (R. O. Tilman)

HANNA, WILLARD ANDERSON.   Sequel to
colonialism; the 1957-60 foundations
for Malaysia, an on the spot examination of the geographic, economic,
and political seedbed where the idea
of a federation of Malaysia was
germinated.   New York, American Universities Field Staff, 1965.
   AS 5 (1965) 169-170.
   JAS 25 (1965-6) 167-8. (R. O.
   Tilman)
   PA 38 (1965) 205-6. (K. G.
   Tregonning)

HARDJADIBRATA, R. R.   Word count; a
computer aided investigation, a
pilot study.   Clayton, Indonesian
and Malay section, Monash Univ.,
1968.
   AR 6 (1973) 230-233. (H. Chambert-
   Loir)

Harootunian, Harry D.   *See* DEAN, VERA
   MICHELES.   West and non-West

HARRISON, KENNETH.   Brave Japanese.
   Adelaide, Rigby, 1966.
   PA 40 (1967) 385-6. (O. L. Roberts)

HARRISSON, THOMAS HARBETT.   Borneo
writing and related matters.   Kuching,
Sarawak Museum, 1966.   (Sarawak
Museum. Journal. Vol. 13, no. 27)
   AP 10 (1967) 168-9. (S. Gill)

HARRISSON, THOMAS HARNETT.   Excavations
of the prehistoric iron industry in
west Borneo, by Tom Harrisson and
Stanley J. O'Connor.   Ithaca, South-
east Asia Program, Cornell Univ.,
1969. 2v.   (Cornell Univ. Southeast
Asia Program. Data paper, no. 72)
   AP 12 (1969) 131-133. (W. G.
   Solheim)
   JSAS 3 (1972) 158-161. (W. G.
   Solheim)
   SOAS 34 (1971) 187-8. (W. Watson)

HARRISSON, THOMAS HARNETT.   Gold and
megalithic activity in prehistoric
and recent west Borneo, by Tom Har-
risson and Stanley J. O'Connor.
Ithaca, Southeast Asia Program, Cor-
nell Univ., 1970.   (Cornell Univ.
Southeast Asia Program. Data paper,
no. 77)
   AP 16 (1973) 203-206. (I. de
   Beauclair)
   BIJ 130 (1974) 185-188. (Ajatro-
   haedi)
   JSAS 3 (1972) 158-161. (W. G.
   Solheim)
   SOAS 35 (1972) 413-415. (I. C.
   Glover)

HARRISSON, THOMAS HARNETT.   The Malays
of south-west Sarawak before Malaysia, a socio-ecological survey.   London, Macmillan, 1970.
   MAS 7 (1973) 310-1. (A. J. N.
   Richards)

Harrisson, Thomas Harnett. The Malays

PA 45 (1972) 140. (H. E. Jacobson)
SMJ 18 (1970) 420-422. (G. Dixon)

HARRISSON, THOMAS HARNETT. Prehistory of Sabah, by Tom and Barbara Harrisson. Kota Kinabalu, Sabah Society, 1971. (Sabah Society journal, 4)
JAS 32 (1972-3) 746-748. (W. G. Solheim)
JMBRAS 45 pt. 1 (1972) 122-3. (M. Sheppard)
SMJ 19 (1971) 379. (B. Sandin)

* HART, DONN VORHIS. Annotated bibliography of the theses and dissertations on Asia accepted at Syracuse University, 1907-1963. Syracuse, Syracuse Univ. Library, 1964.
PS 12 (1964) 756-7. (J. M. Saniel)

HART, DONN VORHIS. Annotated bibliography on barrio councils, by Donn V. Hart, Mario D. Zamora and Mary R. Hollnsteiner. Manila, Presidential Assistant on Community Development, 1965.
JAS 26 (1966-7) 547-549. (D. V. Hart)

HART, DONN VORHIS. Bisayan Filipino and Malayan humoral pathologies: folk medicine and ethnohistory in Southeast Asia. Ithaca, Southeast Asia Program, Cornell Univ., 1969. (Cornell Univ. Southeast Asia Program. Data paper, no. 76)
BIJ 127 (1971) 403-406. (R. Rosaldo)
JAS 31 (1971-2) 468-9. (R. W. Lieban)
JSAS 3 (1972) 333-4. (Mohd. Taib Osman)
PA 44 (1971) 469. (H. E. Jacobson)
PS 20 (1972) 678.

HART, DONN VORHIS. Riddles in Filipino folklore, an anthropological analysis. Syracuse, Syracuse UP, 1964.
JAS 25 (1965-6) 175. (L. Casper)
PA 40 (1967) 166-7. (H. E.

Jacobson)
UN 37 (1965) 161-2. (A. F. Villanueva)

HART, DONN VORHIS. Southeast Asian birth customs, three studies in human reproduction, by Donn V. Hart, Phya Anuman Rajadhon and Richard J. Coughlin. New Haven, Human Relations Area Files, 1965. (Behavior science monographs)
BIJ 124 (1968) 409-413. (C. H. M. Nooy-Palm)
JAS 25 (1965-6) 797-8. (J. R. Hanks)
JSAH 8 (1967) 330-1. (J. Siegel)
UN 39 (1966) 314-5. (A. Panizo)

HARTENDORP, A. V. H. History of industry and trade of the Philippines. Manila, American Chamber of the Philippines, 1958.
PS 8 (1960) 427-438. (B. Legarda y Fernandez)
Author's reply: PS 8 (1960) 439-446.

HARTENDORP, A. V. H. History of industry and trade of the Philippines, the Magsaysay administration, a critical assessment. Manila, Philippine Education Co., 1961.
PA 35 (1962) 194-5. (F. H. Golay)
PS 9 (1961) 701-706. (V. R. Jayme)

HARTENDORP, A. V. H. Japanese occupation of the Philippines. Manila, Bookmark, 1967. 2v.
PA 43 (1970) 306-7. (G. K. Goodman)
PS 17 (1969) 352-354. (J. M. Saniel)

HARTENDORP, A. V. H. Santo Tomas story. New York, McGraw-Hill, 1964.
PA 40 (1967) 407-409. (I. B. Powell)

HASAN BIN MUHAMMAD ALI. Mustafir. Kuala Lumpur, Dewan Bahasa dan Pustaka, 1959.
BIJ 117 (1961) 300-302. (A. Teeuw)

Heimbach, Ernest E. White Meo-English

HASSLER, ALFRED. Saigon, U.S.A. New York, Baron, 1970.
  PA 43 (1970) 625-630. (A. Woodside)

HASTINGS, PETER. New Guinea, problems and prospects. Melbourne, Cheshire, 1969.
  PA 43 (1970) 473-4. (D. G. Bettison)

HATTA, MOHAMMAD. Past and future, an address delivered upon receiving the degree of doctor honoris causa from Gadjah Mada University at Jogjakarta on November 27, 1956. Ithaca, Modern Indonesia Project, Southeast Asia Program, Cornell Univ., 1960. (Cornell Univ. Modern Indonesia Project. Translation series)
  JAS 21 (1961-2) 565-567. (G. J. Pauker)

HAUPT, GEORGES. La Deuxieme Internationale et l'Orient, par G. Haupt et Madeleine Reberioux. Paris, Cujas, 1967. (Collection vie politique et politique internationale)
  FA 21 (1966) 600.

HAWAII. UNIV., HONOLULU. CENTER FOR CULTURAL AND TECHNICAL INTERCHANGE BETWEEN EAST AND WEST. INSTITUTE OF ADVANCED PROJECTS. Student problems in Thailand and Vietnam; translations from the periodical press. Honolulu, East-West Center, 1966. (Hawaii (State) Univ., Honolulu. Center for Cultural and Technical Interchange between East and West. Research translations. Occasional papers. Translation series, no. 12)
  JAS 26 (1966-7) 539-540. (F. H. Tucker)

HAWKINS, EVERETT DAY. Entrepreneurship and labour skills in Indonesian economic development: a symposium. Contributors: E. D. Hawkins, Leslie H. Palmer and H. W. Guthrie. Introduction by B. H. Higgins. New Haven,

Yale Univ., Southeast Asia Studies, 1961. (Yale Univ. Graduate School. Southeast Asia Studies. Monograph series, no. 1)
  JAS 21 (1961-2) 416-7. (B. Glassburner)
  MER 8 pt. 2 (1963) 133-4. (D. J. Blake)
  PA 35 (1962) 429-430. (J. A. C. Mackie)

HAY, STEPHEN N. Southeast Asian history; a bibliographic guide, by Stephen Hay and Margaret H. Case. New York, Praeger, 1962.
  JAS 22 (1962-3) 491. (C. Hobbs)
  SOAS 26 (1963) 461-2. (D. G. E. Hall)

HEALEY, PHYLLIS M. Agta grammar. Manila, GPO, 1960.
  JAS 21 (1961-2) 569-570. (C. Lopez)
  SOAS 27 (1964) 487-489. (E. M. Mendelson)

Heekeren, H. R. van *See* THAI-DANISH PREHISTORIC EXPEDITION, 1960. Archaeological excavations in Thailand

HEEREN, H. J. Het land aan de overkant. Transmigratie van Java naar Sumatra. Meppel, Boom, 1967.
  BIJ 125 (1969) 273-275. (M. A. Jaspan)

HEIDER, KARL G. Dugum Dani; a Papuan culture in the highlands of west New Guinea. Chicago, Aldine, 1970. (Viking Fund publications in anthropology, no. 49)
  BIJ 128 (1972) 509-511. (L. F. B. Dubbeldam)
  PA 44 (1971) 317-8. (D. G. Bettison)

HEIMBACH, ERNEST E. White Meo-English dictionary. Ithaca, Southeast Asia Program, Cornell Univ., 1969. (Cornell Univ. Southeast Asia Program. Data paper, no. 75)
  JAS 30 (1970-1) 503-4. (Kun Chang)

Held, Gerrit Jan. The Papuas of

HELD, GERRIT JAN. The Papuas of Waro-
pen. The Hague, Nijhoff, 1957. (Instituut voor Taal-, Land- en Volkenkunde. Translation series, no. 2)
  PA 33 (1960) 97-8. (L. Pospisil)
  SOAS 23 (1960) 180-1. (G. B.
    Milner)

HELMS, LUDVIG VERNER. Pioneering in
the Far East and journeys to California in 1849 and to the White Sea
in 1878. London, Dawsons of Pall
Mall, 1969. (Colonial history
series)
  JSAS 1 pt. 2 (1970) 145. (D. K.
    Bassett)

Hemery, Daniel See CHESNEAUX, JEAN.
Tradition et revolution au Vietnam

Henderson, Eugenie J. A. See CONFER-
ENCE ON LINGUISTIC PROBLEMS OF THE
INDO-PACIFIC AREA, SCHOOL OF ORIEN-
TAL AND AFRICAN STUDIES, UNIV. OF
LONDON, 1965. Indo-Pacific linguis-
tic studies

HENDERSON, EUGENIE J. A. Tiddim Chin,
a descriptive analysis of two texts.
London, Oxford UP, 1965. (London
Oriental series, vol. 15)
  JAS 25 (1965-6) 547. (R. Burling)
  SOAS 29 (1966) 421-423. (E. G.
    Pulleyblank)

HENDERSON, WILLIAM. Southeast Asia:
problems of United States policy.
Cambridge, MIT Pr., 1963.
  AS 4 (1964) 774-5.
  JAS 24 (1964-5) 169-170. (D. A.
    Wilson)
  PA 38 (1965) 86-7. (J. D. Legge)
  PS 13 (1965) 371-381. (R. N.
    Quintos)

HENDON, RUFUS S. Phonology and morphology of Ulu Muar Malay, Kuala
Pilah District, Negri Sembilan, Malaya. New Haven, Dept. of Anthropology, Yale Univ., 1966. (Yale
Univ. Dept. of Anthropology. Publi-

cations in anthropology, 70)
  BIJ 125 (1969) 509-511. (J. C.
    Anceaux)

HENDON, RUFUS S. Six Indonesian short
stories. New Haven, Yale Univ.,
Southeast Asia Studies, 1968. (Yale
Univ. Graduate School. Southeast Asia
Studies. Translation series, no. 7)
  AS 9 (1969) 397.
  JAS 29 (1969-70) 490-1. (A. M.
    Stevens)

Hendrix, W. J. See DOORN, JACOBUS
ADRIANUS ANTONIUS VAN. Ontsporing
van geweld

HENDRY, ROBERT S. Atlas of the Philippines. Manila, Phil-Asian Publishers,
1959.
  JAS 21 (1961-2) 245-6. (J. E.
    Spencer)

HENIGE, DAVID P. Colonial governors
from the fifteenth century to the
present; a comprehensive list. Madison, Univ. of Wisconsin Pr., 1970.
  PA 44 (1971) 163-4. (B. Harrison)

HERNANDEZ, AMADO V. Isang dipang langit. Manila, Tamaraw, 1961.
  SLQ 1 (1963) 456-458. (M. O. Ortiz)

HERNANDEZ, AMADO V. Rice grains; selected poems. New York, International Publishers, 1966.
  JAS 26 (1966-7) 129-130. (D. V.
    Hart)

* HERNANDEZ, JOSE MA. Catholic action
marches on, a decade of Catholic action, 1950-1960. Manila, 196-.
  SLQ 1 (1963) 444-447.

HERRFURTH, HANS. Djawanisch-deutsches
Worterbuch. Leipzig, Verlag Enzyklo-
padie, 1972.
  BEF 61 (1974) 375-6. (D. Lombard)

HERSH, SEYMOUR M. My Lai 4; a report
on the massacre and its aftermath.

New York, Random House, 1970.
  PA 44 (1971) 591-595. (D. J.
  Duncanson)

HERZ, MARTIN F. Short history of Cambodia from the days of Angkor to the
  present. New York, Praeger, 1958.
    BEF 50 (1960) 205-209. (B. P.
    Groslier)
    FA 17 (1960) 1551-1557. (B.-P.
    Groslier and C. Meyer)
    SEIB 35 (1960) 738.

HESSEL, EUGENE A. Religious thought
  of Jose Rizal. Manila, Philippine
  Education Co., 1961.
    SJ 10 (1963) 421-423. (P. G.
    Gowing)

HEWITT, ARTHUR R. Guide to resources
  for Commonwealth studies in London,
  Oxford and Cambridge, with bibliographical and other information.
  London, Athlone Pr., 1957.
    SOAS 24 (1961) 181-2.

HEWITT, ARTHUR R. Union list of Commonwealth newspapers in London, Oxford and Cambridge. London, Athlone
  Pr., 1960.
    SOAS 24 (1961) 182.

Hickey, Gerald Cannon *See* LeBAR,
  FRANK M. Ethnic groups of mainland
  Southeast Asia

HICKEY, GERALD CANNON. Study of a
  Vietnamese rural community: sociol-
  ogy. Saigon, Michigan State Univ.,
  Viet Nam Advisory Group, 1960.
    JAS 20 (1960-1) 398-9. (J. Mus-
    grave)

HICKEY, GERALD CANNON. Village in
  Vietnam. New Haven, Yale UP, 1964.
    BEF 56 (1969) 195-199. (N. Louis)
    JAS 25 (1965-6) 174-5. (J. C.
    Donnell)
    JAS 28 (1968-9) 821-831. (J. C.
    Donnell)
    RSA (1965) 178-9. (I. Jadoul)
    SOAS 29 (1966) 427-8. (P. J. Honey)

HICKS, GEORGE L. Indonesian economy,
  1950-1965, a bibliography, by George
  L. Hicks and Geoffrey McNicoll. New
  Haven, Southeast Asia Studies, Yale
  Univ., 1967. (Yale Univ. Graduate
  School. Southeast Asia Studies. Bib-
  liography series, no. 9)
    BIJ 126 (1970) 365-6. (H. J.
    Duller)
    FA 22 (1968) 129.
    MER 12 pt. 2 (1967) 137.

HICKS, GEORGE L. Trade and growth in
  the Philippines, an open dual economy, by George L. Hicks and Geoffrey
  McNicoll. Ithaca, Cornell UP, 1971.
    JAS 32 (1972-3) 384-386. (M. E.
    Abel)
    PA 45 (1972) 146. (S. Kirby)
    SA 2 (1972-3) 387-389. (J. A.
    Storer)
    SA 2 (1972) 488-502. (V. D. Ooms)

Higgins, B. H. *See* HAWKINS, EVERETT
  DAY. Entrepreneurship and labor
  skills in Indonesian economic development

HIGGINS, BENJAMIN HOWARD. Indonesia,
  the crisis of the millstones, by
  Benjamin Higgins with Jean Higgins.
  Princeton, Van Nostrand, 1963.
    JAS 23 (1963-4) 599-600. (D. H.
    Kornhauser)
    PA 37 (1964) 232-234. (C. A.
    Fisher)

Higgins, Jean *See* HIGGINS, BENJAMIN
  HOWARD. Indonesia, crisis of the
  millstones

HIGHAM, CHARLES FRANKLIN WANDESFORDE.
  Prehistoric investigations in north-
  east Thailand 1969-70, preliminary
  report, by C. F. W. Higham, R. H.
  Parker and Pote Keakoon. Dunedin,
  N.Z., Univ. of Otago, 1970.
    JSS 61 pt. 1 (1973) 368-373. (H. H.
    E. Loofs)

HIKAJAT ATJEH. Hikajat Atjeh, die Erzahlung von der Abhunft und den Jugendjahren des Sultan Iskandar Muda von Atjeh (Sumatra). Gesamt uber setzung von Hans Penth. Wiesbaden, Harrassowitz, 1969. (Veroffentlichungen des Ostasiatischen Seminars der Johann Wolfgang Goethe Universitat, Frankfurt/Main. Reihe A: Sudostasienkunde, Bd. 2)
   BIJ 127 (1971) 508-510. (A. Teeuw)
   JSS 58 pt. 2 (1970) 149-155. (D. Lombard)
     SOAS 33 (1970) 675. (E. C. G. Barrett)

HIKAYAT ANDAKEN PENURAT. ENGLISH AND MALAY. Hikajat Andaken Penurat. The Hague, Nijhoff, 1969. (Bibliotheca Indonesia, 2)
     SOAS 33 (1970) 431-2. (A. Sweeney)

* Hikayat Merong Mahawangsa. Kuala Lumpur, Univ. of Malaya Pr., 1970.
     SOAS 34 (1971) 436-7. (A. Sweeney)

HINDLEY, DONALD. Communist party of Indonesia, 1951-1963. Berkeley, Univ. of California Pr., 1964.
   AS 5 (1965) 170.
   JAS 26 (1966-7) 340-1. (R. T. McVey)
   SOAS 28 (1965) 687. (J. Bastin)

Hiranyagarbha, a series of articles on the archaeological work and studies of Prof. Dr. F. D. K. Bosch to which is added the address delivered by him at his retirement from the Univ. of Leiden. Published on the occasion of the 50th anniversary of his doctorate on 14th July 1964. The Hague, Mouton, 1964.
   SOAS 29 (1966) 420-1. (A. Christie)

* His majesty King Rama the Fourth, Mongkut. n.p., Mahamakuta Univ., 1968.
   JSS 58 pt. 1 (1970) 140. (W. Klausner)

HISTORICAL CONSERVATION SOCIETY. Christianization of the Philippines, trans. by Rafael Lopez and Alfonso Felix. Manila, Historical Conservation Society, 1965.
   JAS 27 (1967-8) 440-1. (P. G. Gowing)

Historical interaction of China and Vietnam: institutional and cultural themes, compiled by Edgar Wickberg. Lawrence, Center for East Asian Studies, Univ. of Kansas, 1969. (Kansas. Univ. Center for East Asian Studies. International studies. East Asian series research publication, no. 4)
   JSAS 3 (1972) 164-166. (Vu Duy-Tu)
   PA 44 (1971) 591-595. (D. J. Duncanson)

HLA MYINT. Economic theory and the underdeveloped countries. New York, Oxford UP, 1971. (Economic development series)
   MAS 7 (1973) 311-313. (S. Paine)

HLA MYINT. Economics of developing countries. London, Hutchinson, 1964.
   AS 5 (1965) 320.
   JAS 25 (1965-6) 325. (R. S. Basi)
   MER 10 pt. 1 (1965) 122-125. (H. W. Arndt)

HLA MYINT. Southeast Asia's economy, development policies in the 1970's; a study sponsored by the Asian Development Bank. New York, Praeger, 1972.
   JAS 32 (1972-3) 369-371. (R. C. Rice)

HLA PE. Burmese proverbs. London, John Murray, 1962. (Wisdom of the East series)
   FA 19 (1963) 1067.
   PA 36 (1963) 451-2. (H. Tinker)
   SOAS 26 (1963) 488-9. (D. G. E. Hall)

HLA PE. Narrative of the Japanese occupation of Burma, recorded by U. Khin. Ithaca, Southeast Asia Program,

Cornell Univ., 1961. (Cornell Univ.
Southeast Asia Program. Data paper,
no. 41)
   BIJ 119 (1963) 326-7. (J. Vreden-
      bregt)

HO CHI MINH. On revolution, selected
   writings 1920-1966, edited by Bernard
   B. Fall. New York, Praeger, 1967.
      JAS 27 (1967-8) 435-437. (K. P.
         Landon)
      MAS 3 (1969) 79-82. (R. Smith)
      PA 44 (1971) 585-590. (W. E.
         Willmott)

* HOA BANG. Tac-gia the-ky XIX, Ly Van
   Phuc. Hanoi, Thang-long, 1953.
      BEF 52 (1964) 278-287. (Ta Trong
         Hiep)

HOA MAI. Nhan-van affair. n.p.,
   Vietnam Chapter of the Asian Peoples' Anti-Communist League, 1960.
      PA 34 (1961) 214-5. (B. B. Fall)

HOANG VAN CHI. From colonialism to
   communism, a case history of North
   Vietnam. London, Pall Mall Pr.,
   1964.
      AS 5 (1965) 526.
      SOAS 27 (1964) 667-8. (R. B.
         Smith)

HOANG VAN CHI. New class in North
   Vietnam. Saigon, Cong Dan, 1958.
      PA 34 (1961) 214-5. (B. B. Fall)

HOANG VAN CO. La femme vietnamienne.
   Saigon, Son Hai, 1960.
      SEIB 35 (1960) 734.

Hobbs, Cecil Carlton *See* U.S. LI-
   BRARY OF CONGRESS. ORIENTALIA DIVI-
   SION. Southeast Asia

HOBBS, CECIL CARLTON. Southeast Asia
   field trip for the Library of Congress, 1970-1971. Ithaca, Southeast
   Asia Program, Cornell Univ., 1972.
   (Cornell Univ. Southeast Asia Program. Data paper, no. 85)
      BIJ 129 (1973) 390. (R. S. Karni)

HOBBS, CECIL CARLTON. Understanding
   the peoples of Southern Asia, a bib-
   liographical essay. Urbana, Univ. of
   Illinois Graduate School of Library
   Science, 1967. (Illinois. Univ.
   Graduate School of Library Science.
   Occasional papers, no. 81)
      JAS 27 (1967-8) 443.

HODGKIN, MARY C. Australian training
   and Asian living. Nedlands, Univ. of
   Western Australia Pr., 1966.
      JSAH 8 (1967) 345-6. (Yong Ching
         Fatt)

HOHENBERG, JOHN. Between two worlds;
   policy, press and public opinion in
   Asian American relations. New York,
   Praeger, 1967.
      JAS 27 (1967-8) 615-617. (D. Shoe-
         maker)

* HOKE SEIN. Pali-English dictionary.
   n.p., n.d.
      JBRS 44 (1961) 299.

Hollnsteiner, Mary Racelis *See* HART,
   DONN VORHIS. Annotated bibliography
   on barrio councils

HOLLNSTEINER, MARY RACELIS. Dynamics
   of power in a Philippine municipality. Quezon City, Community Development Research Council, Univ. of the
   Philippines, 1963. (Quezon, Philippines. Univ. of the Philippines. Community Development Research Council.
   Study series, no. 7)
      JAS 23 (1963-4) 632-3. (J. H.
         Romani)
      PS 9 (1961) 707-710. (J. V. Abueva)
      PS 12 (1964) 371-374. (F. L.
         Jocano)

HOLT, CLAIRE. Art in Indonesia, continuities and change. Ithaca, Cornell UP, 1967.
      BIJ 126 (1970) 269-272. (R. S.
         Wassing)

schappen, Amsterdam. Afdeeling, letterkunde. Verhandelingen, nieuwe
reeks, deel 79)
   SOAS 37 (1974) 723-4. (M. C.
     Ricklefs)

HOOYKAAS, CHRISTIAAN. Perintis saste-
ra. Terdjemahan Raihoel Amar gelar
Datoek Besar. Kuala Lumpur, Oxford
UP, 1965. (Pustaka Bahasa dan Sas-
tera)
   SOAS 29 (1966) 206-7.

HOOYKAAS, CHRISTIAAN. Religion in
Bali. Leiden, Brill, 1973. (Iconography of religions. Section 13. Indian religions, fasc. 10)
   SOAS 37 (1974) 755. (M. C.
     Ricklefs)

Hooykaas, Christiaan *See* GOUDRIAAN,
T. Stuti and stava

HOOYKAAS, CHRISTIAAN. Surya-sevana,
the way to God of a Balinese Siva
priest. Amsterdam, Noord-Hollandsche Uitgevers Maatschappij, 1966.
(Akademie van Wetenschappen, Amsterdam. Afdeeling voor de Taal-,
Letter-, Geschiedkundige en Wijsgeerige Wetenschappen. Verhandeling-
en, nieuwe reeks, deel 72, no. 3)
   BIJ 124 (1968) 415-417. (P. Zoet-
     mulder)
   SOAS 30 (1967) 445-6. (J. C.
     Wright)

HOOYKAAS-VAN LEEUWEN BOOMKAMP, JACOBA
HINDRIKA. Ritual purification of a
Balinese temple. Amsterdam, Noord-
Hollandsche Uitgevers Maatschappij,
1961. (Akademie van Wetenschappen,
Amsterdam. Afdeeling voor de Taal-,
Letter-, Geschiedkundige en Wijs-
geerige Wetenschappen. Verhandeling-
en, nieuwe reeks, deel 68)
   BIJ 118 (1962) 285-288. (J. L.
     Swellengrebel)
   SOAS 26 (1963) 219-220.

HORNE, ELINOR McCULLOUGH (CLARK). Beginning Javanese. New Haven, Yale

Houston, Charles Orville. Philippine

UP, 1961. (Yale linguistic series,
3)
   AAS 1 (1965) 173-4. (G. Altmann)
   JAS 21 (1961-2) 568-9. (D. Carr)

HORNE, ELINOR McCULLOUGH (CLARK). Intermediate Javanese. New Haven, Yale
UP, 1963. (Yale linguistic series,
4)
   SOAS 28 (1965) 190. (C. Hooykaas)

HORNE, ELINOR McCULLOUGH (CLARK).
Javanese-English dictionary. New
Haven, Yale UP, 1974.
   JAS 34 (1974-5) 260-1. (S.
     Wojowasito)

HOSILLOS, LUCILA V. Philippine-Ameri-
can literary relations, 1898-1941.
Quezon City, Univ. of the Philippines
Pr., 1969.
   JAS 31 (1971-2) 235-6. (C. O.
     Houston)
   PS 18 (1970) 444-447. (M. A.
     Bernad)

HOSMER, STEPHEN T. Viet Cong repression and its implication for the future. Lexington, Mass., Heath Lexington, 1970. (Studies in international development and economics)
   PA 44 (1971) 641-644. (J. L. S.
     Girling)
   SA 3 (1974-5) 627-631. (C. A. Bain)

Houghton, Neilie Doyle *See* Struggle
against history

HOULISTON, SYLVIA. Borneo breakthrough. London, China Inland Mission, 1963.
   SMJ 15 (1967) 440-445. (V. W.
     Mullen)

HOUSTON, CHARLES ORVILLE. Philippine
bibliography. I. An annotated preliminary bibliography of Philippine
bibliographies since 1900. Manila,
Univ. of Manila, 1960.
   JAS 20 (1960-1) 241-2. (D. V. Hart)
   PA 37 (1964) 116. (E. Moseley)

Houston, Charles Orville. Philippine

HOUSTON, CHARLES ORVILLE. Philippine
   studies: the poor relation in
   American scholarship. Manila, 1957.
      JAS 20 (1960-1) 241-2. (D. V. Hart)

Houston, Charles Orville. *See* NATION-
   AL COLLOQUIUM ON THE PHILIPPINES,
   1ST, WESTERN MICHIGAN UNIV., 1966.
   Research and developmental research
   in the social sciences

HOUTMAN, FREDRIK DE. Le *Spraeck ende
   Woord-Boek* de Frederick de Houtman;
   premiere method de malais parle
   (fin du XVIe s.) presente par Denys
   Lombard. Paris, Ecole Francaise de
   Extreme-Orient, 1970. (Ecole Francaise d'Extreme-Orient. Publications,
   v. 74)
      AR 1 (1970) 198-201. (H. Chambert-
      Loir)

HOWARD, JOSEPH T. Society and culture
   in rural Philippines, by Joseph
   T. Howard, Irene L. Ortigas and Felix B. Regalado. Iloilo City, Central Philippines UP, 1965.
      SJ 16 (1969) 110-1. (H. R.
      Reynolds)

Howe, Irving *See* Dissenter's guide
   to foreign policy

HOYT, EDWIN PALMER. Battle of Leyte
   Gulf, the death knell of the Japa-
   nese fleet. New York, Weybright and
   Talley, 1972.
      PA 46 (1973) 177. (A. D. Coox)
      SA 3 (1974) 948-950. (J. B.
      Hattendorf)

Hsing, Mo-huan *See* POWER, JOHN H.
   The Philippines

HSUEH, SHOU SHENG. Public administra-
   tion in South and Southeast Asia.
   Brussels, International Institute of
   Administrative Sciences, 1962.
      PA 37 (1964) 465-6. (F. W. Riggs)

HTIN AUNG. Burmese law tales, the
   legal element in Burmese folklore.
   London, Oxford UP, 1962.
      JAS 22 (1962-3) 228-9. (G. R. Moran
      and R. E. Knowlton)
      PA 36 (1963) 451-2. (H. Tinker)

HTIN AUNG. Burmese monk's tales. New
   York, Columbia UP, 1966.
      JAS 26 (1966-7) 127-8. (F. M.
      LeBar)
      JAS 27 (1966-7) 225. (D. G. E.
      Hall)
      SOAS 30 (1967) 767. (H. L. Shorto)

Htin Aung *See* NANDADHAJA, SHIN.
   Epistles written on the eve of the
   Anglo-Burmese war

HTIN AUNG. Folk elements in Burmese
   Buddhism. London, Oxford UP, 1962.
      JAS 22 (1962-3) 497-8. (C. Hobbs)
      SOAS 27 (1964) 237. (H. L. Shorto)

HTIN AUNG. History of Burma. New
   York, Columbia UP, 1967.
      JAS 27 (1967-8) 909-910. (D. G. E.
      Hall)
      RSA (1968) 128-9. (I. Jadoul)
      SOAS 31 (1968) 679. (H. Tinker)

HTIN AUNG. Stricken peacock, Anglo-
   Burmese relations, 1752-1948. The
   Hague, Nijhoff, 1965.
      JAS 25 (1965-6) 544-5. (J. F.
      Guyot)
      JSAH 7 (Mar. 1966) 131-2. (D. G. E.
      Hall)
      PA 38 (1965) 430-432. (B. R. Pearn)

HUDSON, ALFRED B. Padju Epat, the
   Ma'anyan of Indonesian Borneo. New
   York, Holt, Rinehart and Winston,
   1972. (Case studies in cultural
   anthropology)
      JAS 32 (1972-3) 752-3. (C.
      Cunningham)
      MAS 8 (1974) 559-560. (J. A.
      Barnes)

Hunt, Frazier.   Untold story of Douglas

HUFANA, ALEJANDRINO G.   Poro Point; an
anthology of lives (poems, 1955–
1960).   Quezon City, Univ. of the
Philippines, 1961.
   PS 10 (1962) 159–163. (Sister
      Marie-Laurentina)

Huff, W. G.   *See* FENICHEL, ALLAN H.
Impact of colonialism on Burmese
economic development

HUFFMAN, FRANKLIN E.   Cambodian system
of writing and beginning reader,
with drills and glossary.   New Haven,
Yale UP, 1970.
   JAS 30 (1970–1) 732–3. (P. N.
      Jenner)
   SOAS 34 (1971) 649–650. (S. Lewitz)

HUFFMAN, FRANKLIN E.   Intermediate
Cambodian reader.   New Haven, Yale
UP, 1972.   (Yale linguistic series)
   JAS 32 (1972–3) 563–4. (J. M.
      Jacob)
   SOAS 37 (1974) 754.

HUFFMAN, FRANKLIN E.   Modern spoken
Cambodian.   New Haven, Yale UP, 1970.
   JAS 30 (1970–1) 730–732. (P. N.
      Jenner)

Hughes, Colin A.   *See* NICOLSON, I. F.
Pacific politics

HUGHES, HELEN.   Foreign investment and
industrialization in Singapore, by
Helen Hughes and You Poh Seng.   Madi-
son, Univ. of Wisconsin Pr., 1969.
   MER 15 pt. 1 (1970) 128–130. (T. R.
      McHale)
   PA 43 (1970) 315–6. (Tae Yul Nam)
   SA 2 (1972) 488–502. (V. D. Ooms)

HUGHES, JOHN.   Indonesian upheaval.
New York, McKay, 1967.
   AS 8 (1968) 347.
   PA 41 (1968) 111–2. (R. K. Paget)
   PA 41 (1968) 610–613. (B. B.
      Hering)
   SJ 16 (1969) 330–332. (P. G.
      Gowing)

HUKE, ROBERT E.   Shadows on the land;
an economic geography of the Philip-
pines.   Manila, Bookmark, 1963.
   JAS 23 (1963–4) 631–2. (L. Casper)
   PA 38 (1965) 89. (J. E. Spencer)
   PS 12 (1964) 374–376. (M. McPhelen)

* Human factors in Philippine rural development.   n.p., n.d. (Xavier Univ.
studies, no. 1)
   PS 16 (1968) 408–9. (J. Gill)

HUMAN RELATIONS AREA FILES, INC.   Laos,
its people, its society, its culture.
Editors: Frank M. LeBar and Adrienne
Suddard.   New Haven, Human Relations
Area Files, 1960.
   BEF 51 (1963) 208–215. (P.–B.
      Lafont)
   PA 35 (1962) 195–6. (E. A. Blais)
   SEIB 36 (1961) 744.
   SEIB 37 (1962) 469. (P. B. Lafont)

HUMBERTCLAUDE, PIERRE.   Un Japonais
martyr a Java en 1579, a propos d'une
lettre inconnue des missions.   Paris,
Imprimerie de Union, 1968.
   BEF 58 (1971) 320–1. (D. Lombard)

HUNT, CHESTER L.   Social aspects of
economic development.   New York,
McGraw-Hill, 1966.
   UN 39 (1966) 644–5. (A. P. Bulos)

Hunt, Chester L.   *See* ESPIRITU,
SOCORRO C.   Social foundations of
community development

HUNT, CHESTER L.   Sociology in the
Philippine setting. Rev. ed.   Quezon
City, Phoenix Publishing House, 1963.
   JAS 24 (1964–5) 172–3. (J. N.
      Anderson)
   PA 37 (1964) 475. (R. S. Milne)

HUNT, FRAZIER.   Untold story of Douglas
MacArthur.   New York, New American
Library, 1964.
   SLQ 3 (1965) 511. (T. L. Modelo)

Hunter, Guy. Modernizing peasant

International Bank for Reconstruction

JAS 21 (1961-2) 407-8. (D. K.
Dohanian)
PA 35 (1962) 197-8. (R. J.
Coughlin)

INDIANA. UNIV. INSTITUTE OF TRAINING
FOR PUBLIC SERVICE. Problems of
politics and administration in Thai-
land, edited by Joseph Lee Sutton.
Bloomington, 1962.
JAS 23 (1963-4) 140-1. (F. C.
Darling)

Indochina in conflict; a political assessment. Edited by Joseph J. Zasloff and Allan E. Goodman. Lexington, Mass., Heath, 1972.
JAS 32 (1972-3) 219-220. (J. Race)
PA 46 (1973) 345-6. (D. J.
Duncanson)

INDONESIA. CONSTITUTION, 1950. Pro-
visional constitution of the Repub-
lic of Indonesia, with annotations
and explanations on each article by
Raden Supomo. Ithaca, Southeast
Asia Program, Cornell Univ., 1964.
(Cornell Univ. Modern Indonesia
Project. Translation series)
JSAH 6 (Sept. 1965) 163-4. (J. M.
Pluvier)

Indonesia, resources and their techno-
logical development, edited by
Howard W. Beers. Lexington, Univ.
of Kentucky Pr., 1970.
JAS 31 (1971-2) 457-8. (J. D.
Clarkson)

Indonesian economics, the concept of
dualism in theory and policy. The
Hague, W. van Hoeve, 1961. (Selected
studies on Indonesia by Dutch schol-
ars, vol. 6)
BIJ 119 (1963) 426-429. (J. J.
Hanrath)
JAS 22 (1962-3) 338-9. (J.
Ahrensdorf)
PA 36 (1963) 283-289. (L. H.
Palmier)
PS 10 (1962) 717-720. (M. McPhelin)

RSA (1965) 111-113. (The Siauw Gap)
SOAS 25 (1962) 641-2. (J. A. M.
Caldwell)

INGER, ROBERT F. Fresh water fishes of
North Borneo, by Robert F. Inger and
Chin Phui Kong. Chicago, Field Muse-
um, 1962. (Chicago. Natural History
Museum. Fieldiana: zoology, v. 45)
SMJ 11 (1964) 603-4. (I. Tomiyama)

INGERSOLL, JOSHENA M. Golden years in
the Philippines. Palo Alto, Pacific
Books, 1971.
PA 45 (1972) 463-4. (C. O. Houston)

INGRAM, JAMES C. Economic change in
Thailand, 1850-1970. 2d. ed. Stan-
ford, Stanford UP, 1971.
AF 4 pt. 4 (1972) 62. (S. Oren)
JAH 6 (1972) 152-155. (G. W.
Wilson)
JAS 31 (1971-2) 728-730. (J. A.
Hafner)
MAS 8 (1974) 276-7. (R. C. Y. Ng)
PA 45 (1972) 480. (T. H. Silcock)

Inoki, Masamichi *See* Japan's future
in Southeast Asia

INSOR, D. Thailand, a political, soci-
al and economic analysis. New York,
Praeger, 1963.
PA 37 (1964) 345. (D. A. Wilson)

INSTITUT BOUDDHIQUE. COMMISSION DES
MOEURS ET COUTUMES DU CAMBODGE.
Ceremonies privees des Cambodgiens.
Edited by Eveline Poree-Maspero.
Phnom Penh, Editions de l'Institut
Bouddhique, 1958.
BEF 50 (1960) 222-3. (B. P.
Groslier)

Institute of Asian Economic Affairs
See AJIA KEIZAI KENKYUJO, TOKYO

INTERNATIONAL BANK FOR RECONSTRUCTION
AND DEVELOPMENT. Public development
program for Thailand; report of a
mission organized by the Internation-

International Bank for Reconstruction

al Bank for Reconstruction and Development at the request of the Government of Thailand. Baltimore,
Johns Hopkins Pr., 1959.
    PA 33 (1960) 199-200. (F. Benham)

INTERNATIONAL CONFERENCE OF SOUTH-EAST
ASIAN HISTORIANS. 1ST, SINGAPORE,
1961. Papers on Malayan history,
edited by K. G. Tregonning. Singapore, Journal of Southeast Asian
History, 1962.
    JSAH 3 (Sept. 1962) 177-179. (W.
    D. McIntyre)

INTERNATIONAL CONFERENCE ON INDUSTRIAL
RELATIONS, 2ND, TOKYO, 1967. Labour
relations in Asian countries; pro-
ceedings of the Second International
Conference on Industrial Relations,
Tokyo, Japan, 1967. Tokyo, Japan
Institute of Labor, 1967.
    PA 41 (1968) 264-5. (S. B. Levine)

INTERNATIONAL CONFERENCE SEMINAR OF
TAMIL STUDIES, 1ST, UNIV. OF MALAYA,
1966. Proceedings. Kuala Lumpur,
International Association of Tamil
Research, 1968.
    JAS 28 (1968-9) 425-6. (S.
    Vaidyanathan)
    JSAH 10 (1969) 358-360. (H. Owen)
    SOAS 33 (1970) 695. (J. R. Marr)

INTERNATIONAL CONGRESS ON RIZAL, 1ST,
MANILA, 1961. Proceedings of the
International Congress on Rizal,
December 4-8, 1961. Manila, Jose
Rizal National Centennial Commission,
1962. (Jose Rizal National Centen-
nial Commission. Publications, v. 12)
    JSAH 6 (Mar. 1965) 133-135. (C. O.
    Resurreccion)

International Cooperative Alliance
    See SEMINAR ON COOPERATIVE LEADER-
SHIP IN SOUTH-EAST ASIA, DELHI, 1960.
Cooperative leadership in Southeast
Asia

International Cooperative Alliance
    See REGIONAL CONFERENCE ON THE ROLE
OF COOPERATION IN SOCIAL AND ECONOMIC
DEVELOPMENT. Proceedings of regional
conference

IONOVA, ALLA IVANOVNA. Musulmanskii
natsionalizm v sovremennoi Indonezii,
1945-1965. Moscow, Nauka, 1972.
    AAS 10 (1974) 205-207. (S. Fatura)

Irikura, James K. *See* BENDA, HARRY
JINDRICH. Japanese military administration in Indonesia

IRWIN, GRAHAM. Nineteenth century
Borneo, a study in diplomatic rivalry. Singapore, Donald Moore, 1965.
    JSAH 7 (Mar. 1966) 142-144. (L. R.
    Wright)

* ISHII, YONEO. Glossary index of the
Sukhothai inscriptions, by Yoneo
Ishii, Osamu Akagi and Noriko Endo.
Kyoto, Center for Southeast Asian
Studies, Kyoto Univ., 1972.
    JSS 62 pt. 1 (1974) 256-258. (M.
    Vickery)

* ISHII, YONEO. Selected Thai bibliography on the reign of King Chulalongkorn, by Yoneo Ishii, Toshiharu
Yoshikawa and Osamu Akagi. Osaka,
Osaka Univ. of Foreign Studies, 1972.
    JSS 61 pt. 2 (1973) 197. (K.
    Breazeale)

ISIDRO Y SANTOS, ANTONIO. Moro prob-
lem; an approach through education.
Marawi City, Univ. Research Center,
Mindanao State Univ., 1968.
    JAS 30 (1970-1) 241-2. (M. Mednick)
    SJ 17 (1970) 350-353. (L. Q. Lacar)

ISIDRO Y SANTOS, ANTONIO. Muslim-
Christian integration at the Mindanao
State University. Marawi City, Univ.
Research Center, Mindanao State Univ.,
1968.
    JAS 30 (1970-1) 241-2. (M. Mednick)

ISIDRO Y SANTOS, ANTONIO. Muslim
  Philippines, by Antonio Isidro and
  Mamitua Saber. Marawi City, Univ.
  Research Center, Mindanao State
  Univ., 1968.
    JAS 30 (1970-1) 241-2. (M. Mednick)

ISKANDAR, TEUKU. Kamus dewan. Kuala
  Lumpur, Dewan Bahasa dan Pustaka,
  1970.
    AR 3 (1972) 212-220. (P. Labrousse)
    BMJ 2 pt. 3 (1971) 177-190. (Asmah
    Haji Omar)

Islam and the trade of Asia, a colloquium, edited by D. S. Richards.
  Oxford, Bruno Cassirer, 1971. (Papers on Islamic history, 2)
    JAS 31 (1971-2) 383-4. (M. N.
    Pearson)
    PA 44 (1971) 598-9. (R. J. Young)
    SOAS 35 (1972) 367-370. (D.
    Latham)

ISOART, PAUL. Le phenomene national
  vietnamien, de independence unitaire
  a l'independance fractionnee. Paris,
  Librairie Generale de Droit et de
  Jurisprudence, 1961. (Bibliotheque
  de droit international, t. 15)
    SEIB 41 (1966) 88.

IYER, RAGHAVAN NARASIMHAN. Glass cur-
  tain between Asia and Europe; a symposium on the historical encounters
  and the changing attitudes of the
  peoples of the East and West. London, Oxford UP, 1965.
    JAS 25 (1965-6) 739-741. (K. G.
    Tregonning)

JACKSON, JAMES C. Chinese in the west
  Borneo goldfields, a study in cultural geography. Hull, Univ. of
  Hull, 1970. (Univ. of Hull. Occasional papers in geography, no. 15)
    JSAS 2 (1971) 251-2. (Lee Yong
    Leng)
    PA 44 (1971) 648-650. (W. E.
    Willmott)

JACKSON, JAMES C. Planters and specu-
  lators: Chinese and European agricultural enterprise in Malaya 1786-
  1921. Kuala Lumpur, Univ. of Malaya
  Pr., 1968.
    JSAH 10 (1969) 367-369. (P.
    Wheatley)
    PA 42 (1969) 536-7. (B. F. Beers)
    SOAS 33 (1970) 433-4. (P. I. Ayre)

JACKSON, JAMES C. Sarawak, a geographical survey of a developing state.
  London, Univ. of London Pr., 1968.
    JSAS 2 (1971) 252-3. (R. D. Hill)
    MAS 3 (1969) 280-1. (R. Ng)

JACKSON, ROBERT NICHOLAS. Immigrant
  labour and the development of Malaya,
  1786-1920. Kuala Lumpur, GPO, 1961.
    JSAH 3 (Mar. 1962) 156-7. (W. L.
    Blythe)
    MER 8 pt. 1 (1963) 125. (T. H.
    Silcock)

JACKSON, ROBERT NICHOLAS. Pickering,
  protector of Chinese. Kuala Lumpur,
  Oxford UP, 1965.
    JAS 26 (1966-7) 533-535. (D. G. E.
    Hall)
    JSAH 8 (1967) 343-345. (E. Thio)
    PA 39 (1966) 219-220. (L. E.
    Williams)
    SOAS 29 (1966) 651-2. (M. Freedman)

Jacob, Judith M. *See* SHORTO, H. L.
  Bibliographies of Mon-Khmer and Tai
  linguistics

JACOB, JUDITH M. Introduction to Cambodian. London, Oxford UP, 1968.
    JAS 28 (1968-9) 651-2. (F. E.
    Huffman)
    SOAS 32 (1969) 652-654. (S. Lewitz)

JACOBS, HANS. Indisch A.B.C., door
  Hans Jacobs [and] Jan Roelands. Amsterdam, De Arbeiderspers, 1970.
    JAS 32 (1972-3) 568-570. (W. H.
    Frederick)

Jacobs, Hubert Th. Th. M. Treatise on

Jacobs, Hubert Th. Th. M. *See*
Treatise on the Moluccas

JACOBS, NORMAN. Modernization without
development, Thailand as an Asian
case study. New York, Praeger, 1971.
JAH 6 (1972) 152-155. (G. W.
Wilson)
JCA 4 (1974) 209-217. (P. F. Bell
and Boonsanong Punyodyasa)
JSS 61 pt. 1 (1973) 327-331.
(Saneh Chamarik)
PA 45 (1972) 144-5. (A. Y.
Dessaint)
SA 2 (1972) 514-517. (H. B. Smith)

Jacobs, Pepita Jimenez *See* GUTHRIE,
GEORGE M. Child rearing in the
Philippines

JACOBY, ERICH H. Agrarian unrest in
Southeast Asia. 2d. ed. Bombay,
Asia Publishing House, 1961.
JSAH 3 (Sept. 1962) 180-182. (Ooi
Jin Bee)
PA 35 (1962) 83-4. (R. A.
Hackenberg)
RSA (1964) 184-5. (K. C. Sen)

* JACOTOT, HENRI. Le docteur Alexandre
Yersin, esquisse de ce quil fut et
de ce qu'il fit. Saigon, Imprimerie
Nouvelle d'Extreme-Orient, 1960.
SEIB 36 (1961) 736.

JACQUOT, JEAN. Les theatres d'Asie;
etudes de Jeannine Auboyer, et al.
Paris, Editions du Centre National
de la Recherche Scientifique, 1961.
FA 19 (1963) 1003. (J. Christan)
RSA (1965) 131-2. (L. Rocher)
SOAS 26 (1963) 237.

JAGOR, FEDOR. Travels in the Philip-
pines. Manila, Filipiniana Book
Guild, 1965. (Filipiniana Book
Guild. Publications, 9)
JAS 28 (1968-9) 194-196. (J. A.
Larkin)

JAIN, RAVINDRA K. South Indians on the
plantation frontier in Malaya. New
Haven, Yale UP, 1970.
JAS 31 (1971-2) 225-6. (C.
Jayawardena)

Jakobson, Leo *See* Urbanization and
national development

* JAMARIS, EDWARD. Singkatan naskah
sastra Indonesia lama pengaruh Islam.
Jakarta, L.B.N., 1973.
AR 8 (1974) 226.

JAN, GEORGE P. International politics
of Asia. Belmont, California, Wadsworth Publishing Company, 1969.
PA 43 (1970) 579. (A. B. Cole)

Janeway, Michael *See* MANNING, ROBERT.
Who we are

Jans, H. *See* Volkenkundige encyclopedie

JANSE, OLOV ROBERT THURE. Archaeological research in Indo-China. La
civilisation de Dong-Son. n.p., n.d.
SEIB 35 (1960) 713-715. (L.
Malleret)

JANSEN, G. H. Afro-Asia and non-alignment. London, Faber, 1966.
JSAH 8 (1967) 347-8. (M. Leifer)

JANSEN, G. H. Non-alignment and the
Afro-Asian states. New York, Praeger
1966.
JAH 5 (1971) 147-8. (S. P. Cohen)

Japan's future in Southeast Asia.
Kyoto, Center for Southeast Asian
Studies, Kyoto Univ., 1966. (Kyoto
Daigaku. Tonan Ajia Kenkyu Senta.
Symposium series, 2)
AS 7 (1967) 212.

JASPAN, M. A. Folk literature of south
Sumatra, Redjang Ka-Ga-Nga texts.
Canberra, Australian National Univ.,
1964.

Jit Kasem Sibunruang.   Contes et

AAS 2 (1966) 165. (G. Altmann)
BIJ 124 (1968) 303-4. (P.
  Voorhoeve)
JSAH 6 (Sept. 1965) 164-166. (T.
  Harrisson)
SOAS 29 (1966) 458-9. (E. C. G.
  Barrett)

JASPAN, M. A.   Traditional medical
theory in South-East Asia.   Hull,
Univ. of Hull, 1969.
  BIJ 127 (1971) 401-403. (T. J.
    Gerold-Scheepers)

JASPERS, REINER.   Die missionarische
Erschliessung Ozeaniens: ein quel-
lengeschichtlicher und missiongeo-
graphischer Versuch zur kirchlichen
Gebietsaufteilung in Ozeanien bis
1855. Munster, Aschendorff, 1972.
(Missionswissenschaftliche Abhandlungen und Texte, 30)
  PS 21 (1973) 395-6. (J. N.
    Schumacher)

JASSIN, H. B.   Amir Hamzah radja Pen-
jair pudjangga baru. Djakarta,
Gunung Agung, 1962.
  BIJ 119 (1963) 471-2. (A. Teeuw)

JASSIN, H. B.   Chairil Anwar, pelopor
Angkatan 45. Disertai kumpulan hasil-
hasil tulisannja. Tjet. 2. Djakarta,
Gunung Agung, 1959.
  BIJ 117 (1961) 398-9. (A. Teeuw)

JAY, ROBERT R.   Javanese villagers;
social relations in rural Modjokuto.
Cambridge, MIT Pr., 1969.
  MAS 6 (1972) 120-123. (C. S.
    Kessler)

JAY, ROBERT R.   Religion and politics
in rural central Java. New Haven,
Yale Univ., Southeast Asia Studies,
1963. (Yale Univ. Graduate School.
Southeast Asia Studies. Cultural re-
port series, no. 12)
  BIJ 121 (1965) 173-179. (J. Prins)
  JSAH 5 (Sept. 1964) 214-5. (D.
    Hindley)

Jayawickrama, N. A. *See* VACISSARA
  THERA.   Chronicle of the Thupa

JEANNENEY, JEAN NOEL.   Le riz et le
rouge, cinq mois en Extreme-Orient.
Paris, Seuil, 1969.
  FA 23 (1969) 113-4.

JEFFRIES, CHARLES JOSEPH.   Whitehall
and the colonial service, an adminis-
trative memoir, 1939-1956. London,
Athlone Pr., 1972. (London Univ.
Institute of Commonwealth Studies.
Commonwealth papers, 15)
  JSAS 5 (1974) 134-136. (C. M.
    Turnbull)

JENNER, PHILIP N.   Southeast Asian
literatures in translation, a pre-
liminary bibliography. Honolulu,
Univ. Pr. of Hawaii, 1973. (Asian
Studies at Hawaii)
  AF 5 pt. 4 (1973) 79-80. (A. W.
    Fergusun)
  SEIB 49 (1974) 349-353. (M. Piat,
    E. Guillon and P. Langlet)

Jenson, George Alexander *See* LENSON,
GEORGE ALEXANDER

JEROMIN, ULRICH.   Die Uberseechinesen.
Ihre Bedeutung fur die wirtschaft-
liche Entwicklung Sudostasiens.
Stuttgart, Gustav Fischer, 1966.
(Hamburg. Universitat. Institut fur
Aussenhandel und Uberseewirtschaft.
Okonomische Studien, Bd. 12)
  PA 39 (1966) 405-6. (J. M. van der
    Kroef)

* Jesuite unmasked, being third in the
  series of extracts from the private
  book collection of M. L. Manich Jumsai. Bangkok, 1969.
    JSS 59 pt. 1 (1971) 270-1. (P. W.
      O'Brien)

JIT KASEM SIBUNRUANG.   Contes et leg-
endes de Thailande. Bangkok, Viparts,
1969.
  JSS 58 pt. 1 (1970) 145-6. (M.
    Smithies)

Joaquin, Nick. The woman who had two

Jose, Francisco Sionil. Pretenders

East, proceedings. Calcutta, UNESCO
Research Centre on the Social Impli-
cations of Industrialization in
Southern Asia, 1957.
  JAS 19 (1959-60) 446-7. (R.
    Murphey)

JOINT UNESCO-IAU RESEARCH PROGRAMME IN
HIGHER EDUCATION. Higher education
and development in South-East Asia;
summary report and conclusions.
Paris, 1965-67. 2v.
Volume I.
  PA 40 (1967) 168-170. (J. Fischer)
Volume II.
  PA 42 (1969) 97-8. (J. Fischer)

JONES, A. M. Africa and Indonesia;
  the evidence of the xylophone and
  other musical and cultural factors.
  Leiden, Brill, 1964.
    AAS 2 (1966) 202-204. (I. Macak)

JONES, DELMOS JEHU. Cultural variation among six Lahu villages, northern Thailand. Ithaca, Cornell Univ.,
  PhD dissertation, 1967.
    JSS 56 (1968) 295-297. (H. J.
      Spielmann)

JONES, HOWARD PALFREY. Indonesia, the
  possible dream. New York, Harcourt
  Brace Jovanovich, 1971. (Stanford
  Univ. Hoover Institution on War,
  Revolution, and Peace. Publications,
  102)
    JAS 33 (1973-4) 159-160. (G. G. van
      Beers)
    PA 45 (1972) 310-1. (J. D. Legge)

JONES, L. W. Population of Borneo, a
  study of the peoples of Sarawak, Sabah and Brunei. London, Athlone
  Pr., 1966.
    JAS 27 (1967-8) 182-3. (G. W.
      Jones)
    SMJ 15 (1967) 437-439. (J. Rawlins)

JONES, ROBERT B. Karen linguistic
  studies: description, comparison
  and texts. Berkeley, Univ. of Cali-

fornia Pr., 1961. (California. Univ.
Univ. of California publications in
linguistics, v. 25)
  JAS 22 (1962-3) 120-1. (T. Stern)
  SOAS 27 (1964) 662-665. (E. J. A.
    Henderson)

JONES, ROBERT B. Thai titles and
ranks; including a translation of
Traditions of royal lineage in Siam
by King Chulalongkorn. Ithaca,
Southeast Asia Program, Cornell Univ.,
1971. (Cornell Univ. Southeast Asia
Program. Data paper, no. 81)
  JAS 32 (1972-3) 374-376. (A. G.
    Epstein)
  JSS 62 pt. 1 (1974) 158-173. (M.
    Vickery)
  MAS 8 (1974) 275-6. (J. H. Kemp)
  PS 20 (1972) 200.

JONGE, BONIFACIUS CORNELIS DE. Herin-
neringen van Jhr. Mr. B. C. de Jonge.
Uitg. door S. L. van der Wal.
Groningen, Wolters-Noordhoff, 1968.
  PA 42 (1969) 537-540. (B. B.
    Hering)
  PA 43 (1970) 317-319. (P. W. van
    der Veur)

JONGMANS, D. G. Anthropologists in the
field, edited by D. G. Jongmans and
Peter Claus Wolfgang Gutkind. Assen,
Van Gorcum, 1967. (Samenlevingen
buiten Europa, 6)
  BIJ 122 (1966) 144-146. (J.
    Beattie)

JORDAN, AMOS A. Foreign aid and the
defense of Southeast Asia. New York,
Praeger, 1962.
  JAS 22 (1962-3) 492. (W. Henderson)
  RSA (1964) 270-1. (I. Jadoul)

Jose, F. Sionil *See* Asian PEN anthology

JOSE, FRANCISCO SIONIL. Pretenders.
Manila, Solidaridad, 1962.
  PS 14 (1966) 653-665. (M. A.
    Bernad)

Jose Rizal on his centenary, being an

Jose Rizal on his centenary, being an
attempt at a reevaluation of his significance by professors of the Univ.
of the Philippines, edited by Leopoldo Y. Yabes. Quezon City, Office
of Research Coordination, Univ. of
the Philippines, 1963.
   PA 39 (1966) 244. (R. S. Milne)

JOSEY, ALEX. Lee Kuan Yew. Singapore,
Donald Moore Pr., 1968.
   JAS 29 (1969-70) 737-8. (J. A.
      Hafner)
   PA 42 (1969) 390. (R. S. Milne)

JOSEY, ALEX. Lee Kuan Yew. 2d. ed.
Singapore, Donald Moore Pr., 1971.
   JAS 32 (1972-3) 216-7. (M. Osborne)
   PA 45 (1972) 479. (R. S. Milne)

JOSEY, ALEX. Lee Kuan Yew and the
Commonwealth. Singapore, Donald
Moore Pr., 1969.
   JAS 29 (1969-70) 737-8. (W. Levy)
   PA 43 (1970) 343-4. (R. S. Milne)

JUDD, LAURENCE C. Dry rice agricul-
ture in northern Thailand. Ithaca,
Southeast Asia Program, Cornell Univ.,
1964. (Cornell Univ. Southeast Asia
Program. Data paper, no. 52)
   BIJ 123 (1967) 178-9. (P. E. de
      Josselin de Jong)

JUMPER, ROY. Bibliography on the political and administrative history
of Viet Nam, 1802-1962. Saigon,
Michigan State Univ., Vietnam Advisory Group, 1962.
   JAS 22 (1962-3) 341-2. (M. L.
      Thomas)

JUMPER, ROY. Notes on the political
and administrative history of Vietnam, 1802-1962, by Roy Jumper and
Nguyen The Hue. Saigon, Michigan
State Univ., Vietnam Advisory Group,
1962.
   JAS 22 (1962-3) 341-2. (M. L.
      Thomas)

JUNUS, UMAR. Perkembangan puisi Melayu
moden. Kuala Lumpur, Dewan Bahasa
dan Pustaka, 1970.
   BIJ 127 (1971) 289-293. (H.
      Aveling)

JUPPENLATZ, MORRIS. Cities in transformation, the urban squatter problem
of the developing world. St. Lucia,
Univ. of Queensland Pr., 1970.
   JSAS 3 (1972) 167-8. (A. F. C.
      Choe)

KÄHLER, HANS. Ethnographische und lin-
guistische Studien uber die Orang
Darat, Orang Akit, Orang Laut und
Orang Utan im Riau-Archipel und auf
den Inseln an der Ostkuste von Suma-
tra. Berlin, Dietrich Reimer, 1960.
(Hamburg. Universitat. Seminar fur
indonesische und Sudseesprachen.
Veroffentlichungen, Bd. 2)
   BIJ 117 (1961) 297-300. (A. Teeuw)
   SOAS 24 (1961) 401-2. (C. Hooykaas)

KÄHLER, HANS. Grammatik der Bahasa
Indonesia, mit Chrestomathie und
Worterverzeichnis. Wiesbaden, Har-
rassowitz, 1956. (Porta linguarum
Orientalium, neue Ser., 2)
   BIJ 118 (1962) 282-285. (J.
      Noorduyn)

KÄHLER, HANS. Simalur-deutsches
Worterbuch mit deutsch-simaluresisch-
em Worterverzeichnis. Berlin, Dietrich Reimer, 1961. (Hamburg. Universitat. Seminar fur indonesische
und Sudseesprachen. Veroffentlichung-
en, Bd. 3)
   SOAS 25 (1962) 421-2. (C. Hooykaas)

KÄHLER, HANS. Texte von der Insel Sima-
lur. Berlin, Dietrich Reimer, 1963.
(Hamburg. Universitat. Seminar fur
indonesische und Sudseesprachen
Veroffentlichungen, Bd. 4)
   SOAS 27 (1964) 661. (C. Hooykaas)

Kartini, Raden Adjeng. Letters of a

KÄHLER, HANS. Vergleichen des Worterverzeichnis der Sichule-Sprache auf
der Insel Simalur an der Westkuste
von Sumatra. Berlin, Dietrich
Reimer, 1959. (Hamburg. Universitat.
Seminar fur indonesische und Sudseesprachen Veroffentlichungen, Bd. 1)
 SOAS 23 (1960) 431.

KÄHLER, HANS. Worterverzeichnis des
Omong Djakarta. Berlin, Dietrich
Reimer, 1966. (Hamburg. Universitat.
Seminar fur indonesische und Sudsee-
sprachen Veroffentlichungen, Bd. 5)
 BIJ 122 (1966) 480-483. (A. Teeuw)
 SOAS 30 (1967) 224-5. (C. Hooykaas)

KAHIN, GEORGE McTURNAN. Governments
and politics of Southeast Asia.
Ithaca, Cornell UP, 1959.
 JAS 19 (1959-60) 223-4. (R.
 Butwell)

KAHIN, GEORGE McTURNAN. Governments
and politics of Southeast Asia. 2d.
ed. Ithaca, Cornell UP, 1964.
 JSAH 6 (Sept. 1965) 136-138. (R.
 S. Milne)
 SOAS 28 (1965) 461-2. (H. Tinker)

KAHIN, GEORGE McTURNAN. Major gov-
ernments of Asia. 2d. ed. Ithaca,
Cornell UP, 1963.
 JAS 23 (1963-4) 458-9. (J. M. Maki)
 JSAH 6 (Mar. 1966) 142-144. (P. J.
 Boyce)

KAHIN, GEORGE McTURNAN. United States
in Vietnam, by George M. Kahin and
John W. Lewis. New York, Dial, 1967.
 FA 23 (1969) 231-235. (P.
 Devillers)
 JAS 28 (1968-9) 821-831. (J. C.
 Donnell)

KAHIN, GEORGE McTURNAN. United States
in Vietnam, by George M. Kahin and
John W. Lewis. Rev. ed. New York,
Dial Pr., 1969.
 JSAS 1 pt. 2 (1970) 133-4. (R. H.
 Haas)

KALB, MARVIN L. Roots of involvement,
the U.S. in Asia, 1784-1971, by Mar-
vin L. Kalb and Elie Abel. New York,
Norton, 1971.
 PA 44 (1971) 599-601. (F. H.
 Soward)

* KAMOL SOMVICHIAN. Pattana gammuang
Thai. Bangkok, Faculty of Political
Science, Chulalongkorn Univ., 1970.
 JSS 60 pt. 1 (1972) 431-433. (Astri
 Suhrke)

KAMPAR, 9TH CENTURY. Sri Paduka, the
exile of the prince of Ayodhya.
Athens, Ohio, Center for International Studies, Ohio Univ., 1969. (Papers in international studies. Southeast Asia series, no. 7)
 JAS 29 (1969-70) 506-7. (S.
 Vaidyanathan)

KANA SERA. Kana Sera, zang der
zwangerschap. Door Donatus P. Dun-
selman. The Hague, Nijhoff, 1955.
(Instituut voor Taal-, Land- en
Volkenkunde. Verhandelingen, deel 17)
 JMBRAS 33 pt. 1 (1960) 120-122. (J.
 Keuning)

KANAPATHY, V. Malaysian economy, prob-
lems and prospects. Singapore,
Donald Moore, 1970.
 JAS 32 (1972-3) 746. (G. D. Ness)

KAPLAN, MORTON A. Revolution in world
politics. New York, Wiley, 1962.
 PA 36 (1963) 463-4. (K. J. Holsti)

Kaplan, Morton A. *See* Vietnam settlement

KARNOW, STANLEY. Southeast Asia. New
York, Time Inc., 1962.
 PA 36 (1963) 195-6. (H. W. Robin-
 son)

KARTINI, RADEN ADJENG. Letters of a
Javanese princess. New York, Norton,
1964. (UNESCO Collection of representative works: Indonesian series)

Kartini, Raden Adjeng. Letters of a

JAS 24 (1964-5) 530-1. (R. Van Niel)

KARTODIRDJO, SARTONO. Peasant's revolt of Banten in 1888. Its conditions, course and sequel. The Hague, Nijhoff, 1966. (Instituut voor Taal-, Land- en Volkenkunde. Verhandelingen, deel 50)
JSAH 9 (1968) 163-4. (R. Van Niel)
PA 41 (1968) 114-5. (J. M. van der Kroef)
SOAS 31 (1968) 428-9. (E. J. Hobsbawm)

KARTODIRDJO, SARTONO. Protest movements in rural Java; a study of agrarian unrest in the nineteenth and early twentieth centuries. Singapore, Oxford UP, 1973.
AR 8 (1974) 227-229. (D. Lombard)

KAUFMAN, HOWARD KEVA. Bangkhuad: a community in Thailand. Locust Valley, Augustin, 1960. (Association for Asian Studies. Monographs, 10)
JAS 20 (1960-1) 119-120. (H. P. Phillips)
PA 34 (1961) 213. (R. Firth)

KAYE, BARRINGTON. Upper Nankin Street Singapore, a sociological study of Chinese households living in a densely populated area. Singapore, Univ. of Malaya Pr., 1960.
JAS 20 (1960-1) 393-395. (M. H. Fried)
PA 34 (1961) 84-5. (G. W. Skinner)

Keakoon, Pote *See* HIGHAM, CHARLES FRANKLIN WANDESFORDE. Prehistoric investigations in northeast Thailand

KEATS, JOHN. They fought alone. Philadelphia, Lippincott, 1963.
PS 12 (1964) 378-381. (T. Daigler)

KEESING, FELIX MAXWELL. Ethnohistory of northern Luzon. Stanford, Stanford UP, 1962. (Stanford anthropological series, no. 4)
BIJ 119 (1963) 453-457. (C. H. M. Palm)
JSAH 5 (Mar. 1964) 202-205. (F. Lambrecht)
PA 36 (1963) 323-4. (R. Firth)
PS 11 (1963) 181-2. (F. C. Madigan)
PS 15 (1967) 496-7. (D. J. Scheans)
RSA (1965) 181-2. (I. Jadoul)
SLQ 2 (1964) 376-378. (F. Lambrecht)

Keesing's contemporary archives *See* South Vietnam; a political history, 1954-1970

KEETON, CHARLES LEE. King Thebaw and the ecological rape of Burma; the political and commercial struggle between British India and French Indo-China in Burma, 1878-1886. Delhi, Manohar Book Service, 1974.
PA 47 (1974) 570-572. (D. G. E. Hall)

KEGLEY, CHARLES W. Politics, religion and modern man; essays on Reinhold Niebuhr, Paul Tillich and Rudolf Bultmann. Quezon City, Univ. of the Philippines Pr., 1969.
PS 18 (1970) 791-793. (J. O'Hare)

KEMP, JEREMY. Aspects of Siamese kingship in the seventeenth century. Bangkok, Social Science Association Pr., 1969.
JSAS 3 (1972) 151-2. (W. F. Vella)
JSS 59 pt. 1 (1971) 239. (Thamsook Numnonda)

KENNEDY, DONALD EDWARD. Security of Southern Asia. New York, Praeger, 1965. (Studies in international security, 8)
JAS 25 (1965-6) 799-800. (T. Ropp)
PA 38 (1965) 396-7. (W. M. Dobell)

KENNEDY, JOSEPH. Asian nationalism in the twentieth century. London, Macmillan, 1968.
AS 8 (1968) 817.
JSAH 10 (1969) 386-7. (Zainal Abidin bin Abdul Wahid)

Kiefer, Thomas M. Tausug armed

KENNEDY, JOSEPH. History of Malaya,
  A. D. 1400-1959. London, Macmillan,
  1962.
    JSAH 4 (Mar. 1963) 115-6. (E.
    Sadka)

KENNEDY, JOSEPH. History of Malaya.
  2d. ed. New York, St. Martin's Pr.,
  1970.
    JAH 6 (1972) 94-5. (M. N. Pearson)
    JAS 30 (1970-1) 736-7. (A. Jones)

KENNEDY, RAYMOND. Bibliography of Indonesian peoples and cultures. 2d.
  rev. ed. Revised and edited by
  Thomas W. Maretzki and H. Th.
  Fischer. New Haven, Southeast Asia
  Studies, Yale Univ., 1962. (Behavior science bibliographies)
    JAS 22 (1962-3) 492-3. (C. Hobbs)

KENWORTHY, LEONARD STOUT. Leaders of
  new nations. Garden City, N.Y.,
  Doubleday, 1959.
    PA 33 (1960) 413.

KERSTIENS, THOM. New elite in Asia
  and Africa, a comparative study of
  Indonesia and Ghana. New York,
  Praeger, 1966.
    PA 41 (1968) 619-621. (J. M. van
    der Kroef)

KESAVAN, K. V. Japan's relations with
  Southeast Asia, 1952-60; with particular reference to the Philippines
  and Indonesia. Bombay, Somaiya,
  1972.
    JAS 32 (1972-3) 738-740. (M.
    Nishihara)
    PA 46 (1973) 143-4. (J. C. Lebra)

Kessle, Gun See MYRDAL, JAN. Angkor

KEYES, CHARLES F. Isan, regionalism
  in northeastern Thailand. Ithaca,
  Southeast Asia Program, Cornell
  Univ., 1967. (Cornell Univ. Southeast Asia Program. Data paper, no.
  65)

BIJ 124 (1968) 413-4. (J. W.
  Minderhout)
JSAH 9 (1968) 169-170. (D. A.
  Wilson)
PA 41 (1968) 616. (P. F. Bell)

KEYES, JANE GODFREY. Bibliography of
  North Vietnamese publications in the
  Cornell University Library. Ithaca,
  Southeast Asia Program, Cornell Univ.,
  1962. (Cornell Univ. Southeast Asia
  Program. Data paper, no. 47)
    BIJ 119 (1963) 448. (L. Sluimers)

KEYES, JANE GODFREY. Bibliography of
  western language publications concerning North Vietnam in the Cornell
  University Library. Supplement to
  Data paper, no. 47. Ithaca, Southeast Asia Program, Cornell Univ.,
  1966. (Cornell Univ. Southeast Asia
  Program. Data paper, no. 63)
    BIJ 123 (1967) 300. (L. Sluimers)

KHANTIPALO, PHRA. What is Buddhism?
  An introduction to the teachings of
  Lord Buddha with reference to the belief in and the practice of those
  teachings and their realization.
  Bangkok, Social Science Pr. of Thailand, 1965.
    JAS 25 (1965-6) 502-3. (B. Morgan)

Khin, U See HLA PE. Narrative of the
  Japanese occupation of Burma

KHOO, KAY KIM. The western Malay
  states, 1850-1873, the effects of
  commercial development on Malay politics. Kuala Lumpur, Oxford UP, 1972.
    JAS 32 (1972-3) 557-8. (C. S. Gray)
    JSAS 4 (1973) 146-7. (C. M.
    Turnbull)

KIEFER, THOMAS M. Tausug armed conflict: the social organization of
  military activity in a Philippine
  Moslem society. Chicago, Philippine
  Studies Program, Univ. of Chicago,
  1968. (Chicago. Univ. Philippine

Kraslow, David. Secret search for

(Bibliotheca Indonesica, 4)
   JSAS 3 (1972) 341-344. (A. H.
   Johns)
   SOAS 34 (1971) 186-7. (C. Hooykaas)

KLIENEBERGER, H. R. Bibliography of
   Oceanic linguistics. London, Oxford
   UP, 1957. (London Oriental bibliog-
   raphies, no. 1)
   BIJ 116 (1960) 393. (E. M.
   Uhlenbeck)

KLIMOVICH, LIUTSIAN IPPOLITOVICH.
   Islam. 2d. ed. Moscow, Izdatelstvo
   Nauka, 1965.
   AAS 3 (1967) 230-1. (V. Kopcan)

KNOEBL, KUNO. Victor Charlie, the
   face of war in Vietnam. New York,
   Praeger, 1967.
   JAS 28 (1968-9) 821-831. (J. C.
   Donnell)

Knuth, Eigil *See* THAI-DANISH PREHIS-
   TORIC EXPEDITION, 1960-62. Archaeological excavations in Thailand.

Koehler, John E. *See* AVERCH, HARVEY
   A. A crisis of ambiguity

Koehler, John E. *See* AVERCH, HARVEY
   A. The matrix of policy in the
   Philippines

KOENTJARANINGRAT. Some social-anthro-
   pological observations on gotong
   rojong practices in two villages of
   central Java. Ithaca, Southeast
   Asia Program, Cornell Univ., 1961.
   (Cornell Univ. Modern Indonesia
   Project. Monograph series)
   JAS 21 (1961-2) 413-4. (C. Geertz)

KOENTJARANINGRAT. Villages in Indone-
   sia. Ithaca, Cornell UP, 1967.
   BIJ 124 (1968) 284-5. (Umar Junus)
   JAH 3 (1969) 85-6. (C. K. Byrd)
   JMBRAS 42 pt. 2 (1969) 225-229.
   (Umar Junus)
   MAS 4 (1970) 179-181. (L. Palmier)

KOLB, ALBERT. East Asia: China, Japan,
   Korea and Vietnam: geography of a
   cultural region. London, Methuen,
   1971.
   JAS 32 (1972-3) 125-6. (B. Boxer)
   MAS 7 (1973) 280-288. (P. Wheatley)

Koninklijk Instituut voor de Tropen
   See Indonesian economics, the concept of dualism in theory and policy

KONINKLIJK INSTITUUT VOOR DE TROPEN.
   The Indonesian town, studies in urban
   sociology, by W. Brand. Amsterdam,
   1959. (Selected studies on Indonesia
   by Dutch scholars, v.4)
   JAS 19 (1959-60) 222-3. (L. H.
   Palmier)

Kooijman, S. *See* NEW YORK. MUSEUM OF
   PRIMITIVE ART. Art of Lake Sentani

KOOIJMAN, S. Ornamented bark cloth in
   Indonesia. Leiden, Brill, 1963.
   (Leyden. Rijksmuseum voor Volken-
   kunde. Mededelingen, 16)
   AP 9 (1966) 171-2. (T. Harrisson)
   BIJ 121 (1965) 378-9. (C.
   Nooteboom)

KOOP, JOHN CLEMENT. Eurasian popula-
   tion in Burma. New Haven, Yale Univ.,
   Southeast Asia Studies, 1960. (Yale
   Univ. Graduate School. Southeast Asia
   Studies. Cultural report series, no.
   6)
   JAS 20 (1960-1) 397. (R. Butwell)
   JSAH 2 (Oct. 1961) 112-114. (G. A.
   Theodorson)

Kooyman, S. *See* KOOIJMAN, S.

Kosinski, Leszek A. *See* SYMPOSIUM ON
   POPULATION PRESSURES UPON PHYSICAL
   AND SOCIAL RESOURCES IN THE DEVELOP-
   ING LANDS, PENNSYLVANIA STATE UNIV.,
   1967. Geography and a crowding
   world

KRASLOW, DAVID. Secret search for
   peace in Vietnam, by David Kraslow

* LA RAW MARAN. Burmese and Jingpho, a
study of tonal linguistic processes.
Urbana, Center for Asian Studies,
Univ. of Illinois, 1971.
    JAS 32 (1972-3) 741-743. (J. A.
    Matisoff)

LABIN, SUZANNE. Sellout in Vietnam?
Arlington, Va., Crestwood Books,
1966.
    PA 42 (1969) 423.
    [Note: First edition (1964) had ti-
    tle: Vietnam, an eyewitness account]

Labin, Suzanne. Vietnam: an eyewitness account *See* LABIN, SUZANNE.
Sellout in Vietnam?

LACH, DONALD FREDERICK. Asia in the
making of Europe. Chicago, Univ. of
Chicago Pr., 1965.
    JAS 27 (1967-8) 371-2. (G. F.
    Hudson)
    JSAH 9 (1968) 342-352. (C. Jack-
    Hinton)
    PA 39 (1966) 151-2. (R. Dawson)

LACH, DONALD FREDERICK. Asia on the
eve of Europe's expansion, edited
by Donald F. Lach and Carol Flaumenhaft. Englewood Cliffs, Prentice-
Hall, 1965.
    PA 39 (1966) 156-7. (C. R. Boxer)

LACHICA, EDUARDO. The Huks, Philippine agrarian society in revolt.
New York, Praeger, 1971.
    JAS 31 (1971-2) 743-745. (B.
    Nussbaum)
    PA 45 (1972) 582-585. (D. Wurfel)
    PS 20 (1972) 531-534. (L. Taruc)
    SA 3 (1974-5) 644-647. (E. Gibbs)

Lacouture, Jean *See* DEVILLERS,
PHILIPPE. End of a war

LACOUTURE, JEAN. La fin d'une guerre:
Indochine 1954, par Jean Lacouture
et Philippe Devillers. Paris, Editions du Seuil, 1960. (Collections
Esprit "Frontiere ouverte")

Lafont, Pierre Bernard. Prieres Jarai

    PA 34 (1961) 375-380. (F. J.
    Corley)
    SEIB 35 (1960) 716-7. (L. Pignon)

LACOUTURE, JEAN. Ho Chi Minh. Paris,
Editions du Seuil, 1967.
    PA 44 (1971) 585-590. (W. E.
    Willmott)

LACOUTURE, JEAN. Ho Chi Minh; a political biography. New York, Random
House, 1968.
    JAS 28 (1968-9) 649-651. (J. T.
    McAlister)

LACOUTURE, JEAN. Le poids du tiers-
monde: un milliard d'hommes, par
Jean Lacouture et Jean Baumier.
Paris, Arthaud, 1962.
    FA 19 (1963) 853-861. (J. Chris-
    tan)

LACOUTURE, JEAN. Vietnam: between two
truces. New York, Random House,
1966.
    PA 39 (1966) 408-410. (D. Wurfel)

LACOUTURE, JEAN. Le Viet-nam entre
deux paix. Paris, Editions du Seuil,
1965.
    FA 20 (1965) 127-129.
    RSA (1966) 276-278. (I. Jadoul)

LACOUTURE, SIMONNE. Cambodge.
Lausanne, Rencontre, 1963.
    RSA (1964) 330-1. (Nguyen Van
    Chien)

LAFONT, PIERRE BERNARD. Bibliographie
du Laos. Paris, Ecole Francaise
d'Extreme-Orient, 1964. (Ecole Francaise d'Extreme-Orient. Publications,
no. 50)
    FA 20 (1965) 133-4.
    SEIB 39 (1964) 300.

LAFONT, PIERRE BERNARD. Prieres Jarai.
Paris, Ecole Francaise d'Extreme-
Orient, 1963. (Ecole Francaise
d'Extreme-Orient. Collection de textes
et documents sur l'Indochine, 8)

Lafont, Pierre Bernard. Prieres Jarai

FA 21 (1966) 137-139. (J. Christian)

LAFONT, PIERRE BERNARD. Toloi Djuat; coutumier de la tribu Jarai. Paris, Ecole Francaise d'Extreme-Orient, 1963. (Ecole Francaise d'Extreme-Orient. Publications, no. 51)
FA 21 (1966) 137-139. (J. Christian)

Lal, Kishori Saran *See* ASIAN HISTORY CONGRESS, 1ST, DELHI, 1961. Studies in Asian history

LA LOUBERE, SIMON DE. Kingdom of Siam. Kuala Lumpur, Oxford UP, 1969. (Oxford in Asia historical reprints)
SA 2 (1972) 502-514. (K. P. Landon)

* LAM BINH LOI. Rung ngap nuoc Vietnam, [by] Lam Binh Loi [and] Nguyen Van Thon. Saigon, Vien khao-cuu nong-nghiep, 1972.
SEIB 48 (1973) 152.

LAMB, ALASTAIR. Asian frontiers; studies in a continuing problem. London, Pall Mall Pr., 1968.
AS 8 (1968) 625.
BIJ 122 (1966) 167. (H. J. de Graaf)
MAS 4 (1970) 291-297. (C. A. Fisher)
PA 42 (1969) 71-73. (H. J. Wiens)
SOAS 32 (1969) 231-2. (H. Tinker)

LAMB, ALASTAIR. British missions to Cochin China: 1778-1822. Kuala Lumpur, 1961. (Royal Asiatic Society of Great Britain and Ireland. Malayan Branch. Journal, v. 34, pts. 3-4)
JAS 22 (1962-3) 117-8. (K. G. Tregonning)
SEIB 39 (1964) 134-136. (P. Brocheux)

LAMB, ALASTAIR. Chandi Bukit Batu Pahat, a report on the excavation of an ancient temple in Kedah. Singapore, Eastern Universities Pr., 1960. (Monographs on Southeast Asian subjects, no. 1)
AP 9 (1966) 173-4. (R. Pearson)
BIJ 117 (1961) 485-490. (F. D. K. Bosch)
JAS 21 (1961-2) 95-6. (G. Coedes)
JSAH 2 (Oct. 1961) 106-110. (H. G. Quaritch Wales)
JTG 15 (1961) 97. (K. S. Sandhu)

LAMB, ALASTAIR. Chandi Bukit Batu Pahat, three additional notes. Singapore, Eastern Universities Pr., 1961. (Papers on Southeast Asian subjects, no. 5)
BIJ 117 (1961) 485-490. (F. D. K. Bosch)

LAMB, ALASTAIR. Mandarin Road to old Hue, narratives of Anglo-Vietnamese diplomacy from the seventeenth century to the eve of the French conquest. Hamden, Conn., Archon Books, 1970.
JAS 31 (1971-2) 229-231. (J. F. Cady)

LAMB, ALASTAIR. Miscellaneous papers on early Hindu and Buddhist settlement in northern Malaya and southern Thailand. Kuala Lumpur, Museums Dept., Federation of Malaya, 1961. (Federation Museums Journal, n.s. v.6)
AP 9 (1966) 172-3. (R. Pearson)
BIJ 118 (1962) 390-394. (F. D. K. Bosch)

LAMB, HELEN BOYDEN. Vietnam's will to win; resistance to foreign aggression from early times through the nineteenth century. New York, Monthly Review Pr., 1972.
JCA 3 (1973) 213-4. (M. Caldwell)

LAMBRECHT, FRANCIS. Hudhud of Dinulawan and Bugan at Gonhadan. Baguio City, St. Louis Univ., 1967. (Saint Louis Quarterly, v.5, pts. 3-4)
AP 12 (1969) 147-8. (H. T. Lewis)

LAN ONG. Thu'o'ng kinh ky su. Hanoi,
Van Hoc, 1971.
    SA 3 (1974-5) 631-635. (Nguyen
    Tran Huan)

* LAN ONG. Thu'o'ng kinh ky su. Paris,
Ecole Francaise d'Extreme-Orient,
1972.
    SEIB 48 (1973) 144-5. (Nguyen The
    Anh)

LANCASTER, DONALD. Emancipation of
French Indo-China. London, Oxford
UP, 1961.
    JAS 21 (1961-2) 98-9. (B. B. Fall)
    JSAH 4 (Sept. 1963) 189-193.
    (Truong-Buu-Lam)
    PA 34 (1961) 375-380. (F. J.
    Corley)
    SEIB 36 (1961) 736.

LANDE, CARL HERMAN. Leaders, factions
and parties; the structure of Philippine politics. New Haven, Yale
Univ., Southeast Asia Studies, 1965.
(Yale Univ. Graduate School. Southeast Asia Studies. Monograph series,
no. 6)
    JAS 25 (1965-6) 548-9. (J. Gross-
    holtz)
    JSAH 7 (Sept. 1966) 145-149. (T.
    Bellows)
    PA 38 (1965) 460-1. (R. S. Milne)
    PS 17 (1969) 605-616. (A. M.
    Geoghegan)

LANDE, CARL HERMAN. Southern Tagalog
voting, 1946-1963; political behav-
ior in a Philippine region. DeKalb,
Northern Illinois Univ., Center for
Southeast Asian Studies, 1973.
(Illinois. Northern Illinois Univ.
Center for Southeast Asian Studies.
Special report, no. 7)
    PA 47 (1974) 254-256. (R. S. Milne)

LANDON, KENNETH PERRY. Southeast Asia,
crossroads of religions. Chicago,
Univ. of Chicago Pr., 1949.
    PA 43 (1970) 121-123. (J. M. van
    der Kroef)

LANG, DAVID MARSHALL. Guide to eastern
literatures. New York, Praeger,
1971.
    JAS 31 (1971-2) 633-4. (F. Richter)
    PA 45 (1972) 481-2. (G. R. Nunn)

LANGER, PAUL FRITZ. North Vietnam and
the Pathet Lao, partners in the
struggle for Laos, by Paul F. Langer
and Joseph J. Zasloff. Cambridge,
Harvard UP, 1970.
    JAS 31 (1971-2) 232-3. (J. Badgley)
    PA 44 (1971) 311. (J. L. S.
    Girling)
    SA 2 (1972) 363-371. (J. Badgley)

LANGLOIS, WALTER G. Andre Malraux, the
Indochina adventure. London, Pall
Mall Pr., 1966.
    JAS 26 (1966-7) 130-1. (T. Ropp)
    JSAH 8 (1967) 334-5. (M. Osborne)

LANIER, LUCIEN. Etude historique sur
les relations de la France et du
Royaume de Siam de 1662 a 1703;
d'apres les documents inedits des Archives du Ministere de la Marine et
des Colonies, avec le fac-simile
d'une carte du temps. Farnborough,
Gregg, 1969.
    JSS 60 pt. 2 (1972) 314-317. (M.
    Smithies)

LANSDALE, EDWARD GEARY. In the midst
of wars; an American's mission to
Southeast Asia. New York, Harper and
Row, 1972.
    PA 47 (1974) 394-397.

* LAO KHAMHAWM. Fah Baw kan. Bangkok,
Suksit Siam, 1969.
    JSS 58 pt. 2 (1970) 175-177. (D.
    Garden)

Laos: war and revolution, edited by
Nina S. Adams and Alfred W. McCoy.
New York, Harper and Row, 1971.
    JAS 32 (1972-3) 121-124. (M.
    Leifer)
    JCA 1 pt. 3 (1971) 108-110. (P.
    Limqueco)

Laos: war and revolution

PA 44 (1971) 641-644. (J. L. S. Girling)
SA 2 (1972-3) 347-356. (U. Mahajani)

LAPENA-BONIFACIO, AMELIA. The short, short life of citizen Juan, a play in three acts. Quezon City, Univ. of the Philippines Pr., 1971.
PS 20 (1972) 524-531. (J. A. Galdon, P. A. Dumol and R. S. Reyes)

Lapid, Virginia *See* BERNABE, EMMA. Ilokano lessons

LAQUIAN, APRODICIO ARCILLA. City in nation building, politics in metropolitan Manila. Manila, School of Public Administration, Univ. of the Philippines, 1966. (Quezon, Philippines. Univ. of the Philippines. School of Public Administration. Studies in public administration, 8)
PS 15 (1967) 188-200. (A. E. Lapitan)

LAQUIAN, APRODICIO A. Slums are for people; the barrio Magsaysay pilot project in Philippine urban community development. Honolulu, East-West Center Pr., 1969.
JAS 31 (1971-2) 748-9. (W. F. Arce)

LARKIN, JOHN A. The Pampangans; colonial society in a Philippine province. Berkeley, Univ. of California Pr., 1972.
JAH 8 (1974) 95-6. (N. P. Cushner)
JAS 33 (1973-4) 162-164. (M. S. McLennan)
PA 46 (1973) 176-7. (N. G. Owen)
SA 3 (1974) 941-944. (L. P. Benson)

Larkin, John A. *See* BENDA, HARRY JINDRICH. World of Southeast Asia

LARTEGUY, JEAN. Yellow fever. New York, Dutton, 1965.
PA 39 (1966) 458. (W. E. Willmott)

Laus, Remigia Carpio *See* CARPIO-LAUS, REMIGIA

LAWLESS, ROBERT. Evaluation of Philippine culture-personality research. Quezon City, Asian Center, Univ. of the Philippines Pr., 1969. (Quezon, Philippines. Univ. of the Philippines. Asian Center. Monograph series, 3)
JAS 31 (1971-2) 747-8. (D. J. Scheans)

Lawrence, Peter *See* BERNDT, RONALD MURRAY. Politics in New Guinea

LAWYERS' COMMITTEE ON AMERICAN POLICY TOWARDS VIETNAM. CONSULTATIVE COUNCIL. Vietnam and international law; an analysis of the legality of the U.S. military involvement. Flanders, N.J., O'Hare, 1967.
PA 41 (1968) 269-273. (L. C. Green)

LE HUY HAP. Vietnamese legends. Rev. ed. Saigon, Khai Tri, 1963.
BEF 56 (1969) 192. (T. C. Leocmach)

* LE NGOC TRU. Chanh-ta Viet-nau. 2d. ed. Saigon, Truong-thi xuat-ban, 1960.
BEF 52 (1964) 247-253. (M. Durand)

* LE NGOC TRU. Viet-ngu Chanh-ta tu-vi. Saigon, Thanh-Tan, 1959.
BEF 52 (1964) 247-253. (M. Durand)

* LE QUY DON. Phu bien tap luc. Saigon, Ministere d'Etat Charge des Affaires Culturelles, 1972.
SEIB 48 (1973) 143-4. (Nguyen The Anh)

* LE QUY DON. Van dai loai ngu. Saigon, Ministere d'Etat Charge des Affaires Culturelles, 1972.
SEIB 48 (1973) 144. (Nguyen The Anh)

Le Tac *See* LI TSE

* LE TRAN DUC. Than The va su nghiep y
  hoc cua Hai Thuong Lan Ong. Hanoi,
  Y Hoc va The duc The thao, 1966.
    BEF 58 (1971) 332-334. (Nguyen
    Tran Huan)

LEACH, EDMUND RONALD. Political sys-
  tems of highland Burma, a study of
  Kachin social structure. Boston,
  Beacon Pr., 1965.
    PA 39 (1966) 243-4. (M. Ames)

Leadership and authority; a symposium.
  Edited by Gehan Wijeyewardene.
  Singapore, Univ. of Malaya Pr.,
  1968.
    JAS 29 (1969-70) 680-1. (J. Gross-
    holtz)
    PA 44 (1971) 306. (R. S. Milne)

LEAR, ELMER NORTON. Japanese occupation of the Philippines, Leyte,
  1941-1945. Ithaca, Southeast Asia
  Program, Cornell Univ., 1961. (Cornell Univ. Southeast Asia Program.
  Data paper, no. 42)
    BIJ 119 (1963) 326-7. (J.
    Vredenbregt)
    PA 36 (1963) 196-199. (F. C.
    Jones)
    RSA (1964) 269-270. (I. Jadoul)

LEASOR, JAMES. Singapore: the battle
  that changed the world. Garden City,
  N.Y., Doubleday, 1968. (Crossroads
  of world history series)
    PA 41 (1968) 623-4. (O. L. Roberts)

LeBAR, FRANK M. Ethnic groups of insular Southeast Asia. Volume 1. Indonesia, Andaman Islands and Mada-
  gascar. New Haven, HRAF Pr., 1972.
    JAS 33 (1973-4) 501. (A. A.
    Yengoyan)

LeBAR, FRANK M. Ethnic groups of mainland Southeast Asia, by Frank M.
  Lebar, Gerald C. Hickey and John K.
  Musgrave. New Haven, Human Relations Area Files, 1964.
    JAS 25 (1965-6) 166-7. (C. Hobbs)

Lee, Sherman E. Ancient Cambodian

    SEIB 40 (1965) 357-8. (R. Legay)

LeBar, Frank M. *See* HUMAN RELATIONS
  AREA FILES, INC. Laos

Le Bonheur, Albert *See* PARIS. MUSEE
  GUIMET. La sculpture indonesienne

LEBRA, JOYCE C. Jungle alliance, Japan
  and the Indian National Army. Singapore, Donald Moore, 1971. (Asia Pacific world library)
    JSAS 4 (1973) 141-143. (K. S.
    Sandhu)

LEE, CHAE JIN. Communist China's policy toward Laos, a case study, 1954-
  67. Lawrence, Center for East Asian
  Studies, Univ. of Kansas, 1970. (International Studies. East Asian series. Research publication, no. 6)
    JSAS 3 (1972) 332-3. (J. J.
    Zasloff)
    PA 44 (1971) 312-3. (J. L. S.
    Girling)

LEE, EDDY. Educational planning in
  west Malaysia. Kuala Lumpur, Oxford
  UP, 1972.
    SAJSS 1 pt. 1 (1973) 136. (Gwee Yee
    Hean)

* LEE, EDWIN. Sarawak in the early sixties. Singapore, Dept. of History,
  Univ. of Singapore, 1964. (Singapore
  studies on Borneo and Malaya, no. 5)
    JAS 24 (1964-5) 339. (J. Silver-
    stein)

LEE, HAHN BEEN. Administrative reforms
  in Asia, edited by Lee Hahn Been and
  Abelardo G. Samonte. Manila, Eastern
  Regional Organization for Public Administration, 1970.
    SA 2 (1972) 529. (R. P. de Guzman)

LEE, SHERMAN E. Ancient Cambodian
  sculpture. New York, Asia Society,
  1969.
    JAS 32 (1972-3) 753-4. (G. Tarr)
    JSS 58 pt. 2 (1970) 178-184. (H. W.

LEIFER, MICHAEL. Dilemmas of state-
hood in Southeast Asia. Vancouver,
Univ. of British Columbia Pr., 1972.
   JAS 33 (1973-4) 328-9. (K. G.
      Machado)
   PA 46 (1973) 342-3. (M. Osborne)
   SA 3 (1974) 923-927. (L. G. Noble)

Leifer, Michael *See* Nationalism,
revolution and evolution in South-
East Asia

LEIGH, MICHAEL B. Checklist of holdings on Borneo in the Cornell University Libraries. Ithaca, Southeast Asia Program, Cornell Univ.,
1966. (Cornell Univ. Southeast Asia
Program. Data paper, no. 62)
   BIJ 124 (1968) 279-280. (G. N.
      Appell)

LEIGH, MICHAEL B. Chinese community
of Sarawak; a study of communal relations. Singapore, Malaysia Publishing House, 1964. (Singapore
studies on Malaysia, no. 6)
   JSAH 6 (Sept. 1965) 149-150.
      (J. P. L. Jiang)
   PA 38 (1965) 224. (W. E. Willmott)

LENSEN, GEORGE ALEXANDER. World be-
yond Europe. An introduction to the
history of Africa, India, Southeast
Asia, and the Far East. 2d. ed.
Boston, Houghton, Mifflin, 1966.
   JAH 3 (1969) 58. (C. R. Boxer)
   PA 41 (1968) 263-4. (J. Davidson)

Lent, John A. *See* Asian newspapers
reluctant revolution

LENT, JOHN A. Philippine mass communications before 1811 and after 1966.
Manila, Philippine Pr. Institute,
1971.
   JAS 32 (1972-3) 571-2. (B. Nuss-
      baum)

LENTIN, ALBERT PAUL. La lutte tricon-
tinentale, imperialisme et revolution apres la conference de La

Lev, Daniel S. Transition to guided

Havane. Paris, Maspero, 1966.
   FA 21 (1966) 497.

LE PAGE, ROBERT BROCK. National lan-
guage question, linguistic problems
of newly independent states. London,
Oxford UP, 1964.
   BIJ 122 (1966) 192-196. (J.
      Knappert)
   RSA (1964) 328-9. (L. Rocher)

LE PREVOST, JOHN. Malay word counts.
London, Univ. of London Pr., 1953.
   AR 6 (1973) 230-233. (H. Chambert-
      Loir)

LERNER, DANIEL. Communication and
change in the developing countries,
by Daniel Lerner and Wilbur Schramm.
Honolulu, East-West Center Pr., 1967.
   PA 40 (1967) 349-350. (T. B.
      Bottomore)

LESTER, ROBERT C. Theravada Buddhism
in Southeast Asia. Ann Arbor, Univ.
of Michigan Pr., 1973.
   PA 46 (1973) 599-600. (J. F. Cady)

LEV, DANIEL S. Islamic courts in Indo-
nesia; a study in the political bases
of legal institutions. Berkeley,
Univ. of California Pr., 1972.
   AR 7 (1974) 205-6.
   JAS 33 (1973-4) 160-1. (J. L.
      Peacock)
   JSAS 4 (1973) 311-314. (G. W.
      Bartholomew)
   PA 46 (1973) 349-350. (C. A. O. van
      Nieuwenhuijze)

Lev, Daniel S. *See* FINCH, SUSAN.
Republic of Indonesia cabinets

LEV, DANIEL S. Transition to guided
democracy: Indonesian politics,
1957-1959. Ithaca, Modern Indonesia
Project, Southeast Asia Program, Cornell Univ., 1966. (Cornell Univ.
Modern Indonesia Project. Monograph
series)
   JSAH 9 (1968) 356-7. (J. A. C.
      Mackie)

Levinson, Joseph Richmond.   European

LEVENSON, JOSEPH RICHMOND. European
expansion and the counter-example of
Asia, 1300-1600. Englewood Cliffs,
Prentice-Hall, 1967. (Global history series)
    PA 41 (1968) 263-4. (J. Davidson)

LEVERHULME CONFERENCE, 4TH, UNIVERSITY
OF HONG KONG, 1969. Development of
Japanese studies in Southeast Asia,
proceedings. Edited by Frank H. H.
King. Hong Kong, Centre of Asian
Studies, Univ. of Hong Kong, 1969.
    JAS 30 (1970-1) 226-7. (L. Olson)

LEVI, WERNER. Challenge of world politics in South and Southeast Asia.
Englewood Cliffs, Prentice-Hall,
1968.
    AS 8 (1968) 1027.
    JAS 29 (1969-70) 487-8. (Chae-Jin
      Lee)
    PA 42 (1969) 392-394. (D. R.
      Sardesai)
    SA 2 (1972-3) 148-9. (R. S. Milne)

LEVIN, JONATHAN V. Export economies,
their pattern of development in historical perspective. Cambridge,
Harvard UP, 1960.
    PA 35 (1962) 299-301. (F. N.
      Trager)

LEVINSON, GEORGII ILICH. Filippiny
mezhdu pervoy i vtoroy mirovymi
voynami. (The Philippines between
the First and Second World Wars)
Moscow, 1958.
    BIJ 121 (1965) 179-183. (L.
      Sluimers)
    JAS 22 (1962-3) 89-94. (T. Friend)

LEVINSON, GEORGII ILICH. Filippiny
vchera i segodnia. (The Philippines
yesterday and today) Moscow, 1959.
    JAS 22 (1962-3) 89-94. (T. Friend)

LEWIS, HENRY T. Ilocano rice farmers;
a comparative study of the Philippine

barrios. Honolulu, Univ. of Hawaii
Pr., 1971.
    JAS 33 (1973-4) 505. (A. A.
      Yengokan)

Lewis, John Wilson *See* KAHIN, GEORGE
McTURNAN. United States in Vietnam

LEWIS, MARTHA BLANCHE. Sentence analysis in modern Malay. London, Cambridge UP, 1969.
    AAS 7 (1971) 145. (V. Krupa)
    JAS 29 (1969-70) 736-7. (Amran
      Halim)

LEWIS, PAUL. Akha-English dictionary.
Ithaca, Southeast Asia Program, Cornell Univ., 1968. (Cornell Univ.
Southeast Asia Program. Data paper,
no. 70)
    JAS 28 (1968-9) 644-5. (J. A.
      Matisoff)

LEWIS, REBA. Indonesia, troubled paradise. London, Hale, 1962.
    PA 37 (1964) 115. (J. A. C. Mackie)

Li, Alice *See* NEVEDOMSKY, JOSEPH JOHN.
Chinese in Southeast Asia

LI TSE. An-Nam chi-lu'o'c. Hue, Vien
Dai-hoc, 1961.
    JSAH 4 (Mar. 1963) 120-122.

Lian The *See* THE, LIAN

Liang, Dapen *See* LIANG, TA-PENG

LIANG KIM BANG. Sarawak, 1941-1957.
Singapore, Dept. of History, Univ. of
Singapore, 1964. (Singapore studies
on Borneo and Malaya, no. 5)
    JAS 24 (1964-5) 339. (J. Silver-
      stein)

LIANG, TA-PENG. Philippine parties and
politics; a historical study of national experience in democracy. New
ed. completely rev. and enl. San
Francisco, Gladstone, 1971.
    AF 5 pt. 4 (1973) 76. (M. D. Zamora)

Lich Su Viet Nam. Tap I. Sach bien
soan duoi su chi dao truc tiep cua
Uy Ban Khoa Hoc Xa Hoi Viet Nam.
Hanoi, Nha Xuat Ban Khoa Hoc Xa Hoi,
1971.
   JAS 33 (1973–4) 338–340. (K.
   Taylor)

* LICHFIELD, WHITING, BROWNE ASSOCIATES.
Bangkok-Dhonburi city planning proj-
ect, historical growth. n.p., n.d.
   JSS 48 pt. 2 (1960) 117–8.

LIDDLE, R. WILLIAM. Ethnicity, party,
and national integration, an Indone-
sian case study. New Haven, Yale
UP, 1970.
   AS 11 (1970) 301–2.
   JSAS 3 (1972) 153–155. (M. A.
   Nawawi)
   PA 45 (1972) 618–620. (H. Feith)

LIE, T. S. Introducing Indonesian.
Sydney, Angus and Robertson, 1965–6.
2v.
   BIJ 124 (1968) 545–551. (Soebardi)
   SOAS 31 (1968) 182–3. (N. G.
   Phillips)

LIEBAN, RICHARD WARREN. Cebuano sor-
cery; malign magic in the Philip-
pines. Berkeley, Univ. of California
Pr., 1967.
   JAS 27 (1967–8) 439–440. (C. Kaut)
   PA 41 (1968) 118–9. (H. E. Jacob-
   son)
   SJ 14 (1967) 495–499. (L. P.–R.
   Makil)
   SOAS 32 (1969) 236.

LIGHTFOOT, KEITH. The Philippines.
New York, Praeger, 1973. (Nations
of the modern world)
   PA 47 (1974) 403–4. (C. O. Houston)

LIJPHART, AREND. Trauma of decolonization; the Dutch and West New Guinea. New Haven, Yale UP, 1966.
(Yale studies in political science,
17)
   JAS 26 (1966–7) 341–2. (R. Van

Niel)
   PA 39 (1966) 418–420. (J. M. van
   der Kroef)

LIM, BEDA. Malaya, a background bib-
liography. Kuala Lumpur, 1962.
(Royal Asiatic Society of Great Brit-
ain and Ireland. Malayan Branch.
Journal. v. 35, pts. 2–3)
   BIJ 120 (1964) 479–481. (R. S.
   Karni)
   JSAH 5 (Sept. 1964) 208–210.
   (Hedwig Anuar)

LIM CHONG YAH. Economic development of
modern Malaya. Kuala Lumpur, Oxford
UP, 1968.
   MER 13 pt. 2 (1968) 130–1. (A. H.
   H. Tan)
   PA 41 (1968) 449–450. (K. J.
   Pelzer)

Lim Chong Yah See YOU POH SENG.
Singapore economy

Lim, So Jean See Trends in Thailand

LIM TAY BOH. Development of Singapore's economy. Singapore, Eastern
Universities Pr., 1960. (Background
to Malaya series, no. 14)
   MER 5 pt. 2 (1960) 85–87. (R. Ma)

Limqueco, P. See COATES, KEN. Prevent the crime of silence

Lin, Tsung-Yi See ASIAN SEMINAR ON
MENTAL HEALTH. Reality and vision

LINDHOLM, RICHARD WADSWORTH. Viet-nam,
the first five years; an internation-
al symposium. East Lansing, Michigan
State UP, 1959.
   JAS 19 (1959–60) 220–1. (R. G.
   Scigliano)
   PA 33 (1960) 94–5. (H. Tinker)

Linguistic comparison in South East
Asia and the Pacific. Editor: H. L.
Shorto. London, School of Oriental
and African Studies, 1963. (Collect-

Linguistic comparison in South East

ed papers in Oriental and African
studies)
   BIJ 121 (1963) 384-388. (J. Gonda)
   JSS 52 (1964) 241-244. (W. A.
     Smalley)
   SEIB 42 (1967) 353. (M. Piat)
   SOAS 27 (1964) 483-4. (C. J. E.
     Ball)

* LITERARY APPRENTICE (INDEXES). Literary apprentice, cumulative index,
1927-58, by Catalina A. Nemenzo.
Quezon City, Univ. of the Philippines, 1961.
   JAS 23 (1963-4) 316-7. (D. V. Hart)

Literature at the crossroads; 3 symposia on the Filipino novel, Filipino poetry, the Filipino theater,
edited by Leonard Casper. Manila,
Florentino, 1965.
   SLQ 4 (1966) 464-467. (C. F.
     Bautista)

LLAMZON, TEODORO A. Makabagong bala-
rila ng wikang Tagalog, nina Teodoro
A. Llamzon, Fe Laura del Rosario at
Marinella Sanchez. Quezon City,
Ateneo de Manila UP, 1974.
   PS 22 (1974) 212-215. (F. Aldave-
     Yap)

LLAMZON, TEODORO A. A subgrouping of
nine Philippine languages. The
Hague, Nijhoff, 1969. (Instituut
voor Taal-, Land- en Volkenkunde.
Verhandelingen, 58)
   SOAS 34 (1971) 211-2. (N. G.
     Phillips)

Local level politics: social and
cultural perspectives, edited by
Marc J. Swartz. Chicago, Aldine,
1968.
   PA 42 (1969) 263-4. (R. S. Milne)

Locsin, Cecilia See LOCSIN, LEANDRO.
Oriental ceramics

LOCSIN, LEANDRO. Oriental ceramics
discovered in the Philippines, by
Leandro and Cecilia Locsin. Rutland,

Tuttle, 1967.
   AP 17 (1974) 76-7. (K. Hutterer)

LOH KENG AUN. Fifty years of the Anglican Church in Singapore Island,
1909-1959. Singapore, Dept. of History, Univ. of Singapore, 1963.
(Singapore studies on Borneo and Malaya, no. 4)
   JAS 24 (1964-5) 338-9.

LOH, PHILIP FOOK SENG. The Malay
states 1877-1895, political change
and social policy. Singapore, Oxford
UP, 1969. (East Asian historical
monographs)
   JAH 6 (1972) 93-4. (C. K. Byrd)
   PA 44 (1971) 146. (K. G.
     Tregonning)

Lombard, Denys See HOUTMAN, FREDRIK
DE. Le spraek ende Woord Boek

LOMBARD, SYLVIA J. Yao-English dictionary. Ithaca, Southeast Asia Program, Cornell Univ., 1968. (Cornell
Univ. Southeast Asia Program. Data
paper, no. 69)
   JAS 28 (1968-9) 441-443. (Kun
     Chang)

London. Univ. School of Oriental and
African Studies See Linguistic
comparison in South East Asia and the
Pacific

LONGACRE, ROBERT E. Discourse, para-
graph and sentence structure in selected Philippine languages. Santa
Ana, Summer Institute of Linguistics,
1968-9. 3v.
   AAS 7 (1971) 144. (J. Genzor)

LOOFS, HELMUTH. Elements of the mega-
lithic complex in Southeast Asia; an
annotated bibliography. Canberra,
Centre of Oriental Studies, 1967.
(Australian National Univ., Canberra.
Centre of Oriental Studies. Oriental
monograph series, no. 3)
   SOAS 32 (1969) 651-2. (H. R. van
     Heekeren)

Lyon, Margo L. Bases of conflict in

Loory, Stuart H. *See* KRASLOW, DAVID.
Secret search for peace in Vietnam

LOOS-HAAXMAN, J. DE. Dagwerk in Indie,
hommage aan een verstild verleden.
Franeker, T. Wever, 1972.
BIJ 128 (1972) 395-397. (J. H.
Maronier)

Loosely structured social systems;
Thailand in comparative perspective.
New Haven, Southeast Asia Studies,
Yale Univ., 1969. (Yale Univ. Grad-
uate School. Southeast Asia Studies.
Cultural report series, no. 17)
AS 10 (1970) 177.
BIJ 126 (1970) 358-361. (J. Bunnag)
JAS 29 (1969-70) 415-419. (A. A.
Yengoyan, C. F. Keyes and J. N.
Anderson)
JSAS 2 (1971) 230-232. (F. K.
Lehman)
JSS 58 pt. 1 (1970) 142-144.
(Patya Saihoo)
PA 43 (1970) 308-9. (J. L. S.
Girling)

Lopez, Rafael *See* HISTORICAL CONSER-
VATION SOCIETY. Christianization of
the Philippines

LORD, DONALD C. Mo Bradley and Thai-
land. Grand Rapids, Eerdmans, 1969.
JSS 59 pt. 1 (1971) 273-276. (M.
Smithies)

LOUKA, KATHRYN T. Role of population
in the development of Southeast Asia.
Washington, Population Research
Project, George Washington Univ.,
1960.
JSAH 3 (Sept. 1962) 182-3. (Ooi
Jin Bee)

LOVESTRAND, HAROLD. Hostage in Djakarta. Chicago, Moody Pr., 1967.
PA 41 (1968) 294. (B. B. Hering)

LUCE, DON. Vietnam; the unheard
voices, by Don Luce and John Sommer.
Ithaca, Cornell UP, 1969.
JAS 29 (1969-70) 498-9. (F. Fitz-
Gerald)
MAS 4 (1970) 373-375. (R. B. Smith)
PA 43 (1970) 127-8. (P. J. Honey)

LUCE, GORDON HANNINGTON. Old Burma,
early Pagan. Locust Valley, N.Y.,
Augustin, 1969-70. 3v.
JAS 31 (1971-2) 717-719. (W. M.
Spink)
JSS 59 pt. 2 (1971) 260-1. (H. W.
Woodward)
SOAS 35 (1972) 181-183. (H. L.
Shorto)

LY CHANH TRUNG. Introduction to Viet-
namese poetry. Saigon, GPO, 1960.
(Vietnam culture series, no. 3)
SEIB 35 (1960) 734.

LY QUI CHUNG. Between two fires, the
unheard voices of Vietnam. New York,
Praeger, 1970.
PA 44 (1971) 309-311. (M. E.
Osborne)
SA 2 (1972-3) 363-371. (J. Badgley)

LY TE XUYEN. Viet dien u linh tap. Le-
Huu-Muc-dich. Saigon, Khai-Tri,
1960.
BEF 52 (1964) 290-292. (Nguyen Tran
Huan)

LYNCH, FRANK. Social class in a Bikol
town. Chicago, Univ. of Chicago,
Dept. of Anthropology, Philippine
Studies Program, 1959. (Chicago.
Univ. Philippine Studies Program.
Research series, no. 1)
PS 8 (1960) 461-463. (V.
Encarnacion)

LYON, MARGO L. Bases of conflict in
rural Java. Berkeley, Center for
South and Southeast Asia Studies,
Univ. of California, 1970. (Califor-
nia. Univ. Center for South and
Southeast Asia Studies. Research

Lyon, Margo L. Bases of conflict in

Mackeen, Abdul Majeed Mohamed

Groslier)
SEIB 35 (1960) 738.

MACDONALD, RODERICK ROSS. Student's
reference grammar of modern formal
Indonesian, by Roderick Ross Mac-
donald and Soenjono Darjowidjojo.
Washington, Georgetown UP, 1967.
   AAS 7 (1971) 146-7. (V. Krupa)

MACEDA, MARCELINO N. Culture of the
Mamanua, northeast Mindanao, as
compared with that of the other
Negritos of Southeast Asia. Manila,
Catholic Trade School, 1964. (San
Carlos publications. Ser. A. Human-
ities, no. 1)
   JAS 25 (1965-6) 549. (F. L.
   Wernstedt)

McGARVEY, PATRICK J. Visions of victory; selected Vietnamese communist
military writings, 1964-1968. Stanford, Hoover Institution on War, Revolution and Peace, Stanford Univ.,
1969. (Stanford Univ. Hoover Institution on War, Revolution and Peace.
Publications, 81)
   PA 43 (1970) 630-1. (P. J. Honey)

McGEE, T. G. Petaling Jaya; a socio-
economic survey of a new town in
Selangor, Malaysia, by T. G. McGee
and W. D. McTaggart. Wellington,
Dept. of Geography, Victoria Univ.
of Wellington, 1967. (Pacific view-
point monograph, no. 2)
   JAS 27 (1967-8) 682-3. (K. J.
   Pelzer)

McGEE, T. G. Southeast Asian city.
London, Bell, 1967.
   FA 22 (1968) 127.
   JAH 3 (1969) 85. (C. K. Byrd)
   JSAH 9 (1968) 365-367. (D. W.
   Fryer)
   PA 41 (1968) 441-2. (K. J. Pelzer)
   SOAS 31 (1968) 184-5. (H. Tinker)

McGEE, T. G. Urbanization process in
the third world, exploration in

search of a theory. London, Bell,
1971.
   JAH 6 (1972) 134-5. (L. K. Caldwell)

McHale, Mary C. *See* BOWDITCH,
NATHANIEL. Early American-Philippine
trade

McHale, Thomas R. *See* BOWDITCH,
NATHANIEL. Early American-Philippine
trade

McINTYRE, WILLIAM DAVID. Imperial
frontier in the tropics, 1865-1875:
a study of British colonial policy in
west Africa, Malaya and the South
Pacific in the age of Gladstone and
Disraeli. London, Macmillan, 1967.
   JSAH 9 (1968) 370-372. (C. M.
   Turnbull)

McKAUGHAN, HOWARD P. Ilocano, an in-
tensive language course, by Howard
McKaughan and J. Foster. Grand
Forks, N.D., Summer Institute of Lin-
guistics, 1957.
   AAS 3 (1967) 181-2. (R. Raczynski)

McKAUGHAN, HOWARD P. Inflection and
syntax of Maranao verbs. Manila,
Institute of National Language, 1958.
   PS 8 (1960) 902-3. (R. J. Hemphill)

McKAUGHAN, HOWARD P. Maranao diction-
ary, by Howard McKaughan and Batua A.
Macaraya. Honolulu, Univ. of Hawaii
Pr., 1967.
   AAS 6 (1970) 231. (V. Krupa)
   PS 17 (1969) 177-8. (T. A. Llamson)

MACKEEN, ABDUL MAJEED MOHAMED. Contem-
porary Islamic legal organization in
Malaya. New Haven, Yale Univ.,
Southeast Asia Studies, 1969. (Yale
Univ. Graduate School. Southeast Asia
Studies. Monograph series, no. 13)
   BIJ 126 (1970) 367-8. (W. R. Roff)
   JMBRAS 42 pt. 2 (1969) 233-4.
   (Ahmad Ibrahim)
   JSAS 3 (1972) 161-163. (G. W.

MacKeen Abdul Majeed Mohamed

Bartholomew)
PA 43 (1970) 636. (L. C. Green)
SOAS 34 (1971) 211. (R. B.
Serjeant)

McKeen, Dale L. *See* JOHNSON, ROSALL
JAMES. Business environment in an
emerging nation

McKINLEY, JAMES F. Betrayed and be-
friended, by James F. McKinley and
Elizabeth M. McCabe. Quezon City,
New Day, 1970.
SJ 17 (1970) 78-80. (P. G. Gowing)

McLANE, CHARLES B. Soviet strategies
in Southeast Asia, an exploration
of eastern policy under Lenin and
Stalin. Princeton, Princeton UP,
1966.
JAS 27 (1967-8) 430-1. (C. M.
Foust)
SOAS 30 (1967) 446-7. (R. B. Smith)

McLEOD, ALAN LINDSEY. Commonwealth
pen; an introduction to the literature of the British Commonwealth.
Ithaca, Cornell UP, 1961.
PA 34 (1961) 417-8. (G. Woodcock)

M'LEOD, JOHN. Voyage of the Alceste
to the Ryukus and Southeast Asia.
Rutland, Tuttle, 1963.
JAS 24 (1964-5) 144. (S. Sakamaki)

MacMICKING, ROBERT. Recollections of
Manilla and the Philippines during
1848, 1849 and 1850. Manila, Filipiniana Book Guild, 1967. (Filipiniana Book Guild. Publications, 11)
JAS 27 (1967-8) 917-8. (D. V. Hart)
PA 42 (1969) 118. (I. B. Powell)

McNicoll, Geoffrey *See* HICKS, GEORGE
L. Indonesian economy

McNicoll, Geoffrey *See* HICKS, GEORGE
L. Trade and growth in the Philippines

McPHEE, COLIN. Music in Bali, a study
in form and organization in Balinese
orchestral music. New Haven, Yale
UP, 1966.
PA 40 (1967) 202-3. (E. Weisgarber)

MACRIDIS, ROY C. Modern political systems. Volume II. Asia, edited by Roy
C. Macridis and Robert E. Ward. Englewood Cliffs, Prentice-Hall, 1963.
JAS 23 (1963-4) 458-9. (J. M. Maki)

McVEY, RUTH THOMAS. The Calcutta Conference and the Southeast Asia uprisings. Ithaca, Modern Indonesia
Project, Southeast Asia Program, Cornell Univ., 1958. (Cornell Univ.
Modern Indonesia Project. Interim reports series)
BIJ 116 (1960) 290-1. (J. Vredenbregt)
JAS 21 (1961-2) 409-411. (D.
Hindley)

McVey, Ruth Thomas *See* BENDA, HARRY
JINDRICH. Communist uprisings of
1926-1927 in Indonesia

McVEY, RUTH THOMAS. Indonesia. New
Haven, Human Relations Area Files,
1963. (Survey of world cultures, 12)
BIJ 121 (1965) 477-484. (W. F.
Wertheim)
JAS 23 (1963-4) 634-5. (J. Peacock)
MER 11 pt. 1 (1966) 128-131. (D. J.
Blake)

McVEY, RUTH THOMAS. Rise of Indonesian
communism. Ithaca, Cornell UP, 1965.
JAH 1 (1967) 190-1. (J. M. van der
Kroef)
JAS 26 (1966-7) 342-344. (H. J.
Benda)
JSAH 8 (1967) 320-322. (J. D.
Legge)
MAS 1 (1967) 102-104. (M. Leifer)

McVEY, RUTH THOMAS. Soviet view of the
Indonesian revolution; a study in the
Russian attitude towards Asian na-
tionalism. Ithaca, Modern Indonesia

Majul, Cesar Adib.   Political and

Project, Southeast Asia Program,
Cornell Univ., 1957. (Cornell Univ.
Modern Indonesia Project. Interim
reports series)
    BIJ 116 (1960) 291. (J. Vreden-
      bregt)
    JAS 21 (1961-2) 409-411. (D.
      Hindley)

MADIGAN, FRANCIS C. Screening for
college aptitude; predicting success
in a Mindanao college by objective
tests, by Francis C. Madigan and
Manuel Gapud. Cagayan de Oro City,
Research Institute for Mindanao Culture, Xavier Univ., 1968. (Xavier
Univ., Cagayan, Mindanao, Philippines. Xavier Univ. studies, no. 2)
    PS 17 (1969) 179. (J. F. Culligan)

Magdamo, Patricia Ling See ELWOOD,
DOUGLAS J. Christ in Philippine
context

MAHAJANI, USHA. Philippine nationalism, external challenge and Filipino
response, 1565-1946. St. Lucia,
Univ. of Queensland Pr., 1971.
    JAS 31 (1971-2) 993-995. (P. W.
      Stanley)
    JSAS 3 (1972) 335-337. (D. J.
      Steinberg)
    PA 45 (1972) 308-9. (M. Meadows)
    PS 19 (1971) 434-436. (M. A.
      Bernad)
    RSAS 1 pt. 4 (1971) 48-50. (Cheng
      Siok Hwa)
    SA 2 (1972) 522-527. (R. V. Cruz)

MAHAJANI, USHA. Role of Indian minorities in Burma and Malaya. Bombay,
Vora, 1960.
    JAS 20 (1960-1) 395-6. (H. Tinker)
    JSAH 3 (Mar. 1962) 143-147. (K. S.
      Sandhu)
    PA 34 (1961) 208-9. (F. N. Trager)

Mahamakut Royal Academy Foundation
  See WAT BOWONNIWET. Phraprawat
somdet phramahasamanachao kromphraya
wachirayanwarorot

MAHATHIR BIN MUHAMMAD. Malay dilemma.
Singapore, Donald Moore, 1970.
    BIJ 128 (1972) 384-389. (The Siauw
      Giap)
    JAS 31 (1971-2) 223-225. (G. D.
      Ness)
    JSAS 2 (1971) 243-4. (Mohd. A.
      Nawawi)
    PA 44 (1971) 303-305. (R. S. Milne)

Majid, Abdullah See RICE, OLIVER.
Modern Malay verse

* MAJUL, CESAR ADIB. Apolinario Mabini,
revolutionary. Manila, National
Heros Commission, 1969.
    GEJ 7 (1964) 232-235. (M. P.
      Fabella)

MAJUL, CESAR ADIB. Critique of Rizal's
concept of a Filipino nation. Diliman, 1959.
    PS 8 (1960) 464-5. (G. S. Abad)

MAJUL, CESAR ADIB. Mabini and the
Philippine revolution. Quezon City,
Univ. of the Philippines, 1960.
(Philippine studies series, 4)
    JAS 21 (1961-2) 417-8. (L. Casper)

* MAJUL, CESAR ADIB. Muslims in the
Philippines. Quezon City, Univ. of
the Philippines Pr., 1973.
    AST 11 pt. 2 (1973) 1-5. (A. A.
      Melchor)
    PS 21 (1973) 482-486. (J. N.
      Schumacher)
    SLURJ 4 (1973) 480-483. (F. T.
      Asuncion)

MAJUL, CESAR ADIB. Political and constitutional ideas of the Philippine
revolution. Rev. ed. Quezon City,
Univ. of the Philippines Pr., 1967.
    JAS 28 (1968-9) 915-6. (G. K.
      Goodman)
    PA 42 (1969) 98-9. (R. S. Milne)
    PS 16 (1968) 793-4. (J. N. Schu-
      macher)

Makarenko, Vladimir Afanasevich

MAKARENKO, VLADIMIR AFANASEVICH. Ta-
galskoe slovoobrazovanie. Moscow,
Nauka, 1970.
    AAS 10 (1974) 199. (J. Genzor)

Malalasekera, George Peiris *See*
Encyclopedia of Buddhism

MALAYSIA. DEPT. OF STATISTICS. Report
on West Malaysian family survey,
1966-67. Kuala Lumpur, National
Family Planning Board, 1968.
    JAS 28 (1968-9) 904-5. (W. P.
    Mauldin)
    SJ 16 (1969) 326-330. (H. R.
    Reynolds)

* MALAYSIA. NATIONAL ARCHIVES. Report,
1967. Kuala Lumpur, GPO, 1968.
    SAA 1 (1968) 54. (L. Loh)

* MALAYSIA. NATIONAL OPERATIONS COUNCIL.
May 13 tragedy, a report. Kuala
Lumpur, 1969.
    JAS 31 (1971-2) 734-736. (G. D.
    Ness)

Malefijt, Annemarie de Waal *See* DE
WAAL MALEFIJT, ANNEMARIE

MALLERET, LOUIS. L'archeologie du
delta du Mekong. Le Cisbassac.
Paris, Ecole Francaise d'Extreme-
Orient, 1962. (Ecole Francaise
d'Extreme-Orient. Publications, v. 43)
    AP 9 (1966) 177-179. (W. G.
    Solheim)
    SEIB 39 (1964) 123-129. (L.
    Bezacier)

MALLERET, LOUIS. L'archeologie du
delta du Mekong. La civilisation
materielle d'Oc-eo. Paris, Ecole
Francaise d'Extreme-Orient, 1960.
(Ecole Francaise d'Extreme-Orient.
Publications, v. 43)
    AP 6 (1962) 31-2. (W. G. Solheim)
    FA 17 (1960) 1993-1999. (L.
    Jeanselme)
    SEIB 36 (1961) 723-726. (L.
    Bezacier)
    SOAS 24 (1961) 388-9. (A. Christie)

MALLERET, LOUIS. L'archeologie du
delta du Mekong. La culture du Funan. Paris, Ecole Francaise d'Extreme-Orient, 1962. (Ecole Francaise d'Extreme-Orient. Publications,
v. 43)
    AP 9 (1966) 177-179. (W. G.
    Solheim)
    SEIB 39 (1964) 123-129. (L.
    Bezacier)

MALLERET, LOUIS. L'archeologie du
delta du Mekong. L'exploration archeologique et les fouilles d'Oc-eo.
Paris, Ecole Francaise d'Extreme-
Orient, 1959. (Ecole Francaise
d'Extreme-Orient. Publications, v. 43)
    AP 4 (1960) 64-5. (W. G. Solheim)
    FA 17 (1960) 1993-1999. (L.
    Jeanselme)
    SOAS 24 (1961) 161-163. (A.
    Christie)

MALM, WILLIAM P. Music cultures of the
Pacific, the Near East and Asia.
Englewood Cliffs, Prentice-Hall,
1967.
    AAS 6 (1970) 194-196. (I. Macak)
    PA 40 (1967) 430-1. (E. Weisgarber)
    SJ 15 (1968) 134-137. (A. L.
    Faurot)

MALMGREN, HARALD B. Pacific basin development, the American interests.
Lexington, Mass., Lexington Books,
1972.
    PA 46 (1972) 114-5. (K. Taira)

MANICH JUMSAI, M. L. History of Anglo-
Thai relations. Bangkok, Chalermnit,
1970.
    JSS 59 pt. 2 (1971) 264-268. (A.
    Epstein)

MANICH JUMSAI, M. L. History of Thai-
land and Cambodia, from the days of
Angkor to the present. Bangkok,
Chalermnit, 1970.
    JSS 59 pt. 2 (1971) 262-264. (D. P.
    Chandler)

MANICH JUMSAI, M. L.   King Mongkut and
Sir John Bowring (from Sir John
Bowring's personal files, kept at
the Royal Thai Embassy in London).
Bangkok, Chalermnit, 1970.
  JSS 60 pt. 2 (1972) 307-309. (V.
  Kennedy)

* MANICH JUMSAI. Ramayana Thai. Bangkok, Chalermnit, 1970.
  BEF 59 (1972) 332-3. (L. Gabaude)

* MANICH JUMSAI, M. L.   Understanding
Thai Buddhism. Bangkok, Chalermnit
Pr., 1971.
  BEF 59 (1972) 327-8. (L. Gabaude)

MANIK, LIBERTY. Batak Handschriften.
Wiesbaden, Franz Steiner, 1973.
(Verzeichnis der orientalischen
Handschriften in Deutschland. Bd.
28)
  SOAS 37 (1974) 755. (M. C.
  Ricklefs)

MANILA. LOPEZ MEMORIAL MUSEUM. Catalogue of Filipiniana materials in
the Lopez Memorial Museum. n.p.,
1962.
  JAS 23 (1963-4) 316-7. (D. V. Hart)

MANLEY, TIMOTHY M.   Outline of Sre
structure. Honolulu, Univ. of
Hawaii Pr., 1972. (Oceanic Linguis-
tics, special publication, no. 12)
  JAS 33 (1973-4) 152-155. (F. E.
  Huffman)
  SEIB 48 (1973) 538. (D. Thomas)

MANNING, ROBERT. Who we are; an At-
lantic chronicle of the United
States and Vietnam, by Robert Man-
ning and Michael Janeway. Boston,
Little Brown, 1969.
  PA 43 (1970) 309-311. (G. Duncan)

MANUEL, E. ARSENIO. Philippine folklore bibliography, a preliminary
survey. Quezon City, Philippine
Folklore Society, 1965.

Maring, Ester G.   Historical and

  JAS 26 (1966-7) 547-549. (D. V.
  Hart)

Manuud, Antonio G. *See* Brown heritage

MARCHAL, HENRI. Nouveau guide d'Ang-
kor. Phnom-Penh, Office National du
Tourisme Khmer, 1961.
  SEIB 36 (1961) 743.

MARCHE, ALFRED. Luzon and Palawan.
Manila, Filipiniana Book Guild, 1970.
(Filipiniana Book Guild. Publica-
tions, v. 17)
  JAS 31 (1971-2) 998-9. (M. S.
  McLennan)
  PA 44 (1971) 483. (E. Wickberg)

MARCOS, FERDINAND EDRALIN. Today's
revolution: democracy. Manila,
1971.
  SA 2 (1972) 529-530. (R. P. de
  Guzman)

MARCUS, RUSSELL. English-Lao, Lao-
English dictionary. Bangkok, 1968.
  BEF 57 (1970) 238. (P.-M. Gogneux)

Maretzki, Thomas W. *See* KENNEDY,
RAYMOND. Bibliography of Indonesian
peoples and cultures

Marillier, Andre *See* RHODES,
ALEXANDRE DE. Cathechismus pro iis

* MARILLIER, ANDRE. Phep giang tam
nygay, cathechimus in octo dies divisus. Saigon, Groupe Litteraire
Tinh-Viet, 1961.
  SEIB 36 (1961) 108-9.

Maring, Ester G. *See* MARING, JOEL M.
Historical and cultural dictionary of
Burma

MARING, ESTER G.   Historical and cultural dictionary of the Philippines,
by Ester G. and Joel M. Maring.
Metuchen, N.J., Scarecrow Pr., 1973.
(Historical and cultural dictionaries
of Asia, no. 3)

Maring, Joel M. Historical and

JAS 33 (1973-4) 506-7. (C. O.
Houston)

MARING, JOEL M. Historical and cul-
tural dictionary of Burma, by Joel
M. and Ester G. Maring. Metuchen,
N. J., Scarecrow Pr., 1973. (His-
torical and cultural dictionaries of
Asia series, no. 4)
PA 46 (1973) 606-7. (D. G. E.
Hall)

Maring, Joel M. *See* MARING, ESTER G.
Historical and cultural dictionary
of the Philippines

MARKS, HARRY JULIAN. First contest
for Singapore, 1819-1824. The Hague,
Nijhoff, 1959. (Instituut voor
Taal-, Land- en Volkenkunde. Ver-
handelingen, deel 27)
JAS 19 (1959-60) 475-6. (R. Van
Niel)
JSAH 2 (Mar. 1961) 117-119. (G.
Irwin)
PA 33 (1960) 200-1. (D. G. E.
Hall)

MARR, DAVID G. Vietnamese anticoloni-
alism, 1885-1925. Berkeley, Univ.
of California Pr., 1971.
AAS 10 (1974) 209-213. (J. Mucka)
JSAS 4 (1973) 305-6. (E. Thio)
MAS 7 (1973) 747-754. (M. Osborne)
PA 44 (1971) 591-595. (D. J.
Duncanson)
SA 2 (1972-3) 374-377. (W. B.
Dunn)
SOAS 35 (1972) 412-3. (R. B.
Smith)

* MARSCHALL, WOLFGANG. Metallurgie und
fruhe Besiedlungsgeschichte Indonesiens. Sonderdruck, Ethnologica,
n.d.
AR 6 (1973) 211-214. (D. Lombard)

MARSDEN, WILLIAM. History of Sumatra.
3d. ed. Kuala Lumpur, Oxford UP,
1966.

JAS 26 (1966-7) 545-6. (R. Van
Niel)
MAS 4 (1970) 371-373. (C. A.
Fisher)
PA 40 (1967) 165-6.. (D. G. E.
Hall)

MARSHALL, SAMUEL LYMAN ATWOOD. Battles
in the monsoon; campaigning in the
central highlands, Vietnam, summer
1966. New York, William Morrow,
1967.
PA 42 (1969) 424.

MARTELINO, EDUARDO L. Someday Malay-
sia. New York, Pagent Pr., 1959.
PA 33 (1960) 215.
PA 34 (1961) 100. (F. J. Corley)

MARTINEZ DE ZUNIGA, JOAQUIN. Histori-
cal view of the Philippine Islands.
Manila, Filipiniana Book Guild, 1966.
(Filipiniana Book Guild. Publica-
tions, 10)
JAS 28 (1968-9) 194-196. (J. A.
Larkin)

MARYANOV, GERALD SEYMOUR. Decentralization in Indonesia as a political
problem. Ithaca, Modern Indonesia
Project, Southeast Asia Program, Cornell Univ., 1958. (Cornell Univ.
Modern Indonesia Project. Interim reports series)
JAS 19 (1959-60) 471-473. (H. J.
Benda)

MARZOUK, GIRGIS A. Economic develop-
ment and policies. Case study of
Thailand. Rotterdam, Rotterdam UP,
1972.
JSS 62 pt. 2 (1974) 337-342. (W. A.
McCleary)

* MASAMICHI, ROYAMA. Philippine polity,
a Japanese view, by Royama Masamichi
and Takeuchi Tatsuji. New Haven,
Southeast Asia Studies, Yale Univ.,
1967. (Yale Univ. Graduate School.
Southeast Asia Studies. Monograph
series, no. 12)
SA 1 (1971) 275-6. (L. Thomas)

Means, Gordon Paul. Malaysian politics

Maspero, Eveline Poree *See* POREE-
MASPERO, EVELINE

MASSELMAN, GEORGE. Cradle of colonialism. New Haven, Yale UP, 1963.
    BIJ 121 (1965) 271-274. (I.
     Schoffer)
    JAS 23 (1963-4) 636-7. (J. K.
     Irikura)
    JSAH 7 (Sept. 1966) 120-122. (D. K.
     Bassett)
    PA 37 (1964) 471-2. (C. D. Cowan)
    SOAS 28 (1965) 434-5. (J. Bastin)

MASSON, ANDRE. Histoire du Vietnam.
Paris, Presses universitaires de
France, 1960. (Que-sais-je? no.
398)
    FA 20 (1965) 125-6. (Nguyen Tran
     Huan)
    JAS 20 (1960-1) 115-6. (J. F. Cady)
    SEIB 36 (1961) 735.

* MATISOFF, JAMES ALAN. Proto-Lolo
Burmese. Ann Arbor, Dept. of Linguistics, Univ. of Michigan, 1969.
    JAS 30 (1970-1) 230-1. (R. B.
     Jones)

MATTHEW, HELEN G. Asia in the modern
world. New York, New American Library, 1963.
    FA 19 (1963) 1067-1069.
    JAS 23 (1963-4) 598-9. (G. H.
     Green)

Matthews, Noel *See* WAINWRIGHT, M. D.
Guide to western manuscripts and
documents in the British Isles relating to South and South East Asia

Maung Htin Aung *See* HTIN AUNG

MAUNG MAUNG. Aung San of Burma. The
Hague, Nijhoff, 1962.
    PA 36 (1963) 451-2. (H. Tinker)

MAUNG MAUNG. Burma and General Ne Win.
New York, Asia Publishing House,
1969.

AS 10 (1970) 177-8.
JAS 29 (1969-70) 987-8. (J.
  Badgley)
PA 44 (1971) 302-3. (J. Silver-
  stein)

MAUNG MAUNG. Burma's constitution.
The Hague, Nijhoff, 1959.
    PA 33 (1960) 91-2. (H. Tinker)

MAUNG MAUNG. Burma's constitution. 2d.
ed. The Hague, Nijhoff, 1961.
    SOAS 27 (1964) 502. (H. Tinker)

MAUNG MAUNG. Law and custom in Burma
and the Burmese family. The Hague,
Nijhoff, 1963.
    PA 37 (1964) 93. (R. Allen)
    RSA (1965) 126-7. (L. Rocher)

MAUNG MAUNG. Trial in Burma: the
assassination of Aung San. The
Hague, Nijhoff, 1962.
    JAS 24 (1964-5) 701-2. (C. Hobbs)

MAUNG, MYA. Burma and Pakistan, a comparative study of development. New
York, Praeger, 1971.
    JAS 31 (1971-2) 719-722. (R. L.
     Feldberg)

MAXWELL, LESLIE F. Legal bibliography
of the British Commonwealth of Nations. Volume 7. The British Commonwealth, excluding the United Kingdom,
Australia, New Zealand, Canada, India
and Pakistan. 2d. ed. London, Sweet
and Maxwell, 1964.
    SOAS 28 (1965) 206. (S. A. de
     Smith)

May, Derwant *See* Chepu Kenchana

Mayer, Rudolf *See* Gluck und Wohlergehen

MEANS, GORDON PAUL. Malaysian politics.
London, Univ. of London Pr., 1970.
    JAH 6 (1972) 155-6. (G. W. Wilson)
    JAS 31 (1971-2) 221-223. (A. A.
     Shantz)

Means, Gordon Paul. Malaysian politics

JSAS 2 (1971) 244-246. (J.
MacDougall)
PA 44 (1971) 305-6. (Chan Heng
Chee)

Mears, Leon A. *See* JOHNSON, ROSALL
JAMES. Business environment in an
emerging nation

MEARS, LEON A. Economic project evaluation, with Philippine cases. Quezon City, Univ. of the Philippines
Pr., 1969. 2v.
PS 21 (1973) 249-250. (G. S. Abad)

Mears, Leon A. *See* Rice economy of
the Philippines

MEDWAY, GATHORNE GATHORNE-HARDY. Mammals of Borneo, an annotated checklist. Singapore, Malaysian Branch
of the Royal Asiatic Society, 1965.
SMJ 11 (1964) 602.
SMJ 14 (1966) 341-345. (M. P. L.
Fogden)

MEETING ON SINO-TIBETAN RECONSTRUCTION,
2D, COLUMBIA UNIV., 1969. Papers on
Tibeto-Burman historical and com-
parative linguistics. Edited by F. K.
Lehman. Urbana, Dept. of Linguistics,
Univ. of Illinois, 1971. (Wolfenden
Society on Tibeto-Burman linguistics,
v. 2)
JAS 31 (1971-2) 987-8. (Kun Chang)

MEILINK-ROELOFSZ, MARIE ANTOINETTE
PETRONELLA. Asian trade and European
influence in the Indonesian archi-
pelago between 1500 and about 1630.
The Hague, Nijhoff, 1962.
BIJ 119 (1963) 432-438. (H. J. de
Graaf)
FA 19 (1963) 847-851. (J. M. van
der Kroef)
JAS 23 (1963-4) 139-140. (J. R. W.
Smail)
PA 36 (1963) 320-1. (J. Bastin)
SEIB 41 (1966) 88.
SOAS 26 (1963) 464-466. (D. G. E.
Hall)

MENDES PINTO, FERNAO. Voyages and ad-
ventures of Fernand Mendez Pinto.
London, Dawson's, 1969.
BIJ 127 (1971) 285. (J. Bastin)
JMBRAS 45 pt. 2 (1969) 234. (J.
Bastin)
JSAS 2 (1971) 237-8. (D. K.
Bassett)

Meneses, Francisco de Sa de *See* SA DE
MENESES, FRANCISCO DE

MENOUX, MARCEL. Le dos du tigre;
roman. Paris, Duca, 1959.
SEIB 35 (1960) 736.

MENOUX, MARCEL. Sequences jaunes.
Paris, Societe d'Editions Exterieures
et Coloniales, 1959.
SEIB 35 (1960) 740-1.

* MERCADO, LEONARDO N. Elements of Fili-
pino philosophy. Tacloban City,
Divine Word Univ. Publications, 1974.
PS 22 (1974) 384-386. (N. S. Abueg)

MERTON, THOMAS. Asian journal of
Thomas Merton. New York, New Direc-
tions, 1973.
JSS 62 pt. 2 (1974) 363-4. (S.
Sivaraksa)

MEULEN, D. VAN DER. Ik stond er bij:
het einde van ons koloniale rijk.
Baarn, Bosch en Keuning, n.d.
PA 42 (1969) 537-540. (B. B.
Hering)

Meunier, Achille Dauphin *See* DAUPHIN-
MEUNIER, ACHILLE

MEYER, CHARLES. Derriere le sourire
Khmer. Paris, Plon, 1971.
JAS 31 (1971-2) 730-1. (D. P.
Chandler)
JSS 61 pt. 1 (1973) 310-325. (L.
Summers)
PA 45 (1972) 314-316. (J. L. S.
Girling)

MEYER, MILTON WALTER. Diplomatic his-
tory of the Philippine republic.
Honolulu, Univ. of Hawaii Pr., 1965.
JAS 25 (1965-6) 373-4. (D. J.
Steinberg)

MEYER, MILTON WALTER. Southeast Asia,
a brief history. Totowa, N.J.,
Littlefield, Adams, 1965.
PA 40 (1967) 158-9. (B. Harrison)

MEYER, MILTON WALTER. Southeast Asia,
a brief history. 2d. ed. Totowa, N.
J., Littlefield, Adams, 1971.
PA 44 (1971) 656-7. (N. Tarling)

MI MI KHAING. Burmese family.
Bloomington, Indiana UP, 1962.
PA 36 (1963) 201-2. (H. G. Trager)

MICHIGAN STATE UNIV., EAST LANSING.
VIETNAM PROJECT. What to read on
Vietnam, a selected annotated bibli-
ography. 2d. ed. New York, Institute
of Pacific Relations, 1960.
JSAH 3 (Mar. 1962) 142-3. (Truong
Buu Lam)

MIDDELKOOP, PIETER. Head hunting in
Timor and its historical implications. Sydney, Univ. of Sydney,
1964. (Oceanic Linguistics monograph, no. 8)
BIJ 124 (1968) 280-282. (R. E.
Downs)

MIGOT, ANDRE. Les Khmers, des origines d'Angkor au Cambodge d'au-
jourd'hui. Paris, Le Livre contemporain, 1960.
SEIB 35 (1960) 737.

MILLER, CHARLES CONSTANT. Black Borneo. New York, Modern Age Books,
1942.
SMJ 15 (1967) 440-445. (V. W.
Mullen)

MILLER, HARRY. Short history of Malaysia. New York, Praeger, 1965.
JAS 26 (1966-7) 338-9. (J. F. Cady)

Milne, Robert Stephen. Government and

MILLER, HARRY. Story of Malaysia.
London, Faber and Faber, 1965.
JAS 25 (1965-6) 801-2. (G. P.
Means)
PA 39 (1966) 218-9. (L. E.
Williams)

MILLER, JAMES INNES. Spice trade of
the Roman empire, 29 B.C. to A.D.
641. Oxford, Clarendon Pr., 1969.
BIJ 128 (1972) 401-2. (J. J. M.
Taeymans)
JAS 29 (1969-70) 677-8. (P.
Wheatley)
SOAS 33 (1970) 387-8. (A. K.
Irvine)

Miller, Norman *See* National liberation

MILLS, LENNOX ALGERNON. British Malaya,
1824-67. Singapore, Nanyang Printers,
1961. (Royal Asiatic Society of
Great Britain and Ireland. Malayan
Branch. Journal, v. 33 pt. 3)
JSAH 8 (1967) 352-3. (C. M.
Turnbull)

MILLS, LENNOX ALGERNON. Malaya, a
political and economic appraisal.
Minneapolis, Univ. of Minnesota Pr.,
1958.
MER 5 pt. 1 (1960) 28-30. (U. A.
Aziz)

MILLS, LENNOX ALGERNON. Southeast
Asia: illusion and reality in poli-
tics and economics. Minneapolis,
Univ. of Minnesota Pr., 1964.
AS 4 (1964) 1071.
PA 38 (1965) 199-200. (D. G. E.
Hall)
PS 13 (1965) 892-3. (J. M. Juco)
SOAS 28 (1965) 461. (H. Tinker)

MILNE, ROBERT STEPHEN. Government and
politics in Malaysia. Boston, Hough-
ton Mifflin, 1967.
JAS 27 (1967-8) 179-180. (K.
Mulliner)
JSAH 9 (1968) 161-163. (J. H.

Milne, Robert Stephen. Government and

    Beaglehole)
    PA 40 (1967) 164. (R. O. Tilman)

Milne, Robert Stephen *See* RATNAM, K.
    J. Malayan parliamentary election
    of 1964

MILNE, ROBERT STEPHEN. Planning for
    progress, the administration of eco-
    nomic planning in the Philippines.
    Manila, Univ. of the Philippines,
    Institute of Public Administration,
    1960. (Quezon, Philippines. Univ.
    of the Philippines. Institute of
    Public Administration. Studies in
    public administration, no. 6)
      PA 35 (1962) 192-194. (F. H. Golay)

Milner, George Bertram *See* CONFER-
    ENCE ON LINGUISTIC PROBLEMS OF THE
    INDO-PACIFIC AREA, SCHOOL OF ORIEN-
    TAL AND AFRICAN STUDIES, UNIV. OF
    LONDON, 1965. Indo-Pacific linguis-
    tic studies

MILONE, PAULINE DUBLIN. Urban areas
    in Indonesia; administrative and
    census concepts. Berkeley, Insti-
    tute of International Studies, Univ.
    of California, 1966. (California.
    Univ. Institute of International
    Studies. Research series, no. 10)
      PA 39 (1966) 417-8. (O. D. van den
      Muijzenberg)

* MIN BIN JAMALUDDIN. History of Port
    Swettenham. Singapore, Dept. of
    History, Univ. of Singapore, 1963.
    (Singapore studies on Borneo and
    Malaya, no. 3)
      JAS 24 (1964-5) 338-9. (J.
      Silverstein)

MINN LATT YEKHAUN. Modernization of
    Burmese. Prague, Oriental Institute
    in Academia Publishing House of the
    Czechoslovak Academy of Sciences,
    1966. (Orientalni ustav, Prague.
    Dissertationes orientales, v. 11)
      SOAS 31 (1968) 649-651. (J. Okell)

MINNEY, R. J. Fanny and the regent of
    Siam. London, Collins, 1962.
    JSS 50 (1962) 62-3.

MINTZ, JEANNE S. Indonesia: a pro-
    file. Princeton, Van Nostrand, 1961.
    JAS 21 (1961-2) 564-5. (H. Feith)
    PA 35 (1962) 184-5. (B. Crozier)

MINTZ, JEANNE S. Mohammed, Marx and
    Marhaen, the roots of Indonesian so-
    cialism. New York, Praeger, 1965.
    AS 5 (1965) 170.
    JAS 25 (1965-6) 170-1. (R. C. Bone)
    PA 38 (1965) 425. (D. S. Lev)

MINTZ, MALCOLM W. Bikol grammar notes.
    Honolulu, Univ. of Hawaii Pr., 1971.
    (Hawaii. Univ., Honolulu. Pacific and
    Asian Linguistics Institute. PALI
    language texts)
      AAS 10 (1974) 200. (J. Genzor)

MIRIKITANI, LEATRICE T. Kapampangan
    syntax. Honolulu, Univ. of Hawaii
    Pr., 1972. (Oceanic Linguistics.
    Special publication, no. 10)
      SOAS 37 (1974) 281. (N. G.
      Phillips)

MITCHELL, ROBERT EDWARD. Levels of
    emotional strain in Southeast Asian
    cities; a study of individual re-
    sponses to the stresses of urbaniza-
    tion and industrialization. Taipei,
    Orient Cultural Service, 1972. 2v.
    (Asian folklore and social life mono-
    graphs, vol. 27-28)
      JSAS 4 (1973) 320-322. (Riaz
      Hassan)

MITCHISON, LOIS. Overseas Chinese.
    London, Bodley Head, 1961.
    PA 34 (1961) 307-8. (W. E.
    Willmott)

MODELSKI, GEORGE A. New emerging
    forces: documents on the ideology of
    Indonesian foreign policy. Canberra,
    Dept. of International Relations, Re-
    search School of Pacific Studies,

Institute of Advanced Studies, Aus-
tralian National Univ., 1963. (Aus-
tralian National Univ., Canberra.
Dept. of International Relations.
Documents and data paper, no. 2)
  JAS 24 (1964-5) 531. (J. C. Nahm)

MODELSKI, GEORGE A. SEATO: six
  studies. Melbourne, Cheshire, 1962.
    JAS 23 (1963-4) 122. (J. H.
    Badgley)
    JSAH 7 (Mar. 1966) 152-3. (G. G.
    Thomson)
    PA 37 (1964) 228-230. (R. C. Nairn)

Modern Singapore. Edited by Ooi Jin
  Bee and Chiang Hai Ding. Singapore,
  Univ. of Singapore, 1969.
    JAH 5 (1971) 80-1. (G. W. Wilson)
    PA 43 (1970) 637. (K. S. Sandhu)

MOEBIRMAN. Wajang purwa (le jeu
  d'ombres d'Indonesie). Djakarta,
  Editions Ichtiar, 1960.
    BIJ 118 (1962) 394-396. (G. D.
    van Wengen)

MOERMAN, MICHAEL. Agricultural change
  and peasant choice in a Thai village.
  Berkeley, Univ. of California Pr.,
  1968.
    AP 12 (1969) 139-140. (A. Y.
    Dessaint)
    AS 8 (1968) 433.
    JAS 28 (1968-9) 906-7. (C. F.
    Keyes)
    JSS 57 (1969) 373-4. (M. W.
    Amadeus)
    PA 42 (1969) 103-4. (T. H. Silcock)
    SA 1 (1971) 276-282. (J. L. S.
    Girling)

MOERTONO, SOEMARSAID. State and
  statecraft in old Java, a study of
  the late Mataram period, 16th to
  19th century. Ithaca, Modern Indonesia Project, Cornell Univ., 1968.
  (Cornell Univ. Modern Indonesia
  Project. Monograph series)
    AS 8 (1968) 1027.
    BIJ 125 (1969) 393-396. (H. J. de

Mole, Robert L. Montagnards of South

  Graaf)
    JAS 28 (1968-9) 910-912. (P.
    Wheatley)
    JSAS 1 pt. 1 (1970) 116-7. (M. C.
    Ricklefs)

MÖRZER BRUYNS, A. Kamus singkatan dan
  akronim jang dipergunakan di Indonesia. Glossary of abbreviations and
  acronyms used in Indonesia. Djakarta, Ichtiar, 1970.
    AR 4 (1972) 250-252. (P. Labrousse)
    BIJ 126 (1970) 366-7. (J. W. de
    Vries)

MOFFAT, ABBOT LOW. Mongkut, the King
  of Siam. Ithaca, Cornell UP, 1961.
    JAS 21 (1961-2) 406-7. (W. F.
    Vella)
    JSAH 5 (Sept. 1964) 205-207. (E.
    Thio)
    JSS 50 (1962) 64.
    PA 35 (1962) 302-3. (D. G. E. Hall)

MOHAMED ARIFF BIN OTHMAN. Philippines
  claim to Sabah, its historical, legal
  and political implications. Singapore, Oxford UP, 1970.
    AS 11 (1970) 301.
    JSAS 3 (1972) 142-3. (L. R. Wright)
    PA 44 (1971) 142-3. (L. C. Green)
    PA 45 (1972) 156. (R. S. Milne)

MOHAMED SUFFIAN. Introduction to the
  constitution of Malaysia. Kuala Lumpur, GPO, 1972.
    JAS 32 (1972-3) 558-9. (W. R. Roff)

Mohammad Hatta *See* HATTA, MOHAMMAD

MOITESSIER, BERNARD. Un vagabond des
  mers du sud. Paris, Flammarion,
  1960.
    SEIB 35 (1960) 736-7.

MOLE, ROBERT L. Montagnards of South
  Vietnam, a study of nine tribes.
  Rutland, Tuttle, 1970.
    PA 43 (1970) 626-630. (A. Woodside)

MORISON, SAMUEL ELIOT. History of
United States naval operations in
World War II. Volume XIII. Libera-
tion of the Philippines: Luzon,
Mindanao, the Visayas, 1944–45. Bos-
ton, Little Brown, 1959.
  JAS 19 (1959–60) 478–9. (L. Casper)
  PS 8 (1960) 469–472. (R. H. Smith)

MORRISON, GAYLE. Guide to books on
Southeast Asian history, 1961–1966.
Santa Barbara, American Bibliographi-
cal Center, 1969.
  SA 2 (1972–3) 138–143. (S. Saito)

MORRISON, HEDDA HAMMER. Life in a
longhouse. Kuching, Borneo Literature Bureau, 1962.
  SOAS 29 (1966) 460. (G. B. Milner)

* MORRISON, HEDDA HAMMER. Sarawak.
Detroit, Cellar Book Shop, 1968.
  PA 44 (1971) 466–7. (R. S. Milne)

Morrison, Hedda Hammer *See* WRIGHT,
LEIGH R. Vanishing world

Morrow, William *See* WEST, MORRIS L.

MORTIMER, REX ALFRED. Indonesian communism under Sukarno; ideology and
politics, 1959–1965. Ithaca, Cornell UP, 1974.
  PA 47 (1974) 574–576. (D. Hindley)

MORTIMER, REX ALFRED. The Indonesian
Communist Party and land reform,
1959–65. Clayton, Vic., Centre of
Southeast Asian Studies, Monash Univ.,
1972. (Monash papers on Southeast
Asia, no. 1)
  JCA 4 (1974) 365.

MORTIMER, REX ALFRED. Showcase state:
the illusion of Indonesia's accelerated modernisation. Sydney, Angus
and Robertson, 1973.
  PA 47 (1974) 387–8. (J. M. van der
  Kroef)

MORTON, DAVID. Traditional music of
Thailand; introduction, commentary,
and analyses. Los Angeles, Univ. of
California, Institute of Ethnomusi-
cology, 1968.
  JSS 57 (1969) 375–6. (M. W.
  Amadeus)

MOSHER, ARTHUR THEODORE. Getting agriculture moving, essentials for development and modernization. New York,
Agricultural Development Council,
1966.
  SJ 15 (1968) 313–4. (O. J. Tayko)

Moss, Laurence A. G. *See* GRANT,
JONATHAN S. Cambodia; the widening
war in Indochina

MOSSMAN, JAMES. Rebels in paradise,
Indonesia's civil war. London,
Jonathan Cape, 1961.
  PA 35 (1962) 428–9. (G. McT. Kahin)

MOUHOT, HENRI. Diary: travels in the
central parts of Siam, Cambodia and
Laos during the years 1858–61.
Abridged and edited by Christopher
Pym. Kuala Lumpur, Oxford UP, 1966.
  JAS 26 (1966–7) 533–535. (D. G. E.
  Hall)
  JSAH 9 (1968) 170–172. (C. M.
  Turnbull)
  SOAS 30 (1967) 474. (H. Tinker)

MOUSNY, ANDRE. Economy of Thailand, an
appraisal of a liberal exchange pol-
icy. Bangkok, Social Science Associ-
ation Pr. of Thailand, 1964.
  JAS 24 (1964–5) 336–7. (L. D.
  Stifel)
  MER 11 pt. 1 (1966) 101–113. (T. H.
  Silcock)

* MOUSSAY, GERARD. Dictionnaire Cam-
Vietnamien-Francais. Phanrang, Cen-
tre Culturel Cam, 1971.
  AR 6 (1973) 205–207. (D. Lombard)
  SEIB 48 (1973) 135–139. (Nguy Van
  Nhuan)

Mpu Tanakarun

Mpu Tanakarun *See* Siwaratrikalpa of Mpu Tanakarun

* Muc luc chau ban trieu Nguyen. Hue, Comite des traductions des documents historiques de l'Universite de Hue, 1960.
    BEF 51 (1963) 215-6. (M. M. Durand)

MUHAMMAD RABI'IBN MUHAMMAD IBRAHIM. Ship of Sulaiman, translated by John O'Kane. London, Routledge and Kegan Paul, 1972. (Persian heritage series, no. 11)
    AF 5 pt. 3 (1973) 132-3. (W. K. Archer)
    JAH 8 (1974) 169-170. (C. R. Boxer)
    JSS 62 pt. 1 (1974) 151-157. (D. K. Wyatt)
    SOAS 36 (1973) 714-716. (D. K. Bassett)

Muhammad Shamsul Huq *See* SHAMSUL HUQ, MUHAMMAD

MULDER, JAN ANTON NIELS. Monks, merit and motivation, an exploratory study of the social functions of Buddhism in Thailand in processes of guided social change. DeKalb, Center for Southeast Asian Studies, Northern Illinois Univ., 1969.
    JAS 33 (1973-4) 738-9. (J. Bilmes)
    JSAS 2 (1971) 232-234. (J. Bunnag)
    JSS 59 pt. 2 (1971) 280-282. (D. Lancaster)

MUNOZ, ALFREDO N. Filipinos in America. Los Angeles, Mountain-View, 1971.
    JAS 31 (1971-2) 749-750. (D. V. Hart)

* Mural paintings at Wat Rakang. Bangkok, Thai Watana Pr., 1970.
    JSS 59 pt. 1 (1971) 271-2. (Euayporn Kerdchouay)

MURDOCK, GEORGE PETER. Africa, its people and their cultural history. New York, McGraw-Hill, 1959.
    AP 4 (1960) 61-2. (W. G. Solheim)

MURDOCK, GEORGE PETER. Social structure in Southeast Asia. Chicago, Quadrangle Books, 1960. (Viking Fund publications in anthropology, no. 29)
    JAS 20 (1960-1) 546-548. (L. H. Palmier)
    PA 34 (1961) 216-7. (M. Freedman)

MURTI, BHASKARLA SURYA NARAYANA. Vietnam divided; the unfinished struggle. New York, Asia Publishing House, 1964.
    AS 5 (1965) 527.

MUS, PAUL. Guerre sans visage; lettres commentees du sous-lieutenant Emile Mus. Paris, Seuil, 1961.
    FA 18 (1962) 107. (J. Lacouture)
    FA 18 (1962) 109-111. (M. Roth)

Mus, Paul *See* McALISTER, JOHN T. The Vietnamese and their revolution

MUSCAT, ROBERT J. Development strategy in Thailand; a study of economic growth. New York, Praeger, 1966.
    AS 8 (1968) 148.
    JAS 26 (1966-7) 345-347. (M. F. Long)
    JSS 55 (1967) 299-301. (L. Sternstein)
    PA 40 (1967) 159-160. (C. Belshaw)

Musee Guimet *See* PARIS. MUSEE GUIMET

Musgrave, John K. *See* LeBAR, FRANK M. Ethnic groups of mainland Southeast Asia

MUSEUM PUSAT. Guide to the ceramic collection, Museum Pusat, Djakarta, edited by E. W. Orsoy de Flines. 2d. ed. Djakarta, 1969.
    AR 3 (1972) 200-1. (D. Lombard)

MUSKENS, M. P. M. Indonesie. Een strijd om nationale identiteit. Nationalisten, Islamieten, Katholieken. Bussum, P. Brand, 1969. (De grote

oecumene. Interreligeuze ontwikke-
lingen)
    BIJ 127 (1971) 497-505. (E. Allard)
    BIJ 127 (1971) 505-507. (H. G. S.
      Nordholt)

Mya Maung *See* MAUNG, MYA

MYLIUS, NORBERT. Indonesia Textil-
kunst: Batik, Ikat und Plangi.
Vienna, Verlag Notring der Wissenschaften Verbande Osterrichs, 1964.
    BIJ 121 (1965) 379-380. (C.
      Nooteboom)

MYLIUS, NORBERT. Kulturhistorische
Abhandlungen. Amsterdam, Nabrink,
1970.
    BIJ 128 (1972) 500-1. (R. S.
      Wassing)

MYRDAL, GUNNAR. Asian drama, an inquiry into the poverty of nations.
New York, Twentieth Century Fund,
1968. 3v.
    JAH 3 (1969) 179-180. (A. K. Ho)
    JAS 28 (1968-9) 391-2. (K. Nair)
    MAS 5 (1971) 80-85. (B. L. C.
      Johnson)
    PS 17 (1969) 359-362. (M.
      McPhelin)

MYRDAL, JAN. Angkor; an essay on art
and imperialism, by Jan Myrdal and
Gun Kessle. New York, Pantheon,
1970.
    PA 44 (1971) 313-4. (R. Garry)

* NAFIS AHMAD. Economic resources of
the Union of Burma. Natick, Mass.,
United States Army Natick Labora-
tories, n.d.
    JAS 32 (1972-3) 743-4. (R. E. Huke)

NAGAZUMI, AKIRA. Dawn of Indonesian
nationalism; the early years of the
Budi Utomo, 1908-1918. Tokyo, Institute of Developing Economics,
1972. (Ajia Keizai Kenkyujo, Tokyo.
I.D.E. occasional papers series, no.
10)

Nash, Mannning. Anthropological studies

    AR 6 (1973) 224-226. (F. C.
      Blanchard)

NAIRN, RONALD C. International aid to
Thailand, the new colonialism? New
Haven, Yale UP, 1966. (Yale studies
in political science, 19)
    AS 8 (1968) 347.
    JAS 26 (1966-7) 759-760. (W. F.
      Vella)
    PA 40 (1967) 405-6. (F. C. Darling)

NAKAHARA, JOYCE. Development and conflict in Thailand, by Joyce Nakahara
and Ronald A. Witton. Ithaca, Southeast Asia Program, Cornell Univ.,
1971. (Cornell Univ. Southeast Asia
Program. Data paper, no. 80) (Cornell
Univ. Thailand Project. Interim report series, no. 14)
    JAS 32 (1972-3) 376-378. (C. F.
      Keyes)
    JSS 61 pt. 1 (1973) 332-339. (Serin
      Punnahitanond)
    PS 20 (1972) 678.

NAKHODA MUDA. De biografie van een
Minangkabausen peperhandelaar in de
Lampongs, naar een Maleis handschrift
in de Marsden Collection te London,
uitg. vertaald en ingeleid door G. W.
J. Drewes. The Hague, Nijhoff, 1961.
(Instituut voor Taal-, Land- en
Volkenkunde. Verhandelingen, deel 36)
    SOAS 26 (1963) 676-7. (E. C. G.
      Barrett)

Nakpil, Carmen Guerrero *See* GUERRERO
NAKPIL, CARMEN

NANDADHAJA, SHIN. Epistles written on
the eve of the Anglo-Burmese war,
translated and introduced by Htin
Aung. The Hague, Nijhoff, 1968.
    PA 42 (1969) 118-9. (D. G. E. Hall)
    SOAS 32 (1969) 235-6. (J. Okell)

Nash, Manning *See* CONFERENCE ON
THERAVADA BUDDHISM, UNIV. OF CHICAGO,
1962. Anthropological studies in
Theravada Buddhism

Nash, Manning. Golden road to

NASH, MANNING. Golden road to modernity, village life in contemporary
Burma. New York, John Wiley, 1965.
  AS 5 (1965) 574.
    JAS 25 (1966) 550-1. (J. F. Brohm)
    RSA (1967) 311-313. (I. Jadoul)

NASUTION, ABDUL HARIS. Fundamentals
of guerrilla warfare. New York,
Praeger, 1965.
    JAS 25 (1965-6) 371-2. (G. J.
      Pauker)
    PA 38 (1965) 426-7. (D. S. Lev)

NATIONAL COLLOQUIUM ON THE PHILIPPINES,
1ST, WESTERN MICHIGAN UNIV., 1966.
Research and development research in
the social sciences; proceedings.
Edited by Charles O. Houston. Kalamazoo, Institute of International
and Area Studies, 1969.
    JAS 29 (1969-70) 992-3. (R. W.
      Lieban)

National liberation; revolution in the
third world, edited by Norman Miller
and Roderick Aya. New York, Free
Pr., 1971.
    JAS 32 (1972-3) 508-510. (D.
      Callaway)

Nationalism, revolution and evolution
in South-East Asia. Zug, Switzerland, Inter-Documentation Co., 1970.
(Hull monographs on South-East Asia,
no. 2)
    JAS 31 (1971-2) 985-6. (R. K.
      Paget)
    JSAS 3 (1972) 146-148. (G. S.
      Maryanov)
    MAS 6 (1972) 123-125. (S. Rose)
    PA 44 (1971) 460-462. (R. Emerson)
    SA 1 (1971) 400-402. (R. S. Milne)

Natsionalno-osvoboditelnoe dvizhenie v
Indonesii: 1942-1965 [edited by A.
A. Guber et al.]. Moscow, Nauka,
1970.
    SA 2 (1972) 530. (V. M. Fic)

NATURAL AND APPLIED SCIENCES BULLETIN
(INDEXES). Natural and applied sciences bulletin, index to volumes I-
XVII, 1930-60, compiled by Catalina
A. Nemenzo. Quezon City, Univ. of
the Philippines, 1961.
    JAS 23 (1963-4) 316-7. (D. V. Hart)

Navarrete, Domingo Fernandez *See*
FERNANDEZ NAVARRETE, DOMINGO

Nayagam, Xavier S. Thani *See* THANI
NAYAGAM, XAVIER S.

NEDERLANDS GENOOTSCHAP VOOR INTERNA
TIONALE ZAKEN. Indonesia's struggle
1957-1958; a report. The Hague,
1959.
    JSAH 1 (Sept. 1960) 116-118. (J. D.
      Legge)

NEDERLANDSCHE OOST-INDISCHE COMPAGNIE.
Generale missiven van gouverneur-
generaal en raden aan Heren XVII der
Verenigde Oostindische Compagnie,
uitg. door W. Ph. Coolhaas. The
Hague, Nijhoff, 1964-
Volume II.
    BIJ 123 (1967) 382-3. (H. J. de
      Graaf)
    JSAH 7 (Mar. 1966) 150-1. (R. Van
      Niel)
Volume III.
    BIJ 124 (1968) 554-5. (H. J. de
      Graaf)
    JSAH 10 (1969) 360-362. (S.
      Arasaratnam)
Volume IV.
    BIJ 128 (1972) 499-500. (H. J. de
      Graaf)

Needham, Rodney *See* Rethinking kinship and marriage

NEEDHAM, RODNEY. Structure and sentiment; a test case in social anthropology. Chicago, Univ. of Chicago
Pr., 1962.
    BIJ 118 (1962) 476-7. (H. T.
      Fischer)

NEILL, STEPHEN CHARLES. Concise dictionary of the Christian world mission, by Stephen C. Neill, Gerald H. Anderson and John Goodwin. Nashville, Abingdon Pr., 1971. (World Christian books)
    PS 20 (1972) 345-6. (F. X. Clark)

NEILL, WILFRED T. Twentieth century Indonesia. New York, Columbia UP, 1973.
    JAS 33 (1973-4) 741-2. (W. H. Frederick)

Nemenzo, Catalina A. *See* DILIMAN REVIEW (INDEXES)

NEMENZO, CATALINA A. Flora and fauna of the Philippines, 1851-1966; an annotated bibliography. Quezon City, Univ. of the Philippines, 1967. (Natural and Applied Science Bulletin, vol. 21 pts. 1-2)
    JAS 30 (1970-1) 741. (D. V. Hart)

Nemenzo, Catalina A. *See* LITERARY APPRENTICE (INDEXES)

Nemenzo, Catalina A. *See* NATURAL AND APPLIED SCIENCES BULLETIN (INDEXES)

NESS, GAYL D. Bureaucracy and rural development in Malaysia. Berkeley, Univ. of California Pr., 1967.
    JAS 27 (1967-8) 431-433. (W. S. Hunsberger)
    MER 13 pt. 1 (1968) 130-1. (A. Degani)
    PA 40 (1967) 398-9. (R. S. Milne)

NEVADOMSKY, JOSEPH JOHN. Chinese in Southeast Asia, a selected and annotated bibliography of publications in western languages, 1960-1970, by Joseph J. Nevadomsky and Alice Li. Berkeley, Center for South and Southeast Asia Studies, Univ. of California, 1970. (California. Univ. Center for South and Southeast Asia Studies. Occasional paper, no. 6)
    BIJ 127 (1971) 296-299. (Go Gien

Nghiem Tham. Esquisse d'une etude sur Tjwan)
    PA 44 (1971) 657-8. (E. Wickberg)
    PS 20 (1972) 190-192. (C. J. McCarthy)
    SJ 17 (1970) 349-350. (H. S. Reynolds)

NEVERMANN, HANS. Stimme des Wasserbuffels; malaiische Volkslieder. Eisennach, Erich Roth, 1956.
    BIJ 116 (1960) 483-485. (C. Hooykaas)

NEW YORK. MUSEUM OF PRIMITIVE ART. Art of Lake Sentani, text by S. Kooyman. New York, 1959.
    BIJ 117 (1961) 302-3. (B. A. L. Cranstone)

NEWBOLD, THOMAS JOHN. Political and statistical account of the British settlements in the Straits of Malacca. Singapore, Oxford UP, 1971. 2v.
    PA 45 (1972) 138. (D. G. E. Hall)

NEWELL, WILLIAM HARE. Treacherous river: a study of rural Chinese in north Malaya. Kuala Lumpur, Univ. of Malaya Pr., 1963.
    JAS 25 (1965-6) 168-9. (W. E. Willmott)
    PA 37 (1964) 236-238. (D. E. Willmott)
    SOAS 27 (1964) 486-7. (G. B. Downer)

NGHIEM DANG. Vietnam; politics and public administration. Honolulu, East-West Center Pr., 1966.
    AS 6 (1966) 657.
    JAS 26 (1966-7) 543-4. (D. Wurfel)
    PA 39 (1966) 452-3. (R. S. Milne)

NGHIEM THAM. Esquisse d'une etude sur les interdits chez les Vietnamiens. Saigon, Ministere de la Culture et de Education, 1965. (Publications de l'Institut de recherches archeologiques. So. 8)
    BEF 57 (1970) 242-3. (N. Louis)

Nginn, Somchine P. Dictionnaire

* NGINN, SOMCHINE P. Dictionnaire
  Francais-Lao. Bangkok, Ruang Ratna
  Pr., 1969.
    BEF 57 (1970) 236-7. (P.-M.
    Gagneux)

NGO VINH LONG. Before the revolution,
  the Vietnamese peasants under the
  French. Cambridge, MIT Pr., 1973.
    JCA 4 (1974) 502-504. (T. Shanin)

* Ngoc Kien Le. Hue, Institut de Litterature Vietnamienne de la Faculte
  de Lettres, 1961.
    BEF 52 (1964) 278-287. (Ta Trong
    Hiep)

* NGUYEN BAT TUY. Ngon ngu hoc Viet Nam.
  Saigon, Ngon Ngu, 1959.
    SEIB 36 (1961) 738.

* NGUYEN CHUNG ANH. Hat vi Nghe-Tinh.
  Hanoi, Van Su Dia, 1958.
    BEF 52 (1964) 256-275. (Le Van
    Hao)

NGUYEN DANG LIEM. Vietnamese pronunciation. Honolulu, Univ. of Hawaii
  Pr., 1970. (Hawaii. Univ. Pacific
  and Asian Linguistics Institute.
  PALI language texts)
    AAS 8 (1972) 195-198. (J. Mucka)

NGUYEN, DANG THUC. Democracy in traditional Vietnamese society. Saigon,
  GPO, 1960. (Vietnam culture series,
  no. 4)
    SEIB 35 (1960) 734.

NGUYEN DINH HOA. Read Vietnamese, a
  graded course in written Vietnamese.
  Saigon, Vietnamese-American Association, 1966.
    JAS 26 (1966-7) 544. (F. H.
    Tucker)

NGUYEN DINH HOA. Vietnamese language.
  Saigon, GPO, 1960. (Vietnam culture
  series, no. 2)
    SEIB 35 (1960) 734.

* NGUYEN DONG CHI. Hat dam Nghe-Tinh.
  Hanoi, Tan Viet, 1944.
    BEF 52 (1964) 256-275. (Le Van
    Hao)

* NGUYEN DONG CHI. Hat Giam Nghe-Tinh,
  [by] Nguyen Dong Chi [and] Ninh Viet
  Giao. Hanoi, Vien Su-hoc, 1962.
    BEF 52 (1964) 256-275. (Le Van
    Hao)

* NGUYEN DONG CHI. Kho tang truyen co
  tich Viet-nam. Hanoi, 1958.
    BEF 52 (1964) 243-4. (M. Durand)

* NGUYEN DONG CHI. Kho tang truyen co
  tich Viet-nam. 2d. ed. Hanoi, Vien
  Su Hoc, 1961. 2v.
    BEF 52 (1964) 275-278. (Le Van
    Hao)

NGUYEN DONG CHI. Luoc khao ve than
  thoai Viet-Nam. Hanoi, Van Su Dia,
  1956.
    BEF 52 (1964) 253-256. (Le Van
    Hao)

NGUYEN DU. Kim Van Kieu. Paris, Gallimard, 1961. (Connaissance de
  l'Orient; collection UNESCO d'oeuvres
  representatives, 12)
    SEIB 36 (1961) 730-1.

NGUYEN DU. Tale of Kieu. New York,
  Random House, 1973.
    JAS 33 (1973-4) 743-4. (M. Ross)

* NGUYEN DU. Tho chu Han Nguyen Du.
  Hanoi, Nha xuat-ban Van-Hoa, 1959.
    BEF 50 (1960) 556.

Nguyen Duc Dan *See* DAN, NGUYEN DUC

Nguyen Duc Hiep *See* THOMPSON,
  LAURENCE C. Vietnamese reader

Nguyen Hien Le *See* TRUONG VAN CHINH.
  Khao Luan ve ngu phap Viet-Nam

Nguyen Huu Trong *See* NGUYEN TAN LONG. Viet-Nam Thi nhan tien chien

* NGUYEN HUY. Hien-tinh kinh-te Viet-nam. Saigon, Lua-Thieng, 1972. 2v.
  SEIB 48 (1973) 150-152. (Quach Thanh Tam)

NGUYEN HUYEN ANH. Viet-nam danh nhan tu-dien. Saigon, Hoi Van-Hoa Binh-Dan, 1960.
  BEF 52 (1964) 562-567. (N. Louis)

NGUYEN KHAC KHAM. Introduction to Vietnamese culture. Saigon, GPO, 1961. (Vietnam culture series, no. 1)
  SEIB 35 (1960) 734.

NGUYEN KHAC NGU. Mau-he cham. Saigon, Trinh-Bay, 1967.
  BEF 55 (1969) 266-270. (T. C. Leocmach)

* NGUYEN KHAC VIEN. Tradition and revolution in Vietnam. Berkeley, Indochina Resource Center, 1974.
  JAS 34 (1974-5) 261-2. (J. K. Whitmore)

NGUYEN KHAC VIEN. Le Vietnam traditionnel; quelques etapes historiques. Hanoi, XunHaSaBa, 1969. (Etudes vietnamiennes, no. 21)
  AAS 7 (1971) 158-160. (I. Dolezal)

NGUYEN KIEN. Le Sud Viet-Nam depuis Dien-bien-Phu. Paris, Francois Maspero, 1963.
  FA 19 (1963) 1047-1051. (J. Christan)

* NGUYEN MANH BAO. Luc-thao Nguyen ban cua Khuong-Thai-Cong. Saigon, Xuat-ban Co-Kim an-quan, n.d.
  SEIB 36 (1961) 738-9.

* NGUYEN MANH BAO. Tam luoc Truong Tu Phong (Truong Luong) va Quan chinh doi Duong do Ly-Ve-Cong Ly-Tinh (Xuat ban Co-Kim an quan). Saigon,

Nguyen Thuy Anh. Luoi dang ou madraque 1959.
  SEIB 36 (1961) 738-9.

* NGUYEN NGOC TINH. Binh thu Yeu luoc, [by] Nguyen Ngoc Tinh [and] Do Mong Khuong. Hanoi, Khoa Hoc Xa Hoi, 1970.
  BEF 58 (1971) 335-6. (Nguyen Tran Huan)

* NGUYEN TAN LONG. Viet-nam Thi nhan tien chien [by] Nguyen Tan Long [and] Nguyen Huu Trong. Saigon, 1967-8. 2v.
  BEF 56 (1969) 211-2. (Nguyen Tran Huan)

NGUYEN THAI. Is South Vietnam viable? Manila, 1962.
  PA 37 (1964) 472-3. (F. J. Corley)

NGUYEN THANH NHA. Tableau economique du Viet-Nam aux XVIIe et XVIIIe siecles. Paris, Bibliotheque Bich-Thanh-Tuu, 1966.
  BEF 55 (1969) 298-301. (N. Louis)
  JAS 30 (1970-1) 922-3. (A. Woodside)
  JSAS 2 (1971) 260-1. (J. K. Whitmore)

NGUYEN THE ANH. Bibliographie critique sur les relations entre le Viet-Nam et l'Occident (ouvrages et articles en langues occidentales). Paris, Maisonneuve, 1967.
  FA 21 (1966) 499-500. (P. Grison)
  SEIB 44 (1969) 195. (P. Langlet)
  SOAS 31 (1968) 454. (R. B. Smith)

Nguyen Thi Hue *See* JUMPER, ROY. Notes on the political and administrative history of Viet Nam

* NGUYEN THUY ANH. Luoi dang ou madraque vietnamienne dans la region de Khanh-hoa (Nha-trang). Etude technologique, economique et sociale. Saigon, Societe des Etudes Indochinoises, 1966. (Societe des Etudes Indochinoises. Bulletin, n.s. XLI pt. 3/4)
  BEF 56 (1969) 182-188. (P. Y. Manguin)

Nguyen Trai. Uc-Trai Tuong-cong tap

NGUYEN TRAI. Uc-Trai Tuong-cong tap.
Saigon, Min. d'Etat Charge des Affaires Culturelles, 1972.
    SEIB 48 (1973) 149-150. (Nguyen
    The Anh)

Nguyen Tran Huan *See* DURAND, MAURICE
M. Introduction a la litterature
vietnamienne

NGUYEN VAN MINH. Duoc tinh chi nam.
Saigon, Ky-Lao Ai-Huu, 1964-67. 4v.
    BEF 57 (1970) 269-273. (Nguyen
    Tran Huan)

* NGUYEN VAN MIHN. Phuong phap xem mach
theo dong phuong. Saigon, 1965.
    BEF 57 (1970) 273-275. (Nguyen
    Tran Huan)

NGUYEN VAN PHONG. La societe vietnamienne de 1882 a 1902 d'apres les
ecrits des auteurs francais. Paris,
Presses Universitaires de France,
1971. (Paris. Universite Faculte
des lettres et sciences humaines.
Serie recherches, t. 69)
    JAS 32 (1972-3) 380-1. (A. Wood-
    side)
    JSS 62 pt. 1 (1974) 250-1. (D. P.
    Chandler)

Nguyen Van Thon *See* LAM BINH LOI.
Rung ngap nuoc Viet-nam

NHA-TRANG CONG-HUYEN-TON-NU. Vietnamese folklore, an introductory
and annotated bibliography. Berkeley, Center for South and Southeast
Asia Studies, Univ. of California,
1970. (California. Univ. Center for
South and Southeast Asia Studies.
Occasional paper, no. 7)
    JSAS 3 (1972) 152-3. (M. W. Ross)
    PA 45 (1972) 156. (H. E. Jacobson)
    PS 20 (1972) 199.

Nhat Thanh *See* VU VAN KHIEU. Dat le
que thoi

NICOLSON, I. F. Pacific politics;
Asian, Australasian, Oceanic, by I.
F. Nicolson and Colin A. Hughes.
Carlton, Victoria, Pitman, 1972.
    JAS 32 (1972-3) 556-7. (B. Nuss-
    baum)
    PA 45 (1972) 635. (R. S. Milne)

NIEUWENHUYS, ROB. Oost Indische Spiegel wat Nederlandse schrijvers en
dichters over Indonesie hebben geschreven, vanaf de eerste jaren der
compagnie tot op heden. Amsterdam,
Querido, 1972.
    BIJ 130 (1974) 381-384. (I.
    Schoffer)

NIGHSWONGER, WILLIAM A. Rural pacification in Vietnam. New York, Praeger, 1966.
    AS 7 (1967) 273.
    JAS 28 (1968-9) 821-831. (J. C.
    Donnell)

NIHAL SINGH, S. Malaysia, a commentary. New York, Barnes and Noble,
1971.
    JAS 33 (1973-4) 333-4. (R. O.
    Tilman)
    PA 46 (1973) 173-4. (G. P. Means)

NIKULIN, NIKOLAI IVANOVICH. V'etnam-
skaia literatura. Kratkii ocherk.
Moscow, Nauka, 1971.
    AAS 9 (1973) 199-205. (J. Mucka)

NIMMO, H. ARLO. Sea people of Sulu, a
study of social change in the Philippines. San Francisco, Chandler Publishing Co., 1972. (Studies in social and economic change)
    JAS 33 (1973-4) 343-4. (J. Beckett)

Ninh Viet Giao *See* NGUYEN DONG CHI.
Hat Giam Nghe-tinh

* NINH VIET GIAO. Hat phuong voi, dan
ca Nghe-Tinh. Hanoi, Van-hoa, 1961.
    BEF 52 (1964) 257-275. (Le Van Hao)

NITISASTRO, WIDJOJO. Population
trends in Indonesia. Ithaca, Cornell
UP, 1970.
   AR 4 (1972) 248-250.
   IND 10 (1970) 183-189. (B. Glass-
      burner)
   JAS 30 (1970-1) 916-918. (G. B.
      Simmons)
   PA 44 (1971) 144-5. (W. F.
      Wertheim)
   SA 1 (1971) 406-7. (D. S. Paauw)

No more Vietnams, the war and the
future of American foreign policy,
edited by Richard M. Pfeffer. New
York, Harper and Row, 1968.
   AS 9 (1969) 75.
   PA 43 (1970) 125-127. (J. L. S.
      Girling)

* NO NA PAK NAM. Five months among the
ruins of Ayudhya. Bangkok, Suksit
Siam Pr., 1967.
   JSS 56 (1968) 118-124. (V.
      Kennedy)

NOER, DELIAR. Modernist Muslim move-
ment in Indonesia, 1900-1942. Singa-
pore, Oxford UP, 1973.
   AR 8 (1974) 229-231. (D. Lombard)
   JAS 33 (1973-4) 342-3. (J. L.
      Peacock)
   JCA 4 (1974) 365.
   SOAS 37 (1974) 507-8. (W. R. Roff)

Nordholt, H. G. Schulte *See* SCHULTE
NORDHOLT, H. G.

NORODOM SIHANOUK VARMAN, KING OF CAM-
BODIA. L'Indochine vue de Pekin.
Paris, Seuil, 1972. (L'Histoire
immediate)
   JSS 61 pt. 1 (1973) 357-359. (D.
      P. Chandler)

NORODOM SIHANOUK VARMAN, KING OF CAM-
BODIA. My war with the C.I.A.:
Cambodia's fight for survival, by
Norodom Sihanouk as related to Wil-
fred Burchett. London, Penguin,
1973.

Nyce, Ray. The kingdom and the country
   JAS 33 (1973-4) 336-7. (D. P.
      Chandler)
   JCA 3 (1973) 215-217. (Lek Hor Tan)

NOWELL, CHARLES E. Magellan's voyage
around the world, three contemporary
accounts. Evanston, Northwestern UP,
1962.
   PA 38 (1965) 448-9. (J. G.
      Beaglehole)

NUECHTERLEIN, DONALD EDWIN. Thailand
and the struggle for Southeast Asia.
Ithaca, Cornell UP, 1965.
   AS 5 (1965) 574.
   FA 20 (1965) 406-7. (V. Phakdikun)
   JAH 1 (1967) 182-3.
   JAS 25 (1965-6) 551-2. (K. P.
      Landon)
   MAS 1 (1967) 106-7. (S. Simmonds)
   PA 40 (1967) 392-3. (L. Na Ranong)

NUNN, GODFREY RAYMOND. Asia, a selected
and annotated guide to reference
works. Cambridge, MIT Pr., 1971.
   JAS 31 (1971-2) 470.
   PA 45 (1972) 413. (E. Birnbaum)

NUNN, GODFREY RAYMOND. Asian libraries
and librarianship, an annotated bibliography of selected books and periodicals, and a draft syllabus. Metuchen, Scarecrow Pr., 1973.
   PA 47 (1974) 209-210. (E. Birnbaum)

NURGE, ETHEL. Life in a Leyte village.
Seattle, Univ. of Washington Pr.,
1965. (American Ethnological Soci-
ety. Monograph, no. 40)
   AP 9 (1966) 175-6. (W. G. Davis)
   AS 6 (1966) 186.
   JAS 26 (1966-7) 357-8. (F. M.
      LeBar)
   PA 41 (1968) 117-8. (H. E. Jacobson)
   PS 15 (1967) 206-209. (W. G. Davis)

NYCE, RAY. The kingdom and the country,
a study of church and society in
Singapore. Singapore, Institute for
Study of Religions and Society in
Singapore and Malaysia, 1972.
   JSAS 4 (1973) 140-1. (F. Thomas)

Nydegger. Corinne. Tarong

the world called *Il milione*.
Berkeley, Univ. of California Pr.,
1960.
    SOAS 25 (1962) 200-1. (C. R.
    Bowden)

O'NEILL, ROBERT JOHN. General Giap:
    Praeger, 1969.
    JAS 30 (1970-1) 239-240. (M.
    Osborne)

ONGKILI, JAMES P. Modernization in
    east Malaysia, 1960-1970. Kuala
    Lumpur, Oxford UP, 1972.
    JCA 4 (1974) 111.
    JSAS 4 (1973) 322-3. (G. P. Means)
    PA 46 (1973) 174-5. (R. S. Milne)

ONORATO, MICHAEL PAUL. Brief review
    of American interest in Philippine
    development and other essays. Ma-
    nila, MCS Enterprises, 1972.
    SA 3 (1974) 792-3. (M. Cullinane)

ONORATO, MICHAEL PAUL. Leonard Wood
    as Governor General; a calendar of
    selected correspondence. Manila,
    MCS Enterprises, 1969.
    PS 20 (1972) 193. (J. N. Schu-
    macher)

ONORATO, MICHAEL PAUL. Philippine
    bibliography, 1899-1946. Santa
    Barbara, ABC-Clio Pr., 1968.
    AAS 7 (1971) 157-8. (J. Genzor)
    PA 43 (1970) 483. (E. Wickberg)
    SA 2 (1972-3) 139-143. (S. Saito)

ONSLOW, CRANLEY. Asian economic de-
    velopment. New York, Praeger, 1965.
    AS 5 (1965) 574.

OOI JIN BEE. Land, people and economy
    in Malaya. London, Longmans, 1963.
    MER 9 pt. 2 (1964) 83-91. (W. D.
    McTaggart)
    RSA (1965) 123-4. (I. Jadoul)

Ooi, Jin Bee *See* Modern Singapore

Osborne, Milton E. French presence in

OOSTERS GENOOTSCHAP IN NEDERLAND. Acta
    orientalia neerlandica: proceedings
    of the congress of the Dutch Oriental
    Society held in Leiden on the occa-
    sion of its 50th anniversary, edited
    by P. W. Pestman. Leiden, Brill,
    1971.
    SOAS 35 (1972) 701.

OPLT, MIROSLAV. Bahasa Indonesia,
    Ucebnice indonestiny, Indonesian lan-
    guage. Prague, Statni Pedagogicke
    Nakladatelstvi, 1960.
    BIJ 116 (1960) 492. (A. Teeuw)
    SOAS 24 (1961) 400-1. (C. Hooykaas)

Orsoy de Flines, E. W. *See* MUSEUM
    PUSAT. Guide to the ceramic collec-
    tion

Ortigas, Irene L. *See* HOWARD, JOSEPH
    T. Society and culture in rural
    Philippines

ORTIZ ARMENGOL, PEDRO. Intramuros de
    Manila, de 1571 hasta su destruccion
    en 1945. Madrid, Ediciones de Cul-
    tura Hispanica, 1958.
    PS 8 (1960) 672-674. (N. P.
    Cushner)

OSANKA, FRANKLIN MARK. Modern guerril-
    la warfare: fighting communist guer-
    rilla movements, 1941-61. New York,
    Free Press of Glencoe, 1962.
    JSAH 5 (Sept. 1964) 242-247. (L. W.
    Pye)
    PA 36 (1963) 214. (R. N. Broome)

OSBORNE, MILTON E. French presence in
    Cochinchina and Cambodia, rule and
    response, 1859-1905. Ithaca, Cornell
    UP, 1969.
    BEF 58 (1971) 352-355. (P.
    Brocheux)
    BIJ 126 (1970) 361-365. (L.
    Sluimmers)
    JAH 5 (1971) 65-67. (D. Hemery)
    JAS 29 (1969-70) 991-2. (Truong Buu
    Lam)
    JSAS 2 (1971) 247-8. (D. G. Marr)

Osborne, Milton E.   French presence in

PA 43 (1970) 469-470. (J. F. Cady)
SOAS 33 (1970) 676-7. (R. B. Smith)

OSBORNE, MILTON E.   Politics and power in Cambodia, the Sihanouk years. Melbourne, Longmans Australia, 1973. (Studies in contemporary Southeast Asia)
JAS 33 (1973-4) 742-3. (D. P. Chandler)

OSBORNE, MILTON E.   Region of revolt, focus on Southeast Asia. Harmondsworth, Eng., Penguin Books, 1971.
JSAS 3 (1972) 146-148. (G. S. Maryanov)
PA 46 (1973) 168-9. (U. Mahajani)
RSAS 1 pt. 3 (1971) 64-5. (Mohd. A. Nawawi)

OSBORNE, MILTON E.   Singapore and Malaysia. Ithaca, Southeast Asia Program, Cornell Univ., 1964. (Cornell Univ. Southeast Asia Program. Data paper, no. 53)
JSAH 6 (Sept. 1965) 148-9. (R. Gamer)

OSBORNE, MILTON E.   Strategic hamlets in South Vietnam, a survey and comparison. Ithaca, Southeast Asia Program, Cornell Univ., 1965. (Cornell Univ. Southeast Asia Program. Data paper, no. 55)
BIJ 123 (1967) 522-524. (L. Sluimers)
JAS 25 (1965-6) 552-3. (J. T. Dorsey)
JSAH 8 (1967) 326-329. (A. Short)

OTA, TSUNEZO.   Biruma ni okeru Nihon gunseishi no kenkyu. Tokyo, Yoshikawa Kobunkan, 1967.
JAS 27 (1967-8) 918. (T. Winant)
MAS 3 (1969) 177-181. (L. Allen)

Otanes, Fe T.   See SCHACHTER, PAUL. Tagalog reference grammar

OTTO, ARCHDUKE OF AUSTRIA.   L'extreme-Orient, n'est pas perdu.   Paris, Hachette, 1962.
FA 19 (1963) 853-861. (J. Christian)

Owen, Norman G.   See Compadre colonialism

PAAUW, DOUGLAS S.   Financing economic development, the Indonesian case. Glencoe, Free Pr., 1960.
JAS 20 (1960-1) 388-9. (H. O. Schmitt)
PA 34 (1961) 57-62. (N. Keyfitz)

PAAUW, DOUGLAS S.   Prospects for east Sumatran plantation industries, a symposium.   New Haven, Yale Univ., Southeast Asia Studies, 1962.   (Yale Univ. Graduate School. Southeast Asia Studies. Monograph series, no. 3)
JAS 22 (1962-3) 120. (E. D. Hawkins)
JSAH 4 (Mar. 1963) 116-118. (D. J. Blake)
PA 35 (1962) 429-430. (J. A. C. Mackie)

Pacific Science Congress, 12th, Canberra, 1971 See Countries and peoples of the Pacific basin

PACIS, VICENTE ALBANO.   President Sergio Osmena; a fully documented biography. Manila, Philippine Constitution Association, 1971.
SA 3 (1974) 783-785. (G. E. Sheeler)

PADILLA, AMBROSIO.   Public addresses. n.p., 1954-59. 2v.
PS 8 (1960) 219-220. (J. Bernas)

PÄTZOLD, KLAUS.   Die Palau-Sprache und ihre Stellung zu anderen indonesischen Sprachen.   Berlin, Reimer, 1968. (Hamburg. Universitat. Seminar fur indonesische und Sudseessprachen. Veroffentlichungen, Bd. 6)
SOAS 33 (1970) 700-1. (H. L. Shorto)

* Pages d'histoire, 1945-1954.   Hanoi, Xunhasaba, 1965.   (Etudes vietnam-

Paris. Musee Guimet. La sculpture

iennes, 7)
   AAS 6 (1970) 240-243. (I. Dolezal)

PALLEGOIX, JEAN BAPTISTE. Description
du royaume Thai ou Siam. Farnborough, Gregg International, 1969.
2v.
   JSS 60 pt. 2 (1972) 310-1. (C. M.
   Wilson)

PALM, C. H. M. Tjikoneng; een lampungs
dorp in Banten, West-Java, Indonesie.
Amsterdam, 1967.
   PA 41 (1968) 295-6. (J. M. van der
   Kroef)

PALMER, INGRID. Textiles in Indonesia,
problems of import substitution.
New York, Praeger, 1972.
   JAS 32 (1972-3) 372-3. (R. C. Rice)
   PA 45 (1972) 621-623. (B. Glass-
   burner)

PALMIER, LESLIE H. Communists in Indonesia, power pursued in vain.
Garden City, Anchor Books, Doubleday,
1973. (History of communism)
   PA 47 (1974) 572-574. (R. K. Paget)

Palmier, Leslie H. *See* HAWKINS,
EVERETT DAY. Entrepreneurship and
labor skills in Indonesian economic
development

PALMIER, LESLIE H. Indonesia. New
York, Walker, 1965. (New nations
and peoples)
   JSAH 7 (Sept. 1966) 130-1. (B.
   Grant)
   PA 38 (1965) 425-6. (D. G. E. Hall)

PALMIER, LESLIE H. Indonesia and the
Dutch. London, Oxford UP, 1962.
   FA 19 (1963) 853-861. (J.
   Christan)
   JAS 22 (1962-3) 227-8. (G. S.
   Maryanov)
   JSAH 4 (Mar. 1963) 118-120. (J. D.
   Legge)
   PA 36 (1963) 290-293. (J. M. van
   der Kroef)

PALMIER, LESLIE H. Social status and
power in Java. London, Athlone Pr.,
1960. (London School of Economics.
Monographs on social anthropology,
no. 20)
   BIJ 117 (1961) 509-512. (W. F.
   Wertheim)
   JAS 20 (1960-1) 392-3. (R. R. Jay)
   JSAH 2 (Oct. 1961) 101-104.
   (Sartono Kartodiradjo)
   PA 36 (1963) 450-1. (D. Hindley)
   SOAS 24 (1961) 179-180. (F. G.
   Bailey)

PANG CHENG LIAN. Singapore's People's
Action Party, its history, organiza-
tion and leadership. Singapore, Ox-
ford UP, 1971.
   JAS 32 (1972-3) 749. (G. D. Ness)
   JSAS 3 (1972) 143-4. (G. R. B.
   Currey)
   MAS 7 (1973) 757. (S. Rose)
   PA 44 (1971) 648. (L. E. Williams)

PANGANIBAN, JOSE VILLA. Concise
English-Tagalog dictionary. Rutland,
Tuttle, 1969.
   JAS 29 (1969-70) 499-501. (A. M.
   Stevens)
   SA 2 (1972) 520-522. (N. Asunsion-
   Lande)

PARANAVITANA, SENARAT. Ceylon and Malaysia. Colombo, Lake House Investments, 1966.
   JAS 27 (1967-8) 189. (G. J. Lerski)

PARET, PETER. French revolutionary
warfare from Indochina to Algeria;
the analysis of a political and military doctrine. New York, Praeger,
1964.
   JAS 24 (1964-5) 681-2. (G. K.
   Osburn)

PARIS. MUSEE GUIMET. La sculpture indonesienne au Musee Guimet, catalogue
et etude iconographique, par Albert
Le Bonheur. Paris, Presses Universitaires de France, 1971. (Paris.
Musee Guimet. Etude des collections,

Paris. Musee Guimet. La sculpture

t. 1)
AR 2 (1971) 253-4. (D. Lombard)
BIJ 128 (1972) 398-401. (P. H.
Pott)
JAS 31 (1971-2) 740-1. (U. Bates)
JSS 60 pt. 1 (1972) 446-448.

Parker, Robert H. *See* HIGHAM, CHARLES
FRANKLIN WANDESFORDE. Prehistoric
investigations in north-east Thailand

PARKINSON, CYRIL NORTHCOTE. British
intervention in Malaya, 1867-1877.
Singapore, Univ. of Malaya Pr., 1960.
BIJ 119 (1962) 227-8. (H. J. de
Graaf)
JAS 20 (1960-1) 538-9. (L. A.
Mills)
SOAS 26 (1963) 220-1. (C. D. Cowan)

PARKINSON, CYRIL NORTHCOTE. British
intervention in Malaya, 1867-1877.
London, Oxford UP, 1965.
JAS 26 (1966-7) 535-6. (G. P.
Means)
JSAH 2 (Mar. 1961) 119-122. (D. G.
E. Hall)
RSA (1966) 266-7. (I. Jadoul)

PARMENTIER, HENRI. Angkor; guide.
Saigon, Portail, 1957.
SEIB 36 (1961) 112. (L. Malleret)

PARMER, J. NORMAN. Colonial labor
policy and administration, a history
of labor in the rubber plantation
industry in Malaya, c.1910-1941.
Locust Valley, N.Y., Augustin, 1960.
(Association for Asian Studies.
Monographs, 9)
JAS 20 (1960-1) 539-540. (F. W.
Riggs)
JSAH 1 (Sept. 1960) 110-112. (C.
Gamba)
MER 6 pt. 1 (1961) 81-84. (C. R.
Wharton)
PA 35 (1962) 190-1. (V. L. Allen)
SOAS 23 (1960) 615-6. (J. A. M.
Caldwell)

PATANNE, E. P. The Philippines in the
world of Southeast Asia, a cultural
history. Quezon City, Enterprise,
1972.
SA 3 (1974) 794-796. (J. J. Green)

Patimokkha, 227 fundamental rules of a
Bhikkhu. Bangkok, Social Science
Association Pr., 1966.
JAS 26 (1966-7) 540-1. (Agehananda
Bharati)
JSS 55 (1967) 117-121. (R. Exell)

* Patimokkha. 2d. ed. Bangkok, Mahamaku-
tarajavidyalaya, 1969.
JSS 58 pt. 2 (1970) 201. (P. M.
Sathienpong)

PEACOCK, JAMES L. Indonesia, an anthro-
pological perspective. Pacific Pali-
sades, Goodyear Pub. Co., 1973.
BIJ 130 (1974) 384-5. (E. Postel-
Coster)
PA 47 (1974) 101-2. (M. A. Jaspan)

PEACOCK, JAMES L. Rites of moderniza-
tion, symbolic and social aspects of
Indonesian proletarian drama. Chi-
cago, Univ. of Chicago Pr., 1968.
JMBRAS 43 pt. 1 (1970) 171-182.
(Umar Junus)
PA 42 (1969) 242-244. (C. Holt)

PEARSON, JAMES DOUGLAS. Oriental and
Asian bibliography: an introduction
with some reference to Africa. Lon-
don, Lockwood, 1966.
JAH 2 (1968) 50. (G. R. Nunn)
PA 39 (1966) 454. (P. Wilson)

PECSON, GERONIMA T. Tales of the
American teachers in the Philippines,
by Geronima T. Pecson and Maria Racelis. Manila, Carmelo and Bauer-
mann, 1959.
JAS 20 (1960-1) 124. (D. V. Hart)

PEDELABORDE, PIERRE. The monsoon.
London, Methuen, 1963.
SOAS 27 (1964) 238-9. (J. H. G.
Lebon)

PEDERSEN, PAUL BODHOLDT. Batak blood
and Protestant soul, the development
of national Batak churches in north
Sumatra. Grand Rapids, Eerdmans,
1970. (Christian world mission book)
JSAS 2 (1971) 239-240. (E. M.
Bruner)

PEFFER, NATHANIEL. Transition and
tension in Southeast Asia. White
Plains, N.Y., Fund for Adult Education, 1957.
PA 33 (1960) 89. (A. D. C. Peter-
son)

PELZER, KARL JOSEF. West Malaysia and
Singapore, a selected bibliography.
New Haven, Human Relations Area
Files Pr., 1971. (Behavior science
bibliographies)
PA 46 (1973) 186. (R. S. Milne)
SA 3 (1974) 797-8. (R. F. Austin)

PENDLETON, ROBERT LARIMORE. Thailand:
aspects of landscape and life. New
York, Duell Sloan and Pearce, 1962.
(American Geographical Society hand-
book)
JAS 23 (1963-4) 484-5. (K. J.
Pelzer)
JSS 53 (1965) 126. (L. Sternstein)
PA 35 (1962) 426-7. (K. J. Pelzer)

* Pentagon papers, the secret history of
the Vietnam war. Chicago, Quadrangle
Books, 1971.
PA 45 (1972) 268-272. (M. Leifer)

Penth, Hans *See* HIKAJAT ATJEH

PEPER, BRAM. Grotte en Groei van
Java's inheemse bevolking in de
negontiende eeuw. Een andere visie,
in het bijzonden op de period 1800-
1850. Amsterdam, Anthropologisch-
Sociologisch Centrum, Universiteit
van Amsterdam. (Amsterdam. Universiteit. Anthropologisch-Sociologisch
Centrum. Afdeling Zuid- en Zuidoost
Azie. Publicatie, no. 11)
BIJ 125 (1969) 272-3. (W. Brand)

* PERALEJO, CEZAR C. Ang Kodigo sibil ng
Pilipinas. Quezon City, Mars, 1964.
PS 12 (1964) 545-6. (J. M. Juco)

* PERALTA, CRESENCIO. Toward general
education in the Philippines, by the
Magsaysay Committee on General Educa-
tion, edited by Cresencio Peralta and
Florentino B. Valeros. Manila, Univ.
of the East, 1960.
SJ 7 (1960) 325-327. (L. Q.
Arquiza)

* PEREIRA, CLAUDE. Perspectives sur
l'administration regionale et locale du
Laos. Vientiane, 1962.
SEIB 37 (1962) 466-7. (P. B. Lafont)

Peringatan Sejarah negeri Johor; eine
malaiische Quelle zur Geschichte
Johors im 18. Jahrhundert, hrsg. von
Ernst Ulrich Kratz. Wiesbaden, Har-
rassowitz, 1973. (Frankfurt am Main.
Universitat. Ostasiatisches Seminar.
Veroffentlichungen, Reihe A: Sudost-
asienkunde, Bd. 3)
AR 7 (1974) 204-5.

PEROTIN, YVES. Manual of tropical ar-
chivology. Paris, Mouton, 1966. (Le
Monde d'outre-mer, passe et present.
Quatrieme serie: Bibliographies et
instruments de travail, 7)
SOAS 31 (1968) 199-200. (A. D. H.
Bivar)

Pestman, P. W. *See* OOSTERS GENOOT-
SCHAP IN NEDERLAND. Acta Orientalia
Neerlandica

PETERS, HERMANDUS LAMBERTUS. Enkele
hoofdstukken uit het sociaal-religi-
euze leven van een Dani-groep. Venlo,
Dagblad voor Noord-Limberg, 1965.
BIJ 122 (1966) 398-400. (L. F. B.
Dubbeldam)

* PFEFFER, PIERRE. L'Asie. Paris,
Hachette, 1970.
AR 1 (1970) 227-229. (D. Lombard)

Pfeffer, Richard M. No more Vietnams

Pfeffer, Richard M. *See* No more
Vietnams

PHADNIS, URMILA. Documents on Asian
affairs; select bibliography, by
Urmila Phadnis and S. Dakshina
Moorthy. New Delhi, 1959- (Indian
Council of World Affairs, Delhi. Li-
brary. Bibliographical series)
  PA 33 (1960) 99.

* PHAM THAI. So-kinh tan trang. Hanoi,
Van-hoa, 1960.
  BEF 52 (1964) 287-290. (Ta Trong
  Hiep)

* PHAM VAN HUYEN. Nouveau dictionnaire
scientifique, francais-anglais-
vietnamien. n.p., n.d.
  SEIB 35 (1960) 734.

* PHAN HUY CHU. Lich trieu hien chuong
loai chi. Saigon, Min. d'Etat
Charge des Affaires Culturelles,
1972.
  SEIB 48 (1973) 148. (Nguyen The
  Anh)

PHAN THI DAC. Situation de la personne
au Viet-Nam. Paris, Editions du
C. N. R. S., 1966. (Travaux du Centre d'etudes sociologiques)
  BEF 55 (1969) 294-298. (N. Louis)

Phan Tran; roman en vers. Texte, tra-
duction et notes par Maurice Durand.
Paris, Ecole Francaise d'Extreme-
Orient, 1962. (Ecole Francaise d'Ex-
treme-Orient. Collection de textes
et documents sur l'Indochine, 7.
Textes nom, no. 1)
  FA 20 (1965) 124-5. (P. Grison)
  RSA (1963) 61-2. (Nguyen Tran Huan)

PHAYRE, ARTHUR PURVES. History of
Burma including Burma proper, Pegu,
Taungu, Tenasserim, and Arakan, from
the earliest time to the end of the
first war with British India. New
York, Augustus M. Kelley, 1969.
  JAS 30 (1970-1) 228-9. (D. K.
  Wyatt)
  PA 43 (1970) 648-9. (B. Harrison)

PHELAN, JOHN LEDDY. Hispanization of
the Philippines: Spanish aims and
Filipino responses, 1565-1700. Madi-
son, Univ. of Wisconsin Pr., 1959.
  JSAH 2 (Mar. 1961) 122-127. (G. F.
  Zaide)
  SJ 8 (1961) 118-120. (P. V. Flores)

PHILIPPINE CENTER FOR LANGUAGE STUDY.
Beginning Tagalog, a course for
speakers of English. Berkeley, Univ.
of California Pr., 1965.
  AAS 6 (1970) 226-7. (J. Genzor)

PHILIPPINE CENTER FOR LANGUAGE STUDY.
Intermediate readings in Tagalog,
edited by J. Donald Bowen. Berkeley,
Univ. of California Pr., 1968.
  AAS 7 (1971) 143. (J. Genzor)
  SOAS 32 (1969) 465. (R. H. Robins)

PHILIPPINES (REP.) MAGSAYSAY COMMITTEE
ON GENERAL EDUCATION. Toward general
education in the Philippines, report.
Manila, Univ. of the East, 1960.
  SJ 7 (1960) 325-327. (L. Q. Arquiza)

* PHILIPPINES (REP.) NATIONAL ARCHIVES.
Cedulario de Manila: a collection of
laws emanating from Spain which gov-
erned the city of Manila, 1574-1832.
Manila, 1971.
  PS 22 (1974) 211-2. (V. L. Badillo)

Philippines (Rep.) National Economic
Council *See* UNITED NATIONS. SECRE-
TARIAT. Population growth and man-
power in the Philippines

PHILLIPS, HERBERT P. Thai peasant per-
sonality, the patterning of interper-
sonal behavior in the village of Bang
Chan. Berkeley, Univ. of California
Pr., 1965.
  BIJ 122 (1966) 466-468. (G. Jahoda)
  JAS 26 (1966-7) 683-686. (R. B.
  Textor)

* PHRA RATANAPANNA THERA. Jinakalamali.
  London, Pali Text Society, 1962.
    JSS 50 (1962) 54-62.
    JSS 58 pt. 1 (1970) 137-139. (Phra
      Khantipalo)
    SOAS 26 (1963) 484-5. (P. S. Jaini)

* PHRA RATANAPANNA THERA. Jinakalamali,
  epochs of the conqueror. London,
  Pali Text Society, 1968.
    JSS 58 pt. 1 (1970) 137-139. (Phra
      Khantipalo)

PHRA RATANAPANNA THERA. Sheath of
  garlands of the epochs of the conqueror; being a translation of
  Jinakalamalipakaranam of Ratanapanna
  Thera of Thailand. Translated by
  N. A. Jayawickrama. London, Luzac,
  1968. (Pali Text Society, London.
  Translation series, no. 36) (UNESCO
  collection of representative works)
    SOAS 32 (1969) 171-2. (K. R.
      Norman)

PHROMWOHAN, PHRAYA. Poem in four
  songs, a northern Thai tetralogy,
  by Phayaphrom. Lund, Studentlitter-
  atur, 1971. (Centralinstitut for
  nordisk asienforskning. Monograph
  series, no. 7)
    JSS 62 pt. 1 (1974) 259-269. (H.
      C. Purnell and Phairat Waree)
    SOAS 36 (1973) 188-191. (P. J. Bee)

* PHUANGKASEM, CORRINE. Thailand and
  SEATO. Bangkok, Faculty of Political
  Science, Thammasat Univ., 1973.
    JSS 62 pt. 2 (1974) 331-336. (W.
      S. Thompson)

* PHUNG TAT DAC. Giai-thoai Lang Nho.
  Saigon, 1966.
    BEF 55 (1969) 305-307. (Nguyen
      Tran Huan)

* PHUNG TAT DAC. Le Han van tinh-tuy.
  Saigon, 1965.
    BEF 55 (1969) 302-305. (Nguyen
      Tran Huan)

Pike, Douglas Eugene. War, peace and

PIGEAUD, THEODORE G. TH. Java in the
  14th century: a study in cultural
  history. *The Nagara-kertagama* by
  Rakawi Prapanca of Majapahit, 1365
  A.D. 3d. ed. The Hague, Nijhoff,
  1960-63. 5v. (Instituut voor Taal-,
  Land- en Volkenkunde. Translation
  series, 4)
    SOAS 27 (1964) 658-661. (C.
      Hooykaas)

PIGEAUD, THEODORE G. TH. Literature of
  Java. Catalogue raisonne of Javanese
  manuscripts in the library of the
  University of Leiden and other public
  collections in the Netherlands. The
  Hague, Nijhoff, 1967-70. 3v.
  Volume I.
    BEF 55 (1969) 252-3. (J. Filliozat)
    JAS 27 (1967-8) 683-4. (J. Musgrave)
    JSAH 10 (1969) 381-384. (Soebardi)
    SOAS 31 (1968) 422-424. (C.
      Hooykaas)
  Volume II.
    AR 1 (1970) 195-197. (N. Siberoff)
    JSAS 2 (1971) 234. (Soebardi)
    PA 42 (1969) 540-1. (J. M. van der
      Kroef)
    SOAS 32 (1969) 654-5. (C. Hooykaas)
  Volume III.
    AR 1 (1970) 195-197. (N. Siberoff)
    SOAS 34 (1971) 185-6. (C. Hooykaas)
  [Note: Volumes II and III are
  listed as being part of the following
  series: Leyden. Rijksuniversiteit.
  Bibliotheek. Codices manuscripti, no.
  9]

PIKE, DOUGLAS. Viet Cong: the organization and techniques of the National
  Liberation Front of South Vietnam.
  Cambridge, MIT Pr., 1966. (Massachusetts Institute of Technology. Center
  for International Studies. Studies in
  international communism, no. 7)
    JAS 28 (1968-9) 821-831. (J. C.
      Donnell)
    MAS 2 (1968) 82-3. (R. B. Smith)

PIKE, DOUGLAS EUGENE. War, peace and
  the Viet Cong. Cambridge, MIT Pr.,

Pike, Douglas Eugene. War, peace and

1969.
  JAS 30 (1970-1) 925-6. (F. N.
  Trager)
  MAS 4 (1970) 373-375. (R. B. Smith)
  PA 43 (1970) 127-8. (P. J. Honey)

Pinto, Fernand Mendez *See* MENDES
PINTO, FERNAO

* PIRES, BENJAMIN VIDEIRA. A viagem de
  comercio Macau-Manila, nos seculos
  XVI a XIX. Macao, Imprensa Nacional,
  1971.
    PS 20 (1972) 677-8.

Pires, Tome *See* Travel accounts of
the islands

PIRIYA KRAIRIKSH. Buddhist folk tales
depicted at Chula Pathon Cedi. Bangkok, 1974.
  JSS 62 pt. 2 (1974) 376-7. (H. D.
  Ginsburg)

* PLATER, CHARLES DOMINIC. Maikling
  banal na Pagsasanay. Manila, Bookmark, 1964.
    PS 12 (1964) 760-762. (B. San Juan)

PLION, RAYMOND. Fetes et ceremonies
de Thailande. Bangkok, Assumption
Pr., 1969.
  JSS 58 pt. 1 (1970) 145-6. (M.
  Smithies)

Plion-Bernier, Raymond *See* PLION,
RAYMOND

PLOEG, A. Government in Wanggulam.
The Hague, Nijhoff, 1969. (Instituut
voor Taal-, Land- en Volkenkunde.
Verhandelingen, 57)
  PA 43 (1970) 475. (A. Strathern)
  SOAS 33 (1970) 679-680. (R. T.
  McVey)

De Plurale samenleving; begrip zonder
toekomst? Meppel, Boom, 1966.
  BIJ 122 (1966) 151-153. (C. Baks)

PLUVIER, JAN M. Confrontations, a
study in Indonesian politics. Kuala
Lumpur, Oxford UP, 1965.
  JSAH 7 (Sept. 1966) 131-133. (J. D.
  Legge)

PLUVIER, JAN M. Handbook and chart of
South-East Asian history. Kuala Lum-
pur, Oxford UP, 1967.
  JAS 28 (1968-9) 196. (D. J. Stein-
  berg)
  JSAH 9 (1968) 363. (D. G. E. Hall)

POCOCK, TOM. Fighting general: the
public and private campaigns of
General Sir Walter Walker. London,
Collins, 1973.
  BMJ 3 pt. 2 (1974) 310-312. (T.
  Harrisson)

POERWADARMINTA, W. J. S. Bahasa Indonesia untuk karang-mengarang. Jogjakarta, Indonesia, 1967.
  BIJ 125 (1969) 269-270. (A. Teeuw)

POERWADARMINTA, W. J. S. Kamus umum
bahasa Indonesia. 3d. ed. Djakarta,
Balai Pustaka, 1961.
  BEF 52 (1964) 197-203. (L.-C.
  Damais)

POETZELBERGER, HANS ANDREAS. Einfueh-
rung in das Indonesische. Wiesbaden,
Harrassowitz, 1965. (Sudostasien-
kunde, Bd. 1)
  AAS 4 (1968) 136-140. (H. Spitz-
  bardt)
  BIJ 122 (1966) 401-404. (R.
  Roolvink)
  JAS 25 (1965-6) 800-1. (J. U.
  Wolff)

POGUE, FORREST C. George C. Marshall.
Volume III. Organizer of victory,
1943-45. New York, Viking Pr., 1973.
  PA 46 (1973) 571-2. (J. F. Melby)

Politika kapitalisticheskikh derzhav:
natsionaljno-osvoboditel'noe Dvizhenie
v IUgo-Vostochnoj Azii, 1871-1917,
Dokumenty i Materialy [by] A. A.

Guber. Moscow, 1965. 2v.
  BIJ 122 (1966) 470-477. (L.
  Sluimers)

Polotan, Kerima *See* CARLOS PALANCA
MEMORIAL AWARDS FOR LITERATURE.
Prize stories

POMEROY, WILLIAM J. American neo-
colonialism, its emergence in the
Philippines and Asia. New York,
International Publishers, 1970.
  PA 43 (1970) 641-2. (I. B. Powell)
  PS 21 (1973) 242-244. (J. N.
  Schumacher)

POMEROY, WILLIAM J. Forest, a personal record of the Huk guerrilla
struggle in the Philippines. New
York, International Publishers,
1963.
  JSAH 6 (Mar. 1966) 129-131. (J. V.
  Abueva)

POMEROY, WILLIAM J. Guerrilla war-
fare and Marxism; a collection of
writings from Karl Marx to the pres-
ent on armed struggles for libera-
tion and for socialism. New York,
International Publishers, 1968.
  JSAH 10 (1969) 375-377. (D. S.
  Gibbons)
  PA 42 (1969) 503-4. (J. L. S.
  Girling)

POMONTI, JEAN CLAUDE. Des courtisans
aux partisans, essai sur la crise
cambodgienne, par Jean Claude Pomonti
et Serge Thion. Paris, Editions
Gullimard, 1971. (Collection Idees,
230. Idees actuelles)
  JAS 31 (1971-2) 730-1. (D. P.
  Chandler)
  PA 45 (1972) 314-316. (J. L. S.
  Girling)

POOLE, PETER A. Expansion of the
Vietnam war into Cambodia: action
and response by the governments of
North Vietnam, South Vietnam, Cambodia and the United States. Athens,

Poree-Maspero, Eveline. Etudes sur les
Ohio Univ., Center for International
Studies, 1970. (Papers in interna-
tional studies. Southeast Asia se-
ries, no. 17)
  SA 2 (1972-3) 363-371. (J. Badgley)

POOLE, PETER A. The United States and
Indochina from FDR to Nixon. Hins-
dale, Dryden Pr., 1973. (Berkshire
studies in history)
  PA 47 (1974) 247-8. (D. J. Duncanson)

POOLE, PETER A. Vietnamese in Thai-
land, a historical perspective.
Ithaca, Cornell UP, 1970.
  JAS 30 (1970-1) 725-6. (F. C.
  Darling)
  JSAS 3 (1972) 163-4. (M. Osborne)
  JSS 59 pt. 1 (1971) 253-255.
  (Yongyuth Yuthavong)
  PA 44 (1971) 465. (J. L. S.
  Girling)

* Population research in Thailand, a re-
view and bibliography. A joint pub-
lication of the East-West Population
Institute, East-West Center and the
Institute of Population Studies,
Chulalongkorn University. Honolulu,
East-West Center, 1973.
  JAS 33 (1973-4) 501-2. (J. A.
  Hafner)

Poree-Maspero, Eveline *See* INSTITUT
BOUDDHIQUE. COMMISSION DES MOEURS ET
COUTUMES DU CAMBODGE. Ceremonies
privees des Cambodgiens

POREE-MASPERO, EVELINE. Etudes sur les
rites agraires des Cambodgiens.
Paris, Mouton, 1962- (Le Monde d'
outre-mer passe et present. 1 ser.
Etudes, 14)
Volumes I and II.
  PA 38 (1965) 436-7. (W. E.
  Willmott)
Volume III.
  PA 44 (1971) 314-5. (W. E.
  Willmott)
  SOAS 34 (1971) 439-441. (P. J. Bee)

Power, John H.   The Philippines

Queljoe, David H. de. Preliminary

QUELJOE, DAVID H. DE. Preliminary
  study of some phonetic features of
  Petani, with glossaries. DeKalb,
  Center for Southeast Asian Studies,
  Northern Illinois Univ., 1971.
  (Illinois. Northern Illinois Univ.,
  DeKalb. Center for Southeast Asia
  Studies. Special reports series, no.
  5)
    BIJ 128 (1972) 377-382. (A. Teeuw)

QUEZON, MANUEL LUIS. The good fight.
  New York, Appleton-Century, 1944.
    PS 20 (1972) 323-341. (M. A.
      Bernad)

QUEZON, PHILIPPINES. UNIV. OF THE
  PHILIPPINES. COMMUNITY DEVELOPMENT
  RESEARCH COUNCIL. Masagana/Margate
  system of planting rice: a study of
  an agricultural innovation, by P. R.
  Covar. Manila, 1960. (Quezon, Philippines. Univ. of the Philippines.
  Community Development Research Council. Study series, no. 5)
    JAS 20 (1960-1) 399-403. (F. C.
      Madigan and D. V. Hart)

QUEZON, PHILIPPINES. UNIV. OF THE PHIL-
  IPPINES. COMMUNITY DEVELOPMENT RE-
  SEARCH COUNCIL. Report, 1959-60.
  Diliman, 1960.
    JAS 20 (1960-1) 399-403. (F. C.
      Madigan and D. V. Hart)

Quezon, Philippines. Univ. of the Philippines. Interdepartmental Reference
  Service *See* Index to Philippine
  periodicals

QUEZON, PHILIPPINES. UNIV. OF THE PHIL-
  IPPINES. INTERDEPARTMENTAL REFERENCE
  SERVICE. Union catalogue of Philippine materials of sixty-four government agency libraries of the Philippines. Maxima M. Ferrer, editor.
  Manila, 1962.
    JAS 23 (1963-4) 487-8. (D. V. Hart)

QUEZON, PHILIPPINES. UNIV. OF THE PHIL-
  IPPINES. INTERDEPARTMENTAL REFERENCE

SERVICE. Union list of serials of
  government agency libraries of the
  Philippines. Rev. and enl. ed. Manila, 1960.
    JAS 20 (1960-1) 549-550. (D. V.
      Hart)

QUEZON, PHILIPPINES. UNIV. OF THE PHIL-
  IPPINES. LIBRARY. Classified list of
  Filipiniana books and pamphlets in
  the main library, Univ. of the Phil-
  ippines, as of December 1958. Quezon
  City, Univ. of the Philippines, 1959.
    PS 8 (1960) 197-8. (R. J. Suchan)

QUEZON, PHILIPPINES. UNIV. OF THE PHIL-
  IPPINES. SCIENCE EDUCATION CENTER.
  Plants of the Philippines. Quezon
  City, Univ. of the Philippines, 1971.
    PS 20 (1972) 346-7. (F. M. Perez)

QUEZON, PHILIPPINES. UNIV. OF THE PHIL-
  IPPINES. SOCIAL SCIENCE RESEARCH CEN-
  TER. Annotated bibliography of Phil-
  ippine social sciences. Volume II,
  pt. 1: Sociology, by Reginaldo F.
  Arceo. Quezon City, Univ. of the
  Philippines, 1957.
    JAS 19 (1959-60) 479. (D. V. Hart)

QUIASON, SERAFIN D. English country
  trade with the Philippines, 1644-
  1765. Quezon City, Univ. of the Philippines Pr., 1966.
    PS 15 (1967) 532-534. (H. de la
      Costa)

* QUIRINO, CARLOS. Maps and views of old
  Maynila. Manila, Maharnilad, 1971.
    PS 19 (1971) 551-553. (M. A. Bernad)

QUIRINO, CARLOS. Philippine cartography, 1320-1899. 2d. ed. Amsterdam,
  N. Israel, 1963.
    JAS 24 (1964-5) 171-2. (D. E.
      Sopher)

QUIRINO, CARLOS. Quezon, Paladin of
  Philippine freedom. Manila, Filipini-
  ana Book Guild, 1971. (Filipiniana
  Book Guild. Publications, v. 18)

Ralix, Max. *See* Factors related to

JAS 31 (1971-2) 995-997. (M.
  Cullinane)
PA 45 (1972) 462-3. (I. B. Powell)
PS 20 (1972) 323-341. (M. A.
  Bernad)
SA 3 (1974) 783-785. (G. E.
  Sheeler)

QUIRINO, CARLOS. Young Aguinaldo,
  from Kawit to Biyak-na-Bato. Manila,
  Bookmark, 1969.
    JAS 29 (1969-70) 501-2. (J. A.
      Larkin)
    PS 17 (1969) 637-640. (M. A.
      Bernad)

QUIRINO, LIESEL COMMANS. Like the
  wind I go, a novel. Quezon City,
  Garcia, 1968.
    PS 17 (1969) 332-336. (M. A.
      Bernad)

Quito, Gil *See* DUMAL, PAUL. Ang
  puting timamanukin

* QUOC SU QUAN. Minh-Menh chinh yen.
  Saigon, Min. d'Etat Charge des
  Affaires Culturelles, 1972.
    SEIB 48 (1973) 148-9. (Nguyen The
      Anh)

* Quoc trieu chanh bien toat yeu. Saigon, Nhom Nghien-cuu Su-Dia Viet-
  Nam, 1972.
    SEIB 48 (1973) 147-8. (Nguyen The
      Anh)

RABUSHKA, ALVIN. Politics in plural
  societies; a theory of democratic
  instability, by Alvin Rabushka and
  Kenneth A. Shepsle. Columbus, Ohio,
  Merrill, 1972.
    PA 46 (1973) 435-444. (R. S. Milne)

RABUSHKA, ALVIN. Race and politics in
  urban Malaya. Stanford, Hoover Institution Pr., 1973. (Hoover Institution studies, 35)
    PA 46 (1973) 603-4. (G. P. Means)

RACE, JEFFREY. War comes to Long An;
  revolutionary conflict in a Vietnamese
  province. Berkeley, Univ. of California Pr., 1972.
    MAS 7 (1973) 747-754. (M. Osborne)
    PA 45 (1972) 469-470. (A. E.
      Goodman)

RADAIC, ANTE. Jose Rizal, romantico
  realista; anatomia literaria de *Noli
  y Fili*. Manila, Univ. of Santo Tomas
  Pr., 1961.
    UN 35 (1962) 149. (A. M. Molina)

RAFFEL, BURTON. Anthology of modern
  Indonesian poetry. Berkeley, Univ.
  of California Pr., 1964.
    AAS 4 (1968) 140-147. (R. Stiller)
    BEF 53 (1966) 695-703. (L.-C.
      Damais)
    JAS 24 (1964-5) 531-2. (D. Carr)
    SOAS 28 (1965) 433-4. (E. C. G.
      Barrett)

RAFFEL, BURTON. Anthology of modern
  Indonesian poetry. Albany, State Univ.
  of New York Pr., 1968.
    JAS 28 (1968-9) 444-5. (D. Carr)

RAFFEL, BURTON. Development of modern
  Indonesian poetry. Albany, State
  Univ. of New York Pr., 1967.
    JAS 28 (1968-9) 444-5. (D. Carr)

RAFFEL, BURTON. Forked tongue; a study
  of the translation process. The
  Hague, Mouton, 1971. (De proprietat-
  ibus litterarum. Series maior, v. 14)
    BIJ 128 (1972) 372-374. (H. Aveling)

RAFFLES, THOMAS STAMFORD. History of
  Java. Kuala Lumpur, Oxford UP, 1965.
  2v. (Oxford in Asia historical reprints)
    MAS 1 (1967) 104-106. (C. A. Fisher)
    PA 43 (1970) 637-8. (H. J. Benda)

Rahmann, Rudolf *See* Dr. H. Otley Beyer

Rajaretnam, M. *See* Trends in Thailand

Ralix, Max. Factors related to

Ralix, Max *See* CORNELL UNIV. DEPT.
  OF SOCIOLOGY AND ANTHROPOLOGY.
  CROSS-CULTURAL METHODOLOGY PROJECT.
  Factors related to acceptance of
  innovations

Rajaretnam, M. *See* Trends in Thailand

Rama, V, King of Thailand *See* CHULA-
  LONGKORN, KING OF THAILAND

RAMA RAU, SANTHA. View to the Southeast. New York, Harper, 1957.
    PS 8 (1960) 472-3. (A. G. Manuud)

Ramadhan, K. H. *See* ROSIDI, AJIP.
  Anthologie bilingue de la poesie
  indonesienne contemporaine

* RAMADHAN, K. H. Rojan revolusi. Djakarta, Gunung Agung, 1971.
    AR 3 (1972) 223-235. (B. Milcent)

* RAMAKIEN. Ramakien, a prose translation of the Thai Ramayana, by Ray A.
  Olsson. Bangkok, Praepittaya, 1968.
    BEF 59 (1972) 330-1. (L. Gabaude)
    JSS 58 pt. 2 (1970) 162-165. (J.
    Cadet)

RAMOS, MAXIMO D. Creatures of Philippine lower mythology. Quezon City,
  Univ. of the Philippines Pr., 1971.
    PS 20 (1972) 348. (F. Lynch)

RAMOS, TERESITA V. Tagalog dictionary.
  Honolulu, Univ. of Hawaii Pr., 1971.
  (Hawaii. Univ., Honolulu. Pacific
  and Asian Linguistics Institute.
  PALI language texts)
    AAS 10 (1974) 200-1. (J. Genzor)

RAMOS, TERESITA V. Tagalog structures.
  Honolulu, Univ. of Hawaii Pr., 1971.
  (Hawaii. Univ., Honolulu. Pacific
  and Asian Linguistics Institute.
  PALI language texts)
    AAS 10 (1974) 200-1. (J. Genzor)

RAMOS-SHAHANI, LETICIA V. The Philippines in pictures. Rev. ed. New

York, Sterling, 1969. (Visual geography series)
    PS 20 (1972) 677.

RANDLE, ROBERT F. Geneva, 1954: the
  settlement of the Indochinese war.
  Princeton, Princeton UP, 1969.
    JAS 30 (1970-1) 510-1. (A. E.
    Goodman)
    PA 43 (1970) 467-469. (D. J.
    Duncanson)

RAS, J. J. Hikajat Bandjar, a study in
  Malay historiography. The Hague,
  Nijhoff, 1968. (Bibliotheca Indone-
  sica, 1)
    JSAS 3 (1972) 156-158. (J. L.
    Swellengrebel)
    SOAS 34 (1971) 436. (N. G. Phillips)

RASSERS, WILLEM HUIBERT. Panji, the
  culture hero; a structural study of
  religion in Java. The Hague, Nijhoff, 1959. (Instituut voor Taal-,
  Land- en Volkenkunde. Translation series, 3)
    SOAS 24 (1961) 163-165. (E. M.
    Mendelson)

Ratanapanna *See* PHRA RATANAPANNA
THERA

RATNAM, K. J. Communalism and the political process in Malaya. Kuala Lumpur, Univ. of Malaya Pr., 1965.
    AS 5 (1965) 527.
    FA 18 (1965) 268-9. (M. Osborne)
    JSAH 7 (Sept. 1966) 135-137. (R. O.
    Tilman)
    PA 42 (1969) 104-5. (B. Harrison)
    RSA (1965) 274-276. (I. Jadoul)
    SOAS 29 (1966) 426-7. (J. H.
    Beaglehole)

RATNAM, K. J. Malayan parliamentary
  election of 1964, by K. J. Ratnam and
  R. S. Milne. Singapore, Univ. of Malaya Pr., 1967.
    PA 42 (1969) 534-536. (R. O. Tilman)

Rau, Santha Rama *See* RAMA RAU, SANTHA

Regime interne et politique exterieure

RAUF, MOHAMMED A. Brief history of
Islam with special reference to Ma-
laya. Kuala Lumpur, Oxford UP, 1964.
   AAS 3 (1967) 185-187.

Ravello, Sofia A. *See* BERAN, JANICE
A. Physical activities for the
Filipina

RAVENHOLT, ALBERT. The Philippines:
a young republic on the move.
Princeton, Van Nostrand, 1962.
   JAS 23 (1963-4) 631. (C. O.
      Houston)
   PA 36 (1963) 202-204. (R. S. Milne)
   PS 11 (1963) 454-457. (M. R.
      Hollnsteiner and F. Lynch)
   UN 36 (1963) 164-166. (A. Panizo)

RAWSON, PHILIP S. Art of Southeast
Asia: Cambodia, Vietnam, Thailand,
Laos, Burma, Java, Bali. New York,
Praeger, 1967.
   JAS 27 (1967-8) 918-920. (E. Lyons)
   PA 41 (1968) 296-7. (C. Holt)
   SJ 15 (1968) 134-137. (A. L.
      Faurot)

RAWSON, ROBERT REES. Monsoon lands of
Asia. Chicago, Aldine, 1963.
   JAS 24 (1964-5) 145-6. (R. B. Hall)
   PA 37 (1964) 334-5. (J. E. Spencer)

RAY, JAYANTA KUMAR. Portraits of Thai
politics. New Delhi, Orient Longman,
1972.
   JAS 33 (1973-4) 739-740. (A.
      Howard)
   JSS 62 pt. 1 (1974) 232-237. (M.
      Getzendaner)
   PA 47 (1974) 103-4. (F. C. Darling)

RAY, SIBNARAYAN. Vietnam seen from
east and west: an international
symposium. New York, Praeger, 1966.
   JAS 26 (1966-7) 761-2. (J. H.
      Badgley)

RAZZAQI, SHAHID HUSAIN. Indonishiya.
Lahore, Institute of Islamic Culture,
1963.
   SOAS 27 (1964) 687. (Aziz Ahmad)

Realities of Vietnam; a Ripon Society
appraisal, edited by Christopher W.
Beal. Washington, Public Affairs
Pr., 1968.
   JAS 28 (1968-9) 647-8. (G. McT.
      Kahin)

Rebadavia, Consolacion B. *See* BIBLIO-
GRAPHICAL SOCIETY OF THE PHILIPPINES.
Checklist of Philippine government
documents

Reberioux, Madeleine *See* HAUPT,
GEORGE. La Deuxieme Internationale
et l'Orient

Recits de la resistance vietnamienne,
1925-1945, par Vo Nguyen Giap, et al.
Paris, Maspero, 1966.
   FA 21 (1966) 599-600.

Recits de la resistance vietnamienne,
1925-1945, par Vo Nguyen Giap, et al.
Paris, Francois Maspero, 1971.
   PA 45 (1972) 142-3. (J. L. S.
      Girling)

Recueil des inscriptions (du Siam) par
George Coedes. Troisieme partie. Prachum sila charuk, phak thi 3. Bangkok, Commission for the Publication
of Historical, Cultural and Archaeological Records, Office of the Prime
Minister, 1965.
   JAS 26 (1966-7) 344-5. (D. K.
      Wyatt)

REDDI, V. M. History of the Cambodian
independence movement, 1863-1955.
Tirupati, Sri Venkateswara Univ.,
1970.
   JSAS 5 (1974) 136-7. (D. P.
      Chandler)

Regalado, Felix B. *See* HOWARD, JOSEPH
T. Society and culture in the rural
Philippines

Regime interne et politique exterieure
dans les pays d'Asie. Paris, Librarie
Armand Colin, 1966. (Cahiers de la

Regime interne et politique exterieure

REUTER, FRANK THEODORE. Catholic influence on American colonial policies, 1898-1904. Austin, Univ. of Texas Pr., 1967.
  PS 16 (1968) 596-598. (J. N. Schumacher)

* REUTER, JAMES B. UNDA conference for Asia. Makati, Cultural Printing Pr., 1967.
  PS 16 (1968) 189-197. (C. A. Arnaldo)

Revatoris, Rosvida *See* BORLONGAN, ERLINDA. Catalogue of Filipiniana materials

Revolusi mental. Disusan oleh Senu Abdul Rahman. Kuala Lumpur, Penerbitan Utusan Melayu, 1971.
  RSAS 1 pt. 1 (1971) 58. (Tham Seong Chee)

REYNO, ADRIANO C. Political, social and moral philosophy of Apolinario Mabini. Manila, Catholic Trade School, 1964. (San Carlos publications. Ser. A. Humanities, no. 2)
  JAS 26 (1966-7) 133. (M. J. Fisher)

RHODES, ALEXANDRE DE. Cathechismus pro iis qui volunt suscipere Baptismum in octo dies divisus. Phep giang tam ngay. Cho de muon chju Phep rua toi ma vao dao Thanh Duc Chua Troi. Reedite a l'occasion du tricentenaire de la mort de l'auteur avec introd. et notes par Andre Marillier. Saigon, Group Litteraire Tinh-Viet, 1961.
  SEIB 36 (1961) 108-9.

RHODES, ALEXANDRE DE. Rhodes of Viet Nam; the travels and missions of Father Alexander de Rhodes in China and other kingdoms of the Orient. Westminster, Md., Newman Pr., 1966.
  PA 39 (1966) 225. (D. G. E. Hall)

Rhodius, Hans *See* SPIES, WALTER. Schonheit und Reichtum des Lebens

RIBADENEIRA, MARCELO DE. Historia del Archipielago y otros reynos. History of the Philippines and other kingdoms. Manila, Historical Conservation Society, 1970. 2v. (Historical Conservation Society. Publication, 17)
  JAS 32 (1972-3) 381-2. (J. L. Phelan)
  PA 45 (1972) 146-7. (I. B. Powell)
  PS 19 (1971) 747-749. (J. S. Arcilla)

RICE, OLIVER. Modern Malay verse, 1946-61, selected by Oliver Rice and Abdullah Majid. Kuala Lumpur, Oxford UP, 1963. (Seri sastera timur dan barat)
  AAS 4 (1968) 140-147. (R. Stiller)
  SOAS 28 (1965) 191-2. (Kassim Ahmad)

Rice economy of the Philippines, by Leon A. Mears, et al. Quezon City, Univ. of the Philippines Pr., 1974.
  PA 47 (1974) 580-1. (J. E. Spencer)
  SLURJ 5 (1974) 298. (F. Buen)

Richards, D. S. *See* Islam and the trade of Asia

RIFFAUD, MADELEINE. Dans les maquis Vietcong. Paris, Rene Juliard, 1965.
  RSA (1966) 267-269. (I. Jadoul)

RIGGS, FRED WARREN. Thailand, the modernization of a bureaucratic polity. Honolulu, East-West Center Pr., 1966.
  JAS 26 (1966-7) 347-349. (R. Braibanti)
  PA 39 (1966) 410-412. (R. S. Milne)

* RIVAI APIN. Dari dua dunia belum sudah. Penang, Universiti Sains Malaysia, n.d.
  AR 5 (1973) 311-2. (H. Chambert-Loir)

RIVERA, JUAN F. Congress of the Philippines; a study of its functions and powers and procedures. Manila, Pedro B. Ayuda, 1962.
  PS 11 (1963) 374-5. (J. M. Juco)

Rizal y Alonso, Jose.   El filibusterismo

RIZAL Y ALONSO, JOSE.   El filibuster-
ismo (subversion).   London, Longmans,
1965.
  PS 15 (1967) 204-5. (M. A. Bernad)
[Note: see also reviews under his
The subversive]

RIZAL Y ALONSO, JOSE.   Lost Eden (Noli
Me Tangere).   Bloomington, Indiana
UP, 1961.
  JAS 21 (1961-2) 246-7. (L. Casper)

RIZAL Y ALONSO, JOSE.   One hundred letters of Jose Rizal to his parents,
brother, sisters, relatives.   Manila,
Philippine National Historical Society, 1959.
  JAS 20 (1960-1) 242. (M. J. Fisher)

* RIZAL Y ALONSO, JOSE.   Poems.   Manila,
Far Eastern Univ., n.d.
  UN 34 (1961) 113-116. (C. J.
  Colayco)

RIZAL Y ALONSO, JOSE.   The subversive
(El filibusterismo).   Bloomington,
Indiana UP, 1962.
  JAS 23 (1963-4) 488-9. (F. W.
  Riggs)
[Note: see also reviews under his
El filibusterismo]

Rizal: theme and variations.   Manila,
Univ. of Santo Tomas Pr., 1961.
  UN 34 (1961) 118. (E. Syquia)

ROBB, WALTER JOHNSON.   Filipinos, pre-
war Philippines essays.   Rizal,
Araneta UP, 1963.
  JAS 23 (1963-4) 632. (D. V. Hart)

ROBBINS, JOHN.   Too many Asians.   New
York, Doubleday, 1959.
  PS 9 (1961) 378-9. (M. McPhelin)

Roberts, Chester F. *See* GINSBURG,
NORTON SYDNEY.   Malaya

ROBINSON, HARRY.   Monsoon Asia, a geographical survey.   New York, Praeger,
1967.

  JAS 27 (1967-8) 865-6. (R. B. Hall)
  PA 41 (1968) 416-7. (J. E. Spencer)

ROBINSON, RICHARD H.   Buddhist religion;
a historical introduction.   Belmont,
Dickenson Pub. Co., 1970.   (The reli-
gious life of man)
  JAS 30 (1970-1) 167-8. (W. L.
  Highfill)

ROBLES, ELIODORO G.   The Philippines in
the 19th century.   Quezon City, Malaya Books, 1969.
  AR 5 (1973) 294-297. (O.
  Demeulenacre)

Robson, S. O. *See* WANBAN WIDEYA.
Wanban wideya

ROCES, ALEJANDRO R.   Of cocks and kites,
and other short stories.   Manila,
Regal, 1959.
  JAS 19 (1959-60) 477. (D. V. Hart)

RODITI, EDOUARD.   Magellan of the Pacific.   London, Faber and Faber,
1972.   (Great travellers)
  PA 46 (1973) 351-2. (H. Livermore)

RÖDER, JOSEF.   Felsbilder und Vorge-
schichte des MacCluer-Golfes, West-
Neuguinea.   Darmstadt, Wittich, 1959.
  BIJ 119 (1963) 217-225. (K. W.
  Galis)

ROEDER, O. G.   Who's who in Indonesia;
biographies of prominent Indonesian
personalities in all fields.   Djakarta, Gunung Agung, 1971.
  AR 4 (1972) 254.

Roelands, Jan *See* JACOBS, HANS.   Indisch ABC

Roelofsz, Marie Antoinette Petronella
Meilink *See* MEILINK-ROELOFSZ, MARIE
ANTOINETTE PETRONELLA

ROEM, MOHAMAD.   Bunga rampai dari se-
djarah.   Djakarta, Bulan Bintang,
1972.

AR 5 (1973) 309-310. (H. Chambert-
Loir)

ROFF, WILLIAM R. Bibliography of
Malay and Arabic periodicals publish-
ed in the straits settlements and
peninsular Malay states, 1876-1941;
with an annotated union list of hold-
ings in Malaysia, Singapore and the
United Kingdom. London, Oxford UP,
1972. (London Oriental bibliogra-
phies, v. 3)
   JAS 33 (1973-4) 155-6. (C. A.
   Lockard)
   JSAS 5 (1974) 279-282. (Yusof A.
   Talib)
   SOAS 36 (1973) 751-2. (R. Jones)

ROFF, WILLIAM R. Origins of Malay
nationalism. New Haven, Yale UP,
1967. (Yale Southeast Asia studies,
2)
   AR 1 (1970) 201-203. (D. Lombard)
   AS 7 (1967) 592.
   BIJ 125 (1969) 270-272. (E. C. G.
   Barrett)
   JAS 27 (1967-8) 180. (R. S. Milne)
   MAS 3 (1969) 86. (E. Chew)
   SOAS 31 (1968) 455. (H. Tinker)

ROLA-BUSTRILLOS, NENA. Food management
practices of homemakers in the rural
areas. Quezon City, Community Development Research Council, Univ. of
the Philippines, 1961. (Quezon,
Philippines. Univ. of the Philippines. Community Development Research
Council. Study series, no. 12)
   JAS 22 (1962-3) 342-345. (D. V.
   Hart)

ROMEIN, JAN MARIUS. Asian century; a
history of modern nationalism in
Asia. London, George Allen and Unwin, 1962.
   PA 36 (1963) 295. (H. Tinker)

ROMULO, CARLOS PENA. Clarifying the
Asian mystique. Manila, Solidaridad,
1970.
   JAS 31 (1971-2) 381-2. (C. Hobbs)

Rose, Saul. Socialism in Southern Asia

   SA 3 (1974) 930-933. (J. L.
   Bonpua)

ROMULO, CARLOS PENA. Contemporary nationalism and the world order. Bombay, Asia Publishing House, 1964.
   PS 14 (1966) 181-2. (J. M. Juco)

ROMULO, CARLOS PENA. I walked with
heros, the autobiography of General
Carlos P. Romulo. New York, Holt,
Rinehart and Winston, 1961.
   PS 9 (1961) 551-2. (M. A. Bernad)

ROMULO, CARLOS PENA. Mission to Asia:
the dialogue begins. Quezon City,
Univ. of the Philippines, 1964.
   PS 12 (1964) 548-9. (J. M. Juco)

Rong Syamananda *See* SYAMANANDA, RONG

Roolvink, Roelof *See* BASTIN, JOHN
STURGUS. Malayan and Indonesian
studies

Roop, D. Haigh *See* CORNYN, WILLIAM
STEWART. Beginning Burmese

ROOP, D. HAIGH. Introduction to the
Burmese writing system. New Haven,
Yale UP, 1972. (Yale linguistic se-
ries)
   JAS 32 (1972-3) 205-6. (R. B. Jones)
   SOAS 36 (1973) 188. (A. J. Allott)

Rosario, Fe Laura del *See* LLAMZON,
TEODORO A. Makabagong balarila

ROSE, SAUL. Britain and Southeast
Asia. London, Macmillan, 1963.
   PS 13 (1965) 408-411. (N. Bayne)

ROSE, SAUL. Politics in Southern Asia.
London, Macmillan, 1963.
   JSAH 7 (Mar. 1966) 153-155. (J. N.
   Parmer)
   PA 37 (1964) 464-5. (F. R. von der
   Mehden)

ROSE, SAUL. Socialism in Southern Asia.
London, Oxford UP, 1959.

ROZENTAL, ALEK ARON. Finance and de-
velopment in Thailand. New York,
Praeger, 1970.
JAS 30 (1970-1) 504-5. (E. B.
Ayal)
JSS 60 pt. 1 (1972) 421-423. (L.
D. Stifel)
PA 44 (1971) 462-3. (T. H. Silcock)

Rubinstein, Alvin Z. *See* BERTON,
PETER ALEXANDER MENQUEZ. Soviet
works on Southeast Asia

* RUBIO, MARIANO. Tomas de Habito y
profesiones de la Provincia de San
Gregorio de Filipinas, 1583-1736.
Madrid, 1961.
PS 10 (1962) 506. (J. N.
Schumacher)

RUDNEV, VLADIMIR SERGEEVICH. Malaia,
1945-1963. Moscow, Izdatelstvo
vostochnoi literatury, 1963.
AAS 2 (1966) 170-1. (R. Raczynski)

RUNCIMAN, STEVEN. White rajahs, a
history of Sarawak from 1841 to
1946. Cambridge, Univ. Pr., 1960.
JSAH 3 (Mar. 1962) 160-165. (T.
Harrisson)
PA 36 (1963) 98-9. (R. O. Tilman)

Rupen, Robert Arthur *See* Vietnam and
the Sino-Soviet dispute

Russell Tribunal *See* TRIBUNAL
RUSSELL, 1ST. STOCKHOLM, 1967

RYAN, N. J. Making of modern Malaya,
a history from early times to the
present. Kuala Lumpur, Oxford UP,
1963.
JAS 29 (1969-70) 491-2. (T. R.
Fennell)
MAS 4 (1970) 93-4. (E. Chew)
PA 39 (1966) 216-218. (J. M. van
der Kroef)

RYAN, N. J. Making of modern Malaya,
a history from earliest times to
independence. 2d. ed. Kuala Lumpur,
Oxford UP, 1963.

Saenluang, Ratchasomphan. Nan chroni-
JAS 29 (1969-70) 491-2. (T. R.
Fennell)
MAS 4 (1970) 93-4. (E. Chew)

RYAN, N. J. Making of modern Malaysia
and Singapore; a history from earliest times to 1966. 4th ed. rev.
Kuala Lumpur, Oxford UP, 1969.
PA 44 (1971) 321. (B. Harrison)

RYAN, N. J. Malaya through four centuries, an anthology 1500-1900. London, Oxford UP, 1959.
JAS 19 (1959-60) 366-7. (D. G. E.
Hall)

Saber, Mamintua *See* ISIDRO Y SANTOS,
ANTONIO. Muslim Philippines

SA DE MENESES, FRANCISCO DE. Conquest
of Malacca. Kuala Lumpur, Univ. of
Malaya Pr., 1970.
JAS 32 (1972-3) 748. (J. G. de
Casparis)

Sadec, Caopraya *See* SOMDEJ, CAOPRAYA

SADKA, EMILY. Protected Malay states,
1874-1895. Kuala Lumpur, Univ. of
Malaya Pr., 1968.
JAS 30 (1970-1) 237-8. (W. R. Roff)
PA 43 (1970) 316-7. (B. Harrison)

SEADAG rural development seminar *See*
Agricultural revolution in Southeast
Asia

* SAENGSOM KASEMSRI. History of the
Ratanakosin period, first through
third reigns, by Saengsom Kasemsri and
Wimol Phongphiphat. Bangkok, Thai
History Revision Committee, 1972.
JSS 62 pt. 2 (1974) 369-370. (L.
M. Gesick)

SAENLUANG, RATCHASOMPHAN. Nan chronicle, translated by Prasoet Churatana,
edited by David K. Wyatt. Ithaca,
Southeast Asia Program, Cornell Univ.,
1966. (Cornell Univ. Southeast Asia
Program. Data paper, no. 59)

Saenluang, Ratchasomphan. Nan chroni-

JAS 26 (1966-7) 541-2. (W. F. Vella)
JSAH 9 (1968) 172. (I. W. Mabbett)

SAIMONG MANGRAI, SAO. Shan states and
the British annexation. Ithaca,
Cornell Univ., Southeast Asia Pro-
gram, 1965. (Cornell Univ. South-
east Asia Program. Data paper, no.
57)
JAS 25 (1965-6) 549-550. (J. F.
Cady)
JSAH 7 (Sept. 1966) 127-8. (Cheng
Siok Hwa)
PA 38 (1965) 430-432. (B. R. Pearn)

SAINTENY, JEAN. Face a Ho Chi Minh.
Paris, Seghers, 1970.
FA 24 (1970) 207-8.
PA 44 (1971) 585-590. (W. E.
Willmott)

SAITO, SHIRO. Philippine ethnography:
a critically annotated and selected
bibliography. Honolulu, Univ. Pr. of
Hawaii, 1972. (East-West bibliogra-
phic series)
AAS 10 (1974) 203-4. (J. Genzor)
JAS 33 (1973-4) 507-8. (R. W.
Lieban)
SA 3 (1974) 938-941. (C. O.
Houston)

SAITO, SHIRO. Preliminary bibliography
of Philippine ethnography. Quezon
City, Institute of Philippine Culture,
Ateneo de Manila, 1968.
PS 16 (1968) 795-797. (M. A.
Bernad)

* Sajak2 modern Perancis dalam dua
bahasa. n.p., Pustaka Jaya, 1972.
AR 5 (1973) 311. (H. Chambert-
Loir)

SALAMANCA, BONIFACIO S. Filipino re-
action to American rule, 1901-1913.
Hamden, Conn., Shoe String Pr.,
1968.
PS 18 (1970) 429-435. (J. N.
Schumacher)

SALGADO, PEDRO V. Social philosophy in
the Philippine context. n.p., 1972.
PS 21 (1971) 231-233. (V. R.
Gorospe)

SALISBURY, HARRISON. Behind the lines:
Hanoi, December 23, 1966-January 7,
1967. New York, Harper and Row,
1967.
PA 42 (1969) 423.

SALZNER, RICHARD. Sprachen atlas des
Indopazifischen Raumes. Wiesbaden,
Harrassowitz, 1960.
AAS 1 (1965) 202. (V. Krupa)
SOAS 24 (1961) 607-8. (G. B.
Milner)

* SAMANA, PIERRE. Anthologie de la
poesie vietnamienne. Tananarive,
1962.
BEF 56 (1969) 188-191. (Nguyen Tien
Lang)

Samonte, Abelardo *See* LEE, HAHN BEEN.
Administrative reforms in Asia

SAN JUAN, EPIFANIO. Carlos Bulosan and
the imagination of the class struggle. Quezon City, Univ. of the Philippines Pr., 1972.
PA 47 (1974) 102-3. (C. O. Houston)
PS 21 (1973) 215-222. (J. A.
Galdon)

SANCHEZ, CONCORDIA. Philippine school
libraries, their organization and
management. Manila, MCS Enterprises,
1971.
PS 20 (1972) 350-1. (R. J. Suchan)

Sanchez, Marinela *See* LLAMZON, TEO-
DORO A. Makabagong balarila

SANDERS, ALBERT J. Evangelical ministry
in the Philippines and its future.
Manila, National Council of Churches
in the Philippines, 1964.
JAS 24 (1964-5) 706-708. (G. H.
Anderson)
SJ 12 (1965) 234-5. (P. T. Lauby)

SANDERS, SOL. Sense of Asia. New
  York, Scribner, 1969.
    PA 43 (1970) 91-2. (L. Hobbs)

SANDHU, KERNIAL SINGH. Indians in
  Malaya, some aspects of their immi-
  gration and settlement, 1786-1957.
  London, Cambridge UP, 1969.
    JAS 30 (1970-1) 233-4. (R. W.
      Tellander)
    JSAS 1 pt. 2 (1970) 136-7. (S.
      Arasaratnam)
    MER 15 pt. 1 (1970) 126-128. (T. R.
      McHale)
    SA 1 (1971) 402-406. (U. Mahajani)
    SOAS 33 (1970) 432. (J. C. Jackson)

SANDIN, BENEDICT. The Sea Dyaks of
  Borneo before white rajah rule.
  London, Macmillan, 1968.
    BIJ 125 (1969) 275-279. (J. B.
      Ave)
    JAS 28 (1968-9) 657-8. (D. Freeman)
    JSAS 1 pt. 1 (1970) 112-115. (R.
      M. Pringle)

SANGERMANO, VICENTIUS. Description of
  the Burmese empire. London, Santiago
  de Compostela, Susil Gupta, 1966.
    JAS 30 (1970-1) 228-9. (D. K.
      Wyatt)
    PA 43 (1970) 648-9. (B. Harrison)

Saniel, Josefa M. *See* ASSOCIATION
  FOR ASIAN STUDIES ON THE PACIFIC
  COAST. Filipino exclusion movement,
  1927-1935.

SANIEL, JOSEFA M. Japan and the Philippines, 1868-1898. Quezon City,
  Univ. of the Philippines, 1962.
    GEJ 5 (1963) 221-223. (M. H.
      Rocamora)
    JAS 24 (1964-5) 334. (C. O.
      Houston)
    JSAH 6 (Mar. 1966) 135-137. (W. E.
      Cheong)
    PA 44 (1971) 141-2. (E. Wickberg)

SANSOM, ROBERT L. Economics of insurgency in the Mekong delta of Vietnam.

Santos-Villanueva, Patrocino. Value of

Cambridge, MIT Pr., 1970.
    JAS 30 (1970-1) 508-510. (C. Wolf)
    JOSA 8 (1971) 131-2. (K. G.
      Tregonning)
    MAS 5 (1971) 187-191. (R. B. Smith)

SANTA MARIA, LUIGI. I prestiti porto-
  ghesi nel Malese-Indonesiano. Naples,
  Instituto orientale, 1967. (Naples.
  Instituto orientale. Seminario di
  indianistica. Pubblicazioni, 1)
    BEF 57 (1970) 224-227. (D. Lombard)
    SOAS 33 (1970) 430-1. (E. C. G.
      Barrett)

SANTIAGO, CORAZON DAMO-. Century of
  activism. Manila, Rex Book, 1972.
    PS 21 (1973) 396-398. (M. D.
      Litonjua)

SANTOS, BIENVENIDO N. Brother, my
  brother; a collection of stories.
  Manila, Benipayo Pr., 1960.
    PS 8 (1960) 880-882. (M. A. Bernad)

SANTOS, BIENVENIDO N. The day the
  dancers came; selected prose works.
  Manila, Bookmark, 1967.
    PS 16 (1968) 798-802. (M. A.
      Bernad)

SANTOS, BIENVENIDO N. Villa Magdalena.
  Manila, Erehwon, 1965.
    PS 14 (1966) 182-185. (V. O.
      Olaguer)

SANTOS, BIENVENIDO N. Volcano. Quezon
  City, Phoenix, 1965.
    PS 14 (1966) 299-309. (M. A. Bernad)

SANTOS, ENRIQUE B. Philippine wings; a
  short history of commercial aviation
  in the Philippines. Manila, Philippine Air Lines, 1969.
    JAS 32 (1972-3) 761-2. (J. D.
      Williams)

SANTOS-VILLANUEVA, PATROCINO. Value of
  rural roads. Quezon City, Community
  Development Research Council, 1959.
  (Quezon, Philippines. Univ. of the

Santos-Villanueva, Patrocino. Value of

Philippines. Community Development
Research Council. Study series, no.
2)
JAS 20 (1960-1) 399-403. (F. C.
Madigan and D. V. Hart)

SarDesai, Bhanu *See* SarDESAI, D. R.
Theses and dissertations on Southeast Asia

SarDESAI, D. R. Indian foreign policy
in Cambodia, Laos and Vietnam, 1947-
1964. Berkeley, Univ. of California
Pr., 1968.
AS 8 (1968) 872.
JSAS 2 (1971) 259-260. (V. M. Fic)
PA 42 (1969) 558-9. (D. P. Singhal)

SarDESAI, D. R. Theses and disserta-
tions on Southeast Asia, an interna-
tional bibliography in social sci-
ences, education and fine arts, by
D. R. and Bhanu D. SarDesai. Zug,
Switzerland, Inter-Documentation
Co., 1970. (Bibliotheca Asiatica, 6)
SA 2 (1972-3) 138-143. (S. Saito)

Sarin Chhak *See* CHHAK, SARIN

Sarkar, Bidyut Kumar *See* SEMINAR ON
INDIA AND SOUTHEAST ASIA, DELHI,
1966. India and Southeast Asia.

SARKAR, HIMANSU BHUSAN. Some contributions of India to the ancient
civilisation of Indonesia and Malaysia. Calcutta, Punthi Pustak,
1970.
JSS 59 pt. 2 (1971) 262. (H. W.
Woodward)

SARKAR, KALYAN KUMAR. Early Indo-
Cambodian contacts, literary and
linguistic. Santiniketan, Visva-
Bharati, 1968.
JSAS 2 (1971) 258-9. (I. W.
Mabbett)
JSS 58 pt. 1 (1970) 140-1.
(Prince Subhadradis Diskul)

SARKISYANZ, EMANUEL. Buddhist back-
grounds of the Burmese revolution.
The Hague, Nijhoff, 1965.
AS 6 (1966) 301.
JAH 3 (1969) 80-82. (F. N. Trager)
JAS 26 (1966-7) 133-135. (J. F.
Cady)
JSAH 8 (1967) 331-2. (H. Tinker)
PA 38 (1965) 427-430. (D. G. E.
Hall)
SOAS 29 (1966) 653-4. (E. M.
Mendelson)

SARKISYANZ, EMANUEL. Sudostasian seit
1945. Munich, Oldenbourg, 1961.
JAS 22 (1962-3) 490-1. (K. J.
Pelzer)
PA 35 (1962) 424-5. (B. Lasker)

Sartono Kartodirdjo *See* KARTODIRDJO,
SARTONO

SARUMPAET, J. P. Introduction to
Bahasa Indonesia, by J. P. Sarumpaet
and J. A. C. Mackie. Melbourne, Mel-
bourne UP, 1966.
BIJ 124 (1968) 545-551. (Soebardi)
SOAS 31 (1968) 182-3. (N. G.
Phillips)

SARUMPAET, J. P. Structure of Bahasa
Indonesia. Melbourne, Dept. of Indo-
nesian and Malayan Studies, Univ. of
Melbourne, 1966.
BIJ 124 (1968) 545-551. (Soebardi)

Saunders, Alexander Morris Carr *See*
CARR-SAUNDERS, ALEXANDER MORRIS

Saunders, Bruce *See* TAKEI, YOSHIMITSU.
Educational sponsorship by ethnicity

SAUNDERS, JOHN JOSEPH. Muslim world on
the eve of Europe's expansion. Englewood Cliffs, Prentice-Hall, 1966.
(Global history series)
PA 41 (1968) 263-4. (J. Davidson)

SAUVAGET, JEAN. Introduction a
l'histoire de l'orient musulman, elements de bibliographie. Edition

refondue et completee par C. Cahen.
Paris, Adrien-Maisonneuve, 1961.
(Initiation a l'Islam, 1)
    SOAS 25 (1962) 357-8. (J.
      Wansbrough)

SAW SWEE HOCK. Singapore, population
in transition. Philadelphia, Univ.
of Pennsylvania Pr., 1970.
    AS 11 (1971) 522.
    JSAS 3 (1972) 359-360. (G.
      Shantakumar)
    MAS 8 (1974) 557-559. (P. Wheatley)

Sawaeng Ratanamongkolmas *See* CHAI-
ANAN SAMUDVANIJA. Sat kan muang

SCALAPINO, ROBERT A. Communist revolution in Asia; tactics, goals and
achievements. Englewood Cliffs,
Prentice-Hall, 1965.
    AS 5 (1965) 527.
    JAS 25 (1965-6) 506-508. (S. R.
      Schram)
    RSA (1967) 313-4. (J. S. Roucek)

SCHAAF, C. HART. Lower Mekong:
challenge to cooperation in Southeast Asia, by C. Hart Schaaf and
Russell H. Fifield. Princeton, Van
Nostrand, 1963.
    JAS 23 (1963-4) 599-600. (D. H.
      Kornhauser)

SCHACHTER, PAUL. Tagalog reference
grammar, by Paul Schachter and Fe T.
Otanes. Berkeley, Univ. of California Pr., 1972.
    AAS 10 (1974) 201-2. (J. Genzor)
    JAS 32 (1972-3) 760-1. (M. L.
      Forman)

SCHÄRER, HANS. Ngaju religion, the
conception of God among a south
Borneo people. The Hague, Nijhoff,
1963. (Instituut voor Taal-, Land-
en Volkenkunde. Translation series,
6)
    JAS 24 (1964-5) 340-1. (D. Riepe)
    SOAS 29 (1966) 424-5. (A. Christie)

Schmitz, Carl A. Festschrift, Alfred

SCHÄRER, HANS. Der Totenkult der
Ngadju Dajak in Sud-Borneo, Mythen
zum Totenkult und die Texte zum
Tantolak Matei. The Hague, Nijhoff,
1966. (Instituut voor Taal-, Land-
en Volkenkunde. Verhandelingen, deel
51)
    PA 40 (1967) 395-6. (T. Harrisson)
    SMJ 15 (1967) 456. (T. Harrisson)
    SOAS 31 (1968) 425-6. (C. Hooykaas)

SCHANCHE, DON A. Mister Pop, the adventures of a peaceful man in a small
war. New York, David McKay, 1970.
    SA 2 (1972-3) 347-356. (U. Mahajani)

SCHIRMER, DANIEL B. Republic or em-
pire; American resistance to the
Philippine war. Cambridge, Mass.,
Schenkman, 1972.
    PA 46 (1973) 185. (I. B. Powell)
    SA 3 (1974) 933-935. (W. G.
      Whittaker)

SCHLEGEL, STUART A. Tiruray-English
lexicon. Berkeley, Univ. of California Pr., 1971. (California. Univ.
Univ. of California publications in
linguistics, v. 67)
    JAS 31 (1971-2) 466-468. (G. W.
      Moore)

SCHLEGEL, STUART A. Tiruray justice,
traditional Tiruray law and morality.
Berkeley, Univ. of California Pr.,
1970.
    JAS 31 (1971-2) 466-468. (G. W.
      Moore)

SCHMID, PETER. Paradies im Drachen-
schlund; Reise durch Hinterindien,
Java und Sumatra. Stuttgart, Deutsche
Verlags-Anstalt, 1956.
    FA 18 (1962) 239. (J. May)

SCHMITZ, CARL A. Festschrift, Alfred
Buhler, herausgegeben von Carl A.
Schmitz und Robert Wildhaber. Basel,
Pharos-Verlag, 1965. (Basler Bei-
trage zur Geographie und Ethnologie.
Ethnologische Reihe, Bd. 2)
    BIJ 123 (1967) 192-3. (C. Nooteboom)

Schmitz, Josef. The Abra Mission in

SCHMITZ, JOSEF. The Abra Mission in
northern Luzon, Philippines, 1598-
1955; a historical study. Cebu City,
Univ. of San Carlos, 1971. (San
Carlos publications. Series D: Occasional monographs, no. 2)
    JAS 32 (1972-3) 382-3. (N. P.
      Cushner)
    SJ 19 (1972) 104-107. (H. R.
      Reynolds)
    SLURJ 3 (1972) 637-8. (A. Paredes)

SCHRAM, STUART R. Le Marxisme et
l'Asie, 1853-1964, par Stuart R.
Schram et Helene Carrere d'Encausse.
n.p., 1965.
    RSA (1966) 136-138. (I. Jadoul)

Schramm, Wilbur Lang *See* LERNER,
DANIEL. Communication and change in
the developing countries

SCHRIEKE, BERTRAM JOHANNES OTTO. Ruler
and realm in early Java. The Hague,
van Hoeve, 1957. (Indonesian sociological studies, selected writings
of B. Schrieke, pt. 2)
    PA 33 (1960) 95-6. (D. G. E. Hall)

SCHULTE NORDHOLT, H. G. Political
system of the Atoni of Timor. The
Hague, Nijhoff, 1971. (Instituut
voor Taal-, Land- en Volkenkunde.
Verhandelingen, 60)
    JSAS 3 (1972) 337-8. (D. Hicks)
    SOAS 35 (1972) 443. (M. C.
      Ricklefs)

SCHULTZ, GEORGE F. Vietnamese legends
adapted from the Vietnamese. Rutland, Tuttle, 1965.
    BEF 56 (1969) 191-2. (T. C.
      Leocmach)
    JAS 26 (1966-7) 135-6. (Nguyen
      Khac Kham)
    SA 2 (1972-3) 389-391. (Nguyen
      Dang Liem)

SCHUMACHER, JOHN N. Father Jose
Burgos, priest and nationalist. Manila, Ateneo UP, 1972.

    JAS 33 (1973-4) 344-5. (D. J.
      Steinberg)
    PS 20 (1972) 657-659. (P. Fernandez)

* SCHUMACHER, JOHN N. The propaganda
movement, 1880-1895, the creators of
a Filipino consciousness, the makers
of the revolution. Manila, Solidaridad Pub. House, 1973.
    PA 47 (1974) 402-3. (I. B. Powell)
    PS 22 (1974) 210-1. (M. A. Bernad)

SCHURZ, WILLIAM LYTLE. Manila galleon.
New York, Dutton, 1959.
    PS 8 (1960) 205-6. (N. P. Cushner)

Scientific problems of the humid tropical zone deltas and their implications; proceedings of the Dacca symposium. Paris, UNESCO, 1966.
(United Nations Educational, Scientific and Cultural Organization.
Humid tropics research)
    JAS 26 (1966-7) 497-499. (K. J.
      Pelzer)

SCIGLIANO, ROBERT G. South Vietnam:
nation under stress. Boston, Houghton
Mifflin, 1964.
    AS 4 (1964) 822.
    JAS 24 (1964-5) 170. (J. C. Donnell)
    RSA (1965) 120-1. (I. Jadoul)

SCOTT, ADOLPHE CLARENCE. Theatre in
Asia. London, Weidenfeld and Nicolson, 1972. (History of the theatre)
    SOAS 36 (1973) 752. (C. J. Dunn)

SCOTT, JAMES C. Political ideology in
Malaysia; reality and the beliefs of
an elite. New Haven, Yale UP, 1968.
(Yale Southeast Asia studies, 3)
    JSAS 1 pt. 1 (1970) 111-2. (Chan
      Heng Chee)

SCOTT, JAMES GEORGE. The Burman; his
life and notions, by Shway Yoe. New
York, Norton, 1963.
    JAS 23 (1963-4) 485. (J. F. Cady)

SCOTT, NORMAN CARSON. Dictionary of
  Sea Dayak. London, School of Oriental and African Studies, 1956.
    JMBRAS 33 pt. 1 (1960) 115-117.
    (E. Banks)

Scott, William Henry *See* BAGUIO RE-
  LIGIOUS ACCULTURATION CONFERENCE.
  Acculturation in the Philippines

SCOTT, WILLIAM HENRY. On the Cordillera; a look at the peoples and cultures of the Mountain Province. Manila, MCS, 1966.
    PS 15 (1967) 536-538. (F.
    Lambrecht)

SCOTT, WILLIAM HENRY. A critical study
  of prehispanic source materials for
  the study of Philippine history. Manila, Univ. of Santo Tomas Pr., 1968.
  (Unitas-Filipiniana series)
    AP 12 (1969) 145-6. (W. G. Solheim)
    JAS 29 (1969-70) 994-997. (D. V.
    Hart)
    JSAS 2 (1971) 255-6. (J. R. Fran-
    cisco)
    SJ 16 (1969) 216-7. (P. G. Gowing)
    SLURJ 1 (1970) 584-587. (F. L.
    Lorente)

SCOTT-KEMBALL, JEUNE. Javanese shadow
  puppets: the Raffles collection in
  the British Museum. London, British
  Museum, 1970.
    BIJ 128 (1972) 501-504. (R. S.
    Wassing)

Sdoeng Chur *See* BEJ SAL. Prajum
  rioen bran khmaer phag 8

SEAH, CHEE MEOW. Community centres in
  Singapore; their political involvement. Singapore, Singapore UP, 1973.
    PA 47 (1974) 579-580. (L. E.
    Williams)

SEBEOK, THOMAS ALBERT. Current trends
  in linguistics. The Hague, Mouton,
  1967-
  Volume II.

    JAS 28 (1968-9) 835-837. (J. A.
    Matisoff)
    SOAS 32 (1969) 434-436. (M. A. K.
    Halliday)
  Volume VIII.
    AAS 10 (1974) 191-193. (V. Krupa)

Seh Bari *See* KITAB BONANG. Admonitions of Seh Bari

SEIDENFADEN, ERIK. The Thai peoples.
  Book I. The origins and habitats of
  the Thai peoples with a sketch of
  their material and spiritual culture.
  Bangkok, Siam Society, 1958.
    JAS 19 (1959-60) 467-8. (H. P.
    Phillips)
    PA 36 (1963) 320. (O. W. Wolters)

SEIN, KENNETH. The great Po Sein,
  chronicle of the Burmese theater, by
  Kenneth Maung Khe Sein and J. A.
  Withey. Bloomington, Indiana UP,
  1965.
    JAS 26 (1966-7) 335-6. (J. F. Cady)
    PA 41 (1968) 454-5. (M. K.
    Mulholland)

SEJARAH MELAYU. ENGLISH. Sejarah Melayu, or Malay annals. Kuala Lumpur,
  Oxford UP, 1970. (Oxford in Asia
  historical reprints)
    JAS 31 (1971-2) 989-990. (J. M.
    Echols)
    SOAS 35 (1972) 662-3. (R. Jones)

* Selected Philippine sermons. Manila,
  National Council of Churches in the
  Philippines, 1967. (Christian
  leaders' series, no. 6)
    PS 16 (1968) 598-600.

Seldon, Mark *See* America's Asia

SELLMAN, ROGER RAYMOND. Outline atlas
  of eastern history. London, E.
  Arnold, 1954.
    JSAH 1 (Sept. 1960) 118-121. (K. S.
    Sandhu)

Selosoemardjan *See* SOEMARDJAN, SELO

Seminar on Constitutionalism in Asia

Shepsle, Kenneth A. *See* RABUSHKA,
ALVIN. Politics in plural societies

SHERIDAN, LIONEL ASTOR. Constitution
of Malaysia, by Lionel Astor Sheridan and Harry E. Groves. Dobbs
Ferry, Oceania, 1967.
    JAS 28 (1968-9) 191-2. (W. H.
      Elsbree)
    PA 41 (1968) 328. (R. S. Milne)

SHERIDAN, LIONEL ASTOR. Malaya and
Singapore, the Borneo territories;
the development of their laws and
constitutions. London, Stevens,
1961. (British Commonwealth; the
development of its laws and constitution v. 9)
    JSAH 3 (Sept. 1962) 145-147. (H.
      E. Groves)

SHERRY, NORMAN. Conrad's eastern
world. London, Cambridge UP, 1966.
    PA 39 (1966) 210-1. (G. Woodcock)

* SHIN OKKANTHAMALA. Commentary on the
poems of Taungoo Min. n.p., n.d.
    JBRS 44 (1961) 297.

SHORTO, H. L. Bibliographies of Mon-
Khmer and Tai linguistics, by H. L.
Shorto, Judith M. Jacob and E. H. S.
Simmonds. London, Oxford UP, 1963.
(London Oriental bibliographies, v.
2)
    BEF 53 (1966) 300-303. (F.
      Martini)
    SOAS 27 (1964) 484-5. (H.-J.
      Pinnow)

SHORTO, H. L. Dictionary of modern
spoken Mon. London, Oxford UP,
1962.
    SOAS 26 (1963) 675-6. (H.-J.
      Pinnow)

SHORTO, H. L. Dictionary of the Mon
inscriptions from the sixth to the
sixteenth centuries, incorporating
materials collected by the late C.
O. Blagden. London, Oxford UP, 1971.

(London Oriental series, v. 24)
    BIJ 129 (1973) 510-513. (B. L.
      Foster)
    JSS 61 pt. 2 (1973) 205-209. (M.
      Vickery)
    SOAS 35 (1972) 411-2. (C. Hooykaas)

Shorto, H. L. *See* Linguistic comparison in South East Asia and the
Pacific

Shway Yoe *See* SCOTT, JAMES GEORGE

Sibayan, Bonifacio *See* BERNABE, EMMA.
Ilokano lessons

SICAT, GERARDO P. Economic policy and
Philippine development. Quezon City,
Univ. of the Philippines Pr., 1972.
    PS 20 (1972) 653-4. (M. McPhelin)

Sicat, Gerardo P. *See* POWER, JOHN H.
The Philippines

SIEGEL, JAMES T. Rope of God. Berkeley, Univ. of California Pr., 1969.
    JAS 29 (1969-70) 740-1. (E. M.
      Bruner)
    JSAS 3 (1972) 340-1. (C. E.
      Cunningham)

SIERKSMA, FOKKE. De mens en zijn goden.
Amsterdam, De Brug, 1959.
    BIJ 116 (1960) 287-289. (H. T.
      Fischer)

SIFFIN, WILLIAM J. Thai bureaucracy,
institutional change and development.
Honolulu, East-West Center Pr., 1966.
    AS 6 (1966) 716.
    JSAH 8 (1967) 333-4. (J. P. L.
      Jiang)
    PA 39 (1966) 410-412. (R. S. Milne)

Siffin, William J. *See* THROMBLEY,
WOODWORTH G. Thailand

Sihanouk, Norodom *See* NORODOM
SIHANOUK VARMAN

Silcock, Thomas Henry.   Commonwealth

Singh, S. Nihal

Graduate School. Southeast Asia
Studies. Monograph series, no. 16)
  JAS 32 (1972-3) 383-4. (D. E.
    Voth)
  PA 45 (1972) 623-4. (J. E. Spencer)

Simmonds, E. H. S. *See* SHORTO, H. L.
  Bibliographies of Mon-Khmer and Tai
  linguistics

SIMON, PIERRE J. Hau Bong; un culte
  vietnamien de possession transplante
  en France, par Pierre J. Simon et
  Ida Simon-Barouh. Paris, Mouton,
  1973. (Cahiers de l'homme: ethnologie, geographie, linguistique,
  nouv. ser., 13)
    SEIB 49 (1974) 159-161. (Le Quang
      Trung)
    SOAS 37 (1974) 497-8. (R. B.
      Smith)

SIMON, SHELDON W. Broken triangle;
  Peking, Djakarta, and the PKI.
  Baltimore, Johns Hopkins, 1969.
    PA 42 (1969) 530-1. (R. C. Horn)

SIMON, SHELDON W. War and politics in
  Cambodia; a communications analysis.
  Durham, Duke UP, 1974.
    PA 47 (1974) 398-9. (J. L. S.
      Girling)

Simon-Barouh, Ida *See* SIMON, PIERRE
  J. Hau Bong

SIMONIIA, N. A. Overseas Chinese in
  Southeast Asia, a Russian study.
  Ithaca, Southeast Asia Program, Cor-
  nell Univ., 1961. (Cornell Univ.
  Southeast Asia Program. Data paper,
  no. 45)
    BIJ 120 (1964) 475-477. (W. Brand)
    PA 36 (1963) 317-320. (W. E.
      Willmott)
    PS 11 (1963) 593-598. (J. Amyot)
    RSA (1966) 140-142. (The Siauw
      Giap)

Simpson, Donald Herbert *See* ROYAL
  COMMONWEALTH SOCIETY. LIBRARY. Biography catalogue

SINCO, VICENTE G. Education in Philippine society. Quezon City, Univ. of
  the Philippines Publication Office,
  1959.
    PS 8 (1960) 474-476. (J. J. Meany)

SINGAPORE. MIN. OF NATIONAL DEVELOPMENT.
  Singapore sample household survey,
  1966, report no. 1, tables relating
  to population and housing, by the
  Ministry of National Development and
  the Economic Research Centre, Univ.
  of Singapore. Singapore, GPO, 1967.
    MER 13 pt. 1 (1968) 128-9. (P. M.
      Hauser)

Singapore. Univ. Economic Research Centre *See* SINGAPORE. MIN. OF NATIONAL
  DEVELOPMENT. Singapore sample household survey

SINGAPORE. UNIV. LIBRARY. CATALOGUING
  DEPT. Catalogue of the Singapore/
  Malaysia collection. Boston, G. K.
  Hall, 1968.
    JSAS 1 pt. 2 (1970) 146-7. (J. M.
      Waller)

SINGH, L. P. Colombo plan, some politi-
  cal aspects. Canberra, Dept. of
  International Relations, Research
  School of Pacific Studies, Australian
  National Univ., 1963. (Australian
  National Univ., Canberra. Dept. of
  International Relations. Working
  paper, no. 3)
    JAS 23 (1963-4) 629-630. (J. C.
      Nahm)
    RSA (1963) 296-7. (L. Rocher)

SINGH, LALITA PRASAD. Politics of eco-
  nomic cooperation in Asia, a study of
  Asian international organizations.
  Columbia, Univ. of Missouri Pr., 1966.
    AS 7 (1967) 82.
    JAS 26 (1966-7) 687-8. (C. J.
      Stokes)

Singh, S. Nihal *See* NIHAL SINGH, S.

Singh, Vishal. Indonesia's struggle

Singh, Vishal *See* NEDERLANDS GENOOT-
SCHAP VOOR INTERNATIONALE ZAKEN.
Indonesia's struggle

SINGHAL, D. P. Annexation of Upper
Burma. Singapore, Eastern Universi-
ties Pr., 1960.
　　JAS 20 (1960-1) 396-7. (J. F.
　　Cady)
　　JSAH 1 (Sept. 1960) 113-116. (H.
　　Tinker)
　　PA 35 (1962) 301-2. (F. N. Trager)
　　SOAS 24 (1961) 622. (C. D. Cowan)

SINHA, KRISHNA KISHORE. Problems of
defense of South and East Asia.
Bombay, Manaktalas, 1969.
　　JAS 29 (1969-70) 684-5. (L. P.
　　Singh)

Sisouk Na Champassak *See* CHAMPASSAK,
SISOUK NA

SITHI-AMNUAI, PAUL. Finance and bank-
ing in Thailand; a study of the com-
mercial system, 1888-1963. Bangkok,
Thai Watana Panich, 1964.
　　MER 11 pt. 1 (1966) 101-113. (T.
　　H. Silcock)

SITHIPORN KRIDAKORN, M. C.　Some
aspects of rice farming in Siam.
Bangkok, Suksit Siam, 1970.
　　JSS 58 pt. 2 (1970) 189-190. (L.
　　Stifel)

SITSAYAMKAN, LUANG. Some useful in-
formation on the Buddhist religion
as it is taught and practised in
Thailand. Bangkok, 1963.
　　JSS 52 (1964) 115-117. (M. C.
　　Subhadradis Diskul)

SIVARAM, M. Vietnam war: why?
Rutland, Tuttle, 1966.
　　SJ 14 (1967) 94-5. (C. C. Gayo)

SIVARAMAMURTI, C. Le stupa du Barabudur. Paris, Presses universitaires de France, 1961. (Paris.
Musee Guimet. Recherches et docu-

ments d'art et d'archeologie, t. 8)
　　JAS 21 (1961-2) 96-7. (J. M. Rosen-
　　field)
　　SEIB 36 (1961) 755.
　　SOAS 24 (1961) 389-390. (A.
　　Christie)

Siwaratrikalpa of Mpu Tanakun. An old
Javanese poem, its Indian source and
Balinese illustrations. The Hague,
Nijhoff, 1969. (Bibliotheca Indone-
sica, 3)
　　JSAS 2 (1971) 236-7. (J. Gonda)
　　SOAS 33 (1970) 672-674. (C.
　　Hooykaas)

Six perspectives on the Philippines,
edited by George M. Guthrie. Manila,
Bookmark, 1968.
　　PS 17 (1969) 350-352. (M. A. Bernad)
　　SLQ 6 (1968) 520-523. (F. L.
　　Lorente)

SJAHRIR, SOETAN. Our struggle.
Ithaca, Modern Indonesia Project,
Southeast Asia Program, Cornell Univ.,
1968. (Cornell Univ. Modern Indonesia
Project. Translation series)
　　AS 8 (1968) 1027.

SKINNER, CYRIL. Civil war in Kelantan
in 1839. Singapore, Malaysian Branch,
Royal Asiatic Society, 1966. (Royal
Asiatic Society of Great Britain and
Ireland. Malaysian Branch. Monographs,
2)
　　BIJ 124 (1968) 553-4. (R. Roolvink)
　　JAS 27 (1967-8) 433. (W. F. Vella)
　　MAS 2 (1968) 277-8. (D. K. Bassett)
　　SOAS 31 (1968) 183-4. (Amin Sweeney)

Skinner, Cyril *See* AMIN, ENTJI.
Sjair Perang Mengkasar

SKINNER, GEORGE WILLIAM. Local, ethnic
and national loyalties in village
Indonesia, a symposium. New Haven,
Yale Univ., Southeast Asia Studies,
1959. (Yale Univ. Graduate School.
Southeast Asia Studies. Cultural re-
port series, 8)
　　JAS 19 (1959-60) 363-4. (C. DuBois)

Smith, Robin V. F.   New Guinea; a

SLAMETMULJANA, R. B.   Kaidah bahasa
  Indonesia.   Djakarta, Djambatan,
  1956-7. 2v.
    BIJ 116 (1960) 485-488. (A. Teeuw)

SLAMETMULJANA, R. B.   Politik bahasa
  nasional. Pidato penerimaan djabatan
  guru besar dalam bahasa Indonesia
  pada Fakultas Sastra Universitas
  Indonesia diutjapkan pada tanggal 16
  Mei 1959.   Djakarta, Djambatan, 1959.
    BIJ 116 (1960) 488-9. (A. Teeuw)

SLIMMING, JOHN.   Malaysia, death of a
  democracy.   London, John Murray,
  1969.
    JAS 31 (1971-2) 734-736. (G. D.
      Ness)
    PA 44 (1971) 303-305. (R. S. Milne)

SMAIL, JOHN R. W.   Bandung in the
  early revolution, 1945-1946; a study
  in the social history of the Indonesian revolution.   Ithaca, Southeast
  Asia Program, Cornell Univ., 1964.
  (Cornell Univ. Modern Indonesia
  Project.   Monograph series)
    JAS 24 (1964-5) 710-1. (J. D.
      Legge)
    JSAH 6 (Sept. 1965) 161-163. (J. M.
      Pluvier)

SMALLEY, WILLIAM ALLEN.   Outline of
  Khmu structure.   New Haven, American
  Oriental Society, 1961.   (American
  Oriental Society. American Oriental
  series, essay 2)
    SOAS 27 (1964) 203-4. (H. L.
      Shorto)

SMETS, PAUL F.   De Bandoeng a Moshi,
  contribution a l'etude des confer-
  ences afro-asiatiques 1955-1963.
  Brussels, Universite Libre de
  Bruxelles, Institut de Sociologie,
  1964.   (Brussels. Universite Libre.
  Institut de Sociologie. Etudes
  Africaines)
    RSA (1965) 124-5. (I. Jadoul)

Smith, Arthur K.   See WELCH, CLAUDE
  EMERSON.   Military role and rule

SMITH, BRUCE LANNES.   Indonesian-
  American cooperation in higher education.   East Lansing, Institute of Research on Overseas Programs, Michigan
  State Univ., 1960.
    PA 34 (1961) 309-311. (W. F.
      Wertheim)
    PA 35 (1962) 65. (W. F. Wertheim)

SMITH, DATUS CLIFFORD.   Land and people
  of Indonesia.   Philadelphia, Lippincott, 1961.
    PA 37 (1964) 115. (L. H. Palmier)

SMITH, DONALD EUGENE.   Religion and
  politics in Burma.   Princeton, Princeton UP, 1965.
    FA 20 (1965) 523-4. (F. Cayrac)
    JAS 26 (1966-7) 136-7. (F. R. von
      der Mehden)
    PA 38 (1965) 427-430. (D. G. E.
      Hall)

SMITH, GEORGE EDWARD.   POW-two years
  with the Vietcong.   Berkeley, Ram-
  parts Pr., 1971.
    JCA 2 (1972) 317.

Smith, Harold E.   See Thai rural
  families

SMITH, RALPH BERNARD.   Vietnam and the
  west.   London, Heinemann Educational,
  1968.
    JSAH 10 (1969) 364-367. (D. M. Ray)
    SA 2 (1972) 517-8. (A.-G. Marsot)
    SOAS 32 (1969) 201-2. (A. Woodside)

SMITH, ROBERT ROSS.   Triumph in the
  Philippines.   Washington, GPO, 1963.
  (U.S. Dept. of the Army. Office of
  Military History. United States Army
  in World War II)
    JAS 23 (1963-4) 486-7. (G. K.
      Goodman)

SMITH, ROBIN V. F.   New Guinea; a journey through 10,000 years, by Robin

Smith, Robin V. F.   New Guinea; a

Smith, with text by Keith Willey.
Melbourne, Lansdowne Pr., 1969.
   PA 43 (1970) 473-4. (D. G.
   Bettison)

SMITH, ROGER M.   Cambodia's foreign
policy.   Ithaca, Cornell UP, 1965.
   AS 5 (1965) 528.
   JSAH 7 (Sept. 1966) 137-8. (G.
   Modelski)
   PA 38 (1965) 435-6. (M. Leifer)
   SOAS 30 (1967) 225-6. (W. E.
   Willmott)

SMITH, RONALD BISHOP.   First age of
the Portuguese embassies, naviga-
tions and peregrinations to the
kingdoms and islands of South East
Asia, 1509-1521.   n.p., Decatur Pr.,
1968.
   BEF 61 (1974) 380-383. (P.-Y.
   Manguin)
   JSS 58 pt. 2 (1970) 155-157. (P.
   J. S. Young)

SMITH, RONALD BISHOP.   Siam, or the
history of the Thais from the earliest times to 1569 A.D.   Bethesda,
Md., 1966.
   PA 41 (1968) 152-3. (D. G. E. Hall)

SMITH, T. E.   Elections in developing
countries; a study of electoral pro-
cedures used in tropical Africa,
South-East Asia and the British
Caribbean.   London, St. Martin's
Pr., 1960.
   JSAH 2 (Mar. 1961) 137-139. (K.
   Jeyaratnam)

SMITH, T. E.   Malaysia, by T. E. Smith
and John Bastin.   London, Oxford UP,
1967.
   JAS 28 (1968-9) 646-7. (G. D. Ness)
   PA 41 (1968) 153-4. (R. S. Milne)

SMITH, WINFIELD SCOTT.   Art of the
Philippines, 1521-1957.   Manila,
Associated Publishers, 1958.
   PS 8 (1960) 224-228. (A. G.
   Manuud)

Smithies, Michael   *See*   TEJ BUNNAG.   In
memoriam, Phya Anuman Rajadhon

SNYDER, LOUIS LEO.   New nationalism.
Ithaca, Cornell UP, 1968.
   PA 42 (1969) 568-9. (F. Marzari)

SOBREPENA, ENRIQUE C.   That they may be
one. 2d. ed.   Manila, United Church
of Christ in the Philippines, 1964.
   JAS 24 (1964-5) 706-708. (G. H.
   Anderson)
   SJ 12 (1965) 236-7. (G. H.
   Anderson)

Soedjatmoko   *See*   SUDJATMOKO

Soekmono, R.   *See*   FONTEIN, JAN.
Ancient Indonesian art

SOEMARDJAN, SELO.   Dynamics of commu-
nity development in rural central and
west Java, a comparative report.
Ithaca, Modern Indonesia Project,
Cornell Univ., 1963.   (Cornell Univ.
Modern Indonesia Project. Monograph
series)
   JSAH 6 (Mar. 1965) 108-9. (D.
   Hindley)

SOEMARDJAN, SELO.   Social changes in
Jogjakarta.   Ithaca, Cornell UP,
1962.
   JSAH 6 (Sept. 1965) 154-157. (M. A.
   Jaspan)
   PA 37 (1964) 469-471. (L. Palmier)
   SOAS 27 (1964) 237. (J. A. M.
   Caldwell)

Soemarsaid Moertono   *See*   MOERTONO,
SOEMARSAID

Sørensen, Per   *See*   THAI-DANISH PREHIS-
TORIC EXPEDITION, 1960.   Archaeological excavations in Thailand

* SOERJONO, R.   Gedanke der block Frei-
heit in Sudostasien.   Stuttgart,
Kohlhammer, 1964.
   PA 38 (1965) 422-424. (J. M. van
   der Kroef)

Soetan Sjahrir *See* SJAHRIR, SOETAN

Sointseva, Nina Vasilevna *See* AKA-
DEMIIA NAUK SSSR. INSTITUT NARODOV
AZII. Iazyki IUgo-vostochnoi Azii

SOLHEIM, WILHELM GERHARD. Archaeology
at the eleventh Pacific Science
Congress: papers presented at the
XIth Pacific Science Congress,
Tokyo, August-September 1966. Honolulu, Social Science Research Institute, Univ. of Hawaii, 1967. (Asian
and Pacific archaeology series, no.
1)
    AP 12 (1969) 137-8. (J. D.
    Jennings)

SOLHEIM, WILHELM GERHARD. Archaeology
of central Philippines: a study
chiefly of the iron age and its relationships. Manila, GPO, 1964.
(Philippines. National Institute of
Science and Technology, 10)
    JAS 24 (1964-5) 704-706. (I.
    Rouse)
    SEIB 39 (1964) 531-2. (E. Saurin)

SOLICH, EDUARD J. Die Uberseechinesen
in Sudostasien. Frankfurt am Main,
Metzner, 1960. (Institut fur Asienkunde. Schriften, Bd. 7)
    JAS 21 (1961-2) 238. (M. Freedman)
    PA 34 (1961) 308-9. (B. Lasker)

* SOLIDUM, ESTRELLA D. Towards a Southeast Asian community. Quezon City,
Univ. of the Philippines Pr., 1974.
    SLURJ 5 (1974) 615-6. (F. L.
    Lorente)

Solyom, Bronwen *See* SOLYOM, GARRETT.
Textiles of the Indonesian archipelago

SOLYOM, GARRETT. Textiles of the Indo-
nesian archipelago, by Garrett and
Bronwen Solyom. Honolulu, UP of
Hawaii, 1973. (Asian studies at
Hawaii, no. 10)
    JAS 33 (1973-4) 740-1. (M.
    Gittinger)

SOMCHAY. La porte d'ivoire. Compiegne,
Impr. de Compiegne, 1959.
    SEIB 35 (1960) 740.

SOMERS, MARY F. Peranakan Chinese
politics in Indonesia. Ithaca, Southeast Asia Program, Cornell Univ.,
1964. (Cornell Univ. Modern Indonesia
Project. Interim reports series)
    JSAH 6 (Sept. 1965) 157-8. (W. R.
    Roff)

Somm, A. F. *See* WOLGENSINGER, MICHAEL.
Siam

Sommer, John *See* LUCE, DON. Vietnam;
the unheard voices

SONG ONG SIANG. One hundred years'
history of the Chinese in Singapore;
being a chronological record of the
contribution by the Chinese community
to the development, progress and pros-
perity of Singapore; of events and
incidents concerning the whole or
sections of that community; and of
the lives, pursuits and public service
of individual members thereof from the
foundation of Singapore on 6th February 1819 to its centenary on 6th February 1919. London, Murray, 1923.
    JAS 28 (1968-9) 402-3. (P. Wheatley)

SOPHER, DAVID EDWARD. Sea nomads; a
study based on the literature of the
maritime boat people of Southeast
Asia. Singapore, GPO, 1965. (Singapore. National Museum. Memoirs, no. 5)
    JAS 27 (1967-8) 920-1. (J. D.
    Clarkson)
    PS 15 (1967) 209-212. (H. A. Nimmo)

South and Southeast Asia, enduring
scholarship selected from the Far
Eastern Quarterly - The Journal of
Asian Studies, 1941-1971. Tucson,
Univ. of Arizona Pr., 1972.
Volume III.
    JAH 8 (1974) 189.
    JAS 32 (1973-4) 148-9. (A. T.
    Kirsch)
    PA 46 (1973) 343. (P. Harnetty)

South Moluccas; rebellious province or

hrsg. von Hans Rhodius. The Hague,
1964.
  BEF 53 (1966) 704-720. (L.-C.
  Damais)

SPINKS, CHARLES NELSON. Ceramic wares
of Siam. Bangkok, Siam Society,
1965.
  AP 9 (1966) 174-5. (R. Pearson)

Spinola, Maria Lourdes Diaz-Trechuelo
See DIAZ-TRECHUELO SPINOLA, MARIA
LOURDES

SPIRO, MELFORD E. Buddhism and soci-
ety, a great tradition and its
Burmese vicissitudes. New York,
Harper and Row, 1970.
  BIJ 128 (1972) 520-524. (B. Dahm)
  JAS 31 (1971-2) 373-380. (F. K.
  Lehman)
  JSAS 4 (1973) 309-311. (M. G.
  Swift)
  JSS 60 pt. 1 (1972) 436-438. (J.
  Bunnag)
  MAS 6 (1972) 483-494. (R. Gomrich)
  PA 46 (1973) 604-5. (J. F. Cady)
  SOAS 35 (1972) 665-667. (J. Okell)

SPIRO, MELFORD E. Burmese supernat-
uralism; a study in the explanation
and reduction of suffering. Engle-
wood Cliffs, Prentice-Hall, 1967.
  JAS 28 (1968-9) 903-4. (C. Hobbs)
  JSS 57 (1969) 377-8. (B. J.
  Terwiel)
  MAS 6 (1972) 483-494. (R. Gomrich)
  PA 41 (1968) 297-8. (E. Leach)

* SPOEHR, ALEXANDER. Zamboanga and
Sulu, an archaeological approach to
ethnic diversity. Pittsburgh, Dept.
of Anthropology, Univ. of Pittsburgh, 1973. (Ethnology monograph,
no. 1)
  JAS 34 (1974-5) 258-260. (K. L.
  Hutterer)

Spoelstra, Nyle *See* Economic interdependence in Southeast Asia

SPRUYT, J. History of Indonesia, the
timeless islands. Rev. ed. Melbourne,
Macmillan, 1973.
  JCA 4 (1974) 365.

STANFORD RESEARCH INSTITUTE. Land reform in Vietnam. Menlo Park, 1968.
5v. in 7.
  MAS 5 (1971) 187-191. (R. B. Smith)

STANLEY, PETER W. A nation in the
making: the Philippines and the
United States, 1899-1921. Cambridge,
Harvard UP, 1974. (Harvard studies
in American-East Asian relations, 4)
  PA 47 (1974) 401-2. (I. B. Powell)
  PS 22 (1974) 217-219. (J. N.
  Schumacher)

STARLING, LUCY. Dawn over temple
roofs. New York, World Horizons,
1960.
  JSS 48 pt. 2 (1960) 111-2.

STARNER, FRANCES LUCILLE. Magsaysay
and the Philippine peasantry, the
agrarian impact on Philippine politics, 1953-56. Berkeley, Univ. of
California Pr., 1961. (California.
Univ. Univ. of California publications
in political science, v. 10)
  JAS 21 (1961-2) 244-5. (D. Wurfel)
  PA 36 (1963) 202-204. (R. S. Milne)
  PS 9 (1961) 718-9. (J. U. Montemayor)

STAUFFER, ROBERT B. Development of an
interest group; the Philippine Medical Association. Quezon City, Univ.
of the Philippines Pr., 1966.
  JAS 27 (1967-8) 184-5. (J. Grossholtz)
  PS 15 (1967) 188-200. (A. E.
  Lapitan)

STAVORINUS, JOHAN SPLINTER. Voyages
to the East Indies. London, Dawsons,
1969. 3v. (Colonial history series)
  JSAS 2 (1971) 238-9. (A. Reid)

Steinberg, David J. Cambodia: its

Subbiah, Rama. Lexical study of Tamil

STIRLING, ALFRED THORPE. On the
fringe of diplomacy. Melbourne,
Hawthorn Pr., 1973.
   PS 21 (1973) 475-479. (M. A.
   Bernad)

STÖHR, WALDEMAR. Die Religionen Indo-
nesiens von Waldemar Stohr und Piet
Zoetmulder. Stuttgart, Kohlhammer,
1965.
   BIJ 122 (1966) 460-462. (K. A. H.
   Hidding)
   JAS 26 (1966-7) 344. (F. R. von
   der Mehden)

* STOJKOVIC, IVAN. Les problemes du
transport et du transit au Laos.
Vientiane, United Nations, 1962.
   SEIB 37 (1962) 465-6. (P. B.
   Lafont)

Strany i narody Vostoka. Vyp. XIII.
Stranyi i narody basseyna Tikhogo
Okeana. Kniga 2. [Edited by] D. A.
Olderogge. Moscow, Izdatelstvo
Nauka, 1972.
   SOAS 37 (1974) 282.

STRATHERN, ANDREW. One father, one
blood, descent and group structure
among Melpa people. Canberra, Australian National UP, 1972.
   SOAS 36 (1973) 504-5.

STRATHERN, MARILYN. Women in between;
female roles in a male world, Mount
Hagen, New Guinea. London, Seminar
Pr., 1972.
   BIJ 129 (1973) 518-520. (J. van
   Baal)

STRONG, ANNA LOUISE. Cash and vio-
lence in Laos. Peking, New World
Pr., 1961.
   AAS 1 (1965) 207-210. (I. Dolezal)

Struggle against history: U.S. foreign policy in an age of revolution,
edited by Neal D. Houghton. New
York, Wellington Square Pr., 1968.
   PA 42 (1969) 264-5. (J. F. Melby)

STUCKI, CURTIS W. American doctoral
dissertations on Asia, 1933-1962,
including appendix of master's theses
at Cornell Univ. Ithaca, Southeast
Asia Program, Cornell Univ., 1963.
(Cornell Univ. Southeast Asia Program.
Data paper, no. 50)
   BIJ 122 (1966) 187-8. (P. E. de
   Josselin de Jong)

STUCKI, CURTIS W. American doctoral
dissertations on Asia, 1933-June
1966, including appendix of master's
theses of Cornell University 1933-
June 1968. Ithaca, Southeast Asia
Program, Cornell Univ., 1968. (Cornell Univ. Southeast Asia Program.
Data paper, no. 71)
   PS 18 (1970) 217-8. (J. M. Saniel)

Studies in Philippine anthropology in
honor of H. Otley Beyer, edited by
Mario D. Zamora. Quezon City,
Alemars, 1967.
   PA 42 (1969) 388-390. (H. E.
   Jacobson)

Studies in the social history of China
and South-East Asia; essays in memory
of Victor Purcell. Edited by Jerome
Chen and Nicholas Tarling. Cambridge,
Cambridge UP, 1970.
   JAH 6 (1972) 156-7. (R. H. Brown)
   JAS 30 (1970-1) 163-166. (R.
   Murphey)
   JSAS 2 (1971) 249-250. (S. Leong)
   PA 44 (1971) 272-3. (C. P.
   FitzGerald)
   SA 2 (1972-3) 143-148. (Ka-che Yip)
   SOAS 33 (1970) 699-700. (M.
   Freedman)

Stuers, Cora Vreede de *See* VREEDE DE
STUERS, CORA

SUBBIAH, RAMA. Lexical study of Tamil
dialects in lower Perak. Kuala Lumpur, Univ. of Malaya, Dept. of Indian
Studies, 1966. (Univ. of Malaya.
Dept. of Indian Studies. Monograph
series)

Subbiah, Rama. Lexical study of Tamil

JMBRAS 40 pt. 1 (1967) 157–159.
(T. W. Gething)
SOAS 30 (1967) 471–2. (T. Burrow)

SUBHADRADIS DISKUL. Art in Thailand,
a brief history. Bangkok, Krung
Siam Pr., 1970.
JSS 59 pt. 1 (1971) 263–265. (M.
Smithies)

Suddart, Adrienne *See* HUMAN RELA-
TIONS AREA FILES, INC. Laos

SUDJATMOKO. Approach to Indonesian
history: towards an open future; an
address before the Seminar on Indo-
nesian history, Gadjah Mada Univer-
sity, Jogjakarta, Dec. 14, 1957.
Ithaca, Modern Indonesia Project,
Southeast Asia Program, Cornell
Univ., 1960. (Cornell Univ. Modern
Indonesia Project. Translation
series)
JAS 21 (1961–2) 565–567. (G. J.
Pauker)

SUDJATMOKO. Economic development as a
cultural problem. Ithaca, Modern
Indonesia Project, Southeast Asia
Program, Cornell Univ., 1958. (Cor-
nell Univ. Modern Indonesia Project.
Translation series)
JAS 21 (1961–2) 565–567. (G. J.
Pauker)

SUDJATMOKO. Indonesia; problems and
opportunities, Indonesia and the
world. East Melbourne, Australian
Institute of International Affairs,
1967. (Dyason Memorial Lectures,
1967)
PA 41 (1968) 619–621. (J. M. van
der Kroef)

SUDJATMOKO. Introduction to Indonesian
historiography. Ithaca, Cornell UP,
1965.
JAS 25 (1965–6) 370–1. (J. M. van
der Kroef)
PA 38 (1965) 353–359. (D. G. E.
Hall)

SUKARNO. Marhaen and proletarian;
speech before the Indonesian Nation-
alist Party at the party's thirtieth
anniversary at Bandung, July 3, 1957.
Ithaca, Modern Indonesia Project,
Cornell Univ., 1960. (Cornell Univ.
Modern Indonesia Project. Translation
series)
JAS 21 (1961–2) 565–567. (G. J.
Pauker)

Suleiman, Satyawati *See* FONTEIN, JAN.
Ancient Indonesian art

Sulu studies. Jolo, Sulu, Notre Dame
of Jolo College, 1972.
AR 6 (1973) 214–217. (A. Martenot)

SULZBERGER, CYRUS LEO. Les Etats-Unis
et le tiers monde, une revolution in-
achevee. Paris, Plon, 1966.
FA 22 (1968) 248–255. (P.
Devillers)

SUMET JUMSAI. Seen: architectural
forms of northern Siam and old Siamese
fortifications. Bangkok, Fine Arts
Commission, Association of Siamese
Architects, 1970.
JSS 59 pt. 2 (1971) 258–9. (M.
Smithies)

SUN WICHAI CHAO KHAO. Tribesmen and
peasants in north Thailand. Chiangmai, Tribal Research Centre, 1969.
JAS 30 (1970–1) 726–728. (A. Y.
Dessaint)

* SUNTHON PHU. Nirat Phu Khao Thong,
essai de traduction litteral d'un
poeme Thai, par P. Schweisguth.
Paris, Maisonneuve, 1969.
JSS 59 pt. 2 (1970) 166–172. (Samart
Samphantharak)

Supomo *See* INDONESIA. CONSTITUTION,
1950

Sutan Sjahrir *See* SJAHRIR, SOETAN

Sutomo Tjokronegoro *See* TJOKRONEGORO,
SUTOMO

SUTTER, JOHN O. Indonesianisasi;
  politics in a changing economy,
  1940-1955. Ithaca, Southeast Asia
  Program, Cornell Univ., 1959. (Cornell Univ. Southeast Asia Program.
  Data paper, no. 36)
    JAS 20 (1960-1) 535-6. (B. Higgins)

SUTTER, JOHN O. Scientific facilities
  and information services of the
  Federation of Malaya and State of
  Singapore. Honolulu, Pacific Scientific Information Center, 1961.
    JAS 22 (1962-3) 121-2. (C. Hobbs)

SUTTER, JOHN O. Scientific facilities
  and information services of the
  Republic of Indonesia. Honolulu,
  Pacific Scientific Information Center, 1961.
    JAS 22 (1962-3) 121-2. (C. Hobbs)

SUTTER, JOHN O. Scientific facilities
  and information services of the
  Republic of Vietnam. Honolulu,
  Pacific Scientific Information Center, 1961.
    JAS 22 (1962-3) 122. (C. Hobbs)

Sutton, Joseph Lee *See* INDIANA UNIV.
  INSTITUTE OF TRAINING FOR PUBLIC
  SERVICE. Problems of politics and
  administration in Thailand

* SUWANNEE SUKHONTA. Kao Chue Karn (A
  man called Karn). n.p., Klang
  Wittaya, 1971.
    JSS 60 pt. 1 (1972) 392-395.
      (Mattani Rutnin)

SUZUKI, PETER. Critical survey of
  studies on the anthropology of Nias,
  Mentawei and Enggano. The Hague,
  Nijhoff, 1958. (Instituut voor
  Taal-, Land- en Volkenkunde. Biblio-
  graphical series, 3)
    SOAS 23 (1960) 430.

* SWANN, WIM. Lost cities of Asia. New
  York, Putnam, 1966.
    JAS 27 (1967-8) 173-4. (V. Begley)

Swift, M. G. Malay peasant society in

    PA 40 (1967) 400-402. (S. J.
      O'Connor)

Swartz, Marc J. *See* Local level
  politics

SWEENEY, AMIN. Malay shadow puppets:
  the Wayang Siam of Kelantan. London,
  British Museum, 1972.
    AR 5 (1973) 291-293. (D. Lombard)
    JAS 32 (1972-3) 745-6. (W. P. Malm)
    JMBRAS 45 pt. 1 (1972) 125. (M.
      Sheppard)
    JSS 62 pt. 1 (1974) 272-3. (D.
      Brereton)

SWEENEY, AMIN. The Ramayana and the
  Malay shadow play. Kuala Lumpur,
  National Univ. of Malaysia Pr., 1972.
    JSAS 5 (1974) 148-150. (J. L.
      Swellengrebel)
    JSS 62 pt. 2 (1974) 380-389. (Mat-
      tani Rutnin)
    SOAS 37 (1974) 507. (M. C.
      Ricklefs)

Swellengrebel, J. L. *See* Bali; studies
  in life, thought, and ritual

SWETTENHAM, FRANK ATHELSTANE. Stories
  and sketches, selected and introduced
  by William R. Roff. Kuala Lumpur,
  Oxford UP, 1967.
    JAS 27 (1967-8) 686-7. (J. F. Cady)
    JSAH 9 (1968) 176-7. (J. de V.
      Allen)
    MAS 2 (1968) 276-7. (E. Chew)
    PA 41 (1968) 154. (G. Woodcock)

SWIFT, M. G. Malay peasant society in
  Jelebu. London, Univ. of London
  Athlone Pr., 1965. (London School of
  Economics. Monographs on social
  anthropology, no. 29)
    AS 5 (1965) 528.
    BIJ 122 (1966) 394-396. (P. E. de
      Josselin de Jong)
    JAS 25 (1965-6) 554-5. (F. M. LeBar)
    JSAH 7 (Sept. 1966) 133-4. (E. C. G.
      Barrett)
    MER 11 pt. 2 (1966) 116-7. (J.

Swift, M. G. Malay peasant society in

Purcal)
  PA 40 (1967) 399-400. (W. Newell)
  SOAS 29 (1966) 652-3. (B. E. Ward)

* SYAMANANDA, RONG. History of Thailand.
  Bangkok, Chulalongkorn Univ., 1971.
    JSS 60 pt. 2 (1972) 288-295. (I.
    G. Brown)

SYKES, CHRISTOPHER HUGH. Orde Wingate,
  a biography. Cleveland, World, 1959.
    PA 34 (1961) 62-66. (F. N. Trager)

SYMPOSIUM ON ECOLOGICAL RESEARCH IN
  HUMID TROPICS VEGETATION, KUCHING,
  SARAWAK, 1963. Symposium on ecological research in humid tropics
  vegetation. n.p., 1965.
    AP 12 (1969) 121-124. (W. Clarke)

SYMPOSIUM ON HISTORICAL, ARCHAEOLOGICAL
  AND LINGUISTIC STUDIES ON SOUTHERN
  CHINA, SOUTH-EAST ASIA AND THE HONG
  KONG REGION, UNIV. OF HONG KONG,
  1961. Symposium on historical,
  archaeological and linguistic studies
  on southern China, South-East Asia
  and the Hong Kong region: papers
  presented at meetings held in September 1961 as part of the Golden
  Jubilee Congress of the University
  of Hong Kong, edited by F. S. Drake.
  Hong Kong, Hong Kong UP, 1967.
    AP 10 (1967) 164-166. (Kwang Chih
    Chang)
    BIJ 125 (1969) 378-380. (A. F. P.
    Hulsewe)
    FA 22 (1968) 129-130.
    MAS 4 (1970) 192.
    PA 42 (1969) 417-8. (E. G.
    Pulleyblank)
    SOAS 31 (1968) 645. (M. Freedman)

SYMPOSIUM ON POPULATION PRESSURES UPON
  PHYSICAL AND SOCIAL RESOURCES IN THE
  DEVELOPING LANDS, PENNSYLVANIA STATE
  UNIVERSITY, 1967. Geography and a
  crowding world. Edited by Wilbur
  Zelinsky, Leszek A. Kosinski and R.
  Mansell Prothero. New York, Oxford
  UP, 1970.

RSAS 1 pt. 3 (1971) 62-64. (Yeung
Yue Man)

SYMPOSIUM ON THE MARAGTAS, MANILA, 1968.
  A symposium on the Maragtas held on
  the 27th January 1968 at the Epifanio
  de los Santos Auditorium (National
  Library Building). Manila, National
  Historical Commission, 1970.
    JAS 32 (1972-3) 572-3. (D. V. Hart)

SYMPOSIUM ON THE VIETNAM WAR, EAST
  CAROLINA UNIVERSITY, 1968. Essays on
  the Vietnam war. Greenville, East
  Carolina Univ. Publications, 1970.
    PA 43 (1970) 625-630. (A. Woodside)

* Symposium sur education et developpement dans le Sud-Est de l'Asie.
  Brussels, Universite Libre, Institut
  de Sociologie, 1967.
    PA 42 (1969) 97-8. (J. Fischer)

SZANTON, DAVID L. Estanica in transition, economic growth in a rural
  Philippine community. Quezon City,
  Ateneo de Manila Pr., 1970. (Quezon,
  Philippines. Ateneo de Manila. Institute of Philippine Culture. IPC
  papers, no. 9)
    JAS 31 (1971-2) 746-7. (D. J.
    Scheans)

* TA DUC RAT. Tu Dien Chu Nom. Saigon,
  Faculte des Lettres de Saigon, 1967.
    BEF 56 (1969) 211. (Nguyen Tran
    Huan)

TABOULET, GEORGES. La vie dramatique
  de Gustave Viaud, frere de Pierre
  Loti, par G. Taboulet et J. C. Demariaux. Paris, Edition de Scorpion,
  1961.
    SEIB 35 (1960) 717-8. (S. de
    Labrusse)
    SEIB 36 (1961) 109-111. (L.
    Malleret)

TAKAHASHI, AKIRA. Land and peasants in
  central Luzon, socio-economic structure of a Philippine village. Hono-

lulu, East-West Center Pr., 1970.
JAS 30 (1970-1) 927-8. (B. Fegan)
PA 44 (1974) 140-1. (D. Wurfel)

TAKEI, YOSHIMITSU. Educational sponsorship by ethnicity: a preliminary analysis of the west Malaysian experience, by Yoshimitsu Takei, John C. Bock and Bruce Saunders. Athens, Ohio Univ., Center for International Studies, 1973. (Papers in international studies. Southeast Asia series, no. 28)
PA 47 (1974) 249-250. (R. S. Milne)

Takeuchi, Tatsuji *See* ROYAMA, MASAMICHI. Philippine polity

TAKEYAMA, MICHIO. Harp of Burma. Rutland, Tuttle, 1966. (UNESCO collection of contemporary works)
AS 8 (1968) 516.
FA 22 (1968) 531-2.

* TAM DUONG. Tan-Da khoi mau-thuan lan. Hanoi, Nha xuat-ban Khoa-Hoc, 1964.
BEF 53 (1966) 739-742. (Nguyen Tien Lang)

TAMBIAH, S. J. Buddhism and spirit cults in north-east Thailand. Cambridge, Cambridge UP, 1970. (Cambridge studies in social anthropology, no. 2)
BIJ 128 (1972) 517-519. (M. Ondei)
JAS 31 (1971-2) 724-728. (F. K. Lehman)
JSS 59 pt. 2 (1971) 278-9. (J. Bunnag)
MAS 7 (1973) 121-125. (P. J. Bee, M. Barber and V. T. King)

TAN, ANTONIO G. Study of health, hygenic, and sanitary conditions obtaining among rural homes. Quezon City, 1960. (Quezon, Philippines. Univ. of the Philippines. Community Development Research Council. Study series, no. 10)
JAS 22 (1962-3) 342-345. (D. V. Hart)

Tarling, Nicholas. Britain, the Brookes

TAN, DING EING. Rice industry in Malaya, 1920-1940. Singapore, Dept. of History, Univ. of Singapore, 1963.
JAS 24 (1964-5) 338-9. (J. Silverstein)

TAN, GIOK LAN. Chinese of Sukabumi: a study in social and cultural accommodation. Ithaca, Modern Indonesia Project, Southeast Asia Program, Cornell Univ., 1963. (Cornell Univ. Modern Indonesia Project. Monograph series)
JAS 23 (1963-4) 637. (L. E. Williams)
JSAH 8 (1967) 322-325. (A. Wee)
PA 37 (1964) 234-5. (W. E. Willmott)

TANKOK SENG. Son of Singapore: the autobiography of a coolie. Singapore, Univ. Education Pr., 1972.
AR 8 (1974) 223-225.

Tan, Lek *See* CALDWELL, MALCOLM. Cambodia in the Southeast Asian war

TAN, TJIN KIE. Sukarno's guided Indonesia. Brisbane, Jacaranda Pr., 1967.
MAS 7 (1973) 296-305. (L. Parmer)
PA 41 (1968) 451-2. (R. K. Paget)

TANHAM, GEORGE KILPATRICK. War without guns; American civilians in rural Vietnam. New York, Praeger, 1966.
AS 6 (1966) 406.

TANTRI, KTUT. Revolt in paradise. New York, Harper, 1960.
PA 34 (1961) 211. (C. D. Cowan)

TARLING, NICHOLAS. Anglo-Dutch rivalry in the Malay world, 1780-1824. Cambridge, Cambridge UP, 1962.
JSAH 6 (Mar. 1966) 116-118. (W. D. McIntyre)
SOAS 28 (1965) 190-1. (C. D. Cowan)

TARLING, NICHOLAS. Britain, the Brookes and Brunei. New York, Oxford UP, 1971.
BMJ 3 pt. 2 (1974) 306-309. (D. E. Brown)

Tarling, Nicholas. British policy in

JAS 32 (1972-3) 214-5. (I. D.
  Black)
JSAS 4 (1973) 326-7. (E. Chew)
PA 45 (1972) 460-1. (K. G.
  Tregonning)

TARLING, NICHOLAS. British policy in
the Malay Peninsula and archipelago,
1824-1871. Singapore, Royal Asiatic
Society, Malayan Branch, 1957.
(Royal Asiatic Society of Great
Britain and Ireland, Malayan Branch.
Journal. Vol. 30 pt. 3)
  BIJ 119 (1963) 225-227. (H. J. de
  Graaf)

TARLING, NICHOLAS. British policy in
the Malay Peninsula and archipelago,
1824-1871. Kuala Lumpur, Oxford UP,
1969.
  MAS 6 (1972) 256. (I. Nish)

TARLING, NICHOLAS. Concise history of
Southeast Asia. New York, Praeger,
1966.
  JAH 2 (1968) 186-7. (J. A. Larkin)
  JAS 27 (1967-8) 174-5. (C. Hobbs)
  JSAS 1 pt. 1 (1970) 106. (B.
  Harrison)
  JSS 55 (1967) 301. (L. Sternstein)
  MAS 2 (1968) 80-1. (D. K. Bassett)
  MAS 2 (1968) 278-9. (D. K. Bassett)
  PA 39 (1966) 402-3. (D. G. E. Hall)
  SOAS   (1967) 766. (H. Tinker)

TARLING, NICHOLAS. Piracy and politics
in the Malay world; a study of British imperialism in nineteenth century
South East Asia. Melbourne, Cheshire, 1963
  BIJ 120 (1964) 472-474. (H. J. de
  Graaf)
  JSAH 7 (1966) 140-1. (Zainal Abidin
  bin Abdul Wahid)

TARLING, NICHOLAS. Southeast Asia;
past and present. Melbourne, Cheshire, 1966.
  BIJ 123 (1967) 386-388. (H. J. de
  Graaf)

TARUC, LUIS. He who rides the tiger,
the story of an Asian guerrilla
leader. New York, Praeger, 1967.
  JAS 27 (1967-8) 441-2. (C. O.
  Houston)
  PA 40 (1967) 409-410. (I. B.
  Powell)
  PS 15 (1967) 699-712. (A. B. Saulo)

TATE, D. J. M. Making of modern South-
East Asia. Volume I. The European
conquest. Kuala Lumpur, Oxford UP,
1971.
  JAS 32 (1972-3) 729-731. (J. R. W.
  Smail)

Tatsuji, Takeuchi *See* ROYAMA, MASAMI-
CHI. Philippine polity

TAYLOR, ALASTAIR MacDONALD. Indonesian
independence and the United Nations.
Ithaca, Cornell UP, 1960.
  JAS 21 (1961-2) 94-5. (G. S.
  Maryanov)
  JSAH 2 (Oct. 1961) 104-106. (J. A.
  C. Mackie)
  PA 36 (1963) 447-449. (T. B. Millar)

Taylor, Alice *See* Focus on Southeast
Asia

TAYLOR, GEORGE EDWARD. The Philippines
and the United States: problems of
partnership. New York, Praeger, 1964.
  JAS 24 (1964-5) 337-8. (L. Casper)
  PA 38 (1965) 202-204. (I. B. Powell)
  SJ 12 (1965) 446-450. (C. L. Hunt)

TAYLOR, JOHN RODGERS MEIGS. Philippine
insurrection against the United States.
A compilation of documents with notes
and introduction. Pasay City, Eugenio
Lopez Foundation, 1971. 4v.
  JAS 33 (1973-4) 503. (D. V. Hart)

TAYLOR, ROBERT H. Foreign and domestic
consequences of the KMT intervention
in Burma. Ithaca, Southeast Asia Program, Cornell Univ., 1973. (Cornell
Univ. Southeast Asia Program. Data
paper, no. 93)
  PA 47 (1974) 252-3. (J. F. Cady)

TEDJASUKMANA, ISKANDAR. Political
character of the Indonesian trade
union movement. Ithaca, Modern
Indonesia Project, Southeast Asia
Program, Cornell Univ., 1958. (Cornell Univ. Modern Indonesia Project.
Monograph series)
    BIJ 116 (1960) 289-290. (J.
    Vredenbregt)

TEEUW, A. Critical survey of studies
on Malay and Bahasa Indonesia. The
Hague, Nijhoff, 1961. (Instituut
voor Taal-, Land- en Volkenkunde.
Bibliographical series, 5)
    AAS 1 (1965) 210-1. (G. Altmann)
    SOAS 25 (1962) 402-3. (J. C.
    Bottoms)

TEEUW, A. Hikayat Patani, the story
of Patani, by A. Teeuw and D. K.
Wyatt. The Hague, Nijhoff, 1970.
(Bibliotheca Indonesica, 5)
    JAH 6 (1972) 191-2. (C. R. Boxer)
    JAS 31 (1971-2) 226-7. (W. R. Roff)
    JSAS 2 (1971) 265-6. (S. O. Robson)
    JSS 60 pt. 1 (1972) 410-414. (B.
    and D. Brereton)
    SOAS 35 (1972) 183-4. (E. C. G.
    Barrett)

TEEUW, A. Leerboek Bahasa Indonesia.
Sleutel Leerboek Bahasa Indonesia.
Groningen, Wolters-Noordhoff, 1971.
2v.
    SOAS 36 (1973) 502-3. (R. Jones)

TEEUW, A. Modern Indonesian litera-
ture. The Hague, Nijhoff, 1967.
(Instituut voor Taal-, Land- en
Volkenkunde. Translation series, 10)
    SOAS 32 (1969) 436-7. (E. C. G.
    Barrett)

* TEJ BUNNAG. In memoriam Phya Anuman
Rajadhon, by Tej Bunnag and Michael
Smithies. Bangkok, Siam Society,
1970.
    JSAS 2 (1971) 253-255. (C. M.
    Wilson)
    JSS 59 pt. 2 (1971) 268-9. (W. F.
    Vella)

TELENGA, SUZETTE. The seduction, by
Susan Yorke. New York, Farrar,
Straus and Cudahy, 1960.
    PS 10 (1962) 511-2. (D. V. Hart)

TERNAUX-COMPANS, HENRI. Bibliotheque
asiatique et africaine, ou catalogue
des ouvrages relatifs a l'Asie et a
l'Afrique qui ont paru depuis la
decouverte de l'imprimerie jusqu'en
1700. Amsterdam, Gruner, 1968.
    JAH 3 (1969) 58. (C. R. Boxer)

TESELKIN, AVENIR STEPANOVICH. IAvanskiy
iazyk. Moscow, Izdatel'stvo vosto-
chnoy literatury, 1961.
    AAS 1 (1965) 212. (G. Altmann)

TESELKIN, AVENIR STEPANOVICH. Old
Javanese (Kawi). Ithaca, Modern Indonesia Project, Cornell Univ., 1972.
(Cornell Univ. Modern Indonesia Project. Translation series)
    AR 5 (1973) 289-291. (D. Lombard)

TEXTOR, ROBERT B. From peasant to
pedicab driver; a study of northeastern Thai farmers who periodically
migrated to Bangkok and became pedicab drivers. 2d. ed. New Haven, Yale
Univ., Southeast Asia Studies, 1961.
(Yale Univ. Graduate School. Southeast
Asia Studies. Cultural report series,
no. 9)
    JAS 21 (1961-2) 240-242. (H. P.
    Phillips)
    PA 35 (1962) 82. (R. C. Nairn)

THAI CONG TUNG. Agricultural develop-
ment planning and zoning in South
Vietnam. Saigon, Min. de la Reforme
Agraire, de l'Agriculture des Pecher-
ies et Developpement de l'Elevage,
Agricultural Research Institute, 1972.
    SEIB 47 (1972) 553-4. (Langlet and
    Quach-Thanh-Tam)

THAI-DANISH PREHISTORIC EXPEDITION,
1960-62. Archaeological excavations
in Thailand. Copenhagen, Munksgaard,
1967-

Thai-Danish Prehistoric Expedition

Volume I.
AP 12 (1969) 124-127. (C. Gorman)
BIJ 125 (1969) 384-389. (C. R. Hooijer)
Volume II.
AP 12 (1969) 127-130. (W. G. Solheim)
BIJ 125 (1969) 384-389. (C. R. Hooijer)
Volume III pt. 2.
AP 17 (1974) 72-3. (M. Pietrusewsky)

Thai rural families: a sociologic and economic survey, by Harold E. Smith et al. Washington, D.C., NCR Microcard Editions, 1971.
JAS 32 (1972-3) 376-378. (C. F. Keyes)

THAI VAN KIEM. The twain did meet, first contacts between Vietnam and the United States of America. Saigon, GPO, 1960. (Vietnam culture series, no. 5)
SEIB 35 (1960) 734.

* THAILAND. FINE ARTS DEPT. New acquisitions of three bronzes from Buriram. Bangkok, 1973.
JSS 62 pt. 2 (1974) 371-375. (H. W. Woodward)

* THAILAND. MIN. OF EDUCATION. DEPT. OF ELEMENTARY AND ADULT EDUCATION. Education in Thailand, a century of experience. Bangkok, 1970.
JSS 59 pt. 2 (1971) 255-258. (Yongyuth Yuthavong)

* THAILAND. OFFICE OF THE PRIME MINISTER. COMMISSION FOR THE PUBLICATION OF HISTORICAL, CULTURAL AND ARCHEOLOGICAL RECORDS. Prachum phra tamra baram rachuthit phua kalpana samai Ayuthaya phak 1. Bangkok, 2510.
JSS 60 pt. 1 (1972) 396-409. (M. Vickery)

* THAILAND. OFFICE OF THE PRIME MINISTER. COMMISSION FOR THE PUBLICATION OF

HISTORICAL, CULTURAL AND ARCHEOLOGICAL RECORDS. Prachum sila charuk phak thi, 3. Bangkok, 2510. (Collected inscriptions, pt. 3)
BEF 57 (1970) 230-236. (C. Jacques)
JSS 60 pt. 1 (1972) 396-409. (M. Vickery)

* THAILAND. OFFICE OF THE PRIME MINISTER. COMMISSION FOR THE PUBLICATION OF HISTORICAL, CULTURAL AND ARCHEOLOGICAL RECORDS. Prachum sila charuk phak thi, 4. Bangkok, 2513. (Collected inscriptions, pt. 4)
JAS 31 (1971-2) 227-8. (D. K. Wyatt)
JSS 60 pt. 1 (1972) 396-409. (M. Vickery)

* THAILAND. OFFICE OF THE PRIME MINISTER. COMMISSION FOR THE PUBLICATION OF HISTORICAL, CULTURAL AND ARCHEOLOGICAL RECORDS. Ru'ang song tang chao prathetsarat krung ratankosint rachakan thi 1. Bangkok, 2514.
JSS 61 pt. 1 (1973) 351-356. (M. Vickery)

* Thailand in transition, the church in a Buddhist country. Brussels, Pro Mundi Vita, 1973.
JSS 62 pt. 2 (1974) 361-2. (W. J. Klausner)

THANH NGHI. Phap-Viet tan Tu-Dien; Minhhoa In lan thu nhat. Saigon, Thoi-The, 1961.
SEIB 36 (1961) 739.

THANI NAYAGAM, XAVIER S. Reference guide to Tamil studies: books. Kuala Lumpur, Univ. of Malaya Pr., 1966.
SOAS 31 (1968) 409. (J. R. Marr)

THANI NAYAGAM, XAVIER S. Tamil studies abroad: a symposium. Kuala Lumpur, International Association of Tamil Research, 1968.
JAS 28 (1968-9) 425-6. (S. Vaidyanathan)
SOAS 32 (1969) 459. (J. R. Marr)

* THANOM ANARMWAT. Relations between
   the Thai, Khmer, and Vietnamese in
   the early Bangkok period. Bangkok,
   College of Education, 2514.
      JSS 60 pt. 2 (1972) 311-313. (D.
      P. Chandler)

* THAWATT MOKARAPONG. History of the
   Thai revolution, a study in political
   behavior. Bangkok, Chalermnit, 1972.
      JSS 61 pt. 2 (1973) 186-196. (B.
      A. Batson)

THE, LIAN. Treasures and trivia, doc-
   toral dissertations on Southeast
   Asia accepted by universities in the
   United States, by Lian The and Paul
   W. van der Veur. Athens, Ohio Univ.,
   Center for International Studies,
   Southeast Asia Program, 1968.
      JAS 28 (1968-9) 901-2. (J. K.
      Musgrave)
      PA 42 (1969) 573. (W. E. Willmott)

THIERRY, SOLANGE. Les Khmers. Paris,
   Editions du Seuil, 1964. (Le Temps
   qui court, 33)
      RSA (1965) 129-130. (L. Rocher)

THIO, EUNICE. British policy in the
   Malay peninsula, 1880-1910. Volume I.
   The southern and central states.
   Singapore, Univ. of Malaya Pr., 1969.
      BIJ 129 (1973) 495-6. (S. L. van
      der Wal)
      JSAS 2 (1971) 263-4. (P. L. Burns)
      PA 44 (1971) 647-8. (B. Harrison)

Thion, Serge *See* POMONTI, JEAN
   CLAUDE. Des courtisans aux
   partisans

THIPHAAKORWON, CAWPHRAJAA. Dynastic
   chronicles, Bangkok era, the fourth
   reign (B.E. 2394-2411; A.D. 1851-
   1868). Tokyo, Center for East Asian
   Cultural Studies, 1965-
   Volumes I-II.
      JSS 54 (1966) 231. (L. Sternstein)
   Volume III.
      SA 2 (1972) 502-514. (K. P. Landon)

THOMAS, DAVID D. Chrau grammar. Honolulu, Univ. of Hawaii Pr., 1971.
   (Oceanic linguistics. Special publication, no. 7)
      AAS 8 (1972) 198-204. (J. Mucka)
      JAS 31 (1971-2) 992-3. (F. E.
      Huffman)

Thomas, David D. *See* Mon-Khmer
   studies

Thomas, William Leroy *See* SPENCER,
   JOSEPH EARLE. Asia, East by South

THOMPSON, LAURENCE C. Vietnamese grammar. Seattle, Univ. of Washington
   Pr., 1965.
      JAS 25 (1965-6) 802-3. (F. H.
      Tucker)

THOMPSON, LAURENCE C. Vietnamese
   reader, by L. Thompson and Nguyen Duc
   Hiep. Seattle, Univ. of Washington
   Pr., 1961.
      SEIB 36 (1961) 739.

THOMPSON, ROBERT GRAINGER KER. No exit
   from Vietnam. London, Chatto and
   Windus, 1969.
      PA 43 (1970) 128-130. (M. Osborne)
      SA 3 (1974-5) 627-631. (C. A. Bain)

THOMPSON, WARREN SIMPSON. Population
   and progress in the Far East.
   Chicago, Univ. of Chicago Pr., 1959.
      JAS 19 (1959-60) 192-194. (P. M.
      Hauser)

* Three old cities of Siam, the monuments
   of Sukhodaya, Sajjanalaya and Gam-
   pengpel. Jaiya, Thai Wattana T.
   Suwan Foundation, 1971.
      JSS 60 pt. 2 (1972) 329-332. (H. W.
      Woodward)

THROMBLEY, WOODWORTH G. Thailand politics, economy, and socio-cultural
   setting, a selective guide to the
   literature, by Woodworth G. Thrombley
   and William J. Siffin. Bloomington,
   Indiana UP, 1972.

Thrombley, Woodworth G.   Thailand

JAS 32 (1972-3) 373-4. (J. K.
Musgrave)

* THUAN PHONG. Ca-dao giang-luan. Saigon, Editions A-Chou, 1958.
BEF 52 (1964) 244-247. (M. Durand)

TIAMSON, ALFREDO T. Mindanao-Sulu
bibliography: containing published,
unpublished manuscripts and works in
progress. A preliminary survey and
W. E. Retana's *Bibliografia de Mindanao,* 1894. Davao City, Ateneo de
Davao, 1970.
JAS 31 (1971-2) 236. (D. V. Hart)

* Tiao Khamman Vongkotrattana. Luang
Prabang, 2507.
BEF 55 (1969) 281-290. (A. and F.
Peltier)

TIEMPO, EDILBERTO K. More than con-
querors. Manila, Ayuda, 1964.
PS 14 (1966) 299-309. (M. A.
Bernad)

TIEMPO, EDILBERTO K. A stream at
Dalton Pass and other stories.
Manila, Bookmark, 1970.
PS 18 (1970) 783-788. (M. A.
Bernad)
SJ 17 (1970) 459-460. (F.
Arcellana)

TIEMPO, EDILBERTO K. To be free, a
novel. Quezon City, New Day, 1972.
PS 21 (1973) 389-393. (J. A.
Galdon)
SLURJ 3 (1972) 636-7. (A. G.
Buenviaje)

TIGLAO, TEODORA V. Health practices
in a rural community. Quezon City,
Community Development Research Coun-
cil, Univ. of the Philippines, 1964.
(Quezon, Philippines. Univ. of the
Philippines. Community Development
Research Council. Study series)
PS 13 (1965) 897-899. (M. Escudero)

TILMAN, ROBERT OLIVER. Bureaucratic
transition in Malaya. Durham, Duke
UP, 1964. (Duke Univ. Commonwealth
Studies Center. Publications, no. 21)
AS 5 (1965) 216.
JAS 25 (1965-6) 169-170. (J. N.
Parmer)
PA 38 (1965) 204-5. (J. P. L.
Jiang)

TILMAN, ROBERT OLIVER. International
biographical directory of Southeast
Asia specialists. Ann Arbor, Inter-
university Southeast Asia Committee,
Association for Asian Studies, 1969.
PA 43 (1970) 650. (W. L. Holland)
SJ 17 (1970) 354.

TILMAN, ROBERT OLIVER. Man, state and
society in contemporary Southeast
Asia. New York, Praeger, 1969. (Man,
state and society)
JAS 31 (1971-2) 985. (J. C. Scott)
JSAS 1 pt. 2 (1970) 138-140. (P. D.
Weldon)

TIMMER, MAARTEN. Child mortality and
population pressure in the D.I. Jogjakarta, Java, Indonesia, a social-
medical study. Rotterdam, Bronder-
Offset, 1961.
JAS 21 (1961-2) 242-3. (G. Missen)

* TIN HLA. Handbook of old handicrafts.
n.p., n.d.
JBRS 45 (1962) 109-110.

TINKER, HUGH. Re-orientations; essays
on Asia in transition. New York,
Praeger, 1965.
AS 7 (1967) 82.
PA 39 (1966) 151. (N. D. Palmer)

TINKER, HUGH. Union of Burma, a study
of the first years of independence.
3d. ed. London, Oxford UP, 1961.
PA 35 (1962) 188-190. (J. F. Cady)
RSA (1968) 127-8. (I. Jadoul)

TINKER, HUGH. Union of Burma, a study
of the first years of independence.

4th. ed. London, Oxford UP, 1967.
  MAS 4 (1970) 191.
  PA 41 (1968) 153. (P. Harnetty)

TINKER, JERRY M. Strategies of revolutionary warfare. New Delhi,
  Chand, 1969.
    AS 10 (1970) 178.

TIURIN, VLADIMIR ALEKSANDROVICH.
  Achekhskaia Voina: Iz istorii
  natsionalno-osvoboditelnogo
  dvizheniia v Indonessi. Moscow,
  Nauka, 1970.
    SA 2 (1972) 530. (V. M. Fic)

* TIXIER, T. La Vallee moyenne du Da-
  Nhim, ecologie et agriculture. Saigon, 1961.
    SEIB 36 (1961) 740.

* TJANDRASASMITA, UKA. Projek penggalian
  di Sulawesi selatan, 1970. The
  south Sulawesi excavation project,
  1970. Djakarta, Jajasan Purbakala,
  1970.
    AR 3 (1972) 202-205. (D. Lombard)

TJERITA RANTJAQ DI LABOEH. Rantjak di
  labueh: a Minangkabau Kaba. A
  specimen of the traditional literature of central Sumatra, based on the
  version of Datuk Paduko Alam and
  Sutan Pamuntjak, as reprinted by
  Firma Soeleiman, Bukit Tinggi, 1951.
  Edited, translated and with an introduction by A. H. Johns. Ithaca,
  Southeast Asia Program, Cornell Univ.,
  1958. (Cornell Univ. Southeast Asia
  Program. Data paper, no. 32)
    JAS 19 (1959-60) 473. (I. Dyen)

TJOKRONEGORO, SUTOMO. Tjukupkah sau-
  dara membina bahasa kesatuan kita?
  Bandung, Eresco, 1968.
    BIJ 125 (1969) 269-270. (A. Teeuw)

Tjurin, V. A. *See* AKADEMIIA NAUK
  SSSR. INSTITUT NARODOV AZII. Ocherki
  iz istorii IUgo-Vostochnoi Azii

* TOAN ANH. Con nguoi Viet-nam. Saigon,
  1965.
    BEF 55 (1969) 307-8. (Nguyen Tran
    Huan)

* TOAN ANH. Lang xom Viet-Nam. Saigon,
  1968.
    BEF 56 (1969) 210-1. (Nguyen Tran
    Huan)

* TOAN ANH. Nguoi Viet Dat Viet [by]
  Toan Anh [and] Cuu Long Giang. Saigon, 1968.
    BEF 56 (1969) 209-210. (Nguyen Tran
    Huan)

* TOAN ANH. Tin-nguong Viet-nam. Saigon,
  Nam Chi, 1967-8. 2v.
    BEF 55 (1969) 308-9. (Nguyen Tran
    Huan)
    BEF 56 (1969) 209. (Nguyen Tran
    Huan)

* TOEM WIPHAKPHOTCHANAKIT. Prawatsat
  Isan. Bangkok, Social Science Pr. of
  Thailand, 1970. 2v.
    JSS 60 pt. 1 (1972) 415-417. (K.
    Breazeale)

TOLAND, JOHN. But not in shame; the
  six months after Pearl Harbor. New
  York, Random House, 1961.
    UN 36 (1963) 324-5. (V. J. A.
    Rosales)

TON THAT THIEN. India and South East
  Asia, 1947-1960; a study of India's
  policy towards the South East Asian
  countries in the period 1947-1960.
  Geneva, Librairie Droz, 1963.
    PA 39 (1966) 430-1. (R. H. Fifield)

Tondel, Lyman M. *See* HAMMARSKJOLD
  FORUMS, NEW YORK, OCT. 18, 1965.
  Southeast Asia crisis

TOOZE, RUTH. Cambodia; land of contrasts. New York, Viking, 1962.
    PA 36 (1963) 204-5. (M. Leifer)

Tormo, Leandro. Lucban; a town the

TRAN MINH TIET. Une federation des pays de l'Asie du Sud-Est dans une grande entente asiatique. Paris, Editions Latines, 1965.
　FA 21 (1966) 498.

TRAN TRONG KIM. Mot Con gio bui. Saigon, Vinh son, 1969.
　BEF 58 (1971) 348-350. (Nguyen Tran Huan)

* TRAN VAN GIAP. Danc san ve the ngoc An-duong mot vai y kien ve An-duong ngoc gian va van de Thuc An-duong vuong. n.p., Van Su Dia (n. 28), 1957.
　BEF 52 (1964) 241-2. (M. Durand)

TRAN VAN KHE. La musique vietnamienne traditionnelle. Paris, Presses universitaires de France, 1962. (Paris. Musee Guimet. Annales. Bibliotheque d'etudes, t. 66)
　BEF 52 (1964) 578-589. (Le Van Hao)

TRAN VAN TUNG. Viet-Nam. New York, Praeger, 1959.
　FA 17 (1960) 2383-2385. (B. B. Fall)

Translation of culture: essays to E. E. Evans-Pritchard, edited by T. O. Beidelman. London, Tavistock, 1971.
　SOAS 36 (1973) 754. (A. Cohen)

Travel accounts of the islands, 1513-1787, by Tome Pires and others. Manila, Filipiniana Book Guild, 1971. (Filipiniana Book Guild. Publications, 19)
　JAS 32 (1972-3) 222-3. (A. L. Reber)

Treatise on the Moluccas (c. 1544), probably the preliminary version of Antonio Galvao's lost *Historia dos Molucas*, edited, annotated and translated into English by Hubert Th. Th. M. Jacobs. Rome, Jesuit Historical Institute, 1971. (Sources and studies for the history of the Jesuits, vol. III)
　BEF 61 (1974) 376-380. (P.-Y. Manguin)
　BIJ 128 (1972) 497-499. (W. P. Coolhaas)
　SOAS 35 (1972) 667-8. (D. K. Bassett)

TREGASKIS, RICHARD WILLIAM. Vietnam diary. New York, Holt, Rinehart and Winston, 1963.
　PA 37 (1964) 243-4. (P. J. Honey)

TREGONNING, K. G. British in Malaya, the first forty years, 1786-1826. Tucson, Univ. of Arizona Pr., 1965. (Association for Asian Studies. Monographs and papers, 18)
　JAS 25 (1965-6) 368-9. (L. R. Wright)
　PA 42 (1969) 104-5. (B. Harrison)

TREGONNING, K. G. History of modern Malaya. London, Univ. of London Pr., 1964.
　PS 13 (1965) 900-902. (N. Tarling)

TREGONNING, K. G. History of modern Sabah (North Borneo) 1881-1963. 2d. ed. Singapore, Univ. of Malaya Pr., 1965.
　JAS 26 (1966-7) 137-8. (G. P. Means)
[Note: first edition entitled: Under chartered company rule: North Borneo, 1881-1946]

TREGONNING, K. G. Home port Singapore; a history of Straits Steamship Company Limited, 1890-1965. Singapore, Oxford UP, 1967.
　JAS 29 (1969-70) 990. (J. D. Clarkson)
　SOAS 33 (1970) 700. (P. I. Ayre)

TREGONNING, K. G. Malaysia. Melbourne, Cheshire, 1964.
　JAS 25 (1965-6) 168. (R. O. Tilman)
　PA 39 (1966) 213-216. (J. M. van der Kroef)

Turpin, James W. Vietnam doctor; the

Program, Cornell Univ., 1974. (Cornell Univ. Southeast Asia Program. Data paper, no. 94)
PA 47 (1974) 578-9. (R. S. Milne)

TRUONG CHINH. President Ho Chi Minh, beloved leader of the Vietnamese people. Hanoi, Foreign Language Publishing House, 1966.
PA 44 (1971) 585-590. (W. E. Willmott)

TRUONG CHINH. Primer for revolt; the communist takeover in Vietnam. New York, Praeger, 1963.
JSAH 6 (Mar. 1966) 127-129. (P. J. Honey)

* TRUONG VAN CHINH. Khao Luan ve ngu phap Viet-Nam, [by] Truong Van Chinh [and] Nguyen Hien Le. Hue, Universite de Hue, 1963.
BEF 53 (1966) 303-305. (M. M. Durand)
SEIB 41 (1966) 316-7. (M. Piat)

TRUONG VAN CHINH. Structure de la langue vietnamienne. Paris, Imprimerie Nationale, 1970. (Centre universitaire des langues orientales vivantes. Publications, 6. ser. t. 10)
SEIB 47 (1972) 517-522. (G. D. Meillon)

TSUJI, MASANOBU. Singapore, the Japanese version. New York, St. Martin's Pr., 1960.
JSAH 2 (Oct. 1961) 91-100. (H. G. Bennett)
PA 35 (1962) 191-2. (M. Howard)

* TU DUC. Tu Duc Thanh Che Tu Noc Giai Nghia Ca. Hong Kong, Chinese Univ. of Hong Kong, 1971.
BEF 61 (1974) 365-371. (Nguyen Tran Huan)

TUBANGUI, HELEN R. Catalog of Filipiniana at Valladolid. Quezon City, Ateneo de Manila UP, 1973. (Ateneo

de Manila Univ. Dept. of History. Bibliographical series, no. 4)
PS 21 (1973) 494-497. (M. A. Foronda)

TUDJIMAH. Asrar al-insan fi ma'rifa al-ruh wa l'Rahman. Djakarta, Penerbitan, 1961.
BIJ 117 (1961) 483-485. (P. Voorhoeve)

TUGBY, DONALD J. Ethnological and allied work on Southeast Asia, 1950-1966, and, Distribution of ethnological and allied work in Southeast Asia, 1950-1966, by Elise Tugby. Brisbane, Australia, 1967.
AAS 5 (1969) 108-9. (L. Renko)

Tugby, Elise. Distribution of ethnological and allied work in Southeast Asia *See* TUGBY, DONALD J. Ethnological and allied work on Southeast Asia

TUGGY, ARTHUR LEONARD. The Philippine church, growth in a changing society. Grand Rapids, Eerdmans, 1971. (Church growth series)
PS 21 (1973) 223-228. (P. S. de Achutegui)

TURNBULL, COLIN. Straits Settlements 1826-67, Indian presidency to crown colony. London, Athlone Pr., 1972. (London. Univ. Historical studies, 32)
BIJ 129 (1973) 496-499. (D. K. Bassett)
JAH 8 (1974) 66-7. (A. T. Embree)
JSAS 4 (1973) 147-149. (Khoo Kay Kim)
PA 45 (1972) 625-6. (K. G. Tregonning)
SOAS 36 (1973) 503-4. (Wang Gungwu)

TURPIN, JAMES W. Vietnam doctor; the story of Project Concern. New York, McGraw-Hill, 1966.
PA 42 (1969) 423-4.

Tuuk, Hermanus Neubronner van der

TUUK, HERMANUS NEUBRONNER VAN DER.
Grammar of Toba Batak. Leiden,
Koninklijk Instituut voor Taal-,
Land- en Volkenkunde, 1971. (Insti-
tuut voor Taal-, Land- en Volken-
kunde. Translation series, 13)
 JSAS 3 (1972) 338-340. (J. L.
 Swellengrebel)
 SOAS 35 (1972) 208. (M. C.
 Ricklefs)

Udom Warotamasikkadit See ANTHONY,
EDWARD MASON. Foundations of Thai

UNESCO REGIONAL SEMINAR ON URBAN RURAL
DIFFERENCES AND RELATIONSHIPS IN
SOUTHERN ASIA, DELHI, 1962. Urban-
rural differences in Southern Asia;
some aspects and methods of analysis,
report on regional seminar, Delhi,
1962. Delhi, UNESCO, 1964.
 MER 11 pt. 1 (1966) 131-2. (R.
 Daroesman)

UHLENBECK, E. M. Aantekeningen bij
Tjan Tjoe Siem's vertaling van de
lakon Kurupati rabi. The Hague,
Nijhoff, 1960. (Instituut voor
Taal-, Land- en Volkenkunde. Ver-
handelingen, deel 29)
 SOAS 24 (1961) 402. (C. Hooykaas)

UHLENBECK, E. M. Critical survey of
studies on the languages of Java and
Madura. The Hague, Nijhoff, 1964.
(Instituut voor Taal-, Land- en
Volkenkunde. Bibliographical series,
7)
 AAS 2 (1966) 164-5. (G. Altmann)
 SOAS 29 (1966) 205-6. (C. Hooykaas)

UHLENBECK, E. M. De systematiek der
Javaanse pronomina. The Hague,
Nijhoff, 1960. (Instituut voor
Taal-, Land- en Volkenkunde. Ver-
handelingen, deel 30)
 BIJ 118 (1962) 277-281. (T. W.
 Kamil)
 SOAS 25 (1962) 422. (C. Hooykaas)

ULBRICHT, H. Wayang purwa; shadows of
the past. Kuala Lumpur, Oxford UP,
1970.
 JAS 30 (1970-1) 919-920. (A. C.
 Scott)
 JSS 60 pt. 2 (1972) 338-342. (B.
 and D. Brereton)

Umar Junus See JUNUS, UMAR

Underdevelopment and economic national-
ism in Southeast Asia, by Frank H.
Golay et al. Ithaca, Cornell UP,
1969.
 JAS 30 (1970-1) 724-5. (J. Badgley)
 PA 43 (1970) 119-121. (E. Van Roy)
 PS 18 (1970) 671-673. (M. McPhelin)
 SA 2 (1972) 488-502. (V. D. Ooms)

Unger, Jonathan See GRANT, JONATHAN
S. Cambodia; the widening war in
Indochina

Union catalogue of Asian publications,
1965-1970. Edited by David E. Hall.
London, Mansell, 1971. 4v.
 SOAS 35 (1972) 683-4. (S. Sutton)

UNITED NATIONS. ECONOMIC COMMISSION FOR
ASIA AND THE FAR EAST. Food and agri-
cultural prices in Asia and the Far
East. Bangkok, 1958.
 PA 33 (1960) 98-9.

UNITED NATIONS. SECRETARIAT. Popula-
tion growth and manpower in the Phil-
ippines; a joint study by the United
Nations and the Government of the
Philippines National Economic Council.
New York, 1960.
 PS 9 (1961) 720-1. (M. B.
 Concepcion)

* UNITED NATIONS EDUCATIONAL, SCIENTIFIC
AND CULTURAL ORGANIZATION. Le role
de l'epargne et de la richesse en
Asie du sud et en occident. Paris,
UNESCO, 1963.
 SEIB 39 (1964) 292-298. (P.
 Brocheux)

United Nations Educational, Scientific
and Cultural Organization. Science
Cooperation Office for Southeast
Asia *See* SYMPOSIUM ON ECOLOGICAL
RESEARCH IN HUMID TROPICS VEGETATION,
KUCHING, SARAWAK, 1965

U.S. CONGRESS. SENATE. COMMITTEE ON
FOREIGN RELATIONS. China, Vietnam,
and the United States, highlights of
the hearings of the Senate Foreign
Relations Committee. Washington,
Public Affairs Pr., 1966.
JAS 26 (1966-7) 762-3. (S. M. Chiu)

U.S. CONGRESS. SENATE. COMMITTEE ON
FOREIGN RELATIONS. United States
foreign policy: Asia. Washington,
GPO, 1959.
JAS 20 (1960-1) 87-8. (A. D.
Barnett)

U.S. DEPT. OF THE ARMY. OFFICE OF
MILITARY HISTORY. United States
Army in World War II. History of the
China-Burma-India theater. Time runs
out in CBI. Washington, GPO, 1959.
JAS 19 (1959-60) 452-454. (M.
Kennedy)

U.S. DEPT. OF THE ARMY. OFFICE OF
MILITARY HISTORY. United States
Army in World War II. War in the
Pacific. Washington, GPO, 1962-3.
2v.
PA 38 (1965) 192-194. (M. Howard)

U.S. ECONOMIC SURVEY TEAM TO INDONESIA.
Indonesia: perspective and proposals
for United States economic aid: a
report to the President of the United
States. New Haven, Yale Univ.,
Southeast Asia Studies, 1963.
JAS 23 (1963-4) 142-3. (E. B. Ayal)
JSAH 6 (Mar. 1965) 109-114. (B. J.
Donaldson)
MER 8 pt. 2 (1963) 129-133. (D. H.
Pond)
PA 36 (1963) 322-3. (D. Hindley)

Utrecht. Centraal Museum. Hedendaagse

U.S. INFORMATION SERVICE, VIENTIANE.
LAOS. Briefing notes on the Royal
Kingdom of Laos. Vientiane, 1959.
BEF 50 (1960) 183-4. (P.-B. Lafont)
SEIB 35 (1960) 739-740. (P.-B.
Lafont)

U.S. LIBRARY OF CONGRESS. ORIENTALIA
DIVISION. Southeast Asia, an annotated
bibliography of selected reference
sources in western languages, compiled
by Cecil Hobbs. Rev. and enl. Washington, GPO, 1964.
JSAH 6 (Sept. 1965) 145-147. (A. F.
Johnson)
PS 14 (1966) 176-178. (C. Lopez)

U.S. LIBRARY OF CONGRESS. ORIENTALIA
DIVISION. Southeast Asia, an annotated bibliography of selected reference sources in western languages,
compiled by Cecil Hobbs. New York,
Greenwood Pr., 1968.
PA 43 (1970) 121-123. (J. M. van
der Kroef)

University of the Philippines *See*
QUEZON, PHILIPPINES. UNIV. OF THE
PHILIPPINES

Urbanization and national development,
edited by Leo Jakobson and Ved Prakash. Beverly Hills, Sage Foundation,
1971.
JAS 32 (1972-3) 210-212. (M. R.
Hollnsteiner)
MAS 7 (1973) 280-288. (P. Wheatley)

UTRECHT, ERNST. Ambon, kolonisatie,
dekolonisatie en neo-kolonisatie.
Amsterdam, Van Gennep, 1972. (Kri-
tiese biblioteek)
BIJ 130 (1974) 483-493. (C. F. van
Fraassen)
JCA 4 (1974) 220-1. (J. Pluvier)

UTRECHT. CENTRAAL MUSEUM. Hedendaagse
kunst van Bali, uit het. eigendom ban
Hare Majesteit de Koningin van de
Rijksuniversiteit te Leiden en de
heer R. Bonnet te Blaricum. Utrecht,

Utrecht. Centraal Museuum. Hedendaagse

1962.
   BIJ 121 (1965) 373-378. (F. D. K.
   Bosch)

VACISSARA THERA. Chronicle of the
Thupa and the Thupavamsa, being a
translation and edition of Vacissa-
ratthera's *Thupavamsa*, by N. A.
Jayawickrama. London, Luzac, 1971.
(Sacred books of the Buddhists,
vol. 28)
   JSS 62 pt. 1 (1974) 284-5. (H. D.
   Ginsburg)

* VAJIRANANAVARORASA. Entrance to the
Vinaya, a translation of the
Vinayamukha. Bangkok, King Maha
Makuta's Academy, 1969.
   JSS 58 pt. 2 (1970) 202-206.
   (Phra Srivisuddhimoli)

VALDEPENAS, VINCENTE B. Protection
and development of Philippine manufacturing. Manila, Ateneo UP, 1970.
   PA 45 (1972) 480-1. (G. B.
   Hainsworth)

Valeros, Florentino B. *See* PERALTA,
CRESENCIO. Toward general education
in the Philippines

VALERIANO, NAPOLEON D. Counter-
guerrilla operations, the Philippine
experience, by Napoleon D. Valeriano
and T. R. Bohannan. New York,
Praeger, 1962.
   PA 37 (1964) 238-9. (I. B. Powell)

VALSAN, E. H. Community development
programs and rural local government,
comparative case studies of India
and the Philippines. New York,
Praeger, 1970.
   PA 44 (1971) 138-9. (K. Nair)

VANDENBOSCH, AMRY. Australia faces
Southeast Asia, the emergence of a
foreign policy, by Amry and Mary
Belle Vandenbosch. Lexington, Univ.
of Kentucky Pr., 1967.
   PA 41 (1968) 475-6. (W. M. Ball)

VANDENBOSCH, AMRY. Changing face of
Southeast Asia, by Amry Vandenbosch
and Richard Butwell. Lexington, Univ.
of Kentucky Pr., 1966.
   JAS 26 (1966-7) 528-9. (J. Grossholtz)

Vandenbosch, Mary Belle *See* VANDEN-
BOSCH, AMRY. Australia faces Southeast Asia

VAN DER KROEF, JUSTUS M. Communism in
Malaysia and Singapore: a contempo-
rary survey. The Hague, Nijhoff,
1967.
   AS 8 (1968) 516.
   PA 41 (1968) 449. (R. S. Milne)

VAN DER KROEF, JUSTUS M. Communist
party of Indonesia; its history, program and tactics. Vancouver, Publications Centre, Univ. of British
Columbia, 1965.
   AS 6 (1966) 186.
   JAS 26 (1966-7) 340-1. (R. T. McVey)

VAN DER KROEF, JUSTUS M. Dialectic of
colonial Indonesian history. Amster-
dam, Van der Peet, 1963.
   JAS 24 (1964-5) 527-8. (J. R. W.
   Smail)
   JSAH 6 (Mar. 1966) 114-5. (J. M.
   Pluvier)
   PA 37 (1964) 471-2. (C. D. Cowan)

VAN DER KROEF, JUSTUS M. Indonesia
after Sukarno. Vancouver, Univ. of
British Columbia Pr., 1972.
   SA 3 (1974) 789-790. (D. Kirk)
   SA 3 (1974) 790-792. (G. M.
   Heneghan)

VAN DER KROEF, JUSTUS M. Indonesian
social evolution; some psychological
considerations. Amsterdam, Van der
Peet, 1958.
   JAS 20 (1960-1) 536-538. (J. L.
   Landgraf)
   JSAH 3 (Sept. 1962) 150-152. (R.
   Van Niel)

VAN DER VEUR, PAUL W. Documents and
  correspondence on New Guinea's
  boundaries. Canberra, Australian
  National UP, 1966.
    MAS 4 (1970) 291-297. (C. A.
      Fisher)
    PA 41 (1968) 143-4. (D. C.
      Bettison)

VAN DER VEUR, PAUL W. Search for New
  Guinea's boundaries, from Torres
  Straits to the Pacific. Canberra,
  Australian National UP, 1966.
    MAS 4 (1970) 291-297. (C. A.
      Fisher)
    PA 41 (1968) 143-4. (D. C.
      Bettison)

Van der Veur, Paul W. *See* THE, LIAN.
  Treasures and trivia

VAN NIEL, ROBERT. Economic factors in
  Southeast Asian social change.
  Honolulu, Univ. of Hawaii, 1968.
  (Asian studies at Hawaii, no. 2)
    JAS 30 (1970-1) 515. (C. O.
      Houston)

VAN NIEL, ROBERT. Emergence of the
  modern Indonesian elite. The Hague,
  W. van Hoeve, 1960.
    BIJ 117 (1961) 388-390. (L. H.
      Palmier)
    JAS 20 (1960-1) 389-391. (A.
      Vandenbosch)
    PA 34 (1961) 57-62. (N. Keyfitz)

VAN NIEL, ROBERT. Survey of historical
  source materials in Java and Manila.
  Honolulu, Univ. of Hawaii Pr., 1971.
  (Asian studies at Hawaii, no. 5)
    AAS 8 (1972) 194-5. (J. Genzor)
    BEF 60 (1973) 425-427. (D. Lombard)
    JAH 6 (1972) 189-190. (C. R. Boxer)
    JAS 31 (1971-2) 471. (J. A. Larkin)
    PA 45 (1972) 156-7. (E. Wickberg)
    PS 19 (1971) 751-2. (J. N.
      Schumacher)

VAN ODIJK, ANTONIO. Elementary grammar of the Bisayan language. 2d. ed.

Vaughan, Jonas Daniel. Manners and
  Opon, Cebu, 1959.
    JAS 21 (1961-2) 247-8. (J. Wolff)

Vanoverbergh, Morice *See* CARRO,
  ANDRES. Iloko-English dictionary

VANOVERBERGH, MORICE. Isneg-English
  vocabulary. Honolulu, Univ. Pr. of
  Hawaii, 1972. (Oceanic Linguistics.
  Special publications, no. 11)
    JAS 33 (1973-4) 167. (F. Eggan)

VAN ROY, EDWARD. Economic systems of
  northern Thailand, structure and
  change. Ithaca, Cornell UP, 1971.
    AS 11 (1971) 718.
    JAS 31 (1971-2) 463-4. (J. A.
      Hafner)
    JSAS 3 (1972) 325-329. (A. Y.
      Dessaint and Chia Lin Sien)
    JSS 60 pt. 1 (1972) 424-427. (G.
      Wijeyewardene)
    PA 45 (1972) 466-7. (T. H. Silcock)
    SA 2 (1972) 514-517. (H. B. Smith)
    SOAS 35 (1972) 663-665. (P. J. Bee)

VASIL, R. K. The Malaysian general
  election of 1969. Singapore, Oxford
  UP, 1972.
    JAS 33 (1973-4) 332-3. (R. O.
      Tilman)

VASIL, R. K. Politics in a plural society, a study of non-communal political parties in west Malaysia. Kuala Lumpur, Oxford UP, 1971. (East
  Asian historical monographs)
    JAS 32 (1972-3) 212-3. (R. O.
      Tilman)
    JSAS 3 (1972) 358-9. (G. P. Means)
    PA 45 (1972) 458-460. (Chan Heng
      Chee)

VAUGHAN, JONAS DANIEL. Manners and
  customs of the Chinese of the Straits
  Settlements. Kuala Lumpur, Oxford
  UP, 1971. (Oxford in Asia historical
  reprints)
    JAS 32 (1972-3) 215-6. (H. K.
      Kaufman)
    PA 45 (1972) 324. (E. Wickberg)

Veen, Bart van. Soekarno tabeh

Veen, Bart van *See* KUIJK, OTTO.
Soekarno tabeh

VEEN, HENDRIK VAN DER. Merok feast of
the Sa'dan Toradja. The Hague,
Nijhoff, 1965. (Instituut voor
Taal-, Land- en Volkenkunde. Ver-
handelingen, deel 45)
   PA 40 (1967) 201. (J. M. van der
      Kroef)
   SOAS 30 (1967) 735-6. (G. B.
      Milner)

VEEN, HENDRIK VAN DER. Sa'dan Toradja
chant for the deceased. The Hague,
Nijhoff, 1966. (Instituut voor
Taal-, Land- en Volkenkunde. Ver-
handelingen, deel 49)
   PA 40 (1967) 201. (J. M. van der
      Kroef)
   SOAS 30 (1967) 736. (G. B.
      Milner)

VEER, PAUL VAN'T. De Atjeh-Oorlog.
Amsterdam, De Arbeiderspers, 1969.
(Achtergronden. Nieuwe reeks)
   JAS 30 (1970-1) 918-9. (P. W. van
      der Veur)

VELLA, WALTER FRANCIS. Aspects of
Vietnamese history. Honolulu, Univ.
Pr. of Hawaii, 1973. (Asian studies
at Hawaii, no. 8)
   AF 6 pt. 2 (1974) 54-5. (F. H.
      Tucker)

VELLA, WALTER FRANCIS. Siam under
Rama III, 1824-1851. Locust Valley,
N.Y., Augustin, 1957. (Association
for Asian Studies. Monographs, 4)
   JAS 19 (1959-60) 468-9. (R.
      Emerson)

* VELLUT, J. L. La politique asiatique
des Philippines. Brussels, Institut
des Relations Internationales, 1963.
(Chronique de Politique Etranger.
Vol. 16 no. 3)
   RSA (1963) 299-301. (I. Jadoul)

VELORO, A. T. Philippine prose and
poetry for appreciation. Manila,
Philippine Book Co., 1964.
   SLQ 2 (1964) 230-1. (M. U. Salenga)

VELOSO, ALFREDO S. Poetica; antologia
de poetas filipinos. 9th ed. Quezon
City, Asvel, 1966.
   PS 14 (1966) 713-715. (A. G. Manuud)

Vereenigde Oostindische Compagnie *See*
NEDERLANDISCHE OOST-INDISCHE
COMPAGNIE

VERGOUWEN, JACOB CORNELIS. Social
organization and customary law of the
Toba-Batak of northern Sumatra. The
Hague, Nijhoff, 1964. (Instituut
voor Taal-, Land- en Volkenkunde.
Translation series, 7)
   JAS 25 (1965-6) 803-4. (R. R. Jay)
   PA 41 (1968) 295-6. (J. M. van der
      Kroef)
   SOAS 29 (1966) 424. (A. Christie)

VERGUIN, JOSEPH. Le Malais. Essai
d'analyse fonctionnelle et structur-
ale. Paris, Mouton, 1967. (Cahiers
de l'Homme: Ethnologie, Geographie,
Linguistique. Nouvelle serie, 7)
   BIJ 124 (1968) 552-3. (A. Teeuw)
   SOAS 31 (1968) 424-5. (M. B. Lewis)

VERHEIJEN, JILIS A. J. Kamus Manggarai.
The Hague, Nijhoff, 1967.
   SOAS 32 (1969) 464-5. (R. H. Robins)

Verzeichnis der orientalischen Handschriften in Deutschland. Supplement
band, 3. Thailandische Miniaturmale-
reien, nach einer Handschrift der
Indischen Kunstabteilung der Staat-
lichen Museen Berlin, von Klaus Wenk.
Wiesbaden, Franz Steiner Verlag, 1965.
   SOAS 30 (1967) 444-5. (E. H. S.
      Simmonds)

* VICHIN PANUPONG. Inter-sentence rela-
tions in modern conversational Thai.
Bangkok, Siam Society, 1970.
   JSS 59 pt. 1 (1971) 245-248. (L. M.
      Beebe)

Vo Duc Hanh, Etienne. La place du

* VIDAL, JULES. La vegetation du Laos.
  Vientiane, 1972.
      SEIB 49 (1974) 156-158. (Pham
      Hoang Ho)

* VIETNAM. INSTITUT DE RECHERCHES
  ARCHEOLOGIQUES. Nhu Vien trong
  Kham-Dinh Dai-Nam Hoi-Dien Su-Le.
  Saigon, Min. of Education, 1965.
      SEIB 41 (1966) 89-90.

Vietnam and the Sino-Soviet dispute,
  edited by Robert Arthur Rupen and
  Robert Farrell. New York, Praeger,
  1967.
      AS 8 (1968) 625.
      MAS 3 (1969) 79-82. (R. Smith)

Vietnam settlement, why 1973 not 1969?
  By Morton A. Kaplan and others.
  Washington, American Enterprise
  Institute for Public Research, 1973.
  (Rational debate series)
      PA 47 (1974) 393-4. (M. Leifer)

VIETNAM VETERANS AGAINST THE WAR. Winter soldier investigation; an inquiry into American war crimes.
  Boston, Beacon Pr., 1972.
      PA 46 (1973) 601-603. (M. Osborne)

Villanueva, Patrocino Santos See
  SANTOS-VILLANUEVA, PATROCINO

VILLAROEL, FIDEL. Father Jose Burgos,
  university student. Manila, Univ.
  of Santo Tomas, 1971.
      PS 20 (1972) 351-2. (J. S. Arcilla)

Villeneuve, Marcel See MENOUX, MARCEL

* VIMOLPHAN PEETATHAWATCHAI. Esarn cloth
  design. n.p., Faculty of Education,
  Khon Kaen Univ., 1973.
      JSS 62 pt. 1 (1974) 270-1. (W. J.
      Klausner)

* VIMOLPHAN PEETATHAWATCHAI. Twelve
  festivals. Bangkok, Mahachon Pr.,
  1973.
      JSS 62 pt. 2 (1974) 390-1. (W. J.
      Klausner)

VIRATA, ENRIQUE T. Agrarian reform:
  a bibliography. Quezon City, Community Development Research Council,
  Univ. of the Philippines, 1965.
      JAS 26 (1966-7) 547-549. (D. V.
      Hart)

VIRAVONG, MAHA SILA. History of Laos.
  New York, Paragon Book Reprint Corp.,
  1964.
      JAS 24 (1964-5) 702-3. (D. K.
      Wyatt)

* VIRAVONG, MAHA SILA. Phongsavadan Lao.
  Vientiane, 2500.
      BEF 50 (1960) 573-4. (P. B. Lafont)

VIRAVONG, MAHA SILA. Vachnanoukrom
  Pahsah Lao: a Laotian dictionary.
  Vientiane, Min. de l'Education Na-
  tionale, 1961.
      JAS 21 (1961-2) 570-1. (A. D. Kerr)

Visid See PRACHUABMOH. Rural and
  urban population of Thailand

VITTACHI, TARZIE. Fall of Sukarno.
  London, Mayflower, 1967.
      JAS 27 (1967-8) 438-9. (L. Castles)
      PA 40 (1967) 393-4. (W. F.
      Wertheim)

VLEKKE, BERNARD HUBERTUS MARIA. Nusantara: a history of Indonesia. Rev.
  ed. Chicago, Quadrangle, 1960.
      AP 8 (1964) 136-7. (W. G. Solheim)
      BIJ 118 (1962) 289-290. (L. Kok)
      BIJ 118 (1962) 290-294. (W. P.
      Coolhaas)
      JAS 20 (1960-1) 387-8. (G. E.
      Williams)
      PA 34 (1961) 210-1. (L. H. Palmier)

VO DUC HANH, ETIENNE. La place du
  catholicisme dans les relations entre
  la France et le Viet-Nam de 1851 a
  1870. Leiden, Brill, 1969. 3v.
      BEF 58 (1971) 318. (J. Filliozat)
      JAS 30 (1970-1) 505-507. (A.
      Woodside)
      SOAS 34 (1971) 438-9. (R. B. Smith)

Vo Nguyen Giap. Banner of people's

VO NGUYEN GIAP. Banner of people's
war, the party's military line.
New York, Praeger, 1970.
   PA 44 (1971) 309-311. (M. E.
   Osborne)

VO NGUYEN GIAP. Big victory great
task, North Vietnam's Minister of
Defense assesses the course of the
war. New York, Praeger, 1968.
   JAS 28 (1968-9) 192-3. (J. J.
   Zasloff)

VO NGUYEN GIAP. National liberation
war in Vietnam; general line,
strategy, tactics. Hanoi, Foreign
Languages Pub. House, 1971.
   JCA 4 (1974) 93-96. (T. Shanin)

Vo Nguyen Giap *See* TRUONG CHINH.
The peasant question

VO NGUYEN GIAP. People's war, peo-
ple's army. New York, Praeger,
1962.
   JAS 22 (1962-3) 340-1. (R. M.
   Smith)
   PA 36 (1963) 444-5. (P. J. Honey)

Vo Nguyen Giap *See* Recits de la
resistance vietnamienne

VO NHAN TRI. Croissance economique de
la Republique Democratique du Viet-
Nam. Hanoi, Editions en Langues
Etrangeres, 1967.
   BEF 58 (1971) 345-347. (C.
   Boulleret)
   JCA 1 pt. 2 (1970) 73-75.

VO THU TINH. Phra Lak Phra Lam; le
Ramayana lao. Vientiane, Vithagna,
1972. (Collection litterature lao,
v. 1)
   SEIB 48 (1973) 142-3. (M. Piat)

* VOEGELIN, C. F. Languages of the
world: Indo-Pacific, by C. F. and
F. M. Voegelin. Bloomington, Archives of Languages of the World,
Anthropology Dept., Indiana Univ.,

1964. (Anthropological Linguistics,
vol. 6 pt. 4)
   AAS 2 (1966) 156-7. (G. Altmann)

Voegelin, F. M. *See* VOEGELIN, C. F.
Languages of the world

* Volkenkundige encyclopedie onder re-
dactie van H. Jans. Ghent, Zeist en
Daphne, 1962.
   BIJ 118 (1962) 473-476. (E. Postel-
   Coster)

* VON DER MEHDEN, FRED R. Local author-
ity and administration in Thailand,
by Fred R. von der Mehden and David
A. Wilson. n.p., Academic Advisory
Council for Thailand, 1970.
   JAS 31 (1971-2) 228-9. (B. Nussbaum)
   PA 44 (1971) 464-5. (R. S. Milne)

VON DER MEHDEN, FRED R. Politics of
developing nations. Englewood
Cliffs, Prentice-Hall, 1964.
   JAS 24 (1964-5) 142-144. (M. L.
   Thomas)

VON DER MEHDEN, FRED R. Religion and
nationalism in Southeast Asia: Burma,
Indonesia, and the Philippines.
Madison, Univ. of Wisconsin Pr., 1963.
   AS 4 (1964) 822.
   JAS 23 (1963-4) 489-490. (D. V.
   Hart)
   JSAH 5 (Sept. 1964) 224-227. (S.
   Rose)
   PA 38 (1965) 64-68. (E. M.
   Mendelson)

VOORHOEVE, C. L. Flamingo Bay dialect
of the Asmat language. The Hague,
Nijhoff, 1965. (Instituut voor Taal-,
Land- en Volkenkunde. Verhandelingen,
deel 46)
   SOAS 30 (1967) 734. (G. B. Milner)

Voorhoeve, Petrus *See* Adat Atjeh

Voorhoeve, Petrus *See* BEATTY, ALFRED
CHESTER. Catalogue of the Batak
manuscripts

VOORHOEVE, PETRUS. Sudsumatranische
  Handschriften. Wiesbaden, Franz
  Steiner, 1971. (Verzeichnis der
  Orientalischen Handschriften in
  Deutschland, Bd. 29)
     SOAS 35 (1972) 700. (C. Hooykaas)

VREEDE-DE STUERS, CORA. L'emancipation
  de la femme indonesienne. Paris,
  Mouton, 1959. (Le monde d'outre-
  mer, passe et present, 1)
     BIJ 117 (1961) 493-498. (J. Prins)
     SOAS 23 (1960) 416-7. (B. E. Ward)

VREEDE-DE STUERS, CORA. Indonesian
  woman, struggles and achievements.
  The Hague, Mouton, 1960.
     PA 36 (1963) 449-450. (D. Hindley)

VU HOANG CHUONG. Communion, Camthong
  Vietnamese poems. Saigon, Nguyen
  Khang, 1960.
     AC 2 (Apr. 1960) 147-8.

* VU HOANG CHUONG. Poemes Tam-tinh
  nguoi dep. Saigon, Nguyen Khang,
  1961.
     SEIB 36 (1961) 739-740.

* VU NGOC PHAN. Truyen Tay-suong.
  Hanoi, Van-hoa, 1961.
     BEF 52 (1964) 278-287. (Ta Trong
       Hiep)

VU VAN HIEN. Che-do tai-san trong
  gia-dinh Viet-Nam. Saigon, Bo Quoc-
  Gia Giao-Duc, 1960. 2v.
     SEIB 36 (1961) 107-8.

VU VAN KHIEU. Dat le que thoi:
  phong-tuc Viet Nam cua Nhat-Thanh
  Vu Van Khieu. Saigon, Duong Sang,
  1970.
     BEF 58 (1971) 350-352. (Nguyen
       Tran Huan)

WADDELL, J. ROBERT E. Introduction to
  Southeast Asian politics. Sydney,
  John Wiley, 1972.
     JAS 32 (1972-3) 731. (D. A. Wilson)
     JSAS 5 (1974) 147-8. (R. Peritz)

Wal, S. L. van der. Het onderwijsbeleid
     JSS 61 pt. 1 (1973) 326. (J. L. S.
       Girling)
     PA 46 (1973) 354. (R. S. Milne)
     SA 3 (1974) 923-927. (L. G. Noble)

WAGNER, FRITS A. Indonesia: the art
  of an island group. London, Methuen,
  1959.
     AP 8 (1964) 135-6. (R. R. Jay)
     JAS 20 (1960-1) 123-4. (M. B.
       Rogers)
     PA 34 (1961) 209-210. (C. Holt)

WAGNER, ROY. Habu: the innovation of
  meaning in Daribi religion. Chicago,
  Univ. of Chicago Pr., 1972.
     SOAS 37 (1972) 266-268. (M. W.
       Young)

WAINWRIGHT, M. D. Guide to western
  manuscripts and documents in the
  British Isles relating to South and
  South East Asia, by M. D. Wainwright
  and N. Matthews. London, Oxford UP,
  1965.
     BIJ 122 (1966) 404. (P. Voorhoeve)
     JSAH 8 (1967) 337-8. (Lim U. Wen)
     RSA (1965) 172-3. (L. Rocher)
     SOAS 29 (1966) 406-7. (H. Tinker)

Wal, S. L. van der *See* JONGE, BONIFA-
  CIUS CORNELIS DE. Herinneringen van
  Jhr. Mr. B. C. de Jonge

Wal, S. L. van der *See* Officiele
  bescheiden betreffende de Nederlands-
  Indonesische betrekkingen

WAL, S. L. VAN DER. Het onderwijsbeleid
  in Nederlands-Indie 1900-1940; een
  bronnenpublikatie. Education policy
  in the Netherlands-Indies 1900-1940.
  Groningen, Wolters, 1963. (Historisch
  Genootschap, Utrecht. Commissie voor
  Bronnen publicatie Betreffende de
  Geschiedenis van Nederlands-Indie
  1900-1942. Uitgaven, no. 1)
     BIJ 121 (1965) 366-373. (W.
       Wertheim)
     JAS 24 (1964-5) 529-530. (R. Van
       Niel)
     PA 42 (1969) 537-540. (B. B. Hering)

WAL, S. L. VAN DER. De opkomst van de
  Nationalistische Beweging in Nederlands-Indie. Een bronnenpublikatie.
  Groningen, Wolters, 1967. (Historisch Genootschap, Utrecht. Commissie
  voor Bronnenpublicatie betreffende
  de Geschiedenis van Nederlands-Indie
  1900-1942. Uitgaven, no. 4)
    PA 42 (1969) 537-540. (B. B.
      Hering)
    PA 43 (1970) 317-319. (P. W. van
      der Veur)

WAL, S. L. VAN DER. De volksrad en de
  staatkundige ontwikkeling van Neder-
  lands-Indie; een bronnenpublikatie.
  Groningen, Wolters, 1964-5. 2v.
  (Historisch Genootschap, Utrecht.
  Commissie voor Bronnenpublicatie
  Betreffende de Geschiedenis van
  Nederlands-Indie 1900-1942. Uitgaven,
  no. 3)
    BIJ 126 (1970) 263-265. (H. J.
      Benda)
    PA 42 (1969) 537-540. (B. B.
      Hering)

WALES, HORACE GEOFFREY QUARITCH.
  Ancient Siamese government and ad-
  ministration. New York, Paragon
  Book Reprint Corp., 1965.
    JAS 25 (1965-6) 555. (W. F. Vella)

WALES, HORACE GEOFFREY QUARITCH.
  Angkor and Rome, a historical comparison. London, Quaritch, 1965.
    JAS 25 (1965-6) 171-2. (J. F.
      Cady)

WALES, HORACE GEOFFREY QUARITCH.
  Dvaravati, the earliest kingdom of
  Siam. London, Quaritch, 1969.
    JAS 29 (1969-70) 493-4. (S. J.
      O'Connor)
    JSS 58 pt. 1 (1970) 126-136.
      (Srisakra Vallibhotama)
    SA 2 (1972) 502-514. (K. P. Landon)

WALES, HORACE GEOFFREY QUARITCH.
  Early Burma-old Siam: a comparative
  commentary. London, Quaritch, 1973.

JAS 33 (1973-4) 735-6. (H. W.
  Woodward)

WALES, HORACE GEOFFREY QUARITCH. In-
  dianization of China and Southeast
  Asia. London, Quaritch, 1967.
    JAS 27 (1967-8) 684-686. (P. R.
      Myer)

WALES, HORACE GEOFFREY QUARITCH. Prehistory and religion in South-East
  Asia. London, Quaritch, 1957.
    BIJ 117 (1961) 291-294. (P. E. de
      Josselin de Jong)
    JSS 48 pt. 2 (1960) 103-106. (C. N.
      Spinks)

WALINSKY, LOUIS JOSEPH. Economic development in Burma, 1951-60. New
  York, Twentieth Century Fund, 1962.
    JAS 22 (1962-3) 496-7. (E. B. Ayal)
    JBRS 47 (1964) 173-181. (Thet Tun)
    PA 36 (1963) 325-327. (H. Tinker)
    RSA (1964) 321-2. (I. Jadoul)

WALKER, GEORGE B. Angkor empire.
  Calcutta, Signet Pr., 1955.
    BEF 50 (1960) 191-197. (B. P.
      Groslier)
    SEIB 35 (1960) 738.

WALLACE, BEN J. Village life in insular
  Southeast Asia. Boston, Little,
  Brown, 1971.
    JAS 31 (1971-2) 990-1. (S. A.
      Schlegel)

WALT, LEWIS W. Strange war, strange
  strategy; a generals report on Vietnam. New York, Funk and Wagnalls,
  1970.
    PA 44 (1971) 641-644. (J. L. S.
      Girling)

WANG, GUNGWU. Malaysia, a survey. New
  York, Praeger, 1964.
    JAS 25 (1965-6) 804-5. (J. N.
      Parmer)
    PA 39 (1966) 213-216. (J. M. van
      der Kroef)

Wangbang Wideya, a Javanese Panji
romance, edited and translated by
S. O. Robson. The Hague, Nijhoff,
1971. (Bibliotheca Indonesica
series, vol. 6)
    JSAS 4 (1973) 139-140. (J. L.
    Swellengrebel)

WARBEY, WILLIAM. Ho Chi Minh and the
struggle for an independent Vietnam.
London, Merlin Pr., 1972.
    JCA 2 (1972) 205.

WARD, ARTHUR BARTLETT. Rajah's serv-
ant. Ithaca, Southeast Asia Program,
Cornell Univ., 1966. (Cornell Univ.
Southeast Asia Program. Data paper,
no. 61)
    BIJ 123 (1967) 531-2. (H. J. de
    Graaf)
    SMJ 16 (1968) 435-437. (B. Sandin)

WARD, BARBARA E. Women in the new
Asia; the changing social roles of
men and women in South and Southeast
Asia. Paris, UNESCO, 1963.
    AS 4 (1964) 1072.
    JAS 24 (1964-5) 344-5. (B. B.
    Lanham)
    SOAS 29 (1966) 429-430. (M.
    McArthur)

WARD, JACK H. Bibliography of Philippine linguistics and minor languages;
with annotations and indices based
on works in the library of Cornell
University. Ithaca, Southeast Asia
Program, Cornell Univ., 1971. (Cornell Univ. Southeast Asia Program.
Data paper, no. 83)
    AAS 8 (1972) 193-4. (J. Genzor)
    JAS 32 (1972-3) 570-1. (A. M.
    Stevens)
    SOAS 37 (1974) 754.

Ward, Robert E. *See* MACRIDIS, ROY C.
Modern political systems

WARES, ALAN CAMPBELL. Bibliography of
the Summer Institute of Linguistics,
1935-1968. Santa Ana, California,

Watabe, Tadayo. Glutinous rice in

Summer Institute of Linguistics,
1968.
    AAS 7 (1971) 123-4. (J. Genzor)

WARNER, DENIS. Last Confucian. New
York, Macmillan, 1963.
    JAS 23 (1963-4) 482-3. (R. Butwell)

WARREN, JAMES FRANCIS. North Borneo
Chartered Company's administration of
the Bajau, 1879-1909; the pacification of a maritime nomadic people.
Athens, Ohio Univ. Center for International Studies, 1971. (Papers in
international studies. Southeast Asia
series, no. 22)
    SMJ 19 (1971) 381-2. (C. Sather)

Warren, William *See* BRAKE, BRIAN.
House on the klong

WARREN, WILLIAM. Legendary American;
the remarkable career and strange
disappearance of Jim Thompson.
Boston, Houghton Mifflin, 1970.
    JSS 58 pt. 2 (1970) 198-200. (M.
    Smithies)

* WAT BOWONNIWET. Phraprawat somdet phramahasamanachao kromphraya wachirayanwarorot, [by] Wat Bowonniwet [and]
Mahamakut Royal Academy Foundation.
Bangkok, Mahamakut Pr., 1971.
    JSS 62 pt. 2 (1974) 365-368. (C. J.
    Reynolds)

* WAT BOWONNIWET. Pramuan phraniphon
somdet phramahasamanachao kromphraya
wachirayanwarorot kan khana song.
Bangkok, Mahamakut Pr., 1971.
    JSS 62 pt. 2 (1974) 365-368. (C. J.
    Reynolds)

WATABE, TADAYO. Glutinous rice in
northern Thailand. Kyoto, Center for
Southeast Asian Studies, Kyoto Univ.,
1967. (Kyoto Diagaku. Center for
Southeast Asian Studies. Reports on
research in Southeast Asia. Natural
science series, no. 2)
    JAS 27 (1967-8) 922. (J. D.
    Clarkson)

Watson, James Kiero. Military

WATSON, JAMES KIERO. Military operations in Burma, 1890-1892, letters from Lieutenant J. K. Watson, K.R.R.C. Ithaca, Southeast Asia Program, Cornell Univ., 1967. (Cornell Univ. Southeast Asia Program. Data paper, no. 64)
  JSAH 9 (1968) 173-4. (T. Blackmore)

WATT, ALAN STEWART. Vietnam, an Australian analysis. Melbourne, Cheshire, 1968.
  JSAH 10 (1969) 363-4. (M. Osborne)
  PA 42 (1969) 533-4. (D. Wurfel)

WATTS, RONALD LAMPMAN. New federations: experiments in the Commonwealth. London, Oxford UP, 1966.
  MAS 2 (1968) 273-4. (W. H. Morris-Jones)
  PA 40 (1967) 207-8. (A. C. Cairns)

WAUGH, ALEC. Bangkok, the story of a city. Boston, Little, Brown, 1971.
  PA 45 (1972) 468-9. (J. F. Cady)

WEATHERBEE, DONALD E. Ideology in Indonesia: Sukarno's Indonesian revolution. New Haven, Southeast Asia Studies, Yale Univ., 1966. (Yale Univ. Graduate School. Southeast Asia Studies. Monograph series, no. 8)
  BIJ 123 (1967) 526-528. (L. Sluimers)
  BIJ 123 (1967) 528-530. (J. H. A. Logemann)
  JAS 27 (1967-8) 177-8. (D. S. Lev)

WEATHERBEE, DONALD E. United front in Thailand, a documentary analysis. Columbia, Institute of International Studies, Univ. of South Carolina, 1970. (South Carolina. Univ. Institute of International Studies. Studies in international affairs, no. 8)
  JSS 60 pt. 1 (1972) 431-433. (Astri Suhrke)

Weidner, Edward W. *See* Development administration in Asia

WEINSTEIN, FRANKLIN B. Vietnam's unheld elections; the failure to carry out the 1956 reunification elections and the effect on Hanoi's present outlook. Ithaca, Southeast Asia Program, Cornell Univ., 1966. (Cornell Univ. Southeast Asia Program. Data paper, no. 60)
  BIJ 123 (1967) 524-526. (L. Sluimers)
  JAS 27 (1967-8) 687-8. (J. H. Badgley)

Weiss, P. *See* COATES, KEN. Prevent the crime of silence

WELCH, CLAUDE EMERSON. Military role and rule; perspectives on civil military relations, by Claude E. Welch and Arthur K. Smith. North Scituate, Mass., Duxbury Pr., 1974.
  JSS 62 pt. 2 (1974) 327-330. (Thak Chaloemtiarana)

WELLS, EVELYN. Carlos P. Romulo: voice of freedom. New York, Funk and Wagnalls, 1964.
  PS 13 (1965) 413. (M. P. Onorato)

WELLS, KENNETH ELMER. Thai Buddhism, its rites and activities. Bangkok, Police Pr., 1960.
  JAS 20 (1960-1) 397-8. (H. P. Phillips)
  JSS 48 pt. 2 (1960) 112-3.

Wening, Rudolf *See* WOLGENSINGER, MICHAEL. Siam

WENK, KLAUS. Restoration of Thailand under Rama I, 1782-1809. Tucson, Univ. of Arizona Pr., 1968. (Association for Asian Studies. Monographs and papers, no. 24)
  JAS 28 (1968-9) 434-5. (D. K. Wyatt)
  JSS 57 (1969) 374-5. (M. W. Amadeus)
  PA 42 (1969) 102. (D. G. E. Hall)
  SA 2 (1972) 502-514. (K. P. Landon)

WENK, KLAUS. Die Ruderlieder-kap he ruo-in die Literatur Thailands.

Wiesbaden, Franz Steiner, 1968.
(Abhandlungen fur die Kunde des
Morgenlandes. Band 37 pt. 4)
   JSS 58 pt. 2 (1970) 157-162.
      (Chetana Nagavajara)

WENK, KLAUS. Thai-Handschriften.
Wiesbaden, Franz Steiner Verlag,
1963. (Verzeichnis der oriental-
ischen Handschriften in Deutschland,
Bd. 9)
   AS 8 (1968) 196.
   SOAS 30 (1967) 444-5. (E. H. S.
      Simmonds)

Wenk, Klaus *See* DIRECK JAYANAMA.
Thailand

Wenk, Klaus *See* Verzeichnis der
orientalischen Handschriften in
Deutschland

WERNSTEDT, FREDERICK L. Philippine
Island world: a physical, cultural,
and regional geography, by Frederick
L. Wernstedt and Joseph E. Spencer.
Berkeley, Univ. of California Pr.,
1967.
   AP 12 (1969) 144-5. (W. G. Solheim)
   PA 41 (1968) 613-4. (A. Kolb)
   PS 17 (1969) 646-7. (M. McPhelin)

Wernstedt, Frederick L. *See* SIMKINS,
PAUL D. Philippine migration

WERTHEIM, WILLEM FREDERIK. East-west
parallels; sociological approaches
to modern Asia. The Hague, van
Hoeve, 1964.
   AAS 3 (1967) 242-3. (R. Raczynski)
   BIJ 122 (1966) 477-480. (R. Van
      Niel)
   JSAH 7 (Sept. 1966) 122-3. (M. A.
      Jaspan)
   PA 39 (1966) 376-7. (J. M. van der
      Kroef)

Wertheim, Willem Frederik *See*
Indonesian economics

WERTHEIM, WILLEM FREDERIK. Indonesian
society in transition: a study of
social change. The Hague, van Hoeve,
1956.
   BIJ 117 (1961) 64-79. (G. W. Locher)
   JAS 19 (1959-60) 470-1. (F. Eggan)
   JSAH 2 (Mar. 1961) 128-131. (R.
      Roolvink)

WERTHEIM, WILLEM FREDERIK. Ketters en
kwezels, regenten en rebellen, door
W. F. Wertheim en A. H. Wertheim-
Gijse Weenink. Drachten, Laverman,
1968.
   BIJ 125 (1969) 397-399. (C. Fasseur)

Wertheim-Gijse Weenink, Annie Hetty
   See WERTHEIM, WILLEM FREDERIK.
Ketters en kwezels

WEST, FRANCIS J. The village. New
York, Harper and Row, 1972.
   PA 45 (1972) 469-470. (A. E.
      Goodman)

WEST, MORRIS L. The ambassator, by
William Morrow. New York, Morrow,
1965.
   PA 38 (1965) 460. (W. E. Willmott)

* WESTERN AUSTRALIA. UNIV. CENTRE FOR
ASIAN STUDIES. Working papers in
Asian studies. Nedlands, 1967.
   AAS 5 (1969) 107-8. (R. Raczynski)

Weston, Maynard *See* DOW, MAYNARD
WESTON

WESTON, RUBIN FRANCIS. Racism in U.S.
imperialism; the influence of racial
assumptions on American foreign
policy, 1893-1946. Columbia, Univ.
of South Carolina Pr., 1972.
   PA 45 (1972) 625. (I. B. Powell)

WHARTON, DOLORES D. Contemporary art-
ists of Malaysia, a bibliographic
survey. Kuala Lumpur, Union Cultural
Organization, 1971.
   BIJ 129 (1973) 368-9. (P. E. de
      Josselin de Jong)

Wheatley, Paul. Golden Khersonese

WHEATLEY, PAUL. Golden Khersonese;
  studies in the historical geography
  of the Malay Peninsula before A.D.
  1500. Kuala Lumpur, Univ. of Malaya
  Pr., 1961.
    JAS 21 (1961-2) 567-8. (J. E.
      Spencer)
    JSAH 5 (Mar. 1964) 222-224. (J. G.
      de Casparis)
    JSS 62 pt. 1 (1974) 174-211.
      (Chand Chirayu Rajani)
    MER 7 pt. 1 (1962) 80-1. (T. R.
      McHale)
    PA 37 (1964) 94. (V. Purcell)
    SOAS 25 (1962) 638-9. (O. W.
      Wolters)

WHEELWRIGHT, EDWARD LAWRENCE. Industrialization in Malaysia. London,
  Cambridge UP, 1965.
    AS 6 (1966) 406.
    JAS 26 (1966-7) 538-9. (G. D. Ness)

WHITTEMORE, LEWIS BLISS. Struggle for
  freedom, history of the Philippine
  Independent Church. Greenwich,
  Conn., Seabury Pr., 1961.
    PS 10 (1962) 684-705. (P. S. de
      Achutegui and M. A. Bernad)

WHYTE, ROBERT ORR. Grasslands of the
  monsoon. New York, Praeger, 1968.
    PA 42 (1969) 415-6. (J. E. Spencer)

WICKBERG, EDGAR. Chinese in Philippine life, 1850-1898. New Haven,
  Yale UP, 1965.
    JAS 25 (1965-6) 556. (Y. Akashi)
    JSAH 7 (Sept. 1966) 144-5. (L. E.
      Williams)
    SOAS 30 (1967) 226-7. (W. E.
      Willmott)

Wickberg, Edgar *See* Historical interaction of China and Vietnam

Widjojo Nitisastro *See* NITISASTRO,
  WIDJOJO

WIENS, HEROLD JACOB. Pacific island
  bastions of the United States.

Princeton, Van Nostrand, 1962.
    JAS 23 (1963-4) 599-600. (D. H.
      Kornhauser)

WIGHTMAN, DAVID. Toward economic cooperation in Asia: the United Nations Economic Commission for Asia
  and the Far East. New Haven, Yale
  UP, 1963.
    JAS 23 (1963-4) 294-5. (A. Z.
      Rubinstein)

Wijeyewardene, Gehan *See* Leadership
  and authority

Wildhaber, Robert *See* SCHMITZ, CARL A.
  Festschrift Alfred Buhler

Wiles, Peter *See* CHALIAND, GERARD.
  Peasants of North Vietnam

Wilkinson, R. J. *See* BURNS, PETER L.
  Papers on Malay subjects

Willetts, William *See* SOUTHEAST ASIAN
  CERAMIC SOCIETY. Ceramic art of
  Southeast Asia

Willey, Keith *See* SMITH, ROBIN V. F.
  New Guinea

WILLIAMS, LEA E. Future of the over-
  seas Chinese in Southeast Asia. New
  York, McGraw-Hill, 1966. (United
  States and China in world affairs)
    JAS 27 (1967-8) 175-177. (R. J.
      Coughlin)
    JSAH 8 (1967) 348-350. (Png Poh-
      Seng)

WILLIAMS, LEA E. Overseas Chinese nationalism: the genesis of the Pan-
  Chinese movement in Indonesia, 1900-
  1916. Glencoe, Free Pr., 1960.
    BIJ 119 (1963) 229-232. (A. F. P.
      Hulsewe)
    JAS 20 (1960-1) 353-362. (G. W.
      Skinner)
    JSAH 3 (Mar. 1962) 157-160. (Wang
      Gungwu)
    PA 34 (1961) 205-6. (Giok Po Oey)

Wilson, Peter J. Malay village and

WILLIAMS, MASLYN. Five journeys from
  Jakarta; inside Sukarno's Indonesia.
  New York, Morrow, 1966.
    PA 41 (1968) 116-7. (L. Palmier)

WILLIAMS, MASLYN. Land in between;
  the Cambodian dilemma. New York,
  Morrow, 1970.
    PA 44 (1971) 149-150. (M. Leifer)

WILLIAMS, THOMAS RHYS. The Dusun: a
  North Borneo society. New York,
  Holt, Rinehart and Winston, 1965.
  (Case studies in cultural anthropol-
  ogy)
    JAS 26 (1966-7) 353-4. (P. R.
      Goethals)
    SMJ 14 (1966) 376-388. (G. N.
      Appell)
    SMJ 14 (1966) 389-392. (C. A.
      Sather)
    SMJ 14 (1966) 393-395. (P. R.
      Goethals)

WILLMOTT, DONALD EARL. Chinese of
  Semarang: a changing minority community in Indonesia. Ithaca, Cornell UP, 1960.
    BIJ 117 (1961) 502-504. (Tjan Giok
      Bwee)
    JAS 20 (1960-1) 353-362. (G. W.
      Skinner)
    JSAH 3 (Mar. 1962) 157-160. (Wang
      Gungwu)
    PA 34 (1961) 380-389. (S. Lyman)
    SOAS 25 (1962) 639-641. (B. E.
      Ward)

WILLMOTT, DONALD EARL. National status
  of the Chinese in Indonesia, 1900-
  1958. Rev. ed. Ithaca, Cornell Univ.
  Modern Indonesia Project, 1961.
  (Cornell Univ. Modern Indonesia Project. Monograph series)
    JAS 21 (1961-2) 414-416. (E. J.
      Ryan)
    PA 35 (1965) 181-183. (V. Purcell)

WILLMOTT, WILLIAM E. Chinese in Cambodia. Vancouver, Publications Centre, Univ. of British Columbia, 1967.

AS 8 (1968) 516.
    JSAH 9 (1968) 174-5. (J. P. L.
      Jiang)
    PA 40 (1967) 404-5. (M. Leifer)

WILLMOTT, WILLIAM E. Political structure of the Chinese community in Cambodia. London, Athlone Pr., 1970.
  (London School of Economics. Monographs on social anthropology, no. 42)
    BIJ 127 (1971) 406-411. (P. J.
      Simon)
    JAS 31 (1971-2) 731-733. (R. J.
      Coughlin)
    MAS 4 (1970) 368-371. (C. A.
      Fisher)
    SA 2 (1972-3) 377-379. (M. Ebihara)

WILLOQUET, GASTON. Histoire des Philippines. Paris, Presses Universitaires de France, 1961. (Que sais-
  je? 912)
    SEIB 36 (1961) 756.

Wilson, David A. *See* VON DER MEHDEN,
  FRED R. Local authority and administration in Thailand

WILSON, DAVID A. Politics in Thailand.
  Ithaca, Cornell UP, 1962.
    JAS 22 (1962-3) 337-8. (F. C.
      Darling)
    RSA (1964) 267-269. (I. Jadoul)

WILSON, DAVID A. The United States and
  the future of Thailand. New York,
  Praeger, 1970.
    JAS 30 (1970-1) 729-730. (K. P.
      Landon)
    JSS 59 pt. 2 (1971) 252-255. (Kobkua
      Suwannathat)
    PA 44 (1971) 147-8. (J. L. S.
      Girling)

WILSON, JOHN ANTHONY BURGESS. Long day
  wanes; a Malayan trilogy. New York,
  Norton, 1964.
    PA 38 (1965) 206-7. (G. Woodcock)

WILSON, PETER J. Malay village and Malaysia; social values and rural devel-

Wilson, Peter J. Malay village and

opment. New Haven, Human Relations
Area Files Pr., 1967.
   AS 7 (1967) 752.
   JAS 27 (1967-8) 688-9. (J. D.
   Clarkson)

WILSON, RICHARD GARRATT. Future role
of Singapore. London, Oxford UP,
1972.
   JCA 4 (1974) 111.

Wimol Phongphiphat *See* SAENGSOM
KASEMSRI. History of the Ratanakosin period

* WIN PE. Shwe dagon. Rangoon, Printing and Publishing Corp., 1972.
   SEIB 49 (1974) 155-6. (E. Guillon)

WINKS, ROBIN W. Historiography of the
British Empire-Commonwealth; trends,
interpretations, and resources.
Durham, Duke UP, 1966.
   JAH 3 (1969) 92.
   JSAH 8 (1967) 342-3. (N. Tarling)
   PA 39 (1966) 447-449. (J. E. Flint)

Winks, Robin W. *See* BASTIN, JOHN
STURGUS. Malaysia

WINSTEDT, RICHARD OLOF. History of
classical Malay literature. Singapore, 1961. (Royal Asiatic Society
of Great Britain and Ireland. Malayan Branch. Monographs on Malay subjects, no. 5, rev. ed.)
   JSAH 6 (Mar. 1966) 120-122. (A. H.
   Johns)

WINSTEDT, RICHARD OLOF. History of
classical Malay literature. Kuala
Lumpur, Oxford UP, 1969. (Oxford in
Asia. Historical reprints)
   JAS 30 (1970-1) 737-8. (A. Teeuw)

WINSTEDT, RICHARD OLOF. History of
Malaya. Rev. and enl. ed. Singapore,
Marican, 1962.
   JSAH 4 (Sept. 1963) 184-187. (E.
   Sadka)

WINSTEDT, RICHARD OLOF. Kamus bahasa
Melayu. Singapore, Marican, 1960.
   BIJ 117 (1961) 391-393. (A. Teeuw)
   SOAS 25 (1962) 192-3. (J. C.
   Bottoms)

WINSTEDT, RICHARD OLOF. Start from
alif; count from one, an autobiograph-
ical memoire. Kuala Lumpur, Oxford
UP, 1969.
   JSAS 1 pt. 2 (1970) 137-8. (Tham
   Seong Chee)
   SOAS 33 (1970) 675-6. (E. C. G.
   Barrett)

WINSTEDT, RICHARD OLOF. Unabridged
English-Malay dictionary. 2d. ed.
Singapore, Marican, 1960.
   BIJ 117 (1961) 391-393. (A. Teeuw)

WINSTEDT, RICHARD OLOF. Unabridged
Malay-English dictionary. 3d. ed.
Kuala Lumpur, Marican, 1959.
   BIJ 117 (1961) 391-393. (A. Teeuw)

WINT, GUY. Asia, a handbook. New
York, Praeger, 1966.
   PA 39 (1966) 453. (P. Harnetty)
   RSA (1966) 279. (M. Subhan)

WIRZ, PAUL. Kunst und Kult des Sepik-
Gebietes Neu-Guinea unter besonderer
Berucksichtigung einer daselbst in
den Jahren 1950 und 1953 erworbenen
Sammlung. Amsterdam, Koninklijk In-
stituut voor de Tropen, 1959.
(Koninklijk Instituut voor de Tropen,
Amsterdam. Afdeling Culturele en
Physische Anthropologie, no. 62)
   PA 33 (1960) 200. (L. Pospisil)

Wisdom gone beyond, an anthology of
Buddhist texts. Bangkok, Social Sci-
ence Association Pr., 1966.
   JAS 26 (1966-7) 540-1. (A. Bharati)
   JSS 55 (1967) 122-124. (D.
   Sweetbaum)
   JSS 57 (1969) 361, 364-5. (J.
   Blofeld)

WISEMAN, HERBERT VICTOR. Cabinet in
the Commonwealth; post-war developments in Africa, the West Indies and
South-East Asia. London, Stevens,
1958.
    SOAS 23 (1960) 197-8. (A. Gledhill)

WIT, DANIEL. Thailand, another Vietnam? New York, Schribners, 1968.
    JAS 28 (1968-9) 435-437. (J. C. H.
    Om)
    JSS 57 (1969) 376-7. (M. W.
    Amadeus)

Withey, Joseph A. *See* SEIN, KENNETH.
The great Po Sein

WITHINGTON, WILLIAM A. Southeast Asia,
by William A. Withington and Margaret
Fisher. Grand Rapids, Fideler, 1963.
    PA 38 (1965) 100-1. (W. E.
    Willmott)

Witton, Ronald A. *See* NAKAHARA,
JOYCE. Development and conflict in
Thailand

WOJOWASITO, S. Kamus bahasa Indonesia-
Inggeris, oleh S. Wojowasito, W. J.
S. Poerwadarminta dan S. A. M.
Gaastra. 3d. ed. Djakarta, Versluys,
1959.
    BEF 52 (1964) 196-7. (L.-C.
    Damais)

WOLF, ERIC ROBERT. Peasant wars of
the twentieth century. New York,
Harper and Row, 1969.
    JAS 30 (1970-1) 162-3. (G. Bennett)

WOLFENDEN, ELMER. Intensive Tagalog
conversation course, by Elmer Wolfenden and R. Alejandro. 2d. ed. Grand
Forks, Summer Institute of Linguistics, Univ. of North Dakota, 1958.
    AAS 2 (1966) 161. (J. Genzor)

WOLFF, JOHN U. Beginning Cebuano.
New Haven, Yale UP, 1966-7. 2v.
(Yale linguistic series, 9)
    BIJ 123 (1967) 297-8. (J. C.

Anceaux)
    SOAS 32 (1969) 236.

* WOLFF, JOHN U. Beginning Indonesian.
Ithaca, Southeast Asia Program, Cornell Univ., 1971.
    JAS 32 (1972-3) 565-567. (Marmo
    Soemarmo)

WOLFF, JOHN U. Dictionary of Cebuano
Visayan. Ithaca, Southeast Asia Program, Cornell Univ., 1972. (Cornell
Univ. Southeast Asia Program. Data
paper, no. 87)
    AAS 10 (1974) 202-3. (J. Genzor)
    JAS 33 (1973-4) 166-7. (A. M.
    Stevens)
    PS 20 (1972) 654-657. (M. A. Bernad)
    SOAS 37 (1974) 754-5.

WOLFF, LEON. Little brown brother:
how the United States purchased and
pacified the Philippine Islands at
the century's turn. Garden City,
Doubleday, 1961.
    JAS 20 (1960-1) 540-1. (L. Casper)
    PA 34 (1961) 394-5. (F. C. Jones)
    PS 11 (1963) 460-1. (J. N.
    Schumacher)
    UN 35 (1962) 283-4. (V. J. A.
    Rosales)

WOLGENSINGER, MICHAEL. Siam, pays des
merveilles, 90 photographies par
Michael Wolgensinger; texte par
Rudolf Wening et A. F. Somm. Zurich,
Editions Silva, 1959.
    JSS 48 pt. 2 (1960) 113-116.

WOLTERS, O. W. Early Indonesian commerce; a study of the origins of Srivijaya. Ithaca, Cornell UP, 1967.
    BIJ 124 (1968) 291-294. (P.
    Wheatley)
    JAH 3 (1969) 84. (C. K. Byrd)
    JSS 62 pt. 1 (1974) 174-211. (Chand
    Chirayu Rajani)
    MAS 4 (1970) 94-5. (M. Caldwell)
    SEIB 42 (1967) 355-362. (M.
    Brocheux)
    SOAS 31 (1968) 646-7. (D. K. Wyatt)

Wolters, O. W. Early Indonesian

WRIGGINS, WILLIAM HOWARD. Ruler's
  imperative, strategies for political
  survival in Asia and Africa. New
  York, Columbia UP, 1969. (Columbia
  Univ. Southern Asian Institute.
  Southern Asian Institute Series)
    PA 43 (1970) 422. (R. S. Milne)

WRIGHT, HAROLD RICHARD CHARLES. East-
  Indian economic problems of the age
  of Cornwallis and Raffles. London,
  Luzac, 1961.
    BIJ 119 (1963) 429-432. (W. P.
      Coolhaas)
    JSAH 4 (Sept. 1963) 179-183. (J.
      M. van der Kroef)
    SOAS 25 (1962) 627-8. (K. N.
      Chaudhuri)

WRIGHT, LEIGH R. Origins of British
  Borneo. Hong Kong, Hong Kong UP,
  1970.
    JAS 31 (1971-2) 459-460. (M.
      Heppell)
    JSAS 4 (1973) 326-7. (E. Chew)
    PA 45 (1972) 138-140. (N. Tarling)

WRIGHT, LEIGH R. Vanishing world;
  the Ibans of Borneo, by Leigh Wright,
  Hedda Morrison and K. F. Wong. New
  York, Weatherhill, 1972.
    JAS 32 (1972-3) 227.

WU, CHUN-HSI. Dollars, dependents and
  dogma, overseas Chinese remittances
  to Communist China. Stanford, The
  Hoover Institution on War, Revolution and Peace, 1967. (Hoover Institution publications, 55)
    PS 21 (1973) 250-253. (C. J.
      McCarthy)

Wyatt, David K. *See* TEEUW, A.
  Hikayat Patani

Wyatt, David K. *See* SAENLUANG RATCHA-
  SOMPHAN. Nan chronicle

WYATT, DAVID K. Politics of reform in
  Thailand: education in the reign of
  King Chulalongkorn. New Haven, Yale

Yap, Elsa Paula. Cebuano-Visayan

UP, 1969.
    JAH 6 (1972) 92-3. (G. W. Wilson)
    JAS 32 (1972-3) 744-5. (W. F. Vella)
    JSAS 1 pt. 2 (1970) 129-130. (Tej
      Bunnag)
    JSS 59 pt. 1 (1971) 240-244.
      (Ekavidya Nathalang)
    MAS 4 (1970) 367-8. (P. Bee)
    PA 43 (1970) 633-4. (J. Fischer and
      Juree Namsirichai)
    SA 2 (1972) 502-514. (K. P. Landon)

YABES, LEOPOLDO Y. In larger freedom;
  studies in Philippine life, thought
  and institutions. Quezon City, Univ.
  of the Philippines, 1961. (Philippine Studies series, 6)
    JAS 21 (1961-2) 418-9. (C. O.
      Houston)

YABES, LEOPOLDO Y. Jose Rizal: sage,
  teacher and benefactor of humanity.
  Quezon City, 1961.
    JAS 21 (1961-2) 418-9. (C. O.
      Houston)

Yabes, Leopoldo Y. *See* Jose Rizal on
  his centenary

YAHAYA ISMAIL. Satu kajian mengenai
  karya2 Ahmad Talu. Kuala Lumpur,
  Dewan Bahasa dan Pustaka, 1970.
    BIJ 127 (1971) 288-9. (R. Roolvink)

Yahya Ismail *See* YAHAYA ISMAIL

Yap, Elsa Paula *See* BUNYE, MARIA
  VICTORIA R. Cebuano for beginners

Yap, Elsa Paula *See* BUNYE, MARIA
  VICTORIA R. Cebuano grammar notes

YAP, ELSA PAULA. Cebuano-Visayan dictionary, by Elsa Paula Yap and Maria
  Victoria R. Bunye. Honolulu, Univ.
  of Hawaii Pr., 1971. (Hawaii. Univ.,
  Honolulu. Pacific and Asian Linguistics Institute. PALI language texts)
    AAS 10 (1974) 196-7. (J. Genzor)

Yap-Diangco, Robert T.   The Filipino

YAP-DIANGCO, ROBERT T.   The Filipino
    guerrilla tradition.   Manila, MCS
    Enterprises, 1971.
        PS 20 (1972) 677.

* Yazyki kitaya i Yugo-vostochnoi Azii
    Problemy sintaksisa.   Moscow, Nauka,
    1971.
        AAS 9 (1973) 198-9.   (V. Krupa)

YEGER, MOSHE.   Muslims of Burma, a
    study of a minority group.   Wiesbad-
    en, Harrassowitz, 1972.   (Heidelberg.
    Universitat. Sudasien-Institut.
    Schriftenreihe)
        JAS 33 (1973-4) 329-331.   (M. E.
        Spiro)
        JSAS 4 (1973) 318-320.   (K. S.
        Sandhu)

YEO KIM WAH.   Political development in
    Singapore, 1945-1955.   Singapore,
    Singapore UP, 1973.
        JSAS 5 (1974) 278-9.   (M. Osborne)
        PA 47 (1974) 251.   (R. S. Milne)

Yimsiri, Khien See CHAND, EMCEE.
    Thai monumental bronzes

YIP YAT HOONG.   Development of the tin
    mining industry of Malaya.   Kuala
    Lumpur, Univ. of Malaya Pr., 1969.
        JSAS 3 (1972) 352-355.   (F. K. Chan)

YOINGCO, ANGEL Q.   Fiscal systems and
    practices in Asian countries, by
    Angel Q. Yoingco and Ruben F. Trini-
    dad.   New York, Praeger, 1968.
        AS 8 (1968) 818.
        PA 41 (1968) 580-1.   (E. S. Kirby)

Yong Mun Cheong See Trends in Indo-
    nesia

Yong Mun Cheong See Trends in Malay-
    sia

YOON, WON Z.   Japan's scheme for the
    liberation of Burma: the role of
    Minami Kikan and the thirty comrades.
    Athens, Ohio Univ., Center for In-
ternational Studies, 1973.   (Papers
    in international studies. Southeast
    Asia series, no. 27)
        PA 47 (1974) 252-3.   (J. F. Cady)

Yorke, Susan See TELENGA, SUZETTE

Yoshikawa, Toshiharu See ISHII, YONEO.
    Selected Thai bibliography on the
    reign of King Chulalongkorn

You Poh Seng See HUGHES, HELEN.
    Foreign investment and industrializa-
    tion in Singapore

YOU POH SENG.   Singapore economy, by
    You Poh Seng and Lim Chong Yah.
    Singapore, Far Eastern Universities
    Pr., 1971.
        SA 2 (1972) 488-502.   (V. D. Ooms)

Young, Gordon See YOUNG, OLIVER
GORDON

YOUNG, OLIVER GORDON.   Tracks of an
    intruder.   New York, Winchester Pr.,
    1971.
        JAS 31 (1971-2) 733-4.   (D. Miles)

YULE, HENRY.   Narrative of the mission
    to the Court of Ava in 1855.   Kuala
    Lumpur, Oxford UP, 1968.
        JAS 29 (1969-70) 985-987.   (M. E.
        Spiro)
        JSAH 10 (1969) 355-6.   (D. G. E.
        Hall)
        PA 42 (1969) 391-2.   (F. N. Trager)
        SOAS 33 (1970) 430.   (C. D. Cowan)

YUNESUKO HIGASHI AJIA BUNKA KENKYU
SENTA, TOKYO.   Survey of bibliogra-
    phies in western languages concerning
    East and Southeast Asian studies, pt.
    2.   Tokyo, Centre for East Asian Cul-
    tural Studies, 1969.   (Yunesuko
    Higashi Ajia Bunka Kenkyu Senta,
    Tokyo. Bibliography, 4)
        PA 43 (1970) 482.   (W. L. Holland)

ZACK, ARNOLD.   Labor training in devel-
    oping countries; a challenge in re-

sponsible democracy. New York,
Praeger, 1964.
>JAS 24 (1964-5) 144-5. (H. A.
>Levine)

ZAGORIA, DONALD S. Vietnam triangle;
Moscow, Peking, Hanoi. New York,
Pegasus, 1967.
>JSAH 10 (1969) 364-367. (D. M. Ray)
>PA 41 (1968) 446-7. (P. J. Honey)
>PA 43 (1970) 631-2. (K. H. Khanh)

ZAGORSKI, ULRICH. Burma. Tokyo,
Kondansha International, 1972.
(This beautiful world, v. 32)
>PA 45 (1972) 616-7. (J. F. Cady)

ZAINUDDIN, AILSA GWENNYTH. Short
history of Indonesia. North Melbourne, Cassell Australia, 1968.
>JAH 6 (1972) 191. (C. R. Boxer)
>JAS 33 (1973-4) 158-9. (J. S.
>Mintz)
>JSAS 1 pt. 1 (1970) 115-6. (Sar-
>tono Kartodirdjo)
>PA 44 (1971) 143-4. (D. G. E.
>Hall)

Zamora, Mario Dimarucut *See* HART,
DONN VORHIS. Annotated bibliography
on barrio councils

Zamora, Mario Dimarucut *See* Studies
in Philippine anthropology

ZARINA, XENIA. Classic dances of the
Orient. New York, Crown, 1967.
>PA 41 (1968) 454-5. (M. K.
>Mulholland)

Zasloff, Joseph Jermiah *See* Indochina in conflict

Zasloff, Joseph Jermiah *See* LANGER,
PAUL FRITZ. North Vietnam and the
Pathet Lao

Zelinsky, Wilbur *See* SYMPOSIUM ON
POPULATION PRESSURES UPON PHYSICAL
AND SOCIAL RESOURCES IN THE DEVELOP-
PING LANDS, PENNSYLVANIA STATE UNIV.,
1967. Geography and a crowding
world

ZENOFF, DAVID B. Private enterprise in
the developing countries. Englewood
Cliffs, Prentice-Hall, 1969.
>JAS 29 (1969-70) 682-684. (J. N.
>Anderson)

ZIDE, NORMAN H. Studies in comparative
Austroasiatic linguistics. The Hague,
Mouton, 1966. (Indo-Iranian mono-
graphs, vol. 5)
>SOAS 30 (1967) 732-734. (H. L.
>Shorto)

ZOBEL, FERNANDO. Philippine religious
imagery, by Fernando Zobel de Ayala.
Manila, Ateneo de Manila, 1963.
>PS 11 (1963) 434-438. (B. Legarda
>y Fernandez)

Zoetmulder, Petrus Josephus *See*
STÖHR, WALDEMAR. Die Religionen
Indonesiens

Zuniga, Joaquin Martinez de *See*
MARTINEZ DE ZUNIGA, JOAQUIN

Author Index to Articles

AUTHOR INDEX TO ARTICLES

Title Index to Book Reviews

A la recherche d'un Etat independant. GREINDL, LEOPOLD

Aantekeningen bij Tjan Tjoe Siem's vertaling van de lakon Kurupati rabi. UHLENBECK, E. M.

Abra Mission in northern Luzon. SCHMITZ, JOSEF

Acculturation in the Philippines. BAGUIO RELIGIOUS ACCULTURATION CONFERENCE

Acheen and the ports of the north and east coasts of Sumatra. ANDERSON, JOHN

Achekhskaia Voina. TIURIN, VLADIMIR ALEKSANDROVICH

Acta orientalia neerlandica. OOSTERS GENOOTSCHAP IN NEDERLAND

Adat Atjeh. TITLE ENTRY

Adat laws in modern Malaya. HOOKER, M. B.

Administration and development in Malaysia. ESMAN, MILTON JACOB

Administrative reforms in Asia. LEE, HAHN BEEN

Admonitions of Seh Bari. KITAB BONANG

Africa and Indonesia. JONES, A. M.

Africa, its people and their cultural history. MURDOCK, GEORGE PETER

Afro-Asia and non-alignment. JANSEN, G. H.

After imperialism. BROWN, MICHAEL BARRATT

Agama tirtha. HOOYKAAS, CHRISTIAAN

Agrarian reform. VIRATA, ENRIQUE T.

Agrarian unrest in Southeast Asia. JACOBY, ERICH H.

Agricultural change and peasant choice in a Thai village. MOERMAN, MICHAEL

Agricultural development in Asia. SHAND, RICHARD TREGURTHA

Agricultural development planning and zoning in South Vietnam. THAI CONG TUNG

Agricultural involution. GEERTZ, CLIFFORD

Agricultural revolution in Southeast Asia. TITLE ENTRY

Agta grammar. HEALEY, PHYLLIS M.

Aguinaldo and the revolution of 1896. ACHUTEGUI, PEDRO S. DE

Akha-English dictionary. LEWIS, PAUL

Alexander Dalyrmple. FRY, HOWARD TYRRELL

Alternative in Southeast Asia. BLACK, EUGENE ROBERT

Ambassador. WEST, MORRIS L.

Ambon, kolonisatie, dekolonisatie en neo-kolonisatie. UTRECHT, ERNST

Ambonese adat. COOLEY, FRANK L.

Americains face au Vietcong. GIGON, FERNAND

American doctoral dissertations on Asia. STUCKI, CURTIS W.

American experience in Indonesia. BEERS, HOWARD WAYLAND

American imperialism and the Philippine insurrection. GRAFF, HENRY FRANKLIN

American institutions and organizations interested in Asia. ASIA SOCIETY

American neo-colonialism. POMEROY, WILLIAM J.

American trade with Asia and the Far East. CONFERENCE ON AMERICAN TRADE WITH ASIA AND THE FAR EAST, MARQUETTE UNIV., 1958

Americans in Southeast Asia. FIFIELD, RUSSELL HUNT

Americans in Sumatra. GOULD, JAMES W.

America's Asia. TITLE ENTRY

Amir Hamzah radja penjair pudjangga baru. JASSIN, H. B.

An-Nam chi-lu'o'c. LI TSE

Analysis of Malay magic. ENDICOTT, KIRK MICHAEL

Analysis of the social effects of donated radios on barrio life. COLLER, RICHARD WALTER

Analysis of the syntax and the system of affixes of the Bisaya' language of Cebu. BERGH, J. D. VAN DEN

Anam Sayam yut. KULAP, K. S. R.

Anatomy of a crisis. FALL, BERNARD B.

Anatomy of Philippine Muslim affairs. FILIPINAS FOUNDATION, INC.

Ancient Cambodian sculpture. LEE, SHERMAN E.

Ancient Indonesian art. BERNET KEMPERS, AUGUST JOHAN

Ancient Indonesian art of the central and eastern Javanese periods. FONTEIN, JAN

Ancient Siamese government and administration. WALES, HORACE GEOFFREY QUARITCH

Andre Malraux, the Indochina adventure. LANGLOIS, WALTER G.

Anecdotal history of old times in Singapore. BUCKLEY, CHARLES BURTON

Angels and fugitives. TORRES, EMMANUEL

Angkor. MacDONALD, MALCOLM

Angkor; an essay on art and imperialism. MYRDAL, JAN

Angkor, an introduction. COEDES, GEORGE

Angkor and Rome. WALES, HORACE GEOFFREY QUARITCH

Angkor empire. WALKER, GEORGE B.

Angkor et le Cambodge. GROSLIER, BERNARD PHILIPPE

Angkor; guide. PARMENTIER, HENRI

Anglo-Dutch rivalry in the Malay world. TARLING, NICHOLAS

Annexation of Upper Burma. SINGHAL, D. P.

Anniversary contributions to anthropology. TITLE ENTRY

Annotated bibliography of Javanese folklore. DANANDJAJA, JAMES

Annotated bibliography of Philippine social sciences. QUEZON, PHILIPPINES. UNIV. OF THE PHILIPPINES. SOCIAL SCIENCE RESEARCH CENTER

Annotated bibliography of the history of the sugar industry in Panay and Negros. ABRERA, JOSEFA B.

Annotated bibliography of the theses and dissertations on Asia accepted at Syracuse University. HART, DONN VORHIS

Annotated bibliography on barrio councils. HART, DONN VORHIS

Annuaire statistique retrospectif du Cambodge. CAMBODIA. MINISTERE DU PLAN

Anthologie bilingue de la poesie indonesienne contemporaine. ROSIDI, AJIP

Anthologie de la poesie vietnamienne. TITLE ENTRY

Anthologie de la poesie vietnamienne. SAMANA, PIERRE

Anthology of modern Indonesian poetry. RAFFEL, BURTON

Anthropological studies in Theravada Buddhism. CONFERENCE ON THERAVADA BUDDHISM, UNIV. OF CHICAGO, 1962

Anthropologists in the field. TITLE ENTRY

Antologia literatury malajskiej. STILLER, ROBERT

Apolinario Mabini. MAJUL, CESAR ADIB

Approach to Indonesian history. SUDJATMOKO

Archaeological research in Indo-China. JANSE, OLOV ROBERT THURE

TITLE INDEX TO BOOK REVIEWS

Natsionalno-osvoboditelnoe dvizhenie v Indonesii.
  TITLE ENTRY
Natural and applied sciences bulletin. NATURAL AND
  APPLIED SCIENCES BULLETIN (INDEXES)
Nederlandsch-Indie onder Japansche bezetting.
  GRAAF, HERMANUS JOHANNES DE
Negritos of the Philippines. GARVAN, JOHN M.
Netherlands India. FURNIVALL, JOHN SYDENHAM
New acquisitions of three bronzes from Buriram.
  THAILAND. FINE ARTS DEPT.
New class in North Vietnam. HOANG VAN CHI
New elite in Asia and Africa. KERSTIENS, THOM
New emerging forces. MODELSKI, GEORGE A.
New federations. WATTS, RONALD LAMPMAN
New Guinea. SMITH, ROBIN V. F.
New Guinea, problems and prospects. HASTINGS, PETER
New nationalism. SNYDER, LOUIS LEO
New states of Asia. BRECHER, MICHAEL
New universities overseas. CARR-SAUNDERS, ALEXANDER
  MORRIS
New voyage round the world. DAMPIER, WILLIAM
New writings from the Philippines. CASPER, LEONARD
New Year ceremony at Basak. ARCHAIMBAULT, CHARLES
Ngaju religion. SCHÄRER, HANS
Ngoc Kieu Le. TITLE ENTRY
Ngon ngu hoc Viet Nam. NGUYEN BAT TUY
Nguoi Viet dat Viet. TOAN ANH
Nhan-van affair. HOA MAI
Nhu Vien trong Kham-Dinh Dai-Nam Hoi-Dien Su-Le.
  VIETNAM. INSTITUT DE RECHERCHES ARCHEOLOGIQUES
Nhung dai le va vu khuc cua vua chua Viet-nam. DO
  BANG DOAN
Nimboran language. ANCEAUX, JOHANNES CORNELIS
Nineteenth century Borneo. IRWIN, GRAHAM
Nineteenth century Malaya. COWAN, CHARLES DONALD
Nirat Phu Khao Thong. SUNTHON PHU
No exit from Vietnam. THOMPSON, ROBERT GRAINGER KER
No more Vietnams. TITLE ENTRY
Non-alignment and the Afro-Asian states. JANSEN,
  G. H.
Non Nok Tha. BAYARD, DONN T.
North Borneo Chartered Company's administration of
  the Bajau. WARREN, JAMES FRANCIS
North Borneo, the first 10 years. BAKER, MICHAEL H.
North Vietnam, a documentary. GERASSI, JOHN
North Vietnam and the Pathet Lao. LANGER, PAUL FRITZ
Northern Thai reader. DAVIS, RICHARD
Notes on the 1973 Philippine constitution. CLAUSTRO,
  FELIX B.
Notes on the political and administrative history of
  Vietnam. JUMPER, ROY
Noun substitutes in modern Thai. CAMPBELL,
  RUSSELL N.
Nouveau dictionnaire scientifique francais-anglais-
  vietnamien. PHAM VAN HUYEN
Nouveau guide d'Angkor. MARCHAL, HENRI
Nusantara. VLEKKE, BERNARD HUBERTUS MARIA

Oceanian art. BODROGI, TIBOR
Ocherki iz istorii IUgo-Vostochnoi Azii. AKADEMIIA
  NAUK SSSR. INSTITUT NARODOV AZII
Of cocks and kites. ROCES, ALEJANDRO R.
Officiele bescheiden betreffende de Nederlands-
  Indonesische betrekkingen. TITLE ENTRY
Old Burma. LUCE, GORDON HANNINGTON
Old Javanese. TESELKIN, AVENIR STEPANOVICH
On revolution. HO CHI MINH
On the Cordillera. SCOTT, WILLIAM HENRY
On the fringe of diplomacy. STIRLING, ALFRED THORPE

On the old Javanese Cantakaparwa and its tale of
  Sutasoma. ENSINK, J.
On thrones of gold. BRANDON, JAMES R.
Onderwijsbeleid in Nederlands-Indie. WAL, S. L. VAN
  DER
One father. STRATHERN, ANDREW
One hundred letters of Jose Rizal. RIZAL Y ALONSO,
  JOSE
One hundred years' history of the Chinese in Singa-
  pore. SONG ONG SIANG
One morning in the war. HAMMER, RICHARD
Ontsporing van geweld. DOORN, JACOBUS ADRIANUS
  ANTONIUS VAN
Oost Indische Spiegel. NIEUWENHUYS, ROB
Opkomst van de Nationalistische Beweging in
  Nederlands-Indie. WAL, S. L. VAN DER
Orang Abung. FUNKE, FRIEDRICH W.
Orde Wingate. SYKES, CHRISTOPHER HUGH
Organization of Thai society in the early Bangkok
  period. AKIN RABIBHADANA, M. R.
Oriental and Asian bibliography. PEARSON, JAMES
  DOUGLAS
Oriental Asia. SPENCER, JOSEPH EARLE
Oriental ceramics discovered in the Philippines.
  LOCSIN, LEANDRO
Oriental world. AUBOYER, JEANNINE
Origin and evolution of Thai murals. BIRASRI, SILPA
Origins of British Borneo. WRIGHT, LEIGH R.
Origins of Malay nationalism. ROFF, WILLIAM R.
Origins of the modern Chinese movement in Indonesia.
  KWEE TEK HOAY
Origins of trade unionism in Malaya. GAMBA, CHARLES
Ornamented bark cloth in Indonesia. KOOIJMAN, S.
Osten nach der Erdkarte al-Huwarizmis. DAUNICHT,
  HUBERT
Our struggle. SJAHRIR, SOETAN
Our tropical possessions in Malayan India. CAMERON,
  JOHN
Outline atlas of eastern history. SELLMAN, ROGER
  RAYMOND
Outline of Khmu structure. SMALLEY, WILLIAM ALLEN
Outline of Philippine mythology. JOCANO, F. LANDA
Outline of Sre structure. MANLEY, TIMOTHY M.
Overseas Chinese. MITCHISON, LOIS
Overseas Chinese in Southeast Asia. SIMONIIA, N. A.
Overseas Chinese nationalism. WILLIAMS, LEA E.
Ownership and control in the Malayan economy.
  PUTHUCHEARY, JAMES J.

POW-two years with the Vietcong. SMITH, GEORGE
  EDWARD
Pace and pattern of Philippine economic growth.
  GOODSTEIN, MARVIN E.
Pacific basin development. MALMGREN, HARALD B.
Pacific island bastions of the United States. WIENS,
  HEROLD JACOB
Pacific politics. NICOLSON, I. F.
Pacific, then and now. BAHRENBERG, BRUCE
Pada sebuah kapal. DINI, NH.
Padju Epat. HUDSON, ALFRED B.
Pages d'histoire. TITLE ENTRY
Pagoda war. STEWART, ANTHONY TERENCE QUINCEY
Palau-Sprache und ihre Stellung zu anderen
  indonesischen Sprachen. PÄTZOLD, KLAUS
Pali-English dictionary. HOKE SEIN, U
Pampangans. LARKIN, JOHN A.
Panji. RASSERS, WILLEM HUIBERT
Panorama der Volken. EMST, PETER VAN
Papers on Malay subjects. BURNS, PETER L.

TITLE INDEX TO BOOK REVIEWS